Praise for *PRESIDENT CARTER*

"President Carter anticipated many of the programs that his successor Ronald Reagan embraced. He fostered major deregulation of transportation, communication, and banking, and, most importantly, appointed Paul Volcker, one of the most committed inflation fighters, to the chairmanship of the Federal Reserve. Stuart Eizenstat succeeds in offering a more balanced view of the Carter presidency than is conventional. Splendid read."
—**Alan Greenspan, Chairman of the Federal Reserve, 1987–2006, appointed by President Ronald Reagan, and Chairman of the Council of Economic Advisers under President Gerald Ford**

"'People never did understand me and still don't,' Jimmy Carter has said. Stuart Eizenstat disproves the claim in this ultimate insider's account of our 39th President, which does for Carter what Robert Sherwood did for FDR, and Ted Sorensen for JFK. His access equaled by his objectivity, Eizenstat places the first New Democrat in historical perspective as a self-confident moralist impatient with incrementalism, uncomfortable with Washington's status quo and the politicians who defer to it. Clearly more consequential, and legislatively successful, than it appears in popular memory, Carter's presidency put a lasting stamp on energy and environmental policy, human rights and the tortuous pursuit of peace in the Middle East. Eizenstat makes it all matter in this highly readable narrative forty years in the making, and well worth the wait." —**Richard Norton Smith, Pulitzer Prize finalist for *Thomas E. Dewey and His Times***

"President Carter is an extraordinary reassessment of the first 'New Democrat's' presidency, combining Stu's recognized domestic and international policy range and depth with wonderful political, personal, institutional, and societal insights. This book is much more than a well-written and researched history: Stu reminds that Jimmy Carter was the first modern president who ran as an anti-Establishment populist, navigating currents of alienation that have continued to swirl around American politics."
—**Robert B. Zoellick, former President of the World Bank, US Trade Representative, and Deputy Secretary of State**

"At a time when Americans are yearning for moral leadership, this is exactly the right book written by exactly the right person. Jimmy Carter was not a perfect president but he came close to being a saintly president. Stu Eizenstat, his right-hand assistant on domestic and other affairs, draws from more than five thousand pages of notes he took at the time to draw a balanced, insightful, and uplifting portrait of a president whose moral courage we miss today."
—**David Gergen, presidential adviser, political analyst, and codirector of the Center for Public Leadership at the Harvard Kennedy School**

"Jimmy Carter may well be due for a revisionist wave. If so, Stu Eizenstat's important book will be seen as its cutting edge. As anyone who knows him would expect, Eizenstat's book is tough minded, thorough, and thoughtful in making the case for a new view of the Carter Presidency. It deserves the close attention of anyone concerned with American history or politics." —**Lawrence Summers, Secretary of the Treasury under President Clinton and former chairman of President Obama's National Economic Council**

"History may judge Jimmy Carter guilty of too much humanity, but he lacked neither courage, nor conviction, nor, in the final analysis, real and lasting achievements. This is an important and long overdue assessment." —**Ted Koppel, broadcast journalist, former anchor of ABC's *Nightline***

"What better time than now for a reevaluation of Jimmy Carter's presidency? And who better to initiate it than Stuart Eizenstat, Carter's domestic policy director and one of his top advisors on the Mideast? No apologist, Eizenstat acknowledges Carter's political weaknesses and studiously avoids excessive claims of greatness. President Carter is thus a first-rate work of analysis and history and a much-needed retrospective on a president who reflected great personal credit on the office he held and the country he served." —**Stanley Cloud, former White House correspondent and Washington Bureau Chief for *Time* magazine**

"Stu makes it impossible not to see Carter's genuine accomplishments at home and abroad and his daring to tackle problems others wouldn't touch. It is a rare pleasure to read such a fair-minded and truthful book." —**Leslie H. Gelb, President Emeritus, Council on Foreign Relations**

"An admiring but also very frank account of Jimmy Carter's presidency by the ultimate insider, Stuart Eizenstat. He's honest about Carter's weaknesses, as well as his strengths, and he reveals some details that have never been reported before. His summation of 'what ifs' at the end of the book makes haunting reading. This memoir reminds us that during the Carter years, we had a smart, decent but unlucky man in the Oval Office." —**David Ignatius, columnist, *The Washington Post***

"An unflinchingly honest, comprehensive description and analysis of Jimmy Carter's presidency. Eizenstat's reconstruction of Carter's term offers detailed treatment of foreign and domestic policy issues, along with intriguing analysis of the politics of it all. He was a participant observer and activist who knew the players well. History benefits, as will scholars and other readers of this crisply written, carefully researched volume." —**Charles O. Jones, Hawkins Professor Emeritus of Political Science, University of Wisconsin, Madison**

"The Kennedy administration had, as its inside historian, Arthur Schlesinger. Reagan had James Baker, and now Jimmy Carter has Stuart Eizenstat. And readers have the best history of Carter's consequential, one-term presidency, and it's about time. Written by an insider, capable of seeing—and appreciating—Carter's accomplishments as well as his flaws, *President Carter* is rich in detail and insight, absolutely fair-minded and informative, a welcome reassessment of a president who deserved a fresh look."
—**Marvin Kalb, former network correspondent, Edward R. Murrow Professor Emeritus at Harvard University, author of *The Year I Was Peter the Great***

"This book provides an important corrective to the history of the Carter administration. Written by one of the president's closest and most influential advisers, it portrays the intricacies of presidential politics in compelling, balanced, and extremely readable prose. The discussion of events leading up to and through the Camp David peace accords is fascinating." —**Stephen J. Wayne, Professor of Government, Georgetown University**

"If you believe you know the full truth about the Presidency of Jimmy Carter, you'll think twice after you read Stu Eizenstat's fascinating, richly researched, insider accounts. Eizenstat has filled in a lot of blanks about the administration he loyally served. While he fully acknowledges major mistakes by Carter and his aides (including himself), the author makes a strong case that Carter's four years in the Oval Office are due a serious reevaluation, and that Carter achieved far more than he is often credited with in the shorthand style of current history and commentary." —**Larry J. Sabato, professor, founder and director of the University of Virginia Center for Politics**

"Stuart Eizenstat has written an important book, a richly detailed account of the events and people of Jimmy Carter's presidency, which may very well lead to history's reevaluation of the 39th President." —**Stephen H. Hess, Senior Fellow Emeritus, The Brookings Institution**

"Eizenstat has given us a seminal reminder of the kind of president that we need in this dangerous world—and of the contribution a candid insider's account can give to history's understanding of a widely misunderstood president. As Eizenstat writes, Jimmy Carter was 'not a great president,' but he was a darned good one and, at the head of a functioning U.S. government, accomplished much more than many others who have filled that post." —**Douglas Besharov, Norman and Florence Brody Professor at the University of Maryland School of Public Policy**

"No matter one's assessment of Carter's presidency, one admires his convictions that the human condition must be improved and that America must contribute to this quest. This is a thoughtful book about a principled president and an honorable man."

—Dr. Henry Kissinger, Secretary of State under Presidents Nixon and Ford

"A masterpiece—presidential biography as it should be written. Eizenstat delivers the fly-on-the-wall authenticity of an insider, while providing the arm's-length perspective and historical context of a skilled biographer."

—Fred Kempe, President and CEO of the Atlantic Council

"Helps us better understand the true historical significance of Carter's presidency, and show how, even with its flaws, it stands as a beacon of hope and achievement in politically and economically troubled times. A highly insightful and timely read!"

—Klaus Schwab, Founder and Chairman of the World Economic Forum

"This is a massive book, not just in scale, but in both ambition and achievement. Carter emerges as a highly consequential, albeit flawed president."

—Martin Wolf, Chief Economics Commenator at the Financial Times

"This book is highly instructive today, both for its lessons about governing at a time of political division—within and between parties—and for its account of the complexities of economic policy decisions."

—Robert E. Rubin, Former U.S. Treasury Secretary

"Carter was a much better and more consequential president than the first cut of history has given him. This book corrects the record. It's an exhaustive examination of the successes and failures of those four years by an insider who spares neither himself nor Carter from criticism, but whose work will surely elevate respect for the important accomplishments of the president he serves."

—Sam Donaldson, broadcast journalist and former news anchor

"Comprehensive, compelling, and readable. Eizenstat is no sycophant or apologist for Carter; his book chronicles the mistakes and stumbles just as he outlines the accomplishments. This book should, and will, alter the historical record and place the Carter presidency in a significantly better light."

—Norman Ornstein, author of *One Nation After Trump*

ALSO BY STUART EIZENSTAT

The Future of the Jews: How Global Forces Are Impacting the Jewish People, Israel, and Its Relationship with the United States

Imperfect Justice: Looted Assets, Slave Labor, and the Unfinished Business of World War II

Andrew Young: The Path to History
(with William Barutio)

PRESIDENT CARTER

THE WHITE HOUSE YEARS

STUART E. EIZENSTAT

FOREWORD BY
MADELEINE ALBRIGHT

THOMAS DUNNE BOOKS ✖ ST. MARTIN'S PRESS NEW YORK

THOMAS DUNNE BOOKS.
An imprint of St. Martin's Press.

www.thomasdunnebooks.com
www.stmartins.com

Designed by Steven Seighman

The Library of Congress Cataloging-in-Publication Data is available upon request.

ISBN 978-1-250-10455-7 (hardcover)
ISBN 978-1-250-10457-1 (ebook)

Our books may be purchased in bulk for promotional, educational, or business use. Please contact your local bookseller or the Macmillan Corporate and Premium Sales Department at 1-800-221-7945, extension 5442, or by email at MacmillanSpecialMarkets@macmillan.com.

First Edition: April 2018

10 9 8 7 6 5 4 3 2 1

*To my wonderful loving wife, Fran, who, for forty-five years,
including the challenging Carter White House years, was my selfless life
partner, my closest adviser, and my most ardent supporter.
She is deeply missed.*

*And to my parents, Leo and Sylvia, firstborn-generation Americans,
who took great pride that their son could work in the White House.*

CONTENTS

It is not the critic who counts: not the man who points out how the strong man stumbles or where the doer of deeds could have done better. The credit belongs to the man who is actually in the arena, whose face is marred by dust and sweat and blood, who strives valiantly, who errs and comes up short again and again, because there is no effort without shortcoming, but who knows the great enthusiasm, the great devotion, who spends himself for a worthy cause; who, at the best, knows, in the end, the triumph of high achievement, and who, at the worst, if he fails, at least he fails while daring greatly, so that his place shall never be with those cold and timid souls who knew neither victory nor defeat.

—THEODORE ROOSEVELT, "CITIZENSHIP IN A REPUBLIC,"
SORBONNE, PARIS, APRIL 23, 1910

FOREWORD

I worked on the staff of Jimmy Carter's National Security Council, and it was there that I first got to know Stuart Eizenstat. I have always admired his work ethic, his fine brain, and warm heart—qualities that mirrored those of our boss. I have also always counted on Stu to tackle challenges with unimpeachable integrity and complete honesty. That is precisely how he approached this book. Forty years after Carter's inauguration, the time is ripe for a reappraisal of his presidency. No one could be better suited to undertake such a project. Stu helped lead Carter's historic 1976 campaign and served with distinction as his chief domestic policy adviser in the White House.

He does not argue that Jimmy Carter was a perfect president, nor does he overlook the shortcomings and faults of our thirty-ninth president. But Stu makes a compelling case that Carter's four years in the White House deserve far more credit than he generally receives. Those who dismiss Jimmy Carter's considerable accomplishments as president are doing a disservice to the historical record, and to the country.

This is particularly true in the realm of foreign policy. President Carter was idealistic; he wanted America to present a morally untainted image to the world. His national security adviser, Zbigniew Brzezinski, distrusted the Kremlin leaders and had no illusions about our struggle with the Soviet Union. But both agreed that we would be more successful in countering Communism if we made respect for human rights a fundamental tenet of our foreign policy and in our national interest.

Four months after taking office, Carter explained America's new approach in a speech at Notre Dame, rejecting rigid moral maxims but declaring that the United States had so much faith in democratic methods that we should no longer have an "inordinate fear of Communism"; embrace dictators simply because they fought Communism; or "adopt the flawed and erroneous principles and tactics of our adversaries, sometimes abandoning our own values for theirs. We have fought fire with fire, never thinking that fire is better quenched with water. This approach failed, with Vietnam the best example of its intellectual and moral poverty." President Carter's commitment to human rights made me proud to serve in his administration. It also contributed mightily to the credibility of U.S. leadership and to the eventual expansion of democracy in Latin America, Asia, Africa, and Central Europe. By declaring America's opposition to apartheid and brokering the historic Middle East Peace Accords at Camp David, Carter proved himself to be both a proactive and a principled president.

One foreign-policy accomplishment that remained elusive was a nuclear arms reduction agreement with the Soviet Union. As director of legislative relations for the National Security Council, I was deeply involved in the effort to obtain the Senate's consent to the SALT II Treaty. We probably would have succeeded if on Christmas Day 1979 Soviet troops had not invaded Afghanistan. The Carter administration pushed back against this act of aggression economically by halting grain shipments and by banning the transfer of advanced technology. It responded politically by boycotting the Moscow Olympics and reinstating draft registration.

At the same time the administration's attention was equally focused on Iran, where militants backed by a revolutionary Islamic regime seized our embassy and held our diplomats hostage. President Carter was consumed with saving their lives, but the public quickly grew disenchanted; the press was brutal in its focus on the hostages; and all this fed into a feeling of national helplessness that was soon exploited by Ronald Reagan. He proved a far more formidable adversary than many Democrats predicted, and in my eternal optimism I thought we could beat him. I was wrong.

Although the verdict of the voters was clear, history's verdict on Carter is still being debated. He laid the foundations for conserving energy as a national policy and normalized relations with China. He poured out a cornucopia of good ideas, but they spilled out so swiftly and simultaneously that Carter obscured his own priorities, sending Congress more than it could handle, and foreign leaders and the American people more than they could absorb.

With the benefit of hindsight, public perceptions have begun to change, and with Stu Eizenstat's important contribution, my hope is that those perceptions will continue to evolve so that Jimmy Carter will be recognized as the consequential and successful president that he was. I will always think of him as one of our most intelligent chief executives, who showed a fierce dedication to conflict prevention and individual human dignity, both during and after his term in office. He is a great man, and our country was lucky to have him as our leader.

—Madeleine Albright, former Secretary of State

PREFACE

I never expected to participate in Jimmy Carter's 1970 run for governor of Georgia. But I had contracted an incurable political bug at the University of North Carolina, participating in student government, writing articles on policy issues for the student newspaper, hearing President Kennedy challenge my generation to public service at a 1962 speech in Kenan Memorial Stadium, and in 1963, undergoing a transformative experience serving as a congressional intern in Washington in a university-sponsored program. During the summer of 1964 I worked on the political staff of Postmaster General John Gronouski, the first Polish American in a presidential cabinet. Under the direction of Robert L. Hardesty, I drafted speeches for President Johnson's election that were transliterated into phonetic Polish for him to wow his audiences with his nonexistent Polish skills. I did double duty working at the National Young Democrats of America. That earned me a trip to my first National Democratic Party Convention at Atlantic City, where my sole contribution was joining my fellow Young Democrats—at the instruction of Lyndon Johnson's chief of staff, Marvin Watson—in occupying the seats of the Mississippi Democratic Party and, he emphasized, not leaving even to go to the bathroom until the Rules Committee decided whether to seat the all-white or the racially mixed Mississippi delegation.

In the summer of my first year at Harvard Law School I made my first trip to Israel, to see my aging grandfather, Esor Eizenstat, who had emigrated ("made Aliyah") in 1952 from Atlanta. In the summer of 1966, I worked in the civil rights division of the Office of Education at the then Department of Health, Education, and Welfare, volunteering at night in Head Start's civil rights section. After graduating from Harvard Law School,

I followed Hardesty to Johnson's White House staff, drafting speeches for members of Congress—in English, this time—to support LBJ's legislative initiatives, working on presidential messages to Congress, and attending congressional relations meetings at the White House. When LBJ occasionally appeared, with his massive size and fierce visage, it was like the Lord himself entreating everyone on an important vote. When Johnson pulled out of the 1968 race, I became the research director of Hubert Humphrey's unsuccessful presidential campaign.

After his narrow loss, I returned home to Atlanta and made a beeline for the impressive law office of Carl Sanders, the prohibitive favorite for a new term as governor after sitting out for four years. He had been a successful, popular, moderate governor, with a formidable war chest and the backing of the press and the business and political establishment. He was handsome, well-tailored, and the epitome of what I expected from a senior partner at one of Atlanta's most prestigious firms. After he left office, Sanders had turned his service in the State House into considerable wealth, and I offered to help his campaign, pointing to my work in Washington and my roots in Atlanta. He was a progressive on racial issues, at least by Georgia standards, and an owner of the Atlanta Hawks NBA basketball team, which I thought might help because I had been an All-City and Honorable Mention All-American basketball player at Atlanta's Henry Grady High School (albeit with a large asterisk, playing in a segregated all-white league). Sanders seemed only mildly interested.

Shortly after that meeting, Henry Bauer, Jr., a high school friend, told me he was supporting someone he described in glowing terms as a bright, young, and very impressive former state senator from southwest Georgia, Jimmy Carter, who was taking Sanders on. I told Henry I had committed to Sanders, but he pestered me unmercifully, and so I met Carter at an office across from the federal courthouse, where I was serving as a law clerk to U.S. District Court Judge Newell Edenfield. What I saw was the polar opposite of Sanders and his sumptuously appointed law office: a small room with nothing but a folding table and lamp and two other pieces of furniture, one metal folding chair on which Carter sat, and a second for me. There were no suits, ties, or cuffs. Carter wore khaki pants and an open-collared tan shirt, with brown work boots. It did not take long to see what had drawn Henry to Carter.

He was slight in build and height, but he reminded me of JFK, with his handsome face, full head of sandy hair, and captivating smile. He told me he was running for governor and "did not intend to lose." What initially interested me, however, was that he was a politician from a tiny hamlet in southwest Georgia who nevertheless had a great understanding of the needs of Atlanta, even mass transit. He seemed to be a possible bridge from the historic hostility of rural Georgia, as he spoke forcefully about the environment and his progressive positions on education for all Georgia citizens, black and white. Still, his campaign was a long shot.

Within a few days, he asked to meet again. This time he told me directly that he needed my experience in shaping policies and wanted me to organize and lead a group to provide ideas for his campaign and as governor. I was sold. Sanders had no real interest in me; Carter did. I take no substantial credit for Carter's victory over Sanders in the all-important Democratic primary and finally in the general election. The group I assembled produced some useful policy papers on education, the environment, and reorganizing and streamlining Georgia's sprawling bureaucracy. I could hardly imagine that my modest contribution to the campaign would be only the start of more intense work on a national stage that put me at the right hand of the thirty-ninth president of the United States.

During the long presidential campaign I coordinated all of his domestic and foreign-policy positions, and between his nomination and inauguration I was the only staff person who attended CIA briefings with him. During the administration he called on me for advice on a variety of issues outside my field as domestic-policy adviser, including the Middle East peace process. And when he held his first national call-in program from the Oval Office with the television legend Walter Cronkite as moderator, he asked me to sit with him. He took a personal interest in my health, frequently expressing concern that I was working too hard, invited my son Jay to jog with him at Camp David, and Jay, Brian, and Fran to join him in attending the lighting of the first large Hanukkah menorah (supplied by the Chabad-Lubavitch movement) in Lafayette Park, across from the White House. I deeply admired his intellect, his commitment to the public good, and his political courage from the first day I met him in 1969, when he was running for governor, until his last hours in the White House, on January 20, 1981.

INTRODUCTION

E very four years a handful of talented men and women, mainly elected
public officials or business leaders, have the audacity, self-confidence,
and determination to put themselves and their families through
the hell of a presidential campaign in the belief that they are fit to make
decisions that affect the lives of hundreds of millions in the United States
and billions more people around the world. Their motives are as varied as
their personalities, but all are consumed with ambition to accomplish great
things. They see the presidency as the way to mark the world with their
deepest convictions.

It is conventional wisdom that Jimmy Carter was a weak and hapless president. But I believe that the single term served by the thirty-ninth president
of the United States was one of the most consequential in modern history.
Far from a failed presidency, he left behind concrete reforms and long-lasting
benefits to the people of the United States as well as the international order.
He has more than redeemed himself as an admired public figure by his post-
presidential role as a diplomatic mediator and election monitor, public health
defender, and human rights advocate. Now it is time to redeem his presidency
from the lingering memories of double-digit inflation and interest rates, of
gasoline lines, as well as the scars left by the national humiliation of American diplomats held hostage by Iranian revolutionaries for more than a year.

Let me be clear: I am not nominating Jimmy Carter for a place on Mount
Rushmore. He was not a great president, but he was a good and productive
one. He delivered results, many of which were realized only after he left office. He was a man of almost unyielding principle. Yet his greatest virtue
was at once his most serious fault for a president in an American democracy

of divided powers. The Founding Fathers built our government to advance incrementally through deliberation and compromise. But Carter took on intractable problems with comprehensive solutions while disregarding the political consequences. He could break before he would bend his principles or abandon his personal loyalties.

An extraordinarily gifted political campaigner, he nevertheless believed that politics stopped once he entered the Oval Office and that decisions should be made strictly on their merits. Carter reflected later that it was "a matter of pride with me not to let the political consequences be determinant in making a decision about an issue that was important to the country . . . because the political consequences are not just whether I am going to get some votes or not, but how much public support I will have for the things I'm trying to do. And I have to say that I was often mistaken about that."[1]

To be truly effective, a president cannot make a sharp break between the politics of his campaign and the politics of governing if he wants to nurture an effective national coalition. This Carter not only failed to achieve—he did not want to. Time and again he would say, "Leave the politics to me," while in fact he disdained politics. He believed that if he only did "the right thing" in his eyes, it would be self-evident to the public, which would reward him with reelection. However, politics cannot be parked at the Oval Office door, to be brought out only at election time, but must be kept running all the time by cultivating your political base and mobilizing the broader public, its elected representatives, and the interests they speak for, on behalf of clearly defined priorities. They can never be ignored in order to solve problems and to do good. The presidency is inherently a political job: The president is not only commander in chief but politician in chief.

Carter was so determined to confront intractable problems that he came away at times seeming like a public scold—a nanny telling her charges to eat their spinach, for example when he urged Americans to turn down their thermostats to reduce dependence on imported oil. When he summoned outside advisers to Camp David to help him right his ship of state, one young first-term governor from another Southern state advised him: "Mr. President, don't just preach sacrifice, but that it is an exciting time to be alive." The advice came from none other than William Jefferson Clinton, the new governor of Arkansas.[2] This was not a natural instinct for Carter, who focused

more on the obstacles to a better country and safer world than on the rewards that could be enjoyed.

Presidents who leave the White House under a cloud can emerge in the
clear with the perspective of history. Who today pays attention to contemporaneous charges that Harry Truman was corrupt and soft on Communism, leaving the White House with an approval rating hovering close to
a mere 20 percent, when we now appreciate that he helped construct an
international order that lasted for half a century?[3] The remarkable domestic
legacy of President Lyndon Johnson, on whose White House staff I served,
was totally overshadowed by Vietnam—until the fiftieth anniversaries of his
landmark bills led to new reflection about his presidency. Bill Clinton, in
whose administration I also served, paid a heavy price for a tawdry personal
affair. But his significant accomplishments and extraordinary political gifts
helped restore him to a position of affection. His immediate predecessor,
George H. W. Bush, was dismissed as a silver-spoon president who lost the
support of his own party by reversing his commitment never to raise taxes,
but it is now evident that he deftly managed the end of the Cold War and
avoided the triumphalist trap of chasing Saddam Hussein back into his lair
in Baghdad.

Nevertheless critics still disregard the breadth of Carter's accomplishments and accuse him of being an indecisive president. That is simply not
true; if anything, he was too bold and determined in attacking too many
challenges that other presidents had sidestepped or ignored, such as energy,
the Panama Canal, or the Middle East, while nevertheless achieving lasting results. He reflected that if he had concentrated on a "few major issues, it
would have given an image of accomplishment."[4] The art of presidential compromise rests on the ability to obtain at least half of what the administration
proposes to Congress and then to claim victory. President Carter was maladroit at this political sleight of hand largely because he was uncomfortable
with compromising what seemed to him so obviously the right course.

He was also unable to develop the close relationships necessary to persuade others who might not fully share his principles, despite having weekly
Democratic congressional leadership breakfasts without fail when he was in
town, and many with the Republican leadership. Yet because of his vision
and determination, he actually came away with much of what he wanted,

while obtaining it in a manner that made it appear he had caved to pressure and lost.

One reason his substantial victories are discounted is that he sought such broad and sweeping measures that what he gained in return often looked paltry. Winning was often ugly: He dissipated the political capital that presidents must constantly nourish and replenish for the next battle. He was too unbending while simultaneously tackling too many important issues without clear priorities, venturing where other presidents felt blocked because of the very same political considerations that he dismissed as unworthy of any president. As he told me, "Whenever I felt an issue was important to the country and needed to be addressed, my inclination was to go ahead and do it."[5]

In advancing what is admittedly a revisionist view of the Carter presidency, my perspective benefits not only from the passage of time but from my White House position as his domestic-policy director. I have admired him since I first worked as his policy adviser during his successful 1970 campaign for governor of my home state of Georgia, as well as in his presidential campaign, and I was proud to serve him as one of his closest presidential aides. I was at his side as he made the kinds of decisions that only presidents are called upon to make, where there are often no good options. I was only one of a handful of aides with direct phone lines to the president in my office and home. Every domestic and economic issue passed across my desk, as well as every major piece of legislation. In foreign policy I was kept informed of many decisions even when I was not directly involved. And I was significantly involved in the Middle East, particularly relations with Israel, as a back channel, and with American Jewry, stemming from the president's peace initiatives, as well as with the sanctions arising from the Iranian hostage crisis, and those against the Soviet Union after it invaded Afghanistan.

Inside the White House I was renowned—or, more accurately, the butt of jokes—for my yellow legal pads. There were more than one hundred of them, over five thousand pages, on which I took detailed, often verbatim notes of every meeting I attended and all my telephone conversations, not with the thought of writing a book but as a discipline to stay on top of the issues that it was my job to coordinate. The pads have been essential in writing this book. Over more than three decades, I also conducted more than

350 interviews of almost every major figure in the administration and many outside with a special perspective, including five with Carter himself, two with Rosalynn Carter, and several with Vice President Walter Mondale. I have also been granted access to now-declassified documents at the Carter Presidential Library, including my private memos as well as those of other key officials. These newly released documents also include the daily Evening Reports from Secretary of State Cyrus Vance and Weekly Reports from National Security Adviser Zbigniew Brzezinski.

This level of access, at once both wide and intimate, gives this book its authority. I knew from the outset that it could be taken seriously only if I also accepted the responsibility of telling an unflinchingly honest story of Carter and his administration. I have not shirked analyzing the failures and limitations of his presidency (including my own), secure in the knowledge that they are already better known than his lasting accomplishments. The risk is that skeptics may conclude this only confirms their impressions of Jimmy Carter. On the contrary, I count showing the negatives along with the positives as a sign of my credibility as both participant and author of a book that is part memoir and part an effort to set the historical record right.

But even with Carter's limitations, I refuse to let the mistakes overwhelm the achievements. We still benefit from his vision of the challenges faced by our country and the world; from his willingness to confront and deal directly with them regardless of the political cost; and finally from his essential integrity. He gained the presidency in a post-Vietnam and post-Watergate era of cynicism about government with a personal pledge that "I will never lie to you"—a promise that he worked hard to keep, and is now more important than ever in a new era of "fake news" and post-truth political rhetoric.

It is impossible to understand Carter's term in the Oval Office without appreciating the nature of the 1970s. It was an epic period of change in the American political landscape. The centrist political consensus of the postwar era was unraveling under the combined pressures of a ruinous decade of the Great Stagflation and military defeat in Vietnam—indelibly punctuated by the ignominious image of an American helicopter abandoning the U.S. Embassy with the fall of Saigon in 1975, as desperate South Vietnamese

struggled to board their last lifeline to escape the victorious North Vietnamese troops. Jimmy Carter told me there was a personal element: He saw
his son Jack, who volunteered to serve in Vietnam, come home on leave, "and
was not honored or welcomed, but derided."[6]

At home, social norms were in flux with the rise of the consumer and
environmental movements, women's rights, gay rights, abortion rights, and
affirmative action for black Americans. This led to a counterrevolution of
Nixon's "silent majority" and the rise of the Christian evangelical movement
as a potent political force, which Ronald Reagan skillfully made a key part
of his winning political coalition, and which remains ascendant today.

Abroad, the Cold War was raging, with aggressive Soviet expansionism,
especially in Africa, through Cuban proxies; support for Western European
Communist parties; along with a crackdown on the stirrings of change by
Soviet democratic dissidents and Jewish refuseniks, and a significant military buildup. American intercontinental missiles were challenged by Soviet
technological advances in long-range rocketry; the Soviet Navy was approaching superiority as the number of new American ships declined; and the Red
Army's buildup of conventional ground forces in Europe put NATO at a
disadvantage.

At the same time, a Polish-born pope came into the Vatican, offering hope
to the oppressed peoples in the Communist bloc, as did Jimmy Carter's
human rights campaign. A new great power was rising in China under a
new reformist leader, Deng Xiaoping, who was determined to take the first
halting steps to integrate his country into the world economy. Latin America was largely controlled by military autocracies, but democratic movements
were arising, and Carter helped catalyze them. And the first Islamic republic was created in Iran after the fall of America's decades-long ally, the shah
of Iran, leading to a debilitating hostage crisis and ushering in a new era
of Islamic radicalism and state-sponsored terrorism, with which we struggle
today.

Carter was attacked from the right within his own fractured Democratic
Party by a group of former New Deal liberal defense hawks, who were called
neoconservatives. More debilitating, he was attacked from the Democratic
left for being too conservative on domestic and economic issues. He had
won the Democratic nomination through an outsider's nonideological

appeal to restore trust and confidence in the presidency rather than a promise of the second coming of the New Deal and Great Society. A traditional liberal Democrat could not have been elected in 1976, and in the White House he tried to drag the Democratic Party into a new political reality although he never felt comfortable with his party and regarded it as an "albatross." Flinty in his personal habits ("tight as a tick," Jody Powell joked), and believing, as he flatly told Democratic congressional leaders, that "the Achilles heel of the Democratic Party was fiscal irresponsibility,"[7] he opposed a wave of new spending in an era of high inflation—not what the liberal and labor wing of the party expected after eight lean Republican years.

These ideological and political upheavals not only hindered the substantial accomplishments of the Carter administration, but overshadowed them in the perspective of history. In the diplomatic field, I discuss his success in permanently placing human rights on the domestic and international agendas, by which future presidents are still measured; his influence on the decline of the Soviet Union and the rise of China; establishing a new, positive relationship with Latin America; and his crown jewel, giving birth to the first peace between Israel and one of its Arab neighbors, Egypt. He blunted Soviet interests in the Middle East and Persian Gulf and strengthened U.S. relations with moderate Arab nations.

At home Carter laid the foundation for this century's revival of the domestic energy industry by deregulating crude oil and natural gas prices, championing bills that placed alternative energy and conservation firmly on the nation's agenda, profoundly reformed electricity generation for the benefit of consumers, and laid the foundation—with three major energy bills—for our growing independence from foreign oil producers. One of his most satisfying accomplishments was setting aside huge tracts of public lands for national parks, doubling the size of our National Park System for public enjoyment.

He made government and private corporations more transparent and accountable after Watergate, through the Foreign Corrupt Practices Act. Carter transformed the American transportation industry through deregulation, and he began to loosen federal constraints on the communications and financial industries. He helped save both Chrysler and New York City from bankruptcy through federal loan guarantees, but only after being the first president to demand new management, major labor concessions, and formal oversight before putting federal money at risk. And finally, fully aware that he was putting his own reelection at great risk, Carter set in motion the successful battle against the ruinous inflation of the 1970s, which increased to double-digit levels on his watch, by appointing Paul Volcker chairman of the Federal Reserve and giving him free rein.

Even this abbreviated list of accomplishments far outpaces those of other one-term presidents, and not just Warren G. Harding, Calvin Coolidge, or Herbert Hoover, but the underestimated George H. W. Bush and even my first political hero, John F. Kennedy. Indeed, I believe that they equal or exceed some two-term presidents—Bill Clinton, whom I served for eight years and regard as an outstanding president, and Barack Obama, in whose administration I held an advisory position dealing with Holocaust-related issues, and whose place in history remains to be determined. And while there is also no question that Ronald Reagan decisively changed the ideological debate and political direction of the country, many of the measures put in place by Carter only matured during the early years of the Reagan administration—controlling inflation, increasing military spending, arming the mujahedeen to fight the Soviets in Afghanistan, negotiating a nuclear arms reduction agreement, catalyzing the democratic movement in Latin America, and laying the foundations for Ronald Reagan's signature policies of decreasing government regulation.

Public recognition of Carter's legacy of accomplishments has been obscured by inexperience in the critical early stage of the administration; iconoclastic, idiosyncratic decision making; double-digit inflation and interest rates; internal Democratic Party strife; and the Iran hostage crisis. But, like the successes of Truman, Clinton, and the senior Bush, Carter's achievements shine brighter over time, few more than his unique determination to put human rights at the forefront of his foreign policy from the start of his presidency.

At the time, this shift from the realpolitik of Richard Nixon and Henry Kissinger was derided by some as utopian, and indeed some events demanded responses that did take precedence over human rights. But when backed by actions like cutting military aid to Latin American dictatorships such as Chile and Argentina, his human rights policies helped convert most of our Latin American neighbors from authoritarian rule to democracy. The administration's public advocacy of human rights also weakened the Soviet empire by attacking its soft underbelly—its domestic repression. No less than Anatoly Dobrynin, the longtime Soviet ambassador to Washington, conceded that Carter's human rights policies "played a significant role in the . . . long and difficult process of liberalization inside the Soviet Union and the nations of Eastern Europe. This in turn caused the fundamental changes in all these countries and helped end the Cold War."[8] First enshrined during the Ford administration—even as he soft-pedaled them—in the Helsinki Final Act in 1975, human rights have been established as an essential element of American and international diplomacy. Although several later presidents have given less emphasis to human rights, because of Carter they were not free to ignore them totally, without risking public criticism.

As an Annapolis-trained submarine officer, Carter was no pacifist but was nevertheless very cautious—perhaps excessively so—about deploying American military power until the Soviet invasion of Afghanistan. No American soldiers were killed in combat on his watch. He signed the second and most ambitious Strategic Arms Limitation Treaty (SALT II) with the Soviet Union, which served as the basis for future arms limitation agreements. At the same time he did not hesitate to support cutting-edge weapons technology.

Despite his campaign promise to cut defense spending, he in fact increased it by an annual average of almost 3 percent in real terms, and proposed further increases after the Soviet invasion of Afghanistan. Major new weapons systems such as the MX missile and the Stealth bomber were green-lighted, thus providing the foundation upon which Ronald Reagan built the strong U.S. defense posture that his supporters claim as the principal cause of the Soviet Union's collapse. But it was Carter, not Reagan, who reversed the post-Vietnam decline in military spending and began upgrading America's defenses. "The Reagan revolution in defense spending began during the later years of the Carter Administration," concludes the Pentagon's authorized history of the tenure of Carter's Defense secretary Harold Brown.[9]

Despite allied resistance, Carter persuaded European governments to begin deploying middle-range nuclear weapons in Europe to counter the Soviets' new mobile missiles. Mikhail Gorbachev, the last Soviet leader, later called this allied response a significant factor in convincing him that his predecessors' policies of military threats to the West should be replaced by disarmament and accommodation.[10]

Though Carter was ambivalent about Soviet intentions during a signficant part of his administration, torn between the hard-line Brzezinski and the dovish Vance, the Soviet invasion of Afghanistan dispelled any remaining doubts. He acted firmly with tough sanctions and armed the Afghan mujahedeen in a war that lasted nine years and bled Soviet resources. After the Soviet invasion he promulgated the Carter Doctrine in his January 1980 State of the Union Address, declaring that an attempt by an outside force like the Soviet Union to gain control of the Persian Gulf region "would be regarded as an assault on the vital interests of the United States of America, and such an assault will be repelled by any means necessary, including military force."[11] This permanently expanded the U.S. naval presence in the Gulf and the Indian Ocean, and created the Rapid Deployment Joint Task Force, which became the U.S. military's Central Command three years later.

In another bold step, taken over ferocious and emotional opposition from conservatives, his administration negotiated a treaty with Panama that yielded American sovereignty over the canal, avoiding an almost certain guerrilla war by Panama against this vital sea link, while fully protecting America's priority use of the vital seaway. It led to a giant step in elevating U.S. relations with Latin America. And while Nixon and Kissinger deserve great credit for their dramatic outreach to the People's Republic of China, they could go no further because of fierce opposition from the Taiwan lobby, a major force in the Republican Party. It fell to Carter to take the lasting step of normalizing diplomatic relations with the most populous nation in the world as it grew into a power that could not be ignored.

If ever there was an area in which Carter's strengths as well as his limitations were evident, it was the Middle East. He increased arms sales to solidify our alliances with moderate Arab states against the Soviet Union, despite angry objections from Israel and vehement opposition by the American Jewish leadership. At the same time he was a Middle East peacemaker par excellence, building on Egyptian president Anwar el-Sadat's historic trip to

Jerusalem. Carter stepped in to break the impasse in negotiations between Israel and Egypt by summoning both sides to his retreat at Camp David in Maryland's Catoctin Mountains, near Washington. This was a courageous, almost reckless gamble of his presidential influence, against the virtually unanimous opposition of his own advisers. But the accord negotiated over thirteen cliff-hanging days in 1978 represented one of the greatest feats of personal presidential diplomacy in American history. He then took the risky step of going to the region in a last-ditch attempt to salvage the peace effort and convert the Camp David Accords into a binding treaty that removed Israel's strongest Arab neighbor from the battlefield after five wars and has remained the foundation of American foreign policy in the Middle East for almost forty years.

Carter's accomplishments in domestic policy have also stood the test of time, despite his distant attitude toward Congress. Yet by the reckoning of the respected CQ Almanac and the Miller Center of Public Affairs at the University of Virginia, the Carter administration's success rate in passing major legislation is one of the highest of any modern president beginning with Dwight Eisenhower, and by one estimate, with a success rate of over 70 percent, not far below that of his most immediate Democratic predecessor, Lyndon Johnson, the storied master of Congress.[12] Senate Majority Leader Robert C. Byrd, who had seen many presidents in action, concluded that too many commentators slight his legislative accomplishments, when in fact, with an "extensive and ambitious" legislative agenda, "he won more often than he lost," and "could be justly proud of his legislative accomplishments. History will be more kind to Mr. Carter than were his contemporaries."[13]

The measures most directly affecting ordinary Americans brought lower air fares and cheaper goods to homes and businesses by deregulating the airline, trucking, and railroad industries, and beginning the restructuring of the communications and banking industries. Carter revolutionized America's energy future before other political leaders saw the dangers of America's growing dependence on Middle East oil. He persuaded Congress to pass three major energy bills in four years, which set the United States on a new, revolutionary course of conservation, alternative energy sources, and greater production of traditional American fossil fuel resources. The ending of federal price controls, together with the creation of a Department of Energy, soon allowed the United States to reclaim its position as one of the world's leading producers of natural gas and crude oil.

Carter was also the greatest environmental president since Teddy Roosevelt, and none since have come close to his accomplishments. He set more land aside for national parks than had all his predecessors combined, overriding persistent demands by the Republicans and oil companies to open huge swaths of Alaskan land to oil drilling. Over the strenuous objections of the automobile industry, he issued far-reaching fuel efficiency standards, forcing America's automakers to produce cars that could compete with Japan's.

The man who made the improbable journey from Plains, Georgia, to the Oval Office by running against Watergate and the Washington status quo put in place major reforms that survive to make government more accountable. Independent inspectors general were installed in every department of the executive branch. In the most important reform of the federal civil service since its founding, Carter established the Senior Executive Service, a more highly paid and flexible career track to attract and retain top-quality candidates into public service based upon merit, which it does to this day. It also shielded civil servants from partisan political pressures, and was invoked to protect government employees from a 2016 Trump transition team request for the names of those engaged in climate change work under President Obama.[14] Walter Schaub, Jr., the nonpartisan head of the Office of Government Ethics, created by Carter's 1978 Ethics in Government Act, resigned over what he saw as the Trump administration's repeated flouting of laws and standards.[15]

He tightened disclosure rules for incoming federal officials (setting a standard that eventually led to the resignation of his most valuable adviser and confidant, Bert Lance); passed an ethics bill with a hair-trigger special prosecutor for serving senior officials (which unfairly caught up his chief of staff, Hamilton Jordan); with congressional support instituted a unique bipartisan system for selecting his nominees for federal judgeships on the basis of legal competence; imposed strict gift rules for senior officials in office; and restricted the "revolving door" that allowed outgoing top officials to lobby their former departments. By signing the Foreign Corrupt Practices Act in his first year in office, Carter fulfilled his campaign pledge to abolish bribery and similar crookedness by American multinational corporations to obtain foreign contracts. In any given year, major cases are brought against American companies trying to evade the law. Carter also signed a tough law to prevent American corporations from joining the Arab boycott of Israel, which I helped negotiate with business groups and Jewish organizations on his behalf. We then issued stringent regulations to ensure the law was strictly enforced.

Carter also created the modern vice presidency by giving authority and access to Walter Mondale, in historic contrast to his predecessors' often humiliating and even crippling exclusion from secret information and the presidential decision-making process. He moved the vice president's office from the Executive Office Building to the West Wing of the White House and granted Mondale full access to the paper flow, including intelligence analyses and other classified documents. With variations to suit each personal relationship, this pattern has held ever since. And Jimmy and Rosalynn Carter elevated the position of first lady to greater importance than it occupied since the days of Eleanor Roosevelt, setting a path for Hillary Clinton and other first ladies.

More broadly, Carter was the first "New Democrat"—more conservative on spending than the traditional base, a social and civil rights progressive, and an engaged liberal internationalist seeking diplomatic rather than purely military solutions. In the end he was too conservative for the liberals and too liberal for the conservatives. He departed from Franklin Roosevelt's New Deal without abandoning it, and supported Johnson's Great Society without expanding it, thus creating a new framework for the Democratic Party. This was a difficult political balancing act he could not always master in the White House, although he campaigned brilliantly as a Southerner reaching out to the northern white working class. Carter constantly had to tack between the domestic spending demands of his party's congressional leadership and its liberal wing, and his own and his Southern supporters' inherent fiscal conservatism—a reflection of their historic rejection of federal power.

It would be left to Bill Clinton, another Southerner and a natural politician with an extraordinary grasp of policy, to deploy his rhetorical mastery in articulating and holding a centrist path for the party, better than the man who had begun to map the way under the worst possible economic circumstances—Jimmy Carter the engineer, businessman, and stern moralist.

Notwithstanding Carter's mishandling of the political challenge posed by the activities of his closest friend, Bert Lance, as a small-town banker before he joined the government, Jimmy Carter ran an honest administration. He did not resort to the illegal activities of the Nixon administration, he reined in their CIA excesses, and he did not yield to the temptation of secretly selling arms to Iran to free American hostages in the manner of the Reagan administration's convoluted deal.

Like his idol, Harry Truman, whose favorite slogan, "The Buck Stops Here," he kept on his Oval Office desk, Carter left the White House a widely unpopular president. But Truman now is recognized more for his achievements than his faults, and I hope this book will contribute to a similar reassessment of Jimmy Carter's term in the White House. His administration was consequential, and America became a better and more secure country because of it. As his vice president, Walter Mondale, put it, in words now exhibited in the Carter Presidential Library: "We told the truth, we obeyed the law, we kept the peace."[16]

PART I

INTO THE
WHITE HOUSE

1

THE 1976 CAMPAIGN

James Earl Carter, Jr., was born on October 1, 1924, in Plains, Georgia, a town of some 550 people in the deeply segregated South, and was raised there and in the nearby village of Archery, where he spent part of his childhood. Few had indoor plumbing or electricity, and mule-drawn wagons were more common than automobiles. Whites were a distinct minority, only about one-third of the residents, and young Jimmy played baseball with black children and worked with them in the fields. But his was no log cabin upbringing. His family occupied the top rung in a hierarchical society. James Earl Carter, Sr., owned 350 acres of his own land, raised peanuts, and sold them through his own warehouse. Even during the Great Depression, the father of the future president prospered. By the late 1930s he employed more than two hundred workers, and five black sharecropper families lived on his farm. As in many Southern homes of the era, the maids and cooks were black and cared for the children, including Jimmy and his siblings, and his playmates were often the children of his family's black workers.[1]

As a boy, Jimmy developed an early love of the outdoors, playing hide-and-seek in the woods, fishing, and hiking.[2] He also enjoyed listening to baseball games on the family's battery-powered radio, and absorbing discussions of politics, which ran in the family. His maternal grandfather went into politics simply because he enjoyed it, and his father served in the Georgia legislature because he wanted to protect the rural electrification system established under Franklin Roosevelt's New Deal. As he recalled decades later, the arrival of electricity "had as much of an impact on me as any single event. When people ask me what is the most notable event of your life, I have a hard time not saying the day I married Rosalynn or my appointment to

Annapolis; but very few days in my life were more important than the day they turned the lights on in our home, and I saw the federal government giving me a better life."[3]

As a young boy he wanted most to please his father, a stern taskmaster, by helping around the farm. While James senior held traditional Southern segregationist views on race, his wife, "Miss Lillian," was a registered nurse who insisted on equal treatment for black and white people, and spent a great deal of time helping deliver babies and caring for poor, sick people of both races in their homes across the county, often paid in chickens or vegetables.[4] Jimmy saw his mother resist strong pressure to conform to racial norms and never forgot her example. As he said, "She never apologized for it, and I never knew anyone else when I was growing up who had that willingness to circumvent the segregated racial society. She was my inspiration to look beyond what was then the separate but so-called equal society to a more moral environment."[5] At the age of sixty-eight the indomitable Lillian Carter enrolled in the Peace Corps and served in a community hospital in India on the outskirts of Mumbai (then Bombay). She was a captivating personality who came into my life during the early stages of the Carter presidential campaign. Her hair had turned totally white, and her skin was wrinkled, but her youthful enthusiasm and translucent smile seemed to emanate from the inside. I found her sparkling, warm, and loving, always with a hug and good word for me, my wife, Fran, and my boys, Jay and Brian.

There was good reason for Carter to win a disproportionate number of black votes against far more liberal opponents in Democratic primaries on the road to the White House: He understood black Americans as individuals, while they viewed blacks as a group. Still, as Georgia and the other Southern states required, he attended the all-white Plains High School while there was no high school at all for black children. He explained it to me in searing, highly personal terms: "I grew up with blacks. I got to know them, and I could see the ravages in their lives of a second-class existence," especially when contrasted with his own. His father was determined that he finish high school and go on to college, a rarity even for a privileged white boy during the Depression, especially for one who was the first in his family even to graduate from high school. He began a lifelong, ceaseless commitment to educational self-improvement, making all As in school, while playing basketball and joining the book club.[6]

From the time he was five years old, his ambition was to attend the U.S. Naval Academy, which he eventually reached only by a circuitous route. Through his father's political connections, Jimmy won an appointment through the local congressman but first had to wait a year because the slot had been promised to another candidate. So he studied engineering at Georgia Southwestern Junior College, and when the Navy asked for additional engineering courses, he made the honor roll at Georgia Tech and studied nuclear physics at Union College in Schenectady, New York.[7] His determination to qualify for the Naval Academy went beyond extra study; concerned that his flat feet and skinny frame would disqualify him, he rolled his feet over Coca-Cola bottles to strengthen his arches and went on a banana diet to bulk up.[8]

Carter's four years at Annapolis opened a world far wider than the rural hamlet where he was raised. As he told me, "When I went to the Naval Academy I was a different person from what I am now. I was smart. I never had any problem with studies, but I spent a lot of my time reading great literature and philosophical books, and sailing and flying airplanes, and I studied classical music. I could name almost every piano concerto that had ever been written, and I could listen to a record and I could tell which artist was playing. I stood fifty-sixth in a class of eight hundred." A squib in his academy yearbook read, "Jimmy Carter never opened a book, unless it was to help one of his classmates study." While Carter dismissed this backhanded compliment as untrue, he did tell me that the "point is that I was learning more than just how to tie knots and how to run a steam turbine, and how to navigate a ship."[9]

He also befriended and defended the only black midshipman, Wesley A. Brown, the sixth black man in the academy's history and the first to graduate, his predecessors having been hounded out during their first year by racial harassment. White midshipmen refused to sit next to him, he was barred from joining the choir, and so many racial epithets were thrown at him by his classmates that he considered quitting every day he was there. What led him to stick it out was the support of a small handful of midshipmen who intervened. Carter, then an upperclassman, visited Brown in his dorm to encourage him to hang on and hang tough against seniors who gave him demerits with the aim of forcing his discharge. "If not for that, I'm not sure I would have made it," said Brown. The two were runners on the cross-country team, and in a speech Carter made at a Naval Academy event in 2011, he described his encounters with Brown as "my first personal experience with total integration." That was in 1945, three years before President Truman desegregated America's armed forces.[10] Carter recalled to me that Brown, who retired eventually as a lieutenant commander, "was a better runner than I was, and so I defended him to anyone. It didn't seem like any courageous thing, but when he wrote his biography, he pointed out that I was the midshipman who came and helped him."[11]

RICKOVER'S PROTÉGÉ

After graduating, the young naval officer married his local sweetheart, Rosalynn Smith, in 1946, and together they escaped the confining environment of rural southwest Georgia in a career that took him and his young wife to assignments in Norfolk, Pearl Harbor, submarine training in Groton, San Diego, and Washington, D.C. Great opportunity knocked in 1952, when he applied to join the new nuclear navy headed by then captain (later admiral) Hyman Rickover, who became another formative force in his life. During his initial interview he proudly told Rickover that he had finished in the top 10 percent of his Naval Academy class. Unimpressed, Rickover asked: "Did you always do your best?" The young officer stammered and admitted he had not. "Why not?" Rickover asked, turning his back and ending the interview. Carter continued sitting on an uncomfortable chair that Rickover had prepared with the front legs two inches shorter than the back ones, and then stumbled out of the room, certain he had washed out. Rickover brought him on board, however, and Carter always assumed it was because of his honesty. This seminal event was memorialized in the title of his presidential-campaign book, *Why Not the Best?*

Working in the nuclear navy was itself transformative, recalling that Rickover "drove all of us to levels of effort that we had never before contemplated, and he set an example for us, and he did as much or more than we did."[12] Carter remembered taking off for an eleven-hour flight to Seattle with Rickover aboard an old Constellation prop airplane, and working as hard as he could but nevertheless dozing off. When they landed, Rickover was still working. Carter said: "He was obsessed with his work, very demanding, and I responded well to it, although he never said a congratulatory word to me until after I was governor. He would find something wrong, if possible, with which to condemn me publicly in front of my men, or if he couldn't find anything wrong, he wouldn't say anything. . . . I still think he was the greatest engineer who ever lived, because he made sure that things were designed right, built right, worked right, and operated safely."[13] In a nuclear submarine there was no room for error, and I believe that Carter's own relatively reclusive lifestyle was shaped by his time in the Silent Service. It was normal to stay submerged for thirty days or longer in the notoriously tight quarters of a nuclear submarine.

But his most harrowing experience as a submarine officer came during a storm, as he stood watch on the bridge after midnight, when a huge wave washed him overboard into the Pacific. He managed to swim back to the sub, grab onto its five-inch gun and clamber back on board. If the boat had been traveling just a few degrees at an angle to the waves instead of directly into them, he would have been lost at sea. The storm damaged the radio antenna, so the captain was unable to check in at the usual eight-hour interval, and for the three days it took to reach an island base, the USS *Pomfret* was listed as lost, and next of kin were notified. Fortunately for Rosalynn, she was in Georgia at the time and never got the news.[14] While he never used this incident in his political campaigns, it showed him the fragility of life.

Rickover was unsmiling and always parsimonious in praising his officers, a trait his most famous acolyte shared in dealing with us on his staff. There was a lot of Hyman Rickover in Jimmy Carter. They were both slight in stature, and they both made it to the top the hard way. Rickover was born Chaim Godalia Rickover, into a Jewish family in Russian-controlled Poland, not exactly the normal background for a rise to rear admiral in the U.S. Navy, while Carter through intelligence and diligence vaulted from a town of five hundred people in rural Georgia. Both men had a fierce commitment to public service and to principle, as well as personal austerity and an abhorrence of waste, especially of public money. When Rickover's office was moved from the old Navy Building to nearby Crystal City, the navy wanted to build a wall to block the view from nearby high-rises to protect the classified papers on his desk; Rickover said he would simply close the blinds. He also patched the decrepit linoleum instead of replacing it, and when he brought in projects under budget, he enjoyed testifying before Congress that he was returning the unused funds to the Treasury.[15]

Both Carter and his mentor had a ferocious certitude about their goals and plowed through individuals and other obstacles to achieve them. To Rickover's consternation (as he expressed during some of his visits to my office), he felt his protégé did not always demand the highest level of performance from some of his closest staff and maintained almost a family relationship with some of them, disregarding the foibles Rickover would never have tolerated in his subordinates.

HIS FATHER'S SON

After six years of service he earned a prize post as the senior officer on the nuclear submarine USS *Seawolf*, and his career path to senior ranks in the navy seemed assured.[16] Then came an unexpected turning point in his life, without which he would never have been a resident of the White House: His father contracted cancer—a disease that ran in his family but did not strike him until his ninetieth year. Lieutenant (j.g.) Carter decided to leave a career he loved and return to Plains to take over his father's peanut warehouse. This provoked one of the few significant personal disagreements in his long, loving, successful marriage to Rosalynn. After traveling the world with Jimmy in the navy, the last thing she wanted was to return to the narrow life of a small, mosquito-ridden Southern town.[17] He bluntly admitted he made the decision without her approval, "in fact with very strong disapproval!"[18] "She almost quit on me," he later said.[19] It was one of the few times he acted without her input,[20] and she barely spoke to him on the long trip from Hawaii back to Plains.[21]

Carter idolized his father, who was a model town squire as well as the town's principal employer. As he sat by the bedside of his dying father, he was struck by the stream of blacks and whites who came by to thank him for his private acts of generosity.[22] More than anything else Jimmy Carter wanted to live up to his namesake and follow in his footsteps. After his father's death in 1953, while serving his first term in the Georgia legislature, the seat was offered to his mother, who refused. Jimmy discovered only after his father's death that—although a successful businessman—the senior Carter had extended so many loans to his workers and townspeople to tide them over hard times that when his remaining assets were divided among his children, there was little left for Jimmy and Rosalynn. They lived for a year in government-subsidized public housing.[23] Another serious family problem was Jimmy's younger brother, Billy Carter, who felt he should have taken over the business. Billy's resentment would come back to bite his older brother when he became president.

A more serious obstacle immediately facing Carter as he tried to salvage the family business was the pervasive issue of race. About fifteen of his father's former customers, who were members of the local White Citizens Council, paid him a visit and told him he was the only white man in Plains who had not joined their virulently antiblack organization. He refused, and they even offered to pay his five-dollar membership fee. "I told them I would take the five-dollar bill and flush it down the toilet," he recalled, whereupon they threatened to boycott his business and pressure his suppliers as well. That included the owner of the local gas station, who refused to fill the tank on his pickup truck, so Carter installed his own gas pump at the warehouse. His customers gradually started returning, and the business thrived because of his good service.

Almost immediately he plunged into politics as chairman of the Sumter County Board of Education in 1955, in his own words, "almost exclusively to protect the public school system" from being closed down to evade the historic 1954 Supreme Court decision, *Brown v. Board of Education*, ordering the racial integration of the nation's public schools. This began a life-long passion to improve public education for blacks as well as whites; he was shocked to discover books in the separate but supposedly equal black schools that had been discarded a decade earlier by the white school system. Black children walked to school while school buses whizzed by them carrying white pupils, and sixteen-year-old black students had to sit on "little tiny chairs for three-year-olds." He said, "I was not only angry but embarrassed, and I felt from that moment on a responsibility, and I believed that my concern was so genuine that there was no subterfuge. And I think that black people, even though they were suspect at first, soon realized that I was genuine, and I felt at home with them, and I didn't feel like I was an alien when I was in a black church, whereas I didn't feel at home speaking to the AFL-CIO annual conventions."[24]

In 1962 he ran for state senate, in part to get support for establishing a four-year college in impoverished southwest Georgia, where one million people had access only to a community college and vocational schools. Carter lost by sixty votes, but his senate race was corrupted by ballot stuffing organized by the Quitman County political boss, Joe Hurst, who wanted Jimmy's opponent to win. He and his crowd watched as voters put their paper ballots into an Old Crow liquor box. Carter was determined to muster the evidence to challenge the results, despite a visitor's frightening warning to Rosalynn at the warehouse that the last time anyone had crossed Joe Hurst, his business had burned down.[25] The loss was overturned through the efforts of an Atlanta lawyer, Charles Kirbo, who found out through a drunken local ne'er-do-well that 123 blank ballots had been taken home by a supporter of Carter's opponent and filled in. That was the giveaway: The ballots added up to more than the number of registered voters. Thus began Carter's political rise, sealing Kirbo's relationship with him for life and demonstrating that his client was a dogged fighter.

Mr. Kirbo, as we called him, was a legend among those around Carter. A partner in Atlanta's leading law firm of King & Spalding, he was tall, balding, conservative, and spoke as slowly as molasses in January—as the local expression went—but tersely, colloquially, and as elliptically as the Greek oracle at Delphi; you had to strain to hear him and grasp his meaning.

After Carter was elected president he asked Kirbo several times to move to Washington. The Atlanta lawyer flew to the capital about twice a month to discuss problems and perform occasional missions. But his wife did not want to move, and he later regretted staying in Atlanta because he felt he could have accomplished much and enjoyed government.[26] When Bert Lance was forced to resign as budget director, the absence of a senior eminence and a resident wise man like Kirbo, whose conservatism and Southern ties could have balanced Vice President Walter Mondale's liberalism—and to a degree mine—was a grievous loss.

As president, Carter once assigned him to study the growth of government pension programs, and after a year, Kirbo reported: "We've talked about it and reviewed it with statisticians, and I think the best thing is just sit on it." Incredulous, the president said, "What!?" Kirbo repeated, "Let it sit." That was the end of it. Carter so trusted Kirbo's judgment that he would never have accepted such unadorned advice from anyone else.[27]

After running unopposed for a second term as state senator in 1964, the only reelection in his political career, Carter announced his intention to seek an open congressional seat for the 1966 election, for which he would have been the front-runner. But fate intervened when former governor Ernest Vandiver, the favorite in the gubernatorial race, had a heart attack. To the dismay of his supporters—especially Rosalynn, who was looking forward to escaping from Plains and moving to Washington—he suddenly decided to announce for governor. Carter faced two major candidates: a liberal former governor, Ellis Arnall, and an archsegregationist, Lester Maddox, famous in Georgia for wielding an ax handle to prevent blacks from eating in his restaurant after the 1964 Civil Rights Act barred discrimination in public facilities. Not for the last time did Carter take the most difficult road. Given his late entry, he ran a slapdash campaign, but another problem put him at great disadvantage.

In the midst of this 1966 gubernatorial race, his solidarity with blacks led to a shift in his own church affiliation at the Plains Baptist Church, where his parents had prayed and he was a deacon. When local blacks asked to join, Carter was the only one of twelve deacons who voted to admit them. When the whole church voted, Carter remembered that some of the white members argued that blacks were inferior, as descendants of Ham. Carter and his family cast the only votes to admit blacks, along with one man who was thought to be hard of hearing. The family left the church that had been so much a part of their lives and joined the nearby Maranatha Baptist Church, which was willing to integrate. To this day they remain members, and Carter teaches Sunday school classes, now overflowing with visitors, including myself on one occasion.[28]

These were the choices of a principled antipolitician, almost ending his political career before it began. Carter ran an indefatigable campaign, attacking Arnall as too liberal while aggressively seeking the black vote and courting black ministers.[29] He finished a strong third to Arnall and Maddox, getting just under 21 percent of the vote to Maddox's 23.5 percent and Arnall's 29 percent, but he returned to Plains depressed at having turned down a safe congressional seat to gamble and lose a bid for the governorship, while also losing twenty-two pounds and taking on $66,000 in debt.

THE GEORGIA MAFIA

This sobering experience taught Carter never to enter another race without careful advance planning. He also met several supporters who would become the core of his presidential campaign. Foremost among them was Hamilton Jordan, his youth coordinator, later the brilliant strategist for his insurgent presidential campaign and his top White House aide. Robert Lipshutz, a lawyer and prominent member of Atlanta's Jewish community, would become a leading fund-raiser in his presidential campaign, and then White House counsel. On a campaign swing that coincided with a regional planning commission meeting, he met Bert Lance, who would become his highway commissioner when he finally was elected governor, follow him to Washington as his budget director, and ultimately become a huge political problem. Frank Moore, who headed the Northwest Georgia Planning Commission, succeeded Ham as executive secretary, and became White House congressional liaison.

One other benefit flowed from the political loss: The campaign hired Gerald Rafshoon, a young, New York–born, irrepressible Atlanta advertising executive, to oversee media. Rafshoon—we all called him that, perhaps because he was so irreverent—would eventually take a similar role in the White House. Jody Powell, whose father was a peanut farmer in Vienna, near Plains, became Carter's driver, personal assistant, and de facto press secretary, the position he would formally hold in the White House. This became the heart of Carter's "Georgia Mafia," as the press would dub them.

There was also a spiritual dimension to Carter's depressing loss. His sister Ruth Carter Stapleton, a charismatic evangelical faith healer with a degree in religion, told her brother that one way to deal with his painful loss was to recommit himself to Jesus Christ. This led him to his born-again faith, a process that as a Jew I could never understand but respected, and that became an essential part of his personal and political life. He put his reinvigorated faith into action, going door-to-door in lower-income neighborhoods in Pennsylvania and Massachusetts to ask voters to accept Christ in their lives and offer them Bibles.

He spent a good part of the next four years preparing for his successful 1970 gubernatorial campaign. He was an indefatigable campaigner, hitting factory shifts early in the morning, knocking on doors, going into shops in the smallest towns around the state. Charles Kirbo recalled that "Rosalynn would pack a lunch, Jimmy would drive to some town, stop in the woods to eat, then go to a local rally and make a folksy speech using the same joke he had told at another site a while before."[30]

But it took more than burning shoe-leather to beat Carl Sanders, the popular former governor. Carter and his team knew that—while still holding on to a substantial percentage of the black vote—they needed to win the white working-class, rural, small-town, conservative, and segregationist vote Lester Maddox had captured in beating Carter in 1966. So they focused their attacks on the wealth that Sanders had accumulated after his term as governor, becoming the senior partner at a prestigious Atlanta law firm, and owning a share of the Atlanta Hawks professional basketball team. They called him "Cuff-Link Carl," and said he was supported by the big money in Atlanta, while portraying Carter as the hardworking peanut farmer from Plains. One particularly scurrilous TV spot showed Sanders celebrating a Hawks victory in the locker room surrounded by his team's black players. I was disturbed enough to ask Rafshoon about it, but he simply shrugged and insisted Carter had never reviewed it. Carter also opposed mandatory school busing and, even more disturbing, promised to invite Alabama's segregationist governor, George Wallace, to speak in Georgia.

This populist, antiestablishment campaign was a model for his presidential campaign. The appeal to conservative whites was mirrored by Carter's 1976 comment about maintaining the "ethnic purity" of working-class white neighborhoods in the northern industrial states. The 1970 campaign against Sanders reflected another aspect of Jimmy Carter, repeated in his biting attacks against Gerald Ford in 1976 and Ronald Reagan in 1980: He was a brass-knuckled, no-holds-barred campaigner for office. But after winning, he abjured the same type of tough politics when governing, parking politics at the governor's and then the Oval Office door.

Carter was often ferried around by David Rabhan, a Savannah native and amateur pilot of his own twin-engine Cessna 360. One of his first plane rides had a momentous impact: It petrified Carter but led to one of the most important political statements he would make in his home state. One evening, flying from Brunswick to the little Georgia town of West, David napped and let Jimmy fly the plane. The engines suddenly cut out and, petrified, Jimmy screamed, "David! David!" as Rabhan pretended to be sleeping. "So I knocked the heck out of him with my elbow. I said, 'Wake up, the plane's going down.'" David grinned, reached over, and turned the knob that kicked in the gas supply from the backup tank. "He thought it was very funny. I was really pissed off."

Carter, greatly relieved, conceded that he had helped him in many ways, not least flying him around Georgia at no charge, and asked if he could ever do anything to repay these many favors—"win or lose." Rabhan then grew solemn, and asked the future governor for a pencil and paper. After Carter reached behind the seat and pulled out a small map of Georgia that located all the state's airports, he told his passenger to write: "I want you to promise that if you are elected Governor you will say that the time for racial discrimination is over."[31]

As a Jewish businessman, Rabhan had known discrimination and felt great sympathy for the black citizens of Georgia, who were treated far worse than were the Jews. He had trained Israeli pilots secretly at an airfield in Athens, the home of his alma mater, the University of Georgia. But he had another reason: His parents ran a bakery in Savannah and were partners in building nursing homes with Martin Luther King, Sr.—"Daddy King," as he was affectionately known. Carter had not yet met King's legendary son, but he obtained something far more important early in his political career. During the campaign Daddy King introduced him to the politically influential black ministers who helped deliver the black vote across Georgia. With the election secured, Carter was free to fulfill Rabhan's request.

In his brief inaugural speech he declared that he had traveled the state widely, and "I say to you quite frankly that the time for racial discrimination is over. Never again shall a black child be deprived of equal rights to education, health or social services." He might have made that pledge without that harrowing experience aloft, because he well knew that there would be no future for him in the national Democratic Party without a demonstrated commitment to civil rights. Carter insists Rabhan's request was the catalyst, and further, "That statement got me on the front cover of *Time* magazine."[32] He was not far wrong. The editors were looking for a face representing what was seen as a more tolerant New South, and in Carter they found it. While the statement gave the new governor of Georgia national prominence, it was a politically courageous and deeply unpopular sentiment among white voters in his own Deep South state. That did not stop Carter from hanging a portrait of the martyred civil rights leader Martin Luther King, Jr., in Georgia's Capitol, or from criticizing the very Sumter County School Board on which he had served for "driving white children from the public school system."[33] He appointed record numbers of women and blacks and reformed the criminal justice and mental health systems, which were heavily biased against blacks.

For good or ill, Carter's presidency was foreshadowed by the way he governed in Georgia. He showed his determination to address tough issues by abolishing and combining three hundred state agencies, boards, and commissions into twenty-two. At the same time he left the necessary backroom bargaining with the state legislature to Bert Lance, his highway commissioner, allowing Carter to avoid the messy political compromises he found distasteful. Bert was all too happy to promise new or repaired roads, highways, and bridges to win over recalcitrant legislators.

Carter also showed his commitment to the environment by an unprecedented decision (with shades of the water wars he would fight in Washington) to block the Sprewell Bluff Dam, a job- and park-creating project of the Army Engineers that would have damaged the swamps, streams, and wild rivers Carter prized as God's creation. No governor in any state had ever blocked a water project fully paid for by the federal government. His willingness to take on vested interests, combined with his stellar civil rights record, made it unlikely that he would have been reelected if the Georgia Constitution had permitted governors to serve two consecutive terms.[34] But Carter was already setting his sights higher than that.

"GOVERNOR, WE HAVE COME TO TALK TO YOU ABOUT YOUR FUTURE"

Shortly after his inauguration as governor in January of 1971, the presidency of the United States clearly was coming onto Carter's personal horizon, although among his cronies and even in the privacy of their fishing trips the only term they used was "national office."[35] Indeed, Carter was so determined to become president that at the 1972 Miami Democratic Convention, he instructed Ham to start a movement to promote him as Senator George McGovern's running mate, even though he had been a leader in the anti-McGovern elected officials at the convention.[36] Ham recalled that when they went to Miami they "had this crazy idea of getting Carter on the ticket as VP. We tried to have it both ways. We tried to get on the ticket but not get caught trying."[37] Chance favored Carter in McGovern's crushing defeat. He also met Patrick Caddell, McGovern's brilliant young pollster, just out of Harvard and already a major figure in national Democratic politics— but not to the taste of Kirbo, who recalled that it was "the first time I saw that damn pollster with the long hair."[38] But gradually the Carter team coalesced into a fighting force with awesome political skills.

Carter's ambition to gain the presidency was reinforced by measuring himself against the stream of potential candidates who visited him at the governor's mansion seeking his support. He remembered that "after spending several hours with them drinking beer and so forth, I didn't see that they were any more qualified than I was. . . . I was amazed at how parochial they were and how narrow-minded they were." As governor he had to implement laws they had put through Congress, which Carter said they could barely remember.[39] Still, it seemed presumptuous—even absurd in Ham's view—for Carter to think or at least talk openly about the presidency until prompted by supporters outside his inner circle. The first formal memorandum came from Dr. Peter Bourne, a physician who had helped draft speeches for Carter's gubernatorial campaign. With the Vietnam War dragging to a close and Watergate further coloring the voters' suspicion of Washington, Bourne correctly realized that the forthcoming 1976 presidential campaign might be a time for an outsider with a fresh approach. He wrote Carter a long letter in the summer of 1972, arguing that this was his moment and that he needed to start building a political base. He urged him to travel the country campaigning for Democratic congressional candidates and to write an autobiography; Carter did both.[40]

This sparked a series of meetings in Atlanta throughout the 1972 presidential campaign with Ham, Rosalynn, and his cousin Don Carter, a journalist with Knight-Rider newspapers. The regulars at the mansion joined in. On October 17, Ham started off lightly: "Governor, we have come to talk to you about your future. I don't know any other way to say this, and it's hard to bring myself to say the words, but I guess I will just have to say it." After hesitating for a second, he got it out: "We think you should run for president."[41] Carter put off his decision until the day after McGovern's overwhelming defeat. When she realized he intended to run, Rosalynn called his sister Ruth and exclaimed, " 'Jimmy's going to run for p-p-p . . .' I couldn't even say the word, it was so unreal to me."[42] On November 5 he convened another meeting of his inner circle at the mansion; they realized they needed a concrete plan, and Carter asked Ham to pull together all the ideas in their recent meetings into one memorandum. The result was Ham's seventy-two-page outline of his brilliant strategy for catapulting the unknown governor of a medium-size Southern state to the White House. It became one of the most famous campaign blueprints in modern American political history.

William Hamilton McWhorter Jordan (pronounced "Jerdan") was born in 1944 in Charlotte, North Carolina, but grew up in Albany, Georgia, not far from Jimmy Carter's Plains. He had been Carter's youth coordinator in his unsuccessful 1966 gubernatorial campaign; his campaign manager when

Carter was elected governor in the 1970 race; and then his gubernatorial executive secretary. Ham fought in the Vietnam War when many in our generation sought every means to avoid it. Almost certainly his exposure to Agent Orange, a defoliant used by the American military against the Viet Cong, would later lead to multiple battles with cancer and a premature death. Now he was the unchallenged manager for what looked like an impossible presidential campaign. To Carter "Ham was just like one of my own children."[43]

Ham, as everyone called him, was movie-star handsome, with a thick shock of black hair and an impish smile. He had the most analytical political mind of anyone I ever met. He never bragged about himself, and in all our years together, I never heard a cross word from him. He supported my work on policy, was unfailingly kind to my wife, Fran, and championed me during a crucial showdown during the postelection transition. One of the most remarkable parts of the Carter presidential campaign—and later the White House years—was the total absence of rancor and competition among Carter's top aides. We each knew our roles, and while I always checked our policy proposals and speeches with Ham, Jody Powell, and Rafshoon, there was rarely much pushback. They respected my sense of where Carter needed to position himself on substantive policy issues, and I respected their expertise on electoral politics and the media.

But there was no doubt who ran the overall campaign. In retrospect, Ham's bold plan seems self-evident, but only because it was visionary. He accurately addressed the political situation and the huge challenges Carter would face as a candidate, and he laid down a precise "Plan of Action," with specific tasks allotted in meticulous detail and an overarching theme—restoring trust in government after Watergate. For Carter to be considered a national rather than a regional candidate, he advised him to make clear his commitment to racial equality while also warning him against dwelling on race lest he risk alienating the whites who had to make important adjustments: "the working class men and women who have traditionally voted Democratic and are still having to cope with certain aspects of racial integration; busing, preferential treatment given some blacks in employment, etc." The trade-off between the social agenda of the Democratic Party and an emphasis on jobs and growth for working-class whites and blacks remains a dilemma for Democratic presidential candidates to this day, as Hillary Clinton learned in 2016.

Assume "a learning posture," Ham wrote. "Don't pretend to have all the answers or know everything . . . a major aspect of your campaign will be to travel the country, listen and learn . . . [but you] are not going to compromise the beliefs and principles you have lived by to be elected." And as a governor rather than a legislator like his congressional opponents, Carter could also argue that his was the best preparation for the presidency; Ham also foresaw an important tactical advantage for Carter. As soon as he left the governor's office at the start of 1975, he would be the only candidate who could commit to a full-time campaign. That would also enable him to make the earliest announcement for president, which would attract "inordinate amounts of coverage and publicity." The reverse side of that was a warning to Carter that he had to be ready both emotionally and physically for a brutal schedule, traveling across the country almost without interruption, returning to Georgia only every other weekend for a few days of rest. He laid out a budget that allowed for "a heavyweight issues man" to work up position papers; initially that was Steve Stark, a talented young journalist with the *Boston Globe,* and soon would be me.

Robert Strauss, the legendary Texas-Washington political guru who was serving as chairman of the Democratic National Committee, convened a meeting of potential presidential candidates and their campaign managers in September 1974. Bob and I became very close in the campaign, regularly sharing advice and concerns. He was a natural politician, respected by both Republicans and Democrats, with a twinkle in his eye, profound and profane, his sentences loaded with four-letter words. His purpose was to explain the Democrats' new rules aimed at taking the nomination out of the hands of the party bosses, as well as the post-Watergate fund-raising regulations that had been issued by the Federal Election Commission. While the other candidates brought smooth, impeccably dressed Washington lawyers to understand the new rules, Ham came wearing an informal blue jacket and khaki pants, accompanied by two young election experts in their twenties. Their minds uncluttered by the baggage of past campaigns, they were quick to understand that the convention of 1976, still two years away, would not be brokered by party bosses in backroom deals, and that their national strategy fitted the new rules. These would democratize the nominating process and open it to more than thirty primaries, where average voters would hold the keys to the nomination—just the kind of process for a newcomer with no other job and a gift for retail politics. Ham also was the first to spot the potential impact of the early Iowa caucuses as an unappreciated engine of momentum for the first-in-the-nation New Hampshire primary.

Then fortune smiled. Late in 1973, well before Carter formally announced for president, Strauss was searching among moderate young Southern governors for a new chairman of the Democrats' Congressional Campaign Committee to help elect members of Congress in the midterm elections. Whoever was chosen would pile up political debts and gain national exposure. Over a few drinks with Kirbo and the governor in the governor's mansion in Atlanta, bells rang in Strauss's head. Thanks to his *Time* magazine cover Carter had more visibility than his Southern colleagues. Kirbo and Carter persuaded Strauss not only to name him to the post, but to give Ham an office at Democratic National Committee headquarters to coordinate Carter's efforts, including his travel. As Carter gleefully recalled, while this was part of his budding attempt to run for president, "we didn't tell anybody"—and certainly not Strauss. In retelling the story, Ham smiled and said, "This was probably the last time we ever put anything over on Strauss."[44] His perch in Washington gave him access to a nationwide database of politically active people in key states, and congressional candidates who would prove invaluable to the still-inchoate, budding presidential campaign.

INTO THE VORTEX

That is when I was drawn into the widening vortex. Early in 1974, Governor Carter called me at my Atlanta law office and invited me to lunch with him in his spacious office in the Capitol. Over an unappetizing tuna salad sandwich on plain white bread, for which I had to pay a few dollars to his secretary, Mary Beasley (I was not alone; even Bert Lance had to pay),[45] an early sign of his frugality, he said that after he left office, he wanted to make something out of his new but normally inconsequential position as chairman of the DNC's Congressional Campaign Committee by going around the country to stump for the party's candidates. With the shadow of Watergate threatening Republican electoral prospects in the 1974 midterm elections, he asked me to undertake a special assignment. Without understanding his underlying motive, I accepted his request to develop positions critiquing the policies of the Nixon administration and suggesting Democratic options on every topic from health and energy to defense and foreign affairs. I reached out for ideas to Democratic staffers in the House and Senate and experts in Washington think tanks, and produced more than twenty-five policy papers, which were sent out under his signature on a "DNC74" letterhead and which I still have. I kept the names of those who helped me during that pre-computer era in a small blue box, alphabetized by issue. Many eventually served in the Carter administration. And when the presidential campaign formally got under way, the policy papers gave us a head start.

When the six-month project ended, I called the governor in October 1974 and asked to take him to lunch at Dante's Down the Hatch, a restaurant in the newly created Underground Atlanta, near the Capitol. Together in a booth, with a burly Georgia state trooper protecting him, I got right to the point, because I knew he regarded small talk as a waste of time. Arguing with what I mistakenly believed was highly original political acumen, I told him that in the wake of the Watergate scandal, Democrats were likely to take the House and Senate in a landslide, for which he would get some measure of credit. I said that he was bound to stand out in a weak Democratic field for president, and that if he won a few Southern primaries, someone might want him on the ticket as vice president. Carter smiled broadly and said, "Stu, I have already decided to run, but I am going to be the Democratic candidate for president, not vice president. Would you like to join my campaign?" I accepted on the spot and broke the news to Fran that night.

I had been a high school basketball star in Atlanta; Phi Beta Kappa and cum laude at the University of North Carolina; a junior aide on LBJ's White House staff straight out of Harvard Law School; and research director for the Humphrey presidential campaign in 1968. I returned to Atlanta to serve as a law clerk to a federal judge; became a young partner in the prominent Atlanta firm of Powell, Goldstein, Frazer & Murphy, and eagerly joined local and state Democratic politics. I served on the Fulton County and Georgia State Democratic Executive Committees; led the drafting of a new charter for the Georgia Democratic Party; and worked on policy issues in the campaigns of Atlanta's first Jewish mayor, Sam Massell, and first black mayor,

Maynard Jackson. The one that was most special was the 1972 congressional campaign of Andrew Young, one of Martin Luther King's closest aides, who became the first black congressman elected from the Deep South since post–Civil War Reconstruction. Fran organized the Northern, mostly white, section of Georgia's Fifth Congressional District. I headed Young's policy group and helped secure Justice Department approval for his Voting Rights Act petition to overturn the racially gerrymandered district that would have denied him success, and coauthored a book about his historic victory.[46] In his memoir Andy fondly remembered the "help from key young whites in the district," highlighting the roles Fran and I played, and noting the major role I would play during the Carter presidency: "I'll always be proud that Stu Eizenstat's initial political involvement was with my congressional campaign."[47]

For the rest of Jimmy Carter's Georgia team, he had been the sole focus of their political lives; as deeply committed to him as I became, I was a relative latecomer. When I was finally admitted to Carter's inner circle on the strength of my policy papers in his run for governor, and later, when he moved into national politics as chairman of the Democratic Congressional Campaign Committee, I was under no illusion that my relationship with him could ever be as deep as the others'. Like Carter himself, they were not only from the South but *of* it, going back generations. Hamilton Jordan's great-great-grandfather was a Confederate general; ten of Jody Powell's relatives had fought against the Union in the Battle of Antietam; and his senior aide Frank Moore's great-grandfather was in the Battle of Chickamauga.

By contrast, my paternal great-grandfather and grandfather had fled Russia early in the twentieth century during the Russo-Japanese War and the Kishinev pogrom—one to Atlanta, the other to Palestine. A little later, my mother Sylvia's family, the Medintz's, emigrated from Lithuania for America, leaving behind three sisters of my maternal grandfather, who were killed in the Holocaust. As a boy in Atlanta, I was a member of another minority group in the South: the Jews. When my mother, Sylvia, took me swimming at Mooney's Lake, we were stopped by a sign reading, "No Blacks, Jews, or Dogs Allowed." This was not my only early experience with racial and religious discrimination. As a twelve-year-old, I bowed to the segregation of Atlanta's buses and failed to give up my seat in the white section to an elderly black women laden with shopping bags. My mother had to look at private schools when Georgia's governor Ernest Vandiver threatened to close the public schools to avoid desegregation. And as a student at the University of North Carolina in 1962, I was blind to the reason for the nation's first sit-in, when students from a nearby black college blocked my access to a nearby Howard Johnson's restaurant. Notwithstanding my academic record, federal judicial clerkship, and White House service, I got only one offer in 1970 from a major Atlanta law firm, Powell, Goldstein, Frazer & Murphy, one of whose founding partners was Jewish. For the others, it was still no blacks and Jews allowed. One of the major things that drew me to Jimmy Carter in the 1970 gubernatorial campaign was his opposition to discrimination, which shaped his courageous civil rights policies as president, to which I contributed.

Over time, I developed my own increasingly close relationship with Carter through his respect for my policy expertise and judgment; rightly or wrongly he called me his "brains."[48] I was buoyed by his comment one evening early in the administration, asking if I liked my job, and telling me I was "the perfect staff member, well organized with excellent judgment," and that he had confided to Stan Cloud of *Time* that "I was doing a superb job," and he "couldn't get along without me."[49] So during the long 1976 presidential campaign, I coordinated all domestic- and foreign-policy positions, and established the major task forces of outside experts on key economic and national security issues.

After Carter won the Democratic nomination, I realized how lucky I was to be at this point in history and to live in this wonderful country. Here I was, thirty-two years old, the only son of Sylvia and Leo, a Jewish small businessman in Atlanta who, together with his brother Berry, ran a small shoe company wholesaling what in Yiddish are called *shmattes* (literally "rags," but in this case low-cost shoes), mostly to small Jewish merchants throughout the South who had also fled what they called "the old country" for a new land of hope. Combined with this emotion was another powerful one. I had the privilege of participating up close in the grandeur of American democracy at work, in a nation filled with remarkably diverse people who had assembled here in history's greatest migration and, while occupied by their own challenges, were held together by common American values.

THE RELIGIOUS POPULIST
AND *ROLLING STONE*

As I worked more closely with Carter, I came to realize that his Southern Baptist religion was deeply woven into the fabric of his and Rosalynn's lives. He began teaching Sunday school when he was eighteen and continued even as governor. A friend gave him a book by the famous liberal theologian Reinhold Niebuhr, *Courage and the Courage to Change*, and, among Niebuhr's other works on theology, it influenced him deeply. From years of working with him, I found that one statement of Niebuhr's seemed to sum up Carter's unusual approach to politics: "The sad duty of politics is to establish justice in a sinful world." He told me he was also influenced by the dilemma posed by the theologian Paul Tillich about "the potential conflicts between a life built on my own faith in Christianity and the . . . pragmatic role of public affairs." As governor and president, he was true to his commitment to keep religion separate from government. While devout, what he objected to were public displays of *religiosity*. He was bothered by Nixon's religious services in the East Room and "by Billy Graham always hanging around the White House and ostentatiously being put forward by President Johnson and others to show that they were church people."[50]

He also discovered early in his presidential term that even approaching the line separating church and state did not go over well inside the high councils of government. At the first of regular weekly White House breakfasts for Democratic congressional leaders, Carter's guests gasped when he asked his Georgia friend and budget director Bert Lance to say grace. At a later breakfast the Democratic majority whip John Brademas, a former Rhodes scholar whose district took in South Bend, Indiana, was asked by Carter to intone the prayer; he concluded with the appeal: "O Lord, if it is just the same to you, please let Notre Dame beat Georgia Tech in the upcoming football game." House Speaker Thomas "Tip" O'Neill, a Boston Irishman, also took a dim view of religious displays. When he debriefed the House

Steering Committee about that first congressional breakfast, he expressed his surprise at the opening prayer but, not to be outdone, closed his eyes and recited a Catholic prayer. When he finished and looked around at his colleagues, he declared, "That will last for the entire session."[51]

Candidate Carter's Baptist beliefs were influential with two disparate voting blocs: Southern white conservative evangelicals, and black voters everywhere. I accompanied him on several campaign trips to black churches from Newark to Cleveland, and he was right at home singing Christian hymns with the impassioned black choirs, while holding hands with their pastors and swaying to the music. Even as a Jew, seeing him bond with these black Americans brought tears to my eyes: Most had left the South to escape the worst of segregation, still suffered from discrimination, and yet retained their patriotism and the strong religious feelings that helped shelter them from a hostile world. Carter connected with them through the shared experiences of his upbringing in ways that the more secular liberal politicians in the North could not.

His Christian religion was a bridge that enabled him to create a unique electoral coalition of conservative Southern whites and disadvantaged blacks around the country. During a campaign swing in North Carolina, he was surrounded by a group of Southern Baptists in a backyard, where one of them asked about his religious faith. Carter recalled: "I just told them very frankly how I felt about it—that I had always been a Christian, that I had taught Sunday school. And they asked if I was 'born again' and I said yes, which is not an extraordinary thing for a Southern Baptist. I mean all of us claim to be born again when we become personally aware of and commit ourselves to Christ." Washington reporters witnessed the exchange, and Carter reflected that "they took the 'born-again' phrase as kind of a weird thought of having revelations from heaven or having contact with or communications or conversations with angels and things like that, and I really deplored it."[52]

He was not guided by the Bible in making his decisions, but his faith helped sustain him during the traumas of office. He fully accepted my Jewish faith and close observance of our holidays and customs, and even participated in our family Passover Seder after the Israel-Egypt Peace Treaty. I was never made to feel uncomfortable with Carter's religion. On the contrary,

Carter once told me: "I think, Stu, my whole life and its priorities [have] been shaped by my Christian faith, as yours has by your Jewish faith. It is a normal thing for someone who is as devout as I am and as you are, to say that without embarrassment."[53]

Another factor in Carter's ascension to the presidency was his populist streak, which appealed to rural voters and a spectrum of urban liberals. Carter's populism was rooted in his family. His grandfather was a close associate of the Georgia populist Tom Watson, a leader in the congressional battle to legislate free rural mail delivery, and Carter claimed that the idea originated with "my granddaddy" when he was postmaster in Richmond, Georgia. Preserving the RFD was a prime political project of Carter's father; Republicans opposed this now-almost-forgotten service that once connected millions of isolated American farms to the world, if only through the Sears Roebuck catalog that came in the mail.[54] Like his idol Harry Truman, he had worked in the fields and plowed behind a mule, and did not hide his suspicions of large institutions, corporations, and organizations favoring the wealthy and well-connected at the expense of ordinary people.

One speech brought national attention to his populism and helped propel him to national recognition, a Law Day speech on justice delivered on May 4, 1974, at the University of Georgia School of Law before the state's legal establishment. Carter followed Senator Ted Kennedy, whose celebrity bulked up the audience, which, by another totally unlikely stroke of luck, included the gonzo journalist Hunter Thompson of *Rolling Stone* magazine.

Instead of flattering his eminent audience, the governor delivered a sharply critical attack of the legal profession at a high intellectual level that few elected officials could have matched. He began on a disarming note, describing himself as a "peanut farmer, an engineer, and a nuclear physicist, not a lawyer," and quoted Niebuhr to the effect that "laws are constantly changing to stabilize the social equilibrium of the forces and counterforces of a dynamic society." There followed a second, more surprising reference with a refrain from "a friend of mine, a poet named Bob Dylan, that 'the times, they are a-changing.'" He then proceeded to awaken his audience by attacking the "inadequacies of a system of which it is obvious that you're so patently proud."

Thompson paid close attention as the governor of Georgia laid into lawyers and the legal system in which "the powerful and the influential have carved out for themselves or have inherited a privileged position in society, or wealth or social prominence for higher education or opportunity for the future. Carter cited his policy of appointing judges on merit; his creation of a commission to hear citizen complaints about judicial performance; and the shockingly inequitable sentences for the indigent. Within the lifetime of many lawyers in the audience, Georgia chain gangs had been a notorious feature of incarceration; Carter called the state's prisons a disgrace and reminded the listeners of his reforms to return 95 percent of the state's prisoners to their homes. He chastised the bar association for failing to greet Martin Luther King, Jr., with "approbation and accolades" when he demanded equal treatment for black as well as white citizens. And he also reminded them that the first speech he gave as a member of the state senate, "representing the most conservative district in Georgia," called for the abolition of procedures that kept black citizens from voting.

Carter remarked that individual lawyers, doctors, teachers, and even his fellow peanut warehousemen were deeply committed to their clients, patients, students, or customers, but that something happened when they organized into pressure groups that reversed their priorities. As a prime example, he mentioned "working people struggling for a decent pay, while the Teamsters Union and others were not only committing crimes, but in effect cheating people who had trusted them." Thompson reported that speech in glowing terms that helped etch Carter's populist profile among the political elite, and validated him as an acceptable Democratic candidate for a party whose base was more liberal than he was on fiscal issues.

Carter never felt comfortable with many of the union leaders he had to deal with in Washington, even though their unions were the organizational backbone of the Democratic Party. Unions were deeply unpopular among his base in the conservative, nonunion South, and he saw them and especially their leaders as part of the entrenched interests against which he railed, although as president he supported much of their agenda, such as reforming labor laws to facilitate organizing workers.

This highlights one problem with populism. In a period of deep voter anger over institutions, as today, it can be a winning campaign formula but not a governing philosophy. It is impossible to govern without co-opting major institutions and their leaders to support a president's agenda and stand behind him in tough times. A president can and must appeal over the heads of Congress to the public to put pressure on its representatives in Washington to support his proposed legislation. But he cannot appeal too often for public support without wearing out his welcome, and at the same time he must reach accommodation with the organized groups inside the Beltway, who too often call the shots via access to their deep congressional connections and carefully targeted campaign contributions.

But to run a populist, antiestablishment campaign, a candidate has to be well known. And, he was still "Jimmy Who?" among the press and public. With Carter's national name recognition at less than 1 percent, he was desperate to get any national attention. He went on the television quiz show *What's My Line?* None of the panel identified him as the former governor of Georgia and a presidential candidate. Henry Owen, the head of foreign-policy studies at the Brookings Institution, who met Carter at briefings I arranged at Brookings, ran into Carter and Jody Powell at New York's LaGuardia Airport and dropped them off on the West Side of Manhattan. As Carter and Powell got out of the taxi, Powell leaned over and told the hardened New York cabby, "You have just driven the next president of the United States." He replied, "Yeah, and I still want to get paid." When they left, the cabby turned to Owen and said, "Who was that kook?"[55]

THE PRIMARIES

But even at that early stage Ham knew that name recognition was less important than winning the Iowa party caucuses, whose potential had not yet sunk in with the political establishment. He concluded that Carter had to work by stealth to become the surprise winner, while most of the better-known candidates were still at work in Congress or their governors' mansions. Between Carter's announcement for the presidency late in 1974 and the caucuses on January 19, 1976, the candidate made an astonishing 110 trips to Iowa, many lasting a full week or even longer. These were amplified through visits by Rosalynn Carter and his remarkable mother, "Miss Lillian," with her personal warmth and a mile-wide smile. When the caucus votes were tallied, some 60 percent were undecided, but that was not the headline newspapers used. Carter was declared the winner with 27 percent, or fewer than fourteen thousand votes. Senator Birch Bayh of Indiana was second with 13 percent.

On to New Hampshire, another small state that trades in retail politics where voters were generally moderate to conservative, take their responsibility seriously, and demand persistent, personal contact with candidates. The man from Plains, his wife, his mother, and their sons and daughters-in-law had spent another hundred days campaigning there at town hall meetings and meet-and-greet sessions. A spunky fellow Georgian, Dot Padgett, came up with the creative idea of organizing a "Peanut Brigade," hundreds of Georgians who fanned out over the state to serve as validators for their former governor. It worked: This time Carter was the clear winner.[56]

The next leg of the early campaign strategy involved knocking out Alabama's segregationist governor, George Wallace, in the first Southern primary, held in Florida on March 9. That would leave Carter the sole Southerner in the race and earn the gratitude of Northern liberals confronting Wallace's divisive racism. Here again Carter's clueless opponents were only too happy to defer to him, let him destroy Wallace, and then pick up the pieces. They failed to realize that another primary victory would propel him into the early primaries in the Northern states with an edge. Carter spent a great deal of time in Florida, the state next to Georgia and thoroughly familiar to him, backed by a superb organization put together by a young aide, Phil Wise, who moved to Florida for months before the primary (and became his White House appointments aide). Washington State senator Henry "Scoop" Jackson made a belated effort to win the senior citizens and Jewish voters in South Florida, but it was too little too late. It was the beginning of the end for Wallace, who was debilitated from the assassin's bullet that had severed his spine while he was running for president in 1972. Campaigning from a wheelchair, he had lost much of the fire that ignited his earlier campaign in 1968 around the South and in blue-collar areas around the country, taking traditionally Democratic votes from Hubert Humphrey in key battleground states, as I painfully watched with Humphrey's senior staff in Minneapolis. Carter narrowly beat him, 34 to 31 percent, with a slogan coined by Rafshoon to resonate across the South: "Send them a president, not a message."

Carter went on to defeat Wallace decisively in the North Carolina primary, whereupon Wallace left the campaign and endorsed Carter.

There were bumps in the primary road, as Carter lost liberal Massachusetts and New York the same day, and narrowly escaped a loss in Wisconsin to representative Morris "Mo" Udall of Arizona, winning 37 to 36 percent when the farm vote came in late, after his promise to raise milk price supports—enabling him to emulate the famous 1948 *Chicago Tribune* headline, "Dewey Beats Truman," as he held up the headline of the *Milwaukee Journal*, with his broadest smile: "Udall Beats Carter." As the campaign rolled on, he had an added weapon: Eleven family members worked in eleven different states to spread his message.[57]

Few campaigns made better use of scarce financial resources than Carter's in its early days. The candidate often stayed free at the homes of supporters in the primary states to save money. He flew economy class with Jody Powell as his most frequent companion. But airplanes are an essential tool even in the ground game of today's politics, and they do not come cheap.

When he began to expand his reach, Carter needed to find a trustworthy pilot near the small town of Plains, where he would retreat on weekends to rest, plan for the coming week, and meet with his Atlanta-based staff. There was no shortage of daredevil crop dusters, but once again, small-town luck was with him. G. Thomas Peterson, former chief test pilot for Aero Commander in nearby Albany, had set up a company in Plains with six single-engine and four twin-engine Cessnas. Peterson Aviation Services bought about one hundred acres of land, which, as Tom explained, could serve as a runway exceeding five thousand feet, "depending upon the amount of mowed grass."[58] On a Sunday afternoon following the 1974 Christmas holidays, he received a call from Governor Carter, who asked Tom to hold on until he could move out of earshot of his state police bodyguards, telling them he was going to look for Indian arrowheads, which they knew was one of his favorite pastimes. He asked Peterson: "Will you consider flying me, not in a big plane? I'm going to be president of the United States." The pilot held his tongue but remembers he almost blurted out, "President of *what*?"

In the beginning our small staff contingent flew in a Cessna 172 that held only three passengers and the pilot; the charge was $25 per seat, and we would leave from a small airport outside Atlanta for the one-hour flight to Plains. The passengers were from Carter's inner circle and me. There was only one engine and no control tower to guide our landing of the plane. As Peterson explained: "People could hear you coming in, and if you could hear them you could land." When the plane was low enough, he got his landing vectors from the instruments. When we landed, I literally felt like kissing the ground—and rightly so, because Peterson recalled one landing at sunset, when the plane was headed straight for the trees at the end of the small runway.

As his pilot, Peterson became familiar with the essentials of Carter's character the rest of the country would come to know, albeit imperfectly. One was Carter's unfettered self-confidence. Another was his insistence on punctuality, which had been imbued in him from his Annapolis days. Even more striking was his deep religious faith. In one of their maiden campaign trips, Carter asked Peterson why he did not attend church regularly and told him about the importance of putting religion in his life. While this left a lasting impression, it did not improve his pilot's church attendance.[59]

With the primary victories and consequent national exposure, the Carter campaign expanded and quickly moved upscale to chartered jets. Once Carter secured the presidential nomination, he graduated to a Boeing 727 with 140 to 150 seats. Some member of the campaign press corps jokingly referred to the plane as "Peanut One." The name stuck, and our barnstorming days were over. Although most of my time was spent developing and coordinating campaign policy from headquarters in Atlanta, I frequently flew on Peanut One.

I can attest from personal experience that there is no activity more physically, intellectually, or emotionally demanding than a presidential campaign in a country as large and diverse as the United States. It is a fit test for a potential president. Campaign staffs are small, and the candidate must take positions literally on the fly as news breaks in the United States or around the world. A sitting president has his White House Staff, supported by an enormous federal bureaucracy, to provide facts and recommendations for key decisions. A misstep can often be reversed or ameliorated by presidential actions down the road. Not so for a new and still largely unknown challenger fresh on the campaign trail, where one mistake can be fatal. The Carter campaign did not have the deep resources available to the incumbent, Gerald Ford, who had the White House Rose Garden as a stage set for showing himself as presidential. Ford could sleep in his own bed while Carter and the traveling staff had to bunk in hotels after brutal twelve-hour days on the road and in the air.

At each stop the local Democratic dignitaries, mayors, governors, and members of Congress typically would wait on the tarmac to greet the candidate. We always had to be sensitive to national issues and avoid being drawn into divisive local politics. I had a full-time staff person, Isabel Hyde, to help avoid these local potholes.

On Peanut One, Carter occupied a small section partitioned off in the front of the plane with a small desk for a work space and a green couch for naps. On a table near the desk lay a well-used Bible, and on the wall a good-luck horseshoe provided by a supporter at a campaign rally. Behind the president's flying office were the ubiquitous Secret Service agents with their special lapel badges and coiled white plastic wires hanging down from their earphones into the backs of their suit jackets. Our staff section came next, and then in the back sat the irreverent, jaded working press. The reporters entered through the rear door of the plane, their section strewn with their papers, tape recorders, and typewriters, along with plastic cups, plates, and napkins. The rear wall was hung with a newspaper photo of Vice President Nelson Rockefeller making an obscene gesture, middle finger up.[60]

POLICY GOALS

In conceptualizing the policy goals of his presidential campaign, I tried to make them compatible with Ham's political strategy. Eventually one of my essential functions in the White House was to keep our policies aligned with our political base, not always successfully. In preparation for the formal launch of his improbable presidential campaign, Carter and I met alone at night or on weekends in the downstairs sunroom off the main foyer of the governor's mansion. He would often be in blue jeans with an open shirt, barefoot, as we discussed issues literally from A (abortion) to Z (Zaire). He had no religious scruples against abortion under certain circumstances, but neither did he feel comfortable encouraging it. The Supreme Court had handed down its *Roe v. Wade* decision only a few months before, and the sharpest question immediately facing any presidential candidate was whether the government should underwrite abortions for poor women. As on so many other issues where Carter tried to bridge a gap, we arrived at a middle position supporting a woman's right to abort but opposing funding it through Medicaid. One "B" issue, school busing, was also a tough call, but while strongly supporting the integration of schools, Carter believed it was bad public policy to require students to be bussed to other districts to achieve racial balance in the classroom.

Carter strove to navigate skillfully in the center between the traditional ideological poles within the Democratic Party and knit together as best he could his diverse and often incompatible winning coalition of Southern conservatives and Northern liberals and blue-collar industrial-state workers and their unions. It became clear that he was a fiscal conservative pledging to balance the budget, but also a social and foreign-policy liberal, for example, pledging to withdraw all American troops from South Korea, and cut billions from the defense budget—neither of which he did as president (only 3,000 of over 40,000 U.S. troops were withdrawn from South Korea, and defense spending was substantially boosted).

On several key issues he took liberal positions more out of political necessity than personal belief. In May 1976, with Carter in the political ascendant, heading for our first major Northern primary in Pennsylvania, Steve Schlossberg, the general counsel of the United Auto Workers, called me with a compelling proposition: The UAW would be the first major union to endorse Carter if he would support their number one issue: universal, mandatory, comprehensive national health insurance.[61] No issue motivated the labor and liberal communities more than this expensive program, which ran contrary to Carter's fiscal conservatism. He gave me the authority to negotiate their endorsement, but insisted that I draw the line at a set of principles, without committing him to timetables and details, to be phased in "as revenues permit."[62] Carter likewise pledged to create a Department of Education in exchange for support from the National Education Association and the American Federation of Teachers. He freely announced his (and Rosalynn's) support for the Equal Rights Amendment, which earned him the backing of liberal women's groups, here exercising his own conscience.

But the Carter campaign was less about detailed issues than the broader themes of restoring the voters' trust in the presidency. As we went through the exhaustive list of issues, these were ones that came from his heart. He alone among the Democratic candidates understood that Democratic voters and the electorate at large were not seeking to expand the New Deal or the Great Society with a burst of new programs.

Carter introduced himself to the nation at Washington's National Press Club by announcing his candidacy on December 12, 1974, followed by an evening kickoff in Atlanta's Civic Center. The speech was one of the earliest in presidential history, and for a Democrat, one of the most conservative, as well as populist. He declared himself "a farmer, an engineer, a businessman, a planner, a scientist, a governor, and a Christian," an early signal to his Southern Baptist base. At the urging of the campaign team, it was more a thematic address than the classic Democratic programmatic speech I would have preferred. But his political advisers were right in capturing the mood of the country. There were no clarion calls for big new spending programs on health, education, or welfare.

It was clear from the speech and our private conversations that his prime domestic goals were conserving energy and protecting the environment, and attacking pork-barrel water projects. The speech contained virtually nothing on foreign policy and national security aside from a brief promise to "protect the integrity of Israel" that I slipped in. A promise for a stronger military would normally have been on the agenda of a candidate who was a Southerner and a former naval officer, but Carter showed his early suspicions and flinty spending habits by simply calling for an "adequate military preparedness" and demanding more efficiency from the defense establishment. His most heartfelt national security appeal was an alert to the danger of the proliferation of nuclear weapons. I helped temper his unrealistic goal in early drafts of a worldwide elimination of all nuclear weapons, by adding as an "ultimate goal."[63]

But the essence of the announcement speech and of the entire primary campaign was a clear anti-Watergate, anti-Washington message. He ham-

mered away at restoring trust in government through reforming the bureaucracy, tearing away secrecy in decision-making, and passing strict ethics laws
to control lobbyists and appoint regulators, senior officials, diplomats, and
judges on merit and not connections. He promised specific ethics reforms
on gifts, financial disclosure, limiting the revolving door of officials leaving
to lobby the agencies they led, appointing judges on the basis of merit, and
barring the appointment of government regulators from the industries they
regulated. For good measure, he advocated universal voter registration; an
end to racial discrimination; and a reform of a tax system he believed was a
"disgrace to the human race" in favoring the rich and powerful over those
who earned their living "with the sweat of manual labor." Although Carter
was accused of being "fuzzy" on the issues, in the course of a long and brutal campaign, he took scores of specific positions, which our policy shop
gathered up after the election at his request, and over our objection, published as a memorandum from me and my deputy David Rubenstein after
the election. But there can be no doubt that it was his thematic message of
trust and reform, underwritten by the promise that he would never lie to the
American people, that had the greatest impact during the campaign.[64]

Nevertheless we had to get through the primary season with my tiny and
inexperienced policy staff of just a few full-time people, only one of whom
besides myself, Al Stern, a professor at Detroit's Wayne State University, a
colleague in the 1968 Humphrey campaign, had ever been in the crucible
of a presidential campaign. We had to take positions on dozens of issues,
foreign and domestic, in preparing campaign speeches and answers to questions that inevitably came from the press and policy-oriented groups.

   To add heft and weight to the domestic- and foreign-policy side of the
campaign, I added several young bright aides from Congress and academia,
including Richard Holbrooke and Robert Hunter (foreign policy), Jerry Ja-
sinowski (economics), Orin Kramer (financial), Kitty Schirmer (energy), and
David Rubenstein as my chief deputy. I also created a series of advisory groups
composed of prominent academics like Lawrence Klein of Wharton to head
our economic task force; to lead our foreign-policy group, Zbigniew Brzezinski

of Columbia, later his national security adviser; along with Cyrus Vance, a New York lawyer and experienced diplomat, later his secretary of state. I regularly consulted on international issues with Brzezinski's Columbia colleague Richard Gardner, who came to Atlanta as early as 1975 and slept on our living-room couch. I worked with Ham, Jody, and Rafshoon to develop broad themes for his speeches. First was establishing what he had done as governor to provide a sound, well-managed state government by never raising taxes and leaving a budget surplus. But his more basic, winning campaign message cut across ideological boundaries: to restore trust in America's government, pledging, as he put it, "I will never lie to you" and "a government as good as its people"—on which he tried to deliver.

"ETHNIC PURITY"

Every presidential campaign has its crises. They usually arise from remarks taken out of context, tangled and ill-phrased statements, and similar self-inflicted wounds. These are impossible to avoid in the hothouse atmosphere and under the unrelenting pressures of nonstop campaigning in different time zones, little sleep, and the press and political opponents ready to pounce on every miscue. Candidates take great pains to stay on message, and drifting off the agreed line can reveal more subtle views of their world than fit easily into oversimplified campaign mode. On April 6, the same day as he eked out a one-point victory over Udall in the Wisconsin primary, Carter was in Indianapolis heading toward Pennsylvania for a crucial test three weeks later. At the urging of Geno Baroni, a Jesuit priest I brought on board to help us understand and reach out to white, urban, largely Catholic voters in the North, he was campaigning in the industrial belt from Wisconsin to New England.

Someone asked Carter if he had any objection to German Americans living in their own neighborhoods and sharing their own language and songs. He said he did not, and if he had stopped there, the issue of race that was hiding under the surface of the question would have stayed unnoticed. But in a clumsy attempt to transfer his support from white Southerners to white

Northern ethnics, he went further in Indianapolis: "I have nothing against a community that is made up of people who are Polish, or who are Czechoslovakians, or who are French Canadians or who are blacks trying to maintain the ethnic purity of their neighborhoods. This is a natural inclination. Government should not break up a neighborhood on a numerical basis or inject black families into a white neighborhood just to create some sort of integration."[65] He later tried to seek shelter from the storm he had brought upon himself by dismissing this as "an offhand statement."[66] But it sounded as if he wanted minorities kept out of traditionally white neighborhoods.

I received a call at home from Jody Powell, telling me that we had a real crisis on our hands. I told him that I would immediately reach out to Andy Young, our black Atlanta congressman whom Fran and I had helped elect, and who had already taken Carter to meet the suspicious Congressional Black Caucus, where he left a good impression by emphasizing his commitment to civil rights and wowing them with the number of blacks in senior positions in his campaign.[67] With as much emotion as I could muster, I appealed to Andy for help. He paused, said he was concerned about the remarks, but knew Carter well enough to believe he was no racist. But that did little to calm the furious reaction. Mayor Maynard Jackson of Atlanta postponed plans to endorse Carter, angrily exclaiming, "Is there no white politician I can trust?" Jesse Jackson went over the top, attacking Carter's remarks as a "throwback to Hitlerian racism." Mayor Richard Hatcher of Gary, Indiana, another rising black politician, was hardly more artful: "We've created a Frankenstein's monster with a Southern drawl, a more cultured version of the old Confederate at the schoolhouse door." Carter's Democratic competitors joined in. "Just who does he want to wall out?" asked Mo Udall. Scoop Jackson accused him of talking differently to different groups.[68]

Ham later tried to explain away his boss's words by saying that "We didn't know, living in south Georgia, what it meant to say 'ethnic purity' in a Pennsylvania or Ohio neighborhood urban ethnic setting."[69] I think otherwise. While it certainly was not scripted, I believe Carter was sending a message to the conservative white, ethnic vote in the North—and he finally had to back down. In a news conference aired on NBC's *Today* show fully three days later, he had to apologize for an "unfortunate" remark, but compounded the crisis by saying that while he supported open housing, he also opposed using federal "force to move people of a different ethnic background into a neighborhood just to change its character."[70]

The belated and qualified apology was not enough. It took a downtown Atlanta rally organized by Andy Young, at which the key speaker—Daddy King—saved Carter's campaign by proclaiming in his booming voice, "I forgive you, governor, and I support you all the way."[71] The incident in its entirety ironically locked in the black vote throughout the country, and Carter swept the Pennsylvania primary, winning all but two of its sixty-seven counties. He was now virtually unstoppable, or so I thought.

THE NOMINATION

As he piled up primary victories in the South and Midwest, liberal Democrats tried to block his nomination and dubbed their group ABC—"Anybody But Carter." The fact was that the outspoken liberals never were with this Southern moderate. I was present when Joseph Rauh, the liberal leader of Americans for Democratic Action, literally pulled Carter off his chair as he tried to speak at their reception.[72] He hardly did much better with the labor movement; the AFL-CIO, suspicious of a candidate from a nonunion state, waited until after the Democratic Convention to endorse him. Nevertheless Carter plugged away, accumulating delegates in the primaries with such regularity that he came close to losing his luster as a new face challenging the old guard. He stumbled toward the end as two fresh faces entered the race late: California's maverick governor, Jerry Brown, and the silver-tongued Senator Frank Church of Idaho, won a bunch of late primaries. But he hung on to win Ohio on the last primary day, buoyed by the unique support of blacks in Cleveland and conservative whites in downstate rural areas. He ran in thirty of the thirty-one primaries and won eighteen of them. Jordan's battle plan was perfectly executed by Carter, winning what had seemed an impossible victory.

The convention in New York was remarkably calm and united, a striking contrast with the 1968 convention in Chicago, literally torn apart by riots against the Vietnam War and tear gas from Mayor Richard Daley's tough police, which I had personally observed as a member of Humphrey's staff.

As Carter's representative to the convention's Platform Committee in 1976, I presented his positions on a wide range of issues and had to debate only a few. The most contentious was amnesty for those who had evaded the Vietnam draft, which I ironed out with the antiwar activist Sam Brown, who eventually joined the administration. The only plank to which Carter objected was the party's traditional pledge to support Jerusalem as Israel's undivided capital, which he felt would tie his hands in any Middle East negotiations. Carter sent me a handwritten note, "Stu., Good Job, JC," on a copy of the final platform.

The delegates overwhelmingly supported his vice presidential choice, the liberal Minnesota senator Walter "Fritz" Mondale, giving the ticket regional and ideological balance. Carter needed an entrée to the inner workings of Congress, and ties to the labor and liberal community, along with the snappy slogan, "Fritz and Grits."

As Jimmy Carter rose to give his acceptance speech and saw the waves of adoration from the delegates in Madison Square Garden, he felt a sense of "achievement, of euphoria." And yet true to form, at this most momentous of occasions, he told me he was privately "hoping that the ceremonies would soon be over," a sentiment few politicians would feel, since they would never want the public adoration to stop. But that was not Jimmy Carter: "You know, the trappings of a convention, the making of a speech on different teleprompters and things like that certainly didn't destroy the good feeling of the time, [but] the accolades even then made me a little bit uncomfortable."[73] He took the rostrum with his trademark toothy grin and greeting: "I'm Jimmy Carter, and I'm running for president!" The Madison Square Garden crowd roared approval.

But the speech itself was hardly a traditional Democratic laundry list of promised programs. He spoke as a political outsider coming to give the government back to the people, and recognizing that "government has its limits and cannot solve all of our problems." He spoke about love as no candidate before or since: "Love must be aggressively translated into simple justice. The test for any government is not how popular it is with the powerful, but how honestly and fairly it deals with those who must depend on it." He bemoaned the link between money and politics, and landed on his favorite campaign cry—a pledge to reform an unfair tax structure that was "a disgrace to the human race." That pledge and others resonate to this day—exposing lobby-ists and ending a double standard of justice that let "big-shot crooks" go free while the poor went to prison. His foreign-policy vision was strikingly idealistic—"to depend in world affairs not merely on the size of an arsenal but on the nobility of ideas" and to commit himself to stamping out international terrorism and preserving human rights. The speech was hardly a liberal war cry, but it clearly laid out the principles that had won him the nomination.[74]

The speech was almost denied TV coverage by a threatened work action by a union of the electrical contractor. After the speech, the hundreds of blue balloons released in celebration touched the newly installed ceiling lights and promptly exploded. It was a metaphor for the forthcoming general elec-tion and his presidency.[75]

THE GENERAL ELECTION

Ironically, this triumphant, nearly unimaginable nomination by an enthusi-astic party marked the high point of what was almost his undoing in the general election. Carter began with a thirty-point lead over Gerald Ford in the polls, and while that surely was unrealistically high, it never should have shrunk to under 1 percent on election night. The Republican Party was as divided as the Democrats were united, a role reversal for our chronically feuding political coalition, as upstart California governor Ronald Reagan came within a hairbreadth of winning the GOP nomination. Ford almost gave the election away by pardoning Richard Nixon.

Our own mistakes contributed mightily to Ford almost pulling off a star-tling comeback. Carter delivered tough personal attacks against Ford as a weak leader and "just a quiescent extension of the policies of Nixon," which backfired against a president widely seen as decent and honest. It also was dissonant with a challenger preaching his own brand of political honesty, national healing, and social unity. Another of Carter's political eccentrici-ties was delivering tough messages to audiences that did not want to hear them. When he vowed to pardon Vietnam draft evaders in a speech at the national convention of the American Legion—of all places—he was soundly booed. These helped him lose 10 points in the polls.[76]

At bottom, as Jordan succinctly put it, "We had spent four years figuring out how to win the nomination, and given very little thought to the general election."[77] Substantively, by the time Carter had won his arduous primary campaign, he was a different kind of candidate—no longer the outsider, the insurgent, the antiestablishment populist with the promise of healing the nation's wounds. Now he was the candidate of the Democratic Party, with all its embedded interest groups and outspoken liberal advocates. Ham Jordan, who knew him best, said that "all of a sudden he went from being this kind of loner who was out there fighting and scrapping, the little guy against the system and the status quo, to wearing the mantle of his party, and neither he nor we in his entourage were emotionally prepared for the role of the establishment candidate, where at a minimum it is essential to look at the political consequences before making a leap of conscience."[78]

Traditionally, Republican presidential candidates run to the right in the primaries and move to the center in the general election to capture independent voters, while Democratic candidates do precisely the opposite— run to the left in the primaries to win the liberal activists and then move to the center in the general election to satisfy the uncertain voters seeking continuity and stability. But Carter had run in the center for the primaries and then moved to the left after his nomination, in hopes of uniting the party and energizing it behind him. He looked more like a traditional than a New Democrat, taking on some of the orthodoxies of the Democratic Party.

In that era it was difficult if not impossible for a Democrat to win the presidency without the big labor unions mobilizing thousands of field-workers to organize on the ground, especially to help turn out the voters on Election Day. Carter realized he was working from an unusual position: "Before the nomination I was kind of a lonely farmer, Southerner, decent, honest, who needed the individual help of voters. Afterward, I was the establishment, I was the Democratic Party in the people's mind, and I was never comfortable with that." As he moved from state to state, he remembered often sharing the stage with local candidates where "I would be wrapped with these unsavory politicians who were running for governor, running for Congress, that I didn't really like." He also had a set of personal priorities that many found puzzling: "People never did understand me and still don't, because I had kind of a dichotomy in my life."[79] Along with his profound commitment to racial equality, he was at heart a populist of a rural, self-improvement variety favoring federal aid to education and special programs such as vocational and job training for the poor and hard-pressed workers.

THE DEBATES

Preparing Carter for three presidential debates, the first in sixteen years since the first and decisive Kennedy-Nixon debate, may have been my biggest campaign challenge—and his, too. A trained engineer, experienced businessman, and seasoned administrator whose strong point was the mastery of detail would be squaring off against an incumbent president who had spent a quarter of a century in Congress, and who was experienced in targeting the heart of an issue and finding the weak point of his opponent's argument with the force of the college football player that Gerald Ford had once been. At least that was how it might be handicapped, and our small policy group felt undermanned and under severe pressure.

I was in charge of preparing the briefing papers and made the mistake of presenting Carter at his home in Plains with a book more than four inches thick, with detailed background materials, suggested answers for likely questions, and attack lines against Ford, in the hope that we would refine the material during practice sessions. Instead he circled typographical errors and grammatical mistakes, as if he were my elementary school teacher, a practice he continued with memos in the White House.

To help me in Atlanta with the mammoth project, I sought out Ted Van Dyk, Hubert Humphrey's talented aide with whom I worked in the 1968 campaign. Together we compiled the book, working seven days a week for two weeks, sleeping three or four hours a night. One Sunday morning I arrived to find a note from Ted: "I am sorry I cannot continue to work for Carter. Now that I know in detail his positions, he is too conservative for me to support."

Van Dyk was not the only one who deserted us because Carter could not satisfy the party's liberal wing. Robert Shrum, a gifted but intense speechwriter, joined the staff in the last weeks of the campaign. Handed a wire-service report that Ford was going to veto a Democratic bill raising spending for a popular social program, Shrum dashed off a strong condemnation for Carter to issue at the next campaign stop, and then handed it to me. I warned him that Carter would likely not agree to such a statement and probably felt closer to Ford on the issue, but I gave the draft to Carter anyway. He read it quickly and wrote "No. JC." Shrum was aghast: How could any Democratic presidential nominee agree with Ford? He declared that he could not work for a candidate with such a conservative fiscal position. I urged him not to judge Carter, whom he barely knew, on the basis of this one issue. But at the next stop Shrum left the plane in a huff. He had lasted nine days.[80]

The economy and domestic issues were the focus of the first of three presidential debates between Ford and Carter in Philadelphia on September 23, 1976.

Even when the most trusted members of the inner circle—Ham, Jody, and Rafshoon—joined me to urge him to prepare through a mock debate, he absolutely refused. This says much about his own supreme confidence (bordering on hubris) in his own intelligence, but not about his adaptability to a major-league debating stage, where he needed to reach out to voters with a wide spectrum of political views. He told me he found it "kind of artificial, and on the issues I felt at ease, I didn't see how practice could have made me deal with the human thing." He also later explained: "I never have been at ease with set speeches or with memorized text. I really like the question-and-answer format, and even at the White House press conferences, I like to speak from a few notes, and the more I'm embedded in an element of rigidity, the more uncomfortable I feel."[81] It was an early sign of his preference for the details of any issue as the route to resolving it. His sharp intellect, his ability to absorb and understand mountains of difficult material, made him feel that he knew better than anyone what he wanted to say and made him stubborn in rejecting advice with which he disagreed. But he paid a price.

I got only a few minutes to go over salient points I thought he should make. One was that prices were rising faster than paychecks, and that real earnings were less than they had been when Nixon took office. Predictably one of Carter's first questions was a softball. Frank Reynolds of ABC-TV noted that he had made job creation a top priority during the campaign and asked:

"Governor, can you say in specific terms what your first step would be next January if you are elected, to achieve this?" Carter stumbled over what should have been the incumbent's weakest point on the economy. Instead of batting it back and knocking it out of the park, his answer was so unfocused that it made me cringe, as I heard him roll out a list of employment, housing, public works, research, taxation, and other eye-glazing proposals. He asserted that they would push down the adult unemployment rate to 3 percent by the end of his first term and balance the federal budget. Four years later when he was preparing for his 1980 debate with Reagan, Carter made a rare admission of vulnerability, that "the worst 20 minutes of my life was the first 20 minutes of the first debate with Ford."[82]

Carter was saved by a remarkable electronic fluke that knocked out the audio transmission and forced a twenty-seven-minute delay, as both candidates stood motionless at their lecterns, like wooden statues. He recovered by attacking Ford for increasing unemployment by 50 percent and doubling the number of small-business bankruptcies. Carter's most effective line was countering Ford's assertion that he had learned how to match unemployment with inflation. Carter fired back: "That's right. We've got the highest inflation we've had in twenty-five years right now . . . and the highest unemployment we've had under Mr. Ford's administration since the Great Depression."[83] Little could we imagine that wicked trade-off would only get worse after Carter was elected. But he turned in only a mediocre performance, with polls showing a slight debate advantage for Ford, in what should have been Carter's strong suit. I did not do much better, as my nationwide TV debut as the designated postdebate "talking head" was marred when my glasses broke, requiring masking tape to put them back together; my horrified mother was concerned I had been in an accident.

Nevertheless, for the second debate, on foreign policy, he refused to practice, not even on the long flight aboard Peanut One to San Francisco. The most we could do was persuade him to allow Brzezinski and representative Les Aspin of Wisconsin, a defense expert, to spend an hour with him in his hotel room reviewing his positions, but—heaven forbid!—not to practice answering possible questions.

That debate turned out to be a decisive event in the campaign, although not because of any detailed mastery by Carter, but a historic blunder by Ford.

There had been great controversy about whether the Nixon-Kissinger policy of détente with Moscow meant that somehow the Ford administration was acquiescent about Eastern Europe being part of the Soviet sphere of influence. Ford apparently had that in mind when Max Frankel of the *New York Times*, one of the panelists, asked whether the Soviet Union was gaining the advantage in a number of areas in the world. He ended the question by declaring: "We've recognized the permanent Communist regime in East Germany. We've virtually signed in Helsinki an agreement that the Russians have dominance in Eastern Europe." Ford's answer not only lost him the debate, it helped him lose the presidency. He replied, "There is no Soviet domination of Eastern Europe, and there never will be under a Ford administration."

Astonished, Frankel said, "I'm sorry. Did I understand you to say, sir, that the Russians are not using Eastern Europe as their own sphere of influence, occupying most of the countries there and making sure with their troops that it is a Communist zone, whereas on our side of the line, the Italians and the French are still flirting with the possibilities?" Ford dug himself more deeply into a hole by replying: "I don't believe, Mr. Frankel, that the Yugoslavians consider themselves dominated by the Soviet Union. I don't believe that the Romanians consider themselves dominated by the Soviet Union. I don't believe that the Poles consider themselves dominated by the Soviet Union. Each of those countries is independent, autonomous, it has its own territorial integrity, and the United States does not concede that those countries are under the domination of the Soviet Union."

In my notes I wrote and underlined "Poles don't consider themselves dominated," and drew a big arrow in the margin to remind me to focus on this with the press after the debate, in what is called the spin room. After all, what were Soviet troops doing in those satellite countries if not ensuring that their rulers followed Moscow's orders? But I did not need to wait. Carter immediately pounced on the advantage, offsetting Ford's supposed foreign-policy expertise and appealing to the ethnic vote in key states. He declared: "I would like to see Mr. Ford convince the Polish-Americans and the Czech-Americans and the Hungarian-Americans in this country that those countries don't live under the domination and supervision of the Soviet Union behind the Iron Curtain."[84]

At first the Republican strategists did not realize how badly their man had been wounded; during the debate itself their instant polls never showed a blip at the exchange. We hammered away at it in our spin, but it was repeated questioning by the press that woke them up. Over at the St. Francis Hotel for what he thought would be a routine postdebate briefing, Ford's chief of staff, Dick Cheney, knew right away they were headed for trouble when Luke Hanna of the *Washington Post* shouted from the back of the room, "Hey, Cheney, how many Soviet divisions in Poland?" What Ford's entourage did not yet know was that he could be as stubborn as Carter. The president refused for several days to admit that he had made a huge mistake, thanks in part to what Cheney (later vice president) felt was a fawning phone call from Secretary of State Henry Kissinger: "Oh, you did a wonderful job, Mr. President, magnificent performance."[85]

"WITH LUST IN MY HEART"

Inside our camp there was an air of exhilaration on the flight back to Atlanta, but it did not last long. Carter soon created his own problems with ill-chosen words that came out of his own mouth to reach a younger audience through *Playboy*. On the cover of the magazine's November issue, on the newsstands during the climactic October weeks of the campaign, was the photo of a provocative model and a headline in bold letters, "Now the *Real* Jimmy Carter on Politics, Religion, the Press and Sex in an Incredible Playboy Interview." Rafshoon and Jody, Carter's chief image makers, had urged him to grant the interview to moderate the impression held by many young voters of Carter as an unbending and moralistic Baptist. Jody even made arrangements for a chartered plane to fly the writer, Robert Sheer, to Plains. He told Carter he was doing a character sketch and promised to let the candidate's staff review the text before publication.[86]

The interview itself was unexceptional. As it concluded, and Sheer was turning off his recorder while Carter showed him out, he asked how Carter dealt with his Baptist belief that people who had sex outside of marriage were inferior. Carter remembered the question as a test of whether he would bring such arrogant beliefs into the White House, responding that Christ warned against judging others, and in the Sermon on the Mount, equated even lust for another woman as equivalent to adultery. Sheer then asked if he had ever lusted for other women, and Carter said he probably had, but that most men were inclined to do so. His actual words were, "Christ said, 'I tell you that anyone who looks on a woman with lust, has in his heart already committed adultery." He then added the fateful words that caused such grief: "I've looked at a lot of women with lust. I've committed adultery in my heart many times. This is something God recognizes I will do—and I have done it—and God forgives me for it. But that does not mean that I condemn someone who not only looks on a woman with lust, but who leaves his wife and shacks up with somebody out of wedlock. Christ says, don't consider yourself better than someone else because one guy screws a whole bunch of women while the other guy is loyal to his wife. The guy who's loyal to his wife ought not to be condescending or proud because of the relative degree of sinfulness."[87]

Carter claimed he did not realize that Sheer's tape recorder was running, which seems likely because he would have immediately realized such remarks would hurt his candidacy if published, and they were. Quite apart from its effect on Carter's electoral base of white, churchgoing Southerners, its target audience of the young and other voters discovered in Carter "a weirdo factor," as Rafshoon pungently put it.[88]

I first learned of the article when Jack Nelson, a friendly reporter from the *Atlanta Constitution*, called me on a Sunday morning at our Atlanta headquarters and asked for a comment, which, shocked as I was, I would not give. I called Jody and Rafshoon, the initiators of this mammoth exercise in bad judgment, and they laughed it off. But it was no laughing matter. Carter was unapologetic and insisted he was simply giving a religious message of how Christ viewed adultery. The real problem was that these supposedly pious and definitely revealing remarks only blurred his image. Was he a liberal or a conservative? A genuinely religious Baptist or an impostor? Carter himself in reflection realized it was "very damaging. . . . I had put forth an image, I hope not totally erroneously, that I was an honest, basically good and moral guy, and here I was lusting after women." On a train trip afterward, he was walking down the aisle, shaking hands with passengers and chatting with reporters, "and all they wanted to talk about was 'lust in your heart' and the *Playboy* interview."[89] Carter belatedly apologized, but the incident remained stuck in the popular imagination.

VICTORY

In the final days of the campaign, Carter's lead over Ford tightened considerably, with Ford's carefully managed "Rose Garden strategy" of looking presidential; vetoing Democratic spending bills; and Ford saying that Carter "wanders, he wavers, he waffles, and he wiggles."[90] As Lance admitted, "He was moderate to the moderates; he was conservative to the conservatives; he was liberal to the liberals; and, in fact, he was all of these things."[91] Pat Caddell's polls told us that Carter was holding on to a sliver of a lead. Our happiest memory aboard Peanut One was the last full day of campaigning: Candidates often spend that day chasing the setting sun, from East to West, finishing in a long sprint to the West Coast. It lasts eighteen hours and is justifiably called the "death march," because it concludes exhausting months of nonstop campaigning. We finished the campaign in Sacramento in a show of party unity alongside Jerry Brown, a vanquished primary opponent. It had been almost two years since Jimmy Carter threw his hat in the ring, the longest presidential campaign in American history. Carter had traveled more than four hundred thousand miles by plane, and delivered over two thousand speeches.[92] An upright piano had been brought on board the rear compartment of the plane, and reporters were belting out songs along with the campaign staff. There was a sense of relief and merriment that the torture of the campaign was over.

On our way back to Plains for the Carters to cast their votes, we thought he would win because of a national impulse for change, and we could feel it coming, especially with the weight of a stagnant economy on Ford's shoulders, as it would rest on Carter's four years later.

We nervously awaited the judgment of tens of millions of our fellow Americans on election night at Atlanta's downtown Omni Hotel. Fran had rented a large suite near the president's, and we invited family and close friends. I was in no mood for chatter as the television networks began a long night of reporting the mixed results, with losses in some key states. The uncertainty lasted into the morning. We won the bellwether state of Ohio, which no Republican elected president has ever lost. Carter made calls throughout the night, one to Richard Daley, the Chicago mayor and political boss who had helped deliver Illinois for Jack Kennedy in 1960—by last-minute ballot stuffing, the Republicans believed. But Daley could not work his magic and told Carter that his state would go for Ford. As midnight came and went, we were still short of the decisive 270 electoral votes and needed Hawaii and Mississippi. We had no doubts about solidly Democratic Hawaii, but Mississippi was the most conservative state of the Old Confederacy, particularly on race. Jimmy and Rosalynn were nervously holding hands in front of the television in their hotel suite when a call came at 3:30 a.m. from the governor of Mississippi, Cliff Finch. He reported that the Palmetto State, the deepest of the Deep South, had gone for Carter by about twelve thousand votes, putting him over the top on electoral votes.

Carter has never been a man who wore his emotions on his sleeve in either triumph or tragedy. Like the submarine officer he had been, he was cool and controlled, and in victory he was as relieved as he was exhilarated. He and Rosalynn hugged each other and their children. He quickly strode out of his suite to greet his thrilled supporters, thank the American people for his victory, and then travel immediately to Plains, where hundreds of friends met him at 5:30 a.m.[93]

Fran and I had no such inhibitions. We hugged, kissed, and cried on each other's shoulders. Two years of hard work had turned an impossible dream into a reality. We instinctively knew how profound a change this would make to our lives and those of our two boys, Jay and Brian, only six and three. Fran would make the biggest sacrifice. She had just been selected for the prestigious Leadership Atlanta program and was slated to be the next president of the Atlanta chapter of the National Council of Jewish Women. But as she would throughout forty-five years of a wonderful marriage, she supported our move and would be my partner in the next great challenge ahead in the White House. But there was little time to savor the moment, because I was told to run down to the hotel ballroom to be on the podium when Carter made his victory statement.

For one last election, Carter had overturned Lyndon Johnson's famous prediction that the Democrats would forever lose the South once he signed the 1964 Civil Rights Act. Carter swept every Southern state of the Old Confederacy except Virginia, although those results reflected mostly Southern pride overcoming white racism. John Stennis, Mississippi's ardent segregationist Democratic senator for almost thirty years, never forgot his grandfather's story of Union troops at the end of the Civil War riding into town and being billeted in the courthouse and the schools "like an occupying army." Reliving the moment of Carter's election, Stennis said: "I wish my grandfather could see this now. A man from Georgia being president of the United States."[94] The election was one of the tightest in modern history. Carter won 297 electoral votes (23 states and the District of Columbia) to 240 for Ford (27 states). Except for Texas, a former slave state straddling South and West, Ford carried every Western state including California. Carter won the popular vote by one million of 81 million cast, although to the chagrin of the Ford campaign, a shift of only ten thousand votes in two states, Ohio and Hawaii, would have given him a victory in the Electoral College.[95]

But Carter was not even thinking about how narrow his victory was. Even then, at the pinnacle of his political life, he was already thinking of the complex task of organizing his presidency. We would rest a few days and then, as he put it, we would be "getting down to work." We did not rest very long.

2

A PERILOUS TRANSITION

The United States is unique among the world's democracies in the length of time provided by our Constitution for the transition from the outgoing to the incoming presidential administration. In parliamentary democracies the transfer of power is instantaneous, with the leader of the victorious opposition and shadow ministers ready to step into place. In the two and one-half months from election to inauguration, the president-elect and his team must choose key White House officials and hundreds of senior appointees for the cabinet and subcabinet; set a course for foreign policy; develop a domestic agenda and budget; and write an inaugural address summing up all this for the nation and the world. And this is happening when the president-elect and his team, giddy with victory but exhausted from the campaign, are under scrutiny as never before for clues about the new administration.

Transitions can be perilous if not handled well. The disastrous Bay of Pigs invasion in the early months of the Kennedy administration was an inheritance from the Eisenhower administration, and the new president was hesitant to stop or even check this doomed scheme lest he be accused of being soft on Communism. The road for the incoming Carter administration was especially difficult and laid the groundwork for many of its problems but also for its successes. It was during the transition that he determined to structure his White House without a chief of staff to set priorities among an overly ambitious set of initiatives on energy and water projects, and developed the $50 rebate he would soon abandon,[1] all with only a skeleton crew, and without the expert interagency review that becomes routine when the president takes office.

Every major party candidate after their nomination receives CIA briefings, which I alone attended with Carter. Three were held at his modest ranch house in Plains during July and August, but after he won, the first top-secret briefing on November 19 was different. It was presented by CIA Director George H. W. Bush (later the first President Bush), and given the vast scope of the challenges ranging from missile placement to oil prices, I felt that the sun, moon, and stars had fallen on us all. On the surface the president-elect was the same Jimmy Carter in casual clothes and work boots, but the trappings of the presidency were all around. Secret Service officers were stationed inside his house and even in the surrounding woods. A makeshift gate and guard-house were quickly erected to control access. During a break in the November briefing, Carter asked me to step outside. He confided that he was considering Brzezinski as his national security adviser and Vance as secretary of state, and asked my opinion. During the campaign I had worked with them on our foreign-policy task force, and I told him that either one would be an excellent choice—but not both, because they held diametrically opposing views on his chief foreign-policy challenge, the Soviet Union. But Vance and Brzezinski had recommended each other to Carter for their respective positions.[2]

Vance felt that negotiations were the best way of managing the complex relationship with Moscow. Brzezinski was more of a tough Cold Warrior, in part because of his family's Polish background, but also his keen sense of history and the role of the United States in combating what was at the time an aggressive Soviet Union. Carter paused for a second and said, "I like hearing different opinions. I can handle it." But their ideological differences were far more difficult to reconcile than he realized, and often gave a Janus-like quality to the administration's stance toward the Soviet Union.

A different and more complex set of circumstances inherited from the campaign bedeviled the transition and, over time, the very nature of Carter's governance. After the nomination seemed within his grasp, he did something that at one level was uniquely farsighted by setting up a transition planning staff headed by Jack Watson, a former marine and smart young partner in Kirbo's law firm. About fifty bright young men and women set to work formulating policy goals; they worked in secret, isolated from the campaign team, lest their existence leak out and make Carter appear over-confident of victory. Watson said he tried to stay in touch with Ham on the campaign trail, but "the last thing they were interested in was talking about policy planning or the transition period."[3]

Three days after the election Watson delivered three large black binders to Plains full of recommendations, duplicating precisely what my campaign policy team had been doing for two years. From Watson's perspective he did exactly what Carter wanted him to—begin planning ahead for victory, and it became one of the most painful experiences of his life.[4]

But from Ham's perspective and mine, Watson had been setting up a government-in-waiting while the rest of us were trying to help Carter win the election. His briefing books made no attempt to examine the political dimension that is an essential element of democratic governance. Their attitude was that they were scholars of government who had studied the issues and understood the direction the Carter presidency should take, while we were political hacks. Our view was that we had won an improbable victory, and now they were carving up the pie. Neither side was right; policy and politics have to be integrated, and voters who had sent Carter to the White House expected that he would make good on his promises, or at least try. Harsh words were exchanged, and Jack felt that Ham dismissed his people as "pointy-headed intellectuals."[5]

Carter further complicated the situation by naming Watson, not Jordan, to be transition director, with a two-million-dollar federal allocation and the responsibility of maintaining liaison with the outgoing Ford administration, organizing briefing teams for each cabinet department, and providing detailed recommendations for each incoming cabinet member. More than policy differences were at stake. In every presidential campaign the winning candidate's staff members expect to be awarded important jobs in the new administration; after all, they are battle tested. When Carter was on the road, which was most of the time, his political operatives ran the campaign with a free hand. What was different this time was that two separate camps were competing, and the president-elect was not clearly defining their responsibilities. More strategic questions did not receive the attention they deserved.

Congressional Democrats had unrealistic expectations about the first president from their own party in eight years. Many had been elected as "Watergate babies" in 1974 and 1976 and had never served in Congress with a Democratic president. Although Carter finally and belatedly intervened and told Watson to yield responsibility for presidential appointments to Ham, he did not resolve the split between the two camps. I had a great deal riding on the outcome, since Watson and I were in effect competing for the job I really wanted, chief White House domestic policy adviser. My hopes were not high because Watson was Kirbo's protégé, but he inadvertently did me a favor by empire building, which was spotted by no less than Carter himself. He later told me that when he won the presidency, "all of a sudden we found that Jack had put together a set of decisions in which neither I, nor you nor Hamilton or others were involved."[6] Jordan cut Watson back to a staff of two, while I was given the leeway to hire a large number of able young people, and that gave Ham a counterweight to Watson's ambitions.

I made a rookie mistake during the transition of telling a *New York Times* reporter, Martin Tolchin, that our legislative agenda would be "modest," remembering President Kennedy's adage that great initiatives cannot be built on slim electoral margins—earning me one of Carter's only personal rebukes in our years together. In fact, at his direction we launched a veritable blizzard of "comprehensive" domestic reforms (a favorite Carter goal that I quickly came to loathe) in energy, welfare, taxes, water projects, hospital costs, along with a major economic stimulus package to jump-start the economy and fulfill his campaign promise to end the "Ford recession." At the same time, he launched negotiations to turn over the Panama Canal by treaty, which numerous presidents before him had begun, but never completed because of the fierce politics involved; a Middle East peace process, which had stalled; arms control negotiations with the Soviet Union; and a radically reoriented American foreign policy, which made human rights a principal focus. What could not be imagined was how many of these would succeed in leaving a lasting imprint on American government, although not without struggles.

THE OUTSIDER MOVES IN

The new president's broad vision was not put in the hands of a staff with broad government experience. In an overreaction to the excesses of Watergate and Nixon's centralization of power, Carter initially decided not to have a chief of staff. He felt such a staff post implied a hierarchy among his top staff he wanted to avoid, but this placed enormous burdens on the president alone to coordinate and prioritize his agenda. He also filled the ranks of his senior White House staff with Georgians and campaign aides who had been with him during the long political campaign, myself included. All had one thing in common: Except for me, not one senior executive aide had ever before set foot in the White House, lived in Washington, or knew anything about the operations of the U.S. Congress or the massive federal government. Our home-grown, inexperienced team did not know its way around Washington and the city's multiple power centers—Congress, interest groups, the press.

At one level this was an unfair criticism. Every new president brings with him the campaign team that has helped him across the finish line, proven loyalists whom he knows and trusts. Jack Kennedy brought in his "Boston Mafia," LBJ his "Texas Mafia," Nixon his Californians and longtime New York confidants, and Ford his congressional staff and senior campaign aides. The difference was that all these presidents had served in Congress, as had many of their aides. President Carter did not leaven the inexperience of his Georgia Mafia by adding a senior eminence, for example Bob Strauss, who knew where to find the hidden levers of power and how to use them. Even Ronald Reagan, a seasoned politician as governor of California and before that as head of Hollywood's Screen Actors Guild, helped make up for his lack of Washington experience by naming James A. Baker his chief of staff. This Princeton-educated Texan, a shrewd lawyer with great political skills and Washington experience at the Commerce Department, had managed the general election campaign of his chief rival for the Republican nomination, George H. W. Bush.

The only Georgia hand with the innate political talent to fill this void was Bert Lance, who eagerly courted the Washington establishment, but with a flamboyance that was alien to the ways of Washington's buttoned-up society and fitted more comfortably into the freewheeling pattern of his banking behavior—which later brought him to grief. During the transition he made his rounds aboard a limousine emblazoned with American flags on its bumper and sporting license plates reading BERT in the front and LANCE in the rear.[7]

During the transition it is traditional as well as useful to meet with your outgoing counterpart. When I visited Ford's domestic adviser, James Cannon, he sat me down in his West Wing office directly above the Oval Office, the office I would soon occupy, and pulled a bottle of expensive whiskey out of a small cabinet. I thought: How gracious of him to toast our victory! But Cannon had no intention of pouring a drink, only of teaching me a valuable lesson. The label read BOTTLED EXPRESSLY FOR JOHN EHRLICHMAN, Nixon's domestic adviser, and Cannon pointed to it as an example of the abuse of the power I would soon inherit. He warned me never to forget that I was only a temporary occupant of my high office, that people would fawn over me, extend invitations for lunches and dinners and other social events, and try to influence me in every way. "Just remember," he said, "those invitations are not to you as a person but to the office you hold, and that all the invitations will cease as soon as you leave your position." This lesson in humility stayed with me, and I passed it on to my successor Martin Anderson, Ronald Reagan's domestic adviser, along with that unopened bottle of booze.

Some of Carter's key Georgia appointees performed their jobs superbly. Most of the White House press corps regarded Jody as a gifted press secretary.[8] Watson did a fine job of working with state and local officials and as cabinet secretary. When Ham left the White House to run the 1980 campaign, Jack became the chief of staff and did an excellent job. We would all have been better off if Carter had appointed him at the start, because he had administrative abilities Ham knew he lacked. Frank Moore, by his own admission, had no experience with Congress, and only learned he would be the chief White House lobbyist days before the inauguration. He stumbled at first by not returning scores of telephone calls from the Hill because he was so understaffed. Later he was unfairly barred from the Capitol for days by House Speaker Tip O'Neill over the president's failure to appoint his friend Robert Griffin to a government post, having to intervene with Tip's wife, Millie, to get the ban lifted.[9] While never a great congressional strategist, Frank had good political instincts, worked hard, built a strong staff of young aides who had worked in Congress, and helped to lead an unrecognized, sterling legislative record for the president.

But nothing better demonstrated the Carter team's ambivalence about Washington norms than its poster boys in the early months of the administration: Ham and Jody allowed themselves to appear on the front cover of *Rolling Stone* as "White House Whiz Kids." Ham wore an open shirt and had a towel over his shoulder, and Jody had an open-collared shirt with his tie pulled down, both looking supremely confident.[10] This was a violation of the long-held tradition that White House staff should not make themselves the story. At about the same time *Time* ran a cover story, "The President's Boys," where they were dressed in cartoon form as South Georgia bumpkins, with overalls and no shirts, holding fishing rods.[11] Hugh Sidey, the magazine's Washington bureau chief, piled on by knocking Carter for wearing unpresidential brown wing-tip shoes. Ham later conceded that "mostly people laughed at us; this kind of confirmed the stereotype of the bumpkins from Georgia [who] don't know how to behave in the Big Leagues." But it also violated an informal code that key White House staff should be as invisible as possible, and made Ham vulnerable to attacks. *Newsweek* reported that at a dinner where Ham was seated next to the well-endowed wife of the Egyptian ambassador, he was said to have remarked: "I have always wanted to see the pyramids." Everyone denied it, but Ham realized that once the story was in print, it did not matter whether it was true or false.[12] Again, Ham was in the news in an unflattering way, even if not of his own making.

Ham was an enigma, who seemed to have a chip on his shoulder from the moment he entered the White House. I and many others felt privileged to work there, walking in the footsteps of American history. But he seemed disdainful of official Washington, sending a message by his behavior that said in effect: We beat you, and we'll show you we don't need to conform to your norms. During much of his first year, he came to work at the White House in an informal khaki shirt and trousers with brown high-top work boots, as if he had just come in from the fields in Georgia. He would often greet colleagues and visitors alike with his boots up on his long desk. Initially he had little interest in being involved in policy decisions and did not organize and preside over White House staff meetings.

Even though he carried the title Political Adviser to the President, he never in four years attended the weekly Democratic congressional leadership breakfasts to join in the discussions of legislative priorities and cultivate personal relationships with the lawmakers who held the fate of the president's program in their hands. He intentionally refused to return congressional phone calls, even from the Speaker of the House and the Senate majority leader, contending that he would have been interfering with Moore in his liaison job.

One mix-up that was not his fault, but that of Tip's personal aide, Leo Diehl, over the Speaker's tickets to the preinaugural gala at the Kennedy Center, prompted Tip to call Ham "Hannibal Jerkin." This mistaken notion of keeping his distance demonstrated Jordan's failure to appreciate his own importance. Members of Congress wanted to be able to say they had talked with the president's top adviser. Hardly a day went by when I did not have multiple calls and meetings with members of Congress and their staffs, without which I could not have done my job.

Presidents must constantly attend to the coalition that elected them. Only Ham could have made the determination of how our policies should be integrated into the president's broader political agenda, the imperative of maintaining the support of his voters, and enlarging that number whenever possible. This left a gap that was never filled. When Ham finally calculated the political cost of a number of foreign-policy decisions, particularly when they touched Israel and the Arab states, he began attending the weekly foreign-policy breakfasts with the national security team. There he made important contributions. Indeed, when Ham put his mind to it, there was nothing he could not do. He superbly organized the strategy and a political war room to secure passage of the Panama Canal Treaty, and a controversial arms sale to Saudi Arabia. But his engagements were sporadic, at least until he was finally named chief of staff midway in the president's term.

The worst of this diffident attitude of disengagement was that it would have been totally unnecessary if he and all of us had understood that Washington protocol sprang from a deep commitment to the power that underwrote it. Around the time of Carter's election, I sent the president a new book by Stephen Hess, a former White House official in the Eisenhower and Nixon administrations and a Brookings Institution scholar of the presidency. It was titled *Organizing the Presidency*, but Carter did not internalize an important part of its message. As Hess told me later: "Carter and his people came to town with an inferiority complex. They didn't realize that they could have taken over the town. They were it. When Reagan came in he had dinner with Kay Graham [owner of the *Washington Post*] and Lane Kirkland [president of the AFL-CIO]. All of these people here in Washington would have died to do that with Carter, when in the early stages of the administration you're new and exciting and you're the people that everybody wants to know about and meet. People around here are here to understand and to help the president. But Carter resisted that. He went to great lengths not to be captive of the establishment, when in fact he should have been the leader of the establishment, and used it for his purposes."[13] But Jody saw the other side of the coin, the resentment and suspicion of the Washington establishment against which Carter had campaigned: " 'They're not us. They're not our kind of folks. We'll show them that this town is tougher than they think.' "[14]

This disparity of attitudes underscored a central dilemma of Carter's presidency: maintaining his status as an outsider fighting for the common good against Washington's entrenched interests, while he was simultaneously the ultimate insider as president trying to bend those interest groups and Congress to his will. Just after the election, Ham, its political mastermind, remarked only half-jokingly that if Vance and Brzezinski, two certified members of the establishment, were named to the top foreign-policy positions, the whole point of Carter's insurgent, antiestablishment campaign would be undercut. Of course the president-elect did just that: How could the security of the United States be put in the hands of novices? Late in the administration, Jody was driving his Volkswagen Beetle past the imposing structure of the Kennedy Center for the Performing Arts, with Pat Caddell as his passenger. Jody ruefully reflected, "Boy, we screwed up. We made a terrible mistake when we came to Washington. We should either have burned it down or we should have totally co-opted it—either dance or burn down the barn. But we should not have done what we did, which was to straddle."[15]

Carter's decision to surround himself with us Georgians was compounded by two other closely related decisions: to act as his own White House chief of staff and to organize a cabinet-style government, which empowered each cabinet officer to choose the department's top officials and initiate its own legislative agenda. The loyalties of the subcabinet officials were first to the cabinet officials who hired them. At the same time we were fighting to hire more women and more minorities, and this policy did not always reach far enough into the departments.

With Carter's aggressive agenda, he needed a powerful White House staff that would reach into the departments, ensuring that the president's loyalists were strategically placed and would drive his program and not theirs. In the immediate post-Watergate era, a more decentralized structure seemed an understandable arrangement, but also turned out to be a disastrous one. After all, Carter had not won the White House on the promise of a specific set of policies but on an anti-Watergate message to end the excesses of Nixon and his inner circle. He understandably did not want his White House to resemble the Nixon administration's centralized control by his chief of staff, H. R. Haldeman, and his principal assistant for domestic policy, John Ehrlichman. During their reign, they were known around Washington as "the Germans," with all the obvious implications of that derisive term in that more immediate post–World War II era. These concerns reached well beyond domestic policy and the Watergate crimes to Kissinger's role as a national security adviser bypassing the State Department and, at Nixon's direction, helping start a secret war by bombing Cambodia. The problem was not a faulty White House structure. It was that Kissinger was seen by his critics to be secretive, and that Haldeman, Ehrlichman, and the president himself were dishonest.

Carter's instinct to denude the White House staff, elevate the cabinet, and serve as his own chief of staff was reinforced by a full day of briefings at Brookings that I had arranged during the campaign. Hess and his predominantly Democratic colleagues tried to explain why he could not run the federal government the way he had run his gubernatorial office. Hess impertinently asked how many people lived in Georgia. When Carter replied five million, Hess told him that five million people, equally divided between civilians and military, worked in the federal government, and that he could not hope to run it like the state of Georgia.[16]

Nevertheless Hess opposed a powerful chief, and recommended slimming down the staff to "scrape off the barnacles that had accumulated over the years" as it morphed into a bureaucracy itself and bred a distrust among the cabinet departments. He remembered the Eisenhower staff was so small that everyone could fit into the White House mess at lunchtime, while eight years later there had to be several sittings separating senior from junior staff.

Moreover, while the Eisenhower staff was composed of people of proven accomplishment for whom public service meant a pay cut, in the Nixon era it was filled with political people working in the "the best jobs they had ever had in their lives." The arc of growth, however, was bipartisan. Liberal presidents like Roosevelt felt the departmental bureaucracy was too conservative, and conservatives like Nixon found it too liberal, leading presidents to bypass the departments through their own loyal supporters, many of whom were barely qualified for White House assignments.

A quantum leap in size had indeed occurred during the Nixon presidency, and Nixon's chief of staff, H. R. Haldeman, had indeed amassed too much power relative to the cabinet. When Ford took office after the Nixon resignation, he initially instituted a "spokes of the wheel" White House structure, which had also been used by Kennedy, where four or five senior aides—the bicycle spokes—would report to the president at the hub. This was the model Hess recommended to President-elect Carter.

But for Ford it had led to a disastrous lack of coordination and was quickly abandoned for a traditional chief-of-staff model. After Ford's defeat Chief of Staff Dick Cheney was given a going-away present at a staff roast—a mounted bicycle wheel with all the spokes except one busted, bent, gnarled, and twisted, with an inscription that read "The spokes on the wheel are a rare form of management artistry, invented by Gerald Ford and modified by Dick Cheney." He left that on his desk for Ham Jordan when he took over the office after the inauguration, along with a note: "Dear Hamilton, beware the spokes of the wheel."[17] This is one piece of advice from Cheney we would have done well to follow.

But Ham knew Carter emphatically did not want one chief of staff, although he felt the new president needed "more than anything to have an organizer of information, controlling his schedule and stuff like that." As it was, Ham admitted he "rarely had significant policy input on things."[18] Indeed Carter made clear he "didn't want to have a homogenous group around me, all of whom felt the same way."[19] He got his wish.

The president said he asked Ham several times to take over as chief of staff, when he recognized the void without one, but each time Ham demurred.[20] Even when he was formally installed as chief of staff later after Carter reshuffled his cabinet, Ham felt he never really had the chance to serve effectively because within weeks he was targeted with outlandishly false drug charges following a brief but ill-advised visit to the Studio 54 nightclub in New York. At most he felt he was "more of a coordinator; I wasn't a Chief of Staff in a sense that you'd send domestic policy papers through me. You'd come to me when you had a problem that you wanted me to help you with politically or evaluate politically."[21] To his credit, recognizing his administrative shortcomings, he brought in Alonzo McDonald, managing director of the global consulting firm, McKinsey & Company, as his deputy and White House staff director. Frankly, the president would have been far better off with a chief of staff from the start.

The cabinet that Carter chose was stronger, more experienced, and abler than most of the White House staff. For the three most important cabinet positions, he chose stars who would have been on the short list of any Democratic president. Vance had served in senior positions at State and Defense in the Kennedy and Johnson administrations. Treasury Secretary W. Michael Blumenthal held a Ph.D. in economics, served as a key trade negotiator in the Kennedy administration, led a major American corporation, and had a quick wit and outgoing manner. Defense Secretary Harold Brown not only had served at the Pentagon in the last Democratic administrations but had been director of the Livermore National Laboratory and came into the cabinet as president of the California Institute of Technology. Carter appointed two respected congressmen to the cabinet, Bob Berglund at Agriculture and Brock Adams at Transportation. Joe Califano, the secretary of Health, Education and Welfare, was a dynamo who had served as domestic adviser to President Johnson, and the secretaries of labor and commerce, Ray Marshall and Juanita Kreps, were respected economists.

One of my personal favorites was Cecil Andrus at Interior, a true environmentalist and former governor of Idaho who understood the West. Patricia Harris, at Housing and Urban Development, was a well-known Washington lawyer, urban activist, and the first black woman ever named to the cabinet. Andrew Young, Carter's top black supporter from Atlanta and the first black congressman elected from the Deep South since Reconstruction, was his UN ambassador, and Robert Strauss, who knew everyone there was to know in Washington, became his special trade representative. The only Georgian, other than Lance, with cabinet status, was Attorney General Griffin Bell, Carter's personal friend, Atlanta lawyer, and a former federal court of appeals judge, as well as the most conservative member of the cabinet.

This was a diverse and pathbreaking cabinet by geography, gender, race, and experience. But precisely because his cabinet was composed of strong individuals, with their own agendas, this led to a dissonance and lack of a clear message and priorities, when combined with Carter's refusal to allow strong White House Staff intervention. For example, Patricia Harris was given the lead in developing a comprehensive urban policy among several agencies. As feisty and turf conscious a cabinet officer as we had, she finally threw her hands up and asked me to take over the interagency process because the other departments would not follow her lead.

Only the White House, which had solely the president's interest in mind, could accomplish that kind of job. James Baker, Reagan's chief of staff, later told me: "Everybody likes cabinet government, particularly the cabinet. But the fact of the matter is, presidents are going to make their decisions on the advice of people they trust and have confidence in. And for the most part those are people who have been through the wars with them and been through the campaign, and they're the people in the White House."[22] While Carter never saw the cabinet as a decision-making body, he gave them so much freedom to name their own top aides and to make policy within their orbits that the critical White House role of integrating and coordinating those decisions was compromised during much of the first year of the administration.

But he also left the door of the Oval Office wide open to the disagreements inevitable among such a high-powered group of appointees. At their first gathering with him in Georgia after the election, Carter announced to the incoming cabinet that he would be available to them "at all times," and that he would be in his office by 6:00 a.m. every morning; that he liked to read, and would welcome receiving their memos. Blumenthal remembered thinking, I wonder whether he realizes what that means? He's going to be inundated. He can't really mean it. But he seems sincere."[23]

"COUSIN CHEAP"

In contrast to this delegation of authority to the cabinet heads, Carter early on gained a reputation as a micromanager, a label that was only partly justified and from which he could have saved himself by appointing a chief of staff. He did bring in his cousin Hugh Carter to take a series of self-defeating actions in reducing the White House staff in size and influence, but without bothering to consult the staffers themselves. "Cousin Cheap," as he was infelicitously dubbed by Jody, ordered a reduction of our already small head count by 30 percent from Ford's level.[24] This edict was easily subverted by eliminating clerks and employing the hoary bureaucratic shuffle of seconding people from federal agencies in order to keep them off the published White House payroll. But there were reductions nevertheless in crucial areas such as congressional liaison. The official head count was reduced from 560 to 485, on paper anyway.

But this was only the start. Hess, who had been appointed to assist Watson in the transition, got a call while watching a Washington Redskins football game on Sunday from Greg Schneiders, a top Carter aide, informing him that "the governor wants to know how to cut the White House motor pool." Appalled that Carter was involving himself in such penny-pinching detail, Hess pointed out that these cars normally ferried staffers from the White House to Capitol Hill to lobby for the president's programs, and to agencies spread across the city for discussions and oversight of their operations. He asked, "Do you want them to hitchhike? Catch a bus?"[25]

The motor pool remained, but the president-elect ended the door-to-door car service to pick up senior White House staff at home early in the morning and return them late at night. This was not a matter of losing prestige but of simple efficiency. Depending on how far a staffer lived from 1600 Pennsylvania Avenue, commuting in his or her own car took up to an hour or more a day, as it did for me, and distracted me from the essential tasks of following a steady flow of documents and returning innumerable phone calls that could not be performed at the wheel in the pre–cell phone era. The most ludicrous outcome occurred when gasoline lines emerged following the Iranian revolution and I had to wait in line for more than half an hour so I could drive to the White House and try to end the shortage (and doing a pretty inadequate job at that).

At the same time, to demonstrate to the common man that he would demystify the presidency, Carter denied himself one of the most helpful presidential perks by selling the presidential yacht *Sequoia* for a paltry $286,000. For decades it had been used to woo members of Congress into supporting the president's programs, reward campaign donors and workers, and influence business or labor leaders during cruises along the Potomac River on balmy evenings. For even the most powerful in Washington these were prized invitations to sip drinks and eat snacks while rubbing shoulders with the president of the United States and his staff, who were not along for the ride but to win loyal friends and influence important people.

Carter even contemplated selling the presidential retreat, Camp David, but Rosalynn intervened to remind him that this mountain lodge would be one of the few places available for them to escape from the pressures of the White House on weekends.[26] (Of course there would have been no Camp David Accords, his signature diplomatic accomplishment, if Camp David itself had been put on the auction block.) The difficulty of translating Carter's post-Watergate turn away from the pomp of the presidency was a constant problem that Carter never quite mastered. During the very first days of his presidency he called me on my secure red phone directly connected to the Oval Office and began, "Stu, this is Jimmy." I said, "No, it is Mr. President.'"

More significant was his decision during the transition to abandon the tradition of playing "Ruffles and Flourishes" and "Hail to the Chief" to signal his arrival at a formal White House ceremony. Watching Carter enter the East Room for a formal event with no fanfare, and reflecting on how stirred I had been to hear those themes when LBJ strode into the same room with his giant Texas steps, I joked to myself that it was hardly worth being president without being announced by these symbols of the power of the greatest elected office on earth. Presidents obviously thought so, too; Jacqueline Kennedy once laughingly observed: "Jack's favorite song is 'Hail to the Chief.'"[27] For several weeks a number of Carter's staffers, joined by no less than House Speaker O'Neill, appealed to him to relent, and he finally did so reluctantly.

Tip also got him to change one other thing. At the first Democratic leadership breakfast, he served coffee and some rolls in his frugal fashion.

Tip, a giant of a man in stature and girth roared, "Mr. President, I have waited eight years to have a Democrat in the White House, and at the next meeting, I expect to have a proper breakfast!" The president got the message, and from then on Tip and his colleagues got the full treatment, from fruit and scrambled eggs to bacon and sweets. This normal hospitality was also extended to regular breakfast meetings with the Republican leadership. We also begged him to abandon his campaign habit of carrying his own luggage and warned it would be especially inappropriate on his first trip abroad as president. He agreed, although he often carried his own small briefcase.

Nixon had certainly carried the notion of the "imperial presidency" to absurd lengths, like his order to dress the marines in Gilbert and Sullivan–style uniforms for special occasions. Carter promptly ended that. But the American people revere the presidency, which is as close to royalty as we allow our Republic to approach. Aside from making him commander in chief of the armed forces, the U.S. Constitution gives the president precious few explicit powers. His influence comes from his ability to use the mystique and electoral legitimacy of the office to rally support from Congress, the American public, and foreign leaders. Carter was certainly elected to be a distinctly different president from Nixon, but the country did not want him to jettison the symbols of the office that help raise any president of the United States from being just another jumped-up politician to a figure who represents the majesty of our country.

CARTER UPGRADES TO FIRST CLASS

On November 6, 1976, only a few days after his election, Jimmy Carter graduated to a new level of luxurious travel, when he actually started work as the nation's chief executive. A Boeing 707-26000 of the presidential fleet picked him up at Robins Air Force base in Georgia for a hard-earned vacation with his family on St. Simons Island, at the splendid Georgia estate of Smith Bagley, a prominent Democrat and supporter. The mansion, with its moss-laden trees and antebellum atmosphere, assured complete privacy. The selection of Bagley's estate was a bit odd, since he was an heir to the Reynolds tobacco fortune, an industry Carter abhorred. When the chief steward, Air Force Sergeant Major Charles Palmer, brought him coffee, the president-elect said, "Sit down, I want to talk with you," something that had not happened before with the other presidents he served. Palmer was at first taken aback. Both soon discovered they had a common connection; they were both natives of Georgia. Jody wandered in and made a remark to Carter that Palmer never forgot: "Well, just think, a couple of years ago we didn't have a penny and now we are on Air Force One."[28] Riding on Air Force Once does come as close to royalty as the greatest democracy in the world can offer, but in an interconnected world, the plane has its essential uses.

This flight was designated a Special Air Mission (SAM), because these sumptuous planes, both the 26000 and 27000 series, carry the call sign of Air Force One only when a sitting president is on board. President Eisenhower, in his final months in office, was the first to have a specially designated president's plane put at his service. Over the years it has become a majestic symbol of the power of the presidency and by extension of the grand global reach of the United States of America.

The iconic image of President Kennedy descending the steps of Air Force One with his elegant first lady helped elevate the mystique of America's best-known airplane. Mrs. Kennedy played a key role in adding cachet and symbolism to the flying Oval Office, hiring one of America's leading industrial designers to create the airplane's distinctive livery. The top was painted white, with the front end a dark robin's-egg blue extending to the cockpit. The fuselage was silver, with a gold-and-blue stripe from the midsection to the tail. The bottom was white to keep the temperature down when the plane was parked on a hot asphalt runway. On the tail was painted a huge American flag, and halfway back on the fuselage was the blue-and-gold seal of the president of the United States, an American eagle holding an olive branch in one talon and arrows in the other. Along the fuselage, televisual capital letters spelled out the words "United States of America." At the time Mrs. Kennedy could not have imagined that the plane would be indelibly imprinted in our national psyche as a symbol of tragedy as well as glory, and then of continuity, when Lyndon Johnson rushed aboard to take the oath of office as president while the body of the slain president lay in the aft cabin and his shocked widow stood alongside her husband's successor in her blood-spattered Chanel suit.

Senior members of Congress, chief executive officers of the world's great companies, and even the most jaded celebrities act like kids in a candy shop when offered a ride on Air Force One. In accordance with his desire to avoid any possible image of special influence in the post-Watergate era, President Carter disallowed companies like Coca-Cola or Pepsi from providing free beverages and cigarette manufacturers from supplying free cigarettes, requiring the air force to pay for them out of its budget. However, he did give passengers souvenir gifts carrying the presidential seal and inscribed, "President Jimmy Carter's guest aboard Air Force One." Like his immediate predecessors he also passed out presidentially engraved gold-leaf cufflinks and tie clasps for men and stickpins for women. For special guests he reserved a small, personally autographed Bible with "Air Force One" embossed on the front. While wine was served with meals and liquor was available, the president himself never drank.[29]

The plane that Carter boarded as president-elect to St. Simons Island, Georgia, and all the other flights he took for the next four years as president, had Palmer in charge of eighteen carefully handpicked crew members. Its two pilots were among the best in the air force. A navigator, two flight engineers, four security guards, and a stenographer were also on board. A White House physician, Dr. William Lukash, accompanied the president fully equipped to deal with medical emergencies. The plane had a state-of-the-art communications center and carried equipment for sophisticated food preparation and elegant service. Before a trip Palmer would go to the White House chef to develop a menu for the president, and the stewards would cook and serve the meals. The president ate from official china, with concentric gold-and-green circles, and the presidential seal, which also adorned the glasses and goblets.

With its customized interior, Air Force One carried a maximum of forty-six passengers, not including crew. The interior was refitted into a presidential work and living space worthy of a private jet. There were two staterooms, one for the president, with a spacious desk and chair, and a couch that could comfortably hold three people, and an adjoining stateroom for the first lady. Behind the presidential quarters was a conference room with a small coffee table and couch for four people, along with a conference table that could seat six. The White House staff would sit in one of eight comfortable seats, four on each side, and there were compartments for ten Secret Service offices, and last, a compartment for ten members of the White House press corps.

Carter held his transition meetings and interviewed prospects for the cabinet and senior White House staff mostly in Plains or Atlanta, far from the Washington press corps and the buzz in the nation's capital. During his immediate postelection vacation, Carter invited his incoming cabinet and White House staff to meet in Atlanta and then go to the Bagley estate in St. Simons, to get to know one another in a private, relaxed environment.

On the brief plane ride I got advice from two legendary Democratic figures. The first came from Ted Sorensen, Jack Kennedy's alter ego, who had grown close to Carter as an early campaign supporter, adviser, and validator for suspicious New York liberals. Carter nominated him as director of the Central Intelligence Agency (CIA), with a mandate to clean up the agency. He pulled me aside and said in a thoughtful voice, "Stu, if you do your job right, the policy people in the administration will think you are being too political, and the political people in the White House will think you are being too much of a policy wonk." From the man who had kept his private thoughts only for the president while writing his public speeches, it was a most helpful preview of the tightrope on which I would be balancing for the next four years. Although neither of us knew it yet, his advice would prove deeply ironic: Sorensen was to find himself caught in a political buzz saw when the CIA's bureaucracy joined senators with old grudges against the Kennedys to force him to withdraw because he had been a conscientious objector during the Korean War—a tragic loss of an enormously talented public servant.

The second conversation was more blunt and equally revealing. It came from Joe Califano, with whom I would be dealing in my new job—the same one that he had held at the White House under President Johnson in molding the Great Society, when he was my ultimate boss. Like LBJ, Joe was brilliant, indefatigable, tough, ebullient, and brusque; qualities belied by his cherubic face and engaging smile. I now would occupy the same spacious West Wing office that had once been his, directly over the Oval Office. Joe was determined that would be the only similarity. With that Califano wink in his eye, he said: "Stu, I am not going to let you and the White House staff treat me the way I treated the Cabinet under LBJ." He was true to his word, developing his own positions, like his antismoking crusade, and on occasion lobbying quietly against presidential initiatives with which he disagreed, such as Carter's decision to carve a separate Department of Education from his Department of Health, Education and Welfare and reduce his turf. When Carter later realized that Califano was operating as a semi-independent cabinet fiefdom he was fired over my objection, along with some others, when the president restructured his cabinet.

DOES THE PRESIDENT NEED
TO KNOW EVERY DETAIL?

The Carter administration plowed through heavy seas during its first year. Jimmy Carter did not have the grace of John Kennedy, the congressional wizardry of Lyndon Johnson, the strategic vision of Richard Nixon, the charm and clarity of purpose of Ronald Reagan, the foreign-policy experience of George H. W. Bush, the supreme political skills of Bill Clinton, the toughness of George W. Bush, or the eloquence of Barack Obama. But he brought to the Oval Office his own unique intellect, inquisitiveness, self-discipline, political courage, and resilience in the face of setbacks. He disregarded the political costs of trying to make the nation and the world a better place in ways that transcended his presidency and often did not come to fruition until he left office. It is precisely because of his qualities that he was determined to confront so many difficult challenges and accomplished so much as we pressed ahead. Presidents also are tested by how they deal with the challenges thrown at them by unforeseen events, and he handled some better than others. But it must be also said that Jimmy Carter had more than his share of bad luck in both domestic and international arenas, from embedded inflation and a deeply divided Democratic Party to oil shocks and a radical Islamic revolution in Iran.

There is no job in the world remotely comparable to that of the president of the United States, where all decisions have worldwide impact. And speaking personally, I can say that no job anywhere matches the excitement of standing at the right hand of the president and sharing the camaraderie of hand-to-hand combat on his and our nation's behalf seven days a week for four eventful years. The pressures of working in the West Wing of the White House are enormous. Every major decision that cannot be made elsewhere, from a city hall to the Congress of the United States to governments abroad, comes at you without surcease. Because the decisions presidents must make are so consequential, and the interests of those who have a stake in those decisions—business, labor, environmentalists, consumerists, foreign governments—are so intense and conflicting, there is no presidential decision that does not involve wicked trade-offs.

But it is precisely because every day is filled with endless meetings to resolve interagency disputes, handle congressional and interest group demands, and endure the pressures they generate from winners and losers alike, that I have tried to step back and appreciate what was done wrong and what was done right, with the perspective of almost forty years since leaving the White House. I intend to give an account not only of President Carter's considerable strengths, which were so admirable, but also of his faults and idiosyncrasies, which were maddening to those closest to him in office.

Chief among them was his compartmentalizing of decisions. He decided during the transition to make a frontal assault on water projects, which were often costly and environmentally damaging boondoggles, but without recognizing their importance in greasing the legislative wheels to help pass his other legislative priorities. Carter also believed that he could and should know as much about every issue as the experts he had chosen to guide his decisions, and he drowned himself in detailed memos and background papers in what eventually became a form of hubris. During his critical first year he refused to set priorities among laudable reformist goals, burying his congressional supporters in a blizzard of presidential proposals, despite repeated pleas from House and Senate leaders to set clear priorities. He stuck with—and stood by—all of us in the Georgia Mafia for too long and only belatedly enhanced us with experienced Washington hands. The man whose campaign biography emphasized competence in its title, *Why Not the Best?* did not always insist on the best from those who served him, unlike his mentor, Admiral Rickover. And in seeking more than our divided political system could deliver, he made the best the enemy of the good, and clouded his own considerable accomplishments.

One of the most potent attacks on Jimmy Carter was his attention to detail, and there can be no question that he reveled in it. He would ask for detailed calculations on the throw weights of missiles or the estimates of world oil reserves in square miles. He would correct typographical errors or poor sentence structure in memos, and minutes of cabinet meetings from Deputy Cabinet Secretary Jane Frank (later Harman),[30] and insist on seeing the background material to lengthy decision memorandums. There is no doubt that reading such a fantastic quantity of material left him much less time to meet with members of Congress, leaders of interest groups, and the public.

But I did not find that his attention to detail blinded or even blurred his broader vision. His insistence on knowing everything about an issue before he made a decision was his quintessential method of governing, and he likened it to the way he performed other jobs before ascending to the presidency: "When I ran Carter's Warehouse, I ran it; I knew what was going on, I knew which trailer had a flat tire, which employee was doing a good job. When I was on the submarine, I did the same thing. So when I became president and had to make the ultimate decision about an issue, I wanted to understand it."[31] There can be no doubt that without his attention to detail there would have been no Camp David Accords, no Panama Canal Treaty, no major energy legislation, no Alaska Lands bill.

But this can be done for only a select number of issues. The presidency is light-years different from running Carter's Peanut Warehouse or serving as an officer on even a nuclear submarine, where one mistake can spell disaster. The breadth and complexity of issues, the excruciatingly difficult trade-offs, the enormous impact of presidential decisions, make the job unique. It is impossible and even unwise to try to master everything. Cabinet departments are repositories of vast expertise, albeit refracted to fit the interests they represent and the congressional committees that oversee and fund their programs—the so-called iron triangle. Cabinet government as a system of collective decision making and shared accountability cannot function in our presidential system as it does in a parliamentary democracy, and Carter did not try it. He did try to delegate power, but he did not develop close relationships with any of the cabinet, and rarely met individually with them or their deputies to discuss and oversee the execution of his priorities.

The job of a president is not to try to understand each argument that comes before him in great detail, but to think strategically and talk freely with all the key actors inside the government and out, whose support will shape his fate.

But that was not Carter's way. He explained it to me: "I wanted to make a judgment based on what I knew, and much of what I knew was what I was told by you and by Harold Brown and others. Even in Austria [where the final SALT II agreement was negotiated and signed], I didn't have to turn around at the negotiating table and say, 'Harold, explain to me what is characteristic of this or that missile.' I knew the missile. And the same way with the negotiations at Camp David." He felt the same way about handling domestic issues. In all, he said he was "intrigued" by issues and had to understand them "when I was the one who had to make the ultimate judgment."[32]

Leadership is an essential element of the presidency. Symbolism matters: The night before his inauguration, the incoming president took his family, his senior aides, and our families to the Lincoln Memorial—the country's first chief executive from the Deep South since Reconstruction paying this special tribute to the Great Emancipator in modern times. Carter likewise exercised leadership by combining a vision of where the country should go on the issues he had chosen as critical, while insisting that we on the White House staff present him with all the options and backup material for his review. At the other end of the spectrum, Ronald Reagan is considered a better leader because he believed in and articulated a few basic principles— smaller government, lower taxes, stronger defense, and literally read from three-by-five-inch cards when he held meetings on specific issues. (And more recently, a president who does not even seem to use these.) Which is the preferred model for presidential leaders? Each president brings a unique style of leadership to the Oval Office.

Yet with all the turbulence of the transition, there was an exhilarating message about American democracy that a man from Plains could be elected to the highest office in the land, as he took the oath of office at the U.S. Capitol, opening with a verse from the prophet Micah, "What doth the Lord require of thee, but to do justly, and to love mercy, and to walk humbly with thy God" (Micah 6:8). His short inaugural address was vintage Jimmy Carter: a tone poem, but with a downbeat note. Rather than a call for the American people to reach for the stars, or a promise to expand the New Frontier, New Deal, and Great Society, for which his party's liberal base was hoping, he urged what he knew was politically unpopular: limits and sacrifice. The country could not afford everything its people wanted, and thinking of the looming energy shortages, he asked for "individual sacrifice for the common good." He emphasized human rights, which "must be absolute," and nuclear arms control, which would frame his key foreign-policy goals. He insisted, over internal disagreement, as he had with his announcement speech more than two years before, on calling for the "ultimate goal" of the "elimination of all nuclear weapons from this earth." Instead of a call to combat Soviet expansionism, the wars he wanted to fight were against poverty, ignorance, and injustice.

He followed his speech with a dramatic break from tradition, which shocked and thrilled the onlookers and the nation watching on television: getting out of his limousine and walking about a mile hand in hand with Rosalynn down Pennsylvania Avenue. The idea originated with Wisconsin senator William Proxmire as a way to emphasize physical fitness and was initially discarded until Carter thought it would send a broader message of openness and closeness to the people after Watergate.[33]

In his first official act on his first full day in the White House, he began a pattern that would be emblematic of his presidency: taking politically unpopular steps he felt were the "right thing to do." Following his campaign promise, his first executive order granted pardons to those who refused to serve in Vietnam. While it helped heal an open wound from the divisive war,[34] it was out of step from the start with his Southern conservative base. Carter was never forgiven by some veterans' groups and many of his fellow Southerners for his pardon. But he championed and signed into law the Vietnam Veterans Memorial Bill in 1980, authorizing the creation of the Vietnam Memorial, and movingly described the "simple and austere grandeur" of its design. He acknowledged its long path to properly honor our Vietnam Veterans, led by Jan Scruggs and supported by the Vietnam Memorial Fund, on which Rosalynn Carter served. It is now one of the most visited and, indeed, treasured sites on Washington's National Mall.[35]

3

THE MAKING OF THE MODERN VICE PRESIDENT

Jimmy Carter and Fritz Mondale created the modern vice presidency, moving a constitutional anomaly out of the shadows of power to a trusted partner of the president and not an object of ridicule. The office of vice president was an afterthought at the Constitutional Convention, which did not foresee the rise of political parties. In a compromise the Founders agreed that the candidate winning a majority of Electoral College votes would become president and the second highest—usually his principal rival—vice president. This arrangement quickly proved untenable, and after the Constitution was amended, electors in 1804 voted on one ballot for president and on the second for vice president, which meant that the vice president had not been a candidate for the highest office and could only aspire to it if the president died in office. It is not hard to imagine the discomfort felt by presidents in seeing their own mortal shadow in the flesh, or to understand why many kept their potential successor at arm's length. His political role was to balance the ticket by region or ideology, and his only formal duties were presiding over the Senate and casting tie-breaking votes.

But otherwise, in the often-bowdlerized words of Franklin Roosevelt's first vice president, the Texas populist John Nance "Cactus Jack" Garner, the office was "not worth a bucket of warm piss." The greatest secret of World War II was concealed from FDR's vice president Harry S Truman, upon whom fell the responsibility of whether to use the atom bomb against the Japanese within a couple of months after taking office. Dwight Eisenhower was asked what major tasks his vice president, Richard Nixon, had performed in office and replied dismissively that he would need a week to think about it. The deliberate and painful marginalization of Lyndon Johnson as vice president by John F. Kennedy and his circle became something of a scandal that Johnson never forgot and—like a father reliving an abusive childhood—inflicted on *his* vice president, Hubert H. Humphrey, the liberal Minnesota senator. Johnson denied Humphrey his own plane; he often found himself bumped by mere staff members; and, his staff told me when I was still working in the Johnson White House, that the vice president was left stewing outside the offices of senior staff, like Joe Califano, waiting to meet them.[1] Richard Nixon's first vice president, Spiro Agnew, became his hatchet man until forced to resign over a scandal dating from his term as governor of Maryland.

When Carter ran for president, his campaign's principal theme of restoring trust in government extended to raising respect for the office of vice president. This began in his process of selecting a prospective running mate. Determined to avoid a last-minute choice under pressure at the convention, Carter turned his attention to finding a running mate a month before the Democrats convened.

Working with Ham, Rosalynn, and Kirbo, he compiled a list of about twenty people. Ham developed an elaborate formula with factors including the traditional ones of adding electoral clout and actually being capable of serving as president. As a Washington outsider, Carter also sought an experienced congressional hand.[2] Some names were put on the list as a signal to voting blocs that one of their own was worthy of consideration but that was mainly for show, for example Representative Peter Rodino, a respected Italian American from New Jersey, who publicly declined because of age but made the speech formally nominating Carter at the convention.

Kirbo was entrusted with the job of meeting with the most serious candidates, all senators. He interviewed them mainly by asking few questions, letting them talk, and making notes afterward. He did not advocate one over another, but he did confide, "There were a lot of them I didn't want to have as vice president." He made numerous treks from Atlanta to Washington, because whenever he felt he had completed the roster, "Jimmy said he had one or two more, so I would see them."[3]

As important as Kirbo was in winnowing the field, the decisive interviews were those Carter held in Plains. Until the very end Frank Church of Idaho, an early critic of the Vietnam War and the CIA, was high on Carter's and Rosalynn's list (but no one else's). Then he blew it by bragging that he was distantly related to William Tecumseh Sherman—definitely the wrong Union general; during the Civil War he cut the South in half, his reviled troops singing their anthem, "Marching Through Georgia," and torched Atlanta. Another candidate declared his love for "blue-eyed peas"—oops, the favorite Southern peas have black eyes.[4] The choice finally narrowed down to Edmund Muskie of Maine, a high-maintenance but brilliant senator known for his titanic ego, and Mondale, a mild-mannered and studious Midwesterner weaned on Minnesota's liberal politics, which he tenaciously promoted in the Senate.[5] When Mondale was considering a run for president in 1976, the delivery of his message on a political trip to Atlanta at Andy Young's home was as impressive as he was. After we drove him back to his hotel, Fran said, "Jimmy Carter may be your candidate, but Fritz Mondale is mine!"

Ironically, Mondale came close to taking himself out of the running for simple and compelling reasons. He loved the Senate, and his trial run for the presidency ended with him pulling out with a parting joke that he was fed up with staying in Holiday Inns. When Humphrey backed away from one last try at the presidency, that freed Mondale—but did he really want the job? Richard Moe, Mondale's closest aide, persuaded him to talk to his political mentor. They met over coffee in the Senate dining room, and Mondale was surprised by Humphrey's reply: "I learned more in the vice presidency than I've learned in a lifetime [in the Senate]. I've had more opportunity to affect public policy down there in one day than I have up here in a decade. Everybody thinks the vice presidency was bad; it changed my life. I stretched my mind, my understanding, my experience. I'm a different and a far better person. You don't realize what a president must do until you have been there."[6]

Mondale then set out to prepare himself at a level that would outshine his Senate rivals. He believed that the selection process would take a "typical Carter approach—methodical and disciplined," so he was the only prospective candidate to read Carter's campaign book, his speeches as governor and presidential candidate, and to research articles about Carter. He prepared for the interviews by learning about the vice presidency from scholars and Humphrey's aides. Mondale also discovered that although he and Carter occupied opposing—although not extreme—ends of their party's political spectrum, they shared a small-town upbringing and religious backgrounds: Carter a Baptist, Mondale the son of a Methodist minister. Both had also served in the military, Mondale in the army during the Korean War. Because Carter had stumbled badly in the late primaries against liberal Democrats, Mondale felt he was "looking for somebody who could do serious business [for him] in northern states . . . was influential on the Hill, and respected by his colleagues"—and that he met all those qualifications.[7]

Mondale successfully ran the gauntlet of interviews with Kirbo and Carter's son Chip—they lasted two hours, longer than expected. But these were essentially auditions. After Kirbo, the Southern conservative, interviewed the liberal Mondale, he told Carter: "Governor, I thought I could get rid of that fellah, but I didn't, and I don't think I will." But he went beyond that to tell him that as impressive as Mondale was and as important as he might be in helping get Carter elected, his conservative base was "going to give him hell" once they were in office.[8]

But Carter formed a personal bond with Mondale in their first interview. Armed with his knowledge of Carter, Mondale emphasized their common values and impressed Carter as the only candidate who had read his book. They talked about a wide range of issues, but Mondale felt that one really connected them—civil rights. "That commitment made it possible for a Northern liberal and Southern conservative to join hands and cross the bridge," Mondale said.

After their morning meeting they joined Joan Mondale and Rosalynn for lunch. The two wives had walked around Plains and also hit it off. After lunch they met for another hour and a half, a session that laid the ground-work for a profound and positive change in the American vice presidency. Before his interview Moe had discussed with Mondale the idea that a vice president could be used more effectively as "an arm of the presidency in terms of policy advice, but also in terms of implementing policy, and as a presidential emissary."[9] Mondale transmitted these general ideas to Carter at the risk of turning him off. He told him that "I was not interested in a ceremonial position. I only wanted to come on board if I could help on substance." Carter immediately replied, "That's the only way we are going to do it."

This initial conversation about his role well before his selection was probably unique in American history. Moreover, Carter did not shy away from the unmentionable. He told Mondale that "a lot of presidents were intimidated by the reminder of life's fragility when their vice president showed up. That doesn't bother me at all; if I can't be here, I want to be sure that my Vice President can take over right then, that the government will work, and that we understand the policies. The more we can cooperate, not just in the election, but in the government, the more you could be with me looking at all the confidential and secret information we need to see; attending every meeting with the president that you wish to attend; having full access to key members of the executive branch; and creating the principle that when the vice president talked to somebody in the administration, it was the president talking." He said he wanted his vice president to be his adviser, a "source of independent information, his personal representative on the Hill and around the country."[10] Far from putting him off, Mondale's active stance thoroughly intrigued Carter with the possibility of making the vice presidency a full-time and productive job.[11]

Carter then took Mondale for a long walk around Plains. They visited Miss Lillian's house; they talked about hunting and about small towns; and like two boys they looked for bottles in the woods near his farm. Then they inspected the Carter peanut factory.

With great self-awareness Carter later explained to me why he picked Mondale to help offset his own political weaknesses: "Fritz had two or three advantages: one was that he was familiar with Washington; secondly, he had an intimate relationship with the activities in the trade union movement, in the Jewish community, the environmental community, the women's movement, that I didn't have. He knew who in Washington you could trust and who you didn't trust; I didn't have that. Fritz was also much more sensitive to the political consequences of a controversy than I was. I would go ahead with something even though it might be politically charged with potential unpopularity. I knew the black community better than Fritz; I knew farming better than Fritz: I knew state government better than Fritz. But among other things, he said he "knew best that Fritz was at the forefront of the expressions of concern to me about the United Nations resolutions against Israel."[12]

Ham meanwhile made a political calculation about Mondale's weight as a "a class act, which he was."[13] The Carter camp had the liberals with them when they went after George Wallace in Florida, they had the UAW with them in Iowa because Carter had successfully wooed the local union leadership. But Ham knew that organized labor was cool to Carter and that the Democrats' liberal wing was never with him. But Mondale had deep roots in the liberal, Jewish, and union communities, and Carter needed them to secure the base of the party in the general election.[14]

Then began an extraordinary integration during the campaign that laid the foundation for their close cooperation in office. Mondale's staff moved to Atlanta so we could work together seamlessly and Mondale and his people could learn about Southern customs. Mondale made his first campaign stop in Beaufort, South Carolina, with Senator Ernest Hollings, who shared the nickname "Fritz" with Mondale but not his liberal attitude. Tall, silver-haired, handsome, and charming, with a deep-baritone Southern accent, he could have come straight out of central casting. At an outdoor event they both were eating bowls of shrimp when Hollings started to laugh out loud. Mondale was biting into the hot shrimp, shell and all, like the Yankee he was. Hollings never let him forget it.[15]

Shortly after Carter's razor-thin victory, Mondale asked Moe to put flesh on the bones of his general points on making the vice presidency a meaningful office, and not just standby equipment to be trundled out for funerals of world leaders. Early in December, Carter and Mondale met at Blair House, across from the White House, and talked in more detail after Mondale had sought advice from Humphrey and from Ford's vice president, Nelson Rockefeller. Mondale told Carter he wanted to be "an across-the-board adviser" without specific responsibilities, lest they interfere with cabinet members', and to "float" wherever the president needed him, which would entail complete access to Carter and to the White House information flow, all of which would be unprecedented.[16] As the meeting ended, Mondale made a personal request. He wanted his wife, Joan, to have a role in promoting the arts, to which Carter readily agreed. In her four years she totally transformed public art in America, bringing it to official and private buildings as never before. (On February 4, 2014, Carter delivered a moving eulogy to Joan, calling her as "fervent and effective [a] champion of the arts as anyone I have ever known," joking that he spent more time listening to her plea for more support for the arts than he did on Middle East peace.)

On their way out, Mondale asked Moe to draft what became an eleven-page, double-spaced memorandum of their discussion with Carter, which Mondale signed and sent to the president-elect early in December of 1976 as the new administration was taking shape. This extraordinary document changed the nature of the office and remains Mondale's principal legacy. The memo starts by remarking on the historic ambiguity, frustration, and even antagonism involved in the vice presidency, followed by Mondale's pledge "to do everything possible to make this administration a success. I fully realize that my personal and political success is totally tied to yours and the achievements of your administration." The concrete proposals that followed may seem like bureaucratic minutiae, but to anyone familiar with the way power is exercised in Washington, they were big and bold, and their legitimacy rested on the fact that he was the only other American public official elected nationwide. Furthermore, the argument for change was based on Mondale's accurate observation that "the biggest single problem of our recent administrations has been the failure of the president to be exposed to independent analysis, not conditioned by what it is thought he wants to hear or often what others want him to hear."

Mondale was not the first to remark on the difficulty of piercing the bubble of sycophancy that threatens to suffocate the judgment of any president, nor would he be the last. But he did not hesitate to voice critical opinions to Carter at their regular, private, weekly lunches, and, at times, to me. His key requests were designed to assure him that he had the facts necessary to make informed recommendations:

- Frequent and comprehensive intelligence briefings from the CIA and other intelligence agencies similar to those received by the president, with advance warning of the major issues to be discussed at meetings of the National Security and Domestic Councils, and other significant presidential advisory bodies. Mondale would also have his own "seasoned, experienced" representative on these groups, as well as in the office of the president's press secretary and his legal counsel.

- A special relationship with other members of the executive branch. Carter would emphasize to his cabinet and other high officials that they were to be as responsive to him as to the president himself, which meant that Mondale's voice would be taken as the president's. "Access to you at a meeting at least once a week for thirty minutes to an hour." This demand was quickly satisfied by regular weekly lunches attended only by the president and vice president.

- General functions would include troubleshooting as problems arose, and he singled out the politically radioactive issue of crime; arbitrating conflicts between government departments; and representing the president abroad not just as a ceremonial mourner but to give "a first-hand assessment of foreign leaders and situations." He would also be a key contact with his former congressional colleagues, and provide advice on the best administration approach.

- Political action to help keep the administration on the offensive with the Democratic Party and with special constituencies, such as labor, as well as with mayors and governors. Mondale asked to take the lead on legislative proposals for campaign finance, voter registration, and laws governing political primaries. All that would help him strengthen his political base to run for the presidency (which he did in 1984 but was overwhelmed by Ronald Reagan).

Mondale later told me that he tried to be "the best assistant to the president I could be. I'm not an alternative to the president. I'm not a deputy president. There was only one president and his name was Carter. My job was to be as candid as I could. And then, . . . a decision having been made, unless I disagreed with it deeply, to implement it. And to bring my experience to bear as a troubleshooter within the administration and with the Congress; to be a spokesman nationally; to hold hands and seek the repair of hurt feelings; and generally to be the fireman around there—but not to get in the position where I was competing in a line function with anybody." He also tried to use this power sparingly and diplomatically: "I often held my voice at meetings because I figured people would think it's a signal [from the president], so I'd shut my mouth."[17]

Carter agreed to all Mondale's demands without change, and went a step further. On his own initiative Carter offered a West Wing office, which came as a complete surprise and turned out to be one of the most important reforms. Not until the Kennedy administration did any vice president even have a place next door in the Executive Office Building (now the Eisenhower Executive Office Building), and the vice president's titular office was in the Capitol almost a mile away. Mondale kept that space and in fact ended up with three offices: the magnificent, largely ceremonial one next to the White House; the one on the Senate side of the Capitol, essential for Mondale to keep alive his many contacts with Congress to lobby for administration programs; and the one in the West Wing.

Why was it so important for Mondale to shift his working base from the huge, chandeliered office in the Executive Office Building, with its historic desk engraved with the signature of every one of his predecessors, to the more modest West Wing office? Just as in real estate, "Location, location, location" is the watchword in politics and government; proximity to the president and his top aides is essential to be in the mix of all critical decisions. Mondale could swap rumors with the small handful of people right around the president, and he could walk down the hall to the Oval Office in a few seconds, rather than the few minutes it takes to cross West Executive Avenue, climb the stairs, and reach the president. As he quipped, "If you're in the Executive Office Building, you might as well be in Baltimore!"[18]

Of course there was a downside to this proximity that was not at first evident: When the administration began unraveling in its last year, Mondale was caught up in it. He joked ruefully that the presidency was like a fire hydrant that everyone "could piss on"—and that included every disgruntled member of Congress and every political-interest group he would have to cultivate in continuing his political career.

But Mondale was comfortable in the "dinky little building" of our seat of presidential power and was wise enough not to overreach. Although Carter offered him any office he wanted, he passed up a prized corner office Ham occupied on one side, and Zbig Brzezinski on the other, and took a smaller, windowless office situated less than ten yards from the Roosevelt Room, the Cabinet Room, and the president's own Oval Office. This modest placement gave rise to a comical quest. One day Mondale called Michael Berman, his legal counsel and political consigliere, about a bathroom that had been outside Henry Kissinger's national security office. It had a coveted private commode and small washbasin that now opened only on the corner office that was occupied by Brzezinski. Mondale asked Berman to find out whether the bathroom had originally opened onto his new office. Had the door been moved by Kissinger? Berman was incredulous, but Mondale told him, "I'm serious." Berman obtained the early-twentieth-century blueprints, and sure enough Mondale's memory was correct: The bathroom door had been switched at about the time Kissinger was serving as Nixon's national security adviser— Brzezinski's distinguished predecessor. Having made this historical discovery, Berman gave Mondale the sound political advice that "there's no way to change this bathroom back again!" So with the fate of the Western world hanging on the decision, for the next four years, the vice president of the United States had to content himself with using a bathroom in the hallway.[19]

Symbolic of the historic nature of the change in the vice presidency was a scene witnessed by Norman Sherman, Hubert Humphrey's former press secretary. Berman observed his visitor's startled appearance and asked what was wrong. Sherman said that he had just passed the secretaries of state and defense sitting on a couch in the small anteroom of Mondale's office, waiting to confer with him. He exclaimed to Berman, "There is no time in Humphrey's entire tenure as vice president that two people of the stature that are sitting on that couch waiting to see Mondale would ever have been sitting outside his office anywhere."[20] There could be no more visible evidence that, for the first time in the history of that once-demeaned office, Carter's vice president had real clout.

It was underwritten by Carter assigning major tasks to Mondale from the start. His most historically important achievement was leading the U.S. delegation at the July 1979 UN Special Refugee Conference, where his stirring speech, written with his chief speechwriter, Martin Kaplan, evoked the 1938 Evian Conference, at which the world refused to liberalize immigration quotas for Jewish refugees. He said the "world will not forgive us if we fail" in saving Vietnamese and South Asian boat people. With Carter's full backing, he got a reluctant Sixth Fleet to rescue them at sea, and got a number of countries, prodded by the United States, which took five hundred thousand onto our shores, to take tens of thousands of others.[21] His staff took the lead on a key set of Carter initiatives on the reform of campaign finance, and later, Richard Moe, his chief of staff, was given the sensitive job of vetting candidates for chairman of the Federal Reserve Board.

Carter had in fact suggested that Mondale might serve as a de facto chief of staff, but Mondale declined, lest the administrative responsibility tie him down. Mondale jujitsued Carter into enhancing the vice president's reach after the president declared he did not want competing presidential and vice presidential staffs, but one united staff for both. "I can't be without a staff," Mondale told Carter, so they agreed on two staffs, "effectively integrated."[22] Moe would remain Mondale's chief of staff but was also given the title Assistant to the President, a rank equal to the top presidential aides, and Carter would also include him in the stream of advice from Ham, the president's closest confidant. This had never happened before. As a result of Carter's kumbaya vision of the White House, the vice president, a canny and experienced Washington hand, was able to place his own man, David Aaron, on Brzezinski's staff as deputy national security adviser, and Bert Carp as one of my two deputies. This happened quickly and with stealth. In the first days of the administration Mondale called me and said he wanted Bert Carp, whom I had never met, to serve as deputy chief of my Domestic Policy Council. I told him I already had a talented deputy, David Rubenstein, whom I hired during the campaign. Mondale said gaily, "Stu, now you have two deputies!" What could I say?

In fact, I never regretted it. Carp expertly directed our two dozen Domestic Policy Staff members; oversaw drafts of the decision memoranda by coordinating the views of all departments and agencies; and, in the end, placed some of Mondale's more liberal imprint on our domestic policy. Rubenstein worked with me to finalize decision memorandums we sent to the president, helped organize my schedule, and served as my eyes and ears in the West Wing and the cabinet departments. In his post–White House career he donated hundreds of millions to education, U.S. landmarks, and the arts from the fortune that he amassed later as cofounder of the Carlyle Group, a Washington-based multibillion-dollar investment fund.

Mondale's weekly one-on-one lunch with the president when both were in Washington lasted an hour or more and established a tradition followed by all future presidents. Moe would propose talking points for Mondale, who would add or delete items and make marginal notes in advance as part of his own careful preparation.[23] Moe regarded these lunches as probably the single most important element in their relationship because the two were able to speak frankly between themselves.[24] As Mondale recounted, "The president was serious about it. I brought the agenda in. He would occasionally bring things up. I would raise the issues, and I'd say this is what I want to talk about. And he was very conscientious about that time. He never crowded me, and he always wanted to listen."

These private lunches were important beyond discussing policy issues. Because the president was so hesitant to permit the open discussion of political considerations in cabinet and other meetings, Mondale used the lunches to talk politics. As he put it: "So when I was alone with him for those scheduled lunches everything was on the table that I wanted on the table, or that he wanted on the table."[25] Mondale found the lunches so valuable that he never risked ending them by disclosing what had passed between them. Carter often talked about his place in history or about how he had handled a problem. Mondale did not hold back his views, however painful. Once he told Carter that the Congress was "laughing at you up there. You've got to veto something fast. You've got to wake them up." Carter replied, "Good, I'll do it." And he vetoed a congressional authorization to build the B-1 bomber, an aircraft of limited use that consistently ran over budget.

Carter also invited Mondale to the weekly White House foreign-policy breakfasts and made certain he was in the intelligence flow. "All the stuff that went into the president's office I saw; I had all the secrets," he said. Of course the president did not always accept Mondale's political advice, which at times had an old-school liberal political quality, given that Carter was more conservative and had been elected on a promise to change the way government acted. For example, Carter envisioned establishing blue-ribbon panels of legal experts and eminent public figures to select the federal judges nominated by all presidents. Mondale said: "Mr. President, I don't agree with that at all. I think the political process has done a very fine job picking judges, and I think you are going to get those special-interest corporate lawyers [to pick them instead]." In Mondale's home state of Minnesota, Carter wanted to pick a Republican as well as a Democrat. Mondale said: "Forget it." He did, but by Executive Order made all of his federal district court judicial appointments from a list provided by bipartisan panels of experts.

During the hours they spent alone in Blair House the day before the inauguration, Carter proposed to make Mondale the first vice president in the chain of command in the event of a military emergency during which the president might be disabled. That same night they signed the formal documents in a room at the Kennedy Center at a preinauguration concert. Mondale came very close to serving as acting president once, when the president had minor hemorrhoid surgery that entailed sedation. But it never happened.[26] There was confusion in the White House when Ronald Reagan was shot by a deranged assassin and the then–vice president, George H. W. Bush, was in Texas for a speech, as Chief of Staff Alexander Haig proclaimed he was in charge. On the day of Osama bin Laden's aerial assault on the Twin Towers and the Pentagon, Vice President Dick Cheney temporarily took power to far greater effect while President George W. Bush was in Florida and remained out of Washington for the rest of the day to avoid a second strike that never came.

Carter also shared one other accoutrement of power: He allowed Mondale to use Camp David on his own. When friends came to Washington, Mondale sometimes gave them an unforgettable treat. He would put them in a helicopter on the White House lawn and fly them to Camp David for an overnight stay. Needless to say, political friends were duly impressed.[27] Such gracious behavior meant a great deal to the vice president, who was especially sensitive in view of Humphrey's humiliations by LBJ and his staff. Before they were sworn in, Mondale told Carter: "My pride is very important to me; my dignity is very important to me. If you can help me protect that, I'll do anything for you, but I will become a pipsqueak if I get pushed around, or if I have to go out and sell something I absolutely cannot sell." There were occasional sharp disagreements, and "he'd get mad at me once in a while, and he'd get irritated and get short with me, but, hell, that's got to happen." But, said Mondale, "he never embarrassed me once [and] our relationship was unprecedented."[28]

POLITICS AND THE PRESIDENCY
(AS SEEN BY THE VICE PRESIDENT)

This remarkably intimate partnership gave Mondale a special insight into Jimmy Carter's strengths and weaknesses as the nation's chief executive; it was a more objective view than that of us Georgians, who had been with him longer. Despite Carter's strong record of legislative accomplishment, Mondale felt that one of his great weaknesses was that "he was terrible at the public education role, and he had no confidence in himself." While we were all struggling to have Congress pass his energy legislation, Carter once told Mondale, "You know, nobody will listen to me." Mondale immediately told him, "Mr. President, you cannot believe that; it will destroy you." They jousted over the often-decisive role of presidential speeches, and while Mondale respected Carter's diligence on substance, he faulted him on conveying it to the public.

The vice president saw up close what many of us did. Carter's great strength was his willingness to tackle what seemed to be insurmountable challenges by dint of eighteen-hour days and self-discipline, and that somehow he could govern because he knew more about a subject than anybody else. "That was his management tool," said Mondale. "He'd take all those mounds of paper and read all night, and he'd read everything. And the word got out, and people started dumping more, and he got tons of stuff. He would read it all. He loved to know what was going on." Mondale saw the engineer in Carter, a man who thought that once the model policy was constructed and clearly displayed, it would carry its own weight and thus be clearly understood, "that intelligent people would add up the numbers—it wasn't oratory. . . . He had contempt for orators," telling Mondale, "Oh yeah, you and Humphrey like to speak; I don't do that."[29]

Mondale was a natural politician who loved being with others of his kind. He was a creature of Congress. The camaraderie, the political gossip, and the stories of battles won and lost were in his blood. Carter did not like politicians and felt uncomfortable with the normal byplay of political compromise as well as the give-and-take relationships between the president and Congress. That was why he brought his Georgia political sidekick Bert Lance to Washington. In some ways Mondale supplanted Lance and could accomplish things on the Hill better than Lance because of his long experience there. But he also found that when members felt they were in trouble, Carter would "not be there to help—even when they had been helping him. And when things really got bad, they weren't with us." He marveled that someone like Carter had gone so far in politics while distrusting "its personal side," adding, "He thought that once you're elected president, you've been spotted a certain advantage: you are commander in chief; you are the chief executive officer, and that required a certain respect and deference that he quickly found out that Congress had no intention of granting him." Mondale loved politics, and believed in stressing the positive. But Mondale said it "would break your heart" when Carter would tell a joyful crowd celebrating his victory in creating a new Department of Education, "This thing won't work as well as you think it will."[30]

Mondale learned to his amazement what we already knew—that political considerations simply were a forbidden subject, and, as Ham widely observed—only half in jest—"The worst way to convince Carter to make a decision you wanted was to say it would help him politically." Mondale further observed, "That soul of his wanted to do right, and in a strange way the very fact that the political system rejected him reassured him that he was right." And yet he found this weakness was also his greatest strength: "Look at Camp David. I don't think any other president could have done what he did. It was sheer, utter grit, drive, and courage that did it."[31] Moreover, Carter had a keener sense of the conservative mood of the country and an earlier awareness of the dangers of inflation than Mondale (or me).

None of this takes away from the remarkable partnership of Carter and Mondale. As we shall see toward the end of the term, it came under severe strain, almost to the point of breaking. But it lasted and we are the better for it today. Joe Biden brilliantly and loyally carried on the Mondale legacy, and it was no accident that the first person he called when Obama asked him to serve as his vice president was Walter Mondale.[32]

4

A NEW KIND OF FIRST LADY

J ust as Carter and Mondale created the modern vice presidency, Rosalynn Carter became one of the most influential first ladies in American history. Rising from humble beginnings in rural Georgia, she carved out her own policy role on mental health and served as a true political partner and even a diplomatic representative of the president, while refusing to be merely a convenient social ornament. She had superb political instincts, gave her husband frank advice that he would have done well to have followed more often, while nevertheless fiercely supporting him throughout his term in office.

If Jimmy Carter was an unlikely president, given his origins in Plains, Georgia, Rosalynn Smith Carter was an equally implausible first lady. Her father farmed and worked as an automobile mechanic and died of cancer when Rosalynn was thirteen, effectively ending her childhood. She and her dressmaker mother had to care for her young brothers and sister. Her mother said she was the kind of young lady who could wear a white dress all day and keep it clean. She was shy, read the Bible daily, and had the same zest for education as her future husband, graduating as valedictorian of her Plains High School class and from Georgia Southwestern College in 1946. Jimmy's sister Ruth was her best friend, and when she saw his picture on her bedroom wall, she thought "he was the most handsome man I'd ever seen. One day I confessed to her that I wished she would let me take the photograph home. Because I just thought I had fallen in love with Jimmy Carter." Not long afterward they met, appropriately after a church meeting, when Jimmy drove up with Ruth, came up to her, and asked her to go to the movies. He kissed her good-bye, and after months of corresponding while he was in Annapolis, she was swept off her feet. After putting his proposal on hold for a year so they could better come to know each other and themselves, they were married shortly after his graduation from the Naval Academy, when she was eighteen and he was twenty-one.[1]

Becoming the wife of a naval officer was her way of breaking out of the confines of her tiny hamlet. Because he was gone for long periods at sea, she was left to manage their home and a rapid succession of children: John William ("Jack"), the year after their marriage in Norfolk; James Earl ("Chip") III, less than three years later in Hawaii; then Donnel Jeffrey ("Jeff") in 1952, in New London, Connecticut. (Amy Lynn was born in 1967, the year after Carter's first gubernatorial race.) This taught her to be independent. As she told me, "Jimmy always thought I could do anything."[2] Only once did they fail to make a major political decision together: Rosalynn learned that Jimmy had decided to run for the Georgia State Senate one morning when he donned dress pants instead of his work khakis, and she asked him where he was going. He replied he was going to file for state senate. That would never happen again, and to this day Carter cannot explain why he did not discuss his decision with her in advance. When he ran, Rosalynn took a correspondence course in bookkeeping to help keep the business thriving, coming to feel that she knew more about the business than he did. She advised him to give up the money-losing corn mill, and he came to rely upon her judgment in business and beyond.

Rosalynn also got satisfaction from making it possible for Jimmy to pursue a political career, and even at this early stage she felt she was more a "political partner than just an appendage as a political wife." Her hardest lesson was learning to cope with the criticisms that were part of political life.[3] As she moved with her husband up the "greasy pole," she learned Eleanor Roosevelt's lesson that anyone in public life must develop "the skin of a rhinoceros." Religion was an important part of both their lives, and she believed it had an impact on his foreign policy, feeling "it was always better to reach a peaceful solution than to go to war."[4]

As a young Southern matron, Rosalynn was painfully shy in public and did not make a single speech in Carter's unsuccessful first race for governor in 1966. When she was unexpectedly asked to speak during his next campaign, at a luncheon in Gainesville in 1970, she stammered that her husband needed the help of the audience and sat down, fearful of what they might think of her. What really terrified her was realizing that she would have to go through it again and again as long as her husband was in politics.[5] But as Rosalynn became an active campaigner, she developed a custom that would lead to one of her more controversial decisions when they reached the White House. She was constantly asked about Jimmy's positions on issues, and would come home to ask him the answers. She insisted, both during the gubernatorial and presidential campaigns, on being fully briefed on the issues so she could respond correctly.

I first came into her life in the fall of 1974, when Governor Carter invited Fran and me to a Sunday lunch at the governor's mansion to thank me for my work with him as chairman of the DNC's Congressional Campaign Committee. She agreed I could bring my parents, Leo and Sylvia, and Fran's parents, Eli and Sarah Taylor, who were visiting from Boston. I found her attractive, quiet, and gracious. This was the first time I saw Georgia's first couple together, and their love and mutual respect were obvious. I saw how naturally they held hands (and continued doing so frequently in the White House). When we finished lunch, Rosalynn took us on a tour of their greenhouse. My mother, Sylvia, bless her heart, saw a beautiful bromeliad flower, and to our great embarrassment at her unmitigated chutzpah, she brashly asked Rosalynn if she could take it home. Rosalynn, betraying no astonishment, reached down with a smile and handed it to her. She kept that plant for decades in Atlanta and brought it with her when she moved to Washington to be with us as her health began failing.

ROSALYNN AS CAMPAIGNER, CABINET OBSERVER, AND CONTINENTAL DIPLOMAT

This shy woman blossomed in the most wonderful way. For eighteen months in the presidential race, she was a relentless campaigner. She went to 105 communities in Iowa, spent seventy-five days in Florida, and became a trailblazer as a presidential candidate's wife by campaigning so vigorously on her own. Tim Kraft, the young Iowa campaign manager (and later top political aide to Jordan in the White House) realized she was a "gold mine" in her uncanny ability to relate to voters.[6] Once the Carters arrived at the White House, it was clear that she wanted to become a different kind of first lady with an agenda of issues that mattered to her, and an office and staff of her own. Presidents' wives had traditionally had an office on the second or third floor in the family quarters; she was the first to have her own office with her own staff in the East Wing of the White House.[7] But she went far beyond moving her office closer to the decision-making arena; she gradually moved into a front-row seat. After several months in the White House, where she handled the personal finances, children's activities, and social events, Rosalynn would meet Jimmy at the end of his day on the elevator to the private living quarters with a list of things she needed his help to decide. She remembered that he dreaded seeing her with those lists, so he suggested they meet every Wednesday for lunch to complement the vice president's regular Monday lunches with the resident. She would arrive with a full agenda of subjects in a brown leather folder, an official French gift inscribed "Monsieur le President Jimmy Carter."

These sessions were not limited to social niceties. As Rosalynn traveled more widely, she continued to be asked where the president stood on various issues. She read news accounts voraciously and tried to sift through the comments about his policies. When he settled into the family quarters every evening after work, she bombarded the new president every night when he came home.[8] One evening only about a month after he had been inaugurated, she raised a question about a commentator's newspaper column. He said, "Why don't you sit in on the cabinet meetings, and then you'll know what's going on and why we make the decisions?" The solution was unique to the Carter presidency: On February 28, 1977, the president's wife began auditing the cabinet meetings as regularly as her own busy schedule allowed.

She sat behind the cabinet table where I sat with the senior White House staff, but by the door leading out of the Cabinet Room so she could leave early if necessary. She took notes and never joined in the discussion. By evening she had a notebook full of questions for her husband and had no compunction about telling him if she disapproved of anything. This process gave her the assurance that she understood the general thrust of what the administration was trying to accomplish and to field questions about it with accuracy and authority as she traveled around the country. It was a testament to her political partnership with the president and her intellectual curiosity. Since she did not actually participate and only observed, I did not think her presence was inappropriate in any way, although she was quickly depicted by her enemies as a pushy wife interfering with her husband's presidential business. She knew she would be criticized but felt it was worth it for something she wanted to do anyway, and with the full support of her husband.

As busy as she was, Rosalynn tried to be in the family quarters by 4 p.m. on school days so she could greet Amy on her return from school. Rosalynn tried to make life as normal as possible for a nine-year-old under the media gaze of the White House press corps. Amy was enrolled in a local public school, the first for an incumbent president since Theodore Roosevelt's son, rather than in one of Washington's elite private institutions. She was allowed to roller-skate down the White House hallways; play in the treehouse her father designed; and get a dog (named Grits for the family's Southern heritage) from her teacher, Verona Meeder. And her best friend was the daughter of the cook at the Chilean Embassy.[9]

The president would leave his West Wing office, and he and Rosalynn would often jog around the track on the South Lawn of the White House or play tennis together in the late afternoon. They would then cool off in the Southern-style rocking chairs he personally designed, on the Truman Balcony of the family quarters, discussing what they had done that day. At 6:30 p.m. every evening when he was not tied up with official business, Carter would sit down for family dinner.

Bizarre as it may seem, while Congress appropriates money to pay staff salaries (ninety-four people in Carter's time) and to foot the bill for official receptions and dinners, presidents must pay for their own and their family's food and drink as well as their personal guests in the personal White House residence and at Camp David. That not only meant daughter, Amy, but sons Jeff and Chip and their wives and children, who lived in the White House full-time; Rosalynn's mother, who visited often; and of course Miss Lillian, who stayed for long periods and often parked herself for several hours at a time in the office of the chief usher, Rex Scouten, chatting with the staff and regaling them with stories. It fell to Scouten on the first night after the inauguration to give the Carters the bad news about their personal living costs, and when he presented the first month's bill, he said they were "in shock." But he stuck with the tradition of having his large family dinners, despite the unexpected cost.

Nevertheless they made themselves at home and took great interest in the presidential mansion. Carter installed a sound system throughout the family residence to listen to his large collection of classical music tapes. (Unlike Nixon's, the system was definitely not to record conversations.) A stickler for punctuality, he insisted on having the antique clocks reset whenever they were jostled off real time, often by a press scrum in the Oval Office. In the evenings Jimmy and Rosalynn often strolled together on the White House grounds under the old trees, which Scouten had labeled as well as the plants. Carter sketched out his own design for Amy's treehouse on the South Lawn down to the last nail, and insisted on paying for it himself. When the National Park Service proposed chopping down one tree to expand the South Lawn maintenance shed, Carter studied the architect's plan, paced the site for half an hour, and redrafted it to save the tree. In August, crabgrass on the manicured lawn turned brown, and Scouten wanted to chop up the sod and sterilize the soil, but Carter demurred: "It looks just like the grass down in Georgia; leave it alone." He was overruled on only one major policy concerning the White House itself—his appeal to the public to save energy by turning down their thermostats to 65 degrees. That regimen lasted only about a year after both Miss Lillian and Rosalynn complained about the cold.[10]

To his credit as well as hers, Carter did not waste time putting his wife to work. In the first months of the administration, she undertook a challenging diplomatic assignment unlike any first lady before or since, a grueling two-week trip to seven Latin American countries—Jamaica, Costa Rica, Ecuador, Peru, Brazil, Colombia, and Venezuela. This arduous journey was not to meet with her fellow first ladies as a goodwill gesture, but to bring to the region, studded with military dictators, the president's new focus on human rights and democracy, nonproliferation of nuclear weapons, and reduction of conventional arms they had come to expect from the United States, regardless of how repressive their regimes. She spoke some Spanish, but to prepare she took language lessons three days a week, immersed herself in the novels, poetry, and history of the region, and absorbed briefings by scholars and government specialists.[11]

Before she left, she and the president were severely criticized. Representative Dante Fascell, a Florida Democrat, complained that "the Latins are macho and they hate gringos and women." Latin diplomats felt she would not be taken seriously. But—accompanied by two top officials, Assistant Secretary Terrence Todman from the State Department and Robert Pastor from the National Security Council—she brought home tangible achievements. Ecuador pledged to sign and ratify the American Convention on Human Rights; the military leader of Peru pledged to give up power and establish a democracy (four years later Rosalynn attended the inauguration of the newly elected president); the president of Colombia interceded with Panama's general Omar Torrijos to help move the negotiations on the Panama Canal. But most of all, she planted the flag of human rights in Latin America in a tangible way and in the president's name.[12]

Latin America was not Rosalynn Carter's only challenging diplomatic assignment. Half of Cambodia's population was murdered by the brutal Pol Pot regime in 1975, and tens of thousands of refugees fled to Thailand. In 1979 she went with an expert group on a twenty-four-hour flight, and was warned by our ambassador Morton Abramowitz to brace herself for the degradation she would see—and smell. Her visit helped draw worldwide attention: She urged the king of Thailand to provide more support, prodded UN Secretary General Kurt Waldheim to appoint a special relief coordinator, pushed the administration to contribute several million dollars to UNICEF, and was instrumental in having food and emergency supplies airlifted to Cambodia by the United States.

Rosalynn had a lifelong passion to help the mentally ill, prompted by the illness of one of Jimmy's cousins. When she campaigned in the 1970 gubernatorial race, she told me the most frequent complaint from voters involved family members who were mentally ill but could only be treated in a deplorable state mental institution. As Georgia's first lady, she worked to shift treatment to community mental health centers. In the White House she persuaded her husband to establish a Presidential Commission on Mental Health, with herself as honorary chair. Federal nepotism rules prevented her from taking an operational position, but she joined hearings around the country to expose the plight of the chronically mentally ill, eventually leading to federal legislation she took the lead in drafting, to integrate mental health services into the overall national health system, with funds for training caregivers at the local level and enlarging housing programs and Medicare and Medic-aid funding.[13] When she testified in its favor, she became the first presidential wife since Eleanor Roosevelt to appear before Congress on a bill. (Hillary Clinton later became the third.) She personally helped obtain the support of the American Medical Association and the American Bar Association and worked closely with congressional Democrats. The Mental Health Systems Act of 1980 was signed into law two months before the presidential elec-tion. But her most solid Washington accomplishment became one of her greatest disappointments when President Reagan refused to fund it.

Also building on her work in Georgia, where Rosalynn had developed an ambitious children's immunization program, she made it a national pri-ority by working through Joe Califano's health department and the Atlanta-based Center for Communicable Diseases to set up immunization programs in all fifty states—something that has recently, remarkably, become controver-sial. At the other end of the age spectrum, she lobbied for the Age Discrimi-nation Act, eliminating mandatory retirement at any age in the federal government and raising the retirement age in the private sector from sixty-five to seventy.

With more general women's issues she worked to find qualified women for major appointments, which helped swell to a record the number of women appointed by Carter to judicial, executive, and regulatory positions.[14] The President's Advisory Committee on Women found that women nominees for federal judgeships were being penalized for their scant experience on the bench in lower courts, often because they had taken time from their careers to raise children. Rosalynn interceded with her husband to have the attor-ney general mitigate this discrimination.[15] Along with her husband, she was less successful with the organized women's movement on one key issue—ratification of the Equal Rights Amendment; but it was not for want of try-ing. The first lady did not last long on the Commission on Women chaired by liberal New York firebrand Bella Abzug. They were furious at Carter for not pulling out all the political stops to obtain ratification of the Equal Rights Amendment and turned every meeting into a denunciation by Bella on the steps of the White House. Rosalynn became so upset over this that she "quit meeting with them."[16]

Despite her quiet demeanor—I never heard her speak loudly or discourteously to anyone—she was a tough-minded, more practical politician than her idealistic husband, in part because she was able to break through the cocoon of the presidential entourage and meet people around the country. She developed a keen ear for people's concerns and conveyed them to her husband in unvarnished form. She loved the politics that she felt were part of her responsibilities. While he enjoyed the problem-solving challenge of being president, she knew he disliked the "pettiness of politics" and did not have "any patience for the give and take"—as if these were not part of the process of addressing the nation's problems. That, she said, was one reason he preferred dealing with foreign over domestic policy—"On foreign policy, the President can act."[17] This is a common affliction of most presidents, who find the allure and relative freedom to act as commander in chief more satisfying than buttering up Congressional egos and rallying interest groups and the public to win their votes.

The president Rosalynn described, who was more than familiar to us on the White House staff from a greater distance, was a highly private man who disliked the socializing that comes with his job. Rosalynn regretted that they turned down all the invitations from the Washington elite—"no matter who it was"—and as a result the Carters never got to know the Washington establishment at all. "If there is one thing Jimmy dislikes more than anything I can think of, it is a cocktail party or reception or dinner every night," she said. For Carter the national capital was a repeat of his term in the Georgia statehouse, far from Atlanta's lively social life. "He just works all day, comes home at night, and doesn't want to go out," she said, recognizing that "we would have been better off if we had cultivated some friends at one point in the social power game."[18]

She felt another major mistake was barring alcohol from White House social events. When she first met with Rex Scouten, he told her he had read that the new first couple might not permit alcohol, and he priced the saving at a million dollars a year. When she told her penny-pinching partner, she said, "That settled it; we wouldn't serve alcohol in the White House." The press leaped on the story of a self-righteous Southern Baptist imposing his values on his official guests. Although the Carters ultimately served wines, cordials, and spiked punch, Rosalynn conceded that the initial stumble created a "stereotype that we never lived down."[19]

Her more persistent and fundamental difference with her husband as president was that he was simply not a traditional politician. On vexed and unpopular issues, particularly the Panama Canal, she would ask him, "Why don't you wait until your second term?" His rejoinder usually was, "Suppose I don't have a second term? Do you want me to go down as a do-nothing president?" She saw her husband as a person who believed that getting those things done was more important than being reelected, and she threw that back at him by replying that reelection was more important "because you can get *more* done for the country." That of course is the way he should have ordered his priorities, and she told me, "We used to have that argument all the time." Even as governor, and then as president, she also felt he was taking on too many challenges at once and would "fuss with him," telling him: "This is unreasonable; you know you ought not try to get so much [done] at one time; you can't get it all [done] at one time [while] irritating everybody" in the process. He would reply that he wanted to enact the best possible legislation and, "Would you rather have me ask for 5 percent of what I want and get it and be a success, or would you rather [I] ask for 100 percent of what I want, get 85 percent, and be a failure?"[20]

The problem with that, of course, was he often would not get even that 85 percent, and should not have drawn the odds so starkly between doing nothing or doing everything. She would argue with him about taking on unpopular causes and damaging his political standing, but for him, she said, if "it needed to be done, he was going to try, no matter how many enemies he made."[21]

Rosalynn was fiercely protective of his political standing. Although admitting they were "a little bit green with a lot to learn in the beginning," she bristled at the criticism of the Georgia Mafia by the press and official Washington, and ranked disloyalty as the most unforgivable sin among his appointees.[22] When she felt that a member of his cabinet was hurting her husband politically, she was not shy in saying so, even if the president would not himself. She directly confronted Califano, who led an antismoking campaign with scathing attacks on the tobacco industry, for hurting the president's standing in North Carolina. And she upbraided her own husband over the behavior of his secretary of state when Vance ignored politics in favor of UN diplomacy on Israel while we were locked in a crucial primary campaign in New York City. Rosalynn also became a trusted conduit for his top political staff—Ham, Caddell, and Rafshoon—to call when they wanted to alert Carter to the unforeseen consequences of some decision he had made mainly on its merits. Pat Caddell, the president's brilliant but hyperbolic young pollster, found her political instincts excellent and said that she had a much better sense of what was going on outside the White House bubble than did the president. "Where she was really influential was her antennae, [and] for being inside that bubble I found unbelievable," said Caddell.[23]

Indeed, Rosalynn belied the Southern stereotype of the "steel magnolia"— a hard-hearted woman with a soft exterior, as her critics contended. Everyone who knew her on the White House staff, and her friends, recognized that even while she was giving her husband plainspoken advice, she was warm hearted and respectful, and did not play political games.

What Rosalynn saw with clear eyes, as Carter at times did not, were the political tricks played by others on her husband—and the ones he could play to his advantage. It was her idea to hold the Middle East peace talks at Camp David because of its beauty and isolation. Of course her advice was not always followed. She spotted the danger of Leonid Brezhnev's enfolding kiss when Carter signed the SALT II agreement in Vienna and immediately realized it would make her husband look weak on television. She opposed his Rose Garden strategy of not campaigning against Ted Kennedy to demonstrate his total commitment to bringing home the hostages from Iran by staying aloof from politics. This placed even more of the burden of campaigning on her shoulders. And in campaigning, she had a fine sense of partisan politics, urging the president to stay on the campaign trail rather than abruptly return to the White House when a final offer came from Tehran on the American hostages on the weekend before the election.

Rosalynn was in many ways the president's eyes and ears to the country, constantly reaching out to the vast number of friends she had made on her own. Like every president, every president's wife is different, as is every presidential marriage. The template for the modern first lady veers from the politically progressive pioneer, Eleanor Roosevelt, to the culturally advanced fashion icon, Jacqueline Kennedy, who championed and elevated the role of culture and the arts on the national agenda. Rosalynn Carter enlarged the importance of the role from that of Mrs. Roosevelt, who put ideas and programs on the public agenda that FDR could and often did dismiss as something floated by "my missus." From FDR's betrayal of his marriage vows to his crippling illness, Eleanor was his partner but not his confidante and built a political network of her own to help him. With the Carters' solid, loving marriage, Rosalynn's actual influence over her husband's policies was probably stronger than Mrs. Roosevelt's over her legendary husband. This model of wife as political partner waxes and wanes, but it is possible that there would not have been a Hillary Clinton running for president, after an active period as first lady, without Rosalynn Carter's demonstration of how to make common cause with her husband.

5

THE INDISPENSABLE MAN

Bert Lance came to Washington with Jimmy Carter as his closest friend, tennis partner, confidant, peer in age and background, and most experienced political adviser. As he put it, "I knew him as Jimmy Carter, not as Jimmy Carter the President."[1] He was the new president's indispensable man, the extroverted, glad-handing deal maker for the introverted and analytical chief executive, the man Carter could least afford to lose. But once Bert's legal problems were exposed, his position as Carter's budget director became untenable. The Lance affair was the first crisis of the new administration. It exposed early weaknesses in the White House staff and ended the traditional presidential honeymoon period. Carter lost his essential liaison to the congressional power brokers as well as his chief link to his Southern political base. Months of focusing on Bert's troubles distracted the president and cast a long shadow over his judgment when he wrapped himself around Bert to defend his friend, who was also his political wingman.

Bert was the Carter administration's most-sought-after guest on the Georgetown social circuit, whose parties he and his wife, LaBelle, loved, and which in those days were an essential part of Washington political life. More than most of Carter's Georgia Mafia—including the president himself—he understood how the administration's agenda could be advanced by sharing tidbits of inside information with the journalists, opinion makers, think-tank gurus, corporate and labor leaders, foreign diplomats, and politicians who clustered at these dinner parties and receptions. Bert had direct access and was one of the only people the president genuinely liked as a personal friend. He was the kind of friend the president knew, as Bert put it in rural Georgia parlance, would "be willing to chase hogs for you in the middle of the night."[2]

Bert could say things to and about the president that no one else could. During one meeting devoted to tax reform, he argued against the president's desire to limit deductions for business lunches—what Lance called the "three-martini lunch." Half jokingly the president asked: "What do you all do at [Atlanta's] Commerce Club?" Bert retorted: "Mr. President, I saw you there in July last year, and I know what you were doing, you were getting a campaign contribution." Undeterred, Carter insisted that the deduction for business lunches be expunged from the tax code. Bert pleaded: "I don't drink martinis. . . . But I never had any business with a fellow who drinks three of them, because he's totally incapable of carrying on afterwards."[3] In the end Congress refused to limit the deduction, but the term "three-martini lunch," which had been bandied about before, passed into the English language, in part with the elevation Carter gave to the inequity of business people being able to deduct their expensive lunches, while working people had no such opportunity.

While Frank Moore was the titular chief of White House congressional relations, Bert was our informal liaison on the Hill and reached out just as effectively to the business and financial community, where he was respected as a former CEO of two banks. Bert had a long face with dark circles under droopy eyes, but he could unveil a smile that would melt steel. He talked with a chuckle and was gregarious in a way that made him almost impossible to dislike. A hulk of a man at six feet five and 245 pounds, he was warm, voluble, emotive, and colloquial, with a ready chuckle. He is credited with coining the phrase "If it ain't broke, don't fix it." By contrast, Carter, cool and analytical by nature, was slight, lithe, and only a shade taller than five feet nine and 155 pounds, but handsome, with penetrating hazel eyes and that famous toothy grin.

Their lifestyles also could not have been more different. Bert lived in a sixty-room mansion on a five-hundred-acre hilltop near Calhoun, Georgia. One side of the house was built to resemble the White House and the other, George Washington's estate at Mount Vernon. It had fifteen bathrooms, twenty bedrooms, and three kitchens. He used his bank's private planes to fly around the state and attend political events around the country. Jimmy and

Rosalynn, on the other hand, lived out their lives in a pleasant but unpretentious one-story redbrick ranch house in Plains. Bert never graduated from the University of Georgia, quitting in his senior year to work as a $90-a-month teller in his young wife's family bank, while Jimmy attended Georgia Southwestern College, took mathematics courses at Georgia Tech, and graduated near the top of his class at the U.S. Naval Academy.

On a deeper level, however, they had far more in common. They shared the background of rural Georgia, Jimmy from the flatlands of the state's southwest, Bert from the mountains of the north. Jimmy's family were peanut farmers, Bert's father an educator and president of Young Harris College. Both knew the pains and values of life on a farm, Bert from what he remembered as the "back-bending work" of picking cotton. He married his childhood sweetheart, LaBelle David; both had attended their local elementary school. In words that would later have national import, Bert recalled that LaBelle's grandfather, the bank's founder, "taught me his ways as a country banker, practices and values which I then applied myself as my banking career got under way." He made loans on his local depositors' character and circumstance rather than their collateral. It was a community banker's code, and banking was in Bert's blood just as much as in LaBelle's family.

By the early 1960s Bert had become the youngest bank president in the United States and a chairman in 1974, until he resigned after Carter's inauguration to follow him to Washington. He quintupled the bank's assets from $11.9 to $54.1 million and likewise its profits by lending to help build the local economy, which benefited from cheap labor that made the district a major center for the carpet industry. He also served as president and director of Atlanta's National Bank of Georgia, likewise increasing its deposits by half and almost doubling its assets. To foster economic development in what was becoming known as the New South, Bert led the effort to form an association of counties and cities into the Coosa Valley Planning and Development District, an organization that brought him in contact with Carter, who had formed a similar organization around Plains. Bert first saw Carter in 1966, when Jimmy was standing in the shade of a large oak tree on the campus of Berry College in Rome, Georgia, when both were attending a meeting of Bert's Coosa Valley Planning and Development District. Jimmy had been elected a state senator and was making a run for governor. Bert was instantly taken by Carter and by his campaign message: "Government ought to be as good as the people it serves."

They shared much beyond their rural Georgia roots. They and their wives were deeply religious born-again Christians, especially LaBelle. Another shared interest was rare among white rural Georgians of that era: support for civil rights for black Americans. (I use this term instead of the current "African American" because it is more authentic to that era.) Bert viewed civil rights pragmatically as a way to improve the economic status of the black population. As he put it, "Opposing the efforts of Dr. King and others harmed your own growth and development. . . . In addition to being morally wrong, it was bad business." For Carter, civil rights were more personal. While there were few blacks in the north Georgia hill country, Jimmy grew up with black children in the fields around Plains and had served with black sailors as a naval officer in the close quarters of submarines. Nevertheless the two political allies came together on one conclusion: Discrimination was holding back the South they loved.[4]

When Carter was elected governor in 1970, Bert was asked to become state highway commissioner, to his great surprise, because it was a job about which he knew nothing. But just as when he was later named by Carter to manage the vast federal budget and its bureaucratic establishment, his task in Georgia was to apply his political skills to make state government work more efficiently. The bloated department that Bert Lance took over in 1971 was virtually a law unto itself. The new governor boldly fired the director, Jim Gillis, who had become the most powerful political figure in the state by directing highway contracts to the districts of key members of the legislature. Statehouse leaders warned that the new governor would need Gillis's pork barrel for the votes required to deliver on his major campaign promise, to reorganize the state government. As Carter later conceded, "I would not doubt or deny that he [Lance] would pave a few miles of road in a propitious place in Georgia to get some votes."[5] While Lance made deals that Governor Carter loathed making himself, they helped them cut and combine more than three hundred agencies and advisory boards into a few dozen.

Lance served as highway commissioner for only three years and resigned at Carter's request to run as the governor's successor to block Lester Maddox from returning to the statehouse. In the 1974 elections Maddox was defeated by George Busbee, a moderate, but in the long run the biggest loser was Lance, who borrowed several million dollars for his failed gubernatorial campaign. He never should have been named to a position requiring Senate confirmation. Instead of running the Office of Management and Budget (OMB), he should have been installed in a West Wing office near the president. There, without the rigors of disclosure and Senate confirmation, he could have provided broad-spectrum political and policy advice that would have been a godsend to the detail-oriented and essentially apolitical president.

Still, Lance's appointment was by no means an irrational choice. He shared the president's fiscal conservatism, and Jimmy wanted Bert as his watchdog over spending. All cabinet departments submit their annual spending estimates to OMB for review and incorporation into the presidential budget. The White House staff often suggests compromises, but the ultimate decision is the president's. Bert himself rarely made the detailed OMB presentations, and, as my deputy, David Rubenstein, wryly noted, there were times when Bert sat next to the president on the side of the large oak table opposite his own OMB team and disagreed with them.[6] In our administration, as in all others, competing factions quickly developed, with the conservative side represented by Bert and Treasury Secretary Michael Blumenthal, and sometimes joined by Charles Schultze, chairman of the Council of Economic Advisers. Vice President Walter Mondale and I balanced the president's conservatism with what we thought was sufficient spending on programs to satisfy the more liberal Democratic members of Congress and key Democratic interest groups. So, after the formal budget appeals process was over, Mondale and I would meet with Carter in his private study to gain his approval to spend a a few billion dollars on programs to help low-income Americans, while staying within Carter's tight budget constraints.

The president also had ambitious plans to reorganize the federal government, and wanted Bert to repeat what he had accomplished with state government in Georgia. OMB, the largest organization within the Executive Office of the President, is separated from the White House by a narrow alley and housed in a magnificent nineteenth-century building pillared like a wedding cake, which was designed to hold the Departments of State, Navy, and War—the last two predecessors to the Pentagon, a sign of the vast growth of the federal government. As OMB director, Lance was ideally placed to persuade Congress to give him the authority to oversee Carter's reform of the federal government. They formed a task force headed by Harrison Welford, a talented former aide to Ralph Nader, and many major reforms are still in effect. Most notably, the reorganization of a number of disparate agencies into the Federal Emergency Management Agency (FEMA), which to this day provides a centralized response to natural disasters.

THE PAST COMES DUE

This was the running start by the Carter administration to fulfill the president's pledge to restore trust in the government. But because of Bert's banking background, it soon stumbled, and not for lack of warnings. A rushed and inadequate vetting process failed to allow Carter and his inexperienced staff—themselves close to Bert—to appreciate the problems posed by sweetheart banking practices that violated standard banking custom. Bert's bank had financed an expansion of the Carter peanut warehouse in 1975 with a loan of $4.7 million, but that was repaid, unlike many more dubious loans. In the early months of the presidency neither appreciated how much appearances matter at the highest level of politics, where they now dwelled, particularly in the harsh lights of post-Watergate press coverage.

During their initial discussion in Plains, Bert very generally mentioned issues that had to be resolved about the funding of his abortive gubernatorial campaign, but they did not seem insurmountable. A Calhoun businessman who had been active in Carter's presidential campaign called to warn against Bert's move to Washington and urge that he remain in Georgia and "take care of his finances; he really is exposed." This warning reached John Moore, a prominent Atlanta lawyer appointed to the transition team to examine the financial background of all nominees for high office and specifically to look for conflicts of interest.[7] But none of the president's young aides, whose principal national experience had been in the bubble of the campaign, could conceive that such a hugely successful banker was in serious financial trouble, perhaps even broke.

Moore took his position seriously, consulting with people who had done the same work for the Kennedy administration and staff members of the Senate committees that would confirm the Carter nominees. He realized that he had to make allowances for the way Bert ran the Calhoun Bank, doing favors like most country bankers because he was friends with most of the people who ran the town, although bending regulations like that would not have passed muster in Atlanta, let alone New York. He reported that Lance always demanded adequate collateral, and the bank never lost money on its loans. His problem was one of a potential conflict of interest: Lance held $5 million worth of stock in Atlanta's National Bank of Georgia, of which he was also the president, and about $2.5 million in other stock. Moore felt it would be improper for the head of OMB to hold stock in any bank, and especially such a large concentration of stock in one. That led to a fateful decision that Carter himself made: Lance had to unload the stock of the big Atlanta bank within twelve months. That immediately depressed its value, which was also the collateral for personal loans that helped Bert maintain his grand lifestyle.

That was only the tip of the iceberg. Lance's family bank in Calhoun was under a year-old federal order by the comptroller of the currency to stop granting him large overdrafts. The propriety of those loans, made through his own bank, was to haunt him when he joined the administration. He had used the money to finance his abortive campaign for governor and repaid hundreds of thousands with interest, but the order had nevertheless been referred to the Justice Department for investigation by the U.S. attorney in Atlanta, John Stokes, a Republican appointed by Richard Nixon. Lance quickly went to the comptroller's Atlanta representative and persuaded him to rescind the order against his Calhoun bank. But the comptroller's Washington headquarters did not take formal note that the order had been lifted, and an FBI investigation loomed on possible bank fraud.

Stokes wanted the probe to go ahead so he could remain in office for several months in order to collect $100,000 in retirement benefits.[8] To make matters worse, the formal letter from the comptroller's Washington office to Senator Abraham Ribicoff, chairman of the Government Affairs Committee that would vote to confirm Lance, never mentioned the campaign overdrafts and declared him "well qualified." Lance was quickly confirmed by the full Senate so he could start work on the budget almost as soon as Carter was inaugurated in January 1977. As the details of a sloppy clearance process by both the Carter transition team and Ribicoff's own committee emerged during the spring, the embarrassed senator felt blindsided. Now the pressure mounted on Lance.

In fact it was disclosed only when Bert's banking problems burst into public view from the Senate hearings that, remarkably, the FBI forensic financial team investigating him never communicated with their FBI colleagues doing the standard background check for his appointment as OMB director. The White House legal counsel's office wanted to release these facts to show the fault lay with the FBI and not the Carter transition team in going forward with Bert's nomination. But the Justice Department counseled against it.[9]

As early as May 1977, the newsmagazines began questioning Bert's banking practices, but it seemed they were only rehashing old news. *Time* contended that Bert had serious financial problems because the National Bank of Georgia was going to write off large loans made during his tenure as chairman, and that would bite into the bank's dividends. Bert warned the president at their regular weekly lunch that the write-offs would make it extremely difficult to honor his promise to sell the stock; the price had already dropped from $16 to $11 a share. Carter shrugged off the warning: "I don't pay any attention to stuff like that, and don't you either." With an added sense of urgency, Bert saw the president early the next morning in the Oval Office and warned that "I've got a major problem that relates to my economic viability." He offered to resign to forestall further controversy, straighten out his finances, and then return if Carter wanted him back. Carter remained unfazed: "I'm not about to hear that. That's foolishness and it doesn't make any sense. We'll get the situation straightened out, and you'll get your stock sold. We'll get the Senate to give you an extension of your deadline for that."[10]

Stocks go up and stocks go down, but Lance's predicament was more complicated than that. Bert did not bother to tell Carter that the stock was collateral for a personal loan of $3.4 million that he had negotiated with an even bigger bank, the First National Bank of Chicago. The drop in value imperiled the loan itself, and if it was called by the Chicago bank, Bert's financial empire would probably collapse. On July 11, Carter wrote the Government Affairs Committee asking the senators to lift the year-end deadline on the ground that a forced sale would impose "an undue financial burden" on Lance.[11] The die was cast. The president, sidestepping staff members who might have warned him to let Lance leave, entangled himself in the imbroglio.

Now the press would not let either of them escape. On July 24, the day before Ribicoff scheduled a hearing on the extension, the *Washington Post* published a detailed story raising questions about the Chicago bank loan, which disclosed a financial pyramid: Bert had used a large part of the Chicago loan to pay off a previous loan from a New York bank. That loan had financed the original purchase of his stock in the National Bank of Georgia.

Although it did not come out at that point that both loans had been underwritten by the same collateral, Bert insisted the Chicago loan was perfectly proper, and the committee unanimously agreed to extend the deadline. But this time Ribicoff sought more assurances than he had in January, and asked John Heimann, the incoming comptroller of the currency, to investigate Lance's banking practices and report by mid-August.

"CARTER'S BROKEN LANCE"

Carter himself was soon drawn in. The *New York Times* reported early in August that Bert had brought Jimmy to the Manufacturers Hanover Bank in New York in 1975, while establishing a relationship with the bank. It did not matter that the bank's executive vice president, Llewellyn Jenkins, was telling the comptroller that business was never discussed at the meeting and that Lance simply wanted to "introduce me to an aspiring candidate for the presidency." But after that meeting Lance's National Bank of Georgia put more than half a million dollars on deposit at Manufacturers Hanover in New York, and Bert drew on the money for himself. This turned out to be part of a pattern for Bert: moving money from the Calhoun family bank as interest-free loans to other banks, which in turn would lend some of it back to Lance himself.

The *Times* led the attack through none other than its columnist William Safire, who was fresh from serving as a Nixon speechwriter and had been hired by the newspaper's publisher specifically to balance its liberal columnists with a conservative voice. Safire won a Pulitzer Prize for his July 21, 1977, column under an obvious pun, "Carter's Broken Lance," published before the Ribicoff hearing or the Heimann investigation; the columnist called Lance "a walking conflict of interest" and outlined the dubious banking relationships and pyramid of loans that were shortly to emerge. He kept the story alive with a relentless series of additional columns from July to October 1977, under the lurid headlines "The Lance Cover-Up," "Lance-gate," "Boiling of Lance," and "Mr. Carter's Confession." Nor did he spare Ribicoff and his senior colleague, Charles Percy, a moderate Republican senator from Illinois, for giving Bert a pass both at his confirmation hearing and on the request for an extension to sell his stock.[12]

No one was more publicly engaged on a daily basis than Jody Powell, who had to fight back against what he felt were unfair attacks against the president and Bert. When the White House got a tip from an Illinois businessman that Senator Percy had himself used a plane owned by Bell & Howell, his former company in Chicago, to fly back and forth to Washington, the press secretary committed the cardinal Washington sin of attacking an individual senator by leaking the story to the *Chicago Sun-Times* and thinking he was off the record, calling Percy a "sanctimonious SOB." Blowing this out of all proportion, television networks played it up and accused Jody of Watergate-style "dirty tricks."[13]

Carter was incensed but did not appreciate how much his own anti-Washington, anti-Watergate campaign had played a role in changing the attitude of the press from deference to skepticism and outright hostility. Jody publicly apologized and, with the president's approval, did so personally to Percy, but the damage was done. Both Bert and Jody knew the incident had hurt Bert badly, and there was a clear reason for the press attention paid to Bert: the high standard set by Carter himself. He had pledged that his preeminent mandate as president was trust, and Bert clearly did not meet that standard.

No player in the Bert Lance drama was thrust into a more thankless role than was John Heimann. Only two days after taking office as comptroller, he was handed the politically charged investigation of Lance's banking practices. Not that he was unprepared: Heimann, a handsome, debonair investment banker and public servant, had been New York State's tough banking superintendent. The comptroller's office was established to regulate national banks in a uniquely independent position from which, although nestled in the Treasury, the comptroller is accountable only to Congress for his semi-judicial decisions and cannot be removed by the president who picked him.

Even so, the phone call from Ribicoff and Percy on his second day in office demanding a full investigation of Lance came as a shock. Heimann quickly realized, as he told me later, "I didn't see how I could win no matter what I did." He was already facing newspaper stories that his predecessor, Robert Bloom, had improperly given Bert a clean bill of financial health, and the new comptroller wondered whether the agency he had just taken over was corrupt, trying to curry favor with the incoming administration, or just sloppy. He knew he had to do a thoroughly straightforward job because, as he told himself, "If you're going to go down, do it correctly, funnels burning, flags flying, the orchestra playing, get in full uniform and don't mess around."[14]

So Heimann made an extraordinary decision. He called in implacable inspectors of the Treasury's own Internal Revenue Service, who quickly concluded—correctly, as it turned out—that Bloom's letter to Congress clearing Lance contained "misstatements." Bloom had not revealed all he knew. Heimann spent his first weekend in office reading the Lance files that had been locked in Bloom's safe. He found that bank examiners had cited Lance for violating numerous banking regulations, although none of the violations were criminal. Heimann then set out on his own investigation, putting sixty officials around the country to work reviewing the many accusations against Lance. Lest he be accused of burying bad news, he delivered his findings to Treasury Secretary Blumenthal, and the information was passed on to Carter through the White House counsel, Robert Lipshutz.

The president slowly buckled under the news. According to a memo by Blumenthal's deputy, Robert Carswell, the president was at first "very controlled" and said nothing, and by the second meeting was clearly "quite unhappy." Finally, Carswell said, Carter "didn't want to have anything to do with this. . . . [It was] out of his control and he deeply resented" the investigation.[15]

Now came the unenviable task of confronting Lance himself. Heimann sought the advice of Attorney General Griffin Bell, who was a friend of both Lance and Carter. Bell told him to take along a Justice Department lawyer and court reporter and read Lance his Miranda rights. He did so at 7:00 a.m. on a hot August morning in a Washington hotel room out of sight of the press, and found it personally traumatic to have to read the standard self-incrimination warning for criminal suspects to "the director of the OMB, the president's best pal. . . . I thought I would die of sheer embarrassment." When he asked Lance about pledging the same collateral for two loans, in good-old-boy fashion Lance admitted to "a mistake and an oversight. A lot of things didn't get done that should have been done. But they were not done on purpose." Heimann decided not to press Lance about using the bank's airplane to fly to the 1976 Democratic National Convention carrying a case of champagne bought with bank funds, one of many borderline practices.[16]

The next day Blumenthal summoned me to his office to inform me that while Heimann had not found anything illegal, his report on Lance would detail "borderline shoddy banking practices," including numerous personal loans that had not been reported to the banking regulators. "Lance can't survive," he said.[17] I told him to inform the president about the facts of the incomplete report but nothing more. I knew Blumenthal was already viewed with suspicion by the president and his political entourage.

Nevertheless Mike visited me in my West Wing office and, with an added sense of urgency, repeated, "I don't see how he can survive." The wise old pol Robert Strauss had also told me something similar. Both were clearly enlisting my help in recommending that the president cut his losses as soon as possible. At a minimum I should have brought the news to Lipshutz and to Ham Jordan. I did not do so in order to protect Mike, but also to avoid appearing disloyal to Bert. Although I understood Carter's strong feelings, I frankly did the president a great disservice in remaining silent.[18]

The comptroller and his team completed two detailed reports within sixty days, both landing in August, while most of official Washington was on vacation. The general tenor could not have been a surprise to the White House, and the reports should have raised enough warning flags to make it clear Bert had to go—and fast. Carswell had already warned the president about Bert's dealings with Manufacturers Hanover—the bank to which Carter had accompanied Lance—although Heimann did not press that case. But he cited "quite inconceivable" banking practices, most egregiously Bert's pledge of the same stock as collateral for two loans, as well as other loans to Bert by banks where his own family bank had deposited money.[19] Heimann tried to make his report "very dry reading" while leaving no doubt that Bert had violated sound banking principles. As Heimann later explained, while Bert shuffled money from one account to another, "he never stuck it in his own pocket." Bert's defense was that small-town bankers and lawyers did that all the time, but Heimann argued that Bert had bent these local norms out of shape and used the bank "as a personal fiefdom rather than as a trustee for other people."[20]

The report was forwarded to the Treasury's Carswell, who sent it to White House Counsel Lipshutz, who had been a real estate lawyer in Atlanta with no expertise in banking regulation. He then sent it to Carter at Camp David with a cover note that completely misread its import, largely absolving Bert and emphasizing that because Heimann found no evidence of outright illegality, it was up to the Justice Department to determine if Bert should be indicted for fraud.[21] When the report reached Carter at Camp David, he read only Lipshutz's cover note and the executive summary.

Carter could hardly be faulted for skipping a detailed regulatory report, though it was an exception to his penchant for reading detailed documents. But he paid dearly for not appointing a Washington veteran as his counsel to give him a full analysis of the report's dire implications in the nation's capital, where appearances matter more than reality, and for not having established a staff structure to prevent him from following his instincts. He marched straight off the helicopter from Camp David into the White House to make himself Bert's prime defender to the world. Jody had drafted a statement saying Lance should be given a chance to defend himself. But in an overabundance of exuberance, the president burst out with an impromptu endorsement that would become the epitaph of the Lance affair: "Bert, I'm proud of you."[22] When Heimann heard this, "I almost died. I couldn't believe it. I called up [Carswell at] Treasury and went bananas, and was sick, sick to my stomach." He blamed Lipshutz, "who clearly misread it and didn't recognize the obvious."[23] Worse was to come.

A FRIENDSHIP TESTED

By Labor Day weekend, before official Washington started to return from the summer break, Carter still could not separate his deep friendship with Lance from the need to protect his presidency. He had a long conversation with Kirbo, his closest outside confidant, and stayed up late agonizing in the hope that Bert could somehow salvage his position by taking a leave of absence to prepare for and survive congressional hearings. That was proving increasingly difficult: More details surfaced about his jaunts to football games aboard the National Bank of Georgia's private plane. The allegations were peeling away like the layers of an onion, each bringing its own tears. The Securities and Exchange Commission (SEC) launched a fresh investigation about whether there had been significant omissions in the stock offering of the National Bank of Georgia.[24] And a bill was introduced in the House of Representatives to create a Watergate-style special prosecutor. The noose around Bert's neck was tightening, and the administration would not escape the indignity of a public hanging.

For me, Labor Day weekend of 1977 was traumatic. *Time* quoted me as saying that I could not see how Lance could survive. It was true that after I had seen Heimann's report, I told Ham that I did feel he could not survive, and that more of the president's popularity drained away each day. But I certainly did not say this to the press, and in any event Carter would have viewed making such a statement as an act of disloyalty.

Ham flew to Bert's vacation home in Sea Island, Georgia, to make it clear that he was in serious trouble. Shortly afterward Bert hired the legendary presidential adviser and Washington superlawyer Clark Clifford to help shape his defense. Ribicoff and Percy met with Carter, who flatly refused to let Bert resign before the hearings because "I want him to have his day in court. . . . I prefer an expeditious hearing to let all the facts come out."[25]

Dismayed, Ribicoff felt that Carter was making a serious mistake by not cutting his losses, even though he knew the president "would be losing his good right arm."[26] Ribicoff had no choice but to hold a hearing quickly, as Carter demanded. Ribicoff feared for the president's campaign agenda of post-Watergate government reforms, which would be coming before his committee: new rules for ethics in government, civil service reform, and the creation of new departments of energy and education. In fact those proposals became law. But to undercut the administration, Republicans tried to trap Heimann into accusing Lance of criminal behavior. Heimann was so upset by the tension that while dining with his wife at a restaurant the evening after his testimony, he walked out and vomited in the street.[27]

Early in the morning of September 15, the day that Bert was to testify, an extraordinary event occurred that illuminated the extent to which Christian faith pervaded the lives of the president and his friend. Lance came to the Oval Office at 6:30 a.m. for brief prayers, having selected four Bible passages. One was Joshua 1:6, "Be strong and of good courage. . . ." Then the great vision of life's change and challenges from Ecclesiastes 3:1–8, "To every thing there is a season. . . ." And from the New Testament's 1 Peter 2:17, "Honor all people. Love the brotherhood. Fear God. Honor the king," and finally from 1 Peter 2:25, "For ye were as sheep gone astray; but have now returned unto the Shepherd and Bishop of your souls."[28] Brzezinski arrived a few minutes later to give the president his daily national security briefing, to find the two men on their knees in the small study off the Oval Office. He found the scene "touching, really."[29]

Whether it was thanks to the power of prayer, Clifford's superb preparation, or Bert's own persuasive charm, Bert's hearing turned out to be a public success—at least as measured by the calls that flooded into the White House, and the fairly favorable newspaper stories. His basic defense was that his banking transactions were typical of a small-town family-run bank; that under his leadership the deposits and assets of both the Calhoun Bank and National Bank of Georgia had increased dramatically; and that no depositor "had ever lost a cent while I was with the banks." This may have resonated with ordinary folks watching the televised hearings, but it did not prevent congressional inquisitors of his own party from pressing him on the overdrafts approved by his banks to his own family and himself for his failed campaign for governor. Ribicoff cited the bank examiners' reports describing the payments as "abusive" and "appalling."

Emboldened by Bert's good showing, Carter was in a fighting mood. He took the highly unusual step of walking across the hall from the Oval Office and interrupting our regular morning staff meeting to demand that everyone show full support for Bert. No one must call for his resignation, the president warned, and said: "I will fire anyone who I know does this." (I felt particularly uncomfortable because of the *Time* story that I had denied.) Later that day he repeated to his cabinet members that he was "proud of Bert." He accused the press of dredging up stories and charges that had not undermined his confidence in Lance, and he looked forward to "Bert explaining his side of the story." He assured the cabinet that Bert's troubles in no way impeded the effectiveness of the OMB—the budget process was moving along under Bert's deputy, James McIntyre.[30] No cabinet member said anything.

As Carter focused on the overdrafts, he realized it was time for Bert to resign. The whole affair was sucking the oxygen out of everything else. After an agonizing weekend and a consultation with Robert C. Byrd, the Senate majority leader, Carter confronted Lance at 6:15 a.m. on the following Monday in the Oval Office, where the president had already been at work for an hour. He told Bert that he had had his chance to defend himself and done well, and now he had a few days to decide on his future before the investigation into his personal finances resumed and possibly spread even more uncomfortably to other government agencies. That night Kirbo, Jordan, Powell, and the rest of the president's Georgia entourage belatedly urged Lance to resign. The next day Carter and Lance played a round of tennis, and Bert agreed that he was ready to go but first had to talk to LaBelle—his fiercely loyal, deeply religious wife. She objected strenuously, giving Carter what he described as "probably one of the worst days I've ever spent."[31]

On Wednesday, Lance arrived in the Oval Office uncharacteristically late by almost an hour. In a positively Shakespearean scene of conflict between political and personal loyalties, Bert begged the president to help him with LaBelle. Because the Oval Office was far too formal for such a painful discussion among three old friends, he then ushered Bert and LaBelle through the adjoining private presidential study next door, where he generally worked when not receiving formal delegations or holding our senior White House staff meetings. It was a small, intimate room, with photos of Rosalynn and their children. Here LaBelle made her last stand. She said she realized that her husband and the president had already made their decision, but disagreed strongly.

In passionate terms LaBelle argued the case for keeping Bert. The president listened carefully but countered that Bert's problems had preoccupied him and diverted the attention of the press just when he was trying to rally public support for the Panama Canal Treaty. He told her that he and Bert had sat for forty-five minutes after a tennis match on a bench by the White House court discussing his prospective resignation, and he had told Bert he would defend whatever decision he made. But LaBelle was still not done. As the president was going to the press conference with Bert's sorrowful letter of resignation in hand, he recalled in his diary that she bitterly accused him of betraying his friend and destroying her husband.[32] Lance's recollection of LaBelle's last words to the president was even worse: "I want to tell you one thing—you can go with the rest of the jackals, and I hope you're happy."[33]

Jody had prepared a statement for the president, but once again he overrode his press secretary and spoke impromptu, defending his friend to the last with evident passion: "He's a good man. . . . I think he's made the right decision, because it would be difficult for him to devote full time to his responsibilities in the future." He added that nothing "has shaken my belief in Bert's ability or integrity," and that as president he felt partly responsible because he wanted Bert to sell all his bank stock and sever his relationship with the financial industry.

At the first cabinet meeting after Bert's resignation, as McIntyre began to talk, Carter tried to sound as if Bert's departure would make no difference in the upcoming fiscal year, interrupting the acting budget director with what seemed were hollow words: "Jim McIntyre speaks with the same voice Bert had and has the same authority to speak for me."[34] However, no one believed Jim would ever command the same authority as Bert, try as he might. The president concluded by complimenting the agencies for proposing their budgets earlier than ever before. The scene had a surreal quality.

As so often happens in the Washington hothouse, once the attackers have accomplished their task, they regroup as designated mourners. Safire sent Bert a copy of his next book, in which he reprinted several of his damaging columns about Lance, and autographed it, "For Bert Lance, with hopes for a strong comeback." Chief Justice Warren Burger phoned Carter to declare himself "overwhelmed with emotion and gratitude that the Bert Lance thing had been handled in such a way as to point out the extreme dangers from the press in subverting justice."[35] When Bert held a farewell reception at the OMB's offices, well-wishers poured in—headed by Jimmy and Rosalynn Carter, members of the cabinet, Burger from the Court, Democratic and Republican congressional leaders, and even the White House police officers. Hundreds of people waited up to two hours to tell Bert how much they regretted his departure. I came early to hug Bert and express my profound-est sorrow at the outcome.

During the balance of the Carter administration and even up to the last months of his life, Bert frequently called me to ask how Fran and our boys and I were doing, despite his own troubles. Lance endured a four-month trial in Atlanta federal court on twelve counts of banking irregularities, includ-ing false statements and sweetheart loans. He was acquitted of nine, and the jury was hung on the other three. The government spent $7 million on the case, and Lance's own legal fees totaled $1.5 million.[36] Even the conservative *American Spectator* exonerated Lance, noting that eight federal agencies conducted investigations and found nothing.[37]

But the harm to the Carter administration was as damaging as it was to Bert himself. Although some political and press enemies compared the Lance affair to Watergate, this was unfair. No one ever criticized him for his behav-ior in office, nor was he identified with any political dirty tricks. Whatever poor political judgment the president exhibited by not cutting loose his friend earlier, Bert had not left behind a whiff of impropriety or illegality in Wash-ington itself. But his banking behavior back home went to the heart of Car-ter's ethical campaign, when he repeatedly cited Watergate as undermining confidence in our government. As candidate and president, Carter held him-self and implicitly his top officials to a higher standard, which Lance's be-havior turned into a double-edged sword against his closest friend, who had promised he would never lie to the American people.

For all its majesty, the presidency has few constitutional powers beyond that of commander in chief of the armed forces. The power of the office comes from his ability to influence others to follow his lead—Congress, friends and foes foreign and domestic, and above all the American public. This, in turn, requires any president to constantly cultivate his popularity and personal authority and avoid dissipating a limited stock of influence on politically hopeless ventures, such as prolonging a vain effort to save Lance. Carter needed a tough enforcer as chief of staff to save him from his understand-able feelings. The task of getting rid of a political liability was complicated by the fact that many of the people who followed Carter to the White

House were close to Bert during Carter's years as governor. To most of them, something like pledging the same block of stock as collateral for two separate loans was just Bert being Bert. But frankly, none of us close to Carter, myself included, had the fortitude to tell the president early enough that the banking irregularities of his best friend and most trusted adviser were so serious that he was a political liability and had to go. Jody later reflected, "It would have been better for the president if we had brought that to an end sooner. It threw us off stride. It made it harder for us to talk about other things, and sort of played into questions about whether we could lead and run the country."[38] Carter's Gallup poll approval ratings dropped some 20 percent from their post-Lance high of over 70 percent.[39]

This points to a broader problem that bedevils all presidencies: reluctance to bring bad news to a president. There is such an aura about any president—"clothed in all this power" as Lincoln once said—and such deference to the office itself, that a particular level of fortitude and confidence is essential to tell the occupant in person when he is going in the wrong direction. Once the president takes the oath of office with the legitimacy of national election he (or eventually, she) becomes something more than a mere mortal. Ironically, Bert Lance had the stature and personal ties to the president to speak truth to power, but not about himself. He did his friend a disservice by accepting the job without privately disclosing his financial situation in full. Carter was never quite the same afterward. As he said, Bert "was compatible with everybody and his leaving really hurt."[40] His poll ratings dropped significantly, but I believe he became a better president. His administration was never again tainted by scandal, and he became steeled to the rough political realities of Washington.

PART II

ENERGY

6

THE MORAL EQUIVALENT OF WAR

Just as he would handle foreign policy by tackling the Middle East head-on, Jimmy Carter jumped into the most contentious, divisive domestic issue, energy, and made it his top domestic priority after the economy, calling for a comprehensive plan to revolutionize every aspect of its price and use. If ever there was an ill-considered decision, and one that took a long-lasting toll on Carter's popularity, it was the one he made as president-elect. Only a month after the November election, at an organizational meeting on energy, for the first time I heard him say, "I am hoping to have a comprehensive energy policy within ninety days." I was floored. He made this announcement without consulting Congress, his incoming White House staff, or his incoming cabinet. Continuing with evident relish, he declared he had to make a "box-load of key decisions" on energy.[1] It was a ninety-day program worthy of Franklin Roosevelt's first hundred days, with the difference that Roosevelt took office with a mandate to confront a national economic crisis.

True to his word, less than three months after his inauguration, the new president gave his first major national address on what he saw as a looming crisis in which the United States was increasingly dependent upon imported foreign oil from the most volatile region of the world, the Middle East. By burning fossil fuels as if America had an unlimited supply, we were mortgaging our foreign policy to OPEC suppliers; swelling the deficit in our balance of payments; and cheapening the U.S. dollar. He put his presidential prestige behind meeting a politically unpopular challenge, appealing to Americans to join him in an urgent effort to reverse the nation's profligate habits of consuming energy in gas-guzzling cars, and overheated, poorly insulated offices, factories, and homes. Four years later, after passage of three major energy packages, he had set the nation on an irreversible course toward regaining its lost energy security, by granting major incentives for greater conservation; market-based pricing of crude oil and natural gas to encourage greater domestic production; beginning the solar, wind, and alternative energy revolution; and bringing competition for the benefit of consumers to the delivery of electricity. But in the process he paid a frightful political price, some self-inflicted.

From the first discovery of crude oil in western Pennsylvania before the Civil War, through the early-twentieth-century creation of the Standard Oil Company by John D. Rockefeller, and the wildcatters who brought in gushers rich with oil and natural gas in Texas, Oklahoma and Louisiana, together with vast amounts of coal, the United States enjoyed energy independence. But in less than a century Americans had gone from energy self-sufficiency to a dramatically different and more troubling energy picture.[2]

The dysfunctional mess that Jimmy Carter inherited was the result of almost a century of political mismanagement, and for years the oil companies operated their own cartel through the Texas Railroad Commission. It parceled out production quotas to prevent oil from dropping back to its ruinous Depression-era lows of four cents a barrel until Texas was eclipsed by Saudi Arabia as the swing producer of the Organization of Petroleum Exporting Countries (OPEC). When major discoveries in Venezuela and Mexico threatened the independent producers in the American oil patch, Congress passed the first tariff on foreign oil in the 1930s. Meanwhile the vertically integrated major oil companies, working in the United States and abroad, focused on obtaining mammoth oil concessions in the Arab Middle East. By 1957 imports had surged to almost one-fifth of domestic consumption, and the independents demanded a stiff protective tariff. The Eisenhower administration resisted, but under their severe pressure President Eisenhower in 1959 reluctantly signed an executive order imposing import quotas in the name of national security; they lasted until the early 1970s, when they were replaced by Nixon's domestic price controls that sealed our dependence on foreign oil.

U.S. crude oil production had been dropping steadily, and the nation no longer could satisfy its growing appetite without increasingly depending on

Middle East suppliers. By the time of Carter's inauguration, 46 percent of all the oil consumed in the United States as gasoline, home heating and industrial fuel, and for chemical feedstock had to be imported, mostly from OPEC countries, while domestic production continued to slide despite new discoveries in Alaska.

Richard Nixon was the first president to feel the full fury of OPEC. Crude oil prices had quadrupled since the Arab members of OPEC demonstrated their power by imposing an embargo in retaliation for U.S. support of Israel during the 1973 war against Egypt. The first oil price shock led to long lines at gasoline stations, with 40 percent increases in gasoline prices; tipped the United States into recession; dramatically increased inflation; and un-balanced the economy by beginning the "stagflation" phenomenon of simul-taneous slow growth and high inflation that would bedevil Nixon, Ford, and Carter; and threw energy policy into disarray. Both production and conser-vation were discouraged by his price controls, which had the perverse effect of subsidizing foreign oil imported at world market prices. The American people were angry at everyone: the president, the Arab oil states, and most particularly the American oil companies, which they accused of organizing a conspiracy to make record profits. *Time* labeled them "oil gougers," and congressional leaders made the oil companies the villains. When a nation and its leaders cannot face up to the truth about their challenges and look instead for scapegoats, it is difficult to develop sensible policies.

But we Americans have short memories, and by the time Carter took of-fice, gasoline lines from 1973 had disappeared. Prices, although higher, were affordable, with the market price suppressed by federal controls. Energy seemed abundant, and it had not been a major issue in the 1976 presiden-tial campaign. As long as gasoline poured out of the pump, drivers knew little and cared less where it came from. James Schlesinger, a Harvard-trained economist who served as Carter's energy secretary, later noted that aside from gasoline rationing during World War II and the first, temporary oil price shock of 1973, energy "was a new domestic problem for the American people outside the context of war."[3]

As a neophyte president, Carter waded into this minefield not fully aware of the political lineup of competing interests and the money behind them. He allied himself with the liberal consumer and conservationist groups, but it was the more conservative producer interests that controlled energy policy in Congress through its most powerful members. Even more, neither Schlesinger, despite all his Washington experience, nor any of us, fully recognized the difference between the more colorful and politically potent domestic independent producers and the vertically integrated giant companies engaged in worldwide extraction, refining, and sales. The multinationals had subsidiaries through which they could shuffle costs and profits to minimize taxes; their interest lay mainly in maintaining predictable rules of the game. Although they were the focus of liberal criticism and public outrage, the real political power of the oil and gas lobby came from the independents and their direct financial support of their senators and congressmen, and not from the bogeyman of Big Oil.

Transforming Carter's vision into congressional action was also extremely difficult because the nation had created a crazy-quilt system of federal price controls on oil and gas. It discouraged production and encouraged overconsumption because of the artificially low prices, along with quotas, tax privileges, and subsidies that showered benefits on the oil and gas industry in those parts of the country rich in fossil fuels, while imposing costs on the rest of the nation.

The politics of energy are brutally divided along regional lines, because we are the only major democracy that is simultaneously a major producer and consumer of energy. The producing regions in the Southwest and West hold great pools of energy underground, and the Northeast and Midwest have few energy resources but a great appetite for energy to power their industries, homes, and cars. Politicians from producing states generally want higher prices and federal incentives to drive up profits for their energy industry, while consuming regions want lower prices for their consumers. Interest groups had formed on all sides of energy pricing. Environmental organizations and liberals urged conservation while pressing for tight controls on the prices and profits of the energy companies, while conservatives and the energy companies sought to end price controls and unleash more domestic production.

In proposing higher prices and new energy taxes and trying to construct a rational system, Carter took on the oil and gas industry on one side and consumer and environmental groups on the other, none of whom were happy with his policy. The battle demonstrated his governing style. He reached for comprehensive solutions to the most intractable problems, taking on power-ful interest groups impervious to the political consequences; ignoring the norms of Washington; making early mistakes and then regaining his foot-ing; and in the end achieving major results of the most profound consequence for the future of the nation.

His domestic campaign mirrored the strategy he adopted to bring peace to the Middle East. The results were similar: historic accomplishments that have withstood the test of time, but at severe political cost. Without fear of exaggeration, I believe that Jimmy Carter did more than any president, past or future, to change U.S. energy policy for the better and to prepare our nation for the sound energy future we now enjoy.

With an overwhelmingly Democratic Congress, party politics were a side issue compared with geography in the fight to enact his long-term presiden-tial vision, embodied in his National Energy Plan. He realized that the forces were closely balanced: "If you line up the conflicting interest groups, oil and gas, and coal producers on the one hand, and basically consumers on the other hand, it's just a fifty-fifty deal. The members of Congress in the middle who had the swing votes didn't want to be involved in it. We had to force it. There was no groundswell of support for it."[4] The energy issue haunted his presidency throughout his term in office, leading to more na-tionwide addresses on energy than on any other domestic issue, and to three major energy packages, the last in the midst of the turmoil caused by the Iranian revolution.

OIL, GAS, AND SAUSAGES

The German chancellor Otto von Bismarck famously remarked, "Laws are like sausages. It's better not to see them made." But I want to do just that, so that the public can follow Carter's iconoclastic, eclectic, but ultimately productive governing style, and better understand the often opaque ways that laws are made through Washington's transactional politics. Though Carter regarded himself as the guardian of the public good against vested interests, and felt that the quid pro quo of political compromises with Congress was almost immoral, he could not avoid them. They provide an insight into how the process looked from inside the administration and from the perspective of Congress, and a view of the interplay among the key interest groups: consumer advocates, the oil and gas interests, and the broader business community. This provides the give-and-take of Washington at work, demonstrating that when an administration sets an important goal, it must balance regional against national interests, and consumers against corporate lobbyists. It also demonstrates how difficult it is to make laws that have to accommodate so many conflicting interests that assert themselves even today, and it is made more difficult when they are overlaid by fierce ideological battles, leaving little room for compromise.

Titanic congressional egos are easily bruised in the backroom deals that so often grind out the legislative sausages. In this struggle the barons of the Senate were at war with one another. On one side Senator Russell Long of Louisiana, the powerful and colorful chairman of the Senate Finance Committee, led the coalition of oil and gas states against Henry "Scoop" Jackson, the stolid chairman of the Senate Energy and Natural Resources Committee (industrial growth in his Washington State was heavily based on cheap, government-financed hydroelectric power). In the House of Representatives, Speaker Tip O'Neill of Boston, one of the most endearing figures in American political life, and the veteran Detroit congressman John Dingell, the tall, tough, powerful chairman of the House Power and Energy Subcommittee, represented consumer interests and the Michigan-based automobile industry. Battles over something as seminal as energy policy, or any other major issue, are not over the forces of good versus the forces of evil. Senators and congressmen try to do what is right for the country, but it is always first refracted by what is best for their own local constituencies.

It is the president's job to forge coalitions of interest behind his legislation, and these will shift from issue to issue. In Washington there are no permanent enemies and no permanent friends: A remark attributed to Harry Truman says it best, "If you want a friend in Washington, get a dog." The truth of this aphorism became all too evident during the epic battle over the Carter energy plan.

To complicate the problem, the battle was not just about Nixon-era controls on the price of oil, but also whether to remove federal price controls from natural gas and make it competitive with the black gold that enriched Texas and propelled its politicians to national stature. Natural-gas pricing was one of the nation's most contentious—and opaque—public policy issues in the postwar era, with Truman vetoing a bill in 1948 to remove price controls, and battles ever since. Gas flowed out of the ground into an inefficient market, regulating prices as soon as it crossed state lines. This was supposed to protect consumers in the nonproducing states from high prices, but actually it made them more dependent on oil. There was little incentive for the energy companies to extend gas pipelines nationwide when they could only sell gas across state lines at a tiny fraction of what they could charge in the state where it came out of the ground, in an unregulated, free market.

Inside the borders of producing states, natural gas flowed freely. But once it crossed their boundaries, the gas came under federal price control in the shivering Northeast and Midwest and traded at about one-third of the price in the producing states. What producer would ship his gas across the state line to sell at a controlled low price? Across the oil fields, natural gas that hissed out of the wells as the oil was being pumped to the surface was largely burned off in huge flares—and wasted.

I knew Carter felt strongly about energy as a matter of national security, having committed himself to halt the increase in America's oil imports in his announcement speech for president.[5] But as his policy director during his two-year drive for the presidency, I can attest that energy was not a major issue because Americans did not perceive it as one. Until Carter's nomination looked almost certain, I did not hire an energy specialist—Katherine "Kitty" Schirmer, a Wellesley-educated crackerjack who had worked on energy issues on Capitol Hill. The Democratic Party platform, eying the key votes in Appalachia, pledged to increase coal production and to establish a "clean coal" program for this abundant, and abundantly polluting, American natural resource.

But by far the most politically vexing energy issue was the pricing of crude oil and natural gas, long avoided by presidents because it divided the country. We spent a great deal of campaign time trying to balance these interests, just as we would in the administration, and our electoral calculus marked the energy producing powerhouses of Texas, Oklahoma, and Louisiana as must-win states. Although Carter came out of the Democratic Convention leading President Ford in the polls by more than 30 points, by mid-October he cut Carter's lead to a precious few points. I received worried calls from two of Jimmy Carter's earliest supporters, Governors Dolph Briscoe of Texas and David Boren of Oklahoma. Both warned me their states were slipping away and that it was critical for Carter to reinforce his campaign pledge to decontrol the price of newly discovered natural gas. Boren had a portly girth, boyish round face, pleasant manner, and a ready smile, but he was no common politician. He was a Yale Phi Beta Kappa and Rhodes Scholar. Briscoe, a formidable power who at one time was the largest landowner in Texas, with a personal holding of at least one million acres, had endorsed his fellow Southern governor, Jimmy Carter, in a hotly contested Democratic primary, which Carter won.

During the annual Oklahoma-Texas college football game, when the two governors traditionally sit together, they were joined by Bob Strauss, chairman of the Democratic National Committee and a quintessential Texas political phenomenon. At halftime the three began to talk. "And so," Boren continued, "we all agreed that we were in shooting distance in Louisiana, Texas, and Oklahoma, and we just needed another little boost to pull us over." The conversation focused on natural-gas deregulation, and they conceived of the idea of a letter from Carter reaffirming his position. Boren drafted and faxed it to me in Atlanta, and with minor changes I sent it to the campaign plane, where Carter signed it. The key sentence pledged that if elected he would "work with the Congress, as the Ford administration has been unable to do, to deregulate new natural gas." It was released by the governors with much fanfare in Austin and Oklahoma City, and Strauss did his bit by talking it up with the Texas establishment, greased as always by oil money.[6] We won the three key producing states by an eyelash, and they were enough to put us over the top on election night.

Carter's political debt to these three states was still not large enough to explain why he chose energy as his prime domestic priority. He could have staked his political chips on his promise to end what we constantly called "the Ford recession," or on more traditional Democratic priorities, such as comprehensive national health insurance. But he was not a traditional Democrat, and would not have been elected if he had been. He was a fiscal conservative and chose to concentrate on curbing soaring hospital costs, on welfare reform as his prime social program, and on reforming the inequitable tax code. In truth, while he overwhelmed Congress by making all these his priorities at the same time, energy was clearly the first among too many equals. Why?

The simple answer was that as governor of Georgia during the 1973 embargo, Carter saw the impact from the perspective of gas lines and especially the vulnerability of the U.S. economy to OPEC.[7] But nothing is simple in our politics, which combine personality with policy. Enter James Rodney Schlesinger, who, Carter told me, wanted to see it done. Schlesinger did not come without baggage. He had been summarily fired as Defense secretary by Ford, who found him arrogant, insufferable, and unable to get along with key members of Congress, but his intellect appealed to Carter.

Ham had asked Carter to avoid two people during the campaign—Ralph Nader, because he was unpopular with Southern conservatives, and Jim Schlesinger, because he was equally unpopular among Democratic liberals. Carter's typically hard-headed response was to invite Nader to a softball game in Plains and to meet Schlesinger at his home in Plains.

Schlesinger was a defense intellectual with a long history of public service, and he had the further advantage of having clashed with Henry Kissinger over his policy of détente with Moscow. By nature a contrarian and nominally a Republican, Schlesinger had powerful supporters among the Democratic, anti-Soviet wing led by Scoop Jackson, who had pressed his name on Carter. When Carter sought him out, it was not to discuss energy but China. Schlesinger had just returned from Beijing, where he was the first major American figure to meet the new Chinese leadership after the death of Mao Zedong.[8] Seeing a chance for redemption (and possible return to office), Schlesinger leaped at the opportunity. His brilliance and his iconoclastic attitude appealed to the cerebral Carter, who also saw his embrace of Schlesinger as a way of poking a finger in Ford's eye during the closing weeks of an increasingly tight race.

But there were also personal bonds in their shared love of the outdoors. Schlesinger was a devoted bird-watcher with binoculars and boots of the kind Carter used for his outdoor treks. They also shared experience in nuclear energy, Schlesinger as a former chairman of the Atomic Energy Commission.

Both distrusted the establishment and took on causes regardless of the political consequences. Carter decided Schlesinger would be the perfect man to lead the effort to enact a comprehensive, all-encompassing national energy program. What was not known was that the two agreed he would have personal access to the president and that their conversations would not be restricted to energy but range over foreign and defense policy. So on Saturday mornings, as early as 6:00 a.m., Carter and Schlesinger would meet and talk. Carter said: "We never did publicize it, and we would sit like that and drink coffee; and he was very sensitive about my schedule, and I think he never stayed more than an hour, although I didn't tell him to leave."[9]

A decisive factor was the irrepressible Admiral Rickover, who influenced Carter more than anyone except his father and had kept in touch with all his naval protégés as their careers advanced. When Carter was governor, Rickover did an analysis of the global energy situation, which with characteristic originality he calculated in cubic miles. "I have never seen anything since that, which let a peanut farmer envision the reserves of coal and natural gas and oil . . . and how fast we were using it up, without any conservation," Carter shared with me. He thought of his hometown as a circle a half mile in diameter and a mile deep in oil, and world reserves then being depleted by a cubic mile. Rickover calculated that world reserves had been depleted over time from roughly twenty-one to eighteen cubic miles, and we were using up so many cubic miles a year.[10] When they got to the White House, Carter asked for an update in cubic miles, when the universal measurement was barrels of oil per day, and with Schlesinger's small staff working furiously on the complex energy program, Schlesinger worked out the figures.[11]

One last piece of the puzzle was Carter's first CIA briefing as president-elect. I was the only Carter staff person in attendance, delivered in person by then-CIA director and later president George H. W. Bush with patrician elegance and the authority of a former Texas oil operator. His message was that the Saudis would abandon their restraint and join Iran in raising OPEC's prices, resulting in a severe brake on world economic growth. The warning was based in part on a flawed CIA report forecasting that if America's avaricious appetite for oil was not curbed, world demand for oil would exceed supply by 1985—a prediction that collapsed with the oil market itself in that same year. This market collapse helped bring down the Soviet empire, to the complete surprise of American intelligence.[12] Schlesinger, his aides, and my energy and natural resources expert Kitty Schirmer all derided the report for failing to recognize that rising prices would simultaneously nudge discoveries and conservation, thus bringing supply and demand into balance. The CIA report nevertheless galvanized the president, and was among the principal factors that moved energy to the top of his agenda[13] at the first cabinet meeting after the election.[14]

I took a seat just behind the president, with my back to the snow-covered Rose Garden; the cabinet officers were arrayed around the huge, oval-shaped table in order of the creation of their departments, with Secretary of State Vance to his right and the vice president directly across from the president, whose seat was a few inches taller than the cabinet members', each of whom had a plaque on the back of his chair designating his office. There were American flags in the corner of the Cabinet Room to the president's right, with streamers from major battles fought by our armed forces over the course of American history. One would have had to be brain-dead not to be thrilled by this moment after one of the most improbable presidential political campaigns in American history.

The president announced that the cabinet would meet once a week on Mondays, and that "all congressional legislation would go through Stu to me." He admonished his cabinet officers to "involve Congress on the initial stages of legislation," and a month later at the February 20 meeting he instructed them to send copies of their testimony to me. But unfortunately on energy legislation, he did not enforce either admonition. During that cabinet meeting, as each member intoned about his priorities, my former boss in the LBJ White House, HEW Secretary Califano, slipped me a note: "Stu, Welcome to the problems that will drive you crazy. JAC, Jr."[15]

THE FIRST ENERGY CRISIS

We had barely unpacked the boxes in our new White House offices when an energy crisis hit. The winter of 1976–77 was one of the most brutally cold on record, and there was a severe shortage of natural gas in the Northeast and industrial Midwest. Our family was renting the house of the conservative columnist George Will in northwest Washington until Fran could find a permanent home. The snow and hard-packed ice prevented me from getting my car out of the driveway to get to the White House, so I had to get a special waiver from the president's edict against home–to–White House limousine service; it was a one-day headline with a four-year burden.

Poor people were hit hardest by the icy weather, not only because of gas shortages but due to poor insulation and heating. Governors were also complaining—Milton Shapp of Pennsylvania warned me that without some disaster relief he would have to cut off natural gas to certain industries at the beginning of February. Carter immediately called a special cabinet meeting, declared New York and Pennsylvania disaster areas, and sent legislation to Congress giving him emergency authority to order gas fed into interstate pipelines.[16] It was quickly enacted, but this short-term palliative would be the only energy legislation on which Congress acted quickly.

Schlesinger pressed his own gloomy assessments in cabinet meetings and at a February breakfast meeting with the Economic Policy Group (EPG).[17] He warned that the world was "moving out of an era of abundant and cheap energy," and emphasized conservation—raising fuel efficiency standards in vehicles, saving oil by better home insulation, and converting industrial use from oil and gas to coal and nuclear power. Another breakfast with both Republican and Democratic congressional leaders—an innovation that continued throughout the administration but has rarely been followed since—was largely devoted to general discussions of energy legislation.

Carter compounded the problem of setting an arbitrary ninety-day deadline by ordering that the plan be developed in secret in order to catch interest groups unaware before they could organize against it. But if the energy plan was to be drawn up like a wartime offensive, there was no foreign enemy here, only some members of his administration concerned about pushing through a complex plan in only ninety days, without time to calculate the impact of higher energy prices on inflation, as well as leaving some of the most powerful members of Congress feeling excluded from the development of the battle plan.

The leader of Schlesinger's team of smart and experienced experts was Alvin L. Alm, a tall, ungainly, kind, and brilliant assistant administrator in the Environmental Protection Agency, who heard about the deadline on the radio while driving to work. "Boy, I feel sorry for the poor son of a bitch that has to do that!" he thought. When he called Schlesinger to congratulate him on his new job as energy czar, Schlesinger asked him to join the team already at work. When Alm arrived and asked Schlesinger who was running things day to day, Schlesinger replied: "You are!"[18] Working brutally long hours under tremendous pressure, Alm never lost his good humor and found it easier to assemble a package without having to fight through a huge departmental bureaucracy and the interagency consultations that can stifle new ideas with the weight of often-fossilized experience. Reflecting on Carter's decision to take advantage of a presidential honeymoon to attack a huge and intractable problem, he said, "You just couldn't pick all the winners because you didn't know what the winners were. So from an energy point of view, you got more by proposing more. You shoot 113 rockets and a lot of them would come down."[19]

There is something to be said for a closed process: It moves quickly through the minds of experts without distraction. But this turned out to be a mixed blessing typical of Carter's drive to deliver the best possible solution to a problem regardless of the political forces involved. Carter later conceded that to him the deadline seemed "an eon in time" because he was used to calculating by the constitutional limit of the Georgia legislature of an annual thirty-five or forty-five days."[20] But Georgia is not Washington.

There is also something to be said for a president moving quickly on a key priority while his popularity is at a peak, but the president paid a heavy price. In one sense the story was vintage Jimmy Carter seeking comprehensive solutions rather than an incremental approach. But the real disadvantage was that, in producing the package in haste, it became *less* coherent than if it had been assembled strategically. The different moving parts lacked critical balance because the architects were deprived of feedback from those who, however vigorously they might advance their own interests, still had a better understanding of the realities than the cloistered experts.

Initially Schlesinger's team did reach out to the administration's economic and taxation experts, and there were meetings with industry and environmental groups as well as regional energy forums. But they were mainly listening sessions to pick up ideas rather than opportunities to test the team's own recommendations. By presidential order the package was kept secret from anyone in Congress or the executive branch for fear of leaks, depriving the team not only of outside expertise but also of essential public feedback that could have helped shape a more politically acceptable package. And it did not stop the leaks anyway.

Why wasn't the president challenged on his gag order covering the crucial final month? Just as being unwilling to bring the bad news about Lance to Carter proved, therein lies an important lesson about the awe and majesty of the presidency, particularly in his early months in office. It takes a very special person to pierce that veil, even when a subordinate knows that the boss is wrong. The president carries a democratic legitimacy that no appointee or career civil servant can match; few would dare challenge him except in the most unusual circumstances.

Les Goldman was one of Schlesinger's most knowledgeable subordinates, having dealt with oil and gas as a Senate staffer, and he felt "almost an amazing sense of holiness of what the president was saying. We may think it's wrong—but he's the boss and let's go on with it, and do the best we can do. . . . There isn't anybody who is so bright that they can figure out all the angles that will be thrown up against you. . . . You have to test ideas, and particularly when you're dealing with [Congress], you need some level of involvement so that they feel it's theirs, or at least they have a sense of what's coming. . . . It was a very hard thing to express doubts and put your foot down and say, 'No, I'm sorry, this is just nuts, nuts.'" That led to a kind of intellectual insulation instead of the creativity born of an exchange of ideas and interests that lies at the heart of the democratic process.[21]

As Schlesinger's plan began to evolve, however, it bore Jimmy Carter's authentic stamp. Its first priority was not producing more oil and gas but conserving a vital resource through a variety of tax increases and incentives. To him it was a moral issue to waste a precious and declining basic commodity, and a religious belief that God's resources were being fouled. Schlesinger was a conservationist himself; born a Jew, he had converted to the stern virtues of Lutheranism. He correctly saw the president as "a moralizer in regard to energy. . . . He believed that if you only could explain to people how damn wasteful we were, we could have solved that energy problem. . . . It was as much a moral conviction that we should be provident in our use of the resources that have been placed by the Almighty in relation to the energy problem."[22]

Conservation was a passion for Carter and was the first item David Rubinstein and I cited in the energy section of the 1976 brochure of campaign promises we had been ordered to produce by President-elect Carter. He was an outdoorsman and loved to fish in pure streams and hunt in the clear air of his native southwest Georgia, and his sense of conservation extended from the individual to the community to the attitude of government. He abhorred waste, and wasting precious oil and natural gas was unacceptable profligacy. The breadth and controversial nature of the conservation provisions Carter proposed were nothing less than a bold attempt to change the behavior of the American people.[23]

I knew I had achieved the pinnacle of power in Washington when I was visited by the folksinger John Denver, open-shirted with handsome blond locks flowing, whose music I loved. Predictably, he underscored the importance of subsidizing conservation and said he and Robert Redford were willing to do a six-month ad campaign to inform the public of the importance of conserving energy. He called for a "Manhattan-type Project," like the one that produced the atomic bomb, for NASA to loft a giant "solar receiving satellite" into space by 1995 to reflect solar power for the entire world.[24] His ideas may have been close to science fiction, but readiness to commit his and Redford's celebrity status made it clear that in the short space of a month after his inauguration, the new president had indeed attracted star power to help place energy at the center of the nation's agenda.

I was more concerned by the hard facts of a briefing the president arranged for Schlesinger to provide the cabinet and senior staff and our spouses in the White House theater on March 14, only five weeks before the deadline to publish the energy plan.[25] Again Schlesinger underscored that conservation was the key. European countries were already two times more energy efficient per unit of GDP, in part because they had few energy resources of their own except for their almost exhausted coal mines, and had adopted a high-taxation policy to conserve oil. Schlesinger asserted that the transportation sector in America wasted 60 percent of our energy, but in Europe any tourist can see the result of high energy taxes in its small, fuel-efficient cars and heavy investment in rail and other public transport.

With its own resources, America had a different problem, and Schlesinger raised a key question: Would deregulation of prices encourage greater exploration? Flying directly in the face of Carter's campaign pledge, Schlesinger told us that while some argued that greater incentives would produce more gas, he believed that there were not enough gas reserves, and "the free enterprise system would not alone solve our problem." Carter suddenly interjected, "I cannot wait until Jim takes office to attack the energy problem," but then forecast, almost as a badge of honor, that "my own ratings will fall when I attack this problem directly."[26] Throughout his presidency Carter would throw himself into highly complex and politically vexed issues like this and almost take glee in doing so, as if to show his mettle as well as relishing the image of making a political sacrifice for the public good.

The Schlesinger team assembled 290 separate initiatives that were whittled down to about 90, which Schlesinger presented to the president alone in a three-ring binder. Carter read it and returned it to me, with a note that I should share it with no one. It was the first I had seen of the proposed program, even though Schlesinger's office was just down the hallway from my office in the West Wing, and was largely what Carter would present to Congress. I ignored the admonition, and had Kitty Schirmer, who headed natural resources on my Domestic Policy Staff, read it; her reaction was that "we were trying to scratch every single itch."[27]

The secrecy made Schlesinger the fall guy for Congress and others in the administration, which complicated his ability to advocate the legislation he had drawn up. There had been almost no consultation between agencies or even within the White House. Also cut out were the powerful committee chairmen—and not only Scoop Jackson, the Energy Committee chairman, who felt marginalized, but the pivotal chairman of the Senate Finance Committee, Russell Long of Louisiana, for whom legislation was a transactional process among interest groups. Long saw the interests of his home-state oil and gas industry as a mere extension of the national interest, and for him, a presidential message was only the first chapter in a long process, often merely incidental to the deals he struck. To make matters worse, there was a clear jurisdictional overlap: Jackson's committee was responsible for oil and gas pricing, but shaping energy taxes to encourage conservation and production was Long's domain.

This hardly made for comity even in a chamber controlled by Democrats, because the barons were in combat with one another. Senior people in Congress as well as the executive branch have great pride. They accept long hours and low pay because they genuinely want to help pass laws and manage policies to make the country and the world a better place. When they feel shut out of the process, they do not accept it easily, even if a president's policies are not far from their own. Members of Congress may forgive a president proposing something they oppose, but not embarrassing them by making them appear without influence to the people who elected them. Another victim of the closed process was the interest groups, and particularly the energy industry, which could have been enlisted even as reluctant participants in a process that its more enlightened members realized was necessary to reform a broken system.

One of my most important jobs was to ensure a kind of due process in presidential decision making by soliciting a wide spectrum of views from all the agencies, key congressional leaders, and interest groups, and assembling them into what is called a presidential options memorandum. It often contained the perspectives of different government departments, the interest groups with whom they dealt, and the congressional committees through which their budgets and legislation went, the ubiquitous "Iron Triangle," because the three sides hang together to maintain the status quo from which all have profited. But as the only person in Washington who has been sent by the electorate nationwide, the president has the responsibility to adjudicate among conflicting interests. Bringing them into his decision making gives them a stake in it even if it has gone against them, but it also makes them more likely to support and defend it.

I had to assure every agency that even when I disagreed, I would present their views and backup analysis fairly to the president. But early experience of the energy plan, which was neither transparent nor participatory, left me with the conviction that while a fair and open process does not guarantee a good result, without it any administration can expect trouble. The smartest and most senior operatives, and even their leader, often do not understand the full ramifications of what they are proposing. For the energy bill, on which President Carter would stake so much of his reputation, I simply could not do my job and serve him by exposing all the cross-currents of opinion, or the economic and political impact of Schlesinger's options.

It was a supreme irony that a president elected on the promise of rolling back the secrecy that had enveloped the Nixon White House would have approved, indeed required, a closed process to develop his most important domestic policy. Not long after the fiasco of developing the energy package, I sent him a decision memorandum on another issue summarizing the views of all the agencies involved. The president called me on my secure line and said, "I want you to give me your opinion, not just those of others." I wish I had felt that empowered at the time of the first energy debate as the bill headed toward a climax in April 1977.

Too late, the secrecy led to an internal revolt. It came from the administration's most important economic voices, Treasury Secretary Michael Blumenthal and Charles Schultze, chairman of the Council of Economic Advisers. Blumenthal phoned me[28] to appeal for a thirty-day postponement to consider the wider economic implications. At a time when the administration was preparing a tax reform measure to lower rates in return for closing tax loopholes, the energy bill was packed with new tax incentives to promote conservation. More broadly, the energy package was huge, and Schultze had not had time to calculate its full economic impact. The request for a delay was denied, despite the valid, unanswered, economic questions, because the president was so far out on a limb on the ninety-day deadline that he feared a delay would make him look indecisive and subject the program to greater interagency scrutiny that might dilute it.

With only about two weeks left before the public rollout, the president asked me to come to his small study next to the Oval Office.[29] He was worried. Wearing his trademark tan cardigan, he declared that he found Schlesinger's plan complex and difficult, and he said frankly, "I do not fully understand it, and do not know how I can adequately explain it to the American people." As he admitted later, he had not envisioned the multiplicity of issues, the uncertain costs, and how they could be aligned.[30] But at that late date only minor changes were possible.[31]

An eruption was also not long in coming from the nation's elected representatives. At the congressional leadership breakfast,[32] Majority Leader Byrd complained that senators had not been brought into the energy discussions, and this was holding up business. To make his point, he told the group that Senator Muskie of Maine refused to allow the Clean Air Act amendments out of his Environment Subcommittee for a vote by the full Senate on the Senate floor, without first knowing the impact of our energy plan on the environment.

I moved fast and organized a full interagency meeting in the Cabinet Room on the same day.[33] All the major decision makers were there—with Ham to provide political input for the first time—and it produced a healthy debate, with the president engaged and asking good questions. But it should have been convened near the start and not the end of the process.

The president began the meeting by declaring that when his principal advisers disagreed, he would decide—and that if the disagreements remained, that aspect of the plan could be presented in a less detailed manner until details were thrashed out. Schlesinger countered abruptly: "We are going to galley proofs on Monday, and we can't just lay out pious hopes." He wanted decisions on proposed legislative language, but Carter replied defensively that some elements of the plan could be put forward by April 20, but the entire legislative "book" could come a few days later.

Schlesinger's plan called for roughly $1 billion in tax credits to encourage insulation, and he was considering establishing insulation standards below which banks would be prohibited from writing home mortgages. This immediately drew strong objections from Blumenthal and Schultze, who pointed out that it would make banks federal inspectors of home insulation. Schultze also challenged Schlesinger's estimates that his insulation initiatives would save one million barrels of oil a day, since wealthier property owners—the ones who used more fuel—were already retrofitting their homes. That ended bank certification right there.

Schlesinger then discussed a national building code to focus on energy conservation, which would raise constitutional questions by superseding local codes. And who would perform the inspections to ensure compliance? I noted privately in the margin of my legal pad that while we were about to announce a comprehensive national plan, at this late stage we were only beginning to examine such critical issues. Schlesinger was also forced to retreat on mandatory efficiency standards for industrial motors and boilers. Blumenthal and Schultze argued it would be simpler and more effective to require manufacturers to list efficiency ratings so buyers could calculate their own energy-cost savings. Carter weighed in as an engineer: Not only would it be hard to defend specific designs as more efficient, but a bureaucracy would be required to verify the efficiency claims.

Turning to automobiles, Schlesinger proposed to tax gas guzzlers and offer a rebate to buyers of fuel-efficient cars made in America—but not those made in Japan, where auto engines delivered far better mileage than Detroit's products. Blumenthal, who had been a senior trade negotiator in the Kennedy administration, warned that this would violate a number of our international trade obligations to treat foreign and U.S. products equally and could end with the United States paying Japan $6 billion in compensation. The president interjected that he was "not sure it saves enough gas to warrant the extra cost."

Schultze estimated that the plan would raise inflation by half a percentage point, just from the oil and gas provisions, but he had not had time to calculate the impact of the rest. Schlesinger retorted that it was impossible to judge the impact without knowing exactly what the legislation would look like when finally enacted. To me this inconclusive debate showed the wicked trade-off between good energy policy and its economic consequences.

On the day *after* the plan was introduced, the president asked me to resolve interagency disputes on the economic costs. Every agency had its own figures; like most businesses and professions, each one tended to see the world through its own perspective—and as an old Washington adage goes, "Where you stand depends on where you sit." It took me a week to align the different perspectives into one unified estimate, and even then the many variables left it uncertain. Moreover, the lack of consultation meant that we had no earthly idea of the different reactions among the members of Congress, who would be the ones to resolve the fate of the massive legislation on which the president had staked his reputation.

PRICING OIL AND GAS

As we drilled down to bedrock that April day, the problem was not only the plan's inherent conflicts, but how to price crude oil and natural gas. On crude oil we had inherited a complicated three-tier system with different prices for "old oil" from wells currently in production that had already amortized their drilling costs (about half the total), and from newly discovered oil still paying off start-up costs. The third tier was the world price of imported oil. There was a difference of almost eight dollars a barrel between the price of old oil and the world price of about thirteen dollars a barrel; the policy goal was to raise domestic oil prices to world prices to encourage conservation and production.

Schlesinger proposed a tax as ungainly as its name—the Crude Oil Equalization Tax, or COET, in a typically bureaucratic acronym. The government would impose a tax at the wellhead to claw back the difference between old oil and the world price, and as the regulated price of new oil rose, the government would collect the difference and rebate the money to consumers. The producers, of course, wanted to pocket the higher prices so they could drill new wells—or so they said. The natural suspicion was that they simply wanted to pocket the profits, period. Carter asked whether this system would not effectively let OPEC set American prices as well. They already did, Schlesinger replied, because by setting the price of our domestic oil, the federal control system in effect was subsidizing the price of foreign oil. What if OPEC viewed the rise in U.S. market prices as an invitation to jack up world prices again? Carter asked. Schultze suggested that the president could be given authority to reimpose controls if prices rose too fast.

The wellhead tax was a brilliantly designed, but complicated, device to charge Americans market prices for crude oil while preventing the oil companies from gaining all the additional profit. But we never came down squarely on what to do with these large revenues, estimated at $15 billion a year by Schlesinger. It was not necessarily a bad political idea to shift that debate on dividing up the tax revenues to the elected members of Congress. But it opened an unseemly battle among the government departments; each would want a scoop from this new fiscal honeypot and would seek support from its congressional overseers. Its most significant flaw was that COET had no champions in Congress. The liberals opposed anything that raised oil prices, the conservatives and producer-state representatives simply wanted to decontrol crude oil prices.

But the Achilles' heel of Schlesinger's plan was the even more politically radioactive issue of natural-gas prices. No domestic issue was more contentious for a longer period of time. Decades of political pressure combined with eccentric Supreme Court decisions produced a pricing policy that could only have been invented in an insane asylum. The producing states could charge whatever the local market could bear in an unregulated market; but as soon as the gas crossed state lines, the federal government controlled the price at about one-third the state level. The economic effects were perverse, as energy producers had no incentive to ship their natural gas to consuming states in the North and Midwest: Householders and industries in the North were cut off from cheap energy, while the producing states in the South and Southwest attracted chemical and manufacturing industries that prospered on chemical feedstock used to produce plastics and fertilizer, and energy from abundant local gas.[34]

Schlesinger and his staff agreed on the necessity of one uniform nationwide price for gas, but proposed to accomplish this by extending federal controls into the unregulated producing-states' market, rather than deregulating the price wherever natural gas was sold, as we had promised during the campaign. That new regulated price would be hooked to the energy (BTU) equivalent of crude oil and be sufficiently competitive to open new markets to the gas producers.

This was political poison for the energy companies and the producing states. But the idea had great attraction for key members of Schlesinger's team, who had deep connections with Northern liberals in the Senate, and were suspicious of price deregulation as a consumer rip-off favoring the free-market oilmen who already enjoyed huge government tax subsidies. From a policy standpoint the choice between the predictability of government regulation and the risky attraction of market-based prices was one they were not prepared to make.

Schlesinger's staff, largely drawn from the ranks of government, did not see the seismic shift of public and congressional opinion toward the principle of the marketplace as an efficient provider of goods and services—and that placed Jimmy Carter at a turning point in American history. The change in political attitude toward deregulation was one Carter would later ride to success in deregulating transportation, communications, and banking to the benefit of consumers. Schlesinger's proposal satisfied neither of the major combatants in the energy wars. It raised prices higher than consumer groups wanted, but did not provide for an end to federal controls that producers had long advocated, and that we backed in the campaign.

Opposition to the energy package began to bubble up to the highest levels of the government. At a cabinet meeting on April 11, an unusual voice was heard. Brzezinski, who rarely spoke on economic or energy issues, said our allies feared that the energy program would have negative effects on both inflation and growth.[35] At the same time I argued that the plan depended on higher energy costs, and Congress had already rejected that approach. I was also concerned that we were asking for short-term sacrifices for ill-defined long-term benefits. The rapid introduction of the wellhead tax on oil risked an inflationary jolt, yet we did not have a calculation of the impact on middle- and low-income Americans. Our insulation program would be adding government regulation while we were simultaneously talking about deregulation elsewhere. In my notes, I wrote and underlined: "No one knows the impact in macro sense. Need for greater congressional input and time to assess economic impact; changing life-styles, so do more gradually."[36] I presented some of these concerns to the president in a private meeting, but they fell on deaf ears.

Just four days before his deadline, with these issues still unsettled, President Carter called us together on April 16 for a climactic meeting in the Cabinet Room, what Schlesinger called the "big pow-wow."[37] This was the kind of contentious meeting of all hands, representing all administration viewpoints, that should have been held weeks before. The president opened by declaring that he wanted his message to contain clear goals, principles, and as many specifics as possible. He got what he asked for, but the degree of uncertainty about many of the details and effects was unsettling to say the least.[38]

The first issue was what to do with the huge revenues that would come from the COET. How much if any of it should be rebated to the energy industry to encourage more production? Would it be rebated to consumers through reduced Social Security taxes, welfare reform, or tax reform? The president favored a combination of these two. Schlesinger insisted it all had to be recycled back to the people. Blumenthal wanted to use some of the revenues for tax reform. Transportation Secretary Adams put in a claim to have the funds dedicated to the highway trust fund for maintaining the roads. Schultze favored using the money to keep Social Security taxes down. In the end we simply left it to Congress, and our inability to reach a consensus became a fatal flaw.

We next discussed the gasoline tax. Carter expressed the hope that increasing gasoline prices and rebating money to buyers of small cars would encourage the replacement of big cars with small ones. This is exactly what happened, but according to the law of unintended consequences, wealthier drivers bought the more fuel-efficient cars produced abroad, sold their tail-finned monsters to the poor for a pittance, and stuck them with gas-guzzling prices.

Our most contentious debate was over Schlesinger's natural-gas plan. Realizing that it broke our campaign pledge to deregulate natural-gas prices over a five-year period, he proposed that we present it as a step toward deregulation, although prices would continue to be controlled. Despite our campaign pledge, Carter bought into this verbal manipulation, especially after Schlesinger told him he had checked with Governors Briscoe and Boren and had obtained their support for some type of cap on natural-gas prices. (This turned out to be totally untrue.) I questioned Schlesinger, but he held firm and said Boren was willing to describe it as a step toward phased deregulation. A compromise price of $1.75 per million cubic feet was more or less picked out of the air as a median between the local and interstate price levels. Schultze estimated that the natural-gas price would have to rise to $2.25 to be competitive with the price of new oil, and that would surely boost inflation.

Then the president turned to me, and asked, "Stu, you are the keeper of the campaign-pledge flame, what do you think of Jim's proposal?" I sat in the staff seats directly behind the cabinet table, looking out to the Rose Garden, with the spring flowers and trees beautifully in bloom. I rose with my legal pad, came to the table, and reminded him of our visible and frequently repeated campaign promise to decontrol the price of new natural gas, including the letter to Governors Boren and Briscoe, essential to our election. But he backed away from his pledge, and said that was not what he meant by proposing decontrol.[39] Carter stood by Schlesinger and said he wanted to emphasize that this was just the first step toward eventual deregulation. He gave Schlesinger authority to provide additional incentives for deep gas wells, as long as they really were new, and not just old ones redrilled to claim a higher price. Schlesinger later dismissed my painful reminder of the campaign promise as a mere interpretation made by "a good staff person."[40]

Then, after one last reminder to the president of our promise, I conceded—in words I have regretted ever since—that if Schlesinger felt Briscoe and Boren could live with his position, and if, as he claimed, the Democratic leadership opposed deregulation, "I guess, Mr. President, this is one campaign promise we can violate." That was it. Deregulation would not be in our proposal.

Had this episode occurred a few months later, I would have been more assertive and insisted that we needed to know more about how our supporters in the Southwest would react to Schlesinger's new position, as well as a more nuanced view of the congressional reaction. But at the age of just thirty-three, with only a few summer jobs as an intern in Congress and the executive branch, a junior position in the LBJ White House, and my work as research director of the Hubert Humphrey presidential campaign on my résumé—who was I to contradict the great and brilliant James Schlesinger? He had served as a cabinet officer under two presidents, was on a first-name basis with scores of members of Congress, and was a Washington legend. Nevertheless, I gravely doubted Schlesinger's assertions, and I soon learned that my political judgment was better than his.

I wish I had called Boren and Briscoe, but I felt that I could not challenge Schlesinger in an open meeting, or go behind his back to check with them, when we had been banned from talking outside the White House. If I had, I could have given the president a clear view of how shocked they would be at the reversal of a pledge upon which they had relied in campaigning so hard for him and delivering their critically important states. That would be the last time I deferred with barely a whimper to the judgment of a cabinet officer. I have never forgiven myself for not putting up a stronger fight.

In fact Schlesinger had not made any systematic count of the potential votes for deregulation. Early on he did consult with his two closest friends in the Congress, Scoop Jackson in the Senate and John Dingell in the House, who chaired the key congressional panels dealing with oil and gas pricing. They both passionately opposed decontrol and promised to fight against it. Schlesinger, who like Carter had a populist streak and distrusted the energy industry, did not feel the need to do any more vote counting, nor was he given the leeway by the president to do so.

But that climactic meeting also underscored the utter lack of integration of the political and policy aspects of the energy package and indeed more broadly for all the major policy initiatives of the first year of the administration. We had all been told to keep quiet. It was revealing that Ham Jordan, the president's closest political adviser, was not even at the meeting, nor was he asked to calculate the political implications of this decision in the oil patch, where we would have to defend our victories four years hence.

When Boren and Briscoe heard that Carter had reversed himself, they were shocked. Along with other governors who were in town for the March meeting of the National Governors' Association, they had been invited to a briefing on the outlines of the forthcoming energy package by the president and Schlesinger in the Indian Treaty Room of the Executive Office Building. As Boren told me later when he was serving as a U.S. senator from Oklahoma, "I'll never forget when we both realized that pledge was not going to be kept." When Boren turned to Briscoe, he saw that his colleague from Texas had turned pale and become physically ill. Briscoe returned to his hotel and refused to attend the dinner hosted by the president for the governors. Boren remembers Briscoe saying, "'I can't go back to Texas.' He was very, very upset, and I was upset."[41]

What hurt them most was that they had been blindsided. Neither Carter nor Schlesinger gave them any advance notice of the abrupt change in policy. Carter may have thought they were told, Boren said, but they were not. "No, we learned that in a group in which there were governors from all over the country, not just the governors involved, and we learned it in a group, and for the first time. . . . We were upset about the way we learned it, as well as the [substance]." They had no time to prepare an explanation for the press and public "when this hit, this bombshell." As Carter was leaving the briefing room Boren and Briscoe told him they could not understand why he had suddenly changed course and asked, "What in the world do you want us to say?" There was no response. It took Boren several months to repair relations with Carter, and Briscoe never did. Boren had been particularly close to Carter and gone into the political trenches with him early in his candidacy against a nascent stop-Carter movement in the Democratic Party establishment. "We knew each other so well that on two different occasions, when we were alone, we prayed together," Boren said. On one occasion a few weeks before Carter was nominated, "He looked at me and said, do you think I'm good enough to be president?" And they prayed.[42]

A cardinal rule in politics is never to surprise and embarrass another politician who is invested in an issue. If policy changes, allies are owed fair warning and a private explanation so they can crawl back off the limb together. Boren said he had been left out on a limb by Carter more than once, but, "He sort of didn't want to take the time to play the politics of it. . . . [He] could get miffed by some of the details of politics and the pettiness. . . . I think he didn't like politics very much." Carter once made a politician's congratulatory birthday call to Boren but made it on the wrong day. In national politics everything is connected. Months later, Carter called Boren, then still a governor, to ask him to endorse the Panama Canal Treaty. Boren responded, " 'I'll consider it when you call me back and tell me that you've reversed your breach of your pledge on natural gas!' " As he told me, "We had some pretty strong words back and forth about it."[43]

Schlesinger had even less acute political antennae. When the National Governors Association returned to Washington the following year, he and the president again briefed the governors on the energy package. Schlesinger argued that as the price of natural gas rose to an equilibrium level with oil, it would suddenly flatten out. Boren recalled that he presented "the oddest-looking graph, which had a right angle, and then it was absolutely flat." Rising from his chair, Boren asked, "How could that be? What magic occurs?" Schlesinger responded that once all the drilling rigs were working, that would cap new production. "That makes no sense," Boren riposted. "That assumes you can't produce more drilling rigs." And in fact as prices rose, industry started grinding out new rigs, reaching a total of more than four thousand within a few years. But Boren recalled that Schlesinger "got very excited, and he was very angry" when his assumptions were challenged—and he stayed angry. That same evening, at a White House reception for the governors, Boren introduced his new wife, Molly, to Schlesinger, who rudely rebuffed her: "'Oh, no,' he said. 'Your husband's the man who called me a liar to the president.'" Then the energy secretary turned his back and walked off. Boren was so furious that he almost left.

But that was not the end of the tale. In 1979, after Schlesinger's resignation had just been announced and Boren had moved to the Senate, Schlesinger phoned to break many months of silence between them. Boren wondered why Schlesinger was calling: "I thought he must have a little list of people that he wanted to tell to go to hell before he left his job." But instead Schlesinger said, "Well, I just want to tell you . . . I reread all the files, and I looked at the staff studies prepared for me. . . . And I just don't want to leave office without calling you and telling you that you were right, and I was basing this on the faulty assumption that there could be no more rigs. I just didn't want to leave office without clearing the decks.'" Boren laughed and asked, "'How long have you known this, Jim?' He said, 'About six months.'"[44]

DONNING A CARDIGAN TO SELL A BLACK BOX

On the morning of April 18, the very day the president was to address the nation on prime-time television, he was still holding meetings with his speechwriter and his chief economic and energy advisers. He had already complained that the plan was a "hodgepodge" and that the tax-and-rebate arrangements were particularly complex. After hearing the contentious arguments on how to allocate the new revenues, the president closed his eyes and said, "I see now why Nixon resigned." Everyone laughed, but it was no laughing matter.[45] To the president the plan still seemed a black box.

At one point he had grilled Alm in Schlesinger's absence for two hours, with tough questions on which he should have been fully briefed months before.[46] His energy plan had a strong intellectual basis, was put together by a first-rate team, and was substantively defensible. But what it sorely lacked was a political dynamic that could be championed—a national consensus through coordinated communication and congressional outreach. Carter's instinct in seeking a program with something in it for everybody was politically shrewd, but its execution certainly was not. As the program was rolled out in briefings and public presentations, the producers thought it short-changed them in favor of consumers, and the consumers felt exactly the opposite. This added up to a majority with a political instinct to pick apart the whole program.

These political weaknesses were exacerbated by other priorities we had simultaneously thrown at Congress—economic stimulus, tax reform, welfare reform, hospital cost containment, and a list of local water projects he wanted to kill—that infuriated many of the congressional leaders we needed to pass the energy bill. This was simply more than Congress could possibly digest. But when its Democratic leaders almost begged the president to select his priorities, he replied that pressure groups and their congressional supporters would resent being put in a secondary place while Congress was trying to absorb the massive energy bill. At a Democratic leadership breakfast early in June, O'Neill warned that there were only so many weeks left in the session. He told the president he needed priorities for this term, and "You have four years to accomplish your goals." Carter held firm, refusing to set priorities for fear of offending various interest groups.[47]

As the president met to review the last draft of his speech with the vice president, James Fallows, his chief speechwriter, Ham, Jody, Rafshoon, and me, he joked that shortly, "Our energy policy will be in the Congress's hands—and [Saudi] Prince Fahd's."[48] There was much truth to that.

Carter gave a fireside chat modeled after Franklin Roosevelt's radio addresses to rally the nation during the darkest days of the Great Depression. But while Roosevelt spoke in aristocratic cadences to inspire the confidence of a frightened people, Carter, using the contemporary, more intimate medium of television, presented himself as a plain person dressed in a beige cardigan near a flickering fireplace in the ground-floor library of the White House. Rosalynn came downstairs with what she considered a more presidential blazer, but her husband adamantly refused to cast off his sweater for the jacket.[49]

When Roosevelt spoke, it was not from *his* fireside but to the homes of millions of ordinary Americans supposedly gathered around *theirs*, where they welcomed him as an honored visitor offering hope amid the depths of the Depression. But on television Carter's speech came from a president sitting in the comfort of the White House delivering a warning call of energy conservation, higher prices, and sacrifice to an unsuspecting nation. One of the most difficult tasks for any president is calling the nation to arms against a long-term challenge when they could not see the storm clouds on the horizon to which he so ominously pointed, and enjoyed the lowest energy prices in the Western world.

The speech was vintage Jimmy Carter, downbeat and almost apocalyptic, with a hint of hellfire by a preacher to his flock. He began with a line that few presidents have dared to adopt but typified his approach both to energy and governance: "Tonight I want to have an *unpleasant* talk with you about a problem that is unprecedented in our history. With the exception of preventing war, this is the greatest challenge that our country will face during our lifetime." He urged a better balance between the nation's insatiable demand for energy and its rapidly shrinking resources, and warned that many of his proposals would be unpopular, inconvenient, and demand sacrifice—indeed "the sacrifices will be painful—but so is every meaningful sacrifice. It will lead to some higher prices and to some greater inconveniences for everyone."

Among those inconveniences would be lower thermostats to save fuel. Carter offered the public little benefit in exchange for sacrifice, only a warning that "the alternative may be national catastrophe," such as renewed oil embargoes that would test the "character of the American people and the ability of the president and the Congress to govern this nation." Instead of holding out hope—the essential currency of leadership—he doled out criticism of America as "the most wasteful nation on earth."[50]

As solutions Carter offered conservation as a cornerstone of his policy, plus burning more coal and developing solar power and other renewable energy sources. There was barely a word about increasing incentives to produce our most basic energy sources—oil and natural gas—except to say that "prices should generally reflect the true replacement cost of energy. We are only cheating ourselves if we make energy artificially cheap and use more than we can really afford."

The one sentence that captured the essence of his speech was: "This difficult effort will be the 'moral equivalent of war,' except that we will be uniting our efforts to build and not to destroy." Carter's energy program was ridiculed by the supply-side polemicists of the *Wall Street Journal* editorial page, who referred to his key phrase "moral equivalent of war" by its anagram, MEOW. The clever slur caught on, and in his admirable but often humorless devotion to the public interest, Carter had to fight interest groups on both his left and right. I sometimes felt he actually liked warning his congregants to repent—here telling Americans to conserve energy and pay higher prices for it. More significantly, if energy reform really *was* a moral equivalent of war, we had not mobilized ourselves to fight it as a modern army by putting all the resources of the White House on energy as a priority.

Between his televised speech and the one that followed two days later on April 20, to a Joint Session of Congress, I helped strengthen the language on natural-gas pricing in hopes of blunting the anger of Boren, Briscoe, and many of our political allies in the producer states. Carter told the legislators: "We want to work with the Congress to give gas producers an adequate incentive for exploration." Still, the reality remained that Carter was proposing a nationwide price ceiling for all newly discovered gas, and that price would be tied to the price of domestic crude oil. Carter and Schlesinger briefed the cabinet, pledging that the program would slow the increase in energy demand from 2 to 5 percent and would finally belie the notion that oil was cheap and abundant.[51]

Briefings were also held for the Democratic leadership, 50 members of Congress, and the White House staff. But the fact sheets were not ready for the press briefing, and combined with Schlesinger's brusque manner, created a confused and unceremonious atmosphere for the launch of the president's signature domestic program.

A presidential address to a joint session of Congress in the mammoth chambers of the House of Representatives is a unique event.[52] As I sat with Fran in the gallery, I felt a tingle down my spine as Jimmy Carter entered to address this rare assemblage for the first time. We tightly squeezed each other's hands, reflecting on the incredible journey we had taken from his widely derided announcement for president in Atlanta a little over two years before. Most in the audience had at least a general idea of what the president was going to say, and indeed his speech was a reprise in many ways of his televised address to the nation two nights earlier. This meant he had to raise the threat level for inaction, and he engaged in what turned out to be some questionable assertions. Some were drawn from the flawed CIA report that warned the world would run out of oil by the end of the next decade; so he emphasized again: "Our first goal is conservation." He pressed ahead, seeking a tax on gas guzzlers and the authority to impose an emergency gasoline tax if consumption exceeded our national goals, which turned out to be one of the most controversial proposals in his energy plan.

We were catching flak even from friends like Representative Charles Vanik of Ohio, who called to warn me that his powerful tax-writing committee would reject the standby gasoline tax.[53] However tough the younger Democrats might be on oil companies, they had no appetite for a higher gasoline tax that would be passed on to consumers. Doug Fraser, president of the UAW and our earliest union supporter in the Democratic primaries, met with members of the White House inner circle to complain about new auto-emission and fuel-efficiency standards, and then warned: "Don't let the Republicans become the protectors of over one million American auto-related jobs."[54]

The president also repeated the less controversial proposals for encouraging home insulation, efficient appliances, and more flexible pricing by utilities, but then he dropped yet another political bomb—this one right in the backyard of Howard Baker, the Senate Republican minority leader, whose support for the package would be essential. Carter declared that he saw no need for a fast-breeder nuclear reactor on the Clinch River in Baker's home state of Tennessee. As a nuclear engineer by training, Carter supported light-water reactors for electricity, and indeed wanted to streamline their licensing process. But a dangerous by-product of fast breeders is weapons-grade plutonium, and Carter opposed this particular reactor even as a demonstration project lest it encourage the proliferation of nuclear weapons. He thus effectively killed commercial reprocessing and recycling of spent nuclear fuel in what almost became a deal breaker in gaining Republican support for the entire program.

Campaign supporters of all stripes continued to weigh in. Cliff Finch, the Democratic governor of Mississippi, whose postmidnight call delivering his state for Carter sealed his election, called me to point out that a higher percentage of his state's industries were powered by gas and oil than in New England, and converting their boilers to coal would raise utility bills and even bankrupt some businesses that could not afford the conversion. Reasoned criticism also came from Republicans. Governor Jim Thompson of Illinois, a tall, broad-shouldered, impressive man, told me he foresaw "alarming" losses from Carter's fifty-five-mile-an-hour national speed limit, which would increase fuel efficiency and hold down consumption through higher gas prices. But he needed those gas tax revenues for highway maintenance.[55]

Washington, of course, is a city of positive spin. That was what Jody Powell tried to do to protect his boss at the first press conference after the program's grim rollout, and the gifted press secretary went on the offensive.[56] He shifted his emphasis from the somber presidential call to arms and sacrifice, underscored that the plan would make average Americans better off, and argued that tax rebates would cushion the impact on consumers. The press had a field day pointing out the inconsistency of accentuating the positive while asking for sacrifice. But Jody's tactics paid off. The headline over the *Washington Post*'s first story on the Tuesday morning after the fireside chat read, "Carter: Energy Outlook Grim," and the article itself noted correctly that "President Carter is undertaking the most difficult of all exercises in democratic leadership. He is trying to persuade a large and rich nation to prepare for a crisis not yet entirely visible from the street level." But the next day its front-page headline sent a different message: "Future Called Not So Bleak as Depicted." By Saturday the *Post*'s front page literally spun around: "Energy Plan Now Pictured as Consumer Boon," the paper headlined after a few days of briefings.[57]

In major newspapers across the country the editorial judgment was generally positive, although breaking along ideological lines. The more liberal *New York Times* doubted that the incentives were sufficiently robust to help pull more energy from the ground, but it nevertheless applauded the president's plan as tough and necessary. But this was not where the crucial votes lay on Capitol Hill.[58]

7

ENERGIZING CONGRESS

I n America, it is said, "The President proposes; the Congress disposes."
Almost uniquely among the world's democracies, the U.S. Congress has
two coequal divisions in a bicameral legislature, with a House of Representatives and a Senate. Each jealously guards its own prerogatives, generally takes a dim view of actions by the other, and certainly does not regard
them as binding. The two chambers operate under radically different rules.
The Senate's are so notoriously convoluted that regional and even individual interests can gravely wound or even kill a bill that has passed the House
with presidential support. The prerogatives of individual senators are almost
sacred: A single senator can prevent a bill from even getting to the floor by
placing a sometimes anonymous procedural hold on it. And individual senators can try to talk a bill to death with a filibuster that can be broken only
by a supermajority, thus overriding the principle of simple majority rule.

Because of its larger numbers, the 435 members of the House operate
under a tighter leash. The Speaker, the majority leader and their team of whips,
generally one for each region of the country, exercise control through the
Rules Committee, which sets the terms for debating and amending legislation that comes out of committees. The Speaker can exercise almost absolute authority by restricting amendments from the floor.

When Carter presented his energy plan, the Democratic leadership of
the House was ready to help. Just as there was a new Democratic president,
there was a new Democratic congressional leadership led by Speaker Tip
O'Neill, who had moved up from majority leader when his predecessor, Carl
Albert, retired, and wanted to make his mark by helping a Democratic president to succeed. A tall, rotund Boston Irishman, with a shock of white hair,

a bulbous red nose, and an engaging smile, he was a politician's politician bred in the rough-and-tumble of his Boston district. He was both beloved and respected on both sides of the aisle for his fairness and conviviality. Since his wife, Millie, never moved to Washington, he rarely socialized, shared a Capitol Hill apartment with his close Massachusetts friend, Representative Edward Boland, and spent almost every waking hour on House business, directly or indirectly. He also benefited from the post-Watergate reform of the House rules, enhancing his powers; and although committee chairmen now were elected by the entire Democratic caucus instead of ascending by seniority, the Speaker could set timetables for committee business and controlled the Rules Committee that was the traffic cop for the flow of legislation to the House floor. O'Neill took advantage of this shift of power to the fullest, using Carter's energy plan as his first opportunity.[1]

The two Democrats could not have been more different, yet there was something deeply touching in the old pol and the young president. Carter was slight, appearing even more so next to Tip. He was the antipolitician who came out of a rural, one-party Southern tradition, and when a deal had to be cut with the generally pliant Georgia legislature to pass his major initiatives, he would leave it to Bert Lance, who would tell the governor about it later.

Tip was a Massachusetts liberal, a New Deal and Great Society Democrat who believed in the role of government to stimulate economic growth, create jobs, and work for social equality. Carter, by contrast, believed in effective but not big government, the first New Democrat in high office seeking to prune government programs, reduce federal regulations, and pull the Democratic Party from the left to the center. But he was also a populist with an affinity and concern for the poor and a deep commitment to equal rights for minorities and women, which created a bond of sorts with the Speaker. Where they truly parted company, however, was on the president's personal abstemiousness and fiscal conservatism: O'Neill was raised on rewarding his supporters with patronage; Carter abhorred the concept.

But O'Neill was a savvy enough politician to realize that Carter's nomination and election as a moderate Southern Democrat signaled a shift in the political winds, and that he had to accommodate to it as well.[2] While some of the more liberal members expected a Carter presidency to pick up from where the Vietnam War had ended the construction of Lyndon Johnson's Great Society, Tip knew that as much as he might welcome this, it was not going to happen. But what he and the vast majority of Democrats did expect after suffering two Republican presidents, was a kind of intimacy, a sensitivity to their special needs and projects, a personal rapport with a fellow Democrat. This they would also not receive from this cerebral Southern moderate, who neither honed these social and political skills in Georgia nor enjoyed them in Washington.

The Speaker was a master craftsman of the backroom deals and midnight compromises that are elements of the hands-on contact required for presidents to deal with Congress. This Irish Catholic speaker also employed two truly gifted apprentices, both observant Jews fresh out of college and still in their twenties, Ariel "Ari" Weiss and Joseph "Jack" Lew. Weiss turned out to be essential in guiding legislation through every parliamentary twist and turn (and would become prominent in Israel's philanthropic community). Lew was an astute and intelligent draftsman (and would later hold senior positions in the Clinton and Obama administrations, finally as secretary of the Treasury). Tip did not feel that their youthful expertise was mirrored by the top staff at the White House, whose anti-Washington attitude he loathed, along with what he felt was their lack of respect for him and the institution he led. But he turned out to be immensely loyal to the president, who returned his support with respect and deference. I could not help but genuinely love Tip O'Neill, and I believe that in his cool way, Jimmy Carter did, too.[3]

Until he arrived in Washington, Carter never realized the fragmentary nature of the federal legislative process, the lack of party loyalty, and the hurdles faced by any comprehensive piece of legislation. "The governor is really much more powerful in Georgia than the president of the United States is in Washington," Carter reflected.[4] Because of the vast scope of the energy bill, it would normally have to work its way through seventeen House committees or subcommittees, a number that shocked Carter.

But O'Neill had a novel answer, which he had begun developing when he learned that energy would be a domestic priority of the new president. His solution to these overlapping jurisdictions, never used before or since, was to create an Ad Hoc Energy Committee; each of the numerous regular chairmen would be required to report their part of the bill on a tight time-table to this supercommittee, which was certainly not popular with the barons of the House. If there is anything that enrages committee chairmen it is an attempt to weaken their jurisdiction, which they rank with a sneak attack by a foreign enemy.

Although O'Neill could not get everything he wanted, he achieved more oversight than any Speaker before or since. He was unable to win the right for the supercommittee to change recommendations reported to the full House by the five standing committees. But this unique body could still recommend amendments from the floor to keep the omnibus bill stitched together, internally consistent, and as close as possible to the president's proposal. The main idea was to shield the plan's most controversial proposals on oil and gas pricing from being stripped out of the bill on its way to the floor, then wrap them up with more politically popular energy conservation measures and put the package to an up-or-down vote of the whole House.

To chair the unprecedented Ad Hoc Energy Steering Committee, the Speaker named his friend Thomas "Lud" Ashley, a good-natured, well-liked moderate from Ohio, and then stacked it with twenty-seven Democratic loyalists.[5] When the president's 283-page National Energy Act was introduced, the clerk of the House divided it in the traditionally byzantine manner among the Energy and Power Subcommittee of the Interstate and Foreign Commerce Committee; the Banking, Finance, Urban Affairs, and Ways and Means Committees; plus a minor proposal to save gas by pooling vans conveying federal workers to their jobs, which went to the Government Affairs Committee. Remarkably, almost all but the emergency gas tax and a three-cent increase in gasoline prices were piloted through Ways and Means by the Speaker's deadline. It even fended off efforts by Republicans and oil-state Democrats to return the wellhead revenues to the oil companies instead of to consumers. The conservation part of the program passed largely intact.

While Congress was digesting the energy plan, the president used the weekly cabinet meetings to put energy at the top of the agenda. During the spring and early summer, it was open season in Congress (and within the administration) for interest groups either to avoid the higher costs or obtain a larger rebate on the wellhead tax. As Bismarck could have predicted, it was not a pretty picture, and our uncertainty made it worse.

Economists generally wanted the money to help pay for tax reform, and Senator Daniel Patrick Moynihan objected to putting the energy package ahead of welfare reform.[6] Consumer groups wanted to legislate a full rebate and also wanted gas priced according to the industry's own costs and not the OPEC-managed oil price. Farm-state legislators threatened to band together and kill the whole package—and they had the votes to do it—unless the law exempted oil and gas boilers used in agriculture. Prospective developers of synthetic fuel—for example, turning coal into gas—wanted loan guarantees or government subsidies instead of the research and start-up grants. Transportation Secretary Brock Adams made a salient political point in demanding that some of the money from the energy taxes be siphoned into highway maintenance and mass transit, to give mayors and governors a stake in these funds, and develop a national constituency for Carter's energy package.[7] But it contained too many complex and financially uncertain components, and early on, I made a marginal note: "Overloaded circuits."[8]

The Congressional Budget Office (CBO) then gave us what can best be described as a cold shower. The CBO specialists are highly professional, apolitical, and indispensable in providing Congress with analyses of all legislative proposals (as they did with devastating impact in 2017 to the Republican effort to repeal and replace Obamacare), and they informed me that their estimates of energy savings were considerably less optimistic than our own, although still considerable improvements over the current situation.[9] Among other flaws, they said poor people with cars would be hurt.

It was obvious that our congressional opponents would throw the CBO's more pessimistic numbers in our face, particularly their estimate that the plan would increase inflation by 1 percentage point and slow growth by seven-tenths of a point during its initial three years. However important our plan was for the nation's energy security, their calculations would cut against the grain of the issue most important to Carter's political standing—the state of the economy.

As we approached the House vote, we kept hitting speed bumps despite trying to avoid them. Even the tax credits passed by only one vote after our heavy lobbying. In June, Schlesinger began talking about fallback positions—raising the gasoline tax and dividing up the revenue among the states for highways, localities for mass transit, and a half-cent a gallon for research and development.[10] Representative Vanik[11] called to propose a similar allocation of that money from the wellhead tax. Here was an influential liberal Democrat reaching out to explore a deal, but Schlesinger never engaged in this kind of bargaining.

Les Goldman recalled that his phone rang around that time, and to his astonishment, it was the president, who said he had called Schlesinger to "come over and tell me what's going on," but his boss was out of town. Goldman literally ran across the alley from the Executive Office Building to the White House and told Carter it was important that he make half a dozen calls to help nail down an important vote. Carter said he would see what he could do, but "He really wasn't interested in it. . . . It was so clear to me that at that particular moment he didn't really understand how to get those guys [in Congress] on board."[12]

Sometimes it seemed that the president felt he could spread the idea of energy conservation merely by the example of his own frugality. He tried to switch to a less-expensive presidential limousine and also declared at a budget meeting, "It makes me sick to see the waste of money on TVs and radios in the White House."[13] Mondale remembered that he even ordered the air conditioners turned off, until the insufferable Washington summers made it unbearable.[14]

Gradually, around mid-June, we began to see some flexibility. The president breakfasted with Democratic and Republican congressional leaders to seek cooperation, a gesture unimaginable in today's polarized politics. He made a quite remarkable statement to the bipartisan breakfast: "Normally a Republican President is a restraining force on a Democratic Congress. But I will be a restraining force on a Democratic Congress in terms of spending," citing the breeder reactor, where he would allow research and development to continue but save billions by not putting it into production. Byrd gave Carter some sound political advice that would ease movement on both sides by urging him to settle for 75 percent of the energy package now, come back for another 10 percent the following year, and then come back for more later.[15]

With the program moving through the heavily Democratic House by what Schlesinger described to the cabinet as "precarious votes," I was called into the president's study. He showed his populist colors by asking me to do an analysis of the oil companies' special tax advantages because "We may need that to counter their lobbying."[16] He was beginning to learn how to fight hard, Washington-style.

We now were approaching the moment of truth in the House of Representatives. The Rules Committee, which sets the terms for any House vote, limited Republican amendments to a bare minimum and barred any motions to untie the package by striking out separate parts of it. The only way the bill could be defeated would be under an all-or-nothing vote. The climax began on August 1 with a floor debate on the whole package that emerged from the Ad Hoc Committee—O'Neill's procedural brainchild. The Speaker wisely wanted to finish action before the August recess, lest members return home to be besieged by lobbyists trying to dilute or kill the bill. They targeted natural gas, which previous Congresses tried and failed to decontrol by increasingly narrow margins.

This led to some congressional exchanges well above the normal windbag level, thanks in part to Texas congressman Robert Krueger, who stood out in the exceptionally talented class of Watergate babies swept into office in the 1974 midterm elections. A handsome, curly-haired Rhodes Scholar with a doctorate from Oxford, he had just been named at the tender age of thirty-six as dean of arts and sciences at Duke University, where he was a Shakespeare scholar. But when his father came down with cancer, Krueger moved home to care for him and then ran for Congress from Texas to fight OPEC's grip on America's energy. Deregulating natural gas to encourage more domestic production was one way Krueger chose to retaliate. But after Schlesinger gave only lukewarm congressional testimony favoring eventual decontrol sometime in the future, the two faced each other at a White House briefing. Schlesinger said mockingly, "Methought the young Shakespeare professor had a lean and hungry look in the committee meeting earlier this week." Krueger immediately recognized the allusion to Cassius in Shakespeare's *Julius Caesar* and shot back, "You know, Jim, the next lines are, 'He thinks too much. Men like him are dangerous.'" Bested in scholarly combat, Schlesinger turned away.[17]

But the actual backroom arm twisting was considerably more painful than this war of words, and the Ad Hoc Committee realized it was perilously close to losing a floor fight to Krueger and his allies. A key amendment aimed at peeling off members pressing for speedier decontrol was proposed by the liberal, eccentric Texas Democrat, Bob Eckhardt, who could often be seen wearing a light suit and broad-brimmed straw hat while riding his bicycle around Capitol Hill. But he was a serious legislator and was joined by a rail-thin, swaggering friend of the oil and gas lobby affectionately called Texas Charlie Wilson (to distinguish him from California's Charlie Wilson) who had a seemingly inexhaustible supply of attractive blonde aides and secretaries in his Capitol Hill office. His legs were toothpick thin, all the more evident in the tight-fitting blue jeans and tall cowboy boots he often sported. The well-crafted amendment introduced by this incongruous duo would have liberalized the definition of "new natural gas" qualifying for higher prices. Although the real-world effect would have been minor, the political effect would have been major in helping to stave off full deregulation, desired by producer states, by providing more revenue to natural-gas producers, while preserving the administration's plan to regulate the entire natural-gas market.

As the vote approached, I met with leaders of the consumer groups and likewise with the competing major business organization. Our plan was in the crosshairs of conflicting interests. Jim Flug of Energy Action urged us to stand firm against higher gas prices in any form.[18] John Post of the Business Roundtable spoke for the largest American corporations in a more measured tone, and he was my favorite business lobbyist. Bald as an egg and with sad, drooping eyes, he was kind, thoughtful, and sensible. Big Business favored a compromise leading to eventual deregulation of natural gas but wanted certainty; he was flexible on the transition period because he wanted to avoid a drawn-out battle that would hold back investment.[19]

Soon the deregulation forces did an about-face and supported the compromise, including Krueger and others from oil and gas districts. They realized they could not carry the House for full deregulation, and the Eckhardt-Wilson amendment would mean more money for the energy industry, even if not as much as total deregulation. So what looked like a cliffhanger was adopted by a voice vote.

But the deregulation supporters were not giving up. They proposed yet a different complex path toward full deregulation. It was a time of high drama and stirring debate. O'Neill, who in the tradition of Speakers rarely took the floor to speak, lumbered to the well of the House chamber, waved his arms and slapped his hands together for emphasis. He urged his colleagues in his booming Boston Irish voice to vote against big oil: "Never have I seen such an influx of lobbyists in this town. America is watching this legislation more than it has watched any legislation in years. Will the House fail? Can the House act? Can the House pull together an energy policy?"[20] Most Democratic members were mesmerized, then roared and applauded.

It now was time to vote, and as each member came to cast his or her vote, John Dingell greeted them at one end of the chamber with his fierce visage; his formidable fist waved with his thumb emphatically down. At the opposite end stood Krueger, still hoping for more rapid deregulation, holding both arms aloft. The deregulation amendment failed, getting 199 votes to 227 in opposition, with 72 Southern and producer-state Democrats supporting it along with virtually every Republican. This was the first big test of O'Neill's leadership as Speaker, but he did not crow over his victory. His lieutenants heaved a sigh of relief because passage would have dealt a psychologically catastrophic blow to the whole energy plan.

Carter pitched in, although he did throw some curveballs. On the one hand he gave a group of House members the ultimate presidential perk, opening Camp David to them and their wives for a weekend and ferrying them to the mountain retreat aboard his Marine One helicopter. But he could not put his prudishness above politics. Crossed off the guest list was Don Edwards, a liberal California member of the House Ways and Means Committee, then living with a woman who was not his wife. The couple later married, but not even Bill Cable, the White House lobbyist who attended the wedding, ever told him why he had been blackballed.[21]

To his credit, though, Carter could be forgiving to his enemies. Krueger later gave up his safe seat to challenge Republican Senator John Tower. The Texas Republicans created a sham Hispanic party to drain away votes, and Krueger lost by only five thousand votes out of two million cast. Carter invited him to the Oval Office, and said, "Bob, I know how you feel. But let me tell you, it's a lot worse to lose to a man who chases blacks out of his restaurant with an ax handle [Lester Maddox, who defeated Carter in his first run for governor] than it is to lose by less than one percent to an 18-year

Senate veteran." Carter then appointed him special coordinator for Mexican affairs with ambassadorial rank, and Krueger played an important role in negotiating the importation of Mexican natural gas for the first time, another positive legacy of the Carter energy program.[22]

After the smoke cleared, the president, Schlesinger, and the Democratic leadership had accomplished something truly revolutionary through our normally incremental democratic process. The National Energy Act passed by a healthy 244–177 margin on August 5, 1977, only three and one-half months after the president's energy plan was sent to Congress.

Carter had begun to set the United States on a different course on energy, from which the nation benefits to this day: incentives for home insulation and the first tax credits for solar and wind equipment; home inspections mandated for utilities to assess the cost and saving of energy conservation; federal energy efficiency standards for thirteen different kinds of appliances; $300 million to help pay for energy-conservation equipment in schools, hospitals, and government buildings; one uniform, national regulated market for natural gas; homeowners shielded from the immediate impact of rising prices by making industry absorb a disproportionate amount of the increase; minimum national standards for electricity rates to reflect their true costs; a gas-guzzler tax on autos averaging less than thirteen miles per gallon; a Crude Oil Equalization Tax on domestically produced oil, raising its wellhead price to world market levels, with the revenues rebated to taxpayers through lower income-tax withholding; and strong incentives for industries and utilities to shift to coal from natural gas or oil.[23] (This was long before the threat of burning fossil fuels in causing global warning was widely recognized.)

While the Democratic leadership and the administration had won this decisive battle in the House, it turned into a Pyrrhic victory. The Senate later passed a Krueger-style bill decontrolling natural gas. We would have been far better off if we had we lost that fight to Krueger in the House, since the entire energy package would most likely have been passed promptly by the Senate. We thus would have paid our political debts to the oil-patch governors who helped elect Carter, and the whole energy plan would have gotten under way promptly. Instead, the Senate barons wrangled for home-state advantages, and a House-Senate Conference Committee fought for a year to reconcile differences on natural gas between the bills passed by the two chambers.

THE SENATE GRAVEYARD

If the United States were a parliamentary democracy, Jimmy Carter would have been seen as a hero for his accomplishments on energy during his first six months in office. His early mistakes would have been forgotten, and his image as a leader would have been burnished; his Gallup poll approval ratings were over 60 percent after this first hundred days, almost identical to Ronald Reagan's, and higher than those of George H. W. Bush and Bill Clinton, and far higher than Donald Trump's at a comparable time.[1]

But our Constitution created a federal system with two very distinct legislative bodies. The Founders envisioned the Senate as a more deliberative body, a brake on the instincts of the lower house, which presumably would be subject to the caprices of popular opinion, in part because of its members' two-year terms and more localized districts. By contrast, each state elects two senators regardless of population, and senators take their prerogatives so seriously that many seem to act as if they are the plenipotentiary ambassadors of sovereign states. The Senate's rules and prerogatives reflect that illusion. Its offices and staffs are much larger than those of the House, and many senior senators also have magnificently appointed hideaways in the Capitol itself. They are sensitive to the most minor slights from the White House, since at any given time a substantial number believe they should be president; many had actually tried and failed, and a handful had even been outrun by Jimmy Carter in the race for the White House. Even some who had not, felt they deserved to be sitting in the Oval Office far more than a one-term governor from Georgia who had never been part of their exclusive club. The makers of the Constitution succeeded, perhaps more than they might have wished, in creating not just a brake on the actions of the House, but a grave-yard of hopes. This was the fate of the Carter energy bill, which had been moving like a freight train right on schedule through the House, but was stalled in the Senate for a year and almost emasculated.

The man whose task it was to steer the energy bill through the Senate was its majority leader, Robert C. Byrd of West Virginia, a Democrat of humble origins and a deeply read autodidact who rose to the pinnacle of power out of the hills of his beloved West Virginia. He had flirted with the Ku Klux Klan early in his political career, but apologized and deeply regretted it. As the Carter energy package plopped into Byrd's lap, Carter told a September cabinet meeting that Byrd's "overt demonstration of lead-ership was absent." I felt Carter was overly critical of the majority leader, who had far less power over the Senate than O'Neill over a compliant Democratic majority in the House. In any event, leadership essentially lay with the president himself.[2]

Byrd reminded me of a bantam rooster, with purposeful gait and swept-back hairdo. More important, he lacked O'Neill's powers to package the bill and push it through an Ad Hoc Committee, and surely would have faced a revolt if he had tried. Personal egos, perceived slights, opaque Senate rules, Byrd's inability to exercise discipline over the Senate's unruly procedures and independent barons, all came together when the Senate considered the en-ergy bill passed by the House. He shared O'Neill's desire to help the president, but he lacked O'Neill's charisma and his personal rapport with Carter. Byrd's strength lay in his dogged mastery of the arcane procedures of the Senate he loved, but he could push the powerhouses of the Senate only so far. This was further complicated by our deferential attitude toward the Senate and Byrd's sense of its prerogative in doing things in its own way. By his own admission the president did not lobby senators effectively and never met with the Senate committees involved with energy, as he had with the House, where O'Neill was his powerful ally in short-circuiting the parliamentary process.[3]

In significant part this failure arose from Schlesinger's bizarre notion that Carter's relationships with key senators was so negative that meeting with them would only make matters worse. He simply stopped scheduling such meetings for the president.[4] This was not what I saw, however. He played tennis with Lloyd Bentsen, a key senator from the key oil state of Texas; dined with Russell Long, who chaired the Senate Finance Committee, and maintained cool if correct relations with Scoop Jackson, chairman of the Senate Energy Committee. When the president asked to meet with senators on energy, and our White House congressional lobbyists pushed for them, Schlesinger would routinely say that the senators felt it best to wrangle among themselves. He was simply wrong, and his judgment was further aggravated by his unwarranted optimism about the bill's prospects in the Senate.

So the Senate proceeded on its traditional path of dealing with the legislation by sending it to committees in piecemeal fashion. And it also happened that the two key chairmen could hardly have been worse choices for the administration. Jackson was short, solidly built, and universally known by his childhood nickname of "Scoop," a Senate veteran with a straightforward speaking style, from his early experience as a hometown prosecutor. I believe he carried a political grudge against Carter, who whipped him in the 1976 primaries and then passed him over as his vice presidential choice. Domestically Scoop was a liberal New Dealer and environmentalist and in foreign affairs an unreconstructed Cold Warrior, paralleling his friend Jim Schlesinger, whom he had recommended to Carter and who therefore was in his debt. Jackson also represented a state where oil and gas prices were rarely front-burner issues because the Northwest had prospered on cheap hydroelectric power flowing from federally financed New Deal dams.

Russell Long, whose committee would consider all the tax measures in the energy program, was a different and far more colorful personality. He was born into politics as the son of the assassinated Louisiana governor Huey Long, the Depression-era demagogue fictionalized in Robert Penn Warren's classic novel *All the King's Men*. He told me the story of his father coming home late one night to the governor's mansion so shaky from a night on the town that he collapsed in the foyer after struggling to fit his key in the door. Still young enough to hold on to "Mama's apron strings," Russell watched his mother with her arms folded, looking sternly at her husband for a full explanation. Without pause, the governor said, "Mama, I've completed my prepared remarks, and I will now take questions from the floor!"

Politics in Louisiana is a state of mind, and Huey's son had mastered the game as few others had. He was no mossback conservative. There was a pinch of the populism of his storied father and a bit of the rascal of his uncle, Earl Long, who also served as governor of Louisiana with young Russell as his chief of staff, before abandoning government and politics as folderol and running off with a stripper—not an oil well, but a real one named Blaze Starr. One story Russell recounted was that in a bid for reelection, Uncle Earl made lavish promises of roads and bridges to the state's local leaders if they delivered the vote. After he won, they returned to collect what they considered bills due, but were far beyond the state's capacity to afford. Russell went into the governor's office and asked in a quavering voice what he should say. The answer was quickly given, "Russell, tell them your uncle Earl lied!"

Jimmy Carter's pure and principled version of governance simply did not exist in the same moral universe as Russell Long's thoroughly transactional practice of politics, where there was a quid for every quo. Long made no secret of the fact that he served not only the people of Louisiana but the interests of its producers of oil and gas, and that deregulation of natural gas was an overriding priority. No senator held the fate of the president's moral equivalent of war closer to his own chest than Long, through his committee's oversight of taxation. And many of the president's conservation incentives were tax-based.

I once asked Long, a peerless legislator and leader of his committee, what was the key to his success. He replied with an infectious wink, "I find out which way my troops are going and then I get in front of them." By contrast with the stolid and deliberate Jackson, Long was gregarious, avuncular, effusive, and often talked or mumbled in riddles that others had a hard time deciphering. Fellow senators, the White House, and the press hung on every consciously ambiguous phrase. Chairman Long was such an engaging figure that he could be figuratively knifing you in the back while cupping his hand around your shoulder, chuckling and smiling. More important, unlike Jackson, Long spoke for the smaller, independent producers of the Gulf states, who commanded a phalanx of senators with more power in Congress on energy issues than the mistrusted majors.

During the climactic energy battle he viewed his fellow Southerner Jimmy Carter as a Southern liberal: "He did some good things that you couldn't have done at an earlier stage and managed to survive it politically. For example, he put the picture of Martin Luther King up there in the State Capitol Building."

But what Long did not see in the president was either the interest or the ability to engage in the kind of political horse-trading that was his way of getting things done in Congress and anathema to Jimmy Carter, who felt if he made the right decisions for the country, the public and Congress would follow.

Long served under a number of presidents, and his model was one who would say to a senator, " 'If you'll go as far as you can with me, I'll do equally well by you, and there's not much I wouldn't do for you, providing it's mutual.' . . . [With] that kind of understanding, you can just get a lot of good men to really get out there and do battle for you." At the same time, he made clear that a president has to understand that he can ask too much, at which point a senator has the right to say, "Mr. President, I can't do that." He expected to support a president when it was easy to do so, and on the very few occasions when the political cost of supporting a White House was too much for him, it was the president who would have to back away. He made himself sound like the most reasonable fellow, which in reality he was not when an issue touched his most treasured interests—incentives for his oil and gas industry and subsidies for his state's sugar industry. On the contrary, he preferred to do deals.

When President John F. Kennedy's trade bill was hung up in the Finance Committee and the administration was trying to stop a killer amendment proposed by the archconservative Harry Byrd of Virginia, Lyndon Johnson, then Kennedy's vice president, approached Long and asked him innocently: "Are you trying to keep that military base open at Fort Polk [Louisiana]? If you do what I'll tell you to do, you'll get the base open." Johnson then arranged an Oval Office meeting, advising the president in advance that both would benefit if "you help him with the military base, and he helps you where he can help you." Long talked about the military base, and Kennedy about the need for Long's support on the trade bill. But, recalled Long, "He wasn't hearing me [and] President Kennedy said, 'I don't understand what this trade bill has got to do with that military base.'"

Long then lectured the young president in Politics 101: "I think the votes on the committee are equally divided, leaving me out of it, and if I vote with you on that bill, it's going to come out the way you wanted it. And if I don't vote with you, it's going to come out the way Harry Byrd wants it. . . . All I want is Fort Polk to be open and kept open." Long remembers that Kennedy definitely did not like that but said, "Oh, I see your point." Long cast the decisive vote, and Fort Polk stayed open.

With Carter, no such transactional avenues were open, and the results were telling on the energy bill. Long felt that the president would have done far better if he had started off by saying, " 'I need your help, and I'll do anything I can to help you, provided it's mutual. Let me know what it is that you need; I'll try to see that it works out to your advantage; that we can get it for you. By contrast, I'd like to be in the position to call you when I need you and it's something you can do for me, and I'd hope you'd do it.' " But he found Carter was less willing to engage in such trades with Congress than any other president. It was not for lack of courting on the president's part, with private meals and a White House dinner including Carolyn Long and Rosalynn Carter.

But despite their shared Southern heritage, they might as well have been from different planets. As Long put it to me, "Frankly, the situation never got between us where I could really judge as to what extent he would be willing to do. I think he kind of liked to give the impression that he wasn't going to make any deal of any sort."[5]

But he never was given a chance to deal in the formative stages of the energy plan. Long was so frustrated at having been kept out of the loop that when Carter and Schlesinger were briefing members of Congress on the energy package before it was sent to Congress, Long rose to ask a question, and preceded it by announcing sarcastically, "I'm Russell Long, chairman of the Senate Finance Committee."[6]

Naturally one thinks of Lyndon Johnson, Long's model and the legendary majority leader with a Texas-size ego and a checkbook to underwrite it, with campaign contributions from supporters for senators who voted his way. But Byrd was no LBJ. Treasury Secretary Blumenthal, the administration's chief contact with Long, warned that the Senator was creating problems, and Carter passed that on to a Democratic leadership breakfast. Long wanted the wellhead tax revenues rebated to the energy companies; the president said he would agree to divert tax money for conservation—but not for the oil companies.[7]

Jackson's Energy Committee meanwhile approved only slightly diluted versions of conservation and solar energy provisions, but natural-gas pricing, the key to the program, was stuck there in a split of 9 votes to 9. That meant the gas-deregulation provision would be sent to the Senate without a firm committee recommendation, opening the way either to reviving it by compromise or amending it to death. Byrd suggested adding enough provisions to spread around rebates for consumers and research to attract more liberal votes and set off a titanic Senate debate marked by blocking maneuvers worthy of the game of professional football.

Carter, his frustration rising, publicly threatened to veto any bill that simply deregulated natural gas. Undeterred by the threat, oil-state senators introduced a deregulation bill as their lobbyists furiously lined up votes. Whereupon two liberal, proconsumer Democrats, Senators Howard Metzenbaum of Ohio and James Abourezk of South Dakota, began a filibuster. Metzenbaum was a wealthy businessman who became a consumer champion and bitter enemy of the oil and gas industry; tall, stoop shouldered, and white haired, he was a forceful opponent of deregulation. Abourezk was a Lebanese American who had a venomous dislike of the energy industry (and, it seemed, almost everyone else in the Senate).

With time running out on the first session of Congress, the administration was desperate to obtain something from the Senate that could be sent to a House-Senate Conference Committee to tilt the final version toward the House bill. On September 26 supporters of deregulation rounded up more than the sixty votes needed to end the filibuster, but Metzenbaum and Abourezk were not so easily squelched. They filed 508 amendments and began demanding roll-call votes, one after another, tying up the Senate for three days. They also constantly demanded quorum calls that forced a roundup of fifty-one senators, and they objected to every routine request for unanimous consent by which the Senate moves forward, however slowly. Tempers boiled over at their tactics—every one of which was embedded in the Senate's arcane rules. A round of administration-supported counteramendments was introduced the next day, whereupon Russell Long mounted a minifilibuster of his own against them. Metzenbaum and Abourezk resumed their filibuster, throwing all Senate business back into gridlock.[8]

Why did senators of both parties think they could roll Carter and get away with it? The Bert Lance affair had broken in the newspapers just as the Senate was taking up the bill, and it seemed obvious to the old Washington hands on our energy team that it created a perception of vulnerability. Lance's loss was incalculable, not only because he would have been just the man to work with the Senate barons from the South and Southwest like Long, but because the affair tarnished the president's reputation just when it had been enhanced by his victory in the House. It proved a major turning point for the administration—the first widely perceived public signal that Carter's presidency lacked a certain political acuity, that he would not be able to deliver on his promises because he would not play Washington's roughhouse politics.

The righteous aura that marked his "I'll never lie to you" campaign speeches had begun to crack when it became clear that Carter was insensitive to Washington's unforgiving balance between personal loyalty and practical politics. And once a leader is no longer seen as riding high and in command, his major initiatives are in trouble. Lance's departure sent the president's popularity down by more than ten points in the Gallup poll to just above 50 percent, a fact not lost on either the Senate's Old Bulls or the administration's worker bees. Both saw the system seizing up and began to sense that putting through Carter's ambitious programs was going to be harder than they thought. Carter himself soon came to realize this, too.[9]

Byrd called the president and promised that the Senate "will do better and I will help." Later that day Mondale called together Califano, Moore, Ham, and me for ideas on moving the Senate. Califano, a veteran of political battles as Johnson's domestic adviser, said the president needed to tell the American people that "lobbyists are taking over the Senate" and "deregulation of natural gas was a rip-off." He suggested putting out figures on how deregulation would hit individuals because that also would help shift the focus from Lance and show the president in charge. Carter followed this advice at his news conference, but wisely also decided to praise Byrd.[10] Stroking Byrd in public paid off.

Frustrated by the train wreck on the Senate floor, this master of Senate procedure now was determined to use all his arcane knowledge to see that the hundreds of remaining amendments were thrown overboard. First he drew on a parliamentary rule—"No dilatory motion or amendment or amendments not germane shall be in order"—to block the flow of the Metzenbaum-Abourezk amendments. Then he argued that the Senate's presiding officer was obliged to rule all such dilatory amendments out of order. Metzenbaum and Abourezk vociferously objected, but the fix was in for this highly unusual procedure. Byrd arranged for Mondale to arrive in the Senate chamber for the rare exercise of the vice president's constitutional position as presiding officer. His job was to gavel down the parade of Metzenbaum and Abourezk amendments one by one as out of order, as Byrd systemically called them up. Mondale dispatched the first thirty-three in a matter of a few minutes. Byrd remembered that "pandemonium broke loose" as the two senators screamed for recognition to appeal Mondale's ruling, which Byrd denied them. On appeal to the full Senate, they were flattened by a vote of 79 to 21, and their filibuster was over. Byrd and Mondale were in Byrd's words, "severely criticized for the extraordinary actions we had taken." A veteran of more than three decades in the Senate and its reigning historian, he called the filibuster on the natural-gas deregulation bill "the roughest filibuster I have ever experienced," even "more intense, and far more bitter than the 1964 civil rights filibuster."[11]

Abourezk expressed shock and indignation and declared: "Since I've been in politics I've been told that governments lie. One thing I never thought would happen is that Jimmy Carter would lie." This parliamentary steamroller was also criticized by a number of Democratic senators, and the victory came at a cost to Mondale's and Carter's reputation as well as Byrd's. They not only enraged their liberal allies but raised concerns about establishing a precedent for such strong-arm tactics. Carter himself lamented this in a call to Byrd a few days later: "I believe we used the wrong tactic. A little too abrasive. The Senate is not accustomed to that."[12] But it worked.

This uncertainty and inexperience was characteristic, not just of Carter himself but our entire White House staff; but the tactic was the only way to push the energy bill ahead although the result was anger that could be cut with a knife. Al Alm, the chief architect of the package, vividly recalled that the hard feelings "came within an inch of physical blows" by New Hampshire Democratic senator John Durkin in the cloakroom, where "these guys were just irrational on the subject [of natural gas]; it was crazy; everybody felt very strongly; it was rough stuff politically."[13] Worse, even after the filibuster was broken, the amendment deregulating natural gas was approved by the Senate, 50 to 46, similar to our long-abandoned campaign promise.

THE ROAD GROWS LONGER

By early October, Democrats and Republicans alike recognized that the president's energy program was in deep trouble, and as portions of it reached the Senate floor, the press began ridiculing it as "the moral equivalent of chaos." On October 6 the Senate approved a diluted conservation bill from the Energy Committee by an overwhelming vote of 86 to 7, while Long was making mincemeat of the House-passed tax proposals that represented the final leg of the energy plan. Throughout October his Finance Committee systematically rejected the president's Crude Oil Equalization Tax (COET), the tax on gas guzzlers, and the tax on the industrial use of oil and gas.

The only fiscal measure to survive the Senate Finance Committee was a tax credit to homeowners for insulating their homes or installing solar heat, and this expensive credit would benefit mainly high-income householders rather than poor people who needed cash subsidies to help them save energy to heat their modest homes. The defeats were due in part to the fact that, unable to agree among ourselves, the administration could never put together a clear and persuasive program of what we would do with the tax revenues. That made it easier for Long to argue that the money should be rebated to the producers as an incentive to drill rather than to the consumers as a protection against higher prices. During debate on the Senate floor, Long quipped, with a glint in his eye, "Just what do they think we are, a bunch of Houdinis on this Committee of Finance?" In fact he had designed a simple tax giveaway that would have been appreciated by the legendary escape artist.

What he was really doing was freeing his hands to cut a deal in the Senate-House Conference; he would compromise on the House-passed wellhead tax as long as enough of the revenue found its way back home to the producers. Stroking his oil and gas constituency in colorful but politically potent terms, he intoned: "The American people are not willing to pay more taxes unless they can expect to receive more energy. If all they are going to pay taxes for is a two-way ticket for their money to Washington and back, with Washington's expenses deducted on the one end, they are going to think we are a bunch of idiots to pass it, and vote us out of office for imposing it on them."[14]

The president meanwhile had begun to demonize the oil and gas indus-try in ways that were especially offensive to Long, who excoriated him for calling them war profiteers. As we observed to the president in his study,[15] Long had worked out a devilishly clever strategy. He had refused to bring any of the energy-tax measures to the floor to avoid an embarrassing defeat so that he could have a free hand to make a deal with representatives of the House in the closed Conference Committee. And his mastery was complete because he also controlled the members of his Senate Finance Committee, which gave him blanket authority to put all the tax measures in his pocket to deal on their behalf.

Long had also split the House and Senate Democratic leadership and turned them at least temporarily against the president. The anger burst out at a White House breakfast on October 13, when O'Neill complained to Carter: "You have proposed so much legislation, we can't handle it all. You made a lot of campaign promises and you keep sending up messages [de-manding Congressional action]." Then he turned to Byrd and said he had held his troops together and would also tie the House energy bill in one pack-age and refuse to go to conference "until we know what Long will do. We need to see the whole [Senate] package." Byrd, clearly irritated, shot back the Senate had passed four bills and "if we have to wait until Long finishes, we will have lost valuable time." Then he pointed out that despite the presi-dent's efforts to raise the alarm about our growing dependence on OPEC oil, he found it shocking that polls showed that almost half of all Ameri-cans did not know that the nation imported any oil at all.[16] We were under no illusions: The administration had no choice but to support Long's strat-egy if it wanted any bill at all, and we would not get one unless the House and Senate conferees accepted deregulation of natural gas.

As the start of the Senate-House Conference approached, the cabinet con-vened on October 17 in a meeting that was extraordinary for the precision of its agenda and astounding for its candid admissions by the president. He had finally arranged the order of battle with a great sense of urgency. "Suc-cess on many programs is tied to energy, as is my image as a leader," he told his cabinet, instructing them to work "as a unit" to help pass the energy pro-gram. He laid out a detailed plan for cabinet officers and their deputies to make one additional speech per week on energy. In their appeal for support they were to relate energy directly to their department's functions—transportation, defense, commerce, and so on. They were also tasked with persuading influential laymen in their states to contact their senators and argue for the program, and to make a list for Ham of senators and congressmen with whom they had "personal relationships." Showing his desperation, the president admonished his cabinet to do something he had never previously considered—tie federal grant money to votes: "Use your political influence. If they want something for their states, tie it to energy, and say 'Our success in the next three years depends on this.'"

He also instructed them to raise the international implications—for example, to emphasize that the bill was "crucial to Israel's security; that we should not be dependent upon Middle East oil." In the starkest terms I had ever heard him use, Carter laid his own legacy on the line: "If we get whipped on this, then incompetence and weakness will be perceived. This may be unfair, but this will be our image and it will become a reality."

Remarking—as history would show—that his administration's successes would be buried because he had launched so much legislation,[17] he promised to be more selective in setting priorities and be judged "by only a few key things in the next few years." Admitting that he "had slipped" in not meeting with the Senate committees, as he had with the House, Carter canceled a long-scheduled foreign trip to make a full-court press—in vain, as it turned out.

Then he made a startling admission I had never heard before or since from this supremely confident man: "The issues before us are so complicated, it's gotten past me." To soothe the president's feelings, Strauss added, "Frankly, no one understands it." Nevertheless his top aides could provide little news that would make him or anyone else at the meeting feel better. Budget Director McIntyre estimated that the tax incentives and other giveaways that Long had attached to the Senate bill would add $25 to $35 billion to the budget deficit. Schultze warned that without energy reform, oil imports could raise the trade deficit by $100 billion a year, risking "a substantial deterioration of the dollar."

Struck by the way his economic adviser had framed the threat, Carter asked him and Blumenthal to "draft a paragraph and get it to Stu, without causing a run on the dollar." Blumenthal quickly came up with more diplomatic language: "Just say that without the energy bill, the problems of the dollar will get worse." To close the exhaustive and exhausting cabinet meeting, the president barked out our assignments in staccato form like the naval officer he once was: "Stu and Jim are the technical people; Frank [Moore] is the key person with Congress; Jack Watson will help you schedule speeches; Bob Strauss will call you with ideas; and Ham will coordinate the entire effort."[18]

THE CONFERENCE COMMITTEE FROM HELL

The Conference Committee of House and Senate members held its first meeting on the complex energy bill the following day. Their task was to resolve the differences between the two chambers in a compromise package for an up-or-down vote, and then send it on to the president for his signature or veto. For interest groups, a conference committee represents their final opportunity to bend important legislation. They usually start with their maximum demands; the more exalted their motives, the more unbending they tend to be. Business, by contrast, can usually make a rough reckoning of how deeply any compromise will affect costs and profits, and then act accordingly. So can officials and experts, both elected and appointed, because they live with the classic dictum that politics is the art of the possible.

But here was a conference from hell, perhaps the lengthiest, most difficult, most bizarre in congressional history. Agreements among the conferees were reached by paper-thin majorities and then abandoned. Egos clashed over petty peeves as well as grand issues of policy. Angry words were exchanged, and unholy and unlikely alliances were formed to block action. Compromises were cobbled together to attract coalitions by lengthening or shortening the transition period for deregulation or slicing the wellhead tax rebate by different formulas to attract regional votes. None lasted very long. Republicans and producer-state Democrats banded together against compromises ending federal price controls too slowly for the oil patch, while liberal Democrats and consumer groups believed the sky would fall if controls were removed at all. Estimates of the impacts of the many different proposals varied wildly, and even Schlesinger's figures moved dramatically as the conference droned on, month after month. This was Congress at its worst.

Organizing this conference was especially difficult. The gap between the

two chambers was as wide as the state of Texas. The House wanted all conference members to consider the entire package, while the Senate, with its
piecemeal approach, wanted a separate sub-group to consider each bill in
the form it had been passed by the upper chamber. The first compromise
was the organization of informal groups to work on provisions that did not
involve taxation, while the tax measures would be considered separately by
members representing the Senate Finance Committee and House Ways and
Means Committee. More than forty conferees debated the five sections of
the program, and they included many barons of both chambers. In a highly
unusual move symbolizing the stalemate over natural gas, Senator Jackson
named as conferees his entire Energy Committee—eighteen members who
had split into equal halves in voting on whether to continue federal controls.

The president began his efforts by promising the House conferees that
he would make no deals with the Senate on which the House did not agree—a
promise he would not be able to honor in full because he would be forced
to swing toward the Senate's gas deregulation if he wanted any bill at all.
He also told House members his energy plan would achieve a budget surplus
of $7 billion by 1985—so that in the long run it was "cheaper to conserve."
It sounded good in theory, but the decades-long natural-gas impasse was
too high a bar for it to work in practice. When Senator Bentsen came up
with a rebate formula tied to a new government agency to lend money to
the oil and gas industry, Representative Toby Moffett of Connecticut complained bitterly that it would all be at the expense of consumers." The president
retorted, "Tell me if you see this happening; I won't hurt consumers." He
was depending on the Senate meeting the House halfway and assured the
House conferees that "the Senate was acting in good faith and its reputation is at stake." He would eventually have to eat those words.[19]

At the end of another grueling day fighting the energy wars, Mondale
and the top White House staff members met to discuss the priorities for the
coming year. But with great frustration the vice president bemoaned the focus on energy when "the American people are concerned only with jobs and
inflation."[20]

Carter had to continue walking a tightrope at the October 25 Democratic leadership breakfast, which this time included the opposing senators,
Russell Long and Scoop Jackson, who quickly engaged in a dispute over

energy taxes. Said Long: "Let's get a bill to conference and not fight our battles on the Senator floor now." Aware that getting a bill was a do-or-die test for Carter, Long, who also knew he held most of the high cards, promised not to sign on to a compromise that the president would veto, but that was more blather for show than substance. While Byrd confidently explained that the conference had been divided into two groups, one to deal only with taxes, Long refused to convene his tax group until he got what he wanted on natural gas—and that took almost another year. This high-wire act was also played out with congressional liberals.

The next day Toby Moffett and Bob Eckhardt led a delegation of proregulation, proconsumer liberal congressmen into the Cabinet Room. Emotionally overwrought and strident, Moffett warned the president that if "you cave in to Long, you will lose the House."[21] Put on the defensive, Carter told the liberals he shared their beliefs, and on the bill itself he promised, "I won't betray you; I will tell you of all changes." But in the end, to get any energy bill at all, he had to do just that and agree to a modified form of deregulation, despite all his efforts to deploy his cabinet and appeal over the heads of Congress.

Then some of the senior staff decided we needed to intensify the president's meetings with business leaders, and we brought the idea to Commerce Secretary Juanita Kreps. Schultze said it would be better to have him meet less frequently, but spend more time at the meetings, since he tended to "breeze in" for only half an hour and then leave. This prompted a broader criticism from Strauss, which could be extended to Carter's entire approach to the presidency. He agreed that thirty minutes was not enough time and told us that he had failed to persuade him to spend a full hour with groups he brought in to sell the Tokyo Round agreement on international trade. Strauss said in frustration, "He needs to spend more time seeing people and less on learning the details of every issue."[22] This was blowing in the wind. Immersion in details, for better or worse, was Jimmy Carter's modus operandi.

It was not that he was unable to move the government in the direction he wanted; he definitely could do that and had already done so with a number of bills. At a Democratic leadership breakfast on November 1, O'Neill ticked off these accomplishments. Tom Foley of Washington, an extraordinarily wise legislator who would later become Speaker, pleaded for "issues we can win on" so there would be a strong record going into the midterm elections. But Carter did not think that way: A dogged political campaigner, he separated politics from policy in the White House to pursue what he thought was the right policy and was always suspicious of the link between the two. And when he latched onto an issue like energy that he viewed with a moral dimension, he could be so tenacious that other priorities could fade from view and get stuck in a legislative logjam.[23]

One sad personal experience emphasized this as much as any success: a final appearance at the breakfast by one of the party's most liberal, most outstanding, and one of Carter's most supportive legislators, Hubert Humphrey, who was dying of cancer. Rising to the occasion, and mustering as much strength as his emaciated body allowed, he warned that the Republicans were going to try to create divisions between the Congress and the president on energy to "show we don't know how to govern and can't get anything done. Mr. President, you need to scare the daylights out of them." His last words were to urge the president to continue to drive home to the American people the critical importance of the energy bill, or "we will be bankrupt from importing more and more foreign oil." When he finished there was not a dry eye among those tough politicians.

As the meeting ended in the small White House dining room, I told him how proud I had been to work in his 1968 presidential campaign, and he replied in words that still resonate with me, "Stu, I always tell people you worked for me." I choked up later when he called me shortly before he died to thank me again. His death also deprived Carter of a liberal champion who could have helped him counter Ted Kennedy's eventual challenge.

More important, seeing that Humphrey's days were numbered, Carter took the extraordinary step of inviting him to the Oval Office to sit in the president's chair that he told him he deserved to occupy, and then flew with him on Marine One for a night at Camp David—something he had never had as LBJ's vice president.

Then suddenly—and to his great credit—J. Bennett Johnston, the junior senator from Louisiana and the chairman of Jackson's Subcommittee on Energy and Power, came forward with a natural-gas compromise. Although tough minded, moderate, and articulate, he was a most unlikely dealmaker as a representative of an oil and gas state—and even more so because he felt that Carter had repeatedly snubbed him.[24] Johnston had chaired Jimmy Carter's

1976 campaign in Louisiana because he wanted to see a Southerner in the White House, and his support was a factor in Carter narrowly carrying the state. But when Carter got to the White House, Johnston lamented he never reached out—did not invite Johnston to White House social occasions as Nixon had; never once contacted him on the energy bill; and even blocked Johnston's nominee for U.S. attorney for Louisiana because someone spread a false rumor that the man had Mafia connections. Johnston was offended and later discovered that other Democrats suffered the same treatment, including Joe Biden, senator from Delaware and later vice president in the Obama administration, who had been one of the first to come out for Carter.[25]

But as a good Democrat and a public servant, Johnston tried to break the deadlock, using the leverage he was given by Scoop Jackson, who had put him in charge of the Senate energy conferees, because Jackson was more interested in military affairs as a member of the Armed Services Committee. With the Christmas recess looming, Johnston won the backing of a fellow Southern Democrat, Wendell Ford of Kentucky—a coal state—to propose a compromise that would decontrol natural-gas prices over six years. They called it their "Christmas Turkey," which unfortunately is what it turned out to be. Left and right denounced it.

Then Scoop took his revenge on Johnston for upstaging him—and perhaps on Carter, too. Without explanation he bolted out of Washington for the Christmas break at his vacation house near Palm Springs, California, and refused to agree to the compromise in his absence. Schlesinger, with Scoop Jackson's close friend Charles Curtis, head of the Federal Energy Regulatory Commission, in tow, to bolster his case, flew to see his mentor, who told him, "I am through trying to legislate about natural gas. We [will] never pass any natural gas legislation."[26] Schlesinger persuaded him to try again, and it worked, or so it seemed, because the conferees resumed their meetings in January; but the road was long and hard. Schlesinger believed the real reason that Jackson wrung the neck of Johnston's Christmas turkey was a reporter's account of a dismissive remark by Ham when he was asked about the Senate's role in the energy bill: "Oh, we don't care about Jackson, we licked his ass in [the primary in] Pennsylvania."[27] Ham never called to apologize for the remark or to deny it.

While these stories underscore the apolitical nature of the president's approach, failure to attend to Johnson's home-state needs or stroke Jackson's towering ego could be traced to the White House political operation. It is not enough to be both visionary and right on policy; it is also important to operate in the hothouse of Washington politics, where small slights add up to big problems. Politics in general, and presidential politics in particular, is a contact sport. While there are times when a challenge must be met with a fight, it is also essential to build personal relationships with deft touches such as invitations to small dinners, drinks in the private White House quarters, birthday and anniversary phone calls, notes of thanks, tennis games on the White House court followed by locker-room time to schmooze, trips on Air Force One, and many other personal gestures whose principal value lies in the fact that they come from the President of the United States. These were few and far between in the Carter White House.

After the Christmas recess, the president called me on January 25[28] and said Congressman John Dingell, the formidable Michigan Democrat whose principal interest was protecting the auto industry, had asked the White House to set up a "quick turnaround mechanism" to deal with compromises. Negotiations, it was said, were reaching a critical point, and Carter directed me and my staff to work with Schlesinger's to produce answers to congressional questions within fifteen minutes. Schlesinger kept insisting that the president hold his fire with Congress so he could apply the prestige of his office only at the moment of compromise, when it would be necessary to sell a complete package to both houses. He thought that moment might be near when Scoop seemed to throw his weight behind phasing in natural-gas deregulation by 1985—but that was not soon enough for the Republicans.

Schlesinger assured the cabinet on February 7 that the latest compromise looked like it could win approval, but Scoop scuttled it yet again—this time by leaving on a trip to China. A frustrated Carter was forced to tell the Democratic leadership that "I am staying impatiently aloof" from the energy negotiations.[29] It was hard to escape the conclusion that Scoop was trying to sabotage a deal, whether in anger at Carter or Long or simply because he had opposed deregulation of natural gas throughout his career and wanted to postpone the inevitable as long as possible. But, when nine senators agreed on a bipartisan compromise and presented it to their House colleagues on March 9, the man who blocked the deal was Dingell.

CARTER RECONSIDERS HIS APPROACH

The impasse prompted the president to reconsider the way he was governing. He announced at the March 13 cabinet meeting that he was contemplating holding the meetings every other Monday instead of every week, because "at times I get bored."[30] Vance agreed, and Brzezinski suggested choosing specific topics for certain cabinet sessions, but the president rejected this, preferring to discuss what was relevant that day. Housing Secretary Pat Harris suggested that instead of weekly meetings the president meet separately with each member of the cabinet, once each quarter. This seemed reasonable because, as I noted on my pad, "Cabinet Secretaries saw JC very little" anyway. Juanita Kreps made a telling criticism: She said she "shared his boredom [and] proposed less reporting of trivia and getting more direction of the priorities of the president." There were also rumblings close to the top that would reverberate much later in an administration shake-up that seemed close to panic.

On the night of March 14,[31] we had an unusual meeting at Jody Powell's home, with only Jody and his wife, Nan, Ham Jordan and his wife, Nancy, and me and Fran. It lasted from 9:30 p.m. to midnight, and we discussed Ham's plan to shake up the White House staff and the president's desire to put the cabinet and agencies under tighter control to support his priorities, instead of their own narrow departmental goals. Clearly Carter's original plan of decentralized cabinet government was not working; he had overreacted to the discredited model of the powerful Nixon White House and as a result was leading a government whose goals were too diffuse and results too uncertain, and without a chief of staff to try to develop a coherent theme. Earlier that same day Strauss had called me to urge that the administration bring in a few experienced Washington heavyweights from previous Democratic administrations. "People are turning Carter off and have no respect for him. I feel his presidency will be gone without action before the summer," said Strauss.[32]

Carter himself shared Strauss's worries. On Sunday and Monday, April 16, he held an extraordinary stocktaking with senior White House staff and the cabinet at Camp David. I doubt any president before or since has held such a frank and open assessment of his own presidency. Unsmiling, he began by making bullet points from a small notepad on his progress in international affairs and said he believed no previous president, including Franklin Roosevelt in the midst of the Depression, had "ever put forward a series of comprehensive efforts like we have: the Middle East, Panama, Africa, energy, urban policy, tax reform, water policy, Alaska lands, federal lands, irrigation supplies, national health insurance." But he underscored that because "the country has shifted to a more conservative attitude, everything we do is contrary to people's inclinations."

Next came his own self-critique, rare in any president in front of his own appointees: White House decisions came too slowly; Washington experience was lacking; and staff did not communicate well. He then turned on his cabinet, listing a series of complaints—first that "at times you don't support White House policy, when I make final decisions contrary to what you recommend." And further, that he and the White House staff did not always receive advance notice of controversial decisions made by cabinet departments, and did not respond expeditiously to White House requests for action or comment. Finally, in as blunt an admission as I had ever heard him make, he pointed to the midterm elections in November and demanded that every one of them "bend over backwards to help Democrats—to the second mile. If we lose thirty-five votes in the Congress, we'll be castrated."

Then he turned the tables and asked the cabinet to critique his own performance. This was unique and rightly so, because the president should never allow his subordinates to criticize him in front of their peers. Schlesinger began by saying that from his experience with several presidents, "You spend more time on detail than any president in our history. I suggest you spend less time on detail, and use your time wisely." I knew it was his governing style to be as well informed at any meeting as his interlocutors, but Schlesinger's critique went further: It was really a plea for the president to spend more time thinking broadly about his ultimate goals and meeting with leaders of Congress and his own cabinet. Strauss was more direct and much rougher: "I've never seen an administration with so many people willing to speak negatively about it." Meanwhile, he continued, Congress had been sent so many proposals that the president was "positioned in too many places where you'll come out a loser." Schultze, the top White House economic adviser who had earlier served as budget director to that relentless taskmaster Lyndon Johnson, told Carter he was "not tough enough on us." Mondale also urged him to "act tougher." Agriculture Secretary Bob Berglund said that presidents can govern from "two motivating factors, faith and fear," and while Nixon used the latter, Carter had swung too far in the other direction and needed "to crack political heads."

A common thread of criticism was the lack of a theme for the presidency, which made it harder to let the public know how many of Carter's campaign promises he had actually achieved. Commerce Secretary Kreps said everything should be focused on creating jobs and cutting inflation. What was surprising was that only two participants used the opportunity to push their own agendas. Although Brzezinski spoke broadly, saying that the administration's "historical profile is not clear," he really meant that Carter did not take consistent positions, particularly toward the Soviet Union. The cabinet member with the strongest record in pressing his agenda and a press operation actively publicizing it was Joe Califano. He told Carter that while candid communication with the president was important, cabinet members "need friends whom we can call in rough times." Carter eventually fired him.

Ham, to this day the best political mind I have ever encountered, was remarkably frank in front of the cabinet. "We've got an active Democratic president when the mood of the country is passive and nonpartisan. We don't have an obvious and pressing agenda. The public consensus is that this president is not tough and we're not managing well."

I added my two cents: "We have tried too much, too fast, too comprehensively, in foreign and domestic affairs. Moving this way is contrary to the way Congress operates, and makes it difficult for the American people to understand our agenda." I noted that he had a particularly difficult challenge because the American people "had voted for a better not a larger government," and that the country was in a conservative mood. While he talked tough on inflation and spending, we were negotiating an expensive national health care plan and other programs to satisfy Democratic constituency groups.

The president concluded with a Carteresque self-awareness that his domestic policy themes "are not clear in my mind." He continued, "I feel like a referee between the cabinet and the White House staff. Ninety percent of the problems can be resolved by the staff knowing the cabinet better. Once I sign off on a policy, I expect you to carry it out. . . . I could see a deterioration of our esteem in the public eye, and I don't disagree with the public. What has bothered me is a lack of cohesion and team spirit, which is almost inevitable. We have a damn good administration, a fine cabinet, a good staff. I wish you knew each other better."[33] He closed by stating, "I will try to be meaner."

Shortly afterward he summarized the event by saying he had "frank and brutal talks" with his cabinet and White House Staff and admitting that "we were greenhorns when we came into office."[34] I believe that relations between the White House and the cabinet improved, but this was temporary and later provoked a much greater shake-up, again induced by the pervasive political hurdles in forming an energy policy with so many conflicting interests, and by the lack of an overarching theme for the Carter administration that was never solved.

A FINAL ATTEMPT TO FOIL
THE SENATE GRAVEDIGGER

While Carter's mode of governance, indeed his very election as president, represented at least partly a reaction against the Watergate scandals, Congress had been affected, too. In a post-Watergate paroxysm, House-Senate Conference Committee sessions were opened to the public. This sounds good in theory but in practice was highly counterproductive. Lawmakers are reluctant to make tough compromises in public instead of through the give-and-take that is usually possible only in private sessions, because it may involve sacrificing constituent interests to get to "yes."

Ultimately all elected representatives are accountable, and many political careers have been ended by a recorded vote in the public instead of the provincial interest. The energy conferees met in an open forum in front of a standing-room-only crowd. One reporter likened it to the Mad Hatter's tea party in *Alice in Wonderland*.[35] To me it was more like a Gilbert and Sullivan comic opera, except that it was no laughing matter. Of course the senior members arranged in characteristic form to meet in private for serious negotiations, whereupon the full House of Representatives voted overwhelmingly against the private meetings. Having run through their public performance, the conferees continued meeting in private after Lud Ashley pointed out that these gatherings were informal and did not violate House rules.

Pressure mounted for a deal before Carter would attend the annual Group of Seven Summit of Industrial Nations in July to discuss energy and the world economy. By the end of March, Moore and his congressional lobbyists felt we could wait no longer to involve the president. So on April 11 the president met in the White House with the leading energy conferees, urging a compromise. Ashley, the leading House negotiator, warned ominously: "If this is not resolved this week, I will end negotiations."[36]

Several days later, on April 20, a dozen of the forty-three conferees met for thirteen consecutive hours in two small third-floor rooms in the Capitol, equidistant from the Senate and House chambers, until 3:30 a.m. the following day, on natural-gas pricing, which had taken on near-theological dimensions. Schlesinger worked with them tirelessly, jacket off and tie undone, pushing them at every stage, proposing new compromises, and serving as a delivery service for proposals and counterproposals from one side of the Capitol to the other. They doggedly returned at 11:00 a.m. the next morning for another two-hour session, and at 1:25 p.m. there was a burst of applause. It was as if a new pope had been elected, minus the white smoke. I can remember the elation in the White House: The president was going to win, and with a deregulation proposal much like his 1976 campaign pledge.

But no, he wasn't: It was no sale among the full complement of House conferees. A handful of liberals damned it as a sellout to the oil and gas industry, while two congressmen from the oil patch feared that somehow the deal would extend federal controls on gas into their unregulated states. This time the White House was no longer supine. Ham had brought in Anne Wexler as public liaison to mobilize outside support; she was a seasoned Connecticut politician who had run Carter's Washington campaign office with her husband, Joe Duffy. Anyone who questioned whether the Carter White House, now two years into the presidency, had its act together, needed to look no further than this operation, as it reached out to key individuals and groups for the balance of the Carter term to support his initiatives. The president, as I put it in my private note, "goes political." He told the cabinet to work with Ham and Frank Moore to put energy on the top of their agenda.[37]

But at a Sunday-afternoon meeting in his study, while he complimented me for making his job easier, he expressed exasperation that "it is almost impossible to get my points across with the negative press."[38] A reinvigorated White House lobbying team managed to quiet the fears of the oil-patch congressmen. Finally, on May 24, the dam broke. The House conferees narrowly voted for a compromise. Now the unimaginable happened: Defeat was snatched from the jaws of victory by an embarrassing process of entropy during the period from May 24 to July 31. It took that long for the staff and its lawyers to convert the complex compromise into legal language for a bill on which the Senate and House could vote.

Politics is part of nature and like nature abhors a vacuum. Interest groups used the delay to try to destroy the hard-won compromise. The same odd partners that had made it so difficult to achieve a consensus made common cause against the Conference Report—the Chamber of Commerce, the AFL-CIO, and the Consumer Federation of America, which normally do not agree on the time of day, joined to try to kill it. When the conferees read the final language, defections began almost immediately. Members claimed it did not represent what they had agreed to in May. Three of the thirteen House votes reversed their positions on totally opposite readings of the bill. The situation was as bad in the Senate, where four conferees who had approved the May 24 compromise now opposed it.

None of their reasons were new, and the process devolved into a theater of the absurd. On June 7, when presenting the staff's detailed language on an obscure provision defining an "essential agricultural user" as one who produced animal feed using natural gas, Senator Metzenbaum argued that this would protect producers of dog and cat food, which was hardly in the national interest. Informed by the staff that this provision applied to essential agriculture such as beef production, Metzenbaum still insisted that dog- and cat-food producers did not deserve such special protection. What about food for Alaskan huskies? asked Senator John Durkin of New Hampshire. Not to be outdone, Senator Clifford Hansen of Wyoming exclaimed that because of their importance, the food of sheepdogs should also be excluded. The House conference chairman, Harley Staggers, provoked gales of laughter when he told Metzenbaum he opposed his amendment because there were too many dog and cat owners in his district. Such was the nature of the parting gift from the Congress of the United States to the president as he prepared to negotiate at the highest level with the nation's economic partners at the Group of Seven Summit of Industrial Nations.[39]

9

ENERGY AND THE DOLLAR
AT THE BONN SUMMIT

Diplomacy at the highest level directly intruded on our domestic troubles with energy reform. At the 1978 summit, the goal was a grand bargain to help stabilize and relaunch the industrial world's economy toward recovery from the oil shocks of the first part of the decade. This year the summit was to be held in Bonn, Germany, in mid-July under the chairmanship of West Germany's tough chancellor, Helmut Schmidt, an experienced and respected former finance and defense minister known at home as *Der Macher*—someone who could get things done. Since the first oil shock in 1973, the Germans had drastically reduced energy usage by conservation. The French had long ago taken another road to conserving oil through a national program of nuclear energy that would eventually supply more than three-quarters of their electric power.

Americans had the world's largest appetite for energy and as such were the drivers of world oil prices; our closest allies urgently wanted to know what we were doing to conserve. The United States paid foreign producers in dollars for crude oil imports, and this sent our foreign accounts deeply into the red. In only two years our current accounts had switched from plus to minus by $30 billion. The law of supply and demand applies to currencies as well as goods, so the prospect of an endless flood of dollars circulating around the world affected their value. As the dollar dropped, imported goods became more expensive and boosted domestic inflation. This chain of financial events added a threating international dimension that increasingly overshadowed our deadlocked domestic energy debate.

As the U.S. currency declined dramatically, the German and Japanese central banks had to mop up the flood of cheap dollars or watch their own currencies skyrocket and price their exports out of world markets. Our allies blamed one thing for this spiral: subsidized low U.S. oil prices that encouraged energy profligacy and in turn drew in more OPEC oil. From 1972 to 1977, the cost of U.S. oil imports climbed ninefold from $5 billion to $45 billion. The contrast with the other industrialized countries was dramatic: Their oil imports had actually declined. Treasury Secretary Blumenthal was most concerned in expressing to the president that our increasing dependence on foreign oil was accelerating the slide of the dollar.[1]

Nowhere was the institution of the annual summit written into any national law or treaty. It developed after 1971, when Nixon cut the link between the dollar and gold that had served as the financial foundation of postwar stability. The system was devised in 1944 by the wartime Allies at a resort hotel in Bretton Woods, New Hampshire, but was beginning to unravel after almost thirty years of unparalleled prosperity. Liberal-minded statesmen felt the need for a forum to coordinate the economic policies of the world's principal trading countries. From secluded meetings of finance ministers, it quickly evolved into a traveling jamboree of the leaders of the seven leading industrial democracies, representing three-quarters of the world's economic output, with the world's press in tow. In the early weeks of his administration, with only a few months to prepare for his first summit in London in 1977, Carter sent Mondale to Bonn and Tokyo, backed by senior specialists in international economics, to persuade both countries to join the United States as "locomotives" stimulating their own and in turn the international economy. They argued this could be done with only minimal inflation, but this fell on deaf ears with Schmidt, whose thinking was shaped by Germany's traditional fear of inflation and an economic orthodoxy that persists to this day.

Conventional economic wisdom in Germany still holds that inflation *causes* unemployment rather than helping add jobs by stimulating the economy. The German chancellor, who had presided over his country's continuing postwar prosperity, also resented being lectured by what he considered inexperienced American academics. Schmidt had also openly supported Ford against Carter in the 1976 election. He told the visiting Americans, "We owe a lot to Bill Simon"—Ford's hard-money, free-market treasury secretary from Wall Street. To which Mondale shot back: "Yes, we owe Bill Simon everything. Without him we wouldn't have won the election."[2]

The Mondale mission was not an auspicious start. The G7's first attempt to coordinate its policies got under way at the London summit, and the U.S. fielded an experienced team of economic policymakers, all followers of the intellectual father of Bretton Woods, the great British economist John Maynard Keynes. The G7 summits brought out the best in Carter, even humor. He joked that swashbuckling trade negotiator Bob Strauss, who was negotiating tariffs on shoes in London, had been spotted at a swanky London club, and had left only his shoes after the performance.[3]

What Bonn wanted from Washington was not a class in Economics 101 but action to raise U.S. oil prices to the world levels that the others were paying. Until that happened, European commitments to juice their economies and Japanese pledges to do the same and open the country to foreign goods and investment were barely worth the paper they were written on in the final communiqué. The three so-called locomotive countries committed themselves to specific growth targets between 5 and 6 percent, but only America came close to its target, and as German and Japanese trade surpluses mounted, the dollar continued to drop, and mutual finger-pointing increased.

Carter knew he had to try again at the Bonn summit of 1978, or America's role as the world's only growth engine would cause severe distortions to our economy. He had hoped to have his energy program passed into law before the two-day meeting in Bonn on July 16–17. Carter tried to force congressional action by arguing he would be embarrassed and the reputation of the United States diminished if he had to go to Bonn empty-handed, and more practically, that the dollar would continue to plummet. He warned senators in a letter that each percentage point that the dollar declined added one-tenth of one percent to the consumer price index. An energy bill, he argued, would boost the value of the dollar by cutting oil imports and reducing our current account deficit.

French president Valéry Giscard d'Estaing weighed in just before the summit with a warning directed straight at the congressional conferees: "At the present time, an important reduction in [U.S.] oil imports is the precondition for an improvement in the world economy." This sentiment, somewhat exaggerated as it was, offered Carter another avenue to argue for completion of his energy bill: American leadership and the health of the global economy. It also turned Tip O'Neill's famous adage that "all politics is local" on its head: Domestic politics took second place to obligations imposed by global economic forces. But Congress ignored the international dimension and left him with one hand tied behind his back. Meanwhile the dollar fell to record lows, but Congress did not see any connection to its own dilatory behavior. The American team had attempted to obtain leverage at the London summit to pressure Congress to act; now the leverage would be turned against us. We would now have to adjust our own policies to the realities in the rest of the world. That was the essential meaning of policy coordination at the summit, but our members of Congress tend to shrug off the interests of other countries when they impinge on our own.[4]

Carter thus took on another challenge of changing attitudes at home, but this time he had a strategy. From the very first, he knew that Schmidt would be key. So just before his own inauguration, Carter phoned the German chancellor to emphasize that he sought cooperation and consensus with Germany. In office, he appointed Henry Owen as his personal representative to the group of senior officials who prepared the agenda and negotiated what each government was prepared to agree. This group was known as the Sherpas, after the legendary native guides to the summits of the Himalayan mountains. Owen first met Carter through the Trilateral Commission and was director of foreign-policy studies at the Brookings Institution when he joined the government. His white hair and grandfatherly demeanor belied a mind and manner of speech of great precision, and altogether he was the ideal choice because he also was fluent in French and German. Carter's principal opponent, said Owen, was Schmidt—"the only leader who didn't respect him." So Carter's and Owen's strategy had to be based on surrounding and isolating this difficult and egotistical man who was deeply skeptical about the upstart former Georgia governor who was telling Germany to abandon its prudent values of thrift and to print money.[5]

Alone among the G7 countries, and to the great anger of the Europeans and Japan, the United States still supplied about two-thirds of its energy needs from domestic sources—and at prices that were controlled by a complex system to protect the American consumer from the full effects of OPEC's huge price increases. This system, developed (ironically) in the conservative, free-market Republican Nixon administration, encouraged consumption at artificially low prices and thus greater dependence on imported oil. By contrast the Europeans and Japan had allowed their domestic oil prices to rise to the world price level effectively set by OPEC.

Carter's energy plan was stalled in Congress, but he was not the only major player with tight political constraints at home. They also pinched Schmidt, proud, sometimes petulant, but always brilliant; his European partner Giscard d'Estaing, tall and lean, balding, and with the imperious carriage of a French nobleman (which he actually was not); the cautious Japanese prime minister, Takeo Fukuda; James Callaghan, the large-framed British prime minister, whose sparkling personality earned him the nickname "Sunny Jim," but belied his country's condition as the sick man of Europe after the collapse of the pound only two years before. Schmidt, the leader of the Social Democratic Party, labored under Germany's historical fear of the Weimar Republic inflation that discredited its democracy and helped pave the way for the rise of Hitler.

His coalition partner, Economics Minister Count Otto von Lambsdorff, leader of the probusiness, market-oriented Free Democratic Party, was an even more outspoken champion of economic orthodoxy. (Twenty-five years later Lambsdorff was my negotiating partner during the Clinton administration for a $5 billion Holocaust agreement with Germany). The general view of the German economic institutes was 180 degrees different from the Carter administration's reigning Keynesian theory of stimulating a lagging economy with deficit spending. It is important to recognize that early in the administration, there was a broad consensus among mainstream economists of both parties as well as business and organized labor that a stimulus package was essential even though Carter's instincts were entirely more conservative and his aim was achieving a balanced budget.

As Bonn approached, it became clear that Germany and Japan would badly miss the targets to which they had committed in London the previous year. This posed a dilemma for Schmidt as the host. German growth in mid-1977 was an anemic 1.2 percent. At his home in Hamburg, he had told a small group of advisers he would be *blamiert* (shamed) in front of the fellow G7 leaders he would be hosting. He therefore laid the groundwork for a new stimulus package, mostly tax cuts, that passed the Bundestag in the autumn of 1977. But even in the following summit year of 1978, German growth reached only half of his London pledge of 5 percent, while U.S. GDP grew 5.5 percent for 1977, the only country to come even close to its target. In fact the United States was in a sweet spot: Unemployment dropped to a three-year low of 6.4 percent, and inflation in the second half of 1977 moderated to 4.5 percent. (If only this could have been frozen for the next three years, this book might be discussing a second term for Carter in the White House.)

Owen and his fellow Sherpas met several times to try to reach agreement in three areas before the summit began: economic stimulus, U.S. oil prices, and global trade talks. Divisions between the United States and Germany were so sharp that when Blumenthal visited Bonn in February, he suggested Carter might skip the summit entirely unless there was some prior agreement for Germany to stimulate its economy. Schmidt certainly knew this was a bluff, but still privately promised Blumenthal that Germany would move "if you do your part" on energy prices. Though Callaghan worried that a deal only between Germany and America would have dangerous implications for the global economy as well as his own reelection, he then took on the role of honest broker between Schmidt and Carter. Callaghan first suggested what moving parts were needed to mesh together in this complex global game.[6] He visited Bonn and Washington in mid-March to sell a deal on German economic growth in return for raising American oil prices to world levels.

He delivered the message to the president and then met with Owen and Richard Cooper, the State Department's brilliant undersecretary for economic affairs and former Yale provost. Callaghan, he recalled, emphasized that "of course the Germans must expand, and of course the Japanese have to expand, but you Americans have to put something into the pot. You've got to give Schmidt something he can carry away." That something was of course an end to federal price controls on crude oil.[7]

At lunch with Callaghan and Carter in the Cabinet Room, they agreed that the summit would have to produce a set of interlocking commitments, with the economically weaker countries—Britain, France, and Italy—

recommitting themselves to meet their London summit growth targets; Germany stimulating its economy; the United States raising its oil prices to world levels; and concessions for a successful conclusion of the Tokyo Round of trade negotiations, now in their fifth year. But Schmidt remained a major obstacle, and he was getting farther out on a limb by resisting more economic expansion while German opinion was already beginning to change as economic conditions worsened. When Lambsdorff visited Washington, Owen told him, "This whole thing won't work unless Schmidt is willing to play, and I don't want—and I am sure the president doesn't want—to have a summit which is a failure." Lambsdorff assured him that he favored stimulus and promised: "I'm going to go around the country making speeches about this and rousing the business community to demand tax cuts, and that will put the heat on Schmidt"—a remarkable role for Schmidt's own coalition-government partner.[8]

Now it was time for Owen to see Schmidt. So early in April he traveled to the chancellor's office in Bonn and conveyed a clear message from Carter: "Frankly, we don't want to have a summit unless it is a success, and it can't be a success unless you're prepared to follow an expansionist policy." He then handed Schmidt Carter's personal letter making the point more tactfully. But he also knew Schmidt well enough to say that "you don't want to be too tactful with Schmidt." In any event the point was not lost on Schmidt that as the G7 host, he would suffer a grievous political blow if the summit he was to chair on home ground turned out to be a failure. He promptly volleyed the ball back into our court, telling Owen: "I am prepared to follow an expansionist policy, but there is a price for it, and the price has to be oil decontrol on your part."[9]

When Owen returned to Washington, he went directly to a meeting in the windowless, supersecure White House Situation Room in the basement of the West Wing. Everyone was nervous about whether he had made a deal over their heads, and while he assured us he had made no deal, we would nevertheless have to confront a demand by the allies to decontrol oil prices, because without our commitment Schmidt would not commit to stimulating the German economy.

A serious split developed in the administration over how we would fulfill our part of the bargain. In retrospect, I was on the wrong side of the argument, but it was a close call. The internationalist part of our team, led by Blumenthal, Owen, and Cooper, argued for using the Bonn summit as the global stage to meet the demands of our foreign partners. I was part of a domestic group including Mondale and Ham that feared such a commitment in an international forum would undermine whatever faint chance remained of passing the wellhead oil tax, which was the administration's preferred way of raising our oil prices to world levels. A more direct but politically risky way would have been to take advantage of legislation passed during the Ford administration giving the president authority to raise oil prices without congressional consent as early as June 1979. And even if he did nothing at all, price controls on crude oil would automatically expire by October 1981. So we argued, with legislation already on the books: Why take on the political risk of acting earlier at Bonn, particularly when we had an alternative way to achieve the same goal?

The president summoned key members of Congress for a briefing by Owen, which I joined. Owen remembers Metzenbaum, a fierce opponent of decontrol, "behaving like a real horse's ass." The senator snapped at Owen: "Everything you say is wrong." Frustrated, the president snapped back at the liberal Ohio Democrat, "I'm sure glad of one thing: that the power to do this [decontrol oil prices] lies in my hands because if it lay in your hands, it would never get done."

Frequent but inconclusive internal meetings followed to develop our summit position, with sharp divisions over whether the president should commit himself thousands of miles away to a policy that would enrage the liberal wing of his party and complicate congressional passage of his COET legislation. Nothing had been decided before the president left for Bonn, except in his own mind. Owen soon realized why: "Mainly, the president figured he knew what he was going to do, but he didn't want to talk about it; he didn't want to have a big brouhaha."[10]

This was Carter's typically individualistic decision-making process, backing into one of the most far-reaching decisions of his presidency thousands of miles from Washington, where an intense debate on his signature energy plan was under way in Congress, yet making history in a positive way. Just as he abandoned his campaign pledge to decontrol newly discovered natural-gas prices, but finally embraced it to save our beleaguered energy package, now he was going to abandon his campaign pledge to keep controls on crude oil in exchange for a successful promise of economic stimulus by the Germans and the Japanese, and conclusion of the Tokyo Round. He did not tell any of the staff in advance, not even Owen or the cabinet members traveling with him.

The Bonn summit did not start well. The president proposed something general on oil, referring to the COET wellhead tax, which was still alive if on life support. Schmidt was equally general about economic expansion. Each declared the other's proposal to be inadequate, but no good negotiator opens by playing his highest card. So the first day ended in stalemate, and at about six that evening Schmidt left to meet with his inner cabinet and decide how to break the deadlock. He knew he could not push a tax cut through the Bundestag without the excuse of foreign pressure, and had confided to his entourage that he wanted the Americans "to force me to do it—so that I can."[11]

Carter then made his move. He instructed Owen to call Schlesinger in Washington to determine if he objected to Carter pledging an end to price controls on oil as part of a deal with Schmidt. Owen woke Schlesinger in the early hours of the morning, briefed him as instructed, and found him curiously disengaged and nonplussed: "Jim didn't seem to give a damn. You know, his attitude toward the handling of energy summits was really quite detached." Owen also phoned Kitty Schirmer, my energy aide, who was appalled that Carter would make such a sweeping decision without getting more from our partners in exchange.[12] I repeated the same political objections about preparing Congress for our commitment, but it was too late. Carter had already made up his mind.

The president told Owen, "We are going to go the whole way." Owen negotiated with the German Sherpa, Horst Schulmann, until 1:00 a.m. Each had already received instructions from his boss, and together they hammered out language committing the U.S. government to lift controls on oil prices by the end of 1980, and the Germans to expand their economy. Owen gave the proposed communiqué to Carter as soon as he woke up—"which is very early." Carter approved it, so did Schmidt, and the deal was just about done.[13]

Owen then took the communiqué text to Japanese prime minister Fukuda, who "didn't seem terribly interested in energy," but promised that if Schmidt would adopt policies for the German economy to grow an additional 1 percent, Japan would, too. With these pledges on paper, the third leg of the summit was trade, an anticlimax that became the most amusing part of the summit. The United States felt that the Europeans and the Japanese were not opening markets sufficiently in the multilateral trade negotiations, even though the three key trade ministers representing the United States, Japan, and the European Community reported that they had made considerable progress among themselves at Bonn. Giscard, a classic French protectionist, was unhappy with the concessions made in the name of France by Wilhelm Haverkamp, an equally classic German free trader who negotiated on behalf of all members of Europe's trading bloc as the European Community's trade commissioner.

As Owen colorfully described it, "Giscard, who had himself thoroughly confused with Louis XIV, looked down his nose at them and said, 'I think trade negotiators talk too much about their own accomplishments.' There was a deafening pause in the room, and then Carter's trade chief Bob Strauss spoke up in his deep Texas accent—which I am convinced he rehearses in the evening—and said, 'Well, as Dizzy Dean used to say, "If you done it, it ain't bragging."'" The translators did not have an easy time with this, but neither did Giscard. Who was this peasant addressing him, and who or what was this Dizzy Dean? Owen continued: "Giscard was the only head of government who had a military assistant in the summit room, and he beckoned toward this colonel, a cavalry officer, who clanked across the hall with his boots and spurs. Giscard whispered, *Qui est-ce Dizzy Dean, hein?*' ('Who is this Dizzy Dean, huh?'). The colonel clanked around the room and came over to me: *Monsieur, Dizzy Dean, alors; qui est Dizzy Dean?'* I happened to know because my mother's family comes from St. Louis, the city for whose St. Louis Cardinals Dean had been a star. But before I could tell him, Callaghan turned to his foreign secretary, David Owen, and said, 'David, do you know who Dizzy Dean was?' He thought the prime minister didn't know, and he blushed and said, 'No, Prime Minister, I don't.' Callaghan said, 'Well, he was a pitcher for the St. Louis Cardinals, and in 1934 he won the World Series against the Detroit Tigers.'"[14]

Giscard was so mortified that he refused to see Strauss later in Paris during trade negotiations. When the negotiators ran into trouble, and the French wanted to talk to us on the side, Owen had to be sent in place of Strauss. Strauss had a brazen capacity to get away with things no other mortal could have begun to do. After one trade-negotiating round in Paris, Strauss returned home on the Concorde, thereby violating two of the president's edicts: one, by flying first class (the only class); and, two, by flying on a non-American carrier. When he landed at Dulles Airport the press was ready: How could he fly first class against President Carter's economy-class edict? Because, he shot back, "there's nothing better than first class, and if there was, I would have flown that!" End of story.

As for Schmidt, he also never forgot. When I asked him years later for his views on Bonn, Schmidt replied as condescendingly as his haughty French partner: "Jimmy Carter at that time did not have his own judgment on economic questions; he had to listen to advisers who concentrated on naive Keynesian deficit spending. As far as this advice was accepted worldwide, it worked as a continuous invitation to OPEC to further increase oil prices."[15]

It had taken the better part of a year, with numerous bilateral and multilateral meetings, to sort out a framework for action, an unprecedented tripartite bargain at Bonn that was never duplicated. As Putnam and Henning, the leading academic experts on summit history, concluded, "The Bonn deal successfully meshed domestic and international pressures." No one would have predicted this success when the summit process began."[16] Commitments made at Bonn imparted an international blessing that would help each leader implement domestic policies that might not have been successful otherwise. Indeed, what is striking is that at the very same time Jimmy Carter was struggling to bring members of his own congressional Democratic Party in line behind his energy package, even as a virtual novice in foreign policy, he was able to carry the day several thousand miles away against far more experienced leaders.

The Bonn Accord was not filled with empty pledges. Remarkably, virtually all the crucial pledges of the Bonn summit were redeemed. The German government's package of tax cuts was passed overwhelmingly by the Bundestag in the autumn. The Japanese did likewise. The impasse at the Tokyo Round was broken, giving Strauss and the president ammunition to achieve the most sweeping reduction of trade barriers to date. It passed unanimously in the Senate and with only two dissenting votes in the House, leading Strauss to call and ask in his inimitable way, "Eizenstat, who are the two sons of bitches who voted against our deal?" It was another unrecognized legacy of the Carter administration. And although Jimmy Carter did not invent the G7 process, he perfected it and was indispensable to its success; for the first and only time domestic economic policies were coordinated at the international level. Carter set the agenda, drove the discussion, negotiated the agreements, and was better briefed and at least as knowledgeable as the seasoned Schmidt.

Anyone who doubted Carter's ability to play a leading diplomatic role on behalf of the United States of America never saw him perform at the G7 summits. Moreover, Carter liked it. The ground had been more carefully prepared, and among Carter's fellow leaders he found "a camaraderie among us when we were not in front of the cameras that was reassuring, that I enjoyed."[17]

As domestic-policy adviser, it was fascinating to me that Jimmy Carter, who had such an aversion to hand-to-hand combat with the U.S. Congress, could perform such magic abroad but not at home. He did it at Camp David, and here at the Bonn summit. No one could deny his strength of purpose and negotiating prowess. I believe the president excelled when he had a clear goal and when representing the United States; he was considered a first among equals within a circle of key national leaders. But he found it more difficult when confronted with the rough tactics, competing egos, and overlapping jurisdictions in Congress, where a president's influence cannot be as strongly focused as it is with foreign peers. At Bonn he could have hedged on decontrolling crude oil or conditioned his commitment on congressional approval. But he had learned his lesson. He began an irreversible process of raising American oil prices to world levels, in which Ronald Reagan simply completed the last step, and forced Congress to pass a tax on the oil industry's windfall profits the next year. That was politically risky, but it was the way he operated most effectively as a leader.

10

INTO THE PORK BARREL,
RELUCTANTLY

O nce the Bonn summit was over, President Carter had to deliver on his pledge to end price controls and raise energy prices to world levels by the end of 1980, however reluctantly it had been made and inadequate the decision-making process behind it. Pledges by the other participants were made mainly by political leaders of parliamentary parties who could better implement their pledges; the American presidency is one of three separate branches of government, albeit the one with the most power concentrated in one person. But the president's promise had been made in the name of the United States, and even though it was not legally binding, it was made for the whole world to see as part of a deal with our partners, who largely honored their part of the bargain to stimulate growth. So on July 19, only two days after the summit ended, we started to do our part, and it was left to me to coordinate the effort.[1]

Just after the president briefed congressional leaders, I met with Senator Long, which was always an experience. He talked in free flow, moving from one topic to another, but all had a home-state connection: sugar subsidies, welfare payments (more of the former, less of the latter), and finally the wellhead equalization tax (COET) for oil and a recent proposal by Senator Bob Dole, the powerful Kansas Republican, to curb the president's authority to impose oil import fees or quotas. Long was a master of the legislative headcount and informed us that we did not have the necessary 51 votes in the Senate to pass the tax, but we did have 34 votes to uphold a veto of Dole's proposal. Imposing a fee would be "gutsy, but not popular," he said, and immediately shifted ground to his pet project of deregulating natural gas. "Let's get the natural-gas bill behind us before the president acts on oil," he said, quickly adding that he was not committed to the compromise phasing in market prices over a few years. Then, to excuse bailing out even on natural gas, he said in all earnestness, "It helps with liberals if some conservatives are not happy with the gas bill."[2] This was Russell Long at his irrepressible best—or worst. This was one time the master vote counter was wrong. Carter's veto was overwhelmingly overturned in both houses on June 6, 1978, one of the worst legislative setbacks of his presidency, and the first time a Democratic president's veto had been overridden by Congress since Harry Truman in 1952.[3]

The public began to do what we had feared and write off the energy bill as dead. It was mentioned less and less frequently. Other problems captured national attention: inflation accelerated; the Senate fought over ratifying the Panama Canal Treaties; the president attempted to devise a tax reform to close loopholes for the wealthy and tie it to a broad-based tax reduction for the middle class; and a fistful of other controversial initiatives both foreign and domestic. If Carter's pledge was going to be carved up in renewed political infighting at home, no presidential pledge in any area would have had any meaning, especially any American security guarantee to our allies.

And it was also clear that unless we demonstrated to financial markets our genuine commitment to reduce oil imports, upward pressure on inflation would result in renewed downward pressure on the dollar. We held numerous, interminable daily afternoon meetings in the Domestic Policy Staff's conference room between November 1978 and April 1979, facing up to a set of bad options. The president could accelerate the pace of ending price controls, which under a 1975 law would automatically expire by October 1981. But the choice to act quickly entailed an inevitable spike in inflation. How fast should crude oil prices increase, and should they be tied to a tax on the windfall profits from oil in their old wells? Or would the companies avoid the tax by shutting down some wells until prices rose to world levels? These were not easy questions to answer. Since we do not live in a perfect world, all policies involve trade-offs. Good policies by definition make life better for most citizens, but some will lose a privilege or profit that has often been gained at the expense of the majority, and they do not easily surrender it.

In committing himself to carry out his Bonn pledge, Carter had to do so by playing politics and putting his hands into the place he most disliked, the congressional pork barrel. There was so much riding on getting the package approved by the Conference Committee and then through the whole Congress that they knew they could demand a high price. It was time for the full force of the White House to intervene to save the compromise on natural gas, protect his promise on oil, and enact our many conservation measures. We learned that Senator Johnston would sign the Conference Report if his fellow Louisiana Democrat, Representative Joe Waggoner, also did so. The White House also targeted two Republican Senators, Pete Domenici of New Mexico and James McClure of Idaho.

The most difficult was McClure, whose vote was crucial to unlock the natural-gas bill from the Conference Committee, and whose price was continuing the high-level research on breeder nuclear reactors that, not coincidentally, was being performed at a major facility in his home state of Idaho. He demanded an annual research budget of $125 million. Few projects made Jimmy Carter's hair stand on end as this one did, but the project would not die. Strauss, Mondale, and Kitty Schirmer went to see the president, who declared, "I'm not going to compromise on those things." But he knew he had no choice if he wanted the bill, and as Kitty observed, "In the end he did some compromising, but it was so late, it was kind of ungraceful."[4]

In his preparation for a meeting with McClure, the president was clearly agitated. "This sets a precedent in paying McClure $100 million for his vote. I have never done that before," he said. In my notes I underscored that last sentence. Mondale, a seasoned Washington veteran who had long ago lost his innocence about compromises, weighed in to ease the passage to reality: "Mr. President, now is the time to strike; this is a modest price to pay. The gas bill is very important."[5]

It was a moment of truth for Jimmy Carter. I knew he hated this kind of raw politics, but he realized it was now or never. He took a swipe at Mondale, only half joking that he would probably give a senator "one of your vice presidential gardeners to get this bill done,"[6] before soothing his conscience by emphasizing that he was making no commitment to actually build the reactor, and he wanted to ensure that McClure understood that before he committed a specific amount for research.

And that is exactly what he had to do when McClure arrived with Domenici in the historic Map Room in the White House, where Roosevelt had guided Allied progress in World War II.[7] Carter began by arguing that the

Europeans believed that the energy bill was crucial for the stability of the dollar and was a crucial part of the deal he had made at the Bonn summit. McClure countered with a ridiculous statement: "The breeder reactor is more important to the Europeans than the natural-gas bill." Then he got to the heart of the matter: "I'm giving up on my key concern, the escalator on price for natural gas, and I need assurance from the president on the breeder, which is the key item for me." Reminding McClure that he had served as a naval officer on a nuclear submarine, Carter continued: "I favor atomic power. I am committed to a breeder program, but I am concerned with the spending levels."

This made the vice president, Schlesinger, and me hold our collective breath to hear what the president would say next. Finally, with a sigh, the president agreed and, to the visible relief of everyone there, said: "I don't object to what you will work out with Jim." Schlesinger and McClure worked out a compromise to appropriate $100 million for breeder research but no money for construction. McClure wanted the bill to "suspend" instead of "terminate" the project, so that continued research would seem more plausible. Carter substituted the vague word "discontinue," which was consistent with his position on Clinch River—yes to research but no to construction. That is how deals are done in Washington.

Domenici was an easier sell. He told Carter that he "had never worked harder on anything" since coming to the Senate, that his New Mexico consumers and producers both opposed the natural-gas compromise, and he needed the president to fight hard for the bill when it got to the Senate floor. Carter firmly assured Domenici he would do just that. With McClure and Domenici, we had nine of the seventeen Senate conferees, a bare majority. Now we had to persuade a majority of the thirteen House conferees. Without assurances from the conservative Waggoner and the liberal Democrat Henry Reuss of Wisconsin, O'Neill wanted insurance from two other conferees.

That same day the president invited two of the most liberal Democratic congressmen, Harlem's Charles Rangel and James Corman of Los Angeles, for a late-night meeting back in the Map Room. Before going to the White House, they had already been pressured by O'Neill to support decontrol if only on a patriotic basis, however unpopular it surely would be in their districts. O'Neill had warned that a defeat would damage the prestige of the nation and the president, as well as his own—an unspoken but important factor in the minds of politicians hearing from the principal dispenser of patronage and position in the House of Representatives. So with this appeal from the Speaker, they headed to the White House.[8]

We knew Rangel wanted housing money for his Harlem district, but, Schlesinger said, "The president didn't seem interested." Whatever Carter's disdain for such horse-trading, this was too important to stand on principle. I called our chief legislative liaison, Frank Moore, and we arranged on our own for additional HUD funds for Harlem, a poor district that needed the money anyway. Charlie Rangel, a founder of the Congessional Black Caucus and a political power in America's most prominent black community, had a gravelly voice and great charm. He cared deeply about the impact of rising energy prices on poor people in New York and around the country.[9]

Jim Corman was one of the most courteous members of Congress I ever met. I never heard him raise his voice or say anything unpleasant about anyone. He was silver haired and intense and his liberal, proconsumer credentials were unimpeachable. He and Rangel were among my closest friends in Congress, both had opposed the compromise on decontrolling natural-gas prices, and both made a complete about-face after Carter explained that his credibility and political standing at home and abroad were at stake.

The president made no specific promises (Moore and I had taken care of that), but Rangel made it clear that he was "worried about the impact of rising energy prices on the poor, and on consumers in general, and I want to know, Mr. President, that you will take every action at your disposal to protect them." Carter replied by emphasizing the programs in the energy package to help shield low-income Americans from rising prices and to assist poor people to insulate their homes. Bringing in these two liberals helped give them political cover to switch together. Both also agreed that it was better for Carter to depend on them to push the natural-gas bill over the top rather than the fractious and demanding representatives of oil-patch states.[10]

But even with their reluctant support, the House conferees were one vote short of a majority. The best target was none other than swashbuckling Texas Charlie Wilson, and the saga of signing him up was worthy of a Hollywood movie. (Years later, in fact, he would be played by Tom Hanks in the Mike Nichols film *Charlie Wilson's War*, chronicling his bravado campaign to arm the Afghan mujahadeen against Soviet invaders.) At this critical moment he said he had to catch a plane. Wilson told the Speaker's top aide, Ari Weiss, that if he absolutely needed his vote to make the necessary thirteen, he could have his signature as long as he was not the only producer-state congressman supporting the deal. Wilson was depending on Waggoner to offer political cover, but could not have known that after he left for the airport, Waggoner had withdrawn his support under pressure from oil and gas lobbyists. That left Texas Charlie by himself with the unaccustomed company of liberals Corman and Rangel to bring the compromise out of committee. It also left Weiss understandably reluctant to cast Wilson's vote in such politically treacherous circumstances.

Wilson was on a commercial airliner. Weiss dashed from the Map Room to the White House congressional liaison office, where they were celebrating victory—prematurely, as Weiss explained to their horror. The White House switchboard operators, who can find anyone including the proverbial man on the moon (and even the real ones when they landed there), patched Wilson through to Weiss on the pilot's radio so he could explain the sudden turn of events. Wilson temporarily withdrew his proxy and promised to call back after he landed. For more than two hours there was complete silence. No one could find him, not even the White House operator.

Lud Ashley, Schlesinger, Weiss, Kitty Schirmer, and a handful of senior staff including me paced around the vice president's office late into the night. It was like a hospital waiting room full of nervous prospective fathers—except this pregnancy had not taken nine months but almost twice as long. In desperation, Weiss contacted Wilson's fellow Texan, Majority Leader Jim Wright, who found Wilson at the home of an oil company executive, discussing the bill with a handful of producers. As we waited a few more suspenseful moments for Texas Charlie to check with his congressional colleagues, we were finally able to draw breath: Wilson gave Weiss the go-ahead to cast his proxy. Elated but exhausted, we never did find out exactly what Wilson or his oil-patch colleagues had said among themselves in order to free up his essential vote.[11] Once the natural-gas compromise passed the committee, Long quickly reached a deal with his House counterparts. They killed the wellhead oil tax but approved the gas-guzzler tax and other important incentives for conservation and alternative energy through solar power, wind, and biomass.

THE ANTIPOLITICIAN DRAWN
INTO POLITICS

For both houses of Congress to pass the Conference Report into law, we still had to face floor battles that would revisit many of the same issues and reassemble the cross-party coalitions that had marked its tortuous passage so far. Only a few days after the conferees reached agreement, eighteen other senators including opponents and supporters of deregulation joined in a "Dear Colleague" letter opposing the compromise. The irrepressible Abourezk declared he was ready to filibuster the bill. Another obstacle was the compromise on the breeder reactor; some senators would not be satisfied until they saw a stake through its heart, and McClure aroused their suspicions by publicly claiming he had achieved a greater commitment from the president than he actually had. Carter phoned me from Camp David with instructions to prepare a statement declaring that he had made "no commitment to construction of the breeder or to buy component parts for the new plant." The fact was that, under pressure in the negotiations, each side heard what it wanted to. With Schlesinger trying to work out details with McClure, the president directed me to monitor the agreement closely and call him if any dispute arose.[12]

Again, the same bizarre coalition of conservative business and liberal labor and consumer groups formed to kill the Conference Report. Despite these almost insane circumstances, this time it was different. We banded together like the Argonauts in search of the Golden Fleece, and Carter did not bend or break under the pressure but plowed ahead. We brooked no petty compromises at this late stage and pointed out the impact of delay on the already stressed dollar.

During Labor Day weekend Carter called twenty-six wavering senators as he prepared for the Camp David negotiations between Israel and Egypt, including the Iowa Democrat John Culver at 5:00 a.m. during his holiday trip in Alaska. In the midst of the intensive Camp David negotiations, Carter talked with another thirteen senators by phone and marked each one as leaning positive, negative, or open—and thus subject to persuasion. The president did not need to be told that he needed to use the full power and authority of his office or the bill would fail. It was a brutal example of how often a president must switch from one complex subject to another and stay on top of both. His intense personal lobbying by phone was the closest his presidential politics would come to hands-on lobbying. The natural-gas battle was a fight to the finish. Either we won or the Carter presidency was shot.

While Carter would make as many phone calls as we asked, he still seemed unwilling to personally apply the power of his office on plane trips with members of Congress or in most forms of socializing. On an Air Force One flight to New Jersey with eight of the state's congressmen and its Democratic senator, Harrison Williams, only once was the president heard discussing the urgency of the energy bill. Bill Cable, the White House liaison to the House on energy, overheard him talking about it with the state's moderate Republican senator, Clifford Case.[13] I made a terse note on my legal pad: "JC not politician; JC simply not like to be with other politicians; maybe felt he was better" (than them).[14] Dan Tate, Cable's Senate counterpart, was aghast that on "the most critical domestic vote of his presidency" Carter refused to revisit the subject with New Mexico's Dennis DeConcini, nor would he talk with California's acerbic S. I. Hayakawa—the two had caused him problems ratifying the Panama Canal Treaty—or to Senator Edward Brooke, a moderate Republican from Massachusetts, because of a reported wisecrack implying that the president was debasing the dignity of his office by wearing jeans. "And the list gets longer," Tate complained.[15]

Schlesinger later said that Carter's "heart was not in it. He felt himself unclean when he lobbied a senator, and yet when he appeared before constituency groups, he could talk about substance. . . . He could close with, 'We need your support,' and these people were all flattered to visit with the president of the United States."[16]

Schlesinger worked superhuman hours to apply pressure through the energy industry. But this was a full-team effort for the final push. At an Oval Office meeting on August 31 with Mondale and Carter's close advisers, we had only thirty-four certain Senate votes for the natural-gas compromise, and the president was given another list of senators to call—mostly liberal Republicans—as well as the chief executives of Gulf, Texaco, Mobil, and Exxon.[17] I worked with the president on the final draft of an urgent August 31 letter to Congress, invoking a warning from Federal Reserve Chairman G. William Miller that failure to act risked a further decline in the dollar.[18] Miller, a former Textron CEO, publicly injected himself into the debate unlike any previous Federal Reserve chairman. Mondale virtually camped out in his Capitol office just off the Senate floor to buttonhole Senators.

Ham, Rafshoon, Frank Moore, Gail Harrison of Mondale's staff, and I met with Anne Wexler each morning at 8:30 a.m. to develop strategy for a Conference Committee report that was so riddled with compromises no one liked it. At the same time we worked with Anne to develop an outreach strategy for public support on the grounds of patriotism and national pride. She skillfully reached out to companies and unions with plants in the districts of wavering senators and congressmen for White House briefings. She knew how to set up briefings and form coalitions among groups that usually opposed each other, for example industry and the environmentalists. She assembled about two dozen chief executives from a variety of industries in the Roosevelt Room.[19] Not one of them supported the natural-gas bill, but she had organized her own assault squad of top-level talent. Schlesinger opened with multicolored charts and new figures to show how the compromise would increase gas production. Then Anne brought in Bob Strauss as the closer. With his Texas twang and down-home manner, he told the executives they held the fate of the bill in their hands: "This is close enough so a half dozen bankers I had in here this morning and the people in this room could pass or defeat the bill." Several of the executives, particularly those from industries such as textiles that Strauss had helped as trade czar, changed their positions and supported the compromise.[20]

In the weeks before the Senate vote, executives from insurance to automobiles to aerospace were summoned for another half-dozen sessions in the most extensive administration lobbying campaign on a domestic issue since Carter took office. Nothing was spared. A group of bankers was invited for lunch in the family dining room, a special treat. Even a few oil companies such as Atlantic Richfield were persuaded to hold their noses and support the compromise, although deregulation would not be complete until 1985. Exxon, the paragon of an integrated global oil company, was persuaded to stay neutral. Other industries like steel, autos, and the farm groups were split. Republican senator Robert Griffin of Michigan told us that for him to vote in favor, he needed at least one auto manufacturer to support the measure. So we dragooned Chrysler, in financial trouble and in need of a federal bailout we would later give to save the company and tens of thousands of auto workers' jobs. Schlesinger, never one to mince words, remarked later that it had taken the White House "three years to learn that the real power on Capitol Hill is held by industry."[21]

It is important to recall that at that time, we were dealing with mainly a clash of competing interests and not corporate and union campaign payoffs. All were constrained by post-Watergate campaign finance laws aimed at limiting much of the perverse influence of money on politics. Carter and Ford both ran their 1976 campaigns using funds from the income-tax checkoff, rather than raising tens of millions of dollars in private and corporate donations for today's unconstrained super-PACs. Still, the independent oil and gas companies were masters at getting special tax and regulatory breaks by spreading money around irrespective of party. And we had to curry favor with big business to overwhelm the power of their energy suppliers. (Over the years, the constraints on campaign financing laws have been eroded, most recently by the Supreme Court's fatal Citizens United decision, removing virtually all restraints on campaign spending. The huge cost of television campaigning, and the political organizing that once was shouldered mainly by political parties, has pervaded all areas of public policy.)

This alignment of strange political bedfellows on Capitol Hill helped make the battle as fierce as any that Washington had seen in decades. The principal reason for the preponderance of opponents was that the compromises satisfied no one fully. The energy producers and conservatives, arguing that controls were not being removed quickly enough, formed a marriage of convenience to kill the Conference Committee's compromise with consumer advocates fearful that prices would rise too quickly and angry that deregulation would occur at all, although all controls were slated to end in 1985.

So Senator Long, who normally would not have been caught dead with such liberal, proconsumer senators as Metzenbaum and Abourezk, worked with them to kill the compromise. John Tower, a conservative Texas Republican, lined up against the bill with the liberal standard-bearer, Ted Kennedy. Amoco was working hand in glove with its mortal enemy James Flug, my frequent visitor from the consumer group Energy Action. The U.S. Chamber of Commerce, almost always on opposite sides from the AFL-CIO and the UAW in any political battle, coordinated efforts to strike down the compromise and the tax provisions of the bill.[22]

As the floor vote came closer, feelings were raw. Senator Don Riegle, a Michigan Democrat, told me he was leaning against the bill but might shift if it appeared we would lose. But he took a hard and I felt undeserved shot at Schlesinger as "the worst choice for secretary; he can't deal with people."[23] The most colorful comment came from Senator Joe Biden, never known for rhetorical restraint even as he rose to become vice president of the United States. He declared himself "against the bill, but I would like to stick it up Senator Kennedy's ass."[24] He was offended by his fellow liberal's vociferous opposition and told me he might be able to help us keep the compromise alive by voting against any motion to send the bill back to die in the Conference Committee.

For the majority in Congress who had not served on any of the relevant committees, the details of the president's much-compromised program were new and prompted many of the questions we had long debated. We developed a detailed set of talking points to go through the main arguments in favor of this fundamental reform—nationwide availability of natural gas at predictable prices to help substitute for imported OPEC oil; protection for the dollar abroad and against predatory energy prices at home; and much else. We pointed up that opponents had offered no alternatives, had entered into a marriage of convenience to block the bill, and that the continuation of two separate markets for natural gas, one within producing states, the other when gas flowed between states, was harmful because the country needed cheaper gas to fulfill its energy needs from our own resources. These were indeed powerful, irrefutable facts. But the political opposition to deregulation relied on emotion as much as logic.

I was nevertheless impressed how genuinely conscientious and even bipartisan most were about their vote. They realized it was important to the president and the country. John Danforth of Missouri, a tall, impressive ordained Episcopal priest as well as a highly intelligent, thoughtful politician, expressed his belief in decontrol but was concerned that the complex package was an invitation to litigation and uncertainty. I told him the complexity was an inevitable by-product of the competing interests that had to be accommodated to reach a final deal. Then in a spirit totally alien to today's politically divisive atmosphere, this Republican senator said, "If I vote for it, it is because I do not want to hurt the president."[25]

Senator Joe Clark, a Pennsylvania Democrat, called with a number of questions: How much would the plan cost homeowners? Would it help increase the domestic supply of gas, and how would it affect our balance of payments? Would the Federal Energy Regulatory Commission be able to administer such a complex law? I answered his questions and was comforted when he ended the conversation by saying, "You guys are awfully convincing."[26]

But many also had their price. One of the Senate's most notable Republican conservatives, Strom Thurmond of South Carolina, told Schlesinger we would get his vote in exchange for continued federal support for the Barnwell nuclear waste site in his home state. We guaranteed it.[27] Senator John Heinz, a Pennsylvania Republican and heir to the eponymous ketchup fortune, told Treasury undersecretary Tony Solomon that he wanted a "cheap trade" for his natural-gas support,[28] which turned out to be only a request for assurance that we would properly fund the Environmental Protection Agency.[29] Senator DeConcini had a strange request: a White House commitment that the Department of Energy hire no additional employees.[30] This was so bizarre that the best I could offer was a general commitment to review employment levels closely. His underlying message was hardly a courageous one: He would oppose the bill unless we needed his vote to win. And then there was the Clinch River reactor, which had assumed a life of its own. Centrist Republicans Charles Percy of Illinois and Mark Hatfield of Oregon sought and obtained reassurance that Carter had not folded to obtain McClure's vote.[31]

For others, leverage resided in some of the other important and controversial initiatives the president had laid before Congress, without realizing how his proposals made him vulnerable on energy, where every vote counted. The two most controversial proposals would reform the tax system by cutting some treasured deductions and cut pork-barrel spending on local water projects by vetoing the annual public works bill. House Majority Leader Jim Wright warned that if Carter vetoed the public works bill it would cost him thirty to forty votes on deregulating natural gas.[32] Yet when I sat down with the president, vice president, and the congressional relations staff the next day, Carter told us he was going forward with a veto despite Wright's warning. Mondale, obviously not thrilled with the news, said that next year "We must avoid another 'hit list' "—as the first list of pork-barrel water projects was dubbed by its powerful supporters. He urged the staff to pick a small list of genuinely objectionable projects to make Carter's point about wasteful spending.[33]

Other important bills on which the Hill needed to act before the midterm elections involved highways and mass transit, the Small Business Administration, vocational rehabilitation, tuition tax credits, and still more. All would have to be negotiated to obtain the votes of legislators with local interests or face the meat ax of a presidential veto that might kill an entire program. Carter got the point and said: "I will try to avoid vetoes."[34] But in fact he felt he would not avoid a veto over the water projects funded in the public works bill.

The raw politics of the dilemma made a veto a huge risk for the president. To my mind, a half-dozen pork-barrel water projects were far less important when weighed against the energy bill that the entire administration had been pushing for almost eighteen months. But Carter believed his credibility was on the line, after backing away from a veto the previous year. He was caught in intense political cross fire. The next day Corman, the California liberal who had courageously agreed to support the natural-gas compromise, urged the president not to veto the public works bill lest he endanger not only the energy bill but also tax reform and Carter's political standing across the West.[35]

At the same time the reformist Watergate babies came out in favor of a veto of this pork-barrel legislation. The excruciatingly difficult trade-off between the president's strong environmental and fiscal instincts and the imperative of pushing his signature energy package through Congress came to a head in an Oval Office meeting on October 3. All the president's most trusted advisers were there, along with Schultze and Blumenthal of the economic team. Carter clearly felt beleaguered. He said: "I had wanted to move early in my administration with an anti-inflation program but have been convinced by Stu and others not to do so. But I feel strongly about the public works bill; it is wasteful federal spending. I do not want to give up, although the veto count does not look encouraging. I know they would override my veto if I sent the bill back to them today. We need to build up support for a veto with the media and by other means. Time is on our side."[36]

This was Carter at his most politically courageous. With the natural-gas compromise and energy package in the balance, he was willing to make his point to the public and to Congress even if his veto was overridden—a decision contravening those who see Jimmy Carter as politically weak. While his political judgment in vetoing this bill was certainly open to question, no one need question his will and strength of character.[37]

As the political game played out, Carter won both ways. His veto of the water projects held, and did not undercut the natural-gas compromise, although the fight was bitter to the end. During the day of October 4 and after midnight on October 5, the Senate voted 57 to 42 to pass the natural-gas compromise. Abourezk damned it as a "lousy, stinking" bill,[38] but Senate majority leader Byrd had it right, calling the vote a legislative milestone that ended decades of bitter impasse. The bill created the first unified nationwide market for natural gas, as prices of newly discovered gas were allowed to rise by about 10 percent annually, until 1985, when all price controls would be lifted. It created incentives for the production of a clean-burning domestic source of energy, which has been a key part of America's increasing energy independence in the twenty-first century.

I must admit to a bittersweet feeling about the outcome. If we had stood firm on our deregulation campaign promise, and not let Schlesinger persuade the president to abandon it, I believe we could have avoided the eighteen-month impasse that stalled progress on the other elements of our package. The drawn-out battle also changed the perception of the president from a bold and effective leader to an ineffective one. Too often he came to be seen only as a man of symbolic principle that overshadowed his more complex and lasting accomplishments. Years later Schlesinger ruminated that he should have proposed to the president natural-gas deregulation tied to a windfall profits tax, as the president later did with crude oil, to gain liberal support.[39] If only he had had this epiphany when we needed it.

THE LAST PIECES OF THE PUZZLE

With the Senate approval of the natural-gas compromise finally out of the way, we could turn our attention to the last pieces of the puzzle—the tax features of the energy bill and our broader tax reform to close tax loopholes in return for lowering rates. One of the more egregious demands came from Senator Bentsen, who asked to maintain a huge tax break for oil companies. Treasury's tax staff hated the idea,[40] but Secretary Blumenthal reluctantly agreed in hope of obtaining support for the natural-gas bill from oil-patch senators. We had no choice but to yield. Nevertheless, Bentsen was not done. Just before the Senate's natural-gas vote on October 6, he demanded further tax write-offs for drilling wells that came up dry. This was worth tens of millions of dollars to producers. Jim Wright, also from Texas, called me directly and said the dry-hole exemption was critical to correct an error from a 1976 tax bill. Then he made it clear we had no choice: "I made this commitment to our producers, and it is the reason I am supporting the energy bill. I cannot support the energy bill without it." We could hardly ignore the threat from our own Democratic majority leader.[41]

From the start, there was an inherent conflict between the two bills. The tax reform bill tried to limit deductions ranging from a Texas oilman's drilling costs to a Madison Avenue adman's infamous three-martini lunch to make the tax code fairer and simpler, and help pay for middle-class tax cuts. But our energy package was simultaneously adding new tax incentives for alternative energy sources like solar and wind power, and imposing tax penalties and higher prices for oil and gas, and a gas-guzzler tax. We were distracted by the tax reform battle now reaching a climax and working at cross-purposes with the energy tax bill. What had been a balanced revenue plan in the president's original energy plan had been transformed into costly new energy tax credits, thanks to Senator Long and the energy bill conferees.

Meanwhile the tax reform bill was being loaded down with giveaways, in part to win votes for the energy bill. To Russell Long, everything was connected—including the president's energy bill and his tax reform proposals. Robert Shapiro, staff director of the Joint Tax Committee, warned me that "a lot of crap" was being added to the tax reform bill. "Don't worry," he said, "Senator Long will knock out these items in conference." Given what I knew about Long's idea of tax reform, I was not at all as sure as this congressional tax expert.[42]

The energy taxes, which the House had largely passed more than a year before, were eviscerated by Long in the Senate. After a fifteen-hour filibuster by the ornery Senator Abourezk, the Senate accepted all the recommendations of the Conference Committee on each of the five separate measures, ending with a 60–17 endorsement of the tax measure.

Now the final action rested with the House. The Speaker had withstood great pressure to hold off action until the Senate completed votes on all five parts of the president's program, which he would then roll into one bill for an up-or-down vote. He waited impatiently for Abourezk to tire himself out, which he finally did at 12:30 a.m. on October 15. Now came the hour of judgment on O'Neill's bold strategy. At 2:45 a.m. the House began to debate the energy package. The most dangerous hurdle was a determined motion by liberal Democrats and conservative Republicans to split off the natural-gas compromise from the more popular bills, and then kill it.

The House Rules Committee, which the Speaker normally has in his hip pocket, had divided 8 votes to 8 on whether to take up the whole energy package intact as O'Neill wanted. To switch one vote took a day of heavy lobbying by the Speaker and the White House in what the lead Republican, Clarence Brown of Ohio, described as "the most pressurized arm twisting we have since President Carter took office." Once he had the committee's 9 to 5 approval, the bill moved to the floor, and after further pressure on wavering liberal Democrats, the vote in favor of keeping the package intact was a squeaking margin of 207–205.

Suddenly Millicent Fenwick, a tall, slender liberal New Jersey Republican and aristocratic former editor of *Vogue,* who enjoyed puncturing the bloated egos of her male colleagues in both parties and who was reputed to be the model for the fictional congresswoman Lacey Davenport in the *Doonesbury* comic strip, walked elegantly to the well of the House. As everyone watched with suspense, she picked up an orange card, changing her vote from "Aye" to "Present" and throwing the vote into a tie at 206 to 206. It was heart attack time. President Carter had applied special attention to another moderate Republican, Congressman Tom Evans of Delaware. Knowing it would make him an outcast in his party, Evans nevertheless voted "Aye."[43] When Carter called Evans to thank him for his last-minute support, the congressman broke into tears recalling the abuse he had received from his Republican colleagues.[44]

To forestall any more switches, the Speaker banged down his large gavel, and the package was saved. At 7:30 a.m. on October 15, 1978, a bleary-eyed House voted 231–168 to send the completed bill to the president, almost eighteen grueling months after his proclamation of the moral equivalent of war. It seemed an eon ago. An exhausted president had stayed awake following the proceedings through the night. He then went to Camp David, swam, bicycled, read some books, and slept.[45]

Shortly after 9:00 a.m. on November 9, 1978, in the East Room of the White House, flanked by the congressional leaders he had pressured, the president signed the five major energy bills joined together. He said that together they provided about two-thirds of the energy savings originally proposed. The main omission arose from Congress's refusal to authorize a tax on oil that could be refunded to the American people. Carter promised: "This is something we will pursue through administrative or congressional action next year." (He did, and it passed in 1979.) The president declared its passage represented a declaration of "our intent to control our use of energy and thereby to control our own destiny as a nation," and he was right. For the first time the nation had the foundation of a comprehensive energy program, with strong incentives for conservation at its heart.[46]

ENERGY TWO: THE SHAH AND GASOLINE LINES

Any euphoria over signing the energy bill quickly ended as we had to decide how to honor the president's Bonn summit pledge to allow U.S. oil prices to rise to world levels by the end of 1980 without blowing the gaskets on domestic inflation. I summed up the problem in a memo on January 3, 1979, with a question for Carter that only the president of the United States could answer: "Should our energy policies and international commitments on energy be deferred or delayed in their implementation so as to minimize the near-term inflation effects which an increase in U.S. prices to world levels would entail?" I had never seen Carter more troubled, less certain of how to move. He told us the worst political scenario for him would be rising energy prices pushing up inflation further as he faced the people in November 1980.[47]

But events were taking over. Oil prices were already strengthening because of the political upheaval in Iran, and in mid-December, 1978, OPEC took advantage of the situation to announce a 15 percent price increase that threw a dagger at the pledge Carter had made six months before at Bonn to our allies in the name of the United States. That is when ordinary Americans also felt the point of that dagger at the gasoline pump.

There is an old adage that it is better to be lucky than good. It is no excuse to say that luck and good fortune are often as important to a president's success as his own policies. But the gods were against us, because in the midst of these traumatic decisions an era ended on January 16, 1979: The Shah of Iran was deposed and fled Tehran, yielding power to a radical Islamic movement. Iranian oil production came close to a standstill, with Iranian production dropping from almost six million barrels per day in 1976 to a little over one and half million in 1980, a squeeze of more than five percent, in a global oil market of about sixty million barrels per day. We now faced the second oil shock of the 1970s, and we did not manage it well. I would wake up early each day working on how to cope with this added crisis when we still had not resolved how to handle the president's pledge to move to a world price level that no one could have imagined at Bonn.

Within days after the Shah of Iran fled his country, spot-market prices doubled to $22 a barrel in the panic, and by the end of the decade, crude oil would be trading at $42 a barrel—ten times the $4 price ten years before. The president sent Schlesinger to Saudi Arabia, and Carter personally called Crown Prince Fahd to request more production. He responded in a move still famous in the kingdom: Fahd disappeared for two weeks into the desert, and when he surfaced, Saudi Arabia started pumping up to 11 million barrels of oil a day, up from of 8.5 to 9.5 million. This left only a small shortfall in the world energy market. So why was there a price panic that would double energy prices from February 1979 to February of the election year 1980, and lead to pernicious and politically destructive gasoline lines?

The crude oil price shock came largely because oil stocks were running low in 1978 and 1979, with worldwide consumption close to capacity, and companies and countries stockpiled oil for fear of an Iranian cutoff. Oil giants like BP, Shell, and Exxon warned their customers they could no longer guarantee supplies. So brokers and refiners fled to the spot market (the public cash market in which oil and other commodities are traded for immediate delivery) in a panic that drove up the spot price for the additional barrels everyone was fighting to buy. It was the energy equivalent of a run on the bank. OPEC prices were following, not leading the spot market. The problem of the gasoline lines really began at home, and I accept my share of the blame.

For sure, there was a small imbalance between supply and demand, but it was a quirk in the market that cascaded a shortage into a panic. The problem had arisen the previous winter in California when local refineries ran short of distillates—the lighter crude oil by-products that must be mixed into the local gasoline formula to meet the state's tough air-quality standards. To build up stocks during the spring, the refiners distilled more of the lighter petroleum oils instead of compounding gasoline, and a few gas stations ran dry. Word spread, the panic began, and anyone with a car (almost every adult among California's then-forty-million-plus inhabitants) filled up the tank instead of driving around one-quarter or half full. That sucked one to two hundred million barrels of oil out of the tank farms. The news spread across the country, and it became normal to stop at a station and fill up and top off, even if there was plenty of gas left in the tank. The imbalance in the supply chain then shifted from a physical problem of a small actual shortage to a huge psychological problem of gasoline panic that created spot-market shortages around the world. It also did not help politically when California governor Jerry Brown, who had unsuccessfully opposed Carter in the 1976 presidential primaries, started accusing the president of causing the shortage.[48]

The spiraling disaster was compounded by our reaction to it. Rather than rely on the market, we used a government system pushed into law by Senator Bentsen that allocated gasoline based on historic consumption. It sent more gasoline to rural states than they needed; urban and especially suburban areas got much less. Oil companies followed this perverse formula even though they knew it did not correspond to the actual pattern of demand. What we should have done was simply stopped allocating gasoline by fiat, and freed prices. I believe that ordinary Americans would have adjusted to higher prices by driving less, rather than wasting time in long gas lines that were often rambunctious and occasionally worse. Perhaps it was a form of rough justice on federal bureaucrats that the Energy Department formula allocated extra supplies of gasoline to the capital's favorite vacation resorts of Ocean City, Maryland, and Rehoboth, Delaware, while gasoline was so scarce that Washingtonians could not get there.[49] I had to wait half an hour at the Exxon station near my home in Chevy Chase, Maryland, to get enough gas to travel to the White House to try to deal with the crisis—and then not very well.

President Ford exercised his authority to end gasoline price controls in his last days in office, ending the American driver's era of rolling along the nation's highways on gasoline at about 32 cents a gallon—after his electoral defeat. Even while calling for energy sacrifice, Carter disregarded Ford's move. If he had taken advantage of Ford's decree allowing him to free up prices when oil was much cheaper, price hikes would have been smaller and less noticeable than when the market exploded after the Iranian revolution, and there would have been no gasoline lines. While Schlesinger was eager to decontrol gasoline, he was talked out of it by his mentor Scoop Jackson. Natural-gas decontrol was still working its way through Congress, and the senator believed that the public confused natural gas with gasoline. Even emergency gasoline rationing might have been acceptable if fully explained to the public.

There was a dark humor in this. The Ford administration had ordered ration books printed for an emergency, but never used them. It was discovered belatedly that the government ration coupons could be used as legal tender for food stamps and even cash when slotted into cash machines, and the Secret Service had to destroy them.

Scoop Jackson or no Scoop Jackson, Schlesinger had come to the conclusion that the administration must decontrol gasoline prices and allow natural market forces to allocate gasoline. There were deep divisions within the administration. Schultze and Fred Kahn, the anti-inflation czar, philosophically supported decontrol but were concerned about the impact on rising inflation. I was influenced by their concerns about inflation, but also by the political intervention of allies like Sol "Chick" Chaiken, the president of the International Ladies' Garment Workers Union, who urged "gas rationing rather than rationing by price."[50] And Mondale was also politically and philosophically opposed to decontrol.

What is unmistakable is that we would have been better off if we had left President Ford's last-minute decontrol of gasoline prices in place and not reversed his decision, thus putting the unpopular decision on Ford's back while taking advantage of it when the gasoline crisis hit two years later. I also believe that the American driving public would have traded higher prices for punishing thirty- to forty-five-minute waits at their gasoline stations and topping off even when their tanks were still half full, and after an initial bump-up, prices would probably have settled down.

While we were considering decontrolling gasoline and diesel fuel, the Teamsters Union and the long-haul drivers they represented were up in arms against it. Frustrated truckers were literally shooting gas station attendants who had run out of fuel. These burly drivers shut down the Pennsylvania Turnpike, leading to riots injuring more than one hundred people, and more than 150 arrests.[51] They then converged on the White House with their heavy vehicles in a massive demonstration demanding a meeting with the president, or at least someone on the White House staff. As my energy aide, the brilliant Kitty Schirmer, remembered it, Jack Watson "courageously volunteered me to meet with them on the ground that they probably wouldn't hit me because I was a woman. . . . It was an awful meeting . . . and they dropped F-bombs and things like that. They never did hit me, but they certainly beat me up around the head and ears verbally." Schlesinger, with an air of condescension, remembered that Kitty was frightened to death by these truck drivers.[52] Before the meeting in the Roosevelt Room, she promised me and Schlesinger she would not commit the administration to a special allocation of diesel fuel for the trucking industry. But that is exactly what she did. When Schlesinger later asked Kitty, whom he derisively called the "Wellesley girl," why she had caved, Kitty replied: 'Well, you've never sat down next to somebody who is six feet, six inches tall, looks very angry, and has a size 17 neck!"[53]

There was in fact something close to a national hysteria about the oil shortage. Conspiracy theories abounded that the major oil companies were withholding supplies from the market to drive up prices—an absolute myth. Just like sightings of Unidentified Flying Objects, there were supposed sightings of tankers hiding in the coves of North Carolina because their owners were unwilling to discharge the cargos until prices moved even higher.[54] The president's populist rhetoric against the oil companies helped stoke the tales of profiteering. So we responded by dispatching U.S. Coast Guard cutters to search for these ghost oil ships hiding in the Carolina marshes. Of course, none were ever found.

All the major players met often in an Energy Coordinating Committee from mid-December 1978 to March 1979, in the Situation Room, to find a consensus that would square the circle on the Bonn pledge, and to deal as well with the burgeoning domestic energy crisis. Carter decided to act boldly and not mortgage the future of decontrol to legislative caprice. He placed a high-stakes bet against Congress itself, by first letting Congress know that he would use his existing authority to start phasing in higher oil prices no matter what they did, and then ending control entirely by October 1, 1981. Rather than condition decontrol on the uncertain congressional passage of a windfall profits tax, he simultaneously warned that the wrath of the public would fall on Congress if the windfall in higher revenues from old wells in a decontrolled market was not captured for the public instead of the oil companies. The windfall tax package was brilliantly designed to enlist the support of Democratic liberals by creating an "energy security fund" that would redistribute the revenues to the poor to help buffer the impact of higher energy prices. It also served as a substitute for the wellhead oil tax (COET) that had been killed by the industry and Senator Long. Schlesinger nicknamed it "Energy Two."

This time we faced a palpable oil crisis and were careful not to waste it. With the public awakened by lengthening gas lines, we were careful not to repeat the original mistake of assembling our second package in secret, and spent weeks in talks with interests across the economic spectrum and in Congress, as well as with the government agencies that were able to do the economic and budget calculations for the new program. To obtain maximum public and congressional support for the windfall profits tax, we proposed everything but draining the kitchen sink—mass-transit and low-income assistance, alternative energy development in solar and magnetic fusion, and even wood-burning stoves. There was a minority set-aside program for the major construction projects to encourage the Congressional Black Caucus to support the package. Energy Two even won Metzenbaum's vote and out-flanked Ted Kennedy on the left.

The proof of this inclusive process lay in the pudding itself: A much larger percentage of Energy Two was enacted than our 1977 package.[55] The president began the phased decontrol of crude oil, as he promised at Bonn, and through a combination of public anger and adept White House lobbying, Congress passed our windfall profits tax on the energy industry in April 1980, to capture for the public the unexpected revenues from the run-up of OPEC prices—it raised $80 billion through 1988, when it was repealed.[56]

In June 1980 he signed a third energy package, the Energy Security Act, which included a massive synthetic fuels corporation to encourage drilling for oil shale and liquefying coal, decades before the shale revolution of the twenty-first century began to make the United States more energy self-sufficient; a solar bank to commercialize solar energy; and the first major incentives for geothermal and biomass-based energy.

Over four full years Jimmy Carter struggled more than any other president with energy, accomplished far more, and suffered politically for it. He was ridiculed for proclaiming a moral equivalent of war, but when all the smoke had cleared from the battlefield and despite all the mistakes, stumbles, and reversals that are characteristic of any war, he was wounded but he had won, and so had the country. It was only when set against his overambitious standard that the final product paled. Market-based prices sent signals to consumers to use less and to producers to deliver more. It is hard to see how this century's energy revolution could have taken place without his efforts.

By any objective measure Carter's National Energy Plan in 1978, the 1979 decontrol of crude oil tied to a windfall profits tax, and the 1980 Energy Security Act made historic changes in America's energy policy that have stood the test of time.

It set the United States on a new path to a sounder, more secure, more independent energy future. Carter created a rational market-based system of pricing and selling crude oil and natural gas, a cleaner fuel that had too often been burned away in oil-field flares and now was available to industry nationwide, encouraging consumers to use less and producers to deliver more. On a broader public horizon, a conservation ethic was born in the minds of the public that permanently changed the way in which the American people and our industries and utilities consume scarce energy resources. Things we now take for granted, everything from the way we drive to the way we live—from more fuel-efficient cars, homes, and appliances—were embedded in Carter's new laws and eventually in our consciousness.

For the first time we formally recognized that our domestic supply of oil and gas was not limitless, and that our growing dependence on imported oil was a national security risk. And for the first time there were explicit incentives to produce clean alternative energy sources. Carter ended the thirty-year impasse over natural-gas pricing, creating one uniform, efficient national market; reformed to the benefit of consumers the way electricity was provided; and laid the foundation for the shale revolution which has made America more energy independent in the twenty-first century. At the time one of the least appreciated (but in the long run, most important) features of the final package was the revolutionary reform of monopoly electric utilities, through the Public Utility Regulatory Policies Act: A whole new competitive industry was created to produce power from cogeneration or steam and other renewable sources, and the utilities were required to buy it for mainstream distribution. And the president's new Energy Department implemented these laws and gave energy a seat at the cabinet table. Independent studies found Carter "achieved significant reductions in energy consumption and oil imports." [57]

Moreover, he achieved most of what he sought. In a study of the Carter energy program, the Harvard Business School concluded that Congress gave the president good marks with Congress.[58] The energy wars he fought for four years are also a metaphor for the Carter presidency: great accomplishments achieved by unartful means and at great political cost. Carter paid a frightful political price for leading the country to a coherent energy policy. No one realized more than Carter himself the political cost of his focus on energy: "It sapped our strength," he told me.[59] Courageous as he was in pressing ahead, he barely got credit. Many of the benefits to the country of his energy programs were felt only after he left office, as they are even today.

PART III

THE ENVIRONMENT

11

AN EARLY INTEREST

Just as Bert Lance posed Jimmy Carter's first Washington challenge to personal loyalty, Congress posed its first bruising political test to his deepest principles in preserving the environment. He learned from both encounters, but from the second he emerged as the greatest presidential protector of our nation's natural bounty since Theodore Roosevelt, and if measured by acreage preserved and policies enacted, the greatest in America's history. When Roosevelt left office in 1909, he had protected 230 million acres of public land. When Carter left office in 1981, he had more than doubled the total amount of protected public land from Roosevelt and every president since.

He inherited his appreciation of protecting the land from his father, the first farmer he knew to terrace all his land, rotate his crops, and protect wildlife in the hedgerows between his fields. James Earl Carter, Sr., was a leader of the Civilian Conservation Corps, and young Jimmy followed in his footsteps, working fields that drained into Choctawhatchee Creek, where he fished and learned about the outdoors as a member of the Future Farmers of America.[1] He also drew much of his environmental inspiration from his Christian faith. He was at home in nature, and when he was alone in the woods, he felt "closer to God" and developed an appreciation for the protection of the land. As a child he heard sermons on such biblical texts as "The earth is the Lord's, and the fullness thereof." And even in old age, he wrote, "When humans were given domination over the land, water, fish, animals, and all of nature, the emphasis was on careful management and enhancement, not waste or degradation."[2]

The breadth of what he accomplished in a four-year period is astonishing.

One of his first major presidential messages in May 1977 was on the environment.[3] As in so many other areas, he took on established interests oblivious of the political costs and often in ways that were politically maladroit, alienating the bulls of Congress and the powerful Army Corps of Engineers in tackling what he considered environmentally dangerous and economically wasteful water projects; coal mine operators in the Surface Mining Act, twice vetoed by President Ford to limit environmental degradation for strip mining; the chemical industry in passing the first broad-based toxic-waste-pollution controls; the automobile and oil lobbies in strengthening the Clean Air and Clean Water Acts; and implementing tough fuel-efficiency and emissions standards for cars and trucks.

He did all this by substituting for heavy-handed, top-down government regulation a creative new cost-effective means that gave industry flexibility to meet new environmental standards in a so-called bubble. Each plant did not have to meet environmental standards if the entire company did so, and if they did better than the federal standards, they could then engage in free-market trading of credits for the emissions they had saved with companies that failed to meet the standards—a system known as cap-and-trade. This became the model used by Presidents George H. W. Bush and Bill Clinton decades later to deal with sulfur dioxide emissions, and by the European Union and China to meet their greenhouse-gas-emission obligations under the 2016 Paris Climate Change Agreement.[4] As a lame-duck president after his landslide defeat in 1980, he worked with Representative John LaFalce of Buffalo, where Love Canal first brought toxic chemical waste discharges to the public attention, to sign a far-reaching Comprehensive Environmental Response, Compensation and Liability Act (Superfund) to clean up dangerous wastes around the country and have the chemical industry pay a large share of the cost.[5]

Carter was also the first U.S. president to put conservation of the environment on the global agenda, starting in the summer of 1979 for what became the pathbreaking Global 2000 Report released the next year. I worked on it with Gus Speth, the chairman of the White House Council on Environmental Quality, and Thomas Pickering, assistant secretary of state for the Bureau of Oceans, Environment, and Science. It called attention to global environmental trends in ten major areas of activity, such as world population growth, water resources, agriculture, fishing, and forests. In the Clinton administration in 1998, as undersecretary of state I was the lead negotiator of the Kyoto Climate Change Protocol reducing greenhouse gas emissions, and highlighting the need to protect tropical rain forests, which absorb greenhouse gases. Carter's foresight is striking because when he released the Global 2000 Study while president, one proposal was to have the CIA use Landsat satellite photography to track the disappearance of the Amazon Basin forest.[6] The administration took its findings to the United Nations to help it formulate a new international development strategy. Had Carter been reelected or future presidents followed the report's recommendations, we would have a safer planet.

The rise of the modern environmental movement paralleled Jimmy Carter's political rise; he ran for president on a platform of clean air and water and an end to the pharaonic dams that impeded the natural flow of America's rivers and dried up the breeding grounds of hundreds of animal species in its marshes. The older environmental movement of the Sierra Club and Audubon Society, embodied in Teddy Roosevelt, focused on national parks and wilderness preservation and had some victories throughout the early part of the twentieth century and into the Nixon era. But if there was one catalyst for the modern environmental movement, it was Rachel Carson's 1962 book, *Silent Spring*, which exposed the dangers of the pesticide DDT.[7]

The revolutionary advance from the traditional conservation movement to a new focus on health and safety was literally ignited on June 22, 1969, when chemical discharges in Cleveland's Cuyahoga River burst into flame. This helped catalyze the modern activist environmental movement, which was marked by the first Earth Day, initiated by environmental and solar power advocate Dennis Hayes and Wisconsin Democratic senator Gaylord Nelson on April 22, 1970. It was inspired by the model of the teach-ins held by the activists opposing the Vietnam War, and developed into a middle-class movement to reverse industrial degradation by oil spills and pollutants of the air, water, rivers, wetlands, and animal habitats, imperiling the quality of life on the planet. Suddenly environmental groups organized to influence politicians to legislate and regulate on a bipartisan basis; many environmentalists were Republicans.[8]

President Nixon, with his ear to the ground, gave his blessing to Earth

Day, and declared in his first State of the Union message: "Clean air, clean water, open spaces—these should be the birthright of every American."[9] While he did not take the lead, he signed the bills creating the Environmental Protection Agency and the Clean Air and Clean Water Acts. But he eviscerated funding for the EPA and tried to bottle it up.[10]

As governor of Georgia, Carter took on the development and construction companies, which drained wetlands for their projects, a standard procedure that had never been challenged before he took office. When he assumed office, 535 projects for draining wetlands awaited his signature. As he explained, bulldozers "would take a wandering stream through wetlands, and make a straight ditch out of it, and then the farmer could change that wetland into pastureland and eventually into cropland. And I vetoed all of them, there never was one approved." A number of Atlanta's biggest real estate developers also wanted to build shopping centers and homes along the Chattahoochee River—"dig up half of it and put it on top of the other half and then build stores and homes on the top." He stopped that, too.[11]

Building dams and other water projects had become a very visible and politically profitable exercise after World War II, and Carter had initially supported them for power production, flood control, and recreation.[12] But he slowly grew to realize that the dams came at considerable fiscal and environmental costs. From the governor's office he learned how the sordid system worked, through a Washington alliance of political convenience between members of Congress, particularly Southern and Western Democrats; the U.S. Army Corps of Engineers, which built dams east of the Mississippi and focused on flood control and navigation; and the Interior Department's Bureau of Reclamation, which built them in the West to generate power and irrigate agriculture. As he put it in his antipolitical way, "One of a congressman's highest goals in life was to have built in his district a notable dam at federal government expense that would create a lake that could be named for him. The process began when a newly elected legislator went in as a junior member of Congress. He would put his name on the list to get a dam built in his district. That dam might be at the bottom of 500 dams to be constructed in America. But as the congressman got re-elected time after time, eventually his particular project would move up to the top of the list."[13]

12

THE WATER WARS

I n his most formative environmental battle as governor, Carter took on the Corps of Engineers, which planned to build the Sprewell Bluff Dam on the Flint River, not far from his native Plains. The dam was strongly supported by the local congressman, Jack Flint, and was officially justified by supposed recreational benefits. But from Carter's gubernatorial perspective, it would have interfered with the state's longest remaining free-flowing river, the Flint. Fishermen and environmentalists brought him their concerns about the dam. To get a better idea of the consequences of damming up the Flint River, he canoed down the river twice and fished for shoal bass. He had become an avid canoeist and kayaker on the Chattooga River, the setting for the movie *Deliverance*.

Carter met with some fifty different groups, from concrete manufacturers to developers of a large recreation center planned in the area. The local chamber of commerce estimated that as many as two hundred construction jobs would be created, and more for services after the dam was built. There was no question about the position of the congressman who coincidentally actually bore the river's name—and he was furious with Carter for even questioning the dam. But Carter used his powers as governor to stop the dam, and later got the last word. Thinking back on this seminal experience, he wrote in the river's guidebook, "Lakes and dams are everywhere. But to experience something that is undisturbed and has its natural beauty? You hope and pray that it will be there a thousand years in the future, still just as beautiful and undisturbed."[1]

During the presidential campaign Carter captured the spirit and enthusiasm of the environmental movement down to our campaign's green-and-white

colors. He had been explicit in his pledge to halt the construction of unnecessary dams and severely limit the channeling of streams and rivers,
earning him the first-ever endorsement of a presidential candidate by the
League of Conservation Voters.[2] Three strands of Jimmy Carter's unusual
political DNA came together to oppose this long-established practice: his
environmental consciousness; his flinty habit of carefully watching every
penny spent of taxpayer's money; and his moralistic view of government.

As president, Carter appointed a dream environmental team, with Doug
Costle at the Environmental Protection Agency (EPA), Charles Warren and
Gus Speth at the Council on Environmental Quality, and Cecil Andrus, a
two-term governor of the conservative state of Idaho who had run on a strong
environmental platform and taken on the mining and oil and gas industries.[3]
They first met in 1970 as freshman governors and helped each other in fighting the oversold projects that damaged the environment.[4] Tall, lean, and
balding, with a refreshing candor and a quiet, assured manner, Andrus was
the embodiment of the open spaces of the West as well as one of my favorite
cabinet officers. He ran his department well and was loyal to the president,
even when, in a critical battle, his sage advice was ignored. Andrus left no
doubt of his policy toward managing the government's vast landholdings
"in a manner that will make the three Rs—rape, ruin, and run—a thing of
the past." He asserted that he was "making sweeping policy changes to end
the domination of the department by mining, oil, and special interests. . . .
Our President is canceling the blank check which once went to those
who would exploit resources and pollute the environment in the name of
progress."[5]

The Carter administration could hardly have sounded a clearer battle cry
in what became known as the Water Wars. While many worthy projects offered great benefits to local communities by providing everything from electricity to flood control and recreation for families, the process for funding
them had degenerated. Carter learned from his Sprewell Bluff experience as
governor that the Corps had shifted its goals from making objective cost-
benefit analyses to pleasing Congress by computing the benefits of each dam
far in excess of its costs—and environmental damage was not part of the
calculation. To hide the final cost of a project, congressional appropriators
would first devote a small amount of money to study a project; and each

year include only the current costs. For example, the Central Arizona Project to siphon off Colorado River water was started with an appropriation of approximately $1.2 million but its full construction cost in today's dollars was more than $1 *billion*. And once construction started, the game was over and could not be stopped. Efforts going back to the 1950s to extract water projects from the pork barrel and subject them to rational economic calculations had largely failed.[6]

Carter was determined to reassert strict criteria to judge water projects and put a lid on the federal pork barrel. Even before his inauguration, the president-elect tried to transpose his experience with the Sprewell Bluff Dam to the hundreds of water projects awaiting funding in the Congress. He was about to learn that he had been playing in the minor leagues with one single dam, and to appreciate New York senator Pat Moynihan's admonition that in the big leagues, water projects were an "extraordinarily important subject" championed by powerful members of Congress: "You can live without oil and even without love, but you cannot live without water."[7] With his victory over the Sprewell Bluff Dam in mind, he was ready to join battle. As he later wrote, "I began to question those dams. As President, I had the prerogative to veto them, and I began to do that. I wasn't a dictator, and I have to admit that some of the ill-advised projects were approved. But, overwhelmingly, they were disapproved. It created one of the most difficult confrontations between me and members of Congress of anything I did while I was in office."[8]

Carter had an enormous, almost unprecedented opportunity. Although he had barely won, the Democrats in Congress were swelled by the "Watergate babies" elected in 1974 and 1976, many from traditionally Republican districts, still recoiling from the Nixon administration scandals. In the House there were 292 Democrats to only 143 Republicans, one of the most heavily Democratic in modern times. The Senate was a filibuster-proof 62 to 38 Democratic.

But even with a friendly Congress, there are only so many issues a new president can press. Yet in his early months in office he proposed a blizzard of bills. Some were a must, like an economic recovery program. He used his early political capital on enacting a comprehensive energy package, which was highly divisive but critical for the long-term security of the country. But he added welfare reform; a bill to restrain hospital costs; and he was now

frittering away precious political capital on the marginal issue of water projects, rather than seeking other long-term priorities of the Democratic Party
like national health insurance, which he had endorsed in general terms during the campaign.

But wasn't tackling water projects a prime example of what Carter had
campaigned against: pork-barrel spending that despoiled the environment
and cost taxpayers billions? Wasn't he elected to change the status quo and
to shake up Washington? Yes, but the way it was done led to catastrophic
results. The president's head-on attack on an extraordinarily contentious issue exposed every weakness of the new administration. Lacking both his
own Washington experience and his staff's, the new president pressed ahead
in the belief that he could act on dozens of water projects at the congressional level in the same way he had stopped the Sprewell Bluff Dam, by refusing to sign off on the Corps' plan as governor of Georgia. Politically he
lost in every way possible way. The senior House and Senate leaders found
their cherished water projects under attack. The younger members who joined
his crusade climbed out on a limb with him at the risk of their own futures,
only to find it sawed off by the compromising old guard. The environmental community backed him only to find he folded at the last minute.

During the campaign Carter had asked Jack Watson to develop policy
proposals so he could hit the ground running if he was elected. Watson
knew little about water projects but did know of Carter's experience with the
Sprewell Bluff Dam, and Watson's transition team was loaded with environmental advocates. He asked Kathy Fletcher, a scientist who had worked with
the Environmental Defense Fund and later joined my Domestic Policy Staff,
to contribute to a briefing book for the incoming Interior secretary that
would pull together a list of water projects that were suspect in terms of their
environmental impacts and cost. After the election they worked with Don
Crabill, a career budget official who had been waiting for a president like
Carter for years. He handed them a ready-made list of some fifty suspect water
projects compiled by OMB over the years, which failed to meet a cost-benefit
analysis.[9] His was no lone voice: It seemed that everyone in the field had a
list of suspect projects, so there was not just one list but many. One list of
thirty-five projects had been compiled by Kathy Fletcher herself, and even
the Corps of Engineers knew of thirty-seven that did not meet cost-benefit

standards. The lists were so loosely protected that during the transition period the briefing book fell into the hands of a private-sector lobbyist, David Wyman, who passed it on to Andrus's top policy assistant, Guy Martin, by simply knocking on his hotel room door and handing it to him.[10]

It is difficult to imagine a single meeting in which so much political damage was done to an incoming president by his own hand than the one during the transition on December 9, 1976, when we reviewed the transition team's recommendations for energy and the environment with the president-elect. He compounded the problem of trying to rush the development of a comprehensive energy plan within 90 days of his inauguration by instructing his incoming budget officials to identify wasteful and environmentally damaging projects and to "cut back on the water resources budget" for the coming fiscal year.[11] An immediate problem was that we had only one month to change the outgoing Ford administration's budget proposals for the forthcoming fiscal year. This left no time, even if there had been an inclination, to test congressional sentiment.

His haste precluded a careful decision-making process within the administration and shut out Congress, whose sacred cows were slaughtered in secret. Capitol Hill got information only from news leaks, many based on the multifarious lists. The budget office barons worked furiously together to assemble an authoritative list but decided not to share Crabill's carefully argued list lest Carter go with this "macho solution," and try to kill all the projects at once to demonstrate how decisive he was on tough issues. So they whittled it down, but Carter made it clear he wanted more. In a follow-up meeting they reluctantly showed him the whole list and he embraced it.[12]

There is much blame to go around for all of us involved in this process, but this was not driven by a few in-house environmentalists or long-standing budget hawks somewhere down the pecking order, but by Jimmy Carter himself. Leaks about the water projects were the bane of our existence. The process quickly developed the momentum of a runaway train. A leaked copy of the briefing book with its threatened projects was given to a reporter in Andrus's home state of Idaho who coined the term "hit list." That made the early decision to swing for the fences very difficult to back away from, and from the start put the administration in a defensive battle with the press and Congress. Even as we tried to refine the hit list with the Army Corps of Engineers and the Reclamation Bureau, they immediately leaked it to their congressional patrons.[13]

FIRST SHOTS

Thomas Bevill, a tall, handsome, stoop-shouldered, soft-spoken congressman from Alabama, was the powerful chairman of the House Appropriations Committee's Subcommittee on Energy and Water Development. Unfailingly courteous, this conservative Democrat was nevertheless fiercely determined to preserve his own and the Congress's prerogatives of the purse over water projects. Even liberal members felt that there was almost a constitutional right for Congress to approve water projects without interference from the president. Jim Free, one of our best White House lobbyists on the Hill, was passing by the Public Works Committee Room and noticed several high-ranking officers of the Corps talking with Ray Roberts, another powerful congressman who never met a water project he did not favor. He eavesdropped long enough to overhear them laughing about how they were going to beat us at our own game. Battle lines were forming.[14] Kathy Fletcher was said to have met with environmentalists and passed out a list of forty-five water projects marked P or F—pass or fail. The president was outraged and asked me to investigate, and although she was exonerated after a thorough review by me and my two deputies, Bert Carp and David Rubenstein, the leaks continued and made an already complicated problem even greater.[15]

Andrus meanwhile sent the president a memorandum on thirty-five water projects that he agreed were dubious and deserved to be canceled "if political problems can be overcome"—as he ominously warned. Rather than trying to bundle them all into the administration's forthcoming budget, he urged the president first to develop a more rational system, with "improved planning, current discount rates, and more equitable cost-sharing responsibly" so that local communities would share the cost of each project—and possibly think twice about whether they were really needed. He targeted four dubious Western projects under his jurisdiction for review, and wrote, "Mr. President, let me stress again what I mentioned in the Cabinet meeting this morning: If we attempt to alter any of these projects for whatever reason, our action will act as a catalyst to create political coalitions in the Congress. I am not arguing against eliminating some of these projects—some definitely merit action—but I want you to know that there will be political retaliation from the Congress when we do." Andrus urged instead that four or five of the worst projects should be singled out so the attention could be focused only on them. This memo, sent only some three weeks after Carter's inauguration, was as blunt a warning as a cabinet officer can give. Mondale concurred, but they were ignored, even though Andrus repeated it before the entire cabinet.[16] Senate Majority Leader Byrd, who agreed that many were "obsolete and unnecessary," believed like Andrus that the president should pick out a few of the worst projects and marshal "his forces against the worst excesses of the pork barrel," rather than take on the whole package, alienating more members than he attracted.[17]

The next day Carter's inclination toward confrontation when challenged on a principled stand was reinforced by a letter from sixty-two members of the House, and twelve senators, supporting his water reforms.[18] Then he called me from his small study to ask me to work with the budget specialists on a statement for Congress to "delete money for all water resource programs."[19] We came up with several options in a February memorandum to the president, intentionally leaving blank the total number of projects to be killed until we met the next day. They ranged from green-lighting all water projects that had already been funded and stopping only new projects for a review; slowing down all of them but not killing any; killing only all the new ones permanently; allowing most to continue but stopping a few of the worst as a shot across the bow; and, most radically, killing all water projects that had not been completed, and stopping any new ones. In our memo, we also warned that "the more projects chosen for deletion, the more political heat we will face from Congress." More likely, we said, Congress would approve them all, including those on his hit list, and that he had to be prepared to stand up to one of Capitol Hill's most favored programs, and face down many of his own Democratic supporters with a veto. We offered Andrus's preferred outcome as an "Option B"—kill two or three of the outright worst and delay or reduce funding for the rest of the questionable projects pending a policy review.[20]

But fatally, and incorrectly, we concluded on the basis of advice from our chief lobbyist, Frank Moore, that "this option would seem to raise almost as much potential heat as deleting funds for those 35 projects." This was cosmically bad advice, in which I fully implicate myself for not objecting more strongly. In Moore's defense, he had never asked for his job as congressional liaison, was new to it at the time, and admitted that he did not know Congress had any voice in the president's water projects budget.[21] Over the years he redeemed himself, with the help of talented young, Hill-savvy aides.[22] Carter eventually matched the record of any modern president in winning congressional passage of his legislation. But this record never caught up with the bitterness that arose from the fiasco of the water projects in the formative months of the administration.

The key officials met on February 17, less than a month after the inauguration. The heavy snow of that unusually cold winter was still on the ground of the Rose Garden. In the Cabinet Room the banners of major battles hung from the American flag, along with the personal flag of the president of the United States. The fireplace crackled with a newly made fire, but the historic room also radiated with political tension.[23] At the meeting with the president were Secretary of Defense Harold Brown; Secretary of the Army Clifford Alexander, to whom the Corps of Engineers reported; two Corps generals; Bert Lance, just starting out in office; and the staffers like myself who had worked on this issue. Notably absent for such a crucial political decision was Ham Jordan and Jody Powell. Even though government-supported water was the lifeblood of the American West, the president was about to be seen as declaring war on the West. It mattered little that there were an equal number of projects in key states east of the Mississippi.[24]

The president began by declaring that he wanted to be a partner with the Corps but that he nevertheless wanted to delete thirty-five projects from the Ford budget and quickly undertake a study to assess them under "new priorities." A generation ago, he said, no one raised any environmental concerns, but "I am concerned now." Andrus intervened forcefully to argue against deleting all thirty-five projects, only some of which were bad. He prophetically warned of a congressional coalition against Carter, once again recommended picking out several projects as bad examples so that "the rest of the Congress will side with you and we can get rid of some of the big dogs, and that will mark a change in the way we do business in the future."[25] Mondale agreed; Army Secretary Alexander urged the president to start by developing criteria to measure the effectiveness of the water projects and only then decide which ones to delete from the budget. "Otherwise," he said, "it will appear that the thirty-five were arbitrarily chosen." Andrus agreed: "Don't take the heartburn while you are looking at the projects." On the question of money already appropriated by Congress, Carter said he did not simply want to rescind funding; he wanted a total stop to new projects.[26]

So the heavy hitters—Mondale, Lance, Andrus, Alexander, Brown—all came down urging a cautious, incremental approach. Hearing their persuasive arguments, I also recommended against listing such a large number of projects and urged sending a short list to Congress. The president should have listened to this advice but did not, showing his inflexibility on what he considered a matter of principle. He could have made his point by starving a few of the worst projects and setting in motion a policy process with Congress to develop more honest criteria for the rest. This would have avoided the firestorm that would soon engulf us. Instead the president agreed to take fewer than thirty-five but decided to pick out all those that could not be justified on a cost-benefit basis, and ones where work had just started. Where heavy construction was already under way, the projects should not be put up for review. But he ordered, "Stop the ones without large contracts," and his last, fateful directions were to "put as many as possible to delete" and not just sidetrack them for study.

As the president left, the happiest person in the Cabinet Room was Crabill, who spent his career at OMB overseeing egregious water projects he was not powerful enough to kill on his own. But Andrus had a different view. When the president asked him to come up with a list of the worst of the worst, Andrus was happy and went home that night to tell his wife, "We just averted disaster." He planned to send Carter a short, slimmed-down list the following week. But the next morning he flew home to Idaho, and when he landed a reporter shoved a microphone in his face and said, "What's this hit list?" Andrus was dumbfounded and told me later he did not know what the reporter was talking about. He grabbed the wire-service story out of his hands, saw that it contained the full list of suspect projects, and assumed someone at the meeting had leaked the list to the press. We did cut almost by half the number of targeted projects to 19. But now, as Andrus put it, "The fat was in the fire, the hit list came out and then we were fighting a defensive war."[27] Andrus was unfairly blamed for the hit list, and the *New York Times* reported he "is popular with most environmentalists, but in much of the West, environmentalists are as popular as a social disease."[28] This was Jimmy Carter's decision through and through, and he had to live with the consequences.

Carter then formally announced a major review of water resource projects and threw down the gauntlet to Congress by announcing that his budget would cut off funds for nineteen that "now appear unsupportable on economic, environmental and/or safety grounds," and they would be reviewed with a view to saving $5.1 billion. He told Congress he would work closely with members "to develop a coherent water resource policy," but the horse was out of the barn. The hit list had been developed without a moment of consultation with Congress and no opportunity for the champions of the 19 deleted projects to make their case.[29]

One particularly sensitive project not on the list was an obvious sore point for environmentalists and fiscal conservatives, because it carried what looked like a political exemption. The Tennessee Tombigbee Waterway, or TennTom as it was called, ran through Bevill's district and would connect the Tennessee and Tombigbee Rivers, offering a shorter route for Ohio River valley coal and other commodities heading to the Gulf of Mexico for export.[30] Even the president recognized the political problems of trying to kill it. Representative Bob Edgar, a Pennsylvania Democrat allied with Carter in the Water Wars, described the project as "moving more dirt than was moved to build the Panama Canal." And they were just justifying it because they were going to move more coal than existed in Kentucky and Tennessee and rerouting the Tennessee River.[31]

Even worse, keeping it off the hit list did not in the least soften Bevill's intense opposition, because his power depended upon being able to deliver projects for other members of his subcommittee and not just himself as its chairman. By the time the White House started to notify members whose districts and states were directly impacted by the projects on the hit list, they had already read about it three days before the president's announcement in the *Washington Post* under a banner headline, no less inflammatory because it was slightly inaccurate: "Carter Will Ask Hill to Halt Aid to 18 Major Water Projects."[32]

The reaction from the key members of Congress who focused on public works was one of outrage, which was only intensified by the way the White House formally delivered the bad news.[33] Jim Free, the lead White House lobbyist in the House on the water projects, was given a list of congressmen whose projects had been dropped from the president's budget and told to call them. Admitting he was green and did not appreciate the gravity of his message, he recounted that he telephoned Arizona Republican Mo Udall and announced: "Hi, I'm Jim Free from the White House and I'm calling to let you know that the president is eliminating the Central Arizona project." And Udall said, "What is your name?" And for years after that Mo Udall would have fun at dinner parties recounting the story and saying, "I never forgot Jim Free's name."[34]

Bevill maintained his support for the completion of the TennTom project, a boondoggle that took twelve years and cost $2 billion of taxpayer money to complete.[35] Today there is a Tom Bevill Lock and Dam, one of four such structures, and a nearby Tom Bevill Visitors Center at Pickensville, Alabama. Carter had inherited a deficit of $73.7 billion, until then the largest in history, and wanted to reduce it by curtailing pork-barrel spending. If all 19 projects had been deleted, the savings during his first fiscal year would have amounted to a grand total of $289 million, and $5.1 billion over the life of their construction cycle.[36]

If Carter had applied any sort of cost-benefit analysis to the political price of these relatively piddling savings, he might have realized he would come out a huge loser. But he did not, and he lost big. At one meeting about a hundred congressional Democrats told Andrus that this was the worst political development of their careers.[37] At a presidential briefing of congressional leaders, they told him he simply did not understand what a threat this was to them.[38]

We held frequent meetings as we scrambled to develop a strategy. As March began, Carter, Mondale, Lance, Jordan, Moore, Bowman Cutter of OMB, and I held the kind of all-hands meeting that should have been called before any decision was made. But the president was in a feisty mood, calling me the next week to say we should go public with the worst four or five water projects on the list and explain the difficulty of balancing the budget unless we took this on: "I don't want to back off," and "I want to make a public fight of it so Congress sees they can't push me around."[39] He got the fight he wanted.

The president belatedly recognized the political damage and tried to develop a rationale behind the list, and we held numerous meetings trying to come up with one that fit. Lieutenant General John Morris reported that the experts at the Corps he led had tried to pass 55 projects through a screen using the new and more realistic criteria; but there was no way to get down to just five of the worst. He came up with about 30 and pointed out that a number of projects were already well under way and could not realistically be cut out of the budget. I wrote a marginal note: "Shows the problem of barreling ahead w/o thinking through the consequences."[40]

True to his principles, Carter even wanted to continue to keep a water project memorializing the esteemed late Georgia senator Richard Russell on the hit list. He finally agreed to issue a statement late in March that 337 water projects had been reviewed and 305 had been approved for future funding, while the other 32 would be assessed in the future. He instructed us: "Word it positively, but in a businesslike fashion."[41]

Even so, the hit list landed in Congress like a small atom bomb. The gravamen of their complaint was that the president had usurped their congressional prerogatives: Making decisions on local projects was not his business. Bevill, California's Harold "Bizz" Johnson, and Majority Leader Jim Wright, the titans of the Appropriations Committee, went berserk. As Jim Free witnessed, it became a "real mud fight."[42]

I personally got a taste of the raw emotions involved when I was summoned to meet Wright in his magnificent Capitol office with some constituents who would be disadvantaged by cuts in the water projects. The elegance of the setting was quickly forgotten during the tongue-lashing applied to me and the White House for our peremptory action. Wright, a Texan, had a reddish complexion that seemed to turn to beet-purple, with the veins in his neck bulging as he leaned over and sharply criticized our lack of respect and consultation in trying to take away a congressional prerogative. And on the procedure, he was right.[43]

Russell Long, chairman of the Senate Finance Committee, through which much of our domestic legislation would have to pass, was apoplectic. One of the threatened water projects was in his state of Louisiana, and when he met with Carter, Long went so far as to threaten to put the president's economic stimulus package into a "deep freeze."[44] Another of the angriest senior senators was Edmund S. Muskie of Maine, a strong environmental champion and principal author of the Clean Air and Water Acts, who intimated he would hold up consideration of the budget resolution to save a project in his state.[45] "No President should have the right, unilaterally, on his own, to frustrate a policy that has been made a part of the law of this land, in accordance with constitutional processes," said Muskie. "When the executive aborts established procedures, I, as one member of the Senate, am going to look for anything I can fire back." Senate Majority Leader Byrd went ballistic, saying that the president's attempt to suspend projects that had already gone through environmental-impact statements, engineering studies, and cost-benefit analysis "rubs a raw nerve." He was also aggravated by the absence of any prior consultation with senators.[46]

To show that this was not simply a war of words, the Senate on March 1 voted 65 to 24 to rebuff the president by supporting all nineteen water projects on his list that had previously been approved by the Congress. The anger rippled into other complaints—appointing Republicans to key posts in the administration without prior notice to Democratic senators, severely limiting access to the White House, and failing to notify Congress of pending appointments. To further retaliate, the Senate delayed confirmation of Guy Martin, Andrus's key policy aide at the Interior Department. Even his friend, Senator Floyd Haskell from Colorado, withheld his vote until the administration would support the Narrows water project in his state.[47]

All this was particularly painful for Mondale, who had served in the Senate with them for a decade and had to bite his tongue over the amateur behavior of the inexperienced White House. As we tried to contain the congressional fallout, the president reluctantly agreed to exempt cuts from already contracted projects but grumbled, "It makes me sick to waste this kind of money."[48]

The entire episode underscored all the weaknesses of the new president's approach to his job: By compartmentalizing decisions he failed to make connections to other priorities, and this was compounded by his refusal to appoint a chief of staff to help him sort them out. He was leaping off a precipice without considering the political costs and too often stubbornly refused to listen to good advice. In Washington *everything* is connected. It does not mean that tough decisions should be avoided, but that their effect must be weighed against other goals, and only so many can be pursued at the same time. His decisions also highlighted what my deputy David Rubenstein called the president's moralistic bent: "He just thought things were morally wrong. It wasn't just economically or environmentally bad; they were morally wrong and I think he just thought people who were supporting these pork-barrel projects were corrupt people."[49]

As we moved into May, the president asked me to develop a legislative strategy with the vice president to salvage the water projects initiative.[50] The strategy was clear, but it would be difficult: to create a sufficiently large coalition of young, reformist Democrats and budget conscious Republicans in the House for a veto-proof minority to block the entire $10 billion public works bill, of which the water projects were just a fraction. And then to use this to put pressure on the Senate committee to cut as many projects as possible. Now that the president had jumped into the water with alligators, we had to win to show he could mud-wrestle even the establishment of his own party early in his presidency.

He had natural allies in the newly elected Democrats from the post-Watergate classes, who, like Carter, were bent on changing the traditional ways of congressional politics. After the 1974 election, they had forced through major changes in the House of Representatives, most dramatically by ending the established principle that committee and subcommittee chairmen were selected by seniority and demanding they be selected by a vote of the whole Democratic caucus. This unseated five committee chairmen. Many came from traditional Republican districts and were, like the new president himself, New Democrats—fiscally moderate and socially liberal reformers.

Carter reached out to the Democratic young Turks and fiscal conservative Republicans, inviting them to the White House, where they affirmed their support for the hit list of water projects. They left the meeting energized and ready to work with their fellow reformer. They knew they could not get a majority to support Carter, but needed at least 144 votes in the House to sustain a veto and believed they could prevail if he actually did so, sending the bill back to Congress to reopen and examine the barrel of pork buried in the legislation.[51]

The most courageous opponent of the water projects was Butler Derrick, a tall, good-looking, South Carolinian with a syrupy Southern accent and a razor-sharp mind, whose district abutted Georgia. He explained that he, like many of his young colleagues, had no ties to the traditional Democratic Party establishment. The recent law permitting political action committees (PACs) allowed members to raise large sums of money independent of the party, and the new class came into Congress with the mind-set, in Derrick's words, that they "were going to clean out the House and make things honest; everyone was for honesty back then."[52] He even opposed the Richard B. Russell Dam, which had been started in his district before he took office. Just as it was unheard of for a governor to do what Carter had done in blocking the Sprewell Bluff Dam in his state, it was a total break from tradition for a congressman to support a presidential hit list that targeted his own local water project.

To bolster Derrick's courageous stand, Frank Moore assured him and his colleagues that Carter would veto the public works bill if they could muster enough votes to guarantee that his veto would be sustained.[53] Before the climactic vote, Derrick went to the well of the House and delivered a remarkable speech: "I believe I have the credentials to stand before the members on this issue because I have a dam in my district that is going to cost the taxpayers of this country, by the time it is completed, one-half of one billion dollars. You can have it back; we do not want it. The citizens who live in my district and who work in the textile mills—the people who go in every morning and work an eight-hour shift—are going to be paying for these projects for the rest of their lives."

Derrick was joined by Silvio Conte, a Massachusetts Republican, in cosponsoring an amendment to delete the 19 projects on the Carter hit list from the Energy and Water Appropriations Bill. Conte was a serious but colorful legislator who would occasionally wear garish outfits to make his point. This time it was a uniform like that of the captain of the HMS *Pinafore*, hat and all, to mock the artificial lakes that many of the projects would create. The emotions were raw on the day of the vote.

Derrick walked into the cavernous House chamber and saw Ray Roberts of Texas, powerful chairman of the Veterans Affairs Committee and an avid supporter of water projects (for which he was rewarded by having the Ray Roberts Dam and Lake near Denton, Texas, named for him in 1980). "You boys won't get a hundred votes," Roberts said. Derrick replied, "Well, Mr. Chairman, we'll see." Roberts called Bob Edgar, an ordained minister and Carter ally, "The meanest minister I ever met." The confrontations on the House floor became almost violent. Edgar remembers that Phil Burton, a voluble liberal Democrat from California, climbed over chairs to get at him, when "I was going after something in San Francisco he wanted."[54]

DEFEAT FROM THE JAWS OF VICTORY

To everyone's astonishment, the Derrick-Conte amendment got 194 votes, more than enough votes to sustain Carter's promised veto. When the final tally came in, Derrick exulted, "We've won this thing! We've won this thing!"[55] His joy would soon turn to despair and anger because of another rookie mistake by the president. The unexpectedly narrow House defeat of the amendment alerted the Senate Appropriations Committee to move closer to Carter, and they did. The chief concern of the Senate floor manager of the public works bill, the courtly Senator John C. Stennis of Mississippi, was to avoid a presidential veto by passing an acceptable bill that could survive in a conference committee with the House. Stennis urged: "Give the President some solid ground to stand on so he can sign this bill." The bill eliminated funds for nine projects, and followed Carter's recommendations to reduce and modify three. Finally the committee voted not to fund any new water project starts in fiscal 1978.

That left Carter in a good position for a House-Senate conference. The Senate had come halfway toward him, and he had assembled a veto-proof minority in the House. Now disaster came from inexperience and the president's idiosyncratic way of making decisions in the early months of his administration. In lobbying for votes on his bills, he would dutifully call everyone on a list provided by the White House lobbying team, but he rarely horse-traded and would sometimes mistake the ambiguity of the standard congressional response: "Mr. President, I'll do everything I can to help you."[56] And yet he was effective here, and more generally, through sheer force of will and intelligence, and a generally supportive Democratic congressional leadership.

After catalyzing a New Democratic–Republican coalition that stood by him at risk of retribution from their senior members and angry constituents, Carter, in one thoughtless three-minute phone call, threw them overboard without any consultation with his staff or his friends in Congress. I was with him in his private study on another matter when the president received a call from Speaker O'Neill on Friday, July 15. As recorded in the log, it came at 12:22 p.m.[57] I could only hear the president's end of the conversation, but when it was over he told me he had just reached a compromise with Speaker O'Neill on water projects. The House would agree to delete spending on several projects on the hit list, but only for this year, and would fund the rest. In return the president would not veto the public works bill.

I told the president he could not do this to our allies on the Hill; they would be outraged, and the supposed compromise would not actually kill any of the projects. The president had literally grabbed defeat from the jaws of victory. His young New Democratic allies and some moderate Republicans would feel they had been sold out, while the press and public would see him caving in to pressure from the establishment. I was stunned. When I told Frank Moore about it, he was also dismayed, having made a commitment to Derrick, and felt it was a mistake for Susan Clough, the president's personal secretary, to put through the Speaker's call without having others listening in on it.[58]

At my urging, and in order to ensure that Derrick would not read about it on the wire services first, the president called him at 12:27 p.m. for a seven-minute conversation. Derrick related to me his sense of shock when the president told him he would withhold his veto. He told Carter: "Mr. President, I don't believe that. You know Frank Moore told me you would veto the bill." And Carter replied, "I made a sort of arrangement with Tip that has something to do with the [Clinch River] nuclear plant." A shaken Derrick repeated: "Mr. President, I don't believe that. You know

Frank Moore told me that you would veto the bill." He told Carter he was making a "bad mistake, and I think that it will hurt you in your dealing with the Congress for the rest of your administration." Derrick reflected years later that he had been right, and that after this fiasco Carter "did not enjoy the kind of relationship he should have had with Congress."[59] And Derrick's colleagues, who had gone into the trenches with the president, full of what Derrick called "vim and vigor" to end the old order, had bucked the system and came away with nothing to show for it.

Derrick was so angry when he called Moore, he was "sputtering," reminding him of his unfulfilled promise of a presidential veto. Now a dam would be built in his district over his objection and he would get no credit.[60] Derrick gave Moore's assistant Jim Free a tongue-lashing unlike any he ever received before or since[61] and vented his anger to the *Washington Post*.[62] For good measure, Free said that Conte "went even more berserk." The president's environmental allies issued a blistering statement against the compromise he made with the Speaker, calling it a "complete cave-in."[63] Andrus was also mystified, since everyone in his Interior Department and the environmental community had worked so hard to round up enough votes to support the president's position.

Free later pieced the story together from the Speaker's end: Majority Leader Wright had told the Speaker that the president would be able to sustain a veto and urged O'Neill to persuade Carter to back down and accept a deal that would stop a project known as the Clinch River Breeder Nuclear Reactor, which Carter opposed. O'Neill called the president, played on the fact that Carter was new in town, and said something to the effect that they had to work together on many issues but right now there was already blood in the water. He continued: "And you, Mr. President, do not need to veto this." Free concluded that Carter "fell for the story that [it] would be good in the long run for him not to get in this head-on fight with these guys the first quarter he was in town. So he took the deal."[64] O'Neill himself had other fish to fry: He needed federal money for a huge tunnel known as the "Big Dig" to sink an interstate highway underground and revive the Boston Waterfront, and he required the support of Bevill and the other public works appropriators.[65]

But Congress and the press saw the compromise as a sign of weakness, and Moore sadly concluded: "In his first major legislative initiative he caved; everyone saw that he could be pushed around; and after that they said this guy can be rolled."[66] So in his initial confrontation, the president blinked, and let the old politics he had come to change defeat the new politics of the broader public interest he wanted to embody.

There were broader ramifications. Free believed that a new bipartisan coalition had been formed in this battle, and that the president could have deployed it again—including the young Democrats plus Republicans like Conte, David Stockman of Michigan (who would later become President Reagan's budget director), and even future vice president Dan Quayle, all of whom wanted to rein in wasteful spending and change the old ways of Washington. It also opened a gap between young, reform-minded Democrats and the entrenched Democratic leadership. Free felt it confirmed a congressional suspicion that Carter and his Georgia coterie could not be trusted: "They're not one of us; they didn't understand the politics of what they had in their hand, when he just pulled the rug out from under us."[67]

The Senate-House conference report did not permanently kill any of the projects, only delayed funding for one year. To rub it in, one of the nine water projects still funded was the Richard B. Russell Dam. When Carter signed the bill on August 7, he said he did not consider the battle finished. The whole bloody battle would have to resume again next year, sucking out more political oxygen.

LESSONS LEARNED AFTER THE BATTLE

Jimmy Carter does not accept defeat easily, and learned lessons from his retreat. We began early to try to pick up the shattered pieces of our package. It was not easy, given the initial sense of betrayal. And yet, so great was the initial debacle that the steps he took the following year, which had long-term positive environmental and budget benefits for the country, are hardly remembered today—something that might be said of so much of the Carter presidency.

The basic approach in our next budget was to recommend funding only those projects that met our economic and environmental criteria. We warned Carter that the Russell dam was so strongly supported in the Senate that we could not succeed in deleting it without vetoing the entire public works appropriations bill in an election year. We gave him several options, and he chose the most draconian: "Delete all projects funded by Congress against our recommendation"—but he wrote in by hand "with some exceptions." He decided to take an uncompromising approach once again, and when he met in June 1978 with the House and Senate members who had supported him on water projects, Carter conceded he had made a mistake in not vetoing the previous year's appropriations bill.[68]

A series of events at the White House were organized to build pressure on Congress. Recognizing that we were gaining the upper hand, Johnston, Tom Bevill, and Wright asked the president to consider a compromise on the Public Works Appropriations Bill to be sent to Congress in 1978. We told the president that we now felt we were sufficiently strong and advised him not to move far from his position and offer at most a limited compromise, and only after consulting with our House allies.

Our public works strategy was to set strict terms blocking the revival of any projects terminated in the first year, use the administration's new selection criteria for future projects, and under no conditions accept *extremely* bad projects—without creating any kind of politically explosive hit list. We would discuss specific projects *only* if firm agreement was reached first on an acceptable cap on total spending. That meant Congress could no longer open a federal tap and expect it to flow unhindered. The sophistication of this strategy showed how far we had come in our appreciation of how to achieve results. But it still took continuing presidential pressure to establish a new and more economical paradigm for public works: He also had to veto the 1978 public works bill. He did so, and his veto was sustained. While the once-burned Derrick congratulated the president in an October 1978 letter on his "stunning victory," the lingering bitterness of the 1977 episode would not go away. Years later Derrick told me he barely remembered the successful 1978 veto.[69]

The storm-tossed two-year journey over water projects proved to be an early metaphor for the Carter presidency: In the short term it seriously damaged his relationship with Congress and underscored for a skeptical press corps and Washington establishment that the president did not have a first-class White House team to augment his own inexperience. Success eventually came only in the most politically maladroit way.

Yet Carter's vision proved true in the long run. "Ultimately," he noted, "I was able to block many ill-advised projects, as well as bring significant reforms to the system."[70] And the policies he planted bloomed with the help of former representative Stockman when he became Ronald Reagan's budget director. Reagan built on Carter's accomplishments but helped the medicine go down in his own disarming way. Adopting a Carter proposal, in the 1986 Water Resources Development Act, he implemented local cost sharing, which stopped many projects dead in their tracks. Reagan would say, in effect, "I love water projects. I am from the West and I know their importance. But fellas, we just can't afford them all. You understand?"[71]

After all the smoke had cleared, the environmental activist Brent Blackwelder concluded that Carter had achieved a major accomplishment even at a huge political cost. He felt that Carter legitimized the criticism of dams and other environmentally damaging water projects and "unleashed a giant new vision in which the U.S. is number one in the world in protecting its most outstanding rivers."[72] With the veto of the second public works bill, Carter brought rationality to the consideration of new water projects, eliminated a number of costly ones, and saved taxpayers billions of dollars.[73] But there was an even-longer-term benefit, because Carter's battle over water projects was the opening shot at the practice of legislators earmarking local projects that were sacrosanct from review; this ended when Republicans took control of the House of Representatives in 2011, a ban that continues to this day.

Jimmy Carter gets the last word. Years later, he wrote that when he and Rosalynn stopped in Thomaston, Georgia, where the Sprewell Bluff Dam would have been built, "many people come up to me and confess that they cursed me profoundly when I vetoed the dam. But now they are thankful for my having done it. They are glad that the Flint River was saved. Those people have—we all have—a precious possession along that river."[74] What Jimmy Carter reflected on in later life about saving the river in his own backyard can be extrapolated to many places around the United States.

13

ALASKA FOREVER WILD, DESPITE ITS SENATORS

Nothing better demonstrated how far President Carter's legislative and political skills had been honed since the fiasco of the Water Wars than what he accomplished by negotiating, securing passage, and signing into law the Alaska National Interest Lands Conservation Act. And he accomplished it in 1980 as a lame duck president after his loss to Ronald Reagan, with one foot out of the Oval Office door. Without exaggeration it is one of the most important pieces of environmental legislation in the nation's history. Its scope was breathtaking. It added more than 157 million acres of national parks, national wildlife refuges, national monuments, wild and scenic rivers, recreational areas, national forests and conservation areas, created ten national parks and preserves; two national monuments; the huge Arctic National Wildlife Refuge and nine others; two national conservation areas; and twenty-five wild and scenic rivers. But it was balanced legislation, opening 95 percent of the state for unrestricted oil and gas exploration.

Before he could achieve this historic environmental legacy, however, he was faced with a challenge that would have left it stillborn two years earlier. More than eighty million acres of land were set aside for conservation under the 1971 Alaska Native Claims Settlement Act, passed in the Nixon administration to clarify the land rights of the indigenous people after the discovery of oil off Alaska's coast at Prudhoe Bay. An additional forty-five million acres were set aside by Nixon's interior secretary, Rogers C. B. Morton, but would be reopened for development if Congress did not act by December 18, 1978.

Multiple efforts to resolve the outstanding issues foundered in Congress, and in the autumn of 1977 Representative Mo Udall, a committed environmentalist from a pioneer Arizona family, introduced a bill with sweeping conservation provisions designed to protect what he described as the "crown jewels of Alaska." It brought out in full force Alaska's political and business leadership and energy companies, fearing that passage would limit their access to the area's vast natural resources. The state's two senators, Republican Ted Stevens and Democrat Mike Gravel, united against the bill, although they bore both political and personal grievances against each other arising from an airplane crash in 1978 that took the life of Stevens's wife and almost killed him, for which, rational or not, he blamed Gravel for delaying his departure with dilatory action in the Senate. The two rivals joined to write their own limited bill designed to drag out the legislative process until some provisions of the Settlement Act expired, returning the land to eligibility for development. With only two months to the December deadline, Stevens met with Carter in October 1978 to indicate he was willing to negotiate with the White House and blamed Gravel for the impasse. The best the president could obtain was Stevens's commitment to work out a compromise in early 1979, too late to protect the huge area.[1] Carter knew the clock was ticking and thereupon took one of the boldest domestic decisions of his presidency.

Eliot Cutler, in charge of natural resources at OMB, Interior Secretary Andrus, and I developed a defense against the increasing likelihood that Congress would not pass legislation in time, while simultaneously prompting Congress, especially Stevens and Gravel, to act on an issue that had been delayed for eight years. Our plan involved two federal acts, the 1976 Federal Land Policy and Management Act and the Antiquities Act, an environmental weapon of awesome potential. Enacted in 1906 under President Theodore Roosevelt, it gave a president the right to designate objects and land of historic and scientific interest as national monuments without congressional approval, essentially freezing any commercial and other activity, even hunting and fishing. Although draconian in its reach, it had been used more than a hundred times to preserve the Grand Canyon and the Grand Tetons, along with many other natural treasures. But it had never been invoked to protect such a huge swath of pristine territory. Andrus sent the president a memorandum in November 1978, growing out of our interagency review that warned Carter he needed to act now "to assure that these lands are not despoiled while we await congressional action."[2]

The Interior secretary had just withdrawn 105 million Alaska acres from mining and other local exploitation, but that order extended only three years and could be challenged in court. He also warned Carter that he would be criticized as immoderate because "no president has ever taken an action of this magnitude—nor will any future president have the opportunity to do so." Outside Alaska, Andrus explained, "there are no more frontiers, only remnants of our natural heritage." As for congressional objections, he pointed out that the House had passed a bill by the overwhelming bipartisan vote of 277 to 31, setting aside even more acreage than the administration, but it had been filibustered to death by none other than Alaska's Mike Gravel.

Because of the great political risks, I wanted the president to hear every argument, positive and negative. So the next day, in a November 29, 1978, joint memorandum from Andrus, Agriculture Secretary Bob Bergland (whose department managed some of the areas to be protected), and me, we detailed the areas that would be protected under the monuments designation, and summarized the pros and cons. We said it was the strongest tool available, would be the most significant spur to congressional action, could not be blocked by Stevens and Gravel or even by another president, but only by a future Congress. Thus further delays by the two senators would be eliminated. We warned him of the likelihood of future court challenges, but we emphasized to the president that "regardless of the outcome of legislation, his action would be viewed as strong and decisive."[3]

If anyone doubted that Jimmy Carter was tough and now seasoned late in his presidency, they would be dissuaded by the fact that he promptly checked the option for his approval, and issued a formal Designation of National Monuments on the first day of December, before the deadline.[4] (The Trump administration has removed several designations that protect pristine Monument areas elsewhere from economic development.)

Thus outflanking Congress, he warned that the land would "remain permanent Monuments until the Congress makes other provisions for the land." This was designed as a spur to action—which it was, but only after two years of hand-to-hand political combat. The Alaska congressional delegation, in Andrus's words, "went bonkers."[5] It would be an understatement to say that Carter's proclamation was not readily accepted in Alaska. The president was burned in effigy in Fairbanks. Residents in the Cantwell area organized a major act of civil disobedience known as the Great Denali Trespass, entering the park and violating laws by lighting campfires and firing guns. The towns of Eagle and Glennallen, located in the shadow of newly designated monuments, issued official declarations that they would neither respect nor enforce National Park Service regulations, and would shelter those who violated them.

Even months later, in June 1979, Carter expressed concern about landing briefly in Anchorage on the way to a G7 summit in Tokyo. Stevens greeted him as he descended from Air Force One, and to Carter's surprise, Governor Jay Hammond of Alaska gave the president a mule driver's whip, "just in case he needed it," or in Carter's own words, "I might need it to whip somebody's ass."[6] Indeed, it would come in handy for what followed.

Stevens knew the leverage had shifted decisively to the president, and that further delaying tactics would play against the Alaska senators, who would be better off negotiating a legislative solution with more flexibility than the rigid limits in the monuments designations. We rallied support for his controversial use of the Antiquities Act, with a number of events at the White House organized by Anne Wexler, the most memorable of which occurred the following May. The president was given the ultimate compliment by Chief Matthew Fred of the tribes on Admiralty Island for preserving "this island, its natural resources, its wildlife, from time immemorial." On behalf of the people of Angoon, the chief presented the president with a clan vest and a noble name, *Nakoo'woo*, meaning "a great nation in migration." The chief movingly explained: "The name was given birth when my nation was coming back to their beloved coastal home after the ice had receded from the land, and that is a long time ago. You are now my brother of the Raven Beaver Clan and an honorary chief of Angoon and of all Admiralty Island." Carter thanked the chief and the tribe he represented and repeated sentiments about his deep love for nature in its purest state, as well as his apologies on behalf of all the well-meaning leaders including himself for the times they had fallen short.

Joining the White House ceremony was none other than Theodore Roosevelt IV, a New York investment banker and a Republican, who said, "No cause was closer to the heart of my great-grandfather than the conservation of our natural resources. Were he here today, I think he'd be amongst the first to applaud your efforts to preserve our priceless jewels in Alaska for future

Americans, and he would probably use his favorite adjective, 'bully,' to describe your efforts."[7]

To say that the president was involved in the negotiations would also be an understatement. Even while engaged with gaining the release of the Iranian hostages, and following his crushing electoral defeat, he was focused on preserving the Alaska lands before he left office.

One example illustrates Carter's attention to detail—a characteristic that had its pluses and minuses. Stevens was concerned about the designation of a small piece of Alaska land and asked to discuss it directly with Carter. When he arrived for the appointment with the president and Andrus and raised the issue of this obscure parcel, the president countered, "Let's check that," got down on his hands and knees on the floor of the Oval Office, and rolled out his giant map of Alaska with all of his designated monuments and our proposed legislative positions. "No, I don't think you're right," Carter told Stevens. "You see this little watershed here actually doesn't go into that one. It comes over here." In the car going back to Capitol Hill, Stevens told his chief of staff, Jack Ferguson, that Carter "knows more about Alaska than I do! I've been campaigning all over it and representing it for twenty-five years!"[8]

A final deal reached down to the last watershed. It also protected the Arctic National Wildlife Refuge from development unless the president and both houses of Congress allowed it. The ceremony in the East Room of the White House was memorable. When Carter signed the legislation, Mo Udall, his 1976 Democratic primary opponent, declared: "No president has done more, with the possible exception of Theodore Roosevelt, to do things in conservation that need being done, and nobody can ever take that away from you, Mr. President."[9]

For me, there was a personal event twenty years later that gives Carter's victory a special meaning. I took my two sons with their wives and children, and my grandchildren, on an Alaska cruise. We took two side trips on a smaller boat off the cruise liner—one to Glacier Bay and one to Fjords National Park—both areas among the many that had been set aside in the Alaska Lands Act. The craft displayed copies of the president's 1978 Antiquities Act Proclamation and Monuments Designation, and the National Park Service pamphlets handed out to visitors recounted the history of the bills he signed into law. When I told the park ranger that I had worked with President Carter to make this happen, he was incredulous. He said, "This is wonderful; it really is; I hope I can do it justice on this tour." But Cecil Andrus said it all: "It was the only place in the North American continent, if you go around the coastline, where you don't have the industrial footprint of man, and there are just certain things and places that ought to be left alone."[10]

But our environment is dynamic; changes in the air we breathe, the land we till, and the sea around us are constant, and threats can never be ignored. Part of that coastline is now being slowly inundated by rising seas, and some native villages are already being forced to retreat to higher ground.[11] And even during that family Alaska visit, our guide had pointed out the dramatic melting of the glaciers from global warming.

President Carter elevated the environmental movement to the highest political level. He left office with the environment at the forefront of his thoughts, where it remained, and was taken up as a challenge and a cause by political leaders everywhere. The environment, along with nuclear weapons and human rights, was highlighted in his farewell address to the nation on January 14, 1981—the importance of the "stewardship of the physical resources of our planet" and the need to protect against the "real and growing dangers to our simple and most precious possessions: the air we breathe; the water we drink; and the land that sustains us." He did more than any president of the United States before or since to put the nation on a course to protect this precious heritage.[12]

PART IV

THE ECONOMY

14

THE GREAT STAGFLATION

Jimmy Carter entered office in January 1977, at a time of great economic challenge and flux. The entire decade of the 1970s was characterized by a combination of economic phenomena not seen before or since—a painful condition of simultaneously high unemployment, stagnant growth, and high inflation that required a painfully awkward new term to describe it: *stagflation*.[1] It contradicted the prevailing economic theory that higher levels of inflation were related to high levels of growth, and higher unemployment would lead to less inflationary pressures. Consequently, an angry public was caught running in place, economists were baffled, and the administration was divided over what to do about the miseries of an economy with a unique malady for which no one had a clear, painless prescription: fight unemployment and stoke further inflation, or tackle inflation and worsen unemployment?

The new president inherited a witches' brew that began when Lyndon Johnson decided to fund the Vietnam War simultaneously with the Great Society. It was compounded by Nixon's decision to impose wage and price controls, which enabled him to press his Fed chairman, Arthur Burns, to print money that helped ease his way to reelection. Quickly removed after his victory in 1972, the controls were followed by the first oil shock of 1973, prompting the first burst of double-digit inflation. During the 1970s inflation never fell below 5 percent, double the historic average.[2] Experts from Paul Samuelson, the dean of liberal economists whose textbook remains a staple for economic classes the world over, to conservatives like Alan Greenspan, the longtime Federal Reserve chairman, believed the stagflation cycle began with President Johnson's policy of guns and butter without raising taxes to pay for both. As Greenspan told me, "LBJ let the canary out of the cage."[3]

The administration's economic policy was constantly whipsawed between balancing our commitment to lower unemployment while dealing with surging inflation, a struggle that not only divided the administration internally but also from our liberal Democratic constituency groups, which focused only on jobs. It created dissonance in our economic policy and uncertainty among the American public and our key allies abroad.

After stimulating the economy mainly with tax cuts in the first part of his term, Carter realized before most of his advisers, myself included, that inflation was the greatest danger to the nation and its growth. He employed everything from two anti-inflation czars, tight budgets, increasingly tough wage and price guidelines, a labor-management advisory board, and deregulation. These measures were like using a toy gun against a raging elephant. In the end, however, after all else had failed, Carter courageously appointed Paul Volcker to head the Federal Reserve in the full knowledge that this determined public servant would deploy the blunt instrument of tight money and high interest rates. This ultimately squeezed inflation out of the economy at the cost of high unemployment and helped squeeze him out of a second term, but with long-term benefits to the country to this day.

But on the way we made a series of policy errors in which I was directly complicit (although hardly alone). We failed to recognize the seriousness of inflation and inflationary psychology early enough. We were willing to live with the high rates we inherited in the mistaken belief that we could stimulate the economy to drive down unemployment without further spiking inflation. We failed to reinforce the president's own conservative instincts by persuading him not to veto the 1978 tax cut, as he repeatedly told us he wanted to do. All these domestic decisions combined with a "perfect storm" of other events over which we had little control—the second oil price shock of the 1970s, sparked by the Iranian revolution, soaring world food prices, and productivity that sank to unprecedented low levels. All that boosted inflation from its already high level of about 6 percent that he inherited from Ford to double digits four years later.

This created a fear among the American public that the economy was out of control and their livelihoods with it, a fear shared by America's allies and global financial markets, which questioned whether economic leadership of the free world was in sound hands. This withdrawal of confidence sent the dollar plunging, despite tight budgets and deficits that were a fraction of those racked up during the Reagan administration. In retrospect, if Carter had administered the harsh medicine of a recession during his first year to get it out of the way, that would have run contrary to his campaign promise of restoring growth. While it might have led to lower inflation later in the administration, no one could have been sure of that, and in any case it was a policy that no one advised, inside or outside the administration.

The level and force of inflation had not been seen in America since the Civil War. It made a mockery of economic policy making throughout the decade. One Republican president, Nixon, imposed wage and price controls, while the second, Ford, resorted to vetoing Democratic spending bills and a widely derided Whip Inflation Now campaign of cheerleading conferences and their wacky signature WIN buttons. It was politically easier for the Ford administration to switch its focus from reducing unemployment to fighting inflation by citing the Republican mantra of balancing the budget. But neither Nixon nor Ford urged Arthur Burns, their Federal Reserve chairman, to raise interest rates to fight inflation, fearful it would create a recession. Ford got the recession anyway, along with an inflation rate that averaged 9 percent in 1975.[4] This helped elect Carter but did little to enhance understanding by academics or policy makers of the unprecedented phenomenon of stagflation.

Stagflation had bedeviled three successive American presidents during the 1970s and was a major factor in the defeat of two of them. Against Ford in the 1976 election, we employed economist Arthur Okun's invention of a "misery index" that added up the high percentages for both unemployment and inflation—only to have Ronald Reagan throw it back at us four years later. Stagflation also prevailed in all the leading industrial democracies of Europe and Japan. In the end the Carter administration could boast four years of growth and the creation of more than 10 million new jobs. That was more than were created under Nixon and Ford, almost twice the number created during Ronald Reagan's first term, and almost identical to that in his second; nearly four times more than in George H. W. Bush's one term, and just below the job growth in Bill Clinton's first four years, during his golden times in the 1990s.[5] Our budget deficits were a fraction of Reagan's mammoth ones, and federal spending during the first four years of the Reagan administration averaged about 24 percent of gross domestic product (GDP), compared with only 21 percent during the Carter administration.[6]

Early in his term, Carter, a Democrat who was conservative in both personal and public finance, recognized that inflation was a mortal danger but faced a divided administration, unremitting pressure from Democratic congressional leaders and the party's dominant Washington-based liberal wing, plus union, minority, and urban supporters demanding that he expand the economy, create jobs, and ignore inflation. They had been out of power for eight years and were anticipating a big surge in spending on job creating and social programs starved during the Republican years. This pulled in the opposite direction from every conservative fiscal fiber in Jimmy Carter's being. The gap between his own balanced-budget instincts and those of the party whose banner he carried represented a fault line that cut across his administration. The policy tools in the hands of our traditional Keynesian economists had been devised to fight a 1930s Depression through government spending and were not equipped to confront this new economic phenomenon.

We did not appreciate, and as a noneconomist I certainly did not, the degree to which inflationary psychology had embedded itself into the American psyche and economy as prices kept creeping up and then exploding after the first OPEC oil shock in 1973. Companies reacted by raising prices to cover the sudden explosion of energy costs, while workers, particularly those in labor unions, responded by seeking higher wages in a spiral that continued unchecked. In theory this should not have happened. Almost a century of British statistics compiled by A. W. Phillips were supposed to demonstrate a trade-off between inflation and unemployment, so that fewer people at work would put a lid on prices, and higher levels of employment would lead to more inflation. In all recorded economic history, a stagnant economy or a recession would normally lead to falling prices.

But in the 1970s, Professor Phillips's famous curve was bent out of shape. The Kennedy and Johnson administrations first turned to persuasion through "incomes policies," using voluntary wage and price guidelines that were supposed to temper inflation without the pain of workers losing their jobs and their purchasing power. It was not very effective.[7] Carter's instinctive concern with inflation from the earliest months of the administration was compromised not only by pressures from his party, but by his own central campaign promise to end "the Ford Recession." And when he pivoted to give priority to fighting inflation, the policy tools he was handed by his economic experts were not up to the task.

After running as a more conservative Democrat in the primaries, he turned to the left at the time of the Democratic Convention to unite the liberal wing behind him, emphasizing economic growth and job creation. In the campaign we created an Economic Advisory Task Force that I oversaw, including several leading economists who had served in Democratic administrations. It was headed by Lawrence Klein, who in Carter's last year in office won a Nobel Prize for his mathematical models forecasting the behavior of the economy. The group proposed a stimulus program of public service jobs, tax cuts, and other measures. Klein declared that the federal government had an obligation to fund public employment for those the private sector would not hire, and to set a steady target for economic growth of 4 to 6 percent annually, an inflation rate of 4 percent or less by the end of his first term, and that unemployment should never be used as a tool to fight inflation. Carter embraced this policy prescription in the campaign.

True to Democratic Party tradition, sound money was not a top priority. Carter asserted in the campaign that he would control inflation by reducing government regulation, encouraging competition in transportation and other industries, strictly enforcing the antitrust laws and protecting consumers, and keeping interest rates low. Mandatory wage and price controls, like those used by Nixon, were rejected in the campaign and throughout the administration. But the Council on Wage and Price Stability would be given subpoena power to examine excessive wage and price hikes. This was colloquially known as jawboning and was about as effective against raging inflation in the 1970s as the biblical weapon from which it was derived, "the jawbone of an ass."[8]

CONFLICTING ECONOMIC ADVICE

After the election the president-elect tapped two people to be his top economic advisers, and they could not have been of more different temperaments or, as it turned out, taken more different approaches to the economy. Charles Schultze was named chairman of the Council of Economic Advisers, whose principal job was to help the president develop a macroeconomic policy, determine its economic consequences, and project how specific decisions would interact with the real economy. He was at the top of his game as a mainstream economist, and as former budget director under President Johnson, renowned for his knowledge of how government works. After he left the Carter administration, he became president of the American Economic Association.[9] Throughout our White House years I worked as closely with Charlie as anyone in the administration and found him unfailingly congenial, self-effacing, and brilliant—in a word, a prince of a man, to me the nicest person in the entire administration and one of the most broad-gauged and able.

The other senior economic adviser was Michael Blumenthal, Carter's Treasury secretary. There had been five generations of Blumenthals in Germany, and Mike and his family had narrowly escaped death after the forced sale of the family business in Oranienburg, the Berlin suburb next to Sachsenhausen, the Nazis' first concentration camp. They fled across Russia by train to Vladivostok, and then by boat to the free port of Shanghai, where they survived World War II in the impoverished Jewish ghetto. Afterward Blumenthal and his sister arrived penniless in America. Earning his doctorate in economics at Princeton, he became a top trade negotiator in the Kennedy administration, joined the Bendix Corporation, and within five years rose to become its CEO. As a rare Democrat at the top of the business world, this made him an ideal choice for the job.

Mike had a strongly didactic and sometimes prickly personality and was used to giving orders to his corporate subordinates; working with equals was more difficult. But his differences with Charlie lay not just in personality. Schultze was at home in traditional Keynesian macroeconomics and fashioned his policy prescriptions through the lens of the models based on mountains of economic data. He concluded from the statistics that only 75 percent of our industrial capacity was being used, and with unemployment running above 7 percent, the U.S. economy not only needed a jolt to boost it out of the doldrums, but could absorb it without triggering higher inflation. Blumenthal agreed up to a point but was more concerned about runaway prices, as might be expected from someone formed in the shadow of the German hyperinflation that helped propel Hitler to power.

However essential data might be, Blumenthal believed that another vital if not overriding factor was something that could not be neatly quantified: the psychology of businesspeople, workers and organized labor, and financial markets. Did they believe that inflation was under control? Upon their judgments the economy would react. And it was the job of the president to give a clear signal, particularly on inflation. Blumenthal's views on inflation as a threat greater than unemployment ran counter to the ethos of the Democratic Party, as well as Mondale and me within the White House. Blumenthal saw its dangers earlier than any of us except the president.

After considerable infighting, we organized an Economic Policy Group (EPG) of the key departments to coordinate economic policy and avoid cabinet officers making end runs directly to the president, consisting of Treasury, OMB, and state, and me an ex-officio member, as the domestic-policy adviser, initially with three professionals housed at Treasury to help organize the economic decisions. Other departments such as Labor; Commerce; Health, Education, and Welfare; or Agriculture attended only when relevant to their issues; their desire for inclusion and the core group's desire to limit participation was always a source of tension.[10] Ten days after his inauguration we had our first EPG meeting, cochaired by Schultze and Blumenthal.[11]

Soon Blumenthal chafed at sharing the chairmanship, telling me he should have been "more pushy," on the ground that one person should be in charge; Blumenthal wanted it to be him; he was right, given his position.[12] He was very bright, analytical, intellectually open-minded, and as progressive as a secretary of the Treasury could ever be, and I never had a day's problem working with him. But his CEO mentality did not lend itself to forging a consensus to give the president clear options and recommendations. I called Schultze immediately. Charlie, a smart bureaucratic player as well as a gentleman, agreed to trade his cochairmanship, but for a price: a scheduled hour alone with the president every week to discuss the economy. The president readily agreed, and everyone was happy—or so it seemed.

As the months rolled by there were constant increasingly bitter complaints from cabinet officers like Kreps at Commerce and Marshall at Labor, both eminent economists, that they were being frozen out of the group's weekly meetings, even on key issues important to their constituencies.[13] But there was a more profound problem: Carter had no economic coordinator in the White House, a task performed admirably for Gerald Ford by William Seidman, an accountant and banking regulator. He kept matters on track by ensuring that after the meetings of their economic advisers, he would present Ford a summary, even including Democratic views, leading to a possible consensus.[14]

By contrast, our EPG soon fell victim to the warring departments reflecting their own constituencies, with no one to synthesize and mediate differences before the issues went to the president for his decision. I urged Schultze on several occasions to assume this role, but he refused on the ground that trying to forge a consensus policy and advocating for it would undermine his position as Carter's objective economic adviser and academic tutor.

While Carter had a bent for frugality and a determination to balance the budget, like most presidents he did not have a strong economics background or guiding philosophy. We therefore lacked a consistent, coherent policy and had no clear framework within which individual decisions could be made and explained to the public. Barry Bosworth, the chairman of the Council on Wage and Price stability, later put his finger on the problem: "You can afford to be wrong, as long as you have a consistent line of where you are trying to go and what your targets are, because the public is far more tolerant than politicians think. They understand you can't control all these things, as long as you look like you are in charge and you know what you are doing."[15]

A dysfunctional process makes good decisions infinitely more difficult.

Years later, when Bill Clinton was running for office, I recommended creating what became the White House National Economic Council, initially chaired by Robert Rubin, and which continues to this day. After the 2008 financial crash, President Obama pressed for government spending to restart the American economy, and he appointed Lawrence Summers to run the council. When Summers was asked by a reporter to explain his guiding policies for economic revival, he replied with one word: "Keynes."

We were unable to deliver such clarity because we faced the two-headed monster of stagflation, whose genesis and nature were never fully understood and thrashed out among us. We knew it had started under LBJ, and had come to full force with an explosion in oil prices after the 1973 OPEC oil embargo. But what followed did not fit any economic model. Stagflation simultaneously produced high inflation and rising unemployment, which theoretically were incompatible. But when we attacked it by pushing on one side of the problem, we only created more problems on the other.

It was not a matter of ignoring inflation; that was impossible. Our experts estimated that recent OPEC price increases of about 10 percent were passed on in the form of higher prices, which at the same time took about $10 billion out of the pockets of Americans, as if it were a sharp tax increase, slowing growth. But unlike an ordinary tax increase, the money was not cycled back by the U.S. government in public spending, but deposited in the OPEC countries' international banks. This was one major aspect of the dilemma of stagflation. The other was an inflationary push at home. Facing rising prices, several major union contracts—the Teamsters, Electrical Workers, and Rubber Workers—negotiated before Carter took office, averaged annual increases of about 10 percent.

The settlements were additionally augmented by cost-of-living clauses that further escalated wages as the consumer price index increased. These COLAs—also known as escalator clauses—were a principal force behind the wage-price spiral and would bedevil our efforts to control rampaging inflation. More than one-fourth of private-sector workers were unionized in the 1970s (less than one-tenth in 2016). During 1977, Carter's first full year in office, major union contracts were up for negotiation in steel, paper, coal, and construction. Union leaders and workers in those industries had every reason to try to match the 1976 packages. Our arsenal of weapons at this early stage did not match the challenge posed by stagflation. To my chagrin but on the advice of Schultze and Blumenthal during the transition,[16] Carter never sought standby authority to control wages and prices because of the negative experience under Nixon, and thus did not have it ready when it might have been politically useful later in his administration.

A MODEST STIMULUS

During the postelection transition, Schultze was tapped by the president-elect to assemble the economic stimulus package that Carter had promised in the campaign. Even though the recession itself had abated, it left behind high unemployment. On December 1, 1976, only a few weeks after his election, we held a half-day policy seminar at Miss Lillian's Pond House in Plains, built by her children in 1968 when she was away in the Peace Corps, with the best economic minds in the Democratic Party as well as Mondale, Lance, and me. Carter, dressed in his trademark Georgia work clothes, was serious and took copious notes. Schultze presented the case for a stimulus at a time of spare capacity and judged it likely that unemployment would be unchanged through the year unless consumers had more to spend, and that this would not happen by "spontaneous combustion." Blumenthal's very different views focused on increasing business investment, which, he argued, required predictability, stability, and consistency. Lance weighed in with the classic advice of the local banker that he was: "We can't spend our way out [and] we need to get government out of competition with the private sector in the capital market."[17]

In this way the first of many fault lines were exposed as we moved from analysis to action. Carter himself believed that the nation's economic imbalances would be righted by balancing the federal budget—a belief that was shared by many in America and which he stood by to the end. He proposed to achieve balance by the end of his first term through a "quick and effective stimulus" that would not tie his hands during the rest of his term.

As we prepared to come into office, Schultze surveyed top Republican and Democratic economists, and all favored a modest stimulus as a firebreak against a slide into a recession toward the autumn of Carter's first year in the White House.[18]

The new president was the most cautious, as would often be the case throughout the administration. He said: "I am concerned with public confidence and not creating a sense of irresponsibility at the beginning of my administration." Unfortunately, economists had a more exalted view of their forecasting capabilities than they do now. Paul Samuelson, the guru of mainstream American economic thought, wisely saw another dimension beyond mathematical models—unspoken political bias and electoral calculation. Recalling Nixon's efforts to create the best economic conditions for his 1972 reelection, he said Carter had the option of trying to tackle inflation early in 1977 by pressing the Fed to raise interest rates and thus create a stronger economy for his 1980 reelection.

But such Machiavellian management was not open to Carter because, as Samuelson also said, "It's the duty of the Democrats to push for growth and encourage some risks on the inflation side."[19] Carter had run for the presidency against the "Ford recession" and would have been lacerated by his own party if he suddenly did a U-turn and focused solely on inflation rather than unemployment. Nor did any of his economic advisers recommend that he do so at this stage. On December 8, the president was given a briefing book projecting high unemployment, sluggish growth, and high deficits for the years ahead. He realized this was a sober economic outlook, but on the basis of reports from his pollster Pat Caddell, he maintained his optimism and declared: "There is a basic strength in the American economy, and I believe there is a willingness of the American people, whose basic intelligence I trust, to face these challenges."[20] I found it revealing and of some cold comfort that years later Alan Greenspan, who had served as Ford's chief economic adviser, told me that he consoled Ford and his team after their defeat by his forecast that Carter would face stagflation over the next four years.[21]

The next day Schultze delivered a modest recovery plan of $20 billion, with $15 billion of tax cuts and only $5 billion in new spending, representing only 1.1 percent of the American economy, smaller than President Kennedy's 1.7 percent package to "get America moving again," and even less than Ford's stimulus program of 1.5 percent. There would be a onetime $50 rebate of personal taxes paid in 1976 ($200 for a family of four) and a cash payment for low-income people who paid no taxes to get money quickly into the economy, without long-term budget impacts. A small-business tax credit was added as a sweetener to help attract corporate support. The leaders of the Business Roundtable, the chief executive officers of America's leading companies, told Carter that this would boost business confidence, but their chairman, Reginald Jones of General Electric, said that if anything the package was too small.[22] He was not the only one to think this, and the number would grow under pressure from Democratic congressional leaders.

On January 7, 1977, the president-elect met for the first time with the Democratic leadership of the House and Senate, who trooped down to Plains to discuss the stimulus package. To write up his plan for a quick, short-term economic boost, Schultze went to Bert Lance's home in Atlanta the night before, worked until 1;00 a.m. at a police station nearby, and then handed his draft to the president-elect. Mondale had warned us that the leadership wanted more spending and fewer tax cuts. Ray Marshall, Carter's choice for Labor secretary, pushed for more public service jobs for the unemployed. While Schultze replied that the government could not spend money quickly enough to stimulate the economy in the short term, he presented a revised plan with additional money for job training and a small amount for public works.[23]

There were no conference tables at Miss Lillian's Pond House, but soft chairs, couches, and some folding chairs to accommodate the crowd. Each side was warily sizing up the other. Carter's down-home dress of checked shirt, khakis, and work boots presented a vivid contrast to the congressional uniform of coats, ties, and starched white shirts. I learned from these early meetings that Carter had an iron bladder and a steel-trap mind, going long hours without a bathroom break, without losing his focus, and an amazing capacity to absorb huge amounts of complex information. The battle lines on Capitol Hill were evident even at this early stage, forming a grid that overlaid our own, and would complicate policy making throughout the administration.

Even after eight years of serving under Nixon and Ford and yearning for a leader of their own party, the Democratic leaders of Congress could not unite behind a Democratic president. Schultze proposed several billion dollars in job training and public service jobs for young people and veterans, but only $1 billion for the public works that are a honeypot for Congressmen to spoon out to their constituents. House Majority Leader Jim Wright immediately objected. Disingenuously he warned that his own followers would bloat the numbers, as if he had no control over them. Schultze replied that the money would end up in inefficient projects like indoor pistol ranges and marinas in obscure locations. Carter supported him by arguing that even massive public works programs do not employ enough people to jump-start the economy, and that without a cash tax rebate, the whole pump-priming exercise would not create enough jobs to reduce unemployment. Senate Majority Leader Byrd warned that the money from tax cuts would end up in people's bank accounts instead of injecting consumer demand into the economy.

It was clear from their reactions that the congressional leaders were chagrined at having a complete program dropped unceremoniously in their laps, and they complained it was too skimpy to boost the economy. We anticipated that and had met with the president beforehand; he approved an additional amount for the package if they asked. On the spot Carter agreed to a compromise: an additional $4 billion for public works beyond the $2 billion Congress had authorized last year, but to reduce the immediate budget impact, it would be appropriated half in the current fiscal year 1977, and half in fiscal 1978.

But Carter's fiscal conservatism came out clearly: This was not going to be the Great Society redux. He explained that he was proposing a tax cut for low- and middle-income taxpayers, but that he expected it to be paid for, first by tax reform that he would propose later in 1977, and then by higher tax revenues that would be a growth dividend from the stimulus itself. But, he warned, "I will not promise a tax cut until we have the funds to pay for it. I have always been careful to say that we are going to take these actions only as the new revenues come on stream and we meet our objective of achieving a balanced federal budget by the end of my first term." There was silence from the Democratic leaders.[24] This was not the message they expected, although it was entirely consistent with what he had been saying during the campaign.

Pressures also came from our liberal supporters, and they did not abate.

The AFL-CIO lined up with the congressional leadership in demanding several billion dollars more for public works, which they knew would generate unionized construction jobs instead of the lower-paid public and youth jobs in the Carter package. We received similar complaints at a meeting on February 3 with congressional black leaders, who asked for $2 billion more to combat black teenage unemployment. Carter was clearly stung and said he consistently supported affirmative action and recited a long list of his black appointees. He told them bluntly, "Too much criticism creates needless disharmony, and hurts blacks."[25] We tried to accommodate our Democratic critics by slightly enlarging the plan.

After intensive days of deliberation, the president sent a $31.2 billion Economic Recovery Program to Congress on January 31, along with the basic outline Schultze had originally drawn. Together with the additional public works funding, there was a major expansion of public service employment by a whopping 450,000 places, job training and youth employment programs offering an additional 346,000 positions, and a $1 billion increase in federal revenue shared with hard-pressed cities and states. But at the heart of the program stood the progressive tax cuts, especially the rebate and the cash payment for the poor who paid no taxes, adding up to an injection of $11.4 billion to stimulate the economy immediately in 1977.

The plan also recommended a permanent increase in the standard deduction, which would mean that 3.7 million taxpayers would no longer pay any taxes, and tax simplification for four million more, who could take the standard deduction. In our consultations with business leaders, they were divided on whether they preferred an additional credit for investments in machinery and equipment or an income tax cut, so the plan allowed them to choose either. The recovery package was accompanied by a warning that without further stimulus, the economy would grow at an "inadequate" 4.5 to 5 percent in 1977—a level of growth for which an administration these days would sell its soul.[26]

At a cabinet meeting on February 20 to discuss the package, I received another task from the president, who was quickly discovering that his concept of cabinet government was allowing cabinet officers to make end runs to Congress, blurring his agenda and complicating his life. He instructed all cabinet officers to send me copies of their congressional testimony, "so it does not create confusion with my campaign statements. Stu will monitor legislation."[27] Later that day Carter told us at a staff meeting that he was going to take Evelyn Wood's speed-reading course because of the volume of papers that reached his desk. I told him that I had taken the course between high school and college and found it the best investment I had made, aside from the cost of my marriage license for Fran. I should have told him this would be a self-inflicted burden; we were already providing summaries of decisions he needed to make, but he insisted on reading all the details in the backup material that came with them.[28]

The basic question remains whether the stimulus plan was a mistake and actually accelerated the underlying high inflation. Should it have been abandoned to let nature take its course and allow unemployment to move higher, in stark contrast to Democratic Party orthodoxy—and would that have slowed inflation? Most economists, including the conservative Paul Mc-Cracken, President Nixon's top economic adviser, felt that the benefits outweighed any risk of an inflationary impact.[29] Labor and the liberals simply ignored the trade-off, and constantly pushed for more spending on social and jobs programs. The AFL-CIO's Lane Kirkland said: "There's a big difference between having work and being plagued with rising prices, and not having work and being plagued with any prices."[30]

Economic policy is one of the most challenging of all the broad-spectrum decisions presidents have to make. A president's ability to influence the course of the huge and complex American economy is greatly exaggerated. He can affect it at the margins and set a general direction, but other decisions have far greater weight, particularly those by the Federal Reserve, but even more so those by tens of millions of consumers and companies and even the policies of our major trading partners. Economic data are released regularly for the most recent months, but often revised, making managing the economy, in Alan Greenspan's words, like "driving a car by looking at the rear-view mirror."[31]

Moreover, one quarter's figures are rarely enough to indicate underlying trends. In fact the Ford recession was actually over when Carter took office, and figures later showed that a very strong bounce-back of 9.7 percent had taken place at the height of the campaign, although economic growth later fell into the doldrums.

"THROWING $50 BILLS OFF THE TOP OF THE WASHINGTON MONUMENT"

One element in the stimulus program began to take on a political life of its own: The $50 rebate became a lightning rod for criticism within the cabinet and in Congress. At a cabinet meeting a few weeks after the plan was sent to Congress,[32] it was reported that the most popular proposal focused on youth unemployment and the rebate was the most unpopular. Senator Long belittled it as "throwing $50 bills off the top of the Washington Monument"[33]—which was precisely the metaphor used by its academic supporters to describe the simplicity, directness, and absence of long-term budget impact that were its principal virtues. Gradually Carter began to back away from it, while Mondale argued that it was a vital test of the president's command of Congress, and his standing would "unravel" if they rejected it.[34] Slowly but relentlessly the case for the rebate was barely discussed on its merits. Senator Byrd gave the new president a tough message about how Washington works: He brought up the hit list of objectionable water projects that the president aimed to strike from the annual list of pork-barrel projects for friendly members of Congress. Byrd told Carter he only had forty votes for the rebate, and "the damage from the water projects hit list is terrible. Your other battles are more important."[35]

Carter's refusal to subordinate principle to political success began to affect his overloaded legislative agenda. The vote on this once-urgent rebate had slid at least to mid-April. Twice he asked me whether I still favored it, once during a high-level meeting on energy, and again when he summoned me to his private study at 9:30 p.m. after a White House evening with wives.[36] I argued that unless the economic statistics strengthened markedly, dropping the rebate would look like poor economic planning and uncertain leadership.

The rebate did not last long, and Carter paid a political price for abandoning it in a way that showed his inexperience in dealing with Congress. But in the last analysis, it was a decisive turn from emphasizing jobs during the campaign to giving the fight against inflation at least an equal priority. In hindsight, the economy was near what economists call an inflection point—a change in direction, although rarely spotted until it is past.

There seemed little inflationary risk to the tax rebate when unemployment stood at 7 percent, but he sensed it. Critics who feel Carter did not appreciate the threat of inflation early enough fail to see that after only three months in office, he took the politically risky step of reorienting the economic course on which he had pitched his campaign. The decisive moment came on April 13 in the Roosevelt Room, across the hall from the Oval Office, overlooked by portraits of the two Roosevelts, whose political skills would have been of great help at the moment. Carter convened his economic team and his political inner circle around a large oval table and opened by telling us: "The rebate is the only thing I feel queasy about since I was elected." He took pride in having told the Democratic leadership he was not going to trade with Senator Long on sugar imports for his vote on the $50 rebate and said he had offered no deals to anyone except Massachusetts's two senators, Kennedy and Edward Brooke, promising to keep open the army's Fort Devens in their state. Even so, he seemed to apologize: "I feel I should not link things and horse-trade; I have never been able to do this in politics."[37]

This was an amazing statement. During the presidential campaign, he had been perfectly willing to consider the political dimensions of his policies, but now he parked politics at the door of the Oval Office. The presidency is a political job, and there are precious few levers for key proposals beyond the ability to rally public opinion. Extending, maintaining, or threatening to withhold federal benefits is one of the most essential in assembling a congressional vote.

In the end, elected members of Congress must view a president's proposals not only as sound for the nation, but for their own voters and their own political careers. Schultze, the rebate's architect, argued that without it the recovery package would be reduced by $10 billion, leaving only $21 billion at a time of high unemployment. I had talked with Ham Jordan before the meeting to support the rebate, and his comments at the meeting were as politically cogent as ever: "The best policy will be the best politics. We were elected by the poor and middle class. If you withdraw the rebate, it will hurt your image that you care about them. I would hate to see you back off." Only the financial community would be pleased if we pulled the rebate, he said, and if it turned out that we were wrong, the rebate would be a "self-limiting mistake," because it applied for only one year. Worse, he emphasized, dropping the rebate would only create a backlash from labor and congressional Democrats to add other spending programs in its place that would start stimulating the economy only next year, not now.

I expressed concern about seeming to reverse a signature proposal so soon after he argued its importance, and that if the rebate had to die, it would be best to let the congressional leadership announce they lacked the votes to pass it. While the press would play this as a loss, surveys indicated the rebate was popular with the public. After Jody Powell pointed out that withdrawing the individual rebate would also mean dropping the tax cut for business, Carter broadened the debate to the question that framed the entire economic policy for the next four years, and also underscored the difficulty of simultaneously fighting high inflation and high unemployment: "Should we worry about inflation or the dormant economy?" Blumenthal and Lance argued that the rebate was not necessary, as the economy was strengthening, and would be inflationary.[38]

Presidents often have to change course to deal with changed circumstances. But on a high-visibility issue such as this, adopting a new position must be done with finesse. There was little of that here, and it compounded the problem. Within a few hours of the meeting, when I thought the issue was still unresolved, the wire services quoted unnamed White House sources that the president was abandoning the $50 rebate. I assume Carter told Jody to leak his decision, and the result was immediate and painful.

Hell hath no fury greater than an angry senator, and Ed Muskie, a party elder and former Democratic presidential contender, erupted like Vesuvius. As chairman of the new Senate Budget Committee, he took great pride in the process created under the new budget law and had led his committee in creating an extraordinary third budget resolution to accommodate the fiscal effects of the original stimulus package. It was only from the press leaks that he learned his careful work on behalf of the White House had been for naught. As Schultze put it later, Congress felt "you guys don't really know what you're doing," even those who opposed the rebate.[39] Two days later Carter gave a press conference with a series of lame explanations for dropping the rebate, including that it had been a mutual decision with Congress, which of course it was not.[40] A lingering but more damaging price for the precipitous decision showed up two months later in Caddell's poll, which reported that the public was concerned that Carter "changes his mind on issues."[41]

In fact, except for the rebate, Congress passed and Carter signed into law on May 13, 1977, the balance of his Economic Recovery Program virtually intact. This injected more than $20 billion into the economy, together with $4 billion in public works for state and local government projects, an amount close to the midrange of economists' recommendations for lowering taxes and creating jobs and new public works. But like so much of Carter's legislation, passage was often clouded by the breadth of what he initially sought and his politically maladroit way of making a useful compromise look like a defeat.

"I AM *VERY* CONCERNED WITH INFLATION" (BUT BIG LABOR IS NOT)

Jimmy Carter had to live in the real world. It is impossible to be a purist in politics, particularly for a Democratic president whose base in the industrial working class undergirds his party. Whatever he did, it was never enough to satisfy them. Two Wisconsin Democrats, Senator Gaylord Nelson and Representative David Obey, threatened to attack Carter in public if he did not honor a campaign pledge to raise federal price supports for milk. American shoe manufacturers and their unions demanded that Carter impose punitive tariffs on cheap shoes imported from Asia just as he was planning to make his maiden speech on inflation. The shrinking domestic shoe industry was unable to compete in the low-price market, and imposing tariffs would only send the wrong signals to other industries.

Sure enough, we were confronted with a demand by labor leaders to limit imports of television sets from Japan and Taiwan, where efficient production and good design were decimating the American electronics industry. Next came sugar, probably the most protected commodity in America, that sold here at double the world price, thanks to powerful congressional overlords like Russell Long, whose support on broad economic measures was essential as chairman of the Senate Finance Committee. Carter's instincts were clear and correct. "I want as little constraint on imports as possible and I am concerned with inflation," he bluntly instructed Strauss, his trade negotiator. But this did not satisfy Muskie, whose state of Maine was home to many shoe manufacturers.[42]

Combating the strong inflationary pressures built into the system turned out to be one of the most politically debilitating tasks imaginable. Rather than hand out new benefits to traditional supporters, Carter struggled against the impact of one decision after another seeking special benefits; he did the bare minimum to keep any semblance of political support. Even so, he alienated one group after another in choosing the least inflationary alternative in each decision while trying to keep at least one foot in the progressive camp—then an ankle, then a toe, until Kennedy took him on in the presidential primary. One of Carter's solutions was to put in place the first deregulation of major industries, mainly in transport, communications, and banking, which increased competition and eventually helped lower prices and wages, but not quickly enough to help him politically.

Even with all these pressures for small, incremental steps adding to inflation, Carter stayed ahead of his advisers in recognizing its dangers and had come to the point of making a fight against inflation his major economic goal. At a senior White House staff meeting in the Oval Office on March 28, a little more than two months after his inauguration, he told us firmly that in facing pressures to raise minimum wages for workers and increase price supports for farmers, he could not align himself with these goals of the Democratic-controlled committees. He told us, "I am *very* concerned with inflation. . . . It will be *devastating politically* if inflation gets to 8 or 9 percent."[43] It did, and it was.

Large companies and wealthy people are well equipped to protect themselves by pricing power or political pull when the economy swerves in unexpected directions, as it did in the 1970s and again in the financial crash of 2008. Arthur Okun, who bore the scars of trying but failing to stop the financing of the Vietnam War and Great Society programs from running amok as Johnson's chief economic adviser, had a succinct phrase to describe the social damage when inflation suddenly takes hold: "It separates the sharpies from the suckers."

Once he had shifted focus, the president faced a more daunting task in bringing his party and its traditional supporters along with him. He planned to take it public, and on March 31 at 8:30 a.m. he summoned me to his private study and asked me to coordinate an anti-inflation message he would soon deliver. I began immediately, talking with Schultze and Fed Chairman Burns that day.[44] He took the subject to the cabinet on April 4, a meeting at which Schultze delivered a briefing stressing the impossibility of reducing unemployment without controlling inflation—to try to do it, the first step was to impose budget discipline on all the things the government does to support prices. After he reported that the employment figures looked good, Carter warned that the "good news gives a false picture of what the economy is doing."[45] Two days later he took the message to the regular breakfast of the Democratic congressional leadership, for whom fighting inflation was a nonissue. This was the party of jobs, growth, and increased social services for Americans, the reform party of the Roosevelt coalition.

What they failed to realize, but Carter had grasped from the day he started running for president, was that the country had changed and that the party needed to adapt by becoming more fiscally prudent and moderate. He told them he did not want to get into the position of blaming a spendthrift Congress, whose budget proposals were more than $6 billion higher than his. He informed them he would be making an anti-inflation speech and warned: "Democrats have a reputation of irresponsible spending. To control this, it will mean special-interest groups who are our friends can't get all they want. If we do this, it will take away from the Republicans one of their biggest weapons against us." The Democratic Party barons, particularly Tip O'Neill, were visibly upset. Later that day Carter pursued the same message with the National Farmers Union, which did not want to hear it; they argued for higher federal price supports to underwrite their production costs, even if it meant stockpiling unsold grains and milk products in government warehouses at taxpayer expense. And the leaders of the machinists' and electrical workers' unions demanded that Carter limit imports to protect their jobs.[46]

That encounter set the stage for the most uncomfortable meeting I attended during four years in the Carter White House, a lunch on April 6, 1977, in the Roosevelt Room with the senior leadership of the AFL-CIO, led by its president, George Meany,[47] which we later ruefully dubbed the "George Hardy memorial lunch."

Meany was a tough, burly, bald, stern, cigar-smoking, former pipe welder from the Bronx. He and the courteous peanut farmer from Plains came from two different universes. Carter was from a nonunion state and had not mixed with union leaders—there were virtually none in Georgia—nor did he campaign at union halls or speak to their conventions. Carter later told the cabinet that he was particularly upset by Meany's negative personal comments about him despite his efforts to honor labor's requests.

The memorable luncheon meeting also included Mondale, Labor Secretary Marshall, Ham, Landon Butler, who was Ham's liaison to labor, and me, along with several of Meany's top aides.[48] Carter began by warmly welcoming them to the White House with a declaration that "I am eager to work with you. . . . We share common goals." He made it clear that he was eager to support laws to assist unionization by expediting decisions by the National Labor Relations Board to limit corporate barriers to unions. He promised to let union leaders review his upcoming inflation statement and made it clear he would not blame organized labor for inflation when it pushed for higher wages.

Then George Hardy, president of the Service Employees International Union, started telling dirty jokes, perhaps in the mistaken belief that this kind of union-hall bonhomie would lighten the atmosphere. The Southern Baptist president cringed visibly. The off-color language embarrassed him deeply and confirmed his small-town stereotype of labor leaders as more interested in their own position than in the workers they represented.

Meany finally turned the meeting back toward substance, arguing that the priority should be people and jobs, not fighting inflation, and that it was urgent to raise the minimum wage and index it to manufacturing wages, since it now was set to yield a salary below the poverty line. "Nothing since January 20 [inauguration day] indicates this is a priority for you," he asserted, asking, "Why do you not consult with us on the minimum wage?"—totally ignoring that Carter had been working hard on the minimum wage bill for some time, and that we had worked closely with the AFL-CIO staff on what would become a substantial increase by the end of his first year.

Then followed a long duel of polemics, descending into personalities on all of the trade cases, with Meany accusing our negotiators of being clients of foreign countries and Blumenthal of sounding like Arthur Burns of the Fed. "There is no proof wages contribute to inflation. High interest rates and unemployment are inflationary," Meany said in a message straight out of the 1930s.

Carter responded to Meany's diatribe by defending himself with specific proposals he had made to increase the minimum wage and index it to manufacturing wages, albeit at a lower level than Meany and the unions wanted. He also promised to consult with labor, which Meany rebutted or brushed aside. Meany argued that companies continued to lay off workers even though profits were high, and that corporations did not pay enough taxes and had too much political influence under Carter. Union leaders who take bribes go to jail, he said, but not corporate officers. Carter shot back that he had not yet met with the Business Roundtable, and was giving labor priority; and that he was going to issue a statement on oil spills; intended to reform the tax code; and was preparing corporate antibribery legislation.

When the lunch ended, Carter muttered to me as he left for the Oval Office, "Stu, I will never do this again." And he did not. He limited himself to meetings only with the central leadership of the AFL-CIO and their aides, although at times meeting with the presidents of affiliated unions separately. It left a permanent scar on a key element of the traditional Democratic coalition. For myself, I had never seen such disrespect before or since, not simply for Carter himself but for the office of the president of the United States. In my notes I wrote, "This was a disastrous and rancorous meeting. JC uncomfortable in relationship with Meany."

Strauss later volunteered that neither Carter nor his Labor secretary attended the annual AFL-CIO convention in Florida, but Carter replied that he sought Meany's advice and hated to go to labor conventions anyway.[49] Carter and especially his political guru, Ham, realized that organized labor was an essential building block in the Democratic Party's coalition. Unions were the only organization that threw thousands of workers into the get-out-the-vote ground game in key states to elect Democrats. They also had effective pro-Democratic educational programs at union locals and deployed a strong lobbying organization for key legislation in Washington.

Carter bent himself into a pretzel to try to appease Meany and labor, but it never seemed enough. Meany publicly declared that he could not think of one positive thing Carter had done as president, and was widely known to resent the fact that after waiting eight years for a Democrat in the White House, he had to deal with one from the conservative wing of the party.

Early in the administration we started to work with the AFL-CIO on issues like raising the minimum wage. While none of their workers were employed at the minimum wage, an increase would ripple upward and give them more leverage to seek raises for their better-paid unionized workers. Their major goal was legislation that would make it easier for unions to organize workers. Although Carter came from a "right to work" state where, like most Southern states, organizing unions faced huge legal hurdles, he was willing to accommodate labor. But his personal feelings are best captured by his caustic remark when Landon Butler reviewed the labor law proposal with him: "Labor Law Reform? For what is that a euphemism?"[50] Ham recommended that we support labor's broad objectives in any legislation to force them to "keep coming back for our help." And they needed it, as public opinion and local laws drifted against the unions, and their membership was declining as the manufacturing base of the country eroded and the economy shifted to a service-driven model.[51]

"NO MAGIC SOLUTIONS"

With a week remaining to draft Carter's first anti-inflation statement, there was a dearth of original ideas, and even fewer on which we could all agree. At an EPG meeting Carter's conflicting priorities came into painfully plain view. Blumenthal argued that the energy bill soon to be sent to Congress was inconsistent with the anti-inflation message since it was based upon higher energy prices to encourage conservation and production. Mondale told Carter he should delay the bill, but Carter predictably said we should forge ahead. We did agree that after each major wage and price increase, the Council on Wage and Price Stability could make a public statement and hold public hearings, even if labor did not like them meddling in collective-bargaining negotiations.

Carter directed me to meet with Fed chairman Burns. But although he puffed out the stale idea of an "incomes policy" of wage and price guidelines through the smoke of his ubiquitous pipe, he had no better idea than we did on how the government could usefully intervene to hold down wages or prices. Nor was the problem new to him (or to the economics profession). As far back as 1970 he had said publicly: "We are dealing with a new problem—namely, persistent inflation in the face of substantial unemployment—and the classical remedies may not work well enough or fast enough in this case."[52] Burns repeated his mantra that high government spending equaled high deficits, which produced high interest rates. I knew that he wanted Carter to reappoint him, but as he left my office, I thought that even the august chairman of the Fed had no magic bullet to fight inflation.[53] But neither did Jimmy Carter, and he was the first to admit that "there are no magic solutions in the battle against inflation," as he said when he delivered his first anti-inflation message on April 15—income tax day![54]

He was remarkably candid in laying part of the blame on the changing role of the federal government in addressing costs of combating environmental pollution, improving health and safety at work, and pensions and health care for the elderly. He also pointed to the wage-price process: As individuals and businesses began to expect continued inflation, they demanded higher wages to protect themselves, creating a spiral that helped explain why slow growth, high unemployment, unused plant capacity, and inadequate consumer demand—all of which should have slowed prices—did the reverse and caused stagflation. He announced a new labor-management group chaired by labor's George Meany and Reginald Jones, the CEO of General Electric, coordinated by former Ford Labor secretary and Harvard professor John Dunlop, to discuss how to break the vicious wage-price spiral. But it was a toothless tiger, because the AFL-CIO refused to talk about specific numbers or to agree to restrain their wage demands to catch up with inflation.[55]

Unlike a traditional Democrat, he emphasized the importance of spending restraint and pledged to have a balanced budget by the end of his term "in a normal economy." But the president forcefully rejected fighting inflation through high unemployment, which he called "morally unacceptable and ineffective." He promised: "Inflation must not be attacked by causing additional human misery." Carter deserves credit for identifying inflation early on as a major problem, and he followed through with the various initiatives he promised. But given the underlying inflationary forces, which would only become more ferocious with the oil shock that was yet to arrive in 1979, the message was a lost opportunity, and a promise he could not keep. Yet at that time, no one inside or outside the administration was clamoring for much more. We were always one step behind with our anti-inflation weapons—and sending conflicting signals by signing a minimum wage hike, and negotiating the Humphrey-Hawkins Full Employment Bill (backed by pollster Caddell, who felt it was necessary to strengthen liberal and black support, which was "slipping"), albeit only after insisting that an inflation target be added to the unemployment goal. Finally Carter would have no choice but to do what he said we would never do, fight inflation with higher unemployment and slower growth.[56]

TORPEDOED BY BIG STEEL

Just six months into Carter's presidency at the June meeting of our EPG, Schultze made what would be a fateful and incorrect judgment that the economy would need more stimulus in the following year through a second round of tax cuts in 1978.[57] Our margin for economic maneuver narrowed, given the president's strong desire for a balanced budget by the end of his term. Blumenthal said the goals should really be to reach a better balance between low inflation and low unemployment and, mixing his metaphors, avoid making "a balanced budget holy writ when we may have to eat crow." Commerce Secretary Kreps agreed, and said a balanced budget would only be the result and not the cause of the private economy delivering good numbers for the next several years. We realized we were at an economic crossroads in trying to meet the president's fiscal goals, so at the end of June we called another meeting, which included Ham because of its heavy political consequences. Our economic team determined that we should set the fiscal dials to achieve our growth and employment goals with a tax cut, but without achieving the president's deeply held goal of a balanced budget, calculating that the government would be running a deficit of $25 to $35 billion at the end of 1980.[58]

Schultze and Blumenthal brought various painful options before the president a week later, when Carter had to face economic realities and choose his course: achieve a balanced budget regardless of whether we met our economic growth goals; achieve a balanced budget only if there was higher growth and lower unemployment by another tax cut; and achieve our growth and unemployment goals but only by sacrificing a balanced budget. Carter declared unequivocally: "I am more concerned with inflation than unemployment." Blumenthal assured him that additional tax cuts would not appreciably boost prices, "and we can attack inflation with a rifle." As it turned out, inflation psychology was not subject to such careful targeting, and we could only have attacked it with a sledgehammer. At that point no one thought it necessary to swing that hard.

While he pondered these unpalatable options, inflationary pressures continued. U.S. Steel announced a big price hike, and the president asked me to come to his private office to determine what we could do about it. I reminded him of President Kennedy's famous standoff with steel. I immediately called Schultze, who urged us not to threaten antitrust action, and then I told Bosworth that the president wanted him to examine the steel industry's costs and report by September 15 on whether the increase was justified. Bosworth said that if his council held a public hearing, there would be a confrontation, because the steel companies had terrible profit margins.[59] We agreed we had no real tools to roll back prices except by encouraging foreign steel imports, which would only evoke the wrath of management, labor, and their representatives in Congress. And a meeting with the other steel companies to urge restraint would be like whistling in the wind.

After Bosworth's economists completed their study showing that Japanese costs were lower because their steel companies had modernized and ours had not, all stakeholders—management, labor, and members of Congress—gathered on October 13 for an extraordinary meeting with the president, where each performed according to script. Ed Speer of U.S. Steel laced into the government for failing to impose quotas, tariffs, or bilateral agreements to limit foreign steel imports. Lloyd McBride of the United Steelworkers complained that 20,000 layoffs had left the industry with the lowest number of workers since 1976, and he asked the government to delay enforcing new safety and environmental regulations. Senators of both parties from steel-producing states supported management and labor. "We want a strong steel industry, and we won't put up with unfair competition," said John Glenn, the former astronaut and Democratic senator from Ohio.

When Carter spoke, he said sternly that he would enforce the antidumping laws designed to protect American goods from imports priced below their cost of production, but he insisted that domestic manufacturers produce steel at competitive prices.[60] Anyone thinking that Jimmy Carter lacked backbone should have seen him in action, taking on the steel industry, its union, the United Steelworkers, and the bipartisan steel-state congressional delegation. In fact, in 1980 we did put through a recovery program for the industry worth more than $2 billion in faster equipment write-offs, import relief, and other government help. I coordinated the program, and when I announced it to the nation's leading steel manufactures in the Roosevelt Room, I told the new CEO of U.S. Steel, David Roderick, "Dave, I hope you and the industry use this extra money to modernize your plants, and not to go out and buy an oil company." Absolutely, he assured me. Within months U.S. Steel purchased the Marathon Oil Company.

We now faced the worst of both worlds and started grasping at straws. Bob Strauss suggested that the president bring fifty prominent people to the White House every two weeks, which he said would "do wonders for investor confidence." Carter took the first step by inviting a large, bipartisan group of business leaders to meet with him and the economic team in the Cabinet Room. Irving Shapiro of DuPont, the new chairman of the Business Roundtable, recommended a presidential speech on the economy to help restore business confidence. Walter Wriston of Citibank asked for a clear strategy to calm "stock market jitters."

Donald Regan of Merrill Lynch (later Secretary of the Treasury and White House Chief of Staff in the Reagan administration) said the president needed to lay out his reasons for tax cuts and not just give a "quick hype for the market." Reg Jones of General Electric suggested tax cuts for individuals and corporations. At the same time the CEOs of General Motors and JCPenney declared that business was good and public confidence was growing. Carter said there were many causes for the problems of the stock market and advanced several basic reforms in taxation he wanted to tie to tax cuts. So much for high-powered brainstorming sessions.[61]

I became almost apoplectic about our dilemma and pressed Schultze for anti-inflation alternatives. In a conversation on October 19, he said that we could further restrict federal spending, impose Nixon-style wage and price controls, or use the presidential jawbone.[62] But he told me his Brookings Institution friend Arthur Okun had come up with a genuinely original idea: a tax rebate to companies and unions for any collective-bargaining agreement that came in at or below our inflation guidelines; he gave it the catchy name Real Wage Insurance. Its only problem—once again—was political: it would prove difficult if not impossible for Congress to write the idea into law. Blumenthal believed it would get in the way of tax reform. Business leaders regarded it as too close to price controls, and labor saw it as suppressing wage demands—which is precisely what it was intended to do.

This dismal conversation led me to understand later one of the reasons Jimmy Carter would lose the 1980 election. I had the feeling that the administration had lost the capacity to deal with the economy's worst problems through any conventional means short of inducing a recession or imposing Nixon-style wage and price controls. This proved accurate, and I was not alone. The next day, at a breakfast meeting of the EPG, Blumenthal said it was time for the president to give a major speech on the economy. Schultze agreed but argued it needed to be a coordinated message on taxes, inflation, and jobs. But we had no policy to coordinate, and Schultze continued to insist that without another stimulus, growth would slow and unemployment would start rising. His prescription: a $20 billion tax cut. Back to square one.[63]

One by one Carter's campaign promises on the economy and taxes began drifting out of reach. In late October the Budget Office told him there had been a negative $50 billion swing in the budget assumptions since the spring review. He could no longer put off the choice that Schultze presented him between his goal of a balanced budget and a tax cut that would stimulate growth, but leave a budget deficit of $20 billion. The president paused for what seemed like an eternity and then said: "It is devastating to me to give up a balanced budget." Schultze tried to console him by saying we would try to do nothing that would make a balanced budget impossible under high-employment conditions—our preferred strategy.[64]

As we approached the mid-January deadline for Carter's 1978 State of the Union and budget message, we recognized that our anti-inflation tools were not working or would be denied to us by Congress, setting off a frenzied quest for alternatives that simply did not exist. Departments were asked to develop their own anti-inflation policies to set an example to the private sector, but it was an exercise in futility. Blumenthal and Schultze presented modest initiatives like reducing telephone, excise, and sales taxes, and voluntary wage and price guideposts similar to those used by Kennedy and Johnson, in a much lower-inflation environment, and even then to little effect. And Carter himself never gave up on his goal of a balanced budget, which left Blumenthal "surprised at the president's elementary notions of economics"—a condescending remark unlikely to win friends in the administration. It became obvious that the positive economic effect of the stimulus package of tax cuts and tax reform we were developing depended on lower interest rates. This proved a serious mistake and only fanned the flames of inflation.[65]

Carter was fighting a two-front war, facing ideological hurdles within his own party and constituency groups for whom fighting inflation was not a natural proclivity. He tried to put it in terms they might accept at a March 21 congressional breakfast, telling the Democratic leaders he was "most concerned with inflation, but we are ahead of schedule in reducing unemployment." A month later he told the same skeptical group: "I think it helps Democrats to have me out front on fighting inflation, and it will help with the criticism that we Democrats are free spenders." Budget-busting bills, he said, create "an image of irresponsibility."

This was too much for Tip O'Neill, who accused Carter of following the "Republican line that government spending creates inflation. Mr. President, we have been working on a different philosophy since the 1960s." He added that Democratic economists had estimated that a $25 billion deficit would increase inflation by only 0.2 percent. Carter shot back: "Mr. Speaker, we already have a $60 billion deficit."[66] Carter got a more sympathetic ear from the House Budget Committee chairman, Robert Giamo of Connecticut, who agreed that while budget deficits were only one contributor to inflation, and not the most important, they were "the only thing we can control—but most Democrats do not believe this."[67]

BURNS OUT, MILLER IN

The classic way to fight inflation is through higher interest rates. Former Federal Reserve chairman William McChesney Martin famously said that the job of the central bank was to take away the punch bowl once the party got going. It should be the ultimate watchdog against inflation—but the fact was that given the state of the economy, there was hardly any party at all. Nevertheless, in the spring of Carter's first term, Burns had begun to raise interest rates. In August, Burns asked to have lunch with me, and this time I went to the imposing marble Federal Reserve Building on Constitution Avenue.[68] He argued for a tougher line on inflation, but he was also clearly angling for the president to reappoint him. During Carter's first year in office, everyone pressed Burns to run a looser monetary policy to facilitate growth. And as the economy picked up, the central concern was a potential pause in growth later in the year, reflecting a clear Democratic bias toward promoting growth over controlling inflation, until it was too late.

When Schultze and I later met with Burns to solicit his ideas on our inflation package to start Carter's second year in office, he suggested that the president and his top appointees set an example by taking a pay cut of 5 or 10 percent and asking the private sector to join in, led by its top executives. That was our last meeting with Burns as chairman.[69] At an early December meeting of the EPG, Carter declared he would not reappoint Burns when his term ended on December 31 and asked for candidates to replace him. He turned away from the economics profession toward business, and the president decided on G. William Miller, chairman of Textron and head of the National Association of Businesses, where he had encouraged large corporations to hire the needy. A Democrat with a heart and concern for the disadvantaged, Miller was short and pleasant, spoke in a clipped, clear, and direct manner, but proved out of his depth in dealing with the arcana of monetary policy (although he proved to be a more effective treasury secretary).[70]

"GOVERNMENT CANNOT SOLVE
OUR PROBLEMS"

The president delivered his first formal State of the Union Address to a joint session of Congress on January 19, 1978, almost a year to the day after his inauguration. All the late hours, all the pressures of working in the White House, can be forgotten in an instant whenever the president you serve speaks in the vast and beautiful chamber of the House of Representatives. As everyone rises, the clerk of the House announces in solemn tones: "Ladies and gentlemen, the president of the United States." Members come early to get seats on the aisle to be seen on TV shaking the president's hand as he strides into the well of the House.

It is our republic's democratic borrowing of the British tradition of the monarch's annual speech to Parliament presenting the government's program. As such, the president presents his domestic- and foreign-policy priorities before all members of the House and Senate, the cabinet, the Joint Chiefs of Staff, and the Supreme Court, plus ambassadors from every nation with whom we have diplomatic relations. The mandate is written into the Constitution for the president "from time to time to time give to the Congress information on the State of the Union, and recommend to their Consideration such measures as he shall judge necessary and expedient."

Every president has fulfilled it. The shortest message, of only 1,089 words, was the first, delivered by George Washington in writing.[71] Carter's would be much longer, since the State of the Union also serves a unique purpose. Amid all the hurly-burly of American politics, with all the American people's natural focus on their own jobs, families, welfare, and security, this one speech offers the president his sole guaranteed opportunity to speak to them directly about his hopes and dreams, his vision for the country, and how to meet its challenges and opportunities.

Carter's address focused almost exclusively on the need for a further stimulus to the economy by cutting taxes and expanding programs to create jobs. He announced a total tax reduction of $34 billion, offset by $9 billion in tax reforms, most for individuals, for a net cost of $25 billion. There were no details on tax reform, which would be presented the next day in a detailed presidential message. But he emphasized that cuts in personal and corporate taxes must be tied to tax reform because the loophole-closing revenues from reform would provide the fiscal room for lower taxes. On the economy Carter largely brought good news. The president offered barely a glimpse of our anguished internal debates about the simultaneous challenges of high unemployment and high inflation, and precious few tools to fight inflation. From that perspective it was a lost opportunity to educate and prepare the American people for the difficult choices posed by stagflation.

But he was no different from other presidents in accentuating the positive. In detailing previously the challenges we faced in reforming the structure of the nation's energy supply, Carter had been frank. Not here, however. The president asserted: "We reached all of our major economic goals for 1977"—with four million new jobs, inflation down, and wages up. He conceded that inflation was "still too high, and too many Americans still do not have a job." And he offered only a glimmer of our problems of governance by admitting he had no "simple answers." His economic policy, he said, was based on four principles: expanding the economy to produce new jobs and better income; the expansion must be led by private business and not the government; inflation must be brought down because it slows economic growth and hurts the poor; and the United States must contribute to the strength of the world economy.

In outlook the speech was the most conservative economic declaration from a Democratic president in modern times: "There is a limit to the role and the function of government. Government cannot solve our problems. It can't set our goals. It cannot define our vision. Government cannot eliminate poverty or provide a bountiful economy or reduce inflation or save our cities or cure illiteracy or provide energy. And government cannot mandate goodness. Only a true partnership between the government and the people can ever hope to reach these goals."[72]

So he rejected mandatory wage and price controls in favor of a voluntary program in which government, business, and labor would work together to hold the year's wage and price increases below the level of the previous two years. Given the opposition of labor and business to numerical guidelines, I was pleased we could be at least this specific in trying to ratchet down inflation. After all of our work, this was a balanced program for a New Democrat. If we could have frozen in time the economic situation of the country at this shining moment, the country and the president would have been in good shape. But worse lay around a corner that not even the best of our economists could see.

During the spring came new initiatives to slow the wage-price spiral. Carter set a national inflation goal of 5.5 percent, and in an April 1978 speech to the American Society of Newspaper Editors, he set an example for the private sector by placing a 5.5 percent ceiling on federal pay, and freezing the pay of the White House staff and his other executive appointees. He named Robert Strauss special counselor on inflation, whom the press dubbed "Inflation Czar." With characteristic lack of coordination, the president did not bother to inform Blumenthal in advance, and the Treasury secretary bitterly complained to Mondale and me that the appointment would diminish his role as the administration's principal spokesman on the economy and inflation, and further fragment economic decision making. He did not even want Strauss mentioned in the president's anti-inflation speech.[73]

If any human being could talk labor and management into moderating their behavior, it certainly would be Strauss, Washington wheeler-dealer par excellence as former chairman of the Democratic National Committee and successful negotiator of the languishing Tokyo Round of international trade talks. He could be at once charming and tough, informal and theatrical, with four-letter words spewing out naturally. But Strauss was given no authority, no leverage, no staff. He did succeed in at least delaying some raises in the steel and auto industries, "but it was like charging hell with a bucket of water. You couldn't put out the fire," he told me.[74] By the end of August he had succeeded in persuading more than one hundred companies to take "positive steps" to decelerate inflation. But Strauss felt the administration lacked muscle, such as the threat of formal controls, because "you've got to have something to hit them with." The biblical jawbone was simply not enough, and Strauss complained that the Carter program had only a carrot but no stick, let alone a jawbone.

Even though the president himself walked over from the White House to sit in on several Strauss-led meetings with management and labor in the

Old Executive Office Building, and emphasized the importance he attached to fighting inflation, he was not terribly convincing. When Carter, Strauss, and I met with Meany and the AFL-CIO brass on May 10,[75] the president gave away his own leverage when he said: "I do not think wages are the cause of inflation, nor do I intend to stop it by creating unemployment, or by wage and price controls. Nor do I expect you to take the first step." He said business was better able to take the initial steps on prices and asked the unions for a pledge to decelerate wages. But then he let them off the hook by saying it would be "okay to make it contingent on price restraint." He did show some muscle by warning that if they did not cooperate, a Democratic Congress would be less likely to support his proposals for a higher minimum wage and tougher labor laws that would make it easier to organize workers.

Strauss then assured them that the business leaders would fall into line. Meany expressed his support for the president's efforts to fight inflation but claimed that his hands were tied: "I can't pledge to do what I can't deliver." His excuse was that as the umbrella organization for numerous international unions, the AFL-CIO could not control negotiations with their employers. In Strauss's more blunt recollection, "Meany told the president and us in a nice way to go to hell."[76] The proof of the pudding was soon cooked into the outcome of the year's labor settlements. All the major union contracts during 1978 exceeded the president's targets.

A 110-day miners' strike ended when the coal companies caved in to pressure from Energy Secretary Schlesinger. With Ham Jordan and the White House political staff supporting him, Schlesinger argued that millions of people would be thrown out of work as coal shortages slowed the economy. Schultze countered in vain for the president to hold fast against the miners, but in the end he ruefully agreed that it was the administration as a whole that "caved in."[77] The workers won wage and benefit increases of more than 20 percent for the first year and 36 percent over the three-year contract period. This was a lost opportunity for the president to stand up to outsize union wage demands, as Ronald Reagan would do early in his presidency in breaking the air traffic controllers' strike—although it was much easier to find replacements for the controllers than the coal miners. I certainly did not urge him to take them on. Then, emboldened by the miners' success, electrical workers in San Francisco won a settlement in May worth 30 percent over three years. And just as we were working to deregulate railroads, 120,000 rail workers won a 35 percent wage increase over three years.

With each passing month, the inflation numbers grew worse, but Congress seemed unconcerned. Carter was peeved when Speaker O'Neill brought to the House floor a spending bill for the Health, Education, and Welfare Department that passed while the administration was negotiating a lower number. The president accurately said: "I am being pushed around as the Democratic leadership joins together." Schultze presented dismal inflation forecasts, to which Carter responded: "I am really holding tight on the budget. I was reluctant to veto bills last year, but not now!" For the first time Schultze worried that the Fed would demand drastic action in cutting the budget to avoid further rate hikes. Carter at first shrugged this off but not for long. As he opened the spring budget review on May 16, he complained about the economic forecasts: "Each time we overestimate the need for a stimulus; this is a consistent mistake. We have a real interest in keeping interest rates down and not letting the Fed think they're the only anti-inflation act in town."[78]

Official appeals and mild government pressure had clearly failed. This pointed up a fundamental mistake our team, myself included, made by opposing higher interest rates until it was too late. They could have done more to tame inflation than anything we could have done to cut the budget, but we resisted for fear that either or both would slow growth and tip the economy into recession. We continued to be torn between fears about inflation and unemployment—the stagflation dilemma. At an EPG meeting Schultze neatly summarized our unpalatable options: "Ride it out, or wring it out."[79]

Schultze's explanation to the cabinet in July was about as close as we came to a theoretical understanding of what was happening in the real economy. In the previous months the unemployment rate dropped 2 percentage points and 6.5 million more people had jobs—but the economy had not grown at a rate sufficient to produce that many jobs. This meant that more people were in effect producing less, and that helped feed inflation. Why the lower efficiency? Productivity was falling, and Schultze admitted that not only did he not know why or what to do about it, but neither did his colleagues in the economics profession.

The precipitous drop in the productivity of the American economy showed up only gradually in the statistics, and it was Carter's bad luck that it was becoming evident on his watch.[80] Productivity did not start reviving for another generation through the digital revolution, and by the end of the twentieth century, many of the protections that had been erected to mitigate the inevitable inequities of competitive capitalism had been dismantled or were in disrepair—labor unions, financial regulation, antitrust law, and progressive taxation. When the strong tide of innate American innovation finally did arrive, it no longer lifted all boats, to update President Kennedy's famous metaphor. And mysteriously, by the last part of the Obama administration, productivity again became sluggish.

Against such tectonic changes, almost invisible at the time, it is not hard to understand why Phase 1 of our anti-inflation program was not working—strict but not draconian budgets combined with gentle persuasion of industry and labor for voluntary price and wage restraint.

Chairmen of the congressional economic committees scorned our plan to expand the staff of the Council on Wage and Price Stability. We also looked again at budgetary belt-tightening to see if we could gain the support of the Democratic congressional leadership. At a meeting with the president, Mondale, the liberal champion inside the White House, warned: "They'll strike at the least defensible programs, like liberal social programs." In any event, he argued, federal spending was not a major cause of inflation—a position that put him at odds with the president, a committed budget balancer by instinct.[81]

When it became clear to me that we could be inviting the Fed to undertake a sharp tightening of monetary policy, I called Schultze with the idea of declaring a "year of national austerity," to put a cap on government programs and defer the minimum wage hike.[82] That never went far.

Through the summer we worked on a tougher anti-inflation program but came up with little new, even after calling in the country's leading economists regardless of party. Carter wondered whether inflation, which had averaged 6 percent annually since 1969, had actually made people's lives worse. He also pointed out that it would be hard to sell Congress on postponing a rise on the minimum wage "to give more profits to corporations." The experts brushed aside his musings and reminded him that inflation threatened the stability of the dollar and our ability to manage economic crises, while

Carter worried about the effects of tight policies on working people. He said, "We need to think of the guy that needs $2.70 per hour to live. I want to know what sacrifice business will make." We closed this depressing session by discussing the dollar, which had been drifting down all year. Carter's response was troubling: "I am not convinced it hurts if the dollar declines. I can only sell an anti-inflation program if the country sees it as calling for fair and mutual sacrifice."[83]

TO VOTE OR NOT TO VOTE,
THAT IS THE QUESTION

The president was damned and determined to tie a tax cut to robust reform of the disgraceful tax code. Mondale recommended postponing reform in favor of a straightforward tax cut to push it quickly through Congress and reduce uncertainty in the business community.[84] At a meeting of business leaders,[85] they asked Carter to delay tax reform because it would leave them in a state of suspended animation for months. What they wanted was a tax credit for new investment. The president would have done himself a favor to have listened to his liberal vice president, who was in rare agreement with the businessmen, but Blumenthal also favored at least a modest reform to accompany a cut. Inevitably the two became inextricably linked.

Given what we knew as we came into office early in 1977, it is difficult to argue that we were mistaken in putting forward a stimulus plan for the stalled economy. But it is equally difficult to defend the second jolt that we proposed late in the same year, together with tax reform. Yet Carter had run on the slogan that the tax code was "a disgrace to the human race," as it remains today. By the time tenacious interest groups tighten their grip on their special privileges, reform usually yields less revenue than its backers hope for—and therefore is less help in reducing budget deficits. Carter's brave attempt did not succeed. The reason was best summed up by the aphorism of Senate Finance Committee chairman Russell Long: "Don't tax you; don't tax me; tax that man behind the tree." Everyone theoretically favors closing loopholes in return for lower rates, until it is their own treasured loophole that is threatened.

As Bob Ginsburg of my staff and I worked with Treasury to put Carter's commitment to tax reform into concrete legislative terms for announcement late January 1978, three characteristics became evident. One was his staggering attention to detail. He rose at 5:00 a.m. to study the complex plan we sent him, even the most arcane tax provisions, rather than concentrate on the general principles and political strategies to pass the reforms, which should have been his primary focus.[86]

A second characteristic was his populism. One loophole that particularly struck him was the deduction for "ordinary and necessary business expenses," which had been broadened by use to include country-club dues and even football tickets. During a briefing with Blumenthal and the Treasury's tax experts, Carter exclaimed: "Club dues are a rip-off of the average guy; most club dues are for self-gratification and not legitimate business; I want club dues eliminated entirely."[87] In his message to Congress on January 20, 1978, a year to the day after his inauguration, business deductions would be ended for theater and sporting tickets, yachts, hunting lodges, club dues, and first-class airplane tickets—and only half the cost of the infamous three-martini lunch would be tax deductible. He was particularly eloquent in declaring that the average taxpayer was subsidizing the privileged few who can routinely deduct these kinds of expenses, while the average worker had to pay out of his own pocket with after-tax dollars, for a "rare night on the town."[88] In 2016 Donald Trump's advantage with working-class voters might have been reduced if the Democratic Party had voiced such views.

The third characteristic was his stubbornness. A draft of the reform plan was leaked to the press, and predictably Blumenthal reported that House Ways and Means Committee chairman Al Ullman felt the proposals would stir up the aggrieved special-interest groups, imperiling the reelection of his members. But House members are up for reelection every two years, so Carter felt there would never be a better time for reform, and ignored Ullman's advice for a straight tax cut with no tax reform.

Bending to political reality, however, we did not try to close as many loopholes as Carter would have liked; but there were still enough to stir up a hornet's nest, like curtailing a variety of tax shelters and paper losses that were used by high-income earners, and by strengthening the minimum tax to ensure that everyone paid something no matter how many preferences were claimed. Especially close to Carter's heart was a repeal of the lower tax rate on capital gains, benefiting only those in the highest tax brackets on their investment profits.

The fate of Carter's package spoke volumes about how American democracy was captured then—and still is now—by highly organized special interests that keep their benefits through large donations to ensure that they hold both the ear and the votes of members of Congress. Only the president can appeal over their heads to the common good, and when Carter did so he was neither the first nor the last president to fail on the issue of fiscal fairness and tax justice.

Carter had been itching to veto the tax bill for weeks. On October 14 we had two meetings with the president, the first including Blumenthal, Schultze, and me. He told us: "I am hoping I can veto the tax bill, and use this as an example for my anti-inflation program. Tax reform is so screwed up, I am feeling better knowing I can veto the bill." He explained that the economy was beginning to strengthen and no longer needed to be stimulated by another tax cut, and in any case he was disgusted that a Democratic Congress had eviscerated his tax reform proposals to favor the wealthy. At the second meeting I urged him at least to consult first with his advisers on the economic impact of the bill and consider the political implications of vetoing a Democratic tax bill. But in retrospect he was clearly right, and we were wrong.[89]

The bill provided precious little reform, and a veto would have sent a strong message to the public and financial markets that the president was placing top priority on fighting inflation, and would not accept a dog of a bill simply because it was called tax reform: To mix metaphors, it was little more than a pig with lipstick. But Blumenthal, although sensitive to the inflation concerns, had negotiated the tax reform package, albeit with little to show for it, and felt invested in it, and Schultze felt a second tax cut was necessary to strengthen the recovery.[90] Neither I nor his advisers were willing to take the political risk of the president vetoing a Democratic bill to cut taxes, just before midterm elections.

How did the tax reform bill become so lopsided? Enter Senator Russell Long, who had been in the wings all along, waiting for natural-gas deregulation to be resolved. He had killed the wellhead oil tax, a centerpiece of our energy package, and now his raid on the Treasury through tax cuts went into high gear, under the guise of tax reform. Long had not been consulted from the start on our tax and energy tax packages, although his Finance Committee would be decisive in what went to the Senate floor—or did not. It had been clear from the outset that Long would be the key man on all energy taxes, especially the tax on production by old oil wells, and on tax reform. Late in June, Ham and I urged the president to get to know Long better because we believed he would feel the need to reciprocate the president's friendship. The president did reach out, but there was no reciprocity. As I noted in the margin of my pad, "JC just didn't develop personal relationships," but neither was Long prepared to give up his precious tax benefits for the oil and gas industry.[91]

When Long and I discussed tax reform years later, it was as if he had been looking over my shoulder when I scribbled my note. He reflected in his usual rambling, but pointed and self-justifying style: "My impression is they just sent it [the bill] up there. My advice hadn't been sought. My input's not in it. That's just fine. So I figured I could pretty well do whatever I blessed well pleased about it. If the president had started out by saying, 'Now look, I want to recommend some changes in the tax laws, call it tax reform, call it anything you want to call it, and I just have in mind some things I want to suggest; there might be something that you'd like me to put in that I might be able to put in there that you'd like to see in it. Why don't we talk about it?' I'd have been willing to tell him what I honestly thought about it. If you're going to send that bill up there, and you're not gonna seek my advice, then it's all right. It's perfectly all right with me. But if you aren't going to seek my advice, they're not going to alter it one whit because of my views, one way or the other, and there's not gonna be a bloody thing in there that I asked you to put in there, then I don't know why I shouldn't go ahead and be a totally free agent, with regard to that bill, when it gets there."

He felt if he was in the same party as the president "you ought to go the extra mile to help him, when you can, all things being equal, you ought to help him. But frankly, I don't think Jimmy Carter looked at it that way. I'm not saying I'm right and he's wrong. I'm just saying that I think he'd have been more effective and gotten his way more often, if he had done business that way."[92]

That was the transactional way Long did business, and he could work his will because he was in total command of his committee, and no senator was appointed to it without his approval. As the liberal New York Democrat Pat Moynihan once said to me with mock innocence, he had always wondered why no one won a berth on the Senate Finance Committee without agreeing to support the oil depletion allowance, a notorious tax break for the domestic oil producers.

Meanwhile the president began to waver on cutting taxes, fearing it would add to inflation. The bargain he had proposed of tax cuts together with tax reform had been undermined by Congress, which gave him little help on tax reform and a larger tax cut than he proposed. To rub salt in the wound, a Congress that was nearly two-thirds Democratic voted to support a Republican amendment to lower the capital gains tax on investments in stock and property for the wealthy, rather than restrict it as Carter proposed. It added new tax credits and exemptions for special interests.

The only remnants of our tax reform proposal were an end to deductions for state and local gasoline taxes and for hunting lodges and other facilities when used for business entertainment, although country-club dues continued as deductible business costs. After thirty-four hours of continuous work by a House-Senate conference committee on October 15, Pete Stark, a California liberal Democrat who supported our original reform package, read his colleagues a bit of doggerel he had written in the early hours of the morning while watching major reforms being ground to dust out of public view: "The Speaker had sold all the liberals a bill, and Good Chairman Ullman had swallowed the pill. / With loopholes for dry holes and tax breaks for wine, the deeds of the lobbyists were almost a crime. / They took care of the heirs, and built up the shelters, but for the poor folks Russell [Long] gave us no helpers. / The rich will have Christmas with ill-gotten gains, while others pay taxes with annual pains. / But Scrooging the people is Washington's credo, now what we need, Tiny Tim, is a veto!!"[93]

Carter badly wanted to follow Stark's rhyming appeal. It had been clear for weeks the president wanted a veto to send an anti-inflation message and block the evisceration of his reforms, which Congress not only gutted but turned on their head, favoring the wealthy even more. The Treasury's top tax and congressional staff members Donald Lubick and Larry O'Brien called me to urge a veto because the legislation made the tax code even more unfair than it was before the president sent up his proposals.[94] Thus began an internal tug of war that lasted for weeks. One of the most thoughtful members of the House, Rules Committee chairman Richard Bolling of Missouri, phoned me to say that he also was unhappy about the failure of tax reform but "it would be close to madness to veto the bill . . . [which] will hurt Democrats running for reelection. We couldn't explain it to people who just want a cut in their taxes." That same day the president called and asked if any of us wanted him to veto the tax bill. I told him no.[95]

But the president would not let it go, and showed a prescience on inflation we would have done well to follow. In a meeting the next day with Mondale, Schultze, Jordan, and me, only five days before he planned another major anti-inflation address, he said again, "I am concerned [about] the tax cut; it will not help with fighting inflation." He recognized that we had underestimated the growth of the economy and its impact on inflation. He also unloaded on our Economic Policy Group: "I am disgusted with the bickering in the EPG. I feel there is nothing in the speech, and we'll be laughed at."[96]

Shortly afterward, when a broader group of outside economic advisers joined, his foresight was again evident as he told us the financial markets would be dissatisfied with the content of his anti-inflation speech and the dollar would drop. He felt boxed in, saying he was "depressed": He could not cut defense spending while negotiating a Strategic Arms Limitation Treaty with Moscow, nor could he stop the inflation-indexed increases in such major programs as Medicare and Medicaid. He was ready to wield his veto pen on the tax cut,[97] but Blumenthal and Schultze continued to believe the recovery would stall if he did,[98] and his political and congressional aides, myself included, feared a veto of a popular tax cut just before the midterm election.

Yielding to pressure even from within his own administration, which I was duty-bound to pass on to him in a decision memorandum from all agencies, as well as the entire White House staff, Carter signed the tax-cut bill

without fanfare and with great personal regret on November 6, just before
the midterm elections. As expected, we held our Democratic majority, but
Carter called me up with the most searing criticism I received from him
during our four years in the White House: "I have always depended on
your advice, but you disappointed me on the tax bill." I deserved the rebuke,
as painful as it was.

THE REPUBLICAN SUPPLY-SIDE REVOLUTION:
A LAFFER

While he was struggling over supporting the tax cut, we did not appreciate
that we were on the cusp of the antitax revolution captured by Ronald Reagan
that would turn the Republican party from budget balancers to advocates
of tax-cut-driven supply-side economics to this very day. Out went the uncomfortable Phillips Curve tracking the relationship between unemployment
and inflation, and in came the Laffer Curve. Out went the stingy economics of balanced budgets that were a mainstay of Republican presidents like
Eisenhower and Ford, and in came supposedly self-financing supply-side tax
cuts. This simple curve, developed by the young conservative economist Arthur Laffer, could be drawn on a napkin to prove the argument that lower
taxes would serve as an incentive to more work, more output, and higher
government revenues to fully pay for the lost revenues from tax cuts. It would
need two generations of rising deficits and a rising number of millionaires
at the expense of middle-class taxpayers to demonstrate how false was this
vulgarized Keynesianism. But the public did not see it that way.

In June 1978 they had led the way in California by passing Proposition
13 in a statewide referendum that capped property taxes. Now the popular
mood had swung away from closing tax loopholes to simply slashing taxes.
One Democrat who sensed this oncoming wave was Representative Thomas
Foley of Washington (who would later become Speaker). At a Democratic
breakfast on June 28, he correctly warned everyone that the Proposition 13
victory would create a conservative mood in Congress, and spending and
inflation would be major issues in the November elections.[99]

This impulse was eventually embodied in the massive Kemp-Roth tax cut sponsored by Buffalo's Republican congressman and former Buffalo Bills star quarterback Jack Kemp, and Republican senator William Roth of Delaware in 1981. It was Ronald Reagan's signature economic accomplishment as president and continues to be the dominant economic thread in the twenty-first-century Republican Party—tax cuts do not lose revenues but spur so much growth they pay for themselves. But in fact tax cuts under Ronald Reagan and George W. Bush led to triple-digit budget deficits running into the hundreds of billions.

PHASE II

In the fog of battle it is hard to devise a new strategy for any war, and each tactical thrust encountered its own obstacle. Labor Secretary Marshall came up with an idea for more explicit wage and price guidelines enforced by punishing government contractors that did not comply.[100] But we had only limited authority over existing contracts and would need a large bureaucracy to oversee the new ones.[101]

As we developed ideas for yet another anti-inflation speech, Blumenthal, who thought of himself as the inflation hawk but never liked guidelines, said that he was concerned about the certificate of compliance that government contractors would have to sign under a strengthened wage-price policy we were considering. And Strauss finally threw up his hands as inflation czar and resigned, saying, "I can't go further with only a smile and shoeshine. I need more government help."[102]

As we were preparing the president for a nationwide television address on inflation, we did not want him to speak without having a replacement for Strauss, who had recommended Fred Kahn as his successor. A capable person can be great in one job and miscast in another. This was true for Fred Kahn, and he knew it. He had been a star in helping deregulate the airlines and abolishing his own regulatory agency, but this new challenge was very different. In mid-October 1978, returning from an Italian vacation, he was handed a message to come to the vice president's office. He found himself surrounded by Mondale, Strauss, and Schultze, who gave him the bad news. Kahn demurred, saying he had not finished his job deregulating the airlines and had no experience in dealing with inflation. He protested that Carter did not need an inflation adviser, since he already commanded a talented economic team. In an attempt to make the job more powerful and thus more appealing, they told him he would also be the chairman of a strengthened Council on Wage and Price Stability to enforce new wage and price standards. This had the reverse effect, since he had no interest in such a "messy job" and said that Bosworth was already doing it well.

Kahn avoided seeing the president, which elicited handwritten messages asking, "Why can't I see Fred Kahn?" The answer was that Kahn was otherwise engaged with several eminent economists, including Nobel laureates Robert Solow and James Tobin, who warned him to avoid the job if at all possible. I met Kahn in my office, and a brighter, more able, more personable man one could never hope to meet. But he was deeply reluctant to take the job because "I am a kind of professor" who preferred a specific task backed by law, while an inflation czar must be manipulative, cajoling, and political. Indeed, he was the picture of a professor, with a balding head, heavy glasses, and a low-key manner. Moreover, he said, and we would certainly find this out, "I am very independent, and I say what I believe. I will accumulate a series of enemies."[103]

Just as we should have listened to the president on tax cuts, we should have taken Kahn's misgivings to heart. But there was no other candidate immediately available, and when Carter saw him in the Oval Office, the president asked, "Don't you think inflation is my most serious problem?" To which Kahn could only say yes. "And do you see anything fundamentally wrong with the inflation program I just announced?" And Kahn had to say he did not. He told the president he was not interested in enforcing wage and price standards, and Carter replied that was really Bosworth's job, but he would be able to intervene anywhere he believed there were inflationary pressures, with full presidential support—and that the president needed him. And thus prevailed the truth of the old adage about how hard it is to say no to the president of the United States.

Before his speech he called in the cabinet to present his anti-inflation pitch and was hardly upbeat: "I don't approach this phase of my presidency with a lot of optimism, and we may not show short-term success. But this will be my major domestic undertaking in the next year." When Carter addressed the nation on October 24, 1978, in what would be his fourth major speech on inflation, he declared that more than six million jobs had been created during his first twenty-one months in office, but now inflation was "our most serious domestic problem" and his "central preoccupation." No longer would inflation receive equal billing with unemployment, it would be preeminent. The centerpiece of his anti-inflation program were new and tougher wage and price standards to break the inflation spiral, backed by federal contract authority, as Labor Secretary Marshall had recommended; tough restraints on federal spending to cut the budget deficit in half; no further tax cuts; eliminating unnecessary regulations; and deregulating the transport industries to promote competition and lower prices.[104]

This would come to be known as Phase II. As Carter put it in his address, "Once it's started, wages and prices chase each other up and up—like a crowd standing at a football stadium; no one can see any better than when everyone is sitting down, but no one is willing to be the first to sit down."[105] A neat analogy, but the mechanism for persuading the spectators to resume their seats was our embrace of Art Okun's Real Wage Insurance, so workers who complied with the standards received a tax cut and were not disadvantaged by those who violated them. But this innovative idea was dead on arrival at Capitol Hill.

Carter also announced the next day that Kahn, the master of airline deregulation, would work with him to provide a single voice against inflation. He closed by repeating Winston Churchill's defiant call to his people facing the Nazi threat: "What kind of people do they think we are?" But Carter's rhetoric was no match for Churchill's.

Hardly out of the box, Kahn made it clear he did not want to be the one to enforce what he openly called the "stinking guidelines," a phrase for which he apologized by explaining to business leaders that no one wanted them anyway.[106] He arrived to an empty office in the Old Executive Office Building and some resentment by Bosworth, who headed the Council on Wage and Price Stability, and had his hands full developing detailed guidelines. Kahn's staff did not materialize as promised. He had to struggle with the president's "Cousin Cheap," Hugh Carter, to scrounge for assistants and finally had to intervene at a cabinet meeting on November 20, as Carter was appealing for help in the anti-inflation campaign.[107] He finally was allotted five people to help him identify inflationary regulations and legislation, with particular emphasis on parts of the economy that were major contributors to the rise in the Consumer Price Index, such as health care, energy, and food.

More generally Kahn became a pied piper, the president's chief spokesman in his attempt to highlight his battle against inflation, an effective and credible one, perhaps too credible. When he warned that unchecked inflation might lead to a serious "depression," the unenviable task of asking him to moderate his rhetoric fell to me. Undeterred, he piped an even more discordant note, declaring to the press that he had been told to watch his language, avoid the D-word, and henceforth would warn that the economy might turn into "a banana." When the chairman of the United Fruit Company squawked, the irrepressible Kahn found a different euphemism without a pressure group behind it: He began warning instead of a "kumquat."[108]

But Kahn did his best to take advantage of the strengthened wage and price program. Carter laid down a presidential marker in plain numbers—a ceiling of 7 percent annual wage increases and a 5.75 percent limit for price hikes, which sounded a clearer note and was backed by stronger enforcement. All firms seeking federal contracts had to pledge they would abide by the numerical guideline. The president asserted, "We will use our buying power more effectively to make price restraint and competition a reality."

The program had some limited success. After Church's Fried Chicken raised its prices above the president's numerical ceiling, Kahn issued a stinging release that prompted a drop in the company's walk-in business, whereupon it retreated.[109] A bigger success was achieved when Sears, Roebuck reported it had violated the guidelines and rolled back prices. But this alerted major firms to hire lawyers to vet their certifications and ensure they were technically within the guidelines.[110] While nonunion wages remained largely within the limit, the unions were furious and simply dug in against them—in rare accord with the National Association of Manufacturers. And the effort to use the government's huge purchasing power was partly foiled by the intricacies of federal regulations and especially procurement by the Pentagon, many of whose suppliers had no competition and worked on cost-plus contracts.

There was a further division between large and concentrated industries and those dominated by small firms, over which we had no control. Bosworth explained to the president that there had been an explosion of food prices, with prices of finished goods up strongly and defensive raises by smaller and medium-size firms in the belief that our guidelines were a prelude to mandatory controls. The larger firms were generally complying. Bosworth was able to monitor firms producing just under half of the country's output and recommended extending his oversight so his council could jump on violators of all sizes. Carter agreed and said, "It would be helpful to single out some companies and bust the hell out of them."[111] But all in all financial markets at home and abroad were not impressed by the president's speech or its phase two follow-up.

We now were in a race against time before companies, investors, traders, and speculators lost faith in our economic management. At some point, and there was no way to know when, they might all vote against the dollar, and even with the more rudimentary computers of the day, their votes could move billions across borders in the click of a keystroke.

THE DECLINING DOLLAR

Our economic team, and the Keynesian economists upon whom we relied, had misjudged the ferocity of the underlying inflation and the difficulty of dealing with the phenomenon of stagflation. Despite all our hard work on what we thought was a comprehensive anti-inflation program, the financial markets quickly cast a final vote of no confidence. The dollar immediately dropped to an all-time low in Asia. Europe followed, and within days we faced a dollar crisis after sliding for months, in a policy that the press labeled "benign neglect."[112]

Since the start of the year, America's currency had lost about one-quarter of its value against the world's currency, with inflation still raging. During the weeks following the president's October speech, billions were thrown into the currency markets to halt the dive, but it continued until it blew itself out by year's end.[113] Normally a decline in the value of a nation's currency can stimulate its economy by encouraging sales abroad for its exports at a cheaper price to foreigners. But it can also make imports more expensive, in effect importing more inflation, which was exactly what we did not need at that moment. Blumenthal had first laid down a marker at a July 1977 cabinet meeting.[114] With Carter in office for only six months, he said the dollar had declined more than 1 percent in recent weeks—nothing dramatic yet, but something to watch.

What Blumenthal did not say was that his own ill-chosen words outside the privacy of the cabinet made it appear that he favored a lower dollar—something no Treasury secretary should ever say. His suggestion at a June 1977 meeting of G7 finance ministers in Paris,[115] that the yen and mark should rise against the dollar to help correct the large U.S. trade deficits with Japan and Germany, was widely interpreted as a deliberate policy to talk down the value of the dollar. As Paul Volcker put it later, "Foreigners sensed that for the Carter Administration, a stable dollar was a much lower priority than growth and jobs."[116]

Volcker had been in the front lines during the crisis as president of the Federal Reserve Bank of New York, which operates in the foreign currency markets on behalf of the U.S. government. Blumenthal did not intend to indicate he actually wanted a cheaper dollar, but the suspicion stuck as he declined to support the dollar in the currency markets and claimed that our allies did not want us to do so.[117]

His tone changed toward the end of Carter's first year, when he called me late in December to urgently request a presidential statement, because "there is a risk of a snowballing impact on the dollar."[118] Early in the new year he called again to tell me he was working on a swap with Germany for deutschmarks. Five days later he told the cabinet that the dollar was under attack in world markets: "We are bidding with poor Jacks, and there will be a real problem if our hand is called."[119] Currencies go up and down in international trading without attracting much attention, but this was different. The dollar is the world's reserve currency, and its stability and the policies upon which it depends have been the pillar of the postwar world's financial system. Most international commodity transactions, most crucially the sale of crude oil, also are denominated in dollars. As our purchases of foreign oil sent more dollars abroad, foreign governments were awash with dollars they were no longer able to exchange for gold, after Nixon broke the link between the dollar and gold in 1971.

For several months early in 1978, Blumenthal saw signs of a slow-motion crisis. The stock market was dropping, gold prices were rising, business confidence was collapsing, foreigners were pulling money out of American banks, OPEC prices were rising again, and other countries were freezing their outflows of capital. The dollar's problems could also undercut the hard-won commitments just made at the Bonn summit by America's allies to stimulate their economies, because we would be limited in our ability to do our share by stimulating our own. At a breakfast meeting at Treasury on August 15, Blumenthal, Schultze, Fed chairman Miller, and I reviewed possible emergency measures such as selling gold to mop up dollars and domestic measures like scrapping the tax cut, cutting Social Security taxes, delaying the increase in the minimum wage, imposing a fee on oil imports, and even wartime measures limiting the amount of money Americans could send abroad.[120] None were attractive.

It was nevertheless clear that we had entered a new phase, in which international markets were directly affecting our domestic decisions, and anything and everything had to be reconsidered. After the meeting I called the president and Ham to brief them on the need for urgent action. At a meeting of the National Security Council, Blumenthal said darkly that things had developed into a "psychological semi-panic not due to the underlying situation" and asked for a public statement by the president to calm the markets. Miller made the most dramatic statement: "There is a clear and present danger; financial markets are reacting in a more negative way than even after the assassination of JFK." He warned that the crisis could spread to the world economy, and the administration needed to unveil a comprehensive package and not "dribble it out." The president agreed, but we followed with a replay of our limited options.[121]

Meanwhile, to his great credit, Blumenthal had secretly directed Anthony Solomon, undersecretary of the Treasury for monetary affairs, to develop a package with the Fed that would be so large it would finally exceed even the market's expectations. It was ready when the dollar collapsed after Carter's October speech. If there was a hero in this dollar rescue it was Tony Solomon, holding the key Treasury portfolio with international responsibilities that, in part, was held by Volcker under Nixon, and Tim Geithner under Clinton, during my tenure as deputy Treasury secretary. Aged sixty at the time, this Harvard Ph.D. in economics brought a wealth of experience in the private sector and government, having run a business in Mexico and served under Presidents Roosevelt and Johnson. A man with a slight hunchback, Solomon would at times wear an elegant silk ascot instead of a tie; he had the disposition of an undertaker, dour and crusty, with a gravelly voice and a permanent frown. Opinionated but brilliant, he was right about the link between inflation and the dollar and had little patience either for small talk or for those in the administration he told me he regarded as "Neanderthals regarding international markets."[122]

The next several days were as unnerving as anything I experienced in Washington. Blumenthal called to tell me that traders had begun dumping dollars even before the president spoke and were still doing so, prompting the Fed to increase the discount rate. Solomon called late in the evening of October 26, and asked to see me urgently. I dropped everything and quickly walked across the small path connecting the White House East Wing with the Treasury, thinking to myself that we were close to an economic meltdown. He warned apocalyptically that further declines in the dollar would lead to bank failures and lost prestige abroad.

With an eye toward November's midterm elections, he said that we would need a very large war chest to defend the dollar and simultaneously avoid the high interest rates that would guarantee a recession. He laid out a comprehensive package for coordinated action with our allies: higher bank reserves to make speculation against the dollar more expensive; increasing interest rates substantially; and most crucially, a coordinated U.S.–German–Japanese swap into the currency markets to buy dollars and thus raise their value. I told Solomon this would greatly complicate obtaining labor's cooperation on our new, more stringent wage and price guideline program. He acknowledged that, but recommended that we tell the AFL-CIO that the program would avoid even more pain for workers from a recession. When we finished, I thought how lucky we were to have someone of Tony's talent and experience navigating these treacherous waters, but noted in the margin of my legal pad: "Shows unseen international forces are driving domestic policy."[123]

The next morning, October 27, the president called to ask me to meet with Schultze, Kahn, and Blumenthal; he was still focused on his new antiinflation measures. "I think there is more of a chance of success than I realized," he said. We discussed the dollar crisis, and I told him not to make any precipitous decisions until he had heard everyone out, including Solomon. "I am very much inclined against endorsing higher interest rates," Carter said, and it was clear in a meeting later that day that he put his hopes on enforcing the new wage and price guidelines. He told Kahn and Bosworth to sign up at least five hundred companies and unions using "maximum government and public pressure against those who don't comply." That included compiling a list of government penalties for noncompliance, even enlisting municipal leaders to lean on local industries. Carter was ready to throw himself into the fight. He told his economic team later in the day: "It is better to take our political lumps, but keep credibility on inflation. I want to show black leaders the unemployment consequences of high inflation. The administration's future depends on the success of my anti-inflation program, and I am determined to make it work."[124]

CARTER BONDS

What happened after that meeting would change the course of administration policy, and there would be no turning back. It had all the suspense of an Alfred Hitchcock film and was carried out with great stealth to shock the market. Blumenthal asked to see the president privately, told him that the dollar was sinking badly despite his speech, and then informed him for the first time that Solomon had been working on a rescue plan but had kept it secret in order to first gauge the market reaction to his speech—and now they could not wait.

To avoid any suspicion that the markets would soon be socked by a major intervention, everyone maintained a normal Saturday schedule. Carter campaigned in New England. Miller went to a dinner party at the Georgetown home of Katherine Graham, the owner of the *Washington Post*, but excused himself early. He was sneaked into the White House, where Schultze met him in the room used by the White House chauffeurs.[125] It was more difficult for Solomon, who was hosting a dinner party at his own home, and left early with a hardly credible plea that he had an appointment with an important European steel executive.

I had a personal dilemma. Our synagogue had a long-planned family retreat in the small town of Orkney Springs, Virginia, and I did not want to leave Fran there with the boys, or to have my absence raise questions. But I wanted first to speak to Schultze and then to be plugged in to the afternoon discussion on the plan that would be presented to the president. So it was agreed that I would go through the White House operator and participate by telephone. The problem was that there was only one phone in the place, no desk, and telephone calls were frowned on during the Jewish Sabbath.

What I heard was part of a four-hour discussion about a huge package Solomon had privately outlined to me, with a war chest of $30 billion from the Treasury and the International Monetary Fund to defend the dollar, and an unusually large 1 percent increase in the Fed's discount rate to nudge interest rates higher and encourage foreigners to hold on to their dollars. Miller insisted on selling gold as a gesture, but the decisive American commitment was an offer to finance one-third of the war chest with $10 billion worth of bonds denominated in German marks and Japanese yen. They soon became known as "Carter bonds," and were meant to show that the United States was willing to put its money where its mouth was: If the dollar did not rise, the bonds would cost more to repay in foreign currency.[126] The president returned at 10:00 p.m. in a helicopter from Camp David on the White House South Lawn, shielded by the darkness, arrived at the Map Room unnoticed by reporters, and listened for two hours until just before midnight; then he approved the package.[127]

On Sunday, German, Swiss, and Japanese officials arrived in Washington at Solomon's invitation and went straight to his house. Since it was a weekend, Toyoo Gyohten of the Japanese Finance Ministry had to pay for his plane ticket from Tokyo with his personal credit card and worried that he might not be reimbursed if the negotiations failed.[128]

This "revolutionary" package—Miller's term—was thrown at the markets as soon as they opened at 9:00 a.m. November 1, 1978, after a long European holiday weekend. It worked. Within minutes the dollar rose 7 percent against the mark, 5 percent against the yen, and 7.5 percent against the Swiss franc. The New York Stock Exchange soared to its largest single-day increase

Jimmy Carter, a little-known former state senator, celebrates his November 3, 1970, election as Governor of Georgia, along with his wife, Rosalynn. *(Jimmy Carter Library, photographer unknown)*

Carter is embraced on April 13, 1976, by the Rev. Martin Luther (Daddy) King Sr., who helped save his candidacy by personally defending him after his "ethnic purity" remark, and helped mobilize a supportive network of black churches in the campaign. *(Associated Press)*

President Gerald Ford speaks during the first of three televised presidential debates with Democratic candidate Jimmy Carter at Philadelphia's Walnut Street Theatre on September 23, 1976. *(Associated Press)*

Hand in hand with Rosalynn and their nine-year-old daughter, Amy, Carter was the first president to walk down Pennsylvania Avenue to his new White House home during the inaugural parade. *(Jimmy Carter Library, photographer: Kightlinger)*

The new President and First Lady, along with Vice President Walter Mondale and his wife, Joan, greet the crowd at the inaugural ball, January 20, 1977. *(Associated Press)*

Rosalynn Carter, spearheading mental health legislation, testifies on its behalf before the Senate Human Resources Subcommittee, only the second presidential wife to testify before Congress after Eleanor Roosevelt. *(Jimmy Carter Library, photographer: Fitzpatrick)*

On an unprecedented diplomatic mission for a First Lady, in 1977, Rosalynn tours Latin America to promote her husband's drive for human rights and democracy in the continent's dictatorships. *(Jimmy Carter Library, photographer: Fitzpatrick)*

President-elect Carter, seated near television, gathers his economic team in December 1976 to discuss his initial economic stimulus package of tax cuts and jobs programs at Miss Lillian's Pond House in Plains. Mondale is in the foreground at left, and the author is at the right of the fireplace. *(Associated Press)*

Before the fall: Carter with Bert Lance, his closest friend and political wingman, who was later forced to resign as the President's budget director because of his questionable practices as a Georgia banker. *(Jimmy Carter Library, photographer: Schumacher)*

Press Secretary Jody Powell (left) and Carter's masterful political strategist and Chief of Staff Hamilton Jordan, leaders of the "Georgia Mafia," conferring in the West Wing of the White House. *(Jimmy Carter Library, Photographer: Kightlinger)*

....and as seen in the popular imagination through the eyes of *Time* magazine's editors and the sharp pen of the artist David Levine. *(TIME cover © 1977 Time Inc. Used with permission)*

The author, who served as the Carter campaign's policy director, with the President-elect during the transition for a briefing at Miss Lilian's house. *(Jimmy Carter Library, photographer: Kightlinger)*

Carter, in a cardigan sweater, discussing his 1977 comprehensive energy program with Energy Secretary James Schlesinger. *(Jimmy Carter Library, photographer: Schumacher)*

Charles Schultze, the President's chief White House economic adviser, at his regular weekly meeting with Carter in the Oval Office. *(Jimmy Carter Library, photographer: Schumacher)*

The weekly foreign policy breakfast in the Roosevelt Room with (left to right) Vice President Mondale, Secretary of State Cyrus Vance, Carter, and National Security Advisor Zbigniew Brzezinski. *(Jimmy Carter Library, photographer: Schumacher)*

The weekly Democratic Leadership Breakfast in a small dining room off the State Room, with House Speaker Tip O'Neill on Carter's right, and Senate Majority Leader Robert C. Byrd on his left. *(Jimmy Carter Library, photographer: Kightlinger)*

In the Oval Office, Carter greets his mentor and role model in the Oval Office, Admiral Hyman Rickover, under whom he served in the U.S. Navy's nuclear submarine program. *(Jimmy Carter Library, photographer: Schumacher)*

In the Oval Office with Attorney General Griffin Bell, James Schlesinger, Jody Powell, White House Counsel Robert Lipshutz, Zbigniew Brzezinski, NSC Press Secretary Jerry Schecter, and the author. *(Jimmy Carter Library, photographer: Schumacher)*

in years.[129] Blumenthal called me twice, elated with the good news, and our ambassador to Switzerland, Marvin Warner, told me the president's dollar-rescue program had been "met with ecstasy" throughout Europe.[130]

While no one expected that all the money in the war chest would actually be spent, it cost the equivalent of $6.7 billion through the remainder of the year to support the currency. Solomon wondered aloud to Volcker at one point how long it was worth spending that kind of money, which eventually would have to be paid back.[131] There were other bumps along the way. The Germans at first refused to do their part, but meanwhile medium and short-term interest rates fell and would not have to rise as much as feared.

Solomon kept me apprised and gave me another message that stayed with me throughout my public service: "The Council of Economic Advisers does not understand the psychology of markets, which is critical and cannot be put into their models. Therefore, you need to stroke and pressure money markets. Now we may not need a recession."[132] I only wish he had been correct, and indeed he might have been had not the Iranian revolution intruded. Early in 1979 the dollar settled of its own accord as the trade balance improved—exactly as Solomon had predicted when he started putting the package together, and the dollar crisis ended. I only wish our anti-inflation program could have been as successful.

The dollar rescue was important for other reasons. It ended the locomotive era of stimulating global growth through coordinated pump priming by our key allies. It also proved that the monetarists' free-floating exchange rates did not adjust themselves without an occasional government thumb on the scales of the markets that were supposed to self-correct. It demonstrated how foreign markets can drive domestic decisions. It underscored that the dominance of the U.S. economy during the postwar period had been reduced. But it was also a fundamental turning point for the Carter administration. It showed that in dealing with stagflation, we could not have it both ways—we had to abandon the notion that we could stimulate the economy to lower unemployment without risking rising inflation.

This also unsettled the dominant constituencies of the Democratic Party, which tended to believe that inflation was an issue for Republicans to worry about. What labor and liberals refused to understand was that their opposition to a progressive way of fighting inflation by wage and price guidelines and tighter budgets would inevitably leave brutal monetary policy as the only solution. Key elements of the Democratic Party base simply could not handle persistently high inflation, and were pretending it away, pushing the minimum wage increase and the Humphrey-Hawkins Full Employment Act. We now were on a perilous political course that would lead to a challenge from the left by Senator Kennedy to Carter's renomination.

But even while shifting the goal of his economic policy, Carter could not easily recalibrate the direction of his government to attain it. During the period we were spending billions to defend the dollar, no one was willing to pay the real price of stopping inflation by tightening money. The administration soldiered on with our tougher voluntary policy of anti-inflationary standards. Carter himself wondered why other nations had lower inflation rates, and Schultze explained that their labor markets were not as tight; our lower dollar imported more inflation; and their more disciplined unions were willing to heed their governments.[133] Indeed, in other advanced nations there was a greater sense of social solidarity that eased the application of a voluntary policy—most notably in Germany with its social market economy (*Sozialmarktwissenschaft*), where even captains of industry refer to unions as their "social partners," a model replicated in Scandinavia and to a lesser degree in some other European countries and Japan. All had long taxed petroleum products heavily to encourage conservation, so that when the Iranian revolution created a second worldwide inflationary oil price shock, they were less vulnerable, while we were still struggling to enact our national energy policy.

We hardly started 1979 with holiday cheer. Schultze reported at a January 2, briefing of the president, vice president, and top economic officials[134] that most forecasters expected a recession in late 1979, with a snapback in 1980 that might be avoided if interest rates did not go much higher. All this was enough to leave one breathless and despondent. But it is worth pausing to dispel one myth about inflation, because a movement had arisen for a balanced-budget amendment to the Constitution, as part of the antitax revolt. Carter was in no way a big spender, and failed to achieve his goal of a balanced budget not because of excessive spending but because of inadequate growth and revenues. On the contrary, he followed his conservative instincts whenever possible.

Between the fiscal years of 1976 and projecting into 1980, federal spending increased only by 1.1 percent, excluding defense spending and mandatory Social Security increases. When those figures were presented by Schultze and Budget Director McIntyre, Blumenthal commented that the president needed to tell the American people "the truth, that things are bad." Schultze said that would only backfire because we were facing an inflation that was neither pushed by rising costs nor pulled by high demand—but by external factors like food and energy hikes that suck consumers into a psychological whirlpool where they tend to buy at any price to protect themselves from even higher prices in the future. If the president told the nation that things would only get worse, Americans might rush out to buy more and convert his sober warning into a self-fulfilling prophecy.[135]

The fact is that neither Blumenthal nor any of Carter's other economic advisers presented stronger anti-inflation options that the president himself could actually have adopted. And none focused on monetary policy until too late, because no one wanted to be identified with the increasingly high interest rates and unemployment that tight money would produce. As we moved into the spring of 1979, wholesale prices rose, a reliable harbinger of what consumers would soon be paying.[136] The modest successes of the guidelines had been achieved largely with companies that did business with the government. Oil prices began a steady climb because of the Iranian revolution and would double within a year; food and housing were already growing more costly. Blumenthal could only present tougher and more unpalatable policies: Tighten the guidelines and enforce them by law; squeeze the budget further; and encourage the Fed to raise interest rates. We were near despair. As the cherry trees blossomed in Washington, Bosworth declared: "We've run out of options."[137]

The contemporaneous record, on which I have reflected over the years from my virtually verbatim notes, frequently showed Carter ahead of his advisers. He wanted to veto his own tax cut. He pushed for tough penalties against violations of the government's wage and price guidelines. He ran a tight budget. In the end he had to rescue the sinking American dollar because foreigners and Wall Street lost confidence in our economic program. But no one had a clear answer for inflation, and Carter had the bad luck of governing at a time of deeply embedded inflationary expectations that we did not fully appreciate and could not be neatly modeled in the economists' computers. They drew a statistical picture of dramatically lower growth in productivity, large increases in crude oil prices spiked by the Iran revolution, and a strongly expanding economy that simply did not jibe with their experience or economic equations. Fortunately they also could not account for Jimmy Carter's resilience and his determination to keep trying until he found the answer. When he found it, he was reviled for it.

VOLCKER

On his return home from a successful Tokyo summit at the end of June 1979, in which he was able to coax the G7 nations to adopt import quotas on OPEC oil, he was nevertheless exhausted and dispirited. With lines of cars snaking around gasoline stations, inflation running at 11 percent, and his approval rating at a miserable 30 percent, Carter precipitously canceled a nationwide address on energy, mysteriously retreated to Camp David, rethought and restructured his government, and addressed the nation in what came to be known as the "malaise" speech, although he never uttered the word. The high drama of this extraordinary chapter in the American presidency is recounted later in this book, but suffice it to say here that Carter fired Blumenthal, who was viewed by financial markets as the key anti-inflation fighter, and reshuffled his cabinet without thinking about a replacement. This came just as Blumenthal felt he had at last reached a meeting of the minds with Carter, as they flew home from Tokyo together, but he was derided by Ham and Jody for not being a team player.[138]

The search for successors during a time of high inflation and turmoil in financial markets, as well as in the government itself, was not the most attractive incentive for a quality candidate to succeed Blumenthal at Treasury. We canvassed the usual suspects in the corporate establishment: Reg Jones of General Electric, A. W. "Tom" Clausen, the respected CEO of Bank of America, David Rockefeller of Chase Manhattan, and Irving Shapiro of

DuPont. All refused. Bereft of first-rate outsiders, the president turned to Bill Miller as the default replacement.[139]

Miller had hardly distinguished himself as Fed chairman. He was neither an economist nor an expert in financial markets. He had committed an unprecedented error of leadership in his first months at the Fed by allowing himself to be outvoted on interest rates. His fellow board members begged him to reverse his vote for easier money but he refused.[140] Fearful of creating a recession, Miller was so lax in his monetary policy that in the early weeks of 1979, Schultze and Blumenthal privately met with Miller to urge him to tighten it, an unprecedented appeal by any administration. The two economists started giving background interviews with the press urging higher interest rates until Carter, not yet ready to take this leap, issued Schultze and Blumenthal a written rebuke: "Cease immediately your campaign in the press to get Miller to raise interest rates."[141]

That left a hole to fill as Fed chairman. Dick Moe, the vice president's savvy chief of staff, was quickly asked by Ham and the president to canvass labor, business, and political leaders and economists and compile a list of worthy candidates. In the course of a weekend, he came up with eight to ten names, which he delivered in a black notebook to Carter in the White House residence on Sunday. There were two names at the top of the list: Clausen and Paul Volcker. Volcker was favored by almost everyone he had called as the person most acceptable to nervous financial markets, but there were warnings as well: He would be tough as nails in attacking inflation and might not be a team player. Mondale, Moe's boss, opposed Volcker's appointment in the belief that such tough monetary medicine would lead to a recession as the president was campaigning for reelection. But as Carter went down the list of candidates Moe compiled during the weekend that Miller was asked to move to Treasury, Miller advised the president that Volcker should replace him at the Fed even though the two had clashed over policy.[142] When Miller took Moe to meet Carter in his private study, while Moe did not make a recommendation from the short list, his warning about Volcker caught Carter's attention. As a result, even with Miller's advice, the president soon reached Clausen having breakfast with his wife in San Francisco to determine is he wanted to be considered for the Fed chairmanship. After putting the president on hold to check with his wife, Clausen demurred because, he said, it would "not be a good time to come."[143]

The concerns about Volcker's tough views on fighting inflation were not mere speculation. As president of the New York Fed and vice chairman of the Fed's Open Market Committee that sets interest rates, Volcker had long clashed with Fed chairman Arthur Burns during the Nixon and Ford administrations. "I was always pushing him to be tighter, tighter, tighter to get him to raise the discount rate a quarter of a percent, but he didn't want to raise it at all. . . . Christ!" Volcker said later. As he bluntly put it to me, raising interest rates "isn't fun," so the Fed tended to move cautiously. It lagged the market because it lacked the backbone to get ahead of the traders and speculators, and they had lost confidence in its ability to fulfill its core function of managing America's currency.[144]

But if Volcker felt that Burns moved too little and too late, he felt it in spades about Miller. While he had not been prepared to challenge Burns as directly, Volcker felt that as chairman of a major corporation, Miller was "not a natural choice" to head the Fed: "I don't think he fully appreciated all the sensitivities of central banking." He even voted against Miller on the Open Market Committee, a highly unusual action for the vice chairman. Three other members of the committee joined him in several dissents, and at one point this "Volcker minority" (as the press called them) actually outvoted their own chairman and favored raising the Fed's discount rate.

Volcker remembered that Miller's policy was so loose as inflation raged early in 1979 that Blumenthal and Schultze met with the seven members of the board and pointedly asked why they were not running a tighter policy. "That is nothing that happens every day—when the Administration is concerned about the Federal Reserve being too easy!" Volcker remarked.[145] Miller indirectly confirmed this years later by telling me: "There wasn't a great deal of sentiment at the Fed to be tougher on inflation, because they did not have a desire to throw the economy into a big recession."[146]

Carter knew he needed someone in whom financial markets would have confidence, and Volcker was figuratively and literally head and shoulders above anyone else. Volcker was not simply a default candidate; there were a number of safer candidates to choose from on Moe's list. But I believe that by this time Carter had lost confidence in the anti-inflation remedies his economic advisers had given him during the previous two and a half years and was ready to take a chance on someone committed to administer tough medicine even at his own short-term political peril. Gone was the effort to balance the attack on inflation and unemployment, and to calibrate his conservative instincts against his liberal Democratic constituencies. As he would do after the Soviet invasion of Afghanistan when he took a hard line against Moscow, Carter now was willing to throw in his lot with Volcker and recognize that at this stage there was no remedy for embedded inflation save allowing Volcker and the Fed to painfully squeeze it out of the economy with high interest rates and higher unemployment. He was now doing what he had hoped to avoid: fight inflation through a slowdown or even recession, to the dismay of the core Democrats. It is one reason he was not reelected.

But he still wanted to get the measure of the man in whom he would be placing the fate of the economy, and to a large extent, his own political fate. They met in the Oval Office on July 24. Volcker, a giant of a man, stands six feet seven inches, bald with owlish glasses and a no-nonsense scowl that occasionally lifts for an ironic smile at a foolish idea or a huge laugh at a good joke. Carter, about a foot shorter, barely came up to his chest. Miller, who had served as Fed chairman for only eighteen months, sat in on the meeting. Carter asked if he was interested in being chairman, and Volcker, in typically pointed language and with a nod toward Miller, said: "You've got to understand, if I'm the chairman of the Federal Reserve, I'm going to be in favor of more restrictive policies than that guy."

From Volcker's perspective, the meeting did not go well. He said, "I remember thinking I was kind of an ass, because I did all the talking and he was very nice, and I left." That night he told his wife, "Forget about that, I did all the talking; he isn't going to hire me." And Carter had made no commitments.[147] At a dinner that night with two close friends from the New York University Business School, he said, "I blew it. I said that I attached great importance to the independence of the Federal Reserve and that I also favored a more restrictive monetary policy."[148]

Carter had a parallel and equally vivid recollection of that crucial meeting: "Volcker was sitting, almost lying down in the couch, which was not the normal posture for any visitor to a President, and he had a big cigar in his hand. . . . He acted like he was in his own living room, and he was entertaining a janitor rather than talking to the president of the United States. He said, 'Mr. President, let me tell you now, I think we need to do some things with the economy that are not going to be popular at all, and I would not like to go into the chairmanship with a premise that the White House is going to interfere in what decisions are made by the Federal Reserve.' He told me very plainly, if that was the case, he would not accept the position, and I in effect told him, 'I need to get somebody in here who will take care of the economy—let me take care of the politics.'"[149]

There was no doubt in Carter's mind what he was facing—high interest rates and all they would do to slow the economy in the run-up to the election: "Facing reelection, I was about to make a political decision of momentous importance, and my advisers were very concerned." But he wanted most to have the "strongest effort to control inflation, which was dangerously high and about to go higher."[150] As Carter put it to me, "I decided to go ahead with it, because I thought it was better for the country."[151]

He told Schultze and others of us among his inner circle that he had tried everything else to fight inflation and nothing worked—presidential messages, deregulating transportation, tight budgets, jawboning, two inflation czars, and increasingly tough voluntary wage and price guidelines. He would rather lose the election than leave the country a legacy of high inflation without having taken every possible step, however politically poisonous. Carter also felt since Volcker was so well known and respected that his appointment would calm financial markets at home and abroad. In fact it took much more than the fact of the appointment itself.[152]

A few days later Carter called Volcker while he was still in bed at 7:30 a.m. and told him he would be appointed chairman of the Fed. Volcker flew to Washington that day and met with Mondale, but there was no substantive discussion of monetary policy.[153] Volcker later mused about whether the early-rising president, a naval officer and country farmer, would have appointed him if he had known he was still in bed when he called.[154]

But when he was sworn in at the White House along with Bill Miller on August 6,[155] Volcker felt that the president put on a long face, as Carter made a brief speech warning that a decade of persistent inflation had taken hold of the national consciousness as never before, and "has sapped away the confidence of the American people in the future."[156] As Volcker reflected in his memoirs: "It wasn't quite the malaise speech, but it bore a family resemblance!"[157] Volcker added to the solemnity of the occasion by stating after taking his oath, that "we're face-to-face with economic difficulties really unique in our experience. And we've lost the euphoria we had fifteen years ago, that we had all the answers."[158]

Carter was as good as his word in keeping hands off the Fed; it was not easy for him, and both sides knew it. Fred Shultz, Volcker's vice chairman and close collaborator, told me that he knew Volcker's appointment was difficult and "certainly caused you [in the administration] a great deal of pain, but I'll tell you the truth, I don't think there was a choice, and in my judgment, the situation would have been worse, much worse, than it was had you not appointed Volcker."[159]

Lane Kirkland, who became president of the AFL-CIO following Meany's death, and was a fellow Southerner without Meany's hard edge, developed a much better relationship with Carter, said that on the one hand "Paul Volcker and Ayatollah Khomeini are what I think brought down the Carter administration"—but on the other, Carter had no choice but to pick Volcker and let him loose, because "he had to do it that way in the face of inflation."[160] Charlie Schultze, who never favored Volcker's appointment and "violently disagreed" with his policies at the time, not only praised him as a person who was always "above board, honest, and . . . one of the easiest people to have disagreements with," but finally conceded that Carter "ultimately made the right political choice, which I didn't recognize at the time."[161]

Volcker told me his relationship with Carter was "about right." As Fed chairman he attended regular monthly meetings with Schultze, Miller, and McIntyre of OMB. Kahn would also sit in on these meetings for exchanging information on the direction of the economy, but they were not occasions for the administration to pressure the Fed to back off. Carter also invited Volcker to sit in on several budget meetings, and Volcker sat silently and observed. On the few occasions when Volcker wanted to see the president to give him a heads-up on what the Fed planned to do, a meeting was immediately arranged. As Volcker described his meetings in no uncertain terms, he would warn the president: "Look, things are really steaming up here, and we've got to get tighter." By contrast, when Volcker asked to see President Reagan, the White House staff would say: "'My God, what's he coming over here for?' They'd have nineteen briefings, and then fill him up with some half-page position paper, and when you got beyond the position paper there wouldn't be anything to talk about."[162]

The fact is that Paul Volcker saved the country from economic disaster, and it is another of Jimmy Carter's unheralded legacies that he overrode objections within the highest levels of his own administration to appoint him. Ronald Reagan is given due credit by pundits like Robert Samuelson[163] for standing behind Volcker even under pressure from the ideologues on his Republican team. Yet there is an unwillingness to give Carter anything close to equal billing. I would argue it was harder for Carter to show the restraint he did in an election cycle, never once criticizing Volcker's strong medicine, than for Reagan to do so after his own election and long before he had to face the voters a second time. Certainly Carter was not perfect. Volcker remembers the president remarking at a garden party in Philadelphia during the 1980 campaign, "God, they didn't have to be quite that monetarist." But Volcker nevertheless realized that Carter "had great provocation on historical grounds; it isn't very usual to see interest rates go up like that during an election period."[164]

Volcker did not come to the Fed with a clear blueprint of how to change the operating philosophy of the Fed, and he certainly was not a closet monetarist. Milton Friedman's monetarist followers argued that inflation could be tamed only if the Federal Reserve set a clear and virtually inflexible target for monetary growth, to dampen even the expectations of inflation that had run out of control. When the Fed deviated from his strategy—as it usually did—Friedman would write angry letters to the chairman and attack the central bank in his *Newsweek* column. Unfortunately for the theories of this brilliant polemicist, the real world of finance did not move in straight lines, and one of the Fed's tasks is to act as a corrective, through what Volcker called the "art of central banking." The man Jimmy Carter tapped to head the Fed was a pragmatist, who was convinced that the economic models developed by traditional Keynesians, upon which Schultze and other mainstream economists relied, had no way to account for the psychology of inflation that had become deeply embedded in the American psyche by a decade of inexorably rising prices.

Within a matter of days after taking office at his first meeting as chairman, Volcker engineered a half-point rise in the discount rate at which the Federal Reserve makes loans to banks. This is the time-honored way to signal that the Fed is tightening money, and the market normally responds by raising the federal funds rate at which banks borrow and lend overnight funds to each other, to square up their required reserves at the end of each day's business. But this time the money markets simply ignored the Fed's signal; short-term rates barely moved because the central bank had lost credibility.

Volcker tried again, and on September 18 the board voted to raise the discount rate another half percentage point to a record 11 percent. The vote on the seven-member board was a bare 4 to 3. This did not worry Volcker because he knew he had the votes of Shultz and two other anti-inflation hawks, Henry Wallach and Philip Caldwell. But the markets and the press read the split vote as a sign of hesitation. Up went the price of gold, the traditional hedge against a weak currency.[165]

With exasperation, Volcker recalled his dilemma to me: "We were almost better if we hadn't raised the goddamn discount rate, because they said, 'Aha, they are obviously now at the end of their limit. They only have a four-to-three majority, so next time they will not have a majority for raising it. So we've seen the last of the discount rate increases, or the last of the tightening of any policy.' "[166]

After the first two conventional interest rate hikes, Volcker, Schultze, and Miller met with the president in the Oval Office. Schultze recalls the president plaintively asking Volcker: "Isn't there any way you can control the quantity of money supply without raising interest rates so much?" Volcker told Schultze later that when he went home, he began thinking of controlling the quantity of money, which would be a new mode of operation for the Fed. Years later Charlie Schultze smilingly said he was sure that Carter had no idea what he had started.[167] But it may have helped concentrate Volcker's own mind on attacking market psychology through monetary techniques, and this was where Volcker's creative genius came forward.

Like a general blocked on the battlefield in one direction, he pivoted to take the offensive in another. As he put it, "So I scratched my head and said, 'Goddammit, how do we get some credibility in the policy?'" It is only at this point, seemingly out of ammunition, that he made history. Volker and his vice chairman, Fred Schultz, became convinced that by following the conventional path of raising interest rates, they would never catch up with inflation, which would always stay ahead of them. So they had to do something to break inflationary expectations by controlling the money supply. Schultz said no one on the board, including Volcker, was a "true monetarist," and that "none of us believed in the gospel according to Milton Friedman, which was that all you had to do was control the money supply and the Federal Reserve didn't need to do anything else."[168]

So Volcker began to think along the lines of using the monetarist approach the Fed staff had been debating for a decade. By a law passed under Friedman's influence, the Fed was obliged to announce its money-supply targets six months in advance. It did not supply or withdraw money from the economy directly but did so by moving interest rates up and down and thus fulfilling the Fed's founding mandate of providing "an elastic currency" to feed the economy as much money as it needs to do business, neither more nor less. This is no easy task. The principal lever for regulating the availability of money has been the daily sale or purchase of government bonds in the money markets by the New York Fed acting as the Board's agent. But even its experienced dealers could not hit a target with certainty by aiming at interest rates.

Volcker also knew of the Fed's reluctance to engineer a raise in rates: Easy money can be pulled back, but if higher rates tip the economy into a recession, there will always be a political price to pay. Hence the Fed moves more cautiously when it tightens in order to ensure that rates do not go too high. In normal times this usually works, but at a time of raging inflation such caution looks like mere baby steps. Money markets and business in general see such prudence as a sign of weakness and simply ignore it.[169]

This time Volcker would reverse the normal process. As he put it to me: "Instead of horsing around with the federal funds rate in an attempt to meet our money supply target, we will attempt to meet the money supply target directly, and let the federal funds rate go wherever it goes, because we can't judge what that should be."[170] To accomplish this the Fed would directly regulate the level of bank reserves to be in accordance with the money supply target, and let interest rates go where they might.

So he asked Steve Axilrod, the Fed's staff director, to "brush it out a little bit." The Fed staff recommended restraining growth in bank credit and setting a target for the total supply of money.[171] The shake-up came in October 1979. En route to the annual meeting of the International Monetary Fund in Belgrade, Yugoslavia, he stopped off in Hamburg to visit the irascible Chancellor Helmut Schmidt and the experienced head of Germany's central bank, Otto Emminger. When Volcker hinted at what he planned to do, their conversation left him in no doubt that they had lost patience with the Carter administration. He felt he had to act quickly.

Volcker had already presented the idea to Schultze and Miller for the first time as they crossed the Atlantic together aboard an air force jet. It would be a great understatement to say they were unhappy. Schultze made it clear that given the high inflation, he did not object to increases in interest rates. But in vain he and Miller tried to argue Volcker out of what they considered an inflexible and unproven strategy that would produce volatile interest-rate movements and thrust the U.S. economy into recession."[172]

After they arrived in Belgrade, they sat through a speech by Arthur Burns reflecting on his eight years as Fed chairman and lamenting that the political and economic forces behind inflation made it almost impossible for the Federal Reserve to stop the wage-price spiral. Burns candidly admitted that while the Fed could control inflation, it was only at a cost too politically and economically high (in terms of creating unemployment) to make it feasible.[173]

Volcker viewed Burns's position as a kind of surrender: "Things were fixed so that the central bank could not fight inflation effectively"—that given the power of labor unions, the effect of budget deficits, and the resistance of other institutions, "monetary policy couldn't be expected to maintain price stability under those conditions. . . . He had this impossible standoff that all you could do is slow it down."[174] Volcker was determined to show that Burns was wrong. The Fed could and would not just slow down inflation, but reverse it.

After canvassing foreign sentiment by hinting at what he planned to do, he left the Belgrade meeting a day early, confident of international support for an operation that was new, daring, and risky, but that he was eager to put into effect. Back in Washington on October 4, and armed with his new battle plan to emphasize the supply of reserves, vetted by the Fed's own staff, Volcker talked to his three dissenters. They liked the idea as a way of getting them off the hook by relieving them of the responsibility of constantly voting to increase the discount rate. And they were ready for something new. He then met with his board of governors to try to reach a consensus on his new approach. Meanwhile Miller and Schultze returned, still fearful of the unpredictable results. They consulted with Carter and transmitted his concerns to Volcker. They realized that daily interest rates would fluctuate over a wider range than in the past, and might rise to stratospheric levels.[175]

But the chairman regarded it as significant that the president did not ask to see him. He therefore assumed that Carter was not prepared to overrule a man he had just appointed in a field where the president was no expert and the Fed chairman was.[176]

On Saturday, October 6, Volcker convened an emergency meeting of the Open Market Committee and gravely told its members that financial markets were "ready to crack open, depending on what decisions they see coming out of here."[177] He described the crucial meeting in the no-nonsense lingo he uses in private: "I remember being very careful to be sure they realized what they were voting for. I remember saying: 'goddammit now, before you so enthusiastically vote for this, understand what you're voting for, because I really want to make sure you think this is a good idea, and you are going to stand behind it.'" With only one or two exceptions, he found great enthusiasm in the Open Market Committee.[178]

He announced it to the press that evening, during a Columbus Day weekend that would allow markets an extra day to digest the radical change. It also was a day when the media were focused on the visit of the greatly admired Pope John Paul II to Washington. A CBS producer asked the Fed's press spokesman if he should shift his one-weekend camera crew from the papal visit to cover Volcker's announcement, to which he responded that people would "remember the press conference long after the Pope had left town."[179] And indeed they did.

However arcane, the change was very real—"something unique to the history of central banking; and it is not probably ever going to happen again," said Axilrod.[180] Volcker was key, as Axilrod noted: "No one believed we were going to do it. Paul got out and made speech after speech saying we were going to stick to it. And after about a year, people believed." Volcker explained that he did it because he felt "inflationary psychology was out of control, so we needed to do something dramatic to make people believe you really were going to control inflation, and not only at home, but abroad. The secret was not in what we said the money supply would be; it was that we said we were going to use a different technique, so we actually didn't keep slipping away from the target." He knew that Federal Reserve governors "shrink from voting for tighter money," so by setting a money supply target and staying within it, that would also make it easier for the board to discipline itself, because the cost in credibility from abandoning the experiment might be even higher than that of continuing.[181]

But Volcker was no political babe in the woods. He also knew that this method provided more political cover than directly jacking up interest rates. He applied some legerdemain, although he forcefully argued it was not the political smoke screen some would later allege. As he admitted: "This was certainly an easier way to get public support. You can say that we've got to keep the money supply under control, that's what we're doing; we're not directly aiming at interest rates. Everybody knows that money has something to do with inflation, and that's what we're controlling." He knew he could never politically sustain directly raising rates to the high levels necessary to slay inflation. After his own radical strategy had worked, he was asked directly whether he was a monetarist. He replied with equal directness, "Nah, I just wanted to shake 'em up."[182]

Volcker now had to make his policy work, and he found there were "many slips between fixing the supply of reserves and the actual money supply that come out at the other end of the sausage grinder."[183] He knew short-term interest rates would go up, but he hoped the new policy would have such a psychological impact that the markets and public would come to believe that the Fed really could control inflation. The central bank kept looking for a sign in long-term bond rates. If savers and investors were prepared to park their money in bonds over a period of years at a lower interest rate, it meant they expected inflation to go down and the cost of money along with it. That did not happen, and moreover, short-term rates became far more volatile than he feared, as Charlie Schultze had predicted.

Volcker certainly did not expect interest rates rising close to 20 percent in 1980, while the economy was still barreling along and inflation still sky-high. Volcker called me on April 1 to admit he did not know when interest rates would peak. It could be early, but the economy was still stronger than he thought. We are "caught between overkill and underkill and the two overlap." He said, "I know you're at a point where it hurts, but there is a question whether we have gone far enough."[184] He came face-to-face with embedded inflation psychology when Arthur Levitt, the president of the American Stock Exchange, brought a number of leaders of small and medium-size companies for a visit. Volcker gave the group a pep talk about the Fed's innovative approach to fighting inflation, and the first business-man to respond said he had just agreed to a 13 percent wage increase for his employees over the next three years, and "I'm very happy."[185]

The Carter administration certainly was not pleased. At an EPG meeting in early April 1980, after the Volcker policies had been in operation for half a year and we were heading into an election, I raised concerns that sky-high interest-rate hikes would lead to a deeper recession. Miller agreed and labeled the Fed's last increases "macho." He said he would talk to Volcker, but it came to no avail. On April 8 the legendary financier Felix Rohatyn of Lazard Frères told me he was "more scared than at any time in my career." He explained that banks were fragile and losses in stock portfolios were staggering. He forecast widespread bankruptcies and appealed for a wage-price freeze or mandatory controls instead of Volcker's policy: "His theology is wrong."[186]

The banks meanwhile were making out like bandits, charging their best customers a prime rate of 19 percent while they could borrow the money in the market for half a dozen percentage points less. Carter wanted to know why the prime rate was 19 percent when inflation was 13 percent. Schultze's answer was technical and complex, based on the squeeze we had placed on their loans. "Why can't we jawbone the banks? Why do we need to condone the interest rate spread? We need to manage this carefully or we'll have a massive recession," the president said. Schultze and Miller spoke with Volcker, but he refused to talk down the prime rate and asked the adminis-tration not to do so either.[187]

CREDIT CONTROLS

Still, Carter felt he must show the country—and the electorate—that he was doing whatever he could to curb inflation, and that Volcker's was not the only show in town. On March 14, 1980, the president made yet another nationwide address on inflation. His program contained many elements: a major cut to the budget he had just proposed; a revised wage standard recommended by his labor-management Pay Advisory Committee; and energy conservation measures to halve U.S. oil imports by 1990.

But one key part threw an unanticipated monkey wrench into Volcker's plan. Carter tried to impose controls on consumer credit, which turned out to be a monumentally bad idea, causing a recession in the midst of the election campaign, and temporarily sidetracking Volcker's new interest-rate policy.[188]

This was a pet idea of Fred Kahn's, who argued that inflation was fueled by credit and consumers had gone too heavily into debt. His goal was to restrain consumer spending by restricting credit and thus encourage savings, a risky tactic in an election season.[189] But this had come not only from Kahn. He persuaded others, myself included, that it would help relieve some of the worst pain of high interest rates, while not undermining the Fed's program. And the president had the legal authority to ask the Fed to impose controls anyway.

When the president announced his credit control program, he linked the excessive borrowing that the government must do to fund its deficits with the borrowing individual Americans must do to make ends meet, and asserted that we could not beat inflation with borrowed money: "Inflation is fueled by credit-financed spending" and "Consumers have gone in debt too heavily."

Volcker in the worst way did not want to implement even the limited authority given to him by the president; autos, housing, and durable goods—the principal objects of household credit—were exempt. But since Carter was showing great restraint in not opposing Volcker's tough monetary policy, he felt he owed it to the president to go along, and Carter was "quite insistent." He recalled: "The president hadn't objected to our policy. . . . We could have said, 'Well, Mr. President, you've authorized it, but screw you, we're not going to administer it.' But I thought that was an untenable position."[190] So he told his unhappy board that with the president sitting still for the Fed's very high interest rates and vowing to cut the budget further, "we had to be part of the game and not refuse to do it. But I told everybody I would make it as mild as I could possibly make it."[191] He felt credit controls were a solution in search of a problem, and there actually was no consumer credit problem to be solved: Consumption had already leveled off. What he really feared was that credit controls would kill the momentum of his program. They brought on what Volcker described as "the strangest economic period that I've ever seen." Consumption fell off the table.[192]

After Carter stressed the importance of limiting credit—his instinct to exaggerate was a characteristic trait—he managed to make the public feel it would be unpatriotic to use credit cards.[193] People were so desperate to do their part to fight inflation, they tore up their credit cards as a patriotic act and sent the pieces to Kahn and the White House, accompanied by letters saying: "Mr. President, we will cooperate." Others sent irate letters denouncing Sears, Roebuck for continuing to solicit new credit card accounts. Kahn would write back and say, "No, we don't want you to throw away your credit cards; all we want you to do is restrict your increases."[194] But a policy that is too nebulous and cannot be easily explained is subject to misunderstanding and is not a good policy. So while general retail sales did not fall significantly, sales of big-ticket items fell off by 30 to 40 percent and helped produce a 9 percent collapse in the GDP, the largest single drop in any quarter since the Depression.

Schultze termed it "an absolute freak; it was that psychological reaction."[195] Volcker agreed. Interest rates plunged, frustrating the intent of the Fed's tight money policy because it had to inject money into the banking system to stop the economy from dropping like a stone. Volcker said: "We had a devil of a time getting things back in control again." The whole experience also demonstrated the limits of a short, sharp recession alone to drain inflation from the economy. When credit controls were suddenly imposed, interest rates dropped precipitously to around 9 percent—and shot back into double digits when they were quickly removed. Growth jumped back up too, and inflation was actually higher than before.[196]

MORE BUDGET CUTS

Another key part of the president's anti-inflation program was revising the budget he had just sent to Congress in January 1980, for fiscal 1981, beginning in October, just before the presidential election. This unusual exercise was required because the budget we sent to Congress was met with the proverbial Bronx cheer when our budget office estimated that the deficit for the current fiscal year would likely be twice what we had initially projected. There is nothing worse than fighting raging inflation during an election year, and for a president to tell the American people that his revised budget involves "costs [and] pain, but far less than the still worse permanent pain of constantly rising inflation." When we began a marathon exercise to make additional cuts in the budget, it was as painful as tearing skin from your body. The original budget was already tight. Now, with Senator Kennedy challenging Carter for the Democratic nomination, we were nevertheless going to cut more. We needed to demonstrate even greater fiscal rectitude and remain in sync with Volcker's tougher monetary policy, but we also needed to finance programs designed to protect the most vulnerable Americans, for which Mondale had fought throughout his political career.

Carter asked Volcker to join several of the budget meetings, which were eye-opening in their sharp deliberations. Volcker remained a largely silent observer, but he was particularly critical of my role. As the budgeters presented options for cuts, Carter agreed to most. But on a couple of the more important ones, Volcker noticed that I would object. Years later, as he rehearsed my own behavior back to me: " 'You know the Party's against this, Mr. President, blah, blah, blah,'—and he [Carter] said, 'Well, we'll do it anyway.' And I sat there and I thought what a brash guy: The President said he was willing to do it, and then Eizenstat comes back and tells him, 'You really don't want to do this, Mr. President,' and he'd finally say, 'Cut three-quarters of it,' and you'd come back half an hour later, and he'd say, 'All right, cut a quarter of it.' He started out with cutting the whole thing, and he ended up with a quarter of a loaf. I thought, Well, this is a crazy business. He wanted to restrain but this guy Eizenstat keeps pulling him back."[197]

I plead guilty in part, but it was hardly as dramatic as Volcker colorfully portrays. In the president's message he was proposing cuts of more than

$13 billion to an already stringent budget, mostly in domestic programs at a time we were trying to fend off Kennedy's challenge from the left. This validated Mondale's warning to me in the fall of 1978 that with Carter's stringent budgets "it will be a hard two years with liberals."[198] This allowed the president to realize his wish to propose a balanced budget, even though it would inevitably end up in deficit because of poor economic conditions and congressional action to restore some of the cuts. With Miller and OMB director McIntyre, I helped lead round-the-clock negotiations for ten days with the Congress to sell the package of cuts in record time. They agreed to all the cuts but only delivered half in the end.[199]

Volcker remembers a humorous part of the president's announcement, with himself sitting in the front row in the East Room of the White House, and thus implicitly embracing it. He had an advance copy of the text and noticed that Carter had lost one page, although luckily the previous page ended with a paragraph and the page after the missing one began with another paragraph—so "nobody except me ever realized it." Actually, Miller and Gordon Stewart, the speechwriter, did notice; Carter's usually reliable secretary, Susan Clough, had left the page on the Xerox machine.[200]

But Volcker made a telling point: "I always thought that a real part of the problem was that the president was getting too many diverse views pulling at him in the White House and taking him away from his basic instincts, which were to be fiscally conservative. He always seemed to be compromising between his own instincts and the forces in the party and in the White House pulling at him."[201] Volcker was right, up to a point. But he did not have to work in the hothouse of the West Wing to help the president temper that basic conservatism and hold his liberal base. I strongly supported budget restraint but also wanted to go after many of the federal benefits, from farm subsidies to trade restrictions, that pushed up prices and embedded inflation in our politics and our personal expectations. Kahn, the anti-inflation czar, viewed the traditional Democratic base as favoring constituency policies, particularly those espoused by labor unions, while not realizing that "Democratic inflations are always followed by Republican victories."[202]

More broadly, Carter's budget policies played little role in the stagflation. Carter's budgets were tight. Mondale and I could only affect them at the margins. And as for the wage-price policies, John Dunlop, then the country's leading labor economist and former Labor secretary in the Ford administration, scored some successes as chairman of Carter's Pay Advisory Committee under a national labor-management accord we announced in late September 1979. But in his view, the accomplishments of voluntary guidelines and union-management dialogue under such extreme inflation conditions were "relatively minor."[203]

AFTER THE TURNING POINT

After the election the president met with the economic team on December 17, for almost the last time.[204] Even now Schultze reported that the economy was much stronger than expected, growing by 5 percent during the last quarter of his presidency. Carter said this was fairly good "compared to what the public thinks. But the whole emphasis is on interest rates, and we're getting more blame than we deserve." None of us could have realized that the American economy was at a turning point, and that the coming thirty years would bring stagnant wages and gross disparities in wealth. But there is also a more positive side to the story. In addition to ten million new jobs, while the general perception is that economic growth was terrible under Carter and great during Reagan's "Morning in America," in fact the U.S. economy grew at an almost identical rate during the two presidencies: 3.3 percent under Carter against Reagan's 3.5 percent.[205] Carter did not achieve his dream of a balanced budget, but that was mainly the result of too little revenue rather than too much spending. He added a smaller percentage to the national debt during his four years than did Reagan and the two Bush presidents.[206] His highest budget deficit was almost half of Reagan's lowest.

Yet from his first major national address calling for the "moral equivalent of war" in ending our dependence on imported oil to this last anti-inflation package, Carter's message was sacrifice and pain. When he faced Reagan's message of hope and optimism amid soaring inflation and interest rates, the very contrast itself was painful. And as interest rates mounted even higher after Reagan took office, the new president waved off their side effects and berated the press for writing about unemployment "every time some guy out in South Succotash loses his job."

There is one other key factor in any objective view of the Carter economic performance. In my Yiddish vernacular it is called *mazel*, or luck, and is recognized throughout history; "I chose my marshals for their luck," said Napoleon. And aside from one crucial but courageous choice in Volcker, Carter had no economic luck. He inherited stagflation, and sustained the second oil shock of the decade, a commodity price boom, and a slowdown in productivity that is still not fully understood, and is repeating itself today.

Against these forces, voluntary wage and price guidelines, which had been modestly effective in the Kennedy administration, stood no chance. Nor did the fiscal restraint Carter imposed on an unwilling party. But there was a page from President Kennedy's playbook we should have taken when he faced the coal miners' strike. Kennedy forced the steel companies to retreat from raising prices after granting a modest wage settlement—"My father always told me all businessmen were sons of bitches, but I never believed it until now."[207] Along with Volcker's monetary medicine, Reagan's toughness in firing striking air controllers can be credited with beginning to break the wage-price spiral, although the cost was the erosion of labor union power. These stand in stark contrast to our caving in to a huge wage settlement to end the 110-day coal miners' strike. As Schultze reflected, it would have helped Carter to clobber some unions to show his willingness to be tough on inflationary wage hikes, but he did not feel comfortable doing so,[208] and for better or worse, they were a key part of his Democratic electoral base.

But no set of short-term policies could have blocked the huge run-up in inflation arising from the second oil shock of the 1970s. And just as Nixon suffered double-digit inflation from the first oil shock in 1973, Carter suffered the same from the second in 1979–80.

Many of Carter's economic programs and reforms benefited the country only after he left office, but by far the most important and lasting was his appointment of Paul Volcker. Carter knew there could be no equivocation, whether it meant splitting his party or even forestalling his reelection, both of which it did. It took too long for the president's key economic advisers, Schultze, Blumenthal, and Miller, and certainly for Mondale and me, to come to the realization that in a high-inflation environment, we had given too little emphasis to monetary policy and too much to fiscal policy, failing to recognize that the Federal Reserve was the most important weapon we had to fight inflation and change public psychology.[209] This is dramatically demonstrated by the low-inflation environments of the Reagan and George W. Bush years—even in the face of triple-digit budget deficits far larger than under Carter—because the Fed had assured the public it had inflation under control. Fiscal policies work slowly, and they must also work their way through an often recalcitrant Congress.

Whatever errors we made on the fiscal side, and I have cited them frankly, were overwhelmed by the mistakes of two Fed chairmen—Arthur Burns, appointed by Nixon, and William Miller, appointed by Carter. Neither the best Democratic economists of the era nor the Republican conservatives had a silver bullet, and they were hardly unanimous at the time. When Carter had exhausted all the ammunition his economic advisers provided him, their bullets turned out to be blanks. Even today looking back, most mainstream economists agree that Carter had few realistic alternatives. Today, there is greater consensus on the central importance of monetary policy by the Federal Reserve as the key to a low-inflation environment. During the Carter years some knew that a relentless monetary squeeze would most likely do the job but were reluctant to recommend it: In their profession it was regarded as politically impossible until Paul Volcker came along. Only Carter's willingness to appoint Volcker and allow him to wrestle with the inflation beast no one else was willing to take on turned the corner and set a standard for central banks that has lasted into this new century. Volcker gave Carter the ultimate compliment: 'I always give him a lot of credit in my mind. I may be the only person in the United States who appreciates that he sat there as much as he did, and took a lot of guff on monetary policy."[210]

In the last analysis the choice was not economic but political, and Carter had the courage to make it. It worked too late to help Carter's 1980 reelection, but Ronald Reagan was then the beneficiary, and the country is even now.

15

THE CONSUMER POPULIST

Jimmy Carter was the most consumer-friendly president in the nation's history, channeling his populist instincts in a very different way from all his Democratic predecessors and successors, helping make the U.S. economy more efficient and competitive, with lower long-term inflation. As a small businessman with a deep commitment to his customers, he adopted a sophisticated and forward-looking policy based on competition and not regulation in order to provide maximum choice at the lowest price. For essential health, safety, and environmental protection, he believed in reforms to deter unsafe corporate practices at the least cost possible to industry. In doing so he befriended and publicly embraced the consumer champion Ralph Nader, appointing a number of his activists to high federal regulatory positions.

Carter did more than any president before him to transform regulations that had long since outlived their usefulness, with lasting benefits that became evident only after he left office. Large sectors of the American economy, especially in virtually all modes of transportation and communications, were freed from federal economic regulations dating back to the New Deal and the Progressive era that preceded it. Many had calcified into cozy relationships among the Iron Triangle—powerfully entrenched industries, their federal regulators, and their congressional overseers. Their unions, which were the backbone of the Democratic Party, also gave full support to the status quo.

While deregulation was one strand in the Carter administration's anti-inflation program in producing lower costs, an unexpected result was lower wages and less protection for workers in the industries that were deregulated.

Unionized workers were the biggest losers, realizing organized labor's biggest fear, and most of the benefit accrued to the general public through lower prices and greater choice.[1] Ironically, for all of its success and lasting impact, the Carter presidency also registered the high-water mark of the American consumer movement, which began to lose momentum as corporate America—realizing that its own free-market principles had been deployed against it—struck back.

The reenergized heads of major American corporations for the first time formed their own organization, the Business Roundtable, which mobilized CEOs to directly lobby Congress and the White House, and backed it up with high-caliber position papers and contributions from their newly allowed PACs to punish or reward legislators who had deserted or defended them. Consumerism never recovered from Carter's loss to Ronald Reagan in 1980, which bookended a decades-long growth of the consumer movement. No president before or since, including the Democrats Bill Clinton and Barack Obama, so thoroughly embodied the ethic of the movement and melded its critique of business into government decision making.

In the American political system, issues of social or economic importance usually become politically ripe, and eventually the law of the land, only after withstanding scrutiny in academic and public debate, and then becoming part of the agenda of the president of the United States, the only political figure capable of raising an issue to national and congressional attention. One test of presidential leadership is the ability to discover, define, and elevate issues that are ready for serious consideration. Carter had already defined his approach to consumer protection as governor of Georgia with a Law Day speech that won him national attention through Hunter Thompson in *Rolling Stone* magazine for attacking business organizations and the professional associations representing lawyers and physicians for protecting their members more than the public.

By the force of its logic, deregulation had already moved from the private preserve of academia into the public arena during the Ford administration. But it took a president with small-business experience, who was neither a conservative Republican nor a traditional liberal Democrat, to build a winning coalition that beat back the entrenched opposition of business and labor. That unique and improbable force was composed of free-market conservatives and liberal politicians led by Senator Edward Kennedy. During only one presidential term, Carter's administration led in deregulating the nation's airline, trucking, and railroad industries, and pointed the way toward deregulation of interstate bus lines. But there was more. It also took the first major steps to bring competition to the telecommunications industry, without which the digital revolution of the twenty-first century would have taken place much more slowly. He championed the elimination of Regulation Q and the 1980 Monetary Control Act to lift New Deal–era caps on the interest that banks could pay savers, broke down barriers to interstate banking that protected local banks at the expense of customers, and created variable-rate home mortgages to compete with the traditional long-term fixed-rate mortgages.[2]

These reforms in broad sectors of the economy are not the whole story. Carter put in place systemic regulatory changes across the federal government that weeded out and reshaped obsolete structures enacted in a time of crisis during the Great Depression to save capitalism from its excesses. But as the economy recovered and thrived over the decades, many regulatory structures remained by sheer inertia. Carter moved the pendulum back toward the center, although his successor pushed it further to the right, demonizing almost all government regulation.

In a valedictory signing statement attached to the rail deregulation bill, Carter pulled together his accomplishments. He noted that by executive order, he had mandated that all regulators publicly analyze the costs of major proposals, setting the goal of achieving their objectives in a cost-effective way. He established a sunset-review program to test whether major regulations were still needed after they had been in place a number of years. His paperwork reduction program cut federal paperwork by 40 percent. He created a Regulatory Review Council to eliminate inconsistent regulations and encourage innovative regulatory techniques, saving hundreds of millions of dollars. The president also signed the Regulatory Flexibility Act, which passed the Senate without a dissenting vote, converting into law his 1979 administrative program requiring federal agencies to eliminate unnecessary regulatory burdens on small business. Since the federal government began calculating its benefits, the law is estimated to have saved small business and the economy as a whole more than $200 billion. With all this, Carter was justified in claiming in the signing statement: "We have secured the most fundamental restructuring of the relationship between industry and government since the time of the New Deal."[3]

Why did virtually no one appreciate this then or now? I believe double-digit inflation and interest rates, gasoline lines, and the Iran hostage crisis sucked the political oxygen from the positive effects of deregulation on inflation and competition over the years. Succeeding presidents, Reagan in particular, were the major beneficiaries. His showdown with the air controllers' union demonstrated that Reagan, but not Carter, had taken on powerful unions. And since it was never a traditional Democratic presidential priority to eliminate regulations, Carter was acting out of the party's character—but he was not a traditional Democrat. He was a New Democrat, moderately conservative on fiscal issues and committed to ending regulations shackling private industry, when unconnected with safety. He did more than any president to clear the regulatory underbrush that had imposed costs, inflation, and inefficiencies on the American economy.

Deregulation opened airplane travel to the middle class and made it possible for cargo services like Federal Express (FedEx) and United Parcel Service (UPS) to provide the efficient cross-country delivery that now is part of America's business infrastructure. It permitted low-fare start-ups like Southwest Airlines and JetBlue to thrive. Ending federal controls on trucking and railroads had even greater but less obvious benefits because consumers cannot readily appreciate the billions of dollars saved in more flexible and cheaper transport. The degree to which the Carter administration opened up these basic industries to competition and benefited consumers and businesses through their supply chains is matched only by the energy of Theodore Roosevelt's administration a century ago.

That some of these innovations were later manipulated to endanger the financial system or squeeze consumers is not a criticism of deregulation but of ideologues who treasure the belief that markets can correct themselves without any controls at all, from safety labels to antitrust laws. The general relaxation of antitrust enforcement freed the airlines to merge into a virtual oligopoly, cutting fares to fill planes but skimping on customer service in ways ranging from stuffing passengers into their seats to late arrivals. This demonstrates the truth of one of our democracy's classic rallying cries: "Eternal vigilance is the price of liberty."

Deregulation must always be accompanied by a countervailing policy to protect the consumer from unbridled economic competition, which, without proper oversight, can be turned on its head to the disadvantage of the public, as demonstrated by the financial crash of 2008. Years before, Carter had begun cautiously freeing up the financial sector, but unrestrained regulation of complex financial instruments and nonbanks like Lehman Brothers eventually turned liberties into license and produced disaster. Alan Greenspan, during his remarkable tenure as chairman of the Federal Reserve, justified such financial competition by arguing that informed market participants would police one another and thus protect the consumer and the banking system. After the crash Greenspan was forced to admit to Congress that he had found "a flaw in the model . . . that defines how the world works."[4]

DEREGULATING THE AIRLINES

The airline industry was the first major battlefield for deregulation, and it comes as close as any to a case study of the history of regulation and the benefits of its undoing. The cast of characters that made victory possible was worthy of a Broadway play, with a love story thrown in for good measure. Fred Kahn, Carter's new chairman of the Civil Aeronautics Board, looked the part of an absentminded professor and turned out to be anything but. Kennedy and several of his young lawyers made victory possible by taking on a cosseted political-industrial complex. They were headed by the Judiciary Committee's chief counsel, Stephen Breyer, who was later elevated to the U.S. Supreme Court, and the staff director for the committee's antitrust subcommittee, David Boies, later one of the country's leading litigators. On our side we had my White House Domestic Policy Staff and Mary Schuman, then all of twenty-six years old but as tough and brilliant as she was charming and beautiful, who met Boies during our negotiations and later married him. Presiding over this cast as a sort of producer was no less than the president of the United States, who was willing to risk short-term political costs for the nation's long-term gain—a major theme of the Carter presidency.

The airline industry is virtually a child of the federal government. As an infant industry in the 1920s, United, American, Eastern, and others received subsidies in the form of contracts to carry airmail; the precedent for this was the huge government subsidy to the railroads by giving away millions of acres along the roadbeds that tied together the industrializing nation in the nineteenth century. The airlines easily fell into the lucrative habit of bidding low for the airmail contracts and then claiming they were losing money to obtain more. Congressional investigations led to New Deal legislation regulating entry, prices, and routes through an independent agency later known as the Civil Aeronautics Board (CAB), which also took over airline safety, all designed to protect consumers. Rates were set by the government on the basis of the airlines' costs plus a guaranteed rate of return, which they simply passed along to their passengers long after they had fully matured into profitable companies. The rationale for this arrangement was that competition would endanger safe and reliable service.

While airmail subsidies were phased out during the Eisenhower administration, the CAB staff continued meeting in private with the Airline Transport Association (ATA) to negotiate guaranteed profits on their routes. The government and the industry developed a symbiotic relationship through this cost-plus formula, and passengers had to take it or leave it. On short flights, fares were set low to compete with cars and trains, but on long-haul routes where the airlines had a definite advantage, they were protected by a CAB rule that forced a prospective competitor to show that the existing carrier did not provide adequate service, which was almost impossible to prove.[5]

Ten major trunk airlines carried more than 90 percent of the nation's interstate air traffic, although within California competition thrived, without regulation. From 1969 to 1973 not one new route was approved by the CAB, and it took eight years for Continental Airlines to win approval for a route from San Diego to Denver. As airline seats were limited by an outrageous capacity-control agreement cooked up by American, United, and TWA, ever-higher fares produced more empty seats than profits.

Instead the airlines competed among themselves for the shares of a shrinking market only on frills: serving meals supervised by famous chefs and dressing stewardesses in hot pants. Only business travelers benefited, not just because of the sensory attractions, but because by the time Carter proposed deregulation in 1977, only 55 percent of U.S. airline seats were filled, and business passengers could be fairly well assured of an empty seat next to them to put their briefcase and papers. The CAB oversaw this tight cartel benignly and spent its time regulating even the size of in-flight sandwiches.[6]

Enter stage left, Ralph Nader, the father of the consumer movement, whose harsh exposé of the automobile industry, *Unsafe at Any Speed*, had landed him on the cover of *Time*. Carter shared Nader's suspicion that big industry was anticonsumer, but Ham Jordan vigorously objected when they joined forces because Nader was deeply unpopular with Carter's conservative Southern base. By then, after he was bumped from an oversold Allegheny Airlines flight, Nader had shifted his focus to airlines. He filed a suit for damages charging deliberate overbooking and formed a consumer advocacy group focused on the airline industry.

This raised the visibility of the issue in Congress, where Representative John Moss, a California Democrat, had already formed a congressional consumer caucus and sued the CAB for $265 million on the ground that it had become the industry's partner in setting rates behind closed doors, without public hearings. U.S. District Court judge Skelly Wright agreed and in 1970 threw out the negotiated-rate system.[7] Retreating, the CAB developed a system that fed in the airlines' cost data and automatically spewed out high fares.

At the same time a number of prominent economists allied with both parties presented papers describing the economic inefficiencies of federal airline regulation. But such cries for reform from the ivory tower usually remain unheard unless powerful politicians hear them and act.

TED KENNEDY, STEPHEN BREYER,
AND FROZEN DOGS

In Congress the Massachusetts liberal Ted Kennedy, deeply committed to government action to right what he saw as injustices of the free market, was searching for issues on which to focus. He had become chairman of the nondescript Administrative Practice and Procedure Subcommittee of the Senate Judiciary Committee and, turning to his Harvard brain trust to give it some direction, was recommended to hire Stephen Breyer, a young professor of administrative law. Breyer was initially dubious but decided to use a 1974 sabbatical to take a whirl in the political world, where the laws he taught were being forged. He joined the subcommittee staff and identified 32 sectors of the American economy that could benefit from lighter regulation without affecting health or safety, starting with the airlines. He prepared a list of possible hearings on ten subjects "which nobody's ever heard of . . . [that] would be consumer-oriented and would help people." He impressed Kennedy by simply asking: "Why in heaven's name are you not letting people compete?"[8] The Harvard law professor and the powerful senator realized that the politics of airline and truck deregulation were fierce, with Kennedy recognizing that if Democrats were going to take on the unions, Republicans needed to take on the airlines.[9]

As deregulation hearings got under way in 1975, a constituent from working-class East Boston asked Kennedy why he was holding hearings about airlines when "I've never been able to fly." Kennedy retorted: "That's why I'm holding hearings."[10]

But the Kennedy staff was frustrated by the lack of press attention, which was essential to attract the support of other senators. Finally they scheduled a hearing for what they privately called "frozen dog day"—an exposé of how airlines transported dogs that often arrived frozen stiff after hours in the cargo hold. As the staff foresaw, the press attended the hearing, and, as Mary Schuman recalled, at the same time they "got an earful about airline reform."[11] Eight days of meticulously organized hearings developed tens of thousands of pages of information on the airline industry, with detailed questionnaires for potential witnesses. Predictably, all the airlines testified against any changes, as did the CAB.

But two dazzling star witnesses testified in favor of ending federal regulation. The first was Freddie Laker, the upstart British entrepreneur who pioneered a no-frills, low-cost airline that he dubbed Skytrain. He came up with one of the hearing's best lines, accusing the U.S. government of "Pan-Amania" in trying to save globe-girdling Pan American Airways from competition at all costs. The staff discovered a startling industry-inspired memorandum proposing that U.S. air marshals board Laker's London-bound flight in Tijuana, Mexico, and force it down just across the border to undermine the $135 fare—about one-third of the standard New York–London rate. From the congressional dais came an observation that Laker must be losing money on the route. He proclaimed: "No, I'm making a fortune. Why don't you try it? I mean it's obvious how you do it: You fill up the airplane."[12] Fortunately for the cause of deregulation, Laker appeared before his airline was forced into bankruptcy in 1982 by his own overexpansion and the predatory low-cost fares that his established competitors offered to undercut his popular Skytrain.

No such failure would taint the career of the other star witness, Fred Smith, the future CEO of FedEx. At Yale he had written his senior thesis on setting up a cargo airline; it was graded only a C by his skeptical professor. Smith certainly got the last word. His testimony pointed up the ludicrous regulatory schemes that resulted in what Breyer called "idiot fares," as well as equally senseless regulations that forced the fledgling freight carrier to fly half a dozen small planes wing to wing from FedEx's Memphis hub to its major destinations in order to escape CAB oversight that applied only to large aircraft. Smith struggled on as the Ford administration equivocated over airline reform and the CAB experimented with charter flights by the major airlines.[13]

After the hearings Breyer wrote a book-length report, and in May 1976 Kennedy proposed bipartisan legislation deregulating the airlines, just in time for Carter's presidential campaign. The candidate came out foursquare in favor of competition in the air, even though it meant taking on one of the most important companies in his home state of Georgia, Delta Airlines. He first pledged that reform of all the regulatory agencies would be a major priority if he were elected, and later singled out the airlines by promising them greater freedom on fares, routes, and service while pledging to protect airline access to small communities and the seniority of airline employees—a tall order.[14]

Back in Washington, Kennedy took note of Carter's proposals and remarked to Breyer that they were receiving a very good reception. As Breyer looked back, he said: "There was sort of serendipity: Just by chance a number of people were in the particularly right place at the right time." And that included the president, "a reader in the White House," Breyer said of Carter, who absorbed all the academic arguments favoring airline deregulation and turned them into policy.[15]

An essential element in the story was the president's appointment of Kahn as chairman of the CAB. There were three openings on the five-member board, and Ham Jordan asked Mary Schuman for her recommendations. Enjoying one benefit of even a junior White House position—the most important people instantly return your calls—she canvassed the country and quickly learned that everyone's ideal chairman was Kahn. This Cornell economics professor had written a number of articles on deregulation and was chairman of the New York State Public Service Commission regulating utilities. In that exposed position he had become a veteran of the political wars, and while a sensible deregulator, he preserved a sufficient amount of regulation to protect consumers. Mary reported that back to Ham's office and was told by his secretary Eleanor Connor that Jordan wanted three names, from which he would pick the chairman. Undaunted, she boldly wrote the president's senior adviser a memo proposing three possible candidates for chairman—"Alfred Kahn, Alfred E. Kahn, and Fred Kahn." Realizing he had met his match in this determined young upstart, Jordan called her and said, "I picked the second guy," to which Mary replied, "Hamilton, you're brilliant. That is the guy I would have picked myself." Through such exquisite personal duels is history made.[16]

But it was easier to persuade Ham to approve the nomination than to convince Kahn to accept it. He liked his job in New York, and if he had to go to Washington, he set two conditions—a presidential assurance that he would not have to enforce the existing airline regulations and that he would have a majority on the board committed to overturning them. Mary and I assured him that he would be administering a new deregulation law being pressed by the administration. Kahn, a man of great audacity and humor, would have preferred to chair the Federal Communications Commission (FCC), because he did not "regard it as my highest aspiration to make it easy for people to jet all over the world in a period of energy concern." But he realized that airline deregulation would be the focus of action.

He had never before been invited to the Oval Office or even met a president. But when he was ushered in, Carter, who had his back turned, swung around, and Kahn suddenly saw the president "with his charming smile, and I just loved his air, his kind of modest demeanor and his manifest sincerity." Carter made his commitment to deregulation perfectly clear. Kahn concluded that he was informed and serious, and he took the job.[17]

It was my job to make the initial survey of Congress. When I walked into the Capitol for my first meeting with Ted Kennedy, I had to admit to myself that I was in awe of the last of the Kennedy brothers. President Kennedy's speech in 1962 at the University of North Carolina helped inspired me to go into public service, and when he was assassinated I drove overnight to view his flag-draped coffin in the Capitol Rotunda. Ted Kennedy had the same chiseled face as my idol, his older brother Jack, only larger. In my notes I wrote: "Sen. Kennedy is dynamic, charismatic, very knowledgeable, and hardworking."

I noticed odd contractions of speech, often with incomplete sentences, at this first of innumerable meetings during the following four years. Although he was a fluent, eloquent, and powerful public speaker, in small meetings he spoke almost haltingly, often not completing a sentence or clearly articulating a thought.[18] But Kennedy did have several clear messages to convey to the president. Carter must be specific about exactly what regime he wanted to replace regulation; airline service to small communities must be subsidized, not just to maintain their links to the wider world but to garner the votes of their congressional representatives; once competition in the industry was established, it must be preserved against mergers and backroom deals among the airlines themselves; and finally that the people we appointed to the CAB must be "imbued with the philosophy" of deregulation. With Kahn's appointment we could certainly assure him of his last demand. Thus began a close working relationship during which he became one of the most reliable Senate supporters of Carter's legislative agenda, although he challenged Carter for the Democratic presidential nomination in 1980, partly out of a dynastic sense of entitlement.

Half a dozen Democratic committee chairmen would scrutinize any airline bill, and I met with all of them. It was clear that most would pick at the details, some might try it pull it apart, but that all realized the creaky system was failing the public. They also spotted the dangers. Warren Magnuson, an old New Dealer from Washington State, who by this time shuffled along in an uncertain gait, correctly foresaw that competition would curtail if not kill air service to rural communities. Like Kennedy, he wanted federal subsidies to maintain it at low prices. Howard Cannon, a Nevada Democrat who chaired the Senate Commerce, Transportation, and Science Committee, seemed more concerned with holding his own turf and defending the airlines. Cannon had put in his own narrow reform bill to block Kennedy's broader legislation and suggested that the president limit himself to a message outlining general principles.

These congressional turf wars can be distracting to all but the participants, but they can also move things forward, if only by fits and starts. Cannon's Republican opposite, James Pearson of Kansas, wanted more new carriers but also correctly foresaw the danger of concentration among large airlines, monopolies by a few, and predatory pricing to drive out the new competitors. Representative Glenn Anderson, a pleasant California Democrat who chaired the House Transportation Committee, was a firm supporter of deregulation, but this legislator from east Los Angeles threw a curve ball by insisting that before any deregulation bill passed, Congress must first enact a law limiting aircraft noise.[19]

It became quickly apparent that we were not only facing congressional doubts and demands as well as the united opposition of the airline industry and its unions, but another problem closer to home: Our Transportation secretary, Brock Adams, had been a congressman from Washington State, where Boeing was supreme. He was dead set against ending the cozy relationship between the CAB and the powerful airplane manufacturer's customers. Remarkably, when he was vetted for the Transportation job, he was not quizzed on his position on airline deregulation, although his opposition quickly became obvious. During the transition Simon Lazarus and Mary Schuman on my staff drafted an option memorandum for the president-elect on the issue, a standard procedure in reaching any complex policy decision. But they made the mistake of copying Secretary-designate Adams. It was promptly leaked to the *Washington Post*, almost certainly by Adams, and caused an uproar because it frankly warned Carter that in a free and deregulated market, several of the most important and most cosseted of our airlines might go bankrupt—as indeed some eventually did.[20]

Adams publicly preempted the new president by giving an interview to the *Post* denigrating deregulation and citing the standard list of horrible outcomes—consolidation, bankruptcies, and service disruption. When we showed it to Carter, he was enraged. He summoned Adams to the Oval Office for a dressing-down, opening the meeting by saying: "I see, Brock, that you are opposed to airline deregulation, *which I support!*"[21] He demanded Adams's support as head of the Transportation Department, an early and welcome signal not to mess with the new president. Adams nevertheless continued his opposition in the administration, and his doubts extended into the ranks of his department, where the experts dragged their feet in drafting the deregulation proposal. Tension rose between the White House and Adams, with Mary's youth and vigorous advocacy for the president's position getting under his skin; as he complained to me, she "ordered" him to submit his proposed answers to congressional questions on airline deregulation.[22]

All this gives a picture of the two Washington legs of the Iron Triangle (cabinet departments and congressional committees) that were trying to dismantle our deregulation effort. Initially our cause seemed hopeless. The third leg lobbied hard against deregulation—almost the entire airline industry, its two major unions, and for good measure, the AFL-CIO, for its lack of labor protections. It had attracted little press or public support. When I met with Adams and his staff, he gave deregulation only a 40 to 60 percent chance of congressional approval because there was no constituency for it.[23]

Kennedy phoned me a few days later to warn that his bill was in trouble. He urged Carter to phone Cannon, emphasized the importance the president attached to the bill, and offered to work with him. He only half jokingly said he wished we could put Mary Schuman in the Transportation Department because he was concerned Adams would support a more limited deregulation bill introduced by Republican senator James Pearson and Democrat Howard Cannon.[24] The unions and the airlines worked only that much harder with

Adams. They threw up roadblocks by raising a number of complex issues—the disposition of revenues from a ticket tax devoted to noise abatement, and questioning the validity of a General Accounting Office report reinforcing Kennedy's argument that his deregulation bill would bring lower airline fares. My staff told me that labor and industry were working together hard against airline deregulation, and we would lose if there was a vote now.[25]

Meanwhile Kahn got busy making the most of his eighteen-month tenure as CAB chairman. Stretching his legal authority to a breaking point, he began by allowing a second airline to serve Philadelphia. Then he persuaded his fellow board members not to overturn the experiments begun under his Republican predecessor, John Robson, to introduce discount fares such as American's Super Saver and Continental's Peanuts fares.[26] Under Kahn's leadership the board began to make it easier for an airline to leave an unprofitable route for another where they could attract more passengers with lower fares. He also broke a logjam and overruled airline objections to approve some of the six hundred pending applications for new routes.

In November 1977 the CAB began deregulating air cargo. FedEx and UPS were encouraged to apply for unlimited all-cargo service, and charter freight carriers were permitted, as well as freight carriage by the scheduled airlines. Kahn also helped the president embark on a liberalized international policy now known as "Open Skies," which encouraged foreign carriers to provide greater competition in the U.S. market in return for access by our airlines in theirs. This evolved into agreements allowing foreign and domestic airlines to fly directly between major cities, for example San Francisco to Paris or London to Chicago. Kahn cultivated Congress assiduously and boldly, reminding the conservative senator Barry Goldwater, a devoted pilot in the air force reserve, that he had always championed free markets.[27]

With his quiet charisma and disarming personality, Kahn himself became a spectacular public advocate, deploying candor and ironic wit, a rare combination in Washington. Taking on Delta Airlines at a press conference, he quipped on the airline's slogan by declaring: "No, Delta is *not* ready when we are." When Frank Borman, the former astronaut who headed Eastern Airlines, invited him to inspect its shiny new jets, the former professor of economics tartly responded: "I'm really sorry, Frank, but to me, they're just marginal costs with wings."[28]

MARY SCHUMAN TAKES FLIGHT

Another indispensable factor in reversing the tide was Mary Schuman. As a junior congressional aide, she had been assigned to work on reform of airline regulation precisely because everyone knew that under Senator Cannon it was going nowhere. The Nevada senator, she discovered, was heavily supported by the airlines; their lobbyists spoon-fed him questions during hearings. His modest bill only moved the goalposts slightly by putting the onus on the entrenched airlines to prove they would be hurt by competition rather than, as was then the case, demanding that airlines applying to serve established routes must show that competition would improve travel for the public. The Kennedy bill went much further, essentially dismantling four decades of regulation and permitting free entry of new airlines and market-based pricing under general CAB oversight.

Once Mary moved down to our end of Pennsylvania Avenue to join my Domestic Policy Staff, she took flight in our cause. She organized a broad, diverse, bipartisan deregulation troupe that included Nader's Aviation Consumer Action Project, the Consumer Federation of America, the liberal political lobby Common Cause, the National Association of Manufacturers, the National Federation of Independent Businesses, and even retailers like Sears, Roebuck seeking air shipments to customers,[29] which helped build credibility for airline deregulation.

Kennedy wanted to deregulate at one stroke. But Mary had political smarts far beyond her years. While immediate deregulation might be a fine political coup for the senator, she argued, if things went wrong on the president's watch and the airline industry suddenly collapsed before it could restructure, Carter and not Kennedy would be blamed. So we took the position that the airlines would get five years to phase in a new and more competitive system.

With equal shrewdness, she persuaded me and the president not to submit a detailed administration bill lest it anger the backers of the already-competing Cannon and Kennedy bills, but instead to release a presidential message outlining general principles guiding legislation, while she would try to midwife a compromise bill. (This was a painful lesson we learned from submitting our own detailed energy bills, which quickly became targets, blocking progress for two years.) Carter's message in March 1977 was carefully worded to offend neither Cannon nor Kennedy and their supporters. It asked Congress to allow the airlines to set their own rates and chart their own routes, with only enough government bureaucracy to maintain service to small cities and prevent predatory below-cost fares.[30]

It took weeks of tough negotiations with Congress and within the administration itself, ranging across the experts on the economy, transportation, and the Justice Department's antitrust lawyers. The talented and tough Kennedy legal staff, led by Boies, demanded to know the administration's position on a number of issues. Mary refused, telling us: "If we start negotiating with this guy—no offense—but he's a hundred times smarter than all of us put together. He's going to eat our lunch." She had another reason: If we laid all our cards on the table, some were bound to be unacceptable to Kennedy or Cannon or both. So she saw her role as probing to overcome the differences between them. But compromise came more easily because, as she put it candidly: "I fell in love with David Boies and that helped!"[31]

But like the course of true love, the path of legislation is rarely smooth. The airlines and their unions lobbied vigorously against deregulation. Mary was indefatigable, traveling to Rotary Clubs and Chambers of Commerce in communities represented by key members of Congress; touting the benefits of deregulation to business executives whose actions too often belied their free-market rhetoric; refining testimony for administration officials and buttonholing congressional staffs; and working with Anne Wexler, our public liaison leader at the White House, to organize White House outreach sessions around the country at which the president spoke. Mary helped peel off a couple of the airlines to our side: most notably Herb Kelleher of the no-frills Southwest Airlines, and then United, which made a business decision that it could deal more effectively in an open market than its competitors at Eastern and Braniff. United was right; it thrived, and they failed.

Adams continued to be a problem, proposing we support a weak bill out of committee and then strengthen it later, leading me to ask him to stop blocking a strong bill[32] in the congressional process against what was sure to be massive lobbying—as if he could beat back the lobbyists or would even try. It was a strategy designed to fail. We overrode him, and Carter promptly reassured our supporters in writing that we had no intention of diluting the Senate bill.[33] It took eighteen drafting sessions, called markups, in committee to produce a composite of the Kennedy and Cannon bills, which Mary helped broker. It passed the Senate but almost crashed in the House, weighed down by a last-minute attempt by Glenn Anderson to tack on an antinoise provision that would have given the airlines $3 billion to help retrofit engines or buy new ones. But this giveaway did not have the votes, and a bill approving the most sweeping change in the relationship between the federal government and the airlines literally flew through both houses of Congress over only a handful of negative votes and was signed by a beaming President Carter on October 24, 1978.[34]

Success demonstrated in almost textbook fashion that a determined president (Carter), a gifted regulator (Kahn), an effective member of Congress (Kennedy), and three highly creative and indefatigable staffers (Schuman in the White House and Breyer and Boies in the Senate) could break Washington's ingrained interests. But was all this Washington sound and fury worth it? A passenger crammed into the middle seat in row 36 of a packed redeye flight from LAX to JFK might not think so: His seat is an inch and one-half narrower and four inches closer to the one directly in front.[35]

But without deregulation that uncomfortable traveler might not even be making the trip. Carter's deregulation democratized air travel. Flying economy may be like riding a Greyhound bus, but it is affordable to more people.[36] Delta, originally a fierce opponent, gave Carter and Kahn credit for bringing down fares and boasted that the airline was leading passengers to "flock to airports in record numbers."[37] The number of air passengers leaped from 107 million in 1974, before deregulation, to 721 million in 2010. Before Carter's victory only one-quarter of the public had ever flown; in 2014 three-quarters had.[38]

Fares have come down significantly; airline revenue per passenger adjusted for inflation has halved from 34 cents in 1976, the year before Carter took office, to 17 cents in 2015.[39] The cheapest inflation-adjusted round-trip fare from New York to Los Angeles was then $1,442; now it is $268.[40]

Deregulation also belied the concern that small towns would suffer. A 1996 study by the U.S. Government Accounting Office looked at 87 small- to medium-size markets and found that more than half of them had more flights than before deregulation in 1976, and that 65 of them "enjoyed a combination of lower fares and better service under deregulation."[41] While there may be several reasons beyond deregulation, the expansion of the industry has also led to a substantial increase in the number of jobs created by the U.S. airlines. Airlines for America, the industry's association, reported there were 511,000 full-time and 105,254 part-time workers directly employed by America's airlines in 2016, an increase of 50 percent since 1976.[42]

But the flying public has a right to ask why it faces overcrowded airport terminals, persistent flight delays, poor service, an oligopoly of a few major airlines, and limited service to small airports in rural areas, and then only through the commuter-plane spokes from major hubs. In considering deregulation, it is necessary to face the deficiencies squarely, and offset them against the gains. The balance sheet constantly shifts in a dynamic market, reflecting not only the demand for seats but the extremely high fixed costs of providing them. With only a handful of airlines—all flying full planes and publicly signaling one another not to add more seats via the unfortunate buzzword "capacity discipline"—the Justice Department's trustbusters began investigating under President Obama, as well they might. In the face of the normal business imperative to maximize profits, any government reform of a lopsided market will have only a half-life, just as our own deregulation undid protections that had been designed for an earlier era. The overcrowded airports and flight delays are also due in part to a woeful lack of investment in new terminals and runways, a refusal to spend public money renewing and expanding the nation's infrastructure that is not limited to aviation.

The industry's concentration certainly could have been mitigated through more robust antitrust enforcement. But this was impeded by the disappearance of the independent CAB itself, leaving the Department of Transportation in charge of policy, and wedded to its symbiotic relationship with the airline industry through the department's Federal Aviation Administration. It was derelict in not opposing anticompetitive mergers and indeed "never saw a merger it didn't like," Kahn said. Moreover, antitrust policy barely existed as such during the Reagan administration, with a long list of mergers approved at key hubs, squeezing competition. By then the industry had been restructured on now-familiar lines and the megamergers of this century were only a matter of time. Ten trunk airlines have been merged into a virtual oligopoly of four companies carrying 80 percent of all passengers. The mergers may have been more a symptom of the inability of small carriers to survive than the cause of their disappearance, but another was the major airlines' predatory pricing practices, which were not designed to benefit the consumer but to drive out competition.[43]

The majors also responded to the new competition in ways that barely existed in the regulated world, with computerized reservation systems; hub-and-spoke models offering more connections through a diversified route structure feeding from one spoke to another through the airline's major hub and flying full loads; deeply discounted fares for pinpointed seats likely to be left empty at regular prices; and frequent flyer programs to enhance the market power of carriers dominating their hub. Unseen by most passengers are the special override commissions that airlines give to supposedly independent travel agents to sign on to the majors' computerized reservation services, making their customers virtual captives of the major carrier.

These triple or even quadruple manacles quietly slipped onto their customers by the established carriers have allowed them to offer lower fares than the long-forgotten People Express, even though its costs were lower. Fred Kahn, one of the architects of our airline deregulation, reflected years later that he had not anticipated the turbulence in the industry and the price discrimination that enabled the established carriers to drive away the new boys on the block and keep out all but the most ingenious, such as JetBlue and Southwest, which pioneered low fares, an obsession for efficiency, and consumer responsiveness once deregulation permitted it to jump its Texas borders and fly across the country.[44] Even with the dominance of a few major airlines, Carter's airline deregulation continues to provide opportunities which several start-up airlines are taking for new, low-cost carriers like Spirit Airlines to freely enter the market and provide cheap fares for average travelers, as well as put downward pressure on the fares of the major carriers.[45]

One utterly unexpected beneficiary of airline deregulation was none other than the man who helped start it as a Kennedy aide, Stephen Breyer. A few weeks after Carter's 1980 electoral defeat, the senator phoned me to ask our lame-duck president to appoint this brilliant former Harvard law professor to a vacancy on the First Circuit Court of Appeals, which reviews cases in New England. Flabbergasted, I said: "Senator, you do not need to convince me of Steve's qualifications; I think the world of him, worked closely with him, and know we would never have airline deregulation without him." But I pointed to two hurdles that seemed insurmountable. Kennedy asked me what they were.

First, I said: "There is no love lost by the president for you; he feels that your challenge to his nomination split the party and helped elect Reagan." Kennedy quickly replied: "I know, that's why I called you and not the president." The second was the Democratic loss of the Senate in the election. Strom Thurmond, the archconservative senator from South Carolina, was poised to become the new Republican chairman of the Judiciary Committee. Why, I asked, would Thurmond permit a Democrat to fill a lifetime appellate position just one step below the Supreme Court, when he could wait a few months and confirm Reagan's choice? "Stu," Kennedy said, "you take care of the president; I will take care of Strom."

With some trepidation I went to the Oval Office with all the reasons the president should nominate Breyer written on my trusty yellow legal pad. Before going through my litany, I said: "Mr. President, forget who requested this, but there is a vacancy on the First Circuit, and it would be a tribute to you to nominate Steve Breyer." I then started reading out the reasons, but Carter stopped me. "I agree," he said simply. "I will do it." I called Kennedy to report that I had delivered on my part of the deal—but what about Thurmond? To my amazement he told me that Thurmond would support the nomination and bring the other Republicans along with him. And why, I asked, would he do that? Kennedy explained: "Strom likes Steve and feels he has been fair to him and the Republicans. Even though we are at opposite ends of the political spectrum, we do these kinds of personal favors for each other." In fact, as long as Breyer worked for Kennedy, he and Kenneth Feinberg—a senior Kennedy aide later renowned as the mediator for the 9/11 claims and other cases—breakfasted almost daily with Emery Sneadon of Thurmond's staff to discuss upcoming issues and the different positions of various senators "to try to get things to work out smoothly." They also discussed judicial appointments, and when there were differences, they would also "work out everything" in time for the committee to discuss each nominee in the next closed-door session.[46]

U.S. Supreme Court Justice Breyer has told me he doubts he would have been picked for the high court by President Bill Clinton if he had not already served as an appellate judge. During both confirmation hearings, Thurmond heaped praise so heavily on Breyer that if I had redacted the senator's name from the transcript, I might have imagined Kennedy was speaking. That was a political world far from today's polarized and polluted arena, where what happened to Breyer will be impossible until personal courtesy and congressional comity are restored.

DEREGULATION DOWN TO EARTH

With Jimmy Carter there was no such thing as resting on past achievements. Exhausted by our success with the airlines and the energy wars, we now faced a contentious debate in the Roosevelt Room between the president and the senior White House staff over whether to push to deregulate the trucking industry. This would involve urging the same members of Congress to walk the political plank yet again on another unpopular issue. I argued against it; we already had an overloaded congressional agenda, and we would be facing thousands of trucking firms and the tough and powerful Teamsters Union shaped by Jimmy Hoffa, whose recent disappearance was widely suspected to be revenge by the Mob. His body was said to have been buried in a pillar of fresh concrete at a construction site. The Teamsters were not the equivalent of unions that represented skilled airline mechanics and highly paid pilots. So why risk a likely defeat that would only tarnish our success?

True to form, and fortunately for the country and his legacy, the president ignored our advice. He wanted to maintain his momentum in freeing up the economy, in part because it would help restrain prices at a time of rising inflation. We also had a proven formula of building a coalition of consumer advocates on the left and free-market conservatives on the right, and by appointing a proderegulation chairman of the federal regulatory agency, the Interstate Commerce Commission (ICC). Carter made Darius Gaskins, who had been Kahn's chief economist at the CAB, the first black chairman of any major federal regulatory body in the country's history. This put pressure on Congress. If we did not take advantage of our airline success and confront the opposition head-on, we risked being unable to do it for years to come.

Trucking also was inextricably linked to the railroads as both partner and competitor in the nation's integrated system for moving freight. One was a rising industry rolling its eighteen-wheelers over the newly completed interstate highway system and at the same time loading trailers on flatcars for the long haul and offloading them for local deliveries. The other was an almost bankrupt system that nevertheless carried one-third of the nation's freight and most of our essential bulk commodities, like coal, grain, and chemicals. It was obvious that one industry could not be deregulated without the other, and that if trucking alone were freed to compete, the nation's ailing railroads could only continue as permanent wards of the state.

Both industries were tightly regulated by the ICC, which was created in 1887 to rein in the railroads when they were natural monopolies and cut deals with major shippers that squeezed small ones like farmers. It began regulating trucking during the Depression of the 1930s. Prices were strictly controlled as well as entry into new trucking routes, and Teamster-organized firms had long persuaded the ICC to pass along large union pay increases to the public in higher rates, which in turn were buried in everyday prices at the supermarket and the department store. No sweetheart deal was less noticeable or more costly than the "backhaul" rule: The ICC forbade trucks carrying products from one city to another to pick up a new load and take it back. The trucks had to come home empty.

Carter agreed to a package covering both industries and said he wanted to be personally involved in pushing it forward. The rail message went first because, as Carter warned Congress in March 1979: "Without the changes I am recommending, we will face catastrophic rail bankruptcies, sharply declining service, and massive federal expenditures." This was hardly an exaggeration. Although it was not easy to enact a radical change in railroad operations and pricing—coal companies and their electric utility customers demanded special protection—it was achieved in half a year when the president signed the deregulation law only three weeks before the election of 1980. He crowned it with words not typically found in the lexicon of a Democratic president: "This act is the capstone of my efforts over the past four years to get the Federal government off the backs of private industry by removing needless, burdensome regulation which benefits no one and harms us all." [47]

Railroads could set prices and manage day-to-day operations without ICC interference, and they could more easily abandon unprofitable lines; protections were built in for workers dislocated by these shutdowns or by mergers. This led to reduced rates for most shippers. Freight railroads became profitable, eliminating the need for additional federal subsidies. Railroads were also able to access private capital to invest in maintaining and upgrading the nation's rail system, improving service and safety. The Department of Transportation found that railroad costs and prices were cut in half over a ten-year period. The carriers reversed their historic loss of traffic to the trucking industry and invested almost half a trillion dollars in improving the rail system. [48]

THE TEAMSTERS KEEP ON TRUCKIN'

Deregulating trucking was an entirely different battle. The immovable object was not management but the International Brotherhood of Teamsters, which had organized about half the workforce of the regulated trucking companies and correctly regarded deregulation as an existential threat. As soon as the union heard we wanted to strip the industry of its featherbedding protections, I got a call from its president, Frank Fitzsimmons, Hoffa's successor, who asked me to drop by his office without any staff for a one-on-one meeting so we could get to know each other. A limousine from the White House motor pool drove me to the base of Capitol Hill and the white marble Teamsters building, where I was ushered in—not to Fitzsimmons's private office, but to a giant conference room with a light mahogany table larger than the one at Camp David, where the Middle East peace accords were negotiated.

Arrayed around the table were the regional Teamster presidents from Chicago, Cleveland, Pittsburgh, and other blue-collar cities. I felt like a small running back facing the front line of the Chicago Bears. Each one seemed to have giant biceps leading to steam-pipe necks, with eyes glowering at me but fortunately arms folded and not cocked. I was sharply cross-examined, but at every turn I told them nothing was set in stone—I carefully avoided saying "cement" in deference to Hoffa's memory, and imagined myself encapsulated on one side of a bridge abutment on I-95, with Hoffa on the other, or buried under one goalpost of Meadowlands Stadium with Hoffa a hundred yards away under the other.

I emphasized that we were genuinely interested in hearing their concerns. Fitzsimmons summarized their intense opposition: It would allow small, unsafe, independent, nonunion firms to enter the market and compete unfairly. Unstated was that deregulation would also threaten their cozy relationship with the trucking firms, which was blessed by the ICC and had provided the truckers salaries and pension benefits far higher than those of the average American worker. The hour-long meeting seemed to last an eternity, and by the end, all I could think of was getting out into the sunlight alive.

I followed up this riveting session by hosting a series of meetings on safer grounds at the White House with Teamsters staffers, and Bill Johnston of my staff.[49] We explored the gap between their 600,000 unionized drivers employed by regulated trucking firms and drivers who were hired as "independent contractors" and could not be unionized. The union regarded the independents as outlaws, and defended the industry's rate bureaus that fixed shipping prices with the ICC's blessing as essential to the livelihood of small trucking firms. The Teamsters feared that deregulation would open the way for the big firms to undercut the small ones with predatory prices, driving them out of business and leaving the remaining companies facing less competition in setting their own rates. They were willing to be flexible on rates, but only if our bill contained job and safety protections for the drivers.

I felt that their fears and concerns were legitimate. Deregulation would put pressure on their wages, complicate their ability to organize, and threaten the drivers' jobs. In fact, their fears were not only reasonable, but they became a reality. Their loss was the consumers' gain in lower rates to haul the massive amount of goods across the country. But this was the cruel trade-off between the pressures on their well-paid union workforce and lower prices through more freedom for new firms to compete on routes for the benefit of consumers and shippers.

The companies were equally opposed to ending the protective cocoon they had spun for themselves over the years with the help of the ICC. Representatives of the major trucking firms grouped in the American Trucking Association defended what they called their "collective ratemaking," which they felt was the heart of their ICC regulation, and did not see themselves as being in a competitive business at all. At a meeting with me, they got to the guts of the matter by declaring they were a quasi-public utility, providing safe and stable service to communities large and small.[50] So we faced a phalanx of opposition from both sides, with one exception: the Minority Trucking Association, representing black-owned firms that were systematically frozen out of entering new markets by ICC restrictions. I appreciated their support, but I knew their voice would be drowned out by the big carriers and the Teamsters.[51]

Sheltered from competition by a 1948 law enacted over President Truman's veto giving the trucking industry a special immunity from the antitrust laws, the companies could set prices among themselves through rate bureaus, unlike almost any other industry in the country. The companies and their unions posted about five thousand fixed point-to-point rates for different cargos with the ICC *every day.* We decided that changing the law would work only if the ICC removed this straitjacket and permitted new firms to offer competitive prices, otherwise the firms would simply raise rates and not even post them daily.

After a great deal of interagency disagreement and discussion with the Senate and House, Carter, in June 1979, sent Congress a powerful presidential message seeking legislation freeing this crucial segment of the economy from an "unbelievably mindless scheme of unnecessary government interference [that] contributes to three of the nation's most pressing problems— inflation, excessive government regulation, and the shortage of energy." He enumerated these barriers: The ICC and not the trucking company decides which cities a carrier can serve along with the detailed commodities it may haul; whether its truck must come back empty or not; and whether the driver can take the most direct route, saving time, money, and fuel. The president advanced a vivid example: I-25 directly connects the 440 miles between Denver and Albuquerque, but Garrett Freight Lines was permitted by the ICC to haul freight between the two cities only by way of Salt Lake City, a distance of 730 miles.[52]

The proposed legislation would immediately remove these restrictions and artificial routes, end the industry's antitrust exemption, and abolish the rigged rate bureaus as "price-fixing [which] is normally a felony." We estimated that the current regulatory system cost consumers about $5 billion a year, and that the eight largest trucking companies averaged an annual return of almost 29 percent on their investments. In addition, scarce ICC operating certificates were bought and sold for enormous sums.

To encourage support from members of Congress representing small communities, we proposed that the ICC be directed to improve service to them. We also added interstate buses to the mix, which is why Greyhound is a very different company today and cheap buses ply the interstates between some major cities. As with airline deregulation, Senator Kennedy was an indispensable ally, shielding us from any attacks by Democrats in Congress that we were antiunion.[53]

Removing the restrictions seemed eminently sensible, but that did not stop the large truckers and the Teamsters from exerting all their force in Congress, where we had a long, hard slog against powerful legislators trying to undercut sections of our program. But we got an unexpected break when Howard Cannon, the Senate Commerce Committee chairman, was investigated by a federal grand jury in Chicago for a year for allegedly taking a campaign contribution from the Teamsters, in return for sponsoring a weaker trucking deregulation bill. Although the Justice Department ultimately decided not to charge him (I submitted an affidavit on his behalf, based on what I knew of his activity), Roy Williams, then the Teamsters' president, and Allen Dorfman, a Chicago insurance executive who was close to both the union and to organized crime, were caught on tape admitting that they had tried to bribe the senator and were convicted. I believe the investigation encouraged Cannon to support the tougher deregulation bill being promoted by Carter and Kennedy.

Carter stood firm, and anyone who doubts his determined nature need only look at how relentlessly he pushed trucking deregulation in the face of implacable opposition.[54] There was much blood on the floor, but the Motor Carrier Reform and Regulation Act of 1980 gave him most of the reforms he sought.

The benefits of trucking deregulation are staggering and flow throughout the economy at every level; they have been counted in numerous govern-ment and academic studies. Ending the backhaul rule reduced empty miles by 75 percent among full-load truckers. A 1988 study by the Federal Trade Commission showed that between 1977 and 1982, average interstate rates for trucks carrying full loads fell by 25 percent, despite fuel prices more than doubling during the second oil shock.

A Brookings study demonstrated that by lowering barriers to the entry of new firms, the number of low-cost, nonunion regional carriers more than doubled, with annual benefits to shippers estimated at more than $18 bil-lion.[55] The most pervasive benefit to the economy is the reduction in the costs of holding inventories because of more flexible and quicker delivery times, from 14 percent of GDP in 1981 to 10.8 percent in 1987, an annual saving estimated by the Transportation Department at $38 billion to $56 billion. Another major factor is the growth of piggybacking truck trailers on railroads, which increased by 70 percent from 1981 to 1986.[56]

Arguments by the unions and trucking companies that small commu-nities would be ill served and safety compromised have not been borne out. An Interstate Commerce Commission study found that shipping service to small communities actually improved after the 1980 deregulation, and nu-merous studies found a decrease in trucking accidents and an increase in highway safety.[57]

The Federal Trade Commission found that, far from losing jobs, dereg-ulation sharply increased the number of jobs in the trucking industry, because of the ease of entry of new firms—from 1.368 million workers in 1980 to 1.767 million in 1987, a 29 percent rise.[58]

But one negative prediction has been borne out. With the entry of less expensive, nonunion carriers, the biggest loser was indeed the Teamsters, just as they feared. Deregulation made it easier for nonunion workers to obtain jobs and sharply reduced the pay advantage of unionized workers in the truck-ing industry compared with workers in other industries. The percentage of unionized truckers fell from about 60 to only 28 percent during the first five years of the new law. Their pay fell an average of 10 percent relative to the wages of workers in the general economy. We frankly did not foresee at the time how disruptive deregulation in the trucking industry would be. I wonder if the quintessential liberal Ted Kennedy, who was strongly prolabor, would have been as enthusiastic about trucking deregulation if he had known its impact on unionized workers in the industry.

But I do not believe deregulation alone can be held responsible. While trucking and railroads are not subject to the same foreign competition as U.S. airlines and manufacturers, globalization and foreign competition have put downward pressure on wages in general, particularly for less skilled workers. Unionized workers in the transportation industry could not have been shielded indefinitely from these pressures. The political implications of this have been lasting. Historically Democratic blue-collar workers became Reagan Republicans in the 1980 election against Carter, and many also moved to become supporters of Donald Trump in 2016. But trucking deregulation, like rail and airline deregulation, has stood the test of time and bipartisan scrutiny and led to general price reductions for consumer packaged goods.[59]

THE BEGINNING OF THE SHIFT
FROM MA BELL TO MICROSOFT

Finally, Carter laid the foundations for the telecommunications revolution that began with the dismantling of the telephone monopoly and is still under way in the worldwide digital revolution disrupting all manufacturing and commerce. The industry was just entering a breathtaking technological revolution that caught the interest and the deep commitment of the engineer that lived inside the thirty-ninth president of the United States. He wanted to harness it for the consumer as well as the innovator by removing the regulatory barriers to new technologies, and he made that clear even before he reached the White House.[60] While time expired on his efforts, they nevertheless led the way to freeing electronics for competition and innovation. His first step was the appointment of Charles Ferris as chairman of the Federal Communications Commission.

Ferris was the staff director of the Congressional Democratic Policy Committee and a shrewd lawyer with the politics of his native Boston in his genes. Formed by a Jesuit education at Boston College and its law school, he had the ability to master complex material, and when he met with Carter in the Oval Office, the liberal Irish Catholic and the Southern Baptist found they had much in common, including service in the U.S. Navy and an engineering background.[61] More to the point, Ferris was the first FCC chairman appointed without having been first cleared by the three major broadcasting networks and their voice, Sol Taishoff, the editor of *Broadcasting* magazine. When Taishoff inquired about his credentials for the job, Ferris tartly replied that he had watched television and used a telephone since he was four years old.[62] Carter sent Ferris a letter on April 11, 1978, emphasizing his support for Ferris's actions to promote competition in all areas of communication.[63] He quickly promoted competition among the nationwide radio networks by loosening regulations on local FM stations and then took another huge step by removing the barriers stifling the growth of cable television.

Ted Turner was the pioneer in bouncing ground-based local cable signals off satellites that relayed them to other cable systems across the country, audaciously creating the national (and later international) cable news network CNN, which broadcast around the clock and evaded the complex allocation of time slots and coverage areas that had been enforced by the FCC on behalf of the broadcast networks to protect their national franchises. Ferris swept away these restrictions in 1978. Shortly afterward a senior network executive visited Steve Simmons of my Domestic Policy Staff, pounded on his desk, and shouted: "Cable will destroy broadcasting; it must be stopped. Otherwise, the public will wind up paying for the World Series!"[64] Even as devoted sports fans, we nevertheless backed Ferris to the hilt. Midway in his tenure, and with the president's blessing, I sent my own letter to Ferris in June of 1979 to let him know Carter fully supported him, and that he was "contributing substantially to the President's program of eliminating needless regulation and promoting competition."[65]

Ferris was also instrumental in the erosion of the American Telephone and Telegraph Company's (AT&T) long-distance monopoly, which was tied to its own set of transcontinental wires. This premise was first upended in the 1960s by a revolution in microwave communications that passed multiple signals from amplifying tower to tower across the country. Technology meanwhile was increasingly moving toward a convergence of computers and communications, first through computerized switching equipment and then through the movement of information itself, for example in the

Electronic Funds Transfer system that instantly moved money among the nation's banks.

The FCC maintained an increasingly artificial barrier between AT&T and IBM. The phone company was not permitted to offer computer and data processing services, while IBM was an unregulated corporation and barred from competing in regulated phone lines. Ferris ended this distinction in 1979 through what he felt was one of the most important decisions in modern telecommunications when he permitted AT&T to offer information and data services in competition with IBM as long as Ma Bell did so through completely separate subsidiaries.

This was the essential step in changing AT&T from a regulated monopoly to a competitive corporation, and remains the framework for the explosion in telecommunications services by putting the two titans in a competitive battle. AT&T began to phase out its IBM computers, but more significantly it argued for legislation that would have subjected IBM to regulation on all its equipment and services. We let this self-interested bill die without entering into an unnecessary battle with the phone company and its powerful union.[66]

A second giant step for competition was even more contentious: bringing competition with Ma Bell in long-distance telephone service itself for the first time since AT&T was founded in 1919. One of its most powerful defenses was its control of most access to local phone networks. In a series of antitrust suits dating back to 1947, the Justice Department had tried to limit the company's monopoly power. Gradually a series of consent decrees started prying open long-distance access, the first in 1956, and the last in 1978, which opened the way to competition by MCI with Ferris's support.

But as in other fields, there were limits to what the executive branch and its independent agencies could accomplish without legislation. Representative Lionel Van Deerlin, a California Democrat who chaired the House Subcommittee on Communications, introduced a bill to reform the 1934 Communications Act by opening up the industry to competition. Carter supported it with another presidential message in September 1979, parts of which read then like science fiction but today seem commonplace. Carter described how the new technology was making it possible "to hold meetings, transmit messages, do research, bank, shop and receive a widening variety of information and entertainment—all through electronics." These breakthroughs invalidated the conventional wisdom that telecommunications service was a natural monopoly and led to the core of his message: "Consumers are the final beneficiaries of competition, through lower prices and wider choices."[67]

So close to the presidential campaign, we were in no position to push complex legislation. AT&T introduced its own bill that would only have entrenched its dominant position. With a million employees in nearly every congressional district, the company mobilized a letter-writing campaign that killed any chance for legislative reform under Carter. The president and Van Deerlin were both defeated for reelection in 1980, and Ferris left the FCC. But the battle against the telephone monopoly finally was won in 1982 when AT&T was broken up into seven separate regional operating companies by Judge Harold Greene, a former Justice Department civil rights attorney hearing his first major case on the federal bench, to which he had been nominated by Jimmy Carter.

NADER, CARTER, AND CONSUMERISM

One of the great ironies of the Carter presidency is that although the consumer movement had its greatest friend in the Oval Office, past or present, that was precisely when its decline began. Carter did not invent the modern consumer movement, but he elevated its agenda to the presidential level and attempted to write the consumer interest into law with significant success. In the United States, consumer protection dates from the pure food and drug laws at the start of the twentieth century, to the financial protections of the New Deal in the 1930s, and then to a third wave of automobile and consumer safety laws associated with Ralph Nader.

What is not generally realized is how closely Carter allied himself with Nader and his movement—and how the movement crested, as corporate advocates painted safety, environmental, and financial regulation as onerous to business and damaging to economic growth.

Ralph Nader is a tall, stoop-shouldered, intense, brilliant man from a Lebanese family, for whom smiling and compromise are equally difficult.

But it is hard to think of any American not in public office who had a more profound and positive impact in the second half of the twentieth century. He went to college at Princeton, but early on he was deeply affected by the loss of fellow students in automobile crashes. He did not own a car and hitchhiked everywhere, often with truck drivers who came upon a crash before the police. There he saw "the way the vehicle folded up, crushed people and steering columns, and the fires."[68] At Harvard Law School he wrote a paper on manufacturers' legal liability and reviewed lawsuits against General Motors, more than a hundred involving spins and rollovers of its compact Chevrolet Corvair (my first car). Then he went to the U.S. Patent Office and found that GM had eliminated some engineering stabilizers to save money in producing their sporty Corvairs. The research animated his 1965 bestseller, *Unsafe at Any Speed*, with the Corvair in chapter 1 and a plea for auto safety laws as an overriding theme. In 1966 Congress passed auto safety legislation mandating safety belts and stronger windshields and establishing the National Highway Traffic Safety Administration.

This stunning achievement attracted complaints about other unsafe products such as flammable fabrics. Nader realized he could no longer handle them himself, so he gathered about a hundred young lawyers and founded the Center for the Study of Responsive Law to review unsafe products. It was funded by GM's $465,000 settlement of his lawsuit for invading his privacy by putting detectives on his tail. Then he founded Public Citizen, a separate group that could lobby directly, and his consumer movement mushroomed to some 150,000 members at its height. "Nader's Raiders," as they became known, published books and papers on targets ranging from the Bureau of Reclamation to the Food and Drug Administration. He also developed the concept of "regulatory capture," in which one federal agency after another became the defender of the industry it was supposed to oversee for the benefit of the public.

Carter was thinking along the same lines as the governor of Georgia when their paths first crossed at Agnes Scott College, just outside Atlanta. Nader had gone there to help students start a public-interest research group. The governor told Nader he had tried and failed to have the Georgia legislature enact a consumer protection law. Nader suggested that the consumer movement form groups at universities and felt that Carter was the only governor who actually went out of his way to support it. Their paths crossed again at a food industry convention in Atlanta during the early days of Carter's presidential race. As Nader was sitting at the head table, he heard what became a famous Carter mantra: "I want a government that is as humane and competent and good as are the American people." As the campaign intensified, Carter called Nader to seek his advice and to promise "to take my cues for regulatory appointments" from the consumer activist.[69] And he did.

None of this was a surprise. As early as January 1976, Carter gave a speech to the Consumer Federation of America that I helped shape. Declaring: "I'm an engineer and a scientist and a businessman and a farmer more than I am a politician," he promised if elected to streamline the cumbersome regulatory apparatus that stymied consumers: "I don't want anybody this year to vote for me for President unless you want me as President to completely reorganize the Executive Branch of the nation's government. And, if I'm elected President, I'm going to do it, primarily because the American people are sick of the bureaucratic confusion here in Washington."[70]

The most celebrated encounter between Carter and Nader occurred after Carter was nominated, when he invited Nader to umpire a softball game between the traveling press corps and the Carter staff; Carter was the pitcher. Nader remembered that the biggest excitement came after the game, when a fire broke out at brother Billy's gas station.[71] The relationship was cemented when Nader ate black-eyed peas with Jimmy and Rosalynn, stayed overnight at the ranch house in Plains, and had his breakfast served the next morning by the Democratic presidential nominee. Carter accepted Nader's invitation to address a thousand citizen leaders of consumer, environmental, labor, health, and elder groups, which Nader later remembered was jammed and a great success. Sharing the platform with Nader, he pledged to be the nation's consumer champion: "Consumers will now have a voice in the Oval Office," and "some of you in the audience will be going into the administration."[72] This was not just campaign bluster.

Nader was so close to Carter that he had his personal phone number, and at 2:30 p.m. on election day, when the exit polls showed Carter would win in a close race, Nader called: "Let me be the first to congratulate you!" He told Carter that he was reading his book, *Why Not the Best?* and said,

"I'm going to hold you to it." He said Carter replied, "'I want you to,' just like that." After the election Carter invited Nader back to Plains, this time with James Fallows, a Nader acolyte who became Carter's speechwriter (before his defection). They spoke for three hours, during which Nader tried to map out the hurdles the new president would face in Washington. He urged Carter to spend time at agencies and departments to infuse them with his consumer vision and to develop a strong constituency across the country. Nader observed Carter taking copious notes. For someone who could be cynical in the extreme about politicians after years of contentious public engagement, Nader noted, "I've never had anybody at the top level of politics do something like that."[73]

Carter proved as good as his word in appointing consumer advocates to high regulatory positions, and many were either Nader's Raiders or close allies of his movement: Harrison Wellford went to the Office of Management and Budget to take charge of Carter's project to reorganize and streamline the government. Joan Claybrook was named administrator of Nader's signature agency, the National Highway Traffic Safety Administration; Donald Kennedy was appointed as commissioner of the Food and Drug Administration; Henry Geller was assistant secretary of commerce and led the newly created National Telecommunications Administration; Susan King went to the Consumer Product Safety Commission; Eula Bingham became assistant secretary of Labor in charge of the Occupational Safety and Health Administration; Douglas Costle, administrator of the Environmental Protection Agency; and Michael Pertschuck was tapped as chairman of the Federal Trade Commission.

Carter also made seventy-one-year-old Esther Peterson, from the labor movement and one of the nation's most determined consumer champions, the nation's first and only White House special assistant for consumer affairs—she was also one of the most endearing public figures I have ever met. Said Pertschuck: "Carter was the first and only president to make these appointments without having a business constituency that had made substantial campaign contributions that he had to pay attention to. So he was free to make them with regard to merit." Moreover, he let them do their work and, in Nader's words, "gave them elbow room."[74]

BIG BUSINESS PUSHES BACK

Those appointments, powerful as they were, represented the high tide of the consumer movement in the U.S. government. It began receding when corporate America woke up to what was happening and struck back. Congress refused to enact Carter's proposal for an independent Consumer Protection Agency, one of Nader's public goals for years. It would have established a public consumer advocate in the administrative proceedings of any federal agency. While it would have no power to regulate, it could intervene, debate, and issue studies in the consumer interest and, in extreme cases, bring suit in federal court against an agency that improperly ignored the interests of consumers, and this is what frightened the business community. Their leaders launched a ferocious and effective counterattack that changed forever the way corporate America approached Washington.

This had been several years in the making. In 1971, reacting against the rise of Nader's consumer movement, Lewis Powell, then the president of the American Bar Association and later a U.S. Supreme Court justice, wrote a prescient memorandum, arguing that the consumer movement was imposing enormous costs on American business through consumer, safety, and environmental legislation.[75] Powell urged the chief executives of America's largest corporations to become personally involved with pending legislation and rule making, and not just rely on junior people in their Washington offices. He laid out a detailed program, including the creation of business-oriented research institutions.

This was the genesis of the Business Roundtable, founded in 1972 and it is still influential now. The major business groups joined together in Washington to give the consumer movement, Nader, and Carter a bloody nose and show their strength when laws and regulations were made that affected their companies. Nader grudgingly recognized that "the idea that the CEOs were going down to directly lobby Congress was a master stroke."[76] At the same time he realized that the traditional countervailing force of organized labor had weakened, with its membership declining under an "aging, stagnant leadership, which was self-perpetuating." And the power of business not only was enhanced by chief executives lobbying Congress, but by disbursing money through their PACs.

The effort to pass the Consumer Protection Bill is what soured Nader on Carter. A similar bill had passed both houses of Congress in 1975, but died when President Ford announced he would veto it. When it was reintroduced, Nader thought it would sail through the Democratic Congress once again, this time with a sympathetic White House. The business lobby had already taken dead aim on our tax reform bill when, as Nader put it, "The corporate jets started landing at National Airport and [their passengers] heading for the Hill. And what was a good bill came back as a Swiss cheese operation . . . a monster." Now the business community set its sights on the Consumer Protection Bill. Nader believed the White House consumer advocates had nailed down 60 votes to stop any filibuster in the Senate. The bill was scheduled to come to a vote in the House in November 1977.

But White House congressional liaison Frank Moore, who felt the bill overreached and would alienate the business community and Carter's Southern base, asked Speaker O'Neill at the last minute to delay a vote until early in the new year, without informing Esther Peterson. This gave the business community time to organize opposition in the members' home districts, and when the vote came in February 1978, it was defeated 227 to 189. Nader accused the president of not expending enough political capital to garner the few additional votes that were needed. The legislative defeat was traumatic for him after so many consumer victories in the past few years, and Nader, who wanted all or nothing, turned against Carter.

For her part, Peterson was so outraged at Frank's decision that she boarded a plane to her vacation home in Vermont and had to be reassured by the president that she would have more authority and staff to support consumer interests in all domestic-policy meetings.[77] It was worth her while, because she and the president took dramatic action in the waning days of his administration. Feverishly working around the clock on the Iran hostage crisis, he agreed to meet Esther, who, for two frustrating years, had chaired an interagency group that failed to gain agreement to limit exports of products not approved for use in the United States. When he asked her why he should sign an executive order when everyone in the administration opposed it, she leaned over his presidential desk and said: "Mr. President, because it's the right thing to do, and it's consistent with your promotion of human rights abroad." He did so less than a week before leaving office.[78]

The business community's opposition to Carter's consumer agenda was not enough to deny him lasting accomplishments through his regulatory appointees; on occupational health and safety, automobile airbags, limits on advertising aimed at children, transparency on funeral charges that bilk grieving families; and a National Consumer Bank to make loans for housing, food, clothing, retail, and insurance co-ops. The administration also accelerated the congressionally mandated fuel-efficiency standards the auto industry wanted to delay.

It was commonplace that those for whom President Carter risked his political neck often failed to come to his aid when it mattered—and only realized later what they had lost. Nader told me years later, when this principled activist had had decades to consider the dangers of demanding utopia or nothing in the real world: "I would never have dreamed that I would tell you now that the Carter administration was our last chance. We never did know it. We had a different frame of reference.. . . Little did we know."[79]

SAVING NEW YORK AND CHRYSLER

Two generations ago, New York resembled nothing so much as an exhausted heavyweight on the ropes, with the referee—the president of the United States—ready to stop the fight and let the city go bankrupt. For today's ambitious young men and women drawn to the attractions of the city that never sleeps for jobs in its finance, media, and arts, as well as its after-hours social life, such a presidential thunderbolt seems impossible to comprehend.

While the city was floundering, Gerald Ford was engaged in a life-and-death struggle for the Republican nomination with Ronald Reagan. Bailing out New York City was not the way to capture the conservative Republican vote. Ford never uttered the words in huge capital letters in that celebrated New York *Daily News* headline: "Ford to City: Drop Dead." But he did declare before the press in Washington that he would veto any federal bailout for New York. Instead he proposed legislation to help the city declare bankruptcy, asking why "working people around the U.S. should be forced to rescue those who bankrolled New York City's [profligate] policies for so long—the large investors and big banks."[1] That speech, which inspired the *Daily News* headline, may have been one of the reasons he lost the presidency to Jimmy Carter.

Together with Ford's decision to dump his moderate Republican vice president, former New York governor Nelson Rockefeller in 1976, for a new running mate, the hawkish Kansas senator Bob Dole, the stinging memory of the tabloid headline clearly helped Carter carry New York State in the general election, and helped establish our small-town candidate's urban credentials with Democratic voters across the country. It would have taken much longer for the city to recover if Carter had not moved swiftly, even before his inauguration as president.

New York was and still is the nation's largest city, but with limited taxing power on its own. Its liberal ambitions far outweighed its fiscal reach, and its problems had been accumulating for years. The city had been masking its deficits by accounting tricks, mainly by raiding the capital budget to meet operating costs. Finally, in 1975, when the city's bankers lost all faith in the politicians and balked at again kicking the can into the following year by refusing to renew the municipal credit lines, New York began running out of cash. As the city's lawyers went to the State Supreme Court with bankruptcy papers in hand, the bankers blinked and forked over money at the last minute.[2] This only temporarily averted what would have been the largest municipal bankruptcy in history, with potentially severe repercussions not only for the city but for more than 200 banks around the country that held New York City bonds—and not just for them, either. The city's mammoth municipal workforce would have been in limbo and its pensioners out of luck.

The city had lost about one-fifth of its economy during the previous seven years,[3] and between 1970 and 1978 it lost 600,000 residents, many of them middle class. Woeful mismanagement, white flight to the suburbs, and a declining tax base were exacerbated by the 1975 recession. One million people were on welfare, and the municipal debt load totaled more than $11 billion—about $1,500 for every man, woman, and child in the city. Mayor Abe Beame, a former high school accounting teacher turned clubhouse politician, proposed cutting 38,000 city jobs and denying some 300,000 municipal workers a planned 6 percent raise. In protest, sanitation workers walked out; highway workers blocked traffic on key routes; police officers blocked the Brooklyn Bridge and let air out of the tires of some of the waiting cars. New York's labor leaders had a history of tactical ingenuity. Four years earlier, Victor Gotbaum, leader of the powerful municipal workers' union, had paralyzed the city by the simple expedient of leaving 27 of its 29 drawbridges open, and when the city's financial woes became public and Beame sought concessions, Gotbaum led a protest of 10,000 workers against Citibank, calling it New York's "Number 1 enemy."[4]

So in April 1975, Governor Hugh Carey of New York State provided short-term funds on the condition that the city turn over control of its finances to the New York Municipal Assistance Corporation (Big MAC, as it became known), an oversight body created by the state legislature and headed by Felix Rohatyn, a partner in the famous financial firm of Lazard Frères. Rohatyn, a refugee from the Nazi occupation of France, was a brilliant and creative financier, and a dedicated public servant who dropped everything to help the city that had brought him to prominence. Short and wiry, with a scrub of hair and glasses but a commanding presence despite his relatively diminutive stature, Rohaytn became in effect the city's banker, rolling over the city's ballooning short-term debt while officials struggled to rein in spending.[5]

But even with his credibility and the support of the state, MAC's initial bond offering of July 10, 1975, flopped, and the underwriters had to buy in most of the bonds. The next month the wages of the city's workers were frozen, touching off strikes. In September the state legislature created the Emergency Financial Control Board, appointed to take control of the city's budget and develop a three-year plan to balance it. As things were collapsing, Ford reluctantly signed a bill in December 1975 for a one-time, short-term loan to the city that had to be repaid within a year—like throwing a life preserver to a drowning passenger as the *Titanic* was going down.

"URBAN POLICY FOR THE REMAINDER OF THE TWENTIETH CENTURY"

Seizing an opening during his run for the presidency, Carter delivered a speech in New York City on April 1, 1976, that I coordinated as the campaign's policy director. Titled "Urban Policy for the Remainder of the Twentieth Century," it laid out a comprehensive urban policy for the federal government to work with the nation's cities.[6] Clearly addressing Ford's dismissal of New York, but cautious about singling out the city by name, Carter declared: "Our cities have needed help and the Republicans have turned their backs. Our cities needed financial assistance and the Republicans have given them crumbs. Our cities needed attention and the Republicans have given them neglect." As the race narrowed, Carter took off the gloves in the final televised debate against Ford and said that a "mayor of a city like New York" needed to know that America's cities would be partners with the federal government.

Once elected, the new president came to understand that a partnership would not be an easy arrangement. Mayor Beame called the president-elect and asked for immediate help to avert bankruptcy. Carter called me, and I told him we should be represented by Orin Kramer, a twenty-seven-year-old New Yorker who was my staff specialist in banking and finance. Tall, lanky, swaggering, and provocative in the manner of his hometown, he sported a cigar and knew his way around municipal politics—perhaps too well. New York City politics are a world unto themselves, byzantine and loud, with in-your-face characters, strong union bosses, and an unforgiving press corps. Kramer had worked for a commission investigating a scandal at nursing homes controlled by a Brooklyn rabbi who was close to Stanley Steingut, the speaker of the New York Assembly and one of the most powerful Democrats in the state.

When Carter told Beame he was sending Kramer, the mayor was aghast. Kramer had testified that Steingut had tried to stop the investigation, and the Brooklyn pols complained that Carter was sending the man who "did in Stanley." Beame called back and said he thought Kramer was pretty young and inexperienced. But with my backing, Carter said the appointment had already been announced, and he stood firm. When Kramer arrived at Gracie Mansion, the mayor's official residence, they met in a basement office. Kramer felt he knew "214 facts about New York's financial situation," while Beame, who had previously been the city's comptroller and was elected on the slogan "He knows the buck," had to ask his deputy mayor: "How much debt do we have? Is it $6 billion or $9 billion?" It was neither.[7]

The city's financial plight was so dire that when Carter held his first post-election meeting with the newly named cabinet nominees and White House staff, incoming Treasury Secretary Michael Blumenthal brought along Roger Altman, a young financial wizard who was deeply familiar with the city's problems and the only subcabinet nominee invited. He would soon be named assistant secretary of the Treasury for domestic affairs. The last thing Carter needed coming into office was a financial implosion in the nation's largest city, which could impede his economic recovery plans, and Altman would be working with Kramer to avoid it.[8]

It quickly became clear that we had a stark choice: Help save the city or let it go bankrupt. There really was only one answer, but the question was how to save it for the long term, with minimum federal support and maximum local concessions. During the first weeks of the administration, Beame and the city's comptroller, Harrison "Jay" Goldin (who I found out years later was my distant cousin), came to the White House to remind the president of Beame's support in winning New York, and to collect on the general commitment he had made to help the city. The president called in Blumenthal, who promised to deliver a rescue program within thirty days.[9]

Altman and Kramer talked more than once a day, and I often joined them. They made an odd but effective couple. Altman had an MBA from the University of Chicago, and, within only five years of joining the firm, became a partner at Lehman Brothers in New York. He met Carter in early 1975 when members of the firm were invited to meet the candidate for breakfast and Altman offered to help in his campaign. He was intensely focused, laconic, and a quick study. Working with Kramer, they interviewed labor leaders, bankers, and officials from the governor and mayor on down to sketch out the concessions that each would need to make to obtain federal assistance. They also touched base with key members of Congress who would have to support any program proposed by the president.

The union leaders were especially belligerent. Albert Shanker of the teachers' union, Barry Feinstein of the sanitation workers, and—crucially—Victor Gotbaum, with 110,000 members of the American Federation of State, County, and Municipal Employees, were proud of the middle-class incomes they had negotiated with the city over the years. Gotbaum was a shrewd bargainer but also an expert in raw intimidation. He dismissed Beame as a "basket case," his mayoral successor, Ed Koch, as a "bald-faced liar," and the administration of their liberal Republican predecessor, John Lindsay, as a "disaster."[10]

But the city's abiding problem was that it could not afford its workers' high wages and benefits. A crucial player was Jack Bigel, who over the years had evolved from a union organizer to the financial adviser for the municipal unions. The leaders' confidence in Bigel was essential because he persuaded them to make major wage and pension concessions that they would never have been able to make on their own. While Altman, Kramer, Blumenthal, and Rohaytn met with the unions together, informal and separate meetings were necessary with each union. At each stage, Bigel would tell Altman what he felt each union would be willing to do. But Altman, Kramer, and Blumenthal nevertheless had to cajole and threaten them at endless meetings, with bitter exchanges, table banging, and walkouts.

The crucial break came when Gotbaum finally understood that bankruptcy would be a disaster for the city and his own members. He played a crucial role in persuading the other labor leaders to accept a partial wage freeze that was designed to protect the lowest-paid workers.

Our team and eventually the president himself had to deal with the bankers who held much of the city's debt. They were the bluebloods of New York and American finance—Walter Wriston of CitiGroup, David Rockefeller of Chase Manhattan, and John McGillicuddy of Manufacturers Hanover Trust. Their massive loans to the city were coming due, and they wanted to protect their shareholders from a default. Our plan was to require—not ask, but require—them to convert their short-term finance into long-term loans at a lower interest rate to give the city some breathing space. In all of these intense negotiations, the administration had to work in lockstep with Rohatyn's Big MAC and the state's Emergency Financial Control Board to stiffen the spines of the mayor and his team to stand up to the unions. I also worked to line up support from other cabinet departments, for example by encouraging Transportation Secretary Brock Adams to provide $280 million for New York City's mass transit system, the largest in the country.[11]

When Altman, Blumenthal, and Kramer traveled to New York, the "press attention was insane," in Altman's words. Blumenthal was surrounded by at least two dozen journalists whenever he stepped out of his hotel, which made it difficult to develop a plan. Because the package had to consist of concessions from so many of the city's disparate and warring stakeholders, our recommendations had to be kept strictly among ourselves. By the middle of 1977, our team felt we had sufficient facts to begin to sketch out the details for a plan that we could push through a reluctant Congress. Blumenthal warned the cabinet in November[12] that everyone in New York was going to have to make a major contribution. Ham Jordan, conscious of the politics of the negotiations, implored Blumenthal to avoid telling his interlocutors in the city that they should not expect long-term help from a tight federal budget that might force them to trim urban services.

At the next cabinet meeting, Blumenthal bemoaned the fact that Governor Carey had complicated matters by cutting state taxes and then asking Congress for help.[13] At our weekly EPG meeting at the end of January,[14] I delivered a tough message on the hurdles we faced in Congress. The next day I repeated the warnings[15] to Blumenthal and Ham and reminded them that the president was going to New York on February 5, and would have to clarify his position. This would mean publicly reversing Ford's refusal to provide long-term help. Moreover, trouble loomed with a potential transit strike on March 31; each 1 percent wage hike would cost the city $33 million.

Carter had shrewdly stayed out of the mess as long as possible and did not meet with the labor leaders or the banks. However, he was very much present in the way that a president should be: He laid down a marker of what he expected, kept abreast of developments, and left it to experienced officials to find the right place and time for him to intervene directly, which is exactly what happened. We brought the president into what had become a boiling political cauldron on February 2, 1978, at a meeting with the newly elected mayor, Ed Koch, Comptroller Goldin, and City Council President Carol Bellamy.[16]

The English language is not rich enough to properly describe Ed Koch. He was middle-aged and bald, had won election as mayor after serving several terms as a reform congressman from New York's Greenwich Village. Koch would give a bad name to the Yiddish term "chutzpah," the formal translation of which is unmitigated gall—like someone calling tech support to report a bug on software he pirated![17] He was pompous, prickly, disrespectful, endlessly demanding, while being short on compliments and playing to his constituents in an offensive way, and would eventually stab the president in the back over a UN resolution involving Israel just before the 1980 New York primary, despite Carter's having saved his city. There was no such thing as a private meeting with Koch; everything would be instantly leaked to make him look good. My mother, Sylvia, always taught me to look for the best in people, and I had difficulty finding it in Ed Koch. But his greatest faults became his essential virtue in the city's financial crisis, when he served as an implacable political strategist in standing up to the powerful municipal unions, banks, and other major players.

Koch treated everybody that way, and it was usually how he got what he wanted, which in beleaguered New York City took some political courage. The mayor presented us with a long list of requests, but to his credit he was on his best behavior at his first meeting with the president. More important, he understood the need for sacrifices on his side and put some on the table—reducing and extending the city's short-term credit to $1.2 billion and keeping it there; repairing the city's aging infrastructure by issuing long-term bonds with a government guarantee that underwrote major purchases by the city's union pension funds; reducing municipal workers by 60,000, with another 20,000 if necessary; and finally, ending free tuition at the city's colleges, long a signature of the path toward upward mobility symbolized by the promise of the city itself.

Koch told us point-blank: "I will stand up to the municipal unions; they can't strike. I won't spend more than we have." He pledged to end the pernicious practice of drawing operating funds from the city's capital budget and argued that his plan dealt with all the issues that had locked the city out of the financial markets. It was an impressive performance. When the president joined the meeting, Carter firmly declared: "I do not want New York City to go into bankruptcy, but this must be based upon all the local parties doing their share." He promised that the administration would take a "responsible attitude" at congressional hearings scheduled in three weeks, on February 24.

After the president left, I stayed back with Altman and Kramer to go over further details with Koch and Goldin.[18] From the administration's perspective, we were particularly concerned, and so was Congress, with what economists call "moral hazard"—the realization that once saved, any individual, company, city, or even a nation may feel free to repeat risky financial behavior in the expectation of being bailed out again (a problem that came back in spades when banks were bailed out during the financial crisis of 2008). In this case we were concerned that other cities might follow the example of New York and line up for federal help. The New York delegation understood that fully, and Goldin said they were ready to meet municipal metrics "so substantial, so burdensome, so onerous" that no other city would reach out for federal loan guarantees, unless they were "in extremis" like New York. Koch then asked us to press Governor Carey for more state assistance in a package that would also make demands on the city's unions and banks.

We also wanted to put New York City's problems in the context of a more comprehensive urban policy. During the first half of the 1970s, eleven of the twenty largest metro areas were located in the nation's northern quadrant, and together they had lost 1.5 million residents, including New York City, eroding their tax base.

During Carter's early "cabinet government" phase, Patricia Harris, the secretary of Housing and Urban Development (HUD), was given the lead to coordinate more than a half-dozen agencies to focus funds on urban areas. During that early period, the effort got off to a dubious start in October 1977, when the president and Harris went with Bronx Borough President Robert Abrams to what looked like a war zone in the South Bronx, to draw attention to the plight of inner cities, and to show that a rural Southern president cared about the problems of urban America.[19]

Four years later, however, that same site provided Ronald Reagan a campaign attack when it still looked as empty as when Carter visited. But on the thirtieth anniversary of his appearance, a New York Times article showed a vibrant neighborhood on the very site—although that could hardly be attributed to our urban policy alone.[20]

Harris, a talented but turf-conscious cabinet officer, threw her hands up, and turned the lead over to me and my staff, telling me the other cabinet departments would take orders only from the White House. We worked effectively together to bring the president's urban policy before a group of mayors and county officials in February 1978.[21] Our plan changed federal policy to locate new government facilities in central cities from every department, even the Defense Department; offered public-private partnerships with federal incentives to encourage private investment in cities; and encouraged more state aid and neighborhood self-help projects. The centerpiece was the Urban Development Action Grant Program to leverage federal dollars for private investment.[22]

For New York City we gradually put together a complex package combining state aid for the city's budget, municipal austerity by all parties, and long-term bonds bought by the banks and the unions' pension funds. If there was a hero in New York, it was Rohatyn, who knew the local players and was trusted by all sides. He backed up our demands with his own credibility, and he knew how to handle labor leaders like Gotbaum, who at six feet two inches towered over him. Afterward Rohatyn said: "I trust him, he trusts me. He is somewhat voluble, but so what if he bangs on the table? So does my son. I would make Victor Gotbaum the executor of my estate and the guardian of my children."[23]

But the fulcrum for all negotiations was an innovative demand upon which Carter had insisted from the start: The federal government would not stand behind the bonds without commitments by Koch's new administration, the unions, and the banks to restrain spending, wages, and bank fees. This established a principle that had been ignored in the largest previous government bailout, a $250 million loan authorized by the Nixon administration in 1971 to save Lockheed Aircraft, a major defense contractor.

With Congress skeptical of New York's promises, Blumenthal presented his rescue plan to Carter. Orin Kramer and I then sent the president another memo summarizing the city's perilous situation and the political risks that were vital for Carter to recognize before he approved the plan.[24] The greatest of these, we noted, was that the "package is fraught with contingencies which various parties would regard as difficult or unlikely," the most significant of which was that the city would be unable to borrow cash short-term without federal help and that its unions would not buy a sufficient amount of long-term bonds. Bluntly we told him, "although we are hopeful that Treasury's proposal is sufficient to avert bankruptcy, we are not certain that it is, and neither is Treasury."

We cautioned him to hold fast in negotiations during the months ahead, even if we had to revise the package later to avoid bankruptcy. We recommended a number of steps to which the president agreed: Call Governor Carey and Mayor Koch to endorse the plan, and warn that while it posed difficult choices for the local parties, Congress would nevertheless insist on them before approving government guarantees. We also proposed that the Treasury brief the editorial boards of the major New York newspapers and work closely with the White House to keep pressure on Congress and on New York. I felt I was doing my job combining both substance and politics by noting that "an expression of your personal concern would be very helpful," and that strong public support by Carey and Koch "will improve the political climate for us in New York, and it will assist us in securing the necessary financing commitments."

Suddenly the plan sprang a leak, figuratively anyway. An early version of Blumenthal's plan, less favorable to New York than the one we had finally gotten Carter to accept, appeared on the front page of the *New York Times*, causing a firestorm in New York and making things more difficult for Blumenthal in testifying to Congress on its latest incarnation. I was furious, and Altman was widely suspected. But the story says more about Washington than about either of us. Blumenthal quickly owned up to leaking it himself because, as he explained privately to Altman, he "wanted to know whether this thing [the tighter version] will fly or not."[25]

The essence of our strategy was that long-term financing would replace the city's annual scramble to raise cash from the banks, along with a combination of wage, pension, and job freezes, fresh loans from the New York banks at favorable interest, and spending cuts to balance the municipal budget in four years with the help of $250 to $300 million in state aid.[26]

And, central to its realization: No federal guarantees would be forthcoming without some twenty different certifications that all the local parties were making good on their commitments, including budget approval by the Emergency Financial Control Board. The process itself would be so tortuous and the concessions so painful, that, as Altman put it, repeating what City Comptroller Goldin had said earlier, "Nobody [else] would ever want to do it."[27]

Crucially, Gotbaum, Shanker's teachers' union, and other labor leaders permitted their unions' pension funds to buy more than $3 billion in New York City bonds, avoiding even worse layoffs for municipal workers. As the tug-of-war between Washington and New York was winding down, Gotbaum told a local reporter: "We could stop the collection of millions of dollars a day, turn off the water supply, pull out the ambulance drivers, leave Coney Island without lifeguards. We could rape the city. To me this would be disgraceful for any union to do it. I never think there's validity in destroying the city. I really believe that a union has a responsibility to the public."[28]

The New York City Loan Guarantee Act not only passed the more liberal House with ease, but the Senate as well, 53 to 27, with twenty senators not voting. Most of those would have opposed, but Frank Moore's White House lobbying team was able to persuade them to stand down. The president signed the bill in New York City on August 8, 1978.[29] His signing statement was one of the best short speeches he made in office. He said the importance of the bill extended beyond the limits of the five boroughs of New York City through the entire nation. New York City, he said, was not only the greatest of cities because it was the "focus of ambition," but because it "has long been the center of compassion as well, [offering] welcome and sustenance to generation after generation of newcomers looking for opportunity and for a better life—immigrants from abroad and people from the rural areas of the United States."

He told New Yorkers that the road ahead would not be easy but working together, all could ensure that once again—in the words of E. B. White— "New York is to the nation what the [white] church spire is to the village—the visible symbol of aspiration and faith." I had a lump in my throat when the president referred to that "statue in the harbor [that] holds up her lamp not for New Yorkers alone but for all of us," and I thought of my grandparents, who had come that way in that very century to this remarkable land of opportunity. But I also thought how remarkable a person Jimmy Carter was to have been raised in a hamlet in the Georgia backcountry and still be able to speak with such eloquence about the importance of a city that was light-years from his own—validating one of the things that had initially drawn me to him in his 1970 campaign for governor.

The New York City rescue plan was one of the Carter administration's most important but least heralded accomplishments. The decision-making process worked brilliantly, and the results not only saved New York City, but possibly the entire municipal bond market just as the nation was emerging from the 1975 recession.

It also saved the floundering career of a celebrated laureate of immigrant stock, a son of the Hudson River docks, once the youthful idol of teenaged bobby-soxers and an Oscar-winning actor. Frank Sinatra fished out a song from a 1977 Martin Scorsese movie, gave it his own passionate twist, and launched a new act of a triumphant career with what became one of his signature songs, "Theme from *New York, New York*," signaling the city was back.

"WHEN WE SEE THE COLOR OF YOUR MONEY, WE WILL CONSIDER SOME OF OUR OWN."

One month after Carter signed the New York City bill, I was shocked when John Riccardo, the CEO of Chrysler, came to see me with none other than Felix Rohatyn, this time in his private role as the auto company's Lazard Frères adviser.[30] I had met Riccardo several times in 1977 to hear his complaints about the cost of federal fuel-economy and auto-emissions regulations.[31] Pummeled by the recession and by competition from small Japanese cars that were superior to Chrysler's clunky models, he forecast a cash shortage of almost $2 billion over the next two years. Even after the shortfall had been whittled down to a projected $1.1 billion by the sale of loss-making subsidiaries, Riccardo begged for help. Rohatyn asserted that Chrysler could never raise that kind of money in the private market. On September 22, 1978, I organized an interagency meeting that revealed (unlike the New York rescue) a sharp division over whether we should help private companies at all. The economists argued that under our capitalist system, poor management should pay the price of its own bad decisions.[32]

While we were trying to get our hands around their problem, Rohaytn called me in October with the news that Chrysler would require major federal help early in the New Year, and might not last through the spring. Riccardo met me again in December; he was clearly panicky and depressed, again complaining of the burden of federal regulations and seeking $1 billion of direct federal help over the next two years.[33]

I immediately went to the president's private study to share the grim news. He asked me to join him on his daily run around the South Lawn: "You need to stay in condition and get exercise."[34] While I appreciated the sentiments behind this gesture, I demurred so I could get to work on our newest domestic crisis.

The UAW proposed that the government take an ownership stake in Chrysler because of its importance to the local and national economies, but we swiftly rejected this partial nationalization. Riccardo came to see me again in June 1979, backed by two Midwestern Senate Democrats, Don Riegle of Michigan and Tom Eagleton of Missouri. They brought a further tale of woe: Chrysler's truck and van sales had collapsed, and losses were mounting.[35] Riccardo returned yet again in August.[36]

I convened numerous interagency meetings, but the administration's indispensable player was the new Treasury secretary, G. William Miller. He had been the CEO of the Textron Corporation and then served as a mediocre chairman of the Federal Reserve, before replacing Blumenthal in the cabinet reshuffle. But putting the Chrysler deal together as Treasury secretary was his forte. At the central bank Miller had absorbed a principle enunciated by his predecessor, Arthur Burns, in facing down the presidents of failing banks: "We will see to it that your depositors and borrowers are protected—and we look forward to dealing with your successors."[37] If only more of banking's crowned heads had rolled when the government resolved the financial crisis of 2008, the economic and especially the political history of the United States, with its angry populist turn, might have taken a different course.

This was just the kind of challenge Miller loved. His message was direct and crisp: "This is going to take off and we've got to do something about it."[38] While he felt it was important to avoid a Chrysler bankruptcy when the economy was itself in bad shape, he found Chrysler's demands "ridiculous" and proposed a federal government loan guarantee. Miller and Altman wrenched concessions from the UAW, the banks, and the company, and along with another financial wunderkind on my staff, twenty-seven-year-old Ralph Schlosstein, Altman drafted a Chrysler loan bill closely modeled on the New York City bill with the federal government as the lender of last resort.[39] Carter insisted on stiff conditions. Before the first $500 million of a $1 billion loan guarantee was made, Chrysler's unions had to agree to $1.5 billion in wage and benefit rollbacks; state and local governments had to put up a share of the loan package; and Chrysler's banks had to relax their terms. As Altman colorfully announced: "When we see the color of your money, that's when we will consider some of our own. But not until then; it's up to you."[40]

We also insisted on one other condition: We would seal a Chrysler deal only with new management: On November 2, 1978, Chrysler's board had picked a winner, Lee Iacocca, who had recently been fired as president of Ford Motors, where this marketing genius had helped revive the company's fortunes with the sporty Mustang roadster, but had been spurned by the founding family. Although Riccardo continued to be our interlocutor, he would have to go. Just as the voters of New York had thrown out Beame and elected Koch, Iacocca became a turnaround expert of mythic proportions, aided by a bestselling autobiography with his own name as its title, establishing the cult of the CEO as hero.

Congress passed the Chrysler bill with overwhelming bipartisan support on December 20, 1979, by a vote of 271–136 in the House, led by a dynamic young Detroit area congressman, James Blanchard (later governor of Michigan), and 62–38 in the Senate. A beaming President Carter signed the Chrysler loan guarantee act on January 7, 1980, in the cabinet room, surrounded by the appreciative Michigan delegation, and a deeply grateful (for the moment) Doug Fraser, president of the UAW, tens of thousands of whose good paying jobs were saved.[41] It was the first time a government-led reorganization was done with major labor and management concessions. As I reflect, it is hard to think of a president with so many unheralded and indeed pathbreaking accomplishments who nevertheless got so little political credit for the kudos. Just as Mayor Koch turned against Carter after he saved New York City from bankruptcy, the UAW leadership endorsed Kennedy in the 1980 Democratic primaries, although the president had saved tens of thousands of their union jobs.

PART V

PEACE IN
THE MIDDLE EAST

17

THE CLASH OF PEACE
AND POLITICS

Even at the height of the Cold War, Jimmy Carter made the Middle East peace process his top priority among all the foreign-policy issues confronting the United States. He did so in ways that exemplify the central dilemma of the Carter presidency. By taking on a challenge earlier presidents had feared to confront, he achieved the first peace treaty between Israel and any Arab state. It was an accomplishment of historic proportions, reached by Carter's personal negotiations with Egypt, Israel's most powerful foe in the Middle East, that neither country could have achieved on its own. It was a cold peace but ended the war between the two, creating the diplomatic foundation for Israel's security and American policy in the Middle East for more than thirty years. Today Egypt works closely with Israel against their common foe: radical Islamic groups like Hamas, by sharing intelligence and closing the tunnels to Gaza that were used to smuggle arms to Hamas.

But Carter achieved this by ignoring domestic political constraints, straining relations with a key base of his support, the American Jewish community. Tackling an intractable issue oblivious of its political costs, he stumbled in his initial approach, corrected his course, and with huge and often painful effort achieved lasting results. Except for Cuba, there is no other issue in American foreign policy where domestic politics intrudes more directly than the Middle East. Carter's efforts caused significant schisms even among his advisers. On the one side stood Mondale, Ham Jordan, Bob Lipshutz, and I, seeking a less confrontational posture toward Israel and more sensitivity to domestic political concerns. On the other were Vance and Brzezinski, and usually the president himself, aggressively pushing forward a peace process in ways that often alienated Israel and American Jewish leaders.

The United States has had a moral commitment to Israel's survival since Harry Truman assisted in its birth in 1947 at the United Nations. This was underwritten by American public support, which sees Israel as an island of democracy in a sea of autocratic regimes, the Holy Land, and further reinforced by an American Jewish community determined that Jews surrounded by more than twenty hostile Arab countries would never again stand defenseless and without a refuge to escape another annihilating Holocaust.

But the United States also has strategic and economic interests in the Arab world, which never accepted a Jewish state in its midst. During that Cold War era, America had a powerful interest in reducing Soviet influence in a geostrategic crossroads with huge reserves of crude oil. No American president has been able to avoid prickly relations with the Jewish state, not Carter or even Harry Truman, who in recognizing Israel's independence overrode his revered secretary of state, George Marshall, who threatened to resign, but imposed an arms embargo on Israel during its war of independence. Dwight Eisenhower applied economic pressure to force Israel's withdrawal from the Suez Canal during its 1956 adventure with Britain and France that attempted to topple the Egyptian demagogue Gamal Abdel Nasser, who closed the canal. In 1967, after Israel's lightning victory over the Arab states more than doubled the size of the new nation, Lyndon Johnson negotiated a UN resolution demanding that Israel yield some of the fruits of victory in return for recognition of its right to exist as a sovereign state. The shorthand for this withdrawal policy was an exchange of "land for peace," and only Carter succeeded in negotiating even part of this exchange for a full peace. From time to time Presidents Nixon, Ford, Reagan, and George H. W. Bush all threatened "reassessments" of U.S. policy or reductions in U.S. aid to retaliate against Israel's expansionist policies or other actions, like taking out Syria's nuclear reactor, to little effect. Carter never did.

This is the story of how Anwar el-Sadat alone broke a century of enmity against the Jewish presence in Palestine over the opposition of his Arab allies and of many of his closest advisers. And it is also the story of how Menachem Begin overrode many of his oldest compatriots from the underground Irgun, which fought the British, often by violence, for Israel's independence, as well as his own deep misgivings, to reach a historic accord with Egypt that meant a total military and civilian withdrawal from the Sinai, and granting the Palestinians "full autonomy" after a five-year transition period—which, tragically, was never implemented. Yet he was unable to overcome his ideological attachment to the West Bank, which he called by its biblical names, Judaea and Samaria, to implement the commitment.

CARTER'S AMBITIONS

When Jimmy Carter began to develop the policies on which he planned to run for president in 1976, I knew that while foreign policy could not win the election, it certainly could lose it. Americans rarely vote on international issues unless they feel their own or the country's security is threatened, but they expect their presidents to know about the world and to be capable of projecting American power and working effectively with our allies. Carter was fully aware of this and had begun preparing himself by connecting with the foreign-policy establishment through the Trilateral Commission in 1975, composed of political, business, and academic leaders from Japan, Europe, and the United States, who offered him a place as a progressive Southern governor. This put him in touch with its cochairmen, Brzezinski, a brilliant Columbia University professor of international relations, whom Carter brought into the White House as his national security adviser, and David Rockefeller, a leader of the establishment and banker to oil interests at home and abroad. Even when he was still "Jimmy Who?" to the public and most of the press,[1] Carter was eagerly participating in conferences with the grandees of the industrial nations as well as experts like Harvard Law School professor Jerome Cohen in fields as arcane as Chinese law.[2]

In working with Carter as his principal campaign adviser on policy, I put special emphasis on Israel because of its political sensitivity and its importance to the Middle East, but also my own personal history. I wanted him to know that I had grown up in a home suffused with Jewish learning and culture, and devoted to Israel. My wife, Fran, learned Hebrew during a junior year in Israel, and my paternal grandfather and great-grandfather were buried there. I quickly learned I was pushing on an open door. He told me that since he was a young adult he had taught Bible classes, and support for a state for the Jewish people in their biblical homeland flowed directly from his Baptist upbringing.

He had visited Israel in 1973 as Georgia's governor, and confided to me his admiration of Israel's desert agriculture and its vaunted military, as well as its Cold War importance as a pro-American democratic outpost in the Middle East. But the public campaign was an uphill battle. While I knew that a born-again Southern Baptist would be a hard sell to Jewish voters, the best I could get from him in December 1974, when he announced his run for the presidency, was a bland promise to preserve Israel's "integrity." Even that was a struggle among his political team, who argued against anything that might detract from his basic post-Watergate campaign theme of restoring trust in government.

As the campaign evolved, I knew Carter needed to take more specific positions on the Middle East, and I concentrated on helping draft a speech in June 1976 to be delivered in New Jersey, because it would be crucial to Jews in key northeastern states, as well as Florida and California. He accepted virtually everything I put into the draft, except a phrase describing Israel as an "ally," lest it be taken as an American military commitment. As he reviewed my draft, he paused over several passages and plaintively asked, "Do I really need to say all that?!" I replied that he did, and he agreed to a text in which he expressed many of his private thoughts about the biblical basis for a Jewish homeland, as well as its great accomplishments as a productive state and an open society. And he turned away from the balance-of-power politics played by Henry Kissinger by publicly pledging that the "American people would never sacrifice the security or survival of Israel for barrels of oil."[3]

Much of what he said in the heat of the campaign, he deeply believed and pursued in office—from his pledge to act against the Arab trade boycott of Israel (Congress enacted a law during Carter's first year in office) to his commitment to promote direct Arab-Israeli negotiations (redeemed at Camp David). Unlike any other previous candidate, he cautiously opened his hand to the Palestinians by declaring that their problems had "a humanitarian core which has been neglected too long."

Other pledges had to be modified by events, but the principal thrust of the Carter speeches found its way into the Democratic Party platform, which pledged "consistent support of Israel, including sufficient military and economic assistance to maintain Israel's deterrent strength in the region." He only took exception to the platform's call to move the U.S. Embassy from Tel Aviv to Jerusalem, believing the status of Jerusalem should be decided in negotiations. These reassurances to influential Jewish groups continued through the campaign. In the November election, this Baptist peanut farmer from rural Georgia received 70 percent of the Jewish vote.[4]

In the early weeks following the election, before he named his foreign-policy team, I served as Carter's principal aide during his transition meetings at home in Plains. He held his first meetings on the Middle East separately in December of 1976, with two Jewish Democratic senators, Abraham Ribicoff of Connecticut and Richard Stone of Florida. Ribicoff urged the president-elect to launch a major Middle East peace effort because Egypt was "shattered economically" and needed peace. He also suggested a role in any negotiations for Henry Kissinger on the ground that the Arabs trusted him. Carter politely said he would not rule out Kissinger, but I knew that Carter had no intention of using a man he had publicly criticized for his secret diplomacy, however brilliantly he had operated.

But Carter did an about-face in assuring Ribicoff that he would not call another Geneva conference on the Middle East, when in fact it became an early centerpiece of his policy. Stone urged Carter not to formulate Middle East policy until he met with Prime Minister Yitzhak Rabin, who was seeking reelection as the Labor candidate in Israel's forthcoming elections—advice he would have done well to follow.[5] A month later Stone complained to me about arms sales to Arab nations;[6] he might also have been encouraged by Carter's campaign warnings against matching Soviet arms deliveries to Arab states because, as the candidate declared: "I do not believe arms sales buy lasting friends." In fact Carter had to eat those words and sell fighter jets to Saudi Arabia and Egypt to bolster his diplomacy.

That does not mean that vote-catching campaign promises are worthless and promptly forgotten after the election; but in the Oval Office competing interests come into play. Our campaign was no different. During an election, opportunities for sustained engagement on policy positions are limited. Candidates on the road are mostly cut off from their policy staff at home base, which for us was Atlanta. In addition, presidential campaigns have to concentrate on organizing supporters, coordinating with the media, and, of course, raising money. The role of policy wonks like me is decidedly secondary; making policy in a balanced and considered manner is almost impossible in such political frenzy. Once a president is elected, unanticipated events also can affect the priorities and even change the direction implied by campaign declarations.

More pervasive in foreign policy is the choice of a new president's advisers, who import their own views. Ham warned that bringing in Vance and Brzezinski would undermine the antiestablishment and anti-Washington theme of the campaign, and that is precisely what happened. These appointments were particularly crucial in shaping policy toward Israel. Far from the strongly pro-Israel and anti-Arab campaign rhetoric, they brought what they saw as a more balanced view shaped by the need to reach out to the Arab nations for a mixture of reasons. The most obvious factor was America's dependence on Middle East oil, and another, which particularly drove Brzezinski, was the Cold War. He was convinced that resolving the dispute between the Israelis and the Palestinians was central to enhancing American influence in the Arab world, to the disadvantage of Moscow, and that American influence in the Middle East would rise once this long-standing dispute was settled. As president, Carter bought into this questionable proposition.

By the time Carter was sworn in as president on January 20, 1977, Israel's military dominance of its Arab neighbors had been well established. So had its dependence on the United States, which had to come to Israel's rescue with an emergency airlift to resupply its forces and a presidential hands-off warning by Nixon and Kissinger to Moscow after the surprise Arab attack on Yom Kippur in 1973. That crisis, and the Arab oil embargo that immediately followed, established wholly new conditions in the Middle East. Israel was shown to be potentially vulnerable; the Arab nations had demonstrated their economic leverage over the West; and the potential for increased Soviet influence in the region was recognized as real. Many believed that if the situation in the Middle East were to continue to disintegrate, it could lead to a direct confrontation between the United States and the Soviet Union.

In the preceding decade two UN resolutions had shaped American engagement in reaching a peace agreement following Israel's victory in the Six-Day War of June 1967. UN Resolution 242 codified the land-for-peace formula, but couched it in characteristically ambiguous diplomatic language so it could win passage by the Security Council. The resolution acknowledged the right of "every State in the area . . . to live in peace within secure and recognized boundaries." But how would they be drawn so they would be formally recognized—especially since the resolution refused to admit Israel's wartime conquest, which gave its citizens the space to afford at least a temporary sense of physical security for the first time in the history of the young state?

Indeed, the resolution insisted that peace required a "withdrawal of Israeli armed forces from territories occupied in the recent conflict." But which territories? The English version omitted the definite article, as did the Russian version, written in a language that has no definite article. To make matters more opaque, the French version grammatically read "des territoires"—taken by one side to mean "some territories" and the other "the territories," but in any case not specifying which. Each side seized on the very ambiguity that had made passage of the resolution possible: Israel maintained that it meant Israeli troops should withdraw from *some* of the occupied territories, while the Arabs argued that Israel should withdraw from *all* of them. The United States took a mediator's position that Israel should withdraw from *most* of the territories.

In the aftermath of the next Middle East war in 1973, the United States became more directly involved through a second Security Council resolution, 338, which declared a cease-fire and called for negotiations under "appropriate auspices"—understood to be the United States and the USSR—"aimed at establishing a just and durable peace in the Middle East." The heightened rivalry between the two superpowers was played out at the Middle East conference that was convened, with Kissinger's leadership, under UN Resolution 338 at Geneva in December 1973. But Syria refused to attend, and the Egyptian and Jordanian delegations would not negotiate directly with the Israeli delegation. It adjourned quickly with little progress.

Meanwhile, Soviet influence in the Middle East began to wane despite its role as an arms supplier because many Arab countries began to suspect Moscow's potential to promote radicalism. Anwar el-Sadat, upon taking office in 1970, quickly became dissatisfied with the dominant influence of the Soviet Union. Even though he had fought against Israel with Soviet support, Sadat abruptly changed horses because he saw America as the ascending power and proceeded to expel his Soviet advisers. Saudi Arabia and Jordan joined him in seeking closer relations with Washington; geopolitics thus offered Washington the opportunity to assert leadership in the Middle East. Kissinger skillfully negotiated a series of agreements for Arab and Israeli forces to disengage from part of the Egyptian Sinai desert. When Carter took office, senior members of the new administration recognized that the United States would now have to play a leading role in brokering any peace agreement, and that they would have to move quickly when the new president's influence was strongest. From his first days in office, Carter abandoned Kissinger's incremental path of successive disengagements to seek sweeping, comprehensive peace agreements between Israel and *all* its hostile neighbors, and he revived the idea of the Geneva peace conference. It was an almost utopian program.

Why was the Middle East such a priority for President Carter?[7] Initially he told me it was simply "one of the ten things that Brzezinski and I agreed to do before I was inaugurated." Most of his advisers were not enthusiastic about his getting deeply involved in the Middle East morass, where solutions for a permanent peace had been tried and failed. But seeing growing threats to the U.S. in the region, he decided to make another try, "perhaps overly confident that I could now find answers that had eluded so many others."[8] But there was a more personal connection. Although I never detected any messianic sense, Carter's religion clearly was a factor. As he told me, "I had taught the Bible ever since I was eighteen years old, and exactly half of all my lessons have been from the Hebrew text, and the other half from the New Testament. So I knew the history; I knew the background; and I had a strong religious motivation to try to bring peace to what I call the Holy Land."[9]

He believed that God had ordained a homeland for Jews there, and in the more immediate terms of modern politics he shared the deep bond of a democratic system of government. Moreover, the timing was right—Yitzhak Rabin was prime minister, a son of the kibbutz, a veteran of Israel's war of independence, and a victorious general in the Six-Day War. "Nobody dreamed," Carter later mused, "that Begin would ever be elected; he was a terrorist; a former terrorist."[10]

From working side by side with him for four years in the White House,

I know that Carter cared deeply about Israel's security. But unlike any president before or since, he also had sympathized with the plight of the Palestinians under Israeli occupation of the conquered territories. His feelings were rooted in his own Christianity, which emphasizes Jesus' concern for the poor and downtrodden, in his opposition to discrimination against black citizens in his native South, and in his firm commitment to human as well as civil rights. He never saw an incompatibility between a secure Israel and the Palestinians' right to control their own lives.

He was hardly unaware that not a single Arab nation officially recognized the state of Israel, but he also admitted to me later that his feelings toward the Palestinians developed only after he took office. "When I became president I didn't know anything about the Palestinians; I never talked to a Palestinian, as far as I knew."[11] But during his presidency, he increasingly took up their cause, and even more so since leaving office. He has told me that in his visits to the West Bank, he sees the Palestinians living in conditions like the blacks in the South in which he grew up, but that the Israeli military treats them worse than the white police treat blacks; he finds them not militant or violent, but "just like your mama and daddy were when you were growing up: They want their kids to go to school and maybe get a college education; of course, the college has now been closed."[12]

But at that time there was no way to include Palestinians in the negotiations. After Israel's 1967 conquest, the Arab League made the fateful decision to displace the Hashemite royal family of Jordan, the most moderate Arab state on Israel's border, as the rulers of the Palestinians, and to recognize the Palestine Liberation Organization (PLO) headed by Yāsir Arafat as their sole representative. Arafat insisted on a Palestinian state to enter negotiations about the future of the West Bank and Gaza. But even though the PLO was accorded observer status at the United Nations, it was off limits for our U.S. diplomats because of their terrorist activities and Israeli pressure.

In a secret annex to a 1975 Egyptian-Israeli disengagement agreement negotiated by Henry Kissinger, he bowed to Israeli demands that the United States neither recognize nor even negotiate with the PLO, unless it accepted Israel's right to exist. Kissinger might well have brushed it aside if he felt peace was within his grasp. But in 1976 Congress nailed down the ban in a highly restrictive law: U.S. officials were forbidden to make any contact with the PLO unless it refrained from terrorism and accepted Israel's right to exist through UN Resolution 242. Therefore one of the key protagonists was effectively sidelined, and our diplomacy was hobbled. All this created an enormous barrier to comprehensive peace negotiations.

A ROAD MAP TO PEACE

How was the administration to proceed? Brzezinski had been a member of a Middle East Study Group at the Brookings Institution, along with William Quandt, a veteran of Middle East negotiations under Nixon, Ford, and Kissinger, and he knew Sadat. Carter had an important road map from Brookings—the most senior of the privately endowed think tanks in Washington. These are a uniquely American institution, stuffed with policy-oriented specialists, former officials, academics, and establishment figures waiting for their party to return to power.

Brookings leaned Democratic, and during the campaign I arranged for and accompanied Carter on a full day of briefings on energy, economic, and foreign policy. In December 1975, with the next presidential election in mind, its Middle East Study Group issued a report recommending a comprehensive settlement through negotiations at a formal conference or separate meetings. Any deal that had a chance of lasting, the study group said, would have to guarantee security for all parties, facilitate Israeli withdrawal to boundaries close to those that existed before the Six-Day War, end Arab attacks on Israel, and make progress toward normal relations and Palestinian acceptance of Israel's sovereignty. In exchange the Palestinian territories would either become independent or voluntarily federate with Jordan as an autonomous province. As for Jerusalem, the Brookings group could not define a final political status—even today no one can do so—but it outlined a goal of unimpeded access to all the holy places with no barriers dividing the city itself.

The president-elect bought the Brookings recommendations whole and entire. They could not have been more different from the campaign positions I had help craft for him as a candidate. Gone were the campaign's primary emphasis on Israel's preferred position and its security needs, our opposition to Arab arms sales, and underscoring the dangers from the Arab states. Likewise, out went the domestic political considerations of Middle East policy, and in came the Brookings report, along with two of its key authors, Brzezinski and Quandt. And out I went as the campaign coordinator for all policy, to focus only on domestic issues. But I continued to be involved in Middle East policy, as an acknowledged back channel of information with the Israeli Embassy and in a defensive mode with the American Jewish community, as political difficulties arose from the president's decisions.

Quite separately, Sadat had already realized that he would need American help to regain the Egyptian Sinai from Israel, and that meant he had to settle with Israel if he also wanted to deal directly with the United States. "It was not that he loved the Israelis," Quandt explained to me, "but Sadat realized that he came pretty close to losing [the 1973 war]—and that the war had done what it was designed to do: It had shown that Egypt was not passive and helpless and unable to shake up events. And it triggered the oil embargo, which made people realize that the Middle East crisis was too hot to leave unattended."[13]

Carter had come to the same conclusion, realizing that another Arab oil embargo could wreck the American economy and hurt his chances for reelection. But in a characteristically Carteresque stance of I'd-rather-be-right-than-reelected, he also told us that he felt so strongly about peace in the Middle East that he was willing to lose the presidency to achieve peace for Israel.[14]

At the very first meeting of the National Security Council in the new administration, Carter authorized Vance to visit the Middle East and revive America's dormant diplomacy there. He was responding to signals Washington had been receiving that the Arab leaders were expecting an American approach. As an engineer by training, Carter thought in terms of comprehensive solutions to problems, even though the checks and balances of the American political system made that difficult to achieve. But he aimed high because he genuinely believed that a comprehensive settlement would ensure Israel's security, despite the fears of the American Jewish leadership that it could be undermined by Israel's withdrawal from the West Bank.

Carter was not satisfied with an Egypt-Israel agreement alone; he wanted to forge a comprehensive peace with all the parties to the conflict, and that would not only include Egypt, but Syria, Jordan, and—critically important for Carter—the Palestinians. To do so he needed to revive the moribund 1973 Geneva conference with American and Soviet participation, which Kissinger had launched with the Soviets. This lofty goal was not as unrealistic as it might seem, because few other choices remained. Kissinger's shuttle diplomacy, with partial Israeli withdrawals from the Egyptian Sinai, had played itself out. Israel would make further withdrawals only in exchange for full recognition of Israel. Seventy-six senators—more than even a treaty-size majority—had written President Ford a sharp letter warning against using U.S. leverage to force Israel into more withdrawals.

Vance visited Israel, Egypt, Syria, Jordan, and Saudi Arabia within weeks after Carter's inauguration. The new secretary of state also met his wily counterpart, the long-serving Soviet foreign minister, Andrei Gromyko, to negotiate the terms of the conference. During his first six months in office, Carter personally touched base with Rabin and Begin of Israel, and likewise with Sadat, and then King Hussein and Hafez al-Assad of Syria. In principle everyone was amenable to reconvening the Geneva conference. But Arafat stood fast, without a prior guarantee of Palestinian statehood.

Vance asked Saudi Arabia to pressure Arafat. The administration used outside emissaries, such as John Maroz, president of the East-West Institute, who had close contacts with the PLO. Even Rosalynn got involved through Dr. Landrum Bolling, a personal friend and president of Earlham College, an Indiana school with Quaker roots. He was keenly interested in the possibilities of informal diplomacy and was asked to sound out Arafat: Would he accept UN Resolution 242 and recognize Israel's right to exist? Not unless the United States would guarantee him a Palestinian state, Arafat replied. This closed off that route for the Palestinians to join the conference on their own.

Brzezinski's views were more heavily colored by geopolitics than by the justice of either side's claims. He emphasized quick action lest the Arabs impose another oil embargo. "Time is not on Israel's side," he said.[15] Because the United States had more leverage with Israel than with the Arab states, he felt Israel would have to take more risks by trading off its conquered lands for a peace that would be guaranteed by the superpowers—a guarantee in which few Israelis would place much trust. Even though the PLO was listed as a terrorist organization by the U.S. government, he believed that the Palestinians themselves would welcome a state alongside Israel to facilitate economic development through cooperation with its more advanced Israeli neighbors.

Equally problematic was his belief that the way to neutralize the Russians in the Middle East was to co-opt them into an active peacekeeping role through a joint Soviet-U.S. guarantee, backed by an international force. The conventional wisdom of American experts on the Middle East was that the central problem of the region was the relations between Israel and the Palestinians, and by extension that normalizing them would resolve many of the region's disputes. Brzezinski believed that, too, and articulated his framework in a major article in *Foreign Policy* magazine in the winter of 1975.[16] History has not proved this thesis correct—simply consider the effects of the Iranian revolution of 1979—but for good or ill Carter adopted his position.

"Zbig," as we called him, was an outspoken professor and advocate with a clear worldview. He had sharp, angular features, short-cropped hair, and high-arched brows over narrow eyes that gave him a raptor's appearance commensurate with his hawkish views on the Soviet Union (which I shared). I deeply admired him as a man of ideas and great energy. He saw himself in the model of Kissinger, who had been his academic rival at Harvard, where he failed to earn tenure on the faculty, as Kissinger had, after getting his Ph.D. there and serving on its faculty for seven years. But he became a full professor at Columbia University, and served on the State Department's Policy Planning Staff in the LBJ administration. He spoke with a trace of the Polish heritage that meant so much to him.

His formative years provide insight into the perspective he brought to the Carter White House. He was a firsthand witness to the two great tragedies of twentieth-century European history, Nazism, and Communism. Zbig was born in 1928 in Warsaw, and his father, Tadeusz Brzezinski, was a Polish diplomat posted in Germany during the early years of Hitler's rise. Zbig moved with his family to Moscow where his father served the Polish government during the time of Joseph Stalin's great purge. The family lore is that when his family left for North America, where his father became Polish consul general in Montreal, only ten-year-old Zbigniew was at the back of the boat looking forlornly toward his fatherland.[17] Zbig had little patience for the intrusion of domestic politics into foreign policy, especially by the American Jewish community. He felt the best way to achieve progress was to pressure Israel for consensus, while maintaining a genuine commitment to Israel's security. Contrary to his undeserved reputation among many American Jewish leaders, I can attest that he was neither anti-Israel nor in any way anti-Semitic. In fact, he was proud that as a diplomat his father had saved many Jews from the Nazis before and during World War II.

It did not take long for the Israelis to challenge Brzezinski's views. Shlomo Avineri, former director general of the Israeli Foreign Ministry and Israel's preeminent political scientist, sharply criticized the Brzezinski thesis in a letter to *Foreign Policy*.[18] He argued that no Arab government had been willing to recognize Israel's legitimacy and no Palestinian had been willing to accept a state only on the West Bank. This was the very point that the American Jewish leadership and the Israeli government would make to Carter.

Before Vance left on his maiden trip, the Israeli ambassador, Simcha Dinitz, came to see me. A skilled diplomat who understood how Washington worked, he had been chief of staff to Prime Minister Golda Meir, and used every method including leaks to the press to protect Israel's position, bolstered by a quick wit and a steady flow of stories and jokes. He lamented that the new administration was creating a "poor impression" with several early decisions—reversing the Ford administration's decision to sell Israel high-power concussion bombs and blocking the sale of twenty-five Israeli Kfir fighter jets with their American-made engines to Ecuador's dictatorship. Dinitz exclaimed that he had "never seen an agreement made by one administration reneged upon by another." He was backed up by Al Schwirmer, president of Israel's largest aircraft company, who told me that America's allies in Latin America would turn to the Soviet Union for arms.[19]

When I passed all the back-channel complaints along to Brzezinski, he tried to reassure me that the decisions were not aimed at Israel but were part of the president's new human rights policy of denying arms to Latin American dictators, and placing a ceiling on U.S. arms transfers worldwide. Our leverage with Israel rested in the American components—electronics and engines—in these arms, but our policy clashed with Israel's commercial interests. Still, the Kfir decision was a needless poke in Israel's eye at a time when we were seeking Israel's cooperation to relaunch the Middle East peace process.

Leaving these decisions to foreign-policy specialists was a mistake; I weighed in, and I had at least some initial success. Ham was with me on this; his political antennae were especially sensitive to the risk of alienating the American Jewish community. Israel's supporters made the relaxation of our arms sale policy a litmus test of support for Israel. With the support of Ham, Mondale, and Senator Humphrey, I successfully urged the president and Brzezinski to make an exception to allow Israel more flexibility to export its high-tech arms, containing U.S. components. While we could not offer the privileged position enjoyed by America's NATO allies and Japan, Carter revised the ceiling upward somewhat to help meet Israel's defense needs. These were rearguard actions to prevent American policy from shifting even more strongly against Israel.

When Vance returned from his swing through the Middle East late in February, it was evident that he had received little help from the Arabs in easing the way for the PLO; no Arab government would front for Arafat in public. But he brought even worse news from Tel Aviv. Vance declared that the "Israelis are the major obstacle" to a conference because they would feel outnumbered and preferred to deal with their Arab enemies one at a time, instead of facing them together at a Geneva conference. Moreover, they opposed an independent Palestinian state on the West Bank and insisted on an undivided Jerusalem. Both Carter and Brzezinski believed it was up to the United States to define the terms of any solution—as if one could be imposed. In the margin of my yellow pad I wrote: "Hard times ahead for Israel."[20]

RABIN'S DISASTROUS VISIT

The first Middle East leader to arrive in Washington after Carter's inauguration was Yitzhak Rabin, prime minister of Israel. I had been told by Dinitz, the Israeli ambassador who (with Carter's approval) would become my regular diplomatic interlocutor, that Rabin would be comfortable with either a working dinner or a more formal state dinner. But either way, he wanted a dignified reception on the White House lawn so he could "express greetings on behalf of the Israeli people [and the] special warmth of the relationship, which he wished to keep."[21]

Rabin had every reason to expect such a welcome, and Carter granted it. When Rabin was Israel's ambassador in Washington, he traveled to Atlanta to present Carter with a handsome history of his victorious campaign in the Six-Day War, and invited him to Israel as an official guest. Jimmy and Rosalynn later crisscrossed the lands of the Bible, visiting Jewish as well as Christian holy sites, and immersing themselves as Jesus had done in the Jordan—which, to their surprise, was more a creek than a river.

But Rabin's visit turned out to be a disaster, particularly for the visiting prime minister. Carter had expected him to be warm and flexible, but he was neither. He was facing an unexpectedly tough battle in the forthcoming election from the rising Likud opposition led by Menachem Begin, Rabin's personal and political enemy since the founding of the state of Israel, when Begin had been the commander of the underground terrorist group Irgun Zvai Leumi, which fought the British authorities in Palestine.

Rabin served at first under British command during World War II while a member of the Palmach, shock troops of the prestate army formed by David Ben-Gurion's Labor Zionists. His courage and military capabilities were never in doubt, but the Yitzhak Rabin who came to Washington was in many ways an unlikely political leader. He had a receding hairline even at an early age, and his hair had turned white. He was a heavy smoker, tough and laconic. When he tried to smile, it almost seemed to hurt. He was thoroughly secular and would have been a good, if tough, peace partner for Carter, because he was devoid of religious or nationalist sentiment about the West Bank and saw it only as land providing strategic depth for Israel's defense.

A leader of the left-leaning Labor Party, Rabin barely concealed his support for Nixon's reelection, which did not endear him to the heavily Democratic American Jewish establishment. But it did repay Nixon for his military and diplomatic defense of Israel during the 1973 Yom Kippur War, which led to Golda Meir's resignation the next year. When Rabin was selected by the ruling Labor Party as prime minister in 1974, he was the first native-born Israeli to lead the nation. The Hebrew word for such a person is *sabra*—"prickly pear" in English—the fruit of a tough, spiny cactus plant that is soft and delicious inside: a good description of Rabin that would have served the administration well if the foreign-policy team had thought about it at the time.

Ironically, but for a glitch in normally split-second U.S. military timing, there would have been no need for the elections that constrained Rabin during his visit. Just a couple of months previously, four F-15 Phantom jet fighters were delivered from the United States, usually a cause for rejoicing as the first visible sign of America replacing de Gaulle's France as Israel's principal supplier of advanced weaponry. But they landed just after sundown on Friday and were given an official welcome at the start of the Jewish Sabbath, when all government functions are supposed to shut down. Rather than treat this as a minor mistake, the ultra-orthodox Agudat Israel Party filed a motion of no confidence. Labor's Orthodox coalition partner, the National Religious Party, dared not allow itself to be outflanked and was forced to abstain in the Knesset vote, bringing down the Rabin government and forcing new elections. No one imagined that the winner would be Begin, a perennial loser. Of such quirks is history made.

Rabin had to be much more guarded during the run-up to the Israeli elections than he would have been afterward. But Carter was impatient to start his Middle East diplomacy and, as usual for him when political factors came into play, he found it hard to understand why peacemaking should have to wait for an election. The president pushed hard to obtain Rabin's support for a Geneva peace conference—a poisonous idea to the Israelis because it would have brought the Soviets back into the Middle East through an international conference in which they would face a phalanx of enmity from the Arab states. He also sought Rabin's views on how to include the PLO.

At a White House dinner, Speaker Tip O'Neill, a legendary political magician, was primed by Carter to ask Rabin why Israel could not negotiate with the PLO—just as the United States had talked with the Vietcong, the French with their Algerian rebels, and above all for this Boston Irishman, the British with the Catholic underground movement in Northern Ireland, all to end their countries' wars. Rabin replied that all those groups recognized the countries with whom they agreed to talk, but the PLO did not recognize Israel and was publicly committed to destroy it.[22]

If Rabin was disappointed in Carter, the feeling was mutual. Rabin was his usual gruff self, avoiding pleasantries and small talk. To help establish a personal rapport, President Carter planned to leave the White House dinner early for a private meeting between just the two of them.[23] He told us he set it up just at the time his daughter Amy was going to sleep in the family living quarters, and he would ask Rabin to join him in saying good night to her. After that, in a rare gesture to a foreign leader, he would show the prime minister the Lincoln Bedroom. When the president made the suggestion, Rabin abruptly said no, an almost personal rejection that put Carter off his stride. He nevertheless persisted, escorting Rabin up to the personal residence and trying to pursue a dialogue. Did Rabin have any suggestions about what Carter might propose in forthcoming meetings with the Arab leaders? And especially Anwar el-Sadat, the leader of the Arab world's most populous nation, to which the others would look for leadership if the peace process started anew? Rabin did not respond at all.[24] Carter finally concluded that he simply did not trust the U.S. government any more than Israel's Arab enemies.[25] By the end of Rabin's visit, Carter was angry, and Vance observed that "the two appeared to grate on each other's nerves."[26]

The fact was that many of their differences were deep. While Carter based his strategy on a grand bargain among all the parties, Rabin regarded such a comprehensive settlement as impossible. He had come to Washington with the idea of first concluding a peace agreement with Egypt. "Once we'll finish with one Arab country we'll go to another," he said. Next would be Jordan, and through the Jordanians, and not the PLO, Israel would negotiate the future of the Palestinians and the borders of their territory. Rabin's principal argument against Carter's and Brzezinski's plan to wrap it all into one package was that when attempted, such a negotiation had never succeeded—and the Arabs did not want it any more than the Israelis. At that private session upstairs with Carter in the White House, Rabin recalled to me: "I tried to convince him why any attempt to try to tackle the whole problem in its entirety, will be wrong, because . . . one Arab leader will look over the shoulder of what another will do, and it will not work. . . . I can't say that I convinced him."[27]

PALESTINIAN HOMELAND

It was on the Palestinian dilemma that the public gap between them was deepest, and Carter blithely stumbled into it on Rabin's last day in Washington. Appearing at a town hall meeting in Clinton, Massachusetts, the night of March 16, 1977, with Rabin still in the United States, Carter was asked about the Middle East by a clergyman in the audience. He replied that he was trying to persuade the Arabs to recognize Israel's right to exist and negotiate permanent borders. But then he dropped a totally unscripted blockbuster: "There has to be a homeland provided for the Palestinian refugees who have suffered for many, many years."[28] He in effect outlined the rough shape of that homeland by declaring that there should be "only minor adjustments" to Israel's 1967 borders in any peace agreement. All of this—especially the word "homeland"—was delivered without any advance warning to Rabin or his officials, or for that matter to U.S. officials.

I accompanied the president to that meeting, which was held in an open-air amphitheater. The president was on the stage, and I sat to the side, on the stairs leading up to the stage, taking notes. When I heard him utter these explosive words, I nearly fell off my perch. I mentioned this to the president afterward, but he was unfazed.

Five days before the Israel election he tried to make amends at a press conference with these words: "It's absolutely crucial that no one in our country or around the world doubt that our number-one commitment in the Middle East is to protect the right of Israel to exist, to exist permanently, and to exist in peace. It's a special relationship. . . . And obviously part of that is to make sure that Israelis have adequate means to protect themselves. . . . I'm proud of it—and it will be permanent as long as I'm in office."[29]

But it was the president's use of the term "Palestinian homeland" that enraged Rabin, who was fighting for his political life and felt badly undercut. American Jewish leaders angrily descended upon Carter.[30] They and the Israelis already believed that the new administration was tilting away from Israel. The Likud opposition used Labor's bumpy relationship with the new American administration in its campaign. Rabin came to believe that this was truly a new American stance and that it led to Labor's subsequent defeat in the Israeli election to Begin and the Likud. Carter, for his part, felt he was not making a political statement at all but simply expressing human feelings for the conditions of the Palestinians living under foreign occupation.

The whole episode drove home to Carter's political warriors that the

Middle East was a domestic political issue as much as a matter of foreign policy, and that someone on the domestic political staff should deal with it as such. With Carter's approval, Ham expanded the duties of Mark Siegel, a deputy presidential assistant with a doctorate in political science, as White House liaison to the Jewish community. Siegel originally declined the offer lest he find himself caught between his strong feelings toward Israel and the need to defend administration policy if it diverged from Israel's interests. His loyalty to both would soon be tested.[31]

Carter's statements were actually not all that far from what Rabin really was ready to consider, albeit with variations that he would have had the freedom to advance if he had won the election. At one point in the Washington talks, he was asked how he envisaged Israel's relationship with Jordan, the West Bank, and the Palestinians. He replied like the blunt soldier he was: "Our interest in the West Bank is to ensure that no Arab military can cross the Jordan River without our knowing it and being in a position to stop it. To do that we need some outposts on the high ground of the West Bank to make it possible to see anything that comes to threaten us. That's all we need. It has nothing to do with sovereignty. But I can't say that now [before the elections]."

Rabin said this in front of the NSC's Quandt, who remembered thinking the next day that Rabin had thought through his long-term goals and was prepared to fulfill them.[32] If Rabin had been reelected and stood by his position, Carter would have been vindicated and Israel's own occupation of the West Bank might have been far less complex to negotiate. Rabin had no interest in expanding civilian settlements, although the Labor Party created some in strategic locations in the West Bank after the 1967 war. In 1977 there were only 15,000 Israeli settlers; at the time of this writing there are some 350,000, and growing.

But wading into the Middle East minefield without fully appreciating Israel's sensitivities left Carter open to making statements lacking the nuance that comes from familiarity with the shorthand vocabulary that is part of any long-running dispute. Israel and the United States supported the policy of land for peace that was the basis for UN Resolution 242, but that document contains many deliberate ambiguities. While the resolution called for "secure and recognized borders," what really makes a border secure in a region with a long history of conflict is not just whether it is recognized by diplomats but whether it can be defended by soldiers.

To a military man like Rabin as well as the million-plus Israeli voters who had served in Israel's citizen army and did annual reserve duty for many years after their initial service, a secure border is one that is also "defensible." It is defined in part by geography—high ground, rivers, access for supplies, and by a military presence. Such things would of necessity have required adjustments to the pre-1967 borders as part of peace negotiations.

After Rabin's talks with Carter and his staff, Rabin correctly concluded that they were in fundamental agreement on the sense of UN Resolution 242, if not all the details. He did his best to reassure members of Congress, Jewish leaders in America, and most important, Israeli voters reading about him back home, that he had Carter's support on many key issues. But it did not take long for the question of borders to make its way back to the White House via the press. Reporters wanted to know if Carter had endorsed the concept of *defensible* borders for Israel. No, said Press Secretary Jody Powell, trundling out the traditional party line: "We support secure and recognized borders as called for in UN Resolution 242." Rabin did not hide his dismay.

Carter's unscripted statement and the public misunderstandings that resulted were typical of his first year in office. Foreign policy is rarely best conducted by announcing major shifts in policy through a public megaphone without forewarning, not even to close advisers. And it complicates diplomacy even more when your negotiating partner is caught by surprise. There are certainly times when surprise is necessary, especially in military matters, but in general, leaders and senior legislators abhor surprise, because it makes them look uninformed and left out of important policy decisions.

Long afterward, Carter told me that he realized he had lost a tremendous amount of Jewish support because he talked about a Palestinian homeland and "dealt with very sensitive issues in a politically foolish way. . . . You don't accumulate support from the moderates who say that is a good idea; you accumulate collectively fervent opponents."[33] In fact, the very day after his remarks, I was traveling on Air Force One with him and relayed a private request from Dinitz for Carter and his team to be more prudent in what they said about Israel during the weeks before Rabin faced Israel's voters.

Carter was noncommittal, but asked me to continue to transmit personal messages outside normal diplomatic channels. I remained a back channel with Israeli ambassadors and their senior staff for as long as Carter remained in office, explaining the president's policy, seeking Israeli views, and often passing along ideas at Brzezinski's request.[34] (I was not the only one. Leon Charney, a New York lawyer who was also the American attorney for Ezer Weizman, defense minister during the Camp David talks, served as an essential and unsung channel with White House Counsel Bob Lipshutz to Weizman and Begin, especially in tying up the details of the peace treaty.)[35]

At a cabinet meeting in mid-March, Carter reviewed the situation after Rabin's visit and defended his comments as "proper and necessary to break loose positions on both sides." He said the Arabs were right to insist on the pre-1967 borders for Israel and that Israel had no justifiable claim on the territories it had captured, but at the same time the "Arabs need to get their act together" and agree on ending the state of war with Israel, on new borders, and on settling the future of Palestine.[36]

He was soon to discover how difficult it would be to settle such matters between Israel and only one major Arab state, let alone more than a dozen of them.

SADAT'S TRIUMPHANT VISIT

Early in April, Sadat came to Washington, and the contrast with Rabin could not have been more pronounced. Carter saw Sadat as a "shining light" who brightened the prospects for Middle East peace and, more practically, a potential friend and ally.[37] Rabin had been so cool and reserved that he made Carter look warm—no small feat—and it was easy to be mesmerized by Muhammad Anwar el-Sadat. He was warm, ebullient, loquacious, and jocular—a natural politician who cut a striking figure with jet-black curly hair, wide lapels on his tailored suits, and striking ties. He had an almost regal bearing and, like the general he had been, he stood ramrod straight. He was one of thirteen children born to an Egyptian father and a Nubian mother, who passed on her dark skin color. It was clear from first sight that he was a devout Muslim, since his forehead bore the mark that comes from a lifetime of kneeling with head to the ground during daily prayers.

Although both men had fought to free their countries from their British colonial master, the formation of Sadat's early military career was the exact opposite of Rabin's, who had begun his service with a Jewish unit of the British army. Among Sadat's influences were Kemal Atatürk, who created the modern secular state of Turkey, the non-violence of India's Mahatma Gandhi, and at the other end of the spectrum, Adolph Hitler, less for his violent ant-Semitism than his opposition to the British.

One common thread also connected Sadat and Begin. Each in his own way had resisted the occupation of his country, and each had been arrested or hunted by the British for doing so. But Sadat's path was far different. After World War II, Gamal Abdel Nasser and other disgruntled junior officers including Sadat formed a secret group that overthrew the sybaritic and corrupt King Farouk in a 1952 military coup. Nasser became a hero of the Arab world for his pan-Arab vision and strong opposition to Israel. He appointed Sadat to a succession of senior positions and ultimately as his vice president. When Nasser died in 1970, Sadat succeeded him, and surprised virtually everyone by emerging from Nasser's long shadow. Egypt's early military success in the 1973 Yom Kippur War electrified the Arab world and made Sadat a hero.

But he understood that neither Soviet arms nor Soviet military advisers had saved him, and came to view the Soviet Union as a declining power. He expelled its advisers and pointed Egypt in a Western, specifically American, direction. But Middle East peace was not his first priority when he sat down to dinner with Carter and his advisers; that came later in his private meeting with the president. He made a forceful appeal for U.S. arms to replace those no longer coming from the Soviet Union and to help stop the Soviet incursion in Africa.[38] With the Cold War raging and the Soviets supporting Cuban proxies throughout Africa and the developing world, there was a critical need to support Sadat. Then as now, Egypt was a Middle East linchpin as the largest and most powerful Arab state. To supply Sadat with American arms and resolve the Middle East deadlock by encouraging Israel to withdraw from the Sinai in exchange for peace would not only strengthen Sadat's hand, but significantly enhance Washington's standing and influence at Moscow's expense. This geopolitical dimension was not fully grasped by the Israelis and much of the American Jewish leadership.

As he had done with Rabin, Carter took Sadat upstairs to the private residence, but with more positive results. He assured Carter he would cooperate with his administration but would never have diplomatic relations with Israel and never open the Suez Canal to its ships—but, as Carter later related, "he would be willing to help me."[39] A CIA leadership profile prepared for Carter advised him that Sadat "wants to go down in history as the man who improved the economic and social well-being of the ordinary Egyptian. . . . A consummate politician, he looks at most issues in political terms."[40]

But his closest advisers were not certain about their own leader. Foreign Minister Ismail Fahmy, a friend from their revolutionary days, wrote later that while sincere and direct, Sadat "also seemed to be very isolated, with no special relationship with anybody, in fact, distrustful and contemptuous of those around him."[41] Sadat's ability to stand apart from his own delegation became vital to the peace process. Because Sadat trusted Carter, he was repeatedly willing to take Carter's word that certain steps were necessary. And because Carter truly believed Sadat wanted peace, he was willing to take repeated political risks to maintain the momentum of the negotiating process. For example, while Sadat held out against recognizing Israel, he was open to the possibility of ending Egypt's trade boycott and of establishing demilitarized zones in the Sinai.

THE SWITZERLAND OF THE MIDDLE EAST

About that same time, though, Israeli politics were shifting in a way that would change it and the Middle East, not just during the Carter years, but for the decades that have followed. As Sadat's visit to Washington was ending, Dinitz called me to warn that Rabin's resignation was imminent—even before the elections—although he would stay on until then as caretaker prime minister. The Israeli press had uncovered dollar bank accounts in the name of his wife, Leah, most likely left over from his years as ambassador in Washington. In those years Israel erected strict currency controls, and individual

Israelis had to have official permission to hold money abroad. Even though the law was more honored in the breach than the observance, no Israeli politician could survive such a disclosure in a country where a modest style of life was a foundation of the pioneer culture.

Dinitz added that Shimon Peres, an experienced cabinet minister and protégé of Ben-Gurion, would almost certainly be Rabin's successor and lead the Labor Party list in the elections. I let Brzezinski and the president know immediately.[42] What followed had been foreseen by no one in Washington. Ben-Gurion's party had dominated Israeli politics since independence, but like so many parties too long in power, it suffered from general fatigue in its own ranks and with the public. Rabin's bank account was apparently the last straw for the governing party's leaders.

Thus unfolded a series of exchanges with Dinitz through the month of April into early May. He insisted they must be held in strictest confidence because any leak could lose the election for Labor. Dinitz told me that he had instructions from Rabin and Peres to pass on "reliable Israeli intelligence reports from Cairo" that Sadat had confided to his intimate circle that he interpreted his talks with Carter to mean the president could trade Egypt's cooperation for the territory the country lost in 1967 and obtain a state for the Palestinians in the West Bank, as well. That would mean an Israeli withdrawal from the Egyptian Sinai, one of Sadat's goals to reverse the humiliation of two Egyptian military defeats.

Then we got to the fundamental fear of the Israeli establishment. Dinitz said Israel might be forced into a deal concocted behind its back in Washington: "We can't accept the fact that the U.S. has a plan, as this would foreclose negotiations."[43] I told Dinitz that I could not conceive of the president telling Sadat these things privately, but I would find out. He phoned again the next day with more alarming intelligence: Sadat was telling his people in Cairo that not only would the Americans continue to patrol the demilitarized Sinai as part of a peace agreement but "possibly Russians, too, if both sides wanted it." Even more upsetting—to both of us—was Dinitz's claim that Sadat and Fahmy were saying Carter had assured them the Israelis would accept all this. We knew that they had not even been consulted, and when

I reported to Carter, he instructed me to tell the ambassador his intelligence was "incorrect on borders, the PLO, and the demilitarized zone."[44]

While I cannot say Dinitz was entirely satisfied, he was at least somewhat relieved.[45] Nevertheless the back channel continued humming with another warning from Dinitz that the Arabs were beginning to think "they will get what they want, and if they don't, they can be driven to war." He feared that Carter would publish a peace plan, and with as much emphasis as he could muster, he said: "If the president will devise a formula and Israel will not like it, there will be no reason to negotiate with the Arabs, and we will be on a collision course with the United States. The more public and precise the president is with a plan the worse it is." The American role, he said, should be to consult with all sides and create a framework for negotiations, but not create any plan that would push Israel back to its 1967 borders and accept a Palestinian state: "No Israeli government, however moderate, can accept this."

Dinitz then handed me a three-page paper containing excerpts, marked with ominously underlined sentences, from recent remarks by Carter, Vance, and UN Ambassador Andrew Young, all bearing the imprint of classic American diplomacy. The State Department has long been an Arabist redoubt, if for no other reason than that there is only one Jewish state and 22 Arab states, some with huge oil reserves. In fact America had always moved cautiously; most people forget that Truman, after recognizing Israel following the UN vote, imposed an arms embargo when the fledgling state was fighting its war of independence. In most administrations, the White House counterbalances the State Department's bias because of domestic political considerations or a greater sensitivity to Israel's security needs.

In the Carter administration, while Mondale, Ham, Lipshutz, and I served as ballast, none of us were decisive actors. And without a weighty counterbalance, Carter's instincts mirrored those of the State Department and were reinforced by Brzezinski. Zbig saw almost every issue of foreign policy through the anti-Soviet lens of a true Cold Warrior, and likewise saw Israel standing in the way of a diplomatic process that would weaken Russia's hand in a strategically important part of the world.

Thus I was not surprised when Dinitz alleged that Brzezinski had warned him that, depending upon whether there was a peace agreement, his small and vibrant nation could either be the Switzerland of the Middle East or the region's Vietnam. Dinitz stressed that this warning had been delivered in a "threatening tone regarding Israel moving toward America's views—or else."[46] I wondered if Dinitz had embellished Zbig's comments into a threat.

Meanwhile, Jimmy Carter's first excursion into diplomacy in the Arab world seemed to yield results. On May 9, he met with the brutal dictator of Syria, Hafez el-Assad, in Geneva because Assad had sworn he would never come to the United States.[47] He ruled by murder and assassination, but he was an impressive negotiator and strategist and could turn on his charm when it suited his goals. He could sit across the table for hours without taking a bathroom break, all the while offering heavily caffeinated tea to his American interlocutors. Carter found—or thought he did—a constructive attitude he had encountered in neither Israeli nor Arab leaders. To Carter, Assad was somewhat flexible, and he noted that Assad had told him that a year or two earlier it would have been almost suicidal in Syria to talk about peace with Israel—but they now seemed willing to cooperate.[48] (He later revised this view in his memoirs when it turned out that Assad sabotaged the Geneva peace talks by refusing to attend.)

Returning to Washington, Carter met with Saudi crown prince Fahd, who indicated that the Arab side wanted peace. But what the president ultimately came to recognize in his dealings with both the Arab leaders *and* American Jewish leaders was a "disparity between their private assurances and their public comments." While the Arab leaders were more flexible during private talks about ideas for peace and, aside from Sadat, unwilling in public to acknowledge a willingness to deal with Israel, American Jewish leaders, he said, would privately "deplore Israeli excesses, but in a public showdown on a controversial issue, they would almost always side with the Israeli leaders" and condemn the administration.[49]

For a president who would make Middle East peace his prime goal and a priority for his time and energy, Carter brought little previous experience in the region. He was in no way unsympathetic to the American Jewish community or to the state of Israel, and his deeply held Baptist beliefs honored the place of a Jewish state. But coming from a rural upbringing and a place with few Jews, unlike an urban politician, he had not experienced the organized Jewish community firsthand. Moreover, although he certainly knew about the impact of the two millennia of Jewish exile from Israel—the horrific discrimination, violence, and expulsions of Jews from one nation after another, culminating in the massive Nazi Holocaust, I do not think he fully internalized the collective impact on Israeli attitudes. Nor did he fully appreciate the deep spiritual symbolism of Jerusalem in Jewish prayer, the longing for a return to Zion, and the consequent emotional hold of the new state of Israel on the American Jewish community. To them it had been created almost miraculously out of the ashes of the Holocaust on the very same land where the Jewish religion was born thousands of years before. At a minimum—and usually much more than that—Israel was an anchor against the insecurities of Diaspora Jews, to say nothing of the Israelis themselves surrounded by a sea of armed enemies.

While Carter was engaging the Arabs, I held my first of innumerable meetings with Alex Shindler, a silver-haired and sharp-tongued Reform rabbi who was the president of the umbrella Conference of Presidents of Major Jewish Organizations, representing some forty in all. He suggested a monthly meeting of a dozen or so of the Jewish leaders with Carter's cabinet-level diplomatic and security team—a somewhat unrealistic request. These meetings took place only periodically, although if they had been convened more frequently, we might have avoided some of the political downdraft from the president's aggressive pursuit of Middle East peace.

I received anguished telephone calls about the president's position on Israel from special Atlanta Jewish friends—Cantor Isaac Goodfriend of the synagogue of which my family were longtime members, and who had been invited by Carter at my request to sing the national anthem at the inauguration; and the esteemed Orthodox rabbi Emanuel Feldman, who read me a headline from the *Jewish Press*: "Carter Tilts Toward Arabs."[50] While I assured them of Carter's strong support for Israel, Carter told me that his meetings with Arab leaders had convinced him they "are really willing to have peace with Israel." He confided he had to decide "by the summer whether to make a go-or-no-go on Middle East peace." He felt the time was ripe, and reassured me that the "Arabs don't want an independent Palestinian state and are as concerned as we and Israel about its potential militancy."[51] He repeated this in stronger terms before a meeting with congressional leaders: "The Arabs are not feeding me BS and are serious about peace."[52]

Shortly afterward, I joined Brzezinski for his first meeting with the American Jewish leadership. They were headed by the dean of Jewish leaders, Max Fisher of Detroit—a rather impolitic choice as spokesman because he was an ardent Republican and supporter of Nixon and Ford. I sat in and took notes.[53] Brzezinski began by asking that, in order to encourage frank exchanges, the Jewish leadership keep the substance of their meetings out of the newspapers, a request honored only in the breach. He spoke forcefully of a "special organic relationship with Israel" and reemphasized the administration's commitment to Israel's security. Fisher echoed Israel's official concerns and the apprehensions in the Jewish community over the administration's policy toward Israel. He then referred to a supposed "American plan" for Israel to withdraw from and turn over the conquered territory to "an independent West Bank state headed by the PLO." This was a wild exaggeration, and Brzezinski calmly replied that now that Israel's permanence as a state was secure, it was time to start asking what type of peace Israel should have if the Arabs ended their state of war. He explained that "any change is painful" and that "Israel could become the Switzerland of the Middle East if there was peace," the same phrase Dinitz had reported to me, but without any sense of threat.

This entire exercise quickly demonstrated the special triangular relationship among Israel, the American Jewish leadership, and the Congress in effectively applying pressure on the presidency to modify U.S. policy to Israel's benefit. This is unique in the annals of diplomacy. There are other countries, such as Britain, that have a favored relationship with the United States but exert their influence through traditional diplomacy rather than relying heavily on a domestic American constituency and lobbying Congress. For a vulnerable, small country like Israel, surrounded by enemies, perfecting this unusual brand of political diplomacy was essential. While it existed to a more limited degree before the Carter administration, it was honed to much greater use during our term in office. Since then it has only grown in dimension and intensity to be one of Washington's most effective lobbies. Carter was to discover this through painful experience.

He spent hours in the Cabinet Room and Oval Office trying to explain and demonstrate his commitment to Israeli security to American Jewish leaders. In these private sessions, he ruminated years later, "I would get individual Jewish leaders to say, 'We understand, Mr. President, you have to deal with Palestinian rights.' But then when you get those people in a collective group, they are very reluctant to say the same thing where others can hear." He likened this to other advocacy groups for lawyers, doctors, and even peanut warehousemen. "It is the same way, I think, with the Jewish community . . . you kind of reach the lowest common denominator and consensus is quite often the safest position."[54]

BEGIN THE BEGIN

The Israeli elections of May 17, 1977, were a watershed in Israeli and Middle East political history, and profoundly changed the calculus of Carter's peace policies, while challenging the views of American Jews. I had been warned by the Israeli Embassy to expect gains by Menachem Begin's party, and I was anxiously awaiting the returns aboard Air Force One as we returned from California after discussing domestic problems of drought and energy. I went to the communications center on the president's plane, and was stunned by the news. Begin had run in eight consecutive elections, never garnering enough seats in the Knesset to form a government, and had even sustained a heart attack during the campaign.

But the Likud coalition led by his Herut (Freedom) Party had captured 33.4 percent of the popular vote and enough seats to form a governing coalition with the splinter centrists and the religious parties. But this was no simple political game of musical chairs. It was a historic ideological change of incalculable importance to the peace process affecting the region, the Palestinians, and relations between Israel and the United States ever since. The Israeli television anchor Haim Yavin, announcing the election results to an anxious nation, repeatedly and with disbelief proclaimed: "Ladies and gentlemen, *Mahapach!* Upheaval!"[55]

I raced into Carter's cabin, gave him the results, and warned that this could spell trouble. Begin had distinctly different views on the future of Gaza and the West Bank; indeed, he called the latter by their biblical names, Judaea and Samaria, and saw them as "liberated—not occupied—territories." The president seemed nonplussed but said simply, "I can deal with it." It would not be so simple. The conservative Likud and its nationalist and religious allies remain Israel's dominant political force well into the second decade of the twenty-first century, and during all that period showed little interest in yielding the large parts of its conquered territories that had been its main bargaining chips for peace with the Arabs.

Begin was Israel's first leader from the conservative Revisionist wing of the Zionist movement and brought a profoundly different version of Zionism than that of the dominant socialist Labor Party. The differences went back to the very founding of the modern Zionist enterprise by Theodor Herzl at the World Zionist Congress in 1897 and beyond. Begin was a disciple of Vladimir Jabotinsky from Odessa, who, like Herzl, was convinced by the Drefyus Affair in France and the deadly anti-Jewish Kishinev riots in Moldova in 1903 that European Jewry needed its own state in its ancient homeland. Both sought to found the Third Jewish Commonwealth following two thousand years of exile after the Romans destroyed the Second Temple in Jerusalem.

But Jabotinsky's vision of how to found a Jewish state in what was then Ottoman-controlled Palestine (and was mandated to British control by the allied victors of World War I) was dramatically different from the mainstream secular Zionism of Chaim Weizmann and David Ben-Gurion. At the 1933 World Zionist Congress a bitter battle broke out between Jabotinsky's faction, which wanted to campaign openly for a Jewish state, and Ben-Gurion's majority, which wanted first to build upon and expand the small Jewish community in Palestine known as the Yishuv, already formally recognized by the British and by the Ottomans before them. Although he was not personally religious, Jabotinsky's goal, and that of his young follower Menachem Begin, was fulfilling what they believed was God's biblical promise of a Jewish homeland from the Mediterranean Sea to the Jordan River, and even beyond. Jabotinsky founded the Betar movement in 1923 in Riga, Latvia, which would later become the Herut and then the Likud Party we know today. While the Zionist slogan always was "A land without a people for a people without land," the argument between the two factions was about how to obtain that land and how large it would be—with the status of its Arab inhabitants little discussed.

When Jabotinsky died in 1940, the mantle of leadership passed to Begin. The sharp divisions continued after the end of World War II, as Begin formed a militant underground group, the Irgun, to drive the British out of Palestine by violent means. Their most notorious act was blowing up the British headquarters in Jerusalem's King David Hotel in 1946.

After the United Nations partitioned Britain's Palestine Mandate into Jewish and Arab territories on November 29, 1947, Ben-Gurion proclaimed the state of Israel on May 14, 1948, and accepted the partition, while Begin objected to it as a rump state, and the Arabs rejected it outright and went to war against the new Jewish state. The division between the Revisionists and the Labor Zionists was fierce and at times deadly, because it was based not just on the usual politics that divide parties in any thriving democracy, but on competing visions of the Jewish State. In June 1948 the ship *Altalena*, bringing men and arms for the Irgun, was shelled off the Tel Aviv harbor by the Israel Defense Forces (IDF), as Ben-Gurion was determined to end all prestate militias. The commander of the IDF on the Tel Aviv shore was a young officer, Yitzhak Rabin, whom Begin would succeed as prime minister in 1977, Carter's first year in office.

When Israeli troops conquered the Arab remainder of the partitioned land in their defensive Six-Day War of 1967, for the Labor Party, these territories and the handful of trip-wire settlements they erected in the Jordan Valley were important security buffers that could be traded in part for peace and security guarantees. For Begin and his followers they were much more: a historical redemption of their claim to the whole of the occupied territory, as much a part of Israel as Tel Aviv and Haifa. The Likud-led governments dramatically expanded settlements in the conquered territory, creating facts on the ground to establish the right of Israelis to live there permanently.

The tensions between Carter and Begin and between Israel and the United States today have their roots, in part, in the dominance of Begin's vision.

The internal ideological quarrel was left unsolved at Camp David and festers even now. As Carter would soon learn, Begin held a similar view of the conquered Egyptian territory: Although not a part of what Begin considered the God-given land of Israel, the Israeli settlements that had sprouted in the Sinai after the Six-Day War were also critically important. Had the Carter administration better understood these profound differences, Rabin might have been supported more positively during his first visit to Washington, although that still might not have ensured the election of his successor Shimon Peres as the leader of a tired Labor Party, which had been in power for thirty years.

But no American in authority, nor American Jews who had known only Labor governments since the founding of the state, imagined that Begin might win. He rejected the land-for-peace trade embodied in UN Resolution 242. When the Labor government agreed to participate in the Geneva conference convened by Kissinger in 1973, Begin railed: "Your policy will lead us to destruction."[56] This was the Israeli leader Jimmy Carter faced in Begin's first year in office—and his own.

Like virtually everyone in Washington's high places I was no expert on Menachem Begin, but I knew enough to realize how the election of this classic political outsider would transform the president's Middle East policy. I became increasingly informed about this remarkable man, whose views differed so greatly from what had been for decades established Israeli policy and from the direction in which Carter wanted to move. What I did not immediately appreciate was that Begin's election was not simply a rejection of the fatigued and complacent Labor Party with the baggage of its near-defeat in the Yom Kippur War. It represented a profound demographic and philosophical shift in the Israeli electorate, which increased over the decades.

Although a thoroughly European Ashkenazi Jew, who dressed more formally than most Israelis, with a starched shirt, tie, and suit, Begin appealed to the Sephardic Jews as an outsider. By the hundreds of thousands they had been expelled from the Arab lands of North Africa, Iraq, and Syria, whence they poured into Israel. The Ashkenazi Labor Party establishment, overwhelmed by the flood so soon after the founding of the Jewish state, dumped them into newly built development towns, often barren and windblown, at the edge of the desert. In their native Arab countries, many had been prosperous merchants and professionals with Orthodox beliefs and a distinctive Jewish culture they could trace back many centuries, but here in their homeland they felt abandoned and discriminated against by the successors of the dominant, secular Labor Party pioneers. In Begin they saw a kindred spirit, observant and respectful of their culture, who had skillfully campaigned on providing them equal treatment. With the dramatic growth of the ultra-Orthodox *haredim,* who interpreted literally the biblical injunction to be fruitful and multiply, and the emigration of one million Jews from the former Soviet Union, who brought hawkish Russian views on security with them and applied them to the Arabs, a strong and enduring Likud political base had been built.

This base remains in power right down to the government of Benjamin Netanyahu today, but with significant intervals of moderate governments in between. Begin's most important political move was his choice of foreign minister—Israel's most famous soldier, Moshe Dayan, who was seeking to rehabilitate himself after his forced resignation following the Yom Kippur War. The other fateful choice was his defense minister—Ezer Weizman, the nephew of Israel's first president and architect of its air force. Their appointments were designed to help Begin shake his reputation as an underground terrorist leader.

The American press saw Begin as an extremist. Shortly after the election, *Time's* foreign editor penciled into a story on one of the magazine's signature pronunciation guides: "Begin (rhymes with Fagin)." He later claimed he never realized it would be seen as offensive, but even the magazine's Jewish editor did not stop it from reaching print to an inevitable outcry of anti-Semitism.[57] On May 19, Brzezinski and I met informally with the president in his study to discuss the implications of Begin's election. The president expressed "deep concern" about his views. Brzezinski took an optimistic position that "precisely because Begin is so extreme, the President will be able to mobilize on behalf of a settlement a significant portion of the American Jewish community."[58] I firmly disagreed and warned them that was not how things worked in the organized part of the American Jewish community: Jewish groups would rally to Begin's views as a demonstration of their unyielding support for Israel, and that any effort to peel them away from Begin would be a grave and costly political mistake.

In the long run it made little difference to the initially shocked American Jewish leadership that Israel had exchanged the practical idealism of its Labor Party founders for a new leader who reflected the sharp divisions within the Zionist movement. Ordinary American Jews were hardly aware of the Revisionist wing founded by Begin's idol, Jabotinsky, who died before he could settle in Palestine. But Jabotinsky's goal of a greater Israel was literally sewn into the Irgun flag: it extended even beyond the Jordan to the full territory of the old British Mandate, with a rifle overlaid on the map. Begin publicly kissed that flag at a ceremony when he emerged from hiding. As Carter learned more about Begin through a CIA profile and, shortly after his election, watching him in a televised interview, he found it "was frightening to watch his adamant position on issues that must be resolved if a Middle Eastern peace settlement is going to be realized."[59]

What most observers did not know was that Begin began pursuing better relations with Israel's Muslim neighbors almost immediately after his election. He secretly met with the Shah of Iran in Tehran, then with Nicolae Ceaușescu, the Romanian Communist dictator who had good contacts with the Arab countries. Begin went further, instructing Attorney General Aharon Barak to draft, with Foreign Ministry legal adviser Meir Rosenne, a peace agreement with Egypt, but not a Carter-style comprehensive peace settlement.[60]

Meanwhile, the president told the Democratic leadership in May that the Israeli elections had "done a lot to dramatically moderate Arab leaders' expectations," and that while he frankly did not know what Begin would do, he planned to press ahead toward peace in the Middle East.[61] Later that day we met with Brzezinski, who concluded that it would be better to deal with Begin and his "hawkish coalition," since they could make any agreement stick with the Israeli public. This replay of the Nixon-in-China turnabout simply did not apply here and never would. There was no way that Begin would yield on his principles, as we all would soon learn.

The American Jewish leadership, at least initially, was also worried about the impact of Begin's election. Hyman "Bookie" Bookbinder, the head of the American Jewish Committee's Washington office and a colleague in the Humphrey presidential campaign, called to report "unanimous concern and dismay" at meetings of mainstream American Jewish groups (but not what he called the "ultra-groups"). All were wrestling with the profound change in Israeli politics. But he warned us to avoid any lobbying that might split the Jewish community, whose leaders believed that Carter's own statements had helped cause the political upheaval in Israel.[62] But soon enough the administration's positions would unite the American Jewish leadership behind Begin, whatever qualms may have initially existed. Bookbinder called back in early June to tell me that Ambassador Dinitz was informing them that the Arabs believed Carter would force Israel to withdraw to pre-1967 borders and accept an independent Palestinian homeland.[63] What Carter and Brzezinski did not fully understand was that support for any incumbent Israeli government was the ultimate litmus test of Jewish identity for mainstream Jewish leaders. It remains so, even when sorely tried by Israeli politicians. Many leading American Jews fear that publicly undercutting Israel's leaders would weaken Israel itself and impair their own ties to the Jewish homeland and the Israeli leadership, which is a symbol of their clout.

I began to observe a pattern developing in which the president seemed to overlook negative positions of the Arab autocrats in order to accentuate what he saw as their positive side. At a cabinet meeting on May 23, he applauded Saudi Arabia's restraint on energy prices and declared: "The Saudis have been the most gratifying to me since starting office in every way." I put in my marginal notes "JC's love affair with the Saudis."[64] Things were not going well with Israel. The Israeli press published a so-called fifteen-point American plan supposedly emanating from the White House. Brzezinski told me that there was no such plan, although ideas were being developed, adding that anyone giving them away "was hurting relations."[65]

The political atmosphere was growing heated, and Ham convened a meeting including Brzezinski and several Jews serving in the White House. We decided that to restore calm we had to explain to Jewish groups that our definition of peace for Israel lay well beyond Nixon's and Ford's limited idea of ending Arab belligerency, and extended to full normalization of diplomatic and commercial relations.

The most troubling question since Begin's election was the political status of the West Bank, and we realized that the administration had to back away from Carter's unscripted commitment to a Palestinian homeland, certainly at least until the PLO recognized Israel's right to exist on the other side of an agreed border. I was about to get an up-close-and-personal lesson in how the Jewish community works in Washington and how a White House deals with it.[66]

HAM'S BLUNT WARNING

To achieve the president's goals, we were going to reach out to Vice President Mondale and his political mentor, former vice president, now-senator, Hubert Humphrey, both of whom were trusted champions of Israel. Humphrey issued a helpful press release describing Carter as "an unswerving supporter of the State of Israel, who was carefully moving in the right direction in the Middle East."[67] Mondale had his staff spread it throughout the Jewish community and Congress.

Then, to tamp down tensions, Ham, Mark Siegel, and I met early in June with Morris Amitay, the executive head of the American-Israel Public Affairs Committee, or AIPAC as it is universally known in Washington. With his fierce visage, framed by bushy eyebrows and a thick black mustache, and his blunt manner, he had made AIPAC into the effective spearhead to promote stronger Israel-U.S. ties that it remains to this day. His argument was that "the more secure Israel is, the more willing it is to concede," and he raised the reports of the supposed secret plan to pressure Israel into concessions and split off the West Bank. We told him that there was no such plan, but he continued to stress Israel's need for American support: "The Arabs think the U.S. will push Israel without their doing it, and this makes Israel feel vulnerable. . . . [But] if the Arabs realize the U.S. won't abandon Israel, they'll come to terms with Israel." I was surprised at Ham's candid response conceding that Carter had not given Israel the assurances it needed, adding that the administration wanted to "disabuse the Arabs of the notion that Israel will be pressured into a quick fix."[68] None of this was enough to dampen the increasing nervousness of the Jewish community.

I bundled up the expressions of concern I had received from Jewish leaders and took them to Ham. He was my friend on this issue, because he fully understood the importance of political support from the Jewish community when the president was launching a risky diplomatic venture in the

Middle East. He also had confided that his family had learned his maternal grandmother was Jewish. In an extraordinary memorandum of June 6, 1977,[69] Ham told his boss in no uncertain terms of his concerns about the political impact of Carter's broad foreign-policy initiatives, and in words so direct that he typed the memo himself and locked the only other copy in his office safe. He first warned the president that his foreign policy initiatives were criticized as "consistently 'liberal'" (Carter commented in a written note: "To challenge the Soviets for influence is 'conservative'"). But, focusing on Carter's Middle East initiatives, he tried to take the president's head out of the clouds to face the political implications.

Ham began by pointing out that American Jews vote in greater proportion to their size than any other group; they are predominantly Democratic and have remained so despite economic and educational advances that traditionally lead other groups to change parties. And in key states like New York, the influence of Jews in primaries is often decisive. He noted that Jews also had a tradition of "using one's material wealth for the benefit of others"—in 1976 alone Jewish charities had raised $3.6 billion compared with $200 million by the American Red Cross. More pertinent to politics than charity, 70 of the 125 members of the Democratic National Finance Council were Jews who constituted more than 60 percent of the large donors to the Democratic Party. Then he described the importance of AIPAC—"a strong but paranoid lobby"—in concentrating the political force of all major Jewish organizations on Congress in defense of Israeli interests: "Their collective mobilizing ability is unsurpassed in terms of the quality and quantity of political communications that can be triggered on specific issues perceived to be critical to Israel [and without a] political counterforce that opposes the specific goals of the Jewish lobby." He also ranked the one hundred members of the Senate according to their support for Israel—only three were "generally negative."

In the bluntest terms he discussed the Israeli election and what it meant: Begin's philosophy differed sharply from the past, and for the first time they feared "losing American public support for Israel if the new government and its leaders proved to be unreasonable in its positions." For the president to further his own goals, he would need the support of American Jews. He warned Carter that he had publicly used terms like "defensible borders" and "homeland for the Palestinians" without reassuring elaborations about what he really meant. Most important: "The cumulative effect of your statements on the Middle East and the various bilateral meetings with the heads of state has been generally pleasing to the Arabs and displeasing to the Israelis and the American Jewish community." In fact, Ham said, the press reports on his meetings with four Arab leaders were uniformly described as positive, while his talks with Rabin were reported as unsuccessful and "very cool."

His recommendations followed logically—coordinated consultation with the American Jewish community and the Begin government to emphasize that the Carter administration was not seeking to "impose a U.S. settlement nor attempting any quick-fix solution," and then to lay out the key issues that would be part of a settlement, with concessions on both sides. Then followed recommendations for a detailed outreach program to key members of Congress, the American Jewish press, and Jewish leaders, with Carter personally participating where appropriate.

The president agreed with the program and insisted that his secretary of state join in forging an essential link between foreign policy and domestic politics. The problem was that the policy did not change, and there was no real effort to take into account American Jewish concerns. I sensed that Brzezinski, Vance, and, to a degree, Carter himself saw domestic outreach as a nuisance, and felt that foreign policy in general, and the Middle East in particular, should be insulated from domestic politics. Major decisions were sometimes made without anyone even informing Ham. And the president's lack of political sensitivity was sometimes breathtaking.

SUNDAY SCHOOL

Jimmy Carter had been teaching Sunday school in Georgia since he was eighteen, and he saw no reason to discontinue this fulfilling activity when he arrived in the White House. On the morning of inauguration day, I accompanied him and Rosalynn to a prayer service at the First Baptist Church of Washington, a few blocks north of the White House. There the pastor offered a prayer for him to be blessed with divine strength and wisdom. The president became a communicant and decided to give sermons of his own at the church's couples Bible class until they became an embarrassment. His first mistake was giving a sermon at all, since everything a president says is public, regardless of how private the occasion. The second was his topic: Christ driving the moneylenders from the Temple, leading to his crucifixion. An Associated Press reporter, Casper Nannes, wrote a story innocently head-lined "Learning the Bible with the President." He reported that the president had taught that the confrontation at the Temple was "a turning point in Christ's life. He had directly challenged in a fatal way the existing church, and there was no possible way for the Jewish leaders to avoid the challenge. So they decided to kill Jesus." The article went on to note that Jesus' trial did not provide him with such protections of Jewish law as two witnesses, and it closed by noting: "Carter is the first President to teach a Bible class while in office." He might have added that this sermon persuasively demon-strated why no previous sitting president had ever done so.

It is hard to think of a more remarkable letter written to a president of the United States than the one on May 6, 1977, by the Reverend John F. Steinbruck, pastor of Washington's Luther Place Memorial Church and an ardent participant in interfaith activities. His anguished letter lamented that those Bible class remarks "will undermine progress that has been made in the Christian world removing the basis of deicide charges against the Jewish people." He said that the Catholic Church and other mainstream Christian denominations had long since exonerated the Jews from collective guilt for Jesus' death and urged the president to "reinforce this direction that the Christian world has at long last taken to end false witness against our Jewish neighbors."

Within the week Carter replied with a detailed biblical exegesis that also expressed his thankfulness that Christian denominations "have totally and decisively rejected the charge that the Jewish people as a whole were then or are now responsible for the death of Christ," noting that his own Southern Baptist Convention had declared "anti-Semitism [to be] un-Christian."

Not content with avoiding further damage from this high-wire exercise, the president delivered another sermon at a pre-Christmas Bible class at the First Baptist Church. Again the AP reporter was on the job. This time the president took as his text the raising of Lazarus from the dead and said that

Jesus, by revealing himself as the Messiah, knew he was risking death "as quickly as [it] could be arranged by the Jewish leaders, who were very powerful." A second letter soon arrived from Rev. Steinbruck to White House Counsel Bob Lipshutz, renewing his "plea for Presidential sensitivity on this matter by gently recalling the President's just and forthright declaration on this historically false notion of Jewish responsibility for deicide." When Lipshutz forwarded it to me, I penned a handwritten note: "Bob (1) We've got to write the President a memo & beg him to stay away from this. (2) Can we talk?"[70]

More complaints kept arriving about Carter's explorations of the New Testament. One anguished handwritten note from Bookbinder of the American Jewish Committee asked me why Carter approached the question of the Jews' role in Jesus' death *twice*. Another, from Benjamin Epstein of the Anti-Defamation League, reported a "flood of calls from persons of the Jewish faith from around the country expressing deep concern."[71] I was apoplectic. Why would the president of the United States even address such a topic at a time like this—indeed, why at all? All we could do was to forward Epstein's letter to the president and urge him to stay off the subject. He did, but it was simply inexplicable to me that someone who did not have an anti-Semitic thought in his head could be so insensitive to the way his impolitic Bible lessons would be received.

American Jewish leaders began looking for reassurance about Carter. After meeting twice with Begin, Rabbi Shindler stressed the need for the new prime minister to form a government quickly and make it "broadly representative, so most American Jews could support him." Shindler nevertheless promised that even with Begin as prime minister "there won't be an erosion of American Jewish support for Israel." But he also said ominously: "The American Jewish community is now bothered about Jimmy Carter."[72] Yet he did not indicate that the American Jewish establishment had any concerns about the new prime minister.

With all his obduracy and legalisms, his Revisionist philosophy, his habit of lecturing and not seeming to listen, Begin was an enigma to the president and his foreign-policy advisers, who did not fully appreciate that the prime minister with whom they would have to interact for most of his presidency embodied a history of oppression in his own life. Imprisoned by the

Soviets, a fugitive from Nazi oppression, with an almost mystical commitment to Israel's rebirth, Begin craved acceptance and respect from the president of the United States. He was no longer the shadowy underground Irgun commander derided as a terrorist or a political loser in more than a half-dozen elections, but the prime minister of the Third Jewish Commonwealth. More understanding of Jewish history and of Begin's own suffering might not have fully overcome his inflexibility, nor could it have fully won over the American Jewish community. But it would have helped Jimmy Carter in dealing with American Jewish leaders and Israel, whom he saw through the filter of the Bible, more the New than the Old Testament.

CONFRONTATION WITH
AMERICAN JEWISH LEADERSHIP

Nor did Begin help in easing the way to understanding him. To reassure nervous American Jews about the stiff, scholarly new prime minister, who seemed the exact opposite of the self-confident, bronzed sabra who had reshaped the image of the beleaguered shtetl Jew into an admired kibbutz fighter, Begin dispatched his close friend and former Irgun comrade Shmuel Katz. There has probably never before or since been such a provocative advance man for a visit by a head of government. Justice Department lawyers at first wanted him to register as a foreign agent, but we dissuaded them from insisting.

Katz's meeting with Reform rabbis at the legendary Jewish resort of Grossinger's was captured in a *New York Times* article that Ham forwarded to the president, titled "Katz in the Mountains." It recalled that Katz had first come to the United States to buy arms for the Irgun in April 1948, just days after the organization had been condemned—not only by the Arabs and the British but by Ben-Gurion and even the chief rabbi—for destroying the Arab village of Deir Yassin and allegedly massacring 229 Arab men, women, and children. In answer to a reporter's question if the Irgun had been retaliating against Arab violence to the Jews, Katz answered, "Not enough."[73]

That set the tone for Katz's visit. He turned aside criticism of Begin as a former terrorist as "lurid attacks." But he directed one of his strongest broadsides against the Carter administration only days before Begin was to meet with the president. With Carter pushing for a peace agreement that would envision an Israeli withdrawal from most of the West Bank in return for peace, Katz dismissed it as "recipes for war." When it was suggested that Israel might make peace with the Arabs as the French did by withdrawing from embattled Algeria, Katz told the rabbis: "De Gaulle made peace in Algeria, Nixon went to China, so Begin is the man to commit suicide—he'll give the country away. Never!"

But Katz was just warming up with the liberal Reform rabbis, whom he felt he could eat for breakfast: "I was told I would have a rough time with them. But you see, they're just weak." Moving to a more friendly group of Orthodox rabbis at another borscht belt hotel, Katz was in his element. He invited American Jews to take on their own president: "We are confident that the Jewish community in America will stand out courageously and challenge its government if it becomes necessary." Shmuel Katz may not have been diplomatic, but he was right about American Jews standing up for Israel and accurate in advancing his version of the new prime minister's policies.

Katz's rhetoric—straight out of the Irgun manual—was one reason why Brzezinski and others thought the administration should lay down the law to Begin when he arrived in mid-July.[74] Senator Humphrey suggested a less abrupt approach and proposed that American Jewish leaders try to moderate Begin's views. Carter was more practical. In order to help raise trust, he decided to approve shipments of military equipment to Israel that were caught in a Pentagon bottleneck. Ironically, it was during this time of tension that he signed a landmark Anti-Arab Boycott bill through negotiations that I helped facilitate between American Jewish groups and the Business Roundtable to ban American companies from boycotting Israel, which he had championed since the campaign. We followed up with tough implementing regulations, for which he was given little credit. And Brzezinski informed me that the president had just approved TOW antitank missiles and other military items Israel had wanted.[75]

Thankfully, Carter was also his idealistic self, insisting at a meeting with Mondale, Vance, Brzezinski, Ham, Jody Powell, and me that the Arabs would agree for Israel to deviate from withdrawing back to pre-1967 borders, and opposed an independent Palestinian state. Jody replied that what we tell

Israel is "only bad news for them." But Carter was undeterred: There was a "chance for peace, and we can't let this chance get past."[76]

It dramatized for me that for all his public mistakes in rhetoric—both diplomatic and religious—his determination to achieve peace for Israel regardless of political cost was admirable, and essential. It is even clearer in the decades since, that progress on the same intractable issues with which Carter was struggling forty years ago can come only with a president willing to take enormous domestic political heat and plow ahead. None have done so since with the same combination of his grit and determination—indeed, perhaps because of the political wounds he suffered.

But even as we tried to calm the Jewish community, it was not clear that the president had fully internalized the domestic political dangers. Mondale called me to his office on June 10. Unlike Carter, Vance, and Brzezinski, the vice president believed that foreign policy and domestic politics could not be separated, because the former required support of the latter to be effective. "Stu, we will be in bad shape politically if he gets on the outs with the Jewish community, which is about to blow up over the president's position on Israel," he said, pouring out his frustrations. He felt that Carter had been too public with his positions and "hasn't brought along the Jewish community." I replied that we must try to build support within the Jewish community and Capitol Hill. But apparently Carter did not see the danger Mondale observed, because he had been angered by what he saw as the Jewish leadership's "irrational lobbying."[77]

We were literally besieged with well-intentioned and self-serving advice, warnings, occasionally wise counsel, misunderstandings, and self-inflicted wounds weakening Carter's hand against Begin and further alienating him from the American Jewish community. We first tried to build support among American Jewry with a letter to be signed by senators supporting Carter. But Senator Ribicoff phoned me at home warning against it because Republicans would not sign it "and neither will a lot of Democrats." He warned that Jewish leaders and AIPAC were poisoning the atmosphere for Begin and reiterated: "Be tough! Don't let them think they have the president on the run; tell them off." This was easier said than done.[78]

I passed on the gist of this remarkable outburst from a Jewish senator to Ham, communications director Jerry Rafshoon, and Frank Moore, our congressional liaison. But I feared that confrontation by the president would badly backfire politically. And as it happened, the supportive senatorial initiative died quietly after Humphrey withdrew as a signatory to the proposed letter: AIPAC's lobbying had succeeded. The intensity of feeling increased with each passing day. Rabbi Morris Sherer, president of the Orthodox Agudath Israel of America, an organization with a hundred thousand members and direct ties to the Agudat Israel Party with four seats in the Knesset, assured me he had no connection with Shindler's Conference of Presidents and that his party would be a moderating influence on the Begin government, because "We put life above land."

Shortly after Rabbi Sherer left with his encouraging message, I was informed that George Sherman, the spokesman for the Near East Bureau of the State Department, had been quoted in Israeli papers saying that the administration was trying either to "topple Begin" or to persuade the moderate general and famed archaeologist Yigal Yadin, who led a small center party in Begin's coalition, to become prime minister.[79]

This intrusion, not only on the politics of a friendly country but on *our own* policies, prompted me to dash off a handwritten note to Ham asking if he could take over responsibility for clearing all official statements on the Middle East: "Statement this week has almost put us to point of no return with American Jewish community. Now *we* look like the heavies and Begin the good guy." He replied that the week had been "*disastrous,* we have galvanized public opinion in Israel against us and—I am afraid—alienated in a permanent way the American Jewish community." He confirmed that Sherman's remarks had not been approved by the White House, although they had been presented and accepted as a major statement of U.S. foreign policy. "Hell, I view the statement this week as a self-inflicted wound that serves no good purpose and makes every dimension of this problem more difficult," Ham told me. When the president called, I asked him to contradict the statement, but he only said he knew nothing about it, and we were not supposed to comment anyway. To Carter the incident was "over and done with now, but I'm sorry about it."[80]

There have been many White House meetings with Jewish leaders, but I doubt if any were as intense, substantive, and had as full a complement of senior administration officials as the one in the Cabinet Room on July 6, 1977. Arrayed around the large oval shaped table were about forty presidents of major American Jewish organizations and ten local presidents from the metropolitan areas with the largest number of Jews, led by the eloquent but tart Rabbi Shindler. There were so many people that all the chairs around the cabinet table, plus the high-backed chairs behind them where senior White House staff normally sat, and even the folding chairs among them, were all full. The meeting was scheduled to be unusually long, from 12:30 to 2:30 p.m., with the president attending during the second hour. Our agenda was to open lines of communication, delineate the president's approach, and if possible assuage the apprehensions that he was working against Israel's interests. The principal fear was that the United States was trying to impose a plan that would force Israel back to its 1967 boundaries to create a separate state for the Palestinians on the West Bank.[81]

The event was tightly scripted. Mondale opened by assuring the Jewish representatives that the administration was committed to Israel's survival as a Jewish state and expected "the Arabs to be forthcoming before Israel makes concessions." Vance followed by giving our views on the core issues in considerable detail. Peace, he said, must be "negotiated, not dictated," and Israel must be provided with necessary arms. Brzezinski spoke in a dramatic staccato: "We won't deceive, betray, or compel." As usual, he framed the matter in a geopolitical context: "We have a favorable position for peace; the Soviets are politically out of the Middle East; and we have relatively moderate Arab leaders." But, he warned sharply, "Stalemate without movement to peace will lead to a steady deterioration," while the Arabs were in the process of modernizing their societies and would either become more moderate or radical. Israel, he argued, had an opportunity to help create a more moderate Middle East with a peace settlement. His premise of the Arabs facing a choice was certainly correct, but whether an agreement with Israel at that time would have made them face that choice and in the process unfreeze their authoritarian political structures seems dubious, and remains one of the imponderables of history.

The Jewish leaders responded by accusing us of being too lax in our definition of peace with the Arabs. Some accused the administration of asking more of Israel than of the Arabs, and did not believe the Arabs wanted peace with Israel, in fact just the contrary. Shindler complained that while Israel was being publicly pushed, the Arabs were not being asked to commit to making peace with Israel. Mondale retorted with great conviction that the administration did not expect Israel to withdraw from the territories it acquired in the 1967 war without assurances of real peace. Brzezinski added in plain talk: "Israel needs self-enforcing security arrangements, so it doesn't give up something without getting anything." Shindler remained unpersuaded and complained that Israel had little room for negotiation.

At 1:25 p.m. Carter entered the crowded Cabinet Room, and everyone rose. He thanked them for coming, mentioned his New Jersey campaign speech, and reiterated that its guiding principle was the "peace and security of Israel . . . real peace accepted by Israel and her Arab neighbors—full diplomatic relations, open borders, free travel, and tourism." There was almost a collective sigh of relief when Carter promised to greet Begin as a friend and, contradicting the State Department, added: "I do not question his legitimacy, and I hope to strengthen Israel's esteem in him." He further promised not to impose a settlement and once again drilled down on specific issues in firm language: "No one in my administration has ever drawn a map." But in words no other president has used before or since, he described the problems of the Palestinians as "a cancer which needs to be healed. They need a home and a redress of wrongs."

Then a bizarre thing happened: Rabbi Shindler blessed the president with the traditional Hebrew prayer for heads of state, to which the president audibly said, "Amen." Shindler then said that Carter "was the vessel of two thousand years of Jewish history. We come here with open hearts and grateful hearts." He recalled that as a candidate Carter had met with them and made promises, "and you have fulfilled them much more than anyone could have expected: self-respect for our nation, healing, morality as a factor of government and international relations." He then joked, to laughter from all: "So why do we come here if we are so happy?" He answered his own question: "[Your] words are not perceived as you intended them to be. [The] world is not used to your open diplomacy, and your words are interpreted to be a blueprint to be imposed. We are nervous; this leads to a toughening of the Israeli backbone." Almost as if he had not heard what the administration's policy makers had just said, Shindler read out a statement by Arab leaders indicating that they expected the United States to impose a settlement on the Israelis. Others read out Carter's statements on Israel returning to its 1967 borders, and still others pressed for Israeli coproduction agreements on fighter jets, guidance systems, and other arms.

As we approached the end of the allotted two hours, the president summarized his beliefs, again speaking candidly and earnestly: "The Arabs gain in world opinion when they can emphasize points that further their cause," and "Jews and Israel seldom stress that the U.S. favors a full peace for Israel." Shindler insisted that "Begin has been very forthcoming" and concluded by reporting that Begin felt that "others need to be more flexible to move forward." If time could have been frozen after this extraordinary meeting, much of the tension in American-Israeli relations would have dissipated. But events would raise the temperature back to the boiling point.

BEGIN'S ELEGANT VISIT

On a sweltering July day in 1977, Menachem Begin arrived in Washington for his first official visit as prime minister—after stopping at New York to meet Rabbi Menachem Schneerson, the charismatic leader of the spreading Chabad-Lubavitch movement. Begin had the familiar look of the Eastern European Jews of my grandparents' generation. He was almost completely bald, wore thick glasses, and had a protruding jaw and a face with a sad look that to my eyes made it appear he was carrying the traumas of the Jewish people in Europe through the ages. Yet he bore himself with dignity and pride as the representative of the state of Israel, after his own hard journey in life. His three patient decades on the margins of Israel's political leadership testified to his stubborn perseverance.

We had been advised by U.S. ambassador Sam Lewis to accord him a dignified welcome worthy of his office, and the arrival ceremony took place on the South Portico of the White House accompanied by trumpeted ruffles and flourishes and the two national anthems, our own and Israel's "Hatikvah"—Hope—which I had learned in Hebrew school growing up in Atlanta. We certainly needed every bit of that in the face of a guest who was as tough as he was dignified.

Lewis also warned us that while Begin would be hard to handle, the president should not push him into a corner by laying down the law on giving back all the territory won in the Six-Day War; rather we should try to co-opt him. Lewis believed he would never agree to have the PLO participate in a Geneva conference, but might agree to a mixed delegation of West Bank Palestinians in a Jordanian delegation, and was "ready to sacrifice a lot" for peace with Egypt.[82] Carter followed that advice at this point, and not Brzezinski's get-tough stance. Each greeted the other with public praises and compliments.

At the first meeting in the Cabinet Room on the afternoon of Begin's arrival,[83] all the principal American players were seated around the Cabinet Room oval table with Carter facing Begin. At his side sat Dayan and Dinitz; then Begin's former Irgun comrade and longtime adviser, Yechiel Kadishai, and, both surprisingly and ominously, the same Shmuel Katz of the borscht belt provocations. The president insisted that he wanted to work with Begin toward peace on the basis of the UN land-for-peace resolutions but quickly added that he had "no blueprint, no plan, and no desire to impose one. I want to be a trusted intermediary." Carter said peace meant open borders, exchanges of people, and diplomatic recognition and conceded that not all Arab states were ready to go that far, but Egypt and Jordan were—and they *were* Israel's closest neighbors. When Carter invited Begin to speak his mind, the president got more than he bargained for.

Begin's exquisite and nuanced English had more of a European flavor than a typical Israeli's. His reputation as an orator preceded him, but I was impressed that he spoke knowledgeably without notes on a wide range of complicated topics. He did not reply directly to Carter on the goals and shape of the peace process, but instead emphasized the threats Israel faced from the PLO in southern Lebanon. He then launched into a historical tutorial unlike anything that any Israeli leader had given to a U.S. president. It was a detailed history of grievances—European discrimination against the Jews, British behavior in Palestine, generations of Arab attacks, and heroic and costly defense in Israeli wars—as if he were addressing a class of uneducated students. After independence the Jewish population "lived on a thread," he declared, and until the decisive victory in 1967, Begin said there was "war every day, with fifteen hundred killed in skirmishes." He pulled out a map to demonstrate his tiny country's perilous geography: At its narrowest point,

Israel was only nine miles wide and could be cut in half by a quick military thrust, placing the artillery of a Palestinian state only about twenty-five miles from Israel's main population centers. This took the better part of thirty minutes and sorely tested Carter's patience; he listened politely and attentively, but with a fixed expression that from long experience I recognized barely concealed his frustration.

Begin finally pivoted to the peace process and was obviously well prepared. Instead of agreeing to a multilateral Geneva peace conference dealing with all the Arab states, he announced he favored "face-to-face negotiations without preconditions . . . [and] no prior commitments." He also spoke what Carter thought were the magic words: "I accept UN Resolutions 242 and 338 as the basis for negotiations." To be certain there was no misunderstanding, Carter asked him to repeat it: "Will you say the two UN Resolutions are the basis for negotiations?" Begin replied: "Yes." Carter seemed almost elated.

Later, in private, Carter persisted with his goals of a comprehensive settlement; a trade of conquered land for secure peace; full normalization by the Arab states; and linking a Palestinian homeland to Jordan rather than declaring the West Bank an independent state.[84] But he would find that Begin's definition of what was required of Israel under 242 differed dramatically from the U.S. government's understanding that Israel must withdraw from all of the West Bank, Gaza, and the Golan Heights "with minor modifications" conditioned mainly by security and not settlements. By contrast, Begin was offering only some withdrawal on some fronts.

This was and would remain a persistent source of tension between Carter and Begin, and it was at least partly rooted in the deliberate ambiguity of the UN resolution. I had suggested in preparatory memos that we could try to view Begin's own proposal of a partial withdrawal as the movement of Israeli troops into closed military camps near the 1967 Israel border. When Carter raised the issue, he did not call for dismantling existing settlements, but aligned himself with many American Jewish leaders by bluntly telling Begin: "New settlements on the West Bank might prevent the peace conference itself, as it will foreclose negotiations in the future." Carter's words stand the test of time. Begin set the policy for all his Likud successors. Now, four decades later, the expansion of civilian settlements has vastly complicated the internationally favored solution of two separate states for Jews and

Arabs along with continued Palestinian intransigence. The two-state solution was not even envisioned in 1977 and would bedevil Israeli politics right down to the reelection campaign of Prime Minister Benjamin Netanyahu in 2015 and beyond.

As we continued sorting out our positions, Begin toughened the tone by calling on Shmuel Katz, who was not even a formal member of his government and had been shoehorned into the White House meeting to the surprise of the Secret Service. I blanched at the insensitivity of allowing him to be a spokesman for the prime minister of Israel. Katz launched into his own half-hour diatribe on the centrality of Judaea and Samaria to Israel. Most Palestinian Arabs, he insisted, were only recent immigrants and were hardly even thought of as Palestinian. In his view they had no long-term attachment to the land. As his authority he remarkably cited Mark Twain's nineteenth-century account of his visit to a very sparsely inhabited Holy Land. When he said that their real homeland was Jordan—I thought that King Hussein would be less than pleased to learn that. During the more than twenty years Jordan had controlled the West Bank, the king refused to grant Jordanian citizenship to the Palestinian residents lest they upset his country's delicate balance with the Bedouin, who were mainstays of the army that underwrote his rule. Thankfully, no one on the U.S. side tried to engage Katz in his rant. Carter was furious but listened politely and patiently.

Begin followed up in a far more elegant discourse, but in substance it was almost as uncompromising. While he promised that none of the settlements would be an obstacle to negotiations, he then threw down a potential deal breaker straight out of Jabotinsky: "We cannot prevent Jews from building on land in the original Israel of the Bible." Carter quickly shot back: "This might prevent a Geneva conference and be an indication of bad faith to negotiate under 242. The previous Israeli government discouraged settlements." It made me think back to how Rabin and his Labor Party felt they had been undercut by Carter's declaration on a Palestinian homeland. Carter continued looking for compromise and said almost plaintively: "If you expressed a preference for no new settlements until we determine the attitude of the Arabs at Geneva, it would be a gracious step."

But Begin refused to commit even to such a limited settlement freeze.[85] He stood by his concept of a Geneva meeting, which would actually be a set of direct bilateral negotiations between Israel and each of its neighbors wrapped inside a proposal he called "The Framework for the Peacemaking Process." Later, in private, he presented Carter with the secret portion of his framework. For Egypt, Israel would make a "significant withdrawal from the Sinai" in exchange for a peace treaty. For Syria, Israel would remain on the Golan Heights but would redeploy its troops along a line that would be established as the permanent boundary. As for what he called Judaea and Samaria—the West Bank of the River Jordan—as well as Gaza, Begin refused to countenance any transfer of sovereign authority because of the "historic rights of our nation to this land." Even in private, Begin gave away nothing while repeating the mantra that everything was open for negotiations. But the fact was that within his own tight framework, there was very little room for movement.

Before he left Begin gave evidence of his high character with a generous personal touch. He invited Brzezinski to a private breakfast at Blair House, the official guesthouse across the street from the White House. At one level the two were literally poles apart, and could not have been more different. Begin, a highly formal, quintessential Eastern European Jew; Brzezinski, a sharp-edged Catholic from a country of historically virulent anti-Semitism. But their common Polish heritage created an odd bond. For this breakfast meeting Begin had something special for his guest. He had located documents in a Jerusalem archive that testified to the role of Brzezinski's father, Tadeusz Brzezinski, in saving Jewish lives as a Polish diplomat stationed in Hitler's Germany.[86] Zbig wrote later: "I was deeply touched by this gesture of human sensitivity, especially since it came in the wake of some of the personal attacks on me and on my role [by some American Jewish leaders] in seeking to promote a peace settlement in the Middle East."[87] Although their views clashed, the two developed a grudging respect as opponents because of their shared Polish heritage.

"I MAY HAVE ONLY ONE EYE, BUT I AM NOT BLIND"

At the end of August, the redline on my phone signaled that the president was calling. He asked me to come down to his study and expressed his concern at new Jewish settlements in the West Bank and Begin's refusal to allow any talks with the PLO. "They do not want peace," he said of the Israelis. I questioned that, but he went on that "Assad and Sadat need results to survive," which I felt was a misreading of Assad. He also asserted that Begin had "misled" him on their relationship with South Africa and their help with their nuclear program, which was "clear from our intelligence data." He asked me what to do, and said Senators Byrd and Bentsen were both concerned. He did not ask me to follow up with any action, but his mounting, understandable frustration at Begin was palpable.[88] Vance also reflected Carter's unease by warning a cabinet meeting that the "Middle East was more tense, and this was exacerbated by West Bank developments [settlements] by Israel."[89]

Despite Begin's strictures against the PLO and his insistence on dealing with Arab states one by one, President Carter remained determined to move ahead with a comprehensive Middle East agreement, giving the Palestinians a voice in their own future. The next two months would prove that project a virtual impossibility, and certainly not possible through any route known to classic diplomacy. As we were to discover, only bold strokes could cut through the tangles of faith, ideology, and the bloody history of the Middle East. In the interim, the White House, the State Department, the Israeli team of Begin and Dayan, and—never to be disregarded—the American Jewish leadership, engaged in a chase after a chimera. What mattered is how this diplomatic shadow play set the stage for historic events.

Begin was already moving along his own path toward improved relations with Egypt outside Carter's comprehensive framework. Within six weeks of assuming office he instructed the director of Israel's secret service, the Mossad, to meet with an envoy sent by Sadat. Then, in mid-September, Dayan met in Morocco with Egypt's deputy prime minister, Hassan al-Tuhami.[90] This was one of a series of secret meetings the Israeli foreign minister had with leaders of India, Iran, Jordan, and Morocco. Then he flew to Washington for discussions about the forthcoming Geneva peace conference.

The Moshe Dayan I met in the Oval Office seemed to leap out of the pages of history as the legendary one-eyed hero of the Six-Day War. He was balding, small, and lean, with taut features and an enigmatic smile. His presence as foreign minister in Begin's government was fortuitous for us because of his creativity and courage, but it was also unexpected. Dayan's standing in Israel had gone into eclipse after he was taken by surprise as defense minister when the Arabs invaded in 1973. Forced to resign ignominiously along with Prime Minister Golda Meir, he returned to office in the government of Labor's archenemy Menachem Begin to retrieve his reputation. This enraged his Labor Party colleagues, but Dayan was unconcerned since they had not defended him in his hour of peril. Begin, for his part, needed Dayan in his new, untested government as a symbol of credibility. Begin and Dayan were not strangers. Both had been brought out of the political wilderness by Prime Minister Levi Eshkol to serve in his unity government leading up to the 1967 Six-Day War—Dayan from Ben Gurion's socialist Rafi party as Defense Minister, and Likud conservative Begin as Minister Without Portfolio.

Just as Carter had misplayed his hand with Rabin in their first meeting, he failed to appreciate (until later at Camp David, when he skillfully used Dayan to help forge an agreement) that the Israeli hero, however loyal he might be to Begin at that moment, was far more flexible and highly secular, and was not an adherent of Begin's ideology. For Dayan the principal value of the West Bank and Gaza lay in providing Israel strategic depth, not biblical redemption; they could be traded in part for security guarantees and strategic military outposts. Yet instead of cultivating him, Carter unwittingly left an initial unfavorable impression.

Dayan was accompanied by Ephraim "Eppie" Evron, a skilled diplomat and director general of the Foreign Ministry (and Israeli ambassador to the U.S. later in Carter's term), who particularly remembered the president's "blue cold eyes." He felt that Carter's famous toothy "smile somehow was false, because the eyes didn't smile. . . . He smiled often, but it seemed to be a very artificial smile."[91] Evron felt it was a missed opportunity, because he knew that as a condition of joining Begin's government, Dayan had stipulated that when negotiations were under way, the government would take no unilateral action. "So he [Carter] had an ally there; instead of using him as an ally, as he should have done, he treated him in a manner which upset him and offended him very much," said Evron.

Indeed Dayan, who spoke Arabic as well as Hebrew and English, presented Carter with an opportunity to reach out to the Palestinians through his own experience with their leaders, and offered to meet with them and discuss anything the administration wanted to put on the Geneva agenda. Carter suggested asking if he would accept a referendum for the Palestinians to choose between remaining under Israeli control or forming an association with Jordan, which Dayan rejected as possibly leading to an independent Palestinian state. This may have also been a lost opportunity for Israel, since it would have separated the Palestinians still living in the territories from the exiled leaders of the PLO.

During one of the most revealing meetings in which I participated with Carter, he made an evenhanded admission to the Syrians that would startle many Israeli supporters today. The president was trying to entice the Syrian foreign minister, Abdul Halim Khaddam, to agree to a unified Arab delegation at Geneva including the Palestinians—even, as he put it, "a member of the PLO, but not a well-known or famous person," a clear condition that Yāsir Arafat could not be there. The Syrians wanted the PLO to represent all Palestinians, wherever they lived. Carter emphasized the importance of Syrian acceptance of a joint communiqué with the Soviet Union to convene the conference, and in a last, futile effort to gain Syrian approval, he said: "I am as interested in protecting the legitimate rights of the Palestinians, as Israel's."[92]

Neither Carter nor Vance were able to obtain Begin's advance agreement to the terms of the Geneva conference that were to be announced jointly by the United States and the Soviet Union, nor did they consult Israel about the details. Dayan realized what was happening, and he asked Meir Rosenne for a list of written commitments that previous American administrations had made to Israel. These were largely kept secret, lest their publication tip off the Arabs how closely American policy was tied to Israeli security. They included a letter from Nixon to Golda Meir on August 1, 1970, pledging that "I will not ask you to withdraw one soldier from any territory occupied by Israel since 1967 until there is total peace with all the Arab countries." Another, from Kissinger to Golda Meir on December 20, 1973, just before the abortive first Geneva conference, assured Israel that no parties—read the PLO—would be invited without the approval of all the others. Finally, both the Nixon and Ford administrations had assured Israel of advance consultations before the United States made any major decisions affecting them. Certainly no such consultations had occurred in drafting the latest declaration on a Geneva conference.[93]

When Dayan read the October 1 joint U.S.-USSR communiqué, according to Rosenne, he exploded: "I may have only one eye, but I am not blind!"[94]

Quandt had a different version: that when they showed the proposed announcement to Dayan he asked if they had to agree. "And we said, 'No, this is a US-Soviet statement that would be used to invite parties. You just have to say whether you're going to come or not.' Dayan replied, 'If we don't have to agree to it, you do whatever you want.' "[95]

More likely Dayan intentionally avoided a clear response so he could remain free to rally support against it. If his strategy was trapping the administration, it certainly worked, just as it had often worked on the battlefield. When the joint statement was issued on October 1 convening a conference under American and Soviet auspices, a firestorm immediately arose, orchestrated by Dayan. The American Jewish leadership went into open war against the president in ways rarely seen before or since. The reasons were equally obvious and should have been apparent to Carter and his foreign policy team. The casus belli was not just the lack of prior consultation with Israel but an elevation of the interests of the Palestinians into "legitimate rights"—a phrase no American administration had ever before endorsed.

No one was more outraged than Dayan, who sensed that the superpowers were conspiring to sell out Israel and acknowledge a diplomatic role for the Palestinians. The explosion from American Jewish organizations was equally predictable. The Conference of Presidents of Major Jewish Organizations fired off an angry telegram to Vance accusing him of "an abandonment of America's historic commitment to the security and survival of Israel."[96] AIPAC put out a tough, detailed statement warning that "the U.S. is devaluing commitments to Israel" and organized a congressional letter-writing offensive.[97]

I soon received calls from members of Congress expressing their dismay about the U.S.-Soviet communiqué, and a visit from clearly agitated Israeli ambassador Dinitz, who expressed his grave reservations to Ham, Bob Lipshutz, Mark Siegel, and me.[98] To try to recoup, Carter met with Jewish congressmen on October 6. He defensively explained the rationale behind the joint communiqué with the Soviets as the only way to achieve peace, and tried to reassure them by stating that "I will commit *suicide* [emphasis added] before I abandon Israel." He admitted that it would have "been better if I had briefed Congress in advance, and I will avoid the problem in the future."[99]

The only party that unequivocally supported the declaration was the

PLO, which was pleased with the reference to the "legitimate rights of the Palestinian people"—who now would no longer be seen as just "refugees" and whose leaders felt they would inevitably be recognized as the sole representatives of the Palestinian people.

Political reverberations take time to make their way to the self-confident center of American power. Working inside the White House was like being in the calm at the center of a storm. The thick walls and windows, the Secret Service officers and guards, the setback from the streets behind wide north and south lawns—all create an eerie sense of serenity, quiet, and protection. But the White House is nevertheless where all the contending forces that are engaged in great issues at home and abroad come crashing in, intruding on the inner peace.

Even inside the administration there were angry repercussions. Mark Siegel was driving home from the airport late at night and was so shocked by news of the Soviet-American communiqué that he almost swerved off the highway. He phoned Ham and started screaming at him: "'Goddammit, I'm off in Minneapolis doing your work and at least you could have had the common decency to tell me this, so we could have prepared a strategy.' Ham replied, 'What are you talking about?' And he didn't know [either]. So Hamilton was very quiet, and when Hamilton gets very quiet, he's very, very quiet." The White House political staff had been left out.

The silver lining was that from that point on, Ham began to attend the weekly Friday-morning foreign-policy breakfasts with the president and his national security team. But Siegel would not rest. Two days after the communiqué he sent Ham a memo warning that it had "driven Jimmy Carter's stock in the American Jewish community substantially below any U.S. president since the creation of the state of Israel, and I'm including in that statement Eisenhower's stock after he forced Israel to withdraw from Sinai in 1956." He pointedly reminded Ham, who hardly needed it, of the number of states Carter won with strong Jewish support, and concluded ominously that the "talk in the American Jewish community is getting very ugly. The word 'betrayal' is being used more and more."[100]

The joint communiqué did not sit well with Sadat in Egypt either. After

Mondale later traveled to the Middle East, he recalled that Sadat told him that "he [Sadat] kicked them [the Soviets] out and he wanted to keep them out of there."[101] It took time for Brzezinski to recognize how much he had underestimated the potential domestic impact. Not until years later did the strongest anti-Soviet hawk in the inner circles admit to it: "I did subsequently feel that I had erred in not consulting our domestic political advisers about its likely internal impact and in not objecting more strenuously to the very notion of a joint U.S.-Soviet public statement."[102] And the president did not easily understand it either. He summoned White House Counsel Bob Lipshutz and me, the two senior Jewish White House staff members, and asked us why mainstream Jewish leaders were speaking out against him after he had worked hard to reach out to them. I explained that the declaration had raised several concerns—ones I shared—bringing the Soviets back into the Middle East, handing Syria a virtual veto, and formulating the terms of Palestinian participation in a way that could be seen as a precursor to an independent Palestinian state on Israel's border.[103]

It was becoming increasingly obvious that Carter's plan for a comprehensive, all-encompassing Middle East settlement, presided over by him and the Soviet leader Leonid Brezhnev, was a grand idea that seemed merely grandiose. When Dinitz came to the White House later that day for an urgent meeting with Ham, Bob Lipshutz, Mark Siegel, and me, he foresaw the practical diplomatic possibilities more clearly than America's own diplomats, Vance and Brzezinski included. With emotion building as he spoke, he said that the "best chance for peace is to sit down with the Egyptians, and we can be forthcoming with them. You will never get an agreement if all have to sign!" I wrote a marginal note that "trying to settle all will get nothing; we should be trying to cut a deal with Egypt."[104]

What happened next represented an embarrassing U-turn by the president. One of the world's two superpowers bowed to unprecedented domestic pressure reflecting the views and interests of a small state that was dependent upon the United States for military, political, and diplomatic support. This reflects the unusual relationship that existed for decades and continues today between the world's strongest democracy and one of its smallest, if sturdiest, dependent states, and we were about to get a painful demonstration of how that worked.

When President Carter arrived by helicopter at the UN Plaza Hotel on October 4, he was ambushed at the helipad by Ed Koch, the combative mayor of New York, who had a huge Jewish constituency. Koch handed him a letter angrily protesting the joint declaration and the administration's policies toward Israel; the mayor had already given a copy to the press. The president took a Pollyannaish view of what he insisted was a "friendly" encounter, but it certainly was not meant that way.[105]

The real showdown followed when Dayan met with Carter, Vance, and Brzezinski in the president's suite for an all-night negotiation. Quandt described how the Israelis took advantage of the situation: "Carter walks in and Dayan says, 'I think you have a problem on your hands, Mr. President. And I can perhaps help you with it.' And Carter says, 'What do you mean?' [Dayan] says, 'Well, obviously many people are upset by the October 1 statement. Many of our friends are upset by it, but I think if we could reach a new U.S.-Israeli understanding, and if I were to go out from our meeting tonight and could say that the United States reaffirms all of its previous commitments and so forth and so on, and it doesn't mean such and such and such—by this statement, [I think] that I could help you politically.'"[106]

This was an amazing intrusion into domestic politics by a foreign minister, even from a friendly country. But it had clearly been based on Israel's assiduous cultivation of American Jewish groups and Congress, and left no doubt how closely Middle East policy is intertwined with domestic politics. Carter nevertheless persisted in his plan and argued with Dayan until after midnight. He told Dayan that "of all the nations with whom we had negotiated on the Middle East, Israel was by far the most obstinate and difficult."[107] Dayan did not yield. It is difficult to imagine the foreign minister of any country being as blunt to the leader of its major benefactor, and the president bristled at this threat. He warned that a confrontation would be damaging to Israel and to the support of the American public for Israel, leaving Israel "isolated" and "would cause a cleavage that might be serious."[108] But Dayan held fast in his demand for a joint Israel-U.S. statement in which the president would pledge to adhere to all the agreements between the two countries.

After further wrangling by Dayan with Vance and Brzezinski, Dinitz and Rosenne left at 3:00 a.m. for the office of the Israeli Mission to the United

Nations and typed a statement. The president had told Dayan he should deliver it, but Dayan said no, it was a joint statement. Ham ruefully joked that if there was to be a joint agreement with Israel, he would change his name from Jordan to Judaea and Samaria!

In the early morning hours of October 5, Jody issued a joint statement on behalf of Carter and Dayan, declaring that "Security Council Resolutions 242 and 338 remain the agreed basis for the resumption of the Geneva peace conference and that all the understandings and agreements between them on this subject remain in force"—just as Dayan had demanded. The statement also committed Israel to attend a Geneva conference, but on its own terms.

Dayan gained little standing from his boss when he returned home. Lewis recounted from his post in Jerusalem that Begin felt Dayan had not been tough enough; he wanted the U.S.-USSR agreement canceled entirely! Ultimately Begin acquiesced, as he often did later when negotiations seemed on the brink of collapse; Dayan would work out some arrangement on his own and convince Begin to accept it. However much political and diplomatic cover Dayan provided for Begin, his swashbuckling independence stoked Begin's distrust and helped provoke Dayan's resignation two years later.[109]

But the fact remained that the president of the United States had reversed himself under intense pressure, hurting his credibility with both Israel and the Arab states; Carter had to tie himself into knots to reassure Jewish members of Congress in a White House meeting, even though he had nullified many of what they considered the most egregious aspects of the joint declaration with the Soviets. In the most dramatic statement I ever heard him make about Israel, he told them: "I will commit suicide before I would abandon Israel."[110]

Nevertheless we knew we were in deep political trouble. At a meeting with Brzezinski and me, Ham bemoaned an "irreparable breach with the Jewish community," and Brzezinski understood it looked like a "joint imposition" by the two superpowers.[111] In another with Mondale and me, Ham was in despair at the process and the deteriorating relationship with the Jewish community, while Mondale blasted Brzezinski's role.[112]

Carter compounded his problems in late October when he wanted to follow the State Department's advice to support an Egyptian resolution in the

UN General Assembly condemning Israel's settlement policy as an obstacle to peace.[113] Ham objected to our support on the basis of domestic politics, and proposed that Carter simply issue a statement agreeing that Israel's settlement policy in the West Bank and Sinai was an illegal obstacle to peace, "but only one of many obstacles to peace."

Ham then sent Carter two more memos warning that if we voted for the resolution, it would touch off a political crisis with the Congress and further complicate the president's prospects of a new Geneva conference.[114] Carter sarcastically thanked him politely for his "option paper," but Ham was not the only one to object. In an October 26 meeting with Vance and Zbig, his deputy David Aaron, Lipshutz, Ham, and I, supported by Mondale, jointly weighed in against this kind of public condemnation of Israel and proposed at least abstaining on the vote. I asked Vance what he expected to obtain from the Arabs for supporting the UN Resolution, and he replied, "that at least, we can say we've gone the last mile," but admitted there was no assurance it would lead to greater support. I asked if the United States had ever voted against Israel at the UN, and was told the only time was during the Eisenhower administration over the 1956 Sinai invasion by Israel, Britain, and France. I left the meeting and called the president, who told me he wanted to "go along" with the resolution, but put out a "balanced statement."[115]

Ignoring the advice of his top political aides, Carter at first supported the Egyptian resolution condemning the Israeli settlements. The president was so adamant that they were illegal, and so determined to show Egypt and the Arab world that he was not in Israel's pocket, that he was willing to take the political heat at home and risk further straining relations with Israel. This was quintessential Jimmy Carter, doing what he considered "the right thing" regardless of the political consequences. But at the end of the day, we persuaded him to back off. Ultimately, the United States abstained from voting on the resolution, which was approved, but made little difference to the Begin government anyway.

18

SADAT CHANGES HISTORY

Anwar el-Sadat was a master of the dramatic gesture and knew how to draw the attention of the world. As the first Arab leader to commit himself publicly to direct talks with Israel, he basked in the attention of American television. To Americans, who tend to believe that nothing is real unless they have seen it on TV, it may seem that Sadat's decision to go to Jerusalem was negotiated before their eyes in interviews by two network news stars, Walter Cronkite and Barbara Walters. In fact he had been moving toward his historic break with Egypt's aggressively pan-Arab past for several months.

Our two Middle East ambassadors confirmed it. Hermann Eilts in Cairo said that Sadat "was desperate. Peace was slipping through his fingers."[1] Sam Lewis in Tel Aviv recalled that while the president hoped Sadat would be more flexible on some of the formulations for the conference, the Egyptian leader saw Carter as unable to shape and manage it without help from others, including himself.[2] It certainly did not help when Sadat saw "Carter cave in to Dayan at the UN, where Carter ate crow, almost publicly," as Brzezinski later put it to me.[3]

Others believe that the decisive moment came when Sadat read the joint announcement of the conference and feared the Soviets would be regaining diplomatic influence in the Middle East. He also did not want to give Syria's Assad a veto over his getting back the Sinai from Israel. But none of this fully explains why Sadat decided to take the gamble of publicly reaching out to Israel. He expected his grand gesture of reconciliation would be repaid by Begin in kind—withdrawal of Israeli troops from almost all territory they had conquered in the Six-Day War and progress toward the establishment of a Palestinian state. But Sadat did not fully know his tenacious and ideo-logical opponent; the road to an agreement would be far longer and more tortuous than he could have imagined.

Mark Siegel was accompanying a congressional delegation visiting Cairo, when he heard Sadat tell them: "You know I did not risk my life, and you know we did not break relations with the Soviet Union, and you know hun-dreds of thousands of Egyptian boys did not die—so that the U.S. govern-ment could bring back the Soviet Union to control Egypt." He then threw a political bombshell and declared he would travel to Jerusalem if invited. Siegel rushed to the U.S. Embassy; it was late at night and almost everyone had gone home, so he typed a cable alerting the State Department. Then Siegel called me while I was having lunch with Ham, and finally flew to Jerusalem to urge Lewis to arrange a formal invitation.[4]

But the Carter administration did little to adjust to events as history moved with great speed. Ham instructed Siegel: " 'The president wants you to low-key this. The president doesn't want you to say anything enthusiastic or pos-itive to the press.' " Siegel was shocked: "I said: 'Hamilton, do you know what's going on here? I mean, this is like a miracle taking place, you know. I have to say something positive.' And I was told not to."[5] That was because Carter was still barreling ahead toward a comprehensive Mideast conference, while the only two countries actually interested in negotiating with each other had no interest in his broad-based forum.

Sadat's bold decision did not come out of thin air, but out of domestic as well as diplomatic imperatives that the administration only vaguely under-stood. By early 1977, major public demonstrations, then an exceedingly rare phenomenon in Egypt, left Sadat shaken. He needed to shift toward peace-time investment and lighten the economic burden of maintaining large armed forces. Moreover, Sadat saw a diplomatic opportunity because he believed Begin's hard-line views would help him push through a deal over any do-mestic obstruction. As the Egyptian diplomat Ahmed Aboul Gheit put it to me, the 1973 war showed "how easy it was that you go into battle and you lose in one day 150 to 200 tanks." Sadat had broken with the Soviets and was casting his lot with the Americans. He realized that if he wanted to re-place Soviet weapons with meaningful American military and economic sup-port, he could get it only by making a bold move with Israel, because of his perception of the political influence of American Jews and, more broadly, the support of the American public for Israel.[6]

Sadat took several steps in private before he felt he was ready for Jerusalem. After Begin traveled to Romania, Sadat followed and was advised by Ceauşescu that while Begin was a "tough, strong man, once he had made his mind up, he could deliver." The Shah of Iran gave him similar advice,[7] and Marshal Tito of Yugoslavia also urged him to move forward. Unbeknownst to Washington, King Hassan II of Morocco arranged a secret meeting at his vacation home in Marrakech between Dayan and Hassan al-Tuhami, Egypt's deputy prime minister and one of Sadat's closest confidants.[8] Tuhami, a shadowy mystic and former head of Egyptian intelligence, made fantastic claims that he could stop his heart for long periods of time and could tame lions—an ideal partner for the swaggering Dayan. The Moroccan king also hosted a meeting between the chief of Israel's Mossad, Yitzhak Hofi, and his Egyptian counterpart, Kamal Hassan Ali. As an earnest sign of goodwill, Hofi provided intelligence information of a plot by Libya's Mu'ammar Gadhafi and the PLO to assassinate Sadat. Egyptian intelligence confirmed the information, and this indicated to Sadat that he might be able to trust the Israelis. His idea was to hold an international conference in Cairo with the five permanent members of the UN Security Council presiding over a meeting between him and Begin. Carter warned him: "That won't work; don't do it."[9]

For Sadat that was the last straw. He decided to act on his own, without telling Carter. Within less than three weeks of the ill-fated joint communiqué, Carter's efforts were upended by Sadat's historic visit to Jerusalem. Sadat wiped it all away with a few lines to the Egyptian parliament that shocked even his own foreign minister. "Israel will be stunned to hear me tell you that I am ready to go to the ends of the earth, and even to their home, to the Knesset itself, to argue with them in order to prevent one Egyptian soldier from being wounded."[10] Only then did the administration realize that Sadat meant what he said.

In Washington the reaction was far from jubilant. After all, Carter's grand plan had been derailed. Sadat's bold stroke was at first met with skepticism, which finally gave way to acceptance because there was no other choice. Brzezinski summed up the diplomatic explosion and consequent rush of events: "And then bing! Or bang! came this announcement that he's going to go on his own [to Jerusalem]. So I think by then we were pretty wary . . . [but] within a very short period of time, we concluded that, instead of opposing it, we'd better embrace it, and hopefully give it some broader dimension."[11] At a cabinet meeting in Washington on November 14, only five days before Sadat's historic visit, Vance declared: "Nothing will come out of the Begin-Sadat exchange, but it is good for the atmosphere."[12]

Not so the Israelis. Rabin felt that Sadat's decision was "total desperation" because "all his strategy was on the verge of collapse." Rabin believed Sadat had "burnt his bridges to the Soviet Union"; a "continuation of war with Israel would put a tremendous burden on the Egyptian economy that will lead nowhere"; and while he had caught Israel by surprise in the 1973 Yom Kippur War, it did not end with victory for Egypt, and "he didn't want to continue to stick on the course of the war as the main instrument of Egypt to achieve its goals."[13]

Senior Egyptian officials were also in a state of shock. Foreign Minister Ismail Fahmy resigned.[14] His chief aide Osama el-Baz asked Sadat if he was not afraid that the reaction of the Egyptian people would be negative, to which Sadat responded: "I have no fear whatsoever of this; it is not a matter of life or death."[15]

Begin initially was skeptical, but instructed his communications director Yehuda Avner to draft a welcoming response to be broadcast in Arabic that concluded: "Let us make peace. Let us start on the path of friendship."[16] Lewis then told Begin that Sadat wanted a handwritten invitation. Notwithstanding five wars between the two countries, Begin promptly wrote a warm letter of invitation to Sadat, which he handed to the American ambassador as go-between "in a very public, flamboyant dramatic ceremony in Begin's office at the Knesset."[17]

The president soon realized that he needed to make the most of the radically changed situation and tried to bring in the Palestinians. Years later Carter insisted to me that he had approved of Sadat's gamble,[18] but at the time he sounded very different. As I was heading down the narrow hallway toward the Oval Office with the president going the other way, he pointedly addressed me: "Stu, I think I am going to oppose Sadat's visit. It will be the end of any hope of a comprehensive peace and will result only at best in a bilateral agreement between Egypt and Israel." I was astonished and said, "Mr. President, you can't do that. Sadat's visit will be historic, and it will be catastrophic if you are seen as opposing the first visit of an Arab combatant to Israel since its creation." He grumbled and kept walking.

Carter finally faced reality and threw the weight of the presidency behind Sadat. Had he not done so, said Ephraim Evron, then of the Israeli Foreign Ministry, there would have been no peace agreement because "when we were left alone with the Egyptians, nothing happened." Even so, Evron felt that if the administration had moved more quickly to embrace Sadat's trip, King Hussein of Jordan might have come aboard before Arab extremists had time to rally against it.[19]

On November 17, two days before Sadat's arrival in Jerusalem, I called Hanon Bar-On, the second in command at the Israeli Embassy, to urge that Begin issue a positive statement giving Carter some credit. By 6:00 p.m., he called back and reported that Begin had sent the president a letter saying the visit "would have been impossible without Carter's efforts." Carter put pressure on Begin, the Arabs, and America's European allies as well, to help make Sadat's visit to Jerusalem successful by not condemning it even before it began.[20] He warned Begin in particular to help Sadat with other Arab leaders by not limiting the negotiation to the Sinai. But that limited agenda was precisely what Begin wanted and essentially what he got. As for Egypt, despite Carter's efforts it was suspended from the Arab League, whose headquarters moved from Cairo to Tunis.

"I AM NOT COMING TO ATTACK"

All who gathered to welcome Sadat on November 19 seemed to share the same sense of bearing witness to a unique moment in history. His arrival in Israel was timed after sundown Saturday so it no longer would be Shabbat. The great white Boeing military plane with "Arab Republic of Egypt" on its side appeared out of the dark sky over Ben-Gurion Airport. A seventy-two-man honor guard from every branch of Israel's armed forces dipped its colors and presented arms. Boutros Boutros-Ghali (then minister of state for foreign affairs, later UN secretary general) wrote that as the doors of the plane opened, "I felt I was looking at a page of history being written with letters of fire. Israel seemed as strange to me as a land in outer space. . . . Sadat stood bathed in the glare of what seemed like a thousand floodlights. His presence seemed like a biblical vision."[21] A T-shaped red carpet extended to the place where Sadat's plane would stop. The conductor of the military band could not locate a copy of the Egyptian national anthem and had to transcribe it from a Radio Cairo broadcast.[22] Lewis remembered vividly that as Sadat stepped from his plane: "He stood there at attention with the spotlight on him, wearing a gleaming white uniform while the Egyptian and Israeli national anthems were played. All around us and behind us, among the Israeli dignitaries you could hear some very uncharacteristic sounds of people weeping with joy and amazement."[23]

As he slowly, dramatically descended, Golda Meir remarked to Rabin: "Now he comes! Couldn't he have come before the Yom Kippur War and saved all those dead, his and ours?"[24] When he came face-to-face with her, "they looked at each other solemnly, half-bowing as he took her hand. 'I have wanted to talk to you for a long time,' he said. 'And I have been waiting for you for a long time,' she answered. 'But now I am here,' he said. '*Shalom*. Welcome,' she said." When Sadat reached Ariel Sharon, the commander who led the successful counterattack across the Suez Canal in the 1973 war, Sadat joked: "Aha, here you are! I tried to chase you in the desert. If you try to cross my canal again, I'll have to lock you up."[25] Moving down the receiving line, he also tweaked the army chief of staff, Mordechai "Mota" Gur, the leader of IDF who captured Jerusalem in 1967. He had warned Begin that Sadat's plan was a deceit to throw Israel off guard and urged a general mobilization, but Begin overruled him. "You see," Sadat addressed the celebrated soldier, "I am not coming to attack."[26]

Israel faced a daunting task of protecting its distinguished visitor from assassination—potentially by Syrian, Palestinian, or even Jewish extremists. Israeli security had no armored limousine, so Ambassador Lewis loaned his black Cadillac with the license plate discreetly changed and the

American radio equipment temporarily reset.[27] But that was the limit of America's role.

The next day Sadat addressed the Knesset, and to maintain credibility in the Arab world, he did not publicly deviate from hard-line Arab positions. Defense Minister Ezer Weizman, founder of the Israeli air force, despaired that "I saw no bridge to span this mighty chasm."[28] But what Sadat did offer Israel was normal relations with its mortal enemy and most powerful Arab neighbor. Begin did not fully rise to the occasion. As was his habit, he dwelled on the "tragic history of the Jewish people." Before the Knesset he told Sadat: "No sir, we took no foreign land. We returned to our Homeland." He cautiously appealed for reconciliation between Jews and Arabs and invited King Hussein of Jordan as the "genuine spokesmen of the Palestinian Arabs" to join the peace effort.[29]

This was Begin's only allusion to the Palestinians, a dismissal of their interest that Carter found unfortunate, to say the least. To help take pressure off Sadat, Brzezinski asked me to relay our request that Begin also show his willingness to negotiate with Palestinian Arabs in the joint announcement following the visit. It was my task to send this through Dinitz, as well as to warn of intense reactions to Begin's speech in the Arab world. As Dinitz put it in his cable (which I obtained years later from the Israeli archives), Carter did not want to be perceived as giving advice, since in the president's "opinion the two men [Begin and Sadat] ran their affairs thus far in an exemplary fashion."[30]

At a senior staff meeting the next day in the Oval Office, the president said: "The question is whether Begin remains adamant or will be more flexible." At a cabinet meeting later that morning he made what turned out to be an overly optimistic forecast: "Sadat will help fracture animosities, and there will be no long-term deleterious effects." Carter still had some forlorn hope of reviving the Geneva conference, but conceded that we could fall back on the new ties between Israel and Egypt.[31] That is exactly what happened.

In the first days of November the president gave a speech to try to reassure the American Jewish community and Israel about his commitment to their security and opposition to a Palestinian state. When I called Dinitz to underscore its positive tone, he still found areas to criticize, like the president's emphasis on the "legitimate rights" of the Palestinians, which I later learned he reflected in a top-secret cable to Jerusalem.[32]

I now saw in Jimmy Carter an important aspect of presidential leadership: the ability to pivot out of a dead-end policy, bounce back, and continue to move ahead in utterly unexpected circumstances. Through almost all the first year of his presidency, Carter had staked his Middle East policy on a comprehensive settlement with all of Israel's enemies, through a reconvened Geneva conference. The president, Vance, and Brzezinski had put enormous efforts into achieving this goal, however unrealistic it might have been. Nevertheless Carter had moved the dials and helped unfreeze some positions. In one way or another, his ill-conceived Geneva peace process served as a catalyst for Sadat's trip to Jerusalem, and then he moved to broaden a purely bilateral deal between Egypt and Israel into one that would offer the Palestinians some hope of controlling their own destiny.

But what about the Egyptians? As their delegation was waiting to fly back to Cairo, they engaged in an informal discussion at the airport with Dayan. Egypt's UN ambassador Ahmed Asmat Abdel-Meguid asked Dayan to explain the basis of Israel's claim to the West Bank: "Is it historical? Is it political? Or is it strategic? Tell us." And Dayan did: "No, everything. It is a political claim. It's a security claim." For the crestfallen Egyptians this meant that the Israelis would not accept withdrawal in exchange for an Egyptian offer of political stability and diplomatic recognition.[33]

This dramatized how much Israel's position had been changed by Begin's election. For Labor, the West Bank was a security issue. For Begin and the Likud it was a historical and religious claim. Security can be negotiated; history and religion cannot. Sadat had expected a grand gesture from Begin in exchange for his own, and he was bound to be disappointed—a pattern that extended throughout the negotiations to come.

Still, Sadat had calculated his people's mood correctly. When he arrived in Cairo, millions of Egyptians were lining the streets celebrating his return. He knew he had the support of the military because he could provide them with modern American arms, as well as the support of the intelligence service—"the pillars of authority in our society," as Gheit characterized them to me.[34]

Upstaged by Sadat as a great peacemaker, Jimmy Carter was now faced with the problem of maintaining a leading role if the United States was to keep its leverage in shaping a new order in the Middle East. Kissinger had demonstrated that nothing would be accomplished by the two avowed enemies in Cairo and Jerusalem without American leadership and pressure. This was confirmed by the period of almost a year's drift that followed Sadat's visit to Jerusalem. It fell to Carter to gain Begin's confidence and trust. But Begin not only was an ideologue for a Greater Israel, he maintained all the defenses of a gentleman lawyer including a legalistic mind-set—the exact opposite of the expansive politics practiced by Sadat. American gestures or concessions did not moderate his position, and compromise was made even more difficult by Israeli pressure that was exerted through American Jewish leaders. I explained to Carter that American Jews' nervousness about our Middle East policy was rooted in the bitter memory of American inaction while millions of European Jews were murdered during World War II, and he made it clear that he understood. But it was also difficult for American Jews to understand Carter's strategy of enhancing Israel's security by trying to build bridges to moderate Arabs and the Palestinians. That concept seemed an oxymoron in the American heartland.

Nevertheless the president swallowed hard and praised Sadat's trip as "great and courageous" at a breakfast with Democratic congressional leaders shortly after Sadat returned home. But he quickly followed by saying it would be "good to see how Sadat and Begin do by themselves for the next few weeks."[35] He obviously did not expect to see much and blamed the impasse mainly on Israeli settlements—not only in the West Bank but in the Sinai, where conquest had given Israel strategic depth to throw back any Arab attack.

In fact, little was accomplished in meetings between the two countries, but the reasons are more complicated. As Carter had urged in his letters to Begin and Sadat, Egypt and Israel attempted to settle their differences by themselves. The president stood aside uncomfortably as high-ranking officials began gathering for the first direct negotiations between the two neighboring nations, on the outskirts of Cairo at the fabled Mena House hotel, within site of the Pyramids. But the sense of excitement and even wonder at the new beginning was felt even in the city's teeming bazaars. A member of the Egyptian delegation, Abdel Raouf El Reedy, remembered that it had captured "the eyes and the attention of the Egyptian people that you had an Israeli delegation, Israelis in town, moving around everywhere."[36] An Israeli

member was late because when he went shopping in old Cairo people showered his party with candy, offered tea and coffee, and even refused payment
in the shops.

But all this was bound to lead to disappointment because a principal source
of the popular outpouring of joy was the expectation of getting the Sinai
back, and the Palestinian problem being resolved once and for all. Few knew
that the PLO's Arafat declined Sadat's invitation to participate, because he
refused to accept UN Resolution 242 as a condition of joining the talks.
Israel had already prepared a peace treaty under Dayan's direction, but there
was no hint in the draft of Israeli withdrawal from the Sinai.[37]

The two sides negotiated day and night from December 13 to Christmas Day at the Mena House in rooms with poorly disguised listening devices planted by the Egyptians. Defense Minister Weizman arrived secretly
in Cairo for negotiations, but when he had to telephone Israel, his call had
to be routed through New York, because there was no direct communication
with Jerusalem. The hotel flew the PLO flag prominently, and the Israelis
warned that they would leave if it was not taken down; the Egyptians said the
flag was there only for a photo and then it would be removed. The Egyptians tried linking the talks to the Palestinians, but the Israelis would not
hear of it. The Israeli delegation meanwhile said they were not empowered
to set a date for withdrawing from the Sinai. The hard work was fruitless.[38]

The meeting nevertheless drew such favorable press coverage and congressional reaction that the Carter administration could not be seen as opposing it.[39] Now the onus was on Begin to respond positively to Sadat's opening.
But even before the Mena House talks got under way, Begin had written out
by hand sixteen articles of a proposed treaty and instructed Aharon Barak,
his Foreign Office legal adviser, to "dress it [up] in legal terms."[40] Israel would
offer to withdraw from the Egyptian Sinai in two stages; it would also grant
home rule to Palestinians in the West Bank and Gaza as long as Israel remained
in charge of security for five years, with a review at that time. Sidestepping
Sadat and the Mena House talks, he wanted to take it to Carter in person.

Carter was coming to realize that the Egyptians and Israelis were incapable of making peace without active American engagement, because their opposing positions were so deeply entrenched. While Begin's proposal for
some Palestinian self-government was only a first step, the very fact that he

made it was regarded as significant. The prime minister's own tactics supported Carter's reading of America's essential role as mediator and guarantor of any agreement. He wanted to show his autonomy plan to Carter before showing it to Sadat, and did not even vet it with most of his cabinet before going to Washington just after the Mena talks had begun.

Carter and Brzezinski liked most of Begin's plan for withdrawing from most of Sinai.[41] But they rejected his plan for Palestinian autonomy, feeling it was "a step in the right direction," but inadequate, and Carter warned that it might bring down Sadat. But all in all, Carter appreciated "the flexibility and political courage and was a major reason why I came to believe that I could have a fruitful meeting involving just Begin, Sadat, and me."[42] Brzezinski carefully discussed Begin's proposals with Mondale and me. I was deputed to set up a private meeting between Begin and Brzezinski to discuss details. So I arranged the meeting through Ambassador Dinitz at Blair House. Brzezinski first suggested that Begin adjust the wording by dropping the formal term "autonomy"—which he felt was usually used for a district or region of one's own country—and substituting the more flexible term "self-rule." Begin readily agreed. They then discussed other details to ready the plan for formal presentation to the president in the Cabinet Room.[43]

When Begin came to Washington in mid-December, he gave a bravado performance. In the marginal notes on my yellow pad I wrote: "Begin did almost all the talking. Had maps. Seemed clearly pleased with this forthcoming position." He spoke extemporaneously and without a stop for almost half an hour; included was his almost mandatory dissertation on Jewish history, from the link between the Jewish people and the land of Israel to the Holocaust and the rebirth of the Jewish state. I could see a good deal of fidgeting on the American side of the table, but Carter never once showed the impatience he clearly felt, as Begin inched toward the heart of his proposal. It included a withdrawal from Sinai in three to four years, with a UN force which could not be removed without approval of all the parties (today a multinational force is still there).

For the West Bank, he proposed the creation of a civilian Arab council with continued Israeli military control in military encampments, and leaving open a decision on sovereignty.[44] This was not a bad starting point, but would end up being the high-water mark in loosening Israel's hold over the territories conquered by Israel in the Six-Day War, which Begin became the first Israeli prime minister to always call by their biblical names of Judea and Samaria. It did set the stage for a Camp David accord with Egypt after innumerable twists and turns. Unfortunately, some of those turns were taken by Begin himself as he put forward ideas, dangled them, and then pulled back.

BEGIN AND SADAT FAIL TO
MAKE PEACE ALONE

Shortly after the White House meetings, Begin and Sadat met in Ismailia on December 27. Sadat drove Begin around the Suez Canal Zone to show him the territory. Begin began by lecturing Sadat that the "Arabs and Egypt had been defeated in an aggressive war [and when] people lose wars they lost also territory. My experience in Eastern Europe tells me so." Sadat was taken aback: "I have to remind you, Mr. Prime Minister, that [kind of thinking] led to many, many, many wars, because every time you take territory from this party, the aggrieved party would decide to take back its territory. So if that is your will or wish, then it is strange that we are sitting to discuss this."[45] Not surprisingly, the autonomy plan Begin presented to Sadat was not as liberal as the one he had given to Carter; hawks in the Israeli cabinet argued that it would eventually lead to a Palestinian state. Ismailia, Ambassador Lewis believed, was the beginning of Sadat's ill will toward Begin and "a great missed opportunity." Sadat wanted a general statement of principles to show that he had obtained enough for the Palestinians to defend his negotiations to the Arab world, before his fellow Arabs became too negative and tried to block a deal returning the Sinai to Egypt.[46]

Begin asked to meet Sadat privately, and after twenty minutes alone together, Begin announced they had reached a written agreement on a formula for Palestinian autonomy, which in fact Begin had prepared in advance. "Well, please read it," said Sadat. "No, I prefer you read it," said Begin, and Sadat did so, demonstrating how far he was from his own delegation, which was already deeply suspicious of the entire initiative. And when Sadat read it out in a way that indicated he was close to agreeing, Boutros-Ghali immediately declared:

"This statement is unacceptable." Everyone on the Israeli side was shocked at this outburst, but it clearly reflected the views of Sadat's senior Egyptian advisers, who were trying to protect their bold leader from himself.[47]

To the Egyptians, Boutros-Ghali wrote, Begin's "vision involved a kind of amputated Palestinian entity."[48] Even Mondale, when he learned of Begin's autonomy plan, remarked, "You couldn't even sell that to people in Washington, D.C., (where the residents sought home rule)."[49] And in the end, nothing was agreed. Neither side could reach across to the other to understand his opponent's thinking, and certainly not the pressures against compromise faced by both sides. My own experience in negotiating domestic and international agreements is that it is just as important to know your opposition's problems and bottom lines as it is to know your own. Begin never incorporated Sadat's severe public exposure to Arab intransigence into his own thinking, and Sadat, perhaps feeling he could do better with U.S. pressure on Israel, felt he could overcome them by force of personality and personal vision, without fully recognizing Begin's redlines.[50]

Military and political committees were created and met in January, but nothing materialized. As the Middle East drifted, Ham became concerned that Carter was spreading himself too thin and not investing enough of his resources in his domestic priorities. In a 116-page memo summing up Carter's first year in office, his strongest warning was based in part on the bruising first year of Middle East diplomacy: "Foreign policy and domestic issues bring conflicting political pressures on a President . . . [which] must be continually reconciled." He cited the surveys of Carter's pollster, Pat Caddell, showing that the American people's primary concerns were far from the Middle East—jobs, inflation, and the general condition of the economy.

Ham warned: "The amount of time spent on foreign policy in the last ten months left less time than you needed to deal with domestic issues and maintain an effective political base." In a sharp criticism of the president's lack of priorities, the man who had engineered Carter's election told him as only he could, "You find it difficult—if not impossible—to say that 'this problem is not important enough to merit my personal attention.' As a result, too many policies, programs and issues receive what I describe as excessive Presidential attention and absorb too much of the precious political and moral capital of your Presidency."[51]

The memo had some impact. Ham was later named Carter's first White House chief of staff. Working with me, Brezinski, and our staffs, Mondale was put in charge of what became an effective effort to set strict presidential priorities on issues that demanded Carter's attention, and the rest, which could be handled with White House staff oversight, or by the cabinet members themselves. But one thing that did not change was the extraordinary amount of time and energy Carter devoted to the Middle East, and his willingness to stake out positions that opposed Israeli policies.

Just after the New Year, Carter was off to the Middle East. On January 3 he flew to Saudi Arabia to meet with Crown Prince Fahd to discuss a Palestinian homeland. The following day he arrived in Aswan in Upper Egypt to meet Sadat, only a few days after the Begin-Sadat meeting at Ismailia. In fact Sadat initially praised Begin for a concrete proposal for withdrawal from the occupied territories. But after he met with Carter at Aswan on January 4, the Egyptian press took a hard line, describing Begin as intransigent. Sadat canceled the meetings of the joint Egyptian-Israeli committee that had made considerable progress. Did Sadat believe Carter's pressure on Begin would produce a more favorable outcome? Carter assured Sadat at Aswan that he "agreed with the Arab position that Israel ought to withdraw completely from the occupied territories, with minor adjustments in the western part: that there should be self-determination of the Palestinians short of an independent nation; and genuine peaceful relations between Israel and each of her neighbors."[52]

IT'S THE SETTLEMENTS, STUPID

On January 10 Carter sent Begin a strong message criticizing settlement expansion in the West Bank as "an obstacle to peace."[53] None of this had much effect on Begin or his aggressive new political partner, the military hero Ariel Sharon, who pressed ahead with new settlements, nominally as Begin's agriculture minister. Carter recognized that any progress would require a significant push from Washington and a U.S. plan. Sadat was invited to Camp David to develop a plan under an American strategy in which he would put forward one that would be unacceptable to the

Israelis, and then have the United States moderate it with compromise proposals.[54]

Sadat arrived at Camp David on February 4 with his wife, Jehan, one of the very few occasions that a foreign leader had been invited to the president's retreat. Rosalynn Carter took a snowmobile ride with Sadat, while her husband rode on another with Sadat's wife, Jehan.[55] This was a bonding experience, and it would pay off because Sadat gave the president wide latitude to negotiate with Israel. As Carter noted, in his historic trip to Jerusalem, Sadat had "decided in one fell swoop to accomplish all these Israeli desires and get the U.S. Jew lobby (as he referred to it) off my shoulders. They were not ready for peace and possibly are still not." Carter felt that Sadat was "completely disillusioned with Begin's ridiculous position" at Ismailia of wanting to hold on to settlements in the Sinai.[56]

Sadat warned him that he was going to announce at his National Press Club speech on Monday that Egypt was discontinuing military and political talks; it took every bit of presidential persuasion to get him to back off his threat.[57] This would not be the last time a personal intervention by Carter was necessary to keep Sadat from bolting.

The Israelis also realized they might be forced into a corner. While Carter and Sadat were meeting, Dinitz came to my office and I upbraided him about the new settlements. In a top-secret cable to Dayan I saw years later, Dinitz claimed there was a "hideous campaign" against Israel to "undermine our credibility, by leaks and interpretations directed from above, with the intention to create the impression as though we broke our promise to the President."[58]

The tone of Sadat's visit stood in sharp contrast to the abrasive encounters with Begin. Part was personality. Sadat had a charm, ebullience, and warmth that contrasted sharply with Begin's demeanor. While Begin could be a pedantic lecturer, Sadat spoke in broad generalities, with a sweeping vision and disdain for details, and endeared himself to Carter, calling him "my friend Jimmy." Begin of course had the most to lose in terms of territory and security, so every concession was made grudgingly, while Sadat counted on Carter to protect his interests as long as Egypt regained all of the Sinai and was able to obtain something for the Palestinians. As the months wore on and the administration began preparing for a visit by Begin late in March, the tension heightened, with Sadat angry that Begin had not adequately responded to his grand gesture,[59] and Carter piloting a highly controversial bill through Congress permitting the sale of American fighter jets to Egypt and Saudi Arabia. Caught in the crossfire, Carter blurted out to congressional leaders the day before Begin's arrival that he expected the visit to be "unpleasant" and lamented that "peace hopes have faded."[60]

With all this in mind, the United States and Israel began preparing for a March meeting with Begin. When Dinitz came to my office, I had a harsh message to deliver from Brzezinski, warning that Israel's expansionist policies were untenable.[61] He got the message and cabled home quoting Brzezinski—in capital letters—as warning that "ISRAEL SHOULD NOT BE ALLOWED TO GET AWAY WITH IT." Carter, I said, recommended that Begin start using the term "withdrawal to military encampments" to help Carter sell Sadat on the idea that Israel was showing some flexibility, and Begin eventually accepted this formulation. But the core of the problem was the civilian settlements themselves. To drive home the political danger, I said that Israel's opponents in the administration and even in the White House had fixed on the settlements to "arouse public opinion against you [even among Jews], and to weaken your position in the Congress and in the public." As a friend of Israel, I pleaded with Dinitz to urge Begin not to give ammunition to his opponents. I knew I could not change Begin's long-held views about Israel's right to settle in what he called Judaea and Samaria, but I implored Dinitz to strongly recommend that Begin not exercise that right for the time being so that negotiations with Egypt might succeed. I also urged that Begin reach out to Jordan, which he did, but he did not absorb our basic message.[62]

Begin arrived in Washington in the tense atmosphere of a PLO terrorist attack that killed an American photographer and 35 Israelis and prompted an Israeli attack on a PLO base in southern Lebanon that Carter felt was "a terrible overreaction" and disproportionate in its devastation. This hardened public attitudes about the risks of concessions to Egypt.[63] In the complex history of our relationship with Israel, and as Carter foresaw, there probably has not been a more confrontational meeting with the leader of a friendly country than occurred in the Cabinet Room on March 22, 1978, with the president, vice president, Vance, Brzezinski, and me around the large oval table with Begin, Dayan, and Dinitz. The heart of the bitter dispute lay in

Begin's refusal to agree to yield at least some of Israel's conquests on all fronts, including the West Bank. He did not claim Israeli sovereignty over "Judaea, Samaria and Gaza," but an abiding interest, although he was prepared to offer the Palestinians autonomy, to be reviewed after five years. Brzezinski, seeking compromise, said that if Israel withdrew to military emplacements, as I had told Dinitz, "then your plan could be the basis for a solution, and open the way for peace . . . security yes, political control no."

Carter wasted no time in getting to the heart of what was bothering him: Israel's refusal to follow the terms of UN Resolution 242. Carter spelled out that this meant withdrawal to agreed frontiers and a voice for the Palestinians in their political future. Without giving Begin a chance to reply, Carter expressed his "discouragement" at Israel's refusal to accept these mandates while continuing to establish new Israeli settlements in the occupied territories. Then he warned Begin that he would alert congressional leaders to Israel's unacceptable positions at a meeting only a few hours later.

Carter flatly told Begin that the "obstacle to a peace treaty with Egypt is your insistence on keeping political control over the West Bank and Gaza."[64] Then he icily summed up his understanding of the Israeli position, which came to be called the "six no's"—a play on the Arabs' "three no's" refusing peace with Israel after their 1967 defeat—Israel would not stop building new settlements; would not stop expanding existing ones; would not yield its Sinai settlements; would not withdraw its political authority from the West Bank and Gaza; would not recognize that UN Resolution 242 applied to all the territories; and would not allow the Palestinians to choose between interim self-government or becoming part of Israel or Jordan.[65] After some seconds, which seemed like hours of stony silence, an ashen-faced Begin argued that he *had* been flexible. But despite his attempts to rebut Carter, the president was unrelenting.

Taken aback by the harsh tone, Begin asked Carter to do exactly the opposite—to frame Israel's position positively and convey Israel's willingness to be forthcoming. Begin explained: "We won't agree to halt settlements during the negotiations, as we have the right to settle there, and negotiations could take years." My notes record that "Begin presents a very rigid, unbending position." It was clear that Begin and Carter brought out the worst in each other. Sensing this, Dayan interjected and talked more flexibly about withdrawal to military encampments, and said Israel had a new proposal for using 242 as the basis for negotiations with all of Israel's neighbors. Immediately the president responded: "This is more promising."[66] While I felt that Dayan had salvaged something, from Begin's standpoint the meeting was "nasty," with an absolute stalemate, and hardly improved by the White House spokesman's description of Begin's intransigence.[67]

Shortly afterward, in his private study, the president asked my views. Summarizing Begin's ideology, I told him he would be much more flexible on terms for giving up the Sinai, where he made no historical or biblical claims. I felt the best we could do on the West Bank would be to try to limit the expansion of settlements and develop a plan for Palestinian self-government. I added one other element: As difficult as Begin could be in representing what even the Hebrew Bible described as "a stiff-necked people" (Exodus 32:9), I believed he was totally trustworthy and honest in his beliefs. The president made no comment.[68]

But I received calls offering support for Carter from Jewish members of Congress, including its only Holocaust survivor, Tom Lantos of California.[69] Even my Harvard Law School professor Alan Dershowitz, a staunch supporter of Israel, offered help and warned: "We're creating the wrong [American] Jewish leadership, who are knee-jerk for whatever the government of Israel does."[70] The night of that tense meeting, I sat down with Begin and Yechiel Kadishai in the small den in Dinitz's residence and found Begin morose and upset.

The most useful advice for me came from Lewis, a fine ambassador and one of the American officials most sensitive to Israel's concerns, while nevertheless strongly supporting the president's attempts at peacemaking. Lewis was a Yale-educated career diplomat with a deep understanding of the country where he served. He had earned the trust and confidence of Begin, Dayan, and all the key Israeli government figures, convincing them he was a friend of Israel who also had the president's confidence. The ambassador gave us a biting critique of the president's behavior and the administration, and warned ominously that Begin was "convinced we're trying to do him in." He advised us that the Israelis would be more responsive "if they're convinced we're still their special friends."

Lewis pointed out that the president had sent no personal notes to Begin to help maintain human contact (he rarely did to any foreign or domestic leader). He recommended that the president spend fifteen minutes alone with Begin and show admiration for him as a person despite their differences: "Pump him up." Turning from personal diplomacy to matters of policy, he criticized the way the administration's general reduction of arms sales had meant reneging on promises to Israel, and furthermore that packaging arms destined for Israel with sales to Saudi Arabia and Egypt offended Israel because it tied their needs to the Arabs'—both now and possibly in the future. Taking all these moves together, he explained patiently, "supports Begin's view that Jews are all alone in the world and mustn't give in; it feeds his view of [Jewish] suffering." I welcomed his advice but noted on my legal pad: "JC won't listen and back him up."[71]

I got my chance just before Begin's arrival. On Saturday, April 30, a day of rest for most of the country but a buzz of activity at the White House, I had a lengthy discussion with the president about the many domestic issues in my portfolio, and I was deeply touched by his uncharacteristic thanks and praise: "You are at the top in terms of my estimation of people here. I appreciate your making my job easier." This gave me an opening to talk about Israel, and I summarized many of Lewis's concerns. Carter's response reflected his mind-set: "Begin is solely holding up peace. I have a coldness in my heart toward him after our meetings."[72]

This frank display of feelings sometimes got him in trouble when they tumbled out in public—and it was lucky that this one had not, with its biblical allusion to God hardening Pharaoh's heart against Moses as he sought to lead his people out of Egypt. Carter agreed to be more cordial and met privately with Begin for half an hour the next day, but in his diary entry for that day, it was clear that nothing had changed: "He's a small man with limited vision, and my guess is he will not take the necessary steps to bring peace to Israel—an opportunity that may never come again. I'm determined to put maximum pressure on him but will have to judge the political situation closely to maximize the possibility for success."[73]

After the meeting there was a White House reception for America's religious and lay Jewish leaders. Carter had originally opposed a reception for Begin, but agreed to a ceremony as part of our effort to mend fences. As he confided to his diary: "I finally agreed to meet with two hundred rabbis to celebrate the thirtieth anniversary of Israel. Twelve hundred showed up, and Begin and I made somewhat emotional speeches to them, although brief, and then shook hands with everyone. The result of the whole affair was very positive."[74]

His most positive contribution was a surprise public announcement in Begin's presence, following a written recommendation from Lipshutz and me (based upon the suggestion of Ellen Goldstein of my staff), that he was forming a commission to establish an American memorial for the victims of the Holocaust, to be chaired, at my urging, by Holocaust survivor and famous author Eli Wiesel (another Carter legacy largely forgotten by the more than fifty million people who had visited the United States Holocaust Memorial Museum in Washington by 2017). He focused on Begin's own family's murder at the hand of the Nazis; Begin was clearly moved, and so was I.

But this did not stop intense criticism of Brzezinski among the Jewish leadership, which sufficiently concerned him to send me an extraordinary memo with a summary of his views from 1970 forward on the Middle East, emphasizing his pro-Israeli statements. As much as I disagreed with his tactical decisions in pressing Israel, I replied with a handwritten note that I was "livid at the occasional inference from unnamed members of the organized Jewish community that you are anti-Israel" and promised to help defend him against such calumny. Even New York's strongly pro-Israel senator Daniel Moynihan told me he was "disturbed [that] Jews are responding to demagoguery."[75]

Carter's own family also unwittingly undermined his efforts. His sister Ruth Carter Stapleton had played a prominent part in Carter's becoming a born-again Christian, and had just accepted a speaking engagement at a crusade by the organization Jews for Jesus, whose primary purpose was proselytizing Jews, especially young people. When I heard about this from Rabbi Marc Tanenbaum, who handled interreligious affairs for the American Jewish Committee, I sent Ham a very blunt memo: "This is a group which is despised in the Jewish community, and an appearance by the president's sister will only aggravate the deep feelings in the Jewish community against the administration."[76] I urged him to intervene and explain that her appearance would certainly not help her brother or his administration. He did so, and her appearance was canceled.[77]

A JEWISH CASUALTY OF A SAUDI ARMS SALE

One of the administration's boldest attempts to buy goodwill, if not peace on both sides, was a multibillion-dollar deal to spread American jet fighters around the Middle East, simultaneously enhancing Middle East security and American interests, or so it was argued. It had been arranged by the Ford administration to ensure that the United States would be regarded as a reliable arms supplier capable of replacing the Soviet Union. Sales to Israel were also part of the package that would maintain Israel's qualitative edge. But this did not mollify its supporters in Congress. Israel had legitimate fears that it would start a shift in the strategic balance toward the Arabs. The deal had to be approved by Congress, and this injected fierce opposition by Israel and its American supporters directly into American politics. Overriding Carter's policy of limiting arms sales, the administration wanted to demonstrate to the Saudis and Egyptians that the United States was determined to strengthen ties with them, even in the face of domestic opposition.[78]

The deal provoked one of the most contentious presidential battles with the American Jewish leadership, before or since (perhaps matched by Ronald Reagan's sale of AWACS planes to the Saudis). For the first time—but not the last—AIPAC and the leaders of the American Jewish community went head-to-head against an American president over a congressional vote. They argued that once the jets came into the hands of the Arabs, they would be turned against Israel. Suspicion by AIPAC's executive director, Morris Amitay, turned into sheer ill will over what he considered Brzezinski's high-handed manner. When the administration had first blocked the sale of Israeli-made Kfir jet fighters to Ecuador, Amitay told me he raised the issue after a White House lunch with Brzezinski as they walked into the Rose Garden, and he bluntly replied, 'Next subject,' quote unquote." From then on it was political trench warfare that left permanent scars on both sides.[79]

To provide Israel with greater assurance, and with the backing of Brzezinski and Carter, in an April 20, 1978, meeting with the deputy chief of mission at the Israeli Embassy, Hanon Bar-On, I explored the possibility of crafting a mutual defense treaty to protect Israel from its Arab enemies.[80] Careful to say that I was only putting forward my own informal thoughts,

I told Bar-On that I had heard some "major figures" discuss building a U.S. airbase in the Israeli Sinai and using Israel's ports for our navy as part of a mutual defense agreement. I suggested that the airbase could not only help stabilize relations between our two countries, but also would provide effective protection to the oil resources in Saudi Arabia. Furthermore, I said, Israeli ports for the U.S. Navy could provide reasonable alternatives to our access to Greek and Turkish ports under the NATO treaty.

Bar-On summarized this in a top-secret cable to Dayan that day, but Israel never seriously took up the suggestion.[81] It was a major tenet of Israel's national security posture—as it remains to this day—that the nation can defend itself, although in a crunch it will always ask the United States for help. I believe the reason they demurred was that they felt a U.S. military presence would deter Israel from acting independently—for example against Iraqi and Syrian nuclear facilities, against Hezbollah in Lebanon, or more recently in Gaza. By their calculation the loss of flexibility would be greater than any gain from a formal defense treaty binding the United States.

One immediate casualty of our quarrels with the American Jewish leadership over the Saudi sale was Ham's valued political liaison, Mark Siegel. He had been sent around the country to promote it, and was still a good soldier. The State Department drafted a standard speech emphasizing that the F-15s for Saudi Arabia were only defensive weapons and posed no threat to Israel. Acting on direct orders from Vance, Siegel delivered the speech to the United Jewish Appeal at the Washington Hilton—and was booed. A member of the audience challenged him by holding up a McDonnell-Douglas brochure in which the manufacturer touted the F-15 as "the best offensive attack aircraft in the world." Siegel went to Ham and indicated he wanted to leave, but Ham suggested he remain and just quietly drop his role as Jewish liaison. He did not reject this outright: "I wasn't Joan of Arc. I wasn't a fanatic, and I also had a family." Siegel then asked a good friend, Al Hunt of the *Wall Street Journal*, what he should do. Hunt told him that once a resignation is offered, it can't be withdrawn. Siegel decided to leave, which only served to strengthen the Jewish leadership's belief that the sale

disadvantaged Israel. No one spoke to him during the few days he was packing up his things.

One of the most prized qualities of anyone in a senior White House position is loyalty, no matter whether you agree with the decisions that come
out of the Oval Office. Mark knew he had broken an implicit pledge of
loyalty. He drafted a long letter of resignation, whereupon Carter asked to
see him in the Oval Office, the only time he had been alone there with the
president. Carter said he thought of him as a friend, respected his decision,
but wanted to know more. Siegel expressed his respect for Carter's efforts to
bring peace to Israel but bluntly criticized Brzezinski. He told Carter that at
a formal luncheon in the State Department dining room for Jewish leaders,
Brzezinski snapped at the head of the Jewish Federation of Los Angeles: "You
people better learn that you don't dictate foreign policy." Only after Siegel
left the White House did he go public with his complaints. Humiliated, he
left the White House, and while walking along Pennsylvania Avenue ran
into a reporter, Carl Luebsdorf of the *Dallas Morning News*, who jokingly
said Brzezinski had indicated, "You're not going to meddle in foreign policy
anymore." Now thoroughly rattled, Siegel blurted out that he definitely
would not be involved: He was resigning because he had been told "just
flat-out lies about the offensive capabilities of these aircraft."[82] The White
House then leaked to the press that he had not resigned but been fired,
which of course angered him. Welcome to the world of Washington and
the brutal domestic politics of Middle East policy making.

Siegel's resignation raises the issue of whether it is appropriate for a
senior adviser to a president to resign over a policy difference. My view is that
you have to be prepared that many decisions will not go your way. While
the opportunity always exists to walk out and make a grand statement, this
is not the right course, except in the most extraordinary circumstances. It is
important to stay to fight the next battle. It is a rare privilege to be at the
shoulder of a president of the United States and try to influence decisions that
can have real impact on the way Americans live in our country, and on the
world. It is also important to make your case with force and logic, and I
always tried to do so (with the exception of the Bert Lance case, and its
heavy personal implications). But as the old baseball adage goes: "You win

some, you lose some, and some are rained out." By remaining loyal, even where decisions of great personal importance went against me, I was able to help sway others. I always reminded myself that it was not me but Jimmy Carter who was elected president by the people of the United States.

MONDALE'S MISSION, BAGELS AND ALL

Tensions with Israel and the Jewish community were so high and the negotiations so unpromising that Mondale was sent on a mission to Jerusalem and Cairo from June 30 to July 3, 1978. He had strong pro-Israel credentials and deep relationships with American Jewish leaders, some of whom he brought with him. It was an unusual government mission. For one thing, it was the first trip by any vice president to Israel, and also the first to serve traditional Jewish food on board—lox, bagels, and blintzes for breakfast, courtesy of the White House chef. Only in America could you find a New York City delicatessen on Air Force Two.

I was aboard and was struck by an important difference between Mondale and Carter. On my many trips with the president, he would hold brief conversations with officials accompanying him aboard Air Force One and then retire to his cabin to work. Carter then summoned his aides, myself included, to discuss the issues that we expected to arise on the trip.

But Mondale was a politician's politician. He enjoyed working the cabin, bantering, chatting, schmoozing with the Jewish leaders as we flew across the Atlantic, and then turning serious during a refueling stop in the Azores by trying to comfort them about the president's intentions toward Israel and the peace process. It was a political performance to behold.[83]

The effect of this extraordinary visit on the Jewish leaders was mixed. They were surprised at the depth of feeling against the administration that they encountered in the Israeli leaders they met separately from the vice president's official gatherings. Rabbi Saul Teplitz, president of the Synagogue Council of America, told Ambassador Lewis during a private briefing: "For the first time in 30 years, I got the feeling here that as an American I am somewhat in the enemy camp."[84]

Despite the extensive outreach to the Jewish community, the administration's persistent efforts to wrest concessions from Israel were having a corrosive impact on American Jewish opinion, even though they would be a necessary part of any Middle East peace agreement. A prominent Jewish businessman and campaign supporter of the president warned the White House that unless conditions changed for the better by 1980, "Jewish resources would be used to support a challenge to the President's nomination."[85]

With Jewish leaders lobbying for a stronger voice inside the White House, Ed Sanders, a former president of AIPAC and Los Angeles lawyer, joined the staff, although Carter would have preferred to have him at a distance in the State Department. Sanders demanded a role in launching Middle East policy as opposed to just helping to minimize the damage from the crash landings. He proved a wise colleague, but he was never seriously involved in policy making.[86]

Behind the public imbroglios stood major White House policy disputes that Mondale managed at first to conceal. He had sent the president a draft of his speech to the Knesset, and Carter wrote a tough note in the margins reading in part: "Fritz, be firm on speech points and talking points." At one point in the draft speech, Carter wrote, "Don't weaken these paragraphs, and if questioned, be sure West Bank and Gaza are mentioned." So here at the very start of a goodwill visit to mend a frayed relationship, Mondale received stern presidential instructions not to be accommodating. And just as Mondale was boarding Air Force Two, he received a handwritten message instructing him to include in his speech a declaration that Israel would have to give up almost all of the West Bank as a price of peace. While the note was signed by the president, Mondale was sure that Brzezinski had recommended it, because the same thing had happened to Strauss, another presidential envoy, just as he boarded his flight to Israel. Mondale concluded that that was how Brzezinski avoided debates and got his way on an issue.

The fact of the matter is that Carter was receiving conflicting tactical advice and passing it on to Mondale, and the vice president realized it. He told me later: "Zbig's theory was that in order to get Israel to negotiate, you have to soften them up, you have to weaken them." As for Vance, he had the "traditional State Department feeling that somehow Israel had gotten away with too much."[87]

For me personally the trip was an epiphany. I vividly remembered my first visit to Israel in 1965 at the end of my first year at Harvard Law School. I had come to see my grandfather, then over 90; he's now buried in a cemetery on the outskirts of Tel Aviv, near his father, my great-grandfather. Coming off of Air Force Two with a giant American flag on its tail and the insignia of the vice president on its fuselage, and then being greeted by no less than the prime minister of Israel, gave me an indescribable feeling of how improbable and miraculous it was to have the honor of representing my own country while landing on the sacred soil of my ancestors. But it was no easy task. The tensions within the president's inner circle, and indeed between his own diplomatic goals and political pressures, often pulled us this way and that—rarely more so than on this trip with a planeload of Jewish leaders and a vice president politically committed to Israel who had been sent to soften up Begin.

We were received by Begin and his cabinet in a red-carpet welcome at Ben-Gurion Airport. On the long drive to Jerusalem, Mondale and Begin sat together, and the vice president delivered a personal letter from the president suggesting a foreign ministers meeting at Leeds Castle in England; he later delivered a similar letter to Sadat. His meetings with Begin and Dayan went well in convincing them that they could trust the president to protect Israel's security. And as a guest at a cabinet meeting, an unusual honor for a foreign official, Mondale announced the formal approval of an Israeli sale to Taiwan of Kfir jets with their General Electric jet engines, though a year earlier a similar sale to Ecuador had been scuttled. He asked that America's approval be kept quiet to avoid charges of favoritism to Israel, but privately he told Begin it would be "okay to leak it" to help draw positive attention in the American Jewish community when its distrust of the administration was rising.

But then the president made a remarkably ill-timed statement, restating all his conditions for the Geneva conference. Mondale was beside himself with anger and frustration that this occurred in the midst of his fence-mending visit. As we were getting off an Israeli helicopter at Sde Boker, the desert kibbutz where Ben-Gurion had retired and was buried, Mondale told me he felt that he was beginning to quiet Israeli suspicions, only to be undercut by Carter. He added bitterly: "I think we're finished and we can't recoup."[88]

Normally ebullient and upbeat, Mondale turned all his anger on Brzezinski and blamed him for the president's remarks. Brzezinski, and perhaps the president as well, were concerned that Mondale might somehow deviate from administration policy; but whatever misgivings he had about our position—and he shared my own—Mondale was deeply loyal. When he addressed the Knesset, he was forced to add language about Israeli withdrawal, and hated doing it. "They made my life miserable. . . . Just another gratuitous shot across my bow, and I think it was Zbig," he said later.[89] But years after the administration he felt Carter was also influenced by his reading of the Bible as a devout Baptist.[90]

In his private report to Carter on the Middle East trip, Mondale wrote: "In our first meetings, Begin was unanimated, unsmiling, and without his usual verve or responsiveness to humor. Although fully in command, he is not in good health. By the end of the visit, however, he had begun to smile in response to a steady effort to show respect and warmth toward him. He may be the only man, as Sadat [later] told me, who can deliver Israel on the compromises that would be crucial to peace. I suspect that Begin wants to be a man of peace and there is some possibility of flexibility if we work in a respectful way toward him."[91]

I believe that the trip helped lay the groundwork for a successful Camp David summit, because it helped relieve Begin's suspicions of the president. Mondale recalled that "Begin had lost all confidence in Carter, and I think one thing that I did for Camp David was to spend that time alone with him, nearly three hours explaining Carter to him."[92] But his blunt, handwritten report to the president on the trip reflected his starkly different way of approaching Israel, as a sympathetic supporter rather than someone coming armed with the tough position of Carter and Brzezinski, which they believed would eventually bend Begin's hard line. Mondale concluded: "Our direct confrontation with the Israelis has tended to drive the Israelis together rather than apart. There is a deep feeling in Israel that we have been one-sided in our public statements and Israel is the object of frequent criticism while Sadat isn't."[93]

Despite the vice president's advice, the confrontational approach continued. Yet every president since the Six-Day War has often had to stand firm on America's policy toward Israel, while remaining irrevocably committed to Israel's security. Jimmy Carter was emphatically no exception, because the United States also has broader interests in a region with almost two dozen Arab states.

For all their tough talk, Carter, Brzezinski, and Vance never threatened to reassess policy or cut off American funds, as future presidents would do. Begin was certainly a tough customer, and without Carter's steely determination to push ahead, it is doubtful that as much progress would have been made. But at the same time, Mondale's words ring true. A better mixture of support and empathy, the avoidance of gratuitous insults, and a more balanced view about Sadat and Begin would have been helpful.

One last time, Egyptian and Israeli leaders tried to make progress on their own at Leeds Castle southeast of London, a Norman landmark so beautiful and storied that it is a choice British government venue for high-level conferences. The baronial dining room had been restored with a table about fifty feet long, which occasioned an initial negotiation about whether the Egyptians would eat separately or join the rest on the first night. It became the first time within memory that Israelis and Egyptian officials had dined together. The seating was arranged so that an American was placed next to an Egyptian, and then an Israeli, the alternation of nationalities repeating itself around the table. The group, numbering about 25 or 30, started out very stiffly, but normal human interaction loosened conversation. From then on there was no question of separate tables, but that did little to bridge differences between Israel and Egypt, which remained as wide as the Sinai itself, including the settlements in Sinai under Israeli jurisdiction.[94] Leeds was so unproductive, and Sadat so fed up, that he refused the administration's request for another tripartite meeting and decreed there would be no more of them.

We had reached what appeared to be a dead end to Carter's Middle East diplomacy. He then turned it around in a successful act of personal diplomacy unprecedented in the American presidency.

19

CARTER'S TRIUMPH AT CAMP DAVID

With Sadat angry and Begin intransigent, the president was nevertheless determined to press on with a process in which he had invested so much time and energy. Much of that determination was grounded in Carter's own resolute character as well as his loyalty to Sadat. He did not want to humiliate the man who had risked his office and perhaps his life by opening the path to change in the Middle East. Failing to capitalize on the momentum created by Sadat could have opened the way for the Soviets to return to the region, and Carter believed that events could spin out of control: "Israel was embedded in obdurate positions . . . and Sadat was talking to other Arab leaders about military action."[1]

Once he understood that the peace process was heading toward failure, Carter explained later: "I couldn't see any alternative to bringing Sadat and Begin together." And since he refused to admit failure of such a high-profile project, he also had to jump into it for personal reasons: "Once I had made a decision, I was awfully stubborn about it. I think if I could have one political attribute as a cause of my success to begin with, it would be tenacity. And that may also be a cause of some of my political failures. I just can't say for sure. Stubbornness is never an attractive attribute."[2]

This time, however, it served him well. Against the counsel of his principal administration advisers and the handful of Washington Wise Men he consulted, the staff reluctantly set up a meeting with the modest goal of reintroducing Begin and Sadat to each other and reviewing their positions. Mondale argued that the odds were stacked against success and told Carter: "If you fail, we're done . . . we will sap our stature as national leaders. We've got to find some less risky way of trying to find peace there." Carter replied that he would take the risk.[3]

Carter checked with Ham, Jody, and Rafshoon, and as Rafshoon recounted, Carter reasoned: "If I don't do it there will be a war, because Sadat has told me if his peace initiative fails, he will have to go to war to bring the Israelis back to the negotiating table. If I do it and fail, there will be a war. But I won't fail, because if I can get them together, they won't let me fail."[4] So the president of the United States wrote out personal invitations in his own hand to Sadat and Begin to join him at Camp David, and sent Vance to deliver them in person. That, said Carter, "kind of put them on the spot not to turn it down."[5]

It also put the two Middle East leaders on separate tracks because of their different expectations: Begin envisioned an agenda-setting conference that would demand little commitment, while Sadat calculated that regaining the Sinai and gaining some leverage for the Palestinians would raise his stature in the Arab world and justify his gestures to Israel.

The U.S. ambassador to Egypt, Hermann Eilts, felt that Sadat came to Camp David in a confrontational mood because he felt Begin had shown no appreciation for what he had done.[6] Carter, ever the problem-solving engineer, thought he could bridge their differences in perhaps three or four days by making the two very different leaders see reason. He never imagined it would take almost two weeks to overcome—and then only partly—the suspicions on both sides that were compounded by Begin's searing memories of the European pogroms and the rigid ideology they engendered.[7]

Carter and his wife, who after more than seventy years of marriage disagree on remarkably few things, do not agree on which of them came up with the idea of meeting at Camp David. But each wants to give the other the credit for the brilliant but daring idea of isolating the principals far from the ministrations of officialdom to negotiate an improbable peace agreement. Rosalynn[8] recounted that on a July afternoon when they were walking through the beautiful woods at Camp David, he told her he had an idea: "It's so beautiful here, I don't believe anybody could stay in the place, close to nature, peaceful and isolated from the world, and still carry a grudge. I believe I could get Sadat and Begin both here together, and we could

work out some of the problems between them, or at least we could learn
to understand each other better and maybe make some progress. Everything's
going backward now."

But she told me years later[9] that "I wrote in my book that Jimmy suggested it, but he argues with me still about that, because he said I was the one.
And after he said that, I remember walking around Camp David one day,
and I said, 'I don't see if you brought Begin and Sadat up here—I don't see
how they could do anything [but make progress] it's so peaceful and quiet
and nice up here." Their partnership is so strong that they have often thought
alike.

Whatever the genesis of the decision, once it was made, Carter and his
wife took a boat trip down Idaho's appropriately named River of No Return, then on to the nearby Grand Tetons for a vacation. He was worn out
and needed the break. But he was sent thick State Department briefing books
containing extensive analyses of his two interlocutors—"their psychological
background, their philosophical background, the history of their parents,
what obligations they had made to their friends and allies, what public statements they had made."

When he returned to the White House and read his staff's briefing book
for what they envisioned as an unambitious meeting, he admitted he was
"really pissed off" at the "very timid approach" his advisers wanted him to
take at Camp David. He summoned them angrily to the White House. "I
wanted for them to present to me a maximum possible settlement that we
might reach at Camp David. So I told them to completely revise it."[10]

It cannot be overemphasized how unprecedented this conduct was for
an American president. Time-honored practice is to test the waters before
inviting another head of state—never mind two who so thoroughly distrusted each other—without even knowing whether he or she would accept. Kissinger called the president[11] to warn that a head of state should
never go into a negotiation with a foreign leader unless he knew in advance
how it would come out. He suggested that perhaps someone outside the
administration—read Dr. Kissinger—could negotiate, so a failure would not
hurt the president.

Summits almost always follow a tight script prepared well in advance, with an agreement or joint statement carefully negotiated during weeks or months by trusted aides to avoid the possibility of a failure. None of this existed at Camp David, not even an agreed process for this unique three-way negotiation. It was all done on the fly—a high-wire act of the first order without a net, with uncertain results, and the likelihood of failure far greater than the chance of success. Indeed there was no common understanding even of what success meant, since the leaders of the three countries had different goals. Nevertheless, Carter plunged ahead, and on August 8, 1978, made his surprise announcement to the world convening the meeting.

Sadat jumped at the offer and told Vance he had already realized that a summit meeting was necessary; Begin was also positive but showed no signs of flexibility.[12] For Sadat, failure would bring dangerous repudiation in the Arab world; for Begin, failure could undermine Israel's irreplaceable military and diplomatic support by the United States; for Carter, failure would further damage his already shaky presidency.

Before leaving for Camp David, the president told me to hold down the home front and essentially run the government with the vice president, thinking he would be away for only a few days. This was less grandiose than it might seem. It meant keeping the policy process moving forward on all our issues inside the administration and with Congress, until he could return to make final decisions. Still, it was an unusual time, and I did not want to bother him with anything beyond what he was concentrating on at Camp David day and night.

The issues he faced were staggering: first, securing a withdrawal of all Israeli military forces, bases, and settlements from the Egyptian Sinai in return for full recognition of Israel; second, defining the interim status of the Palestinians in the West Bank in a way that would allow Sadat to present a victory for his Arab brethren. Two others were almost insoluble dilemmas: satisfying Begin's restrictive conditions for controlling what he considered biblical Israel, while limiting Israeli settlement enlargement on the West Bank and Gaza; and, finally, settling the status of Jerusalem—a holy city for the three different religions of the principal participants, Judaism, Islam, and Christianity.

SETTING THE STAGE

Carter deliberately set an informal air to encourage interaction between the delegations and a greater willingness to compromise. Protocol was ignored for seating in the dining room, as was dress and even the manner of speech.[13] Every member of each delegation received a blue Windbreaker with "Camp David" emblazoned in gold letters. Begin maintained his characteristic formality in suit and tie, although occasionally he wore an open-collared shirt. Carter favored faded blue jeans, which some in the Egyptian delegation found improper and unnerving for a president of the United States. The Egyptians in general dressed more formally, and while Sadat usually did not wear a tie, his sports clothes were impeccable, and his aides followed his lead with clothes of studied elegance.[14] This informality did not succeed in breaking down barriers of historical enmity, dating back more than three millennia, when the Jews fled Egyptian slavery in their exodus to the Promised Land. Dayan recorded that "the leaders did not get closer to each other and found no common language."[15] So solutions had to be floated by the Americans shuttling back and forth along the lovely paths connecting the two delegations, and not from the two Middle East leaders working out their problems in concert.

While special kosher arrangements had been made in the dining hall for the Israeli delegation, Sadat brought his own chef and dined alone in his cabin; the Egyptian delegation never ate at the same table with the Israelis. Indeed, the senior Egyptian leaders forbade personal contact with the Israeli negotiators, although unofficial contacts eventually developed between individuals, especially Boutros-Ghali and Weizman.[16] Living space was restricted, and the members of the delegations doubled up in cabins together. The Camp David kitchen was modified to allow for separate sections: one for Sadat's chef to prepare meals in accordance with strict Islamic requirements, the other for kosher meals served to Begin and some of his staff, and one for the rest of the participants.

When members of the Israeli delegation ate with Begin, they ate kosher along with him, but when the prime minister withdrew to his cabin, there were few requests for kosher food.[17] The movie theater doubled as a chapel, mosque, and temple, but when not used for prayers it provided a welcome diversion from the tense negotiations—the projectionist later reported that fifty-eight movies were seen during the thirteen-day period.[18]

Many diplomatic conundrums, all with deeply emotional roots in history, would have to be resolved in that secluded presidential retreat in Maryland's Catoctin Mountains only a half-hour helicopter flight from the White House. The three very different leaders came with vastly different expectations. Sadat, with the erect bearing and charisma of the proud former general that he was, exuded warmth. His prime goal was to regain every inch of the Sinai, and to achieve enough for the Palestinians so he could not be accused in the Arab world of selling them out to protect Egypt. Sadat never went into details, which he left to his delegation—every one of whom was a lawyer except for him. Time and again the Egyptian delegates felt cut off from their leader, whom they found unpredictable and could not restrain. At one point in the negotiations Boutros-Ghali said: "We must offer *al Raiss* [the leader] our advice . . . but the final decision is his," to which his foreign minister objected angrily: "But *al Raiss* is possessed!"[19]

Sadat paid a heavy price for this: Having already lost one foreign minister over his decision to go to Jerusalem, at Camp David he would soon lose his second foreign minister and personal friend, Muhammad Kamel, with whom he was imprisoned during their fight for Egyptian independence from the British. Kamel resigned at Camp David because he felt that Sadat was conceding too much and gaining too little for the Palestinians. But one reason Camp David succeeded was that Sadat overruled all his advisers, almost none of whom believed in his mission, while Begin ultimately acquiesced in certain concessions that his delegation urged on him after Carter pressed for them.[20]

Begin had the most modest expectations. Legalistic, ideological, and burdened by the pain of Jewish history, he neither wanted nor expected the comprehensive agreement that Carter sought. Although his closest associates were privately drafting an outline for Palestinian autonomy, he would never grant the Palestinians an independent state. Nevertheless he came away with the promise of peace with Israel's strongest enemy in a treaty with Egypt, which for two generations remains the anchor of Western policy in the Middle East.

By the time Carter arrived with Rosalynn aboard the presidential Marine One helicopter on Monday, September 4, he was already much closer to Sadat than Begin. His wife was friendly with Sadat's, their children were acquainted, and they had already visited Carter at Camp David as a family. But there was another reason Carter had an easier time with Sadat: *Al Raiss* trusted Carter to an extraordinary degree, and placed ultimate faith in his friend Jimmy to look out for Egypt's interests. Sadat told him at the outset that he would stand with Carter as long as the Sinai was returned and the Palestinians obtained a measure of autonomy. On anything else, he said: "Mr. President, you can just notify me, but I'm flexible on it."[21]

By contrast, when Begin arrived an hour or so after Sadat, he ducked substantive issues. Begin told Carter: "No, this is not the right place; we need to form an outline or framework of what we want to talk about, and that our ministers meet and work out the agreement." Carter realized this would set the tone for the entire meeting. Carter's view of Begin is striking: "Throughout Camp David there were about fifty people on all three sides [and] Begin was by far the most recalcitrant member of the Israeli delegation; Sadat was by far the most forthcoming."[22] How the meeting almost broke up in mutual animosity and how Jimmy Carter then personally broke the deadlock is the essential story of the success of Camp David.

THE CARTER SHUTTLE

Carter began the next day, Tuesday, September 5, by meeting alone with Sadat first, then separately with Begin. Characteristically flamboyant, Sadat said he wanted a complete settlement, asserted that he had his own comprehensive proposal "in my pocket," and accused Begin of not seeking an agreement at all. Carter assured Sadat that he would not put forward any American proposals until the other two could explore their differences; the president was still expecting that he could bring them together by serving as an honest broker. With Begin, Carter was friendly, but both men were ill at ease. In this supposedly relaxed retreat, Begin focused on procedural formalities—the daily schedule, how to keep a record of the sessions, who would be attending them, how many advisers could attend, and so on. Carter found the encounter discouraging.[23]

The next day Sadat told Carter that he was not surprised to learn that the initial discussions with Begin had been unproductive, because he said the Israeli leader was "bitter and inclined to look back in ancient history rather than deal with the present and the future."[24] He portrayed himself as a spokesman for all Arabs and warned that if he betrayed their trust, Egypt would be isolated and the Soviets would win back the Middle East. Sadat agreed that the three leaders should sign a framework for peace and suggested that their aides could draft a peace treaty in three months; but his own proposals clearly were a deal breaker. They amounted to a tired compilation of the more extreme Arab views blaming all previous wars on the Israelis and demanding reparations and a full Israeli withdrawal.

With a sinking heart, Carter realized that it would be a long road and that he would be spending much of his time defending each of the two to the other.[25] His one hope rested on Sadat moderating his demands, but Carter did not want to start out by doing so, lest he undermine Sadat's bargaining position. This was the classic bargaining game of the Middle Eastern souk; so when the president met with Begin in the afternoon of the second day, he warned him not to overreact to Sadat's proposals. The Egyptian then read them out word for word and said Begin should consult his advisers, who included the two military heroes, Dayan and Weizman. For a while after Sadat finished, no one spoke. Then Carter joked that if Begin "was ready to sign the document as presented, it would save us a lot of discussion and debate, and expedite a successful conclusion of Camp David." As the room filled with laughter, Begin asked deadpan: "Would you suggest that I do so?" Carter said no.[26] This turned out to be the last moment of high spirits for eleven more days.

The day's events also forced Carter to recognize that if he was going to be the midwife of a historic agreement, he would have to change his goals on Israeli settlements on the West Bank and Gaza, even though he firmly believed they were illegal and unjustified. On that second day he told the American delegation that he had lost hope of persuading Begin to dismantle them, and the most he could achieve was a freeze on new settlements. This would become one of the most contentious issues after Camp David, and indeed, for successive American administrations until now.

Carter and Sadat realized that it would be increasingly difficult to solve the Palestinian problem if the settlements continued in the years ahead, and they were right. At that time there were perhaps 10,000 in the West Bank, several sponsored by religious groups. Today there are some 350,000 politically powerful settlers. But while Begin was prepared to slow down or even briefly freeze settlements to achieve an agreement, "he was determined not to yield an inch on the principle that Jews could live anywhere—New York, or their ancient homeland, or the conquered territory of the West Bank," as Ambassador Lewis put it.[27]

The next day, Day 3, Carter, Vance, and Brzezinski met with Begin, Dayan, and Weizman. Carter conceded that Sadat's proposals were more rigid than he anticipated,[28] insisting that they were merely a list of maximum demands that could be ignored. Shortly afterward Carter, Sadat, and Begin met alone in one of the cabins, the first and only day of substantive meetings between the two Middle East leaders. It quickly degraded into the kind of deeply principled argument that usually blocks serious negotiation.

From an argument over who defeated whom in the 1973 war, the conversation turned to territory, whereupon Sadat shifted the discussion to UN Resolution 242 and its phrase citing the principle of the "inadmissibility of acquisition of territory by war." Sadat told Begin: "You want land . . . settlements on *my* land." He pounded the table: Land was not negotiable, especially in the Sinai and the Golan Heights. He offered to recognize the state of Israel, end the Arab boycott, and guarantee security: "Security, yes! Land, no!"[29] Begin barely noticed it. For two more hours they wrangled bitterly over incendiary subjects ranging from the drug trade across the Sinai to unrest in Lebanon. Carter's attempts to divert the discussion were futile; the relationship between the two was frayed almost to the breaking point.

It was a depressing exercise, since it meant that all they had accomplished by the morning of the third day was simply to enumerate the issues that had brought them there. Carter realized he would have to meet separately with the Israelis, since the Egyptian delegation refused to have anything to do with them, even socially. When the president and his team met later with the Israelis, it helped him to understand Israeli attitudes. For example, he pressed Begin on whether Israel was willing to withdraw from the occupied territories in exchange for adequate security assurances. Dayan demanded details: "What does withdrawal mean? Troops, settlements? Will I be a foreigner on the West Bank? Will I have to get a visa to go to Jericho? With autonomy, can the Arabs there create a Palestinian state? Can they resettle the refugees from Lebanon to the West Bank? Who will protect us from Jordan? Who will be responsible for controlling terrorists?"[30] Carter seized upon these questions, but once again Begin shifted back to a critique of Sadat's initial hard-line proposal.

When the three leaders reconvened in the afternoon, the strain and tension of the morning meeting had not abated, and they retraced the same rhetorical space. Sadat angrily declared that they had reached a stalemate. He stood up to leave. Carter, desperate, quickly outlined the areas of agreement and the consequences of failure. But Begin retorted that moving the settlers in the Sinai would bring down his government. As the two men moved toward the door, Carter implored them not to break off talks but to let him use his influence and apply his own analysis. They agreed, Sadat more reluctantly, and left without speaking to each other.

That evening the Marines entertained the delegations with music and precision drills, but the atmosphere was strained and unhappy: word spread rapidly through Camp David that the talks had broken down.[31] Sadat especially looked forlorn as the music swept over the crowd. Contemptuous of Begin as his negotiating partner, he later told the first lady: "I have given so much and *that man* acts as though I have done nothing. . . . I have given up all the past to start anew, but that man will not let go of the past."[32]

Begin and Sadat did not meet again for negotiations until their final day at Camp David. Carter's role was no longer that of a mere convener. For another ten days he was a negotiator in two separate and parallel talks. He adopted a technique that he had never expected to use, and was eventually crowned with success. He would draw up a proposal based on his understanding of each side's position and present it to Sadat for approval, which usually came quickly or with a slight modification. Then he would haggle with the Israeli delegation for hours or even days over the same tortured points.[33]

So, on the fourth day, Friday, September 8, Carter worked out a formulation that he hoped would move the negotiations ahead. When he met with Begin that afternoon, the Israeli prime minister complained that the Americans were not acting like mediators, especially in leaning toward Sadat's demand for removing the Israeli settlements in the Sinai. Once again railing against Sadat's proposal, he pulled out a dog-eared copy and declared: "I will never personally recommend that the settlements in the Sinai be dismantled!"

Carter instantly spotted an opportunity in his phrasing: If not Begin, perhaps the Knesset could be persuaded to assume the responsibility. This would in fact become the basis for an agreement. By picking up this nuance, the president demonstrated his ability to move from a small and real-world detail to his larger vision of a settlement. When Begin again implored Carter not to put this in a formal proposal, the president refused because they could not avoid addressing the most contentious issues, "and this is the one on which the entire Camp David talks have foundered so far.'" Begin argued that any proposal stamped "Made in America" might well turn the entire Arab world against the United States. But Carter was willing to take that risk and warned that progress was impossible if it was left to direct negotiations between Israel and Egypt.[34]

Following his new course of personally managing the negotiations, Carter declared that during the following day—the Jewish Sabbath—he would draw up his own comprehensive proposal. Reversing his course of giving Sadat first look, he would show it first to the combative and legalistic Begin so there would be no surprises, and then to Sadat, who preferred to look only at the big picture.[35] The president then walked to Sadat's cabin and presented the timetable for drawing up his own plan, warning that he could not afford to have it rejected by both sides. Convinced that Begin would do so no matter what he presented, he would show it to each side separately and then modify it in search of compromise.

TRYING TO BREAK THE TENSION

With the very nature of the talks changing, the traditional social lubricants of diplomacy also began to be applied to loosen the deadlock; few other options remained. On Friday evening the Carters joined Menachem and Aliza Begin for the first kosher Shabbat dinner ever held at Camp David. Such a gathering had great symbolic value: Throughout Israel and much of the Jewish world, extended families unite around the dinner table on Friday night for nourishment of body and spirit. At Camp David, the Navy's Filipino stewards had been taught in the president's cabin how to prepare kosher meals. Skullcaps (*kippot*), along with gefilte fish and challah, had been brought from Washington.[36] Begin asked Meir Rosenne, the Foreign Ministry's amiable but tough legal adviser, to render Shabbat songs in his beautiful baritone. When he finished, Mrs. Carter asked for a record of the songs, which he sent her. President Carter gave this accomplished but hard-line legal-draftsman-cum-cantor a playful backhanded compliment: "I prefer your singing to your writing."[37] They enjoyed the release from tension and returned to their cabin with their spirits somewhat buoyed.

More gestures were to come from the American side to break the tension of the difficult thirteen days in what Begin called a "concentration camp deluxe."[38] Late one night Rosenne and Simcha Dinitz wanted some coffee. They spotted a woman in the distance at Holly Lodge and, thinking she was a waitress, asked for coffee. It turned out to be Rosalynn Carter, who graciously served them at 2:00 a.m.[39]

All through Saturday, from daybreak to midnight, Carter and the American delegation went through several of what would eventually be twenty-three drafts of a proposal they hoped to sell initially to the Israelis and then to Sadat.[40] Brzezinski broke away to mend fences with Begin by coming to his cabin for a chess match on the porch of Begin's cabin. Both were of Polish origin, but Brzezinski was from a highly educated, urbane Polish diplomatic family, while Begin's roots were in a poor Polish shtetl—"Poles apart," quipped Begin's adviser Yechiel Kadishai to me.[41] They moved pieces in one aggressive game, then another. Word spread about the engagement of the two very different but very sharp minds, and staffers from both sides gathered to watch. Accounts differ about who won the three-game match, or if there were two or three matches. Brzezinski remained diplomatic to the end: In his memoirs he maintains there were two matches, which ended in a one-one tie.[42]

It would take more than chess to make progress, however. Exploratory discussions among officials began gearing up. Not everyone was ready. After Boutros-Ghali and Weizman had a long discussion about how to link Israeli withdrawal from the Sinai to withdrawal from the West Bank and Gaza, the Egyptian diplomat returned to his cabin and found his nervous boss asking him where he had been. He told Foreign Minister Kamel he had been debating with Weizman for the past hour and had succeeded in making some important points. Kamel rebuked him: "Did we not agree not to speak with these people?"[43]

By contrast, the Israeli delegation was flexible—"even indulgent"—although Begin himself remained obstinate. Twice a day he convened his delegation of about a dozen advisers. Not only did he encourage everyone to speak, but he began by asking the opinion of the lowest-ranking staffer and going up the ladder, "so nobody would be a yes man," as Elyakim Rubinstein recounted. At Camp David, Rubinstein was a junior diplomat fresh out of law school (he would later become an Israeli Supreme Court justice), and he said the structure of Begin's meetings gave him the chutzpah to speak up, even though these creative discussions did little to bend Begin's views.[44]

"THE GREAT TASK REMAINING BEFORE US"

The most meaningful effort to relieve tension was initiated by Carter—a Sunday-morning tour of the most important battlefield of the American Civil War at nearby Gettysburg. What better place to emphasize the costs of war and the rewards of peace to two countries that had repeatedly fought each other since Israel's founding? The one ground rule Carter set was a complete ban on any discussions of the peace talks. Carter rode in his presidential limousine to the battleground seated between Sadat and Begin, with Aliza Begin and Rosalynn Carter across from them. The Egyptian and Israeli leaders compared their experiences in a British prison.

Leaving nothing to chance, Carter had already been briefed by the noted Civil War historian Shelby Foote, a fellow Southerner, but his narration of the battle was superfluous for the military men on the tour. Dayan had visited the battlefield before, and Sadat, in his military training, had studied the details of Pickett's charge by the Confederate Army. He explained the Southern leadership's mistakes that lost the decisive battle for the Confederates.

Begin did not join in the excited military discussions shared by the former generals, but when the tour moved to the site of Lincoln's Gettysburg Address, Begin began to speak in a quiet voice. Everyone was shocked and turned reverently silent as he repeated the words by heart.[45] If Carter meant to make the trip an object lesson for his two principal guests, he never said so, but it was obvious: the tremendous cost of another Middle East war and the necessity for peace.

When they returned from Gettysburg, Carter, Mondale, Vance, and Brzezinski met with Begin, Dayan, Weizman, and Barak. Carter's draft sidestepped the specifics of geography and ducked long-term issues of sovereignty for yielding territory, but it was based on the concept of trading land for peace—all the rest, as the rabbis say, is commentary.

Begin understood exactly where Carter wanted to lead him as the president presented the American document, declaring that it "may decide the future of the people of Israel."[46] He told Begin: "There are phrases in it which both you and Sadat will find difficult to accept. . . . My task will be hopeless if you now reject the language of UN [Resolution] 242. Sadat doesn't believe Israel wants to sign an agreement; that you really want land. I told him he was wrong. . . . I would hope you will be flexible and minimize your proposed changes."[47]

But the session soon degenerated into a sterile debate. Begin wanted all three to produce their peace plans in public. Carter quickly pressed forward, explaining that his idea was to have neither side make any substantial changes to this private American draft. The two began to argue over UN Resolution 242. Begin angered Carter with a legalistic argument that the language applied only to wars of aggression, and that the Six-Day War, in which Israel defended its very existence, gave it the right to change its frontiers. Carter responded: "What you say convinces me that Sadat was right—what you want is land." In frustration, Carter adjourned the meeting until later that night in the hope that the Israeli delegation would modify Begin's position. As Carter left, he confided to Ambassador Lewis: "I don't think Begin wants peace. He really doesn't." Lewis wisely advised the president that Begin certainly did want peace, but the more important question was the price Israel was prepared to pay.[48]

When they all reconvened that night, it was to parry back and forth until 3:00 a.m. on Monday morning, with Begin arguing every point tenaciously, including definitions of "sovereignty," "autonomy," "rights," and other disputed words. When they finally adjourned, exhausted, Carter walked to his cabin with Dayan and complained that almost half his time with Begin had been spent discussing the Sinai settlements. As Dayan turned in the dark to leave, the one-eyed war hero walked into a tree. He was shaken, with his nose bleeding, and Carter helped him onto the path to his cabin. Carter later told me it was a poignant reminder of Dayan's heroism in battle.[49] Bone-tired, the president took a brief nap and awoke to make revisions to his text.

When Sadat and Carter met in the morning the president, building on a suggestion by Dayan, proposed allowing Israelis to live in just one settlement while acknowledging it as Egyptian territory. But Sadat refused. Carter argued that Sadat permitted Jews to live in Cairo, so why exclude them from Sinai settlements? Sadat replied: "Some things in the Middle East are not logical or reasonable. For Egypt, this is one of them."[50]

By the eighth day, Tuesday, September 12, Begin was ready to leave Camp David, with only a short, joint general statement. He pulled out a typed draft blandly declaring that the three had met at Camp David, and Israel and Egypt appreciated the invitation from the United States. Or they could simply list the items of agreement and disagreement. Carter said numerous public opinion polls showed that a majority of Israelis were willing to accept a peace treaty as the price for yielding their Sinai settlements, and the conversation grew heated and unpleasant. Carter warned Begin of all he would be giving up if he left: diplomatic recognition and peace with Israel's most formidable enemy, unimpeded access to the Suez Canal, an undivided Jerusalem, and a chance to negotiate with Jordan and others for a comprehensive peace—"all this, just to keep a few settlers in the Sinai."[51]

Facing the prospect of failure, the language of the principals became incendiary. The next day, Lewis met with Begin and other Israelis after lunch and Begin startled him by saying: "Sam, do you know what the President said to me last night? He told me that Sadat had told him that he would never sign an agreement as long as I was Prime Minister. He was asking Carter to have me removed."[52]

Begin furiously called Sadat a hypocrite, reaching a level of personal animosity he had never shown when they were together. Lewis realized that Carter, being too frank, had clearly made a serious error in relaying Sadat's words to Begin, because Begin could see they could be used in Sadat's own defense if Camp David failed and the others tried to blame Israel. Begin also complained to Lewis that he asked Brzezinski where he picked up the term "Palestinian aspirations," and Brzezinski replied it had come from a recent conference convened by Bruno Kreisky, Austria's Socialist chancellor and a Jew, who had put Sadat together with Israel's Shimon Peres. This was hardly reassuring, since Peres was Begin's chief political opponent. In scathing terms, Begin asked what the Socialist International was doing in these negotiations? (The philosophy of this international association of socialist parties, including Peres's and Kreisky's, was light-years from Begin's.) How would he feel if the Republican Party had been drafting position papers for that conference?[53]

It was now obvious that a stalemate had been reached. Carter separately warned Sadat and Begin that time was running out. In what turned out to be a key stratagem, he asked each to designate one man in his delegation to form a working group with him to develop a draft all parties could live with. This proved to be a brilliant tactical move. Fortunately, each side put forward two of their most creative and influential delegates, Osama el-Baz of Egypt and Aharon Barak of Israel. Both had the full confidence of their leaders, and both were brilliant lawyers whose lives were focused on their briefs.

Barak had been a last-minute addition to the Israeli delegation. He had just been elevated to the Israeli Supreme Court, but delayed taking his seat on the bench to join the delegation at Begin's request. His clothes were rumpled and his hands stained with ink from legal drafting, but his appearance belied a creative legal mind—one as imaginative as el-Baz's was meticulous. He had been named dean of the Hebrew University Law School at the age of thirty-eight, while the scholarly Egyptian—slight, diminutive, almost mouselike in appearance—earned two advanced degrees from Harvard and had a Jewish girlfriend while studying with Kissinger and Roger Fisher, the celebrated specialist in techniques of negotiation (*Getting to Yes*). For the president of the United States to sit at a negotiating table across from subordinates, even two such accomplished individuals, but far below his status as a head of state, was unprecedented in American diplomatic annals. This breach of protocol was of no importance to Carter; his mind-set was that of a master builder on his greatest project: He tried to solve problems and get things done.[54]

Without the intimidating presence of Sadat or Begin, the comfort level in Carter's cabin increased measurably. The three sat around the president's desk debating key points in search of acceptable compromises and careful phraseology that might make them more politically palatable. On the issue of UN Resolution 242, they decided that the disputed language proscribing the "acquisition of territory by war" should be deleted from the agreement itself, and that the full text then be placed in an appendix, while the formal agreement would note that "the parties agreed to United Nations Resolution 242 in all its parts." They resolved the arguments over whether to call the territory the "West Bank" (Egypt's preference) or "Judea and Samaria" (Begin's) and "Palestinians" versus "Palestinian Arabs" by deciding to use the appropriate phrase in the Egyptian and English texts and the other phrase in the Hebrew text. All told, they negotiated for eleven hours. But they still could not agree on the disposition of settlements or on full diplomatic recognition, and that was left for the next day.

As they parted, el-Baz startled Carter by telling him Egypt could not agree to grant Israel a veto over which Palestinian refugees could enter the West Bank, which might have opened the way for a return of Yāsir Arafat and the PLO leadership. But Sadat had already agreed to give Israel veto authority. Aghast, Carter asked whether Sadat had reversed himself, and el-Baz admitted he had not discussed that aspect of the refugee question with Sadat. Carter asked him to recheck with his boss so Carter could determine for himself whether Sadat wanted to cause a deadlock. The Egyptians sent word that Sadat had retired and given orders that he was not to be disturbed, although it was still only the middle of the evening and Sadat was a notorious night owl. That night Carter could not sleep. Thinking back to the argument he had witnessed that morning among the Egyptian delegation, he feared for Sadat's safety.[55] Was he at risk from his own delegation? At 4:00 a.m. Carter summoned Brzezinski and his Secret Service agents and ordered them to strengthen security around Sadat's cabin.

"SADAT IS LEAVING!"

The next morning, Thursday, September 14, Carter was greatly relieved to see Sadat emerge from his cabin. Carter joined him on his regular brisk walk, and returned to his cabin to work on the next American draft. Barak was waiting for him and asked the president to meet with Dayan and Weizman to hammer out an agreement for Israel to leave all the settlements in the Sinai. But Begin had refused to agree, and Carter drafted new language to keep the matter open for negotiation for three months. But Sadat refused: he would only negotiate *when*, not *if*, the settlements were disbanded.[56] The Israeli delegation seemed united in refusing to remove the settlers.

That night, as Carter made a list of the remaining differences, they seemed insignificant to him compared with the great advantages of peace. The Israeli delegation was also in despair and seriously considering leaving Camp David.[57] Worse, neither the Americans nor the Israelis realized how increasingly isolated Sadat was from his own delegation. Later that day Kamel abruptly resigned as foreign minister over Sadat's concessions; he remained quietly at Camp David to avoid embarrassing Sadat during the summit. Carter then announced a deadline, a tactical maneuver designed to force a settlement. He instructed Vance to tell the U.S. delegation that, agreement or not, he was going to finish on Sunday and blame the Israelis for the failure. Quandt was assigned to draft a speech. But Carter refused to give up, meeting with Dayan and Weizman and then drafting a new Sinai proposal, with Sadat still insisting that every Israeli must be withdrawn.[58]

With less than seventy-two hours to his self-imposed deadline, Carter awoke Friday morning realizing they could go no further, and proposed drafting a joint communiqué with Sadat and Begin. He already had confided to Rosalynn that the talks had failed and told Mondale to clear his calendar so he could help contain the political damage. Rosalynn said desperately: "I know you're teasing me." He answered, "No, we've failed. We're trying now to think of the best way to present the failure to the public."[59]

Suddenly Vance, who was normally a paragon of establishment restraint, burst into the room, his face drained of blood, and announced, "Sadat is leaving! He and his aides are already packed. He asked me to order a helicopter!"[60] Carter was horrified; it was "one of the worst moments of my life," he confided.[61] A rupture would tilt the Middle East power balance in unpredictable directions; Moscow would certainly try to fill a vacuum that would be left by Sadat's failure and America's inability to help him, even as a great power. Carter went to his bedroom, knelt down, and prayed. He changed from his sports shirt and jeans into a coat and tie and walked to Sadat's cabin, where the entire Egyptian delegation, along with Vance and Defense Secretary Harold Brown, had gathered on the porch.

What followed was one of the most emotional and historic scenes in the highly charged politics and diplomacy of the modern Middle East. Gheit remembered Carter appealing to Sadat "in the most personal way, telling him it would imperil his presidency and his ability to work with Egypt."[62] Carter warned Sadat that breaking off the negotiations would not only inflict severe damage to relations between their two countries, but between the two men as individuals, because Sadat would be violating his word of honor. Sadat remained adamant, so Carter went further. He told Sadat that he had already earned the enmity of Arab rejectionists simply by going to Jerusalem and that acknowledging defeat at Camp David would leave him in "the worst of all worlds," by publicly repudiating his own commitments, damaging his reputation as the world's foremost peacemaker, admitting his visit to Jerusalem had been fruitless, while his enemies would say he had made a foolish mistake. "Give me time to sort it out for you," Carter pleaded.[63]

Sadat explained that he had decided to pull out after Dayan told him the Israelis would not sign any agreement requiring their complete withdrawal from Sinai, which would leave the Egyptians vulnerable not only militarily but diplomatically, because their concessions could be used against them in future negotiations. Carter, thinking quickly, offered to sign a statement declaring that an Israeli rejection of any part of the agreement would nullify all of it. Sadat relented at this promise of a formal pledge and said, "I will stick with you to the end." Some in the Egyptian delegation criticized *al Raiss* for placing too much trust in Carter,[64] others confirmed that Sadat justified overriding their objections by invoking Carter's eminence and power. Nabil Elaraby, legal adviser to the Egyptian Ministry of Foreign Affairs, recalled to me: "He would say, 'I have the promise of the president of the United States.' He kept saying that he thought the president of the United States was all-powerful and whatever he says, it will be done."[65]

No such trust existed among the Israelis. About the same time Carter was confronting Sadat, Weizman burst into a meeting between Vance and Barak. Sadat, he reported excitedly, had pleaded with him not to allow the Sinai settlements to become a deal breaker. Unaware of the confrontation between Carter and Sadat, Weizman reported that he had pulled Sadat back from the brink.[66] Carter had to be summoned, and Weizman told him Sadat had agreed to postpone the question of the settlements for future negotiations. Carter was shocked, since this was not what Sadat had told him. Weizman also predicted that the Knesset would vote to remove the settlements, while Dayan had told Carter the opposite. Carter was exasperated with Begin and showed it.[67] When he next met Sadat, he was assured that Weizman's account was wrong.

This demonstrated how, in the heat of negotiations, two people can come away with their own completely different understanding of the same set of facts. Such misunderstandings would also recur on the equally vexed issue of Jewish settlements in the West Bank, with devastating long-run consequences.

After a rancorous day, the warm feeling that had infused the first Sabbath dinner had evaporated during a week of exasperating negotiations. None of the Americans, not even the Carters, were invited to the second Friday-night dinner. This time Carter dined with Sadat, then they watched the heavyweight championship fight between Muhammad Ali and Leon Spinks, and put in a call to Ali at about one in the morning to congratulate him. Ali said he was going to hold his championship for another six months and retire. Carter invited Ali's ten-year-old daughter to visit Amy at the White House. They had dodged another bullet, although by no means the last one.[68]

Mondale stepped in to play a crucial role. Until that Friday the vice president had been at the White House minding the store with me, but being kept informed by his national security adviser, Denis Clift, at Camp David. Deeply worried that the president would be forever diminished by failure, Mondale was helicoptered from the White House and immediately contacted both leaders. To Sadat he argued forcefully against Egypt's proposal to display an Arab flag on the al-Aqsa Mosque in Jerusalem. He also saw Begin privately and pleaded with him to give up all of the Sinai because the desert buffer between the two countries lacked the religious and political significance of the biblical Judaea or Samaria. He promised Begin to do his utmost to obtain American funds to help relocate Israel's military bases from the Sinai to Israel's Negev Desert. He also offered to set up American surveillance posts in the Mitla Pass, the traditional invasion route across the Sinai from the Suez Canal to Israel and the scene of fierce fighting in previous wars.[69] The early-warning posts remain there to this day.

"OKAY, MY FRIENDS, LET'S PACK AND GO"

The climactic Carter-Begin meeting with Vance, Barak, and Dayan began after sundown Saturday, Day 12, the end of the Jewish Sabbath. It lasted five hours, until half past midnight on Sunday morning, Day 13. The pressure on Begin was intense throughout, not only from Carter but from Dayan, Weizman, and Barak, as the Israeli prime minister fired back in no uncertain terms: "ultimatum," "excessive demands," "political suicide."[70] But for the first time, Begin associated himself with his predecessors on UN Resolution 242: that it applied to all conquered territory, although it did not require a total withdrawal. While Begin wanted to rehash the issue of the settlements, Carter wanted to go over the documents paragraph by paragraph so he could impress on Begin how few differences actually remained. Once again Begin proposed a three-month delay while they negotiated the Sinai withdrawal, after which Begin would submit the proposal to the Knesset. Sadat, however, was insisting on a commitment to remove the settlers *before* any further negotiations. Carter thought the conversation would never end, but quickly realized that Begin had given him an opening.

Although the Sinai settlements did not have the religious or historical significance of those in the West Bank, Begin worried that his political coalition would come apart if he dismantled them and forced out the settlers, who were tightening their emotional grip on the imagination of many Israelis. This was underscored by the popular song "Al Kol Eleh," written by the woman called the First Lady of Israeli Song, Naomi Shemer, which the settlers of Yamit, the largest Sinai settlement, adopted as their anthem: "Do not uproot what has been planted." But there was an even more personal reason: I later learned from Yechiel Kadishai, Begin's closest friend from his underground days and a member of his delegation, that Begin wanted to retire to one of the settlements[71]—instead he retired to his Tel Aviv apartment after the disaster of the 1982 Lebanon war.

Recognizing that dismantling the Sinai settlements would be too painful for Begin to agree to on his own, Carter persuaded him to leave final approval to a vote of the Knesset, backed by Carter's handwritten personal pledge of support. So to diffuse the political burden, Begin agreed to have the Sinai withdrawal approved by Israel's parliament. Carter and Begin both realized that if the Sinai settlements remained the only barrier to a peace treaty, a parliamentary majority to abandon them was certain: The opposition Labor members would vote in favor even if hard-liners in Begin's party would not. To ensure that Begin would not publicly urge the Knesset to turn down the agreement, Carter went a step further: He obtained Begin's promise not to try to sway the votes of the individual members, which meant a suspension of party discipline for a "free vote" on the issue to be held within two weeks. That was a breakthrough—"all that we needed," Carter told me.[72]

The framework for forthcoming discussions about the West Bank and Gaza went more smoothly, and the two sides worked out language that Begin had refused only months before; it referred to "legitimate rights of the Palestinian people" and "full autonomy" for the Palestinians, who had never governed themselves under either Ottoman or Jordanian rule. Dinitz told me immediately after Camp David that he warned Begin he was in effect agreeing to accept a Palestinian state eventually.[73]

But it was at this moment, when success was within reach that the seeds of lasting dissension were sown. Sadat insisted on a settlement freeze during the period needed to convert the Camp David Accords into a legally binding treaty. Carter thought he had persuaded Begin to accept a freeze on new settlements in the West Bank and Gaza during those follow-up negotiations. But which negotiations? Two sets remained, one a relatively brief three months to draft the legally binding Egypt-Israel peace treaty, and the other, drawn out and difficult to define, for Palestinian autonomy during a transitional period of five years. Carter and Vance, a careful lawyer, assumed Begin was agreeing to freeze West Bank settlements for a full five years; but Begin and his delegation, including Barak, also a fine lawyer, understood their commitment to mean a settlement freeze would cover only the three-month period allotted to draft the bilateral treaty.[74]

After only a few hours' sleep, Carter awoke on Sunday, September 17. He briefed Sadat during his morning walk about the agreement with Begin and assured Sadat that the freeze would last for five years, while details of Palestinian autonomy were hammered out. But Day 13 nevertheless turned into a cliffhanger. While redrafting the final agreement to reflect what he thought was a done deal, Carter received a letter from Begin declaring that Israel would adhere to only a three-month freeze. "This is not what Begin agreed to last night!" he fumed. Begin explained that on Saturday night he had only agreed to consider a longer freeze and said he would let Carter know the next morning.

The letter was his response and should have been a red flag, but the president never confronted Begin, perhaps realizing that this explosive disagreement would have blown up the talks, just as everything seemed to be falling into place. Instead he instructed the State Department's Hal Saunders to sort out the matter when they returned to Washington. The misunderstanding would sour the relationship between Begin and Carter for the balance of Carter's term as president and, I believe, colored his relationship with Israel for the rest of his life.[75]

As the clock ticked, Carter also became entangled in an even more emotional and potentially fatal issue—Jerusalem. To Begin and his delegation Jerusalem was the eternal capital of the Jewish state, dating from the rule of King Solomon through the centuries when exiled Jews were accustomed to chant as they do today, "If I forget thee, O Jerusalem, let my right hand wither." Kadishai confided to me that Begin told Carter of a famous rabbi in Mainz, Germany, who was required by the local bishop to convert to

Catholicism. He told the bishop he would give him an answer in three days. When he returned and refused, he was arrested, and asked that his tongue be cut off for even giving the impression that he would consider converting. Begin told Carter he would not emulate the rabbi's mistake. He would pack his bags and leave if Jerusalem was injected.[76]

But Jerusalem is also the site of some of the most revered Muslim symbols, the Dome of the Rock and the al-Aqsa Mosque, as well as home to tens of thousands of Palestinians in the eastern part of the Holy City. On Saturday night general language on Jerusalem seemed to suffice: The city would remain undivided, the holy places would be protected, and its political status would be negotiated later. But Sadat's advisers had convinced him that with all his other concessions, this vague language on Jerusalem's future would inflame the Palestinians and isolate him from the Arab world.

In fact the Camp David language on Jerusalem was hardly very different from the position of the United States from the moment it recognized Israel as a sovereign state in 1948, and has been publicly reaffirmed ever since by the United States, which has maintained its embassy in Tel Aviv and left Jerusalem itself in a sort of diplomatic limbo, down to the Trump administration. Needless to say, this position grated on all Israeli governments and aroused its supporters in America, but Carter was livid at yet another last-minute objection by Begin that Jerusalem was "one city indivisible, the capital of Israel." Several hours of furious wrangling ensued, with much agitated movement and several exchanges among cabins, as all the delegates were getting ready to finish and pack up. Begin reacted decisively: "Okay, my friends, let's pack and go."[77]

Jerusalem was also a sticking point for the Egyptians. Abdel-Meguid, Egypt's UN representative, told Sadat that any exchange of letters was not legally binding anyway. Sadat's response demonstrated that the Palestinians were not his priority: "Listen, Jerusalem's time will come. . . . It is obvious that you do not understand what I am aiming at—saving Egypt from an occupation [in Sinai]. My responsibility primarily is to the Egyptians, so I will free Egypt, and from there we will see how to put added pressure on Israel, supported by our friends, to free Palestine."[78]

Once again Carter seemed trapped between one of Begin's angry demands and Sadat's strategic sense, which the president shared. Carter was down to his last, desperate card. Rather than try to apply last-minute pressure, he ingeniously set the stage for Begin to find a way to reach an agreement. He had asked his secretary, Susan Clough, to prepare eight photographs of himself, Begin, and Sadat together as souvenirs. She called Israel for the name of each of Begin's eight grandchildren. So instead of his usual neutral sign-off of "Best Wishes, Jimmy Carter," the president wrote, "Love and Best Wishes" and addressed the greeting to each grandchild by name. Then he walked the photo packet over to Begin's cabin. Begin greeted him in his usual formal manner. Carter told me: "He turned around and was looking the other way, and he looked at the first photograph and he got emotional; his hand started shaking and he read out the name of his granddaughter. Then he looked at the next one and he read out the name of another grandchild. When he got to about the third one his chin began to quiver and he had a tear. And I got emotional too. He thanked me in a very highly personal way."[79] Carter believed that this simple act of kindness was the turning point for Begin.[80]

Within minutes after he had delivered the photos, there was a knock on his door. It was Barak with a message from Begin: "Why don't we make another effort?"[81] Carter sat down with Barak to work out language on Jerusalem so that, as the president joked, Begin "would not have to [risk] his right arm falling off." In the end the two lawyers, Vance and Barak, worked with Carter to devise an elegant solution that accomplished little legally but resolved a diplomatic conundrum. The side letter simply said that the American position on Jerusalem remained as previously set forth by U.S. ambassadors at the UN, without actually saying what it was. Carter walked the new draft over to Begin and left in a state of apprehension and dejection. As he then moved on to tell Sadat, Begin telephoned: "I will accept the letter you drafted on Jerusalem."[82]

That should have been a wrap, but in the Middle East bringing down the curtain rarely ends the drama. Another session of redrafting commenced with el-Baz and Barak. Again there was a dispute on language concerning precisely how and when the Knesset's approval would trigger Israel's withdrawal from the Sinai. This hairsplitting was really a matter of obtaining maximum leverage to reassure Sadat that the vote would actually take place and the settlers would then leave. Carter tinkered with it and asked Mondale to deliver it to Begin and Sadat. But it was never delivered, because

Mondale emerged to view an extraordinary sight. He found Begin at Sadat's cabin. For the first time in ten days the two were together inside the Camp David negotiating arena, after Carter had given up hope that their fractious relationship could ever be repaired.

Carter recounted to me: "I was in my room getting ready to leave, packing my clothes and so forth, and I heard that Begin had taken a golf cart to Sadat's cabin. I was petrified with fear that they were going to start arguing with each other again. I dashed over there as fast as I could, and I found they were both outside, and they were shaking hands and very friendly."[83] Begin was pleased that Sadat would not insist on pressuring the Knesset. In the relaxed atmosphere, Barak returned to Carter's cabin, and the president rejiggered the language again to stipulate that negotiations and withdrawal were not directly linked. At last Carter had hit on just the right legalism, and at last Begin was satisfied.[84]

"HEVENU SHALOM ALEICHEM"

Announced by a huge thunderclap, a furiously heavy wind-driven rain deluged Camp David, delaying the departure to Washington for the formal ceremony to sign the Camp David Accords. What was one to make of the message that suddenly resounded from above? Said Boutros-Ghali: "The heavens are angry at what has taken place at Camp David!"[85] Many of Sadat's entourage, except for Boutros-Ghali, were to boycott the ceremony, and some even feared for their lives. Elyakim Rubinstein went to the Egyptian delegation seeking signatures on a map of the region as a souvenir, but all refused. They also refused to pose for pictures with the Israeli delegation.[86] The Egyptian Foreign Ministry's legal adviser Elaraby counseled Sadat not to sign, because he had failed to receive ironclad guarantees for the Palestinians and on the status of Jerusalem; but Sadat waved him away: "You and the Ministry of Foreign Affairs, you look at the trees but you don't look at the forests!"[87]

The Israelis felt very different. Ed Sanders, the White House Jewish liaison, was standing with Weizman, and both viewed the storm as some kind of favorable omen: The Israelis were euphoric at the prospect of peace with their most powerful enemy. The three leaders boarded Marine One and called former presidents Nixon and Ford to inform them of their success. They landed at the Washington Monument at 9:45 p.m. Sunday night, September 17, and went straight to the White House, returning from almost two weeks in the rustic environment of Camp David to the glittering East Room of the White House.

Kamel, who had just resigned as foreign minister, was driven to the entrance with part of the Israeli delegation; they urged him to join them, but he refused; in the excitement his absence and that of his subordinates in the East Room went largely unnoticed by the press. Sadat was left alone with only Boutros-Ghali; Hassan al-Tuhami, the Egyptian ambassador to the United States; and his grand chamberlain, Ibrahim Kamel.

When Carter, Begin, and Sadat entered, each had a broad smile, but Carter's face was almost translucent. He had bet his presidency on the unprecedented gamble of bringing together two leaders who deeply distrusted each other. But at least for now the president had beaten the odds and produced a formal document titled "The Framework for Peace in the Middle East." It was signed by Begin and Sadat in the East Room of the White House with the president as witness—and by extension the United States of America as guarantor.

The White House operator telephoned me at home during the afternoon to come down with Fran to witness the occasion from what we regarded as a front-row seat to history. So we were especially moved when Begin remarked that the Camp David conference should be "renamed the Jimmy Carter conference." He addressed Carter directly: "Mr. President, we, the Israelis, thank you from the bottom of our hearts for all you have done for the sake of peace, for which we prayed and yearned for more than thirty years. . . . You inscribed your name forever in the history of two ancient civilizations, the people of Egypt and the people of Israel." He concluded by addressing his countrymen in Hebrew: "Citizens of Israel: When you hear my words, it will be morning, an early hour, and the sun will rise over the land of our forefathers and our sons. We wish to be with you in a matter of a few days and to sing with you 'Hevenu Shalom Aleichem' [We have brought peace unto you]. This can be stated: Just as we have made every possible personal effort in order to bring peace, we will continue, so that the day will come that everyone of us can say, 'Peace has come for our nation and our land not just in this generation, but future generations as well.' With the help of God, we will reach this goal together, and we will be granted good days of building, brotherhood and understanding. May this be His will."[88]

Fran and I were not the only listeners with tears streaming down our faces.

What, then, were the extraordinary circumstances that helped Jimmy Carter pluck a historic victory from almost certain defeat after thirteen brutal days and nights of negotiations? One was Carter's choice of the isolated and bucolic setting. Originally started in 1935 and completed in 1938 by the Depression-era Work Projects Administration (WPA) as a vacation resort for senior government workers and their families, the place was converted into a presidential retreat from the crowded and frenetic wartime White House in 1942 by Franklin D. Roosevelt. He called it Shangri-La after the Tibetan valley of perpetual peace imagined in James Hilton's novel *Lost Horizon*. It was renamed Camp David by President Eisenhower for his first grandson. On its rolling 125 acres sit eleven cabins and a large assembly hall, each named after a species of the majestic hardwood trees in the mountaintop forest, and connected by winding, paved paths. If any setting could encourage some degree of tranquillity, it was that one. Its seclusion was part of the second physical factor in promoting success.

On the very day the meeting was announced, Carter made one of his most important decisions: to tell the press as little as possible while it was under way. He sent his communications director, Gerald Rafshoon, and his press secretary, Jody Powell, identical handwritten notes with his inimitable style of salutation: "To Rafshoon (To Jody): Other than cautious, noncontroversial background briefings, I want *minimal* U.S. Government officials public statements re the Camp David meeting. None until Cy returns & briefs us. I will ask Begin & Sadat to do the same. J.C."[89]

Without this he realized that each side would have used the press to play to its home audience, destroying trust and undermining the flexibility necessary to success. When they received his note, both converged almost immediately on his private study to argue against the edict. Carter's succinct response: "I cannot negotiate in the newspapers."[90] Rafshoon and Jody then reached a compromise with Carter. The press would be kept about thirty miles away at Thurmont, Maryland, and would be fed an official line aimed at damping down expectations and deflecting criticisms while the reporters were locked out.

The administration warned of a deteriorating Middle East situation that could lead to a new war, argued that a settlement could have international economic benefits, defended the personal presidential engagement, and finally expressed the hope that the meeting would narrow differences and encourage all sides to move more directly into continuing negotiations.[91] And so, after each negotiating session, Jody would troop down the mountain to give an anodyne briefing, artfully shielding the press and public from what was happening and allowing Carter sole control of the press.

The press was allowed into Camp David only once, on the third day for three-quarters of an hour. Drinks were set out for a small social gathering at Laurel Lodge, with the guests serenaded by the Marine Corps band and hopefully distracted by an impressive silent drill: A handpicked Marine squad tossed their bayoneted rifles back and forth. When the time came for the bus to take the press away, there were supposed to be fifty reporters aboard, but the head count was an ominous forty-nine. Rafshoon, the president's irrepressible and irreverent communications adviser, took the roll call and found that Barbara Walters was missing. He asked Sam Donaldson, ABC's equally irreverent lead White House correspondent: "Where's Barbara?" Sam retorted: "Am I my sister's keeper? I don't know where the hell she is! Try the ladies' room." And that is precisely where they found her. Her plan had been to hide out and hang back to interview Dayan and Weizman. Rafshoon placed his wife, Eden, outside a stall shouting: "Come out, Barbara, come out!" And as Rafshoon recounted with amusement: "She finally came out with a sheepish grin,"

Decades later, when Rafshoon was producing a play on Camp David, he saw Barbara Walters and she jokingly asked: "Well, who's playing me?" Rafshoon replied: "Nobody." She admitted she had been trying to interview the two Israeli heroes and confided: "You know, I had a love affair with both of them." Was she joking about that? Rafshoon, it seems, took her at face value. It later dawned on him that this might also help explain what was happening when Rafshoon saw Walters with Weizman at the bar of the King David Hotel on the final day of Carter's trip to Egypt and Israel. According to Rafshoon, Walters said that Weizman had told her that they would meet in her room, but then he called her and reversed course: "We're on our way down." "What do you mean?" she asked. Weizman said he meant himself and his wife: "I want her to meet you." Whether or not she was again joking, she was certainly burnishing her acknowledged reputation as an insider among the world's statemen. But in any event, she confided to Rafshoon: "I was so mad. I had bought new lingerie."[92]

Dayan, who feared from the start that Camp David would collapse and Israel would be blamed, circumvented the blackout but did not actually break it. Zalman Shoval, Dayan's Knesset ally and de facto deputy in charge of public diplomacy (later twice Israeli ambassador to the United States), was stationed at the Israeli Embassy, and Rubinstein secretly telephoned elliptical hints about each day's developments. On the next-to-last day Shoval was meeting with John Wallach, the international correspondent for the Hearst newspapers, who told him that the press corps was preparing stories about failure. Shoval warned him away from that theme and said he might be surprised by the outcome. Wallach was grateful for that guidance throughout the rest of his career.[93] By contrast, Wilton Wynn, *Time*'s Cairo bureau chief, had maintained his close contacts with the Egyptian delegation and reflected its warnings of failure in his dispatches. When the reverse proved true in the hours beyond the magazine's normal Saturday deadline, the story had to be rewritten and the cover replaced on Sunday afternoon at great expense.

HOW CARTER UNLOCKED THE COMPROMISES

An unseen but absolutely essential factor was Carter's remarkably detailed preparation. He studied past negotiations, which gave him deep understanding of each side's position and a thorough appreciation of (although at times exasperation over) the personalities of Sadat and especially Begin. This was Jimmy Carter at his best, with one goal, a few key actors, and a complex problem to solve. He involved himself in minutiae and negotiated directly with second-level officials, not only his senior counterparts, unprecedented for a major political leader but indispensable for success. He was both a visionary and a detail man, at once a creative lead negotiator and a careful draftsman, and this gave him extraordinary tools to save the process from foundering at a number of what would otherwise have been choke points.

For a lawyer like Barak, the depth of Carter's participation was both a marvel and a headache: "Sitting with those fellows from the Middle East for ten days out of a total of two weeks—and he was involved. He was a drafter. It was terrible! In the newspapers and the TV he seemed like a weak person; he was not a weak person at all. He was very tough. I begged him to send me a lawyer. [I said] 'I want to negotiate with a lawyer. Then it would come before you as a judge. But don't make it very difficult for me to argue with the president of the United States.' " [94] But Carter did not rely on his lawyers. He engaged directly in negotiations with the Israeli and Egyptian staff, often for hours at a time and literally from dawn until midnight.

Although he was often criticized for excessive attention to minor detail, Carter's mastery of it was essential to his success. Only the president of the United States, with all the prestige of the office, could forge tough compromises, and to accomplish this he had to know as much as the members of his own delegation, as well as the information that was available to the others. He devoted a great deal of study and said later: "I never did regret it. It was not an onerous chore for me; it was kind of an interesting thing for me to do. At the Camp David discussions with Begin and Sadat, I didn't have to turn around to Vance or to Quandt or Harold Saunders and say, 'Would you explain to me the history of this particular issue,' or 'Will you show me on the map where the lines run or where is this town located' because I knew it. And I could negotiate for hours with the subordinates of Begin and Sadat, which I did, with Aharon Barak and with Osama el-Baz." [95]

The two key leaders never actually negotiated face-to-face. Their relationship was so poisonous that Carter quickly realized he had to keep them separated and work through their delegations, where he found flexibility in Begin's deputies if not in him. With Egypt, the negotiations were more complicated, because Sadat did not wish to engage in them at all. Carter did not simply bury his head in briefing books and CIA profiles of Begin,

Sadat, and their aides. He was extensively briefed before going to Camp David by the American ambassadors to Israel and Egypt, Lewis and Eilts, and summoned them to meet not only with him but with Mondale, Vance, Brown, Brzezinski, and Ham. He asked the two ambassadors to gauge the reactions he might expect from Begin and Sadat to various proposals that he ran past them. He even commissioned public opinion polls in Israel to test his proposals so he could defend them in arguments with Begin if the prime minister insisted that his citizens would oppose them.

The president aimed higher for a broader agreement than his advisers thought possible.[96] At the outset of the negotiations, Carter laid out possible solutions to all the major issues and soon discovered that, rather than being a mere facilitator between the two sides by giving legitimacy to deals they made, he would have to draft and introduce his own proposals.[97] In this he had the unified support of the American delegation, which left its disagreements inside the Beltway.[98]

Years later, perhaps because of anger at Carter's increasingly anti-Israel positions after he left office, many Israelis deny him the credit he deserves for his historic peacemaking at Camp David, and for sealing it later by midwifing the treaty between Egypt and Israel. Morris Amitay, the executive director of AIPAC, argued that it would have happened anyway. Not one person on the Israeli or Egyptian delegations shared that view.[99]

Everyone agreed that it was Jimmy Carter who unlocked the compromises to achieve an improbable agreement, not once but twice—at Camp David, and six months later in the treaty itself. This was Jimmy Carter at his best—his attention to detail, his recognition of the limits to which he could push Begin and Sadat, and his appreciation of their starkly different personalities. In diplomatic midstream he recognized that Begin was too ideologically torn to reach an agreement on his own, and quickly began to work around him through Weizman, Dayan, and particularly the unsung hero, Begin's own legal adviser, Aharon Barak. He also sensed that Sadat was so far ahead of his own delegation that he risked losing them, so he sought and obtained the Egyptian autocrat's proxy and thus was accused of being Sadat's agent.

Carter's success was without precedent in American diplomatic history: No president of the United States was so closely engaged in drafting and negotiating agreements, and not just with his international counterparts but with their specialists and subordinates. Theodore Roosevelt won the Nobel Peace Prize for the treaty that ended the Russo-Japanese War in 1905, but he remained in his summer home while the negotiators wrangled and played a generally encouraging rather than an active role. The only possible exception was Woodrow Wilson's personal intervention in the Treaty of Versailles to end World War I. He arrived in France after the Armistice with a list of general principles—his Fourteen Points for a new world order—many of which he not only failed to incorporate in a disastrously punitive settlement but were repudiated at home by American isolationists in Congress and the public.

No president has dedicated himself so exclusively to one project, or taken such a risk to his prestige and standing on a highly uncertain project, or inserted himself so directly in the negotiating minutiae. This saga demonstrates that successful deal-making in the Middle East, perhaps more than anywhere else, demands creative solutions, personal tact, political risks, and above all, tremendous perseverance. President Carter achieved a peace between two former enemies that has lasted into the next century—and without a single violation, as Carter proudly said to me some thirty-five years later.[100] The Camp David Accords also opened the way to Israel's peace treaty with Jordan in 1994 during the Clinton administration, and undergirded the 1993 Oslo Accords for mutual recognition by Israel and the PLO—an agreement that was to fall apart with the assassination of Rabin, the political rise of Benjamin Netanyahu, and the obduracy of the Palestinians, who, in the famous aphorism of Israel's eloquent foreign minister Abba Eban, "never lost an opportunity to lose an opportunity," turning down major Israeli concessions from Prime Ministers Ehud Barak in 2000 and Ehud Olmert in 2008.

20

A COLD PEACE

Almost everyone believes that Camp David was the end of the process, but hammering out a framework proved to be only the beginning—or as Winston Churchill said of Britain's early victories in World War II, "not . . . the beginning of the end. But . . . perhaps, the end of the beginning." Turning the agreed framework into a detailed and legally binding treaty was excruciating and demanded Carter's commitment in time and travel to the Middle East for more personal diplomacy, grinding away at the president's attention to his many other priorities.

It did not take long for the euphoria of Camp David to evaporate. Begin, to protect himself against hard-liners in his own party, as well as skeptical American Jewish leaders, made many bellicose, even defiant, speeches starting the very next day after signing the Camp David Accords. He boasted to them how little he had conceded to Egypt and propounded interpretations that were at wide variance from Carter's understanding on such key matters as new settlements. He also disregarded Carter's urgings to put the best face on the accords to help Sadat quell Arab attacks and give U.S. diplomacy room to sell the agreement, at least to moderates in the Arab world.

One critical ingredient in successful statecraft is to appreciate the internal politics of the nation with whom you are negotiating. In an effort to shore up his own political right-wing, Begin ignored this principle. As Henry Kissinger said after years of negotiating with the Israelis, "Israel has no foreign policy; it only has domestic politics."[1]

Shortly after the signing ceremony in the East Room, I sent the president a memorandum, with copies to Mondale, Brzezinski, and the senior political and congressional advisers, "Regarding the solidification of your

Middle East triumph."[2] I recommended that first we try to persuade Sadat and Begin—but "particularly Begin"—to give the agreement as flexible an interpretation as possible. I pointed out that American Jewish leaders had already warned me that Begin would not only crow about what he had obtained, but would give the agreement the narrowest reading possible, as he had done in a nationally televised interview with Barbara Walters. Second, I recommended that we ask Jewish senators and congressmen to convey to Begin a message of moderation and concern for Sadat. Third, and, perhaps most important, I suggested that we quietly organize a group of senators who supported the sale of arms to Saudi Arabia to remind the Saudi ambassador that this was an important moment for the kingdom to show its support for Sadat. The president's handwritten response was "all done—or better, J."

Begin did keep his promise to secure parliamentary approval of the framework within two weeks. It passed 84–19, with seven of his own party members voting no and an abstention by the Knesset speaker, Yitzhak Shamir, who headed the violent Stern Gang in the underground fight for independence from the British, and succeeded Begin as prime minister.

There was a parallel reaction among the leadership in Egypt. Sadat's close colleagues in the Egyptian delegation were even more upset at the results because they felt he had gone too far and gotten too little. They had already shown their displeasure by refusing to attend the signing, and they harbored it for years afterward in high positions—el-Reedy as ambassador to Washington and Elaraby as head of the Arab League. Sadat rejected all complaints about his vague promises on Jerusalem and the Palestinians and refused Kamel's advice for an Arab League emissary to explain to all members what had been accomplished, and to seek cover from criticism. Why not? asked Elaraby. "I don't need to give you a why," snapped Sadat, waving off his diplomats as small-minded men.[3]

But Sadat was more closely attuned to popular feeling than the sophisticated diplomats in his entourage. When el-Reedy returned to his home near Cairo during Ramadan, a peasant asked if he thought Camp David was a good thing. El-Reedy dutifully replied yes, then asked the villager's views. The humble *fellah* replied: "We got our land back. We got our oil fields back, and there will be no war anymore, so what else do you want?" In his wisdom, the man understood that the problems of the Palestinians lay beyond his horizon.

Sadat intuited this, too, and had told el-Reedy: "We have done for Palestine all that we could, but this problem will never be solved."[4] The Palestinian leadership was predictably unhappy, and in the long run they were the biggest losers. For all the limitations of the autonomy talks, if the Palestinians had been willing to make some compromises and abandon violence, they would have had more leverage on Israeli expansionism in the West Bank.

STUMBLING OVER THE FINE PRINT

After the Accords, hardly a day passed that discord did not arise over their interpretation, most importantly over the length of time Israel would freeze the establishment of new settlements. Assistant Secretary of State Saunders had been assigned the task of working out an acceptable side letter on settlements, while the president wrestled with a side agreement on the status of Jerusalem. Neither made progress. Begin did not submit a new draft of the disputed letter on West Bank settlements until Monday, after the dramatic Sunday night White House signing ceremony. During the time that the president was briefing congressional leaders about the five-year freeze he thought he had obtained, Begin went to the press saying he understood it would last only for the three months it would take to turn the Accords into a binding peace treaty.

In a remarkable backstage scene inside the U.S. Capitol, the president and Sadat berated Begin—to no avail—for the public statements he had just made backing away from Israel's Camp David commitments to withdraw military forces, freeze settlements, and abide by UN Resolution 242.[5] As a beaming Jimmy Carter mounted the historic rostrum of the House of Representatives, the entire Congress burst into cheers. Begin and Sadat, sitting next to each other in the balcony, accepted the acclaim as well. Almost no one knew of the tense confrontation that had just occurred. Carter, although anguished, nevertheless was undeterred and wrote his version of the freeze into the speech.

But Begin was under intense pressure from his Likud Party colleagues and his former Irgun comrades not to yield an inch of conquered West Bank territory—not after three months, five years, or indeed ever. Ed Sanders accompanied Begin and the Israeli party from Washington to New York for their flight back to Israel, and at first, he said, "Everybody was feeling terrific." But then Begin's mood changed dramatically when he read a *Washington Post* report on Brzezinski's statement that the settlement freeze would last five years.[6]

To confirm the three-month suspension, Begin's aides later showed their notes of the Saturday-night meeting to William Brown, the second-ranking American diplomat in Israel, recording a commitment only to signing the treaty when it was formally completed.[7] In Jerusalem, Barak phoned Begin from his Supreme Court chambers, confirmed to the prime minister that he was in the right about a three-month freeze, and then cabled his notes to Carter. Even Sadat was reported to have told the press in Alexandria that the settlement freeze would last only three months.[8] All to no avail. Carter felt Begin had made a commitment on one day and then backed away from it the next. To this day he has not changed his view of bad faith.

I viewed this disagreement firsthand in the Oval Office. I happened to be discussing another matter on the very day the three months were up, when Carter received the news that Begin had authorized new West Bank settlements. Jimmy Carter rarely shows anger, but he certainly did then and accused Begin of misleading him. I said: "Mr. President, there are good reasons to oppose Begin's settlement policy, and I share those reasons with you. However, Begin is an honorable man. I do not believe he would have consciously misled you. There is no way, either philosophically given his views about the West Bank, or politically given his coalition, that he could have agreed to that long a settlement freeze." Carter then went to his desk, reached into the drawer, pulled out a piece of paper, and showed it to me. "These are my notes from my meeting with Begin, here you can see '5-year settlement freeze.' I have checked with Cy [Vance] and he has the same recollection." (In his memoirs, Vance concurred that Begin had finally agreed to five years.)[9] All I could say, rather lamely, was: "Mr. President, there must be an honest disagreement." There certainly was, and it lasted for years—in fact for at least thirty-five of them. As he approached ninety years of age, he lashed out:

"Begin got cold feet almost immediately after we left Camp David, [and made] speeches to Jewish organizations even before we had the Monday night Joint Session of Congress. . . . I'm not accusing Begin of lying. But I'll say he rationalized his position. My belief is [that] until he did, he never would have admitted to himself that he broke his promise. But for me and Sadat and the other people that were there, he broke his promise."[10]

How could two such opposing conclusions have emerged from the same meeting? All those around the table were exhausted after wrestling with the same problems for almost two weeks. The Saturday-night meeting lasted six hours nonstop, into the early hours of Sunday, the thirteenth and final day. The discussions moved back and forth from one disputed point to another. It is not hard to see how one deadline might also have overlapped the other, and that when Begin talked as he did of "the whole process," he and Carter could have misread each other.

The most plausible explanation came from the two diplomats at Camp David with the deepest experience of the close-quarters bargaining, which was rooted in both the bargaining mentality of the Arab souk and Begin's tough negotiating style. State's Hal Saunders called it a "a classic case of that human situation . . . because they were all working from two different mental frameworks."[11] Ambassador Lewis agreed that the misunderstanding arose in part because everyone was worn out "and they were not careful enough. They're very human about this issue." Carter's "dreadful mistake," said Lewis, was made when Begin's letter arrived the next day and the president did not confront him directly, but left Saunders with the impossible task of sorting it out.[12]

Israel's West Bank settlements became the third rail of Middle East diplomacy. It is possible that Carter could have resolved the dispute if he had been elected to a second term, but he was not. Ronald Reagan did not engage himself in the Middle East. But the festering sore of the settlements persisted in various forms through all the American attempts to broker an agreement, including in the Obama administration, when Israeli prime minister Benjamin Netanyahu agreed to a ten-month freeze, but that did not bring the Palestinians to the table to discuss the very same issues that Carter had confronted three decades before.

RISING FURY AT BEGIN

Despite the misunderstandings—and perhaps because of them—the president did not rest on his laurels. He still gets little credit for his efforts to organize Arab support for Sadat's role in making peace with Israel. With no rest after the marathon negotiations, Vance was dispatched by Carter to sell the Accords to the Arab nations, starting with Jordan's King Hussein, disdained by Sadat as the "dwarf king in Amman."[13] Hussein was insulted at not having been invited to Camp David and focused on the ambiguous language in the published agreements, posing nineteen written questions, to which Vance replied in detail and in writing. All that accomplished was to anger Begin, who declared that the United States had no right to give authoritative interpretations of matters that had already been carefully negotiated at Camp David. Zbig told me it was a "big mistake" for Vance to give such specific answers, while at the same time saying that "Begin will end the special relationship with the U.S. the way he is going," and that the administration would never accept only a "separate peace" between Israel and Egypt.[14]

Begin suspected that Carter's goal of an autonomous West Bank was just a smokescreen for an independent Palestine. While that was most likely a distant goal if it came with solid security guarantees for Israel, Carter also realized it was impossible and said so repeatedly. But Begin's speeches and his unbending interpretation of Israel's claims on the West Bank were threatening the accords and deeply irritating Carter.[15] Carter called Begin to urge him not to be abusive toward the Saudis while he was trying to enlist their support.[16] Criticism arose outside normal diplomatic circles, as Doug Fraser, the president of the UAW, snapped: "Begin needs to keep his mouth shut."[17]

At Carter's first breakfast with the Democratic congressional leadership after Camp David on September 28, the president summed up the situation. He described Hussein as "timid, non-committal, and not willing to help"; the Saudis as more constructive (in ways I never saw); and Syria's Assad as "more moderate than his statements." In my marginal note I wrote: "He always puts a better twist on Assad than deserved."[18] Carter wanted to move quickly to the Egyptian-Israel peace treaty and then focus on the West Bank.

After the Camp David success, we were jumping right back into the same political frying pan. Just two days before, Mondale had showed me Carter's draft of what he called a "wildly provocative speech on the Palestinians." I was stunned. To rally Arab support and encourage Palestinian participation in the peace process, the president was going to suggest Palestinian national passports, when there was no Palestinian nation to endorse the Palestinians' right to emigrate to other countries. Further, he was going to support participation in elections about their future by all Palestinians living in the West Bank and abroad, which could include members of the PLO. Mondale told me it exceeded even Sadat's demands on behalf of the Palestinians and of course would be anathema to Israel. "It will be a disaster," Mondale said.[19]

Thus ensued a titanic battle, with Vance arguing that the proposals were essential to obtain support from moderate Arab leaders, despite the opposition of Brzezinski and even Saunders, Vance's own Middle East chief. At one point David Aaron, Brzezinski's deputy and formerly Mondale's foreign-policy adviser in the Senate, had a White House car drive him to the magnificent, sprawling Georgetown home of the Democratic grandee Averell Harriman, where he interrupted a dinner party for Mondale. The vice president exploded when he saw Vance's latest uncompromising draft. I wrote in the margins of my notes on the series of meetings: "Vance was very pro-Arab. Vance was impossible on this issue. Vance felt this was needed to get Arab countries on board of Camp David. V.P. always helpful with Israel; stayed right on top of it. Did much more than recognized."[20]

In the end we managed to bury the speech on the eve of the Knesset debate to ratify the Camp David Accords. Had Carter gone ahead with it, the Israeli parliament would most likely have voted down his greatest diplomatic achievement. But Vance would not let up. Mondale told me before a dinner at his residence that Vance and the State Department were recommending "subtle contacts with the PLO," and that he found that beyond belief. "This would be the end after we've promised not to contact them, and after Carter called them Nazis," Mondale said, promising to advise Carter to stop State's initiative. Mondale did, and the president shut it down.[21]

But Carter's fury at Begin did not abate. When Mondale suggested to Carter at the start of November that he ought to see Begin, the president got angry.[22] He also told the cabinet that while Sadat wanted more food assistance for his hungry people, he did "not want payoffs, but the Israelis do" for the Camp David agreement.[23]

Then, a week later, while I was in his study discussing domestic spending, I realized that what Carter really wanted was to talk about Israel. The Israelis were asking for our financial help to move their military installations out of the Egyptian Sinai and build a new air base on their side of the desert, with roads and other infrastructure to support it. (At Camp David they had only talked about the new air base itself.) "I don't want to be held up on paying for Israeli withdrawal," Carter said, adding that Begin had told him that he needed "to placate his right-wing friends."[24] The money was originally to have been in the form of a long-term government loan with a subsidized rate of interest, but Begin now asked for a combination of grants and loans. When I looked at the price tag, I gulped: $3.3 billion at a time when Carter was trying to trim our own social programs to help balance the budget, over the objections of the liberal wing of the Democratic Party. No wonder he exploded. I had never before seen him hit the table furiously with his fist—as he did at a cabinet-level budget meeting in November warning his appointees against making any commitments to Israel. He had already told me—and I told Ambassador Dinitz—that he would not allow Israel to "buy peace" and he believed Jerusalem was "raising new demands to extort money from the United States."[25] For Carter this was extraordinarily harsh language.

The next day I met with the president and outlined a financing mechanism I had discussed with Dinitz. But, most important, I implored Carter not to jeopardize his historic achievement over an amount of money that was tiny relative to the overall scope of the budget, and even smaller in the perspective of history. He had calmed down and realized that he would have to live with a distasteful link between the money and Israel signing the treaty.[26] Eventually we worked out a deal: The United States paid the cost of the Army Corps of Engineers building the world-class Ramon Air Force Base in the Israeli Negev.[27]

Dinitz realized that Carter's attitude toward Israel was heavily influenced by dealing with Begin. He turned reflective and delivered an astounding statement for a diplomat: "President Carter must understand that Israel is bigger than Menachem Begin, who can make you puke with his rhetoric. I would like to take away [Carter's] anger at Israel. He is dealing with an ally." It is not surprising that Dinitz, who had been nurtured in the Labor Party by Golda Meir, soon completed his long tenure in Washington and left government service.[28]

But Dinitz had put his finger on the fundamental cause of Carter's ambivalent relationship with Begin. On the one hand the prime minister drove everyone to distraction with his inflexibility and legalistic hairsplitting. At the same time, there was a grudging admiration for his negotiating style, which was to wait for the absolute last second to compromise—but never to budge from his core beliefs. These were rooted in Israeli control of the West Bank and Gaza, a central tenet of the Likud Party to this day. It is one reason, together with the Palestinians' refusal to yield what they regard as their right to return to the Jewish state of Israel, and their refusal to negotiate defensible Israeli borders in the West Bank, that a division of the territory into two states is so difficult to achieve.

By mid-November 1978 the glow from Camp David had faded, and the prospects for a treaty were beginning to look desperate. Sadat was ready to abandon his quest for peace if Israel would not agree to elections in the West Bank; he knew that would mean not regaining the Sinai and told Carter he was ready to accept that.[29] This reflected the increased isolation Sadat was facing in the Arab world over what looked like a bilateral agreement with Israel that left nothing tangible for the Palestinians.

Partly because of the stalled talks on Palestinian autonomy, the atmosphere could hardly have been worse when formal work on the language of the treaty began early in October. The president welcomed the Egyptian and Israeli delegations with a brief pep talk urging them to finish within the three-month period set at Camp David. They then went across Pennsylvania Avenue to Blair House to work there, and a few blocks away at the Madison Hotel, which the delegates dubbed "Camp Madison." With the Israeli side led by Weizman and Dayan, tightening the nuts and bolts of the treaty structure actually went well. The two ministers wanted it signed quickly, and within a few weeks they brought their draft agreements on such matters as withdrawal dates and modalities to the Israeli cabinet for approval. Sadat had fewer problems agreeing to the treaty language because he had the powerful support of his armed forces and the public, both tired of war.

Meanwhile Begin began to backpedal. He was furious at Dayan for proceeding without his approval and made sure the cabinet voted down the draft treaty. Dayan threatened to resign but was dissuaded. All this left Sadat feeling betrayed because he had been promised a speedy negotiation. Even worse, at Carter's suggestion Sadat had agreed to exchange ambassadors as a good-will gesture to Begin. He quickly withdrew the offer. Finally, on October 23, with Carter's personal intervention, a tentative agreement was reached on the major issues. Then Begin threw another curve ball—this one from a direction that would become all too familiar to the procession of American and other mediators trying to broker peace in the years to come: He announced plans to expand settlements in the West Bank, advancing the rationale that he had agreed at Camp David to refrain temporarily from building new settlements, but not to limit the growth of existing ones.[30]

WHICH TREATY TAKES PRECEDENCE?

Also impeding progress was a conundrum of the type that only lawyers enjoy, but that was vital to both Israel and Egypt. Under the Arab League Defense Pact, Egypt would automatically be thrown into a nominal state of war if any other member of the league was also at war with Israel. (Technically Syria still was, but more realistically, if Israel and Syria got into a conflict in the Golan Heights, would Egypt be required to aid Syria against Israel?) Now that Egypt wanted to make peace with Israel, Meir Rosenne, the Foreign Ministry's meticulous legal adviser, demanded a provision stipulating that the peace treaty with Egypt would prevail over any others. For Egypt, such an explicit clause would be an unnecessary irritant in the Arab world, and Sadat already had enough of those. Dayan was inclined to override Rosenne: Like Sadat or any other military man, he was trained to grasp the essentials of a fraught situation. Rosenne let it be known that he was ready to resign because "I only have my professional reputation to defend."[31]

Dayan then told Rosenne that he needed support from a non-Israeli lawyer, so they consulted Yale's Eugene Rostow, previously a State Department official and a distinguished conservative legal scholar who had helped draft UN Resolution 242. Rostow flatly told them that if the treaty with Israel did not supersede Egypt's agreements with its Arab friends, "you don't have peace; you have the illusion of peace." This opinion traveled fast.

On a Friday shortly afterward, Dayan, Barak, and Rosenne received a call from the White House summoning them at 7:00 p.m. They were ushered into Carter's private quarters, where they found the president of the United States in jeans, his feet on the table. He asked the State Department's legal adviser, Herbert Hansel, if any precedents existed, but Hansel had found none. Rosenne said he had found no fewer than eight treaties signed by the United States that overrode earlier ones in case of a conflict. Carter testily said: "Mr. Rosenne, you are wasting my time." Rosenne retorted: "Mr. President, I'm sorry to waste your time, but for us it's a vital problem." Dayan cut in sharply: "Meir, you're speaking to the president of the United States." Rosenne said he realized that, but even Rostow supported his position. Carter cut him off: "Mr. Rosenne, go and negotiate your treaty with Eugene Rostow."[32] In the end Israel succeeded in inserting Rosenne's clause into the treaty with Egypt.

"STU, WHAT CAN I DO ABOUT ISRAEL?"

As the three-month period for negotiating the treaty came and went in mid-December, Carter needed to break the deadlock. Although the White House and especially the State Department were tied up with secret negotiations to normalize relations with China and preparing to conclude an arms-limitation treaty with the Soviets, the president nevertheless instructed Vance to undertake shuttle diplomacy between Cairo and Jerusalem.

At this point I again got involved. I told Dinitz we were effectively abandoning any tight linkage between the treaty and Palestinian autonomy, to concentrate on obtaining Egypt's agreement. Carter now decided that to break the logjam, it would be Vance's turn to use Camp David, where the secretary of state met with his counterparts, Dayan and Egypt's Mustafa Khalil, on a bleak February day. They called it Camp David II, but the magic had evaporated. After four days Begin remained the underlying problem;

he refused to delegate any authority to Dayan, who pressed him to join them and urgently wrap up the treaty. Begin refused and castigated his foreign minister for giving away too much. Carter caustically noted that "Khalil is authorized to act, but Dayan will have to go back and report to Begin and the cabinet." He lamented: "For months now the Israelis have refused to negotiate on any reasonable basis. It's hard to understand their motivation."[33]

Carter then invited Begin to Camp David, but at first he refused. Carter was so angry that he declared at a cabinet meeting he was ready to wash his hands of the negotiations and blame Israel. "It is nauseating to see the insignificance of the issues dividing them," he said, citing minor issues like the timing of the exchange of ambassadors. Domestically, he admitted: "We've done nothing but lose politically."[34] He was confident that once an agreement was signed, the moderate Arabs would agree. I noted in my legal pad that he "always overestimated Arabs."

In a desperate attempt to break the impasse, he wrote identical letters to Sadat and Begin, proposing specific compromises and promising explicitly that the United States would serve as guarantor of the treaty.[35] At the end of February 1979, the president met with his top staff members in the Oval Office. At one point he addressed me plaintively: "Stu, what can I do about Israel?"[36] I had no ready answer but promised to relay our consternation to the new Israeli ambassador, Ephraim Evron.

He had arrived just after New Year's Day, and we soon met. I had urged him to develop a personal relationship with Brzezinski, who I felt had the president's ear on the peace process. In a cable to Jerusalem I saw years later, Evron said that I thought "Brzezinski was ready to turn a new page in the relations with us, after I [Evron] have entered into office."[37] "Eppie," as we affectionately called him, quickly endeared himself to Carter, Mondale, Brzezinski, and me. He lacked Dinitz's sharp elbows, knew how to listen, and was determined to improve relations—not just between Israel and the United States in general, but Begin and Carter in particular.

My appeal paid off; Begin arrived on March 1 for a summit meeting he would rather have avoided. Carter found him "moody and sullen" but willing to pursue an agreement despite what he called "Sadat's irresponsible demands," but only after telling the president he had "suffered personally from the Camp David concessions he had made."[38]

Carter emphasized that although the United States and Israel had mutual interests, America also had interests in the region extending beyond Israel. From Carter's perspective the principal threat to Israel no longer came from Egypt or the other Arab states, but from Palestinian militants encouraged by the uprising in Iran. Carter worked on Begin for two agonizing days, climaxing on Saturday night, March 2, in a confrontation so sharp that Begin confided to Carter three days later that he could not sleep that night for fear of a total break with Washington. When Begin came for his last meeting on March 3, two more hours of negotiations proved fruitless.[39]

ANOTHER BIG GAMBLE FOR PEACE

Carter now decided that the only way forward was to take a gamble even more visible than any at Camp David and travel to Israel and Egypt himself to impress upon both leaders what they would be losing if they failed to agree to a peace treaty. By his own admission, making this decision was "the biggest argument I had with my advisers [and], it got kind of ugly."[40] Here was a president traveling halfway across the world, and failure would be far more politically damaging to him and embarrassing to our country, and he knew it. "I don't know how to express it, but I was out on a limb literally, and figuratively, way out on a limb."[41]

Mondale was almost apoplectic about the risks, and Vance and Brzezinski argued against the trip because it was being made in the context of the Iranian revolution and the fall of the Shah. They warned it could be seen as an act of desperation.[42] The domestic political implications were so dire that Ham colorfully told me: "If we come back from the Middle East without a treaty, we can just have Air Force One land in Albany, Georgia [near Plains], and stay there for the rest of [Carter's] term.[43]

The imminent confrontation had a cathartic effect on Begin as he pondered the consequences of a serious deterioration in relations. On March 5, only a few days after leaving Washington, Begin telephoned Carter to give him the welcome news that the Israeli cabinet had accepted the U.S. treaty proposals.[44] It was now up to Sadat, who called Carter to warn that he was under great pressure to join an Arab summit and reintegrate Egypt into the Arab world. It is not an exaggeration that Carter personally salvaged the peace treaty.

As he emplaned for Cairo, Carter felt he had an ace in the hole in Sadat's trust, and his commitment to accept any proposal made by Carter that would not undermine Egypt's fundamental interests.[45] As the president landed, Sadat had organized millions of Egyptians to cheer his train from Cairo to Alexandria, where he met Sadat. Together they drafted side letters about the Palestinians, clarified Egypt's obligations to defend other Arab states, and committed Egypt to sell natural gas to Israel at preferential terms. Carter, mindful of Israel's security needs, told Sadat there was no real need for Egypt to station any tanks in the Sinai or post troops only five kilometers from the Israeli border—but Sadat added helpfully, "Let's make it twenty kilometers because I don't want Prime Minister Begin to be disturbed."[46]

On March 10, just after the end of the Sabbath, Carter landed at Ben-Gurion Airport to a red-carpet welcome but an uncertain outcome. Although Begin and his cabinet had already approved the treaty, he needed them to agree to the adjustments he had made to satisfy Sadat. Alone with Begin in his study after a private dinner, Carter was astounded and recounted that he had "rarely been so disgusted in my life" when Begin told him for the first time that he could not sign any agreement on his own but needed to have the full text submitted to the cabinet and then to permit a Knesset debate of eight to ten days on all the issues. Carter then asked Begin "if he actually wanted a peace treaty, because my impression was he did with apparent relish everything he could do to obstruct it." At these harsh words, Begin "came right up and looked in my eyes about a foot away and said that he wanted peace as much as anything else in the world."[47] His biggest problem of course was the settlements. When Carter left near midnight, the prospects for success were as dark as the night.

At a working meeting the next day, the haggling continued, even down to the meaning of specific English words. Begin objected to "derogate," at which point—in an almost surreal scene—dictionaries and thesauruses were supplied for the president of the United States, the prime minister of Israel, and all their aides to find different combinations of words.[48] At the end of the afternoon the Israelis and the Americans remained deadlocked on all outstanding issues, and Carter realized he needed to outflank Begin with an unprecedented appeal to the Israeli cabinet. Begin for his part realized that a crisis was brewing in which Carter would make him the deal breaker. He asked for an adjournment to consult the Israeli cabinet's seven-member Security Committee. For more than an hour, Carter and his delegation waited in the Cabinet Room, where the president incautiously made unflattering remarks about his host.[49]

When negotiations resumed Begin agreed to convene the full twenty-three-member cabinet to review Sadat's latest modifications. But first the schedule called for a formal dinner at the Knesset, where everyone was on best behavior. The violinists Isaac Stern, a frequent performer at the Carter White House, and Pinchas Zukerman, entertained everyone, with a beautiful Chagall tapestry in the background. Then the U.S. delegation cooled its heels in the lobby of the King David Hotel while the Israeli cabinet met nonstop until 5:30 a.m. Monday. While they accepted parts of the latest U.S. draft, they would not accept all of it. Carter's personal appeal swayed most ministers, but not Begin and Ariel Sharon.

Begin and Carter now were both exhausted. Carter felt that Begin was holding out on trivial issues and that he could not remain longer with so many other problems demanding presidential attention at home. Before leaving, he tried to reassure the Knesset's Foreign Affairs and Defense Committee and the full parliament that they could depend on Egypt. Addressing the Knesset, he witnessed the rough edge of Israeli politics and the intense opposition Begin faced within his own Likud Party—a withering contrast to the respectful attention Begin had received from a joint session of the U.S. Congress. As Begin was introducing Carter, Geulah Cohen, an outspoken, hard-line Likud member, climaxed a hectoring chorus by screaming that her own leader was selling out Israel. After several warnings from the Speaker, she was expelled from the chamber. Carter delivered an eloquent appeal for the preservation of the U.S.-Israel relationship. Ad-libbing a line and looking down at Begin from the rostrum, he said pointedly that national leaders "had not lived up to the aspirations of their peoples."[50] This did nothing to improve Begin's disposition. When Begin spoke he was heckled by other members of his own party, without any prompting from the absent firebrand, Ms. Cohen.

But then Dayan and Weizman joined forces, just as they had in the closing hours at Camp David, to ensure that Carter would not leave empty-handed. After Weizman threatened to resign over Begin's persistent brinks-manship, he and Dayan convened key members of the cabinet to devise new language on a guarantee for Israel's oil supply and other loose ends. Israel and Egypt can be thankful that when Carter awoke from a brief nap, he decided to remain until Tuesday morning, when he heard the surprising news that Begin had told the press that they had made substantial pro-gress. Carter called Begin to thank him for all his efforts and invite him and his wife, Aliza, to breakfast with him and Rosalynn in their presiden-tial suite at the King David Hotel before he left. With Begin fully aware that Carter was going home in defeat, this final gesture of friendship worked like Carter's autographed photos of Begin's grandchildren at Camp David.

About 9:00 a.m. Tuesday, as most of the American delegation was al-ready en route to the airport, and the Israeli airspace was cleared for Carter's departure, Begin and his wife headed for the president's suite. Carter asked for a few minutes for him and Rosalynn to prepare to receive their guests. Rafshoon and Ham were told to entertain them. They found Begin friendly and laughing. "I've always liked the King David Hotel," he said. Unaware of Begin's underground exploits, they agreed it was indeed a very nice place. "You know," he continued, "I blew it up once, using explosives in milk canisters." Shocked, they stared at him. Begin added with a broad smile, enjoying the joke: "Don't worry, I'm not going to do it again."[51]

Breakfast proved more serious and indeed decisive. One hurdle was main-taining a secure supply of energy for Israel, which in those years had no oil and gas reserves and depended in part on the oil fields conquered in Sinai in 1967, which would be returned to Egypt under the treaty. As part of a Kissinger-led agreement in 1975 to withdraw from part of the Sinai and aban-don one oil field, the United States promised to assist Israel for five years in securing its oil supply if it were shut out of buying oil on the world mar-ket.[52] But now Israel would be making a major sacrifice by relinquishing another oil field; Sadat offered to sell crude oil to Israel at market rates, but what if hostilities between the two countries flared again? To make matters worse, a cataclysmic event shook the world: Islamic radicals deposed the Shah of Iran, who had quietly been supplying half of Israel's oil, along with a quarter from Mexico, and the rest from the volatile spot market, in which oil is traded for immediate delivery at current prices. Now Israel demanded American assurances to help maintain a steady supply.

Recognizing their plight, Carter offered to guarantee oil supplies from the United States, which surprised Begin and figuratively helped grease the way to agreement. When Begin showed a bit more flexibility, Carter asked Dayan and Vance to join the breakfast and offered to extend the guarantee for fifteen years, more than the Israelis expected. Carter also told Begin he had Sadat's agreement to pass Israeli ships through the Suez Canal immediately. Now Begin agreed to the treaty in principle.

Then the unimaginable happened to the leader of the free world and the prime minister of Israel. As Carter recalled, Begin "was still huffy. And we started down in the elevator. I didn't know whether he had agreed or not. He was more flexible. [Then] the elevator got stuck. Nobody could get the door open. It was Begin and me and our two wives and two security agents. They finally got a big crowbar and tore the door off. The manager of the hotel got a ladder put up. So we all came down with probably a thousand news reporters with cameras. We came down in a very ignominious way with our butts coming down backwards off the ladder."[53]

On the way to the airport Begin at last said he would accept Carter's final proposals. Carter phoned Sadat to tell him he was bringing new language. When he arrived in Cairo to meet Sadat at the airport, approval was as swift as expected, and Carter confirmed to Begin that all were in agreement.

In fact Begin had never intended to send President Carter home empty-handed, or so Ambassador Lewis was later told by Begin's confidants. The ambassador summed up Begin's brilliant, if almost insufferable, bargaining style, on display both at Camp David and on this last fateful trip: "Begin was simply and purely bargaining; he was going through his usual, very tough, emotional, tenacious, legalistic, annoying bargaining tactics. Begin was a very tough and effective negotiator. He drove everybody crazy, but usually got 90 percent of his objectives. And that, after all, is the test." Begin sent the treaty to the Knesset, which approved it after a spirited debate, despite the defection of some Likud colleagues.[54]

As head of an interagency group of State, Energy, and Treasury Department officials, I was handed the political hot potato of converting Carter's energy pledge into concrete terms. It was not an auspicious moment to be seen guaranteeing Israel's oil supply when four million barrels of Iranian oil had disappeared from the world market during the turmoil of the Iranian revolution, sending spot-market prices to unprecedented heights and creating gasoline shortages that forced cars to line up for hours at gas stations across America. Carter was already being blamed for that.

Not only was timing important because of Israel's imminent withdrawal from the Sinai, but so was the price. Would the oil companies squeeze Israel in a crunch? I suggested that the president give a major speech on energy conservation and to permit the export of Alaska oil and swaps with other countries to balance our supplies. If we buried the guarantees to Israel in this major program, they would be less noticeable. Congress cut this avenue off, prohibiting the export of Alaskan oil to assure domestic supplies.

But at our request Congress authorized the president to export oil to Israel in an emergency. Still, Israel made it clear that they would not sign a treaty without more concrete assurances. The oil issue was not put to bed until the eve of the signing of the treaty. This came in two agreements through the Byzantine interagency process I led. A provision was added to the treaty allowing Israel to bid for Egyptian oil not needed for its domestic needs on the same basis as any other country.[55] After endless meetings and foot dragging by the State Department, in a second agreement we also committed ourselves to supply part of Israel's needs from our own stocks at the prevailing market price for a period of fifteen years, assuring Israel access to U.S. oil at market prices if Israel could not meet its needs from the international market—a pledge the United States had never made before (or since) to any other country. On the same day as the peace treaty was signed, Vance and Dayan also signed a Memorandum of Agreement on oil.

A more detailed oil agreement was consumated well after the treaty was signed, and only two weeks before Carter would face the voters in a bid for reelection. With his Jewish support lagging, I met with Israel's energy minister, Yitzhak Modai, and the Israeli Embassy economic counselor, Dan Halperin. I urgently asked for the deal to be concluded before the election so the president could be seen publicly endorsing it. Then raw American politics intruded. Paul Hall, president of the Seafarers International Union, announced his opposition to sending any American oil to Israel, unless it was shipped in American tankers. Reluctantly I acquiesced. Once the agreement was duly signed, the Israelis pressed us to apply it quickly in order to cement a precedent. We resisted just as strongly to avoid a political outcry.[56]

But after all that effort, the agreement was never invoked by Israel, although it was extended several times and largely forgotten over the years. When it was last extended for another fifteen years in November 2014, the White House had to be reminded of its very existence by an inquiry from the Reuters news agency. Fittingly the renewal was arranged by my cousin Ron Minsk, the energy specialist in the Obama White House.[57]

ENDGAME

For the first time since their brief and strained encounters at Camp David, which seemed eons ago, Begin and Sadat met alone in the large Egyptian Embassy on Massachusetts Avenue, which set a positive mood for the historic signing ceremony the next day.[58] The president and the first lady watched the workers erect the platform on which he, Sadat, and Begin would sign the historic treaty. As a forklift carried a stack of lumber about 10 feet high, he turned and said, "Rosalynn, do you remember when we saved two weeks to buy a sheet of plywood; they're going through it like tissue paper."[59]

On March 26, 1979, a beautiful, cool day, Carter sat between Sadat and Begin on the front lawn of the White House and witnessed their two signatures on the first peace treaty between Israel and an Arab country. The indelible picture of the three leaders clasping hands is one of the great images of American diplomacy. The only cloud on an otherwise cloudless day came in the form of a few protesters across from the White House in Lafayette Park chanting, "PLO, PLO, PLO!"—a harbinger of tougher days ahead.

A giant tent was pitched for a festive dinner with more than a thousand guests, including my wife, Fran, my parents, Sylvia and Leo, and me, and kosher food for observant Jews. It seemed that the entire political and Jewish world had converged on the back lawn of the White House. There was a pervasive sense of joy that the impossible had happened; people could hardly remain at their assigned tables and circulated to hug friends from years past, when peace between Israel and its strongest Arab enemy seemed unimaginable. After five wars with Egypt, the sense of history was palpable. All of my boyhood Jewish education came rushing back to me—Jacob's son Joseph sold into captivity by his jealous brothers, only to become adviser to the Egyptian pharaoh; and then, four hundred years later, Moses leading his people out of Egypt to the Promised Land.

But my most deeply personal link to the treaty was forged just two weeks later, when we hosted a unique and moving Passover seder at our home in suburban Washington, with Jimmy and Rosalynn Carter as the special guests of our family—Fran, our young boys, my parents, Leo and Sylvia, and Fran's sister and her husband, Naomi and Mel Schwartz. Wearing a Jewish head covering—a kippah (or yarmulke, as it was more commonly called then)—the president and his wife stayed for the entire reading of the traditional Passover Haggadah over dinner. He knew not only the story of the Jews' trek to freedom but the seder service itself, which he had attended at the home of a Jewish relative. We needed only one modification for the visiting president. As I moved toward the front door for the ritual of opening it to admit the spirit of the prophet Elijah, a Secret Service officer grabbed me and warned that security prohibited me from doing so. I said it was a religious imperative, and I would open it only a crack, but he was adamant. I finally negotiated a compromise: I would be allowed to open the back door leading to a fenced-in patio. I joked that this would be the only time Elijah would enter through the back door, at which Carter laughed heartily.

If only the story could have ended on such a joyous note, the history of Jimmy Carter's term in office would have been very different. But there are no Hollywood endings in the Middle East. While the Egypt-Israel Peace Treaty remains intact as a major foundation of American policy in the region without one significant violation for more than thirty-five years, Israel and the Palestinians lost what could have been a historic opportunity to use Camp David and the treaty to settle their conflicting claims to the West Bank. Autonomy talks led by Ambassador Sol Linowitz, who negotiated the Panama Canal Treaty, sputtered and died with Carter's defeat in the 1980 election.[60] Each side remains locked in its own historical narrative, and their failure to settle their conflicting claims is the basis for the impasse that has bedeviled every American president since Jimmy Carter. Any hope of achieving Palestinian autonomy and loosening the grip of the Israeli occupation ended with Carter's defeat by Ronald Reagan, who had no interest in the messy peace process.

All the other central figures in the Camp David triumph paid a heavy price. Israel's invasion of Lebanon in 1982 devastated Begin's political career, after he had made such difficult concessions for peace, sending him into self-imposed retirement and almost total seclusion, and bringing an even harder-line successor, Yitzhak Shamir. Four Israeli prime ministers tried to negotiate with the Palestinians by offering various degrees of withdrawal, and none succeeded. Anwar el-Sadat was assassinated on October 6, 1981, while reviewing a military parade when a group of uniformed men broke ranks and shot him to death under a fatwa issued by an Egyptian cleric later convicted for the 1993 bombing of the World Trade Center in New York City. And Carter lost reelection in a landslide, in the process garnering only 40 percent of the Jewish vote, the lowest percentage of any Democratic candidate in modern times. Yet none of the three statesmen who courageously risked so much to change history at Camp David would say their work was of no value; the problem was that so much was left undone after so much effort.

Until his death in 2015, the tough-minded Meir Rosenne telephoned Carter—no matter where either of them happened to be—every year on the March 26 anniversary of the treaty to thank him for the many years of peace between two former enemies.[61] True, it is commonly understood in both countries as a "cold peace"—mainly the absence of war—with little human or commercial traffic from either side but with security guarantees maintained by both. In recent years, with the common threat of Hamas and

Iranian-backed terrorism, Egypt and Israel share intelligence and quietly co-ordinate military actions, although there is little commerical activity, tourism, or public political interaction.

But the peace is a testimony to Carter's willingness to defy conventional wisdom; to take enormous risks for his presidency; and to his negotiating skill and prowess in combining a broad vision with a detailed knowledge of the history, the parties, the personalities, and the legal nuances, all necessary to unlock the promise of peace between two bitter enemies. Jimmy Carter's achievement at Camp David will be indelibly linked with the history of the Middle East and the security of Israel. How many other presidents who have served four or even eight years have come close to matching this singular triumph?

PART VI

PEACE IN THE REST OF THE WORLD

21

THE PANAMA CANAL
AND LATIN AMERICA

Through most of the twentieth century, the Panama Canal had an almost mystical hold over Americans. This miracle of U.S. engineering demonstrated the nation's conquest of nature and its dominance of our own hemisphere, by linking the two oceans that protected it from the ills of the Old World of Europe and threats from Asia. But to the Latin half of our hemisphere, the canal was a painful symbol of "Yanqui imperialism" that threatened their own independence and made them into second-class peoples, whose rights were dispensed at the will of Washington, D.C. Against all the political odds of American national pride, Jimmy Carter changed that for the better. He was not the first president to try, but he was the first to succeed, and once again he paid a political price for doing "the right thing."

The canal signaled America's rise as a world power and was a great legacy of Theodore Roosevelt, the dashing young president who embodied its boldness. By linking the Pacific and Atlantic Oceans, it provided a direct new route for international trade and military transport, cutting almost eight thousand miles off the sea journey between California and New York, and significantly shortening the journey from Europe to the West Coast of the Americas. Shipping through the canal transformed international trade overnight. The canal significantly reduced the costs and time of transportation and positioned the United States as a major player in the international trade, military, and political arenas.

For the Panamanians, the treaty they signed with the United States was both an opportunity and a humiliation. In 1903, only months after declaring independence from neighboring Colombia (with American support, delivered after Colombia rejected a canal treaty), Panama literally signed away its rights, bisecting the new country and granting the United States exclusive and permanent control of a fifty-mile strip across the isthmus. While the treaty did not grant America formal sovereignty, Panama had no access to the new Panama Canal Zone and no right to operate the canal when it opened in 1917; it was built and run by the U.S. Army Corps of Engineers, and Panamanians entered as day laborers.

The Panamanians were unhappy with the arrangement from the start, but lived with it. In 1936, they persuaded President Franklin Roosevelt to modify a treaty provision giving the United States the unilateral right to intervene in Panama's internal affairs to protect the canal. In 1964 students rioted against American control and demanded talks on a new treaty, but President Johnson backed away from the domestic political blowback. President Nixon resumed negotiations, but they were mainly for show, and under President Ford, Henry Kissinger made progress with Panama, negotiating a set of principles. But that initiative withered under the sharp attacks from the Republican right, led by Ford's 1976 primary election challenger, Ronald Reagan. On the stump he scored repeatedly with conservative crowds by holding up a Panama hat and declaring in an aggrieved baritone, "You see this hat? It's mine. I bought it, I paid for it, and I'm gonna keep it. And that's why we oughta keep the Panama Canal." As Ford's campaign manager James Baker ruefully recalled, "Man, the room would erupt."[1]

When I began working on policy with Carter for his campaign, we both knew the canal was a hot political issue, particularly with his Southern political base that never questioned it was anything but part of the United States. Carter mirrored their certainty and turned Ford's good-faith negotiations against him, accusing his opponent of being prepared to cave on eventual sovereignty, while outflanking him from the right. In the presidential debate Carter declared he was ready to negotiate with Panama on physical improvements, tolls, and other practical matters, but "I would not relinquish practical control of the Panama Canal Zone any time in the foreseeable future," repeating that mantra throughout his campaign.[2] So, it came as a surprise to me after he won the election that Carter vaulted one of the most contentious, emotional foreign-policy issues of the era to the top of his priority list. It turned out to be a politically bruising two-year quest to negotiate a new treaty transferring the canal to Panama and struggling for ratification by the constitutional requirement of two-thirds of the Senate. In fact there were several sound reasons for Carter's decision.

In December 1976, Panama persuaded more than half a dozen presidents of other Latin American countries to sign a letter to President-elect Carter emphasizing the need for a new Panama Canal Treaty to improve inter-American relations. Carter was impressed that the Latin countries would put Panama's most pressing issue before their own, a diplomatic rarity anywhere.

Another factor was the threat of violence in the Canal Zone. Before the election there had been a series of nonlethal bombings, which the CIA suggested might be provocations by the Panamanian National Guard. The agency also reported that Panamanians were being trained to commit acts of terrorism.[3]

During the transition Carter also read a report by the Commission on United States–Latin American Relations chaired by Sol Linowitz, former CEO of Xerox. It made two major recommendations to improve relations with Latin America: first to transfer control of the canal to Panama in a new treaty, and then to stress the importance of human rights and democracy in the Americas. The commission's staff director was Robert Pastor, and after the election, he was summoned by Brzezinski to brief Carter about Latin America and the canal for ten minutes. For a young graduate student just finishing his Harvard Ph.D., this was the chance of a lifetime, and Pastor stayed up most of the night preparing.[4] Carter repeated his campaign mantra of negotiating a new treaty without giving away "effective control" and mentioned sharing sovereignty with Panama. But Pastor knew that Panama had never formally relinquished sovereignty and underscored that without a new treaty early in the new administration, violence was inevitable.

Support for this came from no less than Henry Kissinger, who briefed Carter on a range of foreign-policy issues and added that Mexico was even talking about sending troops to Panama's defense if a conflict arose.[5] President Ford put the Panama Canal negotiations ahead of even the Middle East and the Soviet Union in his postelection meeting with Carter.[6] An additional factor was the Cold War. The Soviets already had a foothold in the Western Hemisphere in Cuba and were trying to penetrate other Latin American countries.

The way Carter reacted speaks volumes about how he approached his presidency. If there was a problem, he wanted to tackle it without considering the political consequences or balancing it against other priorities. As he reflected years later: "I have to say I could have put it off to a second term, that's what Johnson had done; that's what Nixon had done: that's what Ford had done, and got away with it. But I didn't think it was right to continue with it."[7] Even when Rosalynn advised him to wait until a second term, he replied, "Suppose there is no second term?"[8] It was not that he was ignorant of the politics of decisions like Panama, but his overriding, guiding principle of presidential governance was to do things that needed to be done, in the certain belief that if he did the "right thing," he would ultimately be rewarded by the American people with another term.[9] But as he later admitted, he underestimated the difficulty of applying this principle to the task in Panama.[10] His insistence on immediately tackling the tough challenges, regardless of political costs and competing priorites, was at once his strength and weakness.

"FAIRNESS, AND NOT FORCE"

Carter, like Pastor and Linowitz, saw a Panama Canal Treaty as the key to opening a new chapter in U.S.–Latin American relations, and crucial to winning friends abroad during the Cold War with the Soviet Union. He also felt correctly that the original treaty was unfair to Panama and had been foisted upon it. Vance, the incoming secretary of state, also read the Linowitz commission report and, in Pastor's words, felt that "Panama's patience machine had run out of gas."[11] Shortly before Carter's inauguration, I accompanied him to a foreign-policy briefing for members of Congress at the Smithsonian "Castle" building on the National Mall. He indicated he wanted to resume negotiations with Panama promptly and hoped for a treaty by June; it was clear he had the bit in his teeth and, in his tenacious style, would not let go.[12] This was accelerated by Brzezinski's decision to hire Pastor as his director for Latin America and instruct him to prepare a memorandum. Drawing heavily on the State Department's expertise, it was highly skeptical that a new treaty could easily be negotiated, let alone ratified by a hostile Senate.

Just before the November election, forty-eight senators had sponsored a resolution declaring that they would never support "giving away the Canal." With Carter in office, Pastor learned that Senator Strom Thurmond, the archconservative South Carolina Republican, was circulating another resolution against even starting negotiations with Panama, and had already obtained the signatures of thirty-four senators. At the request of the White House, the Senate Democratic Whip, California's Alan Cranston, made sure it never came to the floor.[13]

With the battle lines drawn, Vance asked Sol Linowitz to become the lead negotiator and serve for six months; Linowitz insisted that Ellsworth Bunker resume the position he had held as Ford's occasional negotiator and serve with him in bipartisan fashion. He also called me for assurance that Carter was seriously ready to take the intense political heat. I told him that not only was Carter devoted to improving relations with Panama and Latin America, but that he spoke Spanish and read a passage in the Bible in Spanish each night with his wife.[14]

Bunker and Linowitz were the proverbial odd couple: Bunker the tall, elegant, Brahmin model of a diplomat; Linowitz, a shrewd and avuncular Jewish American businessman-turned-diplomat, with an Old World dash of schmaltz. They worked together effectively, but it was Linowitz who discovered the diplomatic keys to success.

When negotiations began in the month following Carter's inauguration, Linowitz never thought an agreement was likely, and certainly not within his six-month assignment. The biggest hurdle would be persuading the Panamanians to extend the most hated aspect of the 1903 treaty, which they had continued to reject during talks with three American administrations over more than a decade: ceding in perpetuity the right to the United States to intervene in Panama if Washington believed the canal's security or neutrality were threatened. Linowitz knew from his congressional consultations that this right of intervention was essential for Senate ratification of any treaty giving Panama operational control of the canal. Session after session, the

Panamanian negotiators repeated their negative mantra. Then Linowitz had what he described to me as a "brainstorm." It was clear that the United States would stop operating the canal in the future but would never give up the authority to act if it was threatened. So, he thought, Why not two treaties?

The first treaty would deal with security, maintaining the canal's permanent neutrality, and giving both Panama and the United States the right to defend it. As Linowitz pointed out, without an agreement on security, any agreement on when and how to turn over control to Panama would be irrelevant. The second treaty would end U.S. operational control on December 31, 1999, and deal with transitional and economic details. But the overriding issue during the tense negotiations with Panama and the bitter Senate and House debates that followed was this: Under what circumstances and where could the United States intervene to protect the canal's neutrality and continued operation? Panama needed a check on the possibility of the American military unilaterally meddling in Panamanian politics under cover of quelling any local unrest that might threaten the canal.[15] Carter sympathized but knew he could never gain congressional approval without a firm guarantee that U.S. ships would have access and the right to defend the canal against *external* threats.[16]

As was his habit, Carter closely followed the negotiations, writing notes in the margins of Linowitz's reports of progress. During those intense months of negotiation, Linowitz developed keen insight into Carter's method of governing. The president had what Linowitz called "an insatiable curiosity about facts; he wanted to know everything about everything, and it was quite clear that he never had enough. If you told him one fact, he'd get another." He would ask Linowitz about such things as the size of some area in the Zone or the shipping volume in the previous year. Linowitz confessed that he often had to lie that he did not know, because if he gave him the answer, Carter would follow up by asking him to break down the amount of traffic in each direction. So he would plead ignorance. And yet Linowitz said that Carter did not micromanage the negotiations themselves. The president instructed him to "find the best deal you can come up with"; "use your judgment"; and then "let me know when you think you've got the best deal you can make."[17]

As the negotiations evolved, the Panamanians reluctantly agreed that under the neutrality treaty, the U.S. could defend the canal militarily but only against external threats, while Panama would protect the canal from dangers arising within its own country.[18] They also agreed that American troops would be stationed in the Canal Zone until the year 2000, but that the U.S. Army would cede operational control to a new Panama Canal Commission, with four American and three Panamanian directors, and that a Panamanian would take charge in 2000.

Linowitz called me on July 1[19] to give me the exciting news that he had made progress beyond his hopes, and that only the financial arrangements remained to be settled. He told me for the first time that Panama had agreed to his idea of two treaties, with the first according the United States the right in perpetuity to preserve the neutrality of the canal—what he called "an invitation to unilateral intervention . . . a great concession by Panama." The second would deal with the economic arrangements, but he warned that they would not approve the treaties without additional U.S government funds, which Carter had to decide. He asked me to arrange a meeting with the president, which I did, but not before giving Sol, in our common vernacular, a hearty *Mazel Tov.*

But his optimism was premature. Toward the end of the month Linowitz called me to say he could conclude a treaty within three weeks, but only if the president sent a personal letter to the mercurial, populist Panamanian dictator, Omar Torrijos, rejecting Panama's absurd demand for a $1 billion lump sum and then $300 million a year, without regard to the canal tolls Panama would collect.[20] I called the president, and it was done thorough a July 29 letter, rejecting the payoff and supporting the agreement Linowitz had reached.[21]

But Panama began backing away from its concessions and reasserting its opposition to an American right to protect the canal "in perpetuity" even after Panama assumed operational control. Now a linguistic distinction without a difference cut the Gordian knot. As Linowitz repeated the need for a perpetual right of protection, his Panamanian translator used the Spanish word *permanente.* Linowitz said yes, and the Panamanians confirmed that it would be "not perpetual" but *permanente.* That quickly wrapped up the security treaty, or so they thought.

When Linowitz and Bunker arrived back in Panama on August 9, the Panamanians sent their final revisions, and the mood had changed. Linowitz said: "It's the most sickening, disheartening thing. They had backed off everything they had committed to in the past two months." He was in a box. His six-month commission ended the next day, his air force plane was ready to take the negotiators back to Washington with what he assumed would be an agreed treaty, and instead Panama had suddenly reneged.[22]

Linowitz called President Carter immediately and told him to have someone start preparing a press statement explaining the failure. When Ham called, Linowitz told him to be sure the statement detailed how far the U.S. side had gone to achieve an agreement, "so the world will know that we acted fairly and reasonably." The next morning, as Linowitz and Bunker arrived for the final session, the Panamanians started by joking he had been "sucking lemons again," a favorite Torrijos line to taunt Linowitz about his gaunt, high-boned face, with its sunken cheeks. But Linowitz was in no mood for jocularity, and snapped back that the United States could not accept any of Panama's changes. Suddenly, on a dime, they agreed to knock out all their modifications—that is what can happen in dictatorships. Linowitz immediately called the president to inform him of the amazing turn of events. Carter's first words were: "Call President Ford and let him know that you want to see him to get him to sign on to the treaty." Linowitz found this very smart, because it gave him the opportunity to get Ford on his side before opponents could get to him.[23]

When they flew back in the afternoon, the president had his presidential helicopter, Marine One, bring them directly to the White House, where, with the cameras rolling, they told the American people and the world that Carter accepted the two treaties with great enthusiasm, marking a new point in relations with Panama and all Latin America. Linowitz marveled that Carter made his declaration even before he had been briefed on the details or seen the treaty drafts. They looked at each other in disbelief, and Linowitz saw Bunker raise his eyebrows, as if to say that Carter had better mean what he said.[24]

But Carter had already committed himself irrevocably. Two days before, he had telephoned or wired all one hundred senators to tell them that the treaties were imminent. Afterward, he sent each senator a handwritten note.[25] Moreover, he had endorsements from Ford and Kissinger in his pocket. Senate Majority Leader Byrd warned him that the treaty was headed for a defeat unless he talked with each senator individually, and Carter actually talked or met privately with every senator, except the leaders of the opposition.[26] Bunker and Linowitz, wise in the ways of Washington, had also kept in touch with the leaders of both Senate and House foreign relations committees as the negotiations proceeded.

The two treaties were signed in Washington on September 7, 1977, at the Pan American Union Building in Washington. Along with former president Ford and Lady Bird Johnson, whom Carter also had as his White House guests the night before, Kissinger and his predecessor as secretary of state under Nixon, William Rogers, were at the ceremony, too. In his remarks Carter framed the treaty in the broad terms of his foreign policy: "fairness, and not force, should lie at the heart of our dealings with the nations of the world." And he pointedly let the Latin dignitaries who attended know that the 1903 treaty had been signed "in a world different from ours today [and which] has become an obstacle to better relations with Latin America," and that the new treaties "can open a new era of understanding and comprehension, friendship, and mutual respect throughtout not only this hemisphere but throughout the world."[27]

THE BATTLE ON CAPITOL HILL

As difficult and contentious as the negotiations were, they barely compared to the battles in the Senate and the House leading up to ratification of the treaties and passage of enabling legislation to finance the deal. It mattered little to diehard conservatives that even the chairman of the Joint Chiefs of Staff, General David Jones, warned that rejection was likely to touch off violence and guerrilla war in Panama—probably threatening the canal even more than a change to local control. In many ways the Panama Canal debate helped foster the New Right within the Republican Party, as Adam Clymer describes in his book *Drawing the Line at the Big Ditch*. As negotiations commenced in February, and even before there was a treaty to examine, the issue became fodder for Ronald Reagan's ascendancy among the Republican Party right, with continuous assaults, including his speech to the Conservative Political Action Conference.

The Senate opponents met regularly in the office of Nevada's Paul Laxalt to trade information on the vote count and get their marching orders from leaders of the conservative insurgents. Paul Weyrich, who coined the term "moral majority" and started the Heritage Foundation, and Richard Viguerie, a brilliant direct-mail fund-raiser with a long list of conservative clients, would become household names from the crucible of their Panama Canal fight.[28] However, one powerful Hollywood symbol of conservative American values lay beyond their reach: John Wayne had a second home in Panama, was friendly with Torrijos, and endorsed the treaty. This helped dilute accusations that the Panamanian was a Communist.

Because of the heavy quotient of partisan politics, Ham Jordan was brought to the front lines. He ran a war room to coordinate our campaign for ratification, and furthermore turned out to be our best primary contact with Torrijos, forming what Brzezinski called a very useful "buddy-buddy relationship,"[29] perhaps because of their shared background as soldiers. We would need an open line to deal with him on the inevitable changes that the Senate would demand as a price for ratification, and Torrijos was not just a standard-issue Latin *caudillo*. He had hopes of developing Panama into a modern country and attracted the interest and support of European writers and intellectuals, most notably the novelist Graham Greene.

Initially there was not even a bare majority in the Senate, let alone the two-thirds necessary to approve any treaty. So our initial lobbying effort was directed at persuading senators to remain neutral and open-minded. Congressional liasion head Frank Moore, Mondale, and Carter divided up the one hundred senators and simply asked them not to commit publicly against the treaty until the administration had the opportunity to defend it before the public and explain how it would protect U.S. interests. This was critical to eventual success, because the temptation of many was to blast the treaty at the first opportunity, on the assumption that it would be political suicide not to do so.

In all our cabinet and senior staff meetings Carter instructed us to underscore that the treaty "opened a new chapter in hemispheric relations, as a gesture of equality"[30]—a very different concept from the realpolitik of Nixon and Kissinger, who had engineered a 1973 CIA-led military coup that killed Chile's popularly elected leftist president, Salvador Allende, and replaced his government with a military junta that murdered its political opposition. But this new era opened Carter to conservative criticism. Sophisticated arguments for ratification paled before our opponents' blunt attack—"Don't Give Away Our Canal"—and polls showed 78 percent of Americans opposed.[31]

The Carter political effort purred to perfection through Ham's war room and slowly began to build support. The president talked with every one of the one hundred senators, and kept a private notebook in his study with every possible bit of information on where each stood and which of their supporters at home might be able to persuade them.[32] They worked in coordination with the congressional leaders. Majority Leader Byrd appointed as Senate floor manager Paul Sarbanes, a Maryland Democrat and a calm, analytical former Rhodes scholar, who partnered with Idaho's silver-tongued Democrat Frank Church to beat back arguments that Torrijos's brother had ties to the drug trade. The allegations came from the hard right, led by Jesse Helms of North Carolina and Nevada's Paul Laxalt, who was close to Reagan.

During treaty debates, it is not unusual for senators to obtain formal clarifications and understandings from the administration. But what happened with the Panama Canal Treaty was virtually unprecedented. For the first time in half a century, key senators forced the two countries to renegotiate and amend the treaty to clarify an essential question: What were the limits to American intervention in Panama? On that issue the fate of the treaties would hinge, and it would require words to dance on the head of a pin.[33]

At the Senate Foreign Relations Committee's first hearing, senators raised what seemed to be discrepancies arising from statements by Panama's chief negotiator, Romulo Escobar. He had been trying to show the Panamanian public that he was succeeding in limiting the right of the U.S. military to intervene, and the priority of American ships to use the canal.[34] Deputy Secretary of State Warren Christopher wrote the committee that Panama and the United States would have the right to defend the canal against any threat to the regime of neutrality established in the treaty, but not to intervene in the internal affairs of Panama. That was still not enough.

Torrijos and Carter met in the White House on October 14, 1977, which led to a Joint Statement of Understanding that same day. The language showed extreme sensitivity on both sides to assuage Panamanian fears of open-ended U.S. intervention. It indicated that *both* Panama and the United States would assure that the canal remained open and secure for all nations. It then said: "The correct interpretation of this principle is that each country shall defend against any threat to the regime of neutrality [and] shall have the right to act against any aggression or threat directed against the Canal or against the peaceful transit of vessels through the Canal." Again, to satisfy Panama, and by extension to help create a new order in Latin American relations, the statement emphasized: "This does not mean, nor shall it be interpreted as a right of intervention by the United States in the internal affairs of Panama. Any United States action will be directed at insuring that the Canal will remain open, secure, and accessible, and it shall never be directed against the territorial integrity or political independence of Panama."[35]

But even this was not enough to push the treaty over the top. Carter felt it would improve both prospects for ratification as well as the conditions of Panama's citizens if he could nudge Torrijos toward expanding democracy and human rights. He correctly viewed Torrijos as a "military dictator" but also saw him as a leader who "genuinely cares for the poor—a sincere populist."[36] His views had some impact on Torrijos, who wrote Senator Byrd early in December[37] that Panama's new Congress would have greatly expanded powers,[38] and that it had repealed laws that allowed summary administrative trials for political opponents with long prison sentences and promised also to roll back a decree limiting press freedom. Byrd was pleased and inserted the letter in the *Congressional Record*. How much further Torrijos would have gone cannot be known, since he died in an airplane crash before his promises could be tested.

One of the most effective ways to sway senators was to fly them to Panama for meetings with Torrijos, who made an almost uniformly positive impression on his visitors, despite his authoritarian nature. Almost half the senators made the trip, organized by Moore and his congressional lobbying team.[39] All the while the president tried to keep Torrijos calm as senators demanded one change after another; Carter even sent him a handwritten note in Spanish.[40] But no visit was more important than the one early in January 1978, by Republican Minority Leader Howard Baker and two colleagues. Baker told Torrijos that the treaties could not pass without changes—and at the same time offered him the prospect that they would pass with them. Torrijos assured Baker he would be flexible and accepted the formalization of his joint understanding with Carter by agreeing to include it in an amended treaty.[41]

Of all the members of Congress with whom I dealt in the Carter White House, none exceeded in stature and in my respect and admiration Howard Baker. He had a homespun Tennessee quality about him, with an arresting smile and a sharp mind. He was short in stature but tall in political courage. During the Watergate hearings, he memorably became the first Republican to ask about Nixon: "What did the president know, and when did he know it?" Baker's father had been a congressman, and his father-in-law, Everett Dirksen, an earlier Republican Senate leader, provided politically difficult and crucial support for President Johnson's 1964 Civil Rights Act. Baker would do the same for the Panama Canal Treaty, almost certainly closing the way for him to secure a Republican presidential nomination. The treaties simply could not have passed without the bipartisan support that he delivered, with the help of his credibility among Republicans.

Slowly the ice began to crack. On January 13 Byrd, who had remained officially neutral to facilitate our lobbying, came out in favor of ratification with the modification of the Carter-Torrijos exchange.[42] At the January 24 congressional leadership breakfast, Baker said the exchange between the leaders needed to be a formal amendment explicitly permitting U.S. intervention to maintain the neutrality of the canal.[43] It would be added as an additional article so that Panama, which had already held a plebiscite, would not have to hold a second one.

When the Senate Foreign Relations Committee voted out the treaties

14–1 on January 30, an essential step to get the treaties to the full Senate, we were still well shy of the 67 votes needed for ratification. New York Senator Pat Moynihan confided to me that by the end of February, only 10 senators genuinely disliked the treaty—but a total of 30 feared that they would lose their seats by supporting it.[44] There were some other profiles in courage. The stately, white-haired Ernest "Fritz" Hollings, a Democrat from South Carolina, with the chiseled profile of an ideal senator and a deep Southern drawl, had announced for the treaties as early as the previous September, and wrote a newsletter to his conservative constituents telling them not only why he was supporting the treaty, but that the opponents were simply afraid.

CARTER APPLIES FORCE

As Carter pulled out all the stops, support increased in fits and starts. Carter told Vance to spend full time on the Hill, and he also asked David Jones, chairman of the Joint Chiefs of Staff, as well as Mondale, Defense Secretary Brown, Energy Secretary Schlesinger, and Interior Secretary Andrus to devote as much time as possible to persuading senators.[45] He asked Kissinger to help, and in a demonstration of bipartisanship sadly lacking today, enlisted former president Ford to call several undecided Republican senators. Carter even called the leadership of the Mormon Church to convert Nevada senator Howard Cannon to the plus side.[46] In March, Carter called me with an update, and then asked if I knew "people who could help, like civil rights leaders, Jewish leaders, and others."[47] I contacted several prominent Jews with whom I had dealt on the anti-Arab-boycott bill, Soviet Jewry, and the Middle East peace talks, as well as civil rights figures.

The president even had Rosalynn call the spouses of wavering senators. But calling in favors was not enough. Senators needed to know that a politically risky vote for the canal treaties would have at least a modicum of support back home. Senators were asked for the names of their key constituents, who were invited to White House briefings with their senators, the negotiators, the national security team, and always a general with his stars glittering. Moore and his congressional liaison team organized these briefings state by state, so we had a Georgia day, an Arkansas day, and so forth. Carter would arrive as cleanup hitter and ask each one to go back home and argue for the treaties.[48]

As important as the merits of the matter might be, senators tried to use the close vote to extract something for their states. It is here that presidents have the advantage through patronage and the government's spending. As Jesse Helms moaned: "I don't want to be crass, but our side can't appoint judges. Our side can't promise a senator he won't have an opponent in the primary." The press jumped on the story of buying votes with federal largesse on everything from routes for Amtrak to new weather stations. There were things we could and would not do. Senator Abourezk wanted us to switch to his side and drop our support for natural-gas deregulation. I got involved with the Agriculture Department when Spark Matsunaga, a Hawaii Democrat, wanted changes in sugar legislation to help his state, and for us to support a farm bill backed by the president's Georgia friend, Senator Herman Talmadge, which we had opposed for budget reasons. We saw the light of day on both, and got their votes. The *Wall Street Journal* editorial page accused us of playing a government version of the popular television program of the time, *Let's Make a Deal.*[49]

Frankly I reveled in the criticism, and wished we had done more of this on other legislation, although some demands took on almost comical dimensions. Florida Democrat Richard Stone, for example, wanted to insert a reaffirmation of the Monroe Doctrine.[50] No president in modern times disliked this kind of horse-trading more than Jimmy Carter, yet here he realized that a defeat of his first major foreign-policy venture would be so serious, and the consequences of a loss so grave for America's prestige, that he had to swallow his distaste.

Carter hated almost all aspects of the politics of his job, especially the stroking of legislators for key votes: "We made a tremendous effort to woo the Congress. Many nights when I was tired and would like to have relaxed, we had a supper for maybe a hundred members of the House, and I would spend two hours in the East Room. describing either domestic or foreign and defense policy. In a way I enjoyed these things, but after you do it time after time after time, it gets tiresome. We had them over in groups ad nauseam. *I mean it was horrible* [emphasis added]. Night after night going through the same basic questions when I was convinced the House members knew they ought to support the Panama Canal legislation. But it was politically damaging for them to do it, and they were tortured. Well, these kinds of efforts that I made, some pleasant, some unpleasant, I think eventually paid dividends, and that was part of being a political leader. But it was more tedious work than being a great communicator. I don't claim to be a great communicator."[51]

The two most difficult senators were the California Republican S. I. Hayakawa and Arizona Democrat Dennis DeConcini, for vastly different reasons. Hayakawa was a brilliant though somewhat flaky professor of linguistics at San Francisco State College who in 1968 had come to fame when, as acting president, he used the police to break up a black student demonstration. A conservative free spirit, during his Senate campaign he famously quipped, in opposing Panamanian control, that the United States "stole it fair and square."

Out of the blue Hayakawa contacted Mondale to say that he might be willing to support the treaty if he could talk regularly with the president and give him foreign-policy advice. Mondale asked him how often, and Hayakawa replied, maybe every two weeks. Carter was alerted, and even now it is hard not to laugh at the president's instant response when Mondale put him on the phone line: "Oh, Senator, I wouldn't want to set it every two weeks. I might want to see you even more often!" He also discussed Hayakawa's best-selling book, *Language in Action*, and praised its brilliance, although he never got beyond skimming the introduction, if that. But stroking this massive ego was what mattered; after securing his vote, Carter never had to meet with Hayakawa after all.[52]

DeConcini presented real problems and became Jimmy Carter's least favorite senator—and that is saying something. Thin and wiry, with a painful smile signaling perpetual worry about reelection, he was serving his first term representing an intensely conservative state. There was nothing subtle about Dennis DeConcini. Arizona was a major copper producer and the government stockpiled copper for its strategic reserve. He insisted that the government prop up the declining price of the metal by buying more, which it did for an additional $250 million. But even this was not enough, or the most serious problem. Senators were introducing amendments galore, some designed to be so unpalatable to Panama that they would kill the treaty, others to show they had toughened it up. DeConcini, insisting on making explicit what had been implicit about the use of American force, added insult to injury by going to the Senate floor and declaring that his amendment was essential to deal not only with foreign attacks but *internal* upheavals that might also affect the operation of the canal, and to do so "in Panama," not just the Canal Zone.

The joint Carter-Torrijos statement was intentionally ambiguous on the nature of the threat that could occasion U.S. intervention, but in proscribing it "in the internal affairs of Panama," both saw clear limits to U.S. action. As Linowitz bemoaned to me, DeConcini "rubbed their noses in it."[53] The president tried in vain to persuade DeConcini to delete the words "in Panama," but he refused.[54] Carter felt he had no choice because DeConcini was bringing along two more senators with him.[55] Not surprisingly this touched the rawest of nerves in Panama: For them the whole point of the treaty was ending the right of the United States to intervene. Carter wanted to consign to history once and for all the arrogant U.S. attitude that made Panama and many other Latin American countries feel that in Washington's eyes they were banana republics. With DeConcini's amendment, Torrijos finally had enough. He was going to renounce the treaty.

The president called Torrijos, who warned him that there would be riots. Carter urged him to make no public statements until he sent Ham to Panama. Ham saved the day by reassuring him, with the backing of both Byrd and Baker, that the impact of the DeConcini amendment would be limited in two ways: It would be added only to the Senate resolution, not the treaty itself, and would be overridden in the second treaty on the operation of the canal by stipulating precisely the opposite of what DeConcini was proposing. Even that did not quiet the senator, who was being threatened by a recall movement in Arizona, and tried to insert even tougher language. Byrd then brought together Sarbanes, Deputy Secretary of State

Christopher, and William Rogers, who was representing Panama as its lawyer.

After hours of bargaining they rewrote the second treaty, indicating that any U.S. action "should be only for assuring that the Canal remains open, secure and accessible, and shall not have as its purpose or be interpreted as a right of intervention in the internal affairs of the Republic of Panama or interference with its political independence or sovereign integrity." This was the exact language in the Carter-Torrijos statement, but omitted DeConcini's phrase "use of military force in Panama." That satisfied Torrijos, but not DeConcini.

Byrd dramatically pulled him aside on the Senate floor and made it clear that DeConcini's status in the Senate depended upon him acting responsibly: "It has to be like this, Dennis, I will not accept any changes." Byrd showed his experience as majority leader: He threw the freshman senator a bone and allowed him to announce the compromise language as his amendment, even though he had played no part in drafting it.[56] Still, no one wanted to cast the decisive sixty-seventh vote, so Byrd and Baker agreed to vote last. But we were still short. Russell Long shouted, "Vote, vote, vote!" But Byrd and Baker were still waiting for Abourezk. He was pressured into a phone booth just off the Senate floor by two fellow liberal Democrats, Ted Kennedy and John Culver, who appealed to him to take a broader view and then literally put the heat on him: They threatened to light a newspaper under the phone booth if he did not come to the Senate floor to support the treaty.[57]

As the roll call proceeded in alphabetical order, the tension was so great it could be cut with a knife; Abourezk voted yes. The Senate unanimously adopted what was known as the "DeConcini amendment" and then approved the second treaty several weeks later, after an equally difficult struggle, by the same one-vote margin provided by Baker and Byrd. The debate had lasted two and one-half months, longer than for any treaty except the Treaty of Versailles ending World War I, which suffered a historic defeat in the Senate. The White House knew that if the Panama treaty had been defeated, the Panamanian national guard was poised to attack. The president confided to the Democratic leadership breakfast on April 18 that if the treaties were not approved, "we would have had 20,000 Panamanians storming the canal."[58]

Still the legislative battle was not over. The House had to enact implementing legislation on the financial costs, and as they began hearings there were rumors, soon substantiated, that Torrijos was supplying arms to Nicaragua's leftist Sandinistas in their fight to unseat the Nicaraguan dictator Anastasio Somoza. This fed allegations that Torrijos was a closet Communist, whose word could not be trusted. The administration asked him to stop because it was unnerving Congress, but Torrijos refused. He hoped to provide the coup de grâce to the Somoza dynasty. The vote in the House was close, 224–202, and came only after several crippling amendments had been defeated by three-vote margins. The bill went back to the Senate, where it finally passed two years after the treaties were signed.

But was all this worth the expenditure of huge amounts of political capital? It diverted energy and attention from other priorities. Seven senators lost their seats in the midterm elections, and another eleven were defeated in 1980.[59] All were treaty supporters, and this was a factor in the erosion of support from Carter's conservative Southern base. Byrd recognized at a congressional breakfast that a defeat "would be a big boost to the New Right."[60] What he did not say was that even their passage would become a victory for them, as well. The treaties became a rallying cry for the new conservative movement that Reagan captured. And Panama's ties to the Sandinistas became ammunition for the small but vociferous neoconservative movement of Democrats that moved sharply right, some into the Republican Party, and made *Commentary* magazine their house organ, with Jeane Kirkpatrick, a Georgetown University professor, as their intellectual leader.[61] Her essay after the final passage of the Panama Canal Treaties, "Dictatorships & Double Standards," argued that Nicaragua was a prime example of undermining pro-American, anti-Communist dictators in favor of leftist movements like the Sandinistas. This helped propel her onto the platform where, as Reagan's ambassador to the United Nations, she continued to defend repressive "authoritarian" regimes such as those in Argentina and Chile, as preferable to "totalitarian" Communist governments.[62]

Such rhetoric was useful in cementing the Republicans' conservative base, but the treaties have stood the test of time, and Reagan never tried to amend them in any way. The Panamanians operated the canal with efficiency and transparency and constructed an expansion to accommodate larger container ships that opened in 2016. Carter correctly saw the treaties as a vehicle to open a new day in U.S.–Latin American relations, ridding Washington of its label by many in the region as a colonialist power, and helping the nations of Latin America shed their dictatorships. He personally ushered it in when he invited every Latin American head of state except for Fidel Castro to attend the elaborate signing ceremony for the treaties—not in the White House but at the Pan American Union Building of the Organization of American States. Organized by our talented U.S. ambassador to the OAS, former senator Gale McGee, the signing was attended by eighteen heads of state, one vice president, and three foreign ministers.[63]

In order to bring them to Washington to witness the signing of a treaty with a third country, the administration had to promise each leader that he would meet personally with the president, a rare occasion for most. During those meetings, which extended over a week, Carter's new Latin American policy was set in motion, as he discussed the concerns of each country and how the United States could help them.[64]

HUMAN RIGHTS AND A NEW ERA IN RELATIONS WITH LATIN AMERICA

But leveraging the Panama treaties into a broader policy based on mutual respect was not a task that could be accomplished through a series of private meetings mainly with dictators, or even by the treaties alone. The most obvious barrier to a new relationship was that the president's policy in Latin America was based upon human rights in a region of autocrats, and, ironically, another was a collision with his liberal Democratic allies in Congress, who pressed principles of human rights beyond the delicate balance the president needed to maintain with American security interests.

Jimmy Carter did not make human rights a key foreign-policy goal at the start of his presidential campaign. When we first fleshed out his positions on national and international issues in the governor's mansion in Atlanta, neither he nor I raised the issue. When he announced his candidacy at the end of 1974, his speech was almost entirely devoted to domestic issues, with an anti-Watergate, reformist twist. There was little on foreign and national security policy, and what there was was focused on efficiency in military spending, the dangers of nuclear proliferation, mutual arms reduction, an obligatory sentence on preserving Israel's integrity (for whose inclusion I fought) and that was it—nothing on human rights. But as the campaign unfurled, we sought to differentiate Carter from the Nixon-Ford-Kissinger policy of realpolitik, which was not based on morality, but on asserting America's national interests and staying out of the domestic affairs of other countries.

Carter's policy began to evolve during the campaign, and it could only have been expected that human rights would become entangled in politics. Like so many American ideals, it rested partly on a political pillar, and I take some credit for helping to cement it there. Carter first pressed the issue in a campaign speech to the Foreign Policy Association in June 1976, just after the Democratic Party platform carried a ringing declaration of human rights. Then in a September campaign speech to B'nai B'rith that I helped draft, he made human rights a central theme for the first time. Patrick Anderson, our chief campaign speechwriter, attributed it to my background as a "devout Jew."[65] But my motives were somewhat less high-minded.

As a principal drafter of the platform, I had made sure that we focused on human rights because it was one of the few foreign-policy issues that united the party's factions—the hard-line anti-Communists led by Scoop Jackson, who wanted it applied to the Soviet Union, and the liberal Democratic followers of George McGovern, who had lost the presidency in the catastrophic 1972 election, and targeted right-wing military regimes. The issue also drew support from the centrist New Yorker Pat Moynihan, who had served in both the Kennedy and Nixon administrations, and Sam Brown, the activist opponent of the Vietnam War.[66] The policy finally came into full voice in Carter's inaugural address: "Because we are free, we can never be indifferent to the fate of freedom elsewhere. Our moral sense dictates a clear-cut preference for those societies which share with us an abiding respect for individual human rights."[67] As president, he applied human rights to both the Soviets and the right-wing autocrats in Latin America.

But Carter did not create a human rights policy on a clean slate. Even before he took office, the new liberal Democratic congressional majority placed human rights on the foreign-policy agenda through initiatives aimed at repressive regimes in Latin America. In 1974 Congress directed the executive branch for the first time to take a country's human rights into account in extending U.S. foreign aid. The next year Congress banned military sales, credits, and training to the brutal Pinochet regime in Chile. In 1976 Congress required the State Department to publish an annual human rights review of countries receiving U.S. assistance. The first annual report (it is still issued today) appeared during the first year of the Carter administration.

The president took human rights to a much higher level, and embedded it in his foreign policy. In his first year in office he appointed Patricia "Patt" Derian, a trailblazing civil rights champion from Mississippi, as the first assistant secretary of state for human rights and humanitarian affairs, and the State Department established the Bureau of Human Rights and Humanitarian Affairs. During his first year the president was also instructed by Congress to end all military assistance to Argentina if its human rights record did not improve; he supported the goal but opposed the congressional mandate, because it limited his flexibility in dealing with the brutal generals running the country.

Until Carter entered the White House, Latin American regimes could obtain the blessing of U.S. administrations by arguing that their repressive policies were necessary to deal with violent, pro-Communist rebels who threatened to provide an opening for the Soviet Union in our own hemisphere. And there were facts to back up their concerns. Inspired by the Castro revolution in Cuba, radical left-wing guerrilla groups had spread throughout the continent. In the spring of 1976, Kissinger met with leaders of Argentina and Chile to warn them of impending change if Carter won the election, and to finish what they were doing quickly.

Change arrived the following year in Carter's human rights speech to the UN General Assembly on March 17 of his first year in office, which made clear that being anti-Communist did not exempt dictators from criticism for their repressive regimes.

To underline his push for human rights, and begin a new era in Western

Hemisphere relations, the president also sent his wife on one of the most unorthodox missions in the history of American diplomacy, a grueling seven-country tour of the region carrying the message that the United States no longer would do business as usual with military dictatorships. The first lady's most significant accomplishments were made in Ecuador and Peru, which in turn set in motion the democratization of Latin America. Peru's military government pledged to establish a democracy, and in 1980 the generals handed power to a democratically elected government whose inauguration Rosalynn Carter attended.[68]

But given the conflicting demands of working with unsavory regimes, it would be devilishly difficult to fashion a clear and uniform human rights policy. There were conflicts within the State Department between Terrence Todman, the assistant secretary for Latin America, and the hard-charging Derian over how far to push the military juntas.

Similar conflicts arose between the White House and human rights champions in Congress on the best balance between security and liberty and the right approach to the harsh realities of the world, with liberals trying to limit presidential negotiating discretion. Following a speech on April 30, 1977, by Secretary of State Vance on human rights, a directive was issued the next month by the National Security Council, establishing the Interagency Group on Human Rights and Foreign Assistance. It met regularly under the chairmanship of Deputy Secretary of State Warren Christopher, and by February 1978 general guidelines had been developed and put into Presidential Directive 30 on such key questions as: When do we use a carrot and when a stick? Which of the numerous countries with severe human rights problems should be targeted? What would provide the greatest leverage to improve their human rights record? The list included our key Middle East oil suppliers with major human rights deficits; the pro-American Latin dictatorships; and the Marcos kleptocracy in the Philippines, our former colony and close Pacific ally.[69]

The tension persists to this day: When Donald Trump attempted to form an antiterrorism coalition of moderate Arab autocracies on his first trip abroad as president in 2017, he decisively shifted the emphasis of U.S. policy by making it clear that their human rights record—or lack of it—would not stand in the way. This was a throwback to the Nixon-Kissinger era, but neither did Carter press those countries on human rights issues, because of their economic and strategic importance adopting a country-by-country approach.[70]

To be clear: Carter did not invent the concept of human rights. If any one person put human rights on the public agenda of the postwar world it was Eleanor Roosevelt. The late president's widow guided the 1948 Universal Declaration of Human Rights through the United Nations, and there it remains as an international ideal. (Ironically, Franklin Roosevelt is still widely quoted as giving a pass to the brutal Nicaraguan dictator Anastasio Somoza on the ground that "He may be a son of a bitch, but he is our son of a bitch.") But Carter was the first American president to apply human rights to U.S. foreign policy as a novel organizing principle, and he had no road map to follow. The result was many inconsistencies in its application; many occasions when Carter's rhetoric did not match his actions; and many instances when he had to restrain members of Congress who wanted to be more absolutist than pragmatic. In areas of strategic significance he had to walk gingerly, which is why the Shah of Iran and Ferdinand Marcos of the Philippines largely got a pass. Carter's human rights policy opened him up to sharp criticism as a naive moralist by conservatives and the neoconservative Democrats adhering to a strongly anti-Communist foreign policy. But Carter was not dewy eyed, and he recognized that a successful foreign policy had to be a blend of ideals and practicalities, a marriage of the best of American values of promoting democracy and human rights with realpolitik. And yet he left with positive if mixed results, and a legacy on human rights that succeeding presidents could not totally ignore without criticism, even when they shifted the ever-changing balance between providing security and promoting freedom.

THE TEST OF HUMAN RIGHTS IN ARGENTINA

In the early months of the administration, four military dictatorships—Brazil, Argentina, El Salvador, and Guatemala—angered by the State Department's report on human rights violations, took the extraordinary step of rejecting U.S. military assistance funds, which decreased our leverage over them. We kept the policy from being a blunderbuss by withholding loans in our own aid program and the World Bank's when they were not focused directly on alleviating poverty. Progress was incremental, but real. When U.S. officials visited military dictatorships, they also met with opposition groups, which had been forbidden in the Nixon-Ford-Kissinger era. In Argentina and Paraguay hundreds of political prisoners were released, although thousands more remained.[71] Chile announced a broad amnesty for political prisoners and asserted that no "disappearances" had been reported.[72]

To support nongovernmental groups, Vance met with Martin Ennals, secretary-general of Amnesty International, and complimented the organization, which had won a Nobel Peace Prize for its human rights work.[73] The State Department hosted a two-day conference for five hundred representatives of such organizations, the first ever held by the U.S. government. They were appreciative, but still criticized our military support to countries engaged in serious human rights violations.[74]

Of all the tough challenges to Carter's Latin American human rights policy, dealing with Argentina was the most difficult. Argentina is a large country heavily endowed with natural resources and self-sufficient in oil. Its capital, Buenos Aires, one of the most beautiful in the world, was the visible result of Argentina's great prosperity, until it came under populist misrule in the middle of the twentieth century and moved toward gross violations of human rights.

During the 1970s the military fought what became known as the "dirty war" against leftists, which they justified as "the first war on terrorism." But the scope of their battle went far beyond radicals and targeted wholesale numbers of moderate-to-liberal political opponents. The ruling junta, which had taken control in a 1976 coup, unleashed its security forces and murdered thousands of innocent people, including priests and nuns; children were taken away from their parents, and in many cases their whereabouts are still unknown.[75]

One favorite form of murder by the military junta was to drop prisoners from airplanes into the broad La Plata Estuary leading to the capital, or to bury them in unmarked graves. The anonymous victims were known in Spanish as *los desaparecidos*—the disappeared. One expert who reviewed the documents of the Argentine intelligence battalion chiefly responsible estimated that between 1975 and the middle of 1976, some 22,000 people were killed and 4,000 others disappeared.[76]

Recently declassified documents[77] show that Kissinger and Vice President Nelson Rockefeller overrode the human rights concerns of the U.S. Embassy in Buenos Aires to green-light an acceleration of the war against subversion by the country's new military rulers, leading to an increase in the number of deaths and disappearances during the last months of the Ford administration in 1976. From 1976 to 1982, about three hundred detention camps were established as sites for torture and murder, and to this day there is no way of knowing the number of victims, with estimates ranging from 30,000 to 50,000. In response, in 1977, Carter's first year in office, Mothers of the Plaza de Mayo, named after the central square in Buenos Aires, was formed by mothers who had lost husbands or children to the death squads. Every Thursday they marched around the Plaza, in front of Casa Rosada, the presidential palace, demanding to know the fate of their loved ones.

Three weeks after Carter was inaugurated, Deputy Secretary of State Christopher met with the senior Argentine official in Washington and told him that while the administration understood Argentina had a serious terrorist problem, it was deeply concerned about torture, witch hunts against opponents, and other gross violations of human rights.[78]

By the end of February the administration cut in half the Ford administration's annual military aid request for Argentina, accompanying the budget request with criticism of the country's human rights record. Negotiations were halted on credits for previously approved military funds, and deliveries of equipment and training agreements slowed. The Carter administration also began to use its voice and vote to curb lending to Argentina by international financial organizations. Angered by the new administration's human rights policy, Argentina announced it would not take up any of its foreign military sales credits for the coming year.[79]

Allen "Tex" Harris, a newly arrived foreign service officer, became a human rights hero on the ground in the U.S. Embassy in Buenos Aires, working under Derian's unique instructions to follow human rights developments closely and maintain close contacts with dissidents, labor leaders, journalists, and the Roman Catholic Church. The embassy opened its doors to victims and their relatives. Every two weeks the embassy also released a regular human rights update, and staffers became experts on the structure of the repressive apparatus, compiling a remarkable database of nearly 10,000 victims, most of whom had disappeared without warrant or public notice.[80]

Senior members of the military junta argued to Harris that they were "spearheading the fight against godless communism" and were not only protecting their own country but "Western civilization itself from the ravages of communism." Harris, far from being persuaded, later was given the State Department's highest award for his work exposing their kidnapping, torture, and murder.[81]

Carter could not avoid meeting with the Argentine ruler, Jorge Videla, when he joined other heads of state to witness the signing of the Panama Canal Treaties in Washington. Pastor and Brzezinski urged the president to invite only the heads of democracies to avoid according an Oval Office meeting to the head of a brutal regime, but Carter believed in meeting with everyone despite the mixed signals that sent. Carter said he found Videla "calm, strong, competent, sure of himself enough to admit Argentina does have problems in the eyes of the world."

Videla promised him that Argentina would finally sign the ten-year-old treaty making Latin America a nuclear-free continent. Carter pressed him on human rights and made a special plea for Jacobo Timerman, a pro-Israel newspaper publisher who later became famous as a prisoner of conscience with his 1981 memoir, *Prisoner Without a Name, Cell Without a Number.*[82] Videla promised Carter to resolve all pending cases by the end of the year and to release many of the four thousand detained without trial under executive decree.[83]

Carter's plea reinforced those of senior members of his administration, especially Patt Derian, who made a game-changing visit to Buenos Aires, publicly criticizing the regime and championing the cause of Timerman and other human rights advocates.[84] Timerman credited her and Carter with saving his life and many others'.

But frankly the publicity Videla generated out of his White House visit was worth more than the concessions Carter extracted from him. For the better part of a year, Videla played a cat-and-mouse game, releasing a few hundred prisoners at a time, and promising to admit a Human Rights Commission of the Organization of American States. But thousands remained in detention, and the commission was never admitted. Although arms deliveries trickled through, they were finally banned starting on September 30, 1978, by a bill the president signed, sponsored by Senators Kennedy and Humphrey. Unfortunately the law was so restrictive that Brzezinski's deputy, David Aaron, complained, "Even if they all became saints tomorrow, we could never resume assistance, because it's been cut off for all time; you have a stick but no carrot—not a very good situation."[85]

Relations with Argentina settled into a nasty stalemate, which was finally broken by war after Carter left the White House. On April 2, 1982, the Argentine junta invaded the small archipelago it claimed as Las Malvinas, which since 1841 had been an English-speaking colony of Britain known as the Falkland Islands. Under the leadership of Prime Minister Margaret Thatcher, Britain retaliated in a long-range amphibious attack, secretly aided by American intelligence, and annihilated the Argentine force. The hated Argentine junta had overreached and was brought down in humiliation by huge public protests.

It took a number of years for Carter's human rights policy to produce lasting change in Latin America, but it came as surely as day follows even the darkest of nights. In November 1983, almost exactly three years to the day from Jimmy Carter's crushing defeat, Raúl Alfonsín won a stunning election restoring democracy to Argentina, and declared that Carter's human rights policy saved thousands of lives in Argentina, possibly including his own.[86] Other Latin American military dictatorships that Carter confronted with his human rights policy—Brazil, Chile, Peru, Ecuador, El Salvador, Bolivia, Honduras, Guatemala, Uruguay—also became democracies, with much higher standards of human rights for their citizens, as validated by America's most respected career diplomat, Thomas Pickering.[87]

The same cannot be said of Nicaragua, where the Somoza regime was overturned by the pro-Communist Sandinistas led by Daniel Ortega, who was nevertheless defeated in a free election monitored by former president Carter and the Carter Center and later returned to power through the ballot box. But because of the strength of the democracies that Carter helped develop throughout Latin America, Ortega is isolated, has cast aside his hardcore Marxism, and presents no danger to his neighbors.

For me, the terrible numbers of those murdered and tortured by Latin dictators took on a personal dimension when I served as U.S. ambassador to the European Union in Brussels during the Clinton administration. There, Fran and I became good friends with the Argentine ambassador, Diego Guelar, whose story gave meaning to the suffering of the era and how much Carter and his team did to change it. Guelar was born on a ranch in the Entre Ríos Province, about 400 miles from Buenos Aires, in an area purchased by Baron Moritz von Hirsch, a German Jewish philanthropist, to finance the first wave of Russian Jews escaping persecution in their czarist homeland. His grandfather arrived in 1885 and became a Jewish gaucho on an Argentine cattle ranch. Guelar won a scholarship in 1966 from the American Field Service, lived in upstate New York, and returned home to graduate from law school in Buenos Aires in 1970. He became involved in a peaceful prodemocracy group opposing the military regime; containing a mixture of Christian Democrats, Jews, and some Marxists, it was outlawed by the government. A paramilitary unit wrecked his small apartment, and he went into hiding from 1971 until 1973, when the ailing former dictator, 82-year-old Juan Perón, returned from exile in Spain and was elected president for a third time.

With Cuban forces active in the region, anti-Communist, anti-Castro military regimes took over in Argentina, Brazil, Chile, Uruguay, Paraguay, and Bolivia. Guelar, like many young people in Latin America, while initially attracted by the Cuban revolution, soon came to see that he and his young friends were being used by the Soviet Union to export the Cold War to Latin America. His life got even more precarious, as he and his law partner received death threats. His law partner went into exile with his family, but Guelar, then 25 years old, decided to stay and run for Congress. Shortly afterward he reaped his reward: Two cars pulled up next to him while he was driving just in front of his law firm, and assailants put 23 bullets into his car. He miraculously survived but went underground a second time, living with false documents until the end of 1981.

When he came out of hiding, he was elected to the Argentine Congress three times, and a democratically elected president made him ambassador to Brazil, the European Union, and then to the United States. In Washington, Fran and I were among those invited to the Argentine Embassy's first kosher barbecue to celebrate the end of the 70-year ban on the import of Argentine beef. In 2016 he became Argentina's ambassador to China. Guelar reflected: "I'm not sure President Carter is aware of how many people's lives were saved thanks to his policy, [but] I can tell you that thousands of people's lives were saved thanks to Carter." The positive relationships built up between the United States and Latin America, he believes, would have been impossible without the Carter policy symbolized by the Panama Canal Treaty, "which is really the cornerstone of the relation between the United States and Latin America." Carter, he said, changed the perception of the United States for millions of Latin Americans, ending what for many was the "idea of the imperial and unjust power of the United States."[88]

22

THE SOVIET UNION

Jimmy Carter came into office with the Cold War at full steam. Soviet power was restrained at the geographic limits created at the dawn of the postwar era by a policy known as containment—the United States and its NATO allies holding the line against Communist expansion until, as indeed finally happened, the Communist vision of the future collapsed from its own internal contradictions and Western solidarity. In the 1970s Moscow had firm control over its Eastern European satellite states and was promoting Communism in Western European countries, especially Spain and Italy, where a local variety known as Eurocommunism had strong public support, especially among intellectuals, because liberal reform parties had been stifled by the extreme right through much of the Cold War.[1]

The Soviets were using Cuban surrogate troops in Africa to foment Communist revolutions. Their military buildup coincided with and was partly induced by the slackening of America's appetite and ability to fight wars abroad after the defeat and disillusion in Vietnam. Moscow had reaped economic and political benefits from détente in the Nixon-Ford-Kissinger era, in which they were regarded as adversaries but equals. The Communists felt that history was on their side.

HUMAN RIGHTS AND SOFT POWER

But in a sharp and profound break with Nixon-Ford-Kissinger realpolitik, Carter was the first American president to make human rights a central feature of his foreign policy, applying it to military dictatorships in Latin

America and to the Soviet Union. For him human rights abroad were the other side of the coin of civil rights at home. Just as he was deeply opposed to the segregation of his native South, he did not want to stand by idly when civil rights were abused abroad, even by some of our friends, particularly in Latin America. As he put it to me: "It was kind of an idealistic thing, and Cy Vance was right in bed with me on that. I can't say Brzezinski was. He wasn't against it, but it was something that I ordained almost unilaterally."[2]

For Carter human rights were not only a morality play. Brzezinski helped marry the moral dimension of human rights with a strategic vision to create a tool to challenge the basis of the repressive Soviet system. Carter envisioned a foreign policy grounded in human rights as an instrument in the raging Cold War to compete more effectively with the Soviet Union for support in the developing world, and as a guiding philosophy reflecting the best ideals of the United States and its Western allies against the soft Soviet underbelly. He meant to exploit it by championing the rights of its oppressed citizens, particularly democratic dissidents and Soviet Jews.

Since the founding of the Republic, the United States has presented its face to the world in alternate directions emblazoned in the Great Seal of the United States depicting an eagle with one talon gripping an olive branch, while the other held together thirteen arrows representing the hand of might of the original thirteen colonies. During the Cold War, Carter embraced this dichtonomy by appointing a negotiator and diplomat (Vance) as his secretary of state; a hard-line anti-Communist (Brzezinski) as his White House national security adviser; and a brilliant, tough-minded scientist (Brown) to run the Pentagon. Carter struggled in the first half of his administration to blend their often conflicting views into one consistent national security policy. His offer of the olive branch to the USSR met its limits in Afghanistan, when Carter seemed surprised by the aggressive nature of Leonid Brezhnev's Soviet Union. Unfortunately, his admission of surprise at the Soviet invasion of Afghanistan overshadowed his steady strengthening of America's defense capability and the defenses of our European allies, as might be expected from a former officer of the U.S. Navy.

He was unfairly accused of waving only the olive branch, while in fact he spent four years improving and expanding the nation's quiver of arrows. Carter reversed the post-Vietnam decline in military spending with average

Carter and Panama's dictator, Brig. Gen. Omar Torrijos, shaking hands after signing the Panama Canal treaties on September 7, 1977. U.S. negotiators Ellsworth Bunker (applauding) and Sol Linowitz are visible behind Carter. *(Jimmy Carter Library, photographer: Kightlinger)*

Israeli Prime Minister Menachem Begin at the Israeli ambassador's residence in Washington, with the author (left) and Yechiel Kadishai (right), Begin's close comrade in the wartime Irgun underground and his chief of staff as prime minister. *(Official White House photograph)*

Israeli Prime Minister Menachem Begin (left) and Egyptian President Anwar Sadat (right) reaching out to each other at the start of the Camp David negotiations with Carter on September 5, 1978. *(Jimmy Carter Library, photographer: Fitzpatrick)*

Sadat, Carter, and Begin shaking hands on the North Lawn of the White House on March 26, 1979, as they completed signing the peace treaty between Egypt and Israel. The peace has lasted for two generations. *(Associated Press)*

After the peace treaty between Israel and Egypt was signed, the Carters joined the Passover seder on April 13, 1979, at the home of the author and his wife, Fran (obscured on the far left, holding their youngest son, Brian). The author stands behind them surrounded by his family. President Carter has his hands on their oldest son, Jay. In front at right are his parents, Sylvia and Leo, with his sister-in-law, Naomi Schwartz, between them. *(Stuart Eizenstat Personal Collection)*

The President with the sons of the author and Fran, Jay (left) and Brian (right) at Camp David, which—uniquely among presidents—Carter opened to his senior staff and their families. *(Stuart Eizenstat Personal Collection)*

With consumer champion Ralph Nader in Plains during the presidential campaign, in August 1976, after being invited against the advice of Carter's political aides, lest his presence offend the candidate's business and conservative supporters. *(Associated Press)*

Lunching on the terrace outside his private West Wing study with AFL-CIO president Lane Kirkland, trying to mend relations with labor after a rocky start with Kirkland's predecessor, George Meany. *(Jimmy Carter Library, photographer: Kightlinger)*

All smiles with political daggers (temporarily) sheathed: Carter in the Oval Office with Ed Koch, mayor of New York City, which he helped save from bankruptcy, and Bella Abzug, feminist fire-brand and ex-congresswoman who was fired as cochair of his National Advisory Committee for Women. *(Jimmy Carter Library, photographer: Schumacher)*

Mary Schuman of the author's White House Domestic Policy Staff and David Boies, senior Kennedy aide, who, while working together on airline deregulation, fell in love and married. *(Mary Boies)*

Carter in the Oval Office with Senate Leader Byrd, a strong supporter of the administration's ambitious legislative program, but who later supported an "open" Democratic Convention during Senator Kennedy's challenge to Carter's 1980 renomination. *(Jimmy Carter Library, photographer: Kightlinger)*

Carter trying to win over colorful Senator Russell Long of the Louisiana political dynasty and chairman of the Senate Finance Committee, which had to clear the President's energy, tax, welfare, and health care proposals. *(Jimmy Carter Library, photographer: Kightlinger)*

With House Speaker Tip O'Neill, the Massachusetts liberal who navigated much of the Carter program through the House, despite his contempt for Carter's inexperienced Georgia Mafia. *(Jimmy Carter Library, photographer: Kightlinger)*

With Health, Education, and Welfare Secretary Joe Califano in April 1977, later fired along with others in the mass Cabinet resignations, for objecting to losing the education portfolio, and keeping up his own Washington political network. *(Associated Press)*

Jimmy Carter announcing the appointment of Andrew Young as UN Ambassador, a key campaign supporter who would later resign over a controversy at the UN regarding the PLO. *(Associated Press)*

Carter with former presidents Ford and Nixon. *(Stuart Eizenstat Personal Collection)*

Carter congratulates Paul Volcker (left) after swearing him in as Chairman of the Federal Reserve, August 6, 1979, along with his predecessor, G. William Miller (right), who moved from the Fed to become Secretary of the Treasury. *(Associated Press)*

With Alfred Kahn, a key figure in airline deregulation and later Carter's outspoken anti-inflation czar. *(Jimmy Carter Library, photographer: Schumacher)*

annual real increases of about 3 percent to help rebuild our forces. He proposed an expanded spending plan of 5 percent annual increases starting in 1980, after the Soviet invasion of Afghanistan, and persuaded our NATO allies to pledge 3 percent of their annual economic output on their own military forces. Carter also persuaded the Europeans to accept American medium-range missiles on their territory as a counterweight to the Soviets' new SS-20 mobile missiles. He initiated the Stealth technology, which remains a crucial element of U.S. national security today. He negotiated a second Strategic Arms Limitation Treaty—known as SALT II—which arrested the Soviet nuclear buildup. Even though it was never ratified by the Senate, it was nevertheless followed by both parties in their mutual interest. And for a variety of reasons, specifically their own excesses—and creative diplomacy, led by the American ambassador to Italy, Richard Gardner—Western European Communist parties began to fade.

In Asia, Carter built on Nixon's opening to China by normalizing diplomatic relations with Beijing, a strategic counterweight to the Soviet Union, over the vigorous objections of the American lobby for the Chinese Nationalists on Taiwan, meanwhile creating an enduring cultural and defense relationship through the Taiwan Relations Act, which protects Taiwan against a military attack by China.[3] Despite fits and starts—Carter's cancellation of the B-1 bomber and a bungled attempt to deploy the neutron bomb in Europe—this is a record of which to be proud, one that hardly anyone appreciates today.

This was the antithesis of the Nixon-Ford-Kissinger concept of balance of power as the organizing principle of world order, a policy based not on emotion or morality but on national interest, and insisting on nonintervention in the domestic affairs of another state. It was therefore in the interest of the United States during the Cold War to build alliances with leaders who were bulwarks against Communism—and if this meant military dictatorships in Latin America or apartheid regimes in southern Africa, based on brutal domestic repression, so be it.

With the Soviet Union, Kissinger pursued détente—a French word implying a relaxation of tension—to establish a productive working relationship; the internal affairs of the Soviet Union were not our business. Well-known human rights abuses in the USSR, specifically concerning the emigration of Soviet Jews, lay outside the Nixon-Kissinger purview, even to a shocking degree. In a recently disclosed White House tape recording, Nixon and his secretary of state were speaking on March 1, 1973, just after a visit by Israeli prime minister Golda Meir, who made a strong pitch for the cause of Soviet Jewry. Nixon, expressing admiration for her, says to Kissinger that the treatment of Soviet Jews is "none of our business," to which Kissinger agreed: "The emigration of Jews from the Soviet Union is not an objective of American foreign policy." Then with exaggeration to make his point, Kissinger says, "And if they put Jews into gas chambers in the Soviet Union, it is not an American concern. Maybe a humanitarian concern." "I know," Nixon responded, "We can't blow up the world because of it."[4]

I know Kissinger well, greatly respect him, and believe that with his record of helping save Israel from defeat in the 1973 Yom Kippur War, and his own background as a German Jewish refugee, such talk should not be taken literally. But the exchange reveals a mind-set: The internal actions of states, however repressive, do not count; what matters is only their external conduct. It is that policy Jimmy Carter ran against in his presidential campaign, and he meant to replace it with a human rights policy. At the same time, given Moscow's aggressive behavior, it proved exceedingly difficult to preserve the Nixon-Ford-Kissinger détente with Russia, even though Carter recognized it could create a more tranquil world.

A milestone upon which Carter would build his global human rights policy and effectively use it against the Soviet Union was the Helsinki Accords of 1975, negotiated by Kissinger, and his boss, President Gerald Ford. From the Soviet standpoint, this agreement among European and American nations was important for implicitly blessing their domination of Eastern Europe, by affirming Europe's postwar borders. However, to gain Western support, the Soviets had to make promises on human rights that they thought they could quietly discard later. These were contained in a section called Basket III, involving freedom of speech and the free movement of people and ideas across borders. Although no one realized it at the time, this marked the beginning of the end for the Soviet Union. The Helsinki Accords laid the groundwork and the legal foundation for negotiation with Moscow on abuses within the USSR's own national borders, of which the Carter administration took full advantage. Although the Soviets formally refused to recognize it, the fact that the Accords had been established as an international norm put significant pressure on Brezhnev to concede to internal reforms. Helsinki Accord monitoring groups cropped up all over the USSR and Eastern Europe in order to hold the Communist governments accountable.

VANCE VS. BRZEZINSKI

Carter's ability to make human rights a major part of his foreign policy critically depended upon his two top foreign-policy advisers. Cyrus Vance, his secretary of state, and Zbigniew Brzezinski, his White House national security adviser. As I had expressed to Carter during the transition, while each was highly able and agreed on many foreign-policy goals, putting them together on the same team was a mistake, because of their major differences in temperament and worldview, particulary on the Soviet Union.

Carter's relationship with Brzezinski was long standing, through his initiative in appointing then governor Carter to the prestigious Trilateral Commission, providing him his first exposure to the foreign-policy elite, and his major help on the election campaign. Every day in the Carter White House officially began with Brzezinski's 7:30 a.m. foreign-policy briefing, and he also saw the president several times a day, more than any other aide. The president felt nearly as close to Zbig as to Jody Powell and Ham Jordan.[5] Brzezinski became his most regular opponent on the White House tennis court, and the Carters and their daughter, Amy, occasionally visited Brzezinski at his home in northern Virginia for quiet dinners with his wife, Emilie, a talented sculptor. Their daughter, Mika, who was close in age to Amy, grew up to be a star television commentator, and their two sons followed in their father's footsteps in government—Mark, as an ambassador, and Ian as a senior Pentagon official.

Carter described himself as an "eager student" of Brzezinski's, particularly on the Soviet Union and Eastern Europe. But Carter recognized his weaknesses as well as his strengths. During the campaign "Zbig put together a constant barrage of new ideas and suggestions, and 90 percent would have to be rejected," Carter said with some exaggeration. He also said that Brzezinski "was always wanting to go somewhere as an emissary, and very seldom did I let him do it. But when he went, he did a good job."[6]

Zbig also was always eager to be the administration's public face on foreign policy, and liked going on the Sunday talk shows or giving background briefings to the press. Because of the enormous amount of time they spent together, Carter found Brzezinski's ideas compatible with his own on many issues, but saw his rhetoric as too provocative and his policy as too hard-line about the Soviet Union.

In many ways the president's relationship with Vance was the mirror image. While he developed a personal relationship with Vance and his wife, Gay, through dinners in the White House family quarters, where they were joined by Rosalynn, Vance was a diplomat who had a vast department to operate and traveled abroad frequently as the nation's premier diplomat. Vance was cautious, perhaps to a fault, while Brzezinski was voluble and aggressive. Philosophically, Carter told me that he was a kindred spirit of Vance, whom he described as a "kind of peacenik" like himself, seeking nonconfrontational diplomatic solutions to such critical problems as saving the hostages in Iran. While he said Vance was "no shrinking violet, when we had a controversial policy to be presented to the public, Cy didn't want to do it."[7]

Carter found Vance valuable in "his orthodox, careful, evolutionary plodding attitude and demeanor," while Brzezinski's attitude was more what he wanted from an adviser, in "giving me a whole range of new ideas and letting me sift through them to see if they were good or bad." Vance was also "extremely protective of the State Department" and would frequently come to see Carter if he felt Brzezinski or his staff was usurping the department's authority or his influence.[8] Carter told me that on four occasions Vance threatened to resign because of some slight, often by Brzezinski. But he saw Vance as a stabilizing factor, a "kind of anchor or screen to hold us back from doing things that were ill-advised; to point out all the reasons why something wouldn't work; and to make sure we didn't take any radical steps."[9]

But Brzezinski was equally protective of his turf and position. One story he shared with me speaks volumes about his relations with Vance, who he felt had a "kind of compulsive anxiety that I was playing more of a role than he felt I should be." On his first day in his office, security officers showed Brzezinski a telephone line he was to answer only when the president called. Then they showed him another special line that would allow the secretary of state to ring him directly in the same way, while other cabinet officers, including the secretary of defense and CIA director, could reach him only through his secretary. Brzezinski asked the security people whether this special line would also ring straight through to Vance if he initiated the call. No, they said, like all the others, any call from Brzezinski would first go through Vance's secretary. "Yank it out," he ordered. "I'm working for the president, not for Vance."[10]

Tensions between the White House and the State Department were nothing new to the Carter administration and persist in every administration down to today. But here disagreements between the two focused mainly on the Soviet Union, which was the central preoccupation of the administration's foreign policy. Vance was a patrician New York lawyer, who felt problems were best examined and solved on a case-by-case basis. The product of the Eastern foreign-policy establishment, the secretary of state had served in senior positions in the Kennedy and Johnson administrations and was handsome, elegantly turned out, and peered intelligently over half-glasses, regarding a disordered world in a methodical manner, with a large ingrained State Department bureaucracy to help him manage it.

Vance was neither ignorant of nor naive about aggressive Soviet actions or the massive buildup of the Soviet military-industrial complex, of which Soviet leader Leonid Brezhnev was a product. But for Vance the Soviets were a problem to be managed separately within the framework of international affairs, and not as America's main adversary, employing diplomacy to maintain détente as best he could, given Carter's human rights campaign, which he fully supported. He argued that Carter should seek increased cooperation with the Soviets and find areas of agreement such as nuclear arms reduction, unlinking other problems from arms-control negotiations.

Zbig saw linkages between events that were not obvious to others, and was a sharp bureaucratic infighter for his views. Brilliant and creative, he was an expert on Soviet policy, and his knowledge of history never let him forget how often his ancestral country had been dismembered and occupied by Russia, most recently in the Cold War. He became increasingly concerned about the political implications of growing Soviet military power and feared that Moscow would be tempted to use it either to exploit turbulence in the Third World or to impose its will in a political contest with the United States.

Zbig constantly urged the president to reject Vance's concept of separate tracks; he wanted to make Moscow pay a price, by linking its misconduct to normalizing relations with China or delaying completion of SALT. Philosophically the president was closer to Vance's than to Brzezinski's line, and tacked away from his secretary of state and decisively aligned himself with Brzezinski only when the Soviet Union invaded Afghanistan, as Carter entered the final year of his presidency. It was this shift, in my opinion, that finally led Vance to resign, and not the mission to rescue the Iranian hostages, which he opposed; that was the last straw of many.

Zbig maintained that cooperation in the face of Soviet aggression served only to make Carter look indecisive and that the Soviets needed to be stopped in their tracks. He was deeply suspicious of the Soviets; gravely concerned at their major military buildup; and eager to counter their aggressive export of revolution in Africa, through their Cuban proxies, in such far-flung places as Angola, Namibia, and Ethiopia, and their support of Western European Communist parties. He believed that opposing them externally would weaken them internally, and told the president that the Soviets were engaged in a "selective détente," only where and when it suited them. The proper response, Brzezinski advised Carter, was not to undermine cooperative relationships "but to increase the costs of Soviet behavior in the malignant category."[11] In the briefest form, this meant continued insistence on human rights as part of the ideological competition, heightening the cost of Soviet interventionism, and more affirmative political initiatives in areas of Soviet sensitivity, such as China. So for Zbig, human rights was not mainly a handmaiden of peace, but a weapon in the Cold War.

Defense Secretary Harold Brown, who worked closely with both Vance and Brzezinski, had a keen analysis of their differences. Vance, he told me, "took a much less confrontational view of the world," and was a "mediator, a negotiator, and not a confrontational person." By contrast, "Zbig is an activist, who sometimes delights in confronting people, not so much on a personal basis, but in intellectual terms, and in deliberately saying shocking things." From Brown's perspective, Zbig "saw himself as an independent player, not either an alter ego for the president or a sage counselor, but as an intiator of ideas." They not only held different views on the Soviet Union, but Vance "had a much friendlier view of the third world than Zbig did."[12]

Carter nevertheless felt that the contest between the two was greatly exaggerated. The Friday-morning foreign-policy breakfasts with the president, Vance, Mondale, Defense Secretary Brown, and Brzezinski were a forum for the president to make decisions after full deliberation, and for Zbig to record and circulate them for comment. In addition, Vance and Brzezinski met weekly to thrash out differences, although Vance had a less charitable view. Vance sent Carter a detailed note of developments around the world every night, and Zbig sent a weekly report, often with biting comments. (I have used both of these for the foreign-policy chapters of this book.)

There are two types of White House national security advisers. In the Kissinger-Brzezinski model the adviser organizes interagency meetings and decisions for the president, but strongly advocates his own ideas. To my mind Brzezinski ran a fair and transparent decision-making process but brought along his own strong views. Brown, for example, never felt Brzezinski suppressed his recommendations.[13] The other model is best exemplified by Brent Scowcroft, President Ford's national security adviser, who saw his role as a coordinator, a synthesizer of inevitable interagency disagreements, but not a forceful advocate. Of course it would have been hard for him to act otherwise with Kissinger also serving as Ford's secretary of state.

THE PERSECUTIONS OF SAKHAROV
AND SHARANSKY

Ultimately the split between Vance and Brzezinski gave a Janus-like quality to the Carter administration's Soviet policy. The former governor of Georgia had not brought a strong worldview to the White House, so he tried to extract the best from his principal advisers and synthesize it, an almost impossible task. Carter appreciated hearing two different sides of an issue, and often believed that both of his advisers' views had merit. He saw himself as at once a moralist and a realist, and saw no inconsistency between the two positions. In his dealings with the Soviets, Carter agreed with Vance that cooperation was key. However, he also accepted some of Brzezinski's ideas. In a commencement speech at Notre Dame after only four months in office, he tried to synthetize the elements of a new foreign policy, with human rights as the fundamental tenet, while taking elements from Vance and Brzezinski. "I believe in détente with the Soviet Union," he proclaimed, but at the same time said he hoped to persuade the Soviet Union that it could not impose its system upon other countries—as Cuban troops in Africa were doing at that moment.

He was trying to lead public opinion to accept a new strategic nuclear arms agreement with the Soviets, SALT II, while at the same time publicly excoriating Moscow for aggressive military activities in Africa. Carter would later write that he rejected the notion of a forced choice "between idealism and realism, or between morality and exertion of power."[14] The subtlety of this was too much to send a clear message to either the American heartland or the Soviet leaders in the Kremlin.

Yet Carter's most controversial line at Notre Dame proved to his conservative critics that he was simply naive about the USSR. In glorifying the virtues of democracy and pointing out that people in India, Portugal, Spain, and Greece had turned their backs on dictatorship within the past few years, he said: "Being confident in our own future, we are now free of that *inordinate fear of Communism which once led us to embrace any dictator who joined us in that fear. I'm glad that's being changed*" [emphasis added].[15] Zbig played a major role in drafting that speech, and agreed the charge of naïveté was undeserved. He later told me "Frankly, I think he was right. Communism was a rotten theory which was already declining, and he deserves credit for saying it, and no one should apologize for that; we shouldn't be fearful of it because it's a rotten theory. And we have a better one, human rights, and he was right."[16]

In retrospect Defense Secretary Harold Brown saw the dangers of such rhetoric. He told me that "Jimmy Carter is a do-gooder, you know, and that's praise, that's not criticism. I think that the more he allowed his own personality and personal attitudes toward what's right and wrong in dealing with the world to be seen, the more he was seen as a wimp, both domestically and by foreign leaders,"[17] however unfairly. More broadly Zbig warned the president at the end of 1978 that, almost two years into his presidency, "we have not dispelled the notion that we are amateurish and disorganized and that our policies are uncertain and irresolute." He saw no remedy short of a "significant shake-up" in the State and Defense Departments and in his own NSC.[18]

I believe that Carter's human rights policy as applied to the Soviet Union gave the United States for the first time an ideological weapon to compete worldwide against the Soviet's tired cry of the international class struggle; and that it began to create fissures in the Soviet Union and its empire that eventually led to its implosion. Far from being a weak and feckless approach to the USSR, it was tougher in some respects than the realpolitik that looked away from Moscow's repressive policies to preserve relations under détente. Emphasizing human rights attacked the Communists in their most vulnerable spot—mistreatment of their own citizens—and helped save the lives of prodemocracy dissidents, as well as promote the freedom of an unprecedented number of Jews to leave the Soviet Union.

We would not have to wait long before the first test came, and it was dramatic. As soon as Carter took office a wave of human rights abuses swept the Soviet Union, perhaps as a warning and a test. Andrei Sakharov, a renowned nuclear physicist and guiding figure in the Soviet nuclear weapons program, had become a human rights activist. This earned him a Nobel Peace Prize in 1975, which the Soviet authorities would not allow him to receive in person. He was attacked by the Soviet press, and his apartment was ransacked. His equally courageous activist wife, Yelena Booner, who founded the Moscow Helsinki Group in 1976, was subject to constant harassment. Both would eventually be imprisoned. Russia's own monitors of compliance with its Helsinki pledge were also harassed, and several other prominent dissidents were arrested.

Less than two weeks after his inauguration, President Carter met with Soviet ambassador Anatoly Dobrynin. He was a tall, imposing man, totally fluent in English, and given more leeway than most Soviet diplomats. His long service in Washington and the wide range of his contacts made him especially valuable to both sides as a reliable link with direct access to the Politburo. Most of their initial meeting was taken up with Carter's ambitions to complete SALT II, but then Carter brought up the Helsinki Accords. He explained that while not interfering in the Soviet Union's internal affairs, the United States understood that when the Soviet Union signed them, it had placed the subject of human rights firmly on the agenda of legitimate discussion between our two nations, and he expected this and all other agreements to be honored.[19] Carter reserved the right to speak out about Sakharov, while Dobrynin countered that Brezhnev had promised not to "test the American president" through confrontation, lest it risk the continuing dialogue with Moscow.[20] Thus the principal difficulty in shifting from realpolitik to idealism was exposed at the highest level during the very first exchange between the two superpowers.

Sakharov wrote a personal letter on January 21, 1977, the day after Carter's inauguration, that dropped into Carter's lap shortly before his meeting with Dobrynin, applauding the new president for making human rights a high priority; stating that his telephone communications were being blocked; naming a number of political prisoners; and urging him to do something about the situation. (A then-unknown young Soviet Jewish dissident, Anatoly—later Natan—Sharansky, translated the letter, which was smuggled out and delivered to the Carter White House by Jewish tourists.) I remember the air of excitement at the White House about how to respond to this early human rights challenge, because it would be a breach of protocol for a president to respond to a communication from a private citizen of another country about his own government's policies. But this was a plea with grave implications from a person of international standing, and following the recommendations of Vance and Brzezinski, Carter replied personally only a few days after the Dobrynin meeting. He wrote Sakharov on February 5, 1977, that he should "rest assured that the American people and our government will continue our firm commitment to promote respect for human rights, not only in our own country, but also abroad."[21]

An official of the American Embassy in Moscow met with Sakharov to inform him of the president's response and tell him that the embassy was willing to accept and transmit documents of a public nature, as well as any letters he might wish to send to members of Congress or the administration. The Kremlin was infuriated when Sakharov posed for photographs holding up the letter and displaying Carter's signature at the bottom. This quickly set the tone of the tense relationship between the two countries.

There was much trial and error in the early going. When Helsinki was first mentioned at a cabinet meeting just a month after the inauguration, on February 28, Carter wanted to be sure the United States was on a firm footing: For years U.S. law had barred known Communists from visiting America, while the Soviet Union had no such barrier against avowed capitalists. Zbig said that the administration's human rights statement should not be pointed only at Russia or "they will see it as an attack against them." At the cabinet meeting Carter gave Vance a clear message: "Don't vacillate on human rights; be moderate and careful, but be consistent, because it is the best thing we can do to restore our world leadership." He warned against singling out the Soviet Union and wanted to remove any stigma in this area, so we should allow Americans to "go wherever in the world they want, and let others come here."[22]

As a lawyer, the secretary of state assured the president early on that Soviet actions and policies violated their Helsinki commitments, and that while the Helsinki Accords recognized their right to determine their own laws, it also stated that human rights " 'derive from the inherent dignity of the human person,' and thus, in our view, these rights transcend national laws."[23] In March, Vance began what would be a regular routine when meeting with his Soviet counterparts. He first presented a list of seven hundred Soviet Jews and appealed on their behalf for permission to leave because of religious discrimination. The issue unified American Jews and was also taken up by Congress, but Vance never received the credit he deserved for his unstinting efforts on behalf of Soviet Jews.

While most of the Russian dissident leadership, like Sakharov, preferred to remain and work for reforms internally, hundreds of thousands of Soviet Jews, who under Soviet law were labeled of "Hebrew" nationality on their identity documents, were not permitted to practice their religion and demanded to emigrate. Their identity and confidence as Jews was raised by Israel's lightning victory in the 1967 Six-Day War, which emboldened Jews worldwide following the devastating Holocaust. They were refused exit visas, itself a violation of the Helsinki Accords, and were called refuseniks—those who were refused permission to leave the Soviet Union.

Many who spoke out were often arrested on trumped-up charges. On February, 24, 1975, ten Soviet Jews demonstrated outside the Lenin Library in Moscow, calling for the release of Jewish prisoners and seeking freer emigration to Israel. Six were arrested and jailed for 15 days, including Sharansky, who was brought before a criminal court and released. From this spark grew a fire of escalating demonstrations and hunger strikes, first in April 1975 by Jewish activists in the Soviet Union who signed an appeal for an international commission to investigate the denial of Jewish emigration, then in Israel, Western Europe, and the United States, including 200,000 demonstrators in New York.[24]

The Soviets did not take these protests lying down. On June 6 a heavy tax was imposed on foreign funds sent to Soviet Jews to assist their emigration, and the Soviets announced that "tourist-Zionists" coming to Russia would be regarded as interfering in Russia's internal affairs. During 1975 and 1976, advocacy organizations were formed in America to defend Soviet Jewry through mass protest and official complaint. This did not go unnoticed by our campaign. I explained to the candidate that the issue had galvanized the American Jewish community like nothing else since the Israeli victory in the 1967 war, and that American Jews, bearing a sense of guilt for doing too little to push President Roosevelt to help European Jewry escape the Nazis, were united under the slogan "Never Again." I helped draft campaign speeches for Carter putting him firmly on the side of Soviet Jewish emigration as part of his own human rights policy. The issue became a cause célèbre among American Jews, and was taken up by Congress and remained a priority on the State Department's diplomatic agenda.

Carter nevertheless continued hoping to build on the policy of détente, and Vance supported him. When Vance told the cabinet on March 14 that the Cubans had approached him about relaxing travel restrictions, Carter responded that the Cubans wanted the trade embargo lifted, and in exchange he would want Cuban troops to withdraw from Africa and release some political prisoners.[25] He clung to the hope that he could have it both ways—sharply criticizing the Soviets on human rights violations, while maintaining an even keel in other areas, particularly SALT II negotiations.

Then, a week later, he told the cabinet that in Brezhnev's private exchanges the Soviet leader indicated "there was progress on SALT; that he might even act on his own to reduce intermediate nuclear forces; and that the Soviet Union was staying out of the Middle East."[26] Vance reported that he had been courted by the Soviets at the UN, and Carter told the cabinet that he welcomed this because he wanted to keep open the lines of communication with Brezhnev, whom he regarded as one of the more moderate Soviet leaders. But he also admitted that "human rights aggravated them more than I anticipated, and I still don't understand it,"[27] exhibiting his inexperience by failing to see how his human rights campaign threatened the Soviets' legitimacy and their need to maintain internal order at all costs. He was so invested in his human rights campaign that he ignored the diplomatic consequences—but in the long run for the better.

LINKAGE?

In Carter's view of the world America was competing with the Soviets in many areas, but he continued to exude optimism, telling the vice president and senior White House staff in July that "things with Russia are better than Brezhnev indicates" in public.[28] He thought he could call Brezhnev directly at the behest of Israeli prime minister Begin, and make a private request to take the pressure off Soviet Jews. Around the same time, Zbig told the cabinet in July that the Soviets were interfering with U.S. telecommunications contacts, and on commercial transactions, as well.[29]

And I also got a whiff of an early version of today's cyberattacks when Senator Moynihan informed me that the Soviets were listening to our White House discussions through the giant antennas on the roof of their nearby embassy, and urged that we use our technology to interfere with their snooping. When I raised this at an NSC meeting, our intelligence agencies, aware of the practice, concluded it was not worth risking retaliation: We got more information on their closed political system from our listening posts, while much of what we were doing was plastered on the front pages of our open press.

Zbig would use every opportunity to point out Soviet misbehavior, but neither side was listening to the other. The Soviets did not seem to comprehend, or care, that the treatment of dissidents was high on the Carter agenda, and Carter did not appreciate that adding human rights and Jewish emigration to his position on SALT II overloaded Brezhnev's political circuits inside the Politburo. As Soviet conduct failed to improve, Carter's attitude began to change. One of the key parts of his Soviet policy, which was shared by Vance, was to avoid linking Soviet behavior in some areas with progress in others, particularly arms control. In March 1978 he told the cabinet that SALT negotiations must go forward, while pressing his campaign against the brutal crackdown on Soviet Jews.[30]

The dilemma was crystallized by Sharansky's arrest on March 15, 1977, on phony charges of spying for the United States and treason, both capital crimes. It would become a test case of the president's human rights policy and profoundly alter the American relationship with the Soviet Union. Sharansky was a particular target because he was both the link between the general dissident community through the Russian Helsinki Watch Committee and the Jewish refuseniks. He also defended Catholic rights, was a key contact to Baptists, and served as a translator for American visitors. His arrest put Carter in a difficult position. Although he knew the charges were utterly false, a president traditionally neither confirms nor denies that persons arrested are spies, because an official statement either way could compromise covert operations, implicate innocent people, and establish an expectation in future cases.

My former Harvard law professor, the combative Alan Dershowitz, came to see me to urge that Carter issue a statement declaring that Sharansky was not an American spy.[31] I had several meetings with Sharansky's wife, Avital, who became an effective champion for him around the world, and made the same plea for a presidential statement of her husband's innocence, which touched me to the core.[32] They had been separated within weeks of their marriage in July 1974, when she was granted an exit visa to Israel and his application was turned down. Carter and Vance initially made clear in private meetings with the Soviets that he was not an American spy.[33] Vance told Dobrynin that we were receiving thousands of letters about his detention and that putting him on trial would undermine public and congressional support for better relations with Moscow.[34]

Vance repeated the warning to Soviet foreign minister Andrei Gromyko in June; he brushed it aside by saying that the case now was in the hands of the court. When Gromyko made his annual visit to America in September for the UN General Assembly meeting, he came to Washington for his regular meeting with the president. There are two differing versions of their September 23 conversation at the White House, but both underline the unyielding Soviet determination to ignore the human rights obligations of the Helsinki Accords. Carter confronted Gromyko with Sharansky's widely publicized case, and as Carter recalled it, Gromyko dismissed Sharansky as "a microscopic dot" of no importance to anyone.[35] According to Dobrynin, Gromyko asked the president: "Who is Sharansky?"—and that ended the matter. But in the car after leaving, Gromyko asked Dobrynin: "Who really is Sharansky? Tell me more about him." Dobrynin did so and discovered that Gromyko had previously instructed his aides not to bother him with such "absurd" matters.[36]

The Sharansky case dragged on for about a year into 1978, and with his trial looming, there was a struggle to persuade the president to make a public statement, while we considered our options to retaliate against Moscow for his expected conviction. On July 7 Brzezinski expressed to me his deep concern that we had reached our limit with the Soviets: "We must fish or cut bait on human rights soon. The Russians don't think we'll back up our words with action." He listed several actions that we might take, which were elaborated at a meeting two days later, including limiting technology transfers and recalling our ambassador.[37] But what he did not say, and what was certainly on Vance's mind, was that any sharp response would slow down, if not derail, the SALT II talks. I was upset to learn that the State Department's senior adviser on Soviet affairs, Marshall Shulman, had persuaded Vance to oppose anything limiting Soviet trade. This was taking the department's notion of unlinking Soviet action against human rights from any other issue to an absurd and politically unsustainable point.

As Sharansky went on trial July 10, the president met in his study with Ham, White House Counsel Lipshutz, and me. I told the president flatly that the human rights issue and his own credibility were at stake if he did not act. I mentioned some of the steps we had been discussing. Defensively he said: "Don't discount what we have already done. *I do not want to resurrect the Cold War*" (emphasis Carter's). He told me he would consider limiting technology transfers and cultural exchanges but added: "We must be measured." Ham and I both cautioned him that he needed to lead the way on Sharansky or Congress would overtake him. He was desperately trying to maintain the fraying ties with Moscow, but most important from his standpoint was somehow to isolate Sharansky's case from SALT II, which he considered—and with good reason—of surpassing importance.[38]

On July 14 Sharansky was sentenced to thirteen years in prison, ten of them in a strict labor camp. Carter did not wait for the conviction, which caused a sensation. With the trial in progress, in an interview with Western European and Japanese reporters on July 11, he made an unprecedented statement that could serve as a guidepost for all future presidents faced with such gross violations of human rights: "The allegation that Sharansky was a spy for the United States is patently false. The Soviets know it to be false. They are prosecuting Sharansky because he represents an element, a small group in the Soviet Union who are fighting for the implementation of international agreements which the Soviet Union itself has signed. . . . These are the things that the Soviets are attacking in the Sharansky trial . . . and others. We deplore this, the actions themselves, and the violation of agreements which the Soviets themselves freely signed." He went on to declare the case an affront to the world, and that it was his responsibility and that of others who had signed the international agreements to point out the violations.[39]

As for Sharansky, his closing remarks electrified the Jewish community and well beyond. He said he was proud to work with other famous dissidents, "but most of all I feel part of a marvelous historical process—the process of the national revival of Soviet Jewry and its return to the homeland, to Israel." He told the packed courtroom that the Jewish people "stubbornly and without reason, say to each other, 'Next Year in Jerusalem.'" Repeating it then to those who would share his hopes everywhere, he turned to the judge and declared: "And to the court, which has only to read a sentence that was prepared long ago—to you, I have nothing to say."[40]

In a rarity, both *Time* and *Newsweek* put Sharansky's picture on their covers, with *Time* adding the backdrop of a crumbled sign reading "détente."

Sharansky's plight gave the issue of dissidents a young and vigorous human face. Committees were formed on American campuses, and congressional resolutions were offered. The Association for Computer Machinery cut ties with the Soviet Union, and by the end of the year 2,400 American scientists, including 13 Nobel laureates, signed a pledge to avoid all contacts with the USSR until Sharansky and other dissident colleagues were freed. In light of the uproar over the conviction, the president had acted just in time. He prohibited the sale of computers to the Soviet news agency, TASS, for use in the 1980 Olympics, and restricted the export to the Soviets of equipment for oil drilling.

Though he declined to cut all trade with the Soviet Union or stop SALT negotiations, he said that "we need to let them know we're concerned. We need to show there are dire consequences of their action, but not impose a total embargo." Senator Jacob Javits, a liberal Jewish New York Republican, supported the president but warned that the Senate would not approve any SALT agreement unless the Soviets liberalized emigration.[41] It had taken Carter a few days to come around, but he did so—and would do much more later after the Soviet invasion of Afghanistan.

I was struck by how the trial of one man had led to these sanctions, even in the midst of the arms-control negotiations. Combined with his sanctions on Latin American dictatorships, Carter's Soviet sanctions were the first time in American history a president employed sanctions to protest human rights violations. To him the Soviet government's adamant hold on Sharansky was indicative of its waning influence on the global stage. It took Sharansky some years and a serious threat to his health for him to become the first Soviet political prisoner released by Mikhail Gorbachev in 1986. When he was finally released across a bridge into the West, Sharansky was ordered by his Soviet captors to walk straight ahead. In a famous gesture of tenacity and unbreakable will, he intentionally walked in a zigzag course to freedom— and then straight into politics in Israel, where he served in several cabinet posts and now heads the Jewish Agency.

In fact the combination of Carter's pressure, and the prospect of a SALT II treaty, led to a major jump in Soviet Jewish emigration from only 14,000 in 1976 to 29,000 in 1978 and 51,000 in 1979. At that point, I got a call from Charles Vanik, the House sponsor of the Jackson-Vanik amendment, which, because of Moscow's restrictive emigration policy, barred our government from offering the Soviet Union the best trade terms we offered other countries. He wanted me to urge the president to waive Congress' own anti-Soviet amendment on a year-by-year basis in order to encourage further progress. Following Carter's instructions, I found American Jewish groups split, but Senator Jackson and his hard-line foreign-policy aide Richard Perle strongly opposed; thus, we were unable to proceed.[42] This was a lost opportunity. With the Soviet invasion of Afghanistan, the Senate roadblock on SALT II, and no prospect of improved trade, Soviet Jewish emigration plummeted to 21,000 in 1980.[43]

POPE JOHN PAUL II

Carter's human rights campaign coincided with an extraordinarily important event in the eventual demise of Communism, the elevation to the papacy of Cardinal Karol Józef Wojtyła as Pope John Paul II on October 16, 1978. His 1979 visit to his native Poland was preceded by Carter's visit in December 1977, his first trip abroad as president. Carter received a wildly enthusiastic reception, exceeded only by the pope's a year and a half later. But it was marred by a series of gaffes, thanks to his State Department translator, Steven Seymour, for whom Polish was only his fourth language. Arriving on December 29, 1977, at 10:40 p.m., Carter and his party were welcomed by the dour Polish Communist leader Edward Gierek. The president declared he was glad to be in Poland, which Seymour mistranslated as Carter expressing his pleasure at abandoning America to live in Poland. Most embarrassing, when Carter said he wanted to learn about the desires of the Polish people, Seymour turned it into "I want to have sex with the Polish people." The Polish press converted that the next morning into "carnal knowledge of the Polish." At the closing banquet Seymour simply gave up and the Polish government's interpreter had to step in.[44]

Things worked more smoothly when the pope visited Washington. In a private meeting with the president,[45] the pope's major message was the need to reach out to Eastern Europe. The head of the Catholic Church had in effect made common cause with the president's human rights agenda.

As Harold Brown put it: "I always felt that the human rights position really got a lot of people in a lot of countries thinking about the difference between the U.S. and the Soviet Union. In a way Carter and Pope John Paul II were the two poles of that."[46] The connection became useful when Brzezinski called the pope to ask that he use his influence when the Soviets were massing troops at the Polish border, late in the administration.[47]

No one can honestly draw a clear line between the collapse of the Soviet Union and Carter's human rights campaign. Every American president after World War II played a role in the bipartisan Cold War policy of containing the spread of Communism, until the Soviet Union collapsed of its own contradictions. This was validated in 1995 by no less than Dobrynin on the American television program *60 Minutes*, who commented that the system had fallen of its own weight: "We did it to ourselves."[48] But Carter played an important role.

Far from being the weak and naive leader his critics asserted, he combined human rights as a tough and effective foreign-policy tool with the beginnings of a military revival brought to its apogee by his successor. This put the Communist world on the defensive, stimulated domestic movements within the eastern bloc, and exacerbated internal divisions by a covert campaign aimed at national groups within the USSR, little known even today. Though not immediately heralded as a success, the human rights campaign became a blueprint in U.S. foreign policy and held every president following Carter to a standard. How large a role human rights play in any specific policy fluctuates with every administration, but it is always a component. Thomas Pickering, who served every president from Nixon to Clinton as an ambassador or senior State Department official, emphasized that "no administration has said the hell with human rights," just because it was some idealistic invention of Carter and the Democrats.[49]

In later years Soviet dissidents would be virtually unanimous in their praise of Carter's policy and its importance in elevating their cause. Robert Gates, who served on Brzezinski's NSC staff, and as Defense secretary in both the George W. Bush and Obama administrations, wrote: "Too bad for Carter that the important impact of his policies would only become known years later, as dissidents fled the East and those affected by his policies would become leaders as their nations became free."[50]

CARTER AND MILITARY POWER

Like human rights and soft power, Jimmy Carter's exercise of hard power began a process that would lead to the implosion of the Soviet Union long after he left office. He significantly increased U.S. defense spending, following a post-Vietnam decline, and pressured our NATO allies to increase theirs; introduced sophisticated Stealth technology in use today that makes U.S. fighter jets, bombers, cruise missiles, and other weapons systems invisible to enemy radar; strenghtened CIA covert action against the Soviet Union; laid the diplomatic groundwork for deploying intermediate-range nuclear weapons in Europe against a Soviet missile buildup; signed SALT II; and reacted with firmness and clarity against the Soviet invasion of Afghanistan. All this helped restrain and ultimately unravel the Soviet empire, as these policies were enhanced by Ronald Reagan.

These historic contributions remain unrecognized, and to this day his Soviet stance is associated with weakness, not strength. This misreading arises from Carter's habit of sending mixed signals, particularly in the first half of his administration. He canceled the B-1 bomber and the neutron bomb while pressing for a military buildup. While pursuing diplomatic détente, he refused to take the Soviets and their Cuban proxies to task as aggressively as Zbig urged for their subversive activities in Africa.

The thread of ambivalence weaving through these contradictions reflected Carter's unwillingness to choose between the contrasting views of Vance and Brzezinski about handling the Soviet Union. From the very start he boldly sought different opinions in the confident conviction that he could synthesize them into a coherent policy, but he had great difficulty doing so. I believe Carter put such a high premium on a nuclear-arms-control agreement that he was willing to unlink, though not ignore, their aggressive activities elsewhere.

From the earliest days of our work together, I was struck by Carter's suspicion of the value of military intervention and his personal dedication to preventing the proliferation of nuclear weapons by working with the Soviet Union to reduce them. The fiscal conservatism of this former naval officer played an important role in his critical evaluation of many highly complex weapons systems, whose costs often outweighed their utility. During the campaign he took dovish views on defense policy, and not simply to appeal to the more liberal Democratic primary electorate. He called for reducing present defense expenditures by $5 to $7 billion;[51] reducing sales of all kinds of weapons abroad;[52] a voluntary moratorium on new nuclear fuel-enrichment plants; and a comprehensive nuclear test-ban treaty with the Soviet Union.[53] He forswore CIA or other covert intervention to overthrow popularly elected governments or change their policies, even Communist regimes.[54] And he sent shock waves through Asia with a campaign statement (never pursued) that American troops and nuclear weapons should be withdrawn from South Korea.[55]

Once in office, when he realized the harsh realities facing him, Carter acted contrary to the campaign's impression that he would gut the defense budget. Far from hollowing out America's military as his opponents had charged (and his liberal supporters hoped), he was the architect of the beginning of its revival, after Americans turned away from pride in military might following the bitter defeat in Vietnam. In the eight years preceding Carter's single term in office, defense spending declined by about one-third after inflation. Carter started the climb back, but as was too often the case, he took less care with appearances. Ford had submitted a deliberately bloated defense budget as he left office, but even after Carter finished cutting it, defense spending had increased by 3 percent in real terms that first year, and 10 percent during his four-year term, with a commitment to a 5 percent annual increase for the following five years, starting in 1980, after the Soviet invasion of Afghanistan.

But the impression stuck that he was soft on defense, in part due to his human rights policies, his strong preference for diplomacy, his initial reluctance to increase defense spending substantially, and his rejection of untried weapons systems while emphasizing arms-control negotiations with the

Soviet Union. Carter spoke of the horrors of a "nuclear holocaust" that would be produced by a nuclear war with a passion he brought to few other problems.[56] He immersed himself deeply in the intricacies of nuclear negotiations, underscored the goal of rough equivalence with the Soviet Union, and was able to discuss with fluency the great U.S. advantage of its triad of land-, sea-, and air-based nuclear weapons, in comparison with the heavier throw weight and increasing accuracy of the large Soviet land-based missiles, concealed in their silos.

When Carter took office, the USSR represented a very real threat that demanded a Western response, and it was Defense Secretary Brown who persuaded the new president to focus on strengthening NATO.[57] The psychological and strategic nuclear balance had changed in the Soviets' favor. While the number of U.S. strategic missile launchers remained relatively stable over a fifteen-year period, the Soviet number grew nearly sevenfold. Through technology that enabled each of these missiles to be loaded with several nuclear warheads, each aimed at a different target, called "MIRVing" (multiple independently targetable reentry vehicles), the United States doubled the number of its intercontinental warheads, but the Soviet Union increased them by nearly twenty times. Carter knew that if the Soviets were to provoke Western aggression, the American people would not want to enter into a military engagement without allied support.

So in May 1977 he appealed directly to NATO defense ministers to increase their budgets by 3 percent annually, to which they agreed in a formal communiqué.[58] American pressure for increased NATO spending remains a thorn in our relationship with them to this day (as President Trump has emphasized), but Carter persuaded them to get started. Not only did this serve to prepare the allies for a potential attack from the East, but it restored vital American leadership in the alliance after we had escaped our entanglement in Vietnam.

GROUNDING THE B-1 BOMBER

Far more complex, both politically and technically, was a divisive debate over whether to build the B-1 bomber, which presents a good lesson in how difficult it is, even for a president with a military background like Carter's, to balance the appetites of what President Eisenhower called "the military-industrial complex" against his own prudent instincts. Only a week after his inauguration, the president met with military and budget officials to discuss whether to fund this technical marvel designed to fly at ground-hugging but supersonic speeds, under Soviet radar, to drop nuclear bombs on enemy territory.[59] The plane was planned to supplement the aging fleet of B-52s that had once been the pride of the Strategic Air Command and was the aerial workhorse of the Vietnam War.

Carter said that he and not the Pentagon would personally decide what to include in the budget and therefore expressed the hope that "before I do, I can assess Soviet intentions." Brown told him he had until the spring, because a new generation of cruise missiles was being built, and the numbers could be increased to serve as negotiating leverage in the SALT II talks. Carter commented: "A commitment to the B-1 says to Russia that we are still committed to the triple method of delivering nuclear weapons, and it will put pressure on them for reductions." Sitting in and taking notes, I felt that these comments reflected a clear desire to move forward with the B-1, and so did everyone else around the table.[60]

But because Carter's campaign statements questioned the utility of the B-1, word was already filtering through to Congress that he was seriously considering killing the plane. In June the president met with a group of the B-1's congressional supporters, including several representing districts where components would be built. They were led by Democratic Representative Sam Stratton, a strong defense advocate from upper New York State, who argued that there were no good alternatives to the B-1 if the United States wanted to maintain the airborne delivery system of the land-sea-air triad. Another argument was that the costs could be trimmed by building fewer than the 249 planes in the Pentagon's plans. Senator John Stennis, a Mississippi power on the Armed Services Committee and a strong supporter of Carter's presidential campaign, took up the diplomatic argument in a slow, Southern cadence. He said construction had already started, and "Mr. President, to delay the B-1 further will put yourself in a hole on SALT."

These arguments were tossed around the table until they reached the superhawk Senator Barry Goldwater, the Arizona Republican and Air Force reserve pilot, who unforgettably promised as a 1964 presidential candidate to "drop one into the men's room of the Kremlin." He stressed that the B-1 could stay in the air for 28 hours and pleaded: "Mr. President, don't make the red [missile] button the only alternative." He said that the B-52 fleet was so old that "the crews flying them now were not born when they started," and in any case it would cost just as much to retool the aging fleet without achieving the speed and penetration promised by the B-1.

Carter listened carefully and then asked a series of questions indicating the depth at which he had examined the options. Since the Pentagon conceded that the B-1 could be easily detected by Soviet radar, he said the CIA indicated that the Soviet Union was far less concerned about the B-1 than about the new cruise missiles, which he supported. These unmanned airbreathing missiles could be fired outside Soviet borders, but penetrate deep into Soviet territory with pinpoint accuracy and less vulnerability to Soviet radar than manned bombers of any type—and by 1980, he asserted, the United States could produce 30 cruise missiles a year. He continued: "The total cost of the B-1 does not bother me, but if the B-52s armed with cruise missiles are as good and cost less, I will go with it." Goldwater countered with a technical argument: It would take years for Soviet radar to be upgraded to detect incoming B-1s, and the planes could approach from any direction while cruise missiles would most likely come only from the direction of Europe.[61]

Three days later, when Senators Ted Kennedy and George McGovern led the congressional opponents of the B-1 in their own meeting with Carter, I was struck that these liberals came nowhere near matching the expertise of their opponents.[62] As well as I thought I knew Jimmy Carter, it also struck me how strange it was that a Southerner, an Annapolis graduate, and nuclear submarine officer would make common cause with this liberal group. I have never believed this arose from his religious convictions, or he would not have chosen a naval career to start with. On the contrary, I think it was his very service aboard nuclear submarines that imbued him with a deep awareness of the incredibly destructive capacity of the nuclear weapons that had been in his own hands. The liberals made many of the arguments Carter himself had already thrown back at the B-1 advocates. They emphasized the enormous cost of the bomber and argued that the money could be better spent on rebuilding our conventional forces or—like true liberals—on domestic programs. They made the political point that his position had been clear in the campaign and that recent polls showed a majority opposing the bomber. Kennedy urged him to focus instead on the country's "human misery." Carter closed the meeting by saying that he now had access to all the secret military information he had lacked as a candidate. As someone who was not a defense specialist, I was impressed by how strong the arguments were on both sides, coming as they did from different perspectives. To me, this is what the presidency is all about: making decisions when arguments are closely balanced.

At the end of June the president called me into his study next to the Oval Office, where he did most of his reading, told me he would oppose the B-1 program—and that I would be the one to tell Brown.[63] But first I would have to review the draft of the public announcement with Brzezinski. Neither of us discussed the merits of the decision Carter had just made, and I did not have the technical competence anyway. I instinctively felt it was substantively correct, but I was certain it was a serious political mistake and an early example of his compartmentalization of decisions.

However deeply the president had considered the technical and fiscal aspects, he had ignored an important diplomatic and political implication: The conservative senators were precisely the ones whose votes he would need to ratify the eventual SALT II arms-control treaty that meant so much to him. He already had the liberals on his side, and he needed to demonstrate to the doubters that he was strong and reliable on defense and thus co-opt them into a coalition that would muster enough votes for the treaty. As far as I know, there was no serious discussion among his national security advisers of the possible relationship between the two issues, nor had his principal political adviser, Ham Jordan, sat in on any of the meetings he held with members of Congress—on this or any other major issue during the Carter presidency.

I never found out why Carter asked me to go to the Pentagon in person and give the news personally to Brown instead of informing him over a secure telephone line. Perhaps he did not want to give Brown one last opportunity to plead the case for the plane. So, in the early morning of June 28, the White House limousine left me off at the Pentagon's River Entrance. This was my first visit to this nation's largest federal building, and by square footage, one of the world's largest, with its five enormous, interlinked corridors. As I walked up the winding staircase toward Brown's office, the sense of history was overwhelming as I passed the paintings of all former Defense secretaries. I was ushered into Brown's huge office, handed him the presidential state- ment drafted by Brzezinski and reviewed by me, and told Brown that the president felt the B-1 was a costly insurance policy, and that while re- search and development on the plane should continue as a backstop, Car- ter's mind was made up. Harold Brown is a brilliant and enormously able man, a physicist who had left the presidency of the California Institute of Technology to join the cabinet, and in my view its best member. He speaks in measured terms, without one superfluous word.

In the four years I worked with him, and in later subsequent government assignments, like the Defense Policy Board in the Obama administration, I had never seen him angry. But it was clear that he was unhappy with the de- cision and—with good reason—by the way it was being conveyed to him. He carefully walked me through the technical, strategic, and fiscal argu- ments and warned in characteristically measured terms: "I will have a hard time supporting *any* of the justifications for killing the B-1 before congres- sional questioning." He went on to recommend that the cancellation statement should start by saying that alternative systems represented "better ways to do the same thing" and should avoid any implication that the B-1 was a complete waste of money.[64] Carter followed this advice when the formal announcement was made on July 30.

DOVE TO HAWK

Carter's transformation from a dove to a hawk on defense spending did not come overnight. Until his shift, the Pentagon's own study of Brown's tenure as Defense secretary ominously noted that the Soviet Union "came closer to matching the U.S. in strategic power than it had in any other period."[65]

Paid for by Soviet oil, as OPEC prices rose sharply in the 1970s, Soviet technology was converted into advanced weapons. Always suspicious of the Pentagon's expense budget requests and expansive promises, Carter rigorously scrutinized them along with his national security team at a critical June 4, 1979, meeting. Intelligence was pouring into the Pentagon about the size and scope of the Soviet military buildup, leading to a new and more pessimistic NSC assessment of Soviet strength. Carter was still suspicious, complaining that the assessment of relative strength was based on a perception of weakness he complained had been created by "people in the room," who in turn created a problem "by their own excessive concentration on our weaknesses." But by the end of the meeting, Carter agreed to deploy theater nuclear weapons in Europe and the MX missile. This was not only because of the unanimous view of his advisers, even the dovish Vance, but as a way to convince conservative hawkish senators to support the forthcoming SALT II arms control treaty. Carter's about-face on significantly raising defense spending thus came well before the Soviet invasion of Afghanistan.[66]

That same day, I gained a personal perspective on how difficult it was to make the shift on defense spending at a senior White House staff meeting. Carter told us the MX missile would cost $78 billion in 1980 dollars, and was "a total waste. . . . I am almost *physically nauseated* [emphasis added] by the NSC deferring to the Joint Chiefs of Staff, and then they sit back and critique my decisions. I need someone on the international side like Stu on the domestic side, who looks at issues from the perspective of being president."[67] However complimented I felt, we were already moving toward the larger military budgets that he had envisioned, but doing so cautiously, not only because of his conservative nature, but his own experience in the military. But change he did, however grudgingly, and in a big way.

Soon afterward, Carter told congressional leaders that while defense spending had declined before he took office, it had now actually risen in real (inflation-adjusted) terms during his presidency and, he promised, would continue to rise until 1985. As a Pentagon study concluded years later, the investments in new weaponry that Carter mapped out at midterm represented the largest increases in defense spending since the Vietnam War and laid the foundation for Reagan's huge defense spending.[68] Carter maintained his pledge to our NATO allies to increase defense spending by an average of 3 percent in real terms, even with high inflation during his term, according to a U.S. Army War College study cleared by the Defense Department decades after he left office.[69] Defense spending during his term increased from 4.7 percent of GDP to 5.2 percent of GDP.[70]

Despite all of its dissonance, Carter eventually developed a coherent Cold War strategy in the second half of his administration, focusing first on new ground weapons systems. Funding for missiles increased by two-thirds as the army received tube-launched, optically-tracked, wire-guided antitank missiles and Roland air-defense missiles. A new wave of armored combat vehicles increased that part of the defense budget by one-quarter, and the president requested funds to accelerate deployment of the army's heavy divisions, to stockpile ordnance in Europe, and to fund reserve units.

It is totally unrecognized that Carter's top priority, given his engineering background, was American strategic superiority over the Soviet Union through technology. After the Soviet Union invaded Afghanistan at the end of 1979, his final budget outlined funding for the XM-1 tanks, armored troop carriers with antitank missiles, stand-alone antitank missiles, howitzers, laser-guided artillery shells that could home in on a tank up to ten miles away, large-scale antitank rockets, antitank attack helicopters, Hellfire missiles, and more accurate target guidance for the army's M-60 tanks.

His goal was not simply to stock up on nuclear bombs, but to maintain superiority through diverse weapons systems and "advanced technology to stay ahead in the arms race,"[71] including new Stealth technology that could not be detected by Soviet radar. To counter the Soviets' larger missile launchers and multiple warheads, Carter and Brown viewed it as essential for the United States to diversify its forces so that no possible combination of attacks would leave the country unable to retaliate. In Brown's strategic view—and he had led development of the submarine-launched Polaris missile while still at Cal Tech—in a nuclear war it would not matter whether you had one hundred or ten thousand warheads. The Soviets were spending all their money on duplicating their forces, but the Carter administration was creating an adaptable military that could retaliate against any attack. Carter was the ideal president to support Brown's innovations because he understood them: One of his assignments had been as an electronic warfare officer testing the navy's latest fire-control systems.[72]

Although wary of spending billions on ineffective weapons systems with fatal strategic flaws like the B-1, Carter nevertheless realized he needed to silence defense hawks to gain their support for SALT II, so he supported the MX missile system. The MX was a massive intercontinental ballistic missile with up to ten independently targeted reentry vehicles, with greater accuracy and range than the aging Minuteman missile, and designed to evade increasingly accurate Soviet guidance systems. In 1979 Carter gave the go-ahead for its development and basing plan, and it was deployed during the Reagan administration.

While Reagan usually gets the credit for overwhelming the Soviet Union with military spending, it was Carter who laid the groundwork for a more balanced force. The Kremlin understood the future implications of Carter's strategic weapons program and began to feel increasingly impotent and isolated. Soviet concern about Carter's military buildup is validated in a book written by the CIA's longtime employee Benjamin B. Fischer and published by the agency's Center for the Study of Intelligence, disclosing secret Soviet KBG documents of the time.[73] They show that the Soviet Politburo recognized it was facing a new reality as the Carter administration began catching up with the Soviet military buildup, a race that Reagan, to his credit, later accelerated. Fischer cites a compelling summary of an interview with then KGB head Yuri Andropov (later General Secretary of the Soviet Communist Party), supported by a top-secret KGB document: "Carter's presidency created great concern in the Kremlin, because he had presented a defense budget of more than $157 billion, which he invested in the MX and Trident missiles and nuclear submarines." This was more than the Soviets and their allies could match.[74]

While Reagan doubled down on all of this, in the view of no less than Bush's and Obama's former defense secretary Robert Gates, who served on the NSC staff in the Carter administration, the perception of revived American strategic power and strength that emerged in the first half of the 1980s was, in fact, "Reagan reaping the harvest sown by Nixon, Ford, and Carter."[75]

THE REAL STORY OF THE NEUTRON BOMB

In the efforts to separate the effective weapons from the duds, none proved more troublesome than an ingenious proposal for a nuclear device under the typically euphemistic label of "enhanced radiation weapon"—soon to be widely known and reviled as the neutron bomb. It had been proposed in Ford's final military budget as an antitank weapon to be deployed in Europe. Only a Dr. Strangelove might have found it innocuous. If it were possible for any nuclear weapon to be relatively humane, it was this one, by killing Soviet tank crews while limiting damage to civilians and Europe's historic cities.[76] This was the reasoning of its inventor, a nuclear physicist named Samuel Cohen, who lobbied the Pentagon for years and finally sold it as a moral and sane weapon to James Schlesinger, then Ford's intellectual Defense secretary and later Carter's energy secretary.

Dr. Cohen's nuclear brainstorm took the incoming Carter administration totally by surprise. The genesis of the weapon lay in NATO's need to counteract a classic Soviet defensive strategy of bunching a mass of tanks like an iron fist, first to break an invasion force from the West and then to counterattack through enemy lines and sweep across Europe's northern plains. That was the way the might of the Red Army defeated the highly maneuverable Panzer divisions led by Hitler's generals in the decisive 1943 Battle of Kursk, the largest tank battle in history. Brezhnev's military buildup raised fears it might happen again, with Warsaw Pact tank forces outnumbering NATO's three to one. A neutron bomb, launched from artillery or airplanes, would force Soviet tank formations to spread out and lose their advantage. Brown also realized it would force Soviet military planners to rethink their entire conventional-war strategy, because the weapon's destructive force came from intense radiation within a small radius.

Walter Pincus, a respected investigative reporter for the *Washington Post*, found the funding for the device buried in the Defense Appropriations Bill, and on June 6, 1977, the newspaper ran a story headlined "Neutron Killer Warhead Buried in ERDA [Energy Research and Development Agency] Budget." This was the first time Vance, Brzezinski, and the president had ever heard of a weapon they would have to decide whether to deploy. Not to be outdone, the *New York Times* referred to it as an "especially ugly weapon."[77] Within days a panicky sense of crisis spread to Western Europe.

As Brown later lamented, if the original headline had read "Bomb Kills Tank Commanders, Leaves Building and Its Inhabitants Undamaged," the result might have been vastly different, although perhaps not. What did not seem to penetrate the walls of the Pentagon was the European fear that this weapon could be a potential trigger for a wider nuclear war on their home-land, and that it could be started by a beleaguered American general on the battlefield without considering the consequences to European lives.[78] It was quickly and angrily rejected by America's European allies as a science-fiction horror that would kill people while leaving their homes standing empty. It became a first-rate embarrassment for the president and his top advisers, gave fodder to those who criticized his hardware buildup, and sowed dissension in the Western alliance it was designed to protect. A moral firestorm arose about the inhumanity of the neutron bomb, as if it was somehow worse than other nuclear weapons.

Mass rallies, petitions, and negative polls across Europe posed a dilemma for a president who had pledged in his inaugural address to move toward the goal of "the elimination of all nuclear weapons from this Earth." It was one thing for the Americans and the Soviets to have intercontinental mis-siles aimed at each other in a Cold War standoff, but it was another for a new and frightening kind of nuclear weapon to be deployed on European—and particularly on German—soil. While the Europeans feared the Soviet buildup and looked to the United States for support, they were wary of what seemed like American callousness; to them it looked like a weapon meant to wage war on European territory while keeping America from suf-fering any real harm. The intense public backlash, egged on by sophisti-cated Soviet propaganda, gave the administration little room to maneuver. The production and deployment of the weapon was seen as a test of Carter's plans to strengthen NATO, yet he was personally torn by the perceived in-humanity of the weapon, indeed of all nuclear weapons.

At a Democratic leadership breakfast in July,[79] Carter urged Congress to approve funding for the bomb while giving him time to decide whether to produce it. But he doubted the concept of a supposedly cleaner bomb, and saw the potential for escalation because "once you go to an atomic war, it will be uncontrollable." That of course was exactly what the Europeans feared. He astutely withdrew to the position that the United States would produce the weapon, but only if European nations agreed to deploy it on their soil.[80]

Thus began one of the most serious decision-making messes of the administration. Vance, Brown, and Brzezinski spent almost a year working together to gain European assent. In October 1977 Brzezinski told the cabinet that the leaders of France, Britain, and Germany opposed its deployment in Europe.[81] But things were more complicated than that. Within each nation there was a severe split between military leaders who wanted the bomb and political leaders who did not.[82] It was easy enough to sell the project to military commanders and defense officials, but not to the politicians who would suffer the backlash from their own voters.

The longer the negotiations dragged on, the more doubtful deployment seemed. Carter had campaigned on a platform of nuclear nonproliferation, and his principal goal with the Soviets was to come to an arms agreement. The festering issue of the neutron bomb was undermining his negotiating position, to say nothing of simply going against his personal values. He was concerned about being remembered as the president who green-lighted a bomb that would kill people but leave property intact.

But Brown, Vance, and Brzezinski continued their complex negotiations to gain European assent. Most difficult of all was the leader most directly involved, Helmut Schmidt of West Germany, whose country stood as the front line against the Soviets, and who seemed to enjoy disparaging Carter as a provincial unfit for international diplomacy. Although able and respected throughout Europe, he was no diplomat himself; one of his nicknames at home was Schmidt *Schnauze* (Schmidt the Lip). He finally agreed to deployment, but only if other allied nations agreed too—not just those who had their own nuclear weapons, like the British, but others whose weak coalition governments were most likely too fragile to bear the political burdens. By mid-March 1978, after what Vance called a "nerve-wracking week of nonstop negotiations,"[83] the British, Germans, French, Dutch, Belgians, and the Scandinavians finally agreed to a NATO alliance statement of collective support for the neutron bomb, an ambiguous declaration worded to protect any individual politician from becoming a target.

A meeting of the North Atlantic Council of political leaders was set for March 20, and two days before, the administration negotiating team sent a joint memo to the president outlining the plan, whereupon he exploded over this final communiqué, so carefully drafted. He was vacationing on the islands off the Georgia coast when he first learned how far his team had come in promising the neutron bomb. He "raised hell about it," seeing it as equivalent to "cluster bombs," obviously thinking the Europeans would never agree to deploy the neutron bomb.[84]

He immediately requested cancellation of the NATO Council meeting, summoning the three exhausted cabinet-level draftsmen for an angry session that lasted four and one-half hours. Carter complained that his cautionary words about the bomb had been ignored, and the ambiguous declaration meant that all the political responsibility for producing it would be placed on him. He told the three that they had backed him into a corner. Angry recriminations and mutual misunderstandings flew back and forth, and at one point Carter said: "I wish I had never heard of this weapon." Zbig confided to me that he was "very low and despondent" that Carter did not support his team's success in finally obtaining European approval, and the president had been unduly cautious only because of "public opinion."[85] Brzezinski made one last try to salvage something from the wreckage, outlining yet another diplomatic course linked to arms-control negotiations. Carter penned a curt reply on the memo: "Zbig, I must say that you never give up."[86]

Militarily not much was lost by cancellation of the project; even if Carter had agreed to produce the bomb it most likely would never have been deployed in Europe. But Carter's ability to lead NATO was attacked, and European governments felt that they had been forced out on a limb and then abandoned. The clumsy handling of the whole affair made it appear to the Europeans that the United States did not know what it was doing, a not-unreasonable conclusion given the painful decision-making process. This was exacerbated by Schmidt's public denunciations when Carter backed out, that he had been made to look like "a fool in the understanding of my countrymen," as Schmidt later put it to me.[87]

Carter himself recognized the breakdown of communication within his own administration, and that he had not made it clear enough that he actually abhorred the weapon.[88] Of such different perspectives is history made. The one thing, however, that emerged intact was Carter's adherence to his moral values and his strength of character in making what he considered the correct choice. But as with so many of his righteous decisions, he paid a frightful political cost at home and abroad.

DIPLOMACY BLUNTS A NEW
SOVIET MISSILE THREAT

One of Jimmy Carter's most sterling attributes was his capacity to bounce back from defeat. He did so in winning allied support to deploy Pershing and cruise missiles in Europe to counter a new Soviet threat. As part of the Soviet military buildup, Brezhnev made the decision during Carter's first year in office to deploy what were called theater or tactical nuclear weapons, in contrast to the intercontinental ballistic missiles targeted by the superpowers at each other. Across Eastern Europe the Soviets were deploying their new SS-20 mobile missiles, carrying multiple warheads that could take out the cities of Western Europe at the press of a button. They could target one country without directly threatening its neighbor, and their deadly accuracy made them ideal for Soviet political blackmail of individual European countries. Brezhnev was testing the limits of Soviet power by putting our NATO allies at risk—one by one if he wished—and seeking to undermine American influence by trying to demonstrate that the United States could not protect its European allies from Soviet power.

Allied governments agreed at the London summit of 1977 that something had to be done in the European theater. But what? Since the 1950s NATO had relied on its combined U.S., British, and French nuclear weapons to offset the Soviet conventional military advantage in tanks, artillery, and manpower. But the NATO nuclear forces, while significant, were composed mainly of aging short- and medium-range tactical weapons, and the alliance had a very limited capability to threaten nuclear retaliation with weapons based in Europe alone.

On August 24 1977, Carter signed a national strategy directive, NSD-18, to counterbalance Soviet influence and military power in Europe, the Middle East, and East Asia.[89] Carter also reaffirmed that the United States would fulfill its commitment to raise the level of defense spending by approximately 3 percent per year along with our NATO allies.[90]

Carter followed this up at the start of 1979 with a summit meeting on the Caribbean island of Guadeloupe with Britain's Callaghan, France's Giscard D'Estaing, and Germany's Schmidt, during which he argued that NATO had to respond to the Soviet buildup. He had been increasingly frustrated that European nations seemed agreeable to U.S. development of new weapons, while no European leader was willing to accept them in his own country. Giscard supported Carter, and Schmidt said he would accept new U.S. weapons only if other leaders would too. Callaghan also supported Carter, adding that the European medium-range systems should be included in negotiations for the overall limitations of nuclear weapons through SALT.

After intensive negotiations the NATO summit on December 12, 1979, adopted the "dual-track" policy of simultaneous preparations to install new intermediate nuclear missiles in Western Europe, and to hold disarmament negotiations with the Soviet Union. The United States would continue to pressure the Soviets at SALT talks to limit or remove their SS-20 nuclear force, and if Moscow refused, a retaliatory nuclear force of 464 new cruise missiles and 108 Pershing II ballistic mobile missiles would be deployed in Europe, where they could strike targets in the Soviet Union from Germany, Italy, Britain, and the Netherlands.[91] The policy required firm American leadership, but those on the diplomatic front lines found themselves facing a new level of skepticism about American motives and power.

Reginald Bartholomew, the senior staffer handling the nuclear brief at the National Security Council (and later a distinguished ambassador to Lebanon and Italy), was dispatched to a NATO meeting in Brussels. He remarked privately to American reporters: "Only a few years back, if we had needed to station some weapons or divisions across NATO, someone would have come from Washington, informed the Europeans, and said, 'You take so many here, and you station some more there, and so on'—and that would be that. Not anymore."[92]

Brezhnev publicly attacked the deployment plans and turned the dual-track strategy against NATO by advocating arms-control negotiations that would disrupt the NATO decision. He launched a major "peace offensive" by announcing unilateral troop and tank withdrawals from East Germany, and offering to reduce the number of Soviet medium-range missiles in exchange for a NATO promise not to deploy any missiles at all.

The administration response was that the Soviets needed to be convinced that their military moves would be met with serious retaliation by NATO, and that this restored balance would in turn lead to restraint on both sides. Carter believed that the United States needed to take a stronger stance against the Soviet offensive, rather than remaining content in the state of détente that preceded his administration; and he followed through with strong allied support. But Carter's position was as unpopular with the European public as the neutron bomb, and there were enormous anti-American, anti-Carter demonstrations in Europe. The administration pressed ahead, and Soviet propaganda proved less effective with elites than with the public. The missiles themselves were finally deployed in 1983 by Ronald Reagan on the basis of the Carter-led 1979 NATO agreement, after negotiations failed to achieve a Soviet withdrawal of the SS-20s.[93]

With Carter's leadership, the steps taken by NATO marked a historic turning point in reaffirming the military and political value of the alliance, as well as an important change in Soviet relations with Washington and Europe, that had been dwindling in influence and importance for several years. Gates gave Carter the credit for "the lion's share of the work and the leadership that shaped an alliance consensus."[94]

A historic figure to attest to this was no less than the last head of the Soviet Union, Mikhail Gorbachev. He would later assert that Brezhnev's deployment of the SS-20s was "an unforgivable adventure," and that the deployment of the Pershing and cruise missiles "was a pistol held to our head" that helped convince him that Brezhnev's aggressive policies needed to be replaced by disarmament and cooperation. As a result, in 1987, he proposed the complete elimination of the SS-20s and the U.S. missiles, a mutual withdrawal that Reagan accepted.

Gorbachev also felt it "represented the first well-prepared step on our way out of the Cold War, the first harbinger of the new times."[95] It does nothing to diminish Ronald Reagan's legacy to place Jimmy Carter's role in proper perspective. Gorbachev's own words could stand as Jimmy Carter's enduring legacy, even if he had done nothing else.

Why, then, is Carter seen as weak on defense to this day? Partly because of his campaign rhetoric to cut the defense budget, when in fact he substantially increased it. But the simple answer is that his more visible decisions to limit the Pentagon's characteristic and expensive programs to develop the ultimate weapon, his opposition to the B-bomber, and a debacle like the neutron bomb, were so highly visible that they overwhelmed progress elsewhere. The president emphasized other military priorities and was so focused on cost-effectiveness that he sent mixed messages. This cut across the rivalry among the Joint Chiefs of Staff for expensive weapons, even when they duplicated those in rival services.[96] It is no surprise that his relationship with his military leaders was never warm and that it spread to their supporters in Congress, where members of the House Armed Services Committee accused Carter of ignoring advice from the Joint Chiefs of Staff. Given their rivalry, it is not hard to understand why.

During the first few months of the administration none of the Joint Chiefs was invited to dinners with visiting foreign leaders, and one incident left a sour taste. Brown was pushing for a pay raise of 4 or 5 percent for the military, many of whom the secretary felt were grossly underpaid. Carter sent Brown a handwritten letter saying that when he served in the Navy, his principal motivation certainly was not money. Brown locked the potentially explosive letter in his safe, but someone in the White House leaked a copy, most likely under the misapprehension that it would demonstrate Carter's humility and hardworking devotion. It did exactly the reverse. Military leaders saw it as a jibe at them for seeking higher pay, and this only helped perpetuate the sense that Carter's values were at odds with their own.[97]

MORE SALT

One of Carter's most heartfelt goals was reducing the threat of nuclear war. He inherited the first Strategic Arms Limitation Treaty, SALT I, between the United States and the Soviet Union, signed in 1972, an essential tenet of the policy of détente. Kissinger, with some hyperbole, declared the agreement's acceptance of mutually assured destruction as "one of the greatest diplomatic coups of all time." It limited the number of ballistic missiles that each nation could deploy to 2,360 for the Soviets and 1,710 for the Americans, and gave the USSR a numerical advantage in the number of land- and sea-based ballistic missile launchers, further enhanced by the number of MIRV missiles mounted on them.[98]

SALT I, which was an interim agreement of five years due to expire in October of Carter's first year in office, did not place a ceiling on the number of heavy bombers or missiles equipped with these MIRVs. A framework agreement for an updated treaty—SALT II—was negotiated by Kissinger and signed by Ford at a summit with Brezhnev in Vladivostok in November 1974 to correct the imbalance in SALT I. The goal was a ceiling on each side of 2,400 for all launchers of strategic nuclear delivery vehicles, of which a maximum subceiling could be 1,320 launchers for MIRV missiles. But politics intervened during the 1976 primaries, when Ronald Reagan challenged Ford for making concessions to the Soviet Union, and Ford backed away from his own agreement.

Like many other Democrats, Carter felt that the treaty had to be renegotiated. But his national security team was divided on whether to use the Vladivostok framework or pursue a more robust agreement with the Soviets to slow the arms race. Carter understood that any American negotiator would have to proceed from a position of military strength, but the Soviets were worried by Carter's strong rhetoric advocating the reduction of nuclear weapons, and his human rights campaign on behalf of Soviet dissidents.

Undeterred, Carter wrote a generally friendly letter to Brezhnev during his first week in the White House emphasizing his goal of improving relations and the importance of arms control. Dobrynin told him at their first meeting that the Soviets had decided not to confront the new president early in his term, but warned that departing from the Vladivostok agreement would create serious problems for the Kremlin in future arms talks.[99] Nevertheless, even in the face of Dobyrin's warning, Carter acted quickly, decisively, and dramatically, setting a characteristically bold course toward comprehensive arms reductions over incremental advances, just as he had on other issues touching his deep personal goals, such as energy and the Middle East.

He faced two options, and again they put Vance and Brzezinski on opposite sides. The new secretary of state saw the advantage of deep cuts in gaining support from defense hawks like Scoop Jackson, but he realized that the Soviets would likely reject them, and argued that Carter should have a backup approach to take advantage of the new administration's momentum and reach a quick agreement based on the Vladivostok formula. Then a third treaty, SALT III, later on, could tackle more contentious issues like limitations on cruise missiles and the new Soviet Backfire bomber.[100] On the contrary, argued Brzezinski, the presidential honeymoon period offered the perfect opportunity to take steps toward long-term security goals by pressing at once for cuts to slow the nuclear arms race, even though it was unlikely that such a demanding negotiation could be completed by the October expiration of SALT I. He later denied he foisted this go-for-broke negotiating strategy of deep cuts on Carter, but that is what the president did—significantly on his own initiative.[101]

Even before making this fateful choice, Carter had made another during the transition as president-elect, when I organized postelection briefings at Miss Lillian's Pond House in Plains. The session on national security quickly devolved into a remarkable half-hour debate between Paul Warnke and Paul Nitze on the decisions looming about SALT II. These were two experienced arms-control experts. Nitze was deeply skeptical about Soviet intentions, and Warnke was certain that a better and more comprehensive agreement could be reached. Both had impeccable credentials, although Nitze's were deeper. Slim, intense, and unsmiling, Nitze had been an investment banker, headed the State Department's policy-planning staff under Truman, and served as navy secretary and deputy secretary of Defense in the Kennedy and Johnson administrations. He had also been a member of the SALT I delegation but resigned because he felt the treaty yielded too much to the Soviets.

Warnke, chunky, smiling, and avuncular, was a distinguished Washington lawyer, and like Nitze had held a senior Pentagon position during the Johnson administration, although he became a skeptic on the Vietnam War and later served as a principal adviser to George McGovern in his 1972 presidential campaign.[102]

They went at each other as if world peace were at stake every bit as much as their next jobs in government. Warnke had published an article in *Foreign Affairs* describing the United States as an offender in the arms race, along with the Soviets, that made both superpowers push for increased defense capabilities, on the ground that aping each other "has meant the absence of restraint." He argued that the United States could present a worthier model and take the first steps toward disarmament, based on his belief that the arms race could be reversed by a strong American commitment. As a nonexpert, I felt Nitze made the best points, and that given his credentials any SALT agreement he could negotiate would have instant credibility in Congress. But Carter was the one who counted, and he saw a kindred spirit in Warnke, whom he named chief arms negotiator and head of the Arms Control and Disarmament Agency to deal with all nuclear issues in the U.S.-Soviet relationship, and beyond.

That choice came at a heavy political cost. An early sign of the trouble for any future arms-control agreement was on vivid display in the Senate's consideration of Warnke's nomination, when no less than Nitze himself testified against his rival. Majority Leader Byrd came away from Warnke's hearing declaring that many senators felt the nominee was "too soft to negotiate with the Soviet Union." Warnke was eventually confirmed by a lukewarm vote of 58–40, which was well below the constitutional two-thirds Senate majority needed to confirm treaties, and lacked the support of Scoop Jackson and other defense hawks. It was a shot across the bow of SALT II; that did not stop Carter from favoring a new and more sweeping approach for nuclear arms. In his view the United States already had more than enough weapons to blow up the world, and stockpiling more was not only irrational, but negotiating cuts in that stockpile would mark a major change in the entire nuclear arms race.[103] Carter believed that the Soviet side was also composed of rational men who would adopt his and Warnke's goal of halting the nuclear arms race for the mutual benefit of the two superpowers and indeed the whole world.

To quiet the contending forces within the administration and to give the Soviets flexibility, Carter sent Vance to Moscow in March with two alternatives—either agree to extending Vladivostok with slightly lower limits on nuclear weapons of about 10 percent on each side, or begin negotiating deeper cuts. But, more important, Vance was to tell the Soviets the deep-cut option was the president's preferred course. Indeed, in a departure from protocol that annoyed the Soviets, Carter had already told the UN General Assembly of his priority before private negotiations began.[104]

Moscow rejected both options. Their sclerotic leadership could not adapt to unexpected changes, and they began stretching out these complex negotiations with moves and counterproposals worthy of a team of chess grand masters. The SALT talks convened, adjourned, and reconvened through the spring and summer in Moscow, Washington, Geneva, and Vienna. By early autumn it appeared that progress could be made in narrowing the gap between the two sides on the number, size, and delivery capabilities of both ICBMs and new bombers.

Roused by news of progress, SALT opponents became more outspoken and warned that the Soviets were deceiving Carter and leading him into unilateral disarmament. Defense hawks and SALT critics released classified materials, published false allegations about U.S. concessions in the secret talks, and accused the Soviets of cheating on the first, interim SALT I agreement. The administration made special efforts to counter the inflammatory rhetoric and cage the congressional hawks by arguing that lower nuclear limits would free up more money to modernize the American military, while playing an essential political role in improving relations with Moscow and disengaging from the arms race. Jackson and his allies were unconvinced and dismissed Carter's approach as naive and dangerous— "McGovernism without McGovern," they called it.[105]

SALT II AND LINKAGE, AGAIN

As the talks dragged on, the diplomatic and political atmosphere was polluted by Moscow's suspicions about Carter's support for Soviet dissidents and Brezhnev's military adventures in postcolonial Africa. Vance was at pains to insist that there was no connection, and that a SALT agreement "should be negotiated on its own merits."[106] Carter also publicly refused to link the war in Angola and the Horn of Africa to the SALT negotiations. But with more than 40,000 Cuban troops serving as Soviet proxies on both sides of the continent, Brzezinski felt otherwise. He argued that it was impossible to decouple these wars from nuclear diplomacy. He urged Carter to warn Brezhnev of the dangers to the superpower relationship if he persisted, with profound impact on American allies. Brzezinski declared on March 1 that Soviet involvement in Africa would inevitably complicate the SALT talks, only to have Carter immediately deny it and refuse to consider any options that might derail his principal goal of negotiating a reduction of nuclear weapons.[107]

But on June 17 Carter met with Brezhnev and changed his tone. Voicing concern at increasing Soviet intervention, he told Brezhnev: "I have tried to achieve peace, but the Soviet leaders have done just the opposite."[108] Brezhnev's response showed total disdain and was laced with outright lies. He baldly asserted that Moscow did not control Cuba's actions in Africa, even though it was funding Fidel Castro's troops, supplying weapons, and even airlifting them into conflict zones. Twisting the knife, he lectured Carter: "Many foreign troops fought with George Washington during your own revolution."[109]

Brzezinski remembered Rosalynn once asking what Jimmy was doing about outrageous Soviet behavior, and he replied that the president had authorized sending a formal protest note to Brezhnev. He continued: "She kind of looked at me and smiled sweetly, and in her soft voice said, 'Well, by now Brezhnev must have a cabinet full of Jimmy's protests'—which I think is a wonderful put-down."[110]

By 1978 the Soviets' actions in the Third World were creating intense political pressure on the administration to take a tougher stance against the USSR, and the push to link the SALT negotiations to other issues was impossible to overlook. Although Carter remained adamant that the talks should move forward without hesitation, others in the administration were more preoccupied with sending a clear message that Soviet aggression would not be tolerated. The contradictory opinions gave the impression that Carter's approach to Moscow was indecisive, disjointed, and ineffective; as with most such issues involving the Soviet Union, the major point of contention lay between Vance and Brzezinski.

Vance believed that the relationship with the Soviets had taken a wrong turn, but could still be salvaged through cooperation that would lead to a new arms treaty. But Brzezinski believed that the Soviets should be kept on a short leash and that their foreign incursions should be condemned even at the cost of a new SALT treaty; failure could then be blamed on Soviet expansionism. He later told me: "Brezhnev and company thought that they had us by the balls, And they were going to write world domination. And I felt that we first had to stop them, and then we could bargain with them. But we had to credibly stop them. And I think Vance felt we could separate these issues . . . and that striking a bargain in the strategic area would help deal with other issues. . . . It goes further than linkage. I felt that we had to stop them in order to really negotiate and then eventually accommodate with them. I frankly never thought SALT was the central issue."[111]

Vance, of course, took a very different view of Soviet adventurism. For him Soviet actions were not part of a grand scheme but opportunities being exploited by them abroad, and the United States should consider each one on a case-by-case basis and deal with it outside of the framework of the East-West conflict. In the long run, he argued, this would lead to cooperation that ultimately benefited U.S. interests.

This conflicting advice, so vigorously expressed and pursued by Zbig, contributed to the widespread sense that the only thing on which the two rival advisers concurred was a lack of clarity in Carter's foreign policies. Recognizing this divergence, the president tried to deal with it in a speech to graduating midshipmen at his alma mater, the U.S. Naval Academy, on June 7, 1978. But it only made matters worse. He took competing drafts written by Brzezinski and Vance and combined them in one speech, without coming down clearly on one side or the other. The first half focused on cooperation and peace between the superpowers, and the second outlined America's strategic superiority and condemned the Soviet view of détente as "a continuing aggressive struggle for political advantage and increased influence in a variety of ways." Robert Hunter, a member of the NSC staff who reviewed both drafts, said that Carter simply stapled them together: "And I could see where the shift was. I could tell where he had gone from one draft to another."[112] My view was that Carter felt so strongly about reducing nuclear arms that he would let no obstacle get in the way.

DENG XIAOPING ADDS PEPPER TO SALT

The internal rivalry intensified as far afield as China. Building on Nixon's opening to Beijing, Carter had decided during his presidential campaign that he wanted to normalize relations with China in order to integrate one-quarter of the world's population into the international order and create a mutual dependency between the two countries. He achieved his goal, pursuing it over the fierce opposition of the American Taiwan lobby and his potential Republican opponent Ronald Reagan—to say nothing of the suspicions of the Soviet Union. The key issue was maintaining relations with Taiwan and selling it weapons.

Normalizing relations with China was pushed by Brzezinski and his China expert, Michael Oksenberg, from start to finish. Brzezinski saw the move as a way to counter Soviet strategy to achieve superiority from Western Europe and the Middle East to Southern Asia and the Indian Ocean, and also to "counter the image of the Carter administration as being soft vis-à-vis the Soviet Union," even at the expense of delaying SALT II. He did so provocatively, going on *Meet the Press* after his first visit to China and blasting Soviet conduct around the world, while Vance was negotiating arms control with them.[113]

Carter himself concluded the China deal completely in secret lest it anger the Russians enough to stop SALT; by his own admission, he never permitted a single message between the White House and Beijing on normalizing diplomatic relations to pass through the State Department.[114] All of this deeply angered Vance, as he was negotiating SALT II.

While preparing for the next round of SALT talks and traveling to the Middle East, Vance obtained Carter's agreement that when negotiations on normalization with China were completed, the announcement would be made on January 1, a week after his next round of SALT negotiations in Geneva. But when the China talks were completed, Carter told him that the agreement with China might unravel, and he would announce it on December 15.[115] Vance did not want it to delay a SALT treaty or intentionally to offend the Soviets, although Brzezinski insists Vance supported the early announcement.[116] Nevertheless it did both.

The announcement referred to mutual opposition by China and the United States to "hegemony"—an incendiary Chinese code word for Soviet global ambitions, which Brzezinski had happily agreed should be included as a signal to the Soviets. Vance would certainly have objected to the language as an unnecessary provocation just as he was about to finalize the SALT treaty with Gromyko—who, in fact, was upset when he saw it.

China's diminutive leader, Deng Xiaoping, took the country by storm when he arrived first in Texas late January 1979 and donned a ten-gallon hat that seemed to consume his whole small face. On January 30 I participated in the meeting in the Cabinet Room, with Deng and the Chinese delegation, the president, Vance, Brzezinski, and other cabinet officials. One of the key points in that meeting for Deng was to obtain the same low tariffs we levied on our traditional trading partners, called "most favored nation" status, which would have been denied to Chinese goods because the Jackson-Vanik Amendment, while directed at the Soviet Union, barred such treatment to all totalitarian countries that limited travel by their citizens. So, disarmingly, he pushed a White House notepad and pencil across the table to Carter and said: "Mr. President, please write on here how many Chinese you would like us to send you each year, one million, two million, ten million?" Everyone laughed. The president quickly replied: "If you want me to receive ten million Chinese to come to the United States, I'd be glad to do so." But in return Carter offered to send Deng 10,000 American journalists![117]

But Carter had to also satisfy our longtime ally Taiwan that it would not be abandoned to its stronger neighbor across the Taiwan Strait. In a tough battle Carter persuaded Congress to pass the Taiwan Relations Act, which to this day remains the basis of our relationship with that country, providing sophisticated arms and guaranteeing its people U.S. protection from any Chinese military attack;[118] the act also set the Taiwanese on a course from a one-party, authoritarian state to a thriving democracy now for more than 35 years.[119]

For all the jollity in the White House, the timing and content of the announcement was one factor in delaying the conclusion of the SALT II Treaty, as Carter later admitted.[120] That eventually proved fatal, contrary to Zbig's belief that formal recognition of China would stop Soviet stalling on SALT and provide strategic leverage in obtaining a better deal for the United States.[121]

Moscow's annoyance contributed to delaying completion of the SALT II negotiations by six months, which—with Carter's foreign policy already buckling under Soviet assertiveness—added more weight than the treaty could bear. Given proper timing, the president might have won approval for the SALT treaty, while waiting a few months to normalize relations with China. Once again the compartmentalization of decisions, however historic, blurred the president's accomplishments. Our White House staff was operating without a fully engaged and experienced chief of staff to keep decisions in a proper order for their effect on diplomacy and domestic politics, and to sequence decisions so they did not conflict. Not only was the message muddled, but policy itself was often adrift. The Vance-Brzezinski rivalry became more incendiary, and was not clarified until the Soviet invasion of Afghanistan forced it, in the most dramatic fashion.

THE SERPENT'S KISS

Despite all the bumps in the road, SALT II was finally signed at a summit with Brezhnev in Vienna on June 18, 1979, a huge step forward in stabilizing U.S.-USSR relations, although not for long. The Soviets gave up more than we did. The limits of missiles for each side were capped at 2,400, but significant constraints were placed on modernizing intercontinental ballistic missiles, the heart of the Soviet nuclear arsenal, while the United States could modernize in every area of our strength; and limits were placed on the number of MIRV missiles.[122] But even then, Carter paid a personal price.

The night before the signing ceremony, the social side of the summit concluded at the Vienna State Opera with a gala performance of Mozart's *The Abduction from the Seraglio*. As Carter and his daughter, Amy, studiously followed an English translation of the libretto, Brezhnev, Gromyko, and several aides could be seen in a neighboring box paying far more attention to the continuing flow of champagne than the opera onstage. Rafshoon took note of this raffish behavior and passed a word of advice to Carter during the intermission. He warned that Russian men have a habit of kissing other males on both cheeks at important occasions or when welcoming them— so he must be careful to avoid a bear hug during the signing ceremony lest it play badly at home, while he was trying to have the treaty ratified by the Senate. The president assured him, "Don't worry, Jerry, it won't happen."

But it did. Brezhnev, a bear of a man, embraced Carter after they both signed the treaty and exchanged pens, and then gave him the traditional Russian kiss. As Rafshoon remembered to his chagrin, it was prominently featured by the Reagan campaign in their ads against Carter. Diplomacy has its uses, but politeness does not always pay: Carter, with his Southern good manners, could not disentangle himself in time from the serpent's kiss seen around the world.[123] But worse was to come.

The treaty was submitted to the Senate on June 22, 1979, four days after it was signed in Vienna. But with the lengthy delay in reaching an agreement, the atmosphere could not have been more foreboding. Carter's popularity was low. The Soviets remained active through their Cuban proxies in Africa. The treaty did not provide the deep Soviet cuts demanded by Jackson and the defense hawks, and Senate Minority Leader Howard Baker had exhausted his political capital with Republican conservatives by supporting the Panama Canal Treaty.

With SALT II already on a knife edge, it received an almost fatal blow from a gross misunderstanding about a routine but callous activity in a supersensitive spot, Cuba. Since the end of the 1962 Cuban missile crisis, some 2,300 Soviet military advisers had remained there with the acquiescence of the Kennedy administration. Over the years the Soviets gradually added a fully equipped defensive brigade with artillery and tank battalions, but no airlift capacity.[124]

Frank Church of the Senate Foreign Relations Committee, up for re-election in conservative Idaho, received a confidential State Department briefing, and then held a shameless news conference in Boise, making it appear that a new security threat existed, and that SALT ratification would be virtually impossible if the brigade was not removed.[125] Carter was livid at Church, but he faced a dilemma. He first declared the Russian presence "unacceptable." Then, after an independent investigation, it was established that the CIA had simply lost track of this small remnant of Russian soldiers, and nothing had changed their lack of offensive capability.

Adm. Stansfield Turner, Carter's Annapolis classmate, appointed to lead the CIA and clean up its dirty-tricks department, later admitted that "we made a terrible mistake on the Soviet brigade in overacting and seeming to give credence to a red herring."[126] In the end Turner's sound assessment prevailed. But whatever momentum remained for SALT was stopped in a surge of public hostility to the Soviet Union. Committee votes made it evident that the treaty did not have sufficient Senate support. Carter asked Byrd to defer action, later describing the withdrawal as his presidency's "most profound disappointment."[127]

Moscow's next move in a faraway country made Senate ratification impossible.[128] Yet SALT II remained another unheralded Carter legacy, because even after the Soviet invasion of Afghanistan put the final nail into the coffin, Ronald Reagan and the Soviet leadership both complied with SALT II throughout its term, as if it had been ratified into law.

AFGHANISTAN

Just six months after the triumph of détente in Vienna, Moscow betrayed Carter's hard-won diplomacy by invading Afghanistan. At Christmastime 1979, Soviet special forces parachuted into the capital city of Kabul, assassinated the prime minister and his family, and put their own man in charge. He was a new and more reliable Afghan leader, supported by 85,000 Soviet troops that had been sent across the border in a massive airlift and ground movement completed in a few weeks.

Carter immediately and correctly saw the Soviet invasion as one of the most difficult challenges of his administration, and it could not have come at a worse time—only weeks after the American hostages were seized in Tehran, and weeks before his first reelection test in the Iowa primary. His bold response ended his straddle between Vance's view of handling the Soviet Union and Brzezinski's: the invasion pushed him firmly across Zbig's hard line.

Afghanistan is less a stable nation than a collection of tribes in constant conflict, which from time to time have served as gravediggers of empires. For three centuries Afghanistan continued to be the chessboard for the "Great Game" of imperialism between Russia and Britain, and was deliberately left to its own devices as a powerless buffer state; the country never conducted a census or built a railroad. By the time Afghanistan became the last battlefield in the Cold War, it had been informally partitioned into spheres of influence, with the Soviet Union dominant in the north, where it extracted natural gas, and in the west in Kabul and the south, where it operated agricultural and civil aid missions, mainly through the United Nations.

In 1973 King Zahir Shah was dethroned in a coup led by his cousin, Mohammed Daoud Khan, who was himself assassinated in another coup on April 27, 1978, led by local Communists of the People's Democratic Party of Afghanistan. This Marxist uprising took Moscow completely by surprise, but the Soviet leaders now had a stake in the stability of a Muslim country on their border, which was itself lined with Soviet provinces that were predominantly Muslim. Afghanistan's new leader, President Nur Mohammad Taraki, remained general secretary of the Communist Party, while Hafizullah Amin became foreign minister and the public face of the new regime, because he spoke fluent English from his days as a student at Columbia University in New York City.

Moscow kept them at arm's length by refusing a mutual defense treaty and full integration into the Soviet economic system. The government was composed of the party's two rival factions: Khalq (masses), which was socialist and tribal, and Parcham (flag), which was urban, Leninist, and closer to the Soviet Union. Sharing power only intensified their bitter internal rivalry, leading to the execution or exile of countless Parcham members, one of whom was the Parcham leader, Babrak Karmal. He was appointed Afghan ambassador to Prague, but never showed up, sheltered by the Soviet Union until its invasion forces put him in power.

Along with violent purges, the regime carried out a series of social and economic reforms that were viewed by the public as opposing Islam, particularly changes in marriage laws and dowries that were the foundation of agricultural credit. Islamic insurgents adopted the mantle of mujahideen—holy warriors—opposing secular reforms. Only a few months after the April revolution of 1978, religious and tribal strife began spreading across the nation. From that time until the Soviet intervention, more than twenty thousand political prisoners were executed.

Amid the chaos, in February 1979 the U.S. ambassador to Afghanistan, Adolph Dubs, was kidnapped as he was being driven to work, and held in a Kabul hotel. The Afghan government refused to negotiate, and its forces stormed the hotel room backed by their Soviet advisers, despite impassioned pleas by the U.S. government and its diplomats on the scene. Dubs was killed in the crossfire. This incident led to a further deterioration of U.S.-Soviet relations. A month later Taraki met with Brezhnev in Moscow to ask for further military aid, but received only token support and a warning to unify his party and prevent an all-out civil war that would inevitably draw in the Soviets.

At the summit to sign SALT II in June 1979, Brzezinski warned Brezhnev about the Soviet presence in Afghanistan. The Soviet leader responded by raising the ruse that the United States was extending its frontiers to the Soviet border.[1] Since the spring Brzezinski had been pressing the president to start a covert program to help the mujahideen. In July, in a decision almost unknown to this day, Carter approved the supply of communications devices and medical and other nonlethal supplies. Fully six months *before* the Soviet invasion, Washington began helping the rebels in the hope of improving their chances of holding Soviet proxy forces at bay.[2]

Several leading Soviet officials, including Foreign Minister Gromyko, opposed intervention, while Soviet advisers in Kabul were urging the regime to move more prudently with its reforms, especially in the countryside. Muslim nations, particularly Pakistan, worried that Soviet intervention might mean further expansion into their territory, and the nervous Saudi government was preparing to formally ask the United States to intervene on behalf of the rebels and block the Soviets.[3] Events escalated rapidly. On September 11 Taraki went to Moscow to discuss replacing Amin. Two days later Amin preempted his dismissal by having Taraki murdered. The Soviets became increasingly suspicious of Amin's motives and loyalty, and suspected him of seeking alliances with Pakistan, China, and even the United States.

On September 14 the CIA sent out an Alert warning that "the Soviet leaders might be on the threshold of a decision to commit their own forces to prevent the collapse of the regime."[4] The White House held an interagency meeting to discuss contingency plans, and on November 3 Brzezinski reported to Carter that Soviet military advisers had been infused at levels from the Afghan Defense Ministry down to divisional commands, and that sizable military and economic aid agreements had been concluded.[5]

Another CIA Alert was sent on December 19, detailing a Soviet buildup along the Afghan borders,[6] and on December 22 Vice Adm. Bobby Inman, director of the National Security Agency, called Brzezinski and Brown to warn that the Soviets would move their forces within 72 hours. Two days later he called again and gave a fifteen-hour warning that proved accurate.[7] The invasion began on Christmas Day 1979, with Soviet propaganda falsely claiming that the troops were moving in response to an Afghan government appeal for help in strengthening its security forces.

Soviet recklessness in invading Afghanistan was a shock for the world. To Carter the invasion represented a real threat to U.S. national security. The administration believed it was plausible for the Soviets to consolidate their hold on Afghanistan and then make a push for the Persian Gulf, through either Iran or Pakistan. Carter's main goals now were to make any such military move as politically costly as possible, and do what he could to stay Brezhnev's hand in the future. He immediately consulted with key allies, nonaligned leaders, and the neighboring Muslim nations, asking them to condemn the Soviets' actions.

Through the Hot Line (a direct link between Washington and Moscow established in the wake of the 1962 Cuban missile crisis to provide instant communication), Carter sent Brezhnev his most strongly worded message ever, strengthening Brzezinski's draft by labeling the Soviet action as a "clear threat to the peace," which "could mark a fundamental and long-lasting turning point in our relations."[8] He also wanted to make it clear that a Soviet intrusion into the Persian Gulf would provoke the same response as an attack on America. With administration leadership, fifty countries signed a letter to the president of the UN Security Council requesting an urgent meeting. Carter worked with congressional and public leaders to ensure that the American people fully understood the gravity of the invasion, which he regarded as the most serious international development on his watch as president. As he explained to me later, unless the Soviets "recognize that it has been counterproductive for them, we will face additional serious problems with invasions or subversion in the future."[9]

Until then Carter's opinion on Soviet matters often aligned with Vance's; but now it was changing. Vance was less certain the invasion presaged a broader Soviet thrust, and he continued to seek cooperation with the Soviet Union to salvage SALT. Brzezinski presented a more menacing view of the Soviet intentions and advocated tougher policies. He needed only to look at the map to envision a potential Soviet pincer movement from Africa on one side and southwest Asia on the other, with the principal artery of the world's oil supply running through the Persian Gulf and the choke point of the Strait of Hormuz.

An excellent chess player, Brzezinski also saw Afghanistan as the perfect place to checkmate Vance in the bureaucratic wars, and win Carter over to his side once and for all on Soviet issues. He told the president that while members of his administration stood solidly behind him against the Soviets, there were two conflicting interpretations—one that saw it as an aberration from Soviet behavior and the other as a clear symptom of it. He did not need to name names.

Brzezinski had been studying Soviet policies for years, and told Carter that Moscow was entering an "assertive phase of its history," characterized by the acquisition of military power that offered the Soviet Union temptations to project it far and wide, first by encouraging and supporting "ideological sympathizers" in Cuba, the Horn of Africa, politically in Western Europe, and now directly in Afghanistan, where Soviet power was supplanting Marxist ideology as the dynamic of Soviet foreign policy.[10]

Brzezinski's geopolitical vision was heady stuff, and it worked. In a year-end television interview, the president declared: "My opinion of the Russians has changed more drastically in the last week than even the previous two and one-half years."[11] Carter's ultimate decision to side with his national security adviser, in my opinion, led to Vance's departure from the administration.

Robert Gates, then the NSC specialist on Soviet affairs, was dismayed by the president's remark because Brzezinski had been sending Carter his weekly Friday reports for two and one-half years focusing on precisely this assertive projection of Soviet power in Africa and Eastern Europe; Gates bemoaned that "it really hadn't clicked with Carter until the Soviets invaded Afghanistan."[12]

The president was severely criticized as naive by hard-liners, but later insisted to me that he had been misunderstood: "We had just agreed to SALT . . . if you look at the actual text I was very clear, but the headlines were 'Carter Surprised at Soviet Aggression,' . . . which made it look as though I thought the Soviets were incapable of aggression—and you know I always knew that the Soviets were capable of aggression and had that inclination."[13]

I believe Carter's views evolved less suddenly. With Soviet adventurism rising in Africa, he was desperately trying to hold on to SALT. Moreover, he felt personally betrayed by Brezhnev after having devoted so much political capital to a conciliatory approach. But Afghanistan was the final piece of evidence that the Soviets represented a tangible threat to American interests and security, and Carter decided that the time for cooperation was over.

THE GRAIN EMBARGO

A full sense of crisis gripped the White House after the Soviet invasion. We had to act quickly and strongly, and the entire decision-making process, covering economic and domestic, as well as foreign and defense policy, was taken over by Brzezinski through a Special Coordinating Committee (SCC) of the National Security Council. In forming his plan to respond, Carter insisted that punitive action had to be clearly defined in order to be broadly supported. America would take the lead, but we would need to work closely with other nations. Within a week of the invasion, in round-the-clock, pressure-packed meetings, we came up with a comprehensive approach, combining political, economic, and military action.

Direct military intervention against the Soviet Union in such a distant and forbidding place was out of the question (until years later, when Al Qaeda made Afghanistan its base for attacks on American facilities abroad and eventually on New York City with 9/11). Still, it was possible to limit Soviet encroachment in the Gulf and Iran. Brzezinski set forth a list of geopolitical measures—creating a unified command structure in the region and staging maneuvers; institutionalizing defense ties with Saudi Arabia; and increasing American access to the military bases in the region, from Kenya and Somalia to Oman and Diego Garcia. Carter quickly expanded the American naval presence in the Gulf and the Indian Ocean, strengthened military and political support to Pakistan to diminish Soviet influence in the region, and built up the Rapid Deployment Force. This was another of the Carter administration's innovations, created in 1979 as a highly mobile strike force that could be moved immediately to areas where there were no existing U.S. bases or friendly countries. In response to the Afghan invasion, Carter made it the Rapid Deployment Joint Task Force, composed of all military services, focused particularly on the Persian Gulf.[14]

Another military component of this strategy, though unknown to the public, was the continued support of the mujahideen against the Soviet-backed Afghan forces. The entire process had to remain covert so as not to provoke the Soviets. In a top-secret operation, to avoid arousing suspicions that the United States was providing aid to Moscow's enemies, the rebels received Soviet-manufactured weapons, which the CIA acquired from Pakistan, Egypt, and Saudi Arabia, and handed them over to the mujahideen, primarily through Pakistan.[15] I found it a sweet irony that the Soviets' own arms were being deployed against them. Military aid continued to increase during Carter's term, including weapons against Soviet tanks and armored personnel carriers, and was enhanced by Reagan, with hand-held Stinger rockets proving decisive in devastating Soviet helicopters.[16]

Of all the actions we considered, the three most contentious were a grain embargo, an Olympic boycott of the 1980 Moscow games, and draft registration. To squeeze the Soviets, the most important economic measure was an embargo on grain sales to the Soviet Union; but it was also the most politically difficult. President Nixon had repeatedly enforced grain embargoes, and the heavily subsidized American farming community argued it was being singled out for an excessive burden in comparison with corporate exporters of manufactured goods. During the 1976 campaign, Carter had called for ending grain embargoes.[17]

We received reports over the Christmas holidays that Moscow did not believe Carter intended to impose an embargo, which only made it a better strategy by showing the Soviets the extent of American conviction. Under a 1975 Ford administration agreement with the USSR, they had the right to buy up to 8 million tons of grain, with discretion to purchase another 17 million tons, for a total of 25 million. Days after their invasion, on January 3, the Soviets protectively ordered 3.8 million tons of wheat, one of their largest purchases yet.

As a farmer himself, questions surrounding a grain embargo hit Carter particularly close to home. America's wheat farmers had been one of

Russia's main grain suppliers since the early 1970s. We knew that agriculture was one of the most vulnerable sectors of the Soviet economy; they were already low on grain, and supplies were available from only a handful of countries. While an embargo was likely to injure them economically and perhaps even stay any further military moves, Carter emphasized that shipping grain to the Soviets now would simply be contrary to American values. But with the Iowa caucuses just weeks away, I feared a backlash from Iowa's farmers. So, when the president called on January 2, I was astonished as he told me he and Brzezinski had already decided on a grain embargo, without the slightest consideration of the legal, economic, and political consequences.[18]

But could he do this with the mere stroke of a pen? It might seem patriotic that the Seafarers Union on the West Coast, from which most U.S. products were shipped to the USSR, were refusing to load any shipments to the Soviet Union. But at least 8 million tons of wheat and corn, mainly for animal feed, had to be delivered to Russia under the agreement negotiated by the Ford administration, and so far only about half of that had been shipped. If even this amount was blocked by presidential order, Brezhnev would know that Carter meant it. But if the shipment was blocked by the union, the presidential sanction would lose much of its diplomatic force because the Russians would believe the White House was using the dockside boycott as a smokescreen to avoid the domestic consequences.

What was our legal obligation to the farmers and grain brokers—the owners of the shipment—if we decreed they could not sell it abroad? And who would be liable if we did not stop the longshoremen's boycott? These questions were not even half of it. I ran down to a meeting in the Roosevelt Room chaired by Vice President Mondale, which seemed to have drawn half the government, including Lynn Daft, my agriculture expert on the Domestic Policy Staff, who was invaluable during this crisis. We discussed the complexities of an embargo and decided that the president had authority under the Export Administration Act to stop all shipments above the basic agreement's 8 million tons without being sued. But we had no legal authority to force longshoremen to load more grain above that limit, and the boycott was spreading to the Port of New Orleans. At the moment, the grain was on barges in the Mississippi River, where it could freeze in the January weather and disrupt the food chain in our own country. As Dale Hathaway, deputy secretary of Agriculture, pointed out, if we could not load or ship the grain that had already been signed for, "it would show the Russians they can disrupt us more than we can disrupt them." That dilemma showed up time and again as we shaped the sanctions regimen.[19]

The next question was how to help the farmers who would lose their market for the remaining grain. Carter knew that cutting off this export market could pile up huge surpluses in our government reserves, which would push down prices. Our meetings addressed this as part of the cost to the Treasury for underwriting the farmers' losses, as well as their reputation as reliable suppliers. The government—meaning the taxpayers—could buy it and put it in a storage reserve; Carter was willing to pay that price.

The immediate question was whether we would be hurting our farmers and the U.S. economy more than we would be hurting the Soviets. The answer depended upon whether they could purchase the grain from other countries. Because the decision was being made so quickly, this vital aspect of the operation received little attention. An even broader issue was whether the president would be using food as a foreign-policy weapon, a slippery slope that we all agreed would hurt our international credibility.

Carter wanted to slap on the grain embargo by the end of the day—January 3, the first working day of the New Year—and demanded an options memorandum by 3:00 p.m. As I pointed out, the legal and economic problems, I had what I described in my notes as a "hot discussion with him." He was visibly uninterested in the details and set 4:00 p.m. for a meeting to make the final decision. With his military sense of punctuality, at 4:00 p.m. and not a minute earlier or later, Carter walked into the Roosevelt Room to face a phalanx of officials. Agriculture Secretary Bob Bergland, a former Minnesota congressman and a no-nonsense Midwesterner with a great knowledge of farm programs and farm politics, gave precise figures on the state of the grain shipments. He warned of the high cost to farmers of an embargo, and not just the $3.5 billion in lost farm income. White House economic adviser Charlie Schultze estimated it would cost the government about $3 billion to buy up the embargoed grain.

In checking with farm groups, Bergland confirmed they would feel unfairly treated unless all exports to the Soviet Union were curtailed, a sweeping ban that was economically and politically impossible. Clearly worried
about how the farmers would be made whole, Bergland was brutally frank:
"Mr. President, we will have to adjust our farm reserve, but there will be
structural damage [emphasis his, as captured in my notes] to our trade position, and as a reliable partner for trade. The embargo will have a greater economic impact here at home than on the Soviets. Mr. President, we will be
shooting ourselves in the foot." More discussion followed, but it clearly washed
over Carter.

The president said, "This is the most serious consequence to world
peace. Afghanistan was not previously a Soviet puppet. We cannot let them
go on with impunity or they might move into Pakistan or Iran. . . . I don't
care if this costs $2 billion, we will save the money elsewhere. . . . I think
the nation's security is involved. For the world to see us pay an economic
cost shows our determination." He soon left the room, leaving no doubt
what he would do, whatever the consequences.[20] The wrangling over alternatives, details, and repercussions continued the next day throughout the
administration—although not in the mind of the determined president.

The speechwriters were already at work on an address Carter would give
to the nation Friday evening, January 4, from the Oval Office. Because he
felt the need to act quickly and decisively, he announced actions that had
not been thoroughly vetted among the key departments. We paid a price
for his haste, but in the end the sprint of several weeks' work at very long
hours was both exhilarating and uplifting, in part because of my pride at
seeing the president act so decisively under duress.

In his address he warned that the Soviet invasion of Afghanistan, a remote country most Americans had never heard of, was an "extremely serious threat to peace" because it could be "a stepping-stone to possible
control over much of the world's oil supplies." The United States had already helped persuade fifty nations to condemn the invasion, and he told
the American people what he was going to do—recall the U.S. ambassador to Moscow, ask the Senate to delay ratification of SALT II, halt or reduce exports to the Soviets in high technology and other strategic products,
severely curtail Soviet fishing in U.S. waters, and embargo grain ship-

ments, which he made clear were to be fed to livestock and not intended for human consumption.

He reassured American farmers that the blocked grain would be bought up by the government to maintain steady prices and expressed confidence that other grain-exporting nations would "not replace these quantities of grain by additional shipments on their part to the Soviet Union." This, unfortunately, was a misplaced confidence. At that point he did not pull out of the summer's Moscow Olympics, but warned that they were also endangered by their hosts' behavior. He closed by reminding Americans that there was "a clear lesson from history learned by the world at great cost: aggression, unopposed, becomes a contagious disease."[21]

Now we had to deal with the consequences of Carter's decisions and further expand sanctions. It was clear to me that if there was a national security crisis abroad, we were on the brink of a different one at home. Economic and political sanctions were particularly difficult to craft, because of intense domestic interests, particularly during a presidential election season. We bumped frustratingly against the legal limits of using economic sanctions in the service of national security, and the necessity of bringing on board all economically important allies for products traded on international markets—a lesson President Obama learned in shaping tough sanctions against Iran's nuclear program decades later.

At a January 9 meeting chaired by Brzezinski, he said we needed to show some visible export cancellations to demonstrate that our program had teeth. State's Richard Cooper countered that if the U.S. canceled a Soviet order and another country picked it up, we would simply "look silly." There were countervailing arguments to everything we examined. Canceling oil-drilling equipment, said Deputy Energy Secretary John Sawhill, would mean the Russians would extract less of their own oil and buy more on the world market, driving up prices even higher. If we banned phosphates, the Soviets would cancel sales of ammonia that we needed for fertilizer. Would the French step in and try to sell their computers in our Russian market? Should we buy corn instead of wheat to stabilize the market and protect Iowa farmers? Bergland argued that if we were going to embargo grain, we should also stop shipping livestock, fertilizer, and soybeans: "If we do any, we should do all."

And so it went on product after product, splitting hairs. It seemed we were "half-pregnant," when we should be persuading our allies to show solidarity by not supplanting our exports.[22] Treasury Secretary Miller separately complained that Brzezinski was "taking over trade policy, and just wants to cancel contracts with the Soviets without thought."[23]

Managing the implications of his grain embargo was particularly testy. The grain-exporting companies demanded full indemnity for their losses, which we had yet to consider in detail. As for the longer term in the markets, I had good reason to urge the president to give us time to consider the economic consequences of the embargo, but he would not hear of it. The ripple effects would go from the farmers to the grain exporters to the grain elevator owners and to the small country banks that had financed different parts of the supply chain. We closed the grain futures exchange while we worked on the details of a program to protect the entire agricultural economy. Bergland succinctly said that we had created a panic and now had a responsibility to fix it.[24]

He then laid out a complex program to avert a meltdown of the agricultural economy, the essence of which was that the U.S. government would take over the Russian contracts, not release the grain on the market, which would depress prices, and put an equivalent amount into the government reserve. It had taken a full, exhausting weekend to work out this plan, which represented only the start of our labors. At the end of the Sunday-night meeting, I felt we had a chance to avert a domestic catastrophe, at least in the farm belt.

At the Monday-morning cabinet meeting on January 7, Vance reported that an estimated 400,000 Afghan refugees had flooded into Pakistan since the invasion. Mondale, always looking at the political implications, said it was important to deny export licenses for high technology and other products, so "farmers won't feel they are alone."

Commerce Secretary Philip Klutznik said he had frozen all applications for strategic exports to the Soviet Union. Carter emphasized the importance of publicizing specific actions, and shifted from international affairs to their effect on domestic politics, announcing he would stick close to the White

House in order to be seen doing his job rather than campaigning. Carter correctly forecast that Reagan would be the Republican nominee, and said that he had not yet seen any deterioration of public support on his handling of the hostage drama in Iran. "What I hear is 'avoid bloodshed and keep us out of war,'" he said. It struck me that a president who was so consciously apolitical in his governance, by trying to do whatever he thought was "right," could turn on a dime when the campaign season began.[25]

DON'T CRY FOR US, ARGENTINA

To have real bite, any U.S. grain embargo had to depend upon our friends denying the Soviets the opportunity to fill in the gap by selling their grain. But in the rush to take action, insufficient attention had been paid to one of the world's greatest grain producers: Argentina, and that left us crying. Arms sales to the military junta had been curbed under the president's human rights campaign, and as the saying goes, everything that goes around comes around. On January 10, Agriculture's Hathaway told me in a state of near-shock that the Argentines had nine million tons of grain, and they were considering selling it to the Soviet Union. The embargo had been announced so precipitously that this was the first time Hathaway told me or anyone at the White House. I called Christopher at State, who declared himself "flab-bergasted" at the size of their stockpile, which he had been told was only six hundred thousand tons.

I learned that in a meeting of grain-exporting countries, the Agriculture Department's representative had found out about Argentina's large stockpile and reported it to state's Richard Cooper, but the correct number was never passed up to me or others at the top, and we therefore did not think of Argentina as a major exporter. I found this unfathomable; but that is what happens when a bureaucracy must suddenly shift course to a new policy under great time pressure, and does not catch up with all the relevant facts.[26]

We then met with Whitney MacMillan, the president of Cargill, the world's largest private grain-trading company. He was totally dismissive of the embargo, asserting that there were plenty of substitutes for the United

States as grain suppliers, and Argentina was only one of them; but Argentina was anxious to take advantage of our embargo and smarting from the human rights pressures we imposed. Cargill had no choice but to help Argentina, he said, or "we will lose our franchise." Moreover, Cargill's foreign subsidiaries needed to be able to maintain their ties with the Soviet Union, "or we will burn our bridges to the USSR to sell U.S. grain." He argued that foreign affiliates of American companies should be free to pursue their normal business abroad without interference from Washington. I knew he had his stockholders to consider, but even though I was no great fan of the embargo, I found his attitude repugnant in showing absolutely no interest in the security challenges our country faced from the Soviet invasion.[27]

Major grain exporters, including Canada, Australia, and Argentina, had agreed to not replace American grain at a meeting in Brussels.[28] But a few days later Argentina reneged on its promise. The Soviets sent envoys to negotiate for the grain, and so did the United States, but our negotiators were waved away by Argentina when we pressed them to support the embargo. The problem would have been significantly worse if Argentina had harvested a better crop that year. It reduced its grain sales to other nations and sold most of its reserves to the Soviets at premium prices. But even so, the Russians were able to buy only an additional seven million tons.

In the end the grain embargo and sanctions program had deeper political results than we could have realized at the time: Together with Carter's direct warning, it helped stay the Soviets' hand against the popular uprising in Poland the following year, when they were poised to invade. But for now, agricultural leaders blamed the president for penalizing farmers more than the Russians, and consumers blamed Carter for raising crop prices. Yet, an analysis of market data showed that wheat and corn grain prices actually fell during this period, and only began to rise after Reagan lifted the embargo in 1981. Ultimately the strategy was very successful, with the prices of grain remaining stable while American grain sales actually reached record highs.

While the embargo caused the United States to lose its dominant share of the Soviet market, by forcing the Soviet Union to diversify its suppliers it achieved its intended aim of retaliating against the Soviet Union by reducing its meat production and forcing it to pay premium prices for grain.

Often they paid nearly 25 percent above international market prices and still were unable to make up even half the seventeen million tons embargoed by the United States. Together with a poor Soviet harvest, that meant less meat on Soviet shelves. Per capita meat consumption fell back to 1965 levels, thwarting an important objective of the Soviet government.[29]

Most important, the administration decided that to promote a united front against Soviet aggression, it was necessary to maintain the embargo even if the Soviets were eventually able to acquire grain elsewhere. By refusing to reverse his position on the embargo in the face of political backlash, Carter proved he was willing to commit himself and the country to a strong stand against aggression, and this in itself was a victory. I should have taken off my domestic adviser's hat in favor of a broader perspective. Carter's resolve and his tough actions against the Soviets were politically popular—even in Iowa, where he decisively defeated Kennedy.[30]

MOSCOW GAMES

In his nationwide address, Carter signaled that the United States would "prefer not to withdraw" from the 1980 Summer Olympics in Moscow, but would have to consider it if the Soviets did not end their aggression in Afghanistan. The issue was first revisited at a January 9 meeting with the president by Mondale, who argued that if people "see Russian ships in our harbors, and American athletes in Russia for the Olympics, it sends the wrong signal."[31]

This time Carter consulted more widely, contacting foreign government and sports federation leaders. He regarded it as immoral for athletes to participate as guests of the Soviet Union while its troops were engaging in a violent suppression in Afghanistan. Extending an olive branch, the administration agreed to attend the games if the Kremlin would make a firm commitment to start withdrawing troops. No such commitment ever came. He sent a personal letter to Brezhnev offering to attend the games after a one-year postponement if the Soviets left Afghanistan. That also was ignored.

The president again raised the question of the Olympics at a senior staff meeting early in January. He said it would be impossible to participate if the Soviets were still in Afghanistan, and "we can't pick it up and move it all to one place; therefore, we should break it into pieces and go to Greece for a permanent place, or we will be killing the Olympics permanently."[32] I knew this troubled him because he was a sportsman, loved playing softball, fishing, and canoeing, and was an avid tennis player.

He simply could not let go of the subject at a meeting later that month with me and our senior White House congressional lobbyists. I told him we were getting ahead of ourselves because the Olympic Games did not take place until August. He forcefully replied in no uncertain terms: "The bottom line is that we're not going if they're still in there." He spent a considerable amount of time with the U.S. Olympic Committee working for the boycott even though he also realized it made him few friends in the world of sport. Although the Winter Olympics were already under way at Lake Placid in upstate New York, he decided not to visit because "I'm too controversial."[33]

A diplomatic tug-of-war began, involving the Soviet Union, our European allies, the International Olympic Committee, and the U.S. government and people, who were surprisingly supportive of a boycott. And like all boycotts, it raised unexpected questions: Should we also bar American companies like Coca-Cola and Levi-Strauss from advertising at the Olympics, while asking our athletes to stay home? We had no legal power to do so. By February, as the Europeans were hesitating, although leaning our way, Carter felt we needed some alternative competition to satisfy the athletes, who had trained for four years and now would be denied an opportunity open to them only during a short window in any young life. He decided to bring the U.S. Olympic Team to the White House to explain the boycott to them in person, appeal to their patriotism, and offer them an alternative.[34]

Although we never mentioned it directly, the dreadful example of American participation in the 1936 Berlin Olympic Games, giving Adolph Hitler a measure of credibility, was certainly on my mind—and I believe on Carter's and Mondale's, too. Congress stood behind the administration with resolutions supporting the boycott by overwhelming bipartisan votes in both houses. So did international leaders, and finally the U.S. Olympic Committee, too, which voted not to participate, although Vance reported "it was a difficult decision."[35]

Polls showed that 55 percent of Americans approved of the Olympic boycott, but Carter knew his plan could backfire and make America look pitiful, unless a majority of national teams also stayed home. Convincing them was a tough slog, led by Vance. Most Olympic bodies are independent and resented being told what to do by their governments. Carter and his top assistants gave interviews, speeches, and made personal appeals to point out that attending would be immoral and unsportsmanlike. Although the decision to boycott the Olympics upset many people, Carter viewed it as an essential political blow against the Soviets. The Moscow games were politically important to the Soviet leadership to showcase and celebrate its achievements. The four most influential nations—the United States, China, Germany, and Japan—did not attend. Several Soviet dissidents and intellectuals said the boycott would send a strong political and ideological message to the Soviet people.

While the Olympic boycott was a blow to sports-mad America and especially its athletes, it was an even harsher one to the prestige of the Soviet leadership. Remarkably, 61 nations chose not to attend the Moscow games, which turned out largely to be an eastern bloc event.[36] A substitute track-and-field event that we encouraged, the Liberty Bell Classic, took place at the University of Pennsylvania on July 16, with 30 countries and 400 athletes participating. Several other events were held internationally and were often referred to as the Olympic Boycott Games. In response the Soviet Union and several of its allies boycotted the 1984 Summer Olympics in Los Angeles and hosted their own "Friendship Games." As for the Olympic movement, it outlasted the Soviet Union itself.

THE MILITARY DRAFT

To further strengthen his stance, Carter also reinstated registration for the military draft. This was another spur-of-the moment decision and was sharply contested inside the administration as essentially unnecessary. I had a fierce debate with the president about adding this measure to the lengthening list of responses to Afghanistan. I argued strenuously that it reversed his campaign promise against registration, that a National Security Council study showed it was unnecessary, that it might look as if we were moving toward a war footing, and that questions remained about whether women should be registered. Carter replied that Defense Secretary Brown said the registration would save six months in raising a conscript army if the nation had to mobilize in response to further Soviet provocations. "It is the only additional military step available," he argued.[37] There was clearly a burr under his saddle.

I did not realize how upset he was at the time, and it is probably better that I did not. He later wrote bitterly of my and Mondale's opposition to draft registration as "practically a rebellion." We argued that he was over-reacting and that reinstating registration would be politically damaging to his reelection. He complained of having to "fight off the draft dodgers in my group," also singling us out for what he considered our timidity about his cabinet reshuffle, his withdrawal from the Iowa primary debate with Kennedy, and the grain embargo.[38]

The fact of the matter was that Jimmy Carter felt he was on a high: His bold actions had reinvigorated him and his style of governance. Just a few days before, he had expressed a certain relief to us that SALT II was off the table for the time being, saying: "[Now] I don't have to kiss every senator's ass." On the contrary, "I need to escalate the rhetoric and bust the hell out of them [the Soviets]. . . . We've been timid because of SALT; the country wants us to be rough."[39] Later in January, grain markets began to stabilize, and Soviet troops soon discovered that Afghanistan was no cakewalk.

When Carter met with the Democratic congressional leaders on the morning of his State of the Union address, the political landscape had changed beyond recognition. Tip O'Neill forecast—correctly—that the president would be greeted warmly by Congress and compared the moment with the period of 1946–47 when the postwar order was being built and America became the guarantor of the world's security. The Speaker dramatically told the president: "America is waiting for direction and wants to know where we stand and what's the stopping point. We are all greatly disturbed, and some people don't think we could beat Mexico or Canada." The president responded: "The Speaker's statement is different than it would have been a year ago, and shows how the country has changed." Carter might have said how much he had changed as well.[40]

THE CARTER DOCTRINE

It was time for the annual State of the Union address, on January 23, 1980—the final one of his presidency, as it turned out. Carter had told us while drafting his speech that he wanted to make the speech "a historic document"—so much so that he thought of distributing advance texts to Congress. Fortunately Mondale warned him against circulating advance copies lest the rustling of pages distract from his message. Moreover, the inevitable leaks to the press would dilute the impact of his dramatic announcement. Carter said he did not want to alienate the Soviets, but he said he knew "the world is frightened and I need to send a clear message to them. Alliances are important, but I am willing to stand alone, if needed. I need a strong speech and [to] preach a sermon, so we let the Persian Gulf countries know we'll be there if the Soviets invade, and let the devil take the hindmost." He closed our meeting by asking me for a few pages on the domestic issues, but dramatically added: "The key to the speech is *here is the line we're drawing* [his emphasis], and if they challenge us, then we'll respond." No one could have had reason to doubt his resolve.[41]

The State of the Union address in the vast chamber of the House of Representatives was the perfect forum for a new Jimmy Carter. Because of the twin crises of Iran and Afghanistan, the air hung so heavily with concern and anticipation it could have been cut with a knife. The president did not disappoint. He began by tying together the two events—"one of international terrorism and one of military aggression." The bulk of the address focused on Afghanistan. He reviewed the containment and détente policies of the previous three decades that had led toward mutual restraint by the two superpowers, but then declared that now the "Soviet Union has taken a radical and aggressive new step."

The heart of his case was that the "Soviet invasion of Afghanistan could pose the most serious threat to the peace since the Second World War." He summarized the package of sanctions designed to make Moscow realize that "its decision to use military force in Afghanistan will be costly to every political and economic relationship it values." He also put the invasion in the regional context of the Middle East oil fields and articulated what became known as the Carter Doctrine, which implicitly invoked the NATO commitment of collective defense: "Let our position be absolutely clear: An attempt by an outside force to gain control of the Persian Gulf region will be regarded as an assault on the vital interests of the United States of America, and such an assault will be repelled by any means necessary, including military force." To provide bulk to his commitment, he noted that he had steadily increased military spending during the past three years, and his new five-year defense program would increase it even more. The speech was repeatedly interrupted by applause, often bringing members of Congress to their feet cheering. As we left the House chamber on a high, it would have been hard to foresee that his standing would fall so far, so fast, and that he could be attacked by Ronald Reagan for a weak national security policy—a false image that lingers to this day.[42]

For the United States the Soviet invasion of Afghanistan effectively meant the end of détente. To drive this home, Zbig made a trip to Pakistan to assure them of administration support. At the famous Khyber Pass dividing Pakistan and Afghanistan, he took a Pakistani guard's rifle, pointed it at Afghanistan, with its Soviet troops, and symbolically said: "Let's hunt some bear." To drive home American backing for the anti-Soviet mujahideen, Zbig proclaimed: "God is on your side"[43] Unfortunately, this is also the fervent belief held by the Taliban, which helps explain why even after the Soviet defeat, this has been a war without end.

For the Soviet Union the invasion was also a pivotal event in the Cold War, as well as a major contributing factor to the collapse of the Soviet regime and its empire. The USSR did not withdraw from Afghanistan until 1989, nine years after their invasion. It takes nothing away from the increased support to the mujahideen by the Reagan administration to underscore that Carter began providing nonlethal assistance six months before their invasion, and afterward promptly provided them with Soviet-made weapons to mask their American origin, at a time when they were so desperate that they had to hike across the mountains into Pakistan early in 1979 to buy bullets in the Peshawar bazaar at $2 each.[44] However, that leads to two broad questions about Afghanistan.

The first is whether by arming the mujahideen the Carter and Reagan administrations inadvertently laid the groundwork for today's Taliban in

Afghanistan, which led to direct American military intervention in 2001, and now ranks as our country's longest war.

The reason American troops first went there was to capture or kill Osama bin Laden, who had been given shelter by the Taliban to plan and direct the 9/11 attacks. We now know that many of the rebels who fought off the Soviets later became the Taliban—literally "students," meaning students of the Holy Quran—and incited a civil war that continues down to the Trump administration.

More than anything else, the Taliban's rise to power was aided by the fact that Western powers all but abandoned the people of Afghanistan as soon as the Soviets pulled out. If the United States had staying power to assist in rebuilding the devastated nation, perhaps the vacuum could have been avoided. But the Taliban seized the opportunity provided by political and social turmoil to assume power over significant parts of Afghanistan and remains a major threat to Afghan peace and security.

The second question is whether the threat of the Soviet invasion was exaggerated? Was it indeed the greatest threat to world peace since the end of World War II—as President Carter repeatedly proclaimed in rousing domestic and global support? Or was it simply a onetime intervention to prevent the collapse of an unruly Communist government on the southern border of the Soviet Union? Would the Soviets really have projected their power into the Persian Gulf? We may never be able to say with certainty. But Carter was correct to assume the worst. If they had occupied Afghanistan with no resistance, it would have profoundly undermined America's influence in the region and given Moscow a green light to extend its military power at a time when they were aggressively building up their military forces and acting through their Cuban client state in the Horn of Africa. The USSR was flexing its muscles everywhere. Carter's tough response restrained them.

Much of the speculation over the ultimate Soviet goals arose because the administration could not be certain of the Soviets' motives for invading Afghanistan in the first place. This was the first time Moscow had used military force to *expand* its sphere of influence since its overthrow of the government of Czechoslovakia in 1948. Although Soviet tanks crushed the

Communist reform movement known as the "Prague Spring" in 1968, it brought no effective international censure. The Russians got away with it and were able to establish the so-called Brezhnev Doctrine, which held that once nations were inside the Soviet orbit they could not leave it. Brezhnev, who told Dobrynin "It'll be over in three or four weeks," may have assumed he could escape censure for Afghanistan as he had for Czechoslovakia.

But for many the Soviets' ambitious mission to salvage their interests in Afghanistan pointed to the decline in their global influence. Desperate to hold on to Communist allies in the face of a stronger U.S. and NATO presence abroad, the Soviets severely miscalculated the costs of inserting themselves into a war with Afghanistan. It was later disclosed that their decision to invade Afghanistan had been a product of an inefficient Soviet decision-making process through which the Politburo pressed ahead with questionable decisions opposed by some generals and others, who dared not argue against them even in the privacy of the highest councils of state.[45]

More to the point, Carter's unhesitating actions had a demonstrable effect on Soviet behavior in the future, and from the very start he made clear that was his goal. At a January 9 meeting of the president, vice president, and a number of cabinet officers, Carter asked them to assess the impact of Afghanistan on their agencies. HUD Secretary Moon Landrieu said that people expected the Soviet troops to pull out shortly and our purpose in acting was not clear. Carter hastened to clarify his purpose: "Brezhnev says his troops are in Afghanistan only temporarily. . . . What we have done is to deter further aggression, not with the expectation it would cause them to withdraw. This is a major threat. We need to punish them. I am doing this to avoid military action."[46] Carter could not have known what an explicit effect on the Soviet leadership his firm stance and his package of sanctions would soon have, however hastily and imperfectly drawn up they may have been.

The following year, continuing strikes in the Gdansk shipyards by Lech Wałęsa's Solidarity trade union disrupted Poland's government. On October 18, 1981, the Kremlin ordered the defense minister, General Wojciech Jaruzelski, to take power as prime minister. The general warned the protesters that he was ready to invoke martial law, backing up his warning with a threat to deploy hated Soviet troops as occupiers. But Moscow refused his demand for reinforcements, and the Kremlin was furious at Jaruzelski for making an idle threat. In staying the hand of Soviet power, Yuri Andropov, the head of the KGB and a future head of the Soviet Union, harking back to the Carter sanctions over Afghanistan, told the December 10, 1981, Politburo meeting: "We do not intend to introduce troops into Poland. Even if Poland falls under the control of Solidarity, that is the way it will be. And if the capitalist countries pounce on the Soviet Union, and you know they have already reached agreement *on a variety of economic and political sanctions, that will be very burdensome for us* [emphasis added]. We must be concerned above all with our own country and about the strengthening of the Soviet Union." That was the beginning of the end of the Soviet empire.[47]

Every American president from Harry Truman through George H. W. Bush played a role in the eventual demise of the Soviet Union and the eclipse of its Communist ideology. But Jimmy Carter's has been least appreciated. His human rights campaign exposed the weakest spot in Soviet society and provided a positive contrast for the United States. Cold War archives now underscore that Carter's human rights policy inspired democratic opposition movements in the Communist bloc, from those led by Václav Havel of Czechoslovakia to Lech Wałęsa of Poland.[48] Obviously there are limits to making human rights a centerpiece of foreign policy; they cannot be applied everywhere, nor can realpolitik be totally replaced in dealing with the autocratic and pro-American Sunni Muslim states in the Gulf. But human rights add a moral element that is consistent with American values and remains to this day an important ingredient that was missing in the Nixon-Ford-Kissinger model and that of the Trump administration, as well. When presidents after Jimmy Carter ignored human rights concerns, they opened themselves to criticism for failing to reflect values that are an element of America's attraction and a source of its power.

At one level the relationship between Moscow and Washington that Carter left after four years in office was in tatters. The Carter administration's Soviet policy presented maddening inconsistencies as the president tried to straddle the unbridgeable gap between his two principal foreign-policy advisers, Vance and Brzezinski. But much of this severe deterioration must be blamed on Brezhnev and his sclerotic comrades, who pushed too aggressively too far, even for a president eager for conciliation and peaceful relations.

Some of Carter's actions, prompted by Soviet misconduct, strained relations in the short term but weakened the Soviet Union in the long term. President Carter started to match their military buildup while mutually limiting the number of nuclear-tipped missiles, normalized the relationship with China as a counterweight, and firmly took a hard line after the Afghan invasion. Economic and political sanctions and the Carter Doctrine could only go so far. In the end, however, Jimmy Carter bent the arc of history away from a Soviet power that seemed to be growing without restraint when he took office, but was, by the time he left it, hopelessly bogged down in Afghanistan, the object of opprobrium across the civilized world as a result of his human rights offensive, and no longer dominant thanks to the trajectory of increased U.S. military spending which he began.[49]

PART VII

THE UNRAVELING: RESIGNATIONS AND RESHUFFLING

24

THE "MALAISE" SPEECH

In the space of ten fateful weeks between the president's return from the Tokyo summit early in July 1979 until mid-September that year, the Carter administration appeared to unravel through a dizzying set of events almost unprecedented in peacetime. As the Iranian revolution erupted, oil prices spiked, and lines threaded around gasoline stations across the nation, Jimmy Carter tried to reset his presidency with boldly unorthodox actions. Suddenly and without public explanation, he canceled a national address on energy, withdrew to Camp David, and then exposed himself to unprecedented flagellation by inviting scores of prominent Americans to come to the mountain and help provide new directions for leading the American people. This resulted in the most successful—but also the most controversial—speech of his presidency, dealing with America's "crisis of confidence," soon labeled by the press as his "malaise" speech. This rhetorical diagnosis was never publicly advanced by Carter, nor did the word appear in his speech. It was introduced in a memorandum to the president by his brilliant young pollster, Patrick Caddell. For a long time it remained a mystery how this negative characterization of an upbeat speech circulated so widely. It can now be said that Caddell passed his memorandum containing the term to Elizabeth Drew of *The New Yorker* immediately after the speech, and she mentioned "malaise" for the first time in print. The word was later widely used by the press as a shorthand description and even now continues to stick to Carter.[1]

Whatever the quality of his rhetoric, the president then stepped on his own best lines by firing his entire cabinet and hiring back most of them, to the confusion of the public he sought to rally behind him. Those dismissed from the administration included his energy secretary in the midst of an oil crisis; his Treasury secretary at a time of soaring inflation; his transportation secretary in the midst of gasoline lines and deregulation of transportation; and his secretary of Health, Education, and Welfare, an experienced Washington hand and key link to the liberal wing of the Democratic Party, who was in the process of negotiating crucial parts of the president's health agenda with Congress. He also suffered a near-mutiny by his valued vice president, who fortunately kept his complaints largely private, even from Carter himself, though not from his own senior staff and not from me.

Although it was during this period that he made perhaps the most significant and lasting economic decision of his presidency by appointing Paul Volcker as chairman of the Federal Reserve, Carter blithely said years later that "none of it" was preplanned.[2] When this ghastly period was over, the Gallup poll of September 14 showed his ratings were the lowest of any president in three decades.[3] And Senator Ted Kennedy saw a clear path to deny the renomination of his party's president.

Very little of this came out of thin air. At its center was a 29-year-old data specialist turned political guru and pollster, who was not even a member of the administration. Pat Caddell was not satisfied with providing poll numbers for the president; he saw deeper trends in American society that he impressed upon the president and first lady with ferocity. He sported a heavy black beard with a streak of white that made it appear he had been touched by lightning—and in a sense he had been. He also wore a perpetual frown under a furrowed brow, and his eyes seemed to be lit by embers of coal, so intense was his visage.

Carter first met this boy wonder, whose unfinished college senior thesis was about changes in Southern politics, when McGovern swung through the South in 1972. Caddell, fresh out of Harvard, worked as the polling expert for the McGovern presidential campaign. Carter and his young Georgia political team sat with Caddell at metal counters in the giant kitchen of the governor's mansion talking politics, particularly Southern politics, until 2:00 a.m. Ties were cemented when Carter learned that Caddell's family roots were those of a Southern Catholic from Charleston, South Carolina, who grew up in the North but whose grandfather had fought on the Confederate side in the Civil War.

When Carter announced for the presidency on the theme of healing the country after war, Watergate scandals, political upheavals, and assassinations, Caddell heard a message of both despair and hope that dovetailed with his own belief that among the American people there prevailed a profound sense of alienation from their government. Caddell told me: "I never saw a candidate in my life connected to people like he was. His instincts were just unbelievable, and he got it from campaigning for two years, living in people's homes; he knew the country." When he came aboard the campaign, this young pollster was more than a number cruncher. He joined Ham, Jody, and Rafshoon in successfully urging Carter to avoid emphasizing traditional Democratic programs, and instead to run a populist campaign for a more responsive and trustworthy government that was "as good as the American people."[4]

Abandoning the traditional formula of running to the left to cement the Democratic base in the primaries and then turning to the center for the general election, Carter did the reverse. As Caddell reflected, "we nearly lost the election," as the nontraditional, thematic candidate took on all the barnacled interest groups and established bosses of the traditional Democratic Party going back to Franklin Roosevelt's presidency. Yet, without the support of the groups that turn out the vote, running a campaign based on some abstract sociological theme most likely would have failed.

Carter assembled a unique but internally contradictory coalition, and barely eked out a victory by holding on to almost half of the white Southern vote while overwhelmingly winning the support of Jews, blacks, liberals, union households, and city dwellers. This posed one of the central dilemmas of the Carter presidency that we never fully overcame: governing effectively with the party's dominant liberal wing demanding more spending than the country could afford, while keeping faith with the more conservative principles that contributed to his victory against President Ford. (By 2016 Caddell had moved into the orbit of Donald Trump and served as pollster and sometime adviser to the candidate and his billionaire backers. Steve Bannon, Trump's political guru, likened Caddell to an "Old Testament prophet" for propounding the same message of voter alienation for a quarter of a century.[5] Caddell was one of the few pollsters to predict a Trump victory, drawing on data showing the same popular suspicion of government as in 1976. In that year Carter had run as an outsider against Washington, just as Reagan did in 1980, and Trump in 2016, albeit with very different messages. (Only the actions of the Trump administration will determine whether his political fate validates Caddell's dark vision.)

Caddell did not join Carter's White House staff but continued running his own firm, Cambridge Survey Research, while spending a week or more each month at the White House. So he was unable to plant himself in the policy flow, but he had his eyes on more visionary concepts. In a memorandum just before the inauguration, he explored ways for Carter to maintain his image as an outsider by serving as a "thematic" rather than "programmatic" president, emphasizing "style over substance."[6] These grand ideas were leaked to the *Washington Post*, but that did not deter Caddell from incessantly pressing his case with end runs to both Carters that I and others on the White House Staff learned about only afterward. He was a catalyst of the dramatic events of this brief but seminal period while we were struggling with the business of governing in the real world of Washington and global challenges. "While we would go home to our wives," recalled Rafshoon, "Pat would be on the phone calling Rosalynn, saying: 'It's all falling apart; you know your husband is in danger; they're not listening to him; this is what he has to do.'" Without the hyperbole, but with a touch of reality, Carter would say the next day: " 'I've decided to do the thing that Pat [recommended].' We said, 'But you said yesterday we weren't going to do it.' And he would say, 'Just do it; I don't want to talk about it.' "[7]

THEME AND FOUNDATIONS

Even as Carter compiled a substantial record of accomplishment in office, Caddell puzzled over the president's diminishing support and concluded he had become captive of the same Washington interest groups he had run against. His surveys picked this up when special interests began blocking Carter's legislative initiatives, particularly his comprehensive energy program, and reining in hospital costs, and he summarized them in a memorandum to the president in October of his first year in office. By the end of that year, Caddell's polls were showing a widening gap between the president's high personal popularity and the increasingly negative attitudes toward his performance in office. Caddell and Rafshoon jointly sent the president a letter to accompany a December 1977 poll, saying that the administration was headed for trouble. Caddell even suggested ordering the hundreds of presidential appointees to submit to an essay examination on the question: "What is the vision and purpose of the Carter Administration?" Then in mid-April 1978, Caddell and Rafshoon met at a sandwich shop in Georgetown just before going to see Rosalynn and presenting her with a memorandum for the president reporting further erosion of public support and urging Carter to return to his thematic campaign style.[8]

In response the president called his cabinet and White House staff together at Camp David on April 16–17, 1978, for a stocktaking.[9] Nearly 20 pages of detailed typewritten minutes of the extraordinary session were taken by Carter's personal secretary, Susan Clough.[10] The principal topic was improving the administration's political performance, and Carter was uncharacteristically blunt in his notes summarizing the frank discussions: "We had problems in the White House; leaks; slow in making many decisions; the lack of Washington experience; the cabinet felt they had inadequate access to me. It took too long to fill subcabinet vacancies. Needed to be more clear on our priorities and themes, particularly in presenting them to the press and the Congress. Need to spend more time cultivating public support and to hold down excessive public expectations. Some of the cabinet members don't always support White House policy. They shared their concerns about leaks from within their departments. How slow it was to get Office of Personnel Management and OMB clearance [for appointments and budget decisions]; the need for more budget discipline."

Carter nevertheless regarded the session as constructive.[11] Two positive outcomes were the appointment of Anne Wexler, an experienced political veteran, to handle public outreach, and to bring in Rafshoon as the president's media adviser. He accelerated Carter's out-of-town trips, organized regular press briefings on Saturdays with regional and local press, and arranged more frequent appearances before the White House press corps to take credit for his legislative achievements. To his chagrin, Caddell, who thought he and Rafshoon would be brought onto the White House staff together, was not invited. The meeting also clarified the role of the White House staff in coordinating administration policy among departments, which empowered me to take more control over the domestic-policy process.

Thus the president ended his experiment with cabinet government, which had encouraged too many disparate voices for coherence in government. Genuine cabinet government cannot work as in Europe, where cabinet members are part of the elected parliament. In our presidential system, only the president and vice president are elected; the cabinet members serve at the pleasure of the president; and members of Congress are elected separately with their own local power base. But the underlying problems remained. The president still did not name a chief of staff, and the White House staff was still showing its inexperience.

Caddell's personal ups and downs with Carter meanwhile mirrored the content of his polls and accompanying memos. By late 1978, when the glow of the Camp David Accords wore off, Caddell's poll showed, in his own pungent words: "We were in deep shit [and] were headed for a very, very precipitous decline." But his polls were picking up more than a drop in the president's own popularity: They were showing "an alarming decline in confidence in the country, both in the political system and in people's expectations for the future, never registered before in data that goes back to the 1940s." In a nation literally founded on the future, he saw "more pessimists than optimists, which is unheard of in America." This was accompanied, he said, by people being "much more hostile, much more greedy, much more short-term, and much more volatile."[12]

To create a theme for the 1979 State of the Union address, Rafshoon, speechwriter Bob Rackleff, Caddell, and I titled the address "New Foundations." In a January 22, 1979, memorandum to the White House Staff, Rafshoon explained that this would be a thematic speech about building a "new foundation for America's future." The goal, he wrote, was to "restore the confidence of our people by building a foundation for a balanced, stable economic growth; we must restore trust to the political process by building a new foundation for competent and compassionate government; we must maintain a stable peace in the world by building a new foundation based upon cooperation and diversity." For an administration that had been groping for a unifying theme, this was a good one. Rafshoon admonished us not to retreat from it lest "six months from now people will say, 'Remember that new foundation thing Carter tried? What ever happened to that?' The theme will hold up in the long run *if we stick with it.*" He put those final words in italics.[13] Even one of the administration's toughest press critics, the conservative *New York Times* columnist (and former Nixon speechwriter) William Safire, applauded the theme as "fitting for this President, since the metaphor helps get across the idea of a return to fundamentals" and helped "pull the speech together."[14] More broadly, the press obliged and picked up this theme in its coverage of the address. But the slogan itself never caught on, in part because once the president enunciated this vision of the future, he failed to follow Rafshoon's admonition, and backed away from using it.[15]

In April 1979 Caddell wrote another memo on continuing problems with the electorate, but said: "Carter got mad at me; he wouldn't talk to me for a long time." He eventually got out of the doghouse at the White House dinner celebrating the signing of the Egypt-Israel Peace Treaty. Carter took him over to meet Anwar el-Sadat: "This is my pollster; he's the person who brings me the bad news—but he always tells the truth, and I love him anyway." Then Carter laughed.[16]

Caddell continued getting around the president by going to Rosalynn. He had a two-hour breakfast with her in April 1979, pouring out his heart about how rising American pessimism was dragging down her husband. On Saturday, April 28, the first lady and her reluctant husband met with Caddell in the Oval Office to give him his day in court—and Jimmy Carter began to come under his spell.[17]

Earlier that day Caddell shared his latest memo with me, but perhaps knowing of my suspicions, did not emphasize the psychosocial themes of public alienation but rather the need for cabinet discipline, policy coherence, and someone on the White House staff to make many of the more routine decisions that fell to the president. The last was the easiest and was music to my ears. According to Carter, Ham Jordan had thrice refused the office of chief of staff[18] because he had little interest in specific policies, except insofar as they affected the president's political standing. This time he accepted the job, doffing the work boots and khaki pants that were part of his rebellious anti-Washington streak in favor of a business suit and tie. Also, another Georgia loyalist, White House Counsel Bob Lipshutz, was replaced by superlawyer and Washington wise man Lloyd Cutler. They all did commendable work but still did not solve Carter's deeper problems.

One Sunday evening in late May 1979, Jimmy and Rosalynn Carter were sipping drinks with Caddell and the Georgia Mafia on the Truman Balcony of the White House residence, overlooking our great national monuments. Caddell found the president in a "foul mood about everything, particularly about politics, about Washington, about the elites."[19] By that time the Carters and my Georgia colleagues had accepted Caddell's thesis and begun to discuss implementing his ideas, especially those on confronting the special interests and returning to the anti-Washington themes of the campaign.

When the president gave Caddell's memo to Mondale, he exploded in anger, telling me Caddell was selling a "bunch of crap" taken from books he might have read in college, and dismissing Caddell's analysis as "crazy," a view shared by the vice president's top staff.[20] Caddell nevertheless pursued his prey relentlessly with a stream of articles, books, and notes to advance his arguments.

Mondale's prescription to reverse Carter's decline was to reach out to the Democratic constituency groups, who felt alienated from the president. I had a more prosaic explanation: Gasoline lines were spreading across the country, and rising prices of fuel and other necessities had reached deep into American pockets. Moreover, the trauma of passing his top-priority energy bill, combined with impressions of an overloaded agenda that was passed in an eviscerated form or not at all by his own overwhelmingly Democratic Congress, gave the president a bloody nose. A CBS/*New York Times* poll found that only 30 percent of Americans approved of Carter's presidency, a level reached by no other president, not even Richard Nixon in the midst of Watergate.[21] The first lady called me on June 2 in great agitation to say that "the situation is desperate." She told me, "We need to get a chief of staff," suggesting former Florida governor Reubin Askew, who was set to become the president's trade represenative. And she added bluntly, "We need to get rid of Schlesinger."[22] It was clear to me that Jim's days were numbered.

Just before the president left for the G7 Tokyo summit in 1979, June 12 became an important day. First he met with his full economic and foreign-policy team, the vice president, and me, to prepare his positions for restraining OPEC oil imports and reducing pressures on spot prices. He then had a feisty meeting with his political advisers. He told us he was concerned that we were discouraged, and said: "I am not. We need to have a fighting attitude and be prepared for even worse news." He demanded loyalty from us and our staffs and warned that "they should leave now if they can't take it." Using his favorite phrase about Kennedy, he said, "I don't care if he runs, I will whip his ass." And he now told us he was willing to make Ham White House chief of staff.[23]

That same evening Caddell organized a dinner in the private residence of the White House for the president to meet with some of the scholars Caddell had cited in his memo. For the first time it was decided to broaden the circle of White House staff to feed Caddell's ideas into administration policy. Caddell invited about ten people, mainly sociologists and political scientists, including notable authors such as Daniel Bell of Harvard and Christopher Lasch, who had just written *The Culture of Narcissism*, a widely read book depicting America as a self-indulgent society, a concept Caddell had already sold to President and Mrs. Carter. When the distinguished dinner guests veered toward giving political advice, Jody Powell tartly steered them away: "You know, folks, we know how to get elected; but that isn't what we're interested in talking about."

Bill Moyers, Lyndon Johnson's former press secretary and now a respected presenter on public television, made the deepest impression with his elegy to the loss of community in America. The president wanted Moyers to see Caddell's memoranda over the past eighteen months, and Moyers later called Caddell to tell him: "Never has anybody in the history of the United States ever been as blunt with the President as you have been with him in this series of writings." So Caddell took what he realized was the biggest gamble in his young life to "refocus and redefine the administration back to what it had been, and not just moving a series of programs in the government."[24]

On the way home from the Tokyo Summit, the Carters had scheduled a sentimental and much-needed vacation in Hawaii to relive a few of their happiest days as a young married couple when he was in the Navy. Both Caddell and I independently implored them to come home at once, fearful of the optics of the television news showing them lounging on the beach while Americans waited in lines at the gas pump and truckers blocked the highways because they were unable to obtain fuel. Gasoline prices had risen more than 50 percent in half a year. Caddell told the president to "come back right away or not come back at all." I was less peremptory, but I was as blunt as any time during my four years in the White House; my urgent memo appealed to him to come home and deliver an energy speech.[25]

I wanted him to press for the energy policy recommendations we had spent months developing in grueling interagency meetings I coordinated. But Caddell believed that the American people had tuned out the president, and that yet another nationwide energy speech, his fifth in less than three years, would fall on deaf ears. I was armed to counter this with numbers from the pollster Louis Harris, who told me that only 35 percent of the public felt there was a serious energy shortage, but 70 percent supported our proposal for a windfall profits tax on the oil companies to be used for alternate energy projects in the United States, which would be a centerpiece of our new energy proposal.[26]

My memo recommended that after a short weekend at Camp David, he spend each day working on the energy crisis, caused by the shortfall in crude oil supplies from the Iranian revolution, which had led to panic buying of oil on the spot market. I emphasized that this was severely affecting our relationship with Congress, and that when Mondale briefed members on the Tokyo summit, we learned that they were literally afraid to go home over the recess, for fear of facing angry constituents over the lengthy gasoline lines. "Nothing which has occurred in the administration to date [has] added so much water to our ship. Nothing else has so frustrated, confused, angered the American people—or so targeted their distress at you personally," I wrote. I then made a number of recommendations. I proposed that, upon landing from Japan, he deliver a tough statement we had drafted that would focus on the latest OPEC price increase as a "watershed event," and use it to our advantage to support increased domestic production of all types of energy. We had to finger OPEC as an enemy, I warned, or we would not convince the public that anything had changed.

I suggested a full day of meetings with our energy advisers to ensure that we were all sending the same signals, and then a briefing for congressional leaders so that he would be seen publicly giving almost total attention to major energy problems. He would also announce a National Energy Mobilization Board to streamline the licensing of major energy projects on wartime schedules. To my lasting regret, I did not include Energy Secretary Schlesinger's proposal to end gasoline lines by decontrolling gasoline prices in place of a clumsy government allocation system that prolonged the gasoline lines. But there was no consensus among our own or the outside economists we consulted, many of whom opposed it because it would spike already soaring inflation.

CADDELL'S END RUN

Two startling things happened after I sent this memorandum. The first, which never occurred at any other time during my four years in the White House, was that it was leaked to the *Washington Post*. Several Republicans attacked me for one phrase in a five-page, single-spaced memorandum: "to shift the cause for inflation and energy problems to OPEC"—as if I were avoiding our own contributions to these problems. The memo had extremely restricted circulation among senior White House staff, so I felt denuded and distrustful of my own colleagues and staff. Leaks are an essential part of official Washington life for officials who want to advance policies or simply to show that the leaker is an insider with access; still it was a painful experience to me. I never leaked and held those who did in disdain. I never discovered the source, but I was buoyed by a call from Representative Sid Yates, a Chicago Democrat, who said he thought the memo was "so good, I think it was consciously leaked" by someone in the White House.[27]

The second and more serious concern was that unbeknownst to me, the president, his wife, and the Jordan-Rafshoon-Powell triumvirate had a very different agenda, driven relentlessly by Caddell. The wunderkind had convinced them that the president had a more basic problem than gasoline lines and double-digit inflation: a loss of confidence among the American public in its own personal, as well as the nation's, future, magnified by a sense of Carter losing touch with the broad message that elected him, as he immersed himself in the petty details of governance. Caddell found that for the first time his surveys showed that Americans felt the future would not be better than what they had now.[28]

But if my leaked memorandum was tough and straightforward, Caddell's was incendiary. In an April 23, 1979, memorandum titled "Of Crises and Opportunities," he warned of frightening damage to the nation's values. America, he wrote, was "a nation deep in crisis . . . a crisis of confidence marked by a dwindling faith in the future [and] growing real despair of elites and ordinary citizens alike as they struggle to articulate in concepts the *malaise* [my emphasis] which they themselves feel." Caddell did not blame Carter, but concluded that the extraordinary personal pessimism about the future was the result of historical forces at work for twenty years and "threatens the stability of the country . . . large majorities believe it doesn't matter who is elected." This created a "psychological crisis of the first order." And he had even consulted psychologists![29]

I found this so hyperbolic, so historically reckless, that it passed the imagination. But it became the predicate for everything that would follow. Some of his observations were on target in citing the nation's recent troubles, from Vietnam to the series of assassinations, the rise of single-issue groups, and what he called the special-interest state fueled by "mail, money, and lobbying." He was also correct that Carter's blizzard of legislative initiatives and foreign-policy challenges lacked an overarching theme that could be grasped by the public.

But the balance of this exceptional memo descended into a sort of collective psychoanalysis, ranging widely to cite Lasch's book as well as the British economist Keynes, Harvard professor James Q. Wilson on the impact of lobbies on Congress, and James MacGregor Burns, another formidable political scientist. Burns made a distinction between traditional leadership that achieves results by trade-offs and compromises, and transformational leadership toward "higher levels of motivation and morality." Transformational leadership, Caddell wrote, was what was needed now, "And that is your opportunity, Mr. President . . . a transforming leader, evolving into a great President who leaves an imprint as great as Washington's, Lincoln's, Wilson's, Kennedy's, or Roosevelt's."

Initially Rafshoon and Ham laughed all this off because they found it self-serving as well as impracticable: One suggestion would have had Carter drop in on average families without telling the Secret Service in advance. More "goofy stuff," said Ham, was Caddell's idea of having Carter announce he had left Washington but not tell the press where he was going. Ham told Rafshoon that once Carter spoke directly to Caddell it would be "the end of Pat, because he's really gone too far." They were wrong, because as Ham put it, Caddell was "almost a Rasputin, he was kind of in Carter's head and in Rosalynn's head.[30]

While Caddell was pursuing the president and first lady, I was coordinating the president's nationwide energy speech to deal with the oil crisis, meeting in my office with Ham, Jody, Caddell, and Rick Hertzberg, the president's chief speechwriter. When Ham asked, "Patrick, can't we just tack some of your stuff at the end of the speech?" he reacted furiously: "Like Hell! You can't do that."[31]

The Carter White House was so compartmentalized that no one at the top was aware that Caddell had sent Carter a draft of his own proposed speech and his updated 107-page memo. Nor did Caddell have any idea that the president would follow his lead and cancel the energy speech. When he left my office with Hertzberg, Caddell was in despair, and as they walked across the driveway to the Executive Office Building, Hertzberg said: "My God, you're not talking about an energy speech; you're talking about a revolution." To which Caddell replied: "Yes, you've got it; that's what it's about."[32]

Carter took Caddell's magnum opus with him to Camp David and arose early on Independence Day to read it. The president called it "one of the most brilliant analyses of sociological and political interrelationships I have ever seen. The more I read it along with Rosalynn, the more I became excited."[33] At 9:30 a.m. on July 4 the president called me from Camp David, said he was reading Caddell's memo, and asked me to deliver the final draft of our energy speech by 1:00 p.m. We scrambled and got the speech to him on time, but with no inkling of what would soon happen.[34]

"I'M NOT GOING TO GIVE ANOTHER ENERGY SPEECH"

After Carter reviewed the last draft of the energy speech I sent him, he wanted a conference call with Rafshoon, Jody, and Ham, but Jody was unavailable, buying a watermelon for a July 4 barbecue. Carter spoke to Rafshoon while Hertzberg listened on an extension to hear the president say he did not want to give another energy speech. Hertzberg said Carter was "rather petulant [and] just didn't damn well want to do it."[35] He made it clear that he had made his decision to cancel the nationwide energy speech after reading Caddell's memo and our new draft speech.

Rafshoon told the president: "We'll get together tonight and we'll work on it some more." Carter said: "No, no, it's not the speech, there's no reason to give this." Rafshoon reminded him the speech had already been publicly announced for the next day. Carter replied brusquely: "Well, unschedule it." Rafshoon said, "Well, it's really not that easy." Carter responded: "Just do it." Rafshoon: "Can you give us a reason?" Carter: "Because the president doesn't want to do it." Still Rafshoon felt he needed to give the public a reason for the cancellation. Carter: "I'm not going to give another energy speech." Rafshoon: "Well, what do we tell them? How can we cancel it?" Carter: "Tell them I'm not going to give a speech." Rafshoon beseeched him for a reason: "Mr. President, we've got to say more than that." Carter yet again said: "No, tell them I'm not going to give a speech."[36]

At 4:00 p.m., while Fran, our boys Jay and Brian, and I were at a July 4 barbecue with friends, Rafshoon reached me to relay the president's decision, and said he had been given no reason. I felt as if a firecracker had just exploded in my hands. Rafshoon did have his own reason: Carter's ratings were down, and "if you talk too much about a problem, you get blamed for the problem, unless you have an immediate, bold solution"—and he saw nothing in our speech that offered such a solution. He had even felt skipping

Hawaii was a bad idea, "because the American people really don't give a damn if anybody takes vacations." He added later: "Frankly, the way they felt about Jimmy Carter, they probably figured he could do less harm on the beach; yeah, he can't fuck us anymore! He's in Hawaii."[37]

First I called Mondale, who said, "Carter is very tired and in a funky mood . . . I don't understand him." I then called Ham, Jody, Rafshoon, and Caddell, expressing my opposition to the abrupt cancellation of the speech, saying that no president had ever done so without warning, and arguing that it would look like a panicky, ill-considered decision.[38]

Rafshoon shared my view. As he put it, "Immediately the country thought, My God, he's not making a speech. He must have cracked up."[39] Jody called Caddell and exclaimed: "What the hell have you done?" But the deed was done. Carter later told me he canceled the speech to "dramatize the issue."[40] Carter was betting his presidency on Caddell's unproved thesis of a nationwide crisis of confidence and his grandiose prescription for solving it.

But now what? The Carters together began to improvise. As he put it to me: "From there we began to say, 'Okay, what can we say?' And Rosalynn and I had private discussions and it was mostly my decision, 'Why don't we bring in folks that will let us understand what is going on in this country? Why can't we deal with what I considered to be a genuine threat to the security of our nation effectively? Why don't people listen to my words about the Moral Equivalent of War, even [though] obviously I had the inclination to exaggerate things."[41]

So the president and Rosalynn decided together to invite to Camp David experts from all walks of life to advise him on how to improve his standing with the American people. He also decided that he would give a speech after all, but a very different kind, and after that he wrote in his diary that he "felt a remarkable sense of relief and renewed confidence."[42] He then instructed Caddell to pass his memo and speech draft to the senior staff. Amazingly this was the first time anyone of high rank in the White House had seen it. Caddell's audacity in going around us to the president without serious discussion of such radical ideas was matched only by the president's decision to follow his advice without consulting anyone but his beloved and trusted wife.

Ripples from the episode, some dangerous, were not far off. If Caddell had wanted to create a sense of mystery, he certainly succeeded. The dollar began dropping like a rock, and money fled into the safe haven of gold, driving the price sky-high. Blumenthal tried unsuccessfully for 24 hours to reach the president at Camp David, and then called Vance and me to emphasize the urgent need for a statement to calm the financial markets.[43] I passed this along to the president, but Blumenthal finally reached Carter only through his military aide. He authorized a Treasury statement, but Blumenthal was fed up: "I'm serious, I really have had it; I really want to go." I told him he was too valuable to lose at this critical time, but he soon got his wish anyway.[44]

A *New York Times*–CBS poll the week after the cancellation found Carter's approval rating had sunk to 26 percent,[45] lower than Nixon's during Watergate.[46] Caddell later admitted to being "scared to death, because now I'm responsible for the collapse of the currency. I'm 29 years old, and I have these awful visions that I am now responsible for the collapse of the Western world. I was terrified, just terrified."[47]

When Mondale was finally able to read Caddell's latest memo and draft speech, he asked me to come to his West Wing office. Gone were the serene, understated Norwegian demeanor and the joy in politics that he usually exuded. He was enraged and even vituperative that a 29-year-old wonder kid was peddling what he considered pop-culture Kool-Aid to the president and first lady based on pseudopsychology. Mondale had a commonsense answer to Carter's problems and no hesitation in describing them in plain language. He called the president a "domestic recluse" and told me he needed to get out and talk with people to understand their real concerns.[48]

I agreed with Caddell that the American people were upset and anxious and that Carter needed to reestablish a personal rapport by emphasizing many of the broader themes he had articulated so well during the campaign. But Caddell failed to realize that the president of the United States has no alternative to governing, and that meant plunging into the political muck and making compromises to enact his legislative program, even with the help of special interests.

Mondale refused to swallow Caddell's thesis that the president's precipitous loss of public support was rooted in some mass psychosis. We both believed that the kind of speech Caddell was asking the president to make seemed to point to a loss of confidence by the people, instead of our own failure to address their serious concerns, ranging from their sagging standard of living to long and aggravating gas lines. Mondale was more direct: If we took Caddell's approach and blamed them instead of ourselves, it would be the end of the administration.[49] I thought Mondale was on the mark.

THE ACHILLES' HEEL OF THE ANTI-POLITICIAN

A showdown with Caddell quickly followed and turned into a contentious and debilitating debate on Carter's leadership. On July 5 the president summoned Mondale, Jody, Ham, Rafshoon, Caddell, and me to join him and the First Lady at Camp David for what became the most ferocious, almost violent, meeting in which I participated during the entire administration, or in any administration since. We met around the large conference table where Israel and Egypt negotiated their peace accords. Mondale and I sat next to each other on one side of the table, and across from us sat Caddell, with Rosalynn on his left and Jody, Ham, and Rafshoon on his right, and the president at the head of the table listening intently to the heated debate. By now everyone had bought into many of Caddell's ideas, except Mondale and me. Caddell was nervous, and Rosalynn gently patted him on the knee to calm him down.[50]

The president opened by explaining for the first time why he had canceled the energy speech. With blunt and raw emotion based on Caddell's poll and lengthy analysis, and using some of the language directly from Caddell's memorandum, he said that we were "irrelevant, and the people don't listen to us." He expressed a "sense of despair in the country that is not helped by passing programs." So he canceled the speech, he explained, to create a sense of drama, as Caddell had advised. He had no objection to the quality of our draft speech on energy, "but it is more of the same—just programs." He expressed concern over the direction of the country and exposed for the

first time, at least to me and to Mondale, the nub of a plan: "I am inclined
to stay up here for a while and then analyze where we are." He went around
the table and asked everyone's opinion.

Rafshoon, his longtime media adviser, now played into the Caddell narrative: "You've become part of the Washington system. You were elected to
kick ass and you haven't."[51] I was bemused by this comment, because certainly official Washington did not feel Carter was at all part of their world. He
never attended Georgetown social events, and almost never asked Washington insiders to the White House for a quiet chat or a social engagement. He
had taken on the lions of Congress over their pet programs and disliked the
traditional Washington backslapping and deal making that lubricate the system. Indeed, it seemed to me that he had tried mightily to maintain the kind
of connection with people that had brought him to the White House through
regular town hall meetings, radio call-in programs, and Saturday-morning
meetings with the local and regional press outside the Washington–New
York–Boston corridor. But an effective president cannot hover at 30,000 feet
aboard Air Force One, far above the messy politics of governing.

I saw Carter up close virtually every working day, and I knew that he
had an unusual view of politics—at least for a politician. He felt that after
winning the election, politics was something that a president put aside and
did not take up again until after his third year in office, when he would be
preparing to seek the approval of the voters. In between, in Carter's vision
of the presidency, what mattered was "doing the right thing" and believing
in a just reward upon returning to face the electorate. So when Rafshoon
proposed a practice session for a major speech, Carter "would make [him]
feel [he] was some kind of whore," in Rafshoon's purple prose, and then grudgingly concede: "All right I'll do it for you, if you think that's more important than the other things I've got to do." This led Rafshoon to the point
where he simply no longer suggested these sessions.[52]

Rafshoon later told a story of how Frank Moore finally persuaded the
president to invite two powerful Democratic senators, Lloyd Bentsen of Texas
and Fritz Hollings of South Carolina, for a game of tennis on the White
House court: "Carter comes down to the tennis court, finishes playing, and
says, 'Well, good-bye,' and goes back into the residence, leaving them sitting there, expecting to be invited up for a drink." When Moore raised this

with Carter the next day, he replied: "'You told me to play tennis with them. I played tennis with them.'" After he lost the election, he confided to Rafshoon that he preferred fishing and hunting, and "I guess I'm antisocial."[53] Rafshoon knew he couldn't change those traits, but felt that Caddell's ideas could break the dynamic of his political free fall, and perhaps reset him as the people's president he had aimed to be in campaign mode.

Caddell then piled on, intoning with a fiery gaze that I could imagine on the face of the prophet Jeremiah decrying the misdeeds of his people. This gave Caddell the visage of someone more than twice his young years. As far back as December 1978, even before the gas lines, his polls had picked up massive pessimism among the American people. To him the fact that there was no positive movement after Carter's Middle East successes meant that "something else was out there." Caddell then waxed eloquent about the broader afflictions of the American body politic. I almost felt I was at a séance, not a serious meeting with the leader of the free world. Caddell divined that "when the country had gotten rich it turned away from its core values" of thrift, hard work, family, and a belief in the common good, citing Alexis de Tocqueville, the French observer of democracy in America in the early days of the American Republic. Then he turned to the president and first lady and told them that until six weeks before, he believed Carter would be reelected because he would stand above the other candidates, "but this has changed."

I argued against an overreaction and urged that we place the president's very real accomplishments in a context, so the American people did not see him as panicking. I also expressed concern that with such dramatic action as Caddell proposed, there would be greater expectations we could not fulfill, since there were no easy answers to the problems posed by energy or inflation, and certainly no quick fixes for his dire assessment of the psychological state of the American people.

If I thought I had been blunt, the vice president, unreconciled and angry, turned not only on Caddell but on Carter himself: "Mr. President, we got elected on the ground that we wanted a government as good as the people; now as I hear it, we want to tell them we need a people as good as the government; I don't think that's going to sell. . . . We are blaming the public, and there are plenty of reasons the public is upset." Mondale brushed aside Caddell's apocalyptic explanation of assassinations, Vietnam, and Watergate, and said plainly that people "can't get gas, interest rates are soaring, basic industry is disappearing; people can't follow what's going on anymore. . . . There's plenty of reasons for the American people to want answers, without having their mental stability questioned. If we do that, I think we're goners."[54]

Mondale's critique of Carter's conduct in office came with a directness that I suspect no vice president before or since has ever used to his president: "You're very tired and this is affecting your thinking." He said that part of Carter's problems with Congress and the public was a "style problem; you can't uplift people." And he also saw a problem with leadership. Carter's own sketchy notes show that he listened carefully to his vice president: "(1) Get tough with Cabinet, W[hite] H[ouse], use a whip. (2) Top people not at conventions, etc. (3) People see me so preoccupied with foreign affairs. (4) Don't withdraw, focus on domestic affairs. (5) Must seize energy issue. (6) President needs to speak to constituents: mayors, NAACP, education, labor."[55]

Toward Caddell, Mondale was merciless. He was visibly upset, and his face became so red with anger that I feared for his health. Looking straight across the table at Caddell, Mondale said his memo "was the craziest goddamn thing I've ever read. There is not a psychiatric problem with America, but real problems with coping economically. The worker making $22,000 a year was slipping." He then ripped into the sources of Caddell's analysis—social scientists talking about theory rather than dealing with the harsh realities faced by ordinary people.

He did not believe that the American people were selfish, but that they wanted a better standard of living for themselves and their families and did not see their hard work paying off. Mondale was particularly incensed about Caddell's suggestion of a new Constitutional Convention—the "worst idea I have ever heard"—which was being advanced by conservative Republicans to require a balanced federal budget.

I was glad the conference table was so large, because I truly feared that Mondale might reach over to choke Caddell in his intense anger. Caddell said later of the tongue-lashing: "I didn't even look up, I was so scared."[56]

Rafshoon tried for a middle ground, while seeking to cool tempers with a dose of calm: "Sometimes the best thing is to do nothing," He argued that we had become too obsessed with policy and tied down in legislative details. He stressed, and with good reason, that while we had a very successful legislative record, it had not helped our political standing at all. As one of the architects of Carter's insurgent campaign, Rafshoon underscored that Carter had not been elected as a traditional programmatic liberal Democrat, but as someone who touched voters through identifying with their broader concerns.[57]

Since I toiled on policy problems, that made me uncomfortable, but Rafshoon was essentially correct. In the campaign we had outlined numerous positions on dozens of issues in many different forums, but they had not won Carter the presidency. He won by offering to heal the country's wounds, reform government, assert the common good over private interests, make the American people feel part of their government, and create jobs and growth. Rafshoon rightly pointed out that now, halfway into his presidency, was the time Carter had to show the voters that he had not forgotten why they elected him.

CADDELL'S PRESCRIPTION

As we prepared to break for dinner, Carter told us he had listened to everyone and declared decisively that he was going to accept Caddell's prescription in its entirety: "I've read it, and I'm going to do it all." Again reflecting Caddell's words, he said: "I think the people have given up on us and turned us off, but I think they would have done this regardless of who was president. . . . We have a good energy program, but it will be five years before it shows results."

Turning to Mondale, he said that his presence at various labor and constituency-group conventions was "not as important to me as it is to you," and "I am inclined to stay up here to arouse the interest of the public. I can't turn around public opinion without drama and mystery"—exactly Caddell's prescription.

What he planned to do before the speech, however, was spend as long as a week at Camp David meeting with mayors and governors, civil rights, business and labor leaders, and listening to new economic voices and political Wise Men to explore solutions to domestic problems. Then he would start spending an average of one week a month outside Washington; however, he did not want to make an energy speech that could be delivered by anyone in the administration. This sent my head reeling. How could he avoid addressing energy when gas lines and soaring prices were a major part of his political problem, but instead launch a philosophical discourse about an ill-defined crisis of confidence?

Then, with the righteous fervor that made Jimmy Carter unique among modern politicians, he said: "The country is not bad off materially, but the problem is with spiritual and moral values . . . I am convinced Pat is correct." I retorted that Caddell's draft was too negative about ordinary Americans, when he had campaigned on heading "a government as good as the American people."

I then proposed what ended up as the accepted compromise. As much as I disagreed with the president acting as the nation's psychoanalyst, I proposed that we tone down Pat's rhetoric to make it clear we were not blaming the American people, but that we took responsibility for the state of the country. The speech would end by giving an abbreviated version of the energy policy speech we had prepared, but in the form of what I urged should be a "call to arms," backed up by a detailed energy fact sheet issued the day after the speech to avoid drowning out the main message. I argued that by tackling our energy challenge and taking on OPEC, we could rally the public with a common purpose, directed at something concrete. The president and everyone else agreed. But when we got to specifics, and I mentioned the possibility of decontrolling gasoline prices to end the lines at gas stations, the president said firmly: "I won't decontrol gasoline."[58]

We were all emotionally tight as drums, and Mondale was inconsolable. Even years later the bitterness of the meeting lingered. Mondale recalled that Carter knew he was so disturbed, because rather than turn his back on Mondale after a stream of accusations, he took him for a walk around the compound to help him recover from a very rough session. Mondale later confided that he knew Carter and his staff were angry at him because he thought Caddell's ideas were "slop," and that we should confront real problems people were facing and ask them to help us.[59]

After Mondale's futile walk around Camp David with the president, Rosalynn took Caddell for a drive in a golf cart and told him that the president had intentionally not disclosed before the meeting with us that he was accepting all of Caddell's plan, because Caddell "was going to be in enough hot water with everybody." Instead, she told him, her husband had read Caddell's memo and speech draft and then decided "he would play his own cards now, he was masterminding that himself. . . . He thought it better not to tell anybody. He would just take charge." Caddell confided to Rosalynn during the short ride that it had been a "terrible 36 hours . . . everybody's on me saying, 'You're to blame.'"[60] After dinner at Holly Lodge we all went to the more informal setting of the president's Aspen Lodge, where we stood around with drinks to watch the TV news, which we were part of in real time.

Now the focus shifted from staying at Camp David to making that stay productive. We began what was a heavily political exercise in choosing whom to invite up to the mountain; any important group that was excluded could immediately become a critic or an outright opponent. What began as an effort to solicit advice on righting Carter's administration turned into a circus because of the necessary inclusion of every major interest group. So energy and economic experts, congressional leaders and governors, labor chiefs and business titans, minority and women's group heads, and even religious leaders, with a careful balance between Christians and Jews, all were summoned for advice in an extraordinary event billed as a "Domestic Summit" setting "Goals for America."

Democratic governors were invited for Friday night. On Saturday came the Washington Wise Men: such eminences as Clark Clifford (top Truman aide and secretary of Defense under LBJ), John Gardner (head of the government watchdog group Common Cause), and Sol Linowitz. On Sunday would come the energy experts; on Monday, the economists in the morning, and the civil and human rights leaders in the evening (including Jesse Jackson, head of Operation PUSH, a black advocacy group focused on jobs for minorities). Tuesday would focus on congressional leaders on energy and the economy. Wednesday would be devoted to meetings with labor leaders (including the UAW's Doug Fraser and Lane Kirkland, head of the AFL-CIO) and others to deal with unemployment, and then finally mayors and county officials. On Thursday he would lunch with the cabinet and White House staff. On Friday the president would schedule visits to a few families in rural Maryland around the Camp David area. Saturday was left open to work on the speech he would deliver Sunday night.

THE WASHINGTON WISE MEN WEIGH IN

I doubt any other American president has subjected himself to such intense scrutiny, soul-searching, and criticism as Carter did during that week—and for good reason. The groups started trooping up to Camp David on July 8. The president was dressed informally. Some meetings were held in his Aspen Lodge residence, some around the large Laurel Lodge cabinet table. He took about a hundred pages of detailed notes in his small, clear handwriting.[61]

These sessions were by no means all fluff and theater. Indeed, the pastoral setting afforded an opportunity for leaders in many fields to engage in serious discussions of two to three hours in front of the president of the United States. But Carter got more than he bargained for by inviting outsiders to unload on him. They unanimously criticized the Georgia Mafia as too immature for their jobs and suggested strengthening the White House staff, advice that was largely ignored.[62] The most cogent critiques were cataloged and included at the introduction of the president's speech, and the sharpness of the criticisms was staggering.

Among the most stinging came from Clifford, former top White House aide to President Truman and secretary of Defense to President Johnson. Before meeting Carter, this most fastidious of men, whose demeanor, expensive wardrobe, and wavy silver hair gave him an elegant, even regal bearing, fell off his bicycle while pedaling with John Gardner of Common Cause.[63] Clifford recoiled from the whole scene, later describing it to me "as unusual a weekend as I have ever spent. The president of the United States was sitting on the floor with a big pad of yellow paper, taking notes while people sat around him, five or six of us, and told him what he was doing wrong."

Clifford urged Carter to give a Churchill-style "blood, toil, tears and sweat" speech, and then sharply criticized Carter for his personnel choices—

Jordan was "not the right man" for the job of chief of staff, and neither was Frank Moore at congressional relations. He also posed a series of rhetorical questions straight out of Political Science 101: "Is there a strong hand on the helm? Is the crew loyal? When decisions are made, is the follow-through there?" As for Carter himself, Clifford told the president that to a certain extent he was "still running against Washington [and] had a lack of understanding of what takes place within the Beltway." This was not altogether surprising advice from one of the most influential and highest-paid lawyer-lobbyists in Washington, D.C.[64]

Gardner called Energy Secretary Schlesinger a "dreadful leader, not a manager and not a politician." Linowitz asked rhetorically: "Can Jimmy Carter govern?" He also had no confidence in Schlesinger, none in Blumenthal, until recently, and felt "Califano was in business for himself." Most congressional criticisms were equally withering. The young Missouri Democrat Richard Gephardt, who would later become House Majority Leader, said: "People are cynical, angry, and desperate, and you need to address this; it is time to tell them we're in a war, an economic war."

The unkindest cut came from House Democratic Majority Leader Wright, who angrily told the president to stop blaming the House of Representatives, since its members had already passed his windfall profits tax and a huge bill to underwrite the development of synthetic fuels. But a more reflective comment came from Representative Morris Udall, who had also been Carter's most formidable opponent in the 1976 primaries. "We are paying a price for overreacting to Nixon," Udall said, and the distrust was "creating a paralysis in decision making, when we should give the president the benefit of the doubt."

When the elder statesmen of Congress and some state governors as well as activists arrived, a certain amount of obvious advice and sheer bloviating was to be expected. Governor Hugh Carey of New York told Carter he was "suffering from overexposure." Others talked of an image of indecision and incompetence for both the president and Congress, and that the American people were not ready for sacrifice because they did not believe there was an energy crisis. Jesse Jackson, of course, focused on urban problems and youth unemployment, and urged a "comprehensive urban policy."

One particularly impressive participant was the 32-year-old first-term governor of Arkansas, Bill Clinton, whose criticism was among the most constructive in proposing that a percentage of public-service jobs be tied to energy conservation. Clinton, showing an upbeat approach that would later serve him well in the White House, advised Carter: "Mr. President, don't just preach sacrifice but liberation—and that it is an exciting time to be alive. Say your program will unleash a burst of energy." In his notes for emphasis, Carter put quotation marks around Clinton's remark about the excitement of life.

With all the criticism of the White House staff, House Speaker Tip O'Neill had given me a strong infusion of oxygen by pulling me aside at the previous week's meeting of congressional leaders on energy to say: "We don't have many things going for us, but you're one of them—stick in there."[65] When Tip spoke to the president, it was to emphasize Congress's limits (vividly on display during the energy debate). He pleaded with Carter not to try to seek legislative authority to ration gasoline because of the "parochialism of people in the House." Senator Bentsen proclaimed: "This is one of the most difficult times since the Civil War" and therefore "the time for action." The one piece of good news came from Russell Long, who pledged passage of a windfall profits tax on newly decontrolled crude oil, but then cautioned that synthetic fuels were three times more expensive than the oil and gas produced by his constituents' industries.

The forum with the energy specialists included Schlesinger and his team, with outside experts from industry and academia. Carter opened with Caddell's litany of Watergate and shocks from the 1960s—the country was suffering, as Caddell had put in his memorandum, from an "American malaise . . . American values are crumbling." This seems not to have made much impression on practical oilmen pursuing profits. Thornton Bradshaw, who headed the Atlantic Richfield oil company, focused on the vast underground shale resources Carter wanted to exploit. Jerome Wiesner, president of MIT, estimated that the United States could produce 3 to 4 million barrels of oil per day from shale without polluting any water. James Akins, a former ambassador to Saudi Arabia and an energy expert, said OPEC's goal was to raise crude oil prices to the cost of alternative fuels like synthetics, to gain more revenues for themselves.[66] Senator Moynihan, the irrepressible Democrat from New York and a distinguished sociologist, said in his puckish way: "Your administration is filled with people who don't agree with you." He urged the president to "emphasize in your speech what OPEC has done to us. . . . Mr. President, get mad at them. What they're doing to us is changing our whole system." Carter made an interesting observation: "I was an OPEC man, but in the last six months I have changed, as I feel they are trying to punish the West." The president played an active role, probing for a new path to lead the country on energy. He was so engaged that supper was served at Holly Lodge and the meeting went well into the night.[67] The ineffable Moynihan privately told me: "Stu, you know the problem with your boss? He's conservative on domestic policy and liberal on foreign policy, and he should be the other way around!"

It would be gratifying to report that experts in other fields offered concrete advice that would be of value to a practical political leader, but the Congressional Inflation Working Group of economic and budget leaders joined with our administration team to retrace our steps over well-trodden ground on the trade-off between inflation versus unemployment, and the effect of skyrocketing oil prices on both. That left us more or less where we started. A two-hour session on July 11 with labor, business, and civil rights leaders considered high and persistent unemployment among youth, especially black teenagers, and focused on the need for economic stimulus and employment and training programs. In many ways this session underscored our central economic dilemma: The base of the Democratic Party was demanding action on jobs and jobs programs, while we tried to keep federal spending tight to deal with high inflation. The UAW's Doug Fraser at least acknowledged the inflation problem, stating that as much as he opposed mandatory wage and price controls, they were better for workers than enduring 13 percent inflation. It was a conflict we could never satisfactorily resolve.[68]

Perhaps the most useful advice on how to proceed came from the Hollywood mogul Steve Ross, who maintained that the entertainment industry best understood the mood of the country and reported that people wanted to know "Who are the good guys?" He urged the president to "make clear who the enemy is" (OPEC), and in military terms to urge sacrifice and energy initiatives on the scale of a new Manhattan Project, which built the atomic bomb. We were doing just that with our $80 billion synthetic-fuels program, but none of these peacetime hawks had thought too deeply about how the leader of a democratic nation could act decisively without building a sturdy base of public support.

Carter ended the Camp David retreat with a gesture engaging ordinary people, as Caddell had suggested. He secretly boarded a small Gulfstream jet to meet with blue-collar families, but threw the press off his trail by sending a mock advance team to the declining Pennsylvania coal-mining cities of Scranton and Wilkes-Barre. Meanwhile he arrived at the opposite end of the state. The White House press corps waited in vain for him to arrive in northeast Pennsylvania. What he heard from the families was what Mondale and I had stressed: how hard it was to break even with high inflation, soaring energy prices, gasoline shortages, and a lack of good jobs.

A CRISIS OF CONFIDENCE

Rafshoon and Hertzberg set to work drafting a new speech to catch the attention of the American people at the start, by distilling many of his visitors' most biting critiques. I drafted the energy section, based on the original energy speech we prepared, but now under Rafshoon's instructions to include "tough, specific rhetoric with an emphasis on individual responsibility, and with a series of brief, clear specific directives and proposals, such as 'I will propose,' 'I will direct.'" He allowed me no more than two pages and told me to outline Carter's concrete energy plan and—as Rafshoon suggested—"unleash the unlimited creativity, ingenuity and enterprise of America to find and develop alternative sources of energy." He also warned me I could only use one number, because I always wanted to cite numerous figures. While I objected, I understood his point about being simple and direct to leave a strong impression.

The president called me on July 14 to make detailed comments on the energy section, and said: "We need to be politically bold and challenging" in setting goals for the centerpiece of the new energy plan—a massive federal and private-sector program to develop synthetic energy—even if we were "not 100 percent certain" we could reach the goals. Rafshoon read the speech to me later that day to be certain the energy section was accurate, but offered no opportunity for further comments on the "crisis in confidence" passages drawn from Caddell. In a covering note to Carter, Rafshoon wrote: "We should consider saying that meeting the threat to America requires a successful war on the energy problem, but more because the threat is deeper than energy alone." Carter wrote, "Okay." When Rafshoon told him that he deleted some of the harsh criticisms of society, Carter replied: "Put more harshness back in." Rafshoon suggested adding the phrase, "We are the generation that will win the energy war," and Carter agreed. The draft contained a stirring call I had recommended and to which Carter agreed: "Energy will be the test of our ability to unite, but it will also be the standard around which we will unite. On the battlefield of energy we can rally our nation to a new confidence and we can seize control of our common destiny."[69] All of this tells a story of how presidential speeches are assembled by officials and talented writers, plus in this case, an unusual number of outside experts summoned to Camp David for the occasion.

The stakes were so high that Carter did something he had never done before. He practiced his delivery in a jerry-built Oval Office mockup in the Camp David theater, where (appropriately for him) church services were held on Sundays. Rafshoon also arranged for a speech coach to improve his delivery. Carter's normal cadence had an unusual singsong quality; he somehow managed to emphasize the wrong words in a sentence and accompany them with facial expressions, including a forced smile, that were unsynchronized with his rhetoric.[70]

This time his speech was delivered flawlessly from his desk in the Oval Office with an intensity that matched the occasion. Framed by the American flag and the flag of the president of the United States, he spoke clearly, forcefully, and without even the trace of a smile, looking directly into the television cameras and thus into the homes of millions of Americans.[71] With great nervousness, I joined the senior White House staff and cabinet in watching from the Roosevelt Room, directly across the hallway from the Oval Office.

Carter opened by recalling that when nominated he promised to be a "president who is not isolated from the people, who feels your pain, and who shares your dreams and who draws strength and his wisdom from you." But he conceded that he had increasingly focused on "what the isolated world of Washington thinks or what the government should be doing, and less and less about our nation's hopes, our dreams and our vision of the future." He then explained that he had precipitously canceled his energy speech because it would have been the fifth time he had laid this urgent problem before the nation while sending his recommendations to Congress—and asked: "Why have we not been able to get together as a nation to resolve our serious energy problem?"

This was the lead into Caddell's section, albeit diluted as Mondale and I had urged, so as not to lay the nation's problems at the feet of the people rather than his own. He answered his own question by saying that the "true problems of our nation are much deeper than gasoline lines or energy shortages, deeper than inflation or recession." He needed the help of the American people, and that was why he reached out at Camp David to almost every segment of our society. He summarized some of their harsh criticisms as no president has done before or since, including having lost the message he delivered to the American people in his campaign, and specifically quoted Bill Clinton's advice.

Now came the Caddell line: a nearly invisible but fundamental threat to American democracy, which gave the speech its title: "Crisis of Confidence." What followed was a passage that could have been lifted from Jimmy Carter's Sunday-school classes in Plains and was at bottom a populist sermon to a "nation that was proud of hard work, strong families, close-knit communities and our faith in God, [where] too many of us now tend to worship self-indulgence and consumption [and are] no longer identified by what one does, but by what one owns."

He cited Caddell's polls detailing the rise of pessimism about the future; traced the growing disrespect for government and the institutions of civil society ranging from churches to the news media back to the upheavals of the 1960s and Watergate, and criticized Congress in terms that could be applied to the present day: "Twisted and pulled in every direction by hundreds of well-funded special interests, [with] every extreme position defended to the last breath by one unyielding group or another. You often see a balanced and fair approach that demands a little sacrifice from everyone abandoned like an orphan."

And how should we deal with this profound crisis of confidence? First was to regain "faith in each other, faith in our ability to govern ourselves, and faith in the future of this nation," and then turn to "the path of common purpose and the restoration of American values [and not] narrow interests, ending in chaos and immobility." Next came the bridge I had urged as a compromise: "Energy will be the immediate test of our ability to unite this nation, and it can also be the standard around which we rally. On the battlefield of energy we can win for our nation a new confidence, and we can seize control again of our common destiny."

Then he focused on the enemy—OPEC; that allowed him to segue into the six-point energy program that had been lifted and condensed from our original speech. In a moving peroration, he reached out to his nationwide audience to help him develop and pass a new agenda for the 1980s and to "take our greatest resources—America's people, America's values, and America's confidence. . . . Let your voice be heard to join hands, and to commit ourselves together to a rebirth of the American spirit. Working together with our common faith we cannot fail."

Even the doubters, myself high among them, were ecstatic. To my utter amazement Caddell and Carter had been right about its impact, and not only had I been wrong, so was even Rick Hertzberg, who wrote the speech.[72] When the president walked into the Roosevelt Room afterward we all rose to give him enthusiastic applause. He glowed that night, having come out of a terribly difficult ordeal. While our reaction was essential to unify the administration, it was the public that mattered, and he had swung them back to his side.

In one night Carter's approval rating jumped 17 points as measured by the Gallup poll, the greatest gain ever recorded by a modern president in such a short time, except for a speech seeking a declaration of war. *Newsweek* stayed open beyond its Saturday deadline to cover the Sunday address, then put Carter on the cover with a halo. On television CBS's normally skeptical Roger Mudd approved of the speech wholeheartedly: "A very strong one, very upbeat."[73] David Broder, dean of the capital's political reporters, wrote in the *Washington Post* that "Jimmy Carter got his voice back tonight. He believed what he said."[74]

What was it about this most unusual presidential speech that drew such a positive response? I must admit that partly it was the mystery he created by canceling his energy speech, followed by the unprecedented, lengthy retreat at Camp David to hear critiques of his presidency and recommendations for changing course. Quite aside from Carter's careful preparation for a decisive moment before the American people, the speech on the whole was positive, much more so than Caddell's original hyperbolic draft. Instead Carter optimistically offered a way to overcome the very conditions he diagnosed. The speech touched people—partly because Carter, unusual for a politician and especially a president, criticized his own failings and partly because they thought the president had captured their concerns. Also, the American people still liked Jimmy Carter and wanted him to succeed. Although disappointed in his performance as president thus far, they believed in his honesty, intelligence, and integrity, and they respected his hard work.

This came clear from some of the Caddell material urging common purpose and national confidence, as I accompanied the president on a short follow-up tour. The very next day, July 16, he spoke to an enthusiastic audience at the convention of the National Association of County Officials in Kansas City, Missouri. And then there was an acid test in Detroit, where he made one of his few addresses to a union audience, the Communications Workers of America. Its president, Glenn Watts, was one of the small number of labor leaders enthusiastically for Carter, and so were his members.

In fact some of the Caddell material urging common purpose and national confidence that had been dropped from the televised address was restored in the Detroit speech.[75] As I watched the rapturous reaction of the labor crowd in Cobo Hall, I said to myself that he had recaptured the magic connection with people from the 1976 campaign. Thunderous applause filled the huge auditorium, and the crowd literally sprang to its feet to cheer Carter. He had obviously touched a nerve I had not seen. Caddell had recognized something I had missed.[76]

I was not the only senior White House staff person happily surprised by the positive reaction to the speech. One clear voice that turned Carter on to Caddell's course after initial doubts was no less than that of Ham Jordan, the brilliant architect of Carter's political success. In an eighty-five-page memo to the president written on July 16, the day after the speech, Ham conceded: "There is no question at the outset that I did largely ignore the merit and brilliance of Pat Caddell's memorandum and analysis. Pat had yelled 'wolf' so many times that I discounted his harsh analysis of our situation as well as his unconventional approach to our problems. However, after exposure to his work and time for reflection, there is no question that Pat's original concept was sound and that many of his suggestions were and are valid."

Having just been informed by Carter he would be named chief of staff, Ham went on to advise his boss to shift his approach to the presidency and become a "leader of society." He wrote: "You have agreed to lead the country instead of manage the government [and to have] greater discipline and accountability in the White House." And then he laid the groundwork for what followed, by advising Carter that "the Cabinet changes are the litmus test."[77]

25

RESIGNATIONS AND RESHUFFLING

As fast as the public turned in the president's favor, the tide turned just as quickly the other way, through his own unforced error. Ham had always been far more interested in imposing White House discipline on the cabinet than in Caddell's high-flown themes. Now was his moment, setting in motion what had not been part of Caddell's playbook. Ham felt that the president needed to fire some of his cabinet to show he was in control of his administration, and like a distant cloud, the threat had hung over the entire episode. As the first lady recalled: "Hamilton kept on saying, 'If you don't fire somebody, people are not going to think you're doing anything about this meeting that you've had, calling up all these people up here [to Camp David]. You've got to get rid of them and you've got to fire them.'"[1] Their prime candidates continued to be Califano, Blumenthal, and Schlesinger. In fact it was Rosalynn in her quiet voice who had sent the first and toughest message during the Camp David deliberations: "You should fire people who are disloyal or no good."[2]

It was no secret that she was thinking of Califano, who had his own powerful liberal connections in Washington and was fighting Carter's plan to divest his agency of education, and make it a separate cabinet department. In my notes of that July 5 exchange, I observed that the "president was *very* subdued."[3] He disliked personal confrontations and was clearly upset by the prospect of firing several members of his cabinet, although one person did get the chop immediately. Carter kicked Caddell out of Camp David as a disruptive presence and refused to talk to him for several days, even though he had been a key architect of the president's successful speech.[4]

Originally the president was strongly opposed to a cabinet reshuffle,[5] when

Ham and Jody raised it during the battle over the speech. But he eventually felt it would show "vigor" if he followed his address with a cabinet shake-up.[6] Now would begin what Jody later called a "bad idea" that "was the final act of the drama" and "turned a lot of people against the whole thing."[7] The president literally stepped on his winning lines.

On July 17 the president unexpectedly joined our early-morning White House senior staff meeting in the Roosevelt Room, which turned out to be one of the most shocking in my four years in the administration. Gone was the triumphant, indeed magnanimous, mood of the week's speeches. He was uncharacteristically blunt, even brutal, as he looked around sternly and said: "We have defects that need to be resolved. I have had time to contemplate these and gotten a lot of advice at Camp David. I heard about the need for a complete reassessment of how we function. I also heard a lot of criticism of the White House staff: that we lack cohesion, that there is too much frag-mentation, that there is excessive sniping at the cabinet. There was also a serious mention of the cabinet."

He repeated to us a specific Camp David critique of himself: that he was too deeply involved in the mechanics of government and in legislation and should spend more time outside Washington. He then announced that he was appointing Ham as chief of staff "with extraordinary power over you and the persons who work under you to coordinate. Ham will not be a peer of yours as before. You will carry out Ham's orders, and if he believes some-one should be replaced he'll talk with you; and if he says you're gone or your assistants are gone then you are."

In all the years I had worked closely with him, I had never heard such a sharp tone. He also said he would make some cabinet changes, but that he had not decided how many. He added that "some are not loyal or effective, and some are damaged, as they have dealt with difficult issues." It was not hard to guess whom he had in mind, and Carter then asked us to give Ham our assessments of the cabinet, just as he would be asking the members of the cabinet to give him their assessments of the White House staff. He hoped to finish this within a week or so.

He then dropped a bombshell: "I may ask all of the cabinet for pro forma resignations," adding that some might be put on probation and fired later if they did not change their conduct. With only eighteen months left in his term of office, Carter recognized that he was constrained by how deeply he could change his administration, but he wanted us on the staff to apply the same rigorous judgment to the work of our subordinates and to "do it quickly."

I was stunned by the threat of a mass cabinet resignation, and I was not the only staff member concerned. To my everlasting regret I did not question Carter, but after he made this startling announcement, he was gone in a flash, with no opportunity for comment. It was not clear how seriously he was considering such a dramatic action. If he wanted to fire a few people, he ought to do so without sowing confusion and doubt about those who remained. When the president left, I whispered to Anne Wexler that foreigners familiar with their own parliamentary system would think the whole government had fallen.

Ham took over without entertaining any questions or comments. "We've had democracy, now we need organization," he declared. He was also frank in saying that the president himself would have to make drastic changes in his own style of governance, but the key would be to protect the president from becoming bogged down in the details of governing. "Let us decide within the White House the disputes between agencies"—and make as many decisions as possible without involving Carter himself. "I will talk for the president to the cabinet."

Then he threw an air of uncertainty into all of us by announcing that personnel changes would soon be made within the White House itself. He handed out forms for us to evaluate all the people reporting to us, and asked us to return them by the end of the week, to "weed out disloyal or incompetent people." The next three or four weeks, he said, would be "difficult and wrenching," and the president would "be a different person than you knew in the past . . . the head of the country" and not just a manager.

All this was a remarkable change for a Carter team that had run against Nixon's centralization of power through his chief of staff, H. R. Haldeman. But it only convinced me that the problem was not the structure of the Nixon White House, but the lack of honesty and integrity among Haldeman, Ehrlichman, and their henchmen.

We certainly needed to avoid having the president immersed in too much detail, but I spoke up and said he needed "to be both the head of government and the head of the country," because that was what it meant to be president. To assert greater control, Ham said he now would also join each week's foreign-policy breakfast and the economic breakfasts (I have no record that he ever attended any), and any other meetings on issues of importance at the time.[8]

Like an avenging angel, Carter moved almost immediately down the hall to the fateful cabinet meeting at 10:30 a.m. Ham, uncharacteristically dressed in a blue suit, shirt, and tie, was the only non-cabinet member present, except for the president himself. Blumenthal has the most detailed account, based on his own notes. Carter explained that he used his long absence at Camp David to review the status of his administration and make a new start that would involve changes in the cabinet, some of whom had been "disloyal . . . [and] not following the administration line." He assured them that he would also take firm action against eight or ten on the White House staff, "whether from Georgia or not." He informed them of Ham's new job as chief of staff and his authority: All cabinet officers would report through him, and all decisions were to be cleared through his office.

About 25 minutes into Carter's talk on the challenges facing the nation, he threw out the hot potato of mass resignations. There is disagreement on exactly what happened next. Carter remembers Attorney General Bell recommending that all cabinet members should submit resignations, so the president could choose those who should leave. But Bell told me Vance offered everyone's resignations, "as if orchestrated," and he was "surprised."[9] Jody believed that the president had primed Vance to make the suggestion before the meeting,[10] and Ham recollected Vance saying: "Maybe we should offer our resignations, so you'll be in the posture of just accepting some resignations, like you're just starting all over again."[11]

But Vance later told me firmly he had no advance warning and that "it came as a surprise, as far as I know, to everybody in the room." Indeed, Vance noted that a president in effect always had everyone's resignation in hand, and by asking his entire cabinet to do this at once, "people are going to think the government is falling apart." He warned: "Don't make a big thing of it, because it is going to be taken all out of proportion."[12]

Blumenthal also recalled that Vance spoke first, telling the president that everyone served at his pleasure; that he did not need to ask everyone to re-sign formally; that the mass resignation was not a good idea; and that he should simply ask for the individual resignations of those cabinet members he wished to depart.[13]

What is clear is that the silence was stunning. The president ignored Vance's advice, asked each one for written letters of resignation, and left the Cabinet Room. Ham handed out questionnaires for cabinet members to grade the effectiveness of their staff, after which the meeting—unlike any other in American history—ended.

Califano remembered that as he, Vance, and Blumenthal left the Cabi-net Room after they had submitted their resignations, he turned to Blumen-thal and said: "Mike, you should call the president and tell him that all hell's going to break loose." Blumenthal laughed and said he was "the last guy to do it," and Califano added, "I certainly was not the guy to do it." Joe cer-tainly called that one right.[14]

Later that same day I met with the president, Ham, and Jody. The pres-ident told me Schlesinger would resign, to be replaced by deputy secretary of Defense, Charles Duncan. He also said he was "inclined" to fire Cali-fano and Blumenthal, which I did not take as a final word.[15]

The next four days were, simply put, like being in hell. I felt everything was unraveling. All the goodwill built up by the retreat to Camp David and the president's speech seemed to be thrown away in a sophomoric effort to look tough. So, instead of a clean break with the past, the process was as messy as the back room of a neighborhood butcher.

The next day I raised the issue of the firings in a small meeting with the president, Ham, and Jody in the Oval Office. I worked closely with and admired Schlesinger but realized he had clearly become a political liability in fighting the energy wars. But I argued strenuously that Carter should keep Califano and Blumenthal. Yes, Joe had his own agenda on issues like our proposal to hive off a separate Department of Education, but he was highly competent, as well as a symbol of reassurance to the liberal wing of the party. He was also in the midst of negotiating a national health care proposal with Senator Kennedy, along with me. I warned that if he was fired, "he'll cut you up with his Washington connections." The president responded, "I am being cut up anyway."[16] Califano was a marked man and had made two enemies that neither Mondale, his original champion, nor I could overcome. One was Rosalynn, who felt he was unhelpful on her mental health initiative and was hurting the president in North Carolina with his antismoking campaign.[17] The other was Ham, who regarded Califano as disloyal and ineffective, despite his cherubic smile and broad Washington ties.

Blumenthal was a harder case for Carter, but especially for me. I told Carter that no one worked more closely with him on a daily and even hourly basis, than I; that he was seen by the financial and business community as a symbol of anti-inflationary rectitude at a time of soaring inflation; and that his dismissal would upset the financial markets. I knew he did not suffer fools gladly, and was not the best consensus builder, but he had earned the respect of our senior economic officials. He had certainly hurt himself with persistent leaks from his press office throughout his tenure. As a childhood refugee from Germany, he had a native fear of runaway inflation and saw the threat in the United States before I and many others did. But he was also targeted by my Georgia colleagues, who wrongly held him responsible for Bert Lance's resignation, because the damaging report on Lance's banking practices came out of the office of the Treasury's quasi-independent comptroller of the currency.

In accepting his resignation, Carter summoned him, spent ten minutes praising his work at Treasury, and blamed friction with some of the White House staff. He concluded by wishing Blumenthal good luck in the future, and asked: "Can I count on your future advice? Will you be sure to come and see me when you're in town." Blumenthal's last words were: "Anytime. I'll come whenever you call." That call never came.[18]

And finally, Transportation Secretary Brock Adams walked out on his own. He disagreed on some presidential policies—airline deregulation and automobile mileage standards—but he had also brought in his own people to run the department. When Ham told him that from now on his deputy, like all others in the cabinet, had to be a White House appointee, Adams retorted: "Ham, for Christ's sake, that's what Nixon did; that's a terrible idea. [Nixon aide Egil] Bud Crowe was indicted for it." When Carter asked him to stay, Adams nevertheless insisted on his own deputy or he would tender his resignation. Carter sighed: "I guess I will have to accept it." Adams said: "Well, that's fine."[19] Actually it wasn't. Tip O'Neill called to complain, and he was not the only Democratic congressman to come to the defense of Adams, a former representative from Washington State.

I had argued with the president that the problem was not the cabinet but the White House staff, as the Washington Wise Men had advised him at Camp David, and that if he wanted to shake things up, he should start with his own staff, "every last one of us." But the White House staff stayed essentially intact. The wrong heads rolled.

In her report the night of the cabinet firings, Lesley Stahl of CBS-TV called them a "slaughterhouse, a purge" that took the glow off Carter's speech in just a few short days.[20] When the shock waves rolled over the White House, there was no lack of finger-pointing. Attorney General Bell, the most conservative member of the cabinet, was ready to resign and return to Atlanta anyway, and was angry that this made it look as if he had been fired, and blamed Vance.[21]

Ham years later simply called the mass resignations a "bad idea."[22] Rafshoon said: "It was really a case of everybody being tired and panicked, and I think the biggest panicker was Caddell, and he had Rosalynn's ear."[23] Rosalynn knew that Bell and Schlesinger were ready to leave, and she was gunning for Califano, but she nevertheless pleaded not guilty: "I think Hamilton was the one who argued that three people—it wouldn't do for one, and it wouldn't do for two . . . it has to be three to go or people wouldn't think there was a change." She added: "I was always skeptical about it."[24]

Caddell said it wasn't him; he feared the firings would divert attention from the message of the speech. He claimed it was Ham, exuberant at the success of the speech, and as usual saw events through his own eyes: Caddell lamented that the firings "devastated" his plan to reposition the president.[25] He certainly shook off any responsibility when his own grandiose term "malaise" made its way into the political vernacular via the media, even though it was never a part of Carter's speech.

If Carter had limited his cabinet changes to a few select members, he would have been seen as acting decisively following his spectacular rise in the polls. But what should have been a targeted effort to reorganize turned into a disastrous overreach, and everyone including Carter belatedly realized it. It certainly suited Carter's temperament, but he later admitted to me ruefully that "it looked like an easy thing for me to do, but I didn't realize that it was just going to be looked upon as a whole cabinet resigning. I was just not as wise as I should have been."[26]

Next came the drive to impose discipline on the subcabinet appointees, the key officials in charge of the daily operations and much of the policy of their departments. Carter summoned some three hundred to the East Room of the White House. By the account of Assistant Secretary of Commerce for Industry and Trade Frank Weil, the president took off his jacket, neatly folded it, and placed it on the floor. Then using Ham's script, he began: "I really have only one thing to say: 'You guys are on my team, but too many of you act as if you're on someone else's team. If you don't like what I'm doing, you can get out. So from now on, you either do it my way or you leave. Any questions?' "

After polite comments from a couple of subcabinet officials, an unidentified voice came from the far corner of the large room: "Mr. President, with all due respect, I don't think you understand the problem." This anonymous official then complained that he and his colleagues work tirelessly on issues, their recommendations are forwarded to the White House, and "then decisions are made that, with all due respect, sir, we don't understand and we don't agree with. We go on struggling because we want to help your administration do things right. And if we ever had a chance to talk with you, we might be able to help get things straightened out, with all due respect, sir." He closed by saying: "For example, Mr. President, this is the first time I've ever been in the same room with you."

As the room fell silent, the president said, "That's impossible. You're my subcabinet. How many people in this room have never been in the same room with me?" Weil recalled that more than half raised their hand.[27] In fact I found that the overwhelming percentage of subcabinet officers, with whom I regularly interacted more than any of Carter's closest advisers, were loyal to the president and his agenda, and worked backbreaking hours to promote them. Fortunately, few beyond the dismissed cabinet members' closest aides departed in the bloodletting, along with their bosses.

Who planted the seed of this drama, and how did it grow into such a calamitous farce? Ham certainly was a major player. But according to his own admission, it was also Rafshoon, of all people, the media maven whose judgment was normally so sound about how the public would view the president's actions and policies. He told me later: "You know Carter will never fire anybody unless he fires everybody. Maybe he should just fire them all and take back the ones he wants to keep. That caught on."[28] He added in another candid moment that "I was that fool who came up with that idea. . . . We didn't realize the impact it would have publicly, and we didn't realize how well the public would receive the speech. We stepped on that news by having the cabinet firings on Tuesday. We wiped it all out. And I regret it."[29]

Quite aside from the uncertainty throughout the administration, Vance and I feared that the mass resignation of a cabinet would be thoroughly misunderstood by foreign leaders. Their own optic was not conditioned by the way the U.S. Constitution separated the legislative from the executive power. In Britain mass resignation is very rare and signals a fundamental change of policy or leadership, as it did when Winston Churchill was named prime minister in the dark wartime days of 1940. In most European nations, governments generally are composed of several parties in coalition, and a mass cabinet resignation would signal the withdrawal of one or several parties, bring down the government, and most likely lead to new elections or a restructured coalition.

In less than a week the rave reception given to the speech began to recede. Quite apart from the collapsing poll numbers, it was possible to watch the tide going out right in the mailroom of the White House, where some of the veterans of this thankless job had worked since the administration of Franklin Roosevelt. One of the women who had been there for decades said that never in their employment there had they seen such an immediate flood of positive mail after a speech—some 30,000 letters in the space of a few days. Normally there was a steady stream of letters or postcards of a paragraph or two (there was no e-mail in those days). Now they reported with great excitement how letters to the president were running five, six, even ten pages long, with the writers telling him how moved they were by his address. Caddell visited the mailroom and took a random sample of about one hundred letters to share with the president and Rosalynn. Many wrote that they had given up on Carter's government, and now they believed in it again. But then the supervisor of the mailroom, with sadness in her voice, told Caddell: "Then he fired the cabinet, and he killed the mail."[30]

MONDALE SERIOUSLY CONSIDERS QUITTING

Although no one outside his immediate staff knew it except me, one of the victims was almost Walter Mondale. He was so disillusioned by the White House antics that he seriously considered falling on his sword and resigning. Normally the vice president was an active and canny politician, more liberal in outlook than Carter. Even for someone of stolid Norwegian heritage, he had a wonderfully understated sense of humor. Often when I came to his office, he would put up his feet on his desk, pull out a cigar (which I never saw him smoke), and schmooze. He once imparted his clever personal secret for returning phone calls that he had to answer but did not want to: He would phone back during lunch hour, usually finding the original caller out of the office, whereupon he would check off the call as dutifully returned, without actually talking to someone he did not want to engage. At Camp David he had no such means of escape. The president tried in vain at Camp David to dissuade him from his warning against Caddell. "What a bizarre guy, my God!" Mondale told his chief of staff, Dick Moe, about Caddell.

Mondale fled the parade of dignitaries to Camp David, leaving Moe to sit in as his proxy and telling him: "I'm not going back there." Clearly Moe was the odd man out. At one point he walked into a staff discussion with Ham, Jody, and Rafshoon about seeking a number of cabinet resignations and remarked that that might look like a "Nixon-type thing." The Carter staffers quickly changed the subject. The entire episode put a temporary strain on what had been a remarkably harmonious relationship between the reflective Moe and the newly empowered Jordan, and at one point they descended into a shouting match.[31] The shake-up represented one of the few occasions that Mondale and his staff had been cut out of a key decision, a violation of his arrangement with Carter that had been honored until then and continued to be for the rest of the administration.

Mondale was not totally blind to what was going on; he knew Califano was in danger and advised Carter that his liberal protégé should be disciplined for insubordination, but not fired. Carter replied: "Well, then, maybe that's the way I'll handle it."[32] It certainly was not. I believe what really enraged Mondale was being frozen out of the broader decision to ask the entire cabinet to submit resignations.

After Carter's nationwide speech, Mondale left Washington to travel the country making speeches to drum up public support for SALT II. He was in Memphis when I phoned to alert him that the president had asked for the resignation of the cabinet en masse, Califano included. He moved on to Nashville and was being interviewed by John Siegenthaler, editor of the *Nashville Tennessean*, when the phone rang. It was Califano, he recalled, "telling me that he had just been fired and that all hell was breaking loose." This was how the vice president of the United States found out about the cabinet firings. For Mondale, it was the last straw: "The bottom line is it looked like a mass execution. It looked like a total pandemonium." And when he arrived in Philadelphia, that is exactly what it was. Mondale recalled he faced "a screaming bunch of reporters who were going to kill me, and we just went from sugar to shit overnight. If we had just held steady, I think we might have pulled it around."[33]

When Mondale returned to Washington, he called me at home at 10:00 p.m. to express his distress. He confided that he was so discouraged by Carter's acceptance of Caddell's ideas at Camp David that he almost walked out, and he said he certainly could not defend the cabinet firings. He felt that Carter's closest advisers were not "plugged into America and its institutions." He was also hurt by Carter's private jabs at him for speaking before labor and other national constituency groups, in the belief that a president "could somehow talk over these groups to reach the general public—when you can't," as Mondale told me.[34]

Mondale asked me to join him for lunch at his favorite Chinese restaurant, the Moon Palace on Wisconsin Avenue, not far from his official residence. He said he could always get a table there, and when I sampled the awful food I understood why. Once again he poured out his heart about the clumsiness of the mass firings and what he saw as the vindictiveness of the inbred staff that surrounded Carter. But he went a serious step further and ended what little appetite I had left by telling me he was seriously considering resigning. The vice president had lost confidence in the president's decision-making ability. It grated that the president had rejected his own political advice in favor of Caddell, whom Mondale considered a young neophyte making an amateur analysis of the nation's psyche by studying himself in the mirror.

He said that there was no question "we were dead in the ditch; we were in terrible shape; something had to be done," and even the candid advice from outsiders at Camp David "was time well spent." But the cabinet firings made him ready to throw in the towel: "My job in the administration had been to keep the progressive side of the party working with us, to avoid a big split; and I could see that falling apart."[35]

If I had believed that his only disagreement with the president had been over following Caddell's line, I would have been less worried. But I had seen over the years an underlying fault line between Mondale's political philosophy and Carter's, which the most recent events had brought to a boil. Mondale was a traditional liberal, responsive to the major interest groups in the Democratic Party—labor, big-city mayors, farm groups, minority leaders, and the Jewish community. He was chosen as Carter's running mate in significant part because of his support by those traditional liberal pillars of the national Democratic Party, balancing Jimmy Carter's weakness with those groups, as a candidate from the South, with no comparable political underpinning. This was bound to create policy differences throughout the administration, with Mondale pressing for traditional Democratic social programs and Carter wary of increases in federal spending.

Indeed, Carter's top campaign staff felt that one reason his exaggerated 30-point lead over Ford almost totally evaporated was that after he became the Democratic Party's nominee he was seen as a more traditional Democrat and lost his sense of freshness. The irony of his razor-thin victory over Ford was that everyone had a claim to it. While Carter could not have won by ignoring the Democratic Party machinery that turned out the vote in the Northeast and industrial Midwest, he could not also have swept every state in the Old Confederacy, except Virginia, if the voters there had simply seen him as another Hubert Humphrey.

Mondale understood this, worked within Carter's ideological framework, and served as the front man facing the increasingly hostile Democratic barons. Precisely because Mondale was not relegated to the sidelines like his predecessors, he weighed-in to keep a modicum of peace with the liberal wing of the party, one reason he had been selected in the first place, by championing more spending for popular and effective social programs like Head Start, higher education, and job training.

I was stunned that Mondale was contemplating a resignation and told him that while I shared his concern about the cabinet firing, he could not simply walk away. He had been elected by the American people, and did not have a cabinet officer's luxury of resigning over a policy issue. There was no constitutional precedent for a resignation, and it would have brought down the administration and, of course, ended his own political career. I emphasized that he must have known there would be decisions with which he would disagree when he accepted the nomination. This might be an extreme event, but he still had an obligation to support the president even though he had not been consulted. I said that together they had created the most powerful vice presidency in American history, and if he resigned, that would be the end of their accomplishment. He listened, but I was not certain if I made any headway.

I believed then, and I believe to this day, that Walter Mondale would never have pulled the trigger, and that he was merely venting his deep frustration. He confirmed this years later, saying he was "never going to quit Carter" and simply needed somebody to "blow smoke off of."[36] But at the time I could not be certain, nor could some of his closest aides. At the very least it showed the depth of his disillusionment, of which the president and his senior political staff were unaware—and might be even now.

Mondale told a few top aides that he was so "depressed he might quit," and this was confirmed to me in talks with his senior staff—Dick Moe, his chief of staff; Michael Berman, his legal counsel;[37] and Jim Johnson, his executive assistant, who spent more time with Mondale day and night than any other staff member.[38] During that blue period Mondale would go home about four o'clock, change clothes, sit in the garden, return phone calls, and play tennis. Often it was just the two of them, Mondale and Johnson, and Jim remembered Mondale going "back and forth around the question of resignation versus not standing for reelection." Berman had begun looking at legal options for resignation. But his most trusted aide, Dick Moe, told Mondale several times the whole idea was ridiculous.[39] Nevertheless, said Johnson, it "was the musing of a man who felt deep distress about the situation he found himself in, with little influence over a ship that seemed to be rudderless."

What finally got Mondale out of his deep funk? Johnson felt it was the likelihood of Ted Kennedy running against Carter for the Democratic nomination. The Caddell cycle had ended, and with the Kennedy challenge looming, Jim Johnson told me that Mondale felt a strong sense of loyalty to Carter and knew his resignation would be an unjustified gift to the Republicans.[40]

CARTER FINALLY REFOCUSES

The bookends to these extraordinary weeks came in two meetings. At an Oval Office staff meeting on August 3, Carter made a comment that spoke volumes about his approach to the presidency, his disdain for public exposure, and his ambivalence about presidential politics.[41] Jody Powell asked him to allow *Time* to do a photo essay of a day in the life of the president, which would mean allowing a *Time* photographer to "hang around with you all week." Then Frank Moore tried to persuade him to meet regularly with three to six senators at the White House. The president got visibly angry and told us "it would take too much time." Three days later he had softened, but only barely. At a meeting of the cabinet and senior staff, he told everyone that "Frank wants me to see three or so senators regularly, and it sends chills down my spine to spend 30 hours of my time that way—but I'll do it."[42]

At the second meeting, which took place in the Blue Room, the appropriate color for this jarring period, Carter spoke with remarkable candor and introspection: "I went to Camp David with deep concerns about myself, my administration, and the country. I felt we were at a historic turning point with a lack of confidence in the future." But he said that all those who gave him advice there "felt the press distorted facts [and] treat me as they do other institutions—they trivialize." Carter felt that he had enumerated the nation's problems well in the past and "had good solutions and a good batting average with Congress." But, he admitted, "I haven't been adequate in some areas and kept away from the people. Whenever we made decisions and worked together, we've prevailed." He told us that the reason for the cabinet changes was that "we need to be united when decisions are made. I do not want subservience, but once I make decisions we need teamwork and this needs to be evident to the public. We have sent mixed signals, which has hurt with the Congress."[43]

This series of totally unplanned and unscripted adventures over several weeks were more than a typical midcourse correction. Faced with the political gallows, the president was forced to change, and he did for the better. He appointed Ham as chief of staff, limited his focus to a few priorities such as energy and SALT II, reduced the mass of his reading material to spend more time on the road connecting with the heartland, and cut the number of Washington news conferences to meet more often with regional and local press.

STUDIO 54

Soon an ominous event occurred that diverted Ham's attention just as he was getting into his new job as chief of staff. While the president and first lady were going down the Mississippi River aboard the *Delta Queen* on a much-derided meet-the-people cruise, the new attorney general, Benjamin Civiletti, called with the stunning news that he had been required to order a preliminary FBI investigation of allegations that Ham had snorted cocaine at Studio 54, the celebrity disco in Manhattan. Jody was also being investigated, even though he had not even stepped inside the infamous drug-laced club. Ham admitted he had been at Studio 54 for about an hour, but strenuously (and accurately) denied using cocaine.[44]

Unfortunately Ham had become too easy a target, with his informal dress habits and an undeserved reputation as a fun-loving, party-going young man—when in fact he worked the same ridiculously long hours we all did at the White House.

The baseless cocaine charges, brought by dubious individuals, occupied months of his time, just as he was organizing his work as chief of staff. By his own admission Ham made a great mistake even entering Studio 54 while serving as chief of staff to the president of the United States.[45] He was unaware that the club's two owners were being investigated for tax evasion, obstruction of justice, and conspiracy. One of them, Steven Rubell, had hired as his lawyer the notorious Roy Cohn, former counsel and hatchet man for Senator Joseph McCarthy during his infamous anti-Communist hearings (he would also be the lawyer who introduced Donald J. Trump to politics in New York City).

Ham declared that Rubell and Cohn, along with Ian Schrager, Rubell's nightclub partner, dreamed up the drug story. Cohn took it to the Justice Department to try to plea-bargain away the indictment on tax evasion, armed with a taped statement from a drug dealer who claimed he had provided cocaine to Jordan, and said Rubell would testify against both Ham and Jody in exchange for immunity, a clear effort to frame Jordan and save his client. There were a number of twists of fate. The National Cancer Institute doctor who treated Jordan's cancer years later was also treating Roy Cohn for AIDS. Rubell and Schrager each served 13 months in prison, the former dying in 1989 and the latter eventually winning a pardon from President Obama.

Ham was the first person ever investigated under the 1977 Ethics Act that Carter championed as part of our post-Watergate reforms. Congress passed it with such a hair trigger to start an investigation that almost any allegation against a senior government official required the appointment of an independent counsel, with no provision for reimbursement of expenses.[46] The investigation proved the allegations baseless. Ham was exonerated by a federal grand-jury vote of 24–0 against an indictment, but it cost him more than $1 million in legal fees, with only a government salary. Walter Cronkite later told Ham that the baseless cocaine charges were "the worst story he ever broadcast."[47]

The Ethics Act was later amended, but the damage was done during a critical time in the Carter presidency, when Ham's great talents were especially needed.[48] It remained on the statute books until it was allowed to expire in 1999, after Kenneth Starr relentlessly pursued President Clinton while serving as a special prosecutor under the amended act.

Such well-intentioned attempts at promoting public morality demand a sense of proportion, whether the issue is grave or petty. I got humorously tangled up in Carter's rule limiting gifts to federal officials to $25 shortly after an article in a business magazine reported that I had a penchant for Tootsie Rolls. I received a giant box of the candy from the Tootsie Roll company, which would have endeared me to my young sons for years. The White House counsel decreed that the gift breached the limit. I argued that the entire box was filled with penny candy that could not conceivably add up to a value of $25. As a compromise I proposed to dump half the candy in the box, just to be arithmetically certain. No, they insisted, under the ethics rules the full box of Tootsie Rolls had to be returned to the company. I accompanied it with a letter of thanks and an explanation of why I could not keep the gift. A few years later, in a story about the Tootsie Roll company, the CEO said I had tried to have it both ways, by making it seem I was following strict ethical standards, while the box that was received from the White House was completely empty. I still wonder which Secret Service agent took my Tootsie Rolls.

TENNIS, EVERYONE?

Stories of supposed White House mischief and maladroitness also made their way into the press at a sensitive preelection period when we should have been organizing for action. Instead, some of Carter's most admirable personal qualities were turned into personal burdens. The most memorable resulted from the widely publicized saga of the White House tennis court, which was turned into an inaccurate caricature of a president who lacked vision, because of his immersion in trivial minutiae. There were two sides to Carter's celebrated attention to detail, and one of them helped him immeasurably in negotiating the Camp David Accords, SALT II, the Alaska Lands Act, and much more. But this was turned on its head when his gifted chief speechwriter, James Fallows, focused on the less admirable aspect shortly after he abruptly quit at midterm. He joined the *Atlantic Monthly* and wrote a sensationalized piece that appeared in May 1979 under the title "The Passionless Presidency: The Trouble with Jimmy Carter's Administration."[49]

In fact, the president was far from passionless. If there was a problem, it was that he had too many conflicting passions, as evidenced by the range of thankless challenges he tackled. But the problem was less the ingratitude of a departed aide than the fact that his politically damaging account was wrong.

The irony is that it never would have happened at all, but for the president's generosity in opening up his many personal presidential perks to members of his staff. He allowed senior aides and their families to use the White House tennis court, gymnasium, hair salon, and even Camp David. But nothing drew the president's ire more than Fallows's account of the way the court, which is nestled on the South Lawn, invisible from the street, was supposedly micromanaged by Carter himself. Carter told me: "He lied. He lied. I don't know if he did it deliberately, but it was a lie. I am an average tennis player, and I played with Dr. Lukash [the White House physician] or with Brzezinski, or with Hamilton. I don't think I ever played with Fallows."

Part of the story is that when Rosalynn started taking tennis lessons, she would go out to play and regularly found staff members on the court. "Damn, when am I going to learn to play?" Rosalynn asked Jimmy.[50]

Fallows was an especially avid player and frequently used the court. (I am glad he had the time for such indulgences, courtesy of the president. I certainly did not!) Matters came to a head very early in the president's term, when he ended a staff meeting at about 4:30 and left to get in a game of tennis. Ten minutes later he returned wearing tennis shorts and carrying his racket. The president explained to the others that "some OMB guys" were using the court. They all agreed it was not right for the president of the United States to be bumped by his own staff.[51]

Carter finally arranged to have his secretary, Susan Clough, check whether the court was clear so that the president would be spared the indignity of personally ordering off anyone in midgame. Susan emphatically told me that he never managed the tennis courts, and that out of politeness, if he drifted down to the court and saw someone playing, "he wouldn't even finish getting there, he'd turn around and go back." She managed the schedule, and later wrote a letter to the *New York Times* on June 22, 1986, explaining that "the responsibility for coordinating court requests was mine," a point Fallows failed to mention.

In Carter's early days in the White House, requests for court time were addressed to the president, most of which he never saw, but when he did, he routed them to Susan Clough, sometimes writing a note of approval.[52] But Fallows's requests were often sent directly to the president as part of covering notes transmitting his speech drafts, which Susan said would help explain why this direct access helped create "myriad problems with the speechwriters." Carter, she said, might put a note on a returned draft either encouraging them to play or to use other facilities. Rex Scouten, the chief White House usher, confirmed that he managed the court with Susan, who forwarded names and proposed playing times to him to ensure that the court would be kept clear when the president and first lady wanted to play.[53] Fallows's botched account of the president as a detail freak followed Carter not just through the election, but for the rest of his life.[54]

THE KILLER RABBIT

Another grossly misread incident arising from Carter's innocent recreational pursuits also helped unfairly trivialize his presidency, the affair of the "killer rabbit." As the president remembered it, in the spring of 1979, he was fishing from a small boat in a one-acre pond not far from Plains.[55] Growing up in rural Georgia, he was accustomed to seeing squirrels, foxes, and rabbits bound out of the woods and swim across the water. So he was not surprised when he heard hounds barking on the side of the pond and saw a "small bunny rabbit" running out of the woods into the pond, and swimming for its life. As the rabbit approached the boat, the president splashed a little water near it with his paddle, and the hunted animal swam to the other shore and ran away.

Back in the White House, the president enjoyed telling this down-home story to Jody Powell, who later shared it over a drink with Brooks Jackson, an Associated Press reporter. But Jody jokingly embellished it in the Southern manner, by suggesting that a large swamp rabbit, in distress or perhaps berserk, tried to take refuge in the presidential rowboat, thus posing a "mortal threat to the Carter presidency."[56] Jody later explained that he told it to many people because "I thought it was a funny goddamn story about this friggin' rabbit."[57] Jackson thought so, too, and put it on the wire in lighthearted style. There was nothing funny about what happened next.

The *Washington Post* front-paged Jackson's story in late August 1979, months after the incident, under the headline "Bunny Goes Bugs: Rabbit Attacks President," with a cartoon parody of the *Jaws* poster, labeled "Paws."[58] The implication was that the story showed up Carter as a weak president. With its usual high seriousness, the *New York Times* ran the story in its main news section, and it spread to the three main television networks like oil on water. Hugh Sidey of *Time* headlined his regular column on the presidency "Rabbits Have No Class." The president tried to make light of it all by joking at a Labor Day picnic with already disaffected union leaders, "I believe in killer rabbits—and killer reporters. But a killer rabbit has never come after me and a killer reporter has."[59]

Suddenly opponents jumped on the incident to belittle the president, linking it to everything that had gone wrong and making it an uncomfortable metaphor for the Carter presidency. Jody wrote disparagingly years later: "As insightful columnists and congressional leaders later pointed out, none of this would have happened to the president if he had been sipping cocktails with them on the presidential yacht *Sequoia* like Presidents are supposed to do, instead of fishing in some godforsaken south Georgia swamp. But Carter had sold the *Sequoia,* and so being attacked by a rabbit was the least he deserved."[60]

All this is also a lesson on the importance of avoiding irony or humorous exaggeration in the White House, when every word can become the focus of examination and ridicule, irrespective of political party. The following year, when Ronald Regan got his environmental chemistry backward and claimed that forests polluted the atmosphere by emitting carbon dioxide, his press secretary, James Brady, joked with the traveling press as they flew over the Pacific Northwest and cried out: "Killer trees! Killer trees!" He almost lost his job.

STILL SEARCHING FOR ANSWERS

As so often happened, Carter summoned the inner strength and tenacity to pick himself up from his low point. The president ended up with a stronger cabinet, with stars like former Portland mayor Neil Goldschmidt (later governor of Oregon) as transportation secretary and Philip Klutznik, an American Jewish leader and prominent Chicago businessman, at Commerce. Carter also shaped a more experienced staff with the addition as White House counsel in October 1979 of Washington superlawyer Lloyd Cutler, who played a key role in the Iran hostage negotiations. But in typical Carter fashion, it was done in an inglorious way. He missed the chance to bring in an experienced Washington political hand like Bob Strauss into the White House and only slightly shuffled the White House staff cards he had brought with him from Georgia.

Moving Miller from the Fed to the Treasury to succeed Blumenthal, after unsuccessfully trying to find his replacement among the upper echelons of American business, left open the key post of central bank chairman. But Paul Volcker was an inspired, even historic, choice. Most important was the change in Jimmy Carter. The president was steeled to set his principal priorities and achieve them. He now knew he had to play an inside political game in Washington, while also emphasizing his continued identification with the common good as the outsider, a difficult balancing task that Ronald Reagan actually managed to achieve.

While introducing fiscal discipline, deregulation, major environmental breakthroughs, and passing our last, major energy bill, Carter had to hold on to the political base of the party's liberals, who did not see any need to change their profligate ways; fend off a challenge from Senator Kennedy to his left; and maintain the support of his conservative Southern base. It was an acrobatic act beyond his or any other mortal at the time, until Bill Clinton applied his magic a decade and a half later. In the meantime, as Caddell artfully put it to me: "You were in the middle of it; you were getting your ass kicked off on both ends, Stu."[61]

Yet, when this extraordinary three-month period was over, a *Washington Post* poll published on September 14 gave Carter the lowest approval rating of any president in three decades.[62] And to insert a visual exclamation point, he collapsed in a ten-kilometer race near Camp David on September 15. This led the press to depict the event as representative of the failing strength of his presidency, even though in characteristic fashion the president recovered quickly and awarded the winner his trophy with a huge smile.

I do not believe that this exceptional period had villains. Caddell's recommendations may have had excesses, but he had put his finger on a major problem with the Carter presidency; Rafshoon may have made a disastrous recommendation for a mass resignation; and Ham's remarkable political antennae may have malfunctioned. But they were looking for ways to follow up his successful speech with dramatic action to show he was reasserting control. Mondale and I misjudged the power of Carter's speech.

But during the storm all the key actors were searching for answers to try to help salvage a presidency at its low point. Everyone acted with the best of intentions, however misguided these actions may appear in the cold light of history. It was an exceptionally tense and difficult time—with an Iranian revolution, gasoline lines, soaring oil prices, energy legislation stuck as special interests battled on all sides, and sinking polls for the president. This kind of environment can produce rash decisions.

Soon an upheaval thousands of miles away in Tehran cruelly prevented the president from building even his modest momentum and from becoming the president who, with a new sense of discipline despite a sour economy, might have reconnected with the American people to gain a second term in office.

PART VIII

IRAN

26

THE RISE OF THE AYATOLLAH

The Iranian revolution of 1979, midway in the Carter presidency, was the most profound geopolitical event of the twentieth century's postwar period, except for the fall of the Soviet Union. The popular uprising brought down the Shah of Iran, one of America's most important allies in the Middle East, cost Carter a distinguished secretary of state, and was a decisive factor in the political demise of his presidency, by creating one of the most humiliating diplomatic traumas in American history. More than fifty American diplomats were held hostage in their own embassy in Tehran for 444 days, serving as a principal lever for Islamic radicals to consolidate their revolution. This ushered radical Islamic theology into a government in the Middle East for the first time in history, turning Iran almost overnight from a key American ally to a sworn enemy.

The challenges born out of the Iranian revolution are as contemporary as today's headlines. Iran remains a hostile theocratic state, in which the ultimate decision makers are not the nominal government figures with whom the Carter administration and its successors have dealt, but a parallel set of organizations: the Council of Elders, the Revolutionary Guard, revolutionary courts controlled by radical Islamic clerics and their adherents, and above it all a grand ayatollah as supreme leader, who does not engage with other sovereign states in the way of the modern world.

Jimmy Carter was the first president to confront this dramatically new and untested reality. Although it was not clear to us at the time—and it rarely is at revolutionary moments—Iran was undergoing a historic upheaval in which the forces that filled the void left by the departure of autocratic rulers initially left their people far worse off, like the early days of the French

Revolution, Russia's Bolshevik Revolution, and the misnamed "Arab Spring" of our century.

The decisions facing Carter on Iran were among the toughest any president could face in peacetime: How to support an increasingly unpopular autocratic leader but a strategically vital ally; whether to block his radical successor and then navigate a new relationship with the unique reality of an Islamic republic; whether to allow the Shah to enter the United States for medical treatment, knowing the risks of inflaming the Iranian public; and finally the worst dilemma of dealing with the unprecedented capture of the American diplomats serving in what was then the largest U.S. embassy in the world. Should the safety of our hostages prevail over American honor and standing as the guarantor of world order?

To appreciate the unique challenges the Carter administration faced, it is important to understand something of Iran's history, in contrast to what Gary Sick, Brzezinski's senior aide on Iran on the National Security Council, called the "unrelieved ignorance" among American foreign-policy makers about such a critical country.[1] Unlike most of the states in the region, which were created by agreements among the colonial powers after World War I, Iran has a long, proud, but troubled history as an independent nation. Iranians have never forgotten their rich ancestry as the Persian empire; in ancient times it was the largest in the known world, extending from what now is Turkey eastward into India. The history of Europe would have been very different if the nascent Athenian democracy had not beaten back King Xerxes' Persian invaders on the plains of Marathon in 490 B.C.E. Like all great empires, the Persian one declined, but its poetry, art, architecture, and even the Persian game of chess remain enduring monuments of civilization and culture.

For Westerners it is worth remembering that Persian history, culture, and language are totally different from the Arabic. When Persians abandoned the Zoroastrian worship of fire for Islam, they adopted the Shia sect, which is founded and still pursued with a sense of grievance over the rightful successor to the prophet Muhammad. Victorian Britain and czarist Russia engaged in the "Great Game" for influence in Central Asia. The British gained a huge oil concession in 1901, which led to a popular revolution forcing the Shah of the ruling Qajar Dynasty in 1906 to accept a constitution with an elected parliament, leaving him as a constitutional monarch. The British posted a wise diplomat to Tehran, Sir Arthur Hardinge, whose prophetic insight should have been known to U.S. intelligence during the entire postwar period of American engagement into the Carter years, and remains pertinent to this day. The religious zeal of the Shiite sect, he wrote, lies in "its resistance to political authority, and its fierce antagonism toward all from the outside world, be they Christians or Sunni Moslems."[2]

Turmoil reflecting this outlook marked the early years of the twentieth century in Iran, as the British sought stability to protect their oil concessions and make the country a buffer between Russia and their colony of India. They installed a commander of the Persian Cossack Brigade as prime minister, and in 1925 he mounted the Peacock Throne as the new Shah, Reza Pahlavi, founding the Pahlavi Dynasty under the 1906 constitution. This authoritarian ruler rapidly modernized what had been a weak and divided country. He curbed the power of the feudal landlords, reformed education, granted significant freedoms to women, and suppressed the powerful religious establishment in a rehearsal for what Carter would confront half a century later with his son.

During World War II Reza Pahlavi was forced into exile for Nazi sympathies, and in 1941 his 21-year-old son Mohammed Reza Pahlavi took the throne. For the next ten years Iran was nominally a constitutional democracy with its own parliament. Since the young Shah had been put on the throne by foreign governments, his legitimacy was questioned. To bolster his position he attempted to negotiate better terms with the Anglo-Iranian Oil Company, with the support of the Americans, who feared that unrest would increase Moscow's leverage in Iran. When Anglo-Iranian finally offered to split profits 50–50, it was rejected as inadequate, and the Shah's handpicked prime minister was assassinated within days after refusing to nationalize the oil company.

The oil minister, Mohammed Mossadegh, no Communist but a nationalist and wealthy aristocrat who had championed nationalization, became prime minister. As far back as the 1920s, he had opposed the Shah's father as an authoritarian ruler. Mossadegh at age 70 transformed himself into an angry populist and mobilized masses of people to demonstrate against the oil company. Foreign intervention followed, serving as a template for Iranian behavior throughout the hostage crisis a quarter-century later. London seriously considered armed intervention to depose Mossadegh, but the United States opposed it lest the USSR be encouraged to move into Iran. The British then embargoed Iranian oil, and Mossadegh roused his countrymen to demonstrate against the British. This left the Shah helpless to combat his popular prime minister, but also deprived Mossadegh of support from the moderate reformers, who saw him as autocratic and dangerous because of his reliance on the mob, and the Shiite clerics, who condemned him as an enemy of Islam for working with the local Communist Party. Mossadegh made a beeline to America to engage the new Eisenhower administration and seek medical help. Aging and ill, he spent forty days in Washington and New York, some of them in the hospital.

When Winston Churchill returned to power in 1951, he turned to his wartime partner, now President Eisenhower, and together they hatched a scheme to get rid of Mossadegh. To implement the plan, the Shah tried to dismiss Mossadegh as prime minister, but the plot failed, and the Shah escaped to Europe. This led to a coup in August 1953 called Operation Ajax, organized by Britain's MI6 (the Secret Intelligence Service) and the CIA under Kermit Roosevelt, Jr., a grandson of Theodore Roosevelt and a career intelligence officer then serving as the agency's Mideast bureau chief. By the end of August, Mossadegh was under house arrest and the Shah was restored to his throne. America's role in ousting an elected prime minister was embedded in the collective memory of the Iranian people, with the United States providing a convenient whipping boy for the ruling clerics, an abiding resonance of the 1953 coup.

Reinstalled in power, the Shah shed his role as a constitutional monarch, grew increasingly autocratic, and appointed only prime ministers who followed his orders. Press censorship grew more severe, no public criticism of his policies was permitted, and the parliament became a rubber stamp.[3] Yet, the Shah was not simply a self-aggrandizing dictator. Flush with money from the huge run-up in oil prices after the 1973 OPEC embargo, and with the best of intentions, he became a reformer and nationalist intent on a great leap forward to lead his country out of poverty and backwardness,[4] with a

White revolution to preempt a Red one by the Communist Tudeh Party. But the process of reform, and especially giving women the vote and breaking up the great feudal estates, was imposed at great speed and created powerful enemies. The Shah abolished political parties and enforced order through the dreaded internal security service, SAVAK—an anagram of the Persian words for Organization of Intelligence and National Security—which ruthlessly pursued and notoriously tortured political opponents.

This led to calls for more freedom. Having alienated the liberal intelligentsia, the clerics, and the landowners in the early 1970s, the Shah also undermined his support among the powerful merchant class by having inspectors impose heavy fines on small businesses. For different reasons, these disparate groups shared the goal of getting rid of the Shah or at least curbing his repressive power with some measure of democratic transparency.

One voice stood above all the rest with a clear message, though it was at sharp variance with the goals of other sectors of Iranian society: The cleric Ruhollah Khomeini, who had great influence as a grand ayatollah, called for the establishment of an Islamic republic along religious lines. In the end these disparate groups coalesced around Khomeini as a way of getting rid of the Shah. Following public speeches by Khomeini in 1963, mass protests against the Shah broke out in Tehran and other major cities. SAVAK and the army quickly put down the demonstrations and killed numbers of people in the streets. The Shah had Khomeini arrested and sent into exile in 1964 just across the Iraqi border in Najaf, a city holy to Shiites. From his Iraqi exile, Khomeini preached against the Shah's corruption, his ties to Israel, and the influence of the United States. He began to develop the idea of an Islamic state based upon Islamic law as interpreted by Islamic clerics in a series of lectures, which were published as a book, *Islamic Government in Persia*.

In putting the reaction of the Carter administration into context, it is important to understand that the concept of a clerically run Islamic state was revolutionary, even in traditional Islamic terms.[5] By the early 1970s, middle-rank clerics throughout Iran became adherents of Khomeini's vision of an Islamic state. Many of these clerics, some leftists, and Mehdi Bazargan, an engineer who would play a central role in President Carter's drama with Iran, were also arrested. They founded the world's first Islamic party as an avowed liberation movement. Khomeini remained above politics, but the Islamic party supported him and developed a set of disciples.[6]

UNKNOWN UNKNOWNS

When Jimmy Carter was inaugurated on January 20, 1977, there was nothing apparent to the administration or our intelligence services—although there should have been—that there was any threat to the Shah's continued rule, now well into its third decade. As the Cold War intensified, he had become the darling of presidents. An enormous pipeline of sophisticated military equipment, managed by Iran with help from Pentagon technicians, and paid for by Iranian oil, supported Iranian power as a Cold War barrier against the USSR and to stabilize the Middle East—$10 billion in arms in just the five years before Carter took office. Nixon and Kissinger, with good reason, staked the protection of U.S. interests in the Persian Gulf on the Shah, and that reliance was deeply embedded in the policy inherited by Carter. The Shah was handsome, with wavy graying hair; he was urbane, suave, wellspoken in fluent English and French, and had a beautiful young empress in his opulent palace and a summer retreat in the mountains above sweltering Tehran.

Because of the bipartisan consensus that put all of America's eggs in the Shah's basket, we did not issue one formal statement or draft one speech for Carter on Iran during the 1976 presidential campaign.

There was certainly no hint of wariness in the elaborate welcome for the Shah when he made a state visit in November 1977. We literally rolled out the red carpet at the White House. Uniformed military buglers welcomed him from the Truman Balcony, along with the Marine Band, and a podium for the Shah and the president to speak was erected on the South Lawn. But trouble was brewing. A well-organized Iran Student Movement, drawn from some 60,000 Iranian students in the United States, donned masks against identification by SAVAK and began demonstrations in Lafayette Park across from the White House for a week before the Shah's arrival. The Iranian Embassy helped organize counterdemonstrations, with frequent clashes and competing bullhorns.

To be closer to the ceremonies, the warring student factions clashed at the Ellipse, just south of the White House, which is normally a quiet place, almost hermetically sealed against the noise of political storms. But it was impossible to ignore the week of angry riots or to avoid the tear gas loosed by the National Park Service during the Shah's arrival. The prevailing wind blew it into the faces of the president and the Shah. The Shah was coughing during his remarks, and the president used a handkerchief to wipe away tears. Carter made light of it during his toast at the formal state dinner that evening: "One thing I can say about the Shah; he knows how to draw a crowd."[7] Everyone laughed, but the events of the day presaged trouble.

Because Carter recognized the Shah's crucial role as an American ally and supplier of half of Israel's oil, he raised concerns about the Shah's iron rule only in a private session after dinner in the small study next to the Oval Office. The Shah pressed for more advanced weapons. Carter tried to deflate his grandiose expectations by pointing out that Iran accounted for almost half of the $11.5 billion in American arms sales abroad.[8] He also told the Shah that he believed SAVAK had attacked the demonstrators, that the Shah was making a serious mistake by clamping down so harshly, and urged him to reach out to dissident groups. Carter remembered that the Shah "completely contradicted" him: "I'm doing what needs to be done against these Communist demonstrators, and the rest of you leaders in the Western world are making a foolish mistake to condemn them." This was the first time Carter had touched on human rights with the Shah, who resented his interference. He believed the Shah was "singularly isolated; he was on a pedestal and he didn't understand what was going on in his country," believing the dissidents represented only a tiny minority.[9]

But it was almost another year before Brzezinski began to suspect that he was not getting the full story from American intelligence. In the autumn of 1978, Brzezinski complained to the president about poor intelligence from the CIA and recommended Carter send a note to CIA Director Turner, whose remit included improving the agency's analytical capabilities. To avoid making it appear that he was pointing a finger solely at Turner, Brzezinski recommended the personal note also go to him and Vance.[10] Carter did so, saying he was "dissatisfied with the quality of political intelligence" on Iran.

Remarkably, the note was leaked to the press and caused a firestorm.[11] The concerns were justified.

One could fill an ocean with what the United States did not know about developments in Iran. It amounted to one of the most massive intelligence failures in American history, attested to later by CIA Director Turner, who admitted his agency "let Carter down badly on Iran,"[12] and more colorfully by the NSC's Iran expert Sick, who concluded the CIA's intelligence was "sheer gobbledygook masquerading as informed judgment."[13]

But there was an underlying reason for the dearth of intelligence about this nation so deeply connected to American security. To seven American administrations the Shah was Iran and Iran was the Shah. He was modern, sophisticated, a reformer of sorts, and a friend. At his insistence Iran was one of the few major countries where we did not position intelligence officers to focus on its internal politics and report on what was actually happening on the ground. The Shah insisted his own SAVAK do that. So while there may have never been a formal directive to avoid contact with opposition groups, there was, as noted by Brzezinski's Iranian specialist Sick, a "clear awareness that the Shah was annoyed and suspicious about such contacts and they gradually dried up."[14] The CIA had assets in Iran, but they were focused across the border on the Soviet Union. As Joint Chiefs of Staff head General David Jones put it, "We will rely" on SAVAK for internal developments.[15] And since the Shah himself depended on SAVAK, he believed his own propaganda when he saw popular demonstrations organized on his behalf.[16]

The result was catastrophic. As Sick told me: "We misjudged the Shah, absolutely. We believed that he was the leader that he portrayed himself as being. We were convinced that he was capable of basic decision making. We did not know of his illness. And we didn't know about his fundamental indecisiveness. By the time we realized he couldn't in fact bring Iran out of this thing, it was really too late."[17] And if it had been admitted even privately to ourselves, it would have meant declaring a generation of American policy toward Iran bankrupt.

The Shah's health played a decisive role in his fall. Although the physical condition of important world leaders is a standard feature of their secret

CIA profiles, it was a total blank in Iran and further evidence of a massive intelligence failure. Not even the Shah's confidant, his dashing ambassador to Washington, Ardeshir Zahedi, knew the ruler was suffering from cancer; the Shah lied that he was plagued by gout. There were sharply conflicting reports: Some had him depressed and appearing sallow, others said that he looked hardy and resolute. To dispel rumors, Ambassador Zahedi arranged to have the Shah waterskiing when Barbara Walters traveled to Iran for a TV interview.[18]

Nor did Carter help the Shah when he made a New Year's Eve visit to Tehran as the last stop on a foreign swing closing out his first year in office. The results belie any notion that he was distancing himself from the Shah, let alone preparing to throw him to the wolves. They settled the details for the civilian nuclear reactors we were selling Iran, and the president also asked for Iran's consolidated shopping list of weapons for the next five years. His briefing papers reminded him of the persistent clashes between student opponents and the police, so Carter was nuanced and cautious on human rights. At the state dinner on the eve of 1978, he gracefully touched on this delicate issue by quoting the revered thirteenth-century Persian poet Saadi: "If the misery of others leaves you indifferent and with no feelings of sorrow, then you cannot be called a human being."[19]

Unfortunately the only thing that was remembered from that formal toast was a phrase of unscripted hyperbole (a regular occurrence that normally brought smiles to those of us who worked with him). Carter tried to boost the Shah's morale by calling Iran *"an island of stability in a turbulent corner of the world"* (emphasis added). At the time he thought of the visit as a "big, wonderful gala" attended by King Hussein of Jordan and press celebrities like the TV anchorman Walter Cronkite, and of himself as the seventh successive president since Franklin Roosevelt who had dealt successfully with the Shah. Nobody, least of all Carter, and certainly not his intelligence agencies, foresaw that riots would rudely push the Shah from his pedestal in the coming year.[20] Later, with 20–20 hindsight, his statement was seen as naive.[21]

The Khomeini forces heard the president's toast in a very different key. Mohsen Zara Sazegara, one of Khomeni's closest aides in exile, told me it only fanned the smoldering flames of revolution.[22] If a revolution can be said to have started on any given day, that would be January 7, 1978, a week after Carter's visit, when the government-controlled newspaper *Tellat* published an article accusing the ayatollah of being a foreign agent. That touched off a spiral of protests starting January 9 in Iran's holy city of Qum, during the Shiite holy month of Muharram, and only two months after the death of Khomeini's son, which some blamed on SAVAK. The police killed several of the Qum demonstrators, and the leading cleric in Iran, Ayatollah Shariatmadari, called the Shah's government anti-Islamic. A month later Khomeini appealed across the border from his exile in Iraq to Iranians to commemorate the killings in Qum, which ignited a large demonstration in Tabriz. This time about sixty demonstrators were killed. In Shiite tradition, the Khomeini forces then commenced memorial demonstrations for the dead at each forty-day interval throughout much of the rest of the year.

Sick sent Brzezinski an ominous memo disputing the official Iranian assertion that the riots were provoked by Communists, and arguing that they originated with "the reactionary Muslim right wing, which finds [The Shah's] modernization program too liberal and moving too fast away from the traditional values of Iranian society."[23] This was also Sazegara's view: It was not America's support but the Shah's own vigorously pursued modernization program that ignited the Islamic opposition.[24]

For the sake of stability Carter was prepared to give the Shah a wide margin for maneuver. Over the objections of Patt Derian, the State Department's designated defender of human rights, the White House on March 28 approved a shipment of tear gas to Iran to control the spreading demonstrations. In April SAVAK bombed the homes of non-Islamic opposition leaders, as the Shah escalated the repression of his domestic opponents. Then the overthrow of the conservative Daoud regime in neighboring Afghanistan reinforced the Shah's belief that he was facing a Communist-Islamic conspiracy, however unlikely such a political alliance may seem.

In the summer of 1978, the Shah expressed the totally unfounded fear to Henry Kissinger, who was visiting him at his vacation palace, that Carter and the Soviets had reached a deal in which Iran would be under Russia's sphere of influence, and Saudi Arabia America's.[25] The Shah soon asked for more U.S. military aid, and in a disastrous news conference appeared indecisive and uncertain about whether to take a hard or soft line to deal with the demonstrations against his rule.

How to best respond to events that called into question four decades of America's unstinting support for the Shah? The president approved most of Iran's military requests. But the summer brought a lull in the demonstrations as the Shah developed a carrot-and-stick policy of sharply repressing the dissidents, while announcing such modest reforms as replacing the head of SAVAK, committing to free elections in 1979, and promising press freedom and space for opposition groups in politics. His opponents had heard all these unfulfilled promises before.

Ambassador William Sullivan, an independent-minded operator who previously had occupied a similar role in Vietnam, returned from Tehran to report that the worst was over and the Shah would survive. But it turned out to be the calm before the storm. The Shah's promises of more liberalization only whetted the appetite of the clerics, who saw weakness instead of confident rule. By backing off even slightly, Sazegara said, the Shah sent a "very significant signal to the people of Iran" that they could push harder.[26] Worse, without realizing it, he helped define the split between secular nationalists who sought democracy, and Islamic fundamentalists who always wanted theocratic rule. When the Shah was eventually forced from power, the two wings grappled to fill the vacuum and the clerics turned out to be the most implacable, as well as ruthless, in exploiting and manipulating the Shah's most extremist opponents, most notably the radicals who later seized the U.S. Embassy.

Widespread demonstrations broke out later in the summer around the country, leading the Shah to impose a curfew on Isfahan and then other cities. Then fire was literally added to the smoldering embers of revolution when 477 people died in the Rex cinema in Abadan, the site of a major oil refinery, on August 19, 1978—another important day leading to the Shah's demise. The Shiite radicals wrongly blamed this theater disaster on SAVAK and the Shah.

When Sullivan returned late in August from a vacation of almost three months—amazing in its length at such a crucial period—he wrote a reassuring assessment of the Shah's promised reforms but concluded that they were not yet recognized by the public. But meanwhile events moved faster than we could. The Shah appointed a new prime minister who was not a strong figure and had a corrupt reputation. More demonstrations filled the streets. On September 5 tens of thousands of Islamists rallied in Tehran's Jaleh Square, and the army opened fire, killing hundreds. The government imposed martial law, but the killings finally registered with the Shah. He announced a shift in priorities, under no pressure from Carter, scaling back his military budget and shifting the money to pay families of those killed in the riots and the Rex cinema fire.

All this resonated far beyond Iran's borders. Iranian ambassador Zahedi[27] met with his longtime friend Israeli foreign minister Moshe Dayan as he was on his way to the Camp David peace talks. Dayan told him the fate of the Shah was more important to Israel than the negotiations with Sadat. At the same time the Shah told Carter there was a plot to take advantage of his liberalization program and asked for Carter's support as he restored law and order. The upshot was a presidential statement reaffirming the close relationship with Iran, regretting the loss of life, and supporting his continued liberalization.[28]

When Sullivan met with the Shah on October 10, he found him "looking drawn and tense, but the conversation was animated," as he expressed concerns about the loyalty of his military.[29] The Shah even considered inviting Khomeini home from exile, which Sullivan told him was a terrible idea.

THE SHAH SEALS HIS FATE

What the Shah next did to Khomeini probably sealed his own fate: He had the radical cleric moved out of his exile in an Iraqi backwater under the thumb of Saddam Hussein to the center of what turned out to be an international media circus in France. Mistakenly believing that pushing the ayatollah far away would lessen his influence by reducing his proximity to Iran, the Shah asked Saddam to squeeze him out of the country. The Iraqi dictator was only too happy to get rid of him, but instead of taking refuge in another Muslim country like Algeria or Syria, he chose France on the recommendation of a young acolyte, Ibrahim Yazdi, a committed Iranian nationalist who had fled Iran because of his activities against the Shah, and who felt Paris would provide Khomeini a world stage.

When Khomeini sought permission to enter France, the French government agreed as long as Iran did not object, and the Shah fatefully did not. Ironically, in Paris, the birthplace of the Enlightenment, the cleric could take advantage of the Western freedom of expression that played no part in his religious scheme of governance. Khomeini and his entourage stayed for only one week in the capital because the neighbors complained of the steady stream of visiting Muslim activists. So they moved to Neauphle-le-Château, a small village only a half-hour's drive outside Paris, and home to an Iranian activist with a small apple orchard where Khomeini liked to stroll. He had an office in the house and slept there, but he held court in a tent erected nearby, where he would meet the world's press, lead Friday prayers, and preach sermons.

Yazdi, who was at Khomeini's side in France, had received a master's degree in philosophy from the University of Tehran, and joined an underground movement after the 1953 coup that deposed Mossadegh and restored the Shah to his throne. In 1961 he moved to the United States, earning a doctorate in biochemistry from Baylor University in 1967, cofounding the Freedom Movement of Iran Abroad, and eventually becoming an American citizen while working for the Veterans Administration. After Carter's election Yazdi flew to Najaf to inform Khomeini that the new president was putting pressure on the Shah to liberalize as part of his human rights campaign, and that Mehdi Bazargan, one of the founders of the Liberation Movement of Iran, planned to write an open letter calling on the Shah to leave Iran. He sought Khomeini's blessing to help him obtain thousands of signatures across the political spectrum from Muslim nationalists to Marxists, and the letter was published. Yazdi, who remained under a form of house arrest in Iran until his death in 2017, at the age of 85, for his work seeking a more democratic Iran, was one of the revolution's many children it devoured. He came to realize that Carter's human rights policies had no effect on the Shah's dealings with the Iranian opposition. (I learned about Yadzi through his son-in-law, Dr. Mehdi Noorbaksh.)[30]

Yazdi threw in his lot with Khomeini and was joined by a few other followers, including Mohsen Sazegara, who gave me a unique perspective on Khomeini and the radical Islamic revolution. Sazegara became an observant Muslim toward the end of high school and recalled that during the 1970s

"SAVAK controlled everything and every activity," even all of Iran's photo-copiers. He attended Sharif University of Technology in Tehran as an Islamic activist, then spent three years at the Illinois Institute of Technology, where he joined the Muslim Student Association. Only a month after Carter's election, Sazegara published an analysis of the new president's human rights policy in the Islamic student newspaper, declaring that it would lead to changes in Iran. He did not expect that the Shah would be overthrown but felt the time had come to spread the Islamic movement. After completing his examinations, he returned home and immediately became involved in activities against the Shah in the mosques and universities in Tehran and Isfahan, which he said had become possible because of Carter. He traveled back and forth between Tehran and Chicago, and always had in his mind the 1953 Anglo-American coup that overthrew Mossadegh.

Soon after Khomeini was ensconced at Neauphle, an aide asked Saze-gara to join the ayatollah. For the young Sazegara it was the chance of a lifetime. He borrowed $200 from an Iranian doctor in Chicago and bought a one-way ticket to Paris, where Yazdi met him at the airport. He joined a group of four students who helped with the arrangements for the flood of press requests: Khomeini held more than four hundred interviews and press conferences, and the students would translate the questions into Farsi and then relay his answers in English or French. Sazegara and his fellow students also read forty or more newspapers and magazines every day and prepared news summaries in Farsi of two or three pages for Khomeini, which they would give him each night. Sazegara told me: "Every night we had a dis-cussion of what Brzezinski said, what Carter said, what the Shah said, and what's the situation."[31]

Volunteers were arriving from Iran and throughout Europe, eager for armed struggle against the Shah, and Sazegara soon had another role. In the small inn adjoining the ayatollah's house he ran four-day courses to train them in techniques of organizing underground guerrilla cells, obtaining weap-ons from army garrisons, and protesting "against a police state." He was in-spired by the Viet Cong and said, "We believed in armed struggle, a long battle with the regime of the Shah and the Americans who support him." Many of these volunteers returned to Iran after the fall of the Shah and were folded into the Revolutionary Guard, which was designed by Sazegara and his colleagues to be exactly what it is today, an army outside the regular armed forces, defending the radical Islamic revolution from internal enemies. In more recent years it has been dispatched to Syria and Iraq to fight for the interests of Iranian Shiism.

At the tender age of 23, Sazegara remained at the ayatollah's right hand when he later returned to Tehran in triumph, and he held a number of high offices in the revolutionary government. He found the 76-year-old Khomeini "very smart . . . [he] listened to whatever you said very carefully, but didn't look at you," while folding his hands together. During the night Khomeini would wake up and pray; he was celebrated as a religious leader for doing this for half a century. This pious behavior, said Sazegara, made the cleric's later conduct of "killing people, torturing people" all the more surprising.[32]

If the CIA knew little about the internal turmoil in Iran, and less about the Shah's terminal illness, it is equally stunning how little they knew about Khomeini's activities in his French exile, from either electronic surveillance or human contacts. Although he was delivering public sermons with the world press in attendance and sending tape cassettes of his fiery sermons back to Iran, neither U.S. nor French intelligence seemed to appreciate his ultimate goal of establishing a fundamentalist Islamic republic, perhaps believing Yazdi's soothing words that Khomeini would remain a spiritual presence while moderate officials would run the government.

A young Afghan-born Ph.D. from Columbia University, Zalmay Khalilzad (later President George W. Bush's ambassador successively to Afghanistan, Iraq, and the UN), told me that he took a New Year's trip to Paris with his new wife and decided on a lark to try to meet Khomeini. He had an introduction to Yazdi, and asked him why a moderate like him would be working for Khomeini against the Shah. Yazdi replied that Khomeini was only a religious figurehead, who, along with his clerical colleagues, would remain on the sidelines when the revolution deposed the Shah. The next day Khalilzad met Khomeini, who was dressed in black clerical robes and sitting unsmiling, cross-legged on the floor in his tent. An aide, initially not realizing that Khalilzad was fluent in Farsi, reminded Khomeini to "tell the

American professor that we want democracy and rights for all—this is what the Americans like to hear."

He asked Khomeini how he planned to govern Iran. After a diatribe against the Shah for not following Islamic law, Khomeini declared that he wanted an Islamic state in which clerics would exercise power through Islamic law, with technocrats implementing the fundamentalist agenda. They were like plumbers, he said, and could be replaced at will if they did not faithfully do their job. This young academic had a clearer understanding of Khomeini's ultimate objectives than did our intelligence services. The ayatollah gave Khalilzad his book, *Islamic Republic*, copies of his speeches and his taped lectures, and pointed to one photograph he said proved the Shah was an "agent of Zionism," because he was supposedly seated next to Israel's Shimon Peres. When Khalilzad looked more closely at the photograph, it showed the Shah at an OPEC meeting not with Shimon Peres, but a very different *Perez,* the president of Venezuela, Carlos Andrés Pérez.[33]

CONFUSION IN WASHINGTON

While the post-Watergate reforms of the CIA ruled out assassinations, many other steps might have been taken to restrain Khomeini. Our diplomats could have urged the French not to permit his return to Iran. Our spies could have asked French intelligence to use electronic surveillance to determine Khomeini's motives and, for example, learn in advance about his plans to call for nationwide strikes.

The Shah and Ambassador Zahedi also dismissed the significance of street protests in Iran, which they attributed to Communist manipulation, and believed differed from "disjointed protests" led by religious leaders. Their suspicions were such that Vance felt compelled to assure Zahedi that "the US was not involved in any respect in the plotting against the Iranian government."[34] When the NSC's Sick was approached by an American academic specialist on Iran who wanted to arrange a meeting with Yazdi, it was vetoed by senior State Department and White House officials lest they give the impression that they lacked confidence in the Shah.[35]

With suspicions rising that the Shah's position was shakier than it seemed, and without sound intelligence on either his motives or Khomeni's, the State Department finished a major analysis for the president, finding that repeated expressions of American support for the Shah were having no effect, and recognizing the limited ability of the United States to influence events.[36] Carter himself had not yet held a single high-level meeting on Iran and was focused elsewhere in the Middle East—on turning the Camp David Accords into a binding treaty between Egypt and Israel.

Brzezinski chaired a Special Coordinating Committee in the White House Situation Room on November 2, 1978, which he opened by stating that Iran's Ambassador Zahedi felt that Sullivan was not sufficiently supportive of the Shah. The meeting reached a consensus, supported by the president, to send Sullivan a clear message that the administration supported the Shah "without reservations" and that the Shah needed to act through the military or form a coalition government.[37]

However, cracks soon developed in the administration's policy. There were three competing camps, and even their positions wavered as power shifted inside Iran. Ambassador Sullivan now felt the Shah should leave as soon as possible and that contacts should be initiated with the opposition in Iran and with Khomeini. Vance continued to emphasize negotiations with the opposition and progress to implement the Shah's reforms, but he was not ready to give up on the Shah.

Brzezinski, a student of history, believed that restoring order was paramount, and that revolutions develop when reforms precede the restoration of order. Vance agreed that order must be restored before further liberalization, but was preoccupied by SALT and Middle East negotiations and delegated Iranian responsibility to others.[38] Brzezinski argued that only a show of force by the Shah could save the day, and he saw Vance and the State Department ready to make concessions to the students, mullahs, and the bazaar merchants to achieve a unity government.

The same division between Vance and Brzezinski that was painfully evident on Soviet policy now hobbled policy making on Iran, with rogue ambassador Sullivan, often acting on his own, added to the mix. Brzezinski later recognized that "sadly there was a duality," and that "it was up to me or

Vance to say one way or the other, but not both ways; but I didn't do it."[39] Sick found the State Department's animosity toward Brzezinski to be of "nearly pathological proportions."[40] No wonder the Shah was confused.

On November 5, 1978, events in Iran took a decided turn for the worse. The army fired at students at Tehran University. Attacks were mounted on Western hotels and businesses by young men encouraged by their mullahs. The British Embassy was overrun and partly burned, and the American Embassy menaced. It is critical to appreciate that the Shah was uneasy about using force against his own people, even though Zahedi pressed him to do so to quell the unrest.[41]

But the next day he named a military government headed by Army Chief of Staff Gholam Reza Azhari, although with a remarkably apologetic statement that indicated his ambivalence. Coming from an absolute ruler who had just turned his government over to his generals, it sent a signal of weakness rather than strength. He expressed his support for the people's revolution, said he had tried unsuccessfully to form a coalition government, and promised to make up for "past mistakes, unlawful acts, oppression and corruption." Simply naming the military government created a period of calm, but General Azhari had no political background or desire to use force. The demonstrations resumed in late November, as oil-field strikes slashed Iran's production from 5 to 1 million barrels a day, touching off the second great oil shock of the 1970s and focusing my attention on America's own domestic turmoil of long lines at the gas pumps that began later in the winter.[42]

Then, on November 9, Sullivan sent a long and explosive top-secret cable to Washington provocatively headed "Thinking the Unthinkable," urging withdrawal of our support for the Shah and forecasting that he could not survive unless the growing unrest was quickly subdued. This was the first in a series of frantic and essentially uncoordinated attempts by Sullivan on his own to prepare moderate Iranian political leaders to fill the vacuum that would be left by what he believed would be the Shah's inevitable departure.[43]

When the cable made its way to the White House, Carter was irate. He asked Brzezinski how the situation could have become so degraded without his knowledge, especially since no one had warned him that the Shah's position was as dire as Sullivan reported directly from Tehran. In response to a personal presidential note, CIA Director Turner later told me he defended his agency by declaring that it concentrated its limited resources on the Soviet threat to Iran, not on internal Iranian politics, which were off-limits to the agency anyway. He blamed the embassy staff for failing to maintain contacts with the opposition and the clergy for fear of offending the Shah.[44]

Carter tried to find his own way out of the confusion by asking Senate Majority Leader Byrd, who was in the region, to make a side trip to Tehran, and also asked Treasury Secretary Blumenthal, who was leaving for a long-planned trip to the Middle East, to meet with the Shah. Both returned with gloomy reports. The Shah told Byrd: "It is a deep internal matter here, and all the best statements from Washington, London and Bonn cannot change that."[45] Blumenthal was even more dramatic. A year before, he had met a confident Shah who lectured him on the permissiveness of Western societies. Now he found Iran's ruler lapsing into embarrassing periods of silence, staring "vacantly into the distance . . ." and seemingly "immobilized by fear and indecision, unable to lead and no longer in control." He plaintively asked his visitor: "What does the president suggest I do?" Blumenthal followed up his written report by meeting with Brzezinski, who asked Blumenthal if he thought the military could contain the opposition, and then told him that no one in Washington really understood Iran well enough to provide a hardheaded analysis.

On Blumenthal's recommendation, and with Brezinski's agreement, George Ball, a Washington lawyer, diplomat, and establishment wise man who also was celebrated for bucking the consensus—as he had when he resigned as Lyndon Johnson's deputy secretary of state because he opposed military escalation in Vietnam—was called in to conduct a full examination of our Iran policy. Ball holed up in the Executive Office Building, read all the cable traffic, and was briefed by State Department's experts as well as those outside the government. To Brzezinski's chagrin, Ball concluded that the Shah could not be saved with his full powers, and that the relatively moderate National Front should be installed to block Khomeini, with the Shah retaining his throne and his control over the military. But the CIA's own report on the National Front offered little hope: It was not a cohesive group, but contained parties ranging from moderates to radical leftists, although not the Communists. The CIA finally got it right, but with a disastrous conclusion: Khomeini commanded the largest support from the demonstrators, and the National Front leaders were moving closer to Khomeini's position.[46]

More decisive than all of Washington's internal maneuvering, however, was an unscripted blunder. At a breakfast meeting with reporters on December 7, Carter was asked if the Shah could survive the radical revolution; the president seemed to back away from the Shah in a devastating way: "This is something that is in the hands of the people of Iran. We have never had any intention and don't have any intention of trying to intercede in the internal political affairs of Iran. We primarily want an absence of violence, and bloodshed, and stability. We personally prefer that the Shah maintain a major role in the government, but that is a decision for the Iranian people to make."[47] This sent an unintended signal that Washington was distancing itself from the Shah and leaving decisions not to him but to the "people of Iran"—the ones who were already in the streets demonstrating against the Shah. Carter's remarks sent the Shah into another round of depression and only emboldened the opposition.

The president nevertheless corrected himself and was upbeat at a December 12 news conference: "I expect the Shah to maintain power in Iran and for the present difficulties to be resolved. The predictions of disaster that came from sources have not been realized at all. The Shah has our support and he also has our confidence." The next day Ball met privately with Carter and was more blunt than in his written report. He said the Shah was finished, and there was "a national regurgitation by the Iranian people" that extended to the professional and middle classes. He urged the transfer of power to "responsible hands before Khomeini comes back and messes everything up." He proposed a council of prominent citizens to pick the leaders of a new government and handed the president the names of several dozen possibilities.

Ball also recommended that the Shah temporarily leave the country but remain as commander in chief of the army. Carter rejected his advice on the ground that "I can't tell another head of state what to do."[48] Critics who argue that Carter failed to support the Shah are wrong; if anything, some like Ambassador Sullivan and George Ball, felt he hung on too long in standing with the Shah and his regime. But Carter certainly stayed in the Shah's corner. Yet the president's continued public expression of confidence in the Shah satisfied no one in the administration. Brzezinski persisted in his hard line: Only the military could save the day by imposing order to give the Shah time to reform his autocracy, and he drafted a letter for Carter to so advise the Shah.

Vance immediately called Carter and warned that Brzezinski's tough language would be interpreted by the Shah as an invitation to mass violence. Carter was caught in the middle, with Vance endlessly seeking diplomatic solutions, and Brzezinski urging the use of military might to accomplish diplomatic ends. Vance edited Brzezinski's proposed letter to make it more ambiguous—not what was needed at this critical time, but in the end the message was never sent.[49] The Shah did not order a crackdown, and Sullivan was furious that his recommendation to commence contacts with the opposition was never approved. The Shah and the United States were woefully outmaneuvered by Khomeini, who masterfully used the youthful Iranian extremist phalanx that soon seized the U.S. Embassy.

CLARITY FROM THE AYATOLLAH

But if the Shah was indecisive and the U.S. government divided, one man was certain of his goals: Grand Ayatollah Ruhollah Khomeini. On November 19, Morteza Motahiri, a celebrated cleric, writer, and Islamic scholar at Tehran University, as well as one of Khomeini's closest friends, left for France with a message: The military crackdown was frightening Iranians away from further strikes and demonstrations, and he urged Khomeini to declare a jihad against the Shah. As a grand ayatollah, he had authority under Shia doctrine, and Sazegara saw Khomeini listen carefully and agree, declaring: "Rise up, get guns, and fight with the Army." As a young revolutionary committed to armed struggle, Sazegara was ready and happy to follow this battle cry and return to Iran and fight.

But Yazdi, a political activist from Mossadegh's nationalist party, had a more effective idea, following a tactical debate among Khomeini's entourage.[50] His goal was establishing a free and open Islamic democracy after

victory over the Shah, with both secular and religious communities supporting Khomeini, whom he originally saw as an advocate of democratic institutions, without a special role for clerics in the Iranian government. Yazdi
routinely met Khomeini every morning and had earned his confidence. He
explained to Khomeini that "the jihad order is your nuclear bomb," that the
threat of using it would be sufficient, and that there was no hurry: "Don't
rush for jihad." Yazdi calmly explained that preparation was essential and
cautioned the ayatollah to develop a more sophisticated and what ultimately
turned out to be a winning strategy. Khomeini realized that if he invited
the Iranian people to wage a holy war, the revolution might not succeed
because ordinary people were unable to get guns. And even if the younger
revolutionaries managed to take up arms, the army would crush them, and
that would be the end of the revolution against the Shah.

Yazdi proposed that before Khomeini announced a holy war against the
Shah, he should first "invite the people to do other things" with far less risk
than death under the guns of a superior military force. The ayatollah agreed
and drafted a strong public letter in the form of a Shiite religious order to
the people of Iran. Rather than engage in open war against the army, the
ayatollah exhorted Iranians not to pay their electricity or gas bills to the
government-owned utilities and to stay home from work, especially if they
held government jobs.

Khomeini also tried to split the armed forces, the pillar of the Shah's
power: He told soldiers to leave their garrisons and directed officers not to
obey their generals as a religious duty. The letter dramatically urged the Iranian people to approach soldiers on the street and ask: "Why do you kill
your brothers?" He even warned the wives of army officers that it was "reli-
giously forbidden to you" for their husbands to obey general orders—and for
good measure commanded the women: "Don't cook anything for them,
this is against religion." Sazegara translated the letter into English and French
for the scores of journalists swarming around Neauphle, just as he had the
ayatollah's other statements.[51]

It worked for Khomeini. People refused to pay their bills. Strikes broke
out around the country; Iranians did not go to work. And they took to the
streets by the tens of thousands, confronting the ubiquitous army. Mothers
brought their young children, carrying some on their shoulders, and gave

red roses to the soldiers, sometimes sticking them in their gun barrels. As Sazegara put it: "You know, it is really difficult for the army to kill such a people." Following Khomeini's directive they shouted: "My brother in the army, why do you kill your brother?!" The phrase "my brother in the army" soon became the title of a popular Farsi song. This went on for less than a month but wore down the army's resistance.[52]

Sazegara was uncertain whether the army disobeyed the Shah's order to kill people on the street or he did not want to order them to shoot to kill civilians at all. But it did not matter, because the rebellion spread unchecked. Even the staff of the government radio and television refused to work. The army tried to take over and get the Shah's message out, but the soldiers were unable to run the studios. The workers in the electric power plant did not want to cast the country into darkness, but they created an electrical blackout every night from 8:00 to 9:00 p.m., when Iranians were most likely to watch the news. Workers in the state-owned oil industries joined the strike, depriving the government of a major source of export revenue and beginning the process of upending the U.S. and world economies with the second oil shock of the decade. In a show of solidarity, even wealthy Iranians, the principal beneficiaries of the Shah's economic reforms, started distributing free food.

It was now clear that General Azhari had failed to calm the country, so the Shah dismissed him and dramatically offered to replace him with a civilian and secular nationalist. That offer was rebuffed after the Shah refused a demand for immediate parliamentary elections. As his regime crumbled, on December 27 the Shah appointed a new prime minister, Shapour Bakhtiar of the largely secular National Front. To counter the new prime minister, Yazdi proposed that Khomeini create a Council of the Revolution, in part to ensure continuity among Islamic militants if anything happened to the ayatollah. It was the skeleton of a parallel Islamic rule that exists to this day.[53]

In a bizarre twist, Bazargan and Mohammed Beheshti, two members of the new revolutionary council, recommended that Khomeini join the United States in endorsing the Shah's choice of Bakhtiar as prime minister. The ayatollah refused as long as Bakhtiar held his appointment from the Shah. He could not serve two masters, and Khomeini demanded that Bakhtiar first resign if he wanted the cleric's endorsement. Sazegara told me they feared that if Khomeini accepted Bakhtiar as prime minister and called off the strikes and demonstrations, the Shah's military forces could regain control and then restore the Shah's regime if he was forced to leave the country—the Shah's flight and return under CIA auspices in 1953 were still a vivid memory. Sazegara remembers Khomeini saying: "This is our only chance; all the people are mobilized, and we can destroy the regime of the Shah."

The Shah believed that the National Front would come up with a suitable cabinet, but as the year ended, his options had narrowed to only two: Leave the country or stay and apply an iron fist to restore order. Bakhtiar held firm as the Shah's appointed prime minister, but his efforts to build a national unity government of moderate secularists and Islamists was proceeding too slowly to catch up with the realities in the street. This was exactly what Khomeini wanted, although not what his young defenders were telling the world's press. Yazdi began a charm offensive indicating that Khomeini was committed to an Islamic republic that would hold free elections, guarantee freedom of speech and the press, support the military, and seek good relations with all countries, including the United States. This line was also conveyed to the administration at a meeting Yazdi held with Henry Precht, the State Department's Iran desk officer, who seemed impressed by the soothing nostrums.

By December 30, 1978, almost a year after the president's toast to Iran as an "island of stability," it was anything but. Ignoring his instructions, and without Washington's approval, Sullivan was trying to strike a bargain with the Khomeini forces.[54] Carter was so furious that he demanded Vance sack him, but Vance pushed back and agreed only to ease him out when the crisis had passed. Carter later said: "I wish I had gone ahead and done it."[55]

At a summit meeting on the French Caribbean island of Guadeloupe in the first week of January 1979, with the leaders of Britain, France, and West Germany, Carter discussed the Iran crisis. He remained supportive of the Shah, his prime minister, Bakhtiar, and the use of the military to support him if the Shah left the country.[56] No one at the White House was willing to force out the Shah, even as his regime was collapsing. Neither the president nor Brzezinski realized that the Iranian military was not willing and indeed barely able to mount a coup. So events unrolled on their own because, to paraphrase Ralph Waldo Emerson, men could not ride them.

The administration desperately tried to save the day, but Sick warned

Brzezinski that a harsh military regime would not work because the fragile Iranian army was being diminished by daily desertions, and that the Shah should limit his powers and become a constitutional monarch under the 1906 constitution. The president approved a cable to Sullivan instructing him to tell the Shah that continued uncertainty was undermining military morale and that a Bakhtiar civilian government was preferable, but if this was in doubt, a strong military government should be chosen. But when Sullivan presented this message, the Shah said the military had not asked to use an iron fist, that the administration's recommendation for a military government would cause more bloodshed, and that he "did not have the heart" for a crackdown on his own people.[57]

THE PEACOCK DETHRONED

Huge crowds of Iranians were taking to the streets all night, without sleep, attacking police stations and military garrisons. At this point there was a united front of all factions to oust the Shah—the nationalists, Communists, the bazaar merchants, and the Islamists. This unity would not last long. On January 16, the very day the Shah was leaving, Carter met with congressional leaders at their regular breakfast and conceded that the United States "couldn't control Iran's internal affairs, and there was no way to forecast developments"[58]—for good reason, as Khomeini attacked Carter from France as "the vilest man on earth." The ayatollah also announced he would return on February 1, calling for Iranians, including soldiers and civil servants, to disobey the government. His messages were broadcast on loudspeakers, and there was little that Bakhtiar, the army, or the United States of America could do about it. From his villa in France, Khomeini announced formally for the first time that he was forming a council for an Islamic republic and would install a government upon his return.[59] He sent cassette tapes to Iran urging the armed forces and the people to unite against foreign "hoodlums."

On January 16, 1979, the Shah's 37-year tenure on the Peacock Throne ended in humiliation with his forced departure from Tehran. Not then or indeed ever did he renounce his monarchy, but he left Iran with a message supporting the Bakhtiar government. He blamed everyone but himself: confusing signals from Washington; lack of direct contact with Carter; even his own ambassador, Ardeshir Zahedi, whom he said had served him badly with "inaccurate reporting." He later reflected that while his generals urged him to use force, "I know today that had I ordered my troops to shoot, the price in blood would have been a hundred times less severe than that which my people have paid since the establishment of the so-called Islamic Republic." But fundamentally the choice was his. He admitted that while a dictator can save his regime with violence, "a sovereign may not save his throne by shedding his countrymen's blood."[60]

Sick saw it from a slightly different and less complimentary perspective, writing later that the Shah was unwilling to order a bloody military crackdown "even to save his own skin."[61] All this undercut Brzezinski's dogged insistence on a military coup to save the Shah, as well as Carter's critics who complained that American force could have saved the Shah.

The day after the Shah fled, the president dispatched General Robert Huyser, deputy commander of NATO, who had long-standing ties with the Iranian military. His mission, in the words of Joint Chiefs chairman Jones, was to "give backbone" to the Shah's generals to stick together—when, no longer if—the Shah left. Huyser was instructed by Carter to inform Iran's generals that the United States felt it was vital for Iran to have a strong, pro-American government, that the military leaders remained in Iran to ensure this, and finally to assure the generals that the United States would support them.[62] But Ambassador Sullivan was still marching to his own drummer.

When Sullivan and Huyser met the Shah, he asked them when he should go—with Sullivan saying as soon as possible and Huyser urging delay to have time to rally his military leaders.[63] This proved to be a mission impossible. The generals feared for their own lives if they remained and the Shah was no longer there to lead and protect them.

New instructions were issued by the administration to Sullivan and Huyser to support the Bakhtiar government, to open lines of communication with the religious community, but to avoid bringing radicals into the government. Huyser and Sullivan interpreted the instructions differently, with Huyser believing his support of the Bakhtiar government included action by the Iranian military if necessary, while Sullivan wanted the military to step aside and let the political forces fight it out.[64] The administration spent hours debating the possibility of a coup against the Khomeini government, but never agreed, in part because the leaderless, divided Iranian military simply was not willing or able to carry out such a difficult and bloody mission.[65]

It is important to avoid viewing this dramatic history with the false assurance of perfect hindsight. Khomeini's Islamic fundamentalism was novel and not well understood at the time. It was difficult to understand the appeal of an aging radical cleric in medieval religious garb, who had been exiled for years by a monarch in a rush to modernize his nation—indeed, as we came to recognize, in too much of a rush. Ironically, this cleric who seemed to come from a distant past pioneered the political use of a new device to rally his followers. American intelligence was clueless about the impact of the tape-recorded cassettes of his venomous sermons circulated clandestinely to mosques, which galvanized support around the country. It was a primitive precursor to the sophisticated use of social media—ranging from direct-mail specialist Richard Viguerie's efforts for Ronald Reagan to today's political campaigns, Donald Trump's use of Twitter, and the sinister deployment of Facebook as a recruiting vehicle by radical Islamic groups. Khomeni's skills had been vastly underestimated. This robed 76-year-old cleric, a ruler of crowds and a pioneer of manipulation by modern electronic media, would be America's new opponent in what was once its client state and an anchor of U.S security in the Middle East.

But did Jimmy Carter "lose Iran"? No. The Shah of Iran, in power for almost four decades, lost his own country. Khomeini, in Brzezinski's words, "crystallized the frustrations" of a wide swath of the Iranian public over the Shah's autocratic, lavish Western lifestyle, SAVAK's repression of all opposition, and the initial appeal of the seemingly humble ayatollah.[66] The Shah refused to cede any authority to the secular opposition and turn himself into a constitutional monarch. To his credit but also to his loss, he refused to order his army to kill demonstrators in large numbers, which probably would only have forestalled the uprising, not ended it. There were limits to what the United States could do to save an unpopular ruler, as the Eisenhower and Kennedy administrations learned in Cuba with Fidel Castro's revolution against Fulgencio Batista, and the Obama administration discovered years later when demonstrators in Cairo drove President Hosni Mubarak from power.

However, the Carter administration certainly did not cover itself with glory. The lack of reliable intelligence was an unacceptable fault in failing to keep the president and his advisers abreast of the nature of events on the ground in real time. The divisions between Vance and Brzezinski and the rogue diplomacy of Ambassador Sullivan impeded the formation of a consistent policy. Although there was consistent support for the Shah, he was not given clear guidance.

A new American face, Bruce Laingen, appeared later as our representative in Tehran. He had been stationed in Iran as a junior diplomat, knew the country, and understood the Shah, who, he said, "lacked the capacity to trust anyone, like all despots."[67] He became a principal figure facing this new and more virulent radical Islamic despotism in the final act of the Carter administration.

27

THE FALL OF THE PRESIDENT

N obody can prevent me," declared Ayatollah Khomeini as he returned from exile to wildly welcoming crowds of Iranians numbering in the millions.[1] The owner of the villa in Neauphle had chartered an airplane from Air France, and when Sazegara asked Khomeini how many people he wanted to accompany him, the ayatollah responded that he wanted not only his entire entourage of about thirty-five people but all of the some three hundred journalists. Air France was concerned that the plane might be turned away from Tehran, so they insisted the airliner carry more fuel and fewer people. Sazegara had the unenviable task of bumping more than half the journalists.

The plane left at midnight from Paris's Orly Airport, with Sazegara the last passenger to jump on as he negotiated until the last minute with journalists begging to join the historic flight. At 9:00 a.m. on February 1, 1979, the Khomeini "Victory Flight," as his adherents in exile called it, landed at Mehrabad Airport in Tehran. General Amir Hossein Rabii had vowed to shoot down Khomeini's plane when it tried to land in Tehran, but only if he had U.S. approval, which he did not receive. He was among the many senior officials under the Shah later shot by the revolutionaries. A new era began in the long history of Iran and its relationship with the United States, and no one could be certain of the outcome at that heady moment.

As the plane's doors swung open, Sazegara found himself looking down on the leaders of the Iranian air force, guns at the ready, and could not be sure what they would do. But he was reassured when Khomeini's brother and his friend Morteza Motahari, who had visited at Neauphle, came running toward the plane. Sazegara let the photographers off first to record the ayatollah's historic return, and the pilot then helped Khomeini down the stairs. Khomeini asked to be driven to a cemetery south of Tehran, where, in Sazegara's words, "the martyrs of the Revolution were buried."

Then Khomeini got down to business and held a press conference at an Islamic high school to announce the appointment of his new prime minister, Mehdi Bazargan, the man who had organized a letter with thousands of signatures opposing the Shah. That put him in direct opposition to Shapour Bakhtiar, a longtime secular opponent of the Shah who nevertheless was not acceptable to Khomeini because he had been named by the Shah. Even before he left France he had directed Dr. Hassan Habibi, an Islamic legal scholar, to begin drafting a new constitution based explicitly on Islamic law. Bakhtiar did not oppose this on principle but insisted that he was the legal prime minister. Khomeini rejected this out of hand, and used the power of public demonstrators to shout: "Independence! Freedom! Islamic Republic!"[2]

The army, trained for decades by the United States and still armed with American weapons, was powerless against the crowds, and gradually switched its loyalty to the ayatollah and his virulently anti-American, anti-Western stance. But it did not happen overnight.

While Brzezinski surreptitiously organized the evacuation of thousands of Americans on C-130 planes, General Huyser for his part spent weeks following the Shah's departure trying to rally the military to support Bakhtiar and block Khomeini's accession to power. The Shah was suspicious of his own military leaders and had never permitted the heads of his air force, army, and navy to meet together. Huyser organized the top six military leaders into an operating group for the first time and did everything he could to stiffen their joint resolve before Khomeini's return. Huyser felt that the military leadership remained willing to work with Bakhtiar and a regency council the Shah had created, but the general constantly had to fight off Sullivan, who lacked confidence in the military.[3]

In the end military support for Bakhtiar evaporated when the soldiers abandoned their units along with the outpouring of public support for Khomeini on his return. In his initial speech he promised to protect the soldiers who supported him and hang as traitors those who did not and remained loyal to Bakhtiar. This promise of amnesty, made by Khomeini's appointed prime minister, Bazargan, ended Huyser's mission.[4] The February 11 cable from the U.S. defense attaché at the embassy captured the reality: "Army surrenders; Khomeini wins. Destroying all classified."[5]

In the words of the last chief of staff of the Shah's armed forces, General Abbas Gharabaghi, we "melt[ed] down like a snowball."[6] With the army neutered, the last vestiges of the Shah's regime were destroyed. Bakhtiar fled to France after only thirty-seven days in power. The State Department's hope of a peaceful transition, upon which Sullivan and State Department Iran desk officer Henry Precht had based their hopes, never had a chance.

WASHINGTON'S FIRST ENCOUNTER WITH RADICAL ISLAM

It became imperative for Washington to establish a relationship with Tehran's new government, or at least to try. The reasons were compelling: the Soviet potential for intervention through its Communist proxy, the Tudeh Party, in a country that was one of the world's largest oil producers, and the security of the Persian Gulf more broadly. Carter was under no illusions about the dangers posed by Khomeini, but because of the long-term interests of the United States in Iran, he immediately established diplomatic relations with the revolutionary government.[7] The Iranian revolution of 1979 followed the same path as the Bolshevik Revolution of 1917. The most ruthless, organized, and radical forces prevailed, even though they did not initially constitute anything like a majority of the opposition to the established order.

This is generally the rule in such upheavals. The moderates are divided and play by more traditional rules that simply do not apply in the vacuum left by the collapse of the established order. Just as the Bolsheviks were never thought to have the staying power to govern post-czarist Russia, so too were the clerical fundamentalists thought to be incapable of establishing control over post-Shah Iran. In both instances there was a great deal of wishful thinking. Brzezinski's own report to the president a day after Khomeini's triumphant return warned him: "Islamic revivalist movements are not sweeping the Middle East and are not likely to be the wave of the future. More concretely, it is worth noting that . . . religious institutions rarely succeed in dominating the political systems of Muslim countries."[8] But in medieval revenge, they executed those top advisers to the Shah who did not flee when he did, beginning a bloodbath of killing anyone associated with him.

Brzezinski's Iran specialist, Gary Sick, later described the situation far more acutely: "Khomeini's call for the establishment of a religious philosopher-king, the *velayat-e faqih*—and clerical management of political institutions according to religious law was so unexpected, so alienating to existing political traditions that it was less a surprise than an embarrassment . . . the notion of a popular revolution leading to the establishment of a theocratic state seemed so unlikely as to be absurd. Unfortunately, there were no relevant models in Western political tradition to explain what we were seeing in Iran during the revolution. . . . The world was surprised not once but twice by the Iranian revolution. It was surprised in the first instance by the breadth and depth of popular opposition to the Shah and the success of revolutionary organization emanating from the mosques." The world was surprised once again when Khomeini was able to sustain his "fanciful" notions of an ideal theocratic state. Nothing quite like this had occurred since the Reformation, and secular observers may be forgiven for their stubborn refusal to believe that this preoccupation with theological niceties in Tehran was anything more than a minor bout of eccentricity that would soon pass."⁹

But at the time, as so often happens, those in power clung to the classic illusion that "this time is different." There was some hope that the new revolutionary government would maintain a relationship with the United States. Bazargan had excellent credentials that made him widely acceptable to the mass of Iranians as prime minister. He had been a minister in the Mossadegh government that was overthrown by Western intelligence. Bazargan and Yazdi, his foreign minister, were members of the more moderate Freedom Movement of Iran. The prime minister was an engineer and technocrat, and while an early and pious supporter of Khomeini, he was Westernized and liberal, and had hopes that once the Shah was deposed, Iran would become a state in which human rights were respected and civil society prevailed, and that Khomeini might be content to serve as a religious but not a political figure.

After the ayatollah's tumultuous reception in Tehran, he quickly left for the holy city of Qum, the "Vatican" of Shiite Islam. Nevertheless huge fights broke out over the direction of the revolution, with Khomeini's clerical followers demanding the formation of the "government of God" he had written about. They trekked to Qum for his word on events, and Ayatollah Khomeini gradually became a political arbiter.[10]

The Carter administration's efforts were designed to build relationships with Bazargan's nonclerical, relatively moderate government, named by Khomeini himself. Washington also tried to strengthen ties with the American-trained and equipped military, using as leverage the backlog of $12 billion in military equipment ordered under the Shah and the continuing need for spare parts. There was also an agreement to resume a small package of $50 million of nonlethal arms like jeeps. But even though Pentagon officials tried to implement it, the diplomatic relationship deteriorated, and the equipment was never delivered. At the start, Carter remembered, the United States had fairly good relations with the new government,[11] but Sick shared Brzezinski's skepticism that the relative moderates would survive. Brzezinski, with his academic knowledge of the Soviet revolution, believed that the radicals would end up in control, and that the Bazargan government was simply an interim arrangement. He was right.

The real battle was an ideological power struggle, played out over the year in drafting the new constitution. The moderates in power argued for a democratic civilian government dedicated to protecting minorities and free speech, as Yazdi had asserted in the final months before the revolution. The Islamists wanted a theocratic government operating under the Islamic law of Sharia. But the moderates were outmaneuvered by the clerics in the constitutional convention. Bazargan famously and courageously remarked that he was like a knife without a handle, unable to get things done.[12] He appealed his case to Khomeini in Qum and lost.

It is barely remembered that on February 14, only two weeks after Khomeini's return, young, left-wing students staged an attack on the U.S. Embassy in Tehran, took hostages, and led Ambassador Sullivan blindfolded out of the embassy as the news photographers clicked. At that time the invaders were efficiently dispatched by the Bazargan government. Foreign Minister Yazdi, recognizing this as a breach of international law and diplomatic protocol, quickly went to the embassy and ordered the release of the

American officials. They were all freed within hours, the Iranian government apologized, and it was over.

This seemed to indicate it was safe for America's diplomats to remain in Tehran and that a realistic chance remained of a correct, if not close, relationship with the new Khomeini-appointed government. Thereafter the government placed guards at the embassy compound, ostensibly to keep order and protect the diplomats. There were actually security squads from separate groups, some aligned with friendly elements from the provisional government to protect them from the organized Revolutionary Guards who were also present, and to whom Bruce Laingen, the ranking American diplomat, referred as "real thugs."[13]

It is only in this political and security context that the seizure of the U.S. Embassy and the hostage crisis that exploded months later on November 4 can be fully understood. It became, in Khomeini's own words, "the second" Islamic revolution.[14] The first had ousted the Shah, and the second used the hostages as pawns in a power play to overturn the civilian Bazargan government Khomeini had appointed as a stopgap measure to consolidate his own power. This led the nation to rally around Khomeini and his clerics. This historic turn away from an intimate partnership of more than three decades helped prompt Khomeini's label of "the Great Satan" for the United States and affixed the slogan "Death to America" in Iran's clerical liturgy. These cries still split the air at rallies to this day, an essential political tool of Iran's clerical leadership and its followers.

Washington wanted to avoid any action that might strengthen the clerics against Bazargan, and the first unnerving hostage episode, brief though it was, had led to a policy review that concluded American security interests in Iran were too important to abandon and that we needed to salvage our relationship with the new revolutionary crowd.

The administration made a continuous effort through contacts with Bazargan's provisional government, but attempts to reach Khomeini himself were rebuffed. Laingen told Washington that the administration needed to send a "quick signal that we were willing to live with the revolution" and make a clean break from the Shah, a message he repeatedly gave to the provisional government, but which was "not enough."[15] One way to accomplish this, he argued, was to name a new ambassador. Finally, in April, the president nominated Walter Cutler, a respected career diplomat, and the Bazargan government gave its formal consent.

But, responding to the new regime's horrific pressure against the Iranian Jewish community, Senator Jacob Javits put through a Senate resolution criticizing the Iranian government's treatment of minorities in general and Jews in particular. This led to angry demonstrations attacking, although not overrunning, the U.S. Embassy; the flag was torn down and graffiti scrawled on the walls. The Iranian government also withdrew its acceptance of Cutler. When the Iranians refused to budge despite our protests, the administration appointed Bruce Laingen as chargé d'affaires with the rank of ambassador in June 1979. He was amazed to see revolutionaries everywhere, many waving their Uzi submachine guns. Banks, theaters, and Western business offices had been burned.[16]

The embassy, with its staff of about 1,100, had been reduced to only 70 people. Bazargan and Yazdi promised to protect it, and on Laingen's orders major security upgrades were made. Heavy steel doors with automatic alarm systems, electronic surveillance cameras, remote control tear-gas devices, bulletproof glass, and steel window grilles were installed, backed up by sand-filled steel boxes to stop projectiles from outside. Food was stored for a long siege, and contingency plans developed for a staged withdrawal if there was an attack. These measures were designed to provide defense for several hours.[17]

Even though the U.S. Marine contingent was enlarged, as I later learned when I was the Brussels-based American ambassador to the European Union in the Clinton administration, embassies are not impregnable fortresses and depend upon the protection of the host country under long-standing international law and practice, and bilateral agreements. Khomeini's forces totally ignored these established norms. Carter depended on precedent to avoid serious abuse or kidnapping of our people, and reflected that "I didn't think it was going to happen. I thought they might have abused or gone into the embassy or something, but I never dreamed that the government would not eventually, maybe over a period of hours, come on in there."[18]

When Laingen first arrived at the 27-acre embassy compound, he saw furniture, cars, and household supplies still piled up following the evacuation of the many members of the American community who had descended on the embassy after the February revolution. At the height of the Shah's reign, there had been some 60,000 Americans living in Tehran, many to manage the large military relationship. As part of his initial focus on strengthening security, he especially wanted the Revolutionary Guards out of the compound, because their mere presence annoyed the marine guards protecting the embassy.

Laingen's immediate mission was restoring the supply chain of military equipment as an earnest indication of his broader goal, which was to implement his instructions of reassuring the provisional government that the United States fully accepted the change of regime and had no intention of bringing back the Shah. His reception by the provisional government was courteous and friendly. It was staffed largely by secular leaders of the National Front, who had made common cause with Khomeini and his clerical followers to overthrow the Shah. He experienced no difficulty meeting with the most senior members of the new government, and was pleasantly surprised at the annual July 4 celebration by the large number of senior ministers who turned out, including Yazdi, although the foreign minister prudently refused to allow himself to be photographed with Laingen in a toast.

Lying in wait, however, was the parallel political structure: Khomeini and his revolutionary council, which never made formal contact with the embassy and was barely visible to it—although not for want of trying. Laingen occasionally met some senior mullahs and one member of the council, Ayatollah Beheshti, and he made it a point to emphasize repeatedly that the United States accepted the revolution and had no intent of reversing it, and that the Shah would not be a factor in making American policy.

In August there seemed to be some improvement. The head of the Iranian security group in the compound, whom Laingen called a "particularly unattractive thug named Mashalla," was forcibly removed by other revolutionary elements. But the chaotic and threatening situation in which Laingen and his colleagues were forced to operate was still unlike that of any U.S. Embassy in the world. One Sunday morning Laingen returned from a swim, clad only in his swim trunks and a bathrobe. When he opened the door to the second floor of his official residence, he was shocked to find several Revolutionary Guards pointing Uzis at him, unaware that they were confronting the senior American diplomat in the country. They entered the residence through kitchen windows at the rear, exploring every corner in search of a competing group of Revolutionary Guards they were trying to evict.[19]

Several of the more friendly Revolutionary Guards and two chagrined marines met with Laingen to sort things out, and this led to a breakthrough. The marines regained control of the compound, and an Iranian police guard was posted outside the walls of the more heavily fortified embassy as a new ring of external security. This was taken as a tangible sign the provisional government wanted to regularize relationships with the Carter administration. But when Vance and Yazdi held the first high-level meeting between the two nations in New York, Yazdi was so full of aggressive revolutionary rhetoric that Vance was unable to pursue his agenda of installing a new ambassador to reopen formal diplomatic relations.[20]

Laingen resolved a number of commercial and consular disputes and facilitated dozens of visits by American business representatives, though he still felt Washington did not fully appreciate the upward trend in relations he saw in Tehran, which was shared by other Western embassies. Three weeks before the hostages were taken, visas started being issued to the thousands of Iranians waiting to come to the United States. There was even a willingness to share military intelligence with the provisional regime of the looming threat from Iraq's Saddam Hussein. American officials felt comfortable traveling outside Tehran.

Only a week before the embassy was seized, American officials worked with the provisional government and the revolutionary committee that controlled the military compound to gain access to the military equipment warehouse, which Laingen regarded as the most important sign that the provisional government really wanted to rebuild the military supply relationship, a goal Laingen considered of overriding importance. The two sides were close to an agreement on a limited resupply of spare parts that was critical for the Iranian air force.[21] What was lost on everyone was a subterranean effort to undermine the Bazargan government by the radicals, who were waiting for the right time to strike.

One of the most fundamental flaws of the U.S. intelligence was its failure to understand the powerful political pull of Islamic fundamentalism embodied in Khomeini, even though a number of Farsi speakers were stationed at the embassy and maintained contacts with lower-level clerics. A type of dual government was developing in Iran that exists even today.

Bazargan spoke frequently on television pleading for cooperation and venting his frustration over his inability to implement his decrees. He complained that the revolutionary committees were undermining his government, operating outside normal administrative channels, and setting up their own roadblocks on streets. He implied that Khomeini was behind this. The ayatollah sat like a potentate in Qum and refused to meet with Laingen. As the latter realized only in retrospect, Bazargan was a reasonable man, but headed a "government without power."[22] The real power lay in the ayatollah, who Laingen later concluded was "so rigidly opposed to any kind of presence of the United States, of 'western toxification,' as to make it impossible ever to have had a relationship with us."[23]

THE SHAH'S POWERFUL FRIENDS
LIGHT THE FUSE

The other major factor in the hostage crisis was the return of the Shah to the United States, and here he and his highly placed American supporters cannot escape their share of the responsibility. As the Shah's regime tottered, Carter offered him an American sanctuary in December 1978 and January 1979, more than a month before Khomeini's return, but the "King of Kings" dithered. The offer was not made out of the goodness of the administration's collective heart, but as an inducement for the Shah to make way for moderate politicians to try to form a less radical government than was likely to be fostered by Khomeini.[24]

The administration made plans for him to stay at Sunnyland, the estate of the media magnate Walter Annenberg in Palm Springs, California; he was to fly there directly and agree to stay out of politics. But to everyone's surprise, he decided first to stop in Egypt, probably because he nursed the illusion that a Khomeini regime would quickly fall and he would be ushered back to his kingdom, just as in 1953. More realistically, he also thought that rushing to America would play into the hands of his Iranian opponents, who considered him a lackey of the United States. In Egypt the deposed Shah stayed with his close friend Anwar el-Sadat, and then went to Morocco at the invitation of King Hassan. There a senior American intelligence officer made contact with him, and reported that while he was a broken man, he believed that he had prevented a bloody military confrontation that might have foreclosed his return.

While counterfactual history is speculative by its very nature, had the Shah accepted the president's first invitation to come to America, I believe it is doubtful there would ever have been a hostage crisis. Khomeini was so pleased to see the Shah leave Iran and clear the way for his return that he initially raised no objections to the Shah going to the United States.[25]

But on February 22, when the Shah informed the American ambassador to Morocco that he would like to enter the United States, it was too late. The next day an NSC committee chaired by Brzezinski assessed the tense political stand-off in Iran and the large number of Iranian students in America who despised the Shah and could be expected to demonstrate against his presence. The CIA officer in Morocco was told to advise the Shah as politely as possible to delay his visit.[26]

Then Brzezinski, prompted by a call from Ambassador Zahedi, had second thoughts about denying immediate entry to a longtime ally and brought them to Carter. But the president was warned by Brzezinski's own deputy, David Aaron, that if the Shah was admitted, American hostages might again be taken, and this time their release might be dependent on extraditing the Shah to Iran to face trial. The president abruptly turned Brzezinski down, pointing out that with Americans already having been held hostage, however briefly, on February 14, he did not want to see pictures of the Shah playing tennis on American soil.[27]

But the Shah was already wearing out his welcome in Morocco and would not take no for an answer. He hired a public relations firm and a lawyer and put tremendous and persistent pressure on Carter, through his good friends Henry Kissinger and David Rockefeller. Both members of the foreign-policy establishment were indignant that such a longtime ally could be kept out of the United States. They arranged for him to take refuge in the Bahamas for an unhappy two months, with little privacy and exorbitant costs, and then he moved to Cuernavaca, a resort outside Mexico City favored by wealthy artists, eccentrics, and, ironically, the retirement home of his nemesis, Ambassador Sullivan.[28] He was allowed to remain there only a few months and then moved on to Panama. Finally Sadat sent a plane to Panama to take him back to Egypt. The Shah's anger at the president grew intense, and he blamed Carter for losing Iran, which was given credence by Henry Kissinger.

Kissinger told me that while he had no particular feeling for the Shah as a person, he felt the United States owed him much because, at some sacrifice to himself, he "was almost alone in helping us in a crisis" in Israel, in offering refueling to U.S. Navy ships in the Indian Ocean, and even in Vietnam. When Kissinger reached an agreement to end the Vietnam War that froze military force levels, the Shah sent all his F-15 fighters—later replenished by the Nixon administration—to beef up the South Vietnamese inventory.

The former secretary of state led an active campaign on behalf of the Shah against the appeals of his own successor, Cyrus Vance, telling me: "I started the ball rolling, as I felt he had been a champion and leader for the U.S. for over two decades, and couldn't see a problem with having him come [here] for a supervised exile, so that he would not engage in Iranian politics."[29] Kissinger started the campaign by going to David Rockefeller, whose Chase Bank was known as "the oil bank" for its deep connections to the industry that was founded by his grandfather, John D. Rockefeller. He also recruited John J. McCloy, lawyer, banker, and de facto chairman of the American foreign-policy establishment. Now Kissinger felt it was time to go public. So in January 1979 he added a paragraph to a speech praising the Shah as a decades-long friend of America who was being treated "like the Flying Dutchman with no place to go." On April 9 the impressive trio of Kissinger, Rockefeller, and McCloy met with Carter, Brzezinski, and Vance.

Kissinger remembers that Vance and Carter rejected their appeal, but Brzezinski let them know he supported it but was constrained by the president's opposition.[30] Carter was upset by the campaign, although he allowed the Shah's children to continue their education in America and was willing to admit the empress for medical care if she wished, so notifying the Iranian government. For the first time the Iranians warned the administration of serious problems if either the Shah or his wife were admitted.

As the brutal nature of the Khomeini regime emerged through torture and summary executions of its opponents, a politically dangerous "Who lost

Iran?" campaign began gathering force as a presidential election year approached. Sentiments within the administration began to change, and even Mondale appealed to Carter in a July 23 memo arguing that "a great nation could not allow these twerps to tell us who could come into our country."[31]

No one in the administration could say they had not been fully warned by the most authoritative American official on the ground. On July 29, Laingen, replying to a request from Vance to assess the possible repercussions of admitting the Shah, sent a secret cable advising against it in half a dozen different ways.[32] He warned that if the Shah took up residence in the next two to three months, it would endanger Americans in Iran unless the political power struggle in Iran was resolved by autumn, which it was not.

Laingen correctly forecast that daily frustrations would increase in the coming months, including a potential "search for scapegoats" for the regime's failure, such as an absurd charge by Khomeini during the previous week blaming the United States for burning agricultural fields throughout Iran. He also reported the frequent intrusions on Bazargan's government by revolutionary groups who were subject to the "whims of the ultimate control of the Ayatollah." Moreover, he chillingly reported that the government still had not replaced the irregular guerrilla force of supposed guards posted by Khomeini around the embassy. Finally he warned correctly that "refuge of the Shah [in the United States] would almost certainly trigger demonstrations against our Embassy . . . [and] Iran's regular police forces remain largely demoralized and cannot yet be relied upon to apply the force that might be needed to prevent violence against us." He concluded: "It is of utmost importance, in my view, that we not inject ourselves in that process by a premature gesture toward the Shah, with all the suspicions about our attitudes and about USG [U.S. Government] interference that this could arouse, and the opportunity it would provide for those revolutionary hotheads who would probably like nothing better than a chance to frustrate the political timetable and take a crack at us at the same time."

Through the late summer and early autumn, Laingen continued sending cables like this with reports that the clerics were heading toward establishing a theocracy, and that the pledges by Bazargan and Yazdi to protect the embassy from attack by the radicals were of diminishing value. Bazargan was publicly critical of the revolutionary committees operating outside the control of his government, and told the celebrated Italian journalist Oriana Fallaci: "For an official point of view the government runs the country, but in an ideological and revolutionary sense Khomeini and his councils control."[33]

If Kissinger, McCloy, and Rockefeller could have read Laingen's stark cables, would they have persisted in lobbying for the Shah's admission? The question underscores the dangers of relying upon even informed Americans offering sensitive advice without full access to all the classified information necessary for a sound decision.

Laingen posed alternatives for the administration and the Shah's advocates. He argued that while the United States had an obligation to admit him at some point, it would be dangerous now, with so much political turmoil, and not until we had demonstrated our acceptance of the Islamic revolution by formally naming someone as ambassador following the aborted nomination of Cutler; until the Iranians largely completed their process of shaping a new constitution; and finally, until the Shah had publicly renounced his and his heirs' claim to the throne—which he never did to his dying day.[34]

Then we learned that the Shah had cancer. Like so many other destabilizing factors in Iran, this secret illness was not uncovered by U.S. intelligence but disclosed on October 18 by David Rockefeller, who must have thought he held a humanitarian trump card by appealing for him to be treated in the United States. Until that moment the Shah had kept his illness a personal and state secret of the highest order. For years since its discovery during a Swiss ski trip in 1974, the Shah had told neither his own family—his wife, Empress Farah, and his twin sister, Ashraf, learned about it only after he went into exile—nor the Iranian government and people, that two French specialists, Dr. Jean Bernard and Dr. Georges Flandrin, had diagnosed him with cancer of the lymph system.

His treatment with the drug chlorambucil kept the cancer in check, but for the CIA to have been unaware for five years of a potentially fatal disease affecting the leader of one of America's major allies and the beneficiary of billions' worth of weapons was another staggering lapse. By the time the Shah had reached the Bahamas, the cancer had flared up. Dr. Flandrin flew to the Bahamas and diagnosed Richter syndrome, a rare and sudden transformation of the Shah's slow-growing cancer into a more aggressive form of lymphoma. Along with the cancer, a case of gallstones and his own reaction to medication made the Shah terribly ill.

As late as September 27, Vance spoke to the Council on Foreign Relations reiterating why security for U.S. diplomats in Tehran precluded the Shah's admission. Dr. Benjamin Kean of New York Hospital made several trips to examine the Shah in Mexico and concluded that the combination of so many maladies, from jaundice to a cancerous spleen and a neck tumor, required immediate attention that he could only receive at a large, sophisticated hospital.

Rockefeller's disclosure had its intended effect. After Vance informed the regular weekly foreign-policy breakfast on October 19, resistance began crumbling. The secretary changed his mind and recommended that the Shah be admitted on humanitarian grounds to deal with this medical emergency. Brzezinski had always advocated his admission as a matter of national honor. As he told me: "How can we have friends in the world if we behave this way?"[35] Journalists began accusing the administration of treating a valued ally like a homeless person.

The president was the last holdout, fearing another attack on the embassy.[36] Carter was the only person who was "skeptical and did not want to let him in," Ham said, and the president was the only person in his inner circle who actually predicted the outcome: "What are you guys going to advise me to do when they overrun our embassy now and take our people hostage?"[37]

Carter told Vance to get a medical opinion on whether the Shah could receive the required medical care abroad. On October 20 the State Department's medical adviser, after reviewing the Shah's records, agreed the Shah could not receive the treatment he needed anywhere in Mexico. Finally Warren Christopher, the deputy secretary of state, told Carter they would obtain an assurance from Bazargan and Yazdi that our diplomats would be protected. So the president said: "Well, if we can get that commitment, okay."

Carter and Brzezinski felt they got that commitment from Bazargan.[38] Ham also recalled they got renewed assurances from the Iranian government that they would protect the embassy as they had the previous February.[39] But it is clear that the Iranians objected to the Shah's entry into the United

States, fearing it was part of a conspiracy to return him to power. There were eight thousand Americans in Iran at the time, plus those seventy-two diplomats.

In fact, however, the commitment was not as binding as it seemed, in part because by that time no one but Khomeini could have made such assurances stick. Carter was at Camp David that weekend, and Brzezinski forwarded Vance's memorandum on admitting the Shah, softening it slightly but crucially. He changed the conditions so that the Iranians would merely be notified and not asked to agree because, as he said "We didn't in effect let Bazargan and Yazdi have a veto power, but we did agree to notify Bazargan and Yazdi through Laingen."[40]

Carter now faced one of the most fateful decisions of his presidency. Vance recommended that before allowing the Shah entry Bazargan should be notified so we could assess the severity of his reaction in advance. But from Camp David, Carter disagreed, and on October 21 decided that the Iranian government should be told he would be admitted for purely medical reasons and no more.[41]

Laingen learned that his advice against admitting the Shah had been ignored when a Marine guard handed him a note two days later as he was having breakfast at the residence. When he read the message, he said, it was a "bit of a shock to all of us in the embassy," and he immediately ordered additional security measures, fearing the worst. Laingen and the Iran desk officer Henry Precht, who was visiting Iran at the time, met with Bazargan and Yazdi, and while the two politicians were unhappy, their response was subdued. They doubted that the real reason was medical, since no one in Iran had ever heard the Shah was ill.[42]

Laingen himself did not have full knowledge of the Shah's condition, and while Bazargan, a dignified man in the Persian tradition, was civil in his response, Yazdi bluntly warned that the Shah's admission to the United States was a very serious step that could have some severe repercussions. They were not ready to believe the Shah had incurable cancer and pressed for a medical evaluation by Iranian doctors, who would fly to the United States to examine the Shah. The State Department and NSC balked and agreed only to inform them of the diagnosis made by the Shah's American oncology team. Laingen asked for assurances that the embassy would be protected, but Bazargan, fearing the worst from the growing power of the radicals, could only say: "We will do our best."[43]

The president faced a classic dilemma. As Ham aptly described it, Carter was being asked: "Mr. President are you going to let him in and get that treatment, or are you going to make him stay in Mexico and possibly have him die and us be blamed for that death?"[44] Public opinion would not have permitted him to deny entry under those dire medical circumstances, and he would have been accused of weakness and betrayal of a valued ally.

But one of the historic ironies of the Carter administration, perhaps the difference between the president serving two terms or only one, was that the president was given an inaccurate medical assessment of the treatment options. He grudgingly agreed to admit the Shah based on the assurance he could only be treated in the United States. But New York was not the only place where the Shah could have been well cared for.

In researching his own book years later, Ham was the only person in the Carter administration who talked to the Shah's French doctors, the two specialists who had originally diagnosed his lymphoma and later examined him when his illness worsened. Bernard and Flandrin were world renowned for their treatment of lymphoma. Jordan also asked several doctors to review the Shah's medical records and concluded that he could have been treated in Mexico City, where many American top medical specialists in all fields do their advanced training. But the crucial medical judgment about whether he needed to be flown to New York's Memorial Sloan Kettering Cancer Center was turned over to Dr. Kean, who was not an oncologist but a pathologist specializing in malaria who had managed the Shah's care in Panama, as well as Dr. Michael DeBakey, the famed cardiovascular surgeon, also not an oncologist. Ham believed that the Shah got "poorer treatment and poorer medical care and attention than you or I would have gotten if we had walked in off the street with the same condition," because with the eyes of the political and medical worlds looking over their shoulders, the Sloan Kettering doctors dared not risk being experimental and bold, but gave their distinguished patient very conservative treatment, which Jordan found to be "uneven and at times contradictory."[45]

From Sazegara's perspective at Khomeini's right hand, the admission of the Shah to the United States was a "powerful trigger" for the second hostage taking. Yazdi felt the same. As Yazdi's son-in-law Professor Noor-baksh told me: "The admission of the Shah to the U.S. was the last blow. Yazdi had warned the U.S. against this act, and said the United States was playing with fire with the Shah's admission to the U.S."[46]

Again the CIA-sponsored 1953 coup loomed large in the minds of Iranians, who were convinced that in admitting the Shah, the United States was on a path to reinstall him. The fateful decision would lead not only to Carter's downfall but to that of Bazargan and Yazdi as well. That is why Yazdi pressed so hard to have one of their doctors examine the Shah. Yet the immediate response on the streets of Tehran and the official media was surprisingly restrained. Even Khomeini simply said: "Let us all hope he dies."[47]

A FATEFUL HANDSHAKE

One final diplomatic event made it almost certain that as the radicals gained control, the revolutionary Iranian regime would turn its back on the United States. In the last few days before the U.S. Embassy was breached on November 4, Brzezinski flew to Algiers at the head of a U.S. delegation to join the celebration of 25 years of Algerian independence from France, with a handful of famous radical figures including General Vō Nguyên Giáp of Vietnam, Raúl Castro of Cuba, Libya's Mu'ammar Gadhafi, and Yāsir Arafat of the PLO, with whom he shook hands at a reception in violation of U.S. policy. For this he was criticized by the White House, but he blithely shrugged it off by saying he had "acted in conformance with the laws of civilized people."[48]

Of more fateful consequence for both sides, Bazargan and Yazdi were also there and asked for a meeting with Brzezinski, which he felt he could not refuse at a time when Washington was trying to open a channel with Iran. He repeated that the United States was willing to open diplomatic relations and resume military sales. But they conveyed another message: Do not provide asylum to the Shah. Brzezinski replied that if he asked for it, "We won't betray him," and that the situation differed from that of the Mossadegh coup of 1953. They repeated their warning, and as they parted, Brzezinski was photographed shaking hands with Bazargan.[49]

This handshake was far more serious. The photograph and the story of the meeting were given massive play on the front pages of the Iranian newspapers even before Bazargan returned from Algiers. While Brzezinski returned home optimistic about doing business with Tehran, to paranoid Iranian radicals—"hotheads," as Laingen called them—it appeared that the civilian government was cozying up to the United States, and this was one more nail in its coffin.

Laingen said flatly that Brzezinski's public embrace of Bazargan in the Algiers meeting "backfired" and "put an end to the provisional government."[50] As the student radicals took to the streets, Brzezinski continued to think their demonstration would turn out to be just one more left-wing revolt against Bazargan and Yazdi.[51] But this time really was different.

A few days before, a group of fervently religious students from Amir Kabir University of Technology had gone mountain climbing, a favorite activity among Iranian students. They decided to show they were more radical and anti-American than the Communist students who had stormed the embassy on February 14, and they contacted Mohammad Mousavi Khoeiniha, a young cleric and close friend of Khomeini's son, imploring him to ask permission from Khomeini. They told Khoeiniha that they did not want to storm the embassy if Ayatollah Khomeini forbade it, and that, in any event, they only intended to stay a few hours or at most a day. Khoeiniha told them the ayatollah would not approve if he was asked in advance. So Khoeiniha advised them to take over the embassy anyway, whereupon he would seek Khomeini's agreement, in effect presenting Khomeini with a fait accompli.[52]

On November 1 more than 1,000 students spent the day marching around the embassy compound walls and posting pictures of Khomeini, drawing graffiti, and slapping on posters denouncing the Shah and the United States. Laingen learned about it the night before, added security, called in the Tehran police chief, and things were under control. There were some tense moments as an embassy security officer ripped down posters with the ayatollah's picture. In view of the warning and the occasional struggles around the gates, it is difficult to understand why the State Department and the White House did not order an immediate evacuation of all embassy personnel.

Laingen had already advised the bulk of the Americans who lived in the vast compound or in apartments behind it to spend the day at the British

Embassy compound in the hills of Tehran. On the evening of November 3, at the invitation of the Iranian Foreign Ministry to its private club, Laingen and most of the diplomatic corps viewed a documentary on the revolution. It included shots of the February breach of the U.S. Embassy, with tanks in the streets. The day had passed in relative quiet, so he decided to reopen the embassy's consular section, after the graffiti were removed.

The difficult events of the previous days seemed to provide evidence that the government meant what it said about providing security. One precaution taken by the staff was a patriotic decision to keep the American flag flying by securing it to the flagpole and greasing the pole itself to make it difficult to climb. The Marines were ordered to keep a state of alert, but business would defiantly go forward.

THE HOSTAGE CRISIS BEGINS

On that fateful November 4, Laingen left the embassy for the Foreign Ministry and a long-scheduled meeting at 10:30 a.m. to arrange for the future reopening of a reduced American military liaison office. He was accompanied by Mike Howland, his security officer, and Victor Tomseth, the senior political officer. As they made their way across town, Laingen noticed several groups of demonstrators heading for the university to commemorate an assault there by the Shah's regime. The meeting, accompanied by traditional cups of tea, was civil and apparently productive. As they were boarding their limousine, Howland, who had a walkie-talkie, relayed the news that the demonstrators had turned toward the embassy compound and that Alan Gola-cinski, a security officer inside the walls, was advising the three diplomats not to return. So they raced up the stairs of the Foreign Ministry seeking Iranian help to block the advancing demonstrators.

They were physically separate but in radio contact. Laingen did not order the marines to fire on the demonstrators, and they did not, but instructed them to use tear gas, which was done. When the alarm bells rang, the Marines raced from Marine House back to the compound, and one or two were captured. The chancery building, the diplomatic heart of the large embassy where the real business takes place and the papers are stored, was surrounded by hundreds of demonstrators. Some had guns, others carried banners; still others were equipped with tools with which they forced open a rear window of the chancery basement. From there they stormed the chancery, even though the Marines used tear gas to try to repel them. The Marines retreated up one floor and then another, to the level where most of the embassy officials were behind locked steel doors.

At the risk of his life, Golacinski, the security officer, went out into the compound to try to negotiate with the demonstrators. He was captured. The embassy's most fluent Farsi speaker, John Limbert, opened the steel door and attempted to talk the students out of their mission, but he too was captured. Smoke was coming through the steel door, suggesting the radicals were trying to burn the chancery. When the diplomats had held out long enough to destroy most of the classified equipment, Laingen ordered them to surrender if they felt they had no other alternative. The radicals then stormed through the open door, tied and blindfolded the staff, and forced them to sit on the floor. The officials in the classified-code room held out longest, but they also were forced to surrender. The security team at the embassy frantically sought to destroy as much sensitive material as possible.

But because of the unexpectedly rapid success of the assault, some of the CIA station chief's highly sensitive papers fell into the hands of the radicals. The CIA stamp alone sent them into a frenzy. As they held the Americans in darkness, they beat some who resisted interrogation, and subjected others to mock executions. The zealous student captors laboriously pieced together many of the documents that had been torn to shreds, and from them they obtained important information for both operations and propaganda. Some documents exposed Iranians who had worked with the United States and helped Khomeini eliminate his opponents. Others were internal diplomatic memoranda, which reported on how Khomeini and his followers demonized the embassy as a "nest of spies."[53]

Remarkably, the embassy's political officer, Elizabeth Ann Swift, was able to give Hal Saunders at the State Department a chilling firsthand account of the assault until the radicals cut the line. When Ham Jordan was informed, his reactions were, "My God, this could mean war," and then, "What will this do to the campaign?" The president's initial worst-case fear was that the revolutionaries might assassinate one hostage every day at sunrise until the Shah was returned.[54]

But Sick believes that the students' original intent, as far as it can be divined, was to stage an American-style sit-in for a relatively short time, a tactic many of the students had learned while studying abroad; they had issued a bulletin announcing that they would hold the hostages for a week. Sazegara agrees and felt that the students expected to be "kicked out of the embassy" in a short time.[55] But there was a danger of escalation: Some students were more radical and wanted to kill some of the hostages during the first hours of the takeover.

During this confused time Yazdi was still on a plane returning from the Algiers celebration, where he had been with Prime Minister Bazargan.[56] Laingen raced up the stairs of the Foreign Ministry to demand that Deputy Foreign Minister Kamal Kharazi immediately take steps to end the siege. He and his staff were as bewildered as the Americans themselves and were frantically trying to get help.[57] Laingen said that Yazdi came from Algiers shortly after the hostage taking and went directly to the Foreign Ministry, where he demanded that the government evict the students. Yazdi tried to duplicate what he had achieved in February, but he clearly had lost his power over the radical students and clerics.

Yazdi's role hardly matters compared with Khomeini's. When did the ayatollah throw his decisive support behind the student seizure of the embassy, and why? The key actors, Sazegara, Yazdi, and Laingen, as well as Carter, agree that the ayatollah did not order the attack. Sick believes that Khomeini must have been briefed in advance of the students' plans but did not intervene in order to determine what the reaction would be.[58]

His son, Ahmad Khomeini, must have played a seminal role because the next afternoon he visited the embassy compound and returned to advise his father to consolidate his power by embracing the radical students.[59] Yazdi and Sazegara learned that Ahmad had gone to see his father at Qum and convinced him that the public would be angry if he did not support the students. So the ayatollah immediately wrote a letter addressing the students and complimenting them for "a great job. You made a second revolution, which is more important than the first revolution." The students became heroes.[60]

The precise timing will probably never be known, but the ayatollah's goal has become absolutely clear: to confirm his power over a revolutionary movement mixing ideologies ranging from Marxism to strict observance of Muslim custom and law, and crucially, to undermine Bazargan's civilian government, which he had initially created but which had been seeking to restore normal ties with Washington. Khomeini knew that he did not have full political control of his country and his movement, and while he was an anti-American revolutionary like many other Shiite clerics, like them he also depended on the support of others, since traditionally they live off donations.

"They very soon understand what the people want, and they say whatever the people want," Sazegara told me. Khomeini, with his ear to the ground, "very soon found out the atmosphere of the country was anti-U.S., and he did not want to lose the majority of the nation who were anti-U.S., angry against the Shah and the U.S., and wanted revenge against the Shah. They wanted the Shah to be delivered to them for trial. So because the people were against the U.S., the ayatollah was against the U.S."[61]

And exactly as Khomeini hoped, the takeover of the U.S. Embassy rallied the public behind him. The ayatollah saw the operation as putting a final wedge between Iran and the United States and other great powers that had intervened in Iranian life over the centuries, after Persia had ceased to be a great empire. The proof of his success came almost immediately.

By Turner's own admission, the CIA was clueless about who the hostage takers were and their objectives.[62] It is now clear that the real goal of the radical students was not to put the Shah on trial but to undermine the Bazargan government's moderate course, destabilize it, and open the way to a more radical, clerical government that had no interest in any reconciliation with Washington. One of the radical chants, based on Yazdi's photo taken in Algiers with Brzezinski, was that he had been negotiating with the Americans. Thus the hostages were really pawns in an internal power struggle.

The diplomats stranded at the Foreign Ministry were in a somewhat more enviable position than their colleagues at the U.S. Embassy, but their situation became far less attractive as the days stretched into more than a year. On the first day Iranian officials gave Laingen a telephone line to communicate with Washington. He sat throughout the day at the side of Yazdi's large desk, determined not to give up the connection. From this unusual place of captivity, Laingen called everyone he could to insist on security for himself and all his colleagues, including those confined in the embassy. The Foreign Ministry officials escorted the three to their elegant diplomatic reception room, fed them from the ministry's kitchen, and let them sleep on the couches. Yazdi came to see them on the second day, and they were kept under guard by older soldiers and not student radicals. As the days wore on, most seemed to become fed up with the revolution and grew friendly, continuing to provide them with adequate food and access to toilets. Yazdi assured Laingen that this was no more serious than the sit-ins at American colleges in the 1960s and would soon be over.

However, when it became clear that Bazargan and Yadzi had no influence over the students, and that power rested solely with the ayatollah, Bazargan, protesting the students' conduct as contrary to Islam and international law, resigned along with Yazdi and his government within 36 hours after the embassy had been seized. This closed off any official channel through which the U.S. government could conceivably conduct normal relations. From then until February 1980, Laingen used the Foreign Ministry telex to communicate with Washington in carefully phrased messages. They were visited by the ambassadors of Britain, Germany, Turkey, Switzerland, and Canada, and it was through them that Laingen could communicate sensitive messages for transmission to Washington.

When Washington finally severed diplomatic relations with Iran in April 1980, the Swiss Embassy became their protecting power and method of communicating with the administration. When the Swiss officials visited, Laingen wrote abbreviated messages to Washington on small bits of paper and handed them over in ways that did not attract the attention of the Iranian guards. Laingen was also allowed periodic telephone contact with the State Department until one day in October 1980 the phone rang with an improbable call from a radio station in Seattle. Laingen told the caller he was in no position to grant an interview, but the station called again, and then a third time. At this point Laingen simply said that negotiations for the hostages' release were at a sensitive stage and the American public needed to keep cool. These brief comments were picked up by the media in Iran and around the world, which led the militants to cut the telephone line for the duration.

From the start of the hostage crisis, the president gave us strict orders to separate it rigorously from the daily demands of governing. In an Oval Office meeting with his inner circle, Carter was explicit about how we were to behave: "I want to compartmentalize this and keep you out of it, so I can deal directly with my cabinet officers on this." I urged him to issue a statement appealing to the American people to be calm and resolute.[63]

In order to keep alive every diplomatic option during that period, Carter allowed the Iranian Embassy on Massachusetts Avenue in Washington to remain open and for their diplomats, unlike ours, to move about freely, until April 6, 1980, when he severed relations. From thousands of miles away, this policy bothered Laingen, but even more so his wife at home. She organized regular Sunday-night prayer vigils from their Washington parish, All Saints Church, and sang the "Battle Hymn of the Republic" standing outside the Iranian outpost on Washington's Embassy Row.

Laingen lived on hope, reinforced when thirteen black and female hostages were released within weeks, following the intercession of the PLO's Yāsir Arafat. He told himself that the Iranians could not possibly keep the hostages through Christmas, but as he poignantly put it later: "Thanksgiving and Christmas came, New Year's came, St. Patrick's Day came, birthdays came, a second Thanksgiving and a second Christmas, even."[64]

Meanwhile the administration frantically approached all our Western European allies, Muslim countries, even Muslim religious leaders, to try to find someone who knew this shadowy figure Khomeini. But it came to naught because no one had a connection to this isolated Shiite radical. We in the White House at first thought that the hostages would be released as quickly as the first batch back in February. But gradually there was a sinking feeling to the contrary as the revolving door of Iran's revolutionary politics threw up and then threw out one unknown individual after another. "It began to dawn on us," said Ham, "that the situation was so chaotic in Iran that maybe it wouldn't be over soon."[65]

Sixty-six Americans were initially taken captive in the embassy, including Laingen and his colleagues in the Iranian Foreign Ministry.[66] But one of the few bright spots was the story of six American diplomats who were away from the embassy in Tehran at the time of the assault. They hid in several different places around Tehran, including in the apartment of Tomseth's Thai cook. Eventually they managed to contact a senior Canadian diplomat who said: "My God, where have you been?! Why didn't you call us before?!"[67]

The Canadians' heroic reception and assistance from the Canadian ambassador, Ken Taylor, and the diplomats' escape in January 1980, through an elaborate CIA masquerade as a Canadian film crew, were memorialized in a book and the Oscar-winning film *Argo*. Canadian foreign minister Flora McDonnell worked with the administration to give the six what looked like authentic Canadian passports. Because it was illegal to issue a false passport, the Canadian parliament had to go into special private session to authorize them. Carter ordered complete secrecy in the White House even after the caper, lest the remaining hostages suffer for its success, even though he could have gotten a political boost if the story had leaked out. Several reporters learned about it, but they were also implored to sit on it, and they did. Even during the Reagan and George H. W. Bush administrations, Carter never revealed his administration's central role: "We gave full credit to the Canadians,"[68] he told me. We too often take our neighbors to the north for granted, but no one could ask for better friends close by than Canada. Nevertheless, the longer the whole miserable story of the hostages lasted, the worse it became.

BLOCKADE, BOMB, OR TALK?

Nothing in his term as president so brutally shone a spotlight on Jimmy Carter as the Iranian hostage crisis, all 444 days of it emblazoned across the nation's front pages and television screens. His reactions showed his great strengths and his weaknesses—his tenacity, his iron will, his deep commitment to bringing back the hostages safely through every nonmilitary means from diplomacy to sanctions, and even a daring if disastrous rescue mission. As with so many of his decisions, foreign and domestic, it also demonstrated his determination to do what he felt was right over what was politically advantageous. But it also exposed the cost of his decision from the start to make their personal safety the paramount concern above the broader reputation of the United States. The hostages themselves must have appreciated the president's choice; Sick told me if he had been a hostage he would have wanted President Carter negotiating for his release.[69] But the broader implications were something they and their families could not fully appreciate.

The problem was that once it became clear that Carter was unwilling to use even a show of military force, he lost possible leverage to release the hostages. And as their captivity dragged on, he relied on negotiations with an Iranian government that did not have the power to make a deal, even when the hostages had served their political purpose and the powers in Iran wanted to get rid of them. Carter could negotiate a historic Middle East peace agreement with Sadat and Begin, but Grand Ayatollah Ruhollah Khomeini so hated the United States that he overrode his own government and refused to negotiate at all. At the root of their extended captivity, Laingen said, was the fact that "Khomeini hated Carter for his involvement with the Shah."[70]

At the dawn of the Islamic fundamentalist movement, Carter and the administration can be forgiven for their meager understanding of this rigidity and deep animus toward the United States. What is much harder to understand is the woefully inadequate intelligence about the movement and Khomeini himself. The manner in which Carter dealt with the hostage crisis provided an open door for Ronald Reagan, who started well behind him in the polls because he was wrongly viewed as a mere movie actor still cast in a shoot-from-the-hip Western, but was able to defeat the Carter administration, in significant part, because the United States was outmaneuvered by an aged Islamic radical.

I sat in on one of the first National Security Council meetings, where a range of options was on the table. From my place in a chair along the wall of the basement-level, windowless Situation Room, I suggested we could effectively shut down the Iranian economy by immediately blockading Kharg Island, from which Iran exported the bulk of its oil. I reminded the

officials that President Kennedy had successfully employed a naval blockade
to force back Soviet ships resupplying Cuba during the 1962 missile crisis,
and I argued that in the early months of the new government, Khomeini
might relent rather than risk his drive to consolidate his power. Defense
Secretary Harold Brown said we could mount a naval blockade, but that a
better option would be to seed mines in the Iranian harbors and not risk
our own warships.[71]

Throughout the crisis, until he overruled Vance on the mission to rescue
the hostages, Carter adhered to Vance's line of negotiations, negotiations,
and more negotiations. They were backed by economic sanctions that lacked
bite because our traditional allies failed to join us at a critical time. In this
Vance was supported by that figure of the legal establishment, White House
Counsel Lloyd Cutler.

From the start, Zbig pressed for some sort of blockade of Kharg Island
as a tourniquet to squeeze the flow of Iran's oil exports—the lifeblood of its
economy. I strongly favored this position, but my role in this crisis was focused on the energy implications and the economic sanctions, as we were
fighting a two-front war to release the hostages and limit the inflationary
fallout of the Iranian revolution. Zbig said it was a "terrible mistake" not to
employ force and talked with me, Ham, and Jody to drum up support for
blockading Kharg Island by mining its harbors. That way the tankers would
be most at risk—and more likely stay away—and we would not have to in-
terpose the U.S. Navy and risk a confrontation with Iranian or possibly
even Soviet warships.[72]

Yet on the first day of the takeover, it was decided not to divert an aircraft carrier group into Iranian waters lest it provide an excuse for the kid-
nappers to kill their hostages. As more than two weeks passed with no sign
that the hostages would be freed, Carter's top advisers held a crucial meeting
at Camp David on November 20 to consider a range of options, including a
naval blockade, mining Iranian harbors, seizing oil stored on Kharg Island,
and bombing the refinery at Abadan. All were militarily feasible, but it was
unclear if any would lead to the release of the hostages.[73] Ham argued
against the blockade because he felt it it would only ratchet up the confrontation and would not bring the hostages home anyway. He continued: "It
might have even resulted in the hostages being killed. And what would we

have done then?"[74] Jody Powell had the same attitude. Defense Secretary Harold Brown later told me that if we decided to mine Iran's harbors, the Soviets might have tried to win the favor of the new regime by confronting the United States and removing any mines.[75]

Brzezinski felt that Carter had a genuine aversion to the use of force, whether it would have been deployed by the Shah's army to put down the rebellion or by the U.S. military to free American hostages: "The president didn't want to, pure and simple. Even at the very last minute, there was an opportunity to knock off Khomeini when he was returning to Iran, and Bakhtiar [the Shah's last prime minister] was willing to do it, and the president wasn't." Carter, he said, "really is a decent person, and I think that decency was perhaps too strong."[76]

And Brzezinski really meant it: He said he would have been willing to "bomb the hell out of Tehran and risk having the hostages killed. There would have been such a surge of patriotism and support for an embattled president, he would have been reelected. But he wouldn't do that. I think he knew he was losing the election in part because of that."[77] Originally Carter had seemed to him a "gutsy type": He solved festering problems before they got worse, and he demonstrated this in the Middle East, Afghanistan, the push to return the Panama Canal, normalizing relations with China, and his advocacy of human rights. But on the other hand, Zbig said Carter had this preoccupation with "quote-unquote 'peace,'" and his national security adviser believed it was based in his religion, so that he could be tough, for example, in his Middle East negotiations "because peace was the objective."[78]

I do not think bombing Tehran would have been wise from any perspective, except as retribution after the hostages had been safely removed. But I believed then, and I believe now, that with all the risks, that either mining or blockading the Iranian harbors, rather than negotiating endlessly with an almost empty hand, would have shown Khomeini that he could not hold the United States or its diplomats hostage. Even if we had moved a significant American naval force into international waters close to Iran, it would have sent a signal that our patience was not infinite and might have made a difference. As for the concern that the radical students would have executed the hostages, it seems to me that when Khomeini was just consolidating his power, even he would have recognized that these murders would have been an act of war and would have led to a fierce response, threatening his regime.

But Carter felt otherwise, so strongly that he closed off some of his own options. When Mondale told the president that everyone he talked to urged toughness and supported an oil blockade, Carter said: "I know that, and I am not going to have it on my conscience that it would kill the hostages." Mondale himself feared that using military power could cost the hostages their lives, but unlike Brzezinski, he saw no evidence of religious scruples in Carter's determination to get them home safely. In any case, no one had come up with any plan that would not in some way risk the hostages.[79]

Six days after the hostages were taken, the president met with their families. Brzezinski told Carter that his biggest mistake was seeing the families the first week, which personalized the crisis. As Rafshoon put it: "They all had faces and he thought about the families."[80] I disagree. He could hardly have avoided them without being publicly savaged for being hardhearted and even unconcerned, despite efforts to free their relatives through every available diplomatic channel. The meeting was on his public schedule, but any comments were supposed to be off the record to avoid disturbing any negotiations.

But when Carter later told the families he would do nothing, including military action, that might lead to the physical harm of the hostages, or "arouse the unstable captors of our hostages to attack or punish them," this was immediately leaked to the press by the anxious families.[81] This sent a clear signal to Iran they had no reason to fear an attack or other retaliation, thus undercutting any threat of force to strengthen the president's negotiating hand.

However comforting that ill-considered statement may have been to the hostage families, it was a serious mistake. At a minimum Carter should have kept Khomeini and the students guessing. At that point Carter believed the hostages would not be held long and would be returned safely, and here religion *did* play a role. He told Rafshoon that Khomeini would not kill the hostages "because he's a religious man; that would be murder." Rafshoon replied: "Well, Mr. President, I think his religion and your religion are two very different things. He believes in retribution, and if he thinks these are evil people, which evidently he does, he would not hesitate to kill them."[82]

Initially, the president and his advisers believed that the hostages would be released in a few days, and, in a bellicose mood that faded as the crisis continued, he was ready to deploy the U.S. military to punish the rebellious upstarts. On November 20, two weeks after the hostages were taken, he agreed with Brown's recommendation to move forces into the area and ordered the aircraft carrier USS *Kitty Hawk* and other military assets closer to Iran. But on December 1, Brown sent a memo to Carter recommending diplomacy and economic sanctions as the best options. The Defense secretary felt that mining the harbors was less risky than blockading them:[83] If sowing naval mines was an act of war, he argued that it was a "bloodless act of war, like invading an embassy and taking hostages." Carter intially agreed to mine the harbors, stating in a note: "Zbig, Harold and I agree completely."[84]

BOXED IN BY BANKERS, DIPLOMATS, AND GEOPOLITICS

But Carter wanted to try economic sanctions first. However, the longer military action was withheld, the less effective it would be. The Iranians were on alert, probably preparing both military and diplomatic retaliation to try to neutralize our actions. Moreover, U.S. sanctions alone, without either coordinated allied support or a credible military threat, or both, is rarely effective. We had neither here. Many years later in the Clinton administration, when I was a leader in dealing with a whole range of sanctions against Iran, Libya, Cuba, and other countries, I learned that for all our economic power, unilateral economic sanctions by the United States are rarely effective in changing the conduct of any target country. And whatever one's view of the nuclear deal with Iran in 2015, there is almost universal agreement that the Iranians came to the negotiating table only because the Obama administration persuaded the European Union to put its economic muscle behind the United States. But during the Iran hostage crisis, we got only fitful cooperation, and to my mind, this was all the more reason to have a military weapon like a blockade or harbor mining, or at least a credible threat, not only to use against Iran, but to spur our allies to join us in a strong coalition.

Beyond freezing billions of dollars of Iran's assets, our multipronged strategy, in which I was deeply engaged, included imposing economic sanctions on Iran. They could only be effective if the major industrial nations joined in, and our European and Japanese allies disgracefully put their pocketbooks before their principles at a time of critical need for their most important ally. I worked almost daily on sanctions through a Special Coordinating Committee (SCC) of the National Security Council. The president and all his national security advisers agreed we should seek a UN Security Council resolution condemning the hostage taking and threatening sanctions. Carter's hope was that a resolution would strengthen our hand in asking major countries to join us in cutting off Iran from international markets. But the Soviet Union vetoed it, and we had to go through the painstaking effort of rallying our allies against Iran.[85] He personally contacted more than 25 world leaders to urge them to pressure Iran to release the hostages, but the real power, the Ayatollah Khomeini, was impervious; no one could reach him.[86]

Carter sent high-level missions to Europe and Japan; but they returned with only limited results. It made little difference that we exchanged expressions of contempt among ourselves for the lack of solidarity by our allies.[87] The Germans criticized the Iranian asset freeze, and Japanese and Canadian companies were doing business as usual. West German banks agreed only to refuse new Iranian deposits in American dollars (solid German marks were acceptable). Switzerland wanted Treasury cooperation to keep the dollar strong so that its safe-haven banks would not be inundated with foreign deposits. The British were willing to be helpful so long as any restrictions on London banks were tied only to the hostages and would be removed as soon as they were released. The French resisted any economic action, and the Italians worried about their oil imports from Iran. Japan continued to be a worrisome outlier, buying oil on the spot market and driving up prices, and Japanese banks were even helping Iran avoid having its assets frozen by refusing to identify Iranian transactions.

The governments were arguing that they had no power over their banks, and the Treasury's Tony Solomon suggested we should publicize their lack of cooperation and warn them it would damage their banking relationships with the United States. With the dollar as the world's major trading currency, this could have bite. Solomon reported that Iran was "awash with money for oil." How were they hiding it? Even though we managed to persuade the European banks to limit dollar transactions, our intelligence found that the Iranian funds were covered up under nominees in Algeria and Libya. State continued patiently to pursue negotiations country by country. Totally frustrated, Solomon, a tough, laconic, but brilliant and experienced official, who had been the driving force in our successful dollar-rescue program, called me to say that we had to use their reliance on America's protective military shield as leverage to persuade them to evacuate their citizens in Iran, whom they were using as excuses for inaction. He said they had to be told the only way to stop us from taking military action like a blockade would be to support tough economic sanctions. I fully agreed and passed this along to Brzezinski, but there seemed to be no disposition by State or the president for such action.[88]

MILITARY OPTIONS

In fact, the decision to mine or blockade with our navy was excruciatingly difficult. There was another consideration in the debate—the Cold War. One of the administration's prime objectives was to keep the Soviets out of the Gulf and away from Iran. There was a very real concern that the Soviets might have tried to win the favor of the new Islamic regime by confronting the U.S. and removing the mines or challenging the blockade, and that we would be driving the Iranian's into the waiting arms of the Soviets.[89] It would also risk a military confrontation with the Soviet Union. As the NSC's Sick dramatically put it to me, "Are we going to shoot at the Russians as they come in and risk the start of a third world war?"[90] If this was not complicated enough, Lt. General John Pustay, top military aide to Joint Chiefs General David Jones, shared with me another concern with mining or a blockade. The Pentagon feared that the Iranians might try to mine the Straits of Hormuz, blocking the sea lanes to *all* oil and commercial traffic through this narrow passageway out of the Gulf, including our own naval forces.[91]

I did not think then, nor do I think now, that these doomsday scenarios were likely. A show of strength might have helped the Soviets understand that we had a right to get our diplomats back. And mining could have avoided a confrontation. But opinions were sharply divided, and the options were brutally difficult.

Vance strongly opposed any show of force, in favor of traditional diplomacy. Laingen favored sanctions and negotiation, although he later said there would have been a good case for using force in the first days as an immediate reaction to an act of war. But he thought force would have led us down a slippery slope. Although he dared not say it from what was in effect his jail cell in the Foreign Ministry, he later reflected that passions in Tehran were running so high that the student militants would have responded by abusing and even executing hostages, just as Carter feared. Moreover, he said: "I believed that the passion was such that Khomeini's vindictiveness, determination, and rigidity [made] it impossible to see him back down." Laingen added: "Military force in dealing with terrorists is a very difficult option that doesn't usually work."[92]

When the hostages finally arrived on the South Lawn of the White House, President Reagan warned of swift retribution if something like this happened on his watch. But his bluster vanished in the first crisis of his presidency: When confronted with the hijacking of a TWA airliner in Beirut, he did not use force to save the passengers but negotiated a solution. Another hostage crisis in Beirut also extended for years, but the Reagan administration could not find a way to deploy military force effectively and struck what later turned out to be a notorious deal to trade arms for the hostages' release. Carter refused to stoop to this subterfuge. Even more dramatic, a 1983 terrorist attack in Beirut killed 241 U.S. Marines in their barracks in Beirut; and an explosion in the U.S. Embassy there almost killed U.S. Ambassador Reginald Bartholomew, with no retaliation and Reagan's decision to withdraw all American officials.

Carter also decided not to engage in a tit-for-tat expulsion of Iranian diplomats; he waited until a few weeks before the failed effort to rescue the hostages. The Iranians had around sixty diplomatic personnel in their Washington embassy, and diplomatic relations, if strained, proceeded correctly because, as he later explained to me: "I always feel, and still do, it is a mistake when the U.S. withholds communication with someone with whom we have a difference."[93] However, only a month after the crisis began he asked Vance to reduce the number of Iranian consulates around the country. The State Department said it was hard to make prompt arrangements to expel everyone and their families. Carter complained: "We treat Libya worse than Iran, without justification."[94]

Carter did threaten military action if any of the hostages was harmed or put on trial, and that worked.[95] A few weeks after they were taken, the president convened a meeting with his foreign-policy team at Camp David and drafted a message warning Khomeini that if the Tehran Embassy hostages were put on trial or harmed in any way, he would take immediate action. The message was passed through the Germans and the Swiss to ensure that it would be read and understood. Carter recounted: "We told him that if a hostage was injured, that we would cut off all trade by sea between Iran and the outside world. And if a hostage was killed that we would launch a military strike against his country." As a result Carter said, "Khomeini was meticulously careful that he never injured or killed a hostage. That was the first time we'd laid down the gauntlet to him."[96] Although it would have helped Carter politically to share this strong and decisive message with the American public, he felt that if word came out Khomeini might have to do the exact opposite to save face. We all had little doubt that Carter's threat ensured that they would survive their captivity physically unharmed.

By April 1980, as the crisis continued unabated, Carter demanded action, and again leaned toward mining the harbors, while his advisers had already moved toward mounting a rescue mission. Brown conceded that neither blockading nor mining Iran's harbors would bring home the hostages. To which Ham Jordan added, "Except in boxes."[97]

As days passed into weeks and then months, Mrs. Carter was the president's eyes and ears to the public during his self-imposed isolation from campaigning. She told him: "Mine the harbors; do something; mine the harbors!" But he would tell her: "And have them take one hostage every day? Line them up before a firing squad and kill them and shoot them?"[98]

When I asked Carter years later on why he did not impose a blockade immediately, he replied: "It would have been an act of war." I countered that they committed an act of war by invading our embassy and capturing our diplomats, and his response was revealing: "Well, I'm not trying to equate the two, but when a navy moves in and blockades all of their ports around an entire country, that is much more authentically an act of war than holding 52 hostages. It was a terrible thing that they did; but they never injured a hostage."[99]

Carter's decision not to deploy the U.S. Navy raises a broader question about his personal beliefs concerning the use of military force. As a Naval Academy graduate and nuclear submarine officer, not only had he experienced the great military might of the United States but he would have been required to use it in the course of duty if commanded to do so. Yet, as commander in chief, he had a great aversion to the demonstration of military force until the Soviet invasion of Afghanistan at the end of 1979, only months after the hostages were taken.

He used to state publicly how proud he was that not one American soldier had died in combat in his presidency. To a degree that is laudable, in contrast to the misjudgments by the George W. Bush administration in invading Iraq, which led to the killing and wounding of thousands of Americans in a needless conflict that upended the Middle East order. Ham, one of the few in the White House who had actually served in combat, used to tell Carter to take care about his boast because it could undermine the use of America's military might. Throughout the hostage crisis, his refusal to threaten robust military action, or at least to keep it as a live option, undercut American diplomatic and economic leverage, and allowed Khomeini to simply play out the string in months of fruitless, debilitating, and humiliating negotiations. But he simply placed the safety of the hostages higher on his scale of priorities than the damage to American prestige and his own political standing.

ROSE GARDEN STRATEGY

As it became clear the hostages would not be released immediately, Carter adopted a domestic stance that had the unintended effect of focusing

American public attention instead of diverting it from what turned out to be a national humiliation. It was called by critics the "Rose Garden strategy." This decision made Carter hostage to the hostage crisis. He announced that he would not leave the country or participate in any campaign activities for his reelection, even though Senator Kennedy was launching a vigorous effort to unseat Carter as the Democratic Party nominee. Initially this proved to be politically wise, as the American people rallied around their president, and the president regained his standing in the polls. There were symbolic and substantive reasons for Carter to stay in the White House and be seen concentrating on the crisis. That not only played well in public, but during the first few weeks was essential. So many things were going on behind the scenes that Carter needed to coordinate them and stay close at hand to make quick decisions.

However, by refusing to campaign during the hostage crisis, Carter had gotten himself into another box of his own making. Carter helped make the hostages into national icons by his singular focus on their fate, raising their value to the Iranians and tying his hands. His explanation was that he knew he would be asked questions about his efforts to free the hostages, and he did not want to tip his hand about secret contacts, some of them seen as disreputable, such as Gadhafi and Arafat: "I didn't want to either mislead the American people or say, 'I can't answer that question,' or be obviously devious."[100] But as time passed, the hostages became a political albatross he could not shake from his shoulders.

Ham said that it was not initially Carter's idea, but his own, for Carter to stay at work in the White House. That began almost immediately with the cancellation of a state visit to Canada at Jordan's urging because of "the fever pitch in the country." Ham explained that we "kind of backed into it. But once we backed into it, there was a legitimate reason for him to be there." But when Carter was faced with an impending Iowa primary debate against Kennedy, he told Ham: "If I go out to debate Kennedy in Iowa, I'm going to go out there as a president and I'm going to come back just as a politician. I need to stay on the high ground." So, said Ham: "We got stuck in that posture, and the thing dragged on and on and on. It looked like an excuse for Carter to hide behind the issue and to avoid the campaign."[101] By election day in November 1980, widespread but unjustified suspicions arose that he was manipulating the crisis for his own benefit as the result of a stay-at-home decision that had been made when no one at the White House imagined it would last longer than a few weeks.[102]

ON TV FOR 444 NIGHTS

The Rose Garden strategy had another unintended and deeply pervasive effect. It totally personalized the crisis in the American media by focusing the responsibility on the Oval Office and showing the terrorists they could put the American presidency itself into dysfunction. Television could not get enough of the story and even invented new platforms for blanket coverage launched into America's living rooms. Foremost among these was ABC's program later established as *Nightline* and hosted by Ted Koppel, an experienced diplomatic reporter.

Another was the decision by Walter Cronkite to end his trusted nightly CBS newscast by reminding viewers how many days the hostages had been held. Neither imagined, any more than Carter himself, that the hostages would be held for 444 days, that their captivity would hold the country's attention for so long, or that Carter by inadvertent word and deed would help keep the attention of the nation on this unprecedented event. After Carter lost the election, Cronkite visited the outgoing president in the Oval Office and "told him how sorry he was that he was the one who started the 'one day, second day of the hostage crisis, third day and so forth.' "[103]

Jody Powell agreed that the story was "an absolute, total negative" for Carter, and as press secretary tried without success to keep it low in public importance.[104] But yellow ribbons sprouted all over the country, and the nation was transfixed. Rafshoon later researched TV usage and calculated that during its fourteen months the hostage crisis astonishingly received more minutes of television time than the Vietnam War, which lasted ten years.[105]

Could the hostage crisis have been handled in ways that did not personalize it so greatly to the president himself? Could the negotiations have been left largely to the State Department and kept away from the president? Judy Woodruff of PBS, who had covered Carter as governor, feels that if he had underscored that the hostage issue was one of many he was handling, he would have seemed "less a victim of it."[106] Andy Glass, the Washington bureau chief for the *Atlanta Journal-Constitution*, who also had covered Carter for years in Georgia, believes that while the president saw the hostages as a humanitarian issue demanding his attention, he could have declared that the White House held Iran responsible for their safety and announced it would have nothing further to say until the Iranians responded to U.S. diplomatic initiatives.[107] After that, said Ted Koppel of ABC News, "the media would soon have found itself with very little on which to report, and certainly not enough to sustain a nightly television program devoted to the hostages, if the administration had not turned it into a crisis from the get-go."

While international relays by satellite had been possible for several years, the high cost of the link made them rare. But with a growing audience, it was worthwhile for Koppel to sit in his Washington studio and serve as a willing conduit for the Iranian foreign minister to give his views from Tehran or to interview a Russian guest in Moscow. The show had started with a producer's exaggerated title, *America Held Hostage*, and then caught the eye of the network's news chief, Roone Arledge, a broadcasting phenomenon who had made his name in sports TV. He had been looking for a vehicle to fill the 11:30 p.m. spot that might help ABC challenge the late-night comedians on the two other major networks, and made a risky but winning bet. *Nightline* became so popular that Johnny Carson, the master of late-night TV on NBC, called Koppel only half jokingly to say: "You're killing me, what the hell are you doing?" Koppel's show drew an average of 7 million viewers and lasted for 6,000 programs before he retired in 2005, long after Carson had gone.

Koppel's program provided the in-depth coverage so rare in television—and also made him a star. For this he gives Carter some of the credit—but he also blames him for his total focus on getting the hostages home safely, including his declaration that their fate was "the first thing I think about in the morning when I get up and the last thing I think about at night." Drawing a verbal picture perfectly suited for television, Koppel explained: "The president is the man dealing with this international crisis. Watch him deal with it. Look how presidential he is. Look how well he's dealing with this crisis. And for the first few days that was just fine. I think it did what you guys intended it to do." But after a few weeks, what became a political asset while Kennedy was campaigning around the country became a liability. In Koppel's view the image changed from "look how presidential he is, [to] look who's the president and look how feckless he is. He's not getting it done; Why are those hostages still over there? How were they able to do that to us?" And this was capped by the failed rescue mission. Koppel concluded: "Everything that could go wrong did go wrong"—even in the balance of forces with Khomeini: "The folks in Tehran got a sense that they had the president by the short hairs."[108]

After leaving office, Carter seemed to agree: "I think the issue would have died down a lot more if I decided to ignore the fate of the hostages, or if I had decided just to stop any statements on the subject. That may have been the best approach."[109] But that was not Jimmy Carter's nature.

GRASPING AT STRAWS

Less effective than the initial stages of the Rose Garden strategy were the administration's attempts—some of them bizarre—to work through special emissaries. On November 7, at the first congressional leadership breakfast after the hostages were taken, the president blamed "religious fanatics" and reported that the UN was working with the PLO to go to Tehran. He said he was sending former attorney general Ramsey Clark, now a left-wing activist sympathetic to the Islamic revolution, to seek an audience with Khomeini.[110] Khomeini refused to see Clark, and he returned to Tehran on his own in June 1980, for the more insidious purpose of participating as an American delegate to the "Crimes of America Conference."

With the military option withheld, Carter took several early constructive steps. He surprised Khomeini by issuing a presidential directive banning all crude oil imports from Iran. Ten days after the hostages were taken, the Iranian government announced that it intended to pull all its deposits out of American and other Western banks, but we were ready. At 8:00 a.m. Washington time that same day, Carter signed an executive order freezing more than 10 billion dollars' worth of Iranian assets in American banks but, controversially and even more effectively, extending it to Iran's dollar deposits in branches and subsidiaries of U.S. banks abroad.[111] Howls of protest arose about America overreaching outside its borders, but the directive worked and it stuck.

There were few other viable options. At the request of the United States, the International Court of Justice ruled that the seizure of our embassy in Tehran was illegal, but the ayatollah could not have cared less about international law.[112]

On November 28, Carter, grasping at straws, suddenly suggested sending none other than Muhammad Ali to Tehran: "He is a Muslim and the most popular person in the world."[113] The great boxer went, but to no avail. As for Arafat of the PLO, he clearly saw an opportunity to ingratiate himself with the United States, while Khomeini saw another chance to divide the American public. Despite the 1975 congressional ban on contacts with the PLO, the CIA activated a long-standing back channel with PLO headquarters in Beirut. It was at Arafat's urging that the ayatollah allowed the release of thirteen hostages during the first few weeks.[114] Iran announced it was releasing the blacks because they lived under American oppression and tyranny.

If the pretext for the embassy assault was the Shah's entry into the United States, then perhaps getting him out would resolve it. So the White House and State Department went all over the world to try to find him another home. The only positive response came from Sadat, and in the end the Shah ended up in Egypt, where he died while the hostages remained immured in the embassy.

As the crisis continued, and the hostages became less of a domestic political lever in Iran and more of a diplomatic burden, Iran's newly elected president, Abolhassan Bani-Sadr, read in *Time* an account of Ham's efforts to move the Shah out of the United States to Panama. Aware that he was Carter's closest aide, he decided that Ham was the person to negotiate a resolution, and reached out to a French lawyer, Christian Bourguet, and an Argentine attorney, Hector Villalon, who had known Khomeini in exile in Paris and were sympathetic to the Islamic revolution. They in turn reached out to Ham, who began months of clandestine negotiations in Paris, London, and even Washington. He met directly with high Iranian officials including Foreign Minister Sadegh Ghotbzadeh (a close aide of Khomeini's during his Paris exile, later executed for supposedly being too close to the United States and trying to overthrow the clerical regime).

Ham flew on the supersonic Concorde to arrive as quickly as possible and avoid detection by going through the luxury jet's special passenger entrance. He joked to Rafshoon: "Don't tell Jimmy, because he would say: 'Can't you fly coach?'" Within the government his mission was coordinated with the State Department's own worldwide campaign instructing every American ambassador to press the host government to appeal to the Iranians to release the hostages. Ghotbzadeh first asked Ham to ban all American press from Iran, which Ham told him was impossible; the foreign minister replied that it certainly could be done because it was a known fact that the Jews ran all the television networks.[115]

Because Ham's face was so well known, when he traveled abroad he went in disguises provided by the CIA, sometimes wearing a mustache and tinted glasses, with a fake passport for a Mr. Thompson. But Ham was also worried, as he colorfully put it, that if it became known he was involved in sensitive diplomatic negotiations, people would say "'My God, we've got this terrible crisis and Carter's got this jerk Jordan involved in it."[116] This was no rogue mission: He teamed with Hal Saunders, the State Department's senior Middle East expert, who had played an important role at Camp David. They worked under very precise written scenarios for resolving the crisis.

The Jordan-Saunders gambit came very close to success in March and then again in April 1980. The administration also worked with the United Nations in a futile effort to end the crisis. Secretary General Kurt Waldheim (whose Nazi past would later be revealed) visited Tehran in January 1980, but was threatened by angry demonstrators.

A UN Commission of Inquiry gave some promise of breaking the impasse. The idea was that it would serve as a vehicle for the Iranians to air their grievances against the Shah, meet with the hostages, move them out of the hands of the radicals in the embassy to the Iranian Foreign Ministry, and to the Iranian government for release. Fifty cots and steel lockers were installed in the Foreign Ministry's reception room. With Ham and Saunders working through Bourguet and Villalon as intermediaries, they won the agreement of what passed for a civilian government headed by Bani-Sadr and Ghotbzadeh. But the frustrated UN commissioners departed when, as always, the stumbling block was Khomeini, who refused to cooperate and asserted that the fate of the hostages would have to await Iran's parliamentary election.[117]

That was the last straw for diplomacy. Protocol had already been abandoned and tempers were short. In April 1980, the Iranian chargé Ali Agah went to the State Department to formalize his departure with Precht, the Iran desk officer, and insisted that the hostages were being treated humanely. Precht responded in most undiplomatic fashion: "That's bullshit!"[118] As Ham told me, in the end, after all their careful checking: "We were dealing with people who claimed to be speaking for Khomeini, but who ultimately didn't. . . . So every time we got close to making something happen, Khomeini would fail to act or fail to bless something happening." Ham realized that the crisis would work itself out only when the Iranians realized they would be better off without the hostages. What belatedly turned things around, he believed, was Iraq's war on Iran. It began late in September 1980, when the Iranians came to understand that holding on to the hostages blocked the shipment of spare parts they needed for their American planes and weapons.[119]

SAVING THE IRANIAN REFUGEES

We did have one unmitigated success with many of the ayatollah's hostages—even if they were not our own. The story has never before been disclosed. The human dilemmas it presented and the bureaucratic delicacy with which they were untangled resonate in today's anti-immigrant fervor. More than fifty thousand Iranian Jews, Christians, and Baha'is escaped Khomeini's Islamic reign of terror against "infidels" and took refuge in America, thanks to our unprecedented and—I must admit—ingenious reading of the immigration rules.

Jewish life in Persia dated back at least to the liberation of the Jews in Babylon by the emperor Cyrus, after their exile following the destruction by the Romans of the First Temple in 586 B.C.E. Over the centuries the Jewish community survived large swings in their status until they reemerged with influence and security under the protection of the Pahlavi Dynasty and were even allowed close ties with Zionism and the new state of Israel.

But the Islamic revolution placed all religious minorities in grave danger, and that was when I entered the fray on behalf of the Carter White House.

Many Iranian Jews began to leave, seeing the unhappy handwriting on the wall. When Khomeini's revolution finally swept the Shah off his throne, all elements seen as sympathetic to his regime began to be purged.

Mark Talisman, the head of the Washington office of the Council of Jewish Federations, arranged a meeting between Habib Elghanian, the leader and symbol of the Iranian Jewish community, and House Speaker O'Neill to describe events in revolutionary Iran. They begged Elghanian not to return, but he believed his standing as an industrialist and philanthropist with close ties to the Muslim clergy would keep him safe and help to reduce danger to Iran's Jews. Instead he was arrested, tried by a revolutionary court as a Zionist, and executed as a spy for Israel. Pictures of his bullet-riddled body, posted prominently in the Iranian press, panicked the Jewish community. Thousands tried to flee, and parents sent out their unaccompanied children by any means possible. With the seizure of the U.S. Embassy, the visa section was shut down. Three days later, at an Oval Office meeting, Carter for the first time discussed deporting all Iranians who were in the United States illegally and revoking all visas for Iranians who were not full-time residents. The president said: "We need to get the bastards out of here."[120]

Executive Order 12172 was issued on November 27, expelling all non-resident Iranians and suspending visas for new arrivals. It extended beyond the militant students to thousands of Iranian Jewish students currently studying in this country; thousands of Iranian Jews, Christians, and Baha'is who had fled Iran and were already in the United States; and tens of thousands who had family here and were fleeing Khomeini's reign of terror. All were at risk of being expelled back to Iran. Carter wanted exceptions made on humanitarian grounds, and although Jody announced this publicly, the order was vague on details.

I received disturbing reports from Mark Talisman that Jews and other minorities had made their way out of Iran to U.S. consulates in Europe, only to be turned back because they did not have proper visas.[121] While the order was being drafted, I discussed it with Attorney General Civiletti, who assured me that the government would not send back anyone "who would be hurt, such as Jewish kids"—but he conceded it would be difficult to distinguish the Jewish students from others, such as pro-Khomeini students.[122] Those in danger if they were forced to return to Iran could seek asylum on the legal grounds of a "well-founded fear of persecution," but that would leave them in limbo.

The U.S. government was not yet ready to declare them refugees outright because we were still hoping—against hope—that we could establish some form of diplomatic relations with the revolutionary government. The urgency of the situation combined with the arbitrary nature of our immigration bureaucracy demanded a clear policy. The problem was magnified because any Iranians who declared to U.S. authorities that they feared persecution under the new government would endanger both themselves and their families in Iran.

To help untangle this dilemma, I organized a series of meetings, starting at the end of January 1980,[123] with Senator Charles "Mac" Mathias, a Maryland Republican; David Crosland, the director of the Immigration and Naturalization Service; Doris Meisner of the Justice Department; David Brody of the American Jewish Congress; and Talisman. Crosland insisted that as long as the Iranian students had entered the United States legally their best protection would be to file an asylum request on the basis of fear of persecution, because it would delay their departure while the request was adjudicated. The requests would be kept secret as they proceeded through the State Department, and the government could also arrange that "they won't proceed," effectively allowing them to stay.

As conditions worsened, a series of crisis appeals arrived at the White House from American and Iranian Jewish representatives seeking leniency or even loopholes in the president's expulsion order. They landed on my desk, and we arranged a White House meeting on April 8 with a delegation composed of 12 Iranian Jews. It was led by Moussa Kermanian and included his son, Sam, speaking for the Iranian students like himself who were at risk of being sent home, and a successful young businessman, Isaac Moradi, who would lose all his assets in Iran as a result of the revolution.[124]

At the meeting on the government side were not only Crosland, who literally held the key to a solution, but a formidable list of officials representing State, Justice, the NSC, and OMB. We met in the large Domestic Policy Staff conference room, and as everyone walked in, each one on our side went around the table to shake the hands of our troubled visitors and help calm their nerves. As we began to discuss how we could help, I was struck by the fact that it was the State Department's representative, Hume Horan, who was the most resistant in arguing that the president's executive order had the force of law and could not be altered. I thought how little had changed since the days before and during World War II, when State also led the government's resistance to admitting Jews fleeing Nazi persecution.

Horan's legalism set off Talisman, rotund and tiny but a ball of talent and energy. His face turned beet-red as he banged his fist on the conference room table—something White House visitors almost never dared to do—and in a torrent of angry words declared that the American Jewish community would never again stay silent as its elders had supinely done in the time of Franklin Roosevelt. Sam Kermanian took the opportunity to point out with logical clarity that "by definition Iranian Jewish students in the U.S. could not be supporters of an Islamic revolution and had not participated in any demonstrations, let alone riots, in support of creating an Islamic republic."[125]

But the complications seemed endless. The passports of many Iranian students in the United States were no longer valid, or their visas had expired. There were 56,000 Iranian students here, 7,000 in violation of their visas, and while most had applied for asylum, some had already been deported. For those whose visas had expired, there could be no extensions unless they had an immediate relative in the United States, required medical attention, or had applied for asylum. I also wanted to have their threatened families admitted to the United States from Iran, but how? On what kind of visa?

As the meeting was finishing, Moussa Kermanian, a trained attorney, turned to me and said with earnestness: "Mr. Eizenstat, we understand that an executive order carries the weight of law, but as a lawyer you would surely agree that all laws are created to serve a purpose. We do not believe the purpose of the president's executive order is to send Iranian Jews back into the hands of the Islamic republic's prosecutors. So in this particular instance, it is not just the letter of the law that needs to be taken into account, but more so it is the spirit of the law that should be followed."

I had already tried to come up with creative solutions that would not require amending the tough executive order, and were based on moral and legal principles. I was also determined to seek special treatment not only for Iranian Jews but other endangered religious minorities as well. I turned to

Crosland and asked what options existed for anyone fleeing persecution. He said they could apply for political asylum. I then asked what would happen to the applications. He replied that if they could establish a reasonable fear of persecution, when their applications were reviewed they would be granted asylum status and residency in the United States. And if they could not they would be deported.

A bell went off in my head. How long did it normally take the INS to process the applications? Was the INS legally compelled to act within a specific time? Crosland said there was no legally mandated period, but the INS usually processed asylum requests as soon as they were received. Then what was the interim status of those waiting for the INS to process their applications? Crosland responded that their legal status was frozen. Then I said: "Considering the nature of the current regime in Iran, it would be reasonable to assume that members of Iranian religious minority groups could face potential persecution and their deportation to Iran could place them in danger, even if they cannot prove a reasonable fear of persecution on an individual basis." I rhetorically asked Crosland, "What if the White House asked that asylum applications for such applicants *not* be processed until the situation in Iran changes or the Shah is restored to power?" Crosland replied, as I hoped he would, that the applicants would remain frozen in their legal status until processing resumed.[126]

That solved the students' problems, but thousands were flooding out of Iran, knocking at the door but left in limbo, their applications delayed or rejected outright by U.S. embassies throughout Europe. I asked Crosland what we could do to help them. Crosland replied that essentially the same rules applied to those outside U.S. borders: They would need to show a reasonable fear of persecution, but this could be presumed if they belonged to religious minorities. With this series of pointed questions from the White House and answers from the INS, Hume of State finally came around.

Colleges and universities were informed that all Iranian students who were members of religious minority groups were exempt from the executive order. All younger children whose parents had applied for asylum or entered the country as refugees were to be allowed to continue their studies or admitted outright, which also took care of those who had graduated and normally would have had to leave. All this had been arranged quietly, quickly, and informally, which shows what government can do to help the world's abandoned people when it wants to extricate them from human-made dilemmas. Carter supported our solution enthusiastically, although he received no political reward from the American Jewish community, which gave him the lowest-ever proportion of its support for any Democrat when he ran for reelection.

When the Reagan administration took office, newly appointed officials at the INS noticed thousands of unprocessed applications for political asylum from Iranian religious minority groups—Jews, Christians, Baha'is, Zoroastrians, Assyrians, Chaldeans, and Sunni Muslims. Unaware of the secret agreement we had reached to avoid Khomeini's brutal retribution, they began processing the applications and denying a significant number. I was back in private practice as a lawyer and was quickly alerted by Sam Kermanian. I contacted Elliott Abrams, a senior member of the Reagan NSC staff, and urged him to continue doing nothing—simply allow the applications to lie dormant until the political situation in Iran became more favorable to religious minorities—which it has not to this day. He agreed. Shortly afterward the processing and denials stopped, and tens of thousands of Iranian minorities made their way to the safety of the United States.

DISASTER AT DESERT ONE

In the early months of 1980, it became apparent that diplomacy, negotiation, and international pressure were having no effect. Carter began working on a very different kind of rescue with his military commanders to free our hostages. On the day of the hostage taking the White House asked the military if an immediate rescue effort could be successfully launched, but the Pentagon replied it could not be successful at that early date. Israel, which had rescued hostages in a daring raid at Entebbe airport in Uganda, concurred. But Brzezinski convened a secret military committee, which met several times every week to plan a rescue mission.[127]

Under the plan that evolved, first a small plane, a twin-engine Cessna, would be sent on what they called an Otter mission[128] to deliver a portfolio of observations of an isolated place within striking distance of Tehran. They had to determine if the ground at a remote site in the desert was firm enough to bear the heavy weight of the C-130 cargo planes that would carry the hostage-rescue team, fuel for the helicopters, and equipment. This was to be the staging point for the mission. Another small plane from Oman landed to test directly if the ground would be firm enough to support landings by large H-53s, the heavy lifters of our helicopter force, to take out more than fifty hostages and, equally important, aerial tankers carrying enough fuel to resupply the helicopters on the long journey from an aircraft carrier offshore. With this information the president decided on the precise location for the place they called Desert One.[129]

The so-called Operation Eagle Claw posed a daunting challenge. The embassy was located in a compound that had been purchased in the 1940s, and was then on the outskirts of the city. But Tehran had spread around it, and the chancery was an unattractive redbrick building that looked like an American high school. Because of its alien architecture and central location, it stuck out as a sore spot to politically sensitive Iranians.

The Pentagon was not fully prepared with a team trained to pluck the hostages from such a place, although hostage operations by other countries during the 1970s made its commanders aware of the need. When the British deployed their Special Air Services commandos to rescue hostages from a London hotel, the Pentagon realized it had no comparable capability, and around 1975 created a top-secret army covert strike group called Delta Force, equipped with about a hundred airplanes and helicopters. The Israelis had a similar elite force, Sayeret Matkal (directorate of intelligence), famed for its hostage rescue at the Entebbe airport. They were called in for an assessment and declared that the location of the embassy in the middle of a major city made the rescue plan unworkable.[130]

One of the few factors favoring the mission was its timing. The date chosen was April 24. The monotony of keeping the captives day after day for half a year had led the captors to let down their guard; they also had little or no professional training or military support, so if Delta Force could actually penetrate the embassy compound, it had a good chance of overwhelming the guards and bringing out the hostages. An early plan also included punitive strikes in Tehran to divert attention and cripple countermeasures by knocking out the city's electric grid. As the rescue plan unfolded, the military pondered whether to mount the strikes in conjunction with the rescue attempt or, if it had to be aborted, then, as the Pentagon's General John Pustay told me, because of the "humiliation of the United States, we would do that just to demonstrate that we still had muscle." The generals later restrained themselves and did not recommend these ancillary strikes in the plan they presented to the president. But Carter would not agree to make this show of force under any circumstances, even if the rescue effort succeeded.[131]

The commander of the ground assault was Col. Charles Beckwith, a large, tough, brave soldier who was one of the creators of the Delta Force. When he met the president in the Situation Room, Carter found out he was from the South and asked if he came from Georgia. Beckwith said: "Even better, Mr. President, I'm from Sumter County"—Carter's home county. Amazed, Carter asked: "Really, who are your folks?" They then started trading stories about who knew whom. But things turned serious as the leadership briefed the president and his top aides on the details. Carter asked Beckwith how many helicopters he needed—six was the minimum, he replied. Afterward Ham turned to Vance and asked if he felt any better about the mission after hearing the briefing. Vance replied that he had sat through more than his share of such upbeat military briefings while serving as Lyndon Johnson's secretary of the army during the Vietnam War, and the one thing he had learned was that "the military will never tell you they can't do something. I just don't believe it."[132]

Secrecy was of paramount concern, so there was no outside review of the plans that had been as carefully constructed as a house of cards. Even before presidential approval, preparations had begun in November 1979, and in December helicopter pilots rehearsed in the desert of the American West. Operation Eagle Claw called for a multiservice force, Delta One, to fly helicopters to an abandoned airstrip in the Iranian desert. There, they would meet up with five C-130 Hercules air transports that had arrived earlier carrying a team of about fifty Army Rangers and huge bladders of aviation fuel. The choppers would refuel and remain at Desert One through the day, hidden under camouflage netting. The Rangers would remain behind to secure the eventual escape route.

The following day the choppers would fly to the next rendezvous point, a mountain hideaway known as Desert Two, about fifty miles northeast of

Tehran. There, they would pick up Green Beret assault troops who had in-filtrated into Iran and had acquired unmarked trucks from Iranian contacts. This force would ride in the trucks to warehouses on the outskirts of Tehran for final intelligence reports and divide into two contingents: one to the Foreign Ministry to retrieve Laingen and his two diplomatic comrades, and the larger Delta Force to the American Embassy compound. Farsi-speaking operatives, rare in the CIA, would help guide them and intervene as neces-sary. A former embassy cook, a Pakistani, had already told CIA agents in Tehran precisely where the hostages were being held inside the building. The assault troops would blow a hole in the embassy wall, free the hostages, and call in the helicopters (already en route from Desert Two). They would land in the embassy parking lot and at a nearby soccer field, pick up the hostages and fly them back, where they would board a C-130 after destroying the helicopters on the ground.

Contrary to almost universal criticism after the fact, the problem with the rescue was *not* too few helicopters. The Joint Chiefs recommended six at a minimum to carry out the mission, and one more as backup in case any-thing went wrong. During the penultimate meeting, David Aaron, Brze-zinski's deputy national security adviser, handed General Jones a handwritten note that said: "Zbig wants to know the long pole in the tent," meaning the most vulnerable part of the mission plan—the pole whose collapse would doom the entire operation. It was that there were only seven helicopters.[133] So to provide an extra margin for safety, Carter ordered an eighth helicop-ter added to the mission, two above the minimum needed.

As Carter later told me: "We felt they were reliable helicopters [and] we originally planned to have one spare just to make damn sure. And I said: 'Why don't we have eight to make double sure?'" That was the maximum that could be held under the deck of the aircraft carrier to avoid Soviet sur-veillance.[134] Zbig carefully noted that it was the civilians and not the mili-tary who raised the number. In his view the problem with the mission was the lack of ancillary strikes: "We weren't prepared in general to use force before or after to back this up or to intimidate the Iranians."[135]

Maintaining secrecy was essential to the element of surprise. There was so much concern about secrecy that General David Jones, chairman of the Joint Chiefs, and General Pustay, his top staff man, would leave the Pentagon for the White House in civilian clothes because they knew that Soviet agents were always watching the White House, and would pick up any suspicious behavior. Pustay also recalled another important intervention just weeks before the risky effort. As everybody stood up to leave, Brzezinski said: "But Mr. President, we haven't firmly established the line of communication." The president replied: "This operation will be conducted by the military," and he would keep abreast of it through General Jones and Defense Secretary Brown. He then added: "If it is successful it will redound to the benefit of the military. And if it is a failure, it would be my failure."[136]

Years later both generals expressed their admiration for Carter's readiness to shoulder the responsibility as commander in chief. As General Pustay put it, "The President stood really, really tall."[137] Jones also said he felt that the number of helicopters was adequate "or we wouldn't have gone." So eight helicopters would be taking off from the U.S. aircraft carrier *Nimitz*, two more than envisioned in the original plan.

After months of fruitless diplomacy, the rescue was seen as a last resort by Carter and his inner circle, with Vance as the one exception. Brzezinski was lukewarm from the start and told me later that "it would have been a miracle if it had worked [but] we were so committed to its success, we did not anticipate all that needed to be done. . . . There were multiple takeoffs and landings; each had to be perfect." While he loyally supported the rescue mission, he insisted he was the only one at the crucial NSC meeting to raise the question "What do we do if it fails?"[138]

He recommended that the scope be expanded to include bombing Iran so that the rescue mission could be presented as part of a retaliatory strike rather than a solitary failure. Carter vetoed that, lest Iranians be killed before the hostages could be saved; he maintained that his primary responsibility as president was "for the lives of Americans." Nevertheless Brzezinski felt strongly that the lives of the hostages, as important as they were, should have carried less weight than the fact that as long as the hostages were held, the country "was being incredibly damaged, and I thought the president was being incredibly damaged."[139]

Vance opposed the mission for two reasons. First, like the president, he felt personally responsible as secretary of state for the safety of the hostages, most of whom were foreign service officers. Second, even if it succeeded—and

Vance was firm in believing it would not and said so on separate occasions to both Carter and Mondale—he felt the mission would only create an even more intense confrontation with Iran. His position was that the hostage crisis would only be resolved when the Iranians decided to let them go, and "we [should] allow them to slowly unravel from an outrageous position."[140]

Carter's recollection is different: "You know, Vance had been completely on board; he was in all the early meetings with the Delta Force commander and with Harold Brown, Brzezinski, and me, and the Vice President."[141] While unaware it was being planned, Laingen later told me he did not favor the rescue mission because it was too complicated and could not have been accomplished without a loss of blood, including that of the hostages.[142]

What happened was this: After the first meeting in the Situation Room, Vance went on vacation. In his absence the national security team met and picked the date, with Vance's deputy, Warren Christopher, voting in favor. When Vance found out about the meeting, he called Christopher and learned that Christopher had voted for the mission, wrongly assuming that was Vance's position. Carter said that when Vance returned from Florida, "he'd had a change of mind; he said now he thought it was an improper thing to do; it had too much of a connotation of an act of war." So Carter held another meeting and another vote, and it was 6–1, with Vance voting no.

While he felt that Vance's philosophy of seeking nonmilitary solutions to problems was close to his,[143] Carter added caustically that Vance had threatened three times previously to resign; this time he was hurt that the president had bypassed the State Department in making a major foreign-policy decision. Carter felt Vance got his chance when they voted at the second meeting. The president decided to go forward, since neither Vance nor anyone else had a better alternative. Carter recalled that Vance "would come to the Oval Office and say I'm going to resign, and I would talk him out of it, and he would go back to work; and that was the fourth time he threatened to resign."[144] This time he felt so strongly that he told the president he was quitting before the operation, regardless of its outcome. From my own observation of Vance during the administration and my later discussion with him out of office, I believe that he was worn down by the constant clashes with Brzezinski, and this daring but risky attempt to rescue the hostages was the last straw.

On the evening of April 24, 1980, after almost a half-year of planning and training, the intricate, complex two-night mission, Operation Eagle Claw, began. It took almost two weeks to get everything in place. It included 132 Delta Force soldiers under Beckwith's command to rescue the hostages in the embassy, and another 13-man army special forces team to free the three U.S. diplomats, headed by Bruce Laingen, in the Iranian Foreign Ministry; 12 Rangers to block the dirt road through Desert One, and manned missile launchers to protect everyone from attack the first night; 15 Iranian and American Persian-speakers to act as truck drivers; six C-130 transport planes, three carrying the Delta Force to free the hostages, and three for logistical supplies; two C-141 Starlifter strategic airlift planes; and eight RH-53 helicopters with sand camouflage and without markings. Three weeks earlier U.S. Air Force Major General John T. Carney, Jr., and two CIA officers had been flown to the Desert One location and successfully prepared an airstrip, taking soil samples, laying hard-packed sand, and installing remotely operated infrared lights and a strobe to establish a landing pattern.[145]

Nonetheless, everything that could go wrong did go wrong. Only two hours after the RH-53 helicopters took off from the *Nimitz*, whose crew had no idea why they had been carrying them for months, they began their night flight of nearly six hundred nautical miles at low altitude to rendezvous with the C-130 planes carrying Beckwith's force and the additional fuel, which left a staging base in Egypt, flying over the Gulf of Oman to Desert One in Iran. Beckwith's Delta Force went with the words taken from the book of Samuel: "So David prevailed over the Philistine with a sling and with a stone" (1 Samuel 17:50).

One helicopter pilot reported that a warning light indicated a possible rotor-blade failure and returned to the carrier. Pustay later noted that the helicopter had a history of false warning lights, yet the pilot followed the military manuals and aborted without seeking authorization.[146]

General Jones, himself an air force pilot, later said that fighter pilots on critical missions like this one generally ignore such warning lights.[147] As the first C-130 approached the landing area, the pilots noted curious patches in the sky. They were two separate haboobs, sandstorms of suspended particles that could extend upward thousands of feet and could last for hours—not a problem for the huge C-130s but a hazard to the helicopters, whose pilots could not be warned in flight because of radio silence. Never briefed on such blinding conditions, they had to break out of their formation to avoid hitting one another.

As the first C-130 approached the landing area, its crew detected something in the isolated desert—a pickup truck coming down the road. The plane landed in soft, ankle-deep sand due to recent weeks of sandstorms, not the hard-packed sand they had been expecting, and lowered its ramp. When the truck spotted the C-130, it quickly turned around and fled. Rangers gave chase but could not catch up, and one of the pursuers fired an antitank missile at the escaping truck, which was loaded with fuel. As it burned bright in the night sky, the men saw one of its occupants jump from the cab and drive away in a jeep the truck had been towing. That intrusion was ignored because they were probably smugglers who thought they were running from Iranian authorities and not Americans, but secrecy may have been compromised nonetheless.

Now the men looked up and saw a bus, piled high with luggage, heading toward them. The passengers, Iranians making a religious pilgrimage through the isolated area, were herded into captivity. After consulting with Brzezinski, who relayed the troubles to the president, it was agreed that the Iranian pilgrims would be flown out on one of the C-130s and returned when the mission was complete.

A second helicopter now experienced navigation and instrument failure in the poor-visibility conditions. At that point Brzezinski called Brown, who was with the president in the Oval Office, and asked if he was willing to proceed. The president told him to do so, since that left six helicopters, using up the margin for error but still enough to complete the mission. Then, remarkably, a third helicopter experienced a partial hydraulic failure, incredibly caused by a crew member who placed his pack over the air blower cooling the systems, which could not be repaired because the spare parts were on the helicopter that had returned to the aircraft carrier. So this helicopter, too, was out of the mission. Air force colonel James Kyle, commander at the Desert One site, felt they could not proceed without that third helicopter.[148] When Beckwith realized they were down to five helicopters, he radioed

Brown for permission to abort the mission, and Brown concurred. As Jones put it: "The president probably knew that this had a serious impact on his future, but he never blinked [and] accepted blame for what went wrong."[149]

Now the problems only grew worse, if that was possible. While repositioning one helicopter to permit another to top off its fuel tanks for the return flight, the pilot lifted it up and hovered about fifteen feet above the ground. Its rotors kicked up a dust storm of the fine, soft sand. The pilot picking up the crew from the disabled helicopter was blinded by the sandstorm, and all he could see was the shadowy figure of the combat controller on the ground, which the pilot then used as his visual point of reference. But the pilot did not notice that the controller had moved next to the wing of the parked C-130. He kept the nose of his helicopter down and turned in the direction of the controller. Suddenly they heard a loud crack. One of the rotors had hit the wing of the C-130. The helicopter lurched forward and crashed into the cockpit of the C-130.

Sparks from the collision ignited a tremendous blaze, immediately engulfing both fuel-filled aircraft in flames. The men in the C-130 opened the back loading ramp, only to be confronted by a wall of flame. The same sight met their eyes when they opened the port troop door. They knew the entire plane could explode within minutes. The starboard troop door was clear of flames and men began crowding around it to escape. Flames were licking the walls of the plane now. As each man escaped from the plane's door, he scrambled in the sand to flee the impending explosion. The ammunition inside the plane began to crack and explode, and finally the entire plane was consumed. The Iranian pilgrims on the bus were freed and the remaining troops fled aboard the C-130s. Eight crew members died, and five other members of the team were injured.

Because of the time difference, the drama encompassed a full working day in Washington—from 10:30 a.m., when the helicopters took off from the carrier, until 6:00 p.m., when the first news arrived of the fatal collision and fire. President Carter and the small group in the White House and State Department that followed the mission maintained a normal work schedule to avoid compromising secrecy. Ham recalled: "I could hardly hide my excitement as the day passed. Every time I looked at my watch, I would try to think what Beckwith and the Delta team would be doing at that moment."

In the Oval Office earlier in the week, the president had admonished Zbig, Jody, the vice president, and Ham to carry out their regular schedules and not do anything out of the ordinary that would arouse suspicion: "And above all, don't tell anyone—not anyone, do you understand? I know that you all have devoted secretaries who know everything about your work, but I don't want them to know about this!'"[150]

At 4:30 p.m., in the midst of a campaign meeting in the Treaty Room planning television spots for the Pennsylvania primary, the president was called to the phone. Ham watched Carter and read his face. The president said nothing, then put down the phone. "Y'all continue. I've got to run to the Oval Office for a minute," Carter said. With that he was gone. About ten minutes later, the phone rang again, and the operator announced: "The President for you, Mr. Jordan." Carter said: "Ham, I want you to get Fritz and Jody and come to the Oval Office at once. Try not to arouse suspicion." When they entered the president's private study, he was standing behind his desk, his coat off, sleeves rolled up, and his hands on his hips. Brzezinski was with him: "I've got some bad news. I had to abort the rescue mission."

Minutes afterward, the phone rang again. It was General Jones, who told him that not only had the mission been aborted because of the shortage of helicopters, but in the process, blinded by the sandstorm, one helicopter had crashed into the C-130 transport, killing eight men and wounding several others; seven helicopters and one C-130 transport were destroyed. The president softly said: "I understand," and explained the tragic outcome to Vance, Brzezinski, and Ham. Vance said painfully: "Mr. President, I'm very, very sorry." Ham was so distraught, knowing that the presidency had potentially gone down in flames with the military equipment, that he rushed into the president's bathroom and, in his words, "vomited my guts out."[151]

One more painful decision faced the president: Whether to send in fighter planes to destroy what was left of the helicopters, which carried the mission's planning documents and other classified information. Bombing them from the air meant that the explosions might kill the busload of Iranians. Carter decided not to order the fire and to save the pilgrims, a humanitarian decision for which he took much criticism.[152]

Rosalynn, who also knew of the rescue plan, was making speeches and campaigning on the fateful day, pretending that nothing special was happening. She remembered: "It was awful. I knew what was going on and I couldn't say that; I could hardly think about what was happening and what I was supposed to be doing." When she got the bad news, "I was actually physically ill. They had it all planned so neatly and if it hadn't been for the accident of the helicopter flying into the plane. . . ." Even years later her voice trailed off in sorrow.[153] The failure was the worst day in the memory of virtually everyone involved. I was called by the White House Operations Center while I was asleep at home. I immediately told Fran that the fate of the hostages and Carter's political future were inseparable: For all practical purposes the election was over.

For Jimmy Carter it was personally devastating. His bold mission failed; eight Americans were dead; the hostages remained captive; and he lost his secretary of state. Within hours the hostages were blindfolded and put in leg irons, then dispersed to every corner of Iran. And the sad result, rather than being seen as the bold and courageous decision that it was, the failed rescue became instead a metaphor for all the problems of the Carter administration. Carter gets no credit for the audacity of the effort. Mondale remembers that after Carter polled everyone about going ahead with it, he asked: "Now, if in the course of this rescue mission our hostages are harmed or killed, would you tell me what policy we should pursue?" When the room fell silent and nobody came forward with an answer or an alternative plan, Carter said: "That's what I thought."[154] Its failure overwhelmed his courageous decision, and as Rafshoon looked back: "Everything just fell apart after the rescue attempt."[155]

In the cold light of hindsight, what made success in such a high-risk operation almost impossible was a mundane reason—lack of practice. Carter, who normally steeped himself in detail, left the planning and execution to the military, and oversight to Defense Secretary Harold Brown, perhaps the smartest and most effective member of his cabinet. But there had been no previous instance when four separate military services—Army Special Forces, Navy ships, Marines and Air Force helicopters, and C-130 planes—

had to coordinate in a joint mission. Fear of leaks prevented joint practice of the entire complex operation. None of the meet-ups and handovers were rehearsed, and the chain of command was unclear among the four separate services. There were no interservice run-throughs, and Brown himself conceded afterward that the mission "was not well rehearsed [because] we were probably overly concerned with security."[156]

There had been no opportunity for joint or integrated training and a full-scale dress rehearsal. The drivers took their trucks over simulated courses in the American desert mountains. The Green Berets whom the drivers were supposed to ferry to the target ran a number of simulations indicating that they could smash into the embassy buildings and retrieve all the hostages within fifteen minutes. But the drivers, the assault troops, and the helicopter pilots who were supposed to pluck everyone from Tehran and fly them to safety never once practiced together.

Colonel Beckwith put the problem in earthy, Southern terms: When the famed Alabama football coach Bear Bryant prepared his team for games, he had all the players working together, from linemen to running backs and the quarterback. "But here the army Delta Force was doing one thing, the air force was doing something else, so we never all trained together."[157]

The official Pentagon Rescue Mission Report concluded that the clandestine operation was consistent with U.S. national security objectives; feasible though high-risk; command and control were excellent at upper echelons but more tenuous at intermediate levels; external resources were not a limiting factor; and planning and preparation were "adequate except for the number of backup helicopters and provisions for weather contingencies"—and "except for the lack of a comprehensive, full-scale training exercise."[158]

At 7:00 a.m., April 25, 1980, a somber president addressed the nation from the Oval Office to share the disastrous news of the failure of the rescue mission. He explained that it had been undertaken because of the "steady unraveling of authority in Iran" and the "mounting dangers" to the American hostages; praised the courage of the rescue team; expressed sorrow to the families of those who died; stressed it was a "humanitarian mission" and was not directed "with any hostility toward Iran or its people"; and accepted full responsibility for the operation and its cancellation.[159]

Now he realized he had to get himself out of the box of his self-imposed ban on traveling and campaigning. And he did it in the most maladroit way possible. At a press conference on April 30, he lamely stated that because the rescue operation was now over and our allies were joining with us to convince Iran to resolve the hostage crisis promptly, sanctions had been imposed against the Soviet Union for their invasion of the Soviet Union; our new anti-inflation proposals had been sent to Congress; our energy legislation was on its way to passage with a windfall profits tax; and the challenges facing the country were "*manageable enough*" (emphasis added) to permit him to resume his outside activities.[160] Watching the press conference, Ham Jordan saw his secretary visibly wince, and said, "We'll catch hell for that" and "We deserved to."[161]

DIPLOMACY UNFROZEN

It is hard to blame Carter alone, and there was one positive and enduring outcome—a change in how the military operated. The Goldwater-Nichols Act of 1986 changed the way the services interact, creating a Joint Special Operations Program involving all the services. This helped make possible the success of the type of daring raid that killed Osama bin Laden during the Obama administration.

There was also a positive and immediate outcome: It unfroze the diplomatic impasse and led to negotiations that ultimately freed the hostages unharmed. It became clear that Khomeini understood he had by now leveraged everything possible out of the hostages to consolidate his own leadership, and that U.S. sanctions and Iran's image as a pariah state presented increasing problems. He had already announced in late February that the hostage crisis would be ended when Iran had an elected government following parliamentary elections.

The Iranian elections were held in August 1980, and when a new government was formed, Khomeini's forces controlled it. The hostages had lost their political value, and U.S. sanctions, imperfect as they were, had begun to bite. The Americans were moved back to Tehran—this time to an Iranian prison where they could hear the screams of others being tortured. A Khomeini emissary contacted the West German government on September 12 to propose negotiations to end the hostage crisis. This was the first time someone with Khomeini's authoritative backing had proposed a negotiated settlement, and the emissary wanted it resolved before the American presidential election on November 4.

Negotiations between the administration and Iran's representative, Sadegh Tabatabai, had begun in earnest in Bonn when they were waylaid by a totally unexpected event: Fearful that a resurgent Shiite Iran would undermine his Sunni political base, Saddam Hussein had the Iraqi army invade on September 22, ostensibly because of a dispute with Iran over territory claimed by Iraq at the head of the Gulf, known as the Shatt al Arab. Tabatabai could not even return from Bonn because the air space was closed. Iran wrongly assumed that the United States was behind the invasion, and the nation now was engaged in a war for survival. The American hostages were no longer the Iranian government's top priority.

Had Saddam not started the war, there is every reason to believe the hostages would have been freed before November. Because I was concerned that the paranoid Iranians would think we had put Saddam Hussein up to it, I quickly called Brzezinski and his deputy, David Aaron, and then Henry Owen to recommend that the president issue a reassuring statement that we were not behind the invasion. Owen said it was a "first-rate idea."[162]

The next day we held a Situation Room meeting with all the military brass, the CIA, and the cabinet members involved with security, including Vance's successor, Edmund Muskie. The new secretary of state said the ultimate threat to the United States lay in the Gulf's busy sea-lanes. We and our allies had naval forces in the area, and the French and Italians believed that Iraq wanted to control the long-disputed territory and bring down Khomeini by destroying Iran's oil resources and its economy. We realized they were in for a long war—it lasted eight years with a million casualties—and we decided to join a formal UN Security Council resolution calling for a cease-fire, as unlikely as that would be.

This put the administration in a tight corner. While we had no sympathy for Khomeini, to say the least, anything that seemed to indicate we favored the invasion might seal the fate of the American hostages. But there was one way that the war might work to the United States' advantage: Providing arms for the Iranian military might give us negotiating leverage in freeing the hostages. In October the administration agreed to release an arms shipment that had been ready for delivery to Iran but was withheld by the political turmoil. While some other military goods were also shipped, highly lethal classified equipment such as radar-guided missiles and high-technology aviation electronics were not. If Carter had as little restraint as Reagan had in the sordid arms deal with Iran, the hostages might have been released well before the election.

I can say without equivocation that Carter never missed a beat on my domestic issues. Decision memorandums were returned just as promptly as ever, and when I asked to meet with him in private to resolve interagency disputes, he was always ready. Campaign speeches were planned, drafted, and edited. I never once saw him lose his composure or seem depressed and downcast, except immediately after the disastrous rescue mission, and at rare moments toward the end.

Brzezinski, who briefed him every day on the hostages and other trouble spots like Afghanistan, saw the same qualities—which he summed up as "serenity." He wondered about the source of this stabilizing quality and concluded that Carter was "a genuinely religious person, who is extremely serious in a thoughtful way about his religion." We both agreed that Rosalynn was also an important source of reassurance and strength, because she was not only close to him but a strong person.[163] Carter never wore his religion on his sleeve, never made me feel uncomfortable about his religion or my own, and that religious devotion, along with his wife's love, support, and advice, sustained him against all the problems that crowded in on him during his last year in office.

Although the final agreement for the hostage release was reached while Carter was in office, as one last humiliation Khomeini allowed the hostages, who had been freed but were still on the ground, to leave Iranian airspace only seconds after Carter's term had officially ended and Reagan was inaugurated. We wondered whether the Reagan election team had struck a deal. Did they offer the Iranians the arms deal they later delivered in order to delay the moment of the release? Sick thought so and laid out the evidence he found in a book, *October Surprise*.[164] Carter told me that he had no independent knowledge beyond what Sick had written in his book, but that at one time during the campaign, George H. W. Bush, who formerly headed the CIA and was Reagan's running mate, "completely disappeared from the American scene and went to Paris."[165]

Hearings were held in the U.S. Senate and House of Representatives, which concluded that there was insufficient evidence to conclude a plot actually occurred.[166] But Sick did note that the Iranians had been expressing a great deal of interest in obtaining spare parts for their American military equipment until they suddenly stopped about a month before the presidential election, despite their pressing need after Saddam's attack. If nothing else the Reagan campaign did an effective job of helping create public cynicism as a firebreak against any surprise release that would have benefited Carter.

Even after losing the election, Carter and his team worked day and night for the hostages' release. On January 12 he briefed the White House staff on the negotiations, correctly forecasting that they would go right down to the wire.[167] The Iranians were contemptuous of Carter, and one of the radical students' favorite sayings was: "Carter can do nothing." They neither forgot nor forgave Carter for his identification with the Shah, and Laingen noted that they wished Carter "ill at every opportunity [and] hoped he would lose to further discredit him and disgrace him, as evidence that God was on their side, too." They got their wish, but they were also unsure about whether Reagan might clobber them and did not want to risk that an hour longer than necessary.[168]

Carter did not go to bed during the last three nights before he left office, sleeping fitfully on the couch in the Oval Office the entire time. He worked through the Algerians, who, he noted, "were the only ones with whom Khomeini would communicate."[169] Christopher was on the ground in Algiers, backed by Lloyd Cutler, the president's White House counsel. Twelve nations were involved, with Britain holding $2 billion in frozen Iranian gold bullion, and the United States $10 billion. Carter let Khomeini know that none of the frozen assets would be exchanged for the hostages, but an international claims court would be established for American contractors and other companies that had built airports, roads, schools, and other projects but had not been paid.

All of this, he said, "I had to orchestrate" with one foot out of the Oval Office. He was determined to obtain the release before he left office or at least to leave his successor a clean slate. As a condition of their release, Carter also made a difficult compromise by blocking the hostages from bringing private suits against Iran for unlawful detention. Carter said he reluctantly agreed, and that "some of the hostages have resented that since then."[170] Could the hostage taking have been prevented? Yes, if the president had been left to follow his own sound instincts and deny entry to the Shah for medical treatment. He was well aware of the risks and presciently asked: "What do you propose to do if they take our diplomats hostage?" No one came up with a coherent answer.

And could the hostages have been released earlier? It is impossible to know. I continue to believe that a stronger show of U.S. military might and shutting off Iran's oil exports would have led to the hostages' release and not to their murder. Khomeini heeded the president's warning that any harm or even show trials of the hostages would be met with the full force of the United States, which is why he did neither. But it is easier for me to say. Carter had to make the terrible choice of weighing the possible loss of life of our diplomats against the loss of the country's prestige in the humiliating impasse with Khomeini.

In providing a fair assessment of the decisions Carter made in dealing with the entire Iranian crisis, little was known at the time about the absolutist, uncompromisingly radical attitude of Islamic fundamentalism, embodied by an unelected, aged ayatollah who did not fit into any historical norms. The Carter administration negotiated with the supposed leaders of the postrevolution government, only to find that they lost their positions and in some cases their lives, and reached agreements overruled by the impervious Khomeini, with whom no one in the U.S. government could even meet, let alone negotiate. Even now, with internal turmoil in Iran, the U.S. still has little insight into, or policies to deal with, the contending internal forces of the more moderate elected government and the radical Islamic clerical regime, which holds the real power.

Carter with Pope John Paul II, October 6, 1979. Together they had a major impact on unraveling the Soviet empire. *(Associated Press)*

The Serpent's Kiss: Warned to keep his distance from Soviet President Leonid Brezhnev, Carter nevertheless succumbed out of Southern politeness to a Russian celebratory embrace in Vienna, Austria, on June 19, 1979, after both signed the SALT II Treaty. *(Associated Press)*

At the Guadeloupe talks, January 6, 1979, are (from left) West German Chancellor Helmut Schmidt, Carter, French President Giscard d'Estaing, and British Prime Minister James Callaghan. *(Associated Press)*

The Shah of Iran wipes his eyes as U.S. Park Police use tear gas to disperse demonstrators trying to disrupt the ceremony welcoming him on his first visit on November 15, 1977. Rosalynn Carter and Empress Farrah stand behind them. *(Jimmy Carter Library, photographer: Schumacher)*

Carter and the Shah later share a social moment in the Blue Room of the White House. *(Jimmy Carter Library, photographer: Schumacher)*

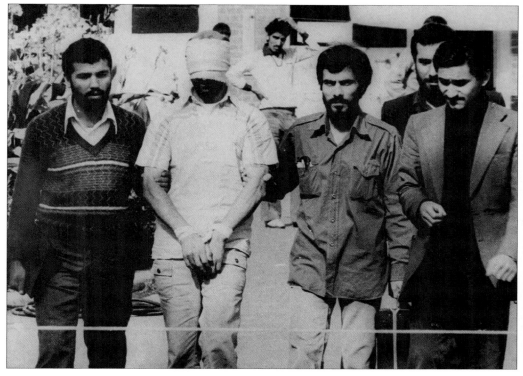

A blindfolded American hostage being led from the U.S. Embassy in Tehran by radical Islamic students who seized it on November 4, 1979. *(Associated Press)*

Carter in the Oval Office in a tense moment, getting the latest report on the hostage negotiations. From right to left: speechwriter Hendrick Hertzberg, Chief of Staff Hamilton Jordan, White House Counsel Lloyd Cutler, pollster Patrick Caddell, and Gary Sick, the NSC's Iran expert, holding documents. *(Jimmy Carter Library, photographer: Fackelman)*

Wreckage of a C-130 U.S. cargo plane at the Desert One site after it was struck by a RH-53 helicopter due to poor weather conditions, in the abortive April 24, 1980, raid to free the hostages in Tehran. *(Associated Press)*

A somber President Carter reports to the nation on April 25, 1980, on the failed rescue mission, seen by some as a symbol of the failure of the Carter presidency. *(Associated Press)*

Ayatollah Ruhollah Khomeini, the Islamic radical leader of revolutionary Iran, who galvanized opposition to the Shah and created the first theocratic Islamic state in February 1979. *(Associated Press)*

Carter and Ronald Reagan at their only debate on October 28, 1980, only days before the election. *(Associated Press)*

Carter inspects the new White House solar hot water heating system he ordered installed, located on the roof of the West Wing, on June 20, 1979. *(Associated Press, Harvey Georges)*

A bitter primary fight ends with a handshake grudgingly extended by Senator Edward Kennedy to Carter at the Democratic National Convention, August 14, 1980. Between them are House Speaker Tip O'Neill (left) and Robert Strauss, Carter's campaign chairman. Behind is New York Congressman Charles Rangel, with Rosalynn and Amy Carter at right. *(Associated Press)*

Carter outside Oval Office with his controversial wunderkind pollster, Patrick Caddell. *(Jimmy Carter Library, photographer: Schumacher)*

The President looks over the author's shoulder as Chief White House Domestic Policy Adviser reviews a paper aboard Air Force One. *(Stuart Eizenstat Personal Collection)*

While on his way to West Germany to meet them aboard Air Force One, an exuberant ex-president celebrates the release of the American hostages and clinks champagne glasses with Chief of Staff Hamilton Jordan; speechwriter Hendrick Hertzberg is between Jordan and Carter. *(Jimmy Carter Library, photographer unknown)*

We had no visibility into his decision-making process, or that of the revolutionary council. In the end the hostages were released partly because of the bite of billions of dollars in frozen assets and imperfect economic sanctions, and partly because even the ayatollah recognized that Iran needed outside help after the Iraqi invasion—but most significantly, because the hostages had fulfilled their role of consolidating Khomeini's power following the August 1980 parliamentary elections and no longer served any useful purpose to a regime whose ways we still do not fully understand decades later.

PART IX

A CATASTROPHIC CONCLUSION

28

"WHERE'S THE CARTER BILL WHEN WE NEED IT?"

National health insurance had been a Democratic dream since Harry Truman's days, and the inability of Jimmy Carter and Ted Kennedy to agree on a plan was a major factor in Kennedy's challenge to the president's renomination. Kennedy rallied the liberal wing of the party and helped weaken Carter against Ronald Reagan in the general election. For three decades—until Barack Obama's presidency—this set back the goal of broad health coverage for the American people that other Western allies adopted after World War II. National health insurance became the major fault line in the party. Kennedy used it as his lodestar in trying to maintain a liberal party supporting huge new social obligations, while Carter, recognizing the rising antigovernment, antitax mood in the nation and struggling to combat rising inflation, tried to create a more centrist party, while holding on to its historic support for the poverty-stricken and the working poor, white and black.

Even at the height of his Great Society programs, Lyndon Johnson did not seek universal coverage but covered the elderly in Medicare and the poor in Medicaid, leaving tens of millions without health insurance unless they were covered through their employers. Ironically the first serious presidential proposal for national health insurance came not from a liberal Democratic president, but from Richard Nixon in his 1971 State of the Union message, when he expected to face Kennedy and needed to outflank him on health care.[1]

When Nixon revived it after Watergate, the unions and liberals shunned the plan, believing they could get a better deal from the Democratic president they expected in the next election. This was a continuing pattern during the Carter administration. Rather than reach a compromise with Carter on a less sweeping bill that would have introduced universal coverage in stages, Kennedy initially aimed for all or nothing, in a comprehensive plan financed by payroll taxes. During lengthy negotiations he made important concessions, but not enough to reach an agreement during a time of high inflation and tight budgets. In the end Kennedy and the nation got nothing. Carter did not share Kennedy's lifelong passion for national health insurance, and during the beginning phase of the Democratic primary campaign did not address it because of its cost, complexity, and because a giant new social program was at odds with his economic focus. This program would have been the mother of them all, and the unions worked with Kennedy to dangle it before Carter as the price for their support.

After capturing several key Southern primaries, the Carter campaign headed to the industrial East and Midwest to test whether the former Georgia governor could be a national and not just a Southern regional candidate. I received a call at our Atlanta headquarters from Steven Schlossberg, the general counsel of the United Auto Workers, who told me the UAW was prepared to endorse Carter if he supported national health insurance—the first union endorsement of any candidate from a nonunion state. While the UAW did not insist that Carter support any particular bill, Schlossberg insisted his statement must include the key principles of universal, mandatory coverage in one law. This had been the union's goal since Walter Reuther, the founding president of the UAW, first approached Kennedy in the 1960s to make it his cause when he was a junior senator. I immediately called Carter and was authorized to negotiate a set of principles, which the candidate instructed me to make as general as possible, and to avoid a specific timetable on something that clearly was not one of his priorities.

So I worked out with Schlossberg a statement that included the key buzzwords demanded by the UAW but heavily hedged. The program would be phased in "as revenues permit," would focus initially on catastrophic coverage to avoid bankrupting families, would first mandate mother-and-child coverage, and would then move toward eventual universal and mandatory participation.[2] There would be an emphasis on quality and cost control. We later issued a separate statement assuring private insurance companies that we envisioned a significant role for them.[3] Thus I had given Carter maximum leeway in committing him to accept the principle but not the details of national health insurance, and in exchange we received both the UAW's endorsement and its union foot soldiers in key battleground states, helping to validate him for the party's wary liberal wing.

Kennedy had eagerly awaited Carter's arrival in the White House in the belief that he had an ally in his life's quest. He called Carter after the election to congratulate him and felt he received assurances that his top priority would also be Carter's.[4] But the senator did not get the speedy attention he expected from the new president. Once elected, Carter shuffled his priorities in a way that would substantially delay and complicate any agreement on health insurance, not mentioning it at all in an early speech on domestic priorities. He was in no rush to propose a massive new entitlement program so soon out of the gate, lest it undermine his campaign's emphasis on fiscal frugality as a major weapon to fight inflation.

On December, 28, 1976, at his transition retreat at St. Simons Island (an 1,800-acre plantation owned by Smith Bagley, a Carter supporter and heir to the R. J. Reynolds fortune), he told the incoming cabinet and White House staff that before proposing any expansion of health coverage, it was essential to control soaring health care costs, starting with hospitals. A sweeping energy plan and welfare reform vaulted to the top of his agenda, sapping both the energy and time of the administration as well as many of the same congressional committees that would have jurisdiction over health insurance. Welfare reform and hospital cost containment fell flat, and national health insurance along with them, while the energy plan took two years to enact.[5]

Containing medical costs was not a diversion from national health insurance; it was an essential condition to include the millions with no coverage at all in a system whose costs were out of control. But it was a sordid object lesson of how Washington's work is stymied by powerful special-interest groups with money and access to influence Congress. A bill was already before Congress to limit Medicare and Medicaid costs, and Carter broadened it to cover private insurance costs. I suggested linking it further to some form of national health insurance, since the expected benefits of an efficient government insurance plan could be a primary selling point for capping hospital costs. But by concentrating only on costs and ignoring coverage, we were proposing a plan with all pain and no gain, a serious strategic mistake that we never adequately discussed and for which I bear equal responsibility with Health Secretary Joe Califano and our political team. The missed opportunity haunts me to this day.

AN EARLY LESSON IN POLITICS AND POLICY

From our earliest days a central failure of the Carter administration was our inability to combine politics with policy in our decision making. The big political questions about health care were never addressed, nor did Califano prompt them. Instead we went ahead blindly, taking on the medical and hospital lobbies, among the most powerful in Washington, without the armor of expanded coverage. Then began an intensive round of discussions inside the administration,[6] and also with outside stakeholders such as the hospital organizations, the American Medical Association (AMA),[7] and the National Association of County Organizations.[8]

We also kept in close contact with Senator Kennedy, who supported our efforts to rein in costs. But when Carter wrote key congressional leaders thanking them for their help, his letters read something like a memorandum: "To Chairman Edward Kennedy: Thank you for your prompt work on hospital cost containment. I am enclosing a copy of a letter on cost containment that I am sending to the other three health subcommittee Chairmen. Sincerely, Jimmy." He rarely personalized his letters by writing in the first names of senators or congressmen or penning a personal inscription at the bottom, which added to their sense of his aloofness, the opposite image from what we saw while working with him daily.[9] With Kennedy's help we moved a bill out of the Senate Human Services Committee to cover privately insured hospital patients as well as those on Medicare and Medicaid.

Then we hit a serious roadblock in the House Ways and Means Committee's Health Subcommittee, chaired by Dan Rostenkowski of Chicago; it was also the home base for the two associations representing for-profit and nonprofit hospitals, where they played their special brand of Washington political hardball. The vote on hospital cost containment, already watered down from the administration's proposal, was tied, and Harold Ford, a Tennessee

Democrat, could not be found, for good reason: He had pledged his vote to both Rostenkowski and to Michael Bromberg, the executive director of the American Federation of Hospitals, which opposed the bill and had written Ford a substantial campaign check. Rostenkowski had a marshal summon Ford to the subcommittee room, where he reluctantly yielded his tie-breaking vote to Rostenkowski. After Rostenkowski gaveled adjournment, Bromberg canceled Ford's check.[10]

Then Rostenkowski decided to call in his own political chit as his price for continued support, as the bill moved to the full Ways and Means Committee. He was furious at the White House for not appointing Chicago's deputy mayor to the Chicago regional office of Califano's department, and vowed: "I'm going to get even."[11] Califano cut a face-saving deal but the president overruled it, saying: "All these guys care about is the head of their regional office. I'm not going to make a deal like that."[12] The unwillingness to trade small favors that can produce big results was emblematic of his distaste for the traditional give-and-take of Washington politics. Rostenkowski was not someone worth crossing on such a minor matter when he was the legislative key to a major initiative.

Bromberg realized that he could not beat something with nothing, so in league with the AMA, he came up with a strategy to pass a bill with only voluntary limits on costs.[13] After first warning me that he supported the voluntary program, Rostenkowski took the bad news directly to the president, urging him to support it, too. The president knew this would eviscerate his bill and refused.[14]

When the bill went to the Health Subcommittee of the Commerce Committee, chaired by an enthusiastic supporter, Paul Rogers of Florida, the vote was also close.[15] Bromberg organized a sophisticated operation that overwhelmed ours with a basic argument that frightened members: Cost controls would mean fewer services, loss of jobs, and they would be blamed if there were not enough hospital beds in a flu epidemic or enough nurses because they had been laid off due to price controls. They also reminded members that hospitals were major employers in their district, and had some of their district's most prominent citizens on their boards. One of the leaders of a Catholic hospital in Chicago was a nun named Sister Sheila. Every time someone mentioned health care to Rostenkowski, he would say: "What does Sister Sheila think? I'll have to check with her."[16] And of course the AMA and the hospital organizations had political action committees that dispersed campaign cash to key members.

The AFL-CIO switched sides, fearing unionized hospital workers would bear the brunt of the cost cutting, and entered into an unholy alliance with the medical lobbies. We adjusted our bill to allow a limited wage pass-through for hospital workers, but it was not enough for organized labor, and Rostenkowski and Rogers rejected our compromise. The key vote to break a tie was held by a strapping, tough young Democratic congressman from Chicago, Marty Russo, a Rostenkowski protégé. Russo met with the hospital heads in his district, and their officials claimed that Illinois hospitals were very efficient and that Califano and Carter were protecting inefficient New England hospitals. Russo suddenly changed his vote and went against the administration's program, which would impose cost controls if nationwide hospital inflation exceeded the overall inflation rate by at least 2 percent.

An angry Paul Rogers escorted Russo into the anteroom off the cavernous committee room, where Califano was also visibly upset. They said: "How the hell can you do this to the president?" and threatened to call Carter, but backed away when they realized that even the president of the United States could not overwhelm Chicago politics.[17] This turned out to be one of the few times Carter retaliated. He pointedly singled out Russo at a White House briefing for Democratic congressmen and at the next Democratic leadership breakfast.[18] Commerce Secretary Kreps canceled her appearance in his district for a small-business meeting Russo had publicized, and he became the House's only Italian Catholic omitted from the White House delegation to the Vatican for the installation of the new pope.

We tried to pick up the pieces in the Senate, where Kennedy was reintroducing the president's original cost containment bill, which now had no chance of passing and, even worse for Kennedy, slowed his drive for national health insurance.[19] Kennedy did not like the signals he was hearing on national health insurance, and asked Califano to dinner at his Virginia home. Califano demurred on pushing forward immediately on the ground that he needed more time and that the key committees were preoccupied with energy, hospital cost containment, and welfare reform. Kennedy was more than mildly irritated. He told Califano that he had been waiting since January, that Carter had made a campaign pledge, and that he intended to hold congressional hearings to put the issue before the public.[20]

Kennedy and Carter spoke on successive days at the UAW's annual convention, with Kennedy charging that health care reform was at risk of becoming "the missing promise" of the Carter administration.[21] After Califano briefed him on Kennedy's barrage, Carter promised to present a proposal early the next year. I then joined him for a meeting with the union's leaders and other health insurance advocates. Carter emphasized that he could not pass national health insurance without containing hospital costs, asked them to help, and said: "We can't get this overnight. If we demand too much and are not fiscally responsible, the whole thing will be rejected. This needs to be politically feasible." For them this was a chilling message and put him at odds with the approach of Kennedy and his labor allies once and for all.[22]

The health insurance advocates led by Kennedy were far in front of most Democrats in Congress in terms of the ambitions—and costs—of the program. The congressional politics were also complicated by the multiple committees in the Senate and House that had overlapping jurisdiction. The special interests that were ferociously circling around health care ranged from labor unions to corporations, hospital and medical associations, insurance companies, and nurses. As we began the laborious effort of developing our own health insurance proposal and trying to marry it with Kennedy's, there were a number of moving parts: the role of private health insurance companies; whether and how to phase in coverage, rather than hold out for the nirvana of universal coverage; and if later phases would be automatic or triggered by economic and budget conditions affecting the huge costs of a comprehensive program. (These same issues bedeviled the Obama administration decades later, when it put together and narrowly passed the Affordable Care Act, often called Obamacare.)

Recognizing the complexity of making massive changes to the American health care system, and our lack of data on it, in April 1977, Califano appointed his talented undersecretary, Hale Champion, to chair a committee of government and private stakeholders.[23] We knew it would be unlikely to have a proposal for at least eighteen months, and on November 9 the president got his first briefing. Twenty-six million Americans had no health insurance and another 28 million had inadequate coverage. Califano underscored that among the prime reasons for the exorbitant costs were the absence of competition among insurance carriers, no cost controls, new technologies, and uninformed consumers. The options extended from a federally run and financed program, as Kennedy was proposing, to various alternatives, including roles for private insurance companies and employer-provided insurance. Carter pointed out that none of these options would work without controlling costs and phasing in coverage.[24]

As we left the meeting Califano and I shared the same concern about pressure from the UAW and Kennedy. He suggested a holding action by announcing a set of broad principles. On November 18, 1977, I met with the senator, his health care expert, Dr. Larry Horowitz, and Dr. Peter Bourne, the president's drug policy adviser.[25] Kennedy had an imposing physical presence, with a shock of hair, a large neck, and a chiseled face sitting on broad shoulders above a barrel chest. He also had the indefinable aura of the Kennedy brothers, whose legacy he consciously tried to preserve. I vividly remembered his brother's stirring 1962 speech on the importance of public service while I was at the University of North Carolina, and my overnight drive to Washington only a year later to see his flag-draped coffin at the Capitol. With us Ted Kennedy was brusque: We would get nowhere if labor opposed the program, and he warned: "I will move it myself if you don't." Delaying a presidential proposal was unacceptable to him because "there never is a right time" to begin, and it would need two or three years to get through Congress. I could see a train wreck ahead.

On December 21 I met with the UAW leadership and its president, Doug Fraser. Normally not a bombastic person, he was quietly seething: "We want national health insurance before the midterm elections [in 1978]. You can't back away!" I raised the idea of including private insurance carriers to broaden the political support and avoid having a total federal system, and this message got through to Kennedy, who set up a conference call with both our staffs. I thought it was the first breakthrough to a possible compromise.[26] Thus began a tug-of-war that neither side won and the nation lost.

When we held our first significant negotiating session with the senior staff of the UAW and AFL-CIO in February 1978, the unions put forward a list that amounted to government-run health care at an even more generous level than most European single-payer systems—a national health care budget administered by a central government authority with no patient deductibles or copayments to help control costs. I thought this was totally unrealistic. They accepted the idea of phasing in coverage starting with those most in need, but only if the law made it clear that the end result would be universal coverage; and they ignored our warning that this would entail massive government costs.[27] At the end of February, Kennedy told me he had reached an "important breakthrough with the unions in accepting a role for private health insurance companies." He asked for a meeting with the president and the labor leadership.[28]

But first Carter, Califano, Blumenthal, and I convened in the Oval Office to discuss the timetable. The two cabinet secretaries wanted to delay formal introduction of a bill because it would clash with reform of taxation and Social Security. Carter emphatically refused: "I made a commitment to the UAW and Kennedy, and I would be lying if I put it off."[29] Later that same day Califano and I met with Kennedy and his union allies, and the senator came part of the way toward our ideas, agreeing to greater private-sector involvement by sharing part of the costs with employers and taking some of the load off the federal budget. He declared: "We have come a long way . . . and we are willing to give up on a big role for the private insurers. But this is our bottom line. The key is universality and comprehensiveness."[30] In one way or another every American would have to be guaranteed full health insurance. His concept was still top-heavy with government involvement: two federally funded corporations to negotiate health care budgets with the states on the one hand, and with doctors and hospitals on the other. Thus began several months that can best be described as a slog through the political weeds with Kennedy and labor.

THE CLASSIC CHOICES IN HEALTH CARE REFORM

With all the options the health insurance experts had laboriously examined, we settled on two basic choices. One was championed by Senators Russell Long and Abraham Ribicoff—one conservative, the other liberal—that called for government protection against catastrophic expenses, combined with the federal government taking over all expenses of Medicaid coverage for poor and low-income Americans. Califano and I favored a plan that would meld Long's approach with a comprehensive program, as the only one consistent with what Carter had pledged in the campaign and repeated several times in office. But ours differed significantly in fiscal effect from Kennedy's plan. We would start by mandating a minimum level of employer coverage, and thus build on the existing system that already covered more than 150 million Americans through the jobs of the family breadwinners. Then coverage would expand in stages, with government support. It did not take long for the press to catch on to a split within the administration, with the *Washington Post* quoting Budget Director McIntyre saying to "heed the lesson of Proposition 13," the antitax referendum in California.[31]

It used to be said that Social Security was the third rail of American politics, but as a lethal issue it has been replaced by health care. We now saw the start of that shift. Kennedy and the unions inhabited a New Deal–Great Society island of their own, oblivious to the growing inflationary and fiscal pressures and the conservative swing in the country. They were far ahead of most Democrats in Congress, especially young Watergate "babies" elected in traditionally Republican districts and Southern Democrats, who were telling us to stay away from it before the 1978 midterm elections. And most Republicans viewed national health insurance as "socialized medicine," which today they demonize as Obamacare.

Concerned about the conflict between congressional reluctance and Kennedy's determination, Califano and I met the president alone in the Oval Office on May 18. Carter was clearly torn, realizing the political stakes on the one hand and the economic and budget realities on the other. He told us his word of honor was at stake, but at the same time instructed us to emphasize controlling costs.[32]

Another meeting on June 1 with the president and the administration's two factions underscored the exquisite box the president was in; both the fiscal and the political boundaries could not have been worse. As Califano reminded him and he surely knew, his own ability and credibility to deliver on his promises were at stake. But OMB's McIntyre and White House economic adviser Charles Schultze stressed the huge costs of a comprehensive bill, from $30 to $40 billion by 1983.

Carter was groping for a way to salvage his campaign commitment and find common ground with Kennedy. Carter had asked whether costs would be kept down by savings through preventive care to tens of millions of Americans who would benefit from full coverage. Treasury Secretary Blumenthal argued it would be "mind-blowing" to control costs with federal regulations. Even Mondale, the liberal voice in the White House, feared the consequences of Carter endorsing Kennedy's comprehensive plan at this time. In the end Carter exclaimed: "It is ridiculous to think about endorsing a bill like Kennedy's. I am not going to destroy my credibility on inflation and budgetary matters!"[33]

In a rational world, Kennedy and the labor unions would have recognized the president's economic constraints and the antitax tide, and agreed on a more limited program that would establish the principle of universal coverage and grow by increments. But there was nothing rational about this debate. One way to square the circle between Kennedy's insistence on wrapping all benefits into one huge bill and our concern about the long-term costs would be to phase in the benefits over a long period of time, starting with coverage of children and catastrophic expenses, and introducing Mondale's creative idea of economic triggers that would give future presidents the right to slow down or postpone each successive phase, depending on what the nation could afford.

After long hours of negotiations over many days in his small but ornate and beautifully appointed "hideaway" Capitol office reserved for senior senators, I reached agreement with Kennedy about phasing in coverage. But he had raised difficulties with anything that would delay eventual universal coverage. I told Ham, who would run Carter's reelection campaign, that I feared Kennedy would pull out of the talks and use his withdrawal as a pretext to contest Carter's nomination. I suggested that we try to rope Kennedy into a partnership on health insurance that would deprive him of a rationale to mount a challenge. Ham replied that Kennedy would base his decision purely on whether he could beat Carter and would find any excuse to challenge him if he thought he could win.

We had a showdown at a June 26 meeting with Kennedy in the Oval Office. Carter told Kennedy he favored a "comprehensive plan but it would take a long time to implement," and that by the end of July he would give a speech on the principles of a bill that would move toward comprehensive coverage in stages, with formal authorizations at each step. Then the president asked Horowitz and me to leave. The accounts of what happened between the two reflect what each wanted to hear.

After Kennedy and Horowitz left the White House, I explained to Carter that while Kennedy was open to phasing in coverage, he wanted all the phases to be mandated in one bill that would define in advance what benefits would be provided in each phase and at what point the nation would move to the next level of coverage. This was far different from Mondale's idea of phasing in the stages depending upon economic conditions.

But when Horowitz called me, he said Kennedy had been pleased by the meeting, had talked to Fraser and Meany, and that while the unions opposed mandated triggers between phases, Kennedy did not oppose them as long as the goals that had to be met at each stage were clearly specified. Horowitz agreed it was "reasonable to see if one phase works before we get into another one" and thought Kennedy could persuade the unions to accept that because "we can't stand a misjudgment on cost" and need to reassure the public that it would not happen again. This was music to my ears, but the tune would soon sound considerably more discordant.[34]

The president was pleased when I told him this in his private study, and said: "I feel it is a way to satisfy my obligation to the UAW without inflation concerns."[35] It seemed that we had resolved our internal debates and that we were also close to an agreement with Kennedy and labor. But no sooner than things seemed to come together, they crumbled into pieces. I believe labor's pressure on Kennedy was the principal force behind the collapse. July became the crucial month to bring it all together—or to break it irrevocably apart. Horowitz carried a jarring message: Kennedy wanted our plan before the midterm elections and felt that he was "losing credibility and getting led along."

Horowitz now said, probably under union pressure, that their version of how a trigger would work was radically different from our conversation a few weeks ago: They would not accept a trigger built into the bill on the basis of general economic conditions, but only one that would give the president limited authority to *request* a delay on the basis of problems with the program or the economy; then Congress would have to approve. This would make any trigger meaningless. The president instructed me to tell Kennedy there would be no complete plan before the midterm elections in November.[36]

The deep divisions were clearly illuminated during the next seventy-two hours and became decisive not only for the relationship between Carter and Kennedy, but for the future of health insurance for a generation. At a July 12, 1978, meeting with the UAW's Steve Schlossberg, with whom I had negotiated our national health principles in return for their endorsement during the 1976 presidential campaign, he was fuming mad at Carter and the administration for being "ineffective eunuchs" on national health insurance.[37]

When I next met with Horowitz, he hardened Kennedy's terms, demanding that the stages leading to universal coverage must kick in almost automatically. The president would have no power to stop them moving forward over the years, and Congress could modify but not stop them from coming into force. Horowitz bluntly told me that by negotiating with us, Kennedy was "los[ing] credibility and getting led along."[38]

Was this the opening salvo in a presidential run? I met on July 26 in his Capitol hideaway office with Kennedy, Horowitz, and Carey Parker, the senator's chief of staff. Kennedy said emphatically: "I want *one bill*, with different ways of phasing in benefits." He said that since it was still unclear if we favored one bill or not, if he delayed his own plan, "I will be caught in the middle." Kennedy did not even want to come to the White House to see the president, but would only talk with him on the phone.[39] This left me thinking: Which of the two was a senator and which the president of the United States? Health care was degenerating into an ominous political brawl within the Democratic family.

Now fed up with Kennedy's demands and his refusal to come to the White House for a meeting, Carter was willing to let Kennedy break off negotiations. Since the senator refused to come to a White House meeting, I had a conference call with him, Horowitz, and Califano. Kennedy hurled accusations: "You've slid on so many timetables, I fear this will slide more. Without one bill we will lose, as we did on hospital cost containment." He drew a hard line on the all-important issue of triggers: "I can't go to the groups [unions] and say we *may* get benefits *if* we meet the triggers. The key is one bill with a minimum of standards. Otherwise opponents can pick it off bit by bit."[40]

I debriefed the president and told him I now believed we could not win with a comprehensive bill, and that my preference was for an incremental approach, starting with an incremental approach, beginning with an affordable first phase of expanded coverage. He agreed.[41]

KENNEDY HOLDS OUT FOR ALL OR NOTHING

If there ever was a political equivalent to Muhammad Ali's "Thrilla in Manila" championship fight against Joe Frazier, it was the confrontation at which Kennedy finally deigned to come to the White House on July 28 and confront Carter. Horowitz, Mondale, Califano, and I served as seconds. The president began by lauding Senator Kennedy's courage and admitting he had "slipped on timing." He said he did not want national health insurance to become a campaign issue in the congressional midterms. He told Kennedy he would release his health care principles on Saturday, but he did not back away from the ideological divide between the two. "The Democratic Party and I need to enhance an image of fiscal responsibility, and the reputation of national health insurance is that it would be irresponsible fiscally." Carter then made a prophetic statement: "It will doom health care if we split. I have no other place to turn if I can't turn to you." He continued earnestly: "I would like to leave office with a comprehensive bill in place, but I must emphasize fiscal responsibility if we are to have a chance."

Kennedy replied that no plan would pass without developing a national constituency: "I want to go around the country and say you are the first president who wants national health insurance. We should give it a fair chance." He insisted on wrapping the program into one bill, so the public could see all the benefits it would receive in the first phase and those that would automatically come later: "They need to understand the program won't be stopped because of unemployment or budget concerns, but only to make [midcourse] corrections. If there is more than one bill, it means the program can be stopped, and the principle of universality has no meaning."

It is one thing for an individual senator, even one like Kennedy, to introduce a broad health care bill when he alone will not have to live with the consequences. It is quite another for a president, who must consider broader interests like the impact on the budget, economy, financial markets, and his other priorities, to embrace costly, transformative legislation. So Carter replied, "I need to have flexibility to stop due to economic conditions." Horowitz put the difference between them in its rawest form: "We need to have an entitlement, and if bad economic or budget conditions come, then you can introduce separate legislation." Carter replied that social programs like this are rarely cut back after they start but are usually expanded. He said he needed the public to trust Congress to be fiscally responsible or the idea of government-backed coverage would die: "If I say national health insurance will happen regardless of what economic conditions are, I'll never get it passed." Kennedy disagreed and told Carter that he was heading in a direction where he would encounter the most political resistance, without rallying support from labor and consumer groups. The senator's only concession was to agree to delay any bill until after the November midterm elections. Otherwise their differences seemed irreconcilable.[42]

This was equally obvious to Kennedy, who immediately called a news conference to denounce whatever the administration would put forward on health insurance. He had called me and Califano to warn us to put out the White House plan first, but Califano said he could not be ready that day. The president was livid, saying that Kennedy "betrayed our trust." I agreed.[43]

At his news conference Kennedy was flanked by the major labor leaders and representatives of senior citizens' and church groups who had formed a Committee for National Health Insurance, which was financially supported by the UAW and AFL-CIO. The senator blamed Carter for a failure of leadership in proposing only a "piecemeal start" that would cripple any program and disappoint millions. He then announced he would introduce his own comprehensive bill. If he wanted an audition for an eventual challenge to Carter's renomination, he could not have organized it better, by stripping away our union support.

SAIL AGAINST THE WIND

In many ways Kennedy's public rollout for his presidential run came on Saturday, December 9, 1978, when Carter also effectively lost control to the senator of his own party's activist liberal and labor base. The Democratic Party held a midterm convention in Memphis—thankfully never repeated since—which gave Kennedy and the liberal constituency groups a forum to challenge Carter's tight anti-inflation budget before he even presented it. Budget Director Jim McIntyre had already proposed severe cuts in a variety of health care programs for the forthcoming budget as part of the administration's anti-inflation program; they were leaked to the press, probably by Califano, to create a backfire.

Shortly before the midterm convention Kennedy suggested that Califano should resign in protest, and Califano responded by assuring him these were only preliminary budget office proposals, which he would appeal to the president. When Carter mounted the convention podium on Friday night to open the event, he did not bring the message liberal activists wanted to hear, even if they needed to understand it. He explained the need for budget stringency but assured the delegates that he would give priority to protecting the poor.[44]

On Saturday afternoon, Califano and I were on a health care panel with Kennedy, moderated by the governor of Arkansas, Bill Clinton. Califano spoke first, reassuring the audience that Carter remained committed to national health insurance, that our differences with Kennedy could be resolved, and that the president had a broad responsibility to deal with inflation and the economy. I remember as if it were yesterday the air of anticipation as Kennedy rose to reply, but also because I became his unwitting foil.

His office had alerted the press that he would be making a major address, and the reporters were there en bloc, even for a late-Saturday-afternoon panel in Memphis.

In our many private meetings, I often found Kennedy's conversation halting, with sentences and thoughts left dangling and incomplete; but when he gave a speech, he was a man transformed by passion, power, and fluency that transfixed his audience. Kennedy said the Democratic Party was not the party of McKinley, Harding, Coolidge, or Hoover, as if somehow Carter fit into this Republican pantheon. Using terms common at his family's summer retreat on Cape Cod to steer directly at the administration's budget cuts, he exclaimed: "Sometimes a party must sail against the wind. We cannot afford to drift or lie at anchor. We cannot heed the call of those who say it is time to furl the sail."

He said the party that had torn itself apart over Vietnam in the 1960s could not afford now to do so by fighting inflation through budget cuts at the expense of the elderly, the poor, the black, the sick, the cities, and the unemployed, while wasteful tax subsidies and inflationary spending continued for defense. Sacrifices must be fair. When he turned to the panel's focus on the urgent need for national health insurance, he emphasized that America stood virtually alone among major countries without it; the rich and members of Congress were covered but not millions of average citizens; and he insisted that only through cost-controlled national health insurance could inflation be brought down and health care be provided to every person. The audience in the large auditorium leaped to its feet and erupted in sustained applause.

I spoke next, feeling like a pinch-hitter fresh from the minors batting right after Ted Williams had hit a grand slam. I cited our support for various health initiatives, including health maintenance organizations (HMOs), and financially distressed medical institutions, including predominantly black ones. At that point Kennedy dramatically pulled out a spreadsheet with a leaked copy of the OMB's proposed cuts. As I finished, Kennedy said: "When the president reviews the budget, I hope Stu gives him the same lecture he gave us." I retorted with a bite: "The president doesn't need a lecture, and I don't lecture him."

Kennedy then held up the OMB spreadsheet in his left hand and laced into me, gesturing with his large right hand, almost shouting, although his target really was the president: "Mr. Eizenstat talked of President Carter's support for HMOs. How much does the OMB budget mark propose for new starts for HMOs? Zero." He then systematically went through the other proposed cuts. At this point Califano came to the rescue, underscoring that these were not President Carter's decisions. As he put it: "OMB makes its recommendations and I make mine. But only the president decides. We should all [with]hold judgment until the president decides." But Kennedy had drawn first blood in what would be the signature issue for his presidential campaign: national health insurance.[45]

TOO LATE, KENNEDY REGRETS

Throughout 1979 we maintained a lengthy and complex effort to develop our own health insurance legislation. In January, Califano sent the president a draft plan melding the Long-Ribicoff plan to insure against catastrophic illness, with expanded and federally financed Medicaid to cover more poor and low-income people with a basic benefit package. For working Americans and their dependents (156 million of the 220 million population at the time), employers would be mandated to provide coverage, paying half the premium cost, with the government picking up the rest. I continued meeting with Horowitz and the unions, the heads of major insurance companies, and congressional leaders, often together with Califano.

Califano tried to narrow our differences at meetings with Kennedy at his home. On May 19, 1979, Kennedy announced his Health Care for All Americans bill and publicly asked President Carter to join him in enacting it. While it was less a government-centered program than Kennedy's previous bills, Califano felt it was not only administratively unworkable but politically unachievable. We continued developing an administration bill through the winter and spring of 1979.[46]

Finally, after more than two years of work, the president unveiled his first-phase bill at a White House briefing with Califano and me on June 12, with the public support of liberal congressmen Charles Rangel of Harlem and James Corman of Los Angeles and conservative senator Russell Long of Louisiana, along with a detailed Message to Congress on our National Health Plan.[47]

In a press conference that followed with me and Califano, he pointed up the contrast with Kennedy's all-or-nothing approach and took note of the fact that no national health insurance bill had ever passed Congress. Califano uttered his most memorable line: Kennedy's approach "had less chance of passing than putting an elephant through a keyhole."[48] To show he had not lost his sense of humor, Kennedy sent Califano a huge poster board with a big keyhole cut out of the center, through which, suspended on a spring was a small stuffed pink elephant.[49]

Although this was only a first phase, Carter's proposal represented a revolutionary change in the American health care system. No American would have to pay more than $1,250 a year in costs, and the government would pay anything above that for catastrophic coverage. Sixty million old, disabled, and poor Americans would be covered with no copayments, while protecting an additional sixteen million people who were not already on Medicare. Employers would be required to provide coverage by paying 75 percent of the premium for their workers and dependents. The remaining nine million Americans, either self-employed or part-time workers, would be able to buy coverage from government health care corporations, as would small companies who could not afford to purchase from private insurers. Prenatal, delivery, and first-year infant care would be provided for all women and children with no cost sharing. Reforms in reimbursements would reduce costs and reorient service toward preventive care. The government's cost was estimated at $18.2 billion in 1980 dollars, and $6.1 billion for employers to cover employees who were not already covered at work by private plans.

Kennedy never tried to move our bill in his committee. In November, Senator Long persuaded a majority of his Finance Committee to support our proposal but eventually abandoned it in 1980 because of a deteriorating economy. More than a quarter of a century later during President Obama's first term, Congress passed a national health insurance bill modeled after our proposal, strongly supported by Kennedy shortly before his death, with not one Republican vote—and later under relentless attack by President Trump and a Republican Congress. The demise of the Carter plan was a political tragedy for the president and a health care tragedy for Americans.

Years later, in 1987, Kennedy invited Karen Davis, one of the key architects under Califano of Carter's first-phase bill, for a discussion of another unsuccessful new national health care bill he was sponsoring. It was also drawn from Carter's first-phase bill, relying on an employer mandate with less federal funding. Wistfully if very belatedly, Kennedy said to her: "Where's the Carter bill now that we need it?"[50]

NO GOOD DEED GOES UNPUNISHED

I t is difficult to conjure up a more catastrophic final year in any American president's term of office than 1980, Carter's last year in the White House—or, to be precise, from November 4, 1979, the day the hostages were seized in Tehran to his defeat for reelection by Reagan on November 4, 1980. In between came the Soviet invasion of Afghanistan, Fed chairman Paul Volcker's decision to apply the monetary brakes, the daring but tragic effort to free the hostages, the disastrous Mariel boatlift of Cubans fleeing the Castro regime, and a scandal surrounding his wayward younger brother that was dubbed "Billygate." In the best of circumstances it would have taken a political magician to sustain the unlikely coalition of Southern and working-class Northern whites, blacks, women, and liberals that had elected him in 1976. But 1980 was hardly the best of times.

Jimmy Carter needed a united Democratic Party, but rumbling up from his presidency were resentment and misunderstanding among all the major building blocks of the winning coalition that had narrowly carried him into the White House four years earlier, and which was now crumbling. His conservative white Southern base; urban, labor, and liberal groups; and Jewish and women's advocates were all after his scalp. In seeking to eliminate pork-barrel water projects, Carter had alienated the congressional old bulls he would need to push through his energy and tax reform programs as well as the idealistic young Democrats who urged him in vain to veto a flawed public works bill. Announcing out of the blue even before assuming office that he would propose a comprehensive energy plan within ninety days of his inauguration, and imposing a ban in sharing drafts of the plan with Congress, led to a debilitating fight lasting two years. He made the Panama

Canal Treaty a top priority, turning it into his bloodiest congressional battle, which not only lost him Southern conservative support but almost all the seats of Democratic senators who voted for the treaty. Killing the B-1 bomber lost him the support of defense hawks, and ironically, personally presiding over the first peace treaty between Israel and any Arab country helped him lose Jewish votes. Appointing Paul Volcker to squeeze out inflation through painfully high interest rates hit everyone.

This is just an abbreviated list of the "right things" Carter accomplished for the long-term benefit of the country while ignoring the great political cost to himself. Add to this his decision to put the lives of the Iranian hostages before all other diplomatic and security considerations, and you have the ingredients that, along with Kennedy's challenge and Reagan's charm, made him a one-term president. It would take a new generation of Democrats to absorb Carter's lessons of fiscal moderation and liberal social and foreign policy and return the Democratic Party to power with Bill Clinton's political magic, powered by an improving economy.

Carter's most loyal constituency remained black Americans, a well-deserved but great irony for a president from the Deep South. Throughout his presidency he carried with him the same ambivalence toward his Democratic Party that he held on the exhilarating night he accepted its nomination: a keen recognition that the liberal base of the party he needed to win the presidency and govern successfully was out of step with the realities of the 1970s and a rising conservative polity.

At the most profound level Carter was a moderately conservative Democrat heading a party dominated by outspoken liberal interest groups. His difficulty in pulling the party to the center was accentuated by a troubled economy, which allotted him fewer federal resources to fund popular social programs. The necessity of budget cuts to fight inflation was resisted by the insatiable demands of the liberal base he saw as an enormous weight around his neck until it finally led Senator Edward Kennedy to challenge his renomination. The middle ground where Carter stood was not the high ground, which was occupied on the left by Kennedy and on the right by Reagan, who built a winning coalition of defense hawks, supply-side tax cutters, and Christian evangelical conservatives that has lasted for two generations.

His anti-Watergate populist campaign had been aimed at reforming

Washington and its established interests, but after winning his party's nomination he said: "The biggest handicap I had politically speaking after the convention was [that] I was immediately saddled with all the gubernatorial candidates, the congressional candidates, and the local candidates of the Democratic Party." He yearned to be the "lonely peanut farmer looking for votes," instead of a man of the establishment wrapped into his party.[1]

Ham believed that one of the reasons Carter lost all but one-half of 1 percent of his big lead over Ford in the 1976 election was that he came to be seen as just another traditional Democrat. But the party's institutional constituents and the Washington establishment, the press, the pundits, and opinion makers, against whom he had run, held great sway over the success of his initiatives as president, and now over his reelection. And for the leaders of such groups, who, wrongly or rightly, felt slighted, Carter's campaign for reelection was payback time.

The disaffection of key elements of the Democratic coalition was no surprise to Ham Jordan. He had prepared for a possible challenge long before the primaries, with a top-secret memo in January of 1979.[2] He laid down several warnings: Though the supposed advantage of presidential incumbency was exaggerated, Carter should still delay declaring his candidacy as long as possible to avoid looking like just another candidate; resist appeasing one wing of the party as Ford had done by dumping the moderate Republican Nelson Rockefeller; "show strength to discourage [primary] opposition"; and win votes in the general election by being a successful president. Ham believed that even though Kennedy had worked with Carter on transportation deregulation and admired his advocacy of civil rights and human rights, there was nothing to be gained politically from meeting the senator halfway on principled issues like health insurance, because that would not buy him off if Kennedy thought he could win.[3]

At a meeting with his top staff and Mondale in the White House Treaty Room on January 28, 1979, Carter showed how he could govern in a nonpolitical way—and then turn on a dime to campaign mode. He said we must "make our platform politically attractive, because in our first two years, I have taken up negative things . . . [and] put the Republicans in a tough position with our support for a balanced budget, controlling the federal bureaucracy, and supporting a strong defense." Mondale urged him to woo the liberals and the unions and not antagonize the responsible left unnecessarily. Rafshoon's message as media adviser was different: Project the image of a prudent president fighting inflation and regain the image of being above party politics and Washington. Carter readily agreed and brought up other eroding elements of the political base, in particular women.[4] This would be a circle we could not square, but Carter remained confident. On June 12, meeting in his White House residence with Rosalynn, Mondale, Rafshoon, Moore, and me, he swaggered: "I don't care if Kennedy runs. I will whip his ass," his favorite macho expression.[5] This choice comment soon made the political rounds, by design.

Why did Kennedy challenge the president of his own party? Ham felt the simple answer was that he felt he could beat Carter and be elected president. But from Kennedy's own entourage there were as many different explanations as there were senior people about whether he should subject himself to the brutal regimen of a presidential campaign against a president of his party. Steve Breyer said Carter's political weakness combined with Kennedy's own feeling "that it was his obligation to be president." Kennedy, inheriting this sense of entitlement from the assassination of his two older brothers, was also the object of a stream of appeals from senators who told him they would go "down the drain unless you run."[6]

Paul Kirk, his senior political aide (and future chairman of the Democratic National Committee), argued against running on the ground that Kennedy was still young and would have other opportunities. In fact Kennedy got off to a bad start in a television interview late in August 1979, when Roger Mudd of CBS asked him flat out to give his rationale for a presidential run and Kennedy could not give a crisp answer. It was remarkable that he was so ill prepared for such an obvious question only two months before he actually announced his candidacy. In the critical three months at the start of 1980, Carter's poll numbers leaped to more than 60 percent approval as voters rallied around the president right after the Soviet invasion of Afghanistan. Over time, the failed hostage rescue and the continued erosion of the economy gave Kennedy a second wind, but too late for him to catch up.

Mondale made one last, futile effort to avert internecine bloodshed, pleading with Kennedy to give Carter a clean shot at Reagan. When Kennedy told him he was going to take the plunge, Mondale replied: "You should know we don't intend to leave voluntarily; we intend to win this thing. This is going to get nasty, and I'm very sorry about that." Mondale concluded that Kennedy never realized how his challenge might help Reagan and shift the country to the right.[7]

Years later I asked Kennedy himself why he had run, and he replied that one element was whether "the federal government was going to be used as actively in terms of dealing with economic issues." Could his challenge have contributed to Reagan's victory? Kennedy replied that events so overwhelmed Carter's chances that "I wonder, given those factors, [if] anybody could have been as successful."[8]

GEORGE MEANY AND THE UNIONS

Carter was acutely uncomfortable with the central leadership of the most powerful of the Democratic Party's major constituency groups, organized labor's AFL-CIO, whose headquarters were just across from the White House. At the time labor represented almost one of every four private-sector workers, and their union dues and members, who helped get out the vote in the key battleground states, provided an indispensable engine for Democratic candidates. But the president of the United States and the president of the AFL-CIO, George Meany—the peanut farmer from Plains and the plumber from the Bronx—had no common history or shared idiom.

Carter's native Georgia had few union members, and he had never campaigned in union halls; their leaders were as foreign to him as their conventions, and he made little effort to attend them. He met frequently with labor's national leadership and supported most of their major initiatives: They ranged from raising the minimum wage; signing the liberal talisman, the Humphrey-Hawkins Full Employment Act; initiating job-training programs; expanding public service employment; and saving the jobs of tens of thousands of unionized autoworkers at Chrysler. But the UAW, the nation's most politically liberal union, gave Carter no credit and even worked against his renomination. This made Carter rightly furious and he exploded at a staff meeting in December 1979, with one of his favorite expletives: "We need to be mean to Fraser [the UAW president] and not kiss his ass."[9] As Carter saw it, Kennedy's attack "led to Doug Fraser's having to choose in a very painful fashion between loyalty to Kennedy, who had been his ally for many years, and loyalty to me."[10] Much later Fraser came to realize the consequences of casting his lot with Kennedy. After Reagan defeated Carter in 1980, Fraser confided to James Blanchard, a Democratic congressman from Michigan (later governor) who led our Chrysler bill in the House: "Jim, that was the biggest political mistake I ever made. If there's one thing I regret, we just assumed that whoever the Democrat was, would win, and it never dawned on me that Reagan could possibly win."[11] It would not be the last time that Democratic leaders would be caught in their own bubble.

The administration also supported labor's top priority, a bill to make it easier for workers to choose to become unionized. It passed the House overwhelmingly, but despite intense White House lobbying was blocked by one vote in a Senate filibuster, and the AFL-CIO blamed Carter rather than themselves for not doing enough to put the law over the top.[12] Despite all our work together, labor's disenchantment sent its leaders into the arms of Teddy Kennedy, setting the stage for one of the most bitter intraparty battles in modern American political history.

BELLA ABZUG AND THE ERA

It is a supreme irony that liberal women activists gave Carter so much grief after he and Rosalynn did so much for their cause. No less an authority than U.S. Supreme Court Justice Ruth Bader Ginsburg proclaimed that "people often ask me, 'Well, did you always want to be a judge?' My answer is it just wasn't in the realm of the possible until Jimmy Carter became president and was determined to draw on the talent of all the people, not just some of them."[13]

As with other disenchanted elements of the Democratic coalition, many of them felt he had not done enough. Promoting equal rights for women was for Carter an extension of civil rights for blacks, Hispanics, and other minorities. Rosalynn was a passionate advocate for women's empowerment. During the 1976 presidential campaign, Carter issued more detailed statements on that issue than on virtually any other topic.[14] In his first year in office Carter created a Presidential Advisory Committee for Women, the first of its kind, to implement the National Action Plan of the 1977 National Women's Conference in Houston. Its two top priorities were increased appointment of women in federal government jobs and ratification of the Equal Rights Amendment (ERA).[15]

When Carter took office in 1977 only one woman was serving among 97 judges in the federal courts. By the time he left in 1981, he had appointed 40 women to judgeships, or five times more women to the federal bench than all previous presidents of the United States combined.[16] He told me that if a Supreme Court vacancy occurred, he would name a woman, almost certainly Judge Shirley Hufstedler, who instead became the nation's first secretary of education.

He also issued an executive order prohibiting sex discrimination in federal employment and appointed a record number of women to top positions in the White House, regulatory agencies, and executive branch departments, even nontraditional positions in the Pentagon. Up to and through the Carter administration, only six women had been appointed cabinet secretaries in U.S. history, and Carter appointed three of them. He appointed three of only five women as undersecretaries, 80 percent of women who ever held the rank of assistant secretary, and the first women ever to serve as general counsels and inspectors general.[17]

So why did relations sour? When the House and Senate approved the ERA in 1971 by huge bipartisan majorities (354–23 and 84–4), it seemed headed for certain approval by the requisite three-quarters of the states. And who could oppose giving equal rights to women? The ERA applied only to government laws and regulations and did not touch private or purely social relationships. By 1977 Indiana became the thirty-fifth state to ratify the amendment, and in 1979, Carter's Justice Department ruled that no state could rescind its approval. To provide more time for the remaining three states, the president obtained congressional approval to extend the deadline for ratification to June 30, 1982. The vote for that was much closer, signaling the success of a rising right-wing opposition on social issues. The Reverend Jerry Falwell's Moral Majority turned the ERA into an attack on the family. It was a remarkable display of the power of the new evangelical coalition against a constitutional amendment that simply read in a few short words: "Equality of rights under law shall not be denied or abridged by the United States or by any State on account of sex."

The president appointed Sarah Weddington, a senior White House staffer, whose office was across from mine in the West Wing, to coordinate all ERA efforts, including weekly strategy meetings with the President's Advisory Committee on Women. He also met regularly with the heads of major women's organizations. The president ordered cabinet officers and agency heads to speak on the ERA in unratified states. The president and first lady, the vice president and Joan Mondale, and the entire White House staff made the ERA a regular topic of our speeches. Briefings were held for opinion leaders in key states and for national business leaders. Both Carters personally called key legislators and individuals.[18]

If only 13 legislators in three states—Florida, North Carolina, and Nevada—had changed their votes, the amendment would have been ratified. The women's groups blamed Carter. They simply could not believe that the president of the United States could not pressure the few remaining recalcitrants to push the amendment over the top. Eleanor Smeal, president of the National Organization of Women (NOW), opposed Carter's nomination even in 1976, and for reasons he could never understand, he could not get along with the group despite his record number of female appointments and his work for women's rights.[19]

But Carter's most persistent and annoying female appointee was the formidable former New York representative Bella Abzug. I first met her under an unusual circumstance at the 1976 New York Democratic Convention, when we were walking in opposite directions along a hallway and she hooked her arm in mine, thrust me against the wall like a wrestler, and began to harangue me about the ERA. Bella was short, heavy, and feisty, and wore one of her huge and garish trademark hats that could literally knock your eye out. After the election she was offered and turned down a variety of senior posts, and finally took the chair of Carter's Advisory Committee on Women. From the start she felt there was not enough contact with the president or his cabinet, so she requested a full-hour meeting with him, but he offered only a quarter of an hour, which she and the committee rejected.[20]

The committee then wrote a report criticizing Carter's cuts to social programs and sent the White House a draft press release in advance of its December 20, 1978, meeting.[21] That meeting was extraordinary, with Bella chastising him for the delay in fixing the date for the meeting. She told him his forthcoming budget would not be good for women and that they "should not be sacrificed to NATO increases." Then she listed a bill of particulars, with public service job cuts and much more. He listened impassively. Years later she told me she felt that the president behaved "rather oddly, and so there were problems between us, but then he kept talking about how we would have a better relationship in the future." She realized that he was "generally annoyed at us," but she found out later the decision had already been made to fire her.[22]

Bella would regularly leave her White House meetings and stage an impromptu press briefing in the portico outside the West Wing to blast Carter's budget cuts. The president himself noted that she and her committee would have productive and friendly meetings with him, and then on three or four occasions she would leave the White House and "condemn me as being insensitive to women's issues."

He finally told Ham to explain that she was supposed to represent him, and that when she criticized him, it made it impossible to accomplish even what they had agreed to do.[23] She told Jordan in effect to get lost. Finally Carter had "a bellyful," as Jody put it, and fired her as committee chair.[24] But as Ham reflected: "Instead of being seen as a tough action, it was seen as callous and chauvinist. We got no credit for all the stuff that we had done."[25] She was replaced as chair by Lynda Johnson Robb, daughter of Lyndon Johnson and wife of Virginia's governor and then senator Chuck Robb, and a strong and effective advocate for women.

Bella had a very different perspective. She felt that Carter did not make a major effort on behalf of the ERA, and the other major grievance, shared with NOW, was Carter's opposition to Medicaid funding for abortions for poor women. When challenged that this was not fair, Carter quoted President Kennedy's famous declaration: "Life is not fair."[26]

So this was another bridge burned with the liberal community, with each side feeling aggrieved. We should have known to expect this kind of confrontation, and it wasn't that we weren't warned—by no less than Rosalynn Carter. With her usually unerring political judgment, the first lady warned

Jody, Anne Wexler, and me at a 1978 meeting in the Map Room of the White House that appointing Bella to head the committee would be a bad idea. We argued that we would need Bella to help us with women in the reelection campaign. Rosalynn was right, and we were wrong.[27]

NORMAN PODHORETZ AND THE NEOCONS

While Carter was being attacked by the left wing of the Democratic Party, he was also attacked from the right by a small but influential group of Democrats who were domestic New Deal liberals but strong anti-Communist hawks on foreign and defense policy. They were called neoconservatives, neocons for short. The movement was started by disillusioned Democrats after Nixon crushed McGovern in the 1972 presidential election. His campaign slogan, "Come Home, America," was taken as a call for withdrawal from international engagement, and they formed a group that initially named itself the Coalition for a Democratic Majority, or CDM, to avert the leftward drift of Democratic foreign policy.[28]

After the election about two dozen committee members, including Norman Podhoretz, the editor of *Commentary* magazine, and Jeane Kirkpatrick, a Georgetown University professor of government, signed an advertisement stressing their disagreement with what they saw as the disastrously soft foreign policy of McGovern and his followers toward the Soviet Union.[29] Among the Democrats who supported them were Max Kampelman, the Carter administration's representative to the Helsinki Accords; Richard Perle, Scoop Jackson's foreign-policy aide; and Ben Wattenberg, an author and commentator who felt the media were so infatuated with the new-wave politics of the left that an intellectual counterweight was urgently needed. (Ben and I had shared an office as staffers in the Johnson White House.) CDM received much of its funding from the AFL-CIO.

Once the Carter administration began settling in, the group began to take issue with the president's appointments, such as former McGovern adviser Paul Warnke as the chief negotiator for the SALT II talks. A few neocons got lesser jobs, but it became clear that those identified with Scoop Jackson were frozen out. Kirkpatrick, an intellectual light of the movement, drew a bright line between right-wing pro-American governments and left-wing anti-American ones, arguing in a now famous November 1979 *Commentary* article, "Dictatorships and Double Standards," that "traditional authoritarian governments are less repressive than revolutionary autocracies" and calling it a historic mistake for the Carter administration to back away from pro-American but anti-Communist dictators.

Stung by the criticism, and hoping to keep their electoral support, the White House arranged a breakfast for CDM's leadership and the president on January 31, 1980.[30] By that time Carter had adopted a harder line toward the Soviets following their invasion of Afghanistan, and all the ingredients of a reconciliation seemed to be in place. There are wildly different accounts of what went wrong, but the guests felt that the president was defensive, did not respond to criticism, and took the position he was doing everything they wanted in foreign policy and could not understand why they had come to complain. I felt to the contrary: My notes show that the president said he had reversed the post-Vietnam defense-spending decline; that there was "unprecedented unity" of the American people following the Soviet invasion of Afghanistan and his strong stand, which had "changed policy"; and that there was a need for greater allied support. He told CDM clearly: "I don't want a return to the Cold War, but I am prepared to take the consequences if our standing firm leads to that."[31]

Podhoretz urged him to orchestrate a vast human rights campaign against the Soviet Union. It surpasses imagination that they could believe the president, who so strongly supported human rights and the cause of democratic dissidents and Jewish refusniks in the Soviet Union and elsewhere, would not have been responsive to their demand for a tough anti-Soviet line: He had already taken the actions Podhoretz recommended. Podhoretz later told me he felt that Carter got red with anger and was "really pissed off."[32]

What Carter said and the tough actions he had taken should have been music to their ears. Instead Josh Muravchik, CDM's director, said that most decided in the weeks after the meeting to support Ronald Reagan, and he wrote a book critical of Carter's human rights record.[33] For some who had been engaged in an eight-year struggle to bring the Democratic Party around to their view, it was the last straw. Wattenberg said they left the meeting "dumbstruck" because they felt the president did not have a clue about their ideas; they felt they were no longer welcome in the Democratic Party.[34] Peter Rosenblatt, who was appointed to a secondary post as Carter's personal representative to Micronesia, in the western Pacific Ocean, and then ignored, said the neoconservative movement was actually born at that meeting. With only limited influence left in the Democratic Party, they gained significant standing inside the Reagan administration, where their hawkishness was welcomed.

JEWS, ANDREW YOUNG, AND THE PLO

How could a Democratic incumbent in 1980 receive the lowest percentage of support from the American Jewish community of any modern Democratic presidential candidate, especially one with such a record of courting and actively supporting causes dear to the hearts of American Jewry? Carter brokered the first peace agreement between Israel and Egypt, its most dangerous foe; strongly supported a new law banning American companies from participating in the Arab boycott of Israel; created the Presidential Commission on the Holocaust headed by Eli Wiesel, and then enthusiastically endorsed by word and deed its recommendation to build the United States Memorial Museum in Washington. He even supported me in overriding the National Park Service's refusal to permit the Lubavitch Chabad movement to erect the world's first giant public menorah in Lafayette Park across the street from the White House, and then personally joined in the Hanukkah lighting with me, my family, and Lubavitch Rabbi Abraham Shemtov, a senior aide to the revered Rebbe, Menachem Mendel Schneerson.

Certainly part of the reason was the tough positions he took with Israeli prime minister Begin to forge a peace treaty with Egypt's Sadat. But the immediate culprit was a series of catastrophically botched diplomatic decisions about UN resolutions on Israel. One involved our UN ambassador, Andrew Young, and another swung Jewish support to Kennedy almost overnight at a critical stage in the Democratic Party primary battle. In politics even one foolish move can overwhelm the best of good intentions, especially when expressed by someone who still seemed somewhat alien to his Jewish supporters.

As a white Southerner, Jimmy Carter would never have been nominated by the Democrats or elected had it not been for the validation he received from prominent figures in the civil rights movement, especially Andy Young. As the quiet and effective counsel at the side of Martin Luther King, Jr., he had negotiated with bullying white sheriffs and judges trying to thwart King's historic marches for racial justice and equality. With significant organizational help from my wife, Fran, policy advice from me, liberal white and overwhelming black support, in 1972 he became the first black since Reconstruction elected from the Deep South to the U.S. House, representing Georgia's Fifth District, in Atlanta.

The more Carter campaigned with Andy at black churches around the country, the more deeply Andy was hooked. "Carter understood better than anybody running the two major problems facing America, race and poverty," Andy told me later.[35] His essential political role in Carter's budding presidential campaign could not have been more forcefully demonstrated than at a meeting Andy arranged with his colleagues in the Congressional Black Caucus. Charlie Rangel of Harlem led the doubters by asking: "Why do you want to bring that Georgia redneck up here and try to sell him as president?" I helped prepare him on the issues, but that was not what swung the day.

As Andy recounted, the meeting was held at the Capitol with more than a dozen members of the Black Caucus. Before Carter could get in a word, Barbara Jordan of Texas jumped on him with questions more hostile than those directed at the parade of previous presidential hopefuls. But the question that threw the others off course was: "How many black people do you have on your staff and what are they doing?" Each of the candidates had only one, and Morris Udall of Arizona had plaintively confessed that he was looking for a black staffer. But Carter replied: "I don't know how many black people I have, but it is at least fifteen or twenty. We don't have a segregated campaign where black people campaign with black people." He had wisely brought along a young black Georgia state senator, Ben Brown, and when Carter turned to him, Brown said: "Governor, at last count we have 27, and they serve in every area of the campaign." That, Andy recalled, "had them stunned."

Andy's support for Carter was crucial not only in the black and liberal white communities, but in the Jewish community as well. I knew from working as Andy Young's policy director during his 1972 campaign that his support for Israel was not empty rhetoric. We developed a strong position on

Israel that appealed to the influential Jewish community in Atlanta, and he carried this with him to Congress, where he compiled an impeccable pro-Israel voting record. After Carter's narrow victory, Andy wanted to stay in Congress and help drive through his legislative program, but the president-elect had grander plans for him: the cabinet-level position as U.S. ambassador to the United Nations. Said Carter, "We need somebody who worked with Martin Luther King, because our human rights policies won't have any credibility if it is just something we are saying, and if we don't have somebody that's really large on the human rights issues." Andy said he would be glad to take up the task in a second term, but insisted he could be more useful now in the House. Carter replied prophetically: "There may not be a second term. I think whatever we are going to do, I think we have four years to get it done."[36]

He asked the new ambassador to visit Africa as soon as he was sworn in and recommend what the new administration could do to advance human rights there. Andy found that hard to turn down, and his wife Jean argued he could have a greater impact taking flight from a world stage at the United Nations. It turned out to be the journey of Icarus. Andy's personal and professional life gave no clue of the lightning rod he would become at the UN. His civil rights biography preceded him, and the knowledge that he had the ear of the president was a known strength but also, as he privately recognized, "my weakness" because it meant—or he thought it did— that he could bypass the State Department bureaucracy. He complained that if he wanted to advocate a change in some amendment to a UN resolution, he needed "seventeen different clearances within the State Department, [and] could go directly to [Secretary of State] Cy Vance and the president and get it changed. And I did that often."[37] This infuriated the hierarchy department at State, a designed to achieve consensus by flattening out sharp views.

Outside the conference rooms of the UN, Andy delivered a stream of unscripted remarks that were nowhere near U.S. policy. In a *Playboy* interview he labeled former Presidents Nixon and Ford as racists because they neglected Africa; in an interview with the French newspaper *Le Matin* he likened the Soviet gulags to American prisons; he called the Ayatollah Khomeini "a saint."[38] Such comments understandably got under Vance's skin.

Of the many ironies in Andy Young's downfall, perhaps the greatest is that he tripped over a deviation from the State Department's diplomatic script in an attempt to protect Israel from a resolution directed against it by no less than the PLO. This time there were no unscripted words. Quite the contrary, Andy operated through a back channel toward a forbidden interlocutor in the hope of helping Israel and Middle East peace. This is exactly the way diplomacy is supposed to operate at the United Nations—by small steps, often hidden from view, in the hope of bringing the world's intractable conflicts into the light of dialogue. He broke an official rule established by Henry Kissinger as secretary of state as part of his interim withdrawal agreements, agreeing with Israel that the United States would not negotiate with the PLO. Carter renewed this pledge during his election campaign to hold on to the Jewish vote, and Congress formalized and broadened the diplomatic ban in 1976.

In the summer of 1979, as Andy Young prepared for a six-month term as rotating president of the Security Council, he was warned by his British predecessor of a resolution being drafted by the Arab bloc demanding recognition of the PLO as the head of a Palestinian state-in-exile. Its capital would be established in Jerusalem and all territory conquered by Israel in the 1967 war would be given up. Such an extreme resolution might force Young into casting an embarrassing U.S. veto while serving as council president, and he set out to modify or delay the draft. For the past several years, the Carter administration's diplomats had been doing backflips to entice the PLO into accepting Israel's existence and joining the Middle East peace process, and Carter himself led the way. When he visited the UN in 1977, Carter conspicuously shook hands with the PLO representative in a reception line, causing great controversy.

On July 25 Andy and his senior staff lunched at his ambassadorial residence in the Waldorf Towers with Arab ambassadors from Kuwait, Lebanon, Egypt, and Syria. They told him the resolution had been written by Yāsir Arafat himself. Young replied that this was a trap for him and the other Arabs, because if the United States cast a veto, it would only prove to the radical opposition to their conservative Arab regimes that America did not want peace; this would give the PLO and the hard-liners just the pretext they needed to justify violence and argue that politics and dialogue were pointless.

Ambassador Abdullah Bishara of Kuwait said the Arabs could not sell a delay to the Palestinians and could no longer negotiate with Young on the PLO's behalf. But as the luncheon was breaking up, Bishara suggested that he could set up a meeting that day at his home to meet with Zehdi Labib Terzi, the Palestinian observer at the UN.[39] Young assured me that all this took place within the hearing of other American officials and was fully reported to the State Department.

Because Bishara had a young son, Andy took along his own six-year-old-son, Bo, and to stress the informality of the meeting, the ambassador wore jeans. Bishara's son did not show up, so there were three adults: Young, Bishara, and Terzi—a tenured professor of English literature at Columbia and, by Andy's description "a very gentle, sophisticated old man." A Christian Arab, he was a member of the PLO, and although the meeting was made out to be chance and informal, there is no question that its purpose not only was entirely benign but actually in the U.S. and indeed the Israeli interest— to persuade Terzi to drop or postpone his provocative resolution.

Andy began the meeting by saying: "If we don't have peace in your lifetime, we're not going to have peace. I do not want to miss this opportunity. But I will have to veto it if you bring it up."[40] Andy won the battle and lost the war. The resolution was postponed, but Andy lost his job trying to help Israel in the process, thanks to the constraints of bureaucracy, diplomatic duplicity, and his own misjudgments about notifying the State Department.

On the one hand, as the American ambassador to the UN he was barely authorized even to acknowledge the existence of any representative of the PLO, let alone meet for a drink in the Delegates' Lounge, the informal birthplace of many diplomatic initiatives that eventually matured into deals among powers great and small. But on the other hand, at the start of the following week Ambassador Young would be taking up his role as president of the Security Council for six months, and was required to meet with all parties to any dispute before the council. Moreover, if his tumultuous years in the civil rights movement had taught him anything, it was the necessity of dealing with white officials who virulently opposed him and his cause. Andy felt: "Not talking to the enemy is the worst possible thing."[41]

Within hours Andy's closest aide Stoney Cooks was told by a press officer at the U.S. Mission that *Newsweek* was on the phone seeking comment on the Terzi meeting. They decided not to comment, partly because they thought the full story was on record at the State Department and they had been in-structed to keep quiet about it anyway. For a while the story died down because *Newsweek* described the meeting as a social encounter. But the lack of official comment fed a press frenzy, as it usually does when reporters smell some kind of internal bureaucratic dispute that might blossom into a scandal.

Hodding Carter, the State Department spokesman, was on vacation, Vance was also away, and when Hodding returned he had to hold a press briefing without top-level guidance and therefore issued a bland statement based upon Andy's assurances that the meeting had been accidental and signified no change in State Department policy.[42] Andy was thus unpro-tected and unprepared, and the press ate him alive. He concluded that his life as an ambassador was "pretty much over, right there."[43] Who was in charge—Ambassador Andy Young or Secretary of State Cyrus Vance? Given Andy's public profile as a loose cannon who refused to be a team player, the answer seemed obvious.

Exactly how the PLO meeting came to light remains a mystery to this day, but much evidence points to the Israelis. The Israeli Ambassador to the UN, Yehuda Blum, hotly denied that the Mossad bugged the homes or offices of anyone involved, but the fact is that almost everyone at the UN spies on one another.[44] Andy gave Blum a detailed briefing about the meeting—more than he gave Vance—admitting it had not been all that casual. Blum, a dour, conservative diplomat who felt his American colleague was a decent man out of his depth, remembered Andy realizing that he was in trouble. Before he left the office that afternoon, Blum cabled an account of their conversation to Jerusalem.

The very next morning Jerusalem time—about midnight New York time—U.S. ambassador Sam Lewis was summoned by Israeli foreign min-ister Moshe Dayan to receive an official protest. By the time Ambassador Blum reached his office in New York the next morning, the affair was front-page news. Ambassador Blum insisted that the Israelis had never asked for Andy Young's resignation. They did not have to: No one knew better than Dayan how to rouse the anger of American Jewry. This set the stage for a round of who said what to whom and when, an exercise in finger-pointing about as useful as trying to identify the culprit behind a screen in a police lineup. But Andy was the most visible: More than a scapegoat, he became a target, to the great detriment of the already fraying relations between the blacks and Jews in Carter's political base.

Andy's future fell into Vance's lap, and the secretary of state, like his boss the president, wanted his word to be trusted. Vance later told me he felt he had no choice but to take this to the White House: "I felt very badly in going to the president, and I was saying that under the circumstances we just could not let the word of the government be treated in this kind of a way. I felt that Andy ought to go."[45] He interrupted Carter jogging on the White House track because, as Carter told me later, Vance could not abide "an ambassador in the UN he could not trust."[46]

At 9:30 p.m. the president called me at home with great agitation in his voice. He summarized events and told me: "Andy must go, and the question is how to do it with a minimum of trouble to Andy, to the administration, and to black-Jewish relations." Jesse Hill, a black Atlanta business leader, had already called him to defend Andy. I urged the president to reconsider and leave it at a verbal reprimand. But Carter was firm: "Cy is making it a choice between Andy and himself, and this it is the eighth or tenth time Andy has caused problems."[47] Andy's provocative statements had tested the patience of not only Vance and the State Department, but of Carter himself. As he told me: "Some of the things Andy said were true, but shouldn't have been said. Andy was truly an unguided missile."[48]

That long night I talked twice with Jesse Hill, Andy's closest friend and adviser, and my colleague in Andy's 1972 congressional race; he warned of "severe repercussions with blacks if Andy goes." He believed that the Arabs had tricked him into the meeting.[49] Andy called me at half past midnight to pour out his side of the story: He said he had been pursuing the department's goal of persuading the PLO to accept Israel and if he had to resign he did not want it to be seen as handing his head on a plate to Vance. I urged him not to act precipitously and to work out a reprimand because he was too valuable to the administration and, in any case, his resignation would severely damage relations between blacks and Jews, just as he feared.

The next morning I tried the same argument on Carter, but he would not accept it: "I love Andy like a brother and I want to guide him. But he has embarrassed us too many times in the past. He acted in contravention of my order and our policy by meeting with the PLO. Plus he lied to the State Department."[50]

Yet, he was clearly torn. The next day he told our senior staff meeting that he should have publicly endorsed Andy's meeting with the PLO as incoming president of the Security Council, but now Andy was "caught in a quandary" after telling the State Department that the meeting was unofficial. Carter recounted that Andy had also told Israeli ambassador Blum, but the Israelis went public.[51] In any case Andy was already on a plane from New York to submit his resignation.

I was left thinking how little personal contact the president had with his UN representative, and how one private meeting between them early on could have helped dial him back to a more acceptable decibel level without silencing his message. But Jimmy Carter did not seek or nurture many close personal relationships. Andy had done a great deal to bring Carter to the Oval Office, but the president barely resisted Vance's ultimatum. Young's firing was not the result of the meeting with the PLO itself, but of the way it offended Vance and his department. "I thought we had to communicate with Palestinians somehow or another," Vance said.[52]

But neither Vance nor Carter could publicly confirm that the real reason Andy had been fired was that he had not told the full story to the State Department, even while trying to advance U.S. policy by stopping an anti-Israel resolution. Vance had to declare it was "absolutely false" that he acted under pressure from the Jewish community, but this only confirmed the suspicions of those who believed that was exactly what he had done, and they were stoked by some in the press. The tabloid *New York Post* quoted "one or two Jewish leaders" under a sensational headline: "Jews Demand, Fire Him."[53]

Theodore Mann, chairman of the Conference of Presidents of Major Jewish Organizations, the umbrella organization for more than thirty American Jewish organizations, called the meeting a "deplorable act," but stopped short of calling for his resignation. Bert Gold, longtime executive director of the American Jewish Committee, perhaps the most prominent national Jewish organization, told the *Post* that if Andy had arranged the meeting without the administration's permission, he "should be fired."[54] Among the most severe remarks were those by Rabbi Joseph Sternstein, president of the conservative American Zionist Federation: "The time has come that Ambassador Young should be dismissed from his post." While even these few calls for Andy's resignation were not directed at him because he was black, the fact remained that only prominent Jews made them and all were supporters of Israel. This was not lost on the black leadership.

In the scramble to fill the vacuum left by Andy's resignation, some black leaders competed with increasingly intense declarations of support for the Palestinians, thus widening the gap with Jews who had supported their fight for civil rights. The ubiquitous Reverend Jesse Jackson announced he would be visiting the Middle East at Arafat's invitation, called Prime Minister Begin a terrorist, and said Israel was "not a democracy but a theocracy." The Reverend Joseph Lowery, president of the Southern Christian Leadership Council, met with Professor Terzi of the PLO and declared his support for "the human rights of all Palestinians, including the right of self-determination in regard to their own homeland." Then Lowery went to Blum's office with an entourage of cameramen, whereupon the Israeli ambassador realized he was a stage prop for the infighting over the leadership of the black community.[55]

When the black leadership met in New York on August 22 to discuss "black grievances against Jews," Andy was not even invited. It became a watershed meeting, which issued a statement, tempered somewhat by the wise judgment of the Urban League's Vernon Jordan, declaring that blacks must express independent views on foreign policy; support the SCLC in opening a dialogue with the PLO as Andy Young had done; and call for a discussion with Jewish leaders to "reassess" the black-Jewish relationship in light of Israel's close relationship with apartheid South Africa. It also declared that many Jews, despite their earlier support for "the aspirations of black Americans for educational, political, and economic equality with other Americans, abruptly became apologists for the racial status quo" by opposing affirmative action.[56]

CYRUS VANCE AND RESOLUTION 465

Then disaster turned into political suicide because of the way an Arab-sponsored UN resolution was handled after Andy had been succeeded by his deputy, Ambassador Donald McHenry, a rare black foreign service officer who knew every step of the State Department ladder. With the New York Democratic primary looming for the nation's largest bloc of Jewish voters, the provocative Arab draft condemned all Israeli settlements, and referred to Jerusalem as "occupied territory." On similar resolutions the Carter administration had abstained and rounded up enough abstentions or negative votes by the lesser powers to let the proposal die.

But Carter's inability to avoid wading into the quicksand of Israeli issues was stunning. Things started well when Vance showed the draft of Security Council Resolution 465 to the Friday-morning foreign-policy breakfast. The president, Jordan, Brzezinski, and Brown all agreed that the United States could not support it as worded, and would abstain. That implied negotiating arcane diplomatic phrases lying in a minefield the administration was unable to cross safely. Even now, with President Trump's public recognition of Jerusalem as Israel's capital, the status of Jerusalem remains as politically and diplomatically explosive as it was then.

McHenry reported later that Friday that he had succeeded in having the language on Jerusalem removed, but not the demand to dismantle the settlements. Vance ordered McHenry to delay a vote until he could check with the president. When the secretary called Carter at Camp David on Saturday, he indicated that the language on Jerusalem was gone. Trusting Vance, the president did not ask for a copy of the last draft. But Vance and the president himself were looking for an opportunity to send a strong signal to Menachem Begin about the impact the expansion of settlements was having on talks about autonomy for the Palestinians. Assuming, incorrectly, that McHenry had deleted the Jerusalem language, he directed McHenry to cast an affirmative vote while expressing strong reservations on dismantling existing settlements.

In fact not all the Jerusalem language had been deleted by McHenry's negotiations. It is remarkable that Vance and Carter, one a world-class lawyer noted for his attention to detail, and the other a president with a penchant for poring over documents, did not insist on seeing the final draft, with its repeated references to Jerusalem, which they knew would contradict an express personal commitment Carter had made to Begin at Camp David not to support any UN resolution dealing with the status of Jerusalem. Carter was furious when Mondale and Ham told him that American Jewish leaders were "extremely upset about the UN vote on the settlements in Jerusalem." He told them he understood references to Jerusalem had been deleted, and when they showed him the resolution with six references to Jerusalem, he told them, "I can't believe it." He called Vance, who was in Chicago, and the secretary told Carter that he also thought references to Jerusalem had been deleted.[57]

Hours before the vote Vance had been forewarned by Israeli ambassador Evron that the resolution contained multiple references to Jerusalem—six, in fact—and on each occasion that settlements in "occupied territories" were mentioned, the phrase "including Jerusalem" accompanied it. Moreover, the resolution clearly called for Israel to dismantle its existing settlements, which even Sadat did not seek at Camp David. Evron bluntly told Vance he would immediately tell Begin he had been misled by the president's promise at Camp David.

It is human nature in remembering events to reorder them in our minds, usually in ways that support our position, and there are as many explanations for the misunderstandings as there were key actors. McHenry cast the affirmative vote in the belief that he had a green light from Vance, who in turn thought he was carrying out the president's wishes. Carter said he had instructed Vance to support the resolution only if the offensive language on Jerusalem was deleted. Ham believed that Carter gave Vance some oral parameters so he could bargain over the language, but to Ham it was also symptomatic of a broader problem: "We were always swinging back and forth between Carter wanting to be tough [on Israel], and the political realities."[58]

Israel's ambassadors in Washington and at the UN were furious, with Yehuda Blum in New York fingering McHenry as a diplomat in the "antiapartheid orbit," who he felt saw Palestinians as "underdogs" and "colored people" like himself.[59] When Carter returned from Camp David Sunday morning, Mondale had the unenviable task of explaining to him what had happened, and letting him know that the campaign staff in New York City was in revolt, with Democratic workers literally walking out of Carter headquarters. Finally scanning the full text, Carter declared that his instructions had not been followed and exploded in anger.[60]

Realizing the force of the gathering political storm, the president issued a statement at 10:00 p.m., March 3, the Monday after the Saturday vote, blaming it on a miscommunication of his instructions to McHenry.[61] When Mondale asked me to come to his office, he told me he was "outraged" about the resolution, which he blamed on an "end-run" by Vance going directly to Carter, when he knew the Jerusalem language was supposed to be deleted but had not been. He was livid and "discouraged," accurately forecasting it had "revived Kennedy" and would cost Carter the New York primary.[62]

Carter continued erupting in successive meetings with all concerned and had the following exchange with McHenry. "The president: 'Don, you know I never realized all those other references to Jerusalem were in there. If I had, I would have ordered you to abstain.' McHenry: 'They weren't new, Mr. President. They were there all along.' The president: 'Nonetheless, I never would have approved it.' McHenry: 'Well, sir, I might have argued with you about them, but of course, I would have voted however you said.'"[63]

Ambassador Evron was asked to meet with Carter in the Oval Office.[64] Wearing his cardigan sweater with a yellow legal pad in hand, the president explained he was assured the Jerusalem language had been excluded and exclaimed: "If my Secretary of State doesn't read the papers that he then talks to me about, what am I supposed to do with him?" In Evron's presence, he called Vance's deputy Warren Christopher and told him he was going to disassociate himself from the resolution—and even suggested Evron draft his statement.[65]

There was confusion then and to this day about who was responsible for the vote, but none whatever about its political implications. As Ham recalled: "The minute that happened, we knew we had a huge mess on our hands, and at that point, we backtracked and we got it both ways."[66]

Mondale became like a man possessed and, realizing the political consequences, called Vance from the campaign trail: "We've got a firestorm, and it is something that we can't live with."[67] Vance said he had talked with McHenry before the vote, and he would take responsibility as McHenry's boss. Mondale replied that it went far beyond blame.[68]

CARTER AND THE PRIMARIES

The howls of outrage from Israel, AIPAC, and major American Jewish leaders reached their highest octave since Carter launched his Middle East peace negotiations and proposed the arms sale to Saudi Arabia. Carter hastily summoned the Jewish leadership to the White House, told them he instructed Vance to abstain if there was any reference to Jerusalem, and stuck to the story of a communications breakdown. He added that while he did not condone the settlements, and believed they were "illegal and an obstacle to peace . . . I never asked Begin to dismantle existing settlements but to stop new ones." The meeting left nerves frayed, but the Jewish community seemed to accept the excuse of a miscommunication and give Carter the benefit of the doubt.[69]

The next week Vance was called before Congress, and the story fell apart. He testified that the resolution was consistent with administration policy and defended McHenry. That was the coup de grace. Rosalynn was campaigning in New York when she saw the headlines in her hotel room and realized they would simply reignite a controversy that had begun to simmer down. She thought: "Heaven knows Cy Vance doesn't have a political bone in his body." She immediately called her husband and pointedly asked: "Doesn't Cy know we're in a campaign?" She told him straight out: "It was bad enough in New York already, but I might as well come home now. We're finished, and I've got to go out and smile at people all day."[70]

At a White House staff meeting on March 24, Carter complained, "The Jewish community has never given me a break, even when Begin is at the far extreme, and other Israelis agree with me."[71] In the primary we suffered massive Jewish defections. Through the early contests against Kennedy, Carter rolled up large majorities of the Jewish electorate and won the votes of about 70 percent of Jewish Democrats in his successful Illinois primary just two weeks before New York. With a 20-point lead in New York's opinion polls, Carter had expected to land the knockout blow against Kennedy. But the senator carried New York with 59 percent of the vote, and neighboring Connecticut the same day.

What was unreported until now is that with Kennedy's full concurrence, his political strategists had been already planning a public withdrawal from the race if he lost in New York. They had drafted a concession and with-drawal statement and reserved a room at a Boston hotel for Kennedy to de-liver it on the morning after the primary.[72] They had just been overwhelmed in Illinois. With a New York defeat, said Carl Wagner, a top Kennedy cam-paign aide, "we would have lost Pennsylvania for certain. The rationale for the candidacy didn't exist."[73]

Carter rebounded and won almost all the remaining primaries, but with losses interspersed, mainly in Pennsylvania and the District of Columbia. The final set of primaries on June 3 was also a mixed bag. But Carter had won 51 percent, or 10 million primary votes, to 37 percent, or 7.3 million votes, for Kennedy, and he ran far ahead in delegates, 2,123 to 1,151.

From the New York primary onward, I believe Carter was left with the view that New York Jews had not only defeated him in the primary but were also a factor in his loss in November.[74] He was also hurt by bitter opposi-tion over the UN vote from New York City's egocentric Jewish mayor, Ed Koch, even after Carter had literally saved his city from bankruptcy. In the 1976 election Jews had been one of the most reliably Democratic groups, giv-ing Carter some 70 percent of their votes. But in 1980 only 45 percent of Jewish voters cast their ballots for him, giving Carter an even lower level of support than McGovern in his landslide loss to Nixon.

Ham attributed the collapse of Jewish support to more than just a botched resolution: "A lot of it was cultural, and Southern Baptist, and there was a huge cultural kind of gap and suspicion of Carter." Another factor Ham identified was that in making a deal in the Middle East, Carter "had to push both sides, and the Jewish community didn't like the fact that he had pushed Israel." And Begin finally contributed to that dislike, and although he spoke graciously about Carter from time to time, he continued making statements to try to rally the Jewish community to him in the peace process.[75] Truly, no good deed goes unpunished.

Carter called Kennedy after the last round of primaries to try to work out a harmonious convention, but Kennedy demanded and Carter rejected a televised national debate between the two. They met at the White House, but it led nowhere. Carter remembers a difficult session with Kennedy, who, rather than withdraw or even attempt to compromise, vowed to press his candidacy at the convention.[76]

"THE DREAM WILL NEVER DIE"

A far more serious threat occurred at the convention, when Kennedy began by appealing to Carter's large majority of delegates to vote their conscience. He won an ally in Senate Majority Leader Byrd, who feared a Reagan landslide would sweep out Democratic senators and give the Republicans a majority, which is exactly what happened. I believe Byrd also vainly hoped that in the event of an impasse the convention would turn to him as its savior. It fell to the Rules Committee to decide whether to unbind delegates and hold what is known as an open convention. But under the chairmanship of Senator Daniel Inouye, a Japanese American war hero from Hawaii who lost one arm in battle, Kennedy's seasoned party operatives lost, and the delegates remained bound by their primary votes. Afterward Inouye went to the suite of Carter's young staff, headed by Tom Donilon (later National Security Adviser to President Obama), complimented them on their victory, and reflected on the bitterness of the fight with a remarkable statement: "I've experienced that kind of scent and that sweat and that smell only one other time in my life, and that was in battle in World War II." That captured the tone of the convention.[77]

Kennedy's next step was to challenge Carter by taking popular liberal positions in a series of platform fights, in the hope that lightning would strike and that the delegates would turn to him.[78] I was in charge of developing the Democratic platform, as I had been in 1976, but this time it was a far more trying task to reach a balance—reaffirming Carter's policies as president, while extending a hand to the Kennedy forces by including as many of their provisions as possible. It failed because they wanted it to fail. They attacked key parts of the president's anti-inflationary budget policies and his position on national health insurance, introducing 60 or 70 minority reports and demanding floor time for separate debates on more than 20 for a public brawl that would have filled prime-time television and delayed the major speakers past midnight.

My two White House deputies, Bert Carp and David Rubenstein, and I met several times with Kennedy's staff, led by his chief policy adviser, Peter Edelman. On June 14, shortly after the last set of primaries, we discovered that compromise was impossible. They demanded an immediate $12 billion economic stimulus and the establishment of a Reindustrialization Corporation, with federal funding and the ability to issue stock and lend money to help industry modernize and improve public infrastructure.[79] These demands were totally divorced from the economic realities of the day, and at the Drafting Committee, the differences between the two factions burst into angry arguments on both sides.[80] Acrimonious meetings continued for several days, and I had frequent meetings with the president and his staff on the emerging platform dispute.[81]

As we faced the Kennedy challenge from the left and the Reagan program of massive tax cuts from the right, we realized we might be dead in the water without our own program. The president's rhetorical marker was "Inflation Robs Jobs," a damp response to Kennedy's bold but unrealistic spending proposals.[82] We had already begun to fashion our own stimulus package with modest tax cuts and some spending programs targeted on creating jobs. Treasury Secretary Miller and I met with Lane Kirkland, who had succeeded Meany at the helm of the AFL-CIO.[83]

The meeting dramatized our dilemma with Kennedy and the party's liberal wing at this time of austerity and high inflation. Their focus was on jobs, jobs, and jobs, and not on inflation at all. Kirkland told us that the Republicans had the initiative in a bad economic situation and the president needed a program, "and he can't do it with chicken shit; it must be substantial." He promised to help broker a compromise if we would embrace Kennedy on a few issues to help him save face. So we searched the Kennedy campaign's minority reports looking for places to meet him halfway, but the best that we could find that would be consonant with Carter's inflation fight was a meager $5 billion targeted tax credit for distressed industries and areas with some help for small business.[84]

But Democratic members of Congress were growing panicky about the political attractiveness of the large income-tax cuts endorsed by Reagan and began proposing their own—especially Russell Long, who was up for reelection in 1980. Carter tried to resist them with smaller, more targeted tax reductions.[85]

Tip O'Neill, who would have to keep his followers in line as presiding officer at the convention, called me on August 12 with a stern message to reach out to Kennedy: "You all need to put aside your Southern pride." He proposed a statement that only a wise, canny old politician could have devised: The president should declare himself in full agreement with the Kennedy minority reports on raising employment—and then promise: "When the Congress of the United States puts a program on my desk, as is the will of this convention, I will sign it."[86]

The president then asked Ham and me to meet secretly with Kennedy's people and work out a deal. We agreed to debate only five of the minority planks, with voice votes on four of them. The only plank to be put to a time-consuming roll-call vote would be Kennedy's $12 billion economic stimulus program, which if seriously considered by Congress would probably blow the gaskets off the financial markets. We won that vote only after a bitter floor debate, during which I was angrily accused on the convention floor of selling out the Democratic Party's values and principles. Some of the Kennedy delegates screamed at me, a brief but sickening rerun of the 1968 Democratic Convention I saw firsthand, which exploded in Chicago over the Vietnam War.

But Kennedy refused to give up; he made the convention his own and not the president's, even though it was Carter running for president and not the last scion of the Kennedys. He delivered a brilliant, barnstorming speech with his vision of the party's direction and no hint that he was endorsing the party's nominee. It was as much an indictment of Carter's direction for the party as it was a critique of Reagan. He gave Carter no credit for anything in the domestic arena, even legislation on which they had worked closely together. The most memorable line was his pledge that "The dream will never die"—Kennedy's dream. Kirk called the speech "very much a personal thing," not a staff recommendation.[87]

After Carter gave a prosaic acceptance speech the following night, Kennedy practically had to be pushed onto the platform to shake his hand. But Kennedy quickly turned away, the president remembered, in "a combination of anger, disappointment, and frustration." There were no traditional joint curtain calls with arms raised in front of millions watching the convention. It was one of the most churlish moments in a storied political career. Carter thought Kennedy had been drinking: "His face was all flushed and when he came up there, he was angry—this was the culmination of his failed campaign."

Kennedy had a very different view: He behaved, he told me later, "more out of sorrow than out of real anger" and blamed the press for exaggerating the story.[88] But Carter felt it "tore the party apart," that the Democrats never came together by the November election, and it could have made a difference if Kennedy "had graciously withdrawn and urged all of his supporters to go with me."

With all the hours we had spent working successfully as partners on many issues, it left me with a cold feeling that Kennedy really did not care who won the general election. It was unfathomable then, and remains so now, that he failed to recognize that his divisive conduct would only help open the Oval Office to someone who profoundly opposed everything for which he had fought. Kennedy finally agreed to do a joint fund-raising event with Carter in Washington on the condition that the Carter campaign and Democratic National Committee assume part of his campaign debts. But as president, Carter felt he was in the role of a supplicant begging Kennedy to help him in the election. Kennedy found it hard to back Carter by name and would say—grudgingly, Carter remembered—that he was "voting for the nominee of the Democratic Party."[89]

Given the hostage crisis, the state of the economy, and the rightward drift of the country, it is by no means certain that Carter would have won the election without the distraction of the hard-fought primaries. One analysis showed that a third of self-identified Democrats rejected the president for another term and an even larger percentage of the self-identified liberals who were the ideological core of the party. He was unable to hold his base. What *can* be said with greater conviction is that the bitter primary battle and Kennedy's minimal support in the general election helped assure Carter's defeat, just as Reagan's challenge to Ford in 1976 was a factor in our victory. It also ended Kennedy's presidential ambitions, which ironically liberated him to become one of the most influential senators of his era, forging bipartisan health and other legislation, and dying a respected, admired American statesman.

30

"ARE YOU BETTER OFF . . . ?"

By mid-1980 Ham foresaw that the protracted primary campaign had badly hurt the president with the electorate by forcing him into a "political posture" so that every decision was placed in a political context by the press. In another crisp, analytical "Eyes Only" memorandum that he typed himself on June 25 for Carter, he warned that the president's greatest personal challenge against Reagan was that in the primaries "support for you based on your being a likeable, well-intentioned, compassionate, and at times atypical politician has been eroded badly." And that, Ham continued, made the president "seem more like the manipulative politician bent on reelection at all costs, than the man and the President that you are."

Carter's challenge, as his chief political strategist saw it, was to dispel the notion that there was no difference between him and Ronald Reagan. Unless he could do so the Democratic coalition would never coalesce, minority voters would stay home, liberals defect, the third-party candidacy of the liberal Illinois Republican congressman John Anderson would flourish, and voters would decide on personal qualities. Here Reagan, with his sunny temperament, had a distinct advantage, and to overcome it Carter would have to present a vision for the future and draw a clear contrast between a prospective Reagan and a Carter presidency.[1]

Reagan was a far more formidable opponent than he seemed when caricatured as a mere former B-movie star who played opposite a chimpanzee in *Bedtime for Bonzo*. He was a Democrat until 1962; had a long public career as president of the Hollywood Screen Actors Guild union in difficult times; was an implacable foe of Communism and conservative spokesman for one of America's largest corporations on *General Electric Theater*; and, most important, a two-term governor of California who made a national name in the heartland as the scourge of rioting students in the 1960s and patron saint of homeowners groaning under high property taxes.

RACE AND POLITICS

But race was and remains a far more important and sensitive dividing line in American society and politics, and therefore a careful balance for any candidate, but especially for a Southerner who was as liberal as Carter on civil rights. This opened the way for Reagan to play the race card, and he soon showed that he knew how to do it. When we first began to run through the tough issues for Carter's first presidential campaign in our meetings in the governor's mansion, school busing to achieve racial balance was one on which we spent a great deal of time. He supported the Atlanta school system's policy that any child could be bused to a different school at government expense, but none could be forced to do so, and that busing must help integrate schools and not result in white flight by students.

Only a little more than a decade after Lyndon Johnson confided to his closest aides that by signing the 1964 Civil Rights Act he was writing off the South for the Democratic Party, Reagan took dead aim at Carter's most vulnerable targets in the Old Confederacy by firing up the issues of race and religion. Ham had long warned that Carter's base would become shaky when the average Southern voter realized that the president was more liberal on social issues than he appeared to be as the down-to-earth, born-again Baptist peanut farmer from Plains.

The other flashpoint was affirmative action to rectify generations of racial discrimination, and it came to a boil in the Supreme Court, where the issue still appears on the docket, to say nothing of the heated political rhetoric in most national elections right down to 2016. The initial test case was brought by Allan Bakke, a thirty-five-year-old white man who had twice been rejected by the University of California Medical School at Davis, which reserved sixteen places in each entering class of one hundred for "qualified" minorities. Bakke contended that his race had excluded him, and that this amounted to unconstitutional reverse discrimination. Although the federal government was not a party to the suit, the Supreme Court was interested in the administration's opinion in the form of a brief known as an amicus curiae—a friend of the court. The Bakke case presented a genuine clash of two American values: the need to override racial discrimination against the commitment to reward individual merit irrespective of race or origin—an enormously difficult political problem that pitted two key Carter constituencies against each other: vocal black supporters of affirmative action, and white working-class voters struggling to move up the socioeconomic ladder.

Nixon had won them over to the Republican side as the "silent majority" in 1968 and 1972. Carter had partly recouped them in 1976, and Reagan now coveted this huge voting bloc. For Bakke's supporters the university had erected a racial quota, and this also drew in several major Jewish organizations to raise the specter of quotas at elite universities that had limited the number of Jews in years past. For black and liberal supporters of the university, the program was designed to rectify a historical injustice to blacks. Vernon Jordan, a friend from Atlanta and president of the Urban League, called to declare that the Bakke case was as important to the black community as *Brown v. Board of Education,* the landmark Supreme Court decision that ended public school segregation.[2]

The initial draft of the brief Attorney General Griffin Bell personally delivered to the president in the Oval Office came down squarely on Bakke's side. Bell explained to Carter, Lipshutz, and me that the slots had been specifically reserved for blacks only, and were an unconstitutional racial quota against white applicants. Bell told us that as a former federal judge who had decided similar cases, he had recused himself and given the task of writing the sensitive brief to the "best black lawyer in America," his solicitor general, Wade McCree.[3] The president told me the next day in his private office that he had read the brief, and "it was not well done." But he was clearly torn, however much he recognized the importance of affirmative action: "We can't go with quotas, and decisions have to be based on the merits of the students." He asked me and Lipshutz to give him our thoughts on how to improve it, and to articulate his views.[4] He elaborated at a cabinet meeting that he felt "race could be a factor, but not the exclusive factor" in admissions.[5]

Mondale, Califano, White House Counsel Lipshutz, and I were appalled at the proposed brief, which we felt was contrary to the president's affirmative-action policy. When I called McCree for an explanation, he told me he had not written the brief but entrusted it to Frank Easterbrook, a conservative holdover from the Nixon-Ford administration and strong opponent of affirmative action (now a Reagan-appointed appeals court judge).

When Bell's draft leaked, all hell broke loose. The Congressional Black Caucus met with the president, Mondale, and me and argued that if the Court ruled against the university's program it would be as bad as the Dred Scott case, in which the high court upheld slavery and contributed to the multiple causes of the Civil War.[6] I was besieged by calls from and meetings with other black leaders. I even went to the White House tennis court to discuss *Bakke* with the president, and he told me he was also getting a lot of anguished calls.[7] I worked with Lipshutz on a memorandum to form the basis for a new brief, which the president approved. We tried, in Solomonic style, to split the baby, supporting affirmative action, opposing racial quotas, but taking no position on whether Bakke should be admitted, instead asking the Supreme Court to send the case back to the California courts to reexamine how the university's program worked in practice.

Fortunately, Drew Days, the assistant attorney general for civil rights—one of many blacks appointed by Carter to important subcabinet positions—took charge and revised the brief, noting that Allen Bakke's lawyers were ignoring the essence of American black history by mistakenly treating him rather than the black applicants as a victim of racial discrimination.[8] Days emphasized Carter's view that race could be a factor in college admission—but not the only one—and also recommended that the case be sent back to the California courts.

Justice Lewis Powell cast the decisive vote to split the baby a slightly different way, by admitting Bakke as the victim of a rigid racial quota that violated the equal protection clause of the Fourteenth Amendment but permitting the use of race as one of several admission criteria. However, the Supreme Court did not resolve a dilemma that remains a legal as well as a political conundrum to this day. There were other difficult civil rights challenges, but none of our proposals for cutting through the dilemma satisfied either the civil rights activists demanding jobs and university places set aside for blacks, or the white middle class that saw itself squeezed by all sorts of government actions to lift minorities but not them. All this undermined Carter's white support in the South and elsewhere, and he knew it. And of course so did Reagan.

It was no coincidence that Reagan staged the first rally after his nomination in Philadelphia, Mississippi, near the site where, in 1964, three young civil rights workers were abducted, murdered, and buried in an earthwork dam by the Ku Klux Klan. He proclaimed fealty to states' rights, the Southern code word for local obstruction of the federal government's efforts to end racial injustice. For disaffected workers nationwide, Reagan invented a code word of his own, "welfare queen," for his fictitious characterization of women breeding children for ever-larger welfare checks so they could supposedly ride around in Cadillacs—when in fact most could barely afford bus fare to find any work at all to support their families.

WHITE EVANGELICALS TURN ON THEIR OWN

Religion was the other powerful arm of Reagan's successful attack on Carter's Southern white base. The president's born-again Baptist beliefs, teaching Sunday school, reading the Bible each night with Rosalynn, often in Spanish, helped carry him to victory in the South in 1976. But in the 1980 election, he was swamped by some two-thirds of the white evangelical Southern Christian vote that was cast for Reagan.[9] Remarkably, this key base of support was shifted to a divorced former movie actor with little or no religious involvement, who fused a number of strands into a potent, durable political force for the first time in the 1980 election.

One strand grew out of the 1973 *Roe v. Wade* Supreme Court decision legalizing abortion early in pregnancy and ignited a movement calling itself "pro-life" in a religious defense of the fetus. Like the debate over affirmative action, the abortion wars are with us to this day. They are not subject to reasoned debate, thanks in part to Nellie Gray, a young Catholic lawyer who left her job in the U.S. Labor Department and organized the initial March for Life in Washington on the first anniversary of the Court's decision. "Pro-life people," she proclaimed, "will not negotiate with baby killers."[10] I met with her and a delegation in the White House in 1978, where they handed me a red flower, and I explained the president's views on abortion, which supported a women's right to choose but opposed Medicaid spending for abortions. But for her it was morally offensive to have any exceptions to a complete ban on abortion, not even for rape.

Abortion alone was not enough of a religious issue to spark a political revolution. Jerry Falwell, an evangelical Baptist pastor from Lynchburg, Virginia, managed to weave it together with white segregationists who had organized private schools to escape the Supreme Court ruling desegregating public schools. In response, President Nixon ordered the Internal Revenue Service to enforce a new policy denying tax exemptions to these segregated private schools.[11] Falwell, whose Bob Jones University denied entrance to blacks, was about to lose his tax exemption in 1975, and in 1978 the IRS under Carter denied tax-exempt status to every one of the all-white private schools. Then a gay-rights measure was approved by a referendum in Miami and surrounding Dade County, and finally the Equal Rights Amendment for women was sent to the states for ratification igniting the evangelical and parts of the Catholic communities.[12]

What had been a religious movement became a political awakening when Falwell formed the Moral Majority in the summer of 1979 as a PAC linked to secular activist conservative groups that flooded supporters with direct mail and raised money, led by Paul Weyrich, Richard Viguerie (a prodigious fundraiser for conservative causes, as a pioneer of direct mail campaigns), Howard Phillips (founder of the Conservative Caucus in 1974, a nationwide, grassroots advocacy group), and Terry Dolan (a New Right activist and leader of the Christian Voice, a conservative Christian lobby). Within a year the Moral Majority had organized in 47 states with the goal of mobilizing ten million evangelical voters for the 1980 election. Its agenda even extended to building the B-1 bomber.[13] For Falwell this represented a shift in strategy and mission from the 1960s, when he believed abortion was not a religious issue, and opposed liberal ministers who included civil rights in their mission. It was not until 1978 that he delivered his first public sermon condemning abortion.

This turn to political activism was part of a broader realignment of the mainstream Southern Baptist Convention, previously a moderate organization that counted Carter as a member, believed in the separation of church and state, opposed prayer in public schools, and stayed out of politics. Falwell met with Reagan as the presidential campaign was beginning, and as Falwell's son put it: "We began to see winning elections as a way to make our country a better moral place."[14]

Carter had never heard of Falwell until he and Rosalynn received a letter from a friend telling them that Falwell frequently took to the radio to condemn Carter and his religious faith. Then the Moral Majority hit the front cover of *Time*, and to Carter "it was just like a signal out of the remote distance."[15] Fallwell's group bought $10 million worth of advertising time on radio and television across the South branding Carter as a "traitor to the South and no longer a Christian." (By contrast, the publicly financed budget for the entire Carter campaign was $26 million). This well-financed invective knew no limits. In a 1980 speech Falwell willfully misquoted the president at a Christian ministers' breakfast at the White House as a supporter of homosexuals on his staff. He only backed off when Carter's liaison to the Christian community, Baptist minister Robert Maddox, produced a tape of the event that made clear the president had said nothing of the kind.[16]

Reagan saw an opportunity and pounced. He embraced the New Christian Right's social agenda and came out for a constitutional amendment banning abortion. One month before Election Day in 1980, Reagan traveled to Lynchburg, Virginia, to speak at Falwell's college, advocating, among other things, the restoration of prayer in public schools.[17] A master of political symbolism, he talked about making America a "shining city on a hill," evoking the Puritan origins of the nation's founding. The marriage of Christian evangelicals and secular conservatives became a significant force behind the Reagan landslide and remains a crucial part of the Republican coalition today.

BILLYGATE

Amid all Carter's other troubles, the last thing he needed in an election year was a family scandal. But when his younger brother, Billy, cozied up to the brutal Libyan dictator Mu'ammar Gadhafi, it became a political nightmare for the president and a personal tragedy for Billy. The youngest of Miss Lillian's children, 13 years his famous brother's junior, she called Billy the smartest of the lot. He was well read and intelligent, but the resemblance

stopped there. Chubby, short, gap-toothed, undisciplined, a college drop-
out, a heavy drinker, and a homey jokester, he was the polar opposite of his
straitlaced, highly disciplined older brother. Their father doted on Billy, and
when James senior died of cancer, 16-year-old Billy was devastated not only
by the loss but by the fact that Jimmy took over the family business, which
Billy admitted being "mad as hell" had not fallen to him.[18]

Billy served four years in the marines, and when Jimmy became governor of Georgia, Billy finally got the chance to run the warehouse, which he
did successfully. He was not the uneducated buffoon many thought (and he
often projected). He was an avid reader, and Chip Carter said that after his
death, more than 20,000 books were found in his attic.[19]

Though he could not abide the national fame that came to his brother,
he reveled in the attention lavished upon him at his gas station, when the
press swarmed into tiny Plains and discovered what great copy Billy made
with his gasoline station. He called himself an authentic American: "I got a
red neck, white socks, and Blue Ribbon beer." He joked about his family:
"My mother went into the Peace Corps when she was 68. My one sister is a
motorcycle freak; my other sister is a Holy Roller evangelist; and my brother
is running for president. I'm the only sane one in the family." As the harsh
national spotlight intensified on Billy, so did his consumption of alcohol.
There is no question the two brothers loved each other deeply; Billy campaigned for Jimmy in the South to help convince voters his brother was the
genuine article.[20] As the president's brother, he went on the talk-show circuit,
cracking self-deprecating jokes and selling a brand of beer to which he lent his
name, "Billy Beer," capitalizing on his image as a Southern "good ol' boy."

But when he tried to take advantage of his brother's Oval Office address
in more serious matters, he nearly pulled everyone down with him. In the
autumn of 1978 Billy made a highly publicized trip to Libya in the company of Georgia officials and business leaders eager to make deals with
Gadhafi, who was anti-American, anti-Israel, and a supporter of terrorism.
In return Billy hosted a delegation of Libyans in Atlanta. Asked why he was
becoming involved with such a nefarious country, he said: "The only thing
I can say is there is a hell of a lot more Arabians than there is Jews." He
complained that the "Jewish media [tore] up the Arab countries full-time"
and defended Libya against charges its government sponsored terrorism by

arguing that "a heap of governments support terrorists and [Libya] at least admitted it."[21]

The president immediately distanced himself from Billy's remarks, telling NBC News that he hoped people would "realize that I don't have any control over what my brother says, and he has no control over me." Out of filial loyalty Jimmy refused to criticize his brother in public but called him to express his concern that many of his talk-show appearances had been canceled because of his intemperate remarks.[22] Ham, who knew Billy well, felt he was "out of control," both loved and resented his famous brother, and had a "perverse need to kind of hurt him."[23]

But this was hardly the worst of it. The warehouse had been placed in trust while the president was in office, and Billy was out of a job. He began drinking more heavily and in March 1979 spent several weeks in an alcohol abuse center. When he was released, jobless, he turned back to the Libyans. Once the American diplomats were taken hostage in Iran, the White House searched frantically for any opportunity to gain their release, and Gadhafi was worth a try. Rosalynn suggested to Brzezinski that Billy's Libyan friends might help.[24] Brzezinski agreed, and then Billy swung into action far above his pay grade. He asked his brother to arrange briefings at the State and Commerce Departments and arranged for the Libyan chargé d'affaires to meet with Brzezinski. That was the first time the Libyans had been in the White House since long before Carter became president, after Gadhafi's forces temporarily seized the U.S. Embassy in Tripoli and the State Department withdrew our ambassador.

Shortly afterward Lloyd Cutler, who became White House counsel after the cabinet shake-up, learned from intelligence sources that Billy was being paid $180,000 by Gadhafi. Cutler insisted that the Justice Department rule on whether Billy should register as a foreign agent, and what, if anything, he had done to earn the money. Suddenly stories about the affair began appearing under headlines containing the word "Billygate."[25]

At our senior staff meeting on July 18,[26] Carter bemoaned the press trying to make this another Watergate, and raised the question of whether Billy had used his influence at the White House improperly. Billy contended the six-figure payment was a loan for oil sales he was supposed to facilitate, and on the eve of his brother's nomination for reelection he belatedly registered as an agent of the Libyan government. In an abundance of caution, Cutler asked Alfred Moses, who was working in the White House on Israeli and Jewish relations and had been a partner at one of Washington's most prominent law firms, Covington & Burling (where I am now senior counsel), to represent the president and Brzezinski.

The Senate held a hearing to determine whether Billy received classified documents for his Libyan trip or if the White House had helped him further his business interests with the Libyans. He conceded that he had brought his notoriety on himself, refused to apologize, and in his defense said: "I considered myself to be a private individual who had not been elected to public office and resented the attention of different government agencies that I began to hear from almost as soon as Jimmy was sworn in." And, he declared, he was not a "buffoon, a boob, or a wacko." The president submitted written testimony that his brother had no influence on U.S. policy in general or Libya in particular, "and he will have no influence in the future." In the end the president thoroughly dispatched all questions at a press conference in a relaxed manner, and the Senate investigators issued a report a month before the election, clearing both brothers. Billy Carter died of cancer in 1988 at the age of 51.[27]

SWAMPED BY THE MARIEL BOATLIFT

Then Fidel Castro piled on. Carter was dedicated to improving relations, but sent a personal message to Castro at the end of 1978 warning that relations could not advance if the Cuban military expanded its role in Africa.[28] Feeling he was riding high, Castro retorted belligerently that America should get out of Europe, but started releasing political prisoners and permitting Cuban Americans to visit their relatives on the island.

This planted the seeds of one of the foreign-policy fiascos in the midst of the presidential campaign: the Mariel boatlift, which created a humanitarian crisis for the U.S. government and a political crisis for Carter. Congress had just amended the Refugee Act to consolidate a number of existing programs and triple the number allowed entry each year under regular asylum and resettlement programs, among them a thousand Cubans a month.

Before the ink was hardly dry on the new law, it was overwhelmed by a surge from Cuba.

On March 28, 1980, some Cubans hijacked a bus, killed a guard at the Peruvian Embassy, and asked for asylum; they were soon joined on the grounds by 10,000 others, egged on by Castro himself. Carter said the United States would accept 3,500 Cubans through Costa Rica. Embarrassed and angry at the number of Cubans eager to leave his Communist "paradise," Castro also emptied his prisons and opened the port of Mariel for more to leave. The Cuban American community in South Florida saw Castro's announcement as a once-in-a-generation opportunity. They sent boats from Florida with lists of Cuban relatives or friends to pick up at Mariel Harbor. When they returned with many of those on their lists, they also carried Cuban political dissidents, mental cases, and even released criminals. Under maritime law the U.S. Coast Guard could not stop them.

This presented Carter with an impossible dilemma: Where to put them? It was impossible to turn them away or send them back to Cuba. More than a half-dozen government departments converged at an emergency White House meeting late in April.[29] Mondale said that the boatlift served as a safety valve for Castro's failing regime, a point that I suggested the president incorporate in a forthcoming speech. On April 27 Carter declared that it was "proof of the failure of Castro's revolution, and a callous, cynical effort by Castro to play on the emotions of the Cuban American community in the U.S."[30] All true, but of little help.

Castro had no intention of allowing an orderly flow of refugees; South Florida's Cuban Americans angrily refused to stop the sealift, and official threats to seize their boats were not taken seriously. Carter then inadvertently undercut his own policy on May 5, when he told the League of Women Voters: "We as a nation have always had our arms open in accordance with American law. Those of us who have been here for a generation or six or eight generations ought to have just as open a heart to receive new refugees as our ancestors were received in the past." I cringed when I heard those impromptu if idealistic remarks; they were interpreted by everyone in Cuba—and voters in America—as an invitation to open the floodgates.[31]

The next day the president declared a state of emergency in South Florida and approved an additional $10 million to reimburse voluntary agencies for assistance in settling the Cubans. Meanwhile the weekly flow of refugees jumped from about 20,000 to 37,000 during the week following his open-arms remarks. We had to move decisively, even if belatedly. The Coast Guard was ordered to get tough and stop small boats plying the ninety-mile strait between Florida and Cuba, but it took most of the month of May to stop the flow. On May 29[32] the president reported that no boats had gone south for two weeks: "It's a mess, but we're doing the best we can." Immigration centers were set up for the Marielitos in south Florida, and when they became overcrowded, a processing center was established at Fort Chaffee in Arkansas. Within eleven days it was filled to capacity with almost 19,000 refugees. As we scattered the Cuban émigrés into military bases in Pennsylvania and Wisconsin, riots erupted at Fort Chaffee, and some detainees escaped.

A human dilemma became a political nightmare. We lost all those states in the Reagan landslide, and young Bill Clinton, running for reelection in Arkansas after his first term as governor, suffered the only loss in his entire political career. I believe it is one reason for the frosty relations between the two ex-presidents to this day. By the end of May the unauthorized boatlift had landed more than 94,000 Cubans. The vast majority were ordinary Cubans, and although only 2,746 were classified as serious or violent criminals and denied American citizenship, the impression lingered across the country that Carter had allowed in an invasive horde of undesirables.

The crisis was unprecedented, and we were slow off the mark. But as with so much of the Carter presidency, there was the unheralded accomplishment of adding some 100,000 law-abiding Cubans to the beautiful mosaic of America, although it was done in the worst possible way. The Cuban American community in Florida gave no credit to Carter and voted heavily for Reagan, damaging beyond repair Carter's chances of winning the state. The cruel irony is that Castro hurt Carter just as he was reaching out in friendship, as no president would do until Barack Obama renewed relations 45 years later. Fidel Castro, in a conversation with Robert Pastor after the Carter administration, acknowledged that he had made a mistake, passing up a chance with Carter that he would never have again.[33]

VOODOO ECONOMICS BEWITCHES
THE REPUBLICANS

As we went into the final months of the election campaign, the Democratic coalition had fractured, while Republicans were united behind Reagan and his aggressive and easily understood brand of conservatism. It no longer preached the party's mantra of austerity and balanced budgets. Conservative think tanks had been laying the ideological groundwork based on the antitax Proposition 13 wave rolling out of Reagan's California and dignified it with their research. He sailed through the Republican primary campaign and latched on to an economic program that to this day remains the basis of Republican orthodoxy: deep tax cuts, particularly for wealthy individuals and corporations. It is based on the proposition that they would spend their tax savings and generate so much economic growth and so many jobs that the tax reductions would be more than made up for by increased revenues. This came out of a dubious theory advanced by a little known economist, Arthur Laffer, whose Laffer Curve offered the American people the possibility of having their cake and eating it—lower taxes, higher growth, and more federal revenues.[34]

Reagan's primary opponent, George H. W. Bush, a businessman who had majored in economics at Yale, derided the idea as "voodoo economics." Yet within a year it was adopted by Reagan and swallowed by Bush after he accepted the vice-presidential nomination to unite Main Street and Wall Street. It became known as supply-side economics, and whatever one thought about it—and I found no more logic in its supposed merits than had candidate Bush—it seemed like an easy nostrum against the curse of stagflation.

Two Republican members of Congress, the earnest true believer Senator William Roth of Delaware, and the telegenic former professional football quarterback Representative Jack Kemp, representing his old team's Buffalo district of New York, proposed a bill codifying Laffer's ideas, which became the principal economic plank of Reagan's campaign and was eventually passed into law in a modified form after his election. Thus the campaign saw a historic reversal of roles. Until then the Democratic Party's candidates and presidents from Roosevelt through Johnson presented programs and initiatives, while Republicans from Hoover through Ford (with the important exception

of Nixon) were budget balancers who argued for a limited role for government. Now a Democratic president was the budget balancer, reducing spending on popular programs and opposing a big tax cut for fear of igniting more
inflation and because, as he told Miller: "I just cannot flip-flop."[35] We presented no attractive new alternative, only thin gruel and more of the same.

Carter was a New Democrat unable to articulate a framework that voters
could understand at a time when households were being squeezed between
higher prices and fewer jobs. The Republicans had become the party of lower
taxes and boundless growth. Reagan's optimistic message was of unlimited
possibilities, while Carter preached sacrifice and limits. Reagan was the pioneer who struck gold in California, Carter was the public scold from the
Bible Belt, preaching the old-time religion of spending cuts and balanced
budgets. Forget that when Congress passed a version of Kemp-Roth in 1981,
it led to billion-dollar budget deficits in triple digits[36] and that the same happened in 2001 after Congress enacted President George W. Bush's proposals
of deep tax cuts on the same theory, blowing through the budget surpluses
that we achieved in the Clinton administration by raising taxes on the wealthy,
restraining government spending, and helping the economy thrive.

But in the 1980 election it was an enormously attractive proposition to
an American public reeling from double-digit inflation and slowing growth.
While we Democrats were fighting among ourselves about the appropriate
level of support for the New Deal and the Great Society programs, the country was changing, and the Republicans were engaging in a whole new and
more revolutionary conversation that would dominate politics for two
generations.

I naively thought Reagan would be easy to defeat because he had made so
many provocative out-of-the box statements: Social Security should be
voluntary; unemployment insurance was "a prepaid vacation plan for free-
loaders"; plants and trees were responsible for most air pollution; the progressive income tax had been invented by Karl Marx; and fascism was the
basis of Franklin Roosevelt's New Deal. Reagan also frequently exaggerated
facts and had stories that turned out to be myths created by his fertile imag-

ination. The fact that voters would turn to such a candidate was a measure of their economic suffering and their resentment at seeing their country humiliated by a band of turbaned revolutionaries in Iran.

But I got a cold shower at a meeting of the senior White House Staff in the Roosevelt Room when Ham arranged for a briefing by Jesse Unruh, chairman of the California Democratic Party and a longtime observer and political opponent of Reagan. Unruh was no amateur—his nickname in the political world was Big Daddy—and his message was blunt: Do not underestimate Ronald Reagan; he is a first-rate, charismatic politician with a compelling message.

We never developed a coherent and positive strategy against Reagan, except stoking fear against him. Without a clear, upbeat message of how the president would lead us out of our economic quagmire and resolve the hostage crisis, the Democratic strategy was largely negative—to make voters fear Ronald Reagan by painting him as a wild-eyed conservative who would tear down the social welfare structure of the country and could not be trusted to keep the peace—and it almost succeeded. When Democrats rolled out the same destructive strategy of trying to frighten voters about their opponent in 2016, it failed again.

Reagan did not rely only on new Republican ideas. He took the bold step of inviting the man who ran the campaigns of two of his Republican Party opponents, Ford in 1976 and Bush in 1980, to run his campaign. There are few people in contemporary American public life more capable than James A. Baker. An elegant Texas lawyer with an impeccable family background and education—the private Hill School, Princeton, and the Marines—he was more moderate than Reagan but remarkably adept politically. Baker realized from Ford's loss, when we promoted Art Okun's misery index, that the economy is *"always the issue."* They threw that index back in our faces. As Baker cogently put it to me later, there were three issues critical to Reagan's chances of defeating a Democratic incumbent who had been elected president, a victory for which there was no modern precedent: "the economy, the economy, and the economy, in that order. I mean, when you look at the misery index, now how the hell could you guys win in the face of that?!"[37]

We might have found our answer to this brilliant and focused political

strategist in Ham Jordan, but he was diverted during long periods of the
campaign in fruitless attempts to negotiate the release of the hostages and
fight the cocaine charges cooked up by the attack-dog lawyer Roy Cohn.

DEBATEGATE

While in recent elections we have come to expect presidential debates, there
had been a 16-year hiatus between the initial Kennedy-Nixon debate and
the one between Ford and Carter. The debate between Carter and Reagan
on October 28, only a week before the November 4 Election Day, was decisive. And we were outfoxed by Jim Baker in agreeing to it so close to the
election. The common wisdom that the Reagan landslide was a foreordained
conclusion is wrong, as Baker himself remembered. The race was close until
the debate put Reagan ahead, and then swung back to Carter until his ill-fated
reaction to a last-minute offer from Iran on the Sunday before the election.

During the Democratic primaries the president refused to debate Kennedy at all, citing the hostage crisis and Soviet invasion of Afghanistan. I
advised him in a meeting in his private study as early as June to debate Kennedy and then Reagan—"anyone and any time"—and run a give-'em-hell
campaign like Harry Truman's.[38] The Carter campaign team repeatedly refused to engage in a three-way debate, fearing that national exposure for
third-party candidate John Anderson would draw votes from Carter. On
September 21 Reagan debated Anderson alone and taunted the president for
refusing to join. He said that Carter knew "he couldn't win a debate even if
it were held in the Rose Garden before an audience of Administration officials with the questions being asked by Jody Powell."[39]

Jimmy Carter on the political attack was never very good at wielding a
stiletto, and his attacks on Reagan became increasingly shrill and personal.
I emphasized to the president in midcampaign that he should quote Reagan's
own words back to him and not engage in personal characterizations. He
agreed, but said that "we should make the strongest rhetorical statement we
can" against the Kemp-Roth tax cuts. While economically sound, politically
it was a little like withholding dessert or a trip to the movies from a rebellious teenager: a punishment with no lasting effect.[40]

As September turned into October, Reagan continued to insist on sharing any debate with Anderson. But our greatest mistake was dragging out our insistence that Carter would take on Reagan only head-to-head, leading with our chins. By contrast Baker confessed that even within his own organization many senior campaign officials feared that Reagan could not stand toe-to-toe against Carter's knowledge of issues and might make an embarrassing stumble. Reagan's pollster, Richard Wirthlin, felt that the race was so close, it was worth the risk to debate. As he put it, "The election is going to hang or fall on that debate." But Baker's was the decisive voice, and his confidence in his candidate may have assured his election, as he was "always impressed with his ability on television."[41]

Reagan's mastery of the medium, not just the message, is what proved decisive. But the broader reason was that without an opportunity to break out from the closely divided electorate, the Republicans could lose. With two weeks to go, the League of Women Voters agreed to exclude Anderson, as the electorate returned to the traditional parties and the third-party candidate's poll numbers fell. Now that Reagan had accepted Carter's terms, Carter was pushed into a box, making the debate at a time dangerously close to the election.

Rafshoon ruefully recalled that as long as Reagan would not accept the one-on-one, "we were on top of it. We were saying he was afraid of one-on-one." When they saw their poll numbers dropping in the final weeks of the campaign, they shifted tactics and agreed to debate Carter alone.[42] Caddell called me on October 18, expressing grave concern that "one of the great mistakes of the campaign was to agree to such a late debate" on October 28, little more than a week before the election.[43]

As I traveled back to Washington with the president on Air Force One from his joint appearance with Reagan at the annual Al Smith Dinner in New York, he was in an expansive mood and even told a ribald joke, the first I had ever heard him make.[44] But he soon turned deadly serious with the crucial debate with Reagan ahead of him. In preparing the debate book for the president, we reached out to the most experienced political operatives, including Bob Barnett, a prominent Washington lawyer and presidential debate coach, and former LBJ White House aides Jack Valenti and Harry McPherson. Their advice was for Carter to be presidential, forget the past, and state that he had learned lessons for a second term from his own mistakes, while reminding voters of Reagan's dangerous stands on subjects from Medicare to nuclear weapons.[45]

When Ham, Jody, Rafshoon, Caddell, and I met Saturday morning, October 25, to review how we would recommend Carter approach the debate, we all agreed he should not have his regular jog around Camp David, because it was wet and cold and we did not want to take a chance on Carter catching a cold. But he would not listen and jogged anyway, leading Jody, who, with Ham, had known him longest, to remark with some admiration, "He's a hardheaded little son-of-a-bitch." He would not have made his improbable journey from Plains to the Oval Office without this stubborn quality. When we met with him, he was no worse for the wear, but he developed laryngitis a day later.[46]

For the first time in his political career, President Carter, realizing the enormous stakes, began sustained debate preparations on October 25 at Camp David's Hickory Lodge, with Jody asking his questions, and then the first lady, Kirbo, Ham, Caddell, David Rubenstein, and I following up, as the reporters would at the debate.[47] During the two practice sessions the next day Carter was in a feisty mood, talking about Reagan's tax cuts as "radical," and a "rich man's tax cut that would flood the country with dollars" like "throwing gasoline on a fire" with already high inflation. When he moved to Reagan's opposition to the SALT II treaty he used terms like "belligerent," "ridiculous," and "dangerous." Ham wrote a note on my legal pad: "Pat's got him excessively combative. He needs to ignore many of Reagan's claims, etc."[48]

For the second session he agreed to a full practice confrontation, with Reagan played by Sam Popkin, a suave, blunt, and analytic professor of political science who worked with Caddell on his polls. "Reagan wins if he shows he does not have a warlike bone in his body," Popkin warned me privately, adding, "Carter wins if he turns the debate to the next four years" rather than attacking Reagan as a person. He cautioned: "Reagan does not have a jugular vein Carter can attack, because he's a free-fly or a butterfly."[49] There were cameras, and mock questions and answers were drawn from our debate book. While we were in practice, Carter, always a tough campaigner, made clear that he understood what he faced: "Reagan is out campaigning like a Democrat, but the people he will appoint are ready to govern as Republicans."[50] But his prescience was no match for the debating skills of the former movie actor opposing him.

On our way to Cleveland for the debate, we made a short campaign stop at Huntington, West Virginia, which I found dispiriting. I put in my notes: "Deadest crowd I've ever seen for the president—no enthusiasm."[51] At our last practice session at the Bond Court Hotel in Cleveland, he was reluctant to handle any questions about the Iranian hostages, telling us: "Iran is hanging by a thread, and I do not want to hit them too hard."

When we asked a question on nuclear proliferation, in a misplaced attempt to personalize the challenge, he responded that he had just talked with his young daughter, Amy, about the scope of this problem. As Rafshoon recalled, everyone thought he was joking, including me, but Carter definitely was not: We winced when he repeated it in the debate. It was one of his most criticized responses.[52]

Reagan gained credibility by a reassuring manner that reached deep into his heartland roots. Few remember the details of the debate itself, but no one in politics can forget that when Carter tried to nail him on his promise to limit Medicare and make Social Security voluntary, Reagan's inimitably soothing baritone simply swatted him away with a perfectly timed interjection: "There you go again." His brilliantly framed closing statement, delivered with an actor's sensibility, has passed into American political discourse: "It might well be if you ask yourself: Are you better off than you were four years ago? If so, vote for four more years of Carter; if not, I suggest another choice that you have."[53]

The reason the debate mattered so much was that Reagan temporarily managed to dispel the fear factor planted by our negative campaign, reassuring the American people that he was not a risky choice. His avuncular manner turned the trick, and the dam broke. Rick Hertzberg, Carter's chief speechwriter, later said, "When people realized that they could get rid of Carter and still not destroy the world, they went ahead and did it."[54]

Going into the debate, which was watched by a record 100 million viewers, average poll data gave Reagan a narrow lead of two or three points. After the debate the lead expanded significantly, and clearly Reagan had won. Caddell's polls showed that the debate added to Reagan's honesty factor and lessened his risk factor.[55] Caddell and his polling colleague, Sam Popkin, called me to say that in the past, presidential debates on average had not moved polls more than 1 percent, but this was an exception. The *New York Times* poll, for example, showed that in the Midwest, Carter had gone from three points ahead of Reagan to six points behind, an unprecedented shift.[56] Caddell reminded me that Ford was ahead of Carter the Sunday before the election, but lost when people took a hard look at Ford being president for the next four years—and this could happen again to Carter, just as it had to Ford. But Caddell said: "We [could] still do it" if Carter followed his strategy of asking voters to contemplate the risks of Reagan in the White House. That remained Carter's campaign strategy in the final week before the election.

What we did not know at the time of the crucial debate and learned only several years later was that Nixon was not the only one to employ dirty tricks. Knowing how high the stakes were for a successful debate, the Reagan campaign obtained a stolen copy of the debate book I had laboriously prepared with my two deputies, Carp and Rubenstein, incorporating the outside advice of the campaign veterans of the Johnson administration and other Democratic insiders on how to deal with specific issues and adopt a winning personal stance against Reagan. As they prepared Reagan for the championship match, our opponents were studying our book as closely as Carter himself, and they knew our strategy. This was confirmed to me by no less than Reagan's campaign manager, Jim Baker. When I told him years later that it was widely believed they had stolen our debate book, he joked: "That's widely believed because it's widely true." He insisted defensively that the information "didn't help us a damn bit [and] wasn't worth a shit."[57]

Maybe so, but Carter believed firmly that it made some difference. I know that we certainly would have liked to have similar information on the strategies of the Reagan camp, although we would not have resorted to thievery to obtain it. After I prepared the debate book, Jim Rowland, my staff administrator, was in charge of assembling and copying the book. He told me later that, starting the night of October 24 and finishing around eleven the next morning, he made copies under the strictest supervision, using the vice president's copying machine.[58] I kept one copy and gave one each to the president, Powell, Rafshoon, and Jordan.

The book contained all our proposed attack lines and answers to Reagan's likely attacks. Baker contended that Reagan's famous comeback to Carter's attacks on his positions on Medicare and other popular programs—"There you go again"—was spontaneous and not part of their debate preparation. Even if this was the case, armed with our plan of attack, he had an advantage that he knew how to exploit.

Baker's account of how our debate book landed in his hands is a story of intrigue that exposes how the Reagan campaign operated—but also reflects the depth of hatred among some of the diehard Kennedy supporters, who simply did not care if Carter lost. Baker was sitting in his campaign office with the debate preparation team when William Casey, the campaign's titular chairman, walked in with a black-bound book, dropped it on Baker's desk, and said: "You might want to give this to your debate prep people." Casey had been the chief of American espionage in Europe during World War II and would be rewarded by Reagan with the directorship of the CIA. As Baker thumbed through the book, he could tell it had come from the Carter campaign. He did not ask where Casey had gotten it and told me that he "probably shouldn't have passed it on—but I did."

The story leaked out in 1983, leading to a ten-month congressional investigation headed by Michigan Democratic Congressman Donald Albosta, during which Baker testified that he had seen the book. But Casey denied that he had ever given it to Baker. The investigators concluded that Baker was telling the truth and Casey was not. Baker admitted to me that the congressional probe "put the fear of God in me, because I know Casey had been out there at the CIA, and he probably knew how to game the polygraph and I didn't—but I knew I was telling the truth. The investigators interrogated hundreds of witnesses and produced a report more than 2,000 pages long, without determining who stole our debate book."[59]

In what was quickly headlined as "Debategate" (initiated by *Time* magazine White House correspondent Laurence I. Barrett) after the election, the FBI examined the book and found the fingerprints of Baker and David Gergen, my Harvard Law School classmate, then working with Baker and later a member of the Reagan White House staff. Rowland also later told me that several strategy memos we sent to the Carter campaign staff were found in the files of David Stockman, then a Republican congressman and later Reagan's OMB director, which Stockman confirmed during the investigation.

Almost 30 years later the truth finally came out. What made it all possible appears to be some rogue elements of the Kennedy clan's intense antipathy toward Carter. Adam Walinsky, a senior speechwriter for Jack Kennedy and Robert Kennedy, justified undermining Carter because he felt his administration had been so "disastrous" that he deserved to be voted out of office even if it meant Reagan's election. So Walinsky responded to a request from Paul Corbin, a member of Ted Kennedy's 1980 campaign team, for a memo he could pass on to the Reagan campaign on how to handle Carter in the debate.[60] (In 2016 Walinsky publicly supported Donald Trump because he felt his own Democratic Party had become warmongers.)

Corbin, a no-holds-bared labor organizer in Wisconsin, was intensely loyal to the Kennedy family and appears to have been the spider at the center of the web orchestrating the theft of the debate book, using Kennedy loyalists on the White House staff as intermediaries. Craig Shirley, a conservative public relations executive, put the pieces together in a book he wrote about the Reagan campaign.[61]

The FBI file on Corbin confirmed him as a shadowy figure who was arrested several times and spent much of his life skirting criminal violations and grand juries. Who actually stole the book is not clear, but based upon Craig Shirley's account, one of the principal players may have been Laurie Lucey, a confidential assistant to Landon Butler, one of Jordan's senior aides, and the daughter of Pat Lucey, a former governor of Wisconsin. Carter appointed him as ambassador to Mexico, but he abruptly quit to help Kennedy challenge Carter. Just days before Lucey resigned, so did his daughter. Around the time she was leaving, Bob Dunn, a longtime friend of Corbin's and a former member of Lucey's gubernatorial staff in Wisconsin, joined the White House as an assistant to Carter's scheduling secretary. It was Corbin who persuaded Lucey to become Anderson's vice-presidential running mate and help divert liberal votes from Carter. According to Craig Shirley, either Dunn or Laurie Lucey may have passed the debate book to Corbin, who joined the Reagan campaign in its last days, for a price. He visited the Reagan-Bush campaign headquarters during September and October and met with Baker and Casey.

What is forgotten is that by all estimates, the momentum had swung back to Carter as his negative campaign ads reignited doubts about Reagan. The campaign used two types of ads—one positive, showing the president as either commander in chief or Camp David peacemaker; the other negative, implying Reagan was a mad bomber in order to stir up fears of him as commander in chief.[62] The week before the election the polls showed a tie—too close to call, with several (Gallup, New York Times–CBS) giving Carter the edge.[63]

But Caddell told us the momentum was on our side. Although Carter's poor debate performance cost him several points, as the halo effect from the debate began to fade he nevertheless began pulling either neck-and-neck or even beating Reagan in several respected polls by taking votes from Anderson. Sam Popkin told me Reagan had lost all his gains from the debate, and "the undecideds are swinging wildly." He believed that if voters went into the booth thinking of foreign policy, Carter would win, but if the economy was on their minds, Reagan would win. Most undecided voters were Democrats or independents who agreed with Carter on the issues but disliked his personal attacks on Reagan or his Rose Garden strategy of staying aloof from the campaign for months after the hostages were taken.[64] Carter now would pay the full price during the last hours of the campaign.

SUCKER-PUNCHED BY THE AYATOLLAH

On Carter's last campaign swing, I accompanied him aboard Air Force One. The sleepless nights working to free the Iran hostages and puzzle out the Soviet motives in Afghanistan had taken a visible toll. The bounce in his walk had disappeared, and he had aged perceptibly. In Houston on October 31 Carter drew his most enthusiastic crowd of the campaign, but I noted that he "absolutely silenced them; he rambled; no coherence."[65] The next day we flew from San Antonio to Miami and then to a fateful stop in Chicago, where the Iranian hostages were thrust back into the faces of voters in the final days of the campaign—and it was Carter who did it. Early Sunday I was roused from sleep at the airport hotel in Chicago at 4:21 a.m. Iran had made another offer. We were all ordered by the White House Operations Center to be ready to leave on Air Force One in fifty minutes, and we were told that the Iranian parliament had voted to release the hostages but set conditions that we might not be able to accept. I scrambled to dress, and we all left, anxious to learn if this would be the final resolution.

That furtive trip back to Washington never should have been made two days before the election. Carter could have examined the Iranian conditions and determined they were unsatisfactory without the drama of canceling his campaign events and returning to the White House. I urged Ham and Jody to tell Carter to stay put, but Ham told me he was reluctant to stop the president because it was "unseemly to campaign now." I disagreed, but I certainly had no chance of beating Hamilton Jordan in an argument about political tactics.[66] I nevertheless went into the president's private cabin on Air Force One and told him I felt strongly that given the history of the hostage issue, if he suspended campaigning it might appear that he was doing so for political purposes. Carter replied: "That's a good point, and that's my feeling." But we were already on our way back.

Someone with uncanny political instincts who had far more influence made the same point to the president. Rosalynn Carter recounted to me that when her husband called her from Chicago that morning to say he had to come back, she pleaded with him: "Why don't you stay? Why do you have to come back? It could mean the election." But he insisted on returning and told her: "I cannot pass up a chance." She was by now fatalistic, given the many Iranian feints built up by the press, only to collapse before the eyes of a weary and skeptical public, which is just what happened. Rosalynn painfully recalled, "We both felt it might be the end, and the reason was because we both knew that the press had built up so many times the fact that the hostages might get out, and every time we built up expectations that were dashed. And I thought the public would think, Here we are doing that again, just to win the election, which is what happened."[67]

Moving into damage-control mode, I jotted down talking points on the Air Force One notepad with "The White House Washington" across the top. "1. The American people resent Iran interfering in our election (they don't believe JC tried to coincide with election, but that Iranians hope to get better terms). 2. They feel strongly JC should say we will not let them interfere in our election, and we will not give them better terms due to election. 3. They feel almost unanimously we should deal with the hostages only after the election as the Iranians will get better terms before it."

When we landed at Andrews Air Force Base on the morning of November 2 and took helicopters to the South Lawn landing pad, we were all in a disheveled state but headed straight to the Cabinet Room. The meeting began at 2:00 p.m. and lasted for an hour.[68] Waiting for the traveling campaign staff were Secretary of State Muskie and his deputy, Warren Christopher; Defense Secretary Brown; Treasury Secretary Miller and his deputy, Bob Carswell; CIA Director Turner; Brzezinski, his deputy, David Aaron, and his Iran expert Gary Sick; and White House Counsel Lloyd Cutler.[69] I have never attended a U.S. government meeting as grim and portentous as this. The fate of the hostages and of the thirty-ninth president hung in the balance. No one in the room failed to realize the gravity of the president's predicament.

Brzezinski said the conditions laid down by the Iranian parliament might be the basis for an agreement with further negotiations, but they could not be accepted outright. Some demands were simply unacceptable, and one was clearly a trap: The Iranians demanded a reply by Monday, the day before the election. The sense of the meeting was not to reject the offer outright but also not to leave the impression that we were chasing a chimera on the eve of an election. To his credit, Carter refused to accept a bad deal at this critical moment in his political life. Instead he decided to give a short statement to the public, but send a longer reply through a neutral ambassador, responding that the offer represented a step forward but did not go sufficiently far for an agreement.

I felt all of that could have been accomplished from the presidential hotel suite in Chicago without breaking stride in the campaign. Callers were flooding radio talk shows with complaints that Iran was interfering in our election and were worried that the president would agree to better terms before the election rather than after. I urged that we wait until after the election to take any action at all, and advised the president to issue a tough statement making absolutely clear to the Iranians that our terms would be no different after the vote than before. Ham and the president agreed.

Carter told us, "We should let the American people know we won't be pushed around and that we are not in a hurry to get them out just before the election." He noted that the Iranian parliament, the Majlis, had used "abusive language for domestic consumption, but their terms weren't unreasonable.

We should do the same." When the meeting broke up, we went into the vice president's office to draft the president's statement, which took another hour, with Christopher in charge as our lead negotiator with Iran.[70] Mondale later concluded that "the ayatollah was needling us; he loved playing Carter and it didn't cost him anything."[71]

Phrasing the reply correctly put us all on a tightrope. Rafshoon argued that a fighting president might have a chance and at least would go out with his head held high. He had long urged that Carter's gloomy public pull-your-socks-up messages about energy, inflation, and diminished expectations should be balanced by the promise to the American people that "we can solve our problems; we can be strong and at peace; we can get control of our energy problems; we can make our economy work."[72] He felt that if Carter had been ready to "bomb the bastards" in Tehran when the embassy was taken, even if the hostages had been put on trial or executed, "we would have won the election."[73]

"IT'S OVER, BOYS"

On that Sunday when we returned from Chicago, the president had one last chance. As everyone was discussing what Carter should say, Rafshoon suggested he "just tell them to go to hell. Really get out there and tell them we're not going to be pushed around anymore." Carter retorted that the Iranians might put one hostage on trial each day until he folded, so he said he would go on television and simply say the Iranians had taken a positive step, but he would not be influenced by the calendar, and things would not happen right away.

His three closest senior advisers—Ham, Jody, and Rafshoon—felt that was too weak. Rafshoon again told the president to give a really angry reply: "I'd tell them to go fuck themselves." Carter retorted: "Will that get the hostages out?" And Ham said no, "but the American people want to hear it." Carter replied: "Oh yeah, what if they decide to take the hostages out in the courtyard and shoot them? And maybe shoot one every hour? I'm not going to let that happen."[74]

So the president went on television, interrupted the Redskins football game, and made a mild statement to let the Iranians' offer work itself out, not influenced by the election. Carter did resume campaigning after his statement, but the sudden break from Chicago, as I feared, reminded the American public in Technicolor of the humiliation of the hostage crisis. When he rejected the offer, the public figuratively threw up its collective hands and gave up on him. I recorded in my notes of November 3 that we had a depressing flight to Oregon and Washington State with "the heavy hand of defeat in the air." But I noted that Carter had given his best speeches in Portland and Seattle, and that "he handled it like a true champion. I felt proud of him."[75]

As we boarded Air Force One and took off for home, the president spoke with the press on the plane and joked that he would favor Mondale over Kennedy for the 1984 Democratic nomination. But then an ominous call came to the plane from Caddell. Four years earlier he had called Peanut One with the news that Carter was likely to win the presidency. Now to Air Force One he reported a massive erosion of support: "It's over, boys," Pat said. He explained that Carter was moving back up in the polls on Saturday; more than half the American people regarded Reagan as a risk, responding to the campaign ads portraying him as a simplistic cowboy who would shoot from the hip.

But then came the latest hostage incident, and it was too much. The focus had shifted back to Carter and Khomeini, and to a sense of frustration and humiliation. The unsuccessful trip back to Washington had driven home the final indignity; as one man told Caddell's polling operation: "That little son-of-a-bitch can't handle a two-bit ayatollah. I'll take my chances on Reagan."[76]

The Republicans played successfully on this feeling by saying that a vote for Carter was a vote for Khomeini; the number of people who felt the hostages would be back home quickly had diminished, and the number who believed the Iranian conditions were unreasonable doubled. Jody with a visible tear in his left eye, said: "Good news means bad news" about the hostages, since the latest offer had been a step forward, although not enough.[77] Americans did not blame Carter for creating the hostage crisis, only for the disgrace of not resolving it.

When the president came out of his stateroom, I rushed up to him, hugged him, and with tears in my eyes said, "Mr. President, we have let you down."

I was overwhelmingly sad that Jimmy Carter had come so far, from tiny Plains to the Oval Office, and now was being rejected after accomplishing so much; that this good man had been rejected by voters who put him into office four years before.

But he was amazingly stoic. He told us not to inform Rosalynn until we landed at home in Georgia to vote. We touched down at 6:45 a.m. on Election Day, and I went into his cabin and told him that no matter what happened, I was proud of him and appreciated the opportunity to serve him. He replied: "You're one of the finest people I've ever known. You're like a son and brother to me." We embraced and wept on each other's shoulders.[78]

When the presidential motorcade arrived at Plains, he spoke at the train depot to his family, friends, and admirers, never hinting that he knew he was going to lose, although his speech reflected it. Fighting back tears, he talked about his roots in Plains and how much they had always meant to him. We then drove to his home, and then helicoptered to the hospital in nearby Americus to visit his mother, Miss Lillian, there. His son Jack and Rosalynn were in front of the helicopter. She was facing me and had obviously been crying, although she tried to keep up appearances. But the voters' verdict was etched in her face, even before the first ballot had been cast—and why shouldn't it have been? It is an odd thing to know the outcome of an election based on polling data before the voting has even begun.

The ride back on Air Force One to Washington was, in a word, depressing. When we landed at Andrews Air Force Base outside Washington and took Marine One back to the South Lawn of the White House that had been his home for four years, Carter spoke to several hundred people assembled from the administration. They were unaware of Caddell's pessimistic report. I called Fran from my office and gave her Caddell's projections—not just a loss, but a massive repudiation.

I then went home totally exhausted, physically and emotionally, not just from the last few days but from the accumulation of four years, knowing that despite all our accomplishments, we had not done enough to win the confidence of the American people for another term. Fran met me at the front door and we sobbed together. She had sacrificed so much to give me this extraordinary experience, raising our two young boys, Jay and Brian, while working part-time to supplement my government salary, never complaining about my ridiculous hours, always there with loving support and sound advice.

My deputy Bert Carp woke me by a phone call at 4:00 p.m. to tell me the exit polls showed Reagan burying Carter in a landslide. I was watching the dismal results with Fran and our two young sons, and we now had the difficult task of answering their questions: "Daddy, why did he lose?" "Why don't people like him?" Then, shortly before nine that evening, I was suddenly told by the White House operator to rush downtown to the Sheraton Washington Hotel ballroom, where the president was going to make his public concession in about half an hour.

When the results came in from the East, South, and Midwest confirming his bleak forecast, Carter, without consulting any of his staff, called Reagan from the White House residence at his home in Southern California at 9:01 p.m. Eastern Standard Time to concede and to congratulate him. I went up on the stage in the hotel ballroom with members of his cabinet and my White House colleagues. Carter shook everyone's hand and then at about 9:30 p.m. made his concession speech, instead of waiting until the polls closed in the West an hour and one-half later. It was the earliest presidential concession since 1904, when Alton Parker lost to Theodore Roosevelt, but there was no radio then to flash the news to the voters.

With a forced grin, the president told the weeping crowd: "I promised you four years ago that I would never lie to you. So I can't stand here tonight and say it doesn't hurt." I made a note to myself: "Hurts Dems in West?" Jody had urged him to wait until 11:00 p.m. so that Democrats on the West Coast would not be discouraged from voting not only for him but for congressional Democrats. Carter refused: "It's ridiculous. Let's get it over with."[79]

Senior Democratic officeholders were furious. Representative Tom Foley of Washington, who would later become Speaker, said: "It was vintage Carter at his dead worst."[80] Tip O'Neill told Frank Moore from his home in Cambridge: "What in God's name is wrong with you people? You guys came in like a bunch of jerks, and I see you're going out the same way."[81]

When a president loses an election, everyone has a reason. The House Majority Whip, John Brademas of Indiana, lost his seat and attributed it to high unemployment. But he caustically said that while Carter had come in as an antiestablishment candidate, once he arrived and settled in, he needed "to loosen up and be part of the give-and-take of politics." Instead, this Rhodes Scholar-turned-practical politician said: "Carter had the attitude of a Calvinist white man's burden regarding politics. He wasn't a good politician."[82]

Reagan won in a landslide, with 480 electoral votes to Carter's 49, the president carrying only six states and the District of Columbia. This was not so much an overwhelming endorsement of Reagan, who took only 50.7 percent of the popular vote, or even a defection to Anderson, as it was a rejection of Carter, the greatest of an incumbent president in modern American history up to that point. Anderson won 6.6 percent of the popular vote, and in Carter's view they were mainly Kennedy supporters seeking an alternative to Reagan. But Anderson got only 5.7 million votes, while Reagan's margin of victory was 8.4 million. Even in the unlikely event that every Anderson voter had switched to Carter, Reagan would still have won by almost 3 million votes.

31

FINAL DAYS

I f" is the cruelest word in the English language, and looking back at the previous four years, we all had our "what-ifs" to contemplate: What if Carter had leavened his talented but inexperienced Georgia Mafia with an experienced chief of staff or senior White House adviser who knew Washington and its players? What if we had not launched a raft of comprehensive legislation in Congress at the outset? What if we had recognized earlier, as Carter did, that inflation was public enemy number one? What if the Iranian revolution had not occurred on his watch and doubled oil prices within a 12-month period? What if there had been an earlier choice between Vance and Brzezinski in dealing with the Soviet Union? What if Carter had followed his own instincts and not allowed the Shah into the United States for medical treatment? Or if he had withdrawn all the embassy personnel after the first aborted attempt by the radical students to overrun the American compound? What if the hostage crisis had been handled differently, with no Rose Garden strategy and more forceful action? What if the bold rescue misson had not been thwarted by a remarkable series of mishaps? What if Kennedy had closed ranks with Carter against Reagan? What if Carter had not left the campaign trail on the last weekend before the election only to receive another inadequate Iranian offer?

Counterfactuals always make an intriguing mental exercise, but they can never rewrite history, and Carter knew that better than anyone. He quickly put an end to such thinking, telling the November 11 senior staff meeting: "We need to stop analyzing our defeat. Everyone is blaming me, and we need to stress our accomplishments. The fact is we just got our ass whipped." He also reassured us: "I feel remarkably good. I've handled the defeat well, and so has Rosalynn. The thing that hurts is the personal rejection." He joked: "I would rather have had an endorsement and then not serve a second term! It's a bitch of a job, and thankless, too."[1]

Two days later at the final Democratic leadership breakfast, he graciously said he had an "overwhelming sense of gratitude for their support and also regret over a number of defeats. We tackled tough problems. . . . We need to tell an accurate history of what we did." Senate Majority Leader Byrd, who lost his post due to the Republican gains in the Senate, said they shared a record of legislative accomplishment "but it continues to escape people. You did the best you could under difficult circumstances." Speaker O'Neill, who had recovered from his election-night pique, also cited the legislative accomplishments and said: "My heart and my door are always open to you. History will treat you well."[2] I hope this book, which has been a labor of love over a quarter of a century, will contribute to making the Speaker's hope a reality.

In a way Carter's departure from office turned out to be one of his finest hours. He gave his farewell address from the Oval Office the night of January 14, 1981, while still struggling to free the hostages. I had worked on the speech with Jody and Gordon Stewart, his speechwriter,[3] and took my older son, Jay, to listen to it with me in the Roosevelt Room. It was a tearjerking episode to hear Jimmy Carter address the nation for the last time as president. In terms reminiscent of what had propelled him from political obscurity four years before, he warned against Americans being "drawn to single-issue groups and special interest organizations" rather than the broader national good. He emphasized, in typical Carter form, three issues he singled out as difficult: the threat of nuclear destruction; the stewardship of the planet; and "the preeminence of the basic rights of human beings." I believe he left a positive legacy in each of these three areas. He closed movingly by saying that "as I return home to the South, where I was born and raised. . . . I intend to work as a citizen, as I've worked here in this office as president, for the values this nation was founded to secure.[4]

But he was not done yet, and exercised the full powers of the presidency until Reagan walked into the White House as his successor. Workaholic to the last, the morning after the devastating loss he asked me to join Rubenstein and Jack Watson in drawing up an agenda of things he could do during his final months as president.

He asked me to meet with journalists for a "historical perspective of our achievements, as they write their assessment pieces." Then he settled some scores. He asked me for a video copy of Reverend Pat Robertson's *700 Club,* a conservative Christian news television program, which aired that morning; he had been told the show was so clearly political that the tax exemption of Robertson's operation should be questioned as "gross and obscene and [transcending] the bounds of religious programming." For good measure, he said: "Something needs to be done to stop the Moral Majority. Your Jewish friends should help protect the country from them."[5]

Far from diminishing the Moral Majority, no less than Israeli prime minister Begin grew closer to it when Carter was out of office. After its founder, Jerry Falwell, visited Israel and expressed his hope that the country would continue to control the West Bank and the "Jews would acknowledge Christ as the Lord," Begin gave him an award named for his own personal Jewish hero, Vladimir Jabotinsky. Thus Begin helped cement an alliance among Israel's expansionist wing, American evangelicals who helped deliver the Republican Party, and conservative American Jews. Those bonds last to this day.

The closing chapter of the Carter presidency was one of his most productive spurts, the equal or better than that of any departing president in a postelection congressional session, when he was the lamest of lame ducks. At a senior staff meeting, he laid down a marker threatening to veto any bill passed by the outgoing Democratic Congress cutting taxes because it would add to the deficit and inflation, and link him to the Kemp-Roth movement. "I want to leave a record of fiscal responsibility; let Reagan make the tax cuts," he said.[6]

He signed the hard-fought Alaska Lands Act, which in a single stroke of his presidential pen doubled the size of our National Park System and protected huge wilderness areas from being despoiled by mining and drilling for oil and gas. He signed another postelection bill he championed that created the Superfund, significantly paid for by the chemical industry, to clean up the worst industrial wastelands.

Nor did he throw up his hands and dump the fate of the Iranian hostages in the lap of his successor. Carter worked to the last moment of his presidency for the agreement permitting the hostages to be released in the first minutes of the Reagan administration, and he sequestered Iranian funds for Americans with claims against Iran. And with a largeness of spirit rare among politicians, he quickly accepted the recommendation his rival Ted Kennedy made through me to appoint Kennedy's former aide Stephen Breyer to an appeals court judgeship that eventually brought him to the Supreme Court. And in an act of bipartisanship virtually unknown in today's polarized politics, Breyer won the support of archconservative, incoming Senate Judiciary Committee chairman, Strom Thurmond, and his Republican colleagues.

LAST HOURS

Early on the morning of Inauguration Day, January 20, 1981, Rafshoon and Ham looked down from the Queen's Bedroom on the second floor of the White House Residence and saw the president and First Lady greet Ronald and Nancy Reagan as they entered the White House for a traditional tea, before proceeding to the Capitol for the ceremony. The two Carter aides then made their way to the Situation Room in the hope that the hostages would clear Iranian airspace before noon. Two phone lines were open, one to the CIA station in Algiers where Christopher was negotiating, the other to Phil Wise, the president's appointments secretary, who was on the inaugural platform with Carter hoping to tell him the hostages were released before the swearing-in, so Carter could announce the good news. It did not happen, the last indignity Khomeini imposed on Jimmy Carter.

Ignoring a warning from Ham's personal secretary, Eleanor Connor, they remained until 12:25 p.m. As she came in to warn them that the Reagan staff people were coming through the South Gate, the two were unceremoniously escorted out of the West Wing for the last time by a Marine guard. He was none too happy that they had literally worn out their welcome because that delayed his own meeting with the new Reagan crew.

In the brief time between the formal end of the Carter presidency and their belated departure down the hallway between the Situation Room and the White House Mess, they were bemused by the speedy removal of all the Carter photographs and their replacement by framed pictures of Reagan. When they arrived at Andrews Air Force Base to board the plane taking Carter back to Georgia, we were all waiting in our seats to accompany him on the final journey. Ham called the Situation Room on the plane's secure phone to find out what had happened to the hostages. The duty officer said: "I am sorry, Mr. Jordan, I cannot tell you," to which Ham replied he was calling from a secure phone. The officer softly said: "Yes, Mr. Jordan, but Mr. Carter is no longer president." The finality of the transfer of power sank in.[7]

As is the custom for a president leaving for home on the inauguration of his successor, Carter boarded a Boeing 707-SAM 27000, designated not as Air Force One but as a Special Air Mission, since he was no longer president. He gave a thumbs-up, indicating that the hostages were free, boarded the plane, and was flown to Georgia's Robins Air Force Base. He gave an emotional speech in the Plains town square for several hundred people. We then walked to his home and presented him with a gift from the staff: a carpentry set to make furniture and other things, which Rosalynn felt he would like. Then Rafshoon, his son, Scott, Anne Wexler, and I returned to Washington on the same plane.

When the U.S. hostages in Iran were released, there would be one last bittersweet ride on Air Force One, when Reagan generously asked the former president to fly on the presidential plane to greet the hostages. So Chief Flight Steward Charlie Palmer and his crew left early the next day, January 21, with Mondale and others who had worked on the hostage deal, and picked up Carter in Georgia for the flight. They landed at Rhein-Main Airbase in West Germany and from there went to the Wiesbaden U.S. Air Force Base Hospital. Many of the hostages tearfully embraced the former president; others, angry at their long captivity, did not.

On the way home Palmer had occasion to sit down with Carter. He recalled flying with Richard Nixon back to Yorba Linda, California, after his resignation. He commented that Nixon hardly communicated with anyone during that raw time. By contrast, Carter had formed a warm friendship with Palmer. By now they had flown hundreds of thousands of miles together, and almost from the beginning Carter affectionately called him "Charlie." On this final flight together, Palmer proposed that he and the former president join in a champagne toast to celebrate the release of the hostages he had sought for 444 days. Little could Palmer, Carter, the country, or the world know that some of his most important accomplishments still lay ahead, through his leadership at the Carter Center in eradicating diseases in Africa, monitoring elections, and promoting human rights and democracy. For all these and his Middle East diplomacy, Carter would be awarded a Nobel Peace Prize in 2002.

Palmer handed over the tulip-shaped glass with the presidential seal, and together they drained their glasses.[8]

ACKNOWLEDGMENTS

This account of the Carter presidency would not have been possible without the confidence that Jimmy Carter bestowed on me to formulate policy during his presidential campaign, and then to serve as his chief domestic-policy adviser in the White House, where I also joined in many foreign-policy decisions. It was the greatest challenge of my life. Although President Carter has been unfailingly helpful with a number of interviews and discussions, and accorded me access to selected personal notes since I began my research in 1981, this is in no way an authorized or official biography. It is my own account of what I observed on the road to the White House and inside the cauldron during the four years we served there. It is heavily based on my own notes and interviews with colleagues and others, whose views are cited or incorporated, and were not always complimentary. At no point did either President Carter or Vice President Mondale seek to influence my narrative or review any part of the book, even though they must have been aware that my inquiries would lead to some information or opinions that would not necessarily be flattering.

From the start, my wonderful wife Fran (of blessed memory) believed in and encouraged this project; my public service with Jimmy Carter shaped our lives and those of our sons, Jay and Brian. I honor her life and our work together and will always mourn her passing. I wish she could have been able to read this account of the administration, in which she felt so invested.

For the substance of this book, I am immensely grateful to Lawrence Malkin. As with my two previous books, Larry has been more than a highly skilled editor and demanding critic; with his wide-ranging experience as an author and journalist for major newspapers and magazines, he has also been a mentor, adviser, and collaborator in helping shape and give voice to this book. Together we have waded through draft after draft of the manuscript to prepare it for publication.

I also deeply thank my publisher, Thomas Dunne, for his perseverance and support and for providing the excellent editorial assistance of his colleagues, Stephen S. Power, Janine Barlow, and Peter Joseph. At St. Martin's Press, we all benefited from the work of John Morrone, the senior production editor; Sue Llewellyn, our tireless copyeditor; Michelle Cashman for marketing; our publicist, Rebecca Lang; the book's designer, Steven Seighman; and Rowen Davis for his book jacket capturing the optimistic Jimmy Carter I knew. My agent, Ronald Goldfarb, brought me to Tom and his colleagues; Ron's sound judgment has been instrumental in finding publishers for three of my books.

Over decades of work, I am grateful to some 325 individuals who were willing to sit for time-consuming interviews, some several times for return visits, leading to over 350 interviews. They include those from inside the administration and outside observers, Republicans as well as Democrats. I benefited greatly from the dedicated assistance of Jay Hakes, David Alsobrook, and, more recently, David Stanhope and his colleagues at the Carter Presidential Library, who helped find key memoranda to the president along with his contemporaneous notes and comments, plus a trove of valuable information in the Evening Reports sent each night to the president by Secretary of State Cyrus Vance or Deputy Secretary of State Warren Christopher, as well as the Weekly Reports to the president from his National Security adviser, Zbigniew Brzezinski. The staff of the Library of Congress was always helpful in promptly accessing my own documents already deposited there. Louise Fischer of the Israeli Foreign Ministry Archives supplied cables of my meetings with Israeli officials, which were expertly translated by Katja Manor in Jerusalem.

After the end of the Carter administration, the Brookings Institution appointed me as a Guest Scholar for several months, which gave me a start on indexing over five thousand legal pad pages of contemporaneous notes of all meetings and telephone calls in which I was involved, and beginning to shape the book. Carolyn Keene, my secretary for 35 years, was invaluable in helping to organize my legal-size notepads and my interviews, arrange (along with Teri Mancini) for their transcription, and organize the work of several young researchers, while we were at the law firm Powell, Goldstein, Frazer & Murphy, then later at Covington & Burling LLP. As the project advanced and my writing began in earnest some three years ago, and deadlines loomed, I am especially grateful to Tim Hester, the Managing Partner at Covington, who granted a leave of absence from my law practice for several critical weeks. The documents staff at Covington transcribed my later interviews, and a number of Covington legal secretaries were helpful, including Pat Adams, Laurina Holte, and Hattie Blackshire. Special thanks go to my current legal secretaries, Michalene Katzer, who helped put my interviews into a format that made them more accessible, and especially to Patrice Jones, whose research skill and remarkably selfless work were indispensable in locating information in my files, interviews, and online.

I have used a talented group of research assistants for each of the major topics. In the early years of the project, Rachel Kogan (Habib), Andrew Schwartz, Stephanie Epstein, Helayna Minsk, Josh Liberson, Mark Brzezinski, and Caroline Lubick Goldzweig did excellent research on several of the topics in my book.

My longest serving and most dedicated research assistant was Lisa Lubick Daniel, who was with me from start to finish, with special emphasis on some of the most complicated subjects—Iran, the Middle East peace process, and energy. In addition, during the final two years, I benefited from essential research and review of my early draft chapters by Sarah Boddy (women's issues, political issues); Michael Blumenthal (airline deregulation); Amy Fisher (economy and taxation); Ruben Karchem (New York City and Chrysler); Shana Krauss (environment); Peter McFarren (Panama Canal Treaty, Latin America, Rhodesia, Horn of Africa, human rights in Latin America, and the Mariel Boatlift); Alexandra Memmott (defense policy, human rights toward the Soviet Union, SALT II, the Soviet invasion of Afghanistan, the neutron bomb and intermediate nuclear weapons in Europe, Angola, and Vietnamese boat people); Randi Michel (China); and Alex Somodevilla (health, education, and welfare reform). A special note of appreciation goes to

Marion Ein Lewin, whose patience, support, kindness, and helpful suggestions during the last phases of this project were vital.

In the end, I bear sole responsibility for the facts, analysis, opinions, and judgments expressed in *President Carter: The White House Years*.

Stuart E. Eizenstat, Washington, D.C.

NOTES

All references to Pad numbers in the notes refer to my legal pads, on which in date order from the beginning to the end of the Carter administration, and in some instances from the campaign and transition, I recorded in chronological order and in virtual verbatim form, all meetings and conversations in which I was a part.

Citations from *Congressional Quarterly* are cited as 1977 CQ Almanac, 95th Congress, 1st Session ... 1977, Volume XXXXIII, Congressional Quarterly, Inc., Washington, D.C.; 1978 CQ Almanac, 2nd Session ... 1978, Volume XXXIV, Congressional Quarterly, Inc., Washington, D.C.; 1979 CQ Almanac, 96th Congress, 1st Session ... 1979, Volume XXXV, Congressional Quarterly, Inc., Washington, D.C.; 1980 CQ Almanac, 96th Congress, 2nd Session ... 1980, Volume XXXVI, Congressional Quarterly, Inc., Washington, D.C. Citations from the Jimmy Carter Presidential Library and Museum can be accessed at www.jimmycarterlibrary .gov; I have been greatly assisted by David Stanhope, director of the Jimmy Carter Library and Museum (David.Stanhope@nara.gov) and Sara Mitchell (Sara.Mitchell@nara.gov).

State Department Evening Reports from Secretary of State Cyrus Vance or Deputy Secretary of State Warren Christopher, and Weekly Reports from National Security Adviser Zbigniew Brzezinski, are in the author's possession. Originals are in the Jimmy Carter Presidential Library and Museum.

Association for Diplomatic Studies and Training, Foreign Affairs Oral History Project, is abbreviated as ADST.

For a detailed list and dates of all interviews, and a bibliography, see the following link: https://us.macmillan.com/static/president-carter-home.html

Introduction

1. Jimmy Carter, interview with the author, October 30, 1991.
2. Pad 59, July 11, 1979.
3. David McCullough, *Truman* (New York: Simon & Schuster, 1992), 873.
4. Jimmy Carter interview, June 4, 1991.
5. Jimmy Carter interview, June 4, 1991.
6. Jimmy Carter, email to the author, August 8, 2018.
7. Pad 14, April 18, 1977; Jimmy Carter interview, November 29, 1992.
8. Anatoly Dobrynin, *In Confidence* (New York: Times Books/Random House, 1995), 352.
9. Edward C. Keefer, *Harold Brown: Offsetting the Soviet Military Challenge, 1977–1981,* Secretaries of Defense Series, Volume IX, Historical Office, Office of the Secretary of Defense, Washington, D.C. 20007. This study was written by a military historian and peer-reviewed by an outside panel of experts, staff historians, and the Chief Historian of the Defense Department, Erin R. Mahan.
10. Mikhail Gorbachev, *Memoirs* (New York: Doubleday, 1996), 442–50.
11. Public Papers of the Presidents, Jimmy Carter, Vol. I, 1980–1981, 197.
12. Willoughby Mariano, "Carter said record with Congress better than most presidents," October 5, 2010, http://www.politifact.com/georgia/statements/2010/oct/05/jimmy -carter-said-record," citing 1980 CQ Almanac, which lists success rates for presidents beginning with Dwight D. Eisenhower, and a survey by the Miller Center of Public Affairs at the University of Virginia. Also Andrew W. Barrett and Matthew Eshbuagh-Soha, "Presidential Success on the Substance of Legislation," University of North Texas, Denton, February 23, 2007, 105, http://prq.sagepub, which likewise gives President Carter high marks.
13. Robert C. Byrd, *The Senate, 1789–1989, Addresses on the History of the United States Senate,* 717.
14. Chris Mooney, "Democrats Want Investigations into Energy Questionnaire," *The Washington Post,* December 17, 2016.
15. Eric Lipton and Nicholas Fandos, "As He Departs, Chief of Ethics Office Offers a Dire Warning," *The New York Times,* July 18, 2017.
16. Wesley G. Pippert, "We Told the Truth, we obeyed the law, and we kept the peace," UPI, June 3, 1982; Allison Sherry, *Star Tribune,* "Minnesota's Elder Statesman Mondale to be Honored Tuesday in Washington, D.C.," October 19, 2015.

PART I

1. The 1976 Campaign

1. *American Experience.* "Jimmy Carter (Part 2)." Episode 174. Directed by Adriana Bosch. Aired on PBS, November 12, 2002.
2. Ibid.
3. Jimmy Carter, interview with the author, June 4, 1991.
4. *American Experience.* "Jimmy Carter (Part 2)." Episode 174. Directed by Adriana Bosch. Aired on PBS, November 12, 2002.

5. Jimmy Carter interview, June 4, 1991.

6. *American Experience.* "Jimmy Carter (Part 2)." Episode 174. Directed by Adriana Bosch. Aired on PBS, November 12, 2002.

7. Jimmy Carter interview, June 4, 1991.

8. *American Experience.* "Jimmy Carter (Part 2)." Episode 174. Directed by Adriana Bosch. Aired on PBS, November 12, 2002.

9. Jimmy Carter interview, September 27, 2013.

10. Paul Vitello, "Wesley Brown, Pioneer as Black Naval Graduate, Dies at 85," *The New York Times,* May 24, 2012.

11. Jimmy Carter interview, September 27, 2013.

12. Ibid., June 4, 1991.

13. Ibid., September 27, 2013.

14. Ibid.; Jimmy Carter, *A Full Life* (New York: Simon & Schuster, 2016).

15. Barry Koe (former Rickover aide), in discussion with the author, February 19, 2017.

16. *American Experience.* "Jimmy Carter (Part 2)." Episode 174. Directed by Adriana Bosch. Aired on PBS, November 12, 2002.

17. Rosalynn Carter interviews, July 13, 1993, and August 13, 2014.

18. Jimmy Carter interviews, June 4, 1991, and September 27, 2013.

19. *American Experience.* "Jimmy Carter (Part 2)." Episode 174. Directed by Adriana Bosch. Aired on PBS, November 12, 2002.

20. Jimmy Carter interview, June 4, 1991.

21. *American Experience.* "Jimmy Carter (Part 2)." Episode 174. Directed by Adriana Bosch. Aired on PBS, November 12, 2002.

22. Ibid.

23. Jimmy Carter interview, June 4, 1991.

24. Ibid.

25. *American Experience.* "Jimmy Carter (Part 2)." Episode 174. Directed by Adriana Bosch. Aired on PBS, November 12, 2002.

26. Charles Kirbo, interview with the author, June 28, 1991.

27. Walter Mondale, interview with the author, April 3, 1991.

28. Jimmy Carter interview, June 4, 1991; Peter G. Bourne, *Jimmy Carter: A Comprehensive Biography from Plains to Postpresidency* (New York: Scribner, 1997), 147.

29. Bourne; Ibid. 158–9.

30. Charles Kirbo, interviews with the author, June 28, 1991, and August 23, 1991.

31. Jimmy Carter interview, June 4, 1991.

32. Ibid.

33. Rick Atkinson, "Segregation Rises Again in Many Southern Schools," *The Washington Post,* April 1, 1984.

34. Hamilton Jordan, interviews with the author, May 11, 1992, and December 23, 1992; Jerry Rafshoon, interviews with the author, January 30, 1990, and August 19, 2003.

35. Charles Kirbo interview, June 28, 1991.

36. Jimmy Carter interview, June 4, 1991.

37. Hamilton Jordan interview, May 11, 1992.

38. Charles Kirbo interviews, June 28, 1991, and August 23, 1991.

39. Jimmy Carter interview, June 4, 1991.

40. Bourne, *Jimmy Carter*, 231.

41. Bourne, *Jimmy Carter*, 233; Hamilton Jordan interviews, May 11, 1992, and December 23, 1992.

42. *American Experience*. "Jimmy Carter (Part 2)." Episode 174. Directed by Adriana Bosch. Aired on PBS, November 12, 2002.

43. Jimmy Carter interview, June 4, 1991.

44. Hamilton Jordan interview, May 11, 1992.

45. *American Experience*. "Jimmy Carter (Part 2)." Episode 174. Directed by Adriana Bosch. Aired on PBS, November 12, 2002.

46. Stuart Eizenstat and William Barutio, *Andrew Young, The Path to History: An Analysis* (Atlanta: Voter Education Project, Inc., 1973).

47. Andrew Young, *An Easy Burden: The Civil Rights Movement and the Transformation of America* (New York: HarperCollins, 1996).

48. Edward Walsh, "Rising Status, Mild Criticism for Eizenstat Policy Staff," *The Washington Post*, December 27, 1977.

49. Pad 13, April 6, 1977.

50. Jimmy Carter interview, June 4, 1991.

51. John Brademas, interview with the author, September 5, 2006.

52. Jimmy Carter interview, June 4, 1991.

53. Jimmy Carter interview, June 4, 1991.

54. Ibid.

55. Henry Owen, interview with the author, July 28, 1989.

56. Dot Padgett, interview with the author, August 8, 2014.

57. *American Experience*. "Jimmy Carter (Part 2)." Episode 174. Directed by Adriana Bosch. Aired on PBS, November 12, 2002. Quoting Chip Carter.

58. Tom Peterson, interview with the author, July 11, 2005; Tom Peterson, emails to author, October 15, 16, 2013.

59. Tom Peterson interview, July 11, 2005; Tom Peterson emails, October 15, 16, 2013.

60. Robert Bentley, "Away from the Madding Crowd, Jimmy Carter Finds Solace on Peanut One," *El Paso Times*, October 9, 1976.

61. Steve Schlossberg, interview with the author, December 21, 1990.

62. National Health Policy Speech by Jimmy Carter, April 16, 1976; *President Carter's Campaign Promises*, Commerce Clearing House, Chicago, June 1977.

63. Jimmy Carter, Acceptance Speech: "Our Nation's Past and Future," Madison Square Garden, New York City, July 15, 1976, www.4president.org/speeches/1976/carter1976acceptance.htm.

64. Jimmy Carter's written Democratic Platform Committee presentation, June 10, 1976, Washington, D.C., *President Carter's Campaign Promises*, printed in Commerce Clearing House, Chicago, 1977, taken from memorandum by the author and David Rubenstein, November 30, 1976, to President-elect Carter.

65. Christopher Lydon, "Carter Defends All-White Areas," *The New York Times*, April 7, 1976.

66. Christopher Lydon, "Carter Issues an Apology on 'Ethnic Purity' Phrase," *The New York Times*, April 9, 1976.

67. Andrew Young, interview with the author, December 17, 1991.

68. *Time*, April 5, 1976, reported by *Time* correspondent Stanley Cloud, cited in *Betsy's Page*, "Jimmy Carter's Projection of Racism," September 21, 2009, betsyspage.blogspot.com /2009/09/jimmy-carter projection of racism.html; *Time*, "The Campaign: Candidate Carter: 'I Apologize,'" April 19, 1976.

69. Jimmy Carter interview, May 11, 1992.

70. *Today*, transcript, April 9, 1976.

71. Jimmy Carter interview, June 4, 1991.

72. Joseph Rauh, interview with the author, December 11, 1992; Jimmy Carter interview, June 4, 1991.

73. Jimmy Carter interview, June 4, 1991.

74. Jimmy Carter, Acceptance Speech: "Our Nation's Past and Future," Madison Square Garden, New York City, July 15, 1976, www.4president.org/speeches/1976 /carter1976acceptance.htm.

75. Stephen Stander, email to author, November 3, 2017.

76. George J. Lankevich, ed., *James E. Carter, 1924-: Chronology, Documents, Bibliographical Aids* (Dobbs Ferry, NY: Oceana Publications, Inc., 1981).

77. Hamilton Jordan, University of Virginia's Miller Center of Public Affairs interview, November 6, 1981.

78. Hamilton Jordan interviews, May 11, 1992, and December 23, 1992.

79. Jimmy Carter interview, June 4, 1991.

80. Robert Shrum, interview with the author, July 21, 1992.

81. Jimmy Carter interview, June 4, 1991.

82. Pad 98, October 25, 1980.

83. *The Presidential Campaign 1976*, Volume Three, The Debates, United States Government Printing Office, Washington, D.C., 1979.

84. Legal Pad "Campaign," October 6, 1976.

85. Dick Cheney, interview with the author, May 29, 2013.

86. Jody Powell, interview with the author, October 16, 1989; and Jerry Rafshoon, interview with the author, August 19, 2013.

87. Robert Scheer, "Playboy Interview: Jimmy Carter," *Playboy*, November 1976, www .playboy.com/articles/playboy-interview-jimmy-carter.

88. Jerry Rafshoon interview, January 30, 1990.

89. Jimmy Carter interview, June 4, 1991.

90. Charles Mohr, "President Asserts Carter Will Say 'Anything Anywhere,'" *The New York Times*, October 17, 1976.

91. *American Experience*. "Jimmy Carter (Part 2)." Episode 174. Directed by Adriana Bosch. Aired on PBS, November 12, 2002.

92. Kandy Stroud, *How Jimmy Won: The Victory Campaign from Plains to the White House* (New York: William Morrow, 1977), 310.

93. Bourne, *Jimmy Carter*, 355.

94. Oral History Project, Carter Library, Frank Moore interview, July 30–31, 2002.

95. James Baker, interview with the author, May 29, 2013.

2. A Perilous Transition

1. Pad 1, December 1, 1976.

2. Jimmy Carter, eulogy for Zbigniew Brzezinski, June 9, 2017.

3. Jack Watson, interview with the author, August 5, 1992; see also, Jack Watson, University of Virginia's Miller Center of Public Affairs interview, April 17–18, 1981; and White House exit interview, December 13, 1980.

4. Jack Watson interview, August 5, 1992.

5. Ibid.

6. Jimmy Carter, interview with the author, June 4, 1991.

7. Harrison Wellford, interview with the author, August 22, 1989.

8. Andy Glass, interview with the author, September 25, 2013; Judy Woodruff, interview with the author, January 15, 2015; Sam Donaldson, interview with the author, May 8, 2013.

9. Frank Moore, interviews with the author, February 1, 2013, July 27, 2013, May 8, 2013, and October 2, 2014.

10. Jimmy Carter interview, May 19, 1977; Joe Klein, "Hamilton Jordan and Jody Powell: The White House Whiz Kids," *Rolling Stone,* May 19, 1977.

11. Ibid.; *Time,* June 6, 1977.

12. Hamilton Jordan, interview with the author, May 11, 1992; Jerry Rafshoon, interviews with the author, April 19, 2013, and February 25, 2014; Hamilton Jordan, *No Such Thing as a Bad Day* (Atlanta: Longstreet Press, 2000).

13. Stephen Hess, interview with the author, July 31, 1992.

14. *American Experience.* "Jimmy Carter (Part 2)." Episode 174. Directed by Adriana Bosch. Aired on PBS, November 12, 2002.

15. Patrick Caddell, interview with the author, January 6, 1993, and April 1, 1993.

16. Stephen Hess, interview with the author, July 31, 1992.

17. Dick Cheney, interview with the author, October 27, 1992.

18. Hamilton Jordan interview, May 11, 1992.

19. Jimmy Carter interviews, June 4, 1991, and September 27, 2013.

20. Ibid., September 27, 2013.

21. Hamilton Jordan interview, May 11, 1992.

22. James Baker, interview with the author, May 29, 2013.

23. W. Michael Blumenthal, interview with the author, September 13, 1990.

24. Hugh Carter, Jr., interview with the author, October 27, 2014.

25. Stephen Hess, interview with the author, July 31, 1992.

26. Rosalynn Carter, interviews with the author, July 13, 1993, and August 13, 2014.

27. Rick Massimo, "10 Things You Didn't Know About John F. Kennedy," *WTOP,* May 22, 2017.

28. Charles Palmer, interview with the author, December 11, 2013.

29. Ibid., October 22, 2015.

30. Jane Harman, interview with the author, May 30, 2017.

31. Jimmy Carter interview, June 4, 1991.

32. Ibid.

33. Jimmy Carter, *Keeping Faith* (Fayetteville, Arkansas: University of Arkansas Press, 1995), 17–25.

34. Public Papers of the Presidents, Jimmy Carter, 1977, 5, Proclamation 4483, Executive Order 11967.

35. President Carter's Remarks on signing the Vietnam Veterans Memorial Bill, July 1, 1980, Public Papers of the Presidents, Jimmy Carter, 1980–1981, 1268–71.

3. The Making of the Modern Vice President

1. See, generally, Robert A. Caro, *The Years of Lyndon Johnson: The Passage of Power* (New York: Alfred A. Knopf, 2012); also the author's discussion with Vice President Humphrey's former senior staff, John Stewart, Ted Van Dyke, and Norman Sherman.

2. Jimmy Carter, *Keeping Faith: Memoirs of a President* (New York: Bantam Books, 1982), 35–40.

3. Charles Kirbo, interviews with the author, June 28, 1991, and August 23, 1991.

4. Hamilton Jordan, interview with the author, May 11, 1991.

5. Charles Kirbo, University of Virginia's Miller Center of Public Affairs interview, January 5, 1983.

6. Richard Moe, interview with the author, October 11, 1991.

7. Walter Mondale, interviews with the author, September 11, 2014, and April 3, 1991.

8. Charles Kirbo interviews, June 28, 1991, and August 23, 1991.

9. Richard Moe interview, October 11, 1991.

10. Walter Mondale interview, September 11, 2014.

11. Richard Moe interview, October 11, 1991.

12. Jimmy Carter, interview with the author, October 25, 1991.

13. Hamilton Jordan interview, May 11, 1992.

14. Ibid.

15. Michael Berman, interview with the author, February 20, 2014.

16. Richard Moe interview, February 18, 2014.

17. Walter Mondale interview, April 3, 1991.

18. Ibid.

19. Michael Berman interview, February 20, 2014.

20. Ibid.

21. Dan Olson, "Mondale's Role in Saving 'Boat People,'" *MPR News,* November 16, 2009.

22. Walter Mondale interview, September 11, 2014.

23. Originals at the Minnesota Historical Society, Manuscripts Collection, Walter F. Mondale papers, Vice Presidential Papers, 1968–2001 (bulk 1975–1981), Finding Aids: MNHS.ORG.

24. Richard Moe interview, October 11, 1991.

25. Walter Mondale interview, September 11, 2014.

26. Ibid., April 3, 1991.

27. Michael Berman interview, February 20, 2014.

28. Walter Mondale interview, April 3, 1991.

29. Ibid., September 11, 2014, and October 6, 2015.
30. Ibid.
31. Ibid., April 3, 1991.
32. Remarks by Vice President Joe Biden, at a reception honoring Walter Mondale, at the vice president's official residence, Washington, D.C., October 20, 2015, heard by author.

4. A New Kind of First Lady

1. *American Experience.* "Jimmy Carter (Part 2)." Episode 174. Directed by Adriana Bosch. Aired on PBS, November 12, 2002.
2. Rosalynn Carter, interview with the author, July 13, 1993.
3. Ibid., August 13, 2014.
4. Ibid., July 13, 1993.
5. Ibid., July 13, 1993, and August 13, 2014.
6. Tim Kraft, interview with the author, June 1, 1993.
7. Rosalynn Carter, interview with the author, August 13, 2014.
8. Ibid., July 13, 1993.
9. *American Experience.* "Jimmy Carter (Part 2)." Episode 174. Directed by Adriana Bosch. Aired on PBS, November 12, 2002.
10. Rex Scouten, interview with the author, November 13, 1995.
11. Rosalynn Carter interview, August 13, 2014; Rosalynn Carter, *First Lady from Plains* (Boston: Houghton Mifflin Company, 1984), 189–91; Robert Pastor, interview with the author, July 13, 2011.
12. Robert Pastor, interview with the author, July 13, 2011.
13. Rosalynn Carter, conversation with the author, June 23, 2017, Lake Tahoe.
14. Rosalynn Carter, *First Lady from Plains*, 289–90.
15. Rosalynn Carter interview, July 13, 1993.
16. Rosalynn Carter interview, July 13, 1993.
17. Ibid.
18. Ibid.
19. Ibid.
20. Ibid.
21. Ibid.
22. Ibid.
23. Patrick Caddell, interview with the author, October 30, 2015.

5. The Indispensable Man

1. Bert Lance, University of Virginia's Miller Center of Public Affairs interview, May 12, 1982.
2. Ibid., 67–8.
3. Ibid., 36.
4. Bert Lance, interview with the author, July 1, 2011; Bert Lance, *The Truth of the Matter* (New York: Summit Books, 1991).
5. Jimmy Carter, interview with the author, June 4, 1991.
6. David Rubenstein, interview with the author, December 11, 1992.

7. John Moore, interview with the author, August 19, 1992.

8. John Stokes, interview with the author, September 3, 1992.

9. Peter Winn, email to the author, April 22, 2017, attaching the opinion of Mary Lawton, Department of Justice to Michael Cardozo, Senior Associate White House Counsel.

10. Bert Lance, *The Truth of the Matter*, 132–3; Bert Lance interviews, April 16, 1990, June 26, 1992, August 15, 2006, and July 1, 2011.

11. E. R. Lanier, "Bert Lance: 1931–2013," *New Georgia Encyclopedia*, www.georgiaency clopedia.org/articles/government-politics/bert-lance-1931-2013.

12. Eric Boehlert, "William Safire's Dubious Legacy," *Salon*, November 22, 2004, www .salon.com/2004/11/22/safire_7/.

13. Jody Powell, *The Other Side of the Story* (New York: William Morrow, 1984), 50–3.

14. John Heimann, interviews with the author, June 23, 1991, and March 30, 1992.

15. Robert Carswell, interviews with the author, April 29, 1991, and June 16, 1992.

16. John Heimann interviews, June 23, 1991, and March 30, 1992.

17. Pad 23, August 11, 1977.

18. Pad 23, August 11, 1977.

19. Robert Carswell, interviews with the author, April 29, 1991, and June 16, 1992.

20. John Heimann interviews, June 23, 1991, and March 30, 1992.

21. Robert Lipshutz, interviews with the author, June 4, 1991, and June 26, 1992.

22. See Haynes Johnson and George Lardner, Jr., *The Washington Post*, September 25, 1977.

23. John Heimann interviews, June 23, 1991, and March 30, 1992.

24. Robert Lipshutz, memorandum to the President, September 12, 1977.

25. Jimmy Carter, *White House Diary* (New York: Farrar, Straus & Giroux, 2010), 89.

26. Richard Wegman (Ribicoff's staff director), interview with the author, December 19, 1991.

27. John Heimann interview, March 30, 1992.

28. Jimmy Carter, *White House Diary*, 98.

29. Zbigniew Brzezinski, interview with the author, March 1, 2014.

30. Pad 24, September 19, 1977.

31. Jimmy Carter, *White House Diary*, 101–2.

32. Jimmy Carter, *White House Diary*, 103.

33. Bert Lance, *The Truth of the Matter*, 13, 148–50.

34. Pad 25, September 26, 1977.

35. Jimmy Carter, *White House Diary*, 103.

36. Bert Lance, *New Georgia Encyclopedia*, by W. B. Woods, "Bert Lance (1931–2013)" August 26, 2013, www.georgiaencyclopedia.org/articles/government-politics-bert-lance -1931-2013. Also Bert Lance, *The Truth of the Matter*, 164–5.

37. Eric Boehlert, "William Safire's Dubious Legacy," *Salon*, November 22, 2004, www .salon.com/2004/11/22/safire_7/.

38. Jody Powell, Miller Center interview, December 17–18, 1981; Jody Powell, interview with the author, October 1, 1989.

39. *American Experience.* "Jimmy Carter (Part 2)." Episode 174. Directed by Adriana Bosch. Aired on PBS, November 12, 2002.

40. Jimmy Carter interview, June 4, 1991.

PART II

6. The Moral Equivalent of War

1. Pad 1, December 9, 1976.
2. Daniel Yergin, *The Prize* (New York: Free Press, 2008), 141, and generally for an excellent history of oil.
3. Dr. James Schlesinger, interview with the author, April 4, 1989.
4. Jimmy Carter, University of Virginia's Miller Center of Public Affairs interview, November 29, 1982.
5. Jimmy Carter, Address Announcing Candidacy for the Democratic Presidential Nomination, National Press Club, Washington, D.C., December 12, 1974, Online by Gerhard Peters and John T. Woolley, The American Presidency Project, www.presidency.ecsb.edu.ws/?pid=77821.
6. Senator David Boren, interview with the author, September 9, 1992.
7. Jimmy Carter, interview with the author, June 4, 1991; George C. Edwards III, interview with the author, Texas A&M University, May 18, 2007.
8. Dr. James Schlesinger, University of Virginia's Miller Center of Public Affairs interview, Presidential Oral History Program, July 19–20, 1984, Charlottesville, Virginia.
9. Jimmy Carter interview, June 8, 1992.
10. Ibid., June 4, 1991, and September 27, 2013.
11. Katherine Cochrane, interview with the author, November 20, 1992.
12. Central Intelligence Agency: "The International Energy Situation: Outlook to 1985," ER 77-10240 U.
13. Pad "Campaign 1976," November 19, 1976, Plains, Georgia.
14. Pad 5, January 24, 1977.
15. Pad 8, February 20, 1977.
16. Pad 6, January 29, 1977.
17. Pad 8, February 20, 1977, and March 7, 1977.
18. Al Alm, interview with the author, August 21, 1989.
19. Ibid.
20. Jimmy Carter interview, June 4, 1991.
21. Les Goldman, interview with the author, July 25, 1991.
22. James Schlesinger, University of Virginia's Miller Center of Public Affairs, interview, July 19–20, 1984.
23. Fact Sheet on the President's National Energy Program, April 20, 1977, Public Papers of the Presidents, Jimmy Carter, 1977, Vol. I, Washington, United States Government Printing Office, 1977, 672–89; Stu Eizenstat and David Rubenstein, memorandum to President-elect Carter, November 30, 1976.
24. Pad 9, February 28, 1977.
25. Pad 10, March 14, 1977.
26. Pad 10, March 14, 1977.
27. Katherine Schirmer Cochrane interview, November 20, 1992.
28. Pad 13, April 8, 1977.
29. Pad 12, March 28, 1977.

30. Jimmy Carter interview, June 4, 1991.

31. Al Alm interview, August 21, 1989.

32. Pad 13, April 6, 1977.

33. Pad 13, April 6, 1977.

34. Summary prepared at the author's request by Professor William C. Boyd at the University of Colorado School of Law, October 1, 2014, referencing Paul W. MacAvoy, "The Natural Gas Market: Sixty Years of Regulation and Deregulation," 2000, and Richard J. Pierce, Jr., "The Evolution of Natural Gas Regulatory Policy," *Natural Resources and Environment,* Summer, 1995.

35. Pad 13, April 11, 1977.

36. Pad 13, April 11, 1977.

37. James Schlesinger interview, March 23, 1989.

38. Pad 14, April 16, 1977.

39. Al Alm interview, August 21, 1989.

40. James Schlesinger, University of Virginia's Miller Center of Public Affairs interview, July 19–20, 1994.

41. David Boren, interview with the author, September 9, 1992.

42. Ibid.

43. Ibid.

44. Ibid.

45. Pad 10, March 14, 1977.

46. Al Alm interview, August 21, 1989.

47. Pad 19, June 9, 1977.

48. Pad 14, April 18, 1977.

49. Rosalynn Carter, interview with the author, July 13, 1993.

50. Jimmy Carter, Address to the Nation on Energy, April 18, 1977, Public Papers of the Presidents, Jimmy Carter, Vol. I, 1977, 656–62.

51. Pad 14, April 20, 1977.

52. Jimmy Carter, Address Delivered Before a Joint Session of Congress on the National Energy Plan, April 2, 1977, Public Papers of the Presidents, Jimmy Carter, Vol. I, 1977, 663–72.

53. Pad 14, April 19, 1977.

54. Pad 14, April 20, 1977.

55. Pad 15, April 27, 1977.

56. Pad 14, April 22, 1977.

57. Edward Walsh, "Carter: Energy Outlook Grim," *The Washington Post,* April 19, 1977, www.washingtonpost.com/archive/politics/1977/04/19/carter-energy-outlook-grim/00060835-8ddc-46c4-b06d-60f308cc47b6/?utm_term=.21e94d051e22.

58. David Herst in "The National Energy Plan," undated draft of case study for Harvard's John F. Kennedy School, Cambridge, Massachusetts, in author's possession.

7. Energizing Congress

1. Bill Cable, interview with the author, August 21, 2013.

2. Ari Weiss, interview with the author, June 25, 2015.

3. Ibid.
4. Jimmy Carter, University of Virginia's Miller Center of Public Affairs interview, (November 29, 1982.
5. 1977 CQ Almanac, 721.
6. Pad 14, April 25, 1977.
7. Pad 18, June 14, 1977.
8. Pad 15, April 27, 1977.
9. Pad 17, June 7, 1977.
10. Pad 17, June 8, 1977.
11. Pad 18, June 10, 1977.
12. Les Goldman, interview with the author, July 25, 1991.
13. Pad 18, June 14, 1977.
14. *American Experience.* "Jimmy Carter (Part 2)." Episode 174. Directed by Adriana Bosch. Aired on PBS, November 12, 2002.
15. Pad 19, June 21, 1977.
16. Pad 19, June 27, 1977.
17. Robert Krueger, interview with the author, April 1, 2015.
18. Pad 16, May 23, 1977.
19. Pad 22, July 22, 1977.
20. Quoted in 1977 CQ Almanac, 725, and Katie Hope, "The National Energy Plan: Congressional Action" (unpublished).
21. William Cable, interview with the author, August 21, 2013.
22. Robert Krueger interview, March 31, 2015.
23. 1977 CQ Almanac, 95th Congress, 1st Session . . . 1977, Volume XXXIII, Congressional Quarterly, Inc., Washington, D.C., 724–5.

Chapter 8

1. Gallup poll, Gerhard Peters, The American Presidency Project, University of California, San Diego, cited in Charles M. Blow, "100 Days of Horror," *The New York Times,* April 17, 2017.
2. Pad 40, September 26, 1978; notes incorporated into a case note for the John F. Kennedy School of Government, Harvard University: "The 1977 Energy Plan: M.E.O.W," by Stuart E. Eizenstat.
3. Jimmy Carter, University of Virginia's Miller Center of Public Affairs interview, November 29, 1982.
4. James Schlesinger, interview with the author, April 4, 1989, and University of Virginia's Miller Center of Public Affairs interview, July 19–20, 1984.
5. Russell Long, interview with the author, January 2, 1991.
6. Senator J. Bennett Johnson, interview with the author, September 12, 2013, who recounted Long's remarks.
7. Pad 24, September 19 and September 20, 1977.
8. 1978 CQ Almanac, 639.
9. Les Goldman, interview with the author, July 25, 1991.
10. Pad 25, September 26, 1977.

11. Robert C. Byrd, *The Senate, 1789–1989, Addresses on the History of the United States Senate*, 153–7. For Senator Abourezk quote, see 1977 CQ Almanac, "Carter Energy Bill," xxxiii, October 3, 1977, 736–37, cited in Joseph M. Bessette and Jeffrey Tobin, *Presidency in the Constitutional Order* (New York: Routledge, 2010); and for an excellent overview of the path of the Carter energy bill through Congress, see 1977 CQ Almanac, 708–45.

12. Jimmy Carter, *White House Diary* (New York: Farrar, Straus & Giroux, 2010), 116; Abourezk quote: 1977 CQ Almanac, "Carter Energy Bill, XXXIII, October 3, 1977, 736–7, cited in *Presidency in the Constitutional Order*, by Joseph M. Bessette and Jeffrey Tulis, https://books.google.com/books/about/Presidency_in_the_Constitutional _Order.html?id=AZMsiyZasEMC; for an excellent overview of the path of the Carter energy bill through Congress, see 1977 CQ Almanac 708–45.

13. Al Alm, interview with the author, August 21, 1989.

14. See Richard Corrigan, "The Energy Tax Bill's Long Road from the Senate to Conference," *National Journal*, November 5, 1977, 1716–9.

15. Pad 25, October 6, 1977.

16. Pad 26, October 13, 1977.

17. Pad 26, October 17, 1977; Jimmy Carter, *White House Diary*, October 17, 1977, 120.

18. Pad 26, October 17, 1977.

19. Ibid., October 18, 1977.

20. Pad 16, October 20, 1977.

21. Pad 26, October 25–26, 1977.

22. Pad 25, October 31, 1977.

23. Pad 26, November 1, 1977.

24. Senator J. Bennett Johnston interview, September 12, 2013.

25. Ibid.

26. Charles Curtis, interview with the author, August 24, 2015; James Schlesinger, University of Virginia's Miller Center of Public Affairs interviews, July 19–20, 1984.

27. James Schlesinger interview, March 27, 1989.

28. Pad 30, January 25, 1978.

29. Pad 30, February 7, 1978.

30. Pad 32, March 13, 1978.

31. Pad 32, March 14, 1978.

32. Pad 32 , March 14, 1978 .

33. Pad 32A, April 16, 1978, from 4:30 p.m. to 6:10 p.m. with President Carter, First Lady Rosalynn Carter, Vice President Mondale, Charles Kirbo, Jack Watson, Frank Moore, Jody Powell, Tim Kraft, and author; April 17, 1978, President and White House Staff with the entire Cabinet; and Jimmy Carter, *White House Diary*, 185–8.

34. Pad 32A, April 17, 1978.

35. 1978 CQ Almanac 648, and for an excellent summary of the entire congressional energy debate and action, 637–67, Library of Congress No. 47-41081, Copyright 1979 by Congressional Quarterly, Inc., Washington, D.C.

36. Pad 32A, April 11, 1978.

37. Pad 32A, April 24, 1978.

38. Pad 32A, April 30, 1978.
39. 1978 CQ Almanac, 95th Congress, 2nd Session . . . Vol. XXXIV, 655.

9. Energy and the Dollar at the Bonn Summit

1. Pad 31, February 27, 1978.
2. Walter Mondale, interviews with the author, April 3, 1991, and April 4, 2002.
3. Henry Owen, interview with the author, July 28, 1989.
4. Ibid.
5. Lord Callaghan, interview with the author, September 5, 1991.
6. Richard Cooper, interview with the author, March 9, 1992.
7. Henry Owen interview, July 28, 1989.
8. Ibid.
9. Ibid.
10. Robert D. Putnam and Henning C. Randall, *The Bonn Summit of 1978: How Does International Economic Policy Coordination Actually Work?* Brookings Papers in International Economics, No. 131 (Washington, D.C.: Brookings Institution, 1980), 67.
11. Katherine Schirmer Cochrane, interview with the author, November 20, 1992; Henry Owen interview, July 28, 1989.
12. Henry Owen interview, July 29, 1989.
13. Ibid.
14. Ibid.
15. Chancellor Helmut Schmidt, email responses to author's questions, October 21, 2013.
16. Putnam and Randall, *The Bonn Summit,* 9.
17. Jimmy Carter, interview with the author, June 8, 1992.

10. Into the Pork Barrel, Reluctantly

1. Pad 36, July 19, 1978.
2. Ibid.
3. CQ Almanac 1980, Vol. XXXVI, "Congress Overrides Veto on Oil Import Fee," 227.
4. Katherine Schirmer Cochrane, interview with the author, November 20, 1992.
5. Pad 38, August 17, 1978.
6. Katherine Schirmer Cochrane interview, November 20, 1992.
7. Pad 38, August 17, 1978.
8. Pad 38, August 17, 1978.
9. Frank Moore, interviews with the author, June 29, 2013, and October 2, 2014.
10. Ari Weiss, interview with the author, June 25, 2015.
11. Ibid.
12. Pad 38, August 25, 1978.
13. William Cable, interview with the author, August 21, 2013.
14. Pad 39, September 20, 1978.
15. Dan Tate, interview with the author, April 17, 2013; Pad 40, September 22, 1978.
16. James Schlesinger, University of Virginia's Miller Center of Public Affairs interview, July 19–20, 1984.

17. Pad 38, August 31, 1978.

18. Ibid.

19. 1978 CQ Almanac, 658, describing a regular 8:30 a.m. White House meeting beginning in mid-August, with Hamilton Jordan, Anne Wexler, top officials from the Department of Energy, Gail Harrison and William Smith of the Vice President's staff, Dan Tate, chief White House Senate lobbyist and William Cable, to White House lobbyist for the House of Representatives.

20. Pad 39, September 8, 1978.

21. James Schlesinger, University of Virginia's Miller Center of Public Affairs interview, July 19–20, 1994.

22. 1978 CQ Almanac, 655.

23. Pad 39, September 9, 1978.

24. Pad 39, September 11, 1978.

25. Pad 39, September 12, 1978.

26. Ibid.

27. Ibid.

28. Pad 39, September 13, 1978.

29. Pad 39, September 18, 1978.

30. Pad 40, September 22, 1978.

31. Pad 39, September 21, 1978.

32. Pad 39, September 20, 1978.

33. Pad 39, September 21, 1978.

34. Ibid.

35. Pad 40, September 28, 1978.

36. Pad 40, October 3, 1978.

37. Ibid.

38. 1978 CQ Almanac, 661.

39. James Schlesinger, University of Virginia's Miller Center of Public Affairs interview, July 19–20, 1984.

40. Donald Lubick, interview with the author, March 29, 2015.

41. Pad 40, October 6, 1978.

42. Pad 40, September 21, 1978; Robert Shapiro, interview with the author, June 16, 2015.

43. 1978 CQ Almanac, 662.

44. Jimmy Carter, *White House Diary*, 252.

45. Jimmy Carter, *White House Diary*, 252.

46. President Carter's Signing Statement, Public Papers of the Presidents II, November 9, 1978. 1978–1985.

47. Stuart Eizenstat Memorandum to President Carter, Carter Presidential Library, January 3, 1979.

48. James Schlesinger, interview with the author, April 4, 1989.

49. Katherine Schirmer Cochrane interview, November 20, 1992.

50. Pad 45, January 8, 1979.

51. *American Experience.* "Jimmy Carter (Part 2)." Episode 174. Directed by Adriana Bosch. Aired on PBS, November 12, 2002.

52. James Schlesinger interview, April 4, 1989.
53. Katherine Schirmer Cochrane interview, November 20, 1992.
54. Ibid.
55. 1979 CQ Almanac, 610.
56. 1980 CQ Almanac, "Carter and Congress: Strangers to the End," 3–9, Cqpress.com /Cqalmanac/Document.Php? Id=Cqa 180-1174637.
57. 1979 CQ Almanac, 610.
58. Robert Stobaugh and Daniel Yergin, *Energy Future* (Cambridge, MA: Harvard Business School, 1979); see also, Alan Webber, "Jimmy Carter: The Statesman as CEO," *Harvard Business Review,* 1988.
59. Jimmy Carter, interview with the author, June 4, 1991.

PART III

11. An Early Interest

1. Jimmy Carter interview, September 27, 2013; https://freedomfightersactualizetruths .wordpress.com/2014/08/08/jimmy-carter/.
2. Jimmy Carter, *Our Endangered Values* (New York: Simon & Schuster, 2005), 177.
3. Jimmy Carter, "The Environment Message to the Congress," May 23, 1977. Online by Gerhard Peters and John T. Woolley, The American Presidency Project, http://www .presidency.ucsb.edu/ws/?pid=7561. Public Papers of the Presidents, Jimmy Carter, 1977, Book I, United States Government Printing Office, Washington, D.C., 967–86.
4. William Drayton, interview with the author, April 9, 1993; William Drayton, "Thinking Ahead," *Harvard Business Review,* 1981.
5. Jimmy Carter, *Keeping Faith,* 581–2. www.ontheissues.org/Celeb/Jimmy_Carter _Environment.htm.
6. "Global 2000 Study Statement on the Report to the President," July 24, 1980, Public Papers of the Presidents, III, Jimmy Carter, 1980–1981, 1415–6. U.S. Government Printing Office, 1982.
7. Rachel Carson, *Silent Spring,* Introduction by Vice President Al Gore (Boston: Houghton Mifflin, 1994).
8. Kathy Fletcher, interviews with the author, September 12, 1991, November 20, 1991, and August 13, 2013; Gus Speth, interview with the author, November 21, 1991.
9. www.usbr.gov/history/HistoryofLargeDams/LargeFederalDams.pdf, 401.
10. www.epa.gov/aboutepa/epa-history-earth-day; Brent Blackwelder, interviews with the author, January 24, 1992, and September 2, 2015; Douglas Costle, interview with the author, October 14, 1992; Eliot Cutler, April 24, 2015, www2.epa.gov/aboutepa /douglas-m-costly-oral-history-interview.
11. Jimmy Carter, interview with the author, September 27, 2013.
12. Jimmy Carter, Foreword, Fred Brown and Sherri M. L. Smith, *The Flint River: A Recreational Guidebook to the Flint River (Georgia) and Environs* (Pleasanton, CA: CI Publishing, 2001).
13. Ibid.

12. The Water Wars

1. Jimmy Carter, Foreword, Fred Brown and Sherri M. L. Smith, *The Flint River: A Recreational Guidebook to the Flint River (Georgia) and Environs* (Pleasanton, CA: CI Publishing, 2001).

2. The Wilderness Statement, Post-Convention No. 178; Message to the Democratic Platform Committee, June 16, 1976, President Carter's Campaign Promises, Commerce Clearing House, Inc., 13–14.

3. Brent Blackwelder, interview with the author, September 2, 2015.

4. Cecil Andrus, interview with the author, March 17, 1992.

5. Margot Hornblower, "A New Breed Shakes Old Order at Interior," *The Washington Post*, April 3, 1977.

6. Don Crabill, interview with the author, October 1, 1991.

7. www.nytimes.com/1986/10/04/us/waterways-plan-nears-agreement.html.

8. Jimmy Carter, Foreword to *The Flint River.*

9. Don Crabill interview, October 1, 1991.

10. Guy Martin, interview with the author, April 15, 1992.

11. Pad 1, December 9, 1976.

12. Bowman Cutter, interview with the author, September 15, 1989.

13. S. A. Frisch and S. Q. Kelly, *Jimmy Carter and the Water Wars: Presidential Influence and the Politics of Pork* (Amherst, NY: Cambria Press, 2008), 51–2.

14. James Free, interviews with the author, May 9, 2013, and December 13, 2013; Frisch and Kelly, *Jimmy Carter and the Water Wars,* citing at page 52, footnote 29; Mark Reisner, *Cadillac Desert: The American West and Its Disappearing Water* (New York: Penguin Press, 1993), 319–20.

15. Stuart Eizenstat memorandum to President Carter, March 21, 1977, in author's possession and Carter Presidential Library.

16. Pad 9, February 14, 1977; Cecil Andrus memorandum to President Carter, February 14, 1977.

17. Robert C. Byrd, *The Senate, 1789–1989, Addresses on the History of the United States Senate* (United States Government Printing Office, 1989), 716–7.

18. Frisch and Kelly, *Jimmy Carter and the Water Wars,* 69.

19. Pad 8, February 15, 1977.

20. Memorandum to the President from Stuart Eizenstat, Jim McIntyre, Eliot Cutler, Bo Cutter, February 16, 1977, in author's possession and Carter Presidential Library.

21. Martin Tolchin, "Byrd Tells Carter Senate Is Angered By Unilateral Acts," *The New York Times*, March 12, 1977.

22. Frank Moore quoted in Frisch and Kelly, *Jimmy Carter and the Water Wars,* 48; also Frank Moore, interviews with the author, February 1, 1993, July 27, 1993, and May 8, 2013; Dan Tate, interviews with the author, November 12, 1991, and April 17, 2013.

23. Pad 8, February 17, 1977.

24. Kathy Fletcher, interviews with the author, November 20, 1991, September 12, 1991, and August 12, 2013.

25. Cecil Andrus interview, March 17, 1992.

26. Pad 8, February 17, 1977.

27. Cecil Andrus interview, March 17, 1992.

28. *The New York Times* News Service, February 21, 1978, https://news.google.com/newspapers ?nid=2199&dat=19780221&id=YU4yAAAAIBAJ&sjid=ZuYFAAAAIBAJ&pg =5311,2801580&hl=en.

29. Public Papers of the Presidents, Jimmy Carter 1977, Vol. I, "Water Resource Projects Message to Congress," February 21, 1977, 207–8.

30. Don Crabill interview, October 1, 1991.

31. Bob Edgar, interview with the author, June 20, 2013.

32. Gaylord Shaw and Paul E. Steiger, "Carter Will Ask Hill to Halt Aid to 18 Major Water Projects," *The Washington Post,* February 18, 1977.

33. Pad 16, May 23, 1977. President Carter meeting with Congressmen Jim Wright (House Majority Leader), Bizz Johnson, and Tom Bevill.

34. Jim Free, interview with the author, May 9, 2013.

35. www.washingtonpost.com/wp-dyn/articles/A14471-2005Mar30.html?nav=E8.

36. Carter Message to Congress, www.presidency.ucsb.edu/ws/?pid=6799; http://usgovinfo .about.com/od/federalbudgetprocess/a/Budget-Deficit-History.htm; Water Resource Projects, Statement Announcing Administration Decisions, April 18, 1977, Public Papers of the Presidents, Jimmy Carter 1977, Book I, 651–4.

37. Guy Martin interview, April 16, 1992.

38. Don Crabill interview, October 10, 1991.

39. Pad 10, March 11, 1977.

40. Pad 10, March 15, 1977.

41. Pad 11, March 21, 1977.

42. Jim Free interviews, December 12, 1991, September 23, 1992, May 9, 2013, and October 18, 2013.

43. Pad 12, March 24, 1977.

44. Frisch and Kelly, *Jimmy Carter and the Water Wars,* 70.

45. Ibid.

46. Martin Tolchin, "Byrd Tells Carter Senate is Angered by Unilateral Acts," *The New York Times,* March 12, 1977.

47. Associated Press, "2 Nominated for Interior," *The Washington Post,* March 11, 1977, https://news.google.com/newspapers?nid=1314&dat=19770311&id=1TtOAA AAIBAJ&sjid=su0DAAAAIBAJ&pg=4655,4125798&hl=en.

48. Pad 14, April 13, 1977.

49. David Rubenstein, interview with the author, February 8, 2014.

50. Pad 15, May 2, 1977.

51. Jim Free interviews, May 9, 2013, and October 13, 2013; Frank Moore interview, May 8, 2013.

52. Butler Derrick, interview with the author, April 22, 2013.

53. Ibid.

54. Bob Edgar interview, April 18, 2013, https://library.cqpress.com/cqalmanac/document .php?id=cqal77-1203898; 1977 CQ Almanac, 113.

55. Butler Derrick interview, April 22, 2013.

56. David Rubenstein interviews with the author, December 11, 1992, and February 8, 2014.
57. The Daily Diary of the President, July 15, 1977, GPO 1977, O-228-197, 3, www.jimmy carterlibrary.gov/assets/documents/diary/1977.
58. Frank Moore interview, May 8, 2013.
59. Butler Derrick interview, April 22, 2013.
60. Frank Moore interview, May 8, 2013.
61. Jim Free interviews, May 9, 2013, and October 13, 2013.
62. Walter Pincus, "Panel Drops 9 Projects on Hit List," *The Washington Post,* July 21, 1977.
63. Ibid.
64. Jim Free interview, May 9, 2013.
65. Bob Edgar, interviews with the author, January 13, 1992, and April 18, 2013.
66. Frank Moore interview, May 8, 2013.
67. Jim Free interview, October 18, 2013.
68. Jimmy Carter, *White House Diary,* 199.
69. Butler Derrick interview, April 22, 2013.
70. Jimmy Carter, *White House Diary,* 23.
71. Daniel McCool, *Command of the Waters* (Berkeley: University of California Press, 1987), 206.
72. Brent Blackwelder interview, September 2, 2015.
73. Carter Presidential Library, Office of Congressional Liaison, Box 45, Public Works Appropriations; and Gus Speth (chairman of the Council of Environmental Quality), interview with the author, November 21, 1991.
74. Jimmy Carter, Foreword to *The Flint River.*

13. Alaska Forever Wild, Despite Its Senators

1. Jimmy Carter, *White House Diary* (New York: Farrar, Straus & Giroux, 2010), 253.
2. Cecil Andrus memorandum to President Carter, November 28, 1978, in author's possession with president's notation, and Carter Presidential Library.
3. Stuart Eizenstat, Cecil Andrus, and Bob Bergland memorandum to President Carter, November 29, 1978, with president's notation, in author's possession.
4. Carter, Designation of National Monuments in Alaska, Statement by the President, December 1, 1978, Public Papers of the Presidents, Jimmy Carter, Book II, 1978, 2111–2.
5. Cecil Andrus interview, March 17, 1992.
6. Jimmy Carter, *White House Diary,* 334.
7. Katherine Fletcher, conversation with author, May 2, 2016.
8. Oral History with Frank Moore, Jimmy Carter Library, July 30–31, 46.
9. Jimmy Carter, Remarks on Signing Alaska National Interest Lands Conservation Act, Public Papers of the Presidents, Jimmy Carter, Book III, 1980–1981, 2756–62.Sources for Alaska Land Act section: www.akhistorycourse.org/articles/article.php?artID=256; www.yosemite.ca.us/john_muir_writings/travels_in_alaska; John Muir: www.alaskacenters.gov/history-public-lands.cfm.
10. Cecil Andrus interview, March 17, 1992.
11. Erica Goode, "A Wrenching Choice for Alaska Towns in the Path of Climate Change," *The New York Times,* November 29, 2016.

12. Public Papers of the Presidents, Jimmy Carter, 1980–1981, Vol. III, "Jimmy Carter's Farewell Address to the Nation," January 14, 1981, 2889–93.

PART IV

14. The Great Stagflation

1. Alan Blinder, interview with the author, June 20, 2015.
2. Alan Blinder interview, June 20, 2015.
3. Paul Samuelson, interview with the author, January 16, 1992; Alan Greenspan, interview with the author, February 27, 2014.
4. "Inflation United States 1975," Worldwide Inflation Data, www.inflation.eu/inflation-rates/united-states/historic-inflation/cpi-inflation-united-states-1975.aspx.
5. Bureau of Labor Statistics data; Federal Reserve Economic Data, Total Nonfarm Employment.
6. Ray Marshall, *Unheard Voices: Labor and Economic Policy in a Competitive World* (New York: Basic Books, 1987), 51.
7. Robert Samuelson interview, May 16, 2015; Robert Samuelson, *The Great Inflation and Its Aftermath* (New York: Random House, 2008).
8. Jimmy Carter, Economic Position Paper, April 22, 1976; *Businessweek* interview, May 3, 1976; Jimmy Carter, Cities Speech April 1, 1976; Jimmy Carter, Democratic Platform Presentation, June 16, 1976; Jimmy Carter, Economic Press Briefing, New York City, July 28, 1976; Jimmy Carter on Economic Issues, Post-Convention No. 133, in "President Carter's Campaign Promises," Commerce Clearing House, Inc., Chicago, June 1977.
9. Joseph Pechman, interview with the author, August 3, 1989.
10. Pad 2, December 16, 1976.
11. Pad 7, January 31, 1977.
12. Pad 13, April 8, 1977.
13. Pad 33A, May 15, 1978; Juanita Kreps, interview with the author, December 10, 1979.
14. L. William Seidman, *Full Faith and Credit* (New York: Times Books, 1993), Chapter 2.
15. Barry Bosworth, interview with the author, August 17, 1990.
16. Charles Schultze, interview with the author, June 19, 1989.
17. Pad 1, December 1, 1976.
18. Lyle Gramley, interview with the author, July 25, 1989; Fred Bergsten, interview with the author, August 19, 1991.
19. Paul Samuelson interview, January 16, 1992.
20. Pad 1, December 8–9, 1976.
21. Alan Greenspan, interview with the author, February 27, 2014.
22. Pad 1, December 9, 1976.
23. Pad 4, January 7, 1977.
24. Pad 4, January 7, 1977.
25. Pad 7, February 3, 1977.
26. Jimmy Carter Economic Recovery Program—Message to the Congress, January 31,

1977, Public Papers of the Presidents, Jimmy Carter, 1977, Book I, 47–55. Also, The American Presidency Project, www.presidency.ucsb.edu/ws?pid=7344.

27. Pad 8, February 20, 1977.

28. Pad 8, February 20, 1977.

29. McCracken quoted in Carl W. Bivens, *Jimmy Carter's Economy: Policy in an Age of Limits* (Chapel Hill: University of North Carolina Press, 2002), 85.

30. Lane Kirkland, interview with the author, December 12, 1989.

31. Alan Greenspan Interview, October 18, 2013.

32. Pad 7, February 7, 1977.

33. Alan Ehrenhalt, CQ Almanac, September 10, 1977.

34. Pad 13, April 5, 1977.

35. Pad 13, April 6, 1977.

36. Pad 13, April 11–12, 1977.

37. Pad 14, April 13, 1977.

38. Ibid.

39. Charles Schultze interview, June 19, 1989.

40. Public Papers of the Presidents, Jimmy Carter, 1977, Vol. I, "Economic Stimulus Package Remarks and a Question-and-Answer Session on the Tax Rebate and Business Tax Credit Proposals," April 14, 1977, 618–22, and "Questions and Answers with Publishers, Editors and Broadcasters," April 15, 1977, 643–51.

41. Pad 18, June 16, 1977.

42. Pad 10, March 10, 1977; Pad 11, March 21, 1977; Pad 12, March 28, 1977; Pad 12, March 31, 1977; Pad 13, March 5, 1977.

43. Pad 12, March 28, 1977.

44. Pad 12, March 31, 1977.

45. Pad 13, April 4, 1977.

46. Pad 13, April 6, 1977.

47. Ibid.

48. Ibid.

49. Pad 13, April 6, 1977.

50. Bill Johnston, discussion and email with the author, July 9, 2017.

51. Pad 12, March 31, 1977.

52. Lawrence Malkin, "A Practical Politician at the Fed," *Fortune,* May 1971, 260. Pad 12, March 31, 1977.

53. Pad 13, April 8, 1977.

54. Jimmy Carter, "Anti-Inflation Program Statement Outlining Administration Actions," April 15, 1977, The American Presidency Project, UCSB; Anti-Inflation Program. Statement Outlining Administration Actions, Public Papers of the Presidents, Jimmy Carter, Book I, 1977, 622–9.

55. Edward Cowan, "A Cautious Administration and the Price-Wage Spiral," *The New York Times,* July 12, 1977.

56. Pad 26, October 14, 1977.

57. Pad 19, June 20, 1977.

58. Pad 20, June 29, 1977.

59. Pad 22, July 23, 25, 1977.

60. Pad 26, October 13, 1977.

61. Pad 24, September 23, 1977.

62. Pad 26, October 19, 1977.

63. Pad 26, October 20, 1977.

64. Pad 26, October 27, 1977.

65. Pad 28, December 15, 1977.

66. Pad 32A, March 21, April 21, May 2, 1978.

67. Pad 33A, May 11, 1978.

68. Pad 23, August 9, 1977.

69. Pad 28, December 17, 1977.

70. Pad 27, December 9, 1977.

71. "State of the Union Address," History, Art & Archives, United States House of Representatives, http://history.house.gov/Institution/SOTU/State-of-the-Union/.

72. Public Papers of the Presidents, Jimmy Carter, 1978, Vol. 1, January 19, 1978, 90–98, with detailed written message, 98–123.

73. Pad 32A, April 11, 1978; Public Papers of the Presidents, Jimmy Carter, 1978, Vol. 1, April 11, 1978, 721–7.

74. Robert Strauss, interview with the author, October 27, 1989.

75. Pad 33A, May 10, 1978.

76. Robert Strauss interview, October 27, 1989.

77. Charles Schultze interview, June 19, 1989.

78. Pad 33A, May 16, 1978.

79. Pad 33A, May 8, 10, 16, 1978; Pad 34, June 21, 1978; Pad 35, June 22, 1978.

80. Pad 35, July 10, 1978.

81. Pad 36, July 23, 1978.

82. Pad 37, August 1, 1978.

83. Pad 38, August 10, 1978.

84. Pad 27, EPG Meeting, November 10, 1977.

85. Pad 24, September 23, 1977.

86. Pad 23, August 4, 1977.

87. Pad 17, June 4, 1977.

88. Public Papers of the Presidents, Jimmy Carter, 1978, Vol. I, January 20, 1978, 158, 160, 184; Edward R. Kantowicz, "The Limits of Incrementalism: Carter's Efforts at Tax Reform," *Journal of Policy Analysis and Management*, vol. 4, no. 2, 1985, 217–23, www.jstor.org/stable/3324625.

89. Pad 41, October 14, 1978.

90. Charles Schultze interview, June 19, 1989.

91. Pad 34, June 21, 1978.

92. Russell Long, interview with the author, January 1, 1991.

93. Robert Kuttner, "Final Passage of the Revenue Act of 1978," *Congressional Record*, 95th Congress, 2nd Session, October 14, 1978, 38638, cited in Edward R. Kantowicz, "The Limits of Incrementalism: Carter's Efforts at Tax Reform," *Journal of Policy Analysis and Management*, vol. 4, no. 2, 1985, 228, www.jstor.org/stable/3324625; 1978 CQ Almanac, "Carter's Reform," 245.

94. Pad 41, October 27, 1978; Larry O'Brien, interview with the author, May 14, 1992.
95. Pad 41, October 18, 1978.
96. Pad 41, October 19, 1978.
97. Pad 41, October 19, 1978.
98. Pad 40, October 6, 1978.
99. Pad 35, June 28, 1978.
100. Pad 36, July 22, 1978.
101. Pad 39, September 7, 8, 1978.
102. Pad 41, October 16, 1978; Robert Strauss interview, October 27, 1989.
103. Pad 41, October 19, 1978; Alfred Kahn interviews, August 26, 1989, and October 24, 1989.
104. Pad 41, October 23, 1978.
105. Public Papers of the Presidents, Jimmy Carter, 1978, Vol. II, "Anti-Inflation Program" with "White House Fact Sheet on Details of the Program," October 24, 1978, 1839–48.
106. Pad 42, November 16, 1978.
107. Pad 42, November 20, 1978.
108. Alfred Kahn, interview with the author, October 24, 1989; Simon Lazarus, interview with the author, January 25, 2016.
109. Joshua Gotbaum, interview with the author, January 29, 2016.
110. Barry Bosworth interview, August 17, 1990.
111. Pad 45, February 22, 1978.
112. Larry Greenberg, "35th Anniversary of Jimmy Carter's Anti-Inflation Speech to the American People," October 24, 2013, http://currencythoughts.com/2013/10/24/35th-anniversary-of-jimmy-carters-anti-inflation-speech-to-the-American-people/.
113. Paul Volcker, *Changing Fortunes* (New York: Three Rivers Press, 1993), 149–50.
114. Pad 22, July 25, 1977.
115. Samuel Rosenberg, *American Economic Development Since 1945: Growth, Decline, and Rejuvenation* (New York: Palgrave, 2003), 202; Hobart Rowen, "Dollar Rescue: Too Successful?" *The Washington Post,* May 20, 1979.
116. Paul Volcker, *Changing Fortunes,* 149.
117. Pad 27, December 4, 1977.
118. Pad 28, December 28, 1977.
119. Pad 28, January 4, 1978.
120. Pad 38, August 15, 1978.
121. Ibid.
122. Pad 41, October 26, 1978.
123. Pad 41, October 26, 1978; see Pad 41, October 25, 1978, for call from Blumenthal.
124. Pad 41, October 27, 1978.
125. Charles Schultze, University of Virginia's Miller Center of Public Affairs interview, January 8, 1992.
126. Pad 41, October 28, 1978, for discussion of package; Fred Bergsten interview, August 19, 1991; Bill Miller, interview with the author, July 28, 1989.
127. Bill Neikirk, "Save Dollar Program Charted in Secrecy at White House," *Chicago Tribune,* November 5, 1978.

128. Paul Volcker, *Changing Fortunes,* 158.
129. Robert D. Putnam and Henning C. Randall, *The Bonn Summit,* 82.
130. Pad 41, November 1, 1978, Blumenthal call; Pad 41, November 3, 1978, Warner call, "and our Ambassador to Switzerland, Marvin Warner, told me the president's dollar rescue program had been 'met with ecstasy' throughout Europe."
131. Paul Volcker, *Changing Fortunes,* 151.
132. Pad 41, November 2, 1978.
133. Pad 54, May 9, 1979.
134. Pad 45, January 2, 1979.
135. Pad 44, December 19, 1978.
136. Pad 48, February 20, 22, 1979.
137. Pad 54, May 10, 1979.
138. W. Michael Blumenthal, *From Exile to Washington* (New York: Overlook Press, 2015), 314–5.
139. William L. Silber, "How Volcker Launched his Attack on Inflation," *Bloomberg News,* August 20, 2012.
140. Lawrence Lindsay, interview with the author, May 24, 1993.
141. Charles Schultze interview, June 19, 1989.
142. Bill Miller interview, July 28, 1989.
143. Richard Moe interviews, February 14, 2014, and June 18, 2017.
144. Paul Volcker interviews, July 31, 1989, and November 11, 2013.
145. Ibid.
146. Bill Miller interview, July 28, 1989.
147. Paul Volcker interview, July 31, 1989.
148. William L. Silber, "How Volcker Launched His Attack on Inflation," *Bloomberg News,* August 20, 2012; William L. Silber, *Volcker: The Triumph of Persistence* (New York: Bloomsbury, 2012).
149. Jimmy Carter interviews, October 25, 1991, and September 27, 2013.
150. Jimmy Carter Miller Center interview, July 31, 1989.
151. Ibid.
152. Bill Miller interview, July 28, 1989.
153. William L. Silber, *Volcker: The Triumph of Persistence,* 164.
154. Paul Volcker interview, November 11, 2013; Fred Schultz, interview with the author, February 1, 1993.
155. Bill Miller interview, July 28, 1989.
156. Public Papers of the Presidents, Jimmy Carter, 1979, Vol. II, August 6, 1979, 1462.
157. Paul Volcker, *Changing Fortunes,* 164.
158. Public Papers of the Presidents, Jimmy Carter, 1979, Vol. II, August 7, 1979, "Volcker Remarks at Swearing-In," August 6, 1979, 1405.
159. Fred Schultz, interview with the author, February 1, 1993.
160. Lane Kirkland interview, December 19, 1989.
161. Charles Schultze interview, June 19, 1989.
162. Paul Volcker interviews, July 31, 1989, and November 11, 2013.
163. Robert Samuelson interview by author, May 16, 2016.

164. Paul Volcker interviews, July 31, 1989, and November 11, 2013.

165. William L. Silber, *Volcker: The Triumph of Persistence,* 165; William L. Silber, "How Volcker Created a Gold Standard Without Gold," *Bloomberg News,* August 21, 2012.

166. Paul Volcker interviews, July 31, 1989, and November 11, 2013.

167. Charles Schultze interview, January 8, 1992.

168. Fred Schultz interview, February 1, 1993.

169. William L. Silber, *Volcker:* Paul Volcker, *The Triumph of Persistence,* 166.

170. Paul Volcker, interview, November 11, 2013.

171. Steve Axilrod, October 26, 1990.

172. Fred Schultze interview, June 19, 1989; Lyle Gramley, interview with author, July 25, 1989; Bill Miller interview, July 28, 1979.

173. Robert Samuelson interview, May 16, 2016.

174. Paul Volcker interview, November 11, 2013.

175. Bill Medley, "Volcker's Announcement of Anti-Inflation Measures," Federal Reserve History, October 1979.

176. William L. Silber, *Volcker: The Triumph of Persistence,* 168–9; Volcker interview, July 31, 1989.

177. William L. Silber, "How Volcker Created a Gold Standard Without Gold."

178. Volcker interviews, July 31, 1989, and November 11, 2013.

179. William L. Silber, "How Volcker Created a Gold Standard Without Gold."

180. Steve Axilrod interview, October 26, 1990.

181. Paul Volcker interviews, July 31, 1989, and November 11, 2013.

182. Paul Volcker conversation with Lawrence Malkin, April 1985.

183. Paul Volcker interviews, July 31, 1989, and November 11, 2013.

184. Pad 81, April 1, 1980; Paul Volcker interview, November 11, 2013.

185. Paul Volcker interview, November 11, 2013.

186. Pad 81, April 8, 1980.

187. Pad 84, May 7, 1980.

188. Public Papers of the Presidents, Jimmy Carter, 1980–81, Vol. I, March 14, 1980, Anti-Inflation Program Remarks Announcing the Administration's Program, 482–3.

189. Alfred Kahn interview, August 26, 1989.

190. Paul Volcker interview, November 11, 2013.

191. Paul Volcker interview, July 31, 1989.

192. Ibid.

193. Charles Schultze interview, June 19, 1989.

194. Alfred Kahn interview, October 11, 1981.

195. Charles Schultze interviews, June 19, 1989, and May 17, 2007.

196. Paul Volcker interview, November 11, 2013; Lyle Gramley interview, July 25, 1989.

197. Paul Volcker interviews, July 31, 1989, and November 11, 2013.

198. Pad 41, November 7, 1978.

199. Bill Miller interview, July 28, 1989.

200. Paul Volcker interview, November 11, 2013; Gordon Stewart exit interview, February 13, 1981; Bill Miller interview, July 28, 1989.

201. Paul Volcker interview, July 31, 1989.

202. Alfred Kahn interview, August 28, 1989.

203. John Dunlop, interview with the author, November 7, 1998.

204. Pad 102, December 17, 1980.

205. Jeffrey H. Anderson, "Economic Growth by President," Hudson Institute, Washington, D.C., August 8, 2016, www.hudson.org/research/12714-economic-growth-by -president, Politicsthatwork.com, BEA, March 29, 2015.

206. Kimberly Amadeo, "U.S. Debt by President: by Dollar and Percent," *The Balance*, April 21, 2016, updated November 2, 2017, www.thebalance.com.

207. Joseph Pechman interview, August 3, 1989.

208. Charles Schultze interview, June 19, 1989.

209. Charles Schultze, interviews with author, June 19, 1989, and May 17, 2007; Schultze, Miller Center interview, January 8, 1992.

210. Paul Volcker interview, July 31, 1989.

15. The Consumer Populist

1. Joshua Gotbaum, interview with the author, January 28, 2016.

2. Orin Kramer, interview with the author, October 2, 2013.

3. Staggers Rail Act of 1980, President Carter's Statement of Signing S. 1946 into law, October 14, 1980, The American Presidency Project, www.presidency.ucsb.edu/us /?pid-45284: Public Papers of the Presidents, Jimmy Carter, 1980–1981, Book III, 2229–31.

4. Alan Greenspan, Testimony before the House Committee on Oversight and Government Reform, One Hundred Tenth Congress, Second Session, Serial No. 110-209, October 23, 2008, http://www.gpoaccess.gov/congress/index.html.

5. Stephen Breyer, interview with the author, November 30, 1992; Mary Schuman Boies, interview with the author, October 16, 2015.

6. Daniel Yergin, "Markets Run into Skepticism—and Regulators," *The Wall Street Journal*, July 18, 2016; Alfred Kahn, interviews with the author, August 26, 1989, and October 24, 1989.

7. CAB v. Moss, 139 U.S. Ap Dec 150, 430 F, 2d 891, 1970.

8. Stephen Breyer interview, November 30, 1992.

9. Edward Kennedy, interview with the author, September 11, 1992.

10. Stephen Breyer, "Airline Deregulation Revisited," *Businessweek*, January 20, 2011.

11. Mary Schuman Boies, interviews with the author, July 25, 1992, and October 16, 2015.

12. Simon Lazarus interview by Emily Soapes, November 24, 1980; email to author, January 25, 2016.

13. Stephen Breyer interview, November 30, 1992; Alfred Kahn interview, August 26, 1989.

14. The Presidential Campaign of 1976, Jimmy Carter 855 (1978); and Andrew Downer Crain, "Ford, Carter, and Deregulation in the 1970s," *Telecomm & High Tech L.* vol. 5, 413–48 (2007); for an excellent discussion of airline and transportation deregulation in the Carter Administration, "Regulatory Reform in the Airline Industry," Carter campaign document, October 30, 1976, published in *Jimmy Carter Campaign Promises* (Chicago, CCH Publishing, 1977).

15. Alfred Kahn interviews, August 26, 1989, and October 24, 1989.

16. Mary Schuman Boies interviews, July 15, 1992, and October 16, 2015.

17. Alfred Kahn interviews, August 26, 1989, and October 24, 1989.

18. Pad 9, March 2, 1977.

19. Pad 9, February 21, 23 and March 2, 1977; Pad 31, February 23, 1978; Pad 32, April 17, 1978.

20. Simon Lazarus, conversation and email to the author, January 25, 2016.

21. Simon Lazarus, conversation and email to the author, January 25, 2016.

22. Pad 10, March 10, 1977; Pad 11, March 18, 1977.

23. Pad 12, March 31, 1977.

24. Pad 13, April 9, 1977.

25. Pad 14, April 22, 1977; Pad 15, May 11, 1977.

26. John Robson, interview with the author, October 20, 1992.

27. Alfred Kahn interviews, August 26, 1989, and October 24, 1989.

28. Simon Lazarus, email to author, January 25, 2016.

29. Mary Schuman Boies interviews, July 15, 1992, and October 16, 2015.

30. Public Papers of the Presidents, Jimmy Carter, 1977, Vol. I, March 4, 1977, 277–8.

31. Mary Schuman Boies interviews, July 15, 1992, and October 16, 2015.

32. Pad 33A, May 8, 1977.

33. Mary Schuman Boies interviews, July 15, 1992, and October 16, 2015.

34. Public Paper of the Presidents, Jimmy Carter, 1978, Vol. II, October 24, 1978, 1837–9.

35. Stephanie Rosenblum, "The Incredible Shrinking Airplane Seat," *The New York Times,* February 29, 2016.

36. William Shughart, "Airline Deregulation Act of 1978," *The Beacon*, October 24, 2014.

37. "Jet Age: 1958–Today," *Delta Air Transport Heritage Museum Magazine,* 2007.

38. Airlines for America, Monthly Passenger and Cargo Yield, 2015.

39. Ibid.

40. Stephen Breyer, "Airline Deregulation, Revisited," *Businessweek,* January 20, 2011; Mary Schuman Boies interviews, July 15, 1992, and October 16, 2015.

41. GAO study cited in John E. Robson, "Airline Deregulation: Twenty Years of Success and Counting," *Regulation Magazine,* Spring 1996.

42. For 2016 employment figures, see www.transtats.bts.gov/employment; for 1998 employment figures, see John Robson, "Airline Deregulation: Twenty Years of Success and Counting," *Regulation Magazine,* 19.

43. Alfred Kahn interviews, August 26, 1989, and October 26, 1989.

44. Ibid.

45. Micah Maidenberg, "How Low-Cost Airlines Alter the Economics of Flying," *The New York Times,* September 1, 2017.

46. Stephen Breyer interview, November 29, 1992.

47. Public Papers of the Presidents, Jimmy Carter, 1979, Vol. I, March 23, 1979, 459–61.

48. Jerry Ellig, "Keeping Rail Deregulation on Track," *RealClearPolicy,* July 20, 2015; Clifford Winston, "The Success of the Staggers Rail Act of 1980," AEI-Brookings Joint Center, October 2005; "The Impact of the Staggers Rail Act of 1980," Association of American Railroads, Washington, D.C., 2011.

49. Pad 42, November 25, 1978; Pad 45, January 10, 1979.

50. Pad 43, November 27, 1978.

51. Pad 44, December 13, 1978.

52. Public Papers of the Presidents, Jimmy Carter, 1979, Vol. I, June 21, 1979, "President's Remarks," 1114–7, "Message to Congress," 1117–25.

53. Pad 45, January 3, 1979.

54. Andrew Downer Crain, "Ford, Carter, and Deregulation in the 1970s," Telecomm & High Tech, vol. 8, 413–48.

55. Thomas Gale Moore, "Trucking Deregulation," *Concise Encyclopedia of Economics,* Liberty Fund, 2002; Stephen Morrison and Clifford Winston, "Regulatory Reform of U.S. Intercity Transportation," *Essays in Transportation Economics and Policy,* Brookings, 477, eds. Jose Gomez-Ibanez, William Tye, and Clifford Winston, 1999.

56. Diane S. Owen, Federal Trade Commission, Bureau of Economics, Deregulation in the Trucking Industry, 1988, cited in "Trucking Deregulation in the United States," submission by the United States to the Ibero-American Competition Forum, September, 2007; Thomas Gale Moore, "Trucking Deregulation," *Concise Encyclopedia of Economics,* 2002, Liberty Fund.

57. Richard Beilock and James Freeman, "Deregulated Motor Carrier Service to Small Communities," *Transportation Journal* (Summer 1984), cited in Ibero-American; "Transportation Deregulation and Safety," Conference Proceedings, June 23–25, 1987, sponsored by the Air Transport Association of America, American Airlines, Inc., American Trucking Associations Foundation, Inc., ENO Foundation, International Brotherhood of Teamsters, Chauffeurs, Warehousemen and Helpers of America, Motor Vehicle Manufacturers Association, United Airlines, Inc., U. Department of Transportation; joint study by the California Public Utilities Commission and the California Highway Patrol; and a 1987 study by Weinstein and Gross of Southern Methodist University, cited on 7 of Ibero-American.

58. Nancy L. Rose, "Labor Rent Sharing and Regulation: Evidence from the Trucking Industry," 95 *Journal of Political Economy,* 1146-78 (1987), cited in Ibero-American Competition Forum.

59. Martha Derthick and Paul Quirk, *The Politics of Deregulation* (Washington, D.C.: Brookings Institution Press, 1985); Thomas Gale Moore, "Rail and Truck Reform: The Record So Far," *Regulation Magazine,* November/December 1988; Organization for Economic Cooperation and Development, International Conference, "Road Transport Deregulation: Experience, Evaluation, Research," November 1988; Dorothy Robyn, *Braking the Special Interests* (University of Chicago Press, 1987); Thomas Gale Moore, "Trucking Deregulation," Library of Economics and Liberty, http://www .econlib.org/library?Enc1/Trucking Deregulation.html.

60. Letter from Richard Neustadt to V. G. Hudson, 3/8/77, White House Central Files, "FG 128, 1/20/77–1/20/81," Box 184, Carter Presidential Library; Letter from President Carter to Charles Ferris, 4/11/78, White House Central Files, "FG 128, 1/20/77– 1/20/81," Box 184, Carter Presidential Library.

61. Letter from President Carter to Charles Ferris, April 11, 1978, White House Central Files, "FG 128, 1/10/77–1/20/81," Box 184, Carter Presidential Papers.

62. Charles Ferris, interview with the author, February 16, 2016.

63. Letter from President Carter to Charles Ferris, April 11, 1978.

64. Steve Simmons interview with the author, January 6, 2014, and conversation and email to the author, February 11, 2016.

65. Stuart Eizenstat letter to Charles Ferris, June 16, 1979, White House Central Files, "FG 128, 1/20/77–1/20/81," Box 184, Carter Presidential Library.

66. Rick Neustadt memo to Stu Eizenstat, February 4, 1979, Domestic Policy staff, Government Reform Neustadt files, Common Carrier Correspondence Folder 6, Box 12, Carter Presidential Library; cited in Crews, 25–6.

67. Presidential Statement to Congress, Reforms to Regulation of Telecommunications, September 21, 1979, *Congressional Quarterly Almanac,* 1979, 58-E-59-E, Washington, D.C., *Congressional Quarterly Almanac,* 1980, http://library.cq press.com/cq almanac /cqa/86126160-1182979.

68. Ralph Nader interviews, August 4, 1993, and November 4, 2013.

69. Ralph Nader interview, August 4, 1993.

70. Speech by Jimmy Carter, January 23, 1976, Sam Bleicher Files, Jimmy Carter Presidential Library, Atlanta, Georgia, in "Agency for Consumer Advocacy, Box 31.

71. Ralph Nader interviews, August 4, 1993 and November 4, 2013.

72. Ralph Nader interviews, October 4, 1993, and November 4, 2013.

73. Ibid.

74. Michael Pertschuck, interview with the author, October 26, 1992.

75. Joan Claybrook, interview with the author, June 3, 1991; Michael Pertschuck interview, October 26, 1992; Edward Cohen, interview with the author, February 26, 2016; Ralph Nader interview, August 4, 1993.

76. Ralph Nader interviews.

77. Emily Soapes interview of Esther Peterson, January 5, 1981.

78. Ed Cohen interview, February 11, 2016.

79. Ralph Nader interview, November 4, 2013.

Chapter 16

1. President Gerald Ford speech to National Press Club, October 29, 1975.

2. Roger Altman, interview with the author, January 27, 2016.

3. Pad 8, February 21, 1977.

4. Steven Greenhouse, "Victor Gotbaum, 93, Dies; Labor Leader Helped Rescue New York City in the 1970s," *The New York Times,* April 5, 2015.

5. 1976 Annual Report of the New York Municipal Assistance Corporation, Baruch College Library, 4.

6. *The Presidential Campaign 1976,* Volume One, Part One, Jimmy Carter (Washington, D.C.: Government Printing Office, 1978), 119.

7. Orin Kramer, interview with the author, November 2, 2013.

8. Roger Altman, interview with the author, January 27, 2016.

9. Pad 9, March 7, 1977.

10. Steven Greenhouse, "Victor Gotbaum, 93, Dies; Labor Leader Helped Rescue New York City in the 1970s," *The New York Times,* April 5, 2015.

11. Pad 25, October 3, 1977.

12. Pad 27, November 21, 1977.
13. Pad 28, January 9, 1978.
14. Pad 29, January 26, 1978.
15. Pad 29, January 27, 1978.
16. Pad 29, February 2, 1978.
17. Guy Kawaski, quoted in Tzvi Freeman, "What Is Chutzpah?" Chabad.org.
18. Pad 29, February 2, 1978.
19. Robert Abrams, interview with the author, April 10, 1991.
20. Manny Fernandez, "When Presidents Visited the South Bronx," *The New York Times,* October 5, 2007.
21. Pad 30, February 12, 1978.
22. Robert C. Embry, Jr. (Assistant Secretary of HUD for Community Development), interview with the author, November 20, 2013.
23. Steven Greenhouse, "Victor Gotbaum, 93, Dies; Labor Leader Helped Rescue New York City in the 1970s," *The New York Times,* April 5, 2015.
24. Pad 30, March 1, 1978.
25. Roger Altman interview, January 27, 2016.
26. Ibid.
27. Ibid.
28. Steven Greenhouse, "Victor Gotbaum, 93, Dies; Labor Leader Helped Rescue New York City in the 1970s," *The New York Times,* April 5, 2015.
29. Public Papers of the Presidents, Jimmy Carter, 1978, II, "Remarks at the Signing Ceremony for HR. 12426," August 8, 1397–1400; Collection Office of Staff Secretary; Series: Presidential Files; Folder, 8/8/78–8/9/78—President's Trip to NYC [1]: Container 88.
30. Pad 39, September 15, 1978.
31. Pad 7, February 1, 1977; Pad 14, April 16, 1977.
32. Pad 40, September 22, 1978.
33. Pad 43, December 4, 1978.
34. Pad 43, December 4, 1978.
35. Pad 57, June 22, 1979.
36. Pad 62, August 8, 1979.
37. Pad 62, August 9, 1979; G. William Miller, interview with the author, July 28, 1979.
38. Pad 57, June 22, 1979.
39. Pad 62, August 9, 1979; G. William Miller interview, July 29, 1979.
40. Roger Altman interview, January 27, 2016.
41. Public Papers of the Presidents, Jimmy Carter, 1980–1981, I, January 8, 1980, 27–32.

PART V

17. The Clash of Peace and Politics

1. Lawrence H. Sharp, "Jimmy Carter and the Trilateral Commission: Presidential Roots," excerpt from the book, *Trilateralism,* ed. Holly Sklar (Boston: South End Press, 1980).
2. Jerome Cohen, interview with the author, August 8, 2014.

3. Jimmy Carter speech, Elizabeth, New Jersey, June 6, 1976, *The Presidential Campaign 1976*, Volume I, Part One, 215–21 U.S. Government Printing Office, Washington, D.C., 1978.

4. CBS poll cited in Peri Deveney, "The City Politics Column: Help for the Republicans," *New York*, December 1, 1976.

5. Pad 1, December 9, 1976.

6. Pad 2, January 13, 1977.

7. Jimmy Carter, *Keeping Faith: Memoirs of a President* (New York, Bantam Books, 1982), 279.

8. Ibid.

9. Jimmy Carter, interviews with the author, June 4, 1991, and September 27, 2013.

10. Jimmy Carter interview, September 27, 2013.

11. Jimmy Carter interview, June 4, 1991.

12. Jimmy Carter interviews, June 4, 1991, and September 27, 2013.

13. William Quandt, interview with the author, September 12, 2013.

14. Jimmy Carter interview, September 27, 2013.

15. Zbigniew Brzezinski, interview with the author, September 16, 1991.

16. Zbigniew Brzezinski, François Duchêne and Kiichi Saeki, "Peace in an International Framework," *Foreign Policy*, Summer 1975, 19, based upon a Trilateral Commission proposal.

17. Ian and Mark Brzezinski speeches at the June 9, 2017 memorial service for their father, Zbigniew Brzezinski.

18. Shlomo Avineri letter and Brzezinski's response were published in "Exchange on the Middle East," *Foreign Policy*, 21, Winter 1975.

19. Pad 7, February 7, 1977.

20. Pad 9, February 20, 1977.

21. Pad 9, February 24, 1977.

22. Yehuda Avner, *The Prime Ministers* (New Milford, CT: Toby Press, 2010), 324–7.

23. Pad 9, March 9, 1977.

24. Jimmy Carter interview, September 27, 2013.

25. Jimmy Carter, *White House Diary* (New York: Farrar, Straus & Giroux, 2010), 31.

26. Cyrus Vance, interview with the author, April 28, 1992.

27. Yitzhak Rabin, interview with the author, July 14, 1991.

28. Pad 11, March 16, 1977; Press conference transcript, March 16, 1977, www.presidency.ucsb.edu/ws/?pid=7180.

29. Jimmy Carter news conference, May 12, 1977, Public Papers of the Presidents, Jimmy Carter, 1977, Vol. I, 86.

30. Kenneth Stein, *Heroic Diplomacy* (New York: Routledge, 1999), 194.

31. Mark Siegel, interview with the author, October 20, 1992.

32. William Quandt interview, September 12, 2013.

33. Jimmy Carter interview, June 4, 1991.

34. Pad 11, March 17, 1977.

35. Leon H. Charney, *Special Counsel* (New York: Philosophical Library, 1984); Robert Lipshutz, interviews with the author, June 4, 1991, June 29, 1992, and July 15, 1993.

36. Pad 10, March 14, 1977.

37. Jimmy Carter, *Keeping Faith*, 282.

38. Pad 13, April 5, 1977.

39. Jimmy Carter interview, September 27, 2013.

40. Personality profile of Anwar Sadat, August 23, 1978, www.foia.cia.gov/carter-camp
    -david/docs/carterPublication.pdf.

41. Ismail Fahmy, *Negotiating for Peace in the Middle East* (New York: Routledge, 2013), 13.

42. Pad 13, April 7, 1977.

43. Pad 14, April 15, 1977.

44. Ibid.

45. Pad 14, April 21, 1977.

46. Pad 15, May 16, 1977.

47. Jimmy Carter interview, September 27, 2013.

48. Jimmy Carter, *White House Diary*, 50.

49. Jimmy Carter, *Keeping Faith*, 286–7.

50. Pad 16, May 19, 1977.

51. Pad 15, May 11, 1977.

52. Pad 15, May 12, 1977.

53. Pad 15, May 16, 1977.

54. Jimmy Carter interview, October 30, 1991.

55. Yehuda Avner, *The Prime Ministers* (New Milford, CT: Toby Press, 2010), 345.

56. Yechiel Kadishai, interview with the author, June 23, 2013.

57. "Israel: Trouble in the Promised Land," *Time*, May 30, 1977, unsigned, but phrase on
    Begin inserted by foreign editor John Elson.

58. Pad 16, May 19, 1977; Zbigniew Brzezinski, *Power and Principle* (New York: Farrar,
    Straus & Giroux, 1983), 96.

59. Jimmy Carter, *White House Diary*, 55–6 for meeting of May 23, 1977.

60. Aharon Barak, interview with the author, May 12, 2013.

61. Pad 16, May 19, 1977.

62. Ibid.

63. Pad 17, June 3, 1977.

64. Pad 16, May 23, 1977.

65. Pad 17, May 17, 1977.

66. Pad 17, May 31, 1977.

67. Jewish Telegraphic Agency archive, www.jta.org/1977/06/14.

68. Pad 17, June 2, 1977.

69. Hamilton Jordan memorandum to President Carter, June 6, 1977, in author's posses-
    sion. Original is in the Jimmy Carter Presidential Library and Museum, Atlanta,
    Georgia, Office of the Chief of Staff Files, Series: Hamilton Jordan's Confidential Files,
    www.jimmycarterlibrary.gov.

70. Letter of Reverend John F. Steinbruck, pastor of Luther Place Memorial Church in
    Washington, D.C., to Robert Lipshutz, White House Counsel. A copy is in author's
    possession, the original in Robert Lipshutz's papers at the Jimmy Carter Presidential
    Library and Museum, Atlanta, Georgia, www.jimmycarterlibrary.gov.

71. Pad 17, June 7, 1977.

72. Ibid.

73. Joseph Lelyveld, "Katz in the Mountains," *New York Times Magazine,* July 10, 1977.

74. Sam Lewis (United States Ambassador to Israel), interview with the author, May 2, 1992.

75. Pad 19, June 25, 1977.

76. Pad 18, June 9, 1977.

77. Pad 18, June 10, 1977.

78. Pad 19, June 26, 1977.

79. Pad 19, June 28, 1977.

80. Pad 20, June 29, 1977.

81. Pad 20, July 6, 1977.

82. Pad 19, June 24, 1977.

83. Pad 22, July 19, 1977.

84. Cyrus Vance, *Hard Choices* (New York: Simon & Schuster, 1983), 81.

85. Yehuda Avner, *The Prime Ministers* (New Milford, CT: Toby Press, 2010), 437.

86. Sam Lewis, interview with Association for Diplomatic Studies and Training, Foreign Affairs Oral History Project (hereinafter referred to as "ADST" interview), August 9, 1998, 59.

87. Zbigniew Brzezinski, *Power and Principle,* 100.

88. Pad 24, September 12, 1977.

89. Ibid.

90. Jon B. Alterman, ed., "Sadat and His Legacy," The Washington Institute for Near East Policy, www.washingtoninstitute.org/uploads/Documents/pubs/SadatandHisLegacy.pdf.pdf, 43.

91. Ephraim Evron (Israeli Ambassador to the United States), interview with the author, June 10, 1991.

92. Pad 25, September 29, 1977.

93. Meir Rosenne, interview with the author, June 13, 2013.

94. Ibid.

95. William Quandt interview, September 12, 2013.

96. Reuters, October 2, 1977.

97. Morris Amitay, interview with the author, July 29, 2014.

98. Pad 25, October 3, 1977.

99. Pad 25, October 6, 1977.

100. Mark Siegel interview, October 20, 1992.

101. Walter Mondale, interview with the author, September 11, 2014.

102. Zbigniew Brzezinski, *Power and Principle,* 110.

103. Pad 25, October 31, 1977.

104. Ibid.

105. Jimmy Carter, *White House Diary,* 112.

106. William Quandt interviews, September 12, 2013, and October 4, 2013.

107. Jimmy Carter, *White House Diary,* 113.

108. Ibid, 213.

109. Sam Lewis, ADST interview, August 9, 1998.

110. Pad 25, October 6, 1977.

111. Pad 25, October 3, 1977.

112. Pad 25, October 6, 1977.

113. Philip Habib memorandum to Cyrus Vance, October 18, 1977.

114. Hamilton Jordan, memorandums to President Carter, container 35, October 26, 1977, in author's possession, originals in the Jimmy Carter Presidential Library and Museum, Office of the Chief of Staff Files, Series: Hamilton Jordan Confidential Files, www .jimmycarterlibrary.gov. President Carter's handwritten notes are revealing. To Ham Jordan's statement that there is some evidence the Syrians or PLO are playing a "disruptive role" in the Middle East, Carter's comment was "I haven't heard this before." To Ham's alternative of abstaining, Carter notes, "It will be unanimous" in the UN Security Council. When Ham asserts supporting the Egyptian resolution would add a "new variable at this critical stage of the negotiations," Carter writes, "not a new variable." When Ham states that a vote against Israel in the UN "could precipitate a political confrontation in the Congress that could be unfavorable to the Administration," Carter responds, "No vote 'against Israel'—the settlements are illegal." This latter statement summarizes Carter's position on Israel. He was *not* anti-Israel, as his critics asserted. He stood strong for Israel's status as a Jewish state and provided an increased amount of military assistance, including some of our country's most sophisticated warplanes and armaments, and civilian aide. But he strongly opposed the building of settlements on land Israel occupied after the 1967 War, an issue that prevails to this date.

115. Pad 25, October 26, 1977.

18. Sadat Changes History

1.   Jon B. Alterman, ed., "Sadat and His Legacy," The Washington Institute for Near East Policy, www.washingtoninstitute.org/uploads/Documents/pubs/SadatandHisLegacy .pdf.pdf.

2.   Sam Lewis, ADST interview.

3.   Zbigniew Brzezinski, interview with the author, September 16, 1991.

4.   Mark Siegel, interview with the author, October 20, 1992.

5.   Ibid.

6.   Ahmed Aboul Gheit, interview with the author, October 2, 2013.

7.   Sam Lewis, ADST interview.

8.   Ahmed Aboul Gheit interview, October 3, 2013.

9.   Jimmy Carter, interview with the author, September 27, 2013.

10. Yehuda Avner, *The Prime Ministers* (New Milford, CT: Toby Press, 2010), 467.

11. Zbigniew Brzezinski interview, September 16, 1991.

12. Pad 27, November 14, 1977.

13. Yitzhak Rabin, interview with the author, July 14, 1991.

14. Ahmed Aboul Gheit interview, October 2, 2013.

15. Abdel Raouf el-Reedy, interview with the author, October 3, 2013.

16. Yehuda Avner, *The Prime Ministers*, 458.

17. Sam Lewis, ADST interview.

18. Jimmy Carter interview, September 27, 2013.

19. Ephraim Evron, interview with the author, June 10, 1991.

20. Jimmy Carter, *White House Diary* (New York: Farrar, Straus & Giroux, 2010), 137.

21. Boutros Boutros-Ghali, *Egypt's Road to Jerusalem* (New York: Random House, 1997), 17–8.

22. Yehuda Avner, *The Prime Ministers*, 460.

23. Sam Lewis, ADST interview.

24. Yehuda Avner, *The Prime Ministers*, 461.

25. Ibid., 461–4.

26. Yitzhak Rabin interview, July 14, 1991.

27. Sam Lewis, ADST interview.

28. Ezer Weizman, *The Battle for Peace* (New York: Bantam Books, 1981), 44.

29. Prime Minister's address, November 20, 1977, 43rd session of the Ninth Knesset, upon the visit of Egyptian President Anwar Sadat, Records of the Knesset.

30. Simcha Dinitz, top secret cable to Israeli Foreign Ministry, November 20, 1977, Archives of the Israeli Foreign Ministry.

31. Pad 27, November 21, 1977.

32. Dinitz, top secret cable to Foreign Office, November 4, 1977, Archives of the Israeli Foreign Ministry.

33. Ahmed Aboul Gheit interviews, October 2, 2013, and October 7, 2013.

34. Ibid.

35. Pad 27, November 29, 1977.

36. Abdel Raouf el-Reedy interview, October 3, 2013.

37. Meir Rosenne, interview with the author, June 17, 2013.

38. Ibid.

39. Sam Lewis, ADST interview.

40. Aharon Barak, interview with the author, May 23, 2013.

41. Zbigniew Brzezinski, *Power and Principle* (New York: Farrar, Straus & Giroux, 1983), 115; Jimmy Carter, *White House Diary* (New York: Farrar, Straus & Giroux, 2010), 150.

42. Jimmy Carter interview, September 27, 2013.

43. Zbigniew Brzezinski, *Power and Principle*, 117.

44. Pad 28, December 16, 1977.

45. Ahmed Aboul Gheit interviews, October 2, 2013, and October 7, 2013.

46. Sam Lewis, ADST interview.

47. Meir Rosenne interview, June 17, 2013.

48. Boutros Boutros-Ghali, *Egypt's Road to Jerusalem*, 45.

49. William Quandt, interviews with the author, September 12, 2013, and October 4, 2013.

50. Clayton Fritchey, "What Derailed the Middle East Talks Last January?" *The Washington Post*, July 8, 1978.

51. Office of the Chief of Staff Files, Series: Hamilton Jordan's Confidential Files; Folder: Administration Review, Goals & Priorities—First Draft of December 1977 Memo, Container 33, Jimmy Carter Presidential Library and Museum, Atlanta, Georgia, www.jimmycarterlibrary.gov.

52. Jimmy Carter, *White House Diary*, 161.

53. Ibid., 161–2.

54. Jimmy Carter, *Keeping Faith: Memoirs of a President* (New York: Bantam Books, 1982), 30; Zbigniew Brzezinski, *Power and Principle*, 243.

55. Rosalynn Carter, interview with the author, August 13, 2014.

56. Jimmy Carter, *White House Diary*, 169–70.

57. Ibid.

58. Pad 29, February 1, 1978, meeting, and Dinitz top secret cable to Foreign Office, February 1, 1978; Pad 29, February 3, 1978, meeting, and Dinitz top secret cable to Foreign Minister, February 3, 1978.

59. Pad 32, March 7, 1978.

60. Pad 32, March 21, 1978.

61. Pad 31, March 1, 1978; Simcha Dinitz, interview with the author, November 9, 1992.

62. Israeli top secret cable from Israeli Ambassador to the United States Simcha Dinitz to Foreign Minister Moshe Dayan, March 1, 1978.

63. Jimmy Carter, *Keeping Faith*, 310.

64. Yehuda Avner, *The Prime Ministers* (Jerusalem, Israel: The Toby Press, 2010), 474–80.

65. Ibid., 480–2; Jimmy Carter, *White House Diary*, 180.

66. Pad 32, March 22, 1978.

67. Yehuda Avner, *The Prime Ministers*, 474–82.

68. Pad 32, March 22, 1978.

69. Ibid.

70. Pad 32A, April 18, 1978.

71. Pad 32A, April 28, 1978.

72. Pad 32A, April 30, 1978.

73. Jimmy Carter, *White House Diary*, 193.

74. Ibid.

75. Pad 33A, May 9, 1978.

76. Pad 33A, May 19, 1978; and memorandum in author's possession and in the Carter presidential library.

77. George Vecsey, "Carter's Sister to Shun Hebrew Christian Meeting," *The New York Times*, June 3, 1978.

78. Israeli cable by Deputy Chief of Mission to the United States Hanon Bar-On on conversation of White House Legal Counsel Robert Lipshutz to Israeli Knesset Member Yosef Rom April 21, 1978. Archives of Israeli Foreign Ministry.

79. Morris Amitay, interview with the author, July 21, 2014.

80. Pad 32A, April 20, 1978.

81. Israeli top secret cable from Israel's Deputy Chief of Mission to the United States Hanon Bar-On to Israeli foreign minister Moshe Dayan, April 20, 1978.

82. White House Interview Program, interview with Mark Siegel by Martha Joynt Kumar, January 6, 2000; Mark Siegel, interview with the author, October 20, 1992.

83. Pad 35, June 31, 1978.

84. Robert Shogan, "Many of Mondale's U.S. Jewish Guests Taken Aback by Tension in Israel," *Los Angeles Times*, July 2, 1978.

85. Robert Shogan, "Carter's Mideast Policies Erode His Jewish Support," *Los Angeles Times,* July 3, 1978.

86. Pad 34, June 15, 1978.

87. Walter Mondale, interview with the author, April 3, 1991; unpublished interview of Walter Mondale by his former staff members Dennis Clift, Gail Harrison, and the author, April 2, 2002, in Washington, D.C., in preparation for the Mondale Lectures on Public Service, Dorsey & Whitney, LLP.

88. Pad 35, July 3, 1978.

89. Walter Mondale interview, April 3, 1991.

90. "Fifty Years: The Mondale Lectures on Public Service," unpublished interview of Walter Mondale by his former staff members, Dennis Clift and Gail Harrison, Washington, D.C., Dorsey & Whitney, LLP, April 2, 2002.

91. Vice President Walter Mondale's top secret report to President Carter, copy in possession of author; original in the Jimmy Carter Presidential Library and Museum, Atlanta, Georgia, www.jimmycarterlibrary.gov.

92. Walter Mondale, interview with the author, April 3, 1991.

93. Dennis Clift, Vice President Mondale's national security adviser, quoting from Mondale's secret report to the president, noted in "Fifty Years: The Mondale Lectures on Public Service," unpublished, Dorsey & Whitney, LLP, Washington, D.C., April 2, 2002.

94. Sam Lewis, ADST interview.

19. Carter's Triumph at Camp David

1. Jimmy Carter, *White House Diary* (New York: Farrar, Straus & Giroux, 2010), 210.

2. Jimmy Carter, University of Virginia's Miller Center of Public Affairs interview, Plains, Georgia, November 29, 1982.

3. Camp David 25th Anniversary Forum, The Carter Center and Woodrow Wilson International Center for Scholars, Washington, D.C., September 17, 2003; see generally for an excellent account of the Camp David negotiations, Lawrence Wright, *Thirteen Days in September: Carter, Begin, and Sadat at Camp David* (New York: Alfred A. Knopf, 2014).

4. Jerry Rafshoon, interview with the author, September 25, 2015.

5. Jimmy Carter, interview with the author, October 30, 1991.

6. Herman Eilts, United States Ambassador to Egypt during the Camp David negotiations, at the Camp David 25th Anniversary Forum, The Carter Center and Woodrow Wilson International Center for Scholars, Washington, D.C., September 17, 2003, 20.

7. Jimmy Carter interview, September 27, 2013.

8. Rosalynn Carter, *First Lady from Plains* (Boston: Houghton Mifflin, 1984), 238.

9. Rosalynn Carter, interview with the author, August 13, 2014.

10. Jimmy Carter interviews, October 25, 1991, and September 27, 2013.

11. Jerry Rafshoon interview, September 28, 2015.

12. Memorandum for Vice President Mondale from William Quandt, August 13, 1978.

13. Moshe Dayan, *Breakthrough: A Personal Account of the Egypt-Israeli Peace Negotiations* (New York: Random House, 1981), 155.

14. Ibid.
15. Ibid., 157.
16. Boutros Boutros-Ghali, *Egypt's Road to Jerusalem* (New York: Random House, 1997), 135.
17. Rosalynn Carter, *First Lady from Plains,* 237.
18. https://aboutcampdavid.blogspot.com/2012/04/camp-david-summit-1978.html.
19. Boutros Boutros-Ghali, *Egypt's Road to Jerusalem,* 142.
20. Sam Lewis, ADST interview.
21. Jimmy Carter interview, September 27, 2013.
22. Ibid.
23. Jimmy Carter, *White House Diary,* 219.
24. Ibid.
25. Jimmy Carter, *Keeping Faith* (Fayetteville: University of Arkansas Press, 1995), 240.
26. Jimmy Carter, *White House Diary,* 223–4.
27. Sam Lewis ADST interview.
28. Jimmy Carter, *White House Diary,* 222.
29. Ibid.
30. Jimmy Carter, *Keeping Faith,* 348.
31. Ibid., 360.
32. Rosalyn Carter, *First Lady from Plains,* 248.
33. "Camp David and U.S. Policy in the Middle East," CIA document, 11, www.foia.cia.gov/carter-camp-david/docs/carterPublication.pdf.
34. Jimmy Carter, *Keeping Faith,* 365–6.
35. Jimmy Carter, *White House Diary,* 217, 229.
36. Ibid., 228.
37. Meir Rosenne, interview with the author, June 17, 2013.
38. Sam Lewis, ADST interview.
39. Meir Rosenne interview, June 17, 2013.
40. Jimmy Carter, *Keeping Faith,* 370.
41. Yechiel Kadeshai, interview with the author, June 23, 2013.
42. Zbigniew Brzezinski, *Power and Principle* (New York: Farrar, Straus & Giroux, 1983), 259.
43. Boutros Boutros-Ghali, *Egypt's Road to Jerusalem,* 138.
44. David Rubenstein, interview with the author, May 23, 2013.
45. Jimmy Carter, *White House Diary,* 230.
46. Ibid.
47. Jimmy Carter, *White House Diary,* 230.
48. Sam Lewis, ADST interview.
49. Jimmy Carter interview, September 27, 2013.
50. Jimmy Carter, *Keeping Faith,* 374, 379.
51. Jimmy Carter, *White House Diary,* 235.
52. Sam Lewis, ADST interview.
53. Ibid.
54. Aharon Barak, interview with the author, May 23, 2013.
55. Jimmy Carter, *Keeping Faith,* 389.

56. Jimmy Carter, *White House Diary,* 236.

57. Sam Lewis, ADST interview.

58. Jimmy Carter, *White House Diary,* 236.

59. Rosalynn Carter, *First Lady from Plains,* 261; Rosalynn Carter, interviews with the author, July 13, 1993, and August 13, 2014.

60. Jimmy Carter, *Keeping Faith,* 391.

61. Jimmy Carter, *White House Diary,* 237.

62. Ahmed Aboul Gheit, interviews with the author, October 2, 2013, and October 7, 2013.

63. Jimmy Carter, *White House Diary,* 137; Jimmy Carter, *Keeping Faith,* 392; Jimmy Carter interview, September 27, 2013.

64. Abdel Raouf el-Reedy, interview with the author, October 3, 2013.

65. Nabil Elaraby, interview with the author, October 1, 2013; Jimmy Carter interview, Sept. 27, 2013; Jimmy Carter, *Keeping Faith,* 391–3.

66. Sam Lewis, ADST interview.

67. Ibid.

68. Jimmy Carter, *White House Diary,* 238.

69. Walter Mondale, interview with the author, April 3, 1991.

70. Jimmy Carter, *White House Diary,* 240.

71. Yechiel Kadishai, interview with the author, June 23, 2013.

72. Jimmy Carter interview, September 27, 1993.

73. Simcha Dinitz, interview with the author, November 9, 1992.

74. Aharon Barak interview, May 23, 2013.

75. Harold Saunders, interview with the author, June 21, 1991.

76. Yechiel Kadishai interview, June 23, 2013.

77. Meir Rosenne interview, June 17, 2013.

78. Ahmed Aboul Gheit interview, October 7, 2013.

79. Jimmy Carter, interview with the author, September 27, 2013.

80. Jimmy Carter, *White House Diary,* 241.

81. Jimmy Carter interview, September 27, 2013.

82. Jimmy Carter, *White House Diary,* 242.

83. Jimmy Carter, interview, September 27, 2013.

84. Jimmy Carter, *White House Diary,* 243.

85. Boutros Boutros-Ghali, *Egypt's Road to Jerusalem* (New York: Random House, 1997), 149.

86. Elyakim Rubenstein interview, May 22, 2013; Meir Rosenne interview, June 17, 2013.

87. Nabil Elaraby interview, October 1, 2013.

88. "Remarks of the President, President Anwar al-Sadat of Egypt, and Prime Minister Menahem Begin of Israel at the Conclusion of the Camp David Meeting on the Middle East," September 17, 1978, Public Papers of the Presidents, Jimmy Carter, 1978, Vol. II, 1519–23.

89. President Carter, memorandum to Jerry Rafshoon and Jody Powell, August 3, 1978, Carter Presidential Library, and in author's possession from Jerry Rafshoon.

90. Author's conversation with Jerry Rafshoon, September 28, 2015.

91. Collection: Office of the Chief of Staff Files, Series: Hamilton Jordan's Confidential Files;

Folder: Middle East Camp David-Israel/Egypt Talks, 9/78; Container: 35, Jimmy Carter Presidential Library and Museum, Atlanta, Georgia, www.jimmycarterlibrary.gov.

92. Jerry Rafshoon interviews with the author, April 2, 2014, and September 28, 2015.

93. Zalman Shoval, interview with the author, October 4, 2014.

94. Aharon Barak, interview with the author, May 23, 2013.

95. Jimmy Carter, University of Virginia's Miller Center of Public Affairs interview, 17.

96. Sam Lewis, ADST interview.

97. William Quandt interviews with the author, September 12, 2013, and October 4, 2013.

98. Sam Lewis, ADST interview, 96; Morris Amitay, interview with the author, July 21, 2014.

99. Morris Amitay, interview with the author, July 21, 2014.

100. Jimmy Carter, interview, September 27, 2013.

20. A Cold Peace

1. Ambassador Samuel W. Lewis interview, The Association for Diplomatic Studies and Training, Foreign Affairs Oral History Project (referred to as ADST interview), August 9, 1998.

2. Stuart E. Eizenstat memorandum to President Carter, September 19, 1978, with copies to Vice President Mondale and National Security Adviser Brzezinski, copies in possession of author, in author's files and files on Camp David summit and Middle East issues, National Archives, Washington, D.C., and Carter Presidential Library and Museum, Atlanta, Georgia. President Carter wrote on my memorandum, "All done—or better."

3. Nabil Elaraby, interview with the author, October 1, 2013.

4. Abdel Raouf el-Reedy, interview with the author, October 6, 2013.

5. Jimmy Carter, interview with the author, September 27, 2013.

6. Harold Saunders, interview with the author, June 21, 1992.

7. Harold Brown, interview with the author, June 6, 1992.

8. Dan Pattir, interview with the author, June 22, 2013; and undated discussion with John Wallach of Hearst newspapers, shortly after the Camp David negotiations were concluded.

9. Cyrus Vance, *Hard Choices* (New York: Simon & Schuster, 1983), 224–5.

10. Jimmy Carter interview, September 27, 2013, on his view of Begin's resumption of settlement expansion following Camp David.

11. Harold Saunders interview, June 21, 1992.

12. Sam Lewis, interview with author, May 20, 1992; Sam Lewis, ADST interview, August 9, 1998.

13. See e.g. Roscoe Suddarth, United States Ambassador to Jordan (1987–1990), interview with Association for Diplomatic Studies and Training, Foreign Service Oral Project, (ADST) March 30, 1990.

14. Pad 44, December 18, 1978.

15. Pad 39, September 17, 20, 1978.

16. Pad 39, September 19, 1978.

17. Pad 40, September 22, 1978.

18. Pad 40, September 28, 1978.

19. Pad 40, September 26, 1978.

20. Pad 40, September 26, 28, 1978.

21. Pad 45, January 10, 1979.

22. Pad 41, November 2, 1978.

23. Pad 40, September 26, 1978.

24. Pad 41, November 7, 1978.

25. Pad 42, November 14, 1978.

26. Pad 42, November 16, 1978.

27. Jimmy Carter interview, September 27, 2013.

28. Pad 42, November 14, 1978.

29. Pad 42, November 15, 1978.

30. Cyrus Vance, *Hard Choices*, 236.

31. Meir Rosenne, interview with the author, June 17, 2013.

32. Meir Rosenne interview, June 17, 2013.

33. Jimmy Carter, *White House Diary*, 296.

34. Pad 49, February 26, 1979.

35. Jimmy Carter, *White House Diary*, 299.

36. Pad 49, February 27, 1979.

37. January 5, 1979, urgent/top secret cable from Israeli Ambassador to the United States Ephraim Evron to the Israeli Foreign Ministry. Archives of the Israeli Foreign Ministry.

38. Jimmy Carter, *White House Diary*, 297.

39. Jimmy Carter interview, September 27, 2013.

40. Ibid.

41. Jimmy Carter, University of Virginia's Miller Center of Public Affairs interview, November 29, 1992.

42. Cyrus Vance, *Hard Choices*, 245.

43. Pad 49, March 7, 1979.

44. Jimmy Carter, *White House Diary*, 299.

45. Jimmy Carter interview, October 30, 1991.

46. Jimmy Carter interviews, October 30, 1991, and September 27, 2013.

47. Jimmy Carter, *White House Diary*, 301.

48. Sam Lewis, ADST interview.

49. Jerry Rafshoon, interviews with the author, January 30, 1990, February 26, 1990, October 30, 1991, January 12, 2007, April 4, 2014, October 18, 2015, and discussions of June 17, 2013, and February 25, 2014.

50. Sam Lewis, ADST interview.

51. Jerry Rafshoon interview, April 4, 2014.

52. Congressional Research Service, May 8, 2014, "1979 Memorandum of Agreement Between the United States and Israel on Oil," memorandum from Jeremy M. Sharp to U.S. Senate Committee on Energy and Natural Resources.

53. Jimmy Carter interview, September 27, 2013.

54. Sam Lewis, ADST interview.

55. Annex III Protocol Concerning Relations of the Parties, to the March 26, 1979,

Israel-Egypt Peace Treaty, copies are in the United States Department of State, the Israeli Ministry of Foreign Affairs, the Egyptian Ministry of Foreign Affairs and the United Nations.

56. Pad 99, October 17, 1980; Public Papers of the Presidents, Jimmy Carter, 1980–1981, III. U.S. Government Printing Office, 1980.

57. Ron Minsk, interview with the author, November 29, 2014.

58. Sam Lewis, ADST interview.

59. Rex Scouten, interview with the author, November 13, 1995.

60. Sol Linowitz, interview with the author, August 26, 1992.

61. Meir Rosenne, interview with the author, June 17, 2013.

PART VI

21. The Panama Canal and Latin America

1. James Baker, interview with the author, May 29, 2013.

2. Jimmy Carter, *Carter's Campaign Promises* (Chicago: Commerce Clearing House, 1977), 57–8.

3. Robert Pastor, interview with the author, transcribed July 13, 2011; Adam Clymer, *Drawing the Line at the Big Ditch: The Panama Canal Treaties and the Rise of the Right* (Lawrence: University of Kansas Press, 2008), 42–3.

4. Robert Pastor, interview with the author, July 13, 2011.

5. Henry Kissinger, interview with the author, June 23, 2013; Adam Clymer, *Drawing the Line at the Big Ditch*, 43.

6. Frank Moore, interview with the author, May 8, 2013.

7. Jimmy Carter, interview with the author, September 27, 2013.

8. Rosalynn Carter, interview with the author, August 19, 1993.

9. Hamilton Jordan, interview with the author, May 11, 1992.

10. Jimmy Carter, University of Virginia's Miller Center of Public Affairs interview, November 29, 1992.

11. Robert Pastor interview, July 13, 2011.

12. Pad 5, January 12, 1977.

13. Robert Pastor interview, July 13, 2011.

14. Sol Linowitz, interview with the author, August 26, 1992.

15. Deputy Secretary of State Warren Christopher, State Department Evening Report to President Carter, May 16 and June 1, 1977, Carter Library.

16. Jimmy Carter, *Keeping Faith*, 157.

17. Sol Linowitz interview, August 26, 1992.

18. Jimmy Carter, *Keeping Faith*, 157–8.

19. Pad 20, July 1, 1977.

20. Pad 29, July 25, 1977.

21. Jimmy Carter, *Keeping Faith*, 158.

22. Sol Linowitz interview, August 26, 1992.

23. Ibid.

24. Ibid.

25. Robert Pastor interview, June 8, 2007.

26. Jimmy Carter, *Keeping Faith*, 165; Pad 21, July 13, 1977.

27. Statement of President Jimmy Carter at signing ceremony for the Panama Canal Treaties, September 7, 1977, Public Papers of the Presidents, Jimmy Carter, 1977, Vol. II, United States Government Printing Office, Washington, D.C., 1978, 1542–6.

28. Adam Clymer, *Drawing the Line at the Big Ditch*, 60.

29. Zbigniew Brzezinski, University of Virginia's Miller Center of Public Affairs interview, February 18, 1992.

30. Pad 24, September 12, 1977.

31. Jimmy Carter, *Keeping Faith*, 159.

32. Ibid., 164.

33. Ibid., 163.

34. Warren Christopher, State Department Evening Report to President Carter, September 26, 1977, Jimmy Carter Presidential Library and Museum.

35. Public Papers of the Presidents, II, Jimmy Carter, 1977, U.S. Government Printing Office, 1973.

36. Jimmy Carter, *White House Diary* (New York: Farrar, Straus & Giroux, 2010), 90.

37. Warren Christopher, State Department Evening Report to President Carter, December 7, 1977, Jimmy Carter Presidential Library and Museum.

38. Jimmy Carter, *Keeping Faith*, 178.

39. Ibid., 163; Frank Moore, interview with the author, October 2, 2014.

40. Jimmy Carter, *White House Diary*, 141.

41. Cyrus Vance, State Department Evening Report to President Carter, January 9, 1978, Jimmy Carter Presidential Library and Museum.

42. January 13, 1978, Warren Christopher, State Department Evening Report to President Carter, Jimmy Carter Presidential Library and Museum.

43. Pad 29, January 24, 1978.

44. Pad 31, February 23, 1978.

45. Adam Clymer, *Drawing the Line at the Big Ditch*, 48–9.

46. Jimmy Carter, *Keeping Faith*, 165–6.

47. Pad 32, March 14, 1978.

48. Frank Moore interviews, June 29, 2013, and October 2, 2014.

49. Adam Clymer, *Drawing the Line at the Big Ditch*, 98.

50. Robert Pastor interview, July 13, 2011.

51. Jimmy Carter Miller Center interview, November 29, 1992.

52. Walter Mondale, interview with the author; also Adam Clymer, *Drawing the Line at the Big Ditch*, 95–8.

53. Sol Linowitz interview, August 16, 1992.

54. Jimmy Carter, *Keeping Faith*, 172–3.

55. Robert Pastor interview, July 13, 2011.

56. Pad 32A, April 10, 1978; Clymer, 98–103.

57. Frank Moore interview, May 8, 2013.

58. Pad 32A, April 18, 1977.

59. Jimmy Carter, *Keeping Faith,* 184.

60. Pad 32, March 7, 1978.

61. Norman Podhoretz, interview with the author, February 26, 2007.

62. Jeane Kirkpatrick, "Dictatorships & Double Standards," *Commentary,* November 1, 1979.

63. Jimmy Carter, *Keeping Faith,* 161.

64. Robert Pastor interview, July 13, 2011.

65. Joshua Muravchik, *The Uncertain Crusade: Jimmy Carter and the Dilemmas of Human Rights Policy* (Lanham, MD: Hamilton Press, 1986), 3–4.

66. Ibid.

67. Inaugural Address of President Jimmy Carter, January 20, 1977, Public Papers of the Presidents, Jimmy Carter, 1977, Vol. I, 1–4.

68. Rosalynn Carter, *First Lady from Plains*; Rosalynn Carter interviews, July 13, 1993, and August 13, 2014; Robert Pastor interview, July 13, 2011.

69. Office of State Department Historian, "Carter and Human Rights," 1977–1981, Office of the Historian, Bureau of Public Affairs, Washington, D.C., history@state.gov.

70. Burton Kaufman, *Presidential Profiles: The Carter Years* (New York: Infobased Publishers, 2006), 155.

71. Zbigniew Brzezinski, NSC Weekly Report to the President, February 19, 1977, Jimmy Carter Presidential Library and Museum.

72. Warren Christopher, State Department Evening Report to President Carter, April 24, 1978, Jimmy Carter Presidential Library and Museum.

73. Cyrus Vance, State Department Evening Report to the President, January 17, 1978, Jimmy Carter Presidential Library and Museum.

74. Cyrus Vance, State Department Evening Report to the President, March 2, 1978, Jimmy Carter Presidential Library and Museum.

75. Robert Cox, "New Argentine Chief Needs Reagan's Help," *The New York Times,* November 3, 1983.

76. John Dinges, quoted in *Argentina-United States Bilateral Relations: An Historical Perspective and Future Challenges,* edited by Cynthia J. Arnson, Washington, D.C., Woodrow Wilson International Center for Scholars, 2003.

77. Kathryn Sikking, quoted in *Argentina-United States Bilateral Relations,* edited by Cynthia J. Arnson, Chapter 3.

78. Cyrus Vance, State Department Evening Report to the President, February 19, 1977, Jimmy Carter Presidential Library and Museum.

79. Cyrus Vance, State Department Evening Report to the President, March 4, 1977, Jimmy Carter Presidential Library and Museum.

80. E. A. Harris, quoted in *Argentina-United States Bilateral Relations,* edited by Cynthia J. Arnson, Chapter 4, 43–4.

81. Ibid., and Harris remarks, at Patricia Derian memorial service, September 25, 2016.

82. Jimmy Carter, *White House Diary,* 94–5.

83. Ibid., and *Argentina-United States Bilateral Relations,* edited by Cynthia J. Arnson, 17.

84. Paul Vitello, "Patricia Derian, Diplomat Who Made Human Rights a Priority," *The New York Times,* May 21, 2016.

85. Exit Interview of David Aaron by Marie Allen, West Wing, White House, on December 15, 1980.

86. Robert Cox, "New Argentine Chief Needs Reagan's Help," *The New York Times,* November 3, 1983.

87. Thomas Pickering, interview with the author, January 26, 2016.

88. Diego Guelar, interview with the author, transcribed June 4, 2016.

22. The Soviet Union

1. Richard Gardner, interview with the author, January 4, 2004.

2. Jimmy Carter, interview with the author, September 13, 2013.

3. Martin B. Gold, *A Legislative History of the Taiwan Relations Act: Bridging the Strait* (New York: Lexington Books, 2016).

4. Adam Nagourney, "In Tapes, Nixon Rails About Jews and Blacks," *The New York Times,* December 10, 2010.

5. Jimmy Carter, eulogy for Zbigniew Brzezinski, June 9, 2017.

6. Jimmy Carter, University of Virginia Miller Center interview, November 29, 1992.

7. Jimmy Carter interview, September 27, 2013.

8. Jimmy Carter, Miller Center interview, November 29, 1992.

9. Jimmy Carter interview, September 27, 2013.

10. Zbigniew Brzezinski interview, October 14, 2015.

11. Zbigniew Brzezinski, NSC Weekly Reports 01–03/1978, Jimmy Carter Presidential Library and Museum.

12. Harold Brown, interview with the author, September 11, 1992.

13. Ibid.

14. Jimmy Carter, *Keeping Faith,* 143.

15. Address at Commencement Exercises of University of Notre Dame, May 22, 1977, Public Papers of the Presidents, Jimmy Carter, 1977, Vol. 1, 954–62.

16. Zbigniew Brzezinski, interview with the author, September 16, 1991.

17. Harold Brown, interview with the author, September 11, 1992.

18. Zbigniew Brzezinski, NSC Weekly Report to the President, December 12, 1978–January 1, 1979, Jimmy Carter Presidential Library and Museum.

19. Robert Gates, *From the Shadows* (New York: Simon & Schuster, 2007), 89.

20. Anatoly Dobrynin, *In Confidence* (Seattle: University of Washington Press, 2001), 390–1.

21. Cyrus Vance, State Department Evening Report to the President, 01–02/1977, Jimmy Carter Presidential Library and Museum; Andrei Sakharov letter to President Carter, January 21, 1977, reproduced in *The New York Times,* www.nytimes.com/1977/01/29/archives/text-of-sakharov-letter-to-carter-on-human-rights.html.

22. Pad 9, February 28, 1977.

23. Cyrus Vance Evening Report, 01–02/1977, 106, 120.

24. Yuli Kosharovsky and Enid Wurtman, Chronology of Events of the Zionist Movement in the Soviet Union, 1975 to 1978, www.SovietJews-exodus.com; www.angelfire.com; kosharovsky.com.

25. Pad 10, March 14, 1977, 28.

26. Pad 12, March 22, 1977, 2.

27. Pad 19, June 20, 1977.
28. Pad 20, July 6, 1977.
29. Pad 22, July 25, 1977.
30. Pad 31, March 6, 1978.
31. Pad 14, April 20, 1977.
32. Pad 36, July 17, 1978, and Pad 50, March 16, 1979.
33. Alan Dershowitz, *The Case Against Israel's Enemies* (Hoboken, NJ: Wiley, 2009), 18.
34. Cyrus Vance Evening Report 04/1977, 82.
35. Jimmy Carter, *White House Diary*, 105.
36. Anatoly Dobrynin, *In Confidence*, 404–5.
37. Pad 35, July 7, 1978.
38. Pad 35, July 10, 1978.
39. Statement of the President, Public Papers of the Presidents, Jimmy Carter, 1978, Vol. II, July 11, 1978, 1232; Thom Shanker, "To the Soviets, a Spy; To the West, a Symbol," *The Chicago Tribune*, February 5, 1986, 224–5.
40. Natan Sharansky, *Fear No Evil* (New York: Random House, 1988), 224–5.
41. Pad 36, July 19, 1978.
42. Richard Perle, interview with the author, July 21, 1991.
43. "What Price a Soviet Jew?" *The New York Times*, February 22, 1981.
44. Marjorie Johnson, *Seeing Fairies* (San Antonio, TX: Anomalist Books, 2014); "Carter, Poland and a Translator," *Beachcombing's Bizarre History Blog*, December 21, 2013, http://strangehistory.net2013/12/21/carter-poland-and-the-translator.
45. Jimmy Carter, *White House Diary*, 358–9.
46. Harold Brown, interview with the author, April 29, 2014.
47. Madeleine Albright, in conversation with the author, June 8, 2017.
48. Interview of Anatoly Dobrynin by Steve Kroft, *60 Minutes*, CBS, October 1, 1995.
49. Thomas Pickering, interview with the author, January 26, 2016.
50. Robert Gates, *From the Shadows* (New York: Simon & Schuster, 2007), 96.
51. Jimmy Carter written Democratic Platform Committee presentation, June 10, 1976, Washington, D.C., *President Carter's Campaign Promises*, printed in Commerce Clearing House, Chicago, 1977, taken from memorandum by the author and David Rubenstein, November 30, 1976, to President-elect Carter.
52. Jimmy Carter Foreign Policy Association Speech, June 23, 1976, New York.
53. Jimmy Carter, San Diego Nuclear Policy Speech, September 25, 1976, San Diego.
54. President Carter's Foreign Policy Speech, Tokyo, Japan, May 28, 1975; President Carter's statement on NBC, July 11, 1976; *Playboy* interview, November 1976.
55. Jimmy Carter Defense Briefing Paper, July 27, 1976.
56. Jimmy Carter Nobel Lecture, Oslo, December 10, 2002, www.nobelprize.org/nobel _prizes/peace/laureates/2002/carter-lecture.html.
57. Zbigniew Brzezinski interview, September 16, 1991.
58. Public Papers of the Presidents, Jimmy Carter, 1977, Vol. I, May 3, 1977, 776–7, and May 10, 1977, 848–54.
59. Pad 6, January 27, 1977.
60. Ibid.

61. Pad 17, June 7, 1977.

62. Pad 18, June 10, 1977.

63. Pad 19, June 27, 1977.

64. Pad 28, June 28, 1977.

65. Edward C. Keefer, *Harold Brown, Offsetting the Soviet Military Challenge, 1977–1981*, Secretaries of Defense Historical Series, Government Printing Office, Washington, D.C., 2017, xvi.

66. Ibid., 545–6.

67. Pad 55, June 4, 1979.

68. Keefer, *Offsetting the Soviet Military Challenge*, 359, 558.

69. Frank L. Jones, "A 'Hollow Army' Reappraised: President Carter, Defense Budgets, and the Politics of Military Readiness," Strategic Studies Institute, U.S. Army War College, Carlisle, PA, October 2012.

70. James Luko, "Carter Revisited," The Nolan Chart, February 4, 2014, www.nolanchart.com.

71. Wesley Morgan, "The B-1 Bomber: The Underappreciated Workhorse of America's Air Wars," *The Washington Post,* December 30, 2015.

72. Jimmy Carter interview, September 27, 2013.

73. Benjamin B. Fischer, "A Cold War Conundrum: The 1983 Soviet War Scare," Center for the Study of Intelligence, Washington, D.C., 1994.

74. Fischer cites KGB No. 373/PR/52 Top Secret, February 1983, Copy No. 1, Attachment 2, excerpt from "The Problem of Discovering Preparation for a Nuclear Missile Attack on the USSR." He also cites Markus Wolf, *Man Without a Face: The Autobiography of Communism's Greatest Spymaster* (Times Books/Random House, 1997), 222. Wolf interviewed his fellow spymaster Andropov.

75. Robert Gates, *From the Shadows,* 111–3.

76. Harold Brown interview, April 29, 2014.

77. Walter Pincus, "Neutron Killer Warhead Buried in ERDA Budget," *The Washington Post,* June 6, 1977; Bernard Weinraub, "What Role for the Neutron Bomb?" *The New York Times,* July 17, 1977; Stuart E. Eizenstat, "Case Study on the Neutron Bomb for the Kennedy School of Government," 1988. See also Sherri Wasserman, *The Neutron Bomb Controversy* (New York: Praeger, 1987).

78. Harold Brown interview, September 11, 1992.

79. Pad 21, July 21, 1977.

80. Robert Hunter, interview with the author, September 29, 2014.

81. Pad 26, October 17, 1977.

82. Jimmy Carter interview, June 8, 1992.

83. Cyrus Vance, *Hard Choices* (New York: Simon & Schuster, 1983), 93–4.

84. Robert Hunter interview, September 29, 2014.

85. Pad 32A, April 10, 1978.

86. Zbigniew Brzezinski, *Power and Principle* (New York: Farrar, Straus & Giroux, 1983), 304–5.

87. Written response by Chancellor Helmut Schmidt, August 28, 2007, to questions posed by the author.

88. Jimmy Carter interview, September 27, 2013.

89. Jimmy Carter, National Strategy Directive, August 24, 1977, 18.

90. Cyrus Vance, State Department Evening Report 06/1977, Carter Presidential Library and Museum; Frank L. Jones, "A 'Hollow Army' Reappraised: President Carter, Defense Budgets, and the Politics of Military Readiness," Strategic Studies Institute (SSI), October 12, 2012, 26, www.strategicstudiesinstitute.army.mil/pdffiles/PUB1125.pdf.

91. Public Papers of the Presidents, Jimmy Carter, 1979, Vol. II, 2232–7.

92. Lawrence Malkin, in conversation with Reginald Bartholomew Brussels, Belgium, 1979.

93. Cyrus Vance, State Department Evening Report, 11/1979, Carter Presidential Library and Museum.

94. Robert Gates, *From the Shadows,* 112; Robert Gates, interview with the author, October 18, 2013.

95. Richard Gardner, *Mission Italy* (New York: Rowman & Littlefield, 2005), 247, 316–7, citing Mikhail Gorbachev, *Memoirs* (New York: Doubleday, 1996), 442–50.

96. Frank Jones, "A Hollow Army," Strategic Studies Institute, 17.

97. Harold Brown, interview with the author, September 11, 1992.

98. Nicholas Thompson, *The Hawk and the Dove: Paul Nitze, George Kennan and the History of the Cold War* (New York: Henry Holt, 2009).

99. Anatoly Dobrynin, *In Confidence,* 390.

100. Cyrus Vance, *Hard Choices,* 48–9; Cyrus Vance, interview with the author, April 28, 1992.

101. Zbigniew Brzezinski, *Power and Principle,* 159; Zbigniew Brzezinski interviews, September 16, 1991, March 10, 2001, July 19, 2006, and October 14, 2015.

102. Paul Nitze, interview with the author, October 8, 1992; Paul Warnke, interview with the author, July 31, 1992.

103. Jimmy Carter interview, September 27, 2013; Cyrus Vance interview, April 28, 1992.

104. Jimmy Carter, *Keeping Faith,* 219; "Address Before the UN General Assembly," Public Papers of the Presidents, Jimmy Carter, Vol. I, March 17, 1977, 446–51.

105. Nicholas Thompson, *The Hawk and the Dove,* 70.

106. Cyrus Vance, *Hard Choices,* 90.

107. Zbigniew Brzezinski, NSC Weekly Report to the President, March 3, 01–03, Jimmy Carter Presidential Library and Museum, 1978; Cyrus Vance, *Hard Choices,* 88.

108. Jimmy Carter, *Keeping Faith,* 254.

109. Ibid., 256.

110. Zbigniew Brzezinski interview, September 16, 1991; and Jerry Rafshoon, interviews with the author, August 13, 2013, and June 16, 2016.

111. Zbigniew Brzezinski interview, September 16, 1991.

112. Robert Hunter interview, September 29, 2014; Public Papers of the Presidents, Jimmy Carter, 1978, Vol. I, Commencement Address at the U.S. Naval Academy, June 7, 1978, 1052–7.

113. Zbigniew Brzezinski interviews, September 16, 1991, July 16, 2006, March 10, 2001, October 14, 2015; *Power and Principle,* 201–23.

114. Jimmy Carter interview, September 27, 2013.

115. Cyrus Vance, *Hard Choices,* 109–10.

116. Zbigniew Brzezinski, *Power and Principle,* 223.

117. Jimmy Carter, *White House Diary,* 285.

118. Martin B. Gold, *A Legislative History of the Taiwan Relations Act: Bridging the Strait* (New York: Lexington Books, 2017).

119. Chris Horton, "Taiwan Fears for Detained Activist," *The New York Times,* July 21, 2017.

120. Jimmy Carter, University of Virginia's Miller Center of Public Affairs interview, November 29, 1982.

121. Zbigniew Brzezinski, NSC Weekly Report to the President, October 5, 1978, Carter Presidential Library and Museum.

122. Cyrus Vance, *Hard Choices,* 135.

123. Jerry Rafshoon interview, June 16, 2016.

124. David D. Newsome, "The Soviet Brigade in Cuba," reviewed in *Foreign Affairs*, Fall 1987, by Gaddis Smith.

125. David Butler, "Russia's Cuban Brigade," *Newsweek*, September 10, 1979.

126. Stansfield Turner, interviews with the author, February 2, 1991, and March 20, 1991.

127. Jimmy Carter, *Keeping Faith,* 265.

128. Ira Shapiro, *The Last Great Senate* (New York: Public Affairs, 2012), 293–7, for an excellent discussion of the Senate consideration of SALT II, and, more generally, the exceptional Senate of that era.

Chapter 23

1. Zbigniew Brzezinski, interview with the author, February 18, 1992.

2. Robert Gates, interview with the author, October 18, 2013.

3. Cyrus Vance, State Department Evening Report, July 1979, 54; December 1979, 53; January 1980, 26, Carter Presidential Library and Museum; Robert Gates, *From the Shadows* (New York: Simon & Schuster, 2007), 132.

4. Robert Gates, *From the Shadows*, 132.

5. Cyrus Vance, Evening Report, October 1979, 11; Zbigniew Brzezinski, Weekly Report, October 12, 1978, 4.

6. Robert Gates, *From the Shadows,* 133.

7. Cyrus Vance Evening Report, December 1979, 28.

8. Zbigniew Brzezinski, *Power and Principle,* 479.

9. Jimmy Carter, interview with the author, September 27, 2013.

10. Zbigniew Brzezinski, Weekly Report, December 21, 1979.

11. Jimmy Carter interview with Frank Reynolds, December 31, 1979, text in Foreign Relations of the United States, 1977–1980, Vol. I, 678, Office of the Historian of the State Department, 2015.

12. Robert Gates interview with the author, October 18, 2013.

13. Jimmy Carter interview, October 25, 1991.

14. Zbigniew Brzezinski, Weekly Report, April 8, 1980.

15. Jimmy Carter interview, September 27, 2013.

16. Jimmy Carter, *White House Diary,* 388–91.

17. Jimmy Carter, Iowa Agricultural Speech, "President Jimmy Carter's Campaign Promises," August 25, 1976, Commerce Clearance House, Chicago, 1977, taken

from the memorandum by the author and David Rubenstein to President-elect Carter, November 30, 1976.

18. Pad 73, January 2, 1980.
19. Pad 73, January 10, 1980; Pad 74, January 15, 1980.
20. Pad 73, January 3, 1980.
21. Public Papers of the Presidents, Jimmy Carter, 1980–81, Vol. I, January 4, 1980, 21–4.
22. Pad 73, January 9, 1980.
23. Pad 73, January 10, 1980.
24. Ibid.; Robert Berglund, interview with the author, January 12, 1990.
25. Pad 73, January 7, 1980.
26. Pad 73, January 10, 1980.
27. Ibid.
28. Cyrus Vance, State Department Evening Reports to the President, January 1980. Carter Presidential Library and Museum.
29. Ibid., 1980.
30. Jimmy Carter, *White House Diary*, 393; for an excellent analysis of the grain embargo, see Roger B. Porter, *The U.S.-U.S.S.R. Grain Agreement* (Cambridge, MA: Harvard University Press, 1984).
31. Pad 73, January 9, 1980.
32. Pad 74, January 13, 1980.
33. Pad 75, January 28, 1990.
34. Pad 77, February 21, 1980.
35. Cyrus Vance, State Department Evening Report, January 1980, 39, 43, Carter Presidential Library and Museum; Jimmy Carter interview, September 27, 2013.
36. Cyrus Vance, State Department Evening Report, January 1980, 54, Carter Presidential Library and Museum.
37. Pad 74, January 22, 1980.
38. Jimmy Carter, *White House Diary*, 394.
39. Pad 74, January 15, 1980.
40. Pad 74, January 14, 1980.
41. Pad 74, January 16, 1980.
42. Public Papers of the Presidents, Jimmy Carter, 1980–81, Vol. I, January 23, 1980, 194–200.
43. David Aaron and Madeleine Albright, conversation with the author, June 9, 2017.
44. Lawrence Malkin, World Policy Institute of the New School University, New York, Fall 2000, 55.
45. Anatoly Dobrynin, *In Confidence* (New York: Times Books/Random House, 1995), 442–6.
46. Pad 73, January 9, 1980.
47. Mark Kramer, *Soviet Deliberations During the Polish Crisis, 1980–1981*, Special Working Paper (Washington, D.C.: Woodrow Wilson International Center for Scholars, 1999). www.wilsoncenter.org/sites/default/files/ACF56F.PDF.
48. David Aaron and Madeleine Albright, conversation with the author, June 9, 2017.

49. Quoting Douglas Brinkley, *American Experience,* "Jimmy Carter (Part 2)," Episode 174. Directed by Adriana Bosch. PBS, aired on November 12, 2002.

PART VII

24. The Malaise Speech

1. Elizabeth Drew, interview with the author, October 6, 2015, and telephone call, October 22, 2017.
2. Jimmy Carter, interview with the author, October 25, 1991.
3. University of Virginia Miller Center of Public Affairs, Timeline for Presidents.
4. Patrick Caddell, interview with the author, January 6, 1993.
5. Jane Mayer, "Trump's Money Man," *The New Yorker,* March 27, 2017.
6. Patrick Caddell memorandum to President-elect Jimmy Carter 19, January, 1977, Carter Presidential Library and Museum; and Patrick Caddell Oral History interview, Miller Center of Public Affairs, April 1, 1982.
7. Jerry Rafshoon, interview with the author, February 26, 1990.
8. Elizabeth Drew, interview with the author, October 6, 2015; see also Elizabeth Drew, "A Reporter at Large," *The New Yorker,* July 18, 1977, and subsequent articles, for a thorough review of this period.
9. Pad 32A, April 16–17, 1977.
10. Copies of minutes taken by President Carter's personal secretary Susan Clough, April 16–17, 1978, of the President's meetings at Camp David with his Cabinet and White House staff, Jimmy Carter Presidential Library and Museum; also Jimmy Carter interview, June 8, 1992.
11. Ibid.
12. Patrick Caddell interviews, April 1, 17, 1993.
13. Jerry Rafshoon memorandum to members of White House staff, January 22, 1979, in author's possession and Carter Presidential Library.
14. William Safire, "The New Foundation," *The New York Times,* January 25, 1979.
15. Charles B. Seib, "Soft Spot for a New Slogan," *The Washington Post,* February 2, 1979.
16. Patrick Caddell interviews, April 1, 17, 1993.
17. Elizabeth Drew, "A Reporter at Large," *The New Yorker,* August 27, 1979.
18. Jimmy Carter interview, September 27, 2013.
19. Patrick Caddell interview, April 1, 1993.
20. Walter Mondale, in conversation with the author, October 20, 2015.
21. George J. Lankevich, editor, *James E. Carter, 1924–: Chronology, Documents, Bibliographical Aids* (Dobbs Ferry, NY: Oceana Publications, 1981), 45–6.
22. Pad 55, June 2, 1979.
23. Pad 56, June 12, 1979.
24. Patrick Caddell interview, April 1993.
25. Stuart Eizenstat Memorandum to the President, Collection: Office of Staff Secretary; Series: Presidential Files; Folder [Trip to Japan and Korea, 6/22/79][1]; Container 122, Jimmy Carter Presidential Library and Museum.

26. Pad 58, July 3, 1979.

27. Pad 58, July 9, 1979.

28. *American Experience.* "Jimmy Carter (Part 2)." Episode 174. Directed by Adriana Bosch. Aired on PBS, November 12, 2002.

29. Patrick Caddell memorandum to the president, "Of Crisis and Opportunities", April 23, 1979, in author's possession, and Jimmy Carter Presidential Library and Museum.

30. Hamilton Jordan, interview with the author, May 11, 1992.

31. Hamilton Jordan, University of Virginia's Miller Center of Public Affairs interview, November 6, 1981.

32. Patrick Caddell interview, April 17, 1993; Hendrick Hertzberg interview, with the author, April 27, 1992.

33. Jimmy Carter, *White House Diary*, 340.

34. Pad 58, July 4, 1979.

35. Hendrick Hertzberg, interview with the author, April 27, 1991.

36. Jerry Rafshoon interview, February 26, 1990.

37. Ibid.

38. Pad 58, July 4, 1979.

39. Jerry Rafshoon, University of Virginia's Miller Center of Public Affairs interview.

40. Jimmy Carter interview, June 8, 1992.

41. Ibid., October 25, 1991.

42. Jimmy Carter, *White House Diary*, 340.

43. Pad 58, July 5, 1979.

44. W. Michael Blumenthal, interview with the author, April 27, 1992; W. Michael Blumenthal, *From Exile to Washington* (London: Duckworth, 2014), 316–7.

45. Ibid., 317.

46. *American Experience.* "Jimmy Carter (Part 2)." Episode 174. Directed by Adriana Bosch. Aired on PBS, November 12, 2002; and *Gallup,* "Presidential Job Approval for Jimmy Carter." www.presidency.ucsb.edu/data/populatiry.php?pres=39; http://www.gallucom /poll/116677/presidential-approval-ratings-gallup-historical-statistic.

47. Patrick Caddell interview, April 1, 1993.

48. Pad 58, July 5, 1979.

49. Ibid.; Walter Mondale, interviews with the author, April 3, 1991, August 8, 1992, and September 22, 2014.

50. Patrick Caddell interview, April 1, 1993.

51. Pad 58, July 5, 1979.

52. Jerry Rafshoon interviews, October 18, 2005, June 17, 2013, and February 25, 2014.

53. Jerry Rafshoon interview, February 26, 1990.

54. Pad 58, July 5, 1979; Walter Mondale, University of Minnesota interview, April 2, 2002; Walter Mondale interview, April 3, 1991.

55. Camp David Domestic Summit, President's notes, July 1979, Folder Citation: Collection: JCPL, Plains Files; Series: Subject Files: Folder: "Camp David Domestic Summit: President's Notes, 7/79," Box 19, www.jimmycarterlibrary.gov/library/finding aids/Plains Files.pdf.

56. Patrick Caddell interview, October 30, 2015.

57. Jerry Rafshoon interview, February 26, 1990.

58. Pad 58, July 5, 1979.

59. Walter Mondale interview, April 3, 1991; Jimmy Carter, *White House Diary,* 341.

60. Patrick Caddell interviews, April 1, 17, 1993.

61. President Carter's notes on Domestic Summit at Camp David, commencing July 8, 1979, original notes are in the Jimmy Carter Presidential Library and Museum; the author has a copy of President Carter's notes.

62. Jimmy Carter interview, June 8, 1992.

63. David Cohen (former head of Common Cause), interview with the author, October 31, 2015.

64. Clark Clifford, interview with the author, October 14, 1991.

65. Pad 58, July 9, 1979.

66. Ibid., July 8, 1979.

67. Ibid., July 9, 1979.

68. Pad 59, July 11, 1979.

69. Ibid., July 14, 1979.

70. Jerry Rafshoon, exit interview conducted by David Alsobrook of the Presidential Papers Staff, September 12, 1979, Old Executive Office Building, Washington, D.C.

71. Public Papers of the Presidents, Jimmy Carter, 1979, Vol. II, July 15, 1979, 1235–41.

72. Hendrick Hertzberg interview, about the impact of the "crisis of confidence" speech, April 27, 1993.

73. Lesley Stahl, *Reporting Live* (New York: Touchstone Books/Simon & Schuster 1999), 100–1.

74. Kevin Mattson, "What the Heck Are You Up To, Mr. President?": *Jimmy Carter, America's "Malaise," and the Speech That Should Have Changed the Country* (New York: Bloomsbury, 2009), citing David Broder's reaction to the speech. The book is reviewed by Dwight Garner, "A President Speaks His Truth and Takes His Licks," *The New York Times,* July 15, 2009; Jerry Rafshoon, Miller Center interview, 34.

75. Elizabeth Drew, "A Reporter at Large," *The New Yorker,* August 27, 1979.

76. Pad 60, July 16, 1977; see also, Landon Butler interview with Hamilton Jordan, University of Virginia's Miller Center of Public Affairs, November 6, 1981, President Carter's speech to the Communications Workers of America in Detroit, July 16, 1979, Public Papers of the Presidents, Jimmy Carter, Vol. II, 1979, 1241–58.

77. Hamilton Jordan memorandum to President Carter, Carter Presidential Library and Museum, Presidential Papers, Staff Offices, Chief of Staff (Jordan) Box 34, July 16, 1979, and in author's possession.

25. Resignations and Reshuffling

1. Rosalynn Carter, interview with the author, August 13, 2014.

2. Pad 58, July 5, 1979.

3. Ibid.

4. Patrick Caddell, interviews with the author, January 6, 1993, April 1 and April 17, 1993, October 30, 2015.

5. Jimmy Carter, interview with the author, June 8, 1992; Jimmy Carter, *White House Diary* (New York: Farrar, Straus & Giroux, 2010), 341.

6. Jimmy Carter interviews, June 8, 1992, and October 25, 1991; Jimmy Carter, *White House Diary*, 341.

7. Jody Powell, interview with the author, October 16, 1989, and University of Virginia's Miller Center of Public Affairs interview, December 17–18, 1981.

8. Pad 60, July 17, 1979.

9. Griffin Bell interview with the author; Jimmy Carter, *White House Diary*, 345.

10. Jody Powell interview, October 16, 1989.

11. Hamilton Jordan, University of Virginia's Miller Center of Public Affairs interview, November 6, 1981.

12. Cyrus Vance, interview with the author, April 28, 1992.

13. W. Michael Blumenthal, interview with the author, April 27, 1992; W. Michael Blumenthal, *From Exile to Washington* (New York: Overlook Press, 2015), 320–1.

14. Joseph Califano, interview with the author, February 20, 1990.

15. Pad 60, July 17, 1979.

16. Ibid., July 18, 1979.

17. Rosalynn Carter interviews, July 13, 1993, and August 13, 2014.

18. W. Michael Blumenthal interview, April 27, 1992.

19. Brock Adams, interview with the author, March 30, 1990.

20. Elizabeth Drew, "A Reporter at Large," *The New Yorker*, July 18, 1977.

21. Griffin Bell, interview with the author, September 6, 1989; Reg Murphy, *Uncommon Sense: The Achievement of Griffin Bell* (Lanham, MD: Rowman & Littlefield, 2001).

22. Hamilton Jordan, interviews with the author, May 11, 1992, and December 23, 1992.

23. Jerry Rafshoon, interview with the author, February 26, 1990.

24. Rosalynn Carter interview, August 13, 1993.

25. Patrick Caddell interview, April 1, 1993.

26. Jimmy Carter interview, October 25, 1992.

27. Frank A. Weil, in conversation and email with the author, October 5, 2015.

28. Jerry Rafshoon interview, February 26, 1990.

29. Jerry Rafshoon, University of Virginia's Miller Center of Public Affairs interview, April 8, 1983.

30. Patrick Caddell interviews, April 1, 1993, and October 30, 2015.

31. Richard Moe, interview with the author, October 11, 1991.

32. Walter Mondale, interview with the author, October 6, 2015.

33. Walter Mondale, interview with the author, April 3, 1991.

34. Pad 60, July 21, 1979.

35. "Fifty Years: The Mondale Lectures on Public Service," Walter Mondale, Richard Moe, Dennis Clift, Bert Carp, Gail Harrison, Ellen Hoffman, and Paul Light, presented April 2, 2002, Minnesota Historical Society, www.mnhs.org/library/findaids/00697 .xml; Minnesota Public Radio, St. Paul, October 11, 2002.

36. Walter Mondale interview, September 11, 2014.

37. Michael Berman, interview with the author, February 20, 2014.

38. Jim Johnson, interview with the author, June 17, 2014.

39. Richard Moe, interview with the author, October 11, 1991.

40. Jim Johnson interview, June 17, 2014.

41. Pad 61, August 3, 1979.

42. Pad 61, August 6, 1979.

43. Ibid.

44. Benjamin Civiletti, interview with the author, October 27, 1992; Hamilton Jordan interviews, May 11, 1992, and December 23, 1992; University of Virginia's Miller Center of Public Affairs, November 6, 1981.

45. Hamilton Jordan interviews, May 11, 1992, and December 23, 1992.

46. Hamilton Jordan interview, May 11, 1992.

47. Hamilton Jordan, *No Such Thing as a Bad Day* (New York: Gallery Books, 2001), 203.

48. Lily Rothman, "The '70s Cocaine Scandal That Could Have Rocked the White House," *Time*, September 3, 2014, written on the 35th anniversary of the original story.

49. James Fallows, "The Passionless Presidency," *The Atlantic*, May 1979.

50. Rosalynn Carter interviews, July 13, 1993, and August 13, 1993; Jimmy Carter interviews, June 4, 1991, and September 27, 2013.

51. Frank Moore, interview with the author, October 2, 2014.

52. Michael Cardozo, interview with author, April 11, 2014; and discussion with the author, April 22, 2017; and Carter's response to Cardozo's memorandum on the use of the White House tennis court; Susan Clough interview with the author, January 6, 1993.

53. Rex Scouten, interview with the author, September 13, 1995.

54. Susan Clough, interview with the author, January 6, 1993.

55. Jimmy Carter interview, October 25, 1991.

56. Jody Powell, *The Other Side of the Story* (New York: William Morrow, 1984), 104–8.

57. Jody Powell interview, October 16, 1998.

58. Brooks Jackson, "Bunny Goes Bugs: Rabbit Attacks President," *The Washington Post*, August 30, 1979.

59. Donnie Radcliffe and Elisabeth Bumiller, "The Picnic: Labor Plays at the White House," *The Washington Post*, September 4, 1979.

60. Jody Powell, *The Other Side of the Story*, 105.

61. Patrick Caddell interview, April 1, 1993.

62. *Washington Post* poll of September 14, 1979, cited in University of Virginia's Miller Center of Public Affairs, Presidential Key Events, Jimmy Carter, https://millercenter .org/president/jimmy-carter/key-events.

PART VIII

26. The Rise of the Ayatollah

1. Gary Sick, *All Fall Down: America's Tragic Encounter with Iran* (New York: Random House, 1991), 5.

2. Quoted in Daniel Yergin, *The Prize: The Epic Quest for Oil, Money & Power* (New York: Free Press, 2008), 138.

3.   Dr. Saul Bakash, interview with the author, October 18, 2013.

4.   Ibid.

5.   Ibid.; Shaul Bakhash, *Reign of the Ayatollahs, Iran and the Islamic Revolution* (New York: Basic Books, 1984 [revised edition]).

6.   Mohsen Sazegara, interview with the author, April 22, 2013.

7.   Jimmy Carter remarks, November 15, 1977, at state dinner for Shah of Iran in White House, Public Papers of the Presidents, Jimmy Carter 1977, 2029.

8.   Edward C. Keefer, *Harold Brown: Offsetting the Soviet Military Challenge, 1977–1981*, Washington, D.C., Historical Office, Office of the Secretary of Defense, 2017, Secretaries of Defense Historical Series, Volume 9, 290.

9.   Jimmy Carter, interview with the author, September 27, 2013; *Keeping Faith: Memoirs of a President* (New York: Bantam, 1982), 416–7.

10. Zbigniew Brzezinski, interview with the author, July 19, 2006.

11. Gary Sick, *All Fall Down*, 90.

12. Stansfield Turner, *Burn Before Reading*, 180–1.

13. Gary Sick, *All Fall Down*, 82–3.

14. Ibid., 32.

15. General David Jones, interview with the author, July 14, 2001.

16. Mohammad Reza Pahlavi, *Answer to History* (New York: Stein & Day, 1980), 154.

17. Gary Sick interview, January 24, 2011.

18. Ardeshir Zahedi, interview with the author, July 13, 2011.

19. Gary Sick, *All Fall Down*, 30.

20. Jimmy Carter interview, September 27, 2013.

21. Judy Woodruff, interview with the author, January 15, 2015.

22. Mohsen Sazegara, interview with the author, April 22, 2013.

23. Gary Sick, *All Fall Down*, 35; and Gary Sick interviews, September 13, 2006, September 25, 2006, July 13, 2011, June 16, 2016; and Gary Sick written answers to author's questions, May 1, 2017 email.

24. Mohsen Sazegara interview, April 22, 2013.

25. Henry Kissinger, interview with the author, April 12, 2006.

26. Mohsen Sazegara interview, April 22, 2013.

27. Ardeshir Zahedi interview, July 13, 2001.

28. Gary Sick, *All Fall Down*, 51.

29. Ibid., 56.

30. Dr. Mehdi Noorbaksh (son-in-law of former Iranian Foreign Minister Ebrahim Yazdi), professor of international affairs at Harrisburg (Pa.) University of Science and Technology, interview with the author, May 17, 2013; and written answers to questions by author, August 12, 2014. Yazdi was a close confidant of Ayatollah Khomeini and his first foreign minister. He became a leading dissident, accusing Khomeini of increasingly using "Stalinist and undemocratic methods," and as a result, being constantly arrested and harassed. He died on August 27, 2017. Dara Elasfar, "Ebrahim Yazdi, Iranian foreign minister turned dissident dies at 85," *The Washington Post*, August 29, 2017.

31. Mohsen Sazegara interview, April 22, 2013.

32. Ibid.

33. Zalmay Khalilzad, interview with the author, April 4, 2016, and Zalmay Khalilzad, *The Envoy* (New York: St. Martin's Press), 50–2.

34. Cyrus Vance, State Department Evening Report to President Carter, September 13, 1978, Carter Presidential Library and Museum, Atlanta, Georgia.

35. Gary Sick interview, June 16, 2016.

36. Gary Sick, *All Fall Down,* 59.

37. Ibid., 67.

38. Ibid., 68, 70.

39. Zbigniew Brzezinski interview, July 19, 2006.

40. Gary Sick, *All Fall Down,* 71.

41. Ardeshir Zahedi interview, July 13, 2011.

42. Gary Sick, *All Fall Down,* 78–79.

43. Scott Armstrong, "Vance Deflects a Call for Toughness," *The Washington Post,* October 28, 1980; Betty Glad, *An Outsider in the White House: Jimmy Carter, His Advisers, and the Making of American Foreign Policy* (Ithaca, NY: Cornell University Press, 2009), 170.

44. Stansfield Turner, interviews with the author, February 8, 1991, and March 20, 1991.

45. Gary Sick, *All Fall Down,* 99–100.

46. Scott Armstrong, "Vance Deflects a Call for Toughness"; W. Michael Blumenthal, interview with the author, March 16, 2016; W. Michael Blumenthal, *From Exile to Washington* (New York: The Overlook Press, 2015), 354–62.

47. Gary Sick, *All Fall Down,* 110.

48. Scott Armstrong, "Vance Deflects a Call for Toughness."

49. Ibid.

50. Dr. Mehdi Noorbaksh interview, May 17, 2013, and written answers to author's questions, August 12, 2014.

51. Mohsen Sazegara interview, April 12, 2013, summarizing Khomeini's letter.

52. Ibid.

53. Gary Sick interview, September 15, 2016; Dr. Mehdi Noorbaksh email to the author, August 14, 2014.

54. Gary Sick interview, September 25, 2006.

55. Jimmy Carter, University of Virginia's Miller Center of Public Affairs interview, November 29, 1993.

56. Jimmy Carter, *White House Diary,* 272–5.

57. Gary Sick, *All Fall Down,* 126.

58. Pad 45, January 16, 1979.

59. Robert Huyser, *Mission to Tehran* (New York: Harper & Row, 1986), 115. See also two files of General Huyser's Iran reports, Carter Presidential Library and Museum, "Iran Reports from General Huyser," Folder Citation: Zbigniew Brzezinski Collection: Series: Geographical Files; Folder: Iran-Reports from General Huyser (1/19–1/31/79); Container 12; and Folder Citation: Collection: Zbigniew Brzezinski Collection: Series: Geographical Files; Folder: Iran-Reports from General Huyser (2/1/79–2/13/79); Container 12.

60. Mohammed Reza Pahlavi, *Answer to History* (Stein & Day, 1980), 167.

61. Gary Sick, *All Fall Down,* 124, 126.

62. Ibid., 132–3.
63. Robert Huyser, *Mission to Tehran,* 89.
64. Gary Sick, *All Fall Down,* 151–3.
65. Edward C. Keefer, *Harold Brown,* 296–7.
66. Zbigniew Brzezinski interview, July 19, 2006.
67. Bruce Laingen interview, Association for Diplomatic Studies and Training (hereinafter referenced as ADST), Foreign Affairs Oral History Program, Georgetown University, January 9, April 7, August 25, 1992; February 17, May 27, 1993.

27. The Fall of the President

1. Mohsen Sazegara, interview with the author, April 27, 2013.
2. Ibid.
3. Robert Huyser, *Mission to Tehran,* 134–5, 141, 148.
4. Ibid., 256.
5. Gary Sick, email to the author, May 1, 2017, answering author's question.
6. Mohsen Sazegara, interview, April 27, 2013.
7. Jimmy Carter, interview, September 27, 2013.
8. Zbigniew Brzezinski, memo to President Carter, February 2, 1979, Carter Presidential Library and Museum.
9. Gary Sick, *All Fall Down,* 164–7.
10. Gary Sick, interviews with the author, September 13, 2006, September 25, 2006, July 13, 2011, June 16, 2016.
11. Jimmy Carter, interview with the author, September 27, 2013.
12. Ervand Abrahimian, *A History of Modern Iran* (New York: Cambridge University Press, 2008).
13. Bruce Laingen, interview with the author, January 10, 2006.
14. Mohsen Sazegara interview, April 22, 2013.
15. Bruce Laingen, interview with the author, January 10, 2006.
16. Ibid., and ADST interviews, January 9, 1992, et al.
17. Bruce Laingen interview with author, January 10, 2006; and ADST interview.
18. Jimmy Carter, University of Virginia's Miller Center of Public Affairs interview, November 29, 1992.
19. Bruce Laingen ADST interviews, January 9, 1992, et al.
20. Ibid.
21. Ibid.
22. Bruce Laingen, interview with the author, January 10, 2006.
23. Ibid.; and ADST interviews, January 9, 1992, et al.
24. Hamilton Jordan, University of Virginia's Miller Center of Public Affairs interview, November 6, 1981.
25. Gary Sick, *All Fall Down,* 177.
26. Gary Sick interview, July 13, 2011.
27. Gary Sick, *All Fall Down,* 178.
28. Gary Sick interview, July 13, 2011.
29. Henry Kissinger, interview with the author, April 12, 2006.

30. Ibid.
31. Walter Mondale, interview with the author, September 22, 2014.
32. Copy of cable from Bruce Laingen to Cyrus Vance, supplied by Bruce Laingen to the author, January 14, 2006, EO 12065; RDS 3, 7/28/79, UR-M.
33. Copy of cable from Bruce Laingen to State Department, provided by Bruce Laingen to the author, January 14, 2006; EO 12065; GDS 10/1/79 (Laingen, L.B.) OR-M.
34. Bruce Laingen, ADST interview, January 9, 1992, et al.
35. Zbigniew Brzezinski, interview with the author, July 16, 2006.
36. Walter Mondale interviews, April 3, 1991, August 8, 1992, and September 22, 2014.
37. Hamilton Jordan interviews, May 11 and December 23, 1992; Hamilton Jordan, University of Virginia's Miller Center of Public Affairs interview, November 6, 1981.
38. Jimmy Carter interview, September 27, 2013; also Jimmy Carter, University of Virginia's Miller Center of Public Affairs interview, November 29, 1982; Zbigniew Brzezinski interview, July 16, 2006.
39. Hamilton Jordan, University of Virginia's Miller Center of Public Affairs interview, November 6, 1981.
40. Zbigniew Brzezinski interview, October 14, 2015.
41. Jimmy Carter, *White House Diary* (New York: Farrar, Straus & Giroux, 2010), 364; Vance interview with the author, April 28, 1992.
42. Bruce Laingen interview with the author, January 10, 2006; and ADST interviews, January 9, 1992, et al.
43. Bruce Laingen, ADST interviews, January 9, 1992, et al.
44. Hamilton Jordan, University of Virginia's Miller Center of Public Affairs interview, November 6, 1981.
45. Ibid.
46. Dr. Mehdi Noorbaksh, interview with the author, May 17, 2013; and August 12, 2014, email answers to author's questions.
47. Bruce Laingen, ADST interview, January 9, 1992, et al.
48. Zbigniew Brzezinski interview, July 19, 1996.
49. Ibid.
50. Bruce Laingen, interview with the author, January 10, 2006; and Laingen ADST interviews, January 9, 1992, et al.
51. Zbigniew Brzezinski interview, July 19, 1996.
52. Mohsen Sazegara interview, April 22, 2013.
53. Bruce Laingen, ADST interviews, January 9, 1992, et al.
54. John Kifner, Terence Smith, Bernard Nossiter, and Paul Lewis, "Putting the Hostages First," *The New York Times,* May 17, 1981.
55. Mohsen Sazegara interview, April 22, 2013.
56. Dr. Mehdi Noorbaksh, written answers to author's questions, August 12, 2014.
57. Bruce Laingen, ADST interviews, January 9, 1992, et al.
58. Gary Sick, interviews with the author, September 13, 2006, September 25, 2006, July 13, 2011, June 16, 2016.
59. Bruce Laingen, interview with the author, January 10, 2006.
60. Mohsen Sazegara interview, April 22, 2013.

61. Ibid.

62. Stansfield Turner, *Burn Before Reading* (New York: Hyperion, 2006), 180–1; Stansfield Turner interviews with the author, February 8, 1991, and March 20, 1991.

63. Pad 68, November 9, 1979.

64. Bruce Laingen, ADST interviews, January 9, 1992, et al.

65. Hamilton Jordan, University of Virginia's Miller Center of Public Affairs interview, November 6, 1981.

66. Jimmy Carter Presidential Library and Museum; for number of U.S. hostages taken in Iran, "Hostage Crisis in Iran," The Jimmy Carter Presidential Library and Museum, www.jimmycarterlibrary.gov/research/hostage_crisis_in-iran.

67. Gary Sick interviews, July 13, 2011, and June 16, 2016; and, generally, *All Fall Down*, 259–60.

68. Jimmy Carter interview, September 27, 2013.

69. Gary Sick interviews, July 13, 2011, and June 16, 2016.

70. Bruce Laingen interview, January 10, 2006.

71. Harold Brown, interview with the author, April 29, 2014; Pad 69, November 15, 1979.

72. Zbigniew Brzezinski interview, September 16, 1991.

73. John Kifner, Terence Smith, Bernard Nossiter, and Paul Lewis, "Putting the Hostages First," *The New York Times,* May 17, 1981.

74. Hamilton Jordan interview, May 11, 1992.

75. Harold Brown interview, April 29, 2014.

76. Zbigniew Brzezinski interview, September 16, 1991.

77. Zbigniew Brzezinski, University of Virginia's Miller Center of Public Affairs interview, February 18, 1992.

78. Zbigniew Brzezinski interview, September 16, 1991.

79. Walter Mondale interview, September 22, 2014.

80. Jerry Rafshoon, interview with the author, April 24, 2014.

81. John Kifner, Terence Smith, Bernard Nossiter, and Paul Lewis, "Putting the Hostages First," *The New York Times,* May 17, 1981.

82. Jerry Rafshoon interviews, June 17, 2013, and February 25, 2014.

83. Harold Brown interview, April 29, 2014.

84. Keefer, *Harold Brown,* 299–300; citing Brown memorandum to Carter, December 1, 1979, folder Alpha Channel, 10/22/79–3/31/80, box 106, Brown papers, L.C., with Carter's comments.

85. Pad 72, December 17, 1979, and December 20, 1979.

86. John Kifner, Terence Smith, Bernard Nossiter, and Paul Lewis, "Putting the Hostages First," *The New York Times,* May 17, 1981.

87. Pad 70, November 30, 1979.

88. Pad 72, December 14, 1979.

89. Harold Brown interview, April 29, 2014.

90. Gary Sick interview, July 13, 2011.

91. John Pustay, interview with the author, July 14, 2011.

92. Bruce Laingen interview, January 10, 2006.

93. Jimmy Carter interview, September 27, 2013.

94. Pad 71, December 6, 1979.
95. Bruce Laingen, ADST interviews, January 9, 1992, et al.
96. Jimmy Carter interview, September 27, 2013.
97. Keefer, *Harold Brown,* 203; Hamilton Jordan, *Crisis* (New York: G. P. Putnam's Sons, 1982), 24.
98. Rosalynn Carter, interview with the author, August 14, 2014.
99. Jimmy Carter, interview, September 27, 2013.
100. Jimmy Carter, University of Virginia's Miller Center of Public Affairs interview, November 29, 1982.
101. Hamilton Jordan, interview with the author, May 11, 1992.
102. Hamilton Jordan, interview with University of Virginia's Miller Center of Public Affairs, November 6, 1981.
103. Rosalynn Carter interview, July 13, 1997.
104. Jody Powell, interview with the author, October 16, 1989; Jody Powell, interview with University of Virginia's Miller Center of Public Affairs, December 17–18, 1981.
105. Jerry Rafshoon interview, August 19, 2013.
106. Judy Woodruff, interview with the author, January 15, 2015.
107. Andy Glass, interview with the author, September 25, 2013.
108. Ted Koppel, interview with the author, July 22, 2014.
109. John Kifner, Terence Smith, Bernard Nossiter, and Paul Lewis, "Putting the Hostages First," *The New York Times,* May 17, 1981.
110. Pad 68, November 7, 1979.
111. EO 12170, November 14, 1979, 2118–20, Public Papers of the Presidents, Jimmy Carter, 1979, U.S. Government Printing Office.
112. Pad 71, November 14, 1979.
113. Pad 70, November, 28, 1979.
114. John Kifner, Terence Smith, Bernard Nossiter, and Paul Lewis, "Putting the Hostages First," *The New York Times,* May 17, 1981.
115. Jerry Rafshoon interview, April 24, 2014.
116. Hamilton Jordan interviews, May 11, 1992, and December 23, 1992.
117. Gary Sick interviews, September 13, 2006, September 25, 2006, July 13, 2011, June 16, 2006; and *All Fall Down,* 266–9; John Kifner, Terence Smith, Bernard Nossiter, and Paul Lewis, "Putting the Hostages First," *The New York Times,* May 17, 1981.
118. Gary Sick, *All Fall Down,* 289.
119. Hamilton Jordan interview, May 11, 1992.
120. Pad 68, November 7, 1979.
121. Mark Talisman, memorandum to the author, November 19, 2015, and subsequent discussions with the author.
122. Pad 69, November 15, 1979.
123. Pad 75, January 31, 1980.
124. Pad 81, April 8, 1980; and Sam Kermanian, memorandum to the author, December 15, 2015.
125. Pad 81, April 8, 1980.
126. Pads 81 and 82, April 9, 11, 15, 1980.

127. John Kifner, Terence Smith, Bernard Nossiter, and Paul Lewis, "Putting the Hostages First," *The New York Times,* May 17, 1981.
128. Jimmy Carter, *White House Diary,* 414.
129. Jimmy Carter interview, September 27, 2013.
130. Jerry Rafshoon interview, April 24, 2014.
131. General John Pustay, interview with the author, July 14, 2001.
132. Jerry Rafshoon interview, April 24, 2014.
133. General David Jones, interview with the author, July 14, 2011; David Aaron, exit interview, December 15, 1980.
134. Jimmy Carter interview, September 27, 2013; Jimmy Carter, *White House Diary,* 411–2, 421.
135. Zbigniew Brzezinski interview, September 16, 1991.
136. General John Pustay interview, July 14, 2011.
137. General David Jones and General John Pustay interviews, July 14, 2011.
138. Zbigniew Brzezinski interview, October 14, 2015, summarized in author's email, November 18, 2015.
139. Ibid. September 16, 1991.
140. Cyrus Vance interview, April 28, 1992; Walter Mondale interview, September 22, 2014.
141. Jimmy Carter interview, September 27, 2013.
142. Bruce Laingen interview, January 10, 2006.
143. Jimmy Carter interview, September 27, 2013.
144. Ibid.; Jimmy Carter, *White House Diary,* 419.
145. Mark Bowden, "The Desert One Debacle," *The Atlantic,* May 2006, www.theatlantic .com/magazine/archive/2006/05/the-desert-one-debacle/304803; Iran Hostage Rescue Report, August 1980, Statement of Admiral J. L. Holloway, III USN (Ret.), Chairman, Special Operations Review Group, https://www.history.navy/mil/research/ . . . /iran-hostage-rescue-mission-report.html.
146. General John Pustay interview, July 14, 2011.
147. General David Jones interview, July 14, 2011.
148. Zbigniew Brzezinski interview, October 14, 2015.
149. General David Jones interview, July 14, 2011.
150. Hamilton Jordan, *Crisis* (New York: G. P. Putnam's Sons, 1982), 270.
151. Ibid., 270–2.
152. See Pentagon Special Operations Review Group Report on the Rescue Mission, August 23, 1980, www.amazon.com/Complete-Operation-HollowayFormerly . . . BOOEY R6MCO.
153. Rosalynn Carter interview, August 13, 2014.
154. Walter Mondale interview, September 22, 2014.
155. Jerry Rafshoon, University of Virginia's Miller Center of Public Affairs interview, April 8, 1983.
156. Harold Brown interviews, April 29, 2014, and October 15, 2015.
157. Jerry Rafshoon interview, April 24, 2014, based upon his discussion with Charles Beckwith for a documentary produced by Jerry Rafshoon.

158. "[Iran Hostage] Rescue Mission Report," Naval History and Heritage Command, August 1980. www.history.navy.mil/research/library/online-reading-room/title -list-alphabetically/iran-hostage-rescue-mission-report.html.

159. Public Papers of the Presidents, Jimmy Carter, 1980–81, Vol. I, April 25, 1980, 772–3.

160. Ibid. 804.

161. Hamilton Jordan, *Crisis,* 287.

162. Pad 96, September 23, 1980.

163. Zbigniew Brzezinski interview, October 14, 2015; Brzezinski, *Power and Principle,* 499, 508.

164. Gary Sick, *October Surprise: America's Hostages in Iran and the Election of Ronald Reagan* (New York: Times Books/Random House, 1991).

165. Jimmy Carter interview, September 27, 2013.

166. Ibid.

167. Pad 103, January 12, 1981.

168. Bruce Laingen, ADST interview, January 9, 1992, et al.

169. Jimmy Carter interview, September 27, 2013.

170. Ibid.

PART IX

28. "Where's the Carter Bill, When We Need It?"

1. www.presidency.ucsb.edu/ws/?pid=3110; Lawrence Malkin and John Stacks, *What If's in American History,* Robert Cowley, ed. (New York: Putnam, 2003), 290.

2. Steven Schlossberg, interview with the author, December 21, 1990; Douglas Fraser (UAW president), interviews with the author, November 14, 1991, and January 6, 1992.

3. Jimmy Carter Campaign, telegram to National Association of Life Underwriters, September 17, 1976, in "President Carter's Campaign Promises," 18 (Chicago: Commerce Clearing House, 1977), based upon a memorandum by Stu Eizenstat and David Rubenstein to President-elect Jimmy Carter, November 30, 1976.

4. Dr. Larry Horowitz, interview with the author, June 5, 1992.

5. Pad 1, December 8, 1976; and Pad 2, December 28–29, 1976.

6. Pad 12, March 24, 1977; Pad 25, October 4, 1977.

7. Pad 14, April 25, 1977.

8. Pad 24, September 4, 1977.

9. Pad 43, October 20, 1977.

10. Michael Bromberg, interview with the author, December 4, 2013.

11. Ibid.

12. Joseph Califano, interview with the author, February 20, 1990.

13. Pad 29, February 1, 2, 1978.

14. Pad 30, February 15, 1978.

15. Joseph Califano, *Governing America: An Insider's Report from the White House and the Cabinet* (New York, Simon & Schuster, 1981), 149.

16. Michael Bromberg interview, December 4, 2013.

17. Martin (Marty) Russo, interview with the author, October 25, 2013.
18. Pad 36, July 24, 1978.
19. Pad 38, August 11, 15, 1978.
20. Dr. Larry Horowitz, interview with the author, January 20, 2014.
21. Joseph Califano, *Governing America,* 97–8.
22. Pad 18, June 16, 1977.
23. Joseph Califano, *Governing America,* 94.
24. Pad 26, November 9, 1977; Joseph Califano, *Governing America,* 100–1.
25. Pad 27, November 18, 1977.
26. Pad 28, December 21, 1977.
27. Pad 29, February 6, 1978.
28. Pad 31, February 28, 1978.
29. Pad 31, March 2, 1978.
30. Ibid.
31. Joseph Califano, *Governing America,* 112.
32. Pad 33A, May 18, 1978.
33. Pad 33A, June 1, 1978; Joseph Califano, *Governing America,* 111.
34. Pad 35, June 26, 1978.
35. Pad 35, June 27, 1978.
36. Pad 36, July 24, 1978.
37. Pad 36, July 12, 1978.
38. Pad 36, July 13, 1978.
39. Pad 37, July 26, 1978.
40. Pad 37, July 27, 1978.
41. Pad 36, July 24, 1978; Pad 37, July 27, 1978.
42. Pad 37, July 28, 1978.
43. Ibid.; Dr. Larry Horowitz interview, June 5, 1992; Jimmy Carter, *White House Diary,* 210.
44. Public Papers of the Presidents, Jimmy Carter, Vol. II, December 8, 1978, 2189–95.
45. Pad 48, December 8, 1978.
46. Pad 47, January 24 and February 13, 1979; Pad 48, April 12, 1979; Pad 51, March 21, 1979; Pad 52, April 11, 1979; Pad 54, May 17, 1979; Pad 55, May 23, 25, 1979; Joseph Califano, *Governing America,* 131; Jimmy Carter, *White House Diary,* 305.
47. Pad 56, June 12, 1979; Public Papers of the Presidents, Jimmy Carter, Vol. I, June 12, 1979, President's Remarks, 1024–8, and President's Message to Congress on the National Health Plan, 1028–31.
48. Joseph Califano interview, February 20, 1990.
49. Joseph Califano, *Governing America,* 135.
50. Karen Davis, interview with the author, December 11, 2015.

Chapter 29
1. Jimmy Carter, University of Virginia's Miller Center of Public Affairs interview, November 29, 1992.
2. Hamilton Jordan, memo to President Carter, January 1979, Carter Presidential Library and Museum.

3. Hamilton Jordan interviews, May 11, 1992, and December 23, 1992.

4. Pad 49, January 28, 1979.

5. Pad 56, June 12, 1979.

6. Stephen Breyer, interview with the author, November 30, 1992.

7. Walter Mondale, interview with the author, September 11, 2014.

8. Edward Kennedy, interview with the author, September 11, 1992.

9. Pad 72, December 21, 1979.

10. Jimmy Carter interview, October 25, 1991.

11. James Blanchard, interview with the author, December 18, 2015.

12. "Filibuster Kills Labor Law 'Reform' Bill," *Congressional Quarterly Almanac,* 1978, http://library.congress.com/cqalmanac/document.php?id+cqal78-1238478.

13. Ruth Bader Ginsburg, quoted in Carmon Iron and Shana Knizhik, *Notorious RBG: The Life and Times of Ruth Bader Ginsburg* (New York: Dey Books, 2015), 77.

14. "Women's Rights," from *President Jimmy Carter's Campaign Promises* (Chicago: Commerce Clearing House, June 1977), reprinted from a memorandum by Stu Eizenstat and David Rubenstein to President-elect Jimmy Carter, "President Carter's Campaign Promises," November 30, 1976, 313–33.

15. Ellen Berlow, Communications Director and Press Advisor to President Carter's Committee for Women, July 2014, comments to author.

16. Mary L. Clark, "Carter's Groundbreaking Appointment of Women to the Federal Bench: His Other 'Human Rights' Record," *American University Journal of Gender, Social Policy & the Law,* vol. 11, no. 3, 2003, 1131–63.

17. Rosalynn Carter, *First Lady from Plains* (Boston: Houghton Mifflin, 1984), 289–90.

18. "Voices for Women," 1980 Report of the President's Advisory Committee for Women, Lynda Johnson Robb, Chair, 16–20.

19. Jimmy Carter, University of Virginia's Miller Center of Public Affairs interview, November 29, 1992.

20. Pad 42, November 22, 1978.

21. Pad 44, December 20, 1978.

22. Bella Abzug, interview with the author, April 8, 1992.

23. Jimmy Carter interview, October 25, 1991.

24. Jody Powell, interview with the author, October 16, 1989.

25. Hamilton Jordan interview, May 11, 1992, and December 23, 1992.

26. Bella Abzug interview, April 8, 1992.

27. Pad 32A, April 24, 1978.

28. Ben Wattenberg, interview with the author, July 21, 1991.

29. Peter Rosenblatt, interview with the author, November 3, 1992.

30. Pad 75, January 31, 1980.

31. Ibid.

32. Norman Podhoretz, interview with the author, July 14, 2011; Justin Vaïsse, *Neoconservatism: The Biography of a Movement* (Cambridge, MA: Belknap Press, 2011).

33. *American Experience.* "Jimmy Carter (Part 2)." Episode 174. Directed by Adriana Bosch. Aired on PBS, November 12, 2002; Joshua Muravchik, *The Uncertain Crusade: Jimmy Carter and the Dilemmas of Human Rights Policy* (Lanham, MD: Hamilton Press, 1986),

197–220, for a critical evaluation by a neoconservative of Carter's human rights record; Jay Winik, *On the Brink: The Dramatic Saga of How the Reagan Administration Changed the Course of History and Won the Cold War* (New York: Simon & Schuster, 1996).

34. Ben Wattenberg interview, July 21, 1991.

35. Andrew Young, interviews with the author, December 17, 1991, and September 14, 2014.

36. Ibid., December 17, 1991, October 5, 2012, and September 27, 2014.

37. Andrew Young interview, September 27, 2014.

38. Pad 48, February 8, 1979.

39. Stoney Cooks, interview with the author, April 29, 1992.

40. Andrew Young interview, September 27, 2014.

41. Stoney Cooks interview, April 29, 1992.

42. Hodding Carter III, interview with the author, June 10, 1992.

43. Stoney Cooks interview, April 29, 1992.

44. Yehuda Blum, interview with the author, July 15, 1991.

45. Cyrus Vance, interview with the author, April 28, 1992.

46. Jimmy Carter interview, October 30, 1991.

47. Pad 62, August 14, 1979.

48. Jimmy Carter interview, October 30, 1991.

49. Pad 62, August 14, 1979.

50. Ibid., August 15, 1979.

51. Ibid., August 16, 1979; Jimmy Carter interview, October 30, 1991.

52. Cyrus Vance interview, April 28, 1992.

53. Andrew Young interview, Atlanta, Georgia, July 25, 1981, Box 140, Item 13, Side 1, Andy Young Oral History Collection, Tulane University Digital Library.

54. Bert Gold, interview with the author, September 19, 1991.

55. Vernon Jordan, interview with the author, November 11, 1991; Pranay B. Gupte, "Civil Rights Leader Backs Cause of PLO After Meeting at U.N.," *The New York Times*, August 20, 1977.

56. Thomas Johnson, "Black Leaders Air Grievances on Jews," *The New York Times*, August 23, 1979.

57. Jimmy Carter, *White House Diary*, 406; Ephraim "Eppie" Evron, Israeli Ambassador to the U.S., interview with the author, December 23, 1992.

58. Hamilton Jordan interviews, May 11, 1992, and December 23, 1992.

59. Yehuda Bloom, Israeli Ambassador to the UN, interview with the author, July 15, 1991.

60. Walter Mondale interviews, April 3, 1991, October 8, 1992, September 11, 2014, October 6, 2015.

61. Terence Smith, "President Terms Anti-Israel Vote in U.N. an Error," *The New York Times*, March 3, 1980.

62. Pad 78, March 3, 1980.

63. Terence Smith, "The U.N. Vote: Snowfall, Missed Signals, Iran and the Other Problems Contributed," *The New York Times*, March 18, 1980.

64. Robert Strauss, interview with the author, October 27, 1989.

65. Ephraim "Eppie" Evron, Israeli ambassador to the United States, interview with the author, December 23, 1992.

66. Hamilton Jordan interviews, May 11, 1992, and December 23, 1992.

67. William Maynes, Assistant Secretary of State for International Organizations, interview with the author, August 26, 1992. Maynes was listening in Cyrus Vance's office at the State Department to the Mondale-Vance telephone conversation and quoted Walter Mondale in his interview with the author.

68. Cyrus Vance interview, April 28, 1992.

69. Pad 78, March 4, 1978.

70. Rosalynn Carter, *First Lady from Plains*, 321–2; Rosalynn Carter, interviews with the author, July 13, 1993, and August 13, 2014.

71. Pad 79, March 24, 1980.

72. Paul Kirk, interview with the author, January 19, 1993.

73. Carl Wagner, interview with the author, August 17, 1992.

74. Ambassador Sam Lewis, ADST interview, August 9, 1998; and Sam Lewis, interview with the author, May 20, 1992.

75. Hamilton Jordan interviews, May 11, 1992, and December 23, 1992.

76. Jimmy Carter interview, October 25, 1991.

77. Tom Donilon, interview with the author, August 9, 2014.

78. Carl Wagner, interview with the author, August 17, 1992.

79. Pad 88, June 14, 1980.

80. Pad 88, June 17, 1980.

81. Pad 88, June 18, 22, 1980.

82. Pad 93, August 7, 1980.

83. Pad 88, June 18, 1980.

84. Pad 95, August 26, 27, 1980.

85. Pad 95, September 10, 1980.

86. Pad 93, August 12, 1980.

87. Paul Kirk interview, January 19, 1993.

88. Edward Kennedy interview, September 11, 1992.

89. Jimmy Carter interviews, October 25, 1991, and September 27, 2013.

30. "Are You Better Off . . . ? "

1. Hamilton Jordan, memorandum to President Carter, June 25, 1980, Carter Presidential Library and Museum.

2. Pad 17, May 31, 1977.

3. Pad 24, September 1, 1977; Griffin Bell, interview with the author, September 6, 1989.

4. Pad 24, September 2, 1977.

5. Ibid., September 12, 1977.

6. Ibid., September 7, 1977.

7. Ibid., September 10, 1977.

8. Drew Days, interview with the author, May 7, 1992.

9. Daniel K. Williams, "Jerry Falwell's Sunbelt Politics: The Regional Origins of the Moral Majority," *Journal of Policy History*, Cambridge University Press, November 2, 2010.

10. Denise Grady, Nellie Gray obituary, *The New York Times,* August 15, 2012.

11. Randall Balmer, "The Real Origins of the Religious Right: They'll Tell You It Was Abortion. Sorry, the Historical Record's Clear: It Was Segregation," *Politico,* May 27, 2014.

12. Max Blumenthal, *Republican Gomorrah: Inside the Movement that Shattered the Party* (New York: Nation Books, 2009), 25.

13. WETA, "God in America: Transcripts: Hour Six—'Of God and Caesar,'" www.pbs .org/godinamercia/transcripts/hour-six-html.

14. Ibid.

15. Jimmy Carter, interview with the author, June 4, 1991.

16. Robert Maddox exit interview, December 8, 1980, by Marie Allen, Presidential Papers; Helen Parmley, "Aide Explains Falwell Talk," The Portal to Texas History, August 7, 1980, in which a spokesperson for Falwell tried to explain away Falwell's allegation that Carter supported homosexuals on his White House staff.

17. Daniel K. Williams, "Jerry Falwell's Sunbelt Politics: The Regional Origins of the Moral Majority," *Journal of Policy History,* (New York: Cambridge University Press, 2010).

18. *American Experience.* "Biography: Billy Carter," www.pbs.org/wgbh/americanexperience /featuresbiographybilly-carter/.

19. *American Experience.* "Jimmy Carter (Part 2)." Episode 174. Directed by Adriana Bosch. Aired on PBS, November 12, 2002.

20. Robert Hershey, Jr., "Billy Carter Dies of Cancer at 51: Troubled Brother of a President," *The New York Times,* September 26, 1988.

21. Ethan Trex, "6 Presidential Siblings and the Headaches They Caused," July 29, 2008, http://mentalfloss.com/article/19202/6-presidential-siblings-and-headaches-they -caused.

22. Jimmy Carter, *White House Diary* (New York: Farrar, Straus & Giroux, 2010), 279.

23. Hamilton Jordan interview, May 11, 1992.

24. Alfred Moses, interview with the author, August 25, 2015.

25. www.washingtonpost.com/wp-srv/politics/special/clintonfrenzy/hart.htm.

26. Pad 91, June 18, 1979.

27. Larry Sabato, "Billygate-1980," washingtonpost.com, July 21, 1998; Robert O. Hershey, Jr. "Billy Carter Dies of Cancer at 51: Troubled Brother of a President," *The New York Times,* September 26, 1988.

28. Robert Pastor, interview with the author, transcribed July 13, 2011.

29. Pad 83, April 23, 25, 1980.

30. Public Papers of the Presidents, Jimmy Carter, 1980–1981, April 27, 1980, 780.

31. Ibid., 834.

32. Pad 86, May 29, 1980.

33. Robert Pastor interview, July 13, 2011.

34. Chris Good, "The Laffer Curve: The Most Powerful and Ambiguous Idea in Tax Politics," *The Atlantic,* August 9, 2010; "Laffer Curve," Dylan Matthews in Ezra Klein's blog, "Where Does the Laffer Curve Bend?" http://voicds.washingtonpost.com/ezra -klein210/08/where_does_the laffer_curve/be.html.

35. G. William (Bill) Miller, interview with the author, July 28, 1989.

36. JEC Report, Joint Economic Committee, Congress of the United States, April 1996.

37. James Baker interview, May 29, 2013.

38. Pad 88, June 9, 1980.

39. Debates, External Video, the Reagan-Carter presidential debate, October 28, 1980, on YouTube.

40. Pad 97, September 30, 1980.

41. James Baker interview, May 29, 2013; Richard Wirthlin statement to Elizabeth Drew, in Morton Kondracke, "Debategate," *The New Republic,* July 18, 1993.

42. Jerry Rafshoon, interview with the author, August 19, 2013.

43. Pad 98, October 28, 1980.

44. Ibid., October 16, 1980.

45. Ibid., October 18, 1980.

46. Ibid., October 25, 1980.

47. Ibid.

48. Pad 98, October 26, 1980.

49. Ibid., October 19, 1980.

50. Ibid., October 26, 1980.

51. Ibid., October 27, 1980.

52. Jerry Rafshoon interviews, April 4, 2014, and October 18, 2015; and discussions with the author, June 17, 2013, and February 25, 2014.

53. www.pbs/org/wgbh/americanexperiencefeatures/general-article/carter-election1980.

54. Hendrick Hertzberg, interview with the author, April 27, 1992; exit interview by Marie Allen, Presidential Projects Papers; *American Experience,* "The Election of 1980, Carter Strategies," November 11, 2002, www.pbs.org/wgbh/americanexperience/film/carter/.

55. Pad 99, October 31, 1980.

56. Ibid., November 3, 1980.

57. James Baker, interview with the author, May 29, 2013.

58. James Rowland, interview with the author, July 14, 1992; Jimmy Carter quote in Craig Shirley, "New Book Pins 'debategate' on Dem," *Politico,* October 15, 2009.

59. James Baker interview, May 29, 2013; Craig Shirley, Ibid.

60. Adam Walinsky, interview with the author, September 19, 1992; Adam Walinsky, "I Was RFK's Speechwriter. Now I'm Voting for Trump. Here's Why," *Politico,* September 21, 2016; Laurence I. Barrett, *Gambling with History: Ronald Reagan in the White House* (New York: Doubleday, 1983).

61. Craig Shirley, "New Book Pins 'Debategate' on Dem," *Politico,* October 15, 2009, www.politico.com/story/2009/10/new-book-pins-debategate-on-dem-028317.

62. Jerry Rafshoon, University of Virginia's Miller Center of Public Affairs, April 8, 1983.

63. Elizabeth Drew, "1980: The Election," *The New Yorker,* December 1, 1980; also quoted in *American Experience,* "The Election of 1980," www.pbs.org/wgbh/americanexperience /featuresgeneral-article/carter-election1980/; Elizabeth Drew, *Portrait of an Election: The 1980 Presidential Election* (New York: Simon and Schuster, 1981).

64. Pad 99, November 3, 1980; Samuel Popkin Popkin (professor at University of California, San Diego), interview with the author, November 11, 1991.

65. Pad 99, October 31, 1980.

66. Ibid., November 2, 1980, 25.

67. Rosalynn Carter, interview with the author, August 13, 2014.

68. Pad 99, November 2, 1980.

69. Ibid.

70. Ibid.

71. Walter Mondale, interview with the author, September 22, 2014.

72. Jerry Rafshoon interview, August 19, 2013.

73. Jerry Rafshoon, University of Virginia's Miller Center of Public Affairs interview, April 8, 1983.

74. Jerry Rafshoon interviews, June 17, 2013, and February 25, 2014.

75. Pad 99, November 3, 1980.

76. Samuel Popkin interview, November 11, 1991; Pad 99, November 4, 1990.

77. Pad 99, November 4, 1980.

78. Ibid.

79. Jody Powell, interviews with the author, December 17, 18, 1981, and October 16, 1989.

80. Douglas Brinkley, *The Unfinished Presidency: James Carter's Journey Beyond the White House,* www.nytimes.com/books/first/b/brinkley-unfinished.html.

81. Tip O'Neill, *Man of the House: The Life and Political Memoirs of Speaker Tip O'Neill* (New York: Random House, 1987), 329; Frank Moore, interview with the author, May 8, 2013.

82. Pad 99, November 11, 1980.

31. Final Days

1. Pad 99, November 11, 1980.

2. Pad 100, November 13, 1980.

3. Pad 103, January 14, 1981.

4. Public Papers of the Presidents, Jimmy Carter, Vol. III, 1980–1981, January 14, 1981, 2889–93.

5. Pad 99, November 5, 1980.

6. Ibid., November 11, 1980.

7. Jerry Rafshoon, interview with the author, October 18, 2015.

8. Charlie Palmer, interview with the author, December 11, 2013; and in conversations, October 21, 22, 2015.

INDEX